First Edition

Rock History
the Musician's Perspective

Dr. Robert Brosh

DDG Publishing

Rock History- The Musician's Perspective
by Dr. Robert Brosh
Copyright © 2018 by DDG Publishing

All rights reserved. No part of this book may be used, transmitted, or reproduced in any form or by any means without the prior written permission of the publisher, except for brief quotations in reviews of the work.

DDG Publishing, PO Box 41, Mt. Laurel, NJ 08054
  www.rockmusicbook.com

The information in this book is accurate and effective to the best of our knowledge but are offered without guarantee. The author and DDG Publishing disclaim

all liability in connection with the use of the information in this book.

Edited by Sarah F. Wimberley
  Mark Griffith
  Robert Brosh
  Jason Gianni

Contributing Writer Mark Griffith

Book Design Concept by Ben Brotman
Page Layout by Sarah F. Wimberley
Illustrations by Aly Castle

This book was made possible in part by a grant from The University of the Arts

Library of Congress Control Number: 2018941736
ISBN: 978-1-5323-7174-5 (hardcover)
ISBN: 978-1-5323-7175-2 (e-book)

Printed in the United States of America

To the memory of my mother, Jeanne Brosh,
who took me to every Genesis, Yes, and Jethro Tull concert possible.

I would like to thank my family;
Patty, Robbie, Kel, and Smidgeon (the dog)
for enduring my obsessive nonsense in the writing and editing of this book.

Contents

Part One Rock Music - The Early Years

Chapter One - The Roots of Rock Music...pg 3

✯ Gospel ✯ The Blues ✯ Country Music ✯ Folk Music

Chapter Two - Elvis Presley and Rockabilly...pg 15

✯ Elvis Presley ✯ Rockabilly Artists ✯ More Elvis

Chapter Three - Early Rock 'N' Roll...pg 25

✯ Early Rock 'n' Roll Artists ✯ Chuck Berry ✯ Fats Domino ✯ Little Richard ✯ Buddy Holly

✯ Roy Orbison ✯ Teen Idols ✯ Surf Rock Artists ✯ The Beach Boys

Chapter Four - The Blues Takes a Trip and the Supergroups...pg 43

✯ British Blues Scene ✯ The Rolling Stones ✯ The Yardbirds ✯ Cream ✯ Led Zeppelin

Chapter Five - The Beatles and the Solo Beatles..pg 57

✯ The Beatles ✯ George Harrison ✯ John Lennon ✯ Paul McCartney ✯ Ringo Starr

Chapter Six - The British Invasion Continues and the American Answer...........................pg 71

✯ British Invasion Artists ✯ The Kinks ✯ The Who ✯ Psychedelic Rock Artists

✯ The Grateful Dead ✯ More Psychedelic Artists ✯ The Doors ✯ Jimi Hendrix

Part Two Rock Finds New Directions

Chapter Seven - Folk Rock-Bob Dylan-Singer/Songwriters..pg 95

★ Bob Dylan ★ Early Folk Rock Artists ★ Simon and Garfunkel ★ CSN&Y ★ Carole King

★ Singer/Songwriters ★ James Taylor ★ Paul Simon ★ Neil Young ★ More Singer/Songwriters

Chapter Eight - Art Rock and Glam Rock..pg 121

★ Pink Floyd ★ Art Rock Artists ★ The Avant-Garde ★ David Bowie ★ Glam Rock Artists

★ Roxy Music ★ Queen ★ More Glam Rock Artists

Chapter Nine - Country Rock and Southern Rock..pg 143

★ Early Country Rock Artists ★ The Flying Burrito Brothers ★ More Country Rock Artists

★ The Country Rock Dylan ★ Alternative Country Rock Artists ★ The Allman Brothers

★ Lynyrd Skynyrd ★ More Southern Rock Artists

Chapter Ten - Heavy Metal and Hard Rock..pg 165

★ Early Heavy Metal ★ Black Sabbath ★ More Heavy Metal Artists ★ Glam Metal Artists

★ The Big Four Thrash Metal Bands ★ Metal Sub-Genre Artists ★ Early Hard Rock Bands

★ Aerosmith ★ Kiss ★ AC/DC ★ Van Halen ★ More Hard Rock Bands

Chapter Eleven - Classic Rock..pg 191

★ Early Classic Rock Bands ★ ZZ Top ★ Derek and the Dominos ★ ELO ★ The Eagles

★ More Classic Rock Bands ★ Journey ★ Dire Straits ★ Toto

Chapter Twelve - Classic Rock Singer - Led Bands..pg 213

★ Elton John ★ Billy Joel ★ Bob Seger ★ Bruce Springsteen ★ Eric Clapton ★ Tom Petty

★ More Classic Singer-Led Bands ★ Sting ★ Jam Bands

Chapter Thirteen - Progressive Rock..pg 233

★ Progressive Rock Roots ★ Musical Characteristics ★ First Wave Bands ★ The Moody Blues

★ Procol Harum ★ Second Wave ★ King Crimson ★ ELP ★ Gentle Giant ★ Genesis

★ Jethro Tull ★ Yes ★ Rush ★ Third Wave Bands

Part Three Rock Gets Angry and Evolves

Chapter Fourteen - Punk Rock and New Wave..pg 255

★ Musical Characteristics ★ Early American Punk ★ The Ramones ★ Origins of British Punk ★ The Sex Pistols ★ The Clash ★ More British Punk Artists ★ Regionalization of American Punk ★ Crossover Thrash ★ Pop-Punk Bands ★ New Wave ★ Devo ★ Blondie ★ The Cars ★ The Pretenders ★ More New Wave

Chapter Fifteen - Pop-Rock..pg 279

★ Michael Jackson ★ Madonna ★ Prince ★ More Pop-Rock Artists ★ Hall and Oates ★ The Bee Gees ★ Phil Collins ★ More Pop-Rock Artists ★ BritPop Artists ★ Power Pop Artists

Chapter Sixteen -The Big Eighties-Grungy Nineties-and the Alternative..........pg 299

★ The Police ★ U2 ★ R.E.M. ★ Arrival of MTV ★ Early Grunge Bands ★ Nirvana ★ More Grunge Bands ★ Post Grunge Bands ★ The Foo Fighters ★ Alternative Rock Bands ★ Radiohead ★ 1990's to Present Alternative Pop Bands

Chapter Seventeen - Important Musical Styles that Mixed with Rock...............pg 325

★ Funk and Funk-Rock Artists ★ Rap-Rock Artists ★ Jazz-Rock and Horn Rock ★ Electronica to EDM ★ New Innovations in Metal ★ Industrial Metal ★ Nu Metal ★ Guitar Slingers

Chapter Eighteen - Rock Music Visionaries..pg 347

★ Frank Zappa ★ The Band ★ Joni Mitchell ★ Steely Dan ★ Brian Eno ★ Peter Gabriel

Artist/Band Index..pg 371
Rock Genres, Sub-Genres and Other Musical Styles Index.................................pg 381
Sources Cited by Chapters..pg 385

Forward

Ethnomusicologists have explored the first traces of music from virtually every culture in the world. Some of these music cultures evolved fairly quickly, while others progressed slowly over hundreds and even thousands of years. When it came to rock music, the songs showed up in the late 1940's to early 1950's. This birth date makes rock music about seventy years old, give or take a few years. When compared to the history of all music from every time period and region of the world, no music style has evolved as rapidly as rock. Advancements in technology, such as sound recording, the radio, sound in movies, television, and the computer has had a lot to do with rock's rapid evolution as well as other styles of music. However, never has a genre grown so quickly and morphed into so many sub-genres as rock. Decades of musical acculturation occurred when American musicians of diverse ethnicity integrated with British musicians to create many rock sub-genres. A prime example would be the blues, born in the rural American south and mixed with young British musicians to form some of the most defining rock music ever created.

The study of rock styles is often done according to a chronological timeline from decade to decade. With so many rock sub-genres to explore, our approach will be based on a concept of parallel streams. This means that a sub-genre such as punk rock will be examined from its infancy throughout its complete evolution. Often, rock sub-genres mixed to eventually form even newer sub-genres. A parallel streams approach avoids the nightmare of attempting to follow the different rock styles in chronological order from year to year and decade to decade. For example, the late 1960's saw the continued development of The Beatles and many blues based rock bands, numerous folk-rock artists, and the beginning of progressive rock. That's a lot of music to juggle at once. Following a specific sub-genre (for example southern rock) from its infancy to current times allows for a clear and focused path of study.

Part One begins with a brief overview of the roots of rock. Although, many music styles played a role in rock's evolution, gospel music, the blues, folk music, and country music exerted the most influence on early rock 'n' roll. We then move to Elvis Presley and rockabilly to early rock 'n' roll artists. Next, we explore how blues shaped the music of the early British supergroups. The Beatles follow, along with the rest of the British Invasion into the American reaction. Part Two begins with folk rock and singer/songwriters and moves to art rock. We quickly shift to country and southern rock and into heavy metal and hard rock. Classic rock bands and singer-led classic rock bands follow. Part two ends with progressive rock. Part Three sees the radical shift to punk rock and new wave and moves to the pop-rock genre. Next, we focus on the Big 1980's, grunge music in the 1990's and alternative rock styles. We follow with a chapter on some of the other significant music styles that influenced and merged with rock. We end with a look at four visionary artists and two bands that have profoundly affected rock music and its potential future.

Our approach to building an understanding of rock music comes from the perspective of the rock musician; both the player and composer. This means that we will examine the great guitar players, the creative drummers, the innovative keyboardists, the virtuoso bass players, unique singers, and influential producers of rock music. Same goes for the brilliant songwriters and their masterful approach to composing melodies and harmonies. Innovative rock bands experiment collaborate. They take chances and create combinations of instrumental sounds that validate their special group sound. When you hear Led

Zeppelin for a few measures or even a few notes, you know it's them. That's the magic of timeless rock music at work. We will place an emphasis on the special songwriting chemistry of some of the masters like Lennon and McCartney, and Richards and Jagger. We will also explore some of the issues that helped to shape rock history such as payola, censorship, and social and political concerns.

Rhythm and blues has often crossed paths with rock 'n' roll and has a important history of its own. This rich history warrants an examination of its own. This book excluded some rock bands and artists, while others were briefly mentioned. Making a complete list of the thousands of rock bands was never our goal. Maybe your favorite rock artist is omitted. Sorry about that. This book has attempted to explore the vast world of the rock artists and bands that have uniquely shaped the ever-evolving course of rock history.

How to Use This Book

Rock History-The Musician's Perspective can be utilized in a variety of ways. By starting with a quick glance at the content pages, the reader can become familiar with how each chapter presents a vast array of rock sub-genres. Chapter one presents a brief background of the source roots of rock music in order to understand its foundation. Each chapter traces the evolution of specific sub-genres and related issues. It is suggested to work through the book in sequential order to best understand the overall chronology of rock's development.

Throughout the book, some of the most influential and groundbreaking albums in rock history are profiled. When reading the narrative for major artists or bands, these album profiles offer more insight into the music of individual artists. Some profiles are about selected individual musicians that changed the course of rock history. Other profiles address various topics and issues connected to rock music. Throughout the book, hundreds of quotes are utilized by many of rock's most influential musicians. We thought it would be best to hear the direct words of many of rock's all-time great musicians. This provides small glimpses into many aspects of rock music. Rock hard facts appear often and serve to provide small tidbits of rock trivia. For many artists and bands, individual songs were selected and briefly detailed. Wherever recordings were highlighted, we analyzed the original versions as the source material. The goal was not to do a theoretical breakdown of songs or albums. Rather, we sought to highlight some of the back-stories, lyrical meanings, recording processes, or other relevant and interesting musical issues found in the significant songs of important artists.

Discussion questions are presented at the midpoint (except chapter eighteen) and at end of each chapter. One approach is to read the discussion question first and keep it in mind while reading the chapter. Discussion questions are there to encourage the reader to think about the musical possibilities and key issues of rock music. They also provide for challenging writing assignments. When utilized as the textbook for a semester-long college course, the chapters of Rock History-The Musician's Perspective can be taught in sequential order. In developing a curriculum, certain chapters (rock genres) can be omitted due to time restrictions. The book's three overall parts flow in a general chronological order, although the parallel streams of each chapter follow their own chronology.

Pictures of musicians do not appear in this book. Within a few key strokes, you can access any photos on your phone or computer. Our rock history icon figure appears in illustrations and embodies the personality of the music of each chapter. However you choose to read this book, have fun with the material! View each part, each chapter, and each artist or band as the individual parts that fill in the enormous puzzle of rock music history.

Part One

Rock Music

The Early Years

Chapter One: The Roots of Rock Music

Rock music evolved from a number of strong musical roots. These included blues, rhythm and blues, jazz, gospel and spirituals, country, folk, and even some popular music such as Tin Pan Alley tunes. Each of these diverse musical styles were developed by different ethnic groups from specific regions of America. The eventual merger of white and African-American cultures that began in the early 1940's through the 1950's resulted in the assimilation of many unique musical characteristics. Before anyone would refer to music as **rock 'n' roll**, many musicians began to experiment by combining existing styles. Sometimes, musicians were merely trying to express themselves in a personal way and their assimilation of different music styles came naturally. Others deliberately fused multiple styles in pursuit of new modes of musical expression. Specifically, the four musical ingredients of **gospel**, **the blues**, **country music**, and **folk music** became the strongest catalysts in the creation of rock music. Each style brought a number of unique musical characteristics that would contribute in different ways. This would define early rock 'n' roll but also facilitate the creation of the many genres of rock music that exist today. In this chapter, we will briefly explore these core music styles that are the defining roots of rock music. We begin with gospel music.

Gospel Music

Gospel music has played an important role in the development of rock music. From the time of the growth of the Pentecostal churches in the late 19th century, African-American gospel was present along with blues, ragtime, and early jazz. Musical sources traced back to slavery have existed for much of the history of America. Nothing could compare to the massive enslavement and exportation of African slaves to North America, South America, and the Caribbean. By the middle of the 18th century there were approximately 300,000 slaves in America. To make matters worse, Africans were denied the right to sing and play instruments. But they continued to do so secretly as a way to cope with the horrible conditions and also to maintain a sense of their culture. Some of the general musical characteristics present in African music were vocal lines sung in call and response phrases, the use of pentatonic tonal centers, and the use of blue notes. African drum and percussion music featured complex rhythms, meters, and polyrhythms. Additionally, the frequent use of ostinato repeated figures and complex timelines of interwoven, dense rhythmic parts made for unique and musical "African qualities." All of this eventually was traceable to jazz, blues, and eventually, rock music.

By the mid-1800's, black sources of American music included the spirituals, field hollers, and street cries that became the blues. **Spirituals** were essentially religious songs of African-American origin that were usually based on Biblical stories of promise and redemption such as the crossing of the river Jordan or Daniel's deliverance from the lion's den. Spirituals combined four-part harmonies often derived from the white hymn texts of Issac Watts and anonymous shape-note hymns. Melodies of spirituals utilized African-American syncopated rhythms, call and response phrases, and blue notes added to enhance vocal expression. African-American slaves and post emancipated African-Americans found solace in Christianity and could identify with the figure of the martyred Christ and the promise of redemption and relief from their plight.

> "I sing gospel music because it makes me feel free... it gives me hope"
>
> –Mahalia Jackson

From West Africa to rock 'n' roll

How did we get from the slave songs and drum ensembles of the Ivory Coast (aka The Gold Coast) of West Africa to early rock 'n' roll such as Jerry Lee Lewis's "Great Balls of Fire?" Centuries ago, Sir John Hawkins in 1562 was the first Englishman to bring slaves to America. Slaves were distributed to plantations, particularly in the south, where they were forced to assimilate European musical traditions. Although their captors wanted to strip Africans of their culture and customs, West Africans refused to be separated from their music, dancing, and dignity. One strong characteristic of West African music was call and response vocal phrasing. An African chorus may sing back a call verbatim or with slightly different responses. They might even respond with a different melodic phrase altogether. Oppressed workers sang about their suffering with great emotional expression. They began to alter melodic lines by singing with flat thirds and sevenths to create "blue" notes.

West African musicians also had a highly developed concept of ostinato patterns (a reiteration of a single rhythmic or melodic pattern) that led to the complex layering of rhythms. Many drum ensembles performed these rhythmic patterns with the result being polyrhythmic and polymetric structures. Complex cross accents were created by overlapping ostinato figures that produced syncopated rhythms (accents played off of the beat). Slaves applied their rhythmic concepts to early spirituals and field hollers. Eventually, all of these incredible musical innovations were a catalyst in the development of the blues, jazz, rhythm and blues, and early rock 'n' roll. The strong syncopation of beats two and four created rhythmic tension and provided the "swing" of jazz and the blues shuffle. This eventually led to an important fundamental attribute of rock 'n' roll, the backbeat.

When you hear the layering of a rock guitar player strumming a repeated pattern over a steady drumset beat and yet another pattern added by a keyboard player; all supporting a burning guitar solo, you begin to understand the African influence on rock music. The process evolved over a long time and may not at first appear obvious. Sometimes musical evolution came slow. European music traditions certainly played a role. But the rhythms of rock 'n' roll melodies, harmonic accompaniments, basslines, and drumset patterns all follow a clear path that came from African music.

The late 19th century saw the rise of the gospel **hymn**. Hymn writing was exploding all over the South. In addition, a wealth of folk music plus the popularity of camp-meeting events created a recipe for both white and black gospel music. The Pentecostal churches of the late 19th and early 20th centuries were the home of black congregations that sang hundreds of gospel hymns. These compositions used a verse-refrain format with simple harmonies and were based on pentatonic scales. More than 700 gospel sermons were recorded in the 1920's and 1930's as blacks sought comfort in Jesus and the Lord and hoped for a better future. The role of the black preacher took on many responsibilities as gospel music continued to evolve in hundreds of churches across America.

Known as the "father of modern gospel music," **Thomas Dorsey** (1988-1993) grew up in Georgia. His father was a minister and his mother was a piano teacher. Dorsey learned blues piano and studied music formerly in Chicago. He soon formed a band called The Wild Cats Jazz Band in 1924 and accompanied blues great Ma Rainey. Dorsey developed into a prolific gospel songwriter and the leading promoter of gospel music throughout the early 20th century. Among Dorsey's most famous compositions was "Precious Lord" written in 1932 that he described with the term "gospel song" (these songs were previously called evangelical songs). Thomas Dorsey had a wide influence on artists across many music genres. His compositions were later performed and recorded by B.B. King, Roy Rogers, Tennessee Ernie Ford, and Johnny Cash among others.

"Take My Hand, Precious Lord"
by Rev. Thomas A. Dorsey

Thomas Dorsey adapted the melody for "Precious Lord" from an 1844 hymn "Maitland" that can be found in many of the old hymnal books. Dorsey wrote the tune in response to his sadness over the death of his wife, Nettie Harper in 1932. The earliest recording was by The Heavenly Gospel Singers in 1937. Marin Luther King Jr. often asked Mahalia Jackson to sing it at civil rights events to inspire the crowd. King's last words right before he was assassinated was his request that "Precious Lord" be performed that night at a mass he would attend. Dorsey would tirelessly perform "Take My Hand, Precious Lord" all across America. Thomas Dorsey's "Take My Hand Precious Lord" was inducted into the Christian Music Hall of Fame in 2007.

Dorsey became a great ambassador for Gospel by traveling extensively from church to church. He helped to promote the careers of many gospel greats such as Sallie Martin and perhaps the greatest female gospel singer ever, **Mahalia Jackson** (1911-1972). Jackson had an incredibly powerful voice that she assimilated with the influence of blues singers Ma Rainey and Bessie Smith. Mahalia, called "The Queen of Gospel," was an internationally known vocalist and an avid civil rights activist. Jackson grew up in New Orleans but moved to Chicago at age sixteen. In 1950, she became the first gospel singer to perform at Carnegie Hall and she began to tour Europe by 1952.

In 1929, Mahalia met gospel pianist/promoter Thomas Dorsey and they began a fourteen-year musical partnership that would help to define modern gospel music in America. She refused to sing secular music, even when presented with lucrative offers, because she believed strongly in gospel's message. She utilized her great talent to sing at countless civil rights rallies, her other great passion. Mahalia Jackson was inducted into the Rock and Roll Hall of Fame in 1997.

"Didn't It Rain"
traditional African-American spiritual/work song

"Didn't It Rain" was a gospel standard in the performance repertoire of Mahalia Jackson. Sometimes called "Oh, Didn't It Rain" it was first written in 1919 by arranger Henry Thacker Burleigh. There are many modern versions of the tune including those by Sister Rosetta Tharpe, Marion Williams, Tom Jones, and Hugh Laurie. In this version, Mahalia's smooth and powerful voice interacts with the boogie-woogie blues-inspired accompaniment of Thomas Dorsey on piano. Many feel that she defined the essence of gospel singing as smooth, yet powerful and extremely expressive. She had it all. Mahalia first recorded "Didn't It Rain" on her debut album for Columbia Records <u>The World's Greatest Gospel Singer</u>. On that landmark recording, Mahalia also recorded Dorsey's

---

> **Rock Hard Fact**
>
> Thomas Dorsey's gospel standard "Take My Hand, Precious Lord" was Reverend Martin Luther King's favorite song.

> "Whether you're drawn to gospel music or church music or honky-tonk music, it informs your character and it informs your talent"
>
> - Bruce Springsteen

"I'm Going to Live the Life I Sing About in My Song," and "Walk Over God's Heaven."

Male vocal ensembles were a significant part of gospel music. From 1910 to 1930, popular male ensembles such as The Dixie Hummingbirds, The Golden Gate Quartet, and the Five Blind Boys of Alabama dominated the modern gospel movement. These groups utilized the male voice as a powerful rhythmic instrument. Another significant group, The Soul Stirrers, featuring the talented Sam Cooke. The Soul Stirrers sang falsetto parts that would later be transformed into **doo-wop** vocals.

Black gospel music had a profound effect on the vocal techniques of rock 'n' roll. Gospel music characteristics eventually crossed over to soul, rhythm and blues, and early rock 'n' roll as heard in the vocal styles of James Brown, Little Richard, Ray Charles, Aretha Franklin, and countless others. Ray Charles reworked gospel classics such as "My Jesus Is All the World to Me" into his secular tune "I've Got a Women." In the 1950's, Elvis Presley defined his style with a clear gospel influence. In the 1960's and 1970's, Mick Jagger and Robert Plant, also defined their styles with strong gospel and blues influences.

The Blues

No musical style has exerted more influence on rock music than **the blues**. As many musicians and writers have noted, the blues still provides the deepest roots of rock music and other styles such as jazz. Without it, you simply don't have The Rolling Stones, Louis Armstrong, Led Zeppelin, Charlie Parker, Eric Clapton or Jimi Hendrix, to name a few. The blues simultaneously developed all over the South in Georgia, North Carolina, Texas, and Tennessee. Early blues can even be found in California. However, the hotbed of the blues was the Mississippi and Louisiana Delta. Bandleaders such as W.C. Handy discovered the blues for themselves while traveling throughout the deep South. Ma Rainey, often referred to as "the Mother of the Blues," added Delta styled blues to her repertory of minstrel songs, spirituals, and rural folk songs. While the Delta was home to some of the richest soil for cotton production and other crops, it was also home to a very pure and rich style of blues. In the late 1800's, the harsh and difficult lifestyles imposed on African-American slaves cultivated genuine feelings of human suffering, and a life that was both desperate and often hopeless. The blues emerged out of these circumstances, and were manifested in the field hollers of oppressed plantation workers. Common themes in blues tunes were poverty, infidelity, loneliness, the forces of good vs. evil, and a sense of wandering and moving on.

By the beginning of the twentieth century, the blues fully assimilated musical elements of West African roots, American spirituals, work songs, and field hollers. These blues roots combined with elements of European song forms. What emerged were clear musical characteristics including; a twelve-bar song form, call and response phrasing, the use of "blue notes," evolving shuffle or "swing" rhythms, and new guitar techniques such as bottleneck style. The format of a twelve-bar form evolved over time and was not set in stone, especially for many Delta musicians. Three phrases, each consisting of four measures, were repeated to make one twelve-bar chorus of a tune. This is referred to as AAB form and both of the A phrases typically used a call of two vocal measures and a response of two instrumental measures. Often the B phrase continued to develop the response from the second A phrase. This was not strictly adhered to because most blues performers took great liberty with the form and even the beat structure of the meter, which was usually in 4/4 time. Each of the three phrases of the blues contained a common chord pattern that came from European hymns. The first A phrase was built with a tonic (I) chord while the second phrase was built on the four chord, also known as the sub-dominant (IV) chord. The third phrase, or B phrase was built on the five chord, also known as the dominant (V) chord. This was open to interpretation and could easily be supplemented with other chords, often on the spot, since improvisation was a large part of every performance. This gave the music both a sense of unpredictability and a great vehicle for self-expression. The ability of a blues musician to spontaneously respond to the vocal call became an art form in itself. The rhythmic element of the blues evolved from a straight eighth-note feel to a triplet-based swung eighth-note feel, often referred to as a shuffle. Not every blues swings, but this feel was a major part of both jazz and early rock music. We will soon examine these musical characteristics in greater detail in the songs of some of the blues greats.

The blues produced by many Delta musicians had unique qualities. When you compare the blues of the aforementioned Carolinas and Texas, the Mississippi Delta blues were more raw and dripping with emotion. Delta bluesmen could make the guitar talk with uncanny speech-like effects, and they delivered their music with a real *punch in the gut!* Of the dozens of important Delta blues musicians, Charley Patton, Eddie "Son" House, and Robert Johnson had the most impact. Between the years of 1923 and 1930 many record companies made field trips to the Delta in search of blues musicians to record. Record company scout Henry C. Speir made a number of discoveries of untapped talent including Charley Patton, Robert Johnson, and Howlin Wolf as well as Skip James. However, most blues musicians never made it out of the Delta or nearby Memphis, Tennessee. Later, the mass migration of African-Americans north to Chicago and other urban areas affected the Delta blues musicians who struggled to adjust to life in the big cities.

Charley Patton (approximately 1881-1943) was considered to be the "father of the Delta blues." Patton started playing the guitar by 1895 against his father's wishes. Patton heard all kinds of music popular in the South at the time such as ballads, ragtime tunes, spirituals, minstrel show tunes, and Tin Pan Alley songs. His other influences included white country music and even some light classical repertory. There was no such thing as the blues yet, at least in the fully formed twelve-measure format. Patten was however, beginning to assimilate elements of the blues in his vast collection of songs. Patton was light skinned, probably of mixed heritage, and therefore, didn't look the part of the typical Delta musician. He was also angry with his father and was abusive to women. His dark moods landed him in jail often but he would go on to inspire just about every blues musician to come after him.

Musically, Patton played with an advanced sense of West African rhythm as he stacked rhythms on top of each other to form a densely layered complexity unlike any of his Delta contemporaries. Although Patton played guitar in a narrow melodic range, his use of microtonal wavering of pitches was evident. Patton didn't always think in terms of chordal harmony, since he didn't often strum full chords on his guitar. The rhythmic flow of his music was strong. He incorporated many one-measure rhythmic patterns influenced by the many drum and fife

---

"Delta blues is a refined, extremely subtle, and ingeniously systematic musical language... bluesmen gave their audience a music they could relate to."

- author Robert Palmer

Rock Hard Fact

Charley Patton often used a slider (slide guitar) when playing blues guitar to imitate his own vocal timbre, diction, and timing.

bands he had heard as a child. He also developed many bass line runs that he coupled with hammered percussive sounds on the body of his guitar. Patton could keep a guitar riff going for half an hour or more and he was an entertaining live performer. Patton's pieces evolved from night to night as he sang about the way in which he lived life.

"34 Blues"
by Charley Patton

Charley Patton recorded "34 Blues" on January 31st, 1934 in New York City on the Vocalion Record label. He performed annually in Chicago but rarely performed outside of the South. The lyrics referred to Dockery, Patton's hometown that was a Delta plantation town. Robert Johnson used the same melody in his tune "Traveling Riverside Blues" and "If I had Possession Over Judgment Day." When Patton sang the lyrics to most of his songs, his powerful voice was said to carry 500 yards without amplification.

Musically, Patton utilizing a simple guitar accompaniment. He strummed chords and utilized single lines to answer each call. Patton's voice, although rough and crude, combined with his percussive approach to create his signature and influential country blues sound. Patton usually kept the melody, guitar patterns, rhythms, and the basic verses of the tune the same while freely injecting new verses. Tunes such as "34 Blues" would evolve from night to night. Muddy Waters and Howlin' Wolf have also recorded versions of "34 Blues." Bob Dylan dedicated his song "High Water (For Charley Patton)," from his 2001 album <u>Love and Thift</u>, to Charley Patton.

Eddie "Son" House (1902- 1988), also from the Delta, was a walking contradiction. He preached his first gospel sermon before the age of sixteen but was convicted of murdering a man at a house party by age twenty. Later, House spent time with Charley Patton and learned much by playing with him. House was not a fancy player, but conveyed a direct and forceful style that moved everyone that heard him. Although his guitar technique was limited, he displayed a strong, gravelly voice that projected a real sense of emotion. House had performed two very powerful blues, "My Black Momma" and "Preachin the Blues" of which the later was very autobiographical. It described the struggle between the church and the devil, an often utilized theme in blues lyrics and a personal source of pain for House. In the early 1940's, House was recorded on location in Mississippi by Alan Lomax for the Library of Congress. House's career went into decline but was later revitalized in the 1960's.

"Preachin the Blues"
reworked traditional blues by Son House

In "Preachin the Blues," House reworked a blues that had been previously played by other Delta blues players. He developed the lyrics to create his own version of the tune. The lyrics explained how House was trying to pray and lead a good life but was being pulled away by women and whiskey, the work of the devil. This theme was much imitated by many artists including Ray Charles. In the lyrics, Son House sang "Oh, I'd-a had religion, Lord, this every day." He repeated the line and then sang "But the women's and whiskey, well, they would not set me free."

"Preachin the Blues" was very personal to Son House. House knew that singing the blues could also function as preaching the blues, which is exactly what he did here. His rhythmic drive combined with an emotional intensity that hit the listener hard. Son House's version of "Preachin the Blues" inspired many future great blues artists from Robert Johnson and Muddy Waters to John Hammond Jr. and Bonnie Raitt.

The blues themes of Son House had a big effect on the early development of the legendary Delta bluesman **Robert Johnson** (1911-1938). Often called the "King of the Delta blues," Robert Johnson developed the blues into a true art form. Robert Johnson was originally from Hazelhurst, Mississippi. He spent most of his childhood in the upper Delta region of Robinsonville. Johnson endured an unsettling childhood with three different stepfathers, often uprooted and given a number of name changes. He became interested in music and began to play the jew's harp and quickly progressed to the harmonica and then to the guitar. One of the first songs he learned on guitar was Leroy Carr's "How Long-How Long Blues." Johnson listened to blues greats Charley Patton, Son House, and Willie Brown to learn the basics of the blues vocabulary. However, when Johnson was still a novice, he was the subject of ridicule by these three bluesmen and he soon disappeared from the Mississippi music scene. When he returned, he was playing at a very high level (see Crossroads profile), displaying stunning guitar technique and singing with an incredible feel. He wandered throughout the Delta his entire career dedicating his life to chasing women, consuming alcohol, and pursuing an endless need to keep moving on.

Robert Johnson at the Crossroads

The legend goes that Robert Johnson made a deal with the devil at a crossroads to obtain his extraordinary musical talent and in return would have only eight more years to live on this Earth. A literal reading of the tune "Crossroads Blues" was a description of Johnson standing at a country crossroads, alone. There was a sense of spookiness describing the crossroads to be dark and very quiet when Johnson waited for the devil to appear. He was not the first to claim to have this supernatural experience but he was its most famous. What probably happened instead, was that Johnson practiced for many hours and listened to many of the popular race records popular at the time. When he returned to the blues scene around a year later, Johnson had made incredible strides as a guitarist, singer, and composer. Son House and Willie Brown were amazed at the progress Johnson had made. He had absorbed their tradition and broadened it enormously by incorporating musical influences from a wide range of sources.

Johnson's songs came out of the already vast repertoire of previous Delta blues singers and was deeply rooted in field hollers, spirituals, and work songs. Blues biographer Robert Palmer recalled that Johnson fused "Ike Zinneman's flowing East Coast style, Leroy Carr's distinctive melodies and chordal figures, and the aggressive single-string picking of Scrapper Blackwell and Lonnie Johnson...He also borrowed heavily from recordings by three more musicians-Kokomo Arnold, Peetie Wheatstraw, and Skip James." #4 Robert Johnson evolved into a stunning guitar player with superior slide technique and virtuosic runs. His revolutionary approach made him sound like a full band. He developed innovative chording and a heavy percussive rhythm with his feet. He also slapped on the body of his guitar which provided a powerful accompaniment for his solo lines. In stunning fashion, Johnson displayed an incredible ability to achieve complete independence of his vocal lines from his guitar accompaniment. The overall effect was a vocal and instrumental sound that sounded like a full band. This brought him to a level never seen before. Musicians were amazed, as the total effect of his blues performances was breathtaking.

Johnson only recorded twenty-nine songs, which is way too little for such a giant. This almost didn't even happen due to the fact that his first recording session was in 1936, only two years before his death. Some of Johnson's classic and often imitated blues were; "I Believe I'll Dust My Broom," "Terraplane Blues," "Love in Vain," and of course, "Crossroads Blues."

"Crossroads Blues"
by Robert Johnson

"Crossroads Blues" was one of twenty-two songs that Robert Johnson recorded for ARC Records over a five day period from November 23rd-27th, 1936. The sessions took place in a hotel room in San Antonio, Texas where two different takes of the song were recorded. This blues in particular showed a darker, more apocalyptic side of Johnson's compositional style. The themes of damnation and redemption were a look into his inner life with all the turmoil and pain he endured. On one level, "Crossroads Blues," has been interpreted as a description of the singer's fear of losing his soul to the devil (in exchange for eight years of supreme talent), although the lyrics don't contain any direct references to Satan. On another level, Johnson was literarily standing at the crossroads in blues history, looking back at his predecessors such as Charley Patton and Son House.

Johnson showed a great sense of elasticity as he freely added and subtracted both beats and entire measures of the standard twelve-bar blues format. Every chorus became an adventure full of unpredictable twists where Johnson truly improvised in the moment. This ability to spontaneously improvise was an inspiration to blues, jazz, and later rock musicians. Johnson showed great rhythmic intensity by hammering and bending a single guitar string, so forcefully that it sounded like an electric guitar, instead of an acoustic. His guitar accompaniment was complex, employing two and three beat figures while he also played driving bass riffs. When Eric Clapton reworked "Cross Roads Blues," he had to closely adhere to the twelve bar form to interact with bassist Jack Bruce and drummer Ginger Baker.

At the end of his life, Robert Johnson moved from woman to woman, town to town, generally trusting no one. Robert Johnson died at the age of twenty-seven (making him the first member of the tragic 27 club which included Jimi Hendrix and Janis Joplin) when he was allegedly poisoned at a juke joint by the jealous husband of a woman Johnson had pursued. Johnson's legacy provided an enormous influence on countless blues and rock musicians. Johnson's guitar riff from his "Dust My Broom" influenced Fleetwood Mac in the 1960's and George Thorogood in the 1970's. The dramatic blues solo phrasing on his "Crossroads Blues" motivated Eric Clapton to rework the song for his band Cream. Robert Johnson also had a profound influence on Muddy Waters, Willie Dixon, Howlin Wolf, B.B. King, Keith Richards, The Rolling Stones, Jimmy Page and Robert Plant of Led Zeppelin, to name just a few. Robert Johnson was inducted into The Rock and Roll Hall of Fame in 1986.

Not all of the important blues musicians were from the Mississippi Delta. **Blind Lemon Jefferson** was an influential blues musician from Dallas, Texas. But Jefferson didn't *just* sing the blues. He worked the street corners and bars of Dallas, Texas singing work songs, hymns and spirituals, and folk songs. Jefferson had an extraordinarily expressive vocal style and his tunes "Match Box Blues" and "That Black Snake Moan" became standards in the repertoire of most country blues musicians all over the South. In the 1920's, Jefferson's country styled blues was responsible for bringing some of the first commercial success to the blues. Between 1926 and 1929, Jefferson recorded more than 100 songs on the Paramount Record label. Jefferson's innovative music combined with Paramount's innovative mail order sales program. This made him their most popular male blues artist. These successful recordings enabled Blind Lemon Jefferson to join Ma Rainey and Bessie Smith (the two most popular female blues singers of the era) in developing a national following.

Some of Jefferson's tunes were the source of both folk and rock tunes by Elvis Presley, Bob Dylan, and The Beatles. Jefferson frequently utilized jazz-like improvisation in his performances. His lyrical content about relationship troubles and homelessness were common experiences of which many southern black men and women could relate. Blind Lemon Jefferson opened the door to commercial viability for early blues artists from all over the South, including the Delta.

From the mid-1940's through the 1950's, at least one quarter of the Mississippi population, including blues musicians, migrated to many urban areas including Chicago, Detroit, New York, Philadelphia, and places as close as Memphis and as far as Los Angeles. However, Chicago became the hotbed for the emerging urban blues style. Many Delta blues musicians made the move including Big Bill Broonzy, Memphis Minnie, Little Walter Jacobs, Elmore James, John Lee Hooker, Lightnin Hopkins, Howlin' Wolf, Willie Dixon, Muddy Waters and later, B.B. King. In Chicago, the emerging style of rhythm and blues and a style called **jump blues** (made popular by Louis Jordan and Lionel Hampton) helped make popular a heavier, more backbeat oriented sound. Bluesman from the Delta were squeezed out that did not adapt to the newer styles. Sonny Boy Williamson #1 (aka John Lee Williamson) was playing with guitar player Robert Nighthawk by 1940. They were adding heavier electric guitar and drumset to Sonny Boy's harmonica sound. Another important musician that helped urbanize the Delta Blues was pianist Sunnyland Slim. His association with Muddy Waters was a key factor in developing Muddy's early career.

McKinley Morganfield (1915-1983) aka **Muddy Waters** was one of the most significant figures in transforming the Delta blues to the urban blues. When Muddy first moved to Chicago in 1943, he thought people only wanted to hear a more modern blues version of his Delta bottleneck blues sound. Muddy met **Phil and Leonard Chess**, the creators of Chess Records, a label that became *the* leading blues record label in the country. Chess Records played a key role in spreading the urban blues across the world, especially in London, England, where we will soon see its effects on many of the early great rock bands. Waters' famous song "Rollin Stone" inspired the name of the successful music magazine *Rolling Stone*, and the name of the superband **The Rolling Stones**, and even the Bob Dylan tune "Like a Rolling Stone." Muddy Waters was inducted into the Rock and Roll Hall of Fame in 1987.

"I tried to copy (Robert) Johnson, but his style of simultaneously playing a disjointed bassline on the low strings, rhythm on the middle strings, and lead on the treble strings while singing at the same time was impossible to even imagine."

– Eric Clapton

Rock Hard Fact

Muddy Waters and his band did not invent electric blues, but they were the first important electric band to use amplification to make the blues more raw and physical.

Willie Dixon (1915-1992) was a bass player and perhaps the greatest blues songwriter of all time. Dixon began his career in Chicago playing bass with the Big Three Trio, which was modeled after the popular Nat King Cole Trio. This led to Dixon playing bass on many early urban blues recordings. His musical knowledge and skillful arranging led him to work as the musical director for Chess records. At Chess, Willie Dixon wore many hats. He led the house band, served as a talent scout, helped develop many of the great recording artists, and oversaw countless recording sessions including sessions by both Chuck Berry and Bo Diddley. Willie Dixon was inducted into the Rock and Roll Hall of Fame in 1994.

The Muddy Water Blues Band and Willie Dixon = urban blues magic

Muddy Waters assembled what may have been the greatest blues band of the urban blues era. The band featured Jimmy Rogers on guitar, Little Walter Jacobs on harmonica, Otis Spann on piano, Elgin Evans on drums, and Willie Dixon on bass (on the recordings-not so much live). Waters cut two important tracks at Chess, "I Can't Be Satisfied" (he originally recorded this in 1941 as "I Be's Troubled" for the Library of Congress) and "I Feel Like Going Home." On these forward thinking tracks, Muddy realized that people still wanted to hear that down home Delta sound but now with the added power boost of a fully electric band. The result was an exciting, powerful blues sound and a key ingredient in the makeup of rock music. Muddy's blues had a heavy rhythmic emphasis and a forceful, danceable beat that stood out from the already popular rhythm and blues style. In 1954, Muddy found a solid backbeat drummer in Francis Clay, who worked with Muddy into the early 1960's. From 1951-1954, Muddy and his band were constantly placing tunes high on the rhythm and blues charts. Even with his great success, Muddy Waters never lost his deep Delta roots and that continued to give him great credibility and depth as an artist.

Willie Dixon may have been the most important musician in the evolution of the urban blues. Dixon was renowned for not just writing a great blues tune, but he would often customize a particular blues to match the personal style of individual artists. Many Dixon tunes were written for the gritty Howlin' Wolf. Others were written for the smoother style of Muddy Waters and yet others for Sonny Boy Williamson #2 or Little Walter. Willie Dixon's genius was his ability to transcend the essence of the blues and combine it with the expressive language of a pop songwriter. This resulted in blues compositions that contained strong melodic hooks. Willie Dixon made frequent use of stop-time riffs, which became part of the rhythmic vocabulary of rock 'n' roll, rhythm and blues, and jazz. When the whole band often phrasing in unison, it sounded something like dah DAH dah dat! This rhythm was featured in the song "Hoochie Coochie Man."

"I'm Your Hoochie Coochie Man"
by Willie Dixon

This classic blues by Willie Dixon was first recorded by Muddy Waters. The tune referred to hoodoo folk magic which dealt with spirituality based on West African culture. It was one of Muddy's first recordings with a full backup band. The tune featured a famous stop time riff that became a standard arranging tool for countless blues and shuffle tunes. "Hoochie Coochie" was a sixteen bar blues that expanded the basic twelve bar format. This expanded form worked well with stop time phrasing where the first eight bars stayed on the tonic before changing chords. It's played as a shuffle in 12/8 time in three full choruses.

Lyrically, "The Hoochie Coochie" man bragged about his good luck and his effect on women. Muddy Waters sang the lines "Don't you know I'm here/Everybody knows I'm here/Well, you know I'm the hoochie-coochie man/Everybody knows I'm here." This song represented Muddy Water's transition to an electrified, yet still traditional Delta based blues sound. The "Hoochie Coochie Man" helped to move the blues forward to the 1950's Chicago blues sound.

Chester Arthur Burnett (1910-1976) aka **Howlin' Wolf** grew up in the Mississippi Delta and was influenced by Charley Patton. He made his way after military service to Arkansas, where Ike Turner discovered him. Wolf recorded at Sam Phillips Sun Studio and his early recordings were released on the Chess label. Wolf moved to Chicago in 1953 and recorded for Chess under the guidance of Willie Dixon. Howlin' Wolf was an electrifying performer and often competed with Muddy Waters on the South Chicago blues scene. Wolf played an aggressive harmonica style and received his name from his yells, moans, and growls onstage. Howlin' Wolf always played with a deep sense of the blues but never really scored many hits on the rhythm and blues charts. Willie Dixon wrote more songs for Wolf than he did for Muddy, especially those with a raw and gritty character. Howlin' Wolf was inducted into the Rock and Roll Hall of Fame in 1991.

"Little Red Rooster"
by Willie Dixon

Written by Willie Dixon for Howlin' Wolf, this is one of the most covered blues by artists as diverse as Big Mama Thornton, Sam Cooke, The Rolling Stones, The Grateful Dead, and many more. Howlin' Wolf first recorded the tune in 1961. Wolf utilized "Little Red Rooster" to display his raw, intense vocal style and his slide guitar playing. The rooster theme was from an early twentieth century folk story in the South where a rooster brought peace to the barnyard. Some interpretations of the song were about an actual rooster in the barnyard. However, most see the meaning of the rooster as representing a woman who was cheating on her man and has not come back home. Many of Willie Dixon's lyrics were ambiguous and had multiple interpretations.

The "Little Red Rooster" recorded version by Howlin' Wolf featured Jimmy Rogers on guitar and the great Willie Dixon on double bass. An important feature of Wolf's version was his distinctive slide guitar performance, accompanied by electric guitarist Hubert Sumlin. Sumlin weaved in and out of the vocal lines and provided the foundation for the song. Also featured on the track were pianist Johnny Jones and drummer Sam Lay. (See the Rolling Stones version in chapter four)

Elmore James (1918-1963) was one of the most influential bottleneck blues guitar players. By 1945, his exciting style introduced musicians in the Delta area to the electric guitar. James used a metal pipe to capture his bottleneck sound, which was often in a falsetto range that matched his voice. James became a favorite of many guitar players such as Stevie Ray Vaughan, Eric Clapton, and B.B. King. Elmore James recording of Robert Johnson's

---

"When you're a kid and you're trying to find your own voice, it's rather daunting to hear somebody like Howlin'Wolf, because you know that you'll never achieve that"

- singer Tom Waits

"I'll Believe I'll Dust My Broom" was shortened to the title "Dust My Broom" and became his signature tune. James collaborated often with **Rice Miller** (1912-1965) aka **Sonny Boy Williamson #2**. It is a mystery how Rice Miller became Sonny Boy Williamson #2 but the original Sonny Boy was named John Lee Williamson. What was not a mystery was the remarkable harmonica playing and radio personality that Sonny Boy #2 developed on the famous King Biscuit Flour Hour blues radio show. This groundbreaking broadcast was heard throughout the Delta and surrounding areas. It was instrumental in bringing the blues to thousands of people throughout the south. Both Elmore James and Sonny Boy #2 deserve much credit for amplifying the Delta blues. Elmore James was inducted into the Rock and Roll Hall of Fame in 1992.

Many other blues artists were true innovators and were also responsible for the development of the urban blues. **John Lee Hooker** (1917-2001) was originally from the Delta but became a mainstay in the Memphis clubs in his thirties. His tune "Boogie Chillen" utilized a one-chord ostinato that extended the guitar boogie-woogie patterns that blues guitar players were copying. Hooker sang in a deep, rich voice that influenced many rock musicians including Canned Heat and George Thorogood. John Lee Hooker was inducted into the Rock and Roll Hall of Fame in 1991.

Aaron Thibeaux Walker (1910-1975) aka **T.Bone Walker** was among the first to use the electric guitar as a solo blues instrument. T. Bone played in the Blind Lemon Jefferson style (T. Bone at one time led Blind Lemon through the streets of Dallas) and developed complex solo guitar lines that filled in between his own vocal phrases. T. Bone's flashy guitar style had an impact on B.B. King, Chuck Berry, and Jimi Hendrix. T. Bone was a strong showman and worked often with jump bands that included a rhythm section and two or more horn players. His style progressed to combine a strong jazz influence with his deep blues roots. T. Bone Walker was inducted into the Rock and Roll Hall of Fame in 1987.

Riley B. King (1925-2015) aka **B.B. King** was born in the Delta and became the greatest champion of the urban blues style. B.B. King came to define the Memphis blues scene with his electric performances. He grew up with a strong gospel influence that can be heard in his vocal and instrumental approach. He first made the rhythm and blues charts with his recording of Lowell Fulson's "Three O'Clock Blues" and later had his biggest hit with "The Thrill is Gone," a huge pop hit in 1970. King's vocal delivery was very soulful and polished. His guitar lines were evolved and were very horn-like which revealed his long time love for big band music. He has won more awards for his blues playing than anyone in music history. B.B. King has long been the true ambassador for the blues and his name is synonymous with the blues genre. B.B. King was inducted into the Rock and Roll Hall of Fame in 1987.

"The Thrill is Gone"
by Roy Hawkins and Rick Darnell and performed by B.B. King

Roy Hawkins recording of "The Thrill is Gone" peaked at number six on the rhythm and blues charts in 1951, but the tune became a major hit for B.B. King. King recorded his version in 1969 on his <u>Completely Well</u> album. His version went to number three on the rhythm and blues charts and crossed over to the pop charts at number fifteen. "The Thrill is Gone" was about moving on from a relationship that had gone bad.

"The Thrill is Gone" was a twelve bar minor blues played with a slow feel that B.B. used to full effect. King utilized a full string section after producer Bill Szymczyk called King at 4:00 am and suggested the addition of string parts. Szymczyk also handled the very polished production on King's recorded version. This helped to bring the blues to a new level of sound quality, often lacking on blues recordings. "The Thrill Is Gone" became B.B. King's signature tune and he always featured it on his thousands of live performances. This song has been covered by Aretha Franklin, Jerry Garcia and David Grisman, Willie Nelson, and many more. B.B. King and Tracy Chapman recorded a duet version of "The Thrill Is Gone" for B.B.'s 1997 album <u>Deuces Wild</u>.

Throughout the history of the country and urban blues there have been countless contributions from hundreds of great blues artists. Space precludes us from discussing all of them including the great blues singers such as Ma Rainey and Bessie Smith whom we associate more closely with jazz. The blues and its great impact on the development of rock music will be a dominant theme moving forward.

Discussion Question

Define the important musical innovations that served to transform the country Delta blues to the urban blues style. Be specific in describing instrumentation and vocal and guitar styles. Cite artists and give examples of important recordings.

Country Music

The country roots of rock music, similar to folk roots, can be traced to seventeenth century immigrants from Europe, particularly The British Isles, Ireland, and Scotland. Immigrants that located to Southern States and the mountains of Appalachia kept strong musical traditions alive. Rhythmic dances such as jigs, reels, polkas, waltzes, hymns, and ballads defined this traditional music. The songs of immigrant settlers were accompanied on acoustic guitars, dulcimers, fiddles, and harmonicas. The African instrument of the banza was adapted by American settlers and developed into the banjo. By the early part of the nineteenth century, the string bass, steel guitar, and autoharp were additional common instruments utilized to accompany simple country songs. When the radio became a luxury in many American homes, early country music became popular throughout the South and eventually the entire country.

By the 1920's, hillbilly music developed a dedicated and growing market throughout the South. One popular radio program was the *Barn Dance Show* in 1925 that eventually developed into the Grand Ole Opry. Nashville, Tennessee became the center of country music where live venues gave promising country stars opportunities to build an audience. Country music developed into a number of sub-genres including; western swing, bluegrass, honky-tonk, and the simple country songs of the early country singer.

The **western swing style** developed primarily in Texas in the 1920's. Early western swing stars were Bill Haley and his Sattlemen band, Tex Williams, Milton Brown, and **Bob Wills and his Texas Playboys.** Western swing was essentially a hybrid between country music and big band jazz. This resulted in a mixture of

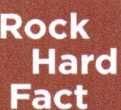

Rock Hard Fact

Gene Autry introduced the first honky-tonk style songs to country music and was the first singing cowboy making his Hollywood debut in 1935.

> "When we went into the New England states, people were talking about the new sound of Flatt and Scruggs, but we had been doing that sound for twenty years."
>
> - Lester Flatt

saxophone, trumpet, and drumset with acoustic guitar, acoustic bass, and the fiddle. Western swing combined the twelve bar blues with syncopated rhythms and stressed the backbeat on two and four. This later evolved further into **hillbilly boogie** with the addition of honky-tonk piano as the style inched closer to early rock 'n' roll and rockabilly. In the early 1930's, western swing gained great popularity. An early star, Bill Haley (covered more in chapter three), started out as a disc jockey and country singer from Michigan. Haley formed The Four Aces of Western Swing and promoted his band on his own radio show. From there, Haley formed The Saddlemen and recorded a number of country songs. The most successful western swing star was Bob Wills. Wills and his Texas Playboys developed a following on the country charts with tunes such as "San Antonio Rose." Wills promoted and toured with his band from Texas to California.

The style of **bluegrass** was an exciting genre of mostly instrumental music that grew out of the tradition of earlier string bands. What was exciting was the emphasis on fast tempos and virtuosic soloists. The most common instrumentation was the fiddle, banjo, acoustic guitar, mandolin, and acoustic bass. The bluegrass style of the 1920's to the 1930's did not have a big an impact on early rock 'n' rock but it would later influence folk rock and country rock.

An important early bluegrass star was **Bill Monroe (1911-1996) and His Bluegrass Boys**. Monroe was a talented bandleader who sang and played the mandolin and guitar. He formed his band in Georgia and moved them to Nashville, where they became part of the Grand Ole Opry. The five-string banjo was a key sound of bluegrass and it was brought to a virtuoso level by **Earl Scruggs** (1924-2002). Scruggs performed with The Blue Grass Boys for three years beginning in 1945 and left to form his own band with singer and guitar/mandolin player **Lester Flatt** (1914-1979). Flatt and Scruggs are known to many for their strong musicianship heard on the theme of *The Beverly Hillbillies* TV series. The song was an immediate hit on the country music charts. Flatt and Scruggs had a twenty-five year musical partnership. They split up in 1969 when Flatt wanted to remain true to his bluegrass roots while Scruggs wished to go in a more mainstream direction. A later bluegrass star was singer and fiddle player Allison Krauss, and her band Union Station. The Charlie Daniels Band is another group that plays with a strong bluegrass influence.

The country singers of the early part of the twentieth-century brought the country song and the image of the country star to a new level. **The Carter Family**, from Tennessee, started a career in 1927 that would see them dominate country music until the early 1940's. Their repertoire included over three-hundred traditional folk, gospel, and blues songs that they recorded for various major record labels. They also recorded many country and bluegrass tunes that would become standards over time. Among them were "Wabash Cannonball," "Wildwood Flower," and "Will the Circle be Unbroken." Their style represented the Appalachian Mountain sound and they sang with a nasal vocal quality accompanied by acoustic instruments. Mother Maybelle Carter was an influential guitar player with a technique that allowed her to pick the melody on the higher strings while strumming chords on the lower strings. Another Carter Family member, Sara Carter, sang in a plain vocal style with a heavy country twang that contributed to their group sound. The simplicity of their mountain songs later influenced The Everly Brothers and Buddy Holly. The Carter Family was inducted into the Country Music Hall of Fame in 1970.

Jimmy Rodgers (1897-1933) became country music's first big star. He became known as "the Father of Country Music." The Mississippi born Rodgers was a railroad worker also known as "the singing brakeman" who assimilated all types of music styles; folk, jazz, blues, Hawaiian music, vaudeville songs, and black work chants. He recorded over one-hundred songs, often African-American blues with a twelve bar form that he learned working on the railroad. He freely fused these songs with hillbilly tunes. Rodgers' unique vocal style, combined with his ability to mix instrument sounds, set him apart from other country artists. On his "Waiting for a Train," he combined his famous train whistle imitation with the dixieland jazz band sound of acoustic guitar, cornet, clarinet, string bass, and steel guitar. Rodgers' signature sound was a vocal style of yodeling in a falsetto voice, gaining him the nickname, "America's Blue Yodeler." His repertoire set the standard for country music. Jimmie Rodgers was recognized and honored by many prominent musicians including Bob Dylan. Jimmy Rodgers was inducted into the Country Music Hall of Fame in 1961 and the Rock and Roll Hall of Fame in 1986.

Country music by now had some very defining musical characteristics. Harmonies were usually simple and triadic. Forms were also simple, often with repeating four or eight bar sections. Basic rhythms were usually played right on the beat. The bass often emphasized the root and fifth. Vocal timbres exhibited a twangy, nasal quality while the lyrics told stories about everyday feelings, people, or events. Songs could be sung either very deadpan and detached or highly emotional, with the performer on the verge of tears.

In the 1930's, another style that emerged in the West was **honky-tonk**. It was named after the bars and saloons, particularly in Texas, where people would listen to music and dance on the weekends. Honky-tonk tunes were loud and upbeat to provide a lively party environment. Often the piano and the acoustic guitar drove a strong dance beat. Honky-tonk harmony was simple and based off of the blues while the form was commonly played in a verse-refrain format. As the style progressed, the electric and steel guitar made more sense for playing honky-tonk than acoustic guitar. An early honky-tonk star was Ernest Tubb. When the style progressed further, major artists such as Hank Williams Sr., Hank Snow, and Lefty Frizzell recorded in the style. Perhaps the biggest beneficiary of honky-tonk was pianist Jerry Lee Lewis (see chapter three) with his driving rhythmic feel and high-energy stage show.

Hank Williams Sr. (1923-1953), from Alabama, was one of country music's giants. Williams started performing in honky-tonks and then went on to establish his career by writing songs for singer Molly O'Day. His early hit, "Lovesick Blues," led to his early performances at the Grand Ole Opry. Hank Williams wrote country songs for his audience that were real and personal. Songs about drinking, lost love, family, and religion connected his music to the everyday person. An incredible slew of hits kept coming with "Honky-Tonkin," "Hey Good Lookin," "Your Cheating Heart," and "I'm So Lonesome I Could Cry." All of these were only a few of his masterpieces.

I'm So Lonesome I Could Cry"
by Hank Williams Sr.

For "I'm So Lonesome I Could Cry," Hank Williams Sr. wrote about his troubled relationship with his wife Audrey Sheppard. The raw emotion and sense of despair Williams sang with was matched by the excel-

---

Rock Hard Fact

Jimmy Rodgers recorded his "Blue Yodel No. 9" with jazz great Louis Armstrong, making him one of the first white stars to work with African-American musicians.

> "I started writing songs after I heard Hank Williams (Sr)"
>
> -Bob Dylan

lent backing musicians on the recording. Hank Williams showed how he could express his intense and personal emotions with what became a country music style trait; a sense of directness and honest storytelling. Recorded in 1949, "I'm So Lonesome I Could Cry" rose to number four on the country charts that same year. Williams, and this song in particular, inspired many of the greats including Bob Dylan who said, "I identified with him. I didn't have to experience anything that Hank did to know what he was singing about…but I could imagine it and it made me sad." #1 Elvis Presley covered "I'm So Lonesome I Could Cry" and often said it was one of the saddest he ever heard.

When Hank Williams Sr. died in 1953, it was way too early. At this time, country music was at an all time high in popularity and Williams' tunes were routinely crossing over onto the pop charts. Williams' personal life was difficult as he battled alcoholism, drug abuse, and marital issues. Many believe that the pain he felt allowed him to express his emotions with genuine conviction. Beginning with his tune "Honky Tonk," a song that sounded very early rock 'n' roll-like, William's songs developed into pop hits for Tony Bennett, Mitch Miller, and Frankie Laine. His music had an enormous influence on Elvis Presley, Carl Perkins, Ray Charles, and Chuck Berry to name a few. Hank Williams Sr. was inducted into the Rock and Roll Hall of Fame in 1987.

The Nashville Sound and the Grand Ole Opry

When rockabilly and Elvis Presley (see chapter three) arrived on the music scene, it was an immediate threat to country music. The sudden popularity of rockabilly stole the young audience of country music. Many country artists jumped onto the rockabilly bandwagon and others saw the opportunity to blend a country sound with the lucrative potential of pop music. In the 1950's and 1960's many country artists altered their sound by making it smoother and more commercial by adding horns, a string section, and background vocals. Country music's hillbilly twangy sound was toned down and the music sounded more contemporary. Guitarist, producer and record executive Chet Atkins (see chapter nine) established the Nashville sound through his playing and musical vision. He played on and produced countless recordings, including those by Elvis Presley, Roy Orbison and Eddy Arnold. The Nashville sound has been popular since the 1960's as country singers appealed to audiences by connecting them to their country roots.

Radio broadcasting in the 1920's was responsible for the growing success of country music. Stars such as Jimmy Rodgers, The Carter Family, and Uncle Dave Macon were brought to New York City to record. As previously mentioned, the radio show called the The Barn Dance Show started in 1925 and soon evolved into The Grand Ole Opry. It is still the longest running radio show in U.S. history. The Opry was dedicated to promoting country music and its history. It featured a mixture of country, bluegrass, gospel, and comedy acts. In the 1930's, the show expanded to four hours and it's directors started to hire only professional musicians. In 1939, it debuted nationally on NBC Radio. The Opry moved to its permanent home, the Ryman Auditorium in 1943. As the Opry developed, so went the country music scene in Nashville. Country music legends Patty Cline, Roy Acuff, The Carter Family, Hank Williams Sr., Bill Monroe, and Minnie Pearl became regulars on the show. The Grand Ole Opry has not lost any steam as it continues to host contemporary country artists such as Dolly Parton, Garth Brooks, Carrie Underwood, Brad Paisley, the Dixie Chicks, and many more. Since 1974, the show has been broadcast from the Grand Ole Opry House in Nashville and it has been occasionally televised.

Johnny Cash (1932-2003) is one of America's most respected musicians of the twentieth century. Cash was a country music icon that sold over ninety million records worldwide. He was a versatile musician that achieved major success as a rockabilly musician (see chapter two) and also wrote songs and sang in gospel, folk, and blues styles. Cash had a deep bass baritone voice and cultivated a persona of a rebellious bad boy image. Some of his signature songs included "Folsom Prison Blues," "I Walk The Line," "A Boy Named Sue," and "Ring of Fire." Johnny Cash's country and gospel themes were about redemption, sorrow, and moral issues. He was known as "the man in black" which he said was about wearing all black in tribute of the many poor and hungry, those affected by drugs, and the forgotten Vietnam War Veterans.

"Hurt"
by Trent Reznor covered by Johnny Cash

Johnny Cash covered songs by a few rock artists toward the end of his life. Originally written and recorded by Trent Reznor, "Hurt" has references to self-harm and heroin addiction. The song has been interpreted to address a man's suicide note or it could serve to describe the struggle he experienced with his depression. In 2002, Johnny Cash covered the song on his album <u>American IV: The Man Comes Around</u>. Reznor's version of his own song was dark and created an eerie mood while Cash's version captured the emotion of despair and pain. Cash utilized a detached delivery to express Reznor's lyrics and therefore, firmly plant his signature on the song.

Cash changed the lyric of "crown of sh**" to "crown of thorns" to reference Christ and his devout Christianity. Reznor was so moved at Cash's version that he said "Wow, I felt like I just lost my girlfriend, because that song isn't mine anymore… It really made me think about how powerful music is as a medium and art form… Somehow that winds up reinterpreted by a music legend from a radically different era and still retains sincerity and meaning-different, but every bit as pure." #2

Johnny Cash starred on his own TV show from 1969 to 1971, where The Carter Family and Carl Perkins were regulars on the show. Cash met June Carter (of The Carter Family) and they married in 1968, forming one of the most famous marriages in country music history. Cash struggled with alcohol and drugs; and for all of the bad boy stories, he never did any significant jail time. He performed many free concerts at prisons and recorded two live albums <u>Johnny Cash at Folsom</u> and <u>Johnny Cash at San Quentin</u>. Cash was also an advocate for the forgotten and oppressed Native American people as he always fought for the poor and neglected. Johnny Cash was inducted into the Country Music Hall of Fame in 1980 and The Rock and Roll Hall of Fame in 1992, among his numerous awards.

We will cover many more country artists in the southern rock and country rock chapter.

> "My doctor tells me I should start slowing it down, but there are more old drunks than there are old doctors so let's have another round"
>
> - Willie Nelson

> "I mean, the genuine roots of culture is folk music."
>
> - John Lydon of The Sex Pistols

Folk Music

The **folk** roots of rock music date back to the earliest American colonists who brought with them a rich tradition of Anglo-Irish-Scottish secular folk songs. Folk music was very simple music of mostly rural origin that was passed down exclusively in an oral tradition. Folk songs underwent constant change as they were retold from generation to generation. These changes included subtle differences in lengths of phrases and forms, rhythms, harmonies and melodies. The ballad was the most common folk medium, usually in strophic form (same music-different lyrics) with stanzas of four lines. Folk music also included work songs, sacred songs, instrumental dance music, and even festive drinking songs. There are at least 300 known British ballads that were brought to America, but the most popular and imitated was the Scottish ballad "Barbara Allen." The Library of Congress Archive of American Folk Songs contains more than 200 transcribed versions of this ballad. Another popular ballad was "The Gypsie Laddie" aka the "Gypsy Davey," well known to most folk singers including Pete Seeger and Woodie Guthrie.

The 1930's saw a strong resurgence of folk music and ethnomusicologists such as John and Alan Lomax visited virtually all parts of America. They recorded and collected 1000's of folk songs, including blues and whatever songs were in a folk musicians' repertoire. This led to an increasing public awareness of singers such as Lead Belly and Woodie Guthrie. A folk song revival was then sparked that delivered hundreds of folk songs into the repertoire of a new generation of folk singers that included Joan Baez, Judy Collins, The Weavers, and the Kingston Trio.

Lead Belly (1888-1949) (aka **Huddie Ledbetter**) was discovered by the Lomax's at a prison in Louisiana where they recorded many of his original folk songs and blues as well as his extensive covers of African-American folk songs. Lead Belly played a twelve-string guitar with a strong rhythmic approach. He also played violin, harmonica, accordion, mandolin, and piano. What made him really unique was that he could sing folk and blues with a rich, powerful voice. His wide repertoire included spirituals, gospel songs, prison songs, pop songs, and of course, hundreds of folk songs and blues. With the help of the Lomax's, Lead Belly moved to New York City where he influenced and collaborated with both Pete Seeger and Woodie Guthrie. Lead Belly's unique voice reached many prominent artists and bands including; Brian Wilson, Bob Dylan, Elvis Presley, Frank Sinatra, The Grateful Dead, and Led Zeppelin who were inspired by his version of the British ballad "The Gallows Pole." Nirvana's Kurt Cobain cited Lead Belly as his biggest influence as well. In 2018, jazz drummer Adam Nussbaum released his album **The Lead Belly Project**, a tribute to the music of this great blues and folk master. Lead Belly was inducted into the Rock and Roll Hall of Fame in 1988.

"Goodnight Irene"
by Lead Belly

Lead Belly sang this song as early as 1908, when he said that he learned it from his uncles. As far back as 1892, singer Gussie Davis sang a song with similar lyrics. By the 1930's, Lead Belly had made the song his own by changing some of the lyrics and changing the rhythm. "Goodnight Irene" told a story about a man's troubled past, and how he was frustrated with his bad relationship with his love, Irene. Lead Belly often performed the song while he was serving various prison sentences, including time served at The Louisiana State Penitentiary.

Musicologists John and Alan Lomax recorded a number of Lead Belly's songs for the Library of Congress, including "Goodnight Irene." Many of Lead Belly's songs covered a wide range of subjects that included racism, prison life, liquor, songs about work, cattle herding, cowboys, and dancing. His lyrics also addressed current events and people in the news such as Howard Hughes, Franklin D. Roosevelt, Adolf Hitler, and many others. "Goodnight Irene," now considered a standard in American popular song, has been covered many times including versions by The Weavers, Frank Sinatra, and by Keith Richards as recently as 2016.

The 1960's brought great unrest to American society over issues of civil rights, drug laws, police brutality, the war in Vietnam, and women's rights. But before this came about, the 1940's saw folk music become a strong force in the social and cultural development of America. The 1950's brought a social awareness of traditional folk music as a force for political and social change. Leading the way were Pete Seeger and Woodie Guthrie, both considered to be the two most impactful folk artists of this time period. They would go on to become *the* most important early 20th century folk songwriters. Another folk singer, **Joan Baez** (1941-) inspired activists and popularized protest music through her powerful voice and strong messages. Baez also was a factor in helping to launch the career of Bob Dylan. She was inducted into the Rock and Roll Hall of Fame in 2017.

The son of a prominent ethnomusicologist, **Pete Seeger** (1919-2014), dropped out of Harvard University to pursue a folk singing career. Seeger was a good banjo player and was in a perfect position to add hundreds of traditional folk songs to his repertoire. He proved to be an important asset by assisting Alan Lomax in documenting numerous folk songs. In 1941, Seeger and Woodie Guthrie formed the Almanac Singers in New York City where the group transformed traditional folk songs with new texts about current political and social issues. In 1948, Seeger went on to form The Weavers, thus creating a harmonized group vocal sound that achieved great popularity. The Weavers sang both traditional folk songs and developed a number of protest songs. The music of both the Almanac Singers and The Weavers were considered controversial, as many right wing politicians believed they were anti-American. Conversely, these left-wing musicians felt a great love for their country and attempted to express it through their songs of protest. Although not a fan of early rock 'n' roll, Pete Seeger was inducted into the Rock and Roll Hall of Fame in 1996.

"Turn!, Turn!, Turn!"
by Pete Seeger

Pete Seeger wrote "Turn!, Turn!, Turn! In the late 1950's. Seeger's lyrics were taken almost verbatim from the book of Ecclesiastes, from the King James Version of the Bible. The Biblical text stated that there was a time for all things including healing and killing and for war and peace. Seeger's version was a call for world peace and he wrote in the closing line, "a time for peace, I swear it's not too late." This line and the song's title were the only parts added by Seeger to the Biblical text. The song was first released in 1962 on the Limeliters' album <u>Folk Matinee</u> and then later on Seeger's album <u>The Bitter and the Sweet</u>. Seeger's lyrics resonated strongly with

---

Rock Hard Fact

Pete Seeger was accused of trying to unplug Bob Dylan's folk-rock band at the Newport Folk Festival in 1965. He claimed that he didn't hate the music but only yelled at the sound crew that Dylan's words weren't clearly audible.

the American public when the Vietnam War began to escalate.

The folk-rock band The Byrds covered the song in 1965 and turned it into an international hit. The Byrds version of "Turn!, Turn!, Turn!" went to number one on the American pop charts. The song was also known to have the oldest lyrics ever for an American song. In The Byrds (see chapter seven) folk-rock version, guitarist Jim McGuinn created a jangly twelve-string Rickenbacker guitar sound that mixed with the Byrds' vocal harmonies, much to the approval of Pete Seeger. Other covers of the song were recorded by Dolly Parton, and Emmylou Harris with Ricky Skaggs for the movie soundtrack of the 2014 film, *The Song*.

Woodie Guthrie (1912-1967) was the most significant American folk singer of the 1930's and 1940's. Born in Oklahoma, Guthrie traveled and performed in almost every state in America where he observed and composed original folk songs about social, economic, and political issues of the day. He was an Okie Walt Whitman who sang about inequality and injustice. Guthrie had a natural ability for internalizing numerous English and Scottish ballads. He often put new texts to many traditional folk songs (many of which were immigrant ballads) that served to transform them into American ballads about American issues. He also learned blues harmonica which supplemented his ability to write guitar melodies and harmonies. As his musical ability evolved, Guthrie's great love for reading would later serve to inform the wide range of topics he would write about. His lyrics became more polished, which shaped his prolific songwriting ability. Countless songwriters have been inspired by Guthrie's impact on American culture. A few included Bob Dylan, Johnny Cash, Bruce Springsteen, Robert Hunter, Joe Strummer, Jerry Garcia, Bob Weir, and many more. Woodie Guthrie was inducted into the Rock and Roll Hall of Fame in 1988.

Woodie Guthrie-A Man of the People

Woodie Guthrie was an advocate for the common man. He knew that his untrained voice gave his music and especially his messages, great credibility. Additionally, he grew to be a good guitar accompanist for his ever-growing folk song texts. Guthrie's 1940 album Dust Bowl Ballads focused attention on the devastating economic effects of the 1930's depression on the American farmer. This recording was considered to be one of the first concept albums. At the time of the dust bowl period, Guthrie joined thousands of Mid-Westerners who migrated to California, all desperate for work and a better way of life. It isn't often that a musician becomes a spokesman for hundreds of thousands of poor and oppressed individuals. Woodie Guthrie was one such musician.

Guthrie served in the military in World War Two. From this experience, he began to compose songs that supported the war cause. When he later wrote songs of war protest, his military background gave him great credibility when he was accused of being un-American. Some of his best-known works were "So Long, It's Been Good To Know You," and "This Land Is Your Land."

In 1940, Woodie Guthrie moved to New York City and lived with Pete Seeger. Guthrie also became friendly with Lead Belly and was a frequent guest on The CBS radio show Back Where I Come From. He used his influence to get an appearance for Lead Belly on the show. Also at this time, Guthrie collaborated with Pete Seeger to compose peace songs for Seeger's newly formed folk-protest group, The Almanac Singers. Guthrie officially joined the Almanac Singers to complete the core members that included Seeger, Millard Lampell, and Lee Hays. Guthrie brought his "heart of America" personality to The Almanac Singers. After Hitler invaded the Soviet Union, The Almanac's and Guthrie wrote many anti-fascist songs. Guthrie went on to write thousands of pages of unpublished poems and prose while he lived in New York. He also wrote his autobiography, Bound for Glory, at this time.

Guthrie spent the last years of his life in a New York City hospital where Bob Dylan was a frequent visitor to his long time mentor. Guthrie, before Dylan, was the American folk singer that was able to truly relate to the common people of America. His more than 1000 original tunes, most of which strongly embody the American spirit, are permanently woven into American life. Songs about fallen heroes, songs of social issues, political unrest, and songs that celebrate America, personify what Woodie Guthrie was all about.

"This Land is Your Land"
by Woodie Guthrie

The composition of "This Land is Your Land" was controversial when Woody Guthrie wrote it in 1940. It's based on the melody of a Carter Family tune "When the World's on Fire." The melody was borrowed from a Baptist gospel hymn called "Oh, My Loving Brother," that The Carter Family had reworked. Guthrie wrote the song while hitchhiking from Los Angeles to New York City. He would often change the lyrics of the verses, as he would apply them to different political activities. Guthrie didn't record the song until 1944, after he had changed the lyrics numerous times. Early performances contained many more verses, that Guthrie paired down for the recording.

Guthrie wrote "This Land is Your Land" as a critical response to Irving Berlin's "God Bless America." Guthrie was tired of the tune (on jukeboxes playing all over the country) and sarcastically wrote "God Blessed America for Me." He then renamed it "This Land is Your Land." Guthrie felt that there should be a tune that championed the poor and hungry whom did not prosper from the American dream. The song has made its way into the repertoire of countless folk singers and specifically that of Bob Dylan, The Kingston Trio, Peter, Paul, and Mary, and The New Christy Minstrels. Pete Seeger and Bruce Springsteen also sang it live in 2009. "This Land is Your Land" is perhaps *the* American folk song!

Discussion Question

If you were a folk singer writing about the social, political, or even ethical/moral issues of today, what would be relevant topics? Would you target any specific groups of people in your lyrical content?

Chapter Two: Elvis Presley and Rockabilly

Rockabilly is a music style that emerged in the 1950's with combined elements of country music, blues, rhythm and blues, honky-tonk, and western swing to create an upbeat musical form that helped to shape early rock 'n' roll. Essentially, it evolved when white singers and instrumentalists from the South were looking to combine the African-American blues with the hillbilly styles of music. The result was fundamentally early country rock, but it was called rockabilly by the record labels. The dominant artist of the rockabilly era was the "King of Rock 'N' Roll," Elvis Presley. In a male dominated field, other significant artists included Eddie Cochran, Carl Perkins, and Jerry Lee Lewis. Another important rockabilly figure was the founder of Sun Records, producer and businessman Sam Phillips. In this chapter, we will examine rockabilly's musical characteristics; it's evolution, it's relationship to early rock and roll, and it's most profound artists and bands.

The rise of Elvis Presley and the genre of rockabilly represent some of the most significant developments in the creation of rock music. The importance that rockabilly music had on early rock 'n' roll was undeniable and unshakable. Paul McCartney impressed John Lennon by knowing the Eddie Cochran song "Twenty Flight Rock" (referencing the fact that The Beatles recorded several Carl Perkins songs), and The Beatles were inspired to take the name The Beatles from the name Buddy Holly's Crickets. These examples reveal that rockabilly music lit a fuse that burned brightly in the creation of rock 'n' roll. It wasn't only The Beatles who drew inspiration from this quickly burning fuse of American angst, rebellion, and musical excitement. In London, The Rolling Stones didn't escape the rockabilly influence either, evidenced by their recording of Buddy Holly's "Not Fade Away." From another part of England there was The Who's exciting cover of Cochran's "Summertime Blues" and Johnny Kidd's "Shakin' All Over."

Rockabilly was around long before Eddie Cochran and Buddy Holly. It was even around before Elvis Presley first popularized the sound of rockabilly with his 1954 recordings "That's All Right," "Blue Moon of Kentucky," and 1955's "Good Rockin' Tonight." But Elvis didn't invent rockabilly. Before Elvis, rockabilly was already being played at local talent contests, modest recording studios, and high school dances throughout the South by groups like The Maddox Brothers and Rose ("The Death of Rock 'n' Roll"), The Collins Kids, ("Beetle Bug Bop"), Johnny Carroll, ("Hot Rock"), and Werly Fairburn ("Everybody's Rockin"). These artists, and others, found a natural combination of Bob Wills and the Texas Playboy's styled western swing, Jimmie Rodgers' southern hillbilly music (later referred to as country), B.B. King's souped up electric Memphis blues, and Meade Lux Lewis' rollicking boogie woogie music. It became known as rockabilly. However, some musicians and writers disliked calling this fledgling music rockabilly, as the hillbilly part came with a negative and backwoods connotation. Many just preferred the term rock 'n' roll.

In October of 1949 a young disc jockey from Memphis' WREC radio station signed a lease for a building at 706 Union Avenue. This man was named **Sam Phillips**, and this building became Sun Recording Studio. In August of 1950, he made the first recordings for his fledgling Phillips record label. That first record was made by one-man-band performer Joe Hill Louis, and was called "Gotta Let You Go." This was the beginning of Sam Phillips' influential career in discovering and

Rock Hard Fact

Rockabilly featured not just male stars. Rockabilly Hall of Fame member Wanda Jackson recorded over twenty albums of country and rockabilly material. She has also been nominated for two Grammy awards.

"The early rockabilly guitarists like Cliff Gallup (with Gene Vincent) and Scotty Moore (with Elvis Presley) were just as important to me as the blues guitarists."

- Jimmy Page

recording music at his Sun Recording Studios. Phillips Records became the home for rockabilly music.

However, Phillips' career didn't begin with rockabilly. He first recorded blues legends like B.B. King (then called Riley King), Howlin' Wolf, and lesser known musicians like "Harmonica" Frank Floyd ("Swamp Root") and Rosco Gordon ("Let's Get High"). Sam Phillips engineered the recordings and he was smart enough to know that he didn't know enough about the record business to continue with his own label. Therefore, Phillips licensed many of his early recordings to bigger record labels like RPM-Meteor in Memphis and Chess in Chicago. In 1951, Phillips recorded what some called the first rock 'n' roll record, Jackie Brenston's "Rocket 88" (which also featured a young Ike Turner, of Ike and Tina Turner fame). It was released by Chess Records, and garnered a good deal of attention, reaching number one on the R&B charts. Eventually, Phillips small self-titled record label became the slightly bigger Sun Records, which meant that even more artists started coming to Sun Studio to record. Blues artists like James Cotton, Willie Nix, and Little Milton were among the many artists who made their first recordings at Sun. There were more popular oriented artists like The Prisonaires ("Just Walking in the Rain"), Rufus Thomas ("Bear Cat" and "Tiger Man"), and Little Junior's Blue Flames ("Mystery Train"). But while many of Sun's artists would go on to become well known, many of their Sun recordings didn't become huge sellers. However, Sam Phillips kept on recording.

Phillips encouraged musical experimentation with his recording artists. When he was recording Warren Smith singing the Roy Orbison composition "So Long I'm Gone," Smith's initial take was in a very predictable traditional country style. It was Phillips who suggested a faster version that almost singlehandedly and instantly created Smith's rockabilly sound. Sam Phillips was responsible for many of the earliest rockabilly records. Phillips recalled those times in the liner notes to the outstanding box set <u>The Sun Records Collection</u> and said, "What I was attempting to do at Sun was to get to a certain area, a certain province, of human emotion. The things that I was exposed to were things that were just kind of laughed at by most people. I didn't set out to revolutionize the world. I wanted to see if what I had thought all of my life-that there was something very profound in the life of people with less means." #1 Phillips slogan for Sun Records was "We record anything, anywhere, anytime."

In July of 1954, Sam Phillips would find out that he was *very* right. That was the date that Elvis, **Scotty Moore** (1931-2016), and **Bill Black** (1926-1965), stepped into Memphis' Sun Studio. They would be listed on their records as "Elvis Presley, Scotty & Bill." That was the day the sound and the popularity of rockabilly came together. But the three musicians weren't novices. Moore and Black had been to Sun earlier to record "My Kind of Carryin' On" with Doug Poindexter and the Starlite Wranglers. And Elvis had already made his television debut in 1955 on the TV broadcast called *The Louisiana Hayride*, plus he had already performed at the Grand Ole Opry.

The King of Rock and Roll, **Elvis Aaron Presley** (1935-1977) was Sam Phillips' most important musical discovery. Elvis embodied the American dream and his life would become the ultimate rags to riches story. His music and lifestyle exerted profound influence on almost every aspect of rock music from the late 1950's until the 1970's. Presley's early sound and musical approach defined the rockabilly style, although later he became much more than just a rockabilly artist. Elvis became a "larger than life" figure for millions of fans worldwide, and his legend is still celebrated with Elvis publications, fan clubs, conventions, videos, books, boxed sets, and every and anything Elvis. Fans from all corners of the Earth still flock to Memphis where tours are given daily at his Graceland estate and the Memphis Sun Studio where his legend began.

Elvis was born in Tupelo, Mississippi in 1935 but the family later moved to Memphis, Tennessee. Growing up in the poor section of Tupelo, Elvis heard rhythm and blues and the Delta blues on the street. A young Elvis developed a strong love of country, blues, and above all, the gospel music that he heard every week at the Pentecostal Church. Elvis found music to be exciting, it gave him a sense of peace that translated into a deep passion for music. For his eleventh birthday, he received an acoustic guitar and sat in with numerous bands on Beale Street in Memphis. Presley listened to the radio daily and heard gospel choirs, jazz, pop, classical, and country (especially the Grand Ole Opry on Saturday nights). Elvis would go to jamborees that were live broadcasts of local musicians. There, he heard other musical styles including African-American field hollers and work songs of farm workers and prisoners from the State Penitentiary, where his father had served a jail sentence. In 1948, The Presleys moved to Memphis. There, he heard more Delta blues and spent much of his time on Beale Street hearing bluesmen Furry Lewis and B.B. King. In Memphis, Elvis felt closer to African-Americans as he shared cultural and financial similarities. He felt out of place in school and surprisingly, did not excel in music. In 1953, Elvis graduated from high school and worked at a number of manufacturing and truck driving jobs.

Because his family was poor, Elvis spent his life trying to become someone special. His father discouraged him from pursuing a career in music, but Elvis had a passion to become a singer. This passion, and his desire to hear how his voice sounded on record, brought Presley to record a few crooning pop songs at Sun Studio. His debut at Sun Records was Elvis and *the trio* ripping through Arthur Crudup's tune "That's Alright (Mama)." Elvis made a good impression on Sam Phillips who was convinced that he had something that would "move both blues and country folk." Their next tunes "Good Rockin' Tonight," "Baby Let's Play House," and "Mystery Train," assured that he was right. Simply put, Sam Phillips finally had recorded some hits.

"That's Alright (Mama)"
by Arthur Crudup

"That's Alright (Mama)" was written and first performed by blues singer Arthur "Big Boy" Crudup. It was also the first single that Elvis Presley released. "That's Alright (Mama)" was recorded in the summer of 1954 and the B-side was another Elvis classic, "Blue Moon of Kentucky." These recordings occurred on Elvis' fifth time in Sam Phillips' studio. On this particular recording session with Scotty Moore and Bill Black, the trio played a few tunes in various styles, but nothing really clicked. The band took a break and Elvis began experimenting with Crudup's obscure blues "That's All Right" in a fast tempo. Bill Black soon joined in on bass, followed by Moore. Sam Phillips took notice and had them stop and quickly begin again once he could get it down on tape.

WHBQ radio in Memphis was the first station to play "That's Alright (Mama)," the day after the trio recorded it. The song quickly caught on in Memphis and just as quickly, it blew up nationally. Local interest was

Before Elvis there was Nothing"

- John Lennon

so strong, that WHBQ's DJ Dewey Phillip (no relation to Sam), interviewed Elvis the very same night the song was aired for the first time. Many felt that "That's Alright (Mama)" was the first ever rock 'n' roll record. Although Johnny Burnette and Fats Domino would take issue with that claim, it was certain that Elvis *had arrived* and the blueprint for rockabilly and the future of rock music was firmly established.

But Elvis didn't do it alone. The recorded sound of Elvis' early trio merged Presley's acoustic strumming, Scotty Moore's fingerpicking telecaster twang, Bill Black's percussive bass with Sam Phillips innovative use of echo. Presley's rhythms were relentless. Moore's guitar solos moved in a different direction than typical blues licks. Black's bass provided an attacking slapping sound (first used by jazz bassist Slam Stewart) that made the drums simply unnecessary. This combination of sounds became the signature sound of rockabilly. Through the integration of these components, the drum-less sound of rockabilly was created. Above all, a song sounded like rockabilly if it was sung with strong emotion, used plenty of echo effects, sounded like Elvis Presley, or was Elvis himself.

The King's Secret Weapons: Scotty Moore and Bill Black

Scotty Moore (1931-2016) developed a ground-breaking guitar sound when he utilized an EchoSonic amplifier that contained a built-in tape loop echo. In Scotty's hands, his Gibson guitar combined with the EchoSonic amp and created a beautiful twang that became the rockabilly sound. Moore first started listening to both country (including bluegrass) and jazz styles. He had a unique finger-picking style like that of country great Chet Atkins, only honed into a rockabilly mode. Additionally, Moore can be credited with helping to bring the electric guitar to play a more dominant role in rock 'n' roll bands, functioning as a lead instrument. After his time with Elvis Presley, Moore worked as a production manager at Sam Phillips Recording Service, supervising all aspects of studio production. In 1964, Scotty Moore released a solo album on Epic Records called The Guitar That Changed the World.

Moore influenced many of the world's great rock guitar players. Keith Richards recalled "Scotty Moore was my icon…Back then, just being able to get through 'I'm Left, You're Right, She's Gone,' that was the epitome of guitar playing. And then "Mystery Train' and 'Money Honey.' I'd have died and gone to heaven just to play like that. How the hell was that done? To this day there's a Scotty Moore lick I still can't get down and he won't tell me. Forty-nine years it's eluded me." #2 Scotty Moore also influenced guitar greats Jeff Beck and George Harrison. He was inducted into the Rockabilly Hall of Fame and The Rock and Roll Hall of Fame in 2000.

Bassist Bill Black began playing the acoustic bass and borrowed his "slap bass" technique from his idol, Fred Maddox. By 1952, Black was working clubs and radio shows with guitarist Scotty Moore. They developed a strong musical relationship performing the country songs of Hank Williams Sr. and Red Foley. When they did their first session backing the young Elvis Presley, Moore and Black were really not very impressed. But when Elvis exploded on the scene, Moore and Black became Presley's backup band and were paid twenty-five percent of his earnings. Onstage, Bill Black had honed his "clowning around" persona. Black and Elvis developed a few on-stage comedy bits.

When Elvis' contract was sold to RCA in 1955, Black went with him. Black played on most of the early Presley classics including "Good Rockin Tonight," "Baby Let's Play House," "Heartbreak Hotel," "Mystery Train," "That's All Right (Mama)," and "Hound Dog." Black was also one of the first bassists to use the Fender Precision Bass in popular music (with Elvis on "Jailhouse Rock"). The trio later was billed as "Elvis Presley and the Blue Moon Boys." The chemistry of Scotty Moore and Bill Black (and later drummer D.J. Fontana) was pure and simple. Bill Black was inducted into the Rock and Roll Hall of Fame in 2009.

The Elvis, Moore, and Black trio would go on to record eighteen more tunes with at least six of them being pure rockabilly, while the others were more in a pure country style. When "That's All Right (Mama)" was released, the flip side was the Bill Monroe classic "Blue Moon of Kentucky." In the Elvis version, the trio converted Monroe's bluegrass song into a rockabilly pop tune. "That's All Right (Mama)" was a powerful statement of a white artist combining black and white style characteristics on an old blues song, thus crossing racial lines in a controversial way that had never been done before. "That's All Right (Mama)" featured Elvis' dynamic voice, sexual energy, and hard driving rhythmic feel. As Phillips had predicted, Elvis captured the essence of both country and the blues, and his music spoke directly to a southern black and white audience.

Presley's Sun singles were all blues songs mixed with country elements and each sold progressively more, from "That's All Right (Mama)" to the last Sun single "Mystery Train." Elvis refined his highly personalized vocal style with hiccups, intervallic leaps, and drawn-out syllables, to create a sense of desperation that mixed perfectly with the instrumental accompaniment of the band. Presley had a strong sense of rhythm that worked well with Moore and Black's frequent use of stop time, and call and response phrasing that they had borrowed from the blues.

"Mystery Train"
by Little Junior Parker

Elvis' cover of Little Junior Parker's "Mystery Train" achieved a balance between country and the blues. Parker had recorded "Mystery Train" at Sun two years prior, but Elvis' version was different. Presley avoided using a saxophone, which was a sound that could be heard on many typical 1950's rhythm and blues tunes. Elvis' version also moved even faster than Parker's, and Elvis increased his vocal density from verse to verse. On "Mystery Train," it had all come together. Elvis, Scotty, Bill and Sam had perfected Elvis' rockabilly sound.

"Mystery Train" varied the standard blues progression by initially using the IV chord. The chord progression was a IV-IV-I-I phrase that was repeated, until a V-IV-I-I phrase was played with a double time feel. "Mystery Train" placed number one on the country charts and stayed there for forty-six weeks. RCA producer Peter Guralnick realized that the Sun recording sessions (including "Mystery Train") produced some of the greatest recording experiences in rock music history. Guralnick said, "The sessions are like these concentric circles, where Elvis and the musicians just wander around and the whole idea is for Elvis to get to that point where he's free. He'll be honing in on something that he can't

Rock Hard Fact

Elvis loved to collect Police badges from every city where he performed. He would sometimes dress in a police uniform and patrol the Memphis freeways wearing one of his badges.

really define and yet when he gets it, the feeling is what defines it. It's nothing to do with a technical perfection... He knows when he had that feeling and that feeling was a loose spontaneity." #3

Eventually Presley's drum-less sound of early rockabilly would be explored to its fullest, and Elvis added drummer D.J. Fontana. Fontana's drumming created yet another level of excitement for rockabilly to explore. Levon Helm, drummer of The Band, recalled Fontana's impact of "building up solos, riding the solos in, and riding them out again...He (Fontana) had incredible technique and fast hands...he played like a big-band (jazz) drummer-full throttle." Now Elvis had a new musical foundation, and he made the most of it. Helm concluded by saying, "D.J. set Elvis free!" #4 It was the band of Elvis, Scotty Moore, Bill Black, and D.J. Fontana who would appear on national television twelve times; six times on *The Jackie Gleason Show*, twice on *The Milton Berle Show*, and three times on T*he Ed Sullivan Show*. D.J. Fontana was induced into the Rock and Roll Hall of Fame in 2009.

However, Elvis and his band weren't the only musicians pushing the boundaries of the rockabilly tradition, and garnering attention. Rockabilly was gaining in national popularity thanks to the same musicians that would create some of the first rock 'n' roll. Many of these musicians would first inspire Elvis, and then ride the musical wave that Elvis Presley created. Artists and songs such as; Buddy Holly's "That'll Be the Day" and "Peggy Sue," Gene Vincent's "Be Bop-A-Lula," Carl Perkins' "Blue Suede Shoes" and "Everybody's Trying To Be My Baby," " Roy Orbison's "You're My Baby," Johnny Cash's "I Walk The Line," and Jerry Lee Lewis' "Whole Lotta Shakin' Goin On" served to continue the musical journey of rockabilly.

Discussion Question

Elvis Presley wasn't the first rockabilly artist but he did become it's most popular and enduring. What were the most important factors in Elvis' long-term success? Be specific and use examples.

Before Elvis Presley, Scotty Moore, Carl Perkins, and Buddy Holly (see chapter three) made the guitar the primary instrument of rockabilly, it was the pianists that created the musical excitement in music. The primary rockabilly pianist was **Jerry Lee Lewis** (1935-). Lewis was a product of the long tradition of the boogie-woogie piano style that originated in Texas and Louisiana. This sound began as far back as 1870 with pianists such as Pine Top Smith, Albert Ammons, James P. Johnson, and Jelly Roll Morton playing songs such as "The Fives," "Tin Roof Blues," "Chicago Stomp," and "Pinetop's Boogie Woogie." Through disciples like Lewis, and later rock 'n' roll and blues pianists such as Johnnie Johnson, Otis Spann, Fats Domino, and Little Richard; this rowdy piano style became an important sound in rockabilly and rock 'n' roll. The boogie-woogie piano style even influenced guitarists such as Bill Haley, Chuck Berry, and John Lee Hooker.

"Great Balls of Fire"
by Otis Blackwell and Jack Hammer

"Great Balls of Fire" was co-written by Otis Blackwell, a prolific songwriter who wrote numerous hits for Elvis Presley. It would become one of the best selling singles in music history. Jerry Lee Lewis originally recorded it at Sam Phillips' Sun Studio in the fall of 1957. Lewis used bassist Sidney Stokes and an unknown session drummer. The song was popular across the charts, reaching number two on the rock charts, number three on the R&B charts, and number one of the country charts.

Musically, "Great Balls of Fire" was filled with sexual innuendo with lines like "let me love you like a lover should," which turned a few heads back in the South in 1957. Lewis grew up in a religious home and his behavior and song lyrics were a constant source of conflict. Jerry Lee Lewis played with a reckless abandon and his driving boogie-woogie piano skills were on full display on this song. "Great Balls of Fire" was one of the most intense of the early rock 'n roll tunes. Jerry Lee Lewis' life story was portrayed by actor Dennis Quaid in the 1989 film *Great Balls of Fire*. In the film, Lewis shocked many when he set the piano on fire.

Like Elvis, Jerry Lee Lewis (aka "The Killer") also started his recording career at Sun Records. Beginning in 1956, Lewis had an early run of success that began with his recording of Ray Price's composition "Crazy Arms." Jerry Lee continued with a string of hits including; "End of the Road," "Whole Lotta Shakin' Going On," "Great Balls of Fire," "Breathless," and "High School Confidential." All of Lewis' Sun recordings sizzle with musical excitement and a wild nature that no other musician could match. Jerry Lee earned his nickname, and when it came to performing electrifying music, Jerry Lee Lewis was *The Killer*. Unfortunately, Lewis' life was marred with controversy. Many of his issues stemmed from an early marriage to an underage woman who also happened to be his cousin. Amid all of the unrest in his personal life, Lewis managed to record a rock 'n' roll masterpiece. In 1964, producer Siggi Loch set up his recording equipment at the Star Club in Hamburg, Germany. The result was a seminal live recording in which Rolling Stone Magazine stated, "Live at the Star Club, Hamburg is not a recording, it's a crime scene. Jerry Lee Lewis slaughters his rivals in this 13 song set." #5 Many consider this recording to be one of rock music's best live recordings of all time.

As well as being an essential solo artist, Lewis was also a vital contributor to many other artists' recordings. One of these sessions was particularly memorable. It was while Lewis was playing piano on Carl Perkins' song "Matchbox," that Elvis and Johnny Cash stopped by Sun Studio to say hello. Suddenly, Sam Phillips was witnessing history. The impromptu gathering of Carl Perkins, Jerry Lee Lewis, Johnny Cash, and Elvis Presley all in the studio at the same time led to probably the most famous jam session in music history (see Million Dollar Quartet profile). Phillips quickly called some of the local press and demanded that the tape recorders be turned on.

The Million Dollar Quartet

The Million Dollar Quarter happened by chance on December 4th, 1956, when a recording session at Sun Studios for Carl Perkins turned into one of the most famous jam sessions of all time. Perkins, accompanied by his brothers Jay and Clayton and drummer W.S. Holland, were recording new materi-

---

Rock Hard Fact

Jerry Lee Lewis did on at least one occasion set his piano on fire using a Coke bottle filled with gasoline by dousing the piano and then setting it on fire during a performance.

al on the heels of Perkins' recently successful "Blue Suede Shoes." Sam Phillips was looking to augment Perkins' sound by bringing in new sensation pianist Jerry Lee Lewis, not yet known outside of the Memphis area. Sometime later that afternoon (after Perkins and company had recorded some tracks), Elvis Presley walked into the studio (formerly a Sun artist and now with the RCA label). Elvis listened to some of Perkins' earlier takes and then sat down at the piano and soon the jam session began. Johnny Cash arrived at the studio at some point, although he claimed to be there much earlier to hear the Perkins' recording session. The recording engineer that day was Jack Clement who quickly set up to record this historic event. Elvis left briefly and Lewis pounded away on the piano but when Elvis returned, the four legends began to play and sing snippets of gospel songs that they had all grown up singing. Elvis, by now internationally famous, was the focal point of the session.

During the session, Sam Phillips called the local newspaper and Bob Johnson, the paper's entertainment editor, went to the studio. He later wrote an article about the event and used the headline "Million Dollar Quartet." In the article Johnson said that the quartet of Carl Perkins, Jerry Lee Lewis, Johnny Cash, and Elvis Presley had a million dollars worth of talent. As the session progressed, which would not be released until 1980, the members of the quartet took turns singing and playing guitar and piano. Presley was heard imitating country singers (Hank Snow and Bill Monroe), and even imitated soul singer Jackie Wilson. They also played the country songs of Bill Monroe, Ernest Tubb, and Gene Autry. The quartet jammed through some current popular country and gospel songs of the day and told stories. They quickly segued between tunes, and rarely completed an entire song. Upon close examination, the recordings showed Cash's involvement to be minimal (legend has it that he slipped out after the press arrived to get some shopping done). But that doesn't detract from this amazing musical happening that could be called music's first super-group. However, there was no super-group marketing plan or record company scheme to make money.

In 1969, Shelby Singleton bought Sun Records from Sam Phillips. He searched the Sun catalogue to explore its depth, listening to more than 10,000 hours of tape. Singleton had also licensed much of the Sun catalogue to the British Charly label for reissue in Europe. Singleton soon realized that a Million Dollar Quartet album with seventeen tracks (mostly the gospel oriented tracks) was previously released in 1980. In 1990, this album was replicated by RCA and released as Elvis Presley-The Million Dollar Quartet. The Million Dollar Quartet was just a group of southern musicians who loved the same music and had great respect for each other. They were simply playing and singing the music that they all loved. The recordings showed Elvis in a rare moment. He was relaxed and in his most natural musical environment. Elvis would later say that he was most happy when he could simply return to his first real love, gospel music.

Rockabilly guitarist, singer, and songwriter **Carl Perkins** (1928-1958) was called "The King of Rockabilly." Perkins was both inspired by, and inspiring to, Elvis. Perkins' songs were recorded by everyone from Elvis Presley and The Beatles, to Ricky Nelson and Jimi Hendrix to George Thorogood and the Destroyers. He even co-wrote the song "Champaign, Illinois" with Bob Dylan. Along with Scotty Moore, Carl Perkins' guitar playing defined the sound of rockabilly. Their use of finger picking and (traditional) guitar imitations of the pedal steel guitar created new guitar timbres. Perkins described the sound of rockabilly this way, "Rockabilly is all about conflict- between rural and urban, between the headfirst sin of Saturday night and the heartfelt repentance of Sunday morning." #6 While Perkins was a gifted country singer and composer (as heard on his tune "Turn Around"), his rockabilly music was his most popular. It was Perkins who wrote "Blue Suede Shoes" (popularized by Elvis), "Everybody's Trying To Be My Baby," "Dixie Fried," and the rockabilly anthem "Matchbox." Perkins' final recording was called Go Cat Go and included duets with Paul Simon, Bono, Tom Petty, and John Fogerty. Perkins was inducted into the Nashville Songwriters Hall of Fame, the Rockabilly Hall of Fame, and the Rock and Roll Hall of Fame in 1987.

"Blue Suede Shoes"
by Carl Perkins

Carl Perkins recorded "Blue Suede Shoes" at Sam Phillips Sun Studio. He was on his way to perform it on national TV when he was in a serious car accident that killed his brother. "Blue Suede Shoes" was released in early 1956 and quickly went to number two on the pop charts. This was the first song to ever hit the pop, country and rhythm and blues charts at the same time. The success of the song put Perkins in great demand for live performances. Elvis Presley's version of "Blue Suede Shoes" was also a huge hit. Elvis shortened Perkins' intro by taking out the pauses after "one for the money" and "two for the show." Perkins' "Blue Suede Shoes" also influenced The Beatles and Johnny Cash.

Carl Perkins wrote "Blue Suede Shoes" after he saw a man get upset when his date scuffed up his shoes while they were dancing together. He took the intro lyric "one for the money, two for the show, three to get ready," etc... from a 1953 Bill Haley song called "Whatcha Gonna Do?" Perkins achieved an authentic rockabilly sound and was very musical in how he phrased the lyrics with short pauses. He employed a number of musical ideas including chords with added ninths and suspensions and he also effectively used stop time. Perkins played an electric hollow body guitar and his band instrumentation featured classic rockabilly acoustic guitar, acoustic bass, and drumset. He used a fair amount of syncopated rhythms and could anticipate chords with his harmonic rhythm. Usually played in A major, "Blue Suede Shoes" utilized basic I, IV, and V chords throughout. Perkins developed a crosspicking approach where he repeated three-note patterns. The accented notes of each pattern would sometimes fall on the beat or off the beat.

More than Carl Perkins, **Johnny Cash** (1932-2003) defined rockabilly as the conflict between rural and urban life. The life of "The Man in Black" (as Cash was called) was filled with personal conflicts and musical duality. The subject of his songs often walked the line between moral shortcomings and spiritual redemption. A musically diverse career led Cash to be elected to the gospel, Rock and Roll, and Rockabilly Halls of Fame. Throughout his long career he released nearly 100 records, and collaborated with musical legends from Willie Nelson to Tom Petty and the Heartbreakers to U2. Like most of the rockabilly greats, Johnny Cash's career began at Sun Records with Sam Phillips behind the glass. Cash remembered his experience at Sun while talking to Robert Hilburn, "Sam didn't have a clock in the studio. He didn't

> "Compassion is something I have a lot of, because I've been through a lot of pain in my life"
>
> - Johnny Cash

make me feel like I was spending anybody's money by just playing new songs. After an hour or two, he'd say, 'OK, what else you got? Let's keep going till we get your best. I loved that in a producer. That's what Sam did with all of us at Sun. He tried to find the uniqueness in each of us." #7 This quote says as much about Cash as it does about Phillips. And it says a lot about the familial musical scene that created so much great music at Sun Studios. Johnny Cash was Sun Records' most consistent and most prolific artist. He was also the first Sun artist to release a long-playing album. Cash eventually left Sun Records due to his insistence to record a gospel record.

Cash was known for his deep religious beliefs, and his deep baritone voice. Instrumentally, he could create a rhythmic guitar effect that simulated the rhythmic clattering of a passing train. This effect was achieved by weaving a dollar bill through the guitar strings to deaden them while strumming the guitar in a normal fashion. Like bassist Bill Black's rhythmic slapping, this guitar technique eliminated the need for a drummer. And like Elvis, Cash's early group (called Johnny Cash & the Tennessee Two) didn't include a drummer. You can hear this effect in Cash's 1956 Sun Records singles "Get Rhythm" and the seminal "I Walk The Line." Believe it or not, there are no drums on either of these recordings, and what is heard in their place is the signature boom-chicka-boom dead string strumming.

"Big River"
by Johnny Cash

"Big River" was one of Johnny Cash's great masterpieces. Cash read an article about himself with the headline stating, "Johnny Cash Has the Big River Blues in His Voice." This inspired Cash to write a rockabilly/country song about a man who was attracted to a woman and her irresistible southern drawl. He pursued her down the whole length of the Mississippi River and missed her at every turn. "Big River" was a story that began at the top of the Mississippi, in St Paul, Minnesota, and ended up in New Orleans. Cash wrote with an intuitive and refined sense of narrative and language. He created a cinematic landscape. It's essentially a piece of American history and part of the legacy of his family and country.

Musically, "Big River" achieved the classic rockabilly sound and feel. Cash originally envisioned the tune as a slow blues. But Sam Phillips recorded Cash at his Sun Studio and approached the song with an uptempo rockabilly attitude. Cash recorded with guitarist Luther Perkins (who played an electrifying solo) and acoustic bassist Marshall Grant. Johnny Cash performed the song with the outlaw country supergroup The Highwaymen, of which he was a member. Bob Dylan thought that "Big River" was an excellent piece of songwriting, noting that Cash was great at giving life to inanimate objects in his lyric writing.

Again, like Elvis, Cash would later add a new texture to his music by adding a drummer to transform The Tennessee Two into The Tennessee Three. Cash's drummer, W.S. Holland, is often referred to as the first country drummer. He came to prominence with Carl Perkins and was the drummer for the Million Dollar Quartet jam session. After joining Cash, Holland would remain for most of Cash's career. During his lifetime, Johnny Cash released disparately themed records such as My Mother's Hymn Book, Johnny Cash Live at San Quentin, Bitter Tears: Ballads of the American Indian, and Johnny Cash Live at Folsom Prison. These contrasting themes and settings could only scratch the surface of Cash's varied musical persona. Cash's musical duality even manifested itself in his chart successes. When his song "Ring of Fire" reached number one on the country charts, it also entered the top twenty on the pop charts. Cash's duality even came to the forefront in his outlaw image. Although Cash was a devout Christian, he was arrested and landed in jail seven times. However, Johnny Cash never spent more than one night in jail, and never served a prison sentence. As his song, and the movie about his life was called… Johnny Cash *walked the line*.

In 1965 Johnny Cash and his wife (musician June Carter Cash) appeared on Pete Seeger's TV show *Rainbow Quest*, and the experience must have been a positive one. Johnny Cash's outlaw image made him a perfect candidate for television roles. Throughout his career he appeared in several TV shows such as *The Partridge Family*, *Columbo*, and *Little House on the Prairie*. In the late 1960's and early 1970's, Cash even hosted his own television show called *The Johnny Cash Show* in which his guests included everyone from Louis Armstrong to Ray Charles to Derek and the Dominoes and Bob Dylan. Cash would even appear on, and write the liner notes for, Bob Dylan's Nashville Skyline record.

Like Dylan, Cash wrote poetic and meaningful lyrics that often took on social and institutional injustice. Through his activism, he spoke for the incarcerated, Native Americans, and peace. In 1997's *Cash: The Autobiography*, Johnny Cash explained his man in black image stating, "I wore 'black' on behalf of the poor and hungry, on behalf of 'the prisoner who has long paid for his crime,' and on behalf of those who have been betrayed by age or drugs…with the Vietnam War as painful in my mind as it was in most other Americans, I wore it 'in mournin'' for the lives that could have been…Apart from the Vietnam War being over, I don't see much reason to change my position…The old are still neglected, the poor are still poor, the young are still dying before their time, and we're not making many moves to make things right. There's still plenty of darkness to carry off." #8

Because of the attention that Elvis' initial success with Sun Records garnered, legends such as Jerry Lee Lewis, Carl Perkins, and Johnny Cash received the attention that they deserved. Elvis opened the door, and many musicians walked through it. However, it wasn't only the household names that deserved fame. Warren Smith's "Ubangi Stomp," Bill Justis' "Raunchy," Roy Orbison's "Ooby Dooby," and Charlie Rich's "Lonely Weekends," were important songs by prominent artists that helped create and ride the rockabilly wave.

Elvis' quick Sun Records success drew the attention of the major record labels. In 1956 Elvis signed with RCA records. He was 25 when he did his first RCA session in Nashville. Elvis' appearance on his first RCA record cover with a guitar hanging around his neck, thrust the guitar to the forefront of rock 'n' roll. His music and image placed rock 'n' roll into the mainstream of popular culture. Beginning with the hit "Heartbreak Hotel" and the film *Love Me Tender*, Elvis began 20 years of hit recordings, TV specials, and feature films.

"Heartbreak Hotel" quickly went to number one on the pop and country charts and number five on the R&B charts. With the support of the RCA songwriting team, Elvis focused on more commercial songs. The hits didn't stop: "Blue Suede Shoes," "Don't Be Cruel," "Love Me Tender," and "Heartbreak Hotel" came quickly. In 1956 alone, Presley's albums sold at a record pace with eleven singles, eight EP's, one double EP, two albums, a movie, and a ton of Elvis souvenirs. With Elvis' good looks, sincerity and good manners, he charmed the public

---

Rock Hard Fact

Even thought Johnny Cash could have his dark side, he also made a recording of the entire New King James version of the New Testament of the Bible.

and became the obsession of thousands of teenage girls. However, some critics denounced his performances, behavior, and music. But this only worked in Presley's favor, as Elvis and rock 'n' roll rose to even greater popularity. After a June 1956 performance on *The Milton Berle Show*, a national controversy exploded when adults were outraged and teenagers were thrilled by Elvis' raw sexuality onstage. Elvis was often filmed from the waist up but the talent, good looks, and undeniable charisma always came through.

"Heartbreak Hotel"
by Mae Boren Axton, Thomas Durden, and Elvis Presley

"Heartbreak Hotel" was the first song Elvis released on his new label, RCA. It reached number one on the country charts and number three on the R&B charts and became Presley's first million selling single. The song was inspired about the suicide of a lonely man who jumped from a hotel window. Mae Boren Axton first offered the song to a popular singing duo, The Wilburn Brothers. However, they turned it down, citing its strange and morbid theme. Axton then showed the song to Elvis at a country music convention in Nashville. Elvis was eager to record it and did so in the winter of 1956 with his band, The Blue Moon Boys (Scotty Moore, Bill Black, and D.J. Fontana). The band was augmented with pianist Floyd Cramer and the legendary guitarist Chet Atkins.

Musically, "Heartbreak Hotel" was built on an eight-bar blues progression. RCA was trying to replicate the sound of Presley's Sun recordings by utilizing heavy reverb on the track. Problems arose in the studio because Elvis always moved around when he sang. RCA producer Steve Sholes insisted that Elvis stay still and sing directly into the microphone. Sholes re-miked the whole studio to allow Presley's voice and guitar to be picked up from anywhere in the room. Now Elvis could move freely. Presley did not write "Heartbreak Hotel," but was credited as a co-writer when Colonel Parker conned Axton into giving up a third of the songs' royalties. Elvis was excellent at interpreting songs. For "Heartbreak Hotel," Elvis (functioning like a producer) changed the tempo, some of the lyrics, the phrasing, and certain elements of the overall sound.

Elvis had a new manager named Colonel Tom Parker and a new emphasis on developing pop songs. He was also trying to cultivate a more wholesome image. By 1957, Elvis Presley was the most famous man in the world, and the undisputed "King of Rock 'N' Roll." He embraced his newfound role of superstar. Elvis flew on private jets, had a fleet of cars, and bought a Memphis estate which he named Graceland. This became the headquarters for the Elvis machine. But in 1958, Elvis was drafted into the U.S. Army. During his military service, RCA kept his popularity high. They released a steady stream of already recorded, yet un-heard, music until Elvis would return home from the service in 1960. While Elvis was away fighting for his country, there was another budding teen idol that was ready to fill the musical void.

Rockabilly's popularity, influence, and rebellion had continued with the emergence of guitarist and singer **Eddie Cochran** (1938-1960). The Cochran family moved from Minnesota to a suburb in Los Angeles when Eddie was fourteen years old. He left school in 1955 and teamed up with Hank Cochran. Undeterred by not being related, they formed a band called The Cochran Brothers. The duo played country music and mostly covers of Hank Williams Sr. and Jimmie Rodgers. Eddie became very infatuated with the sound and style of Elvis Presley, although he never wanted to sound like him. The Cochran duo added some rockabilly to their repertoire and even unsuccessfully auditioned for Sun Records.

In 1955, Eddie met songwriter/drummer Jerry Capehart and now the two Cochrans formed a trio with Capehart. Their sound became increasingly more rockabilly when Eddie's lead guitar combined with acoustic bass, strong piano, and drums. The vocal lines alternated between the Cochrans. In 1956, the Cochran trio split up as Hank wanted to pursue a pure country style and Eddie was going in a rockabilly route. In October of 1956, Eddie Cochran signed with Liberty Records and had a hit with "Sittin In The Balcony." Cochran's other early hits included; "Skinny Jim," "Twenty Flight Rock," "C'mon Everybody," and "Summertime Blues." They prompted his appearance in movies such as *The Girl Can't Help It* and *Untamed Youth*. "Summertime Blues" revealed Cochran's individuality and connected his image to his growing fan base.

What set Eddie Cochran apart was his strong sense of rhythm. He was able to get the instrumental parts of his songs to rhythmically interlock, resulting in infectious grooves. Cochran's sound was defined by his distinctive voice, electric bass, acoustic guitar, and a variety of percussion sounds that included rim shots, loose snares on the snare drum, tambourine and handclaps. He was all about the music, often foregoing guitar solos, even thought he was a talented guitar player. Cochran was also a pioneer in the use of studio effects, becoming one of the first to experiment with echo and reverb. He did many sessions as a guitarist, bassist and producer. At what would prove to his last studio session in January of 1960, Cochran was backed by two members of Buddy Hollies' Crickets, Sonny Curtis on guitar and Jerry Allison on drums.

Eddie Cochran had it all. He was an influential guitarist who appeared on other people's records, a teen idol movie star, a popular bandleader, and talented composer. His success led to extended touring, even to Australia with Gene Vincent and Little Richard. But it was a short-lived stay at the top. In 1959, three of Cochran's innovative rock 'n' roll peers were killed in a tragic plane crash. Buddy Holly, Richie Valens, and The Big Bopper were among the creators of early rock 'n' roll (see chapter three), and their loss hit Cochran hard. Eddie Cochran would die the very next year (1960) in a car accident in the United Kingdom. Eddie had been on his way back to America after a very successful tour with Gene Vincent, who was badly injured but survived the accident.

"Summertime Blues"
by Eddie Cochran and Jerry Capehart

Eddie Cochran's record label was trying to turn him into a crooning teen idol when "Summertime Blues" was first released as a B-side to the ballad "Love Again." On "Summertime Blues," Cochran played all of the guitar parts and sang both the vocal and bass vocal parts. Capehart and Sharon Sheeley played the handclaps, Connie Smith was on bass, and session great Earl Palmer was on drums. This was Cochran's biggest hit, making the top of the pop charts in the summer of 1958. "Summertime Blues" was a powerful, direct, and natural musical statement that contained the essence of rock 'n roll. It represented Cochran as a spokesman for life as a teenager; the parties, summer jobs, cars, weekends, and the opposite sex. Just like Chuck Berry, Eddie Cochran was an authentic voice for the desires and pressures of being a teenager in the 1950's.

> "Had Eddie lived, he would have probably been as important a name in the industry as you could really mention today"
>
> - Jerry Capehart

Rock History - the Musician's Perspective

> **Rock Hard Fact**
>
> "Be-Bop-A-Lula" was the first record Paul McCartney ever bought and he performed it in 1991 on his MTV Unplugged appearance.

There were many cover versions of the tune including; versions by The Beach Boys (1962), American rock band Blue Cheer (1968), and the most famous by The Who (1970). "Summertime Blues" was a staple of The Who's live performances and they recorded at least two studio versions. It came to stand for rebelliousness itself as other artists that wanted a more rebellious image would record it including; Joan Jett, Van Halen, and T Rex. George Harrison cited "Summertime Blues" to be one of his main influences. Harrison carried a picture of Cochran in his wallet.

Another important figure in rockabilly was **Gene Vincent** (1935-1971). Born and raised in Virginia, Vincent made his best known recordings in Nashville. He toured extensively in America, Europe, Africa, Canada, Japan, and Australia. His greatest success came at the beginning of his career when rockabilly was at its peak. In 1952, Vincent joined the Navy but three years later, he was recovering from a motorcycle accident in the hospital. It was there that he wrote his signature tune "Be-Bop-A Lula." In 1956, Vincent formed his backing band, The Blue Caps, and they secured a recording contract with Capital Records. His repertoire included covers of country and rhythm and blues hits. Gene Vincent had a voice that was expressive and musically flexible enough to create much inflection. He often exaggerated his southern accent and his pronunciation was influenced by Elvis Presley.

Vincent was able to create an image of a tough guy who was wild and did whatever he wanted regardless of society standards or the wishes of a girlfriend. This image of a guy with a mean streak that raced cars and lived fast appealed to a mostly young male audience. Gene Vincent had just three more hits that made the pop charts after "Be-Bop-A-Lula." In 1960, he was badly injured in a car crash in England that killed his good friend and fellow rocker Eddie Cochran. After surviving the accident, Vincent continued to tour but rockabilly itself was losing momentum. Vincent appeared on a rock 'n' roll festival in Toronto in 1969. A few years later, he suffered from a bleeding ulcer, caused by alcoholism that ended his life.

"Be-Bop-A-Lula"
by Gene Vincent

"Be-Bop-A-Lula" was a top ten hit selling over 200,000 copies in its first month. It became a rockabilly classic. In this song, Vincent revealed an obvious influence of Elvis Presley in its mood and character. He sounded so much like Elvis on the recording that even Elvis' mother was fooled when she first heard the song. "Be-Bop-A-Lula" was about a boy's feelings for a girl with an unusual name (taken from a comic strip character Little Lulu). In the song, Vincent said, "she's my baby"; mentioned her clothes ("red blue jeans"), her social status ("queen of all the teens"), and her ability to dance ("flying feet" and "got the beat"), and goes on to say how she loves him so much. Vincent pulled the tune off with an intensity and sexual energy that he would display with his charismatic stage presence and strong stage show.

Musically, Vincent used a honky-tonk piano accompaniment and stop-time feel. This created a full arrangement that blended with his twangy guitar sound. Vincent's drummer, Dickie Harrell, impulsively screamed during a live performance of the song, prompting Vincent to do so in the studio version and every time they performed live. "Be-Bop-A-Lula" helped Vincent to develop a large cult following based on his rebel image.

Neither Elvis' two year absence, nor the tragic deaths of Holly, Valens, The Big Bopper, and Cochran could stop the evolution of rock 'n' roll. The beat marched on. The British invasion, the American musical reaction, and the California surf music craze were all on the horizon. The "new" rock 'n' roll music, combined with the blatant serialization of Elvis' rebellious image, combined to hurt his popularity. This prompted Col. Parker (with whom Elvis had signed a personal contract giving Parker twenty-five percent of his total profits) to send Elvis and his entourage to Hollywood to renew his popularity. The result, however, found Elvis trapped in a series of low quality movies that pulled him away from high quality music making. Presley would star in a total of 33 movies, but his success kept him feeling isolated, desperate to become a "real actor," and feeling hopelessly trapped. However, his hit records, popular films, and risqué dancing cultivated the rebellious image of Elvis as a teen idol. This paved the way for rebellious teen idols like Cochran, James Dean, Marlon Brando, and Sal Mineo. Singers such as Frankie Avalon, Fabian, and Pat Boone would soon walk in those footsteps as well. Other singers such as Paul Anka, Ricky Nelson, and Neil Sedaka were marketed in an attempt to create safer images of teen idols. Suddenly it seemed like there was a new teen idol being discovered every month. What had originally made Elvis unique, now made him another one of the ever-growing crowd of teen idols.

Col. Parker had yet another trick up his sleeve. In 1968, Elvis' "comeback special" appeared on national TV, and in 1969 he made his debut at the International Hotel in Las Vegas. Although Elvis had never really gone away, he had returned with the authority of a "King." Interestingly, at a press conference following his Las Vegas debut, a journalist referred to Elvis as "the King of Rock and Roll," which Elvis deflected while gesturing to Fats Domino (who was in attendance) saying, "No, that's the real king of rock and roll." These concerts began the very successful relationship between Las Vegas and Elvis, which continued with many concerts and extended stays for the rest of his life.

While performing in Las Vegas, Elvis heard Freddie Bell and the Bellboys perform "Hound Dog." It was written by the exceptional songwriting team of Jerry Leiber and Mike Stoller, and was first recorded by Willie Mae "Big Mama" Thornton.

"Hound Dog"
written by Jerry Lieber and Mike Stoller (1952)

Hound Dog has been recorded over 250 times, the best known being the Elvis Presley version that sold over ten million copies worldwide. He first performed "Hound Dog" on Milton Berle's television show in 1956 and it became an instant hit. A subsequent TV performance occurred on *The Steve Allen Show*. Because the networks were afraid of Elvis' gyrating hips, they asked him to sing the song to a bassett hound, which he did. Ed Sullivan did't want to book Elvis, but after the incredible reaction to his TV performances, he changed his mind in a hurry.

Jerry Lieber once described his opening line lyric of "You ain't nothin' but a hound dog" as a slang expression that referred to a man who sought a woman to take care of him. Lieber meant the song to be a Southern blues lament and initially wrote it for a woman to sing, reflecting on her selfish and exploitative man. Elvis changed the lyrics to that of a man singing about a woman who had no more worth than a hound dog that can't catch rabbits. This was a different spin from the

> *"The image is one thing and the human being is another, its very hard to live up to an image"*
>
> *- Elvis on being Elvis*

"Big Mama" Thornton version where the man had been cheating on her. Presley's vocal style, lyrical content, and musical background was much different than Thornton's version. Elvis sang "Hound Dog" in a smooth urban blues vocal style. His version used strong backbeats, stop-time, and handclaps. Elvis even added a harmonized male chorus and guitar solos that created a honky-tonk country feel.

Elvis' comeback was a huge success. RCA looked to cultivate his marketability even more. Elvis continued to release a number of successful singles, and RCA successfully transformed him into a crooner with a softer pop sound. Presley found more success recording songs such as 1962's "Can't Help Falling in Love" and 1969's number one hit, "Suspicious Minds." At the same time, Elvis was feeling the effects of making one bad movie after another. He took acting seriously but was forced to accept scripts that limited his roles and potential. Col. Parker's sole focus was making money and producing hit songs that would appear at strategic points in each Elvis film. He never cared about helping Elvis cultivate a real acting career. As for his personal life, Elvis married Priscilla Beaulieu in 1967 and had a daughter, Lisa Marie. Elvis went through extended tough times, and he developed a dependence on prescription drugs. Elvis and Priscilla were divorced in 1973.

"Suspicious Minds"
by Mark James

"Suspicious Minds" was Elvis Presley's great comeback song. It had been seven years since his last hit record. "Suspicious Minds" was the eighteenth and last number one hit of his career. It was written and first recorded by songwriter Mark James, but failed commercially. James felt Presley needed a mature rock song that could bring him back and when Elvis heard it, he knew he could turn it into a hit.

The song told the story about a mistrusting and dysfunctional relationship between a couple. The lyrics found the man pledging his love and pleading that they could find a way to regain trust and save their relationship. Elvis sang was great emotion and conveyed a great sense of desperation. The track built intensity by going back and forth between a half-time feel and a driving four to the bar pulse. Future Grateful Dead vocalist Donna Jean Godchaux sang background vocals on the track. "Suspicious Minds" was a great victory for Elvis Presley. "The King" was back!

The Las Vegas concerts gave Presley the confidence to return to national touring which he continued to do up until 1977. Tragically, it was just before launching a new tour that Elvis Presley died of heart failure at Graceland at the age of 42. Elvis was the first rock idol and will always be "The King of Rock 'N' Roll." Elvis was inducted into the Rock and Roll Hall of Fame in 1986 (Sam Phillip was inducted that same year). From the musician's perspective, Elvis should be remembered for popularizing rockabilly music, for his synthesizing of country, blues, R&B, and (his true love) gospel music into his unique sound. Elvis Presley embodied remarkable musicianship and an electrifying persona. Throughout his career, he recorded country, blues, gospel, rockabilly, and rock 'n' roll. Elvis Presley was *larger than life*, not to mention one of the best selling solo recording artists of all time.

Rockabilly's lasting influence can be heard in the Tiny Bradshaw tune "Train Kept a Rollin" which was famously popularized by rockabilly legends Johnny Burnette and the Rock and Roll Trio. It was subsequently covered by everyone from The Yardbirds to Aerosmith to Twisted Sister.

According to Led Zeppelin biographer Mick Wall, "The Train Kept a Rollin'" was even the first song that Led Zeppelin ever played as a band. In the Led Zeppelin book *When Giants Walked The Earth*, Wall quotes Jimmy Page as saying, "We did 'Train' ... It was there immediately. It was so *powerful* that I don't remember what we played after that. For me it was just like, 'Crikey!' I mean, I'd had moments of elation with groups before, but nothing as intense as that. It was like a thunderbolt, a lightning flash – boosh! Everyone sort of went 'Wow'." #9

"Train Kept A Rollin"
by Tiny Bradshaw

"Train Kept a Rollin" was first written and recorded by Tiny Bradshaw in 1951. It was first played in the style of a jump blues and the lyrics were based on an old cowboy song called "Cow-Cow Boogie." Johnny Burnette and The Rock and Roll Trio interpreted it with a rockabilly styled guitar riff and one of the first appearances of guitar distortion in a rock song. The Trio's guitar player, Paul Burlison, got his signature rockabilly guitar sound by accident when a tube became loose in his amplifier. From that point forward, Burlison would loosen a tube purposely to achieve that sound.

"Train Kept A Rollin" was one of the most covered tunes in rockabilly and rock music history. The Yardbirds recorded it in 1965 when guitarist Jeff Beck introduced it to the group. On their version, Beck imitated the sound of a train whistle by manipulating the volume on his overdriven guitar. Besides the above mentioned Led Zeppelin version, "Train Kept A Rollin" has been covered by Aerosmith, Motorhead, Skid Row, and Twisted Sister, thus appealing to many metal and hard rock bands. Van Halen would also frequently add it to their live performances.

In a strange twist of fate, it was Elvis' first recordings in 1954 that created the popularity of rockabilly, but it was Elvis' later rock 'n' roll recordings on RCA (among other factors) that marked the end of rockabilly's popularity by 1959. Rockabilly's initial stay created an excitement and an energy that was felt for decades and is still being felt today. Rockabilly's instrumentation of lead guitar, rhythm guitar, bass, and (later) drums became the core instrumentation of rock music. Rockabilly's rebellious attitude and distain for authority predates punk music, its energy predates rock 'n' roll, and its fashion statement of blue jeans, t-shirts, and leather jackets is timeless. These attributes are so strong that rockabilly has lived on with popular bands including; Nick Lowe and Rockpile, Dave Edmunds, The Polecats, Brian Setzer and The Stray Cats, and Social Distortion. These bands and others are all keeping the attitude and the musical tradition of rockabilly alive.

Discussion Question

How rock 'n' roll is rockabilly? Compare rockabilly to other more current rock genres and describe what might make it unique. Be specific and use examples.

> "It was like he came along and whispered some dream in everybody's ear, and somehow we all dreamed it"
>
> – Bruce Springsteen about Elvis Presley

Chapter Three: Early Rock 'N' Roll

Rock 'n' roll was a term that evolved in the 1950's to identify an emerging music genre that synthesized the many major root styles of folk, country, blues, gospel, pop, and especially rhythm and blues. The term rock 'n' roll gained acceptance as a counter-term for rhythm and blues and its earlier used term "race music" that was marketed to a black audience. Disc jockey **Alan Freed** (1921-1965) coined the term rock 'n' roll when he marketed this new genre through his radio show (called Moondog's *Rock 'N' Roll Party*) where he played up-tempo rhythm and blues tunes. In 1952, Freed was also credited with hosting the first ever rock 'n' roll concert in Cleveland that he called *The Moondog Coronation Ball*. Freed began to organize early rock 'n' roll concerts that were marketed to a largely white and (mostly) teenage audience. The term rock 'n' roll also came to symbolize sex, a common theme in many songs. In this chapter, we will connect many of the rhythm and blues artists such as Bo Diddley, Chuck Berry, Fats Domino, and Little Richard that were able to cross over to the new emerging genre of rock 'n' roll. We will also explore the 1950's teen idols and the surf rock style.

The Atlantic and Chess record labels played a huge role in the development of rhythm and blues artists. Owner and producer **Ahmet Ertegun** (1923-2006) and writer/producer Jerry Wexler of Atlantic Records shaped the music of Ray Charles, Aretha Franklin, Otis Redding, Wilson Pickett, and many others. **Aretha Franklin** (1942-2018) came out of a strong gospel background and Jerry Wexler helped her refine a style that expressed great emotion and raw power. Her version of Otis Redding's tune "Respect" went to number one on the rhythm and blues and pop charts. Aretha Franklin was inducted into the Rock and Roll Hall of Fame in 1987. **Ray Charles** (1930-2004), another Atlantic recording artist, synthesized country, gospel, blues, jazz, and rhythm and blues to create his unique style of music. Charles made two country albums in 1962 and used some of the typical country texts for his original songs. Ray Charles and the Atlantic Records staff arrangers wrote great big band arrangements for Ray's music utilizing his country, blues, and gospel elements. His 1962 tune "I Can't Stop Loving You," was his biggest hit. Ray Charles was inducted into the Rock and Roll Hall of Fame in 1986. Ahmet Ertegun and Jerry Wexler were inducted the following year.

Using powerful backbeats and a strong rhythmic pulse, rhythm and blues continued to have significant influence on early rock 'n' roll. Rhythm and blues songs were about enjoying life and were performed with energetic and powerful stage shows. Some of the original female "pure" blues singers of the early fifties also sang equally well in the rhythm and blues style. These singers included "Big Mamma" Thornton, Ruth Brown, and Etta James. The impact and influence of Thornton's "Hound Dog" version was revealed in the last chapter. Other great rhythm and blues influences were Ike Turner, Hank Ballard, Big Joe Turner, and **Louis Jordan** (1908-1975) who performed in the jump blues style. Louis Jordan came to rhythm and blues from a different direction. He grew up playing alto saxophone and clarinet in jazz big bands. His high-energy style, also called jump and jive (also known as shuffle boogie), combined blues and a danceable shuffle feel that emphasized strong backbeats. His stage show included a large dose of humor and he had a big impact on Bill Haley, who imitated his shuffles in the early 1950's. Jordan was inducted into the Rock and Roll Hall of Fame in 1987.

> "If you tried to give rock "n' roll another name, you might call it Chuck Berry"
>
> – John Lennon

Bill Haley (1925-1981) was one of the earliest and most successful rock 'n' roll artists. He started in the music business as a country musician influenced by the western swing style of Bob Wills and His Texas Playboys. Haley was working as a disc jockey in Chester, Pennsylvania when he formed a band, The Four Aces of Western Swing. Haley changed the group name to Bill Haley and The Saddlemen in 1949. In 1952 after covering Jackie Brenston's "Rocket 88," Haley saw the money making potential of rhythm and blues music and noticed that it could be played and marketed to the new white teenage audience. Haley dropped his cowboy song repertoire and image, and formed a new group called Bill Haley and the Comets. Haley's next hit was a modified version of the tune "Rock Around the Clock," first recorded by rhythm and blues artist Sunny Dae. Bill Haley and the Comets were the first rock artists to appear on *The Ed Sullivan Show* and the success of "Rock Around the Clock" made him one of rock 'n' roll's first and biggest stars.

"(We're Gonna) Rock Around the Clock Tonight"
by James Myers and Max Freedman
(covered by Bill Haley and the Comets and Big Joe Turner)

"Rock Around the Clock" (later shortened to remove the words "we're gonna" and "tonight") was a twelve bar blues that has a long and complicated history that traced back to blues legend Charley Patton. Patton wrote the song "Going to Move to Alabama" and recorded it in 1929. The basic melody of "Going to Move to Alabama" was borrowed by Hank Williams Sr. for his song "Move it on Over" in 1947. In 1952, James Mayers and Max Freedman co-wrote "Rock Around the Clock." However, the melody of the verses of "Rock Around the Clock" sound a lot like "Move it on Over." Two years later, Sonny Dae and His Knights were the first group to record "Rock Around the Clock," but it achieved only moderate success. It was then recorded by rhythm and blues legend Big Joe Turner with a great "in the cracks" rhythmic feel.

Bill Haley would modify Turner's version by playing it faster and with stronger backbeats. Bill Haley claimed that "Rock Around the Clock" was offered to him to record after he achieved national success with his own tune "Crazy Man, Crazy." Haley began performing "Rock Around the Clock" in his live shows and recorded it for the Decca label in 1954. Haley's version was featured in the 1955 movie *Blackboard Jungle*, but it didn't become a hit just yet. After the movie, Decca reissued the song and its popularity grew. Without the many contributions of Charley Patton, Hank Williams, Mayers and Freeman, Sonny Dae, and Big Joe Turner, there never would have been the song "Rock Around the Clock." Bill Haley's version of the song went on to sell twenty-two million copies worldwide and stayed on the charts for almost six months. Haley's recording of "Rock Around the Clock" was the first rock 'n' roll record to make it to number one on the pop charts.

Haley had another hit when he covered another Big Joe Turner tune called "Shake, Rattle, and Roll." It soon went to number seven on the pop charts. Turner's original version of the song was full of sexual innuendos and never made the pop charts, although it did go to number one on the rhythm and blues charts. Haley's version took out most of the sexual references and was therefore more appealing to the record company and radio stations. Haley did leave in the lyrics in the third verse about a "one-eyed cat in a seafood store" because he thought it would get by the censors, which it did. Haley's appeal waned when Elvis and the other rockabilly singers arrived on the scene. When the style of rockabilly soon declined, so did Haley's career. Although Haley's popularity deteriorated in America, he kept a steady following in Europe. Haley is considered to be the first international rock star. Bill Haley was inducted into the Rock and Roll Hall of Fame in 1987. His band called The Comets was later inducted in 2012.

The artists that achieved early rock 'n' roll success were able to adapt their music and their image to a new teenage audience. This crossover was one of the key developments that stripped early rock 'n' roll of racial boundaries. Although people such as disc jockey and promoter Alan Freed and Sun owner Sam Phillips had monetary motivations, they also saw that listening to and enjoying good music did not require (and should not support) a racial divide. Rock 'n' roll (and rhythm and blues) was an integral part of early racial integration. It also affected the emerging music styles in the northern and southern parts of the country. Two such areas were Chicago and New Orleans.

The Rise of the Disc Jockey and the Payola Scandal

Payola can be defined as payment in the form of cash or gifts in exchange for more radio play or television airtime for specific songs. In the 1950's, payola became common practice among rock 'n' roll disc jockeys that sought to bolster their meager salaries. This practice among DJ's became all too common and allowed new songs to reach a radio audience, no matter how small the label was or how unknown the artist. Payola fueled the success of a number of small independent labels that recorded rock music. It enabled them to shatter the stronghold of the major labels such as RCA, Columbia, and Decca that monopolized the airplay and sales of popular records. Payola was seen as unfair because money could decide the fate of whether or not a record gets to the public's ears rather than an honest evaluation of a song's quality. As songs were heard more often from town to town, the chances of that record being a hit increased. Ultimately though, the listening public would decide a record or artists' popularity.

Songwriters were typically paid from sheet music sales, mechanical fees (for each copy of sold recordings), and public performances fees. The American Society of Composers, Authors and Publishers (ASCAP) was formed in 1914 to collect performance fees and distribute them to the songwriters. After a fight between radio stations and ASCAP over royalty payments, the radio stations boycotted recordings registered with ASCAP. Broadcast Music Incorporated (BMI) was soon founded and most 1950's and 1960's rock songwriters joined them. ASCAP resented the competition from BMI and requested that a U.S. House Legislative Oversight subcommittee investigate corrupt broadcasting practices. This included the practice of payola in radio. The investigation became known as the payola scandal. The subcommittee focused on showing that BMI was responsible for having its records fraudulently made into hits due to payola practices. One of the investigation results exposed the fact that many small labels were dependent on payola practices, and were therefore forced out of business. Another result of the investigation found that some of

---

Rock Hard Fact

Atlantic Records, first known as a rhythm and blues label, went on to sign some of rock's biggest artists including: Led Zeppelin, The Rolling Stones, Bad Company, Cream, and many more.

the DJ's from the Cleveland and Boston area were also guilty of payola violations.

Two high profile figures in the music business were at the center of the investigation, disc jockey and American Bandstand host Dick Clark (1929-2012), and disc jockey Alan Freed. Dick Clark was able to successfully prove that he played records because listeners wanted to hear them and not because he stood to gain financially. Although Clark came away clean, he was forced to sell his share in thirty-three music businesses that presented a conflict of interest to his role of promoting records as a disc jockey and TV icon. Alan Freed was not so lucky. Freed plead guilty to two charges of commercial bribery, thus taking the fall for the payola scandal. Later, he was also convicted of tax evasion. As a result, Freed lost his television show called Dance Party that had promoted rock and rhythm and blues artists.

Bo Diddley (1928-2008) was born in Mississippi but moved to Chicago as a youth. His real name was Ellas Bates. He most likely got his stage name from the African single-stringed instrument called a diddley bow. As a youngster on the south side of Chicago, Bo heard both Delta blues and black gospel music. Diddley also studied both classical violin and blues guitar. Diddley's time in Mississippi and Chicago put him in the right place to absorb the blues of Muddy Waters, Jimmy Reed, and John Lee Hooker. Diddley combined all of these styles with a heavy R&B influence. This enabled him to write some of the legendary early rock 'n' roll songs. His first three hits, all recorded in 1955, were "Bo Diddley," "Diddley Daddy," and "I'm Your Man," which went to number one on the rhythm and blues charts.

The secret to Bo Diddley's success was rhythm. Diddley created a rhythmic groove known as the "Bo Diddley beat." Diddley essentially adapted a rhythm rooted in the African diaspora that made its way around the world (through slave trade) and eventually became integral in the music of Brazil, Cuba, and the United States. To propel Diddley's famous beat, he employed a full time maraca player in his band. That musician, Jerome Green, became an essential part of Bo Diddley's sound. Keith Richards of the Rolling Stones became great friends with Jerome and admired his playing and recalled, "Jerome Green was Bo Diddley's maraca shaker. He'd been with him on all the records…he was almost Bo's partner. They'd been through everything together…there was a lot of call and response phrasing going on…he used to play four in each hand, eight maracas, very African and the sound was incredible." #1

"Bo Diddley"
by Bo Diddley

Bo Diddley performed his namesake tune on *The Ed Sullivan Show* in 1955 and it became a number one hit on the American charts. The song's original name was "Uncle John" but Diddley decided to change the name of the tune in order to better market himself to the public. This song, along with so many of Diddley's compositions, was all about rhythm. So much so, that the whole song was built on only one chord change. Diddley used the bottleneck guitar technique of sliding between frets that he learned from many Delta bluesmen playing around Chicago. This created the illusion that there were more chord changes, especially in the breaks in the melody. The tune "Bo Diddley" featured the aforementioned African influenced rhythm that Diddley learned from church music growing up. Diddley aggressively strummed this rhythm on his guitar as if he was playing it on the drums. Jerome Green's maraca part provided an important continuous rhythmic flow. Diddley's unpredictable vocal phrasing caused the form of the tune to be quite irregular.

The song "Bo Diddley" became an instant hit for the Chicago blues label Chess Records. Everyone from Buddy Holly and The Rolling Stones ("Not Fade Away") to The Who's ("Magic Bus") utilized this infectious rhythm. The Bo Diddley beat has been the source of many later rock beats including; Bow Wow Wow's "I Want Candy," George Michael's "Faith," and Bruce Springsteen's "She's The One." The rhythm is notated: quarter note--two eighth notes--eighth rest--eighth note--quarter note.

Throughout the 1950's, Diddley toured incessantly across the country with other rhythm and blues acts. He was one of the first to appeal to a predominantly white teenage market. After Diddley influenced so many early rock 'n' roll American artists, he continued to do so for the emerging 1960's British blues and R&B bands. When the surf rock movement hit across the country in the early 1960's, Diddley was right there releasing surf albums Surfin' with Bo Diddley and Bo Diddley's Beach Party. Bo Diddley most certainly broke the racial barrier for rhythm and blues artists. Although Diddley had the ability to reach a new rock audience, his only major top forty hit came in 1959 with "Say Man." It reached number twenty on the Billboard pop charts.

Diddley continued to tour in the 1970's and 1980's and even opened for The Clash in 1979. The Animals recorded a tribute to him called "The Story of Bo Diddley," when they honored his legacy and enormous effect on rock 'n' roll. Bo Diddley was inducted into the Rock and Roll Hall of Fame in 1987.

Chuck Berry (1926-2017) has been acknowledged as one of the most significant and creative innovators in the history of rock and all of American music. Berry was the *first* musician to be inducted into the Rock and Roll Hall of Fame in 1986 at their inaugural induction ceremony. He is thought of by many to be "The Father of Rock Guitar." Chuck Berry was born in 1926 in St. Louis, Missouri. His parents were the grandchildren of slaves and they migrated from the rural South to St. Louis during World War I. Berry first encountered music when he sang in his church choir at age six. He became interested in the guitar when he sang the Jay McShann tune "Confessin the Blues" at his school talent show. Berry dropped out of high school, got himself into some trouble, and spent three years in prison. At age 20, he returned to St. Louis where he worked at a number of jobs. He married Themetta "Toddy" Suggs in 1948 and began playing guitar seriously in bands around the St. Louis area. By 1952, he joined a group with pianist Johnnie Johnson and introduced some upbeat country tunes into the band's repertoire. Berry was soon gaining a reputation for his on stage showmanship. Even though his band was playing mostly blues, Berry was incorporating many country music characteristics (heard as a child listening to country music on the radio) into his evolving style. Berry, with the help of Johnnie Johnson, fused these country influences with the blues. The result was a huge step to a new sound, rock 'n' roll.

Not only was Chuck Berry central to creating the new rock style, he was creating new guitar vocabulary. His guitar roots went back to blues masters T-Bone Walker, Muddy Waters, and Carl Hogan (guitarist for Louis Jordan). He also was exposed to jazz guitar in his

> "The big jungle rhythm was the Bo Diddley lick 'Shave and a haircut, two bits' is what the beat's called and what it sounds like"
>
> -Keith Richards

> "My momma always said, 'You and Elvis (Presley) are pretty good, but y'all ain't no Chuck Berry'"
>
> – Jerry Lee Lewis

> "Listening to Chuck Berry had turned me on in a big way to electric blues, and somehow I had managed to persuade my grandparents to buy me an electric guitar."
>
> - Eric Clapton

lessons, particularly the approach of Charlie Christian. Throughout the decade of the 1950's, Chuck Berry continued to combine the musical elements of jazz, country, and rhythm and blues to become a major catalyst in the creation of rock 'n' roll.

Chuck Berry was a *master* rock 'n' roll lyricist. Through his clever lyrics about cars and girls, Berry was able to effectively connect with the (mostly) white teenagers of the 1950's. He had an uncanny ability to musically describe what it was to be a teenager in the quickly changing American culture of the 1950's. Berry has said on numerous occasions that he worked to articulate his lyrics with a clear diction that enabled white audiences to clearly understand what he was saying.

Around 1955, Berry traveled to Chicago looking for a record contract. He met many prominent blues musicians including Muddy Waters, who directed him to approach Chess Records. On Waters' advice, Berry went to Chess with a song he had recently written and recorded called "Maybellene." Chess quickly recorded it and soon Berry followed with a string of hits that would later become rock standards including; "Roll Over Beethoven," "Rock and Roll Music," "Sweet Little Sixteen," and "Johnny B. Goode." Berry sold more records than anyone else on the Chess label when teens were drawn to his simple yet powerful style.

Chuck Berry often recorded his hits with the house band at Chess that included drummer Fred Below. The first Berry sessions involving Below were in 1956 and yielded "Roll Over Beethoven" and "Too Much Monkey Business." Below also played on Berry's classic hits; "School Day," "Rock and Roll Music," "Sweet Little Sixteen," and "Johnny B. Goode." It was here that Below was crucial in helping to shape the rhythmic feel of early rock 'n' roll. Charlie Watts of The Rolling Stones explained, "Freddie Below played shuffles, which is what they did in Chicago. We (The Rolling Stones) turned that into straight eighth-note rhythms and so did Chuck Berry. Freddie played 4/4 swing and the mixture (when it hits right) is incredible, but if it doesn't (mix well), one of you is going to be out of sync. So we learned to play the Freddie Below way." #2

"Maybellene"
by Chuck Berry

This tune was first called "Ida Red" and was included on the audition tape Berry had made for Leonard Chess at Chess Records. Berry was inspired by an old traditional country tune he had heard on a recording from 1938 by Bob Wills and His Texas Playboys. Berry renamed his song "Maybellene" and it reached number one on the rhythm and blues charts and number five on the pop charts. This song was considered by some music historians to be the first true rock 'n' roll song. "Maybellene" featured a unique blend of country guitar licks, a strong Chicago blues flavor, rhythm and blues backbeats, and original narrative storytelling. On the studio recording of "Maybellene," Berry was accompanied by Johnnie Johnson, Willie Dixon, and other members of the Chess Records house band. Berry's lead guitar solo was powerful and influenced many future generations of guitar players. "Maybellene" also captured Johnnie Johnson's melodic piano accompaniment. Johnson's piano playing was a vital component of many Chuck Berry songs.

The lyrics were a prime example of how Berry dealt with teen themes, which helped him work across racial lines. It also helped to establish him as a rock star. The lyrics described a man in his Ford V8 in pursuit of his romantically unfaithful girlfriend, who was driving a Cadillac. This subject matter showed Berry's ability to write songs for an audience half his age that wanted to hear about sex, cars, and freedom. There was some controversy with the authorship of "Maybellene" when DJ Alan Freed was given credit as co-composer. It was widely thought that Freed did not help write "Maybellene" but was receiving royalties in the form of payola for promoting the record. In 1988, "Maybellene" was inducted into the Grammy Hall of Fame as one of the most influential rock 'n' roll songs of all time.

In 1958, Berry released "Sweet Little Sixteen," his most popular tune to date. The song was quickly embraced by the new generation of rock 'n' roll fans. It went to number one on the rhythm and blues charts and number three on the pop charts. Berry utilized a clever lyric writing concept in the song by referencing the cities of New Orleans, Boston, San Francisco, St. Louis, and others. This made people identify even more with the tune. Adding to his many classic songs, Berry embarked on frequent cross-country tours and appearances in rock 'n' roll films. Berry made the films *Rock, Rock, Rock!* in 1956, *Mister Rock and Roll* in 1957, and *Go, Johnny, Go!* in 1958. Berry's influence was felt strongly in Britain, which resulted in the Rolling Stones and The Beatles covering many of his songs.

In 1959, Berry was charged with violating the (vaguely worded) Mann Act, was convicted, and imprisoned from 1962 to 1964. The wording of this law was amended in 1978 and 1986. Some believe that his spirit was never the same afterward but he did make a strong comeback. His 1960's rebirth included the hit "No Particular Place to Go" and in 1972, Berry had a number one hit with the controversial tune "My Ding-a-Ling." By this time, he had stopped touring with a regular band, choosing to use a pickup band at every gig location.

The legacy of Chuck Berry and his music defined rock 'n' roll in the 1950's. Chuck Berry set the stage for thousands of rock musicians to come. He had a heavy influence on rock guitarists including; Keith Richards, Buddy Holly, Carl Wilson, Eric Clapton, and countless others. His ability to synthesize the songwriting styles of country, blues, jazz, rhythm and blues, and pop was groundbreaking. He simply set the standard for the future of rock music. Like Louis Jordan before him, his approach to lyric writing was simple yet highly effective. Chuck Berry had a strong understanding of the feelings and attitude of the youth culture of the 1950's. His showmanship was exciting and unique as thousands of young guitar players copied his famous duckwalk when he moved across the stage. Chuck Berry was the master of creating the pure rock song. His music was simple, powerful, and spoke directly to the common person.

"Johnny B. Goode"
by Chuck Berry

The lyrics of "Johnny B. Goode" provided rock 'n' roll with an archetypal character, a talented country guitar player from Louisiana who had success in the big city and went on to pursue a life of musical fame. "Johnny B. Goode" was the first song about rock 'n' roll stardom. The song peaked at number two on the rhythm and blues charts and went to number eight on the pop charts. "Johnny B. Goode" utilized a twelve bar form with blue notes in the guitar intro and solo. There was call and response phrasing between the guitar and piano parts. The guitar introduction was one of the most copied in rock history and helped establish the tune as one of rock's first great anthems. Berry himself copied the intro from

Rock Hard Fact

The melody of The Beach Boys' "Surfin USA" was so nearly identical to Chuck Berry's 1958 classic "Sweet Little Sixteen," that The Beach Boys were forced to give Berry co-writing credit to avoid a lawsuit.

a guitar riff taken from the song "Ain't That Just Like a Woman" (played by Louis Jordan's guitarist Carl Hogan). Berry overdubbed the intro guitar rhythm and solo parts. "Johnny B. Goode" had an urgency and up-tempo energy that was pure *rock 'n' roll*.

The song could be interpreted to be autobiographical in nature, but Berry has refuted this saying that it's about his musical accompanist Johnnie Johnson, even though pianist Lafayette Leake played piano on the original recording. The lyrics told the story of an illiterate country boy who played guitar as easily as ringing a bell. He might one day have his name in lights; this boy was probably Chuck Berry. The musicians on the recording were Berry, Leake, drummer Fred Below, and bassist Willie Dixon. When Chuck Berry was inducted into the Rock and Roll Hall of Fame, he performed "Johnny B. Goode" backed by Bruce Springsteen and the E Street Band.

In 1987, Chuck Berry's story was finally told. The movie *Hail! Hail! Rock 'n' Roll* featured many talented artists including; Keith Richards and Steve Jordan, movie producer Taylor Hackford, pianists Johnnie Johnson and Chuck Leavell, and special guests Eric Clapton, Etta James, and Linda Ronstadt. They worked to create a documentary about two concerts that commemorated Berry's 60th birthday. It told his legendary story. Incredibly, at age 90, Chuck Berry released his first album Chuck in 38 years on Dualtone Records. Said Berry, "This record is dedicated to my beloved Toddy (his wife Themetta Berry of 68 years), My darlin', I'm growing old! I've worked on this record for a long time. Now I can hang up my shoes." #3 The musicians on Chuck included his longtime backing band members bassist Jimmy Marsala (with Berry for over 40 years), pianist Robert Lohr, and drummer Keith Robinson. His children, guitarist Charles Berry Jr., and harmonica player Ingrid Berry, played on the record. The material on the album Chuck, covered an array of songs that were soul-inspired and, of course, hard driving rockers. Chuck Berry died in 2017. He was inducted into the Rock and Roll Hall of Fame in 1986.

New Orleans pianist, vocalist, and composer **Antoine "Fats" Domino** (1929-2017) became a legendary performer beginning in the late 1940's and 1950's. Domino was born into a musical family. His father was an accomplished violinist and his brother-in-law, Harrison Verrett, played guitar in Fats' band for many years. Domino grew up hearing piano greats Amos Milburn and Professor Longhair in the New Orleans clubs. Bill Diamond, a bandleader who had hired Fats (and gave him his nickname), encouraged him to sing and write his own tunes. The many diverse styles found in New Orleans music including; second-line feels, funeral marches, Dixieland, and the rich tradition of jazz, each contributed to Fats' musical education. Domino soon developed a warm and relaxed vocal style and cultivated a polished stage presence that featured his boogie-woogie piano style.

In 1949, Fats teamed up with composer, producer, trumpeter, and bandleader David Bartholomew (see New Orleans profile) to produce a long succession of rhythm and blues hits that crossed over into the teen rock 'n' roll market. Bartholomew was an experienced producer and wrote strong horn arrangements for Domino's tunes. These arrangements translated well into Domino's high-energy stage show. Domino's career was launched with his hit, "The Fat Man," that sold over twenty-five million records. Fats had an incredible string of sixty-one rhythm and blues hits and sixty-six hits on the pop charts.

"The Fat Man"
by Fats Domino and David Bartholomew

Some people, including Fats, considered this to be the first rock 'n' roll song. Written in 1949 and released in 1950, "The Fat Man" went to number two on the rhythm and blues charts. It became a trademark tune for Domino with its driving shuffle feel. By 1953, "The Fat Man" had sold over one million copies. "The Fat Man" brought together many of the musical elements that would represent Fat's compositions over the next twenty-five years. Fats sang with a sense of self-deprecation and a sense of confidence that made it easy for the listener to like him and his message. Domino sang with his head cocked sideways and had a reassuring simile that made you like him personally.

"The Fat Man" was inspired by a traditional New Orleans tune titled "Junker's Blues." Drummer Earl Palmer has often said that it was the first time a drummer (himself on the recording) had played a backbeat (accents on beats two and four) throughout a recording. Palmer derived his relentless backbeat from the drive he felt from dixieland music. Fats scat sang on a few of the choruses in his characteristic "wah-wah" falsetto that imitated a muted trumpet, similar to a muted dixieland-styled trumpet solo. "The Fat Man" was recorded at Cosimo Matassa's J&M Studio in New Orleans for Imperial Records. Fat's legendary band featured Earl Palmer on drums, Frank Fields on acoustic bass, Ernest McLean on guitar, and a four-man saxophone section.

Throughout the 1950's and 1960's, Fats Domino's presence on the pop charts was almost constant. It began in 1955 with "Ain't That a Shame" and the hits followed in rapid succession with 1956's "Blueberry Hill" and "Blue Monday," 1957's "I'm Walkin," and 1958's "Whole Lotta Lovin." And they kept coming. Both live and in the studio, the Domino and Bartholomew combination featured Fats' smooth, blues inspired boogie-woogie feel along with Red Tyler on saxophone and the legendary Earl Palmer on drums. One of Fats' style traits was his falsetto voice that could imitate the sound of a trumpet. Domino had a soft, non-threatening voice that appealed to both black and white audiences and provided a great contrast to the aggressive, honking saxophones of Bartholomew's band. Over the years, the Domino and Bartholomew partnership continued with musical string arrangements. The excellent production work of their frequent studio engineer, Cosimo Matassa, was another contributing factor to their success.

Fats Domino, along with Jerry Lee Lewis and Little Richard helped to establish the piano as a viable rock 'n' roll instrument. Although he kept an incessant touring schedule, Domino never forgot his New Orleans roots. He often sang about his beloved city with hits such as "Walking to New Orleans" that went to number two on the rhythm and blues charts and six on the pop charts. His wholesome lyrics and family friendly onstage personality was void of the sexual appeal of performers like Elvis Presley and later, Mick Jagger. By 1964, the immensely successful songwriting team of Domino and Bartholomew had run its course, and soon music audiences shifted to more pop, soul, and surf rock.

Over time, many recording artists have dipped into Fats' catalogue of hits. His catchy melodies, lyrics, and musical arrangements lent themselves to many cover versions by artists like John Lennon and Cheap Trick. In 2007, many artists, including Paul McCartney and Elton John, appeared at a tribute concert held for Fats and his

> "Everybody started calling my music rock and roll, but it wasn't anything but the same rhythm and blues I'd been playing down in New Orleans...I don't remember anyone else before me playing that kind of stuff"
>
> – Fats Domino

family. The Domino family had to be rescued when Hurricane Katrina ravaged New Orleans in 2005, destroying their home. A subsequent recording of the concert was called Going Home: A Tribute to Fats Domino. President George W. Bush made a visit to replace the National Medal of the Arts that Fats had received from President Bill Clinton when it was lost in the hurricane. Fats Domino sold more records in the 1950's than any rock 'n' roll star not named Elvis Presley. Fats Domino died in 2017 in his hometown of New Orleans. Fats Domino was inducted into the Rock and Roll Hall of Fame in 1986.

The Sounds of New Orleans

A lot of American popular music was born and raised in the South, particularly New Orleans. The cities' vitality as a center for diverse music styles is reflected in its rich diversity of ethnic groups and their culture elements. For over a century, its strong musical traditions have been alive in music venues that include; dance halls, social clubs, music festivals and parks. Diverse blends of native musical styles, including dixieland and jazz have had a major impact on the development of rhythm and blues. Other examples of specific New Orleans musical styles that impacted America's musical diversity are zydeco, cajun, and the second line rhythms of Mardi Gras parades. These New Orleans styles could fit into a multi-volume set of books.

Throughout the 1940's and 1950's, talent scouts from record companies realized that New Orleans was producing a number of important artists that could sell many records and go on to help shape the course of rock music. The success and influence of bandleaders and recordings coming out of New Orleans, such as Fats Domino and Little Richard, and sidemen like Earl Palmer, Larry Williams, and Dave Bartholomew has left an incredible legacy. Other prominent New Orleans artists included; Lee Dorsey, Earl King, Professor Longhair, Lloyd Price, Huey "Piano" Smith, Guitar Slim, Frogman Henry, Alan Toussaint, Dr. John, The Neville Brothers, and The Meters.

David Bartholomew (Rock and Roll Hall of Fame 1991) led his own dance band in 1946. They were called Dave Bartholomew and the Dew Drippers. After World War Two, he organized some of the best horn players and a rhythm section that featured legendary drummer Earl Palmer. In addition to writing with Fats Domino, Bartholomew directed recording sessions for many New Orleans artists including; Smiley Lewis, Lloyd Price, Roy Brown, and James Booker. Another central figure was the owner and engineer of J&M Studio, Cosimo Matassa. Featuring a simple approach to recording, Matassa recorded dozens of future stars such as Little Richard and Ray Charles utilizing an ambient room sound without any electronic manipulation or overdubbing. The result was an exciting live sound that you either got right or you kept recording take after take.

Professor Longhair, born Roy Byrd, in Bogalusa, Louisiana, transformed the traditional barrelhouse piano style into a bass-centered rhythm and blues approach. He also developed a unique yodeling vocal style mixed with raw blues. Add some Latin, second line, and early rock 'n' roll rhythms, and the result was a musical gumbo that was all his own. Professor Longhair began performing in New Orleans clubs in the late 1940's and his impact on audiences and musicians was powerful. Fess' influence on rock 'n' roll is still felt today. Professor Longhair was inducted into the Rock and Roll Hall of Fame in 1992.

Although The Meters (see chapter seventeen) had over ten rhythm and blues and pop charts hits, they were never a best-selling band. But The Meters' musical influence was felt throughout the musical world. And although they didn't invent funk (that was James Brown), guitarist Leo Nocentelli, bassist George Porter Jr., drummer Joseph "Zigaboo" Modeliste, and organist Art Neville defined New Orleans funk. In the 1960's and 1970's, a live Meters show in New Orleans was the place to be. They were even invited to open for the Rolling Stones in 1975 and 1976. The Meters had a sleek, clean sound where each instrument added rhythms that together created some of the best ensemble grooves in music history. Building on their reputation as an exciting live band, The Meters became an exciting session band, and played on most of producer Allen Toussaint's sessions. They recorded with Dr. John, Lee Dorsey, Robert Palmer, and many more. Bassist George Porter Jr. said "I think we brought New Orleans funk to the rest of the country and the rest of the world…Our tracks are used so much in the hip-hop thing because they were serious rhythm tracks waiting for a melody…It was like having windows without curtains, and our music was serious great windows, but it had room for curtains because we had nice big, gaping holes in the music." #4

The major breakthrough for New Orleans music in terms of rock 'n' roll was in the mid-fifties when rhythm and blues morphed into Little Richard, Fats Domino, and others. The late 1960's brought the New Orleans artist Dr. John and his form of psychedelic, funky music. Later, the 1980's brought The Dirty Dozen Brass Band and current bands such as Stanton Moore and Galactic that continue to fuse New Orleans and rock styles.

Little Richard (1932-) was born **Richard Penniman** in Macon, Georgia. He learned to play piano at his church where he also sang gospel music. Richard adapted gospel vocal characteristics that included embellishments and slides. He incorporated these with the hollers, shrieks, and moans he heard in the early jump blues style. Little Richard cultivated an outrageous and rebellious rock 'n' roll persona with a shocking (especially at the time) appearance and a wild performance style. Richard developed a unique style by ramping up a high-powered R&B sound with his infectious energy and aggressive boogie-woogie influenced piano approach. He introduced cross-dressing and an ambiguous sexuality to the stage that was unimaginable to an American audience in the 1950's. On and offstage, he wore makeup, had a pompadour hairstyle, flashy suits, and lots of jewelry. His performances were exciting as he banged and danced on the piano and took the style of gospel shout singing to a new (screaming) level. His performances were *fun*. He pushed the medium of the live rock stage show into uncharted territory with his aggressive and outrageous behavior.

Little Richard left home in his early teens when he struggled with the lack of public tolerance over his sexuality. He traveled with a minstrel show and performed in clubs throughout the South. He met and began to hang out with Eskew Esquerita, a rhythm and blues singer and pianist (similar to Richard) that influenced Richard's stage presence and racy song lyrics. In 1955, R&B star Lloyd Price suggested to Richard that he send a demo tape to Specialty Records. They were impressed and signed him to a deal and arranged a recording session in New Orleans. In 1955, Little Richard recorded "Tutti

> "When I heard Little Richard, I mean, it just set my world on fire."
>
> – David Bowie

Frutti" in New Orleans at Cosimo Matassa's studio with a group of studio musicians. With slightly cleaned-up lyrics, "Tutti Frutti" featured Richard's furious piano playing and a saxophone-driven, energized rhythm section.

"Tutti Frutti"
by Richard Penniman and Dorothy LaBostrie

Written in 1955, "Tutti Frutti" became Little Richard's fist hit record. Inspired by a drum pattern he had heard, the opening vocal is "A-wop-bop-a-loo-bop-a-wop-bam-boom." Thought by many to be one of the most important songs in rock history, its up-tempo feel and backbeats combined with Little Richard's cutting edge vocal style, thus helping to define early rock 'n' roll. On the recording session, Richard utilized Fat's Domino's backing band, a magic combination that included the legendary musicians Huey Smith on piano, Red Tyler on baritone saxophone, and Earl Palmer on drums.

The tune's original lyrics were sexually provocative. Referring to a homosexual man, the original lyrics contained "Tutti Frutti, good booty-if it don't fit, don't force it-You can grease it, make it easy" making these lyrics risqué even by today's standards. They were replaced with "Tutti, Frutti, aw rooty-Tutti Frutti, aw rooty." The song suggested rocking (sex) with the girls mentioned in the lyrics. "Tutti Frutti" had a boogie-woogie influence and it moved away from a shuffle to a more straight-eight note feel while still maintaining a little bit of swing. The magic of the song was the "in the cracks" feel that was captured by drumming great Earl Palmer and the rest of the rhythm section. The song went to number two on the rhythm and blues charts and number seventeen on the pop charts (while the Pat Boone version went to number twelve).

"Tutti Frutti" sold over three million copies for Little Richard and had an enormous impact on other artists. It was covered by Pat Boone, Elvis Presley, and The Beatles. The Pat Boone version showed how the recording industry at the time was unfortunately looking to cash in on black artists by having prominent and socially accepted white artists cover their material. Even Pat Boone himself did not want to cover the song, but his record company pushed him into doing it. Little Richard said "When Tutti Frutti came out…They needed a rock star to block me out of white homes because I was a hero to white kids. The white kids would have Pat Boone up on the dresser and me in the drawer cause they liked my version better, but the families didn't want me because of the image that I was projecting." #5

A string of Little Richard hits followed with songs that included; "Long Tall Sally," "Rip it Up," "Keep a Knockin," "Good Golly, Miss Molly," "Slippin' and Slidin'," and "Send Me Some Lovin." "Long Tall Sally" went to number one on the rhythm and blues charts and number six on the pop charts. Pat Boone also covered "Long Tall Sally." But, despite record sales figures, audiences were beginning to figure out that they preferred the real deal-Little Richard. While Richard's great talent was undeniable, he owed a lot of his success to stellar New Orleans session players such as tenor saxophonist Lee Allan, baritone saxophonist Alvin Tyler, and especially drummer Earl Palmer. The legendary Palmer often recorded with Richard in both New Orleans and Los Angeles studios.

Just when he was on top of the rock world, Little Richard abruptly left rock 'n' roll to become an ordained minister. Richard enrolled in a Bible college in Alabama after an Australian tour in late 1957. Richard had been thinking of this move for a while but it was still a shock to both his fans and the entire music industry. Speciality Records (his label) quickly drew on a few previously unreleased sessions to release a few more rocking Little Richard singles. However, Little Richard basically disappeared from the music scene.

"Long Tall Sally"
by Richard Penniman, Enotris Johnson, and Robert Blackwell

"Long Tall Sally" was not about a cross-dresser as many have speculated. Little Richard has said many times that Sally was a real life friend of his family who drank a lot of whiskey, claimed to have a cold, and needed the alcohol to make hot toddies to ease the cold. Richard described Sally as tall and ugly, with only two teeth. Sally was having an affair with a man named John, who was married to a woman named Mary, also known as "short fat Fanny."

Richard's producer, "Bumps" Blackwell, had him record the vocals at a fast temp to counter the version Pat Boone *would* copy, in order to make it difficult for Boone to replicate. Richard's rhythm section achieved that characteristic "in the cracks" shuffle feel that leaned in a straight-eighth note direction. The recording featured an inspired saxophone solo by Lee Allen (similar to his solo on "Tutti Frutti"). Richard was in full form on this track with his infectious energy and inspired vocal embellishments. The Beatles recorded a version of "Long Tall Sally," with Paul McCartney singing the lead. Rockabilly star Eddie Cochran wrote a tune inspired by "Sally" titled "Skinny Jim," that actually helped him score a recording contract.

Little Richard next focused his energies on the gospel style, recording a few low-profile albums for Mercury, Atlantic, and End Records in the early 1960's. However, Richard did return to rock 'n' roll by 1962 and toured England to great fanfare. Both the Rolling Stones and The Beatles heard him and were greatly influenced (especially Paul McCartney), as were many other potential British Invaders. Richard went back to Specialty Records and had a small hit with the song "Bama Lama Bama Loo." Richard spent the rest of the 1960's in constant comeback mode. He even recorded a few tracks at various record labels, including Vee Jay Records, where *Jimi Hendrix* was briefly in his band. The rock 'n' roll revival of the early 1970's allowed Richard to work on the nostalgia circuit with success. He also had a marginal hit with his 1970 song "Freedom Blues." In spite of his successful comeback, Richard returned to the church again in the late 1970's. He then eased his way back into rock 'n' roll by the mid-1980's and continued to guest on soundtracks and movies.

Little Richard with his "long tall" pompadour hair, eye mascara, and exciting flamboyant performances made him a living legend. Richard was, without doubt, one of rock musics' most charismatic performers and personalities. Richard has claimed many times that he was the first real rock 'n' roll artist and that he invented rock 'n' roll by combining his vocal techniques with boogie-woogie piano and R&B music. Many people would agree with that affirmation. Jerry Lee Lewis (and others) copied his wild stage antics of playing the piano while standing, banging the keys using different body parts, and bouncing up and down on the piano. Little Richard's extroverted and controversial performances made him one of the most successful rock artists of the 1950's. Among his many awards, Little Richard was inducted into the Rock and Roll Hall of Fame in 1986.

"The first record I bought myself could have been 'Wake Up Little Susie' by The Everly Brothers"

- John Oates (Hall and Oates)

"When I went into the studio to make Born To Run, I wanted to make a record with words like Bob Dylan that sounded like Phil Spector. But most of all, I wanted to sing like Roy Orbison."

- Bruce Springsteen

Collectively, Bo Diddley, Chuck Berry, Fats Domino, and Little Richard were the four giants of 1950's rhythm and blues that were to successfully cross racial barriers and bring early rock 'n' roll to America. They not only helped to invent rock 'n' roll but they changed the course of American popular music.

Another important influence on early rock 'n' roll was **The Everly Brothers** (1957-2005). Don and Phil Everly were the sons of the successful country music performers Ike and Margaret Everly. The Everly family had a radio show where the boys performed at the ages of seven and nine years old. In 1957, Don and Phil Everly were signed to Cadence Records located in Nashville where they showed great potential as a country act. It was at Cadence where label president Archie Bleyer and country division head Wesley Rose, introduced The Everly Brothers to Boudleaux Bryant, who was a prominent songwriter. Recording sessions for the Everly's featured top session sidemen guitarist Chet Atkins and Floyd Cramer on piano. Don and Phil Everly skillfully harmonized their voices together to create a perfect blend with their acoustic guitar sound. The Everly Brothers had a smooth sound and they rehearsed their carefully worked out musical arrangements before every recording session. The Everly style was different from the rockabilly sound and this helped them develop their own unique musical approach. Together, they absorbed the styles of Little Richard and Bo Diddley, and infused them into the prolific songs provided by Bryant, who wrote many of their early hits. The Everly Brothers toured with Buddy Holly in 1957 and 1958. They signed with Warner Brothers Records in 1960 and recorded their biggest hit "Cathy's Clown," before their career began to decline. Phil Everly died in 2014. The Everly Brothers were inducted into the Rock and Roll Hall of Fame in 1986 and the Country Music Hall of Fame in 2001.

"Bye Bye Love"
by Boudleaux Bryant and Felice

Written in 1959, "Bye Bye Love" was written to specifically fit the vocal range and harmonies of Don and Phil Everly. Ten days after the song hit the radio, "Bye Bye Love" went to number two on the U.S. charts and number one on the country charts. The tone of "Bye Bye Love" was non-threatening while catering to an adolescent audience. The Everly Brothers captured a feeling of optimism by singing about love in a way that it cured all problems.

"Bye Bye Love" defined the Everly Brothers' sound of two acoustic guitars, combined with a rhythm section of piano, bass, and drums. This simple instrumentation created an energy that propelled their songs without the need for shouting or hysterics. The smooth flow of the Everly's light melodic lines blended with smooth harmonies that enabled the music to float along seamlessly. Don Everly added the guitar intro to the tune while studio great Chet Atkins played lead guitar on the recording session. Many prominent artists including; George Harrison, Simon and Garfunkel, and Ray Charles covered "Bye Bye Love."

Buddy Holly (1936-1958) was one of the most important figures in early rock 'n' roll history. Holly was born in Lubbock, Texas and learned guitar at an early age while he absorbed country, gospel, and rhythm and blues styles. In 1952, Holly formed his first group Buddy and Bob, with his childhood friend Bob Montgomery. In 1955, Holly had three opportunities to open up for Elvis Presley. When Holly and his band shifted from a mostly country repertoire to rock 'n' roll, they were signed to a recording contract by Decca Records. They soon went to Nashville to record. Frustrated with the recording and production at Decca, Buddy went to New Mexico and re-recorded a demo of the tune "That'll Be the Day" that he wrote with drummer Jerry Allison and his soon to be producer, Norman Petty. Holly next signed to Brunswick Records and released "That'll Be the Day." He credited the song to his new band, which he called Buddy Holly and The Crickets. The song became a hit and was followed by another hit single "Peggy Sue."

In 1957 Buddy Holly and The Crickets released their debut album The Chirping Crickets featuring two more singles, "Oh, Boy," and "Not Fade Away." The album went to number five on the British charts. Holly's singing included a distinct style of vocal hiccups combined with a great ability to move smoothly from his standard voice into a falsetto voice. Holly played his Fender Stratocaster guitar (he was one of the first to use a solid body guitar) with an exciting and percussive feel. After a second appearance on *The Ed Sullivan Show*, Holly toured Australia and Britain, and returned to America for a forty-one city tour as part of Alan Freed's *Big Beat Show*. Holly restructured his band with guitarist Tommy Allsup, drummer Carl Bunch, and future country great Waylon Jennings on bass.

Holly and his new band went on a new tour of America with emerging rock stars Richie Valens and The Big Bopper. After a show in Iowa, Holly boarded a chartered plane that crashed; killing him, Valens, The Big Bopper, and the pilot Roger Peterson. This tragedy became known as the day the music died. Gone at age twenty-two, Buddy Holly defined the classic rock band instrumentation of two guitars, bass, and drums. He was a major influence on many artists including; Elton John, The Rolling Stones, and especially The Beatles. John Lennon and Paul McCartney studied Holly's songs and were fascinated by the image of the shy Texan with the horn-rimmed glasses. Lennon and McCartney were so inspired by Buddy Holly that they named The Beatles based on Holly's band name, The Crickets. Through his songs, Holly had an ability to communicate a real sense of hope in finding true love. He was one of the first rock 'n' rollers to musically convey a sense of optimism combined with an adolescent confidence. Buddy Holly was inducted into the Rock and Roll Hall of Fame in 1986.

"Peggy Sue"
written by Buddy Holly, Jerry Allison and Norman Petty

"Peggy Sue" went to number three on the American charts and number six on the British charts in 1957. Acoustic bassist Joe Mauldin and drummer Jerry Allison accompanied Holly on the recording. The song was originally titled "Cindy Lou," for Holly's niece and later changed to "Peggy Sue," after the girlfriend and future wife of drummer Jerry Allison. Buddy Holly created one of rock 'n' roll's most iconic figures in "Peggy Sue." The very idea of worshiping her seemed to appear in almost every Buddy Holly song.

"Peggy Sue" utilized a modified twelve-bar blues. The instrumentation was an electric solid-body guitar, acoustic rhythm guitar, acoustic bass, and drum set. On the recording, Holly added a guitar solo featuring a Chuck Berry styled strumming pattern. Jerry Allison's drums added a lot of energy to the track with a four to the bar accented sixteenth note tom-tom pattern. Holly's signature vocal hiccup was heard throughout the recording. Buddy Holly wrote a sequel to "Peggy Sue" titled "Peggy

Rock Hard Fact

In 1976 Paul McCartney bought the rights to the entire Buddy Holly song catalogue; and in 1987 McCartney narrated the movie *The Real Buddy Holly Story*.

Sue Got Married" that was recorded as a demo with only his acoustic guitar accompaniment. It was discovered after his death and reworked for the 1986 film *Peggy Sue Got Married* starring Kathleen Turner.

Roy Orbison (1936-1988) was an early rock 'n' roll singer from Vernon, Texas. His father, Orbie Lee, taught Roy to play guitar and he quickly started playing classic songs such as "You Are My Sunshine." Orbison formed his first band, The Wink Westerners, in 1949. They played country tunes but also created string arrangements of big band standards. Roy recorded a tune written by Dick Penner and Wade Lee Moore titled "Ooby Dooby," and attempted to secure a record deal with Columbia Records. It didn't happen. The Wink Westerners did however, have success performing some rock 'n' roll tunes including "Rock Around the Clock" and "That's All Right Mama." This earned them their own radio show. The show became successful and Johnny Cash and Elvis Presley both made appearances.

Next, Roy Orbison formed a new band, The Teen Kings, and focused on learning more rock 'n' roll songs. In 1956, Sam Phillips heard the band and brought them in to record at Sun. They recorded "Ooby Dooby," "Go Go Go (Down the Line)," and "Trying To Get To You." Orbison and The Teen Kings never really fit into the typical rockabilly model that came out of Sam Phillips's stable of stars. Orbison preferred more of the pop style of singing and considered himself more of a ballad singer. However, Orbison and The Teen Kings did develop an energetic stage show and toured with Carl Perkins, Johnny Cash, Jerry Lee Lewis, and other country and rockabilly stars. "Ooby Dooby" peaked at number one on the American charts but his other tunes didn't fair as well. Orbison started to focus more on his songwriting skills. From there, his new tunes, production skills, and performances gradually earned him success.

Roy Orbison had an original compositional style. Songs such as "Dream Baby," "Crying," "It's Over," and "Mean Woman Blues," became top forty hits and Orbison became a top selling American artist with international appeal. In 1964, Orbison recorded his biggest hit and best-known song "Oh Pretty Woman." It was co-written with his new writing partner, Bill Dees, and sold over seven million copies peaking at number one in America and Britain. "Oh Pretty Woman" was most famously covered by Van Halen, becoming the first hit from their Diver Down record. Orbison's personal life was marred by tragedy when his wife and two of his children died. Over time, Orbison went on to recover from this tragedy and had more musical success.

"Oh Pretty Woman"
by Roy Orbison and Bill Dees

"Oh Pretty Woman" was written by Orbison and his writing partner Bill Dees at a writing session at the Orbison family home. They began playing around with some ideas, when Roy's wife, Claudette, came in and said that she was going to town to do some shopping. Roy asked her if she needed any money and she replied, "No." Dees remarked that "pretty woman never need any money." Orbison then sang "pretty woman walking down the street." By the time Claudette returned from shopping, the song was complete. By the following week Orbison recorded it and by the next week it was a hit on the radio.

Musically, "Oh Pretty Woman" featured a driving four to the snare feel and a melodic bassline that Orbison utilized to build his vocal phrases. The guitar part and piano figures were built around the bassline. Of course, Orbison added his famous "catcall growl" to the track. Toward the end of the song, the bassline was partially stated and repeated until the full bassline entered to continue to drive the song. Most people know the song from the movie of the same name, starring Julia Roberts and Richard Gere, and the popular cover version by Van Halen. Roy Orbison also performed an inspired live version of "Oh Pretty Woman" backed by Bruce Springsteen, Jackson Browne, Elvis Costello, Tom Waits, James Burton, and J.D. Souther.

Roy Orbison fostered an eclectic approach to music. He blended his own brand of country music with Latin rhythms and he even borrowed sounds and arrangement techniques from classical music. Orbison also helped to pioneer the use of sophisticated string arrangements. His lush vocal choruses worked well with his own rich and distinctive three-octave voice. Late in his life, Orbison became one of the Traveling Wilbury's (see chapter twelve) which was an impromptu supergroup created by George Harrison and also featured Bob Dylan, Tom Petty, Jeff Lynne, and drummer, Jim Keltner. Orbison is on the first Wilbury's recording but he died at the age of 52 from cardiac arrest before the second Traveling Wilbury's recording. Roy Orbison was inducted into the Rock and Roll Hall of Fame in 1987.

Discussion Question

Did the crossover of rhythm and blues into a new market of popular youth culture serve as a catalyst for the development of early rock 'n' roll or would rock music have developed anyway? Take a position and use musical examples of different artists.

Teen Idols

The tragic day that Buddy Holly died (February 3rd, 1959) marked a clear turning point for rock 'n' roll. Soon after, Elvis Presley joined the Army, Chuck Berry went to jail, Jerry Lee Lewis had his personal and legal issues, Eddie Cochran also died, and rockabilly was fading quickly. There was a musical void that would eventually be filled by The Beatles and the British Invasion. But before the invasion, pop music was temporarily in the hands of record executives, promoters, television personalities, radio programmers, and disc jockeys. Music fans were hungry for new music and from the years, 1959 to 1963, the era of the **teen idol** dominated American pop-rock music. Many powerful individuals in the music business made meaningful musical contributions such as producer Phil Spector, TV personality and DJ Dick Clark, and Brill Building songwriters Carole King, Gerry Goffin, and Neil Sedaka.

In Philadelphia, **Dick Clark's** (1929-2012) legendary TV show *American Bandstand* became a national showcase for rock talent. *American Bandstand* was a daytime program that brought rock 'n' roll music, performers, and dancers directly to a teenage audience. Ed Sullivan's Sunday evening TV show also featured early rock performers, including The Beatles and Elvis Presley. Occasionally *American Bandstand* would give exposure to rockabilly and blues artists, but early on, it mostly spotlighted clean-cut white teen idols. The conservative family images of Pat Boone, Frankie Avalon, Fabian, Annette Funicello, Bobby Rydell, Ricky Nelson, and others

Rock Hard Fact

In addition to launching the careers of many teen idols, Dick Clark's *American Bandstand* later introduced America to Prince, The Jackson Five, Aerosmith, Run D.M.C., and many others.

"The white kids didn't want their mamma to know I was in the house. They'd put Pat Boone's record on the bed and put me in the drawer"

-Little Richard

were perfect since the rebel image of rockabilly stars was rejected by many leaders in the entertainment industry. Many of the emerging teen idols, especially the males, utilized the earlier singing styles of the 1920's and 1930's crooners such as Bing Crosby and Perry Como.

Pat Boone (1934-) was often referred to as a "safe" alternative to Elvis Presley. Pat Boone built his repertoire by singing pop ballads and covers of rhythm and blues tunes. His clean good boy image came to the forefront as he dramatically toned down Little Richards' provocative sound and vocal delivery. In the 1950's, Pat Boone's records charted more than any other rock 'n' roll artist other than Elvis Presley. He still holds the Billboard chart record of 220 consecutive weeks on the pop charts with one or more songs holding a spot each week. The "clean teen" image grew from the support of the movie and television industry. Pat Boone signed a million-dollar deal with Twentieth Century Fox in 1956 and made fifteen feature films. Later, Boone hosted a weekly TV show called *The Pat Boone-Chevy Showroom*. He also toured on the gospel circuit with his gospel-based *Pat Boone Family Show*.

"Two Hearts, Two Kisses (Make One Love)"
by Otis Williams and Henry Stone

"Two Hearts, Two Kisses," written in 1954, was originally recorded and released by a doo-wop vocal group from Cincinnati called Otis Williams and the Charms. It reached the rhythm and blues charts peaking at number eight in 1955. Later, Frank Sinatra, Doris Day, and the Crew Cuts covered it. However, it was Pat Boone that had the most success with the tune. As was customary for Boone, he was able to bring a song to a white teen market that was still unreachable for many deserving black rhythm and blues artists.

The tune had alternating twelve-bar sections with an eight bar bridge. Boone's version was recorded with Lew Douglas and His Orchestra. The groove had a shuffle feel (similar to the Charm's version) with a modified boogie-woogie piano accompaniment. The arrangement featured a tenor saxophone solo in the jump-jive style of Louis Jordan, making Boone's danceable version very popular with the teen-age television market.

In a weird moment, even for rock history, Pat Boone, at age sixty-seven, made an album in 1997 titled In a Metal Mood: No More Mr. Nice Guy. This shocker featured Boone's big band arrangements of covers of Metallica, Van Halen, and Led Zeppelin songs. This album got Boone kicked off the show *Gospel America*, but he was later re-instated.

Teen idol songs were about the happiness and heartbreak of teenage romance. Puppy love and the dreams of finding a perfect mate defined most song lyrics. **Frankie Avalon** (1940-) was born Francis Thomas Avallone in Philadelphia, Pa. He peaked with his hit "Venus" in 1959. In "Venus," Avalon sang in desperation to Venus, the Roman Goddess of love, to provide him with a girlfriend. Avalon was able to musically re-invent himself playing the romantic lead in many teen movies where he often worked opposite of the former Mickey Mouse club star, **Annette Funicello** (1942-2013). Funicello herself had eight hit records on the Walt Disney Vista label between 1959 and 1960. In a world dominated by male teen idol stars, Funicello was able to build her movie career with films such as *Beach Blanket Bingo* in 1965. **Fabian** (1943-) was born Fabiano Forte Bonaparte and was discovered by talent scouts in Philadelphia in 1957. After a few appearances on *American Bandstand*, Fabian became a teen sensation when he released the top forty hit "I'm a Man" in 1959. Fabian cultivated a tough guy, but still safe, image as another answer to Elvis. His other hits included "Tiger" and "Turn Me Loose." **Bobby Rydell** (1942-) was born Bobby Ridarelli and was a drummer before he became a singer. Rydell became a teen idol at age seventeen with his hit "Kissin Time." Another one of his hits, "We Got Love," focused on the high school subject of who was taking whom to the dance. In a five-year period, Rydell achieved more than twenty pop chart singles, most of them making the top forty.

The Brill Building Pop-Rock Songwriting Dynasty

The Brill Building in Manhattan, New York, was the home of a team of early rock 'n' roll and pop music songwriters that changed the course of rock music history. Al Nevins and Don Kirshner's music publishing company, Aldon Music, was located directly across the street from the Brill Building. Nevins and Kirshner saw the growing market for teenage based rock 'n' roll and the need to supply hundreds of new singers with rock songs. Few of these emerging talented singers wrote their own material, so Nevins and Kirshner systematically assembled an incredibly talented group of songwriters. The Brill lineup of songwriters were mostly organized in teams, such as Howard Greenfield and Neil Sedaka, Jeff Barry and Ellie Greenwich, Gerry Goffin and Carole King, Jerry Leiber and Mike Stoller, Barry Mann and Cynthia Weil, and Doc Pomus and Mort Shuman. Other Brill songwriters included Bobby Darin, Neil Diamond, and producer Phil Spector. The artists on many record labels came to rely on the Brill songwriters for material. No record label was larger than Atlantic Records, whose needs were frequently met by the hits written by the great Brill songwriting teams. Atlantic Records became known for having wonderful songs, magnificent artists, and talented producers.

The Brill songwriters were all raised on the Tin Pan Alley tradition of songwriting that was established in the first half of the twentieth century. Competition between the Brill songwriters was strong. Everyone wanted to score the latest hit and compose the most hits. However, this competition manifested into a few common musical and compositional qualities that became the "Brill Building" sound. All of the Brill songwriters found a connection with their teenage audience, writing songs that could appeal to teens. The songwriters related to teenage emotions, teenage interests, and values, but they also composed with a high level of professionalism.

The first of the great Brill songwriting teams was Neil Sedaka and Howard Greenfield. Sedaka and Greenfield wrote in the style of legends such as Cole Porter and Rodgers and Hart. Their lyrics were witty, utilized metaphors and imagery, and were technically refined. Sedaka and Greenfield wrote songs for many artists including; Connie Francis ("Who's Sorry Now," and "Where The Boys Are"), The 5th Dimension, The Monkees, and Frankie Valli.

Among the greatest of the Brill writers were Carole King and Gerry Goffin. In a span of five years, they wrote more than 200 singles, at least half making the charts. Goffin had a lyrical gift of dealing with teenage problems and situations that he combined with a sense of fantasy and realism. King became a

---

Rock Hard Fact

On their first visit to New York, The Beatles made it a point to meet their idols; the Brill Building songwriters Carole King and Gerry Goffin.

first rate melody writer, so good that it delayed her career as a solo artist. When the King and Goffin team called it quits (both musically and in their real life marriage), King (see chapter seven) went on to have great success with a very popular album in the 1970's called Tapestry.

Jerry Leiber and Mike Stoller were central to the creation of pop-rock. They started in Los Angeles in the early 1950's and cultivated a merger of rhythm and blues and pop songwriting. They wrote the hit "Hound Dog" for singer Willie Mae Thornton and began to work with a local act named The Robins. Soon, Atlantic Records signed The Robins and changed their name to the Coasters. Leiber and Stoller then moved to New York and wrote a string of hits for the Coasters and a newcomer named Elvis Presley. Leiber and Stoller also wrote for The Drifters, Lavern Baker, Peggy Lee, Perry Como, and many others. Leiber and Stoller were innovative in their use of strings on rhythm and blues records and also brought Phil Spector to New York to produce The Drifters and Ben E. King.

In their time, The Brill Building songwriters brought an unmatched sense of professionalism and great creativity to the craft of pop-rock songwriting. The teen idol era and the era of girl groups such as The Chiffons, The Shirelles, and The Angels would soon come to an end. With that, so did The Brill Building songwriting empire.

Bobby Darin (1936-1973) (aka Walden Robert Cassotto) was born in New York and entered the teen idol scene in the late 1950's. Darin was successful with the hits "Splish Splash," " Dream Lover," and a number one single, "Mack the Knife." Darin was able to dodge the label of being just a teen idol when he added jazz standards and folk songs to his repertoire. He also enjoyed successful performances in Las Vegas. Bobby Darin was inducted into the Rock and Roll Hall of Fame in 1990.

While Philadelphia was the hotbed for teen idols, New York offered **Paul Anka** (1941-), who became an overnight sensation with his hit "Diana" in 1957. It went to number one on the American pop charts. Anka (born in Canada) was a child prodigy, having written songs and performed at an early age. He wrote most of his own songs including his first hit, written at age fourteen, titled "I Confess." His other hits included "She's a Lady," "Lonely Boy," and "Anytime (I'll Be There)." Anka also wrote film music and acted in a number of films including *The Longest Day*.

"Diana"
by Paul Anka

Paul Anka's number one pop hit "Diana" was recorded in 1957 at RCA studios. It sold more than nine million copies. Anka recorded the tune many times, including a version in Italian. He has said that a girl from his church that he barely knew inspired "Diana." The song has been recorded by many of Anka's teen idol peers including Frankie Avalon and Frankie Lymon and The Teenagers. In 1965, Bobby Rydell also covered "Diana," where it reached number ninety-eight on the charts, eight years after Anka had taken it to the number one spot.

Besides the Italian version, "Diana" has had much international appeal. It has twice been adapted to Hindi film music. Anka sang it as a duet with Latin singer Ricky Martin on the album Amigos. In addition, another Italian cover was done when Anka again sang a duet of "Diana" with Italian singer Adriano Celentano.

Connie Francis (1938-) (aka Concetta Rosa Maria Franconero) was a teen idol vocalist in the late 1950's and early 1960's. Francis's career started slow with a string of moderately successful singles. Her breakthrough came in 1957 with a duet she sang with Marvin Rainater titled "The Majesty of Love." She recorded an album in Italian at Abbey Road Studios in 1959. A hit single emerged from the session titled "Mama." A slew of top forty hits followed including "Second Hand Love," and "Where the Boys Are." Connie Francis went on to star in a number of successful films. Another female teen idol, **Brenda Lee** (1944-) (aka Brenda Mae Tarpley), was a versatile singer that was comfortable singing rockabilly, pop, and country styles. She charted forty-seven hits in the 1960's and was best known in America for her songs "I'm Sorry," and "Rockin' Around the Christmas Tree." Brenda Lee was inducted into the Rock and Roll Hall of Fame in 2002.

Ricky Nelson (1940-1985) started as a child actor playing himself on the TV series *The Adventures of Ozzie and Harriet*. Between 1957 and 1973 he placed 53 songs on the American pop charts. Influenced by Carl Perkins, Nelson released a version of Fats Domino's "I'm Walkin" in 1957. He also released the hit "A Teenager's Romance," that went to number two on the charts. Ricky Nelson was the first of the teen idols to utilize television to promote his career. From 1957 to 1962, Nelson achieved thirty top forty hits, more than any artist other than Elvis and Pat Boone. He could sing rockabilly but his smooth voice made him equally adept at singing ballads. After his rockabilly career was over he became a major country rock music star (see chapter nine). Ricky Nelson was inducted into the Rock and Roll Hall of Fame in 1987.

Bobby Vee (1943-2016) (aka Robert Thomas Velline) was a teen idol in the early 1960's. Vee had thirty-eight chart hits and ten of them made the top twenty. Vee's first hit was "Suzie Baby" and was a tribute to Buddy Holly's "Peggy Sue." Bobby Vee also performed briefly with Bob Dylan when Dylan joined Vee's band for a short period. **Gene Pitney** (1940-2006) was a successful singer and songwriter whose career started in the early 1960's. Pitney saw sixteen of his songs reach the top forty charts and four made the top ten. Pitney was also the beneficiary of the songwriting team of Bert Bacharach and Hal David, who wrote some of his hits. Gene Pitney was inducted into the Rock and Roll Hall of Fame in 2002.

Chubby Checker (1941-) (aka Ernest Evans) was born in South Carolina. The Evans family moved to Philadelphia where Checker sang in a street-corner harmony group at the age of eight. Checker's stage name came while he was working for a man who called him chubby and after doing a Fats Domino impression, someone called him checker, thus Chubby Checker. Chubby had a huge hit in 1960 when he covered the Hank Ballard and The Midnighters' R&B hit "The Twist." It went to number one and became the source of a dance craze by the same name.

"The Twist"
by Hank Ballard (covered by Chubby Checker)

Songs about doing the twist go back to the time of minstrelsy, and have inspired many rhythm and blues variations. Similar songs to Hank Ballard's version include the "Grape Vine Twist." Hank Ballad's version became popular in Baltimore on a local television show in 1960. That got the attention of Dick Clark who tried to book Ballard for *American Bandstand*, but he was un-

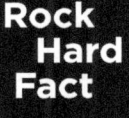

Rock Hard Fact

Guitar legend Jimi Hendrix once opened a show for the Monkees. Brian Wilson, Kurt Cobain, and the band U2, were also big fans of the group.

available. Dick Clark searched for a local artist to record the tune and settled on Chubby Checker, since his voice was similar to Ballard's voice.

By 1962, the twist was a fully established dance craze in America. Checker went on to re-record the tune many times; he even did a version of the tune called "Let's Twist Again." Joey Dee and the Starliters scored a knock off hit called "The Peppermint Twist." In 1988, Checker even did a hip-hop version with the group The Fat Boys called "Yo, Twist." Chubby Checker's "The Twist" was added to the National Recording Registry of the Library of Congress in 2013.

Richie Valens (1941-1959) (aka Richard Steven Valenzuela) was a rock 'n' roll pioneer. His career was tragically cut short when he died in the plane crash that also killed Buddy Holly and J.P. "The Big Bopper" Richardson. Valens was best known for his hit "La Bamba," that he adapted from a Mexican folk song. Valens was signed to Del-Fi Records in Hollywood, California. He recorded with an excellent studio band that included guitarist Rene Hall, bassist Carol Kaye, and drummer Earl Palmer. With them, Valens recorded his hit tunes "Come On, Let's Go," "Donna," and "La Bamba." Richie Valens was inducted into the Rock and Roll Hall of Fame in 2001.

"La Bamba"
traditional Mexican folk song (adapted by Richie Valens)

"La Bamba" became one of rock 'n' roll's best-known tunes. Valens was inspired by a similar melody of a Mexican folk song in the Son Jarocho style that combined Spanish, Mexican, and African musical elements. In the traditional wedding customs of Mexican culture, "La Bamba" is sung and danced by the bride and groom.

In the Richie Valens' version, he combined the traditional tune with strong rock energy and rhythmic drive. Valens was proud of his Mexican heritage, but was hesitant at first to create the rock version. Pleased with the recording of the tune, Valens grew to view the song as a measure of his identity. Los Lobos covered "La Bamba" in 1987 and their version was utilized in the film *La Bamba*.

The Monkees (1965-present) were a band created for television. The idea was to have a sitcom about a struggling band that consisted of four musicians (one British) that wanted to be The Beatles. The Monkees began with a Los Angeles newspaper ad looking for "four insane boys, ages seventeen to twenty-one." The chosen group consisted of child actors Micky Dolenz, Davy Jones, and musicians Peter Tork and Mike Nesmith. The TV show premiered in 1966 and the following year, The Monkees had a (real life) number one album and were a touring band.

Because The Monkees were created for TV, they needed professional studio musicians to write and record most of their songs (Mike Nesmith could really play-see chapter nine). Brill Building songwriters Tommy Boyce, Bobby Hart, and Neil Diamond wrote many of their hits. Top studio musicians contributed to their recordings, especially in the beginning. The four members of the band eventually wrote and continued to record their music through 1971, even though the TV show was canceled in 1968. The Monkees have sold over seventy-five million records worldwide and their hits included "Daydream Believer," and "Last Train to Clarksville."

Surf Rock

While the East Coast of America was pumping out teen idol songs about puppy love and going to the high school dance, the West Coast was generating bands that were creating their own brand of pop called **surf rock**. America knew little about the sport of surfing and its lifestyle of carefree trips to the beach to "hang ten" (get every toe over the surfboard) or to "wipe-out" (crash off the surfboard into a monstrous wave). But teens soon learned that surf rock was synonymous with having a good time and pursuing the dream of freedom. Unlike the East Coast vocalists who were inspired by the old crooner traditions and accompanied by large studio orchestras, the surf rock groups played their own instruments. Surf rock was a return to the rock 'n' roll basics of guitars, bass, and drums, yet it was still pop-oriented. In surf music, the vocals were important but the new sound and style of electric guitar playing was what characterized this new style of rock 'n' roll. Surf music was raw and full of energy. It featured the early guitar styles of **Duane Eddy**, **Dick Dale**, **Link Wray**, and **The Ventures**.

Duane Eddy (1938-) was an early rock 'n' roll guitarist that was influenced by blues and gospel styles. Duane Eddy helped to popularize the electric guitar, and had great success on the American pop charts between 1957 and 1963 with more that fifteen top forty hits. Eddy was also one of the first to record long playing albums instead of just releasing singles. In 1957, his hit "Movin N Groovin" established his sound and was followed by "Rebel-Rouser" in 1958. "Rebel-Rouser" saw Eddy's use of call and response phrasing when his lead guitar lines were answered by saxophone responses. Eddy influenced almost every rock guitar player to follow him, including George Harrison of The Beatles. By sticking with his trademark sound, Eddy's style became dated and he lost popularity with the coming of the British invasion. George Harrison and Paul McCartney, along with Ry Cooder and John Fogerty, helped Duane Eddy make a comeback album in 1987. Duane Eddy sold more than one-hundred million records worldwide and totaled over thirty singles on the pop charts. Duane Eddy was inducted into the Rock and Roll Hall of Fame in 1994.

Dick Dale (1937-) and The Del-Tones were one of the first to popularize the surf sound. He entered the scene in 1958 with his hit "Ooh-Whee-Marie." Dale, himself an avid surfer, released "Let's Go Trippin," in the summer of 1961. "Let's Go Trippin" was often called the first surf rock song, and reached number sixty on the pop charts while helping to fuel an explosion of garage surf rock bands. It was Dick Dale and The Del-Tones that firmly established the surf rock style. Dale was featured in the 1987 movie B*ack to the Beach* with teen idol stars Frankie Avalon and Annette Funicello. Dick Dale was given the title "The King of Surf" and his tremolo sounding guitar style was the most emulated of all the surf rock guitar players.

Early Developments in Guitar Sound and Techniques

There have been many significant developments in electric guitar technology throughout the history of rock. Advancements in guitar technology go hand in hand with innovative performance techniques and styles. Buddy Holly used a Stratocaster guitar that was one of the first solid-body guitars to be utilized in rock music. Solid-body guitars immediately became

---

> "The style of music I developed was the feeling I got when I was out there on the waves...I locked in a tube with the white water caving in over my head... trying to project the power of the ocean to the people. I couldn't get the feeling by singing, so the music took an instrumental form."
>
> – Dick Dale

popular when guitarists were attracted to their tone qualities and noticed they were very different from acoustic guitars and electric-acoustic guitars. From Dave Davies of the Kinks, to the surf rock guitarists, to the tapping techniques of Eddie Van Halen, guitar sound and technique has come a long way. Duane Eddy achieved a "twangy" guitar sound by plucking the strings close to the guitar bridge. Eddy used studio effects to create vibrato (a shimmering or wavering sound), especially when he played on the low guitar strings. This helped to define the "surf rock" sound.

Dick Dale worked with the Fender Guitar Company to develop the first one hundred watt guitar amplifier (after he kept blowing guitar amps up). Dale was one of the first to push the limits of guitar amps to create distortion at previously unheard of volume. Dale's single-note staccato guitar picking technique influenced both Jimi Hendrix and Eddie Van Halen, and set the stage for the "shredding" generation.

Link Wray, another guitar pioneer, was one of the first guitarists to use distortion on a rock recording. Wray was also credited for inventing the power chord. This was a chord consisting of only the root and fifth, and was played while using distortion. The use of distortion was important because it transformed the audio signal of different pitches (root and fifth of a power chord) to create additional partials (pitches) resulting in a full, more bassy and powerful sound. The Fender Stratocaster, Telecaster, and the Gibson Les Paul have become the standard instruments for most rock guitar players from the 1960's and 1970's. This included Jimi Hendrix who used a Fender Stratocaster and Eric Clapton who used a Gibson Les Paul.

Link Wray (1929-2005) was a songwriter, vocalist, and guitarist who gained popularity in the late 1950's. Wray was the first Native American rock star. He began playing a mixture of country, rockabilly, and early rock 'n' roll songs. In 1958, Link Wray and his Ray Men released the single "Rumble" and it eventually went to number sixteen on the pop charts and would sell over a million copies. It also fit into the surf rock instrumental song category. At first, "Rumble" was banned in Boston and New York for concerns that it might insight a riot (something you would not expect from an instrumental song). Link Wray was a strong influence on Neil Young, Iggy Pop, Pete Townshend, and Jimmy Page. Wray had a real rebel attitude and conveyed it in his guitar approach.

The Ventures (1958-present) were formed in 1958 in Tacoma, Washington by guitarists Bob Bogle and Don Wilson. They have sold over one million records worldwide and are the best selling instrumental rock band of all-time. The Ventures were popular in America and Japan in the 1960's when they released their debut album, Walk, Don't Run, which peaked at number eleven on the pop charts.

"Walk, Don't Run"
by Johnny Smith

"Walk, Don't Run" was an instrumental tune written by jazz guitarist Johnny Smith in 1954. Smith was inspired to write the tune after hearing the jazz standard "Softly, as in a Morning Sunrise." Smith used the chord progression from "Softly" when he composed the melody for "Walk, Don't Run." Later, the song was covered by country guitar great Chet Atkins in 1956. It was this version that inspired The Ventures to record the tune.

"Walk, Don't Run" was the Ventures first national release and it quickly went to number two on the pop charts. It had a clean, smooth melody played with a Duane Eddy type guitar sound. The drummer, Howie Johnson, played a typical "surfer beat" and had a brief solo break in the song. "Walk, Don't Run" effectively captured the sound and spirit of the surf rock movement.

The Ventures later released the album Hawaii Five-O in 1969 and it reached number eleven on the pop charts. The title track became known as the theme for the popular TV show *Hawaii Five-O*. The drummer in the band at the time was Mel Taylor, who joined the band in 1962 and stayed until 1996. The Ventures were one of the few surf rock bands that were able to maintain a substantial following all throughout the 1960's. The Ventures were inducted into the Rock and Roll Hall of Fame in 2008.

The Beach Boys (1961-present) were formed in 1961 in Los Angeles, California. Three brothers named Brian, Carl, and Dennis Wilson, their cousin Mike Love, and school friend Al Jardine first started a band called the Pendletones. Within a few months, the group was given the name The Beach Boys (which Brian Wilson detested) by a record label executive. Mike Love and Brian were inspired by Dick Dale and the Del-Tones (and the rest of the local music scene) to write a tune titled "Surfin." By the summer of 1962, The Beach Boys, with the help of the Wilson's father, Murray Wilson (who provided a musical but also abusive home life), helped secure a deal with Capitol Records.

The Beach Boys would soon find success that was comparable to The Beatles. In the 1960's, they triumphed by writing and releasing over fifteen American chart hits and numerous popular albums. The early Beach Boys style was identified by a signature vocal harmony style and Carl Wilson's guitar sound. Brian Wilson became The Beach Boys main composer, arranger, and producer. He was heavily influenced by the vocal harmonies of the group, The Four Freshman. Carl's guitar approach was inspired by Duane Eddy's twangy sound, the tremolo guitar effects of Dick Dale, and the riffs of Chuck Berry. Dennis Wilson lived the surfer lifestyle and played drumset, although studio musicians were sometimes brought in to play some of the drum parts.

In mid-1962, The Beach Boys released their debut album Surfin' Safari and it made the top twenty on the pop charts. Two songs, "Help Me Rhonda" and "I Get Around," both went to number one. Al Jardine temporarily left the group and was replaced by Dave Marks for a short time. By 1963, The Beach Boys had perfected their sound and style with the album Surfin' U.S.A., which went to number two on the American pop charts. Brian Wilson was coming into his own as a composer and record producer. Surfin' U.S.A. saw Brian's use of a rich sounding double track vocal recording technique, which strengthened the groups' already impressive vocal sound.

1963's Surfer Girl, their third studio album, went to number seven in America and number thirteen in Britain. Brian Wilson wrote the title track, "Surfer Girl," and the album marked the first time he was in total charge of the production. By 1964, Brian had quit touring with the band to focus on composing and studio production. The Beach Boys needed a tour replacement for Brian and Glen Campbell was chosen. Bruce Johnston then permanently replaced Campbell, who went on to have a successful solo career. Over the next four years, The Beach Boys cranked out seven more albums, establishing

> "The idea of taking a song, envisioning the overall sound in my head and then bringing the arrangement to life in the studio...well, that gives me satisfaction like nothing else."
>
> – Brian Wilson

Rock Hard Fact

Of the three Beach Boys brothers, drummer and vocalist Dennis Wilson was the only one to actually surf.

them as one of rock music's biggest acts, rivaled only by The Beatles.

The Beach Boys eleventh studio album, Pet Sounds, released in 1966, went to number ten on the American charts and number two in Britain. Not as commercially successful as many of their previous recordings, it was however soon recognized as a masterpiece by both critics and musicians (see Pet Sounds profile). Brian Wilson wrote most of the music, produced, and arranged the entire album. In late 1966, The Beach Boys released the single "Good Vibrations" after the release of Pet Sounds. "Good Vibrations" was an instant hit and was acknowledged as one of the most sophisticated pop-rock studio productions in rock history.

Groundbreaking album Pet Sounds

Brian Wilson experimented with the drug LSD in 1965 and said that he saw God. He then began working on a song cycle that would become the material for the album Pet Sounds. Brian was motivated by an ongoing rivalry with The Beatles. He had heard The Beatles' Rubber Soul and his goal was to make the greatest rock record ever. By creating a unified song cycle with elaborate arrangements and orchestration, Wilson was conceptualizing sounds that were previously unheard of on a rock recording. Wilson was looking to create the massive production approach made popular by Phil Spector and his "Wall of Sound." He even utilized many of the same first call studio musicians, (known as the Wrecking Crew) which were usually in the employ of Phil Spector. When recording Pet Sounds, Wilson would take the individual parts of the entire orchestral arrangement (contained in his mind), and teach the individual parts to each studio musician. Brian was open to advice and collaboration from the Wrecking Crew musicians, which was smart, since they represented the very best in the business.

The unifying concept of Pet Sounds saw Wilson articulate a young person's dreams, hopes, and anxiety about their current and future life. The optimism for life was reflected in the songs "Wouldn't It Be Nice," "I'm Waiting For the Day," and "Don't Talk (Put Your Head On My Shoulder)." The opening song, "Wouldn't It Be Nice," revealed Brian's fantasy theme of marital bliss. Other themes spoke to Wilson's obsession with the human condition of isolation and a hope for finding security. Feelings of being insecure were heard in the songs "I Know There's an Answer," "God Only Knows," and "Caroline, No." The album's conclusion contained a sad tone and dealt with the inevitability of personal change. The song cycle ended with a tone of resignation with "Caroline, No." It was the culmination of Brian Wilson's use of large melodic intervals and his imaginative experimentation with tone colors and studio soundscapes.

For Pet Sounds, Brian Wilson utilized numerous sound effects that included; barking dogs, soda cans, train sounds, and bicycle bells. Wilson also employed the wide array of instrumental sounds of the harpsichord, flute, organ, and Hawaiian string instruments. His vocal harmonies were complex and were voiced in multi-layers. Wilson brought in a new lyricist, Tony Asher, because he wanted to explore doing something completely different with an outside creative force. Pet Sounds had a feeling of psychedelia, not just because of Wilson's previous use of LSD, but also in its haunting and expansive ("trippy" as the Hippies would say) feeling.

Pet Sounds would become known as the first rock concept album, which would become a trend in the late 1960's throughout the 1970's. Previously, concept albums were common in classical and jazz recordings but rock albums were merely collections of individual songs with no connection to each other. Pet Sounds inspired The Beatles to write Sgt. Pepper's Lonely Hearts Club Band and together, these two albums fueled dozens of rock concept albums, especially in the progressive rock genre.

"Good Vibrations"
by Brian Wilson and Mike Love

"Good Vibrations" hit the British charts at number six and quickly went to number one, giving The Beatles strong competition. In America, the song sold over four-hundred thousand copies in only four days as it climbed to number one on the charts. Brian Wilson spent more than $75,000 dollars (making it the most expensive single ever recorded to date) on the multi-layered approach he had developed from his experience recording Pet Sounds. Band member Mike Love wrote the lyrics for "Good Vibrations."

Wilson experimented with numerous instrument combinations including the electro-theremin and cello parts to help to thicken the musical texture. Brian Wilson, much like Phil Spector, was able to utilize the recording studio as an instrument unto itself. "Good Vibrations" would take more than six months to complete with over ninety hours of recorded music and eleven complete versions of the song before Brian was happy with the three and a half minute final version.

The first part of the song used sixteen bar sections in an ABAB structure. The B sections contain the "Good Vibrations" lyrics. The tune moved to an instrumental section and then a closing section in a slower tempo where two melodies were sung simultaneously creating a polyphonic texture. The recording was done in mono, similar to Phil Spector's approach, to avoid the separation of stereo recording. Brian Wilson named the tune after his obsession with the idea of cosmic vibrations, after his mother once told him (as a child) that dogs will bark at people that give off bad vibrations.

In 1967, it appeared that Brian Wilson and The Beach Boys were on top of the musical world, but something was wrong. Brian was becoming less productive and very erratic in his personal life. A new record that would be Brian's crown jewel, to be titled Smile, was to feature a four-part suite. The plan was to release it by Christmas of that year. It remained unfinished. A new song for the album, "Heroes and Villains," was nearly complete, but Brian was working on new pieces and then kept scrapping them. Numerous recording sessions were cancelled and his mental state was deteriorating. Brian had brought in songwriter and composer Van Dyke Parks to collaborate with him on the lyrics for the Smile album, but Parks became frustrated with Brian's behavior. In 1967, The Beach Boys released Smiley Smile with an abridged version of "Heroes and Villains" and material salvaged from the failed Smile sessions. After their next album, titled Wild Honey, The Beach Boys were facing diminished record sales and Brian became less involved in the band's recording output. The Beatles had also recently released Sgt. Pepper's Lonely Hearts Club Band and Brian (very competitive) became more depressed.

Moving forward, The Beach Boys were still successful on the charts and on tours. However, the days of chart domination seemed to be over. Throughout the 1970's, they were still able to establish a new fan base and continue to record new material and tour as a featured act. In 1971, The Beach Boys released their seventeenth studio album, Surf's Up, which saw Carl Wilson emerge to lead the band. The Beach Boys had always felt the pressure to perform their old chart topping material and in 1974 they released Endless Summer, a double album of greatest hits. It went to number one on the American charts and served to revitalize their career. However, Brian was writing music outside of The Beach Boys mold that was dark and moody. Then in the late 1970's, Brian Wilson returned to the stage with The Beach Boys and played a major part in producing a couple of their albums, including The Beach Boys Love You in 1977.

The band was in turmoil in 1981 when Carl Wilson left (he came back a year and a half later) and Brian was fired (he returned the following year). Then, tragically Dennis Wilson drowned while swimming in 1983. Brian Wilson next released his debut solo album in 1988. The Beach Boys did manage to release 1985's The Beach Boys, 1989's Still Cruisin, and 1992's Summer in Paradise. Carl Wilson then died of cancer in 1998. Brian and Al Jardine focused on developing their own bands.

The new millennium saw Brian's long overdue lost album Smile released as well as more Beach Boys compilation records. Brian Wilson's solo career included nine albums that charted in America and Britain. In 2006, the surviving members of The Beach Boys; Brian Wilson, Mike Love, Al Jardine, Dave Marks, and Bruce Johnston reunited for a celebration of the fortieth anniversary of Pet Sounds. In 2011, the Beach Boys released The Smile Sessions, a collection of original recordings to celebrate the band's fiftieth anniversary. The Beach Boys remain active, currently still recording and touring.

Over a long career, The Beach Boys music developed far past their original surf image and suburban myths. The components of The Beach Boys musical sound became legendary. The densely clustered vocals were distinctive with intricate polyphonic motion. Their songs could be either simple or complex, and they were often anthem-like in their message of the American dream. Throughout the 1960's, The Beach Boys painted a picture of beaches, fun parties, and the endless summer. By the end of the decade and into the 1970's, The Beach Boys left behind the themes of youth and explored more serious topics of religion, conservation, and even politics. Similar to Chuck Berry, The Beach Boys came to represent, through their music and lyrics, an entire era of music. Like The Beatles, they found incredible early success and then progressed musically in complex and innovative directions. The Beach Boys were inducted into the Rock and Roll Hall of Fame in 1988.

Jan and Dean were a vocal duo that became popular surf rock and psychedelic rock artists in the early 1960's. Jan was born William Jan Berry (1941-2004) and Dean was born Dean Ormsby Torrence (1940-). Jan and Dean attained hit status in 1963 when their friend, Brian Wilson of The Beach Boys, gifted them the tune "Goody Connie Won't You Come Back Home," which turned into "Two Girls for Every Boy," and finally became "Surf City." The tune "Surf City" was the first surf rock tune to reach number one on the American pop charts. In 1991, Dean convinced town officials to change the name of Huntington Beach, California, to Surf City. Jan Berry went on to become one of the most successful record producers on the West Coast. **The Bel-Airs** (1961-1963) were another surf rock band that developed the surf rock guitar sound. Their best-known tune was the 1961 hit "Mr. Moto." **The Surfaris** (1962-present) were one of the most popular surf rock bands in the early 1960's. They were known for two surf songs; "Surfer Joe" and "Wipe Out" (also covered by The Ventures.)

Phil Spector's Wall of Sound and The Wrecking Crew

In the 1960's, talented musicians, producers, and sound engineers utilized recording studios and music technology like painters used brushes and paint. The studio became not only a place to record music, but also a tool to achieve new creative milestones. The studio became an instrument. The producer became more than someone who gave orders and booked recording sessions. He became a powerful conduit in the artistic process. Top-level studio musicians became in demand when songwriters and artists wanted the highest standard of musicianship to bring their songs to life. This evolution transformed producer Phil Spector, and a collective group of first call Los Angeles studio musicians known as The Wrecking Crew, into the pinnacle of studio production and first-rate musicianship available to musicians anywhere.

Phil Spector (1939-) was born in the Bronx, New York. His family moved to Los Angeles when he was a young boy. Spector played guitar and piano and began writing songs including "To Know Him is to Love Him," which he soon recorded. It became an instant hit. Next, he moved to Philadelphia and appeared on American Bandstand. At age nineteen, Spector returned to New York to be around the many talented songwriting teams at the Brill Building. Eventually, Atlantic Records hired Spector to produce some recording sessions. There, he produced hit singles for Curtis Lee and Ray Paterson and wrote the hit "Spanish Harlem" for artist Ben E. King.

After this early success at Atlantic, Spector founded his own label, Philles (after his partnership with Lester Sill). He moved back to Los Angeles and started to work at Gold Star Studios. At Gold Star, Spector learned his craft from the studio's owners and recording engineers, Stan Ross and Dave Gold. They taught him how to record drums, how to arrange, and how to mix a record. Ross and Gold treated the studio like an instrument itself and Spector further learned how to layer tracks and create larger soundscapes. Spector kept expanding on these recording and production techniques to eventually establish his "Wall of Sound" approach.

The "Wall of Sound" utilized enormous instrumentation and complex arrangements. Spector's approach evolved from his daring and imaginative creative mind. Through the use of multi-tracking, he made his rhythm sections sound like massive armies. Spector controlled every aspect of his recordings and came away with the most intense and explosive rock recordings in the 1960's. Between 1961 and 1966, Spector produced more than two-dozen top forty hits by artists such as; The Ronettes, The Crystals, The Righteous Brothers, Ben E. King, Gene Pitney, and many more. A few of the hit "teen dreams" songs included; "Then He Kissed Me," "Be My Baby," "Baby I Love You," and "You've Lost That Lovin' Feeling."

Phil Spector was rich and on top of the recording business. Then in the mid-1960's, Spector had trouble maintaining his own label and production company. He retired, became a recluse, then returned

Rock Hard Fact

If a rock song came out of a Los Angeles studio between 1962 and 1973, it was probably recorded by some combination of the Wrecking Crew musicians.

to work on some projects, including producing John Lennon's "Imagine." Alan Klein (The Beatles manager) asked Spector to rescue The Beatles album <u>Let It Be</u> when The Beatles had broken up and left only the raw session tapes behind. Lennon and George Harrison were happy with the result (McCartney was not pleased) and this led to Spector co-producing solo records by Lennon and Harrison. Phil Spector, one of the most successful producers in rock music history, had long suffered from mental and personal issues. In 2003, he was charged with murder and was convicted in 2008. He had previously been inducted into the Rock and Roll Hall of Fame in 1989.

Sometimes called the First Call Gang or The Clique, they were often referred to as The Phil Spector Wall of Sound Orchestra. But drummer Hal Blaine named them The Wrecking Crew and the name stuck. The Wrecking Crew was a collection of top studio musicians that worked from the 1960's to 1970's in Los Angeles. Recording in various combinations, they supported numerous rock 'n' roll artists on countless top hits.

The Wrecking Crew played on many of Phil Spector's productions, effectively becoming his house band on his "Wall of Sound" productions. Their reputation spread quickly and they soon became the most requested session musicians in Los Angeles, playing behind; Frank Sinatra, Jan and Dean, The Beach Boys (<u>Pet Sounds</u> and "Good Vibrations"), Sonny and Cher, The Ronettes, The Mamas and The Papas, and countless others. They also appeared without credit on records by Bob Dylan, The Byrds, and The Monkees.

One of the Wrecking crew's great drummers, Hal Blaine, has said that the Wrecking Crew's name came from negative comments made to them by older musicians who did not agree with their support of rock 'n' roll music. A partial list of Wrecking Crew musicians included; guitarists Tommy Tedesco, Barney Kessel, and Glen Campbell, bassist and guitarist Carol Kaye, drummers Earl Palmer and Hal Blaine, keyboardists Larry Knechtel, Dr. John, and Leon Russell, saxophonist Steve Douglas, and others.

Discussion Question

How did the innovations in songwriting and studio production change the face of rock music moving forward? Give specific examples of current rock music (post-1970's) studio albums and link them to some of the artists you learned about in this chapter.

Chapter Three: Early Rock 'N' Roll

"I mean what lyric could possible say it better than this? 'A-wop wop-a loo-mop-a wop bam boom-tutti frutti, aw rootie, tutti frutti'"

- Carole King on the influence of Little Richard

Chapter Four:
The Blues Takes a Trip and the Supergroups

In the 1950's American rock 'n' roll became popular in Britain. So did the Delta and Chicago blues. Many American blues greats began to tour Britain, particularly London, where young hungry to learn musicians such as Jimmy Page, Eric Clapton, Keith Richards and Mick Jagger were just getting on the scene. British blues musicians played with a real passion for the music as they attempted to cover the great tunes of Willie Dixon, Muddy Waters, Howlin' Wolf and others as authentically as they could. This was pivotal in rock history since so many talented young musicians would work together to absorb the pure blues. Their goal was simple but improbable. They tried to replicate exactly what they heard from a completely different culture that was an ocean away.

British blues artists such as Cyril Davies and Alexis Korner's **Blues Incorporated**, **John Mayall's Bluesbreakers**, Peter Green and Mick Fleetwood's **Fleetwood Mac**, **The Animals**, and **The Yardbirds** provided the training ground for many of rock's great bands of the future. Supergroups such as **Cream**, **The Rolling Stones**, and **Led Zeppelin** were all formed and developed as a result of the strong influence of the American blues. This chapter will explore this strong blues influence and the careers of these supergroups.

Almost from its beginning, jazz appealed to audiences all over Europe. Starting in the 1930's, the first American blues also found its way to Britain. Classic blues singers such as Ma Rainey, Bessie Smith, the blues styles of Fats Waller, and the ragtime of Jelly Roll Morton were also exposed to British musicians. Blues artists on major American record labels in the early 1950's became the obsession for a growing blues market in London. The blues soon mixed with the British folk style of skiffle as artists such as Lonnie Donegan became popular using simple homemade instruments. Trombonist Chris Barber led a number of traditional jazz bands and also supported a number of young blues musicians that worked their way through his ensembles. Barber was a catalyst in helping to bring many American blues artists to London including Big Bill Broonzy and Muddy Waters.

Cyril Davies, a harmonica and guitar player, together with guitarist Alexis Korner, formed **Blues Incorporated**. They also ran their own blues club. Blues Incorporated became an important stop for many of the early blues-rock stars to emerge from the London blues scene. Korner, a former member of Chris Barber's Jazz Band, shared the same passion for the blues as did Cyril Davies. In 1954, they first worked as a duo, playing blues in London jazz clubs. The Korner and Davies-led Blues Incorporated became the first blues band to become amplified in England. Later in 1962, Davies left to start his own band, The Cyril Davies All-Stars because he disagreed with Korner's idea of adding a full brass section to the band. Most of the Rolling Stones including Mick Jagger, Keith Richards, and Charlie Watts all played with Blues Incorporated at one time. Future members of the band Cream, Ginger Baker and Jack Bruce, also played in Blues Incorporated.

Another significant British blues band known as **John Mayall and the Bluesbreakers** (1963-1970) (1982-2008) formed in 1962. Mayall developed his blues style with an ever-evolving lineup of hungry blues musicians. Mayall was a singer/songwriter/organist/and guitarist who provided a training ground for

> "I was astounded by what I heard. It took guitar playing, songwriting, and delivery, to a totally different height. And at the same time it confused us, because it wasn't band music, it was one guy."
>
> – Keith Richards on the influence of Robert Johnson

Rock Hard Fact

The Rolling Stones have had a remarkably stable official lineup over their fifty-plus year history with only guitarist Ronnie Wood replacing Mick Taylor who replaced Brian Jones.

"Rock and Roll: Music for the neck downwards"

– Keith Richards

many prominent musicians including; Peter Green, Eric Clapton, Mick Fleetwood, Mick Taylor, John McVie, and Aynsley Dunbar. Mayall had previously released two singles in 1964 titled "Mr. James" and "Crawling Up a Hill." He went on to release John Mayall Plays John Mayall in 1964. After working with so many of Britain's up and coming blues and rock musicians, Mayall and the Bluesbreakers later found some success in America. Much later in 2003, Eric Clapton, Mick Taylor, and Chris Barber reunited with Mayall and The Bluesbreakers for John Mayall's 70th Birthday Concert in Liverpool. Mayall disbanded the Bluesbreakers in 2008 but did record an album in 2009 for Eagle Records.

Guitarist Peter Green and drummer Mick Fleetwood formed the first version of **Fleetwood Mac** (see chapter eleven) in 1967. Fleetwood Mac debuted at the British Jazz and Blues Festival in August 1967. Bob Brunning played bass (John McVie would later join) and slide guitarist Jeremy Spencer also joined the band. Their debut album, Fleetwood Mac was a big hit in England, spending over a year in the top ten on the charts. However, the album was unknown in America. The following year, Fleetwood Mac recorded the album Fleetwood Mac in Chicago with bluesmen Otis Spann and Willie Dixon. They later signed a record deal with Reprise/Warner Bros. Records who also re-released the band's British records. Fleetwood Mac released two albums in 1969, English Rose and Then Play On. However, Peter Green suddenly left the band in 1970 and later released two solo albums over that same decade.

Another British musician that played a prominent role was singer Eric Burdon. Burdon, together with keyboardist and composer Alan Price, formed **The Animals** in 1962. Burdon's powerful voice allowed him to sing the Delta blues style with authority. The Animals covered many American blues and R&B songs and were a part of the soon to be British Invasion (see chapter eleven for more on The Animals).

Throughout the 1950's British musicians focused on Muddy Waters, Howlin' Wolf, and many other Delta and Chicago legends. Those influences and especially the brilliant blues songwriting of Willie Dixon, would become the core roots for four of the biggest supergroups of all time.

On July 12th, 1962 **The Rolling Stones** (1962-present) gave their first public performance at London's Marquee Club. Their original lineup consisted of vocalist/harmonica player Mick Jagger, guitarist/vocalist Keith Richards, guitarist/vocalist Brian Jones, bassist Dick Taylor, drummer Mick Avory (later drummer for The Kinks) and keyboardist Ian Stewart. The Stones were created from members of many popular London blues bands. Mick Jagger had led the group Little Boy Blue and the Blue Boys with Dick Taylor on bass. Brian Jones played with Alexis Korner's Blues Incorporated. Jagger and Richards would occasionally sit in with Blues Incorporated. Bassist Bill Wyman then replaced Taylor and soon after, Charlie Watts replaced Mick Avory on drums.

Early on, Ian Stewart was considered to be the sixth Rolling Stone. However, he was not included in the official lineup because management thought that he didn't look the part fitting the desired image of the Stones. Ian Stewart was responsible for organizing the Stones with rehearsals and influencing them to blend blues with early rock 'n' roll. Richards was inspired by Stewart's strong jazz background, love of Count Basie, and boogie-woogie piano styles. Keith Richards stated, "Stu encouraged me to play the Chuck Berry stuff, while the other guys wanted to play strictly Howlin' Wolf, Lead Belly, and other bluesy material." #1

The Rolling Stones really began when Jagger and Richards met as young teenagers. Both had a strong love of the blues and were open minded about embracing the musical styles of early rock 'n' roll, rhythm and blues, skiffle, American country music, and more. Keith remembered his strong musical connection to Mick when he said, "By the time I met Mick on the train at Dartford, I'd already heard one or two tracks by Muddy Waters, but I didn't actually own any of his records. Mick had a copy of The Best of Muddy Waters. Within a few days of seeing each other, I either went over to Mick's place or he came over to mine. And almost inexplicably, from that one meeting between Mick and myself, with me wanting to know where he'd got his records from, and then as we listened to them together, we realized that we were really in touch-which we still are now, in this weird, bizarre, night and day method of ours. When it comes to music, if we work on it together, there's something that just happens. I don't know how or why: I leave that to the mysteries of alchemy." #2

The Rolling Stones acquired their name in a spontaneous way. Keith explained, "Jazz News had far cheaper ad rates that Melody Maker. Brian (Jones) was on the phone talking to them and said, 'We'd like to place an ad. We're available for work, and you can call us at…' The voice on the other end of the line obviously said, 'What are you called?' Panic. The Best of Muddy Waters album was on the floor-and track one was 'Rollin' Stone Blues.' So the band's name was picked for us by Muddy Waters." #3

The Stones began to play a regular weekly gig at Richman's Station Hotel which was later renamed the Crawdaddy Club after a Bo Diddley tune. Initially, the focus of the band was to study and imitate the styles of blues greats such as Howlin' Wolf, Muddy Waters, and John Lee Hooker. The Stones played these blues standards and their early performances were well attended. Even The Beatles came out to hear them. Much has been written about the contrast between the good boy image of The Beatles with their matching suits and nice boy manners and the bad boy image of The Rolling Stones. The Stones were identified as rebellious and unruly, the guys you would not want your daughter to date. This controversy was largely media driven. The reality was that all of the members of The Beatles and The Stones knew and liked each other, often cooperating with the timing of their record releases. In 1963, Lennon and McCartney actually gave The Stones their first hit on the British charts titled "I Wanna Be Your Man."

Andrew Oldham was signed to manage The Rolling Stones. Oldham was very aggressive, smart, and an observer of Brian Epstein's successful management of The Beatles. Oldham quickly helped The Stones sign their first recording contract with Decca records. It's important to recognize that like other bands from this era, The Stones were permitted to release a number of albums without record company pressure to record original material. This allowed the band to absorb other artists and styles (especially the blues) and most importantly, develop their own sound over time.

The Rolling Stones debut was their self-titled 1964 The Rolling Stones (British release). The American release was titled The Rolling Stones-England's Newest Hit Makers. It consisted of mostly covers of blues greats such as Willie Dixon and Jimmy Reed and a cover of rock legend Chuck Berry's "Carol." Their second release was titled 12 x 5 and contained mixtures of early rock covers, blues, and some original songs. In 1965, The Stones released The Rolling Stones Now! that featured the Willie Dixon tune "Little Red Rooster." This blues was covered by many blues and rock artists including Big Mama Thornton and The Grateful Dead. On a tour of America, the band recorded at Chess Records in Chicago with their hero Willie Dixon in attendance. This was an important milestone for The Stones because Willie Dixon made a huge impact on their approach to the blues.

"Little Red Rooster"
by Willie Dixon

"Little Red Rooster" was a blues standard written by bassist/vocalist/songwriter and producer Willie Dixon in 1961. Dixon wrote the song with Delta blues great Howlin' Wolf in mind for his characteristic vocals and slide guitar style of playing. Dixon borrowed elements from earlier blues tunes and the story came from a southern belief that a rooster helped to keep peace in the barnyard. The rooster was a metaphor for a woman who has left her man and home (the barnyard). Her man was pleading for her to return.

Mick Jagger, Keith Richards, and Brian Jones previously met Howlin' Wolf and had seen him perform at the first American Folk Blues Festival in 1962. Soon after, The Rolling Stones went to Chess Records when they were in Chicago and spent time with Willie Dixon. He encouraged them to play and record his songs. When The Stones recorded "Little Red Rooster," Jagger changed the lyric from "I got a little red rooster" to "I am a little red rooster." Brian Jones played inspired blues guitar and managed to get his guitar to crow like a rooster and bark and howl like a hound dog. Brian Jones was perhaps The Stones biggest blues purist and it showed on this recording. "Little Red Rooster" went to number one on the British pop charts and had the distinction of being the only blues tune to ever get to number one! In addition to the above mentioned artists, "Little Red Rooster" was also recorded by the legendary soul singer Sam Cooke.

Andrew Oldham realized that most successful bands wrote their own material and that the Stones were not doing much writing. Therefore, he forced Mick and Keith to compose original songs. Mick Jagger recalled, "Andrew told Keith and I that 'I should lock you in a room until you've written a song,' and in that way mentally he did lock us in a room, but he didn't literally lock us in." #4 Oldham saw the potential of the Jagger/Richards songwriting combination and he also pushed the band to record and tour at a frenzied pace. All of this led to their first all original recording titled Aftermath. Recorded in 1966, Aftermath contained the songs "Paint it Black" and "Under My Thumb." "Paint it Black" featured the musical experimentation of Brian Jones where he added a sitar part (an Indian instrument). Brian Jones frequently added other timbres to Stones songs like the marimba, dulcimer, autoharp, and Mellotron.

Keith Richards

Keith Richards defines what it means to play rock guitar. Keith admits learning most of what he played off of records. He wasn't a fan of notating music, and felt it was too constricting. Keith never limited himself to the standard roles of having a rhythm guitar play chords and a lead player shredding a solo. Of course, in the Rolling Stones chords are played, and solos are taken. However, Richards heard the interplay of two guitarists much like counterpoint heard in classical composition. Keith never felt the need to dominate the solo spotlight and was always unselfish for the "good of the team." The results? The Stones are about the feel of the music. Whether it was with Mick Taylor or Ronnie Wood, Richards made the rhythmic interplay of two guitars musical and exciting.

Keith Richards is the master of the rock guitar riff. It's never about the flash (except Jumpin Jack). The riffs have built-in melodies. The listener can hear the soul and essence of rock within his guitar approach. Richards worked constantly to incorporate what he heard many of the old blues guitarists play. He then converted it to electric guitar. His goal was to keep the simplicity and the pumping drive achieved by many of the acoustic blues players, but now reinvent it for The Rolling Stones.

Richards also successfully experimented with guitar tunings. He remembered, "In 1968 or early 1969 was when I started playing the open five-string tuning. It transformed my life. It's the way of playing that I use for the riffs and songs the Stones are best known for; 'Honky Tonk Women,' 'Brown Sugar', 'Tumbling Dice,' 'Happy,' 'Start Me Up,' 'Satisfaction,' 'Flash' too… I just really thought I was not getting anywhere from straight concert tuning. I wasn't learning anymore; I wasn't getting some of the sounds I really wanted. I'd been experimenting with tunings for quite a while. Most times I went into different tunings because I had a song going and I was hearing it in my head but I couldn't get it out of the conventional tuning no matter any way I looked at it." #5

There are many legendary stories about Keith's bad boy image and about how he has eluded death on more than one occasion. Richards was on vacation on a private Island off of Fuji during a break from The Stones The Bigger Bang world tour. When Keith was lounging in a tree; he slipped and fell, hitting his head. A few days later, he suffered two seizures from a brain bleed from the fall and almost died. He was air-lifted to New Zealand and had emergency brain surgery by a neurosurgeon. Six weeks later Keith Richards was back on stage with The Stones.

The 1967 album Their Satanic Majesties Request was the Stones' answer to The Beatles Sergeant Peppers Lonely Hearts Club Band. The Stones were not happy with the results, nor was Andrew Oldham, who officially left as the band's manager. This was a difficult time in the band's history. The combination of drug experimentation, lack of direction in the studio with no producer, and inconsistent material led to chaos and problems. One bright spot was the emergence of pianist Nicky Hopkins (he joined the band in the studio) who went on to become one of rock's great piano players.

Groundbreaking album Beggars Banquet
by The Rolling Stones

1968's Beggars Banquet saw a change in the direction of the songwriting for the Stones. New producer Jimmy Miller gave the band a much needed strong focus. Miller was respected as someone who had great ears and was a good musician himself, occasionally adding parts to tracks (including drums and backing vocals). He brought the band to a new level exactly when they needed it. Miller simply had a great feel for the band. Beggars Banquet had a very folk song flavor that also contained a mix of styles including; country, a return to earlier blues roots, and

Rock Hard Fact

One honor that the 74 year-old Keith Richards is proud of is that he has appeared the most on many music magazine's top ten mostly likely to die next lists.

still enough rock 'n' roll to produce two of the Stones greatest classics.

Side one opened with "Sympathy for the Devil," then "No Expectations," "Dear Doctor," "Parachute Woman," and "Jigsaw Puzzle." "Sympathy for the Devil" contained a hybrid Latin groove and a gospel meets R&B piano feel that built with musical intensity throughout. Brian Jones provided a great slide guitar part on "No Expectations," one of his last meaningful contributions to the band.

Side two opened with "Street Fighting Man," then "Prodigal Son," "Stray Cat Blues," "Factory Girl," and "Salt of the Earth." "Street Fighting Man" explored the political turbulence of the late 1960's and was The Stones first song to take a political stance. Keith came up with a breakthrough sound for "Street Fighting Man" by playing his acoustic guitar into a cassette recorder and then distorting the sound by playing it back through a speaker. The only electric instrument on the track was the electric bass. "Prodigal Son" and "Stray Cat Blues" achieved a strong Delta blues feeling. "Factory Girl" utilized an interesting mix of country music and an Indian raga sound (Dave Mason added the Indian reed instrument called a shehnai).

Beggars Banquet included the additional personnel of pianist Nick Hopkins, violinist Ric Grech, Rocky Dijon on congas, Dave Mason on shehnai, and backing vocals by The Watts Street Gospel Choir, Jimmy Miller, Anita Pallenberg and Marianne Faithfull. Beggars Banquet marked a turning point for the Rolling Stones and while reaching back to the blues, they simultaneously found new ways to combine many divergent musical styles.

"Jumpin Jack Flash"
by Keith Richards

1968's "Jumpin Jack Flash" was first recorded by Richards on acoustic guitar using an old cassette recorder and a wooden extension speaker. This created a distorted sound, essentially using the recorder as a pickup mic. This also allowed him to get the sound of both an acoustic and electric guitar simultaneously, by overloading the tape machine. Richards believed that the acoustic guitar (for every tune) was really the foundation, and that he could only get a crisp sound from the acoustic guitar. Richards realized that anytime an acoustic guitar was played into a microphone, the result was some kind of electric sound.

Keith explained the inspiration for "Jumpin Jack Flash" when he recalled, "Mick and I had been up all night, it was raining outside and there was the sound of these heavy stomping rubber boots near the window, belonging to my gardener, Jack Dyer, a real country man from Sussex. It woke Mick up. He said, 'What's that?' I said, 'Oh that's Jack. That's jumping Jack.' I started to work around the phrase on the guitar, which was in open tuning, singing the phrase 'Jumping Jack.' Mick said, 'Flash,' and suddenly we had this phrase with a great rhythm and ring to it. So we got to work on it and wrote it. I can hear the whole band take off behind me every time I play 'Flash'—there's this extra sort of turbo overdrive. You jump on the riff and it plays you." #6 Keith Richards has said many times that if could only play one of his riffs ever again, it would be "Jumpin Jack Flash."

The Songwriting Genius of Mick Jagger and Keith Richards

Over many years Mick Jagger and Keith Richards have learned how to combine their individual approach to songwriting with a shared ability to write songs together. Keith Richards said, "It's been a progression from Mick and I sitting face-to-face with a guitar and a tape recorder... Let me put it this way: I'd say, 'Mick, it goes like this: 'Wild horses couldn't drag me away.' Then it would be a division of labor, Mick filling in the verses. There are instances like 'Undercover of the Night' or 'Rock and a Hard Place' where it's totally Mick's song. And there are times when I come in with 'Happy' or 'Before They Make Me Run.' I say, 'It goes like this. In fact, Mick, you don't even have to know about it, because you're not singing.' When we get together, we see what ideas each has got: I'm stuck on the bridge. 'Well, I have this bit that might work.' A lot of what Mick and I do is fixing and touching up, writing the song in bits, assembling it on the spot." #7

Keith Richards has always learned a lot from writing ballads. He often wrote a ballad and saw where it took him. Mick Jagger also had strong ideas about where certain elements of a song would go. Jagger said, "The problem with song-writing is that at the time you have to think that the song is a good thing, and that at some point it's a wonderful creation, but at the same time it usually isn't wonderful. There are usually one or two things that should be left out, but it's very rare that you have some time to step back from the process, look at the song and think about it, and go 'wait a minute, that is good, but this could be better and that part shouldn't be there.'" #8

Jagger tried to write in the moment and not think too much about the impact a song would have. He understood the transitory nature of songwriting and how it should be an extension of how you feel at the time you are writing the song. Richards understood how different he and Jagger were as individuals and that was a strength they had been able to cultivate and use to complement each other's musical ideas. For years, the relationship between Mick Jagger and Keith Richards had its ups and downs. At times it had threatened to break up the Rolling Stones. Mick Jagger said, "Keith and I have a very complicated relationship. I don't pretend to understand it. I find it quite tricky. He is a very inward person and he was always a very quite and meditative type of person, so to bring out what he really wants to say is, I think, quite a problem for him sometimes. I'm a very outgoing person and very gregarious." #9 However, in the end, the Jagger/Richards musical relationship produced countless musical gems, already rock 'n' roll classics.

After more successful records and tours, tragedy struck when Brian Jones was found dead on July 3rd, 1969. It was only weeks after he had left the group. Beggars Banquet would be his last recording. Some people saw this coming because he had been struggling with his personal demons, and was relegated to a diminished role in the Stones because Mick and Keith had emerged as bandleaders. He was soon replaced by guitarist Mick Taylor, another accomplished blues veteran of John Mayall's Bluesbreakers. The band had entered a rough period plagued by drug problems, issues with their record label and management, and possible tax exile. To make matters worse, on December 6th of that same year at an Altamont Speedway Rolling Stones concert, Meredith Hunter (a

---

Rock Hard Fact

The Rolling Stones named their album Exile on Main Street after they were forced to move to France in 1971 to go into "tax exile," due to the extremely high tax rate in their native England.

member of the audience), was murdered by members of the Hell's Angel's motorcycle gang. The Stones had hired the Hell's Angels to work security. Through all of this tragedy and hardships, The Rolling Stones still managed to produce some of their strongest music.

By the early 1970's, The Rolling Stones became one of the most popular bands in the world; some fans calling them "the world's greatest rock and roll band." What became more and more evident was their assimilation of many diverse music styles. 1971's Sticky Fingers featured a controversial cover of a man's blue jeans crotch with a real working zipper. With Mick Taylor now firmly in the lineup, Sticky Fingers produced the country-sounding ballad "Wild Horses" and the funk inspired "Brown Sugar." In 1972, the Stones released a double album Exile on Main Street. Exile was well received but was mostly pieced together. For a double album, it didn't produce many hits, but Exile still featured the gospel influenced "Tumbling Dice," the hard rocking "Happy," and "All Down the Line." The contributions of brilliant pianist Nicky Hopkins, the gospel feel of organist Billy Preston, and the use of horn arrangements, expanded the sonic possibilities of the band even more. Jimmy Miller was still there to give the band direction. Miller encouraged The Stones to balance the presence of country, gospel, blues, and hard rocking styles. This produced the band's most eclectic work to date.

In 1973, the Stones released the album Goat's Head Soup. One year later the release of It's Only Rock and Roll turned out to be Mick Taylor's last with the band (he left to start a band with bassist Jack Bruce). He was gradually replaced by guitarist Ronnie Wood from Rod Stewart's band, The Faces. Although Wood was a great addition, Keith was especially sad to see Taylor depart because he loved his strong guitar playing and his shared love of the blues. Due to the many drug problems and tax issues, the band had relocated a number of times; including a stint in Jamaica where Keith developed a strong love for reggae music. This appreciation was reflected in both Mick and Keith's utilization of reggae feels on many future Stones and solo albums. A strong reggae feel was evident on the tune "Cherry Oh Baby" from 1976's Black and Blue.

The Rolling Stones had a much-needed hit album in 1978 with Some Girls. The tune "Shattered" was very popular and showed Keith's unique guitar tunings. The song "Miss You" made it to number one on the American charts when the Stones embraced the popular style of disco. The late 1970's almost saw the end of the Stones when Keith was arrested in Canada on a drug possession charge and faced certain prolonged jail time. However, he escaped with community service and the Stones survived when many thought that they had met their demise. 1980's Tattoo You contained the popular tune "Start Me Up" and "Slave," the later featuring a strong funk feel and great saxophone playing from jazz legend Sonny Rollins.

By the time the Stones released Undercover in 1983, Mick and Keith were not getting along very well and the future of the band looked uncertain yet again. Some of the issues were that Keith, now drug free, became more involved with the band both business-wise and musically. This flew in the face of Mick's previous control of the band. Compounding the problem, was Mick's interest in current popular music styles, while Keith was looking to revive the band's strong earlier blues roots. Both decided to develop solo projects and put together their own working bands. Jagger's solo release, She's The Boss, was met with mixed reaction. Keith eventually countered with his debut solo album Talk is Cheap with his band **The X-Pensive Winos**. In 1988, The Stones successfully met to work out their differences and they planned a huge world tour to promote their new record, Steel Wheels, that guaranteed them millions of dollars.

By 1993, original Rolling Stones bassist Bill Wyman officially retired from the band. Wyman's replacement on bass was Darryl Jones (formally with Miles Davis and Sting). Also in that same year, Mick and Keith were inducted in the Songwriters Hall of Fame in New York. In 1994, the band released Voodoo Lounge and played a concert in Dallas, Texas that became the first ever rock concert broadcast over the Internet. At this point, The Rolling Stones would plan a world tour every few years to support each new record release. Massive stage sets were built for each tour which culminated in a world record $437 million dollars gross for their Bridges to Babylon album tour. This would become the highest-grossing music tour of all time.

In 2002, The Rolling Stones released a compilation from their deep repertoire along with a few new songs. A Bigger Bang followed in 2005 and next came a 2013 live record from a performance in Hyde Park, London. With this recording, the band came full circle to the same venue where they had performed decades earlier. Only now, it was in front of one of the biggest crowds ever in British history. In 2016, the Stones completed the circle by releasing the album Blue and Lonesome featuring all blues covers, including four songs by harmonica blues master Little Walter Jacobs. Eric Clapton, who was recording nearby, guested on two of the songs. All of the members of the band had long talked about making a pure blues recording. They knew this was an important opportunity to pay their respects to the music that they all felt to their core.

As seen and heard on their many live DVD's and records, the Rolling Stones are all about *the feel of the music.* Live in concert, The Rolling Stones are all about *emotion and the party.* From Mick's swaggering showmanship to Keith's depth of blues knowledge and mastery of the riff, the band has always been about making music together. The Stones have utilized more diverse styles than any other band in rock history. Stones drummer Charlie Watts summed it up best when he said, "It's not technical, it's emotional, one of the hardest things of all is to get that feeling across." #10 The Rolling Stones were inducted into the Rock and Roll Hall of Fame in 1989.

Mick Jagger

Mick Jagger is known for his charismatic and bold stage presence, meaningful lyrics, sense of stylistic versatility, and a unique voice. These many diverse traits are all housed in the rock 'n' roll personality that is internationally known as simply "Mick." In the span of five decades, Jagger's lyrical abilities rose to a sophisticated and mature level that was central to the Jagger/Richards songwriting team. He has described his songwriting process, lyrics in particular, as an outgrowth of personal experience. However, Jagger has also frequently found his inspiration for lyric writing from different authors. For example, early in his songwriting career, Jagger wrote the lyrics for "Sympathy for the Devil" based on the writings of French poet and writer Charles Baudelaire. Jagger recalled, "I just took a couple of lines and expanded on it. I wrote it as sort of like a Bob Dylan song…there's all these attractions of opposites and turning things upside down (referring to the line 'Just as every cop is a criminal and all the sinners saints') When you write songs, you have

> "We're taking the blues forward and hopefully introducing it to a whole new generation of fans."
>
> – Mick Jagger on the recent Stones record Blue and Lonesome

Rock Hard Fact

Jeff Beck's 1966 recording of the song "Beck's Bolero" included musicians Jimmy Page, John Paul Jones, and drummer Keith Moon (who Page was considering for Led Zeppelin). This planted the seed for the group Led Zeppelin.

---

to first like them yourself, but then you have to make everyone else like them." #11 Over the first decade of The Stones career, Jagger grew from being "just" a lyricist into a complete musician. By the end of the 1960's, he was playing a lot of guitar and developing complete songs with great regularity. More than most musicians, Jagger's compositional process involved working out songs in great detail, before focusing on completing the finished studio product.

Mick Jagger is an electrifying performer on-stage; he uses his physicality to express The Stones music. Jagger remembered, "Of course I copied everyone's moves; you're got to learn from people. At first I copied my grandmother, my mother, and my cousins. Then I copied Little Richard. It isn't really copying them, you just pick up things and you try and do steps you think are going to work for you. You say, 'That's a move I like'." #12 Jagger saw more moves he liked when he accompanied Rolling Stone's drummer Charlie Watts to the Apollo Theater in Harlem to see James Brown perform live in the 1960's. That had a big impact on Jagger because for the longest time, he had only heard James Brown on recordings. But then, he could visually study his moves and see how hard he worked his audience.

Jagger and Richards have kept the Rolling Stones stylistically balanced. Although open to many musical styles, Richards kept The Rolling Stones grounded in the blues. At the same time, Jagger, (also a lover of the blues and a very good blues harmonica player) has been a champion for musical diversity within the Stones. Jagger saw "Miss You" as an opportunity to provide The Stones with an answer to disco. Most Rolling Stones albums featured Jagger singing a country tune, and songs such as "Slave" showed Jagger's ease in singing funk. Jagger's respect for different musical styles enhanced his own singing and songwriting abilities. Perhaps Jagger's most enduring legacy is his unique persona as a singer and a front man. His onstage relationship with the audience is in the league of greats such as Elvis Presley and Frank Sinatra. Jagger has the rare vocal ability to sing gut-bucket blues, authentic country ballads, and then land a knock out punch with hard-hitting rock 'n' roll anthems like "Gimme Shelter," "Brown Sugar," "Shattered," and "Start Me Up."

The Yardbirds (1963-1968) were an important English supergroup that also proved to be an important catalyst for the careers of Cream and Led Zeppelin. In addition, they helped to launch the solo careers of guitarists Jeff Beck and Eric Clapton. The original lineup was fronted by guitarist/vocalist Keith Reif and featured guitarists Chris Dreja and Anthony Topham, bassist Paul Samwell-Smith, and drummer Jim McCarty. The Yardbirds assumed a residency at The Crawdaddy Club when The Rolling Stones left to tour with Bo Diddley. Topham soon left the band and guitarist Eric Clapton joined. Clapton shared a passion with the other Yardbirds in playing the Delta and Chicago blues style. Their most popular cover was Howlin' Wolf's "Smokestack Lightning." The band received a break when it was asked to back up Delta blues star Sonny Boy Williamson II. Eric Clapton recalled asking Sonny Boy, "Isn't your real name Rice Miller? At which point he (Sonny Boy) pulled out a small penknife and glared at me. It went downhill from there." #13 At this time, The Beatles were becoming a worldwide sensation and The Rolling Stones were discovering America. The Yardbirds were now one of the most popular blues bands around London. The Yardbirds approached session guitarist Jimmy Page about joining the band when he would frequently sit in with them. In 1965, they recorded "For Your Love," a big hit in England and America. However, Clapton became disillusioned with the band's desire to write pop hits and he realized that his real love was playing the blues. He soon left to join John Mayall's Bluesbreakers, and would go on to create the supergroup Cream (later in this chapter).

"For Your Love"
written by Graham Gouldman

Graham Gouldman, future member of the band 10CC, wrote this song inspired by The Beatles. He then decided to offer it to The Yardbirds to record. The Yardbirds released "For Your Love" in 1965 as a catchy pop single that immediately did well on the British charts. However, it had a lot of competition from the British Invasion, which was in full swing. Bassist Paul Samwell-Smith was really pushing The Yardbirds into a more commercial direction, but Eric Clapton had misgivings with the song and its overall pop direction.

The Yardbirds recorded the song, augmented with Brian Auger on harpsichord, which was kind of a strange sound for a pop song. Eric Clapton and Chris Dreja added guitar parts only on the double-time middle section. "For Your Love" had a psychedelic meets pop sound and was a complete departure from the previous blues sound of The Yardbirds. Paul Samwell-Smith produced the song and made all of the creative decisions in the studio. "For Your Love" was the first Yardbirds tune to make the charts, but by that time, Eric Clapton had left the band.

Clapton's replacement was the young guitar phenomenon, Jeff Beck. The band continued to write pop tunes, only now with a strong psychedelic edge. Beck played well but proved to be professionally unreliable. The Yardbirds went through some lineup changes and again Jimmy Page was asked to join the band. Page was reluctant at first, but agreed to join as the bassist to replace Paul Samwell-Smith. Jeff Beck remained as the lead guitar player because the idea of two great guitar players was irresistible to him (he knew it only a matter of time until Page switched to guitar). The Yardbirds soon featured both guitarists Beck and Page with Chris Dreja playing bass. However, it didn't take long for Beck to become disinterested in The Yardbirds. Page was able to keep the band focused, but after a disastrous American tour in 1966, Beck was asked to leave.

"Beck's Bolero"
by Jeff Beck and Jimmy Page
inspired by Maurice Ravel's Bolero

Because no official recordings exist of Jeff Beck and Jimmy Page playing together in The Yardbirds, Jeff Beck's 1966 recording of "Beck's Bolero" had significant importance. The song was originally created as the B-side of a single, and was first released in 1966. When Beck included it on his 1968 album titled Truth, it sounded as modern as it did when it was recorded two years earlier. "Beck's Bolero" marked one of the first times that a rock musician would create a combination of the thematic material from a classical work (inspired by composer Maurice Ravel's "Bolero") with the raw energy of rock 'n' roll.

On this recording, Jeff Beck played with his signature melodic fluidity. When this was combined with Jimmy Page's equally strong rhythmic sense, it produced one of the classic guitar recordings in rock history. The end of "Beck's Bolero" also featured one of the first times that backward guitar parts were created through tape manipulation and utilized in a rock composition. The drummer for the session was the legendary Keith Moon. Previously known for his unbridled energy, Moon directed his approach toward the song's repeating rhythmic figure with his march-like snare drum accompaniment. Later, in the recording, Moon played a furious fill that led into the energetic B section of the song. This landmark track was one of rock's first great instrumental recordings.

Jimmy Page assumed leadership of The Yardbirds and soon hired Peter Grant (later manager of Led Zeppelin) to manage the band. After numerous tours and some commercial success, The Yardbirds were finished by 1968. Page remembered, "I tried desperately to keep the band together. The group was almost ashamed of the very name (The Yardbirds), though I don't know why. We were a great band." #14 The Yardbirds were inducted into the Rock and Roll Hall of Fame in 1992. Jeff Beck (see chapter seventeen) was also inducted as a solo artist in 2009.

Discussion Question

So far in this chapter we have explored a successful rock band such as the Rolling Stones. Can you think of another profession where employees are asked to collaborate and produce a product for the betterment of the organization or business? Compare and contrast your own example of a successful collaboration to a successful band (such as the Rolling Stones).

As previously stated, by 1965 Eric Clapton had left the Yardbirds. He was focusing squarely on the Chicago blues style with covers of Buddy Guy, Elmore James, and Willie Dixon. This love of the blues led him directly to John Mayall's Bluesbreakers band. This version of The Bluesbreakers can be heard on the Decca recording Bluesbreakers, John Mayall with Eric Clapton. Even though Clapton was happy playing in a pure blues style, he was also thinking about becoming the front man of his own band. One of England's most respected drummers, Ginger Baker, was playing in The Graham Bond Organization and approached Clapton about forming a group. Clapton informed Baker that he would form a new group only if bassist Jack Bruce was invited to complete the lineup. However, Baker and Bruce had worked together previously and did not get along. But once the trio rehearsed for the first time, they knew that had something special. Clapton still wanted to add a keyboard player. Steve Winwood would be a perfect choice because he composed and sang well. But both Baker and Bruce wanted to work exclusively as a trio. Thus, the supergroup **Cream** (1966-1969) was formed in 1966. The band's name came from their collective opinion that they were the "cream" of the crop of all the musicians in their musical genre.

Cream made a strong impression at the Windsor Festival in England when they performed their high-powered blues influenced covers and original material. All three members demonstrated tremendous solo improvisation abilities. Audiences were stunned at how they could combine jazz influenced improvisation with a commitment to the blues, and yet create a rock style with catchy melodies. Cream was finding a unique musical direction because the power trio was a new concept and much different than the usual quartet or larger ensemble. Clapton explained, "In a trio I had to provide a lot more of the sound, and I found that difficult because I didn't really enjoy having to play so much. My technique altered quite a lot in that I started playing a lot more bar chords and hitting open strings to provide a kind of drone for my lead work." #15

"Sunshine of Your Love"
written by Eric Clapton, Pete Brown, and Jack Bruce

"Sunshine of Your Love" was recorded and released on Cream's Disraeli Gears album in 1967. This song was based around a strong bass riff which functioned as a repeating melodic idea. This riff allowed the guitar and vocals to improvise around a constant structure and at the same time create a hypnotic effect. Jack Bruce was inspired after he saw Jimi Hendrix play live for the first time. Bruce went home and came up with this famous blues-derived riff that came from a minor pentatonic scale with a flatted fifth. It wasn't until Ginger Baker slowed the tempo down in the studio and played a heavy tom-tom pattern, that all the parts came together.

The lyrics were written by a beat poet named Pete Brown, who was a friend of both Ginger Baker and Jack Bruce. Brown wrote the lyric "It's getting near dawn, when lights close their tired eyes," after being up all night and seeing the sun rise. Atlantic Records executive Ahmet Ertegun brought in producer and musician Felix Pappalardi (bassist and vocalist of the band Mountain) for the session, who helped to arrange many of Cream's tunes. Pappalardi went on to produce Cream's 1968 Wheels of Fire and 1969's Goodbye albums. In America, "Sunshine of Your Love" was one of the biggest selling singles in 1968. "Sunshine of Your Love" is still one of Eric Clapton's favorite songs and he continues to play it at many of his live performances.

Cream was more successful in America than in their native England. However, the stress of constant touring and the self-imposed pressure they placed on themselves, created tension within the band. Many believed that the personal issues between Jack Bruce and Ginger Baker were the demise of the band. This was a factor, but Clapton felt that Cream was forgetting the principles that first brought them together. Clapton remembered, "There were times, too, when playing to audiences who were only too happy to worship us, where complacency set in. I began to be quite ashamed of being in Cream, because I thought it was a con. It wasn't really developing from where we were. As we made our voyage across America, we were being exposed to extremely strong and powerful influences, with jazz and rock 'n' roll that was growing up around us, and it seemed that we weren't learning from it." #16 Clapton was also comparing Cream to other bands such as The Band, who had just released their groundbreaking album Music from Big Pink. Clapton was feeling trapped and uninspired because he felt Cream was just showing off their individual skills on their gigs. Cream disbanded in 1968, but have reunited occasionally. Cream was inducted into the Rock and Roll Hall of Fame in 1993. (more about the solo career of Eric Clapton in chapter twelve)

Jack Bruce

John Symon Asher "Jack" Bruce (1943-2014) was one of the première bass players in the early blues

> "It was one of the highlights of my life"
>
> - Dave Grohl on playing with John Paul Jones in the band Them Crooked Vultures

scene in London. Bruce was a vocalist, songwriter, and multi-dimensional musician who played harmonica, piano, cello, and guitar. Born in Scotland, Bruce learned to play acoustic bass in his teens and won a scholarship to study the cello at the Royal Scottish Academy of Music and Drama. The Academy did not approve of his bass playing, so he left to pursue playing the blues and jazz. Bruce moved to London in the early 1960's to join Blues Incorporated that also included Charlie Watts on drums, Alexis Korner on guitar and harmonica player Cyril Davies. In 1962, they served as the house band at the Ealing Cellar, which was England's first rhythm and blues club. In 1963, Bruce helped form The Graham Bond Organization when he switched to electric bass. With Graham Bond, Bruce played with drummer Ginger Baker and guitarist John McLaughlin.

It is well documented that Jack Bruce and Ginger Baker did not get along personally. They would often fight on stage and even damage each other's equipment. Because of this, Bruce left Graham Bond in 1965. He soon joined Manfred Mann's group in 1965 and can be heard on the recording "Instrumental Asylum." That same year, Clapton, Bruce and Baker formed Cream. Baker and Bruce would go on to continue their personal feud. In Cream, Jack Bruce sang most of the lead vocals while Clapton sang backups before eventually assuming lead vocals. Bruce co-wrote two of Cream's biggest hits, "Sunshine of Your Love" and "White Room."

Jack Bruce played the bass with energy and his bass lines were front and center in the music. He tended to stay in a middle range of the bass which worked well in the trio format. He easily moved back and forth between a Fender Bass VI, a Gibson EB-3, and later, a fretless Warwick bass. Bruce's bass playing was tied to his sense of composition. Many of his basslines were syncopated and often utilized elements of dissonance to add to the harmonic complexity of a song. His early classical education lent a sophisticated approach to his thinking. His playing utilized voice leading and counterpoint to give musical depth to his basslines and compositions.

After Cream, Jack Bruce would go on to have a successful solo career releasing many solo records including; Songs For A Tailor, Things We Like, and Harmony Row. He also continued to play in notable bands and do frequent session work. Some musicians Bruce worked with included; Frank Zappa on his 1972 album Apostrophe, Lou Reed on his Berlin album in 1973, Tony Williams Lifetime's 1970 release Turn It Over, and collaborations with John McLaughlin, Gary Moore, and Robin Trower.

In 1968, Jimmy Page and Peter Grant (who had retained the legal rights to the Yardbirds name) were determined to carry on. Page slowly began reforming **The New Yardbirds** to fulfill some contracted performance dates in Europe. The session bassist, keyboardist, composer, and arranger, John Paul Jones (aka John Baldwin) had asked Page about his plans for The New Yardbirds. The two had done many recording sessions together since 1965. On one particular session, Jones told Page that he would like to be a part of Page's new band. But Page told him that he didn't need to join his band. However, if he wanted to join, he was in. The quest for a new lead singer proved to be more challenging. Page and (still current Yardbirds manager) Peter Grant both agreed that they wanted a powerful singer that could rival Page's strong emotional guitar lines. Jimmy Page's first choice was Terry Reid, a solid singer who just committed to another band. Reid had told Page about this tall, blonde singer named Robert Anthony Plant from Birmingham who was really into the Delta blues. Plant had been working with a group called The Band Of Joy and recently worked with another band called Hobbstweedle. Page and Grant went to see Plant at a Hobbstweedle performance and Page came away intrigued saying, "That voice…It had it, that distinctive, highly charged sexual quality that we needed. It was as good a white man's blues voice as Rod Stewart's, but it was even wilder, even a little crazy-sounding." #17 Page had found his singer and frontman.

John Henry Bonham, from Worcestershire, England, had played in a number of bands including an English blues group called The Crawling King Snakes and later in one version of Robert Plant's Band of Joy. Plant and Page had considered other drummers for Led Zeppelin, including English session drummer Clem Cattini who had a stripped down drumming approach. Other more complex drummers were also considered, including; Keith Moon, Aynsley Dunbar, Ginger Baker, and Procol Harum's BJ Wilson. Plant recommended Bonham to Page, who went to see him play with an artist named Tim Rose in a North London pub. Page was instantly impressed and knew then what The New Yardbirds would sound like with Jones, Plant and Bonham. Still it proved difficult to get Bonham to join since his popularity was on the rise and other offers poured in. Page managed to convince Bonham to come to London and see if Page and Plant's Delta blues influence would mesh with Bonham's rootsy and slinky time-keeping approach. Their first rehearsal was held in the basement of a record store on Gerard Street, London. The result was magic. Jones remembered "The first time, we all met in this little room to see if we could stand each other." #18 Page asked the band, "Do you know the blues standard (and Yardbirds theme tune) 'Train Kept A-Rollin'? They said no. Page replied, "It's easy just G and A. I counted it out and the room just *exploded*. We all said, 'Right, we're on, this is it, this is going to work!!!" #19

While the band was brand new, the name of the band wasn't. Earlier in 1968, The Yardbirds were on tour in New York and found themselves hanging out with Keith Moon and John Entwistle of The Who. They were talking about leaving The Who to form a new band with Jimmy Page and Steve Winwood. Entwistle famously said, "Yeah. We'll call it Lead Zeppelin. Because it'll go over like a lead balloon." #20 Jimmy Page remembered the name and soon The New Yardbirds became **Led Zeppelin** (1969-1980).

Their first live shows were still billed as Jimmy Page and the New Yardbirds. Led Zeppelin's first performances were loud and powerful, and were reviewed as "the most exciting new sounds since Hendrix or Cream." In late 1968, Peter Grant was able to obtain a record deal from Atlantic Records in America. Page was in charge and wanted to remain so. Therefore, he asked that Led Zeppelin would have complete control of song publishing, recording, production, cover art, scheduling of live dates, and promotion. Ahmet Ertegun, the head of Atlantic Records, agreed and signed them to a generous deal as the first rock band on Atlantic Records. Led Zeppelin would have full control. Page and Grant delivered the completed (already mixed) tapes of their first album to the record company.

Rock Hard Fact

The Theremin is an electronic instrument first introduced in the 1930's. The Beach Boys used an Electro-Theremin on the 1966 single "Good Vibrations." Eleven years later Jimmy Page used the Theremin during the performances of "Whole Lotta Love" and "No Quarter."

Groundbreaking album Led Zeppelin I
by Led Zeppelin

Led Zeppelin I was released in 1969 after an American tour that had them opening for the band Vanilla Fudge. This debut recording sold very well and made an immediate statement revealing the band's link to the Delta and Chicago blues while simultaneously introducing the world to the unmistakable raw power and energy of Led Zeppelin.

Side one opened with "Good Times Bad Times," then "Babe I'm Gonna Leave You," "You Shook Me," and "Dazed and Confused." The rock world was stunned when they first heard "Good Times Bad Times." John Paul Jones came up with the basic riff while Page wrote the chorus and John Bonham provided the fiery drumset part. "Babe I'm Gonna Leave You" was a cover of a tune by an American singer named Anne Bredon and was also covered by folk singer Joan Baez. Page created a flamenco-like section with acoustic guitar and Plant added a highly emotional vocal part. Zeppelin redefined the Willie Dixon classic "You Shook Me" with a very slow and heavy (metal) feel.

Side two opened with "Your Time Is Gonna Come," then "Black Mountain Side," "Communication Breakdown," "I Can't Quit You Baby," and "How Many More Times." "Your Time is Gonna Come" opened with Jones very ecclesiastic organ intro. "Black Mountain Side" was a short instrumental based on a traditional folk song with added tabla drums by Viram Jasani. "Communication Breakdown" was an anthem for frustrated youth inspired by rockabilly great Eddie Cochran's tune "Nervous Breakdown." The album ended with a version of Willie Dixon's "I Can't Quit You Baby" and "How Many More Times" that was inspired by Howlin' Wolf's tune "How Many More Years." Page knew that radio DJ's wouldn't play a long song (this one was 8:28) so he stated on the album credits that it was 3:30 (to trick DJ's into playing the song on the radio). Led Zeppelin I was a studio reflection of the band's intense live shows that were an all out assault on their audiences. The feel and raw energy heard on this debut album sent tremors through the rock music world.

"Dazed and Confused"
by Jake Holmes (reworked by Jimmy Page)

Jimmy Page built "Dazed and Confused" based on an acoustic song written by folk singer Jake Holmes. When Page was in The Yardbirds, Holmes would play on the same bill at the Village Theatre in New York City. Page eventually paid Holmes for the right to use the melody of the song. The lyrics of this tune were controversial at the time. For example, the phrase "Lots of people talking, few of them know, the soul of a women was created below" was considered offensive to many. Zeppelin's references to subjects, such as strong sexual conquest and the occult, foreshadowed some of the future concepts that would embrace the genre of heavy metal. This song featured a long instrumental improvisation that felt like a drug-induced psychedelic experience, especially when Zeppelin played it live.

"Dazed and Confused" was made up of a long, descending, melodic bassline. Page explained how he developed an idea like "Dazed and Confused" when he said, "A riff will come out of…this whole thing you do when you practice. I played at home, and before I knew it, things would be coming out, and that's those little sections or riffs. At that stage its selection and rejection." #21 "Dazed and Confused" was one of the first songs on which Page utilized a violin bow on his guitar.

By this time, Led Zeppelin had completed many tours of America and Europe. Word had spread that the band and its entourage were wild and out of control. The tour manager, Richie Cole, was at the center of the chaos. The band had to repeatedly pay for damages at hotels and were often banned from returning. Zeppelin was rising to greater popularity with each and every tour. Led Zeppelin (II) was released in late 1969 and further established them as one of the most popular rock bands in the world. The songs on Zeppelin II were written, recorded, and mixed in studios all over North America and Europe. All of the band members were more involved in writing the compositions and arrangements than they were on Zeppelin I. This created more of a group identity. The legendary Glyn Johns engineered Zeppelin I, and the engineer on Zeppelin II was another master, Eddie Kramer. Page's famously distorted "Whole Lotta Love" guitar riff opened Zeppelin II. This became one of the band's best-known tunes. After the opening riff, the song worked its way into an abstract middle section, where Page used a theramin (an experimental instrument). "Whole Lotta Love" was about raw sexuality and aggression. It was also a message to a whole new generation. Led Zeppelin II, often called a masterpiece, displayed musical creativity that included the legendary John Bonham drum solo feature "Moby Dick."

Led Zeppelin did not have a good working relationship with the media. FM radio stations often took out the spacey improvisation middle section of "Whole Lotta Love" to squeeze it into a FM radio friendly format. This did not sit well with Jimmy Page who refused to put out singles from the albums and often by-passed the media and press. Page knew how strong the Zeppelin brand was becoming. He was content to have Zeppelin built their audience through the process of selling albums and concert tickets to their strong live performances. Even the original album cover for Led Zeppelin IV was created void of the song titles or the band's name. This would be a marketing disaster for most bands. Not Led Zeppelin.

Jimmy Page

First and foremost, Jimmy Page is one of the all-time great rock guitar players. Early on, he was exposed to a number of musical influences including everything from skiffle music to rockabilly. Jimmy studied classical and jazz guitar techniques, and the sounds of Les Paul, Gypsy guitarist Django Reinhardt, and especially Elvis Presley's guitarist, Scotty Moore. In many of Jimmy's solos you can hear this wide range of influences.

Jimmy was a first call studio musician in London long before he joined The Yardbirds or Led Zeppelin. Studio experience made him a master of production and sound design. He was one of the first to record the ambient sound of a rock band. Page would also experiment with microphone placement. He often placed a mic ten or fifteen feet behind an amp as well as directly in front. This was known as "distance equals depth" which became very common in rock recording. Page stated, "The whole idea is to try and capture the sound of the room live and the emotion of the whole moment and try to convey that….You've got to capture as much of the room sound as possible. That's the very essence of it." #22

> "Jimmy was the driving force, but I don't think John Paul Jones gets nearly enough credit for his input… John Bonham was an absolute genius… And then you put Plant on top - who'd ever heard anything like him before? It was an amazing combination."
>
> – Legendary producer Glyn Johns on producing Led Zeppelin I.

Page used an enormous collection of guitars throughout his career. Jeff Beck had given Jimmy a 1959 Fender Telecaster when Page first joined The Yardbirds and that became Jimmy's main guitar for quite some time. His guitar sound changed from a Telecaster on Led Zeppelin I to a Les Paul on Led Zeppelin II. After recording some of the "Stairway To Heaven" passages on separate six and twelve string guitars, a problem surfaced. How would Page bring "Stairway to Heaven" from the studio to the concert stage? Page said, "I'd recorded the thing and then wondered how I was going to do it." #23 The solution was found with an incredible instrument that was custom made for him by Gibson, the EDS 1275, which combined a 12 string and a six-string guitar on one double-necked instrument. The EDS 1275 was a 34 lb. cherry mahogany double-necked axe that was as stunning to look at as it was to play. This guitar appeared in many Zeppelin concert photos.

Page became famous for his live use of a violin bow on his guitars to create unique improvised solos and add an eerie, mystical quality to many Zeppelin songs. On an early pre-Yardbirds recording session with the Royal Philharmonic Orchestra, their principle violinist, David McCallum, asked Jimmy if he had ever bowed his guitar. Jimmy replied, "It wouldn't work because the strings aren't arched over the guitar the way they are over the violin. But, McCallum said 'Have a go.' So I tried it and realized there might be something in it. I don't remember if I used it on any sessions, but I certainly used it the minute I was in The Yardbirds." #24

As a songwriter, Page knew what his contributions should be, and limited his input in writing lyrics. Whether it was acoustic or electric, he usually focused on writing the music first. Sometimes he did write the lyrics for songs such as "Good Times, Bad Times." For that tune he wrote the lyrics for the chorus, and Plant wrote the lyrics for the verses. Page gave further insight into Zeppelin's songs when he said, "One of the things that you'll see in Led Zeppelin music is that every song is different from the others. Each one has its own character, musically as much as lyrically. The music was really of paramount importance to setting the scene and most probably inspired the singer, in this case Robert, to get set into the overall emotion, the ambience of the track of what was being presented, and then hopefully inspired him to write the lyrics." #25

Jimmy Page, the complete rock musician.

1970's Led Zeppelin (III) saw the emergence of a new musical side of the band. Zeppelin recorded in the country and was inspired by old folk songs, Celtic folklore, and traditional acoustic guitar sounds. The album still featured the powerful "Immigrant Song" and a return to the blues with "Since I've Been Loving You." This album, although criticized by the press (who weren't open to such musical and cultural diversity), showed that Zeppelin could draw from a wide range of influences. The band was stung by this criticism but refused to compromise their musical tastes and standards. In the long run, Led Zeppelin (III) served to widen the Zeppelin fan base.

1971's Led Zeppelin IV (aka ZOSO) remained on the charts for over 250 weeks and went platinum a dozen times over! This set a record for chart longevity. Each group member designed his own symbol for the album. They refused to say what the symbols actually meant but it did help to identify the album. The rock classic "Stairway to Heaven" was featured and has been the subject of controversy since Page was accused of stealing the melody from a tune by the band Spirit (The dispute was resolved in court and Page was found not guilty). "Stairway to Heaven," as a composition, showed how the band could bridge an acoustic, folkloric direction with a hard rocking second section. The band knew this tune would help to define their legacy. Jimmy Page said, "I thought 'Stairway' crystallized the essence of the band.... It was a milestone for us. Every musician wants to do something of lasting quality, something that will hold up over time." # 26 As usual, Zeppelin would extend this tune at live shows to new performance heights. The band now found a tremendous balance between their hard rocking and acoustic material. This album also featured one of their favorite concert openers, "Rock and Roll," and their use of odd time signatures with the tune "Black Dog."

1973's Houses of the Holy marked even more experimentation, more use of odd meters, and the presence of James Brown inspired funk. This was their first album with an actual title. Page understood the feel of Jimmy Nolen's (James Brown's guitar player) funky strumming and Bonham loved to use beat displacement to create some enormous syncopated drumset feels. This was an exciting new direction for the band. John Paul Jones utilized a Mellotron to get an eerie effect on "The Rain Song." Also, the song "The Ocean" utilized a two bar feel that removed an eighth-note to create an odd time syncopated 15/8 feel. However, the funkiest tune on Houses of the Holy was "The Crunge."

"The Crunge"
written by Led Zeppelin

"The Crunge" was released on Led Zeppelin's Houses of the Holy album and was the B side to D'yer Mak'er" as a single. The song was perhaps Zeppelin's most funky as the influence of James Brown was loud and clear. The song evolved out of a jam in the studio with Bonham starting the feel, soon joined by John Paul Jones and Jimmy Page. "The Crunge" is phrased in a quirky 9/8 time feel of a seven bar pattern ending with a 4/4 bar. It then moved to a repeating second phrase of three 4/4 bars that ended with a 9/8 bar. This made the song tricky to play and unpredictable for the listener. On the recording, Jimmy Page used a Fender Stratocaster guitar and employed the effect of a whammy bar, which became common practice for funk guitar players.

The recording revealed all of the members of Led Zeppelin fully capable of playing with a funky feel. John Paul Jones used a VCS3 synthesizer, in addition to his bass part. On their 1975 American tour, Zeppelin would squeeze "The Crunge" into a major jam part of the show between "Whole Lotta Love" and "Black Dog." "The Crunge" has been covered by jazz saxophonist Joshua Redman.

For the next three years Led Zeppelin was in its prime. At this point many other hard rock and metal bands had emerged, but Zeppelin had set the standard with their musicianship, sense of mystique, and worldwide popularity. In 1973, Zeppelin embarked on their biggest and highest grossing tour of America to date. New stage effects were used. Fog (created by dry ice) was created for John Paul Jones' keyboard feature on "No Quarter," and a state of the art light show brought stadium rock shows to a new level. This tour was not without controversy when the band was robbed of $200,000 dollars from a safe deposit box at a New York Hotel.

1975's Physical Graffiti was Zeppelin's only double album and included fifteen tracks. At the same

---

Rock Hard Fact

John Bonham's massive bass drum sound was a result of his enormous twenty-eight inch bass drum often lined with aluminum foil to further enhance the volume.

time, Zeppelin negotiated a new distribution deal with Atlantic Records and started their own label called Swan Song Records where new acts could be developed and signed. The signature tune from Physical Graffiti was "Kashmir." It featured a Middle Eastern influence and Jones' orchestral sounds on the bridge of the tune. The song "In My Time of Dying" was inspired by an old spiritual that Bob Dylan had reworked years ago. Some of the songs on Physical Graffiti had been previously recorded and were in the can and ready to go. Zeppelin would often record more material than would fit on a standard record. Only occasionally would all of those songs make it onto the current album they were recording. Therefore, some songs wouldn't make it onto any of their albums. The double album format allowed for the inclusion of some of the earlier material.

In 1975, Robert Plant, his wife Maureen, and his children were in a bad car accident. Maureen barely survived and Plant's legs were badly injured. Plant choose to get back to work quickly. The tracks for Zeppelin's next album, Presence, were cut in Munich in only eighteen days. The record included no keyboards or acoustic material and Plant was forced to sing from a wheelchair. Page multi-tracked many of his guitar parts. Presence marked a return to a harder edged Zeppelin sound with the songs "Achilles Last Stand" and "Nobody's Fault But Mine," which was a tune adapted from an old Blind Lemon Jefferson blues. Presence did not sell as well as previous Zeppelin albums, but the band's popularity remained.

Robert Plant

Robert Plant was one of rock's most charismatic frontmen. His sex symbol golden blond hair and bare-chested stage appearance embodied the sexy rock idol. Plant's stage prowess was defined by his hair tossing and his "hands on hips" stance that created swagger and commanded confidence. Plant's stage movements and dancing combined elements of Elvis Presley to go along with his own unique mannerisms. Plant's voice was immediately recognizable with a large and very high range. He utilized an expressive vocal palette molded by the influence of many Delta blues singers. This was seen in Plant's subtle vocal innuendos and enormous power. Plant created the sound that had the most influence on hard rock and heavy metal singers. The hard rock-heavy metal magazine Hit Parader listed him as number one on their greatest metal vocalists of all-time. Rock vocal stars Freddie Mercury, Axl Rose, Geddy Lee, and Sammy Hagar are among the many that cite Plant as a major influence on their vocal styles.

Robert Plant recalled the feeling of Led Zeppelin's first recording session when he said, "That first album was the first time that headphones meant anything to me. What I heard coming back to me over the cans while I was singing was better than any chick in all the land. It had so much weight, so much power-it was devastating. It was all very raunchy." #27 It took time for Robert Plant to mature as a strong lyric writer. At his best, his thematic content was spiritual and mystical and he developed storylines about classical European mythology. But Plant was also intrigued by the writings of J.R.R. Tolkien, which inspired some of his lyrics for early Zeppelin songs. In 1980, Plant was hit particularly hard by the death of his dear friend, John Bonham. He remembered "It was one of the flattening, heartbreaking parts of my life. I had a great, warm, big-hearted friend I haven't got anymore. It was so…final. I never even thought about the future of the band or music." #28

Taking time off and two years to recover, Robert Plant started his post-Led Zeppelin solo career in 1982 with his Zeppelin-like album Pictures at Eleven. With a smoother vocal style than heard on previous Zeppelin records, Plant channeled his energy and refined his sound while his unique vocal qualities remained intact. Over the next few years, Plant would record with a number of great drummers including Phil Collins, Barrimore Barlow, Richie Hayward, and Cozy Powell. 1983's The Principle of Moments would display a lighter and quieter side of Plant's musicianship. In 1984, Robert Plant explored his Elvis and rockabilly side with his new band The Honeydrippers. Plant always had a deep love for early rock 'n' roll. This was evident on The Honeydrippers Vol. 1 where he recorded five golden oldies from the pre-Beatles era. On this album, Plant was joined by Jimmy Page and Jeff Beck to help him to rework tunes such as "Rockin at Midnight."

Refusing to be typecast, Robert Plant went on to make albums experimenting with modern synthesizer embellishments. He also employed diverse musical lineups. Plant reconnected with Jimmy Page on a number of projects from 1994 to 1998. At times, this included John Bonham's son, Jason Bonham on drums. Plant and Page recorded their only post-Zeppelin album of original material, 1998's Walking into Clarksdale. This album was largely unsuccessful. From 2007 to 2008, Plant recorded and performed live with bluegrass star Alison Krauss. In 2010, Plant formed and toured with a new group, using the name of his first group, The Band of Joy. In 2012, Plant formed another band, The Sensational Space Shifter, that would record a mix of originals and reworked Led Zeppelin tunes.

In spite of Led Zeppelin reunion events such as 1985's Live Aid and 2007's Ahmet Ertegun Tribute Concert, Jimmy Page and Robert Plant strongly disagree concerning any long term plans to reunite Led Zeppelin.

On the third leg of their 1977 tour, tragedy struck Led Zeppelin. Robert Plant's son, Karac, died suddenly from a virus. The rest of the tour was cancelled and Led Zeppelin would never play in America again. 1979's In Through the Out Door would be the last Zeppelin album for Page, Plant, Jones, and Bonham. John Paul Jones and Robert Plant took charge of this recording as Page and Bonham were barely functioning due to alcohol and drug issues. This would be Zeppelin's most commercial album with the tunes "All My Love" and "In the Evening." The band did a short tour of Europe in April of 1980. As they prepared for their twelfth tour of America more tragedy ensued, when John Bonham was found dead on September 25th, 1980 at the age of thirty-one. It was determined that he had choked on his own vomit while sleeping after a long day and night of drinking. The band was devastated and issued the following statement: "The loss of our dear friend, and the deep sense of harmony felt by ourselves and our manager, have led us to decide that we could not continue as we were." #29

Jimmy Page released the last Led Zeppelin album entitled Coda in 1982. It collected outtakes and old session tracks from Zeppelin's previous twelve years. The tune "Bonzo's Montreux" was a Bonham drum solo with added Jimmy Page effects. Coda sold well for about a year.

John Bonham

John "Henry" Bonham (1948-1980) is arguably the greatest and most influential rock drummer ever. It is well documented that Robert Plant and Jimmy Page brought a huge amount of Delta blues influence into Led Zeppelin. But Bonham's musical influences were less obvious, but no less important. He provided the rhythmic "yin" to Jimmy Page's "yang" of rhythm guitar. Early on, he was the fire that prevented early Led Zeppelin from becoming "just another" English blues band. As Led Zeppelin evolved, the rhythm section of Bonham, bassist John Paul Jones, and Jimmy Page became a rhythmic steamroller. As a part of that rhythm section, Bonham became the creator of a drumming style that can't be pigeon holed by the words hard rock or heavy metal. Bonham's drumming had it all: power, flash, groove, simplicity, complexity, audacity, and subtlety. You could dance to Bonham's drumming, and you could bang your head to Bonham's drumming. His grooves spoke to your soul, and his solos spoke to your head. His drumming was firmly rooted in the past, while it looked fearlessly into the future.

Bonham's drumming approach was a complex and unique amalgamation of drumming and musical styles that included; jazz, blues, early rock 'n' roll, funk, and the powerful drumming styles already evident on the Birmingham and North London (and American) musical scenes. "Bonzo"(as he was later called) wasn't the only drummer to mix these influences, but he was the first drummer to assemble all of these ingredients into such a seamless and tight package.

Bonham's early love of jazz came through when he was often heard quoting a popular Max Roach drumming phrase (from Roach's "The Drum Also Waltzes") at the beginning of his "Moby Dick" drum solo. His jazz influence also inspired his use of his bare hands on this same solo (the direct influence of jazz drummer Joe Morello and "Papa" Joe Jones). Bonham's blues influence can be heard on the intro of "How Many More Times," the subtle swing of "Celebration Day," and the easy-going "Down By The Seaside."

John Bonham had an appreciation for the roots of early rock 'n' roll drumming. The evidence is heard in a fascinating comparison between his drum intro and groove on Zeppelin's "Rock and Roll," and drummer Charles Connor's intro to Little Richard's "You Keep a Knocking." Also, Bonham's (unison two-handed) "Rock and Roll" groove is almost identical to Earl Palmer's groove on Eddie Cochran's "Something Else." Bonham's funk drumming influences came from American drummers such as Clyde Stubblefield and Bernard Purdie. The sounds of American funk are evident in Bonham's syncopated phrases, hi-hat barks, and quick bass drum patterns heard on the grooves "Good Times, Bad Times," "Royal Orleans," "Fool in the Rain," The Rover," and "Darlene."

John Bonham's drumming thumbprint can be heard in every rock drummer that has picked up a pair of sticks since Bonham's first recordings with Led Zeppelin in 1969. Bonham's musical ideas and his drum grooves borrowed from the past and blazed a trail into the future of music. His unique combination of space and complexity, power and finesse, make him "The Godfather of Heavy Rock Drumming."

Led Zeppelin released a film of concert footage in 1975 called *The Song Remains the Same*. The live footage of the band was interrupted with footage that profiled each of their personalities. In 2003, Zeppelin released a triple CD set of rare concert recordings called How the West Was Won. A DVD compilation of live concerts from 1970-1979 was also released in 2003. These two releases revealed the live power of Led Zeppelin to a whole new generation.

One of the greatest strengths of Led Zeppelin was their tremendous energy. They gave audiences a powerful energy and received it right back. The anticipation of a Zeppelin show created its own energy. When they performed it was magic. A Zeppelin concert was a life force of its own. All four members were stars in their own right but fit together like a well-oiled machine. Led Zeppelin paved the way and inspired many bands and artists. The music critics were hard on Zeppelin over the years but the fans always saw it differently. Although Jimmy Page and many others conceived of Zeppelin as more than "just" a metal band, they did inspire most of the hard rock and metal bands to come. Led Zeppelin was inducted into the Rock and Roll Hall of Fame in 1995.

Discussion Question

Can one band single-handedly define a music genre or does it take a number of bands to create a trend before defining a genre? Be specific by providing examples to support your position.

Chapter Four: The Blues Takes a Trip and the Supergroups

"Led Zeppelin was a band that would change things around substantially each time it played...We were becoming tighter, to the point of telepathy...it was always four musicians at the top of their game, but they could play like a band"

- Jimmy Page

55

Chapter Five: The Beatles and The Solo Beatles

The Beatles

By the late 1950's, rockabilly had lost its appeal with the youth of America, as Elvis moved into movie star mode singing pop ballads. The teen idol movement that had made an impact on rock music was coming to an end. In November of 1963, American culture was in a state of crisis with the assassination of President John F. Kennedy. The nation was is need of healing and something new musically. This would come from a British band that would create an unprecedented impact on music and culture, both American and worldwide. The rules of rock would soon be rewritten while the music of Elvis, Chuck Berry, and Buddy Holly would be used as inspiration for a new British style that would capture a new generation of rock music fans.

The Beatles (1960-1970) grew out of a combination of musical cultures and styles in the late 1950's and early 1960's. Based on the British folk music style called skiffle, and the strong influence of Buddy Holly and the Crickets, John Lennon and Paul McCartney formed one of the greatest songwriting teams in rock history. With the final additions of George Harrison and Ringo Starr, The Beatles took America by storm in 1964 at a time of great political and social upheaval. In their relatively short ten-year career, no band in music history achieved such worldwide success and musically evolved in such dramatic fashion. In this chapter we will trace The Beatles evolution in their different phases and then look at the solo careers of the Fab Four. We will also examine the transitional albums of Rubber Soul and Revolver and do a full breakdown of Sgt. Peppers Lonely Hearts Club Band.

The port city of Liverpool, England was home to a thriving, yet different musical scene than that found in London. One significant difference was that London was visited much more frequently by American blues greats such as Muddy Waters and Howlin' Wolf. Meanwhile, the music scene in Liverpool was influenced more by skiffle musicians. **Skiffle** was a simple style of British folk music that featured guitar or banjo and homemade instruments such as washboard bass and a wooden box. Skiffle drew from simple two and three chord harmonies. It was fairly easy to play and sing basic skiffle folk melodies.

At this same time, a Liverpool resident, sixteen-year-old John Lennon (1940-1980), was intrigued with the sounds of Elvis Presley and Buddy Holly. Lennon, with the help of his mother, Julia, learned to play simple chords on his first guitar. John soon adapted a rebellious image and wore slicked back hair and tight pants. He also heard the single "Rock Island Line" by skiffle singer Lonnie Donegan, and was determined to form his own skiffle group with his friends from his school, Quarry Bank High School. Lennon named the band **The Quarrymen** and they played little gigs around Liverpool. It was then that John was introduced to Paul McCartney (1942-) in 1957 at a Quarrymen gig. Paul was raised in a musical family where his father, Jim, had led a successful society band. He learned to imitate the guitar and vocal styles of Elvis and other rockabilly artists. McCartney also listened to Little Richard and The Everly Brothers. Soon, Paul impressed Lennon with his knowledge of Eddie Cochran, Gene Vincent, and Little Richards' tunes. Within a week, McCartney was asked to join the Quarrymen.

The Lennon and McCartney combination found instant chemistry in the Quarrymen. They shared a love for both rock 'n' roll music and guitars. They also loved art and language, a sign of what was to come. However, they had very different personalities. John was uninhibited and rebellious while Paul worked to establish a "good boy" image and wanted the approval of authority figures. Their similarities and differences contributed to their strong songwriting relationship but

Rock Hard Fact

The Beatles had twenty songs go to number one on the American charts and seventeen on the British charts.

"The Beatles were formative in my upbringing, my education. They came from a very similar background: the industrial towns in England, working class; they wrote their own songs, conquered the world. That was the blueprint for lots of other British kids to try to do the same."

- Sting

would also eventually contribute to the demise of The Beatles. Lennon and McCartney were also smart and they shared an ability to understand the creative approaches of other musicians and composers. By 1957, Lennon had failed out of Quarry Bank and enrolled in the Liverpool Institute where he joined his bandmate, McCartney. At the Institute, Paul was a model student. Later that year, a younger student and friend of McCartney, George Harrison (1943-2001) began to hang around and sit in with The Quarrymen on guitar. Harrison was also absorbing the sounds of American rock 'n' roll, especially Buddy Holly. Harrison soon joined the group. In 1958, tragedy struck when John's mother, Julia, died when hit by a car. John managed to stay in school and continued to gig with The Quarrymen. He soon met his eventual wife, Cynthia Powell.

The Quarrymen were without a bassist (and drummer), until a fellow student and friend of John, Stu Sutcliffe, bought a bass guitar. Sutcliffe was invited to join the band, although he had no idea how to play. What he did do was suggest a name change to the "Beetles" inspired by Buddy Holly's "Crickets." After a short time as "Long John and The Silver Beetles" they settled on The Silver Beatles changing the spelling, a pun on the word *beat*. In 1960, the still drummer-less Silver Beatles were not very good and did not have a stage act. They were learning to play by covering early rock and skiffle songs. George was defining his role in the band as Sutcliffe was faking the bass, barely getting by. Later that year, The Silver Beatles added drummer Tommy Moore, who was a friend of Sutcliffe. In 1962, the band received an opportunity to play in the rebuilt World War II city of Hamburg, Germany. New drummer Moore was not up to a lengthy engagement out of the country and McCartney quickly asked a local drummer, Pete Best, to join the band for its two-month engagement as The Beatles (thus dropping Silver). The demands of a nightly four and a half an hour gig forced the band to develop more material and get its stage act together. Soon, the German police discovered that George was underage to play in clubs and promptly deported him. To compound the problem, The Beatles got into some other minor trouble and soon returned to England. At the same time, Stu Sutcliffe became more interested in painting and less in The Beatles. He was also suffering from severe headaches and soon died of a cerebral hemorrhage. Now without a bassist, Paul quickly moved to become the new bass player in The Beatles.

The Beatles' early stage repertoire at this point was a healthy mix of Buddy Holly, Elvis Presley, Little Richard, The Everly Brothers, and Gene Vincent tunes. They also covered Chuck Berry's "Too Much Monkey Business," Hank Williams Sr's "Hey Good Lookin," and Ray Charles's "Hallelujah, I Love Her So" etc… The first of their original songs included the McCartney songs "Tip of My Tongue," and "Like Dreamers Do," a Lennon tune "Hello Little Girl," and a Lennon /McCartney tune "P.S. I Love You." Thus far, The Beatles had recorded only one original song (it wasn't released until after their initial success) and one cover. These recordings were the Lennon/McCartney original "In Spite of All the Danger," and the Buddy Holly cover "That'll Be the Day."

Back in Liverpool, The Beatles started a residency at the Cavern Club, owned by Pete Best's mother, Mona. It was here that they gained a steady following. A local store manager, **Brian Epstein** (1934-1967), was asked if he sold any Beatles records. That request peaked his interest in The Beatles, who were playing down the street from his store. Epstein befriended the band by going to many of their Cavern Club shows and eventually asked to become their manager in late 1961. He had no managerial experience but quickly learned on the job. However, all of the major record companies including Decca, EMI, and Pye Records rejected Epstein's proposals to sign The Beatles.

Brian Epstein

Brian Epstein was strongly determined to make The Beatles a success. Epstein created an image for them right from the beginning. He made them give up their leather jackets and jeans and embrace a professional look that started with matching, custom-made velvet collared jackets. They sported narrow pants and what became Beatle boots (Cuban-heeled boots handcrafted by a custom shoemaker). Then came the mop-tops, better known as Beatles cut hairstyles. George Harrison was first to adapt this new "Beatles look," (started back in the days of their Hamburg residency) and the others soon followed. Epstein also made them behave. He no longer allowed them to smoke, to swear or eat or drink onstage. He made them bow after tunes to appear humble, especially to win over adults who were disapproving of their hairstyles. Epstein was passionate about promoting the band and simple refused to take no for an answer. While they were becoming a sensation in Britain, Epstein had bigger plans; the musical takeover of America.

Epstein flew to New York in November of 1963 looking for American label support. In Britain, Epstein convinced Capitol to release "I Want to Hold Your Hand" (small labels Vee Jay and Swan had released the first three Beatles singles with none making the top 100) and in January of 1964, Epstein also secured a concert date at Carnegie Hall and two appearances on The Ed Sullivan Show. Epstein was successful as over 70 million people saw The Beatles first Sullivan appearance.

In return, The Beatles were very loyal to Brian Epstein. In 1963, Epstein had The Beatles unfortunately sign a publishing contract with Northern Songs. This publishing company only gave Lennon and McCartney twenty percent each and Epstein nine percent of the publishing rights to their tunes. Epstein was very busy managing The Beatles schedule between 1963 and 1965. After what would be their last live concert, held in 1966 at Candlestick Park in San Francisco, Epstein pressured The Beatles to continue touring but they refused.

Brian Epstein died of an alcohol and sleeping pill overdose in August 1967. He will always be remembered for his aggressive and unwavering ambition that broke The Beatles wide open to the whole world. McCartney always referred to him as a fifth Beatle.

The Beatles returned again to Hamburg for a seven-week engagement at the Star club, a new rock venue. They honed their stage act playing four hours a night, seven nights a week. While The Beatles were still in Hamburg, Brian Epstein set up a meeting with Parlophone Records, a subsidiary of EMI. **George Martin** (1926-2016), the head of Parlophone, liked Epstein but was unimpressed with the quality of the demo that Epstein provided. Martin was looking to make Parlophone a respectable and successful label. Martin was intrigued with The Beatles and was thinking about signing them, since he had come to believe in their potential. However, he was unsure of what to do with them in terms of material. In June of 1962, Martin had The Beatles play through some of their repertoire, and finalized an offer for a contract to record four songs over a one-year period. Later that summer, the band decided that Pete Best was not working out both personally and musically. Brian Epstein fired Best and replaced him with Richard Starkey, aka Ringo Starr (1940-).

Ringo Starr had first started out in a skiffle band called Rory and the Hurricanes. He received the nickname, Ringo, because he wore so many rings. Rory and the Hurricanes were well known around Liverpool and Hamburg. Ringo began to hang out with The Beatles in Hamburg and by August of 1962, The Beatles were complete with Ringo in place. He soon got his own Beatle haircut and shaved his beard to fit into the band's image. The first original songs in The Beatles' repertoire were not profound lyrically but were very simple and musically inventive. The Beatles worked within the conventions of the standard pop market but often added different chord changes. They experimented with key shifts that they learned from their various musical influences. Early Beatles songs were not about personal life events and they knew their lyrics didn't possess much meaning or depth. Soon, they would expand their influences to embrace the sounds of Motown, Marvin Gaye, and the songwriting combination of Gerry Goffin and Carole King. Lennon and McCartney began to write songs for other artists and they envisioned themselves as a songwriting team in the Brill Building style of songwriters.

The Beatles recorded "Love Me Do" and "P.S. I Love You" in the fall of 1962. "Love Me Do" would climb to number seventeen on the British charts by the end of the year. Martin arranged another recording session for the band later that same year. They recorded "Please, Please Me" and Martin knew they had a number one hit. By March of 1963, it went to number one. Martin quickly had them record a full album of songs from their live repertoire. This included a cover version of the Isley Brothers "Twist and Shout." The big hits came quickly with "From Me to You" and 'She Loves You" and they firmly established a new sound that people were referencing as the Mersey sound (named for the river that ran through Liverpool). A slew of television appearances followed, along with a tour of Sweden and a home appearance for the Queen Mother and Princess Margaret. The English version of Beatlemania was up and running. They soon had seven of the top twenty hits on the British charts. However, a full-scale invasion of America was on the horizon.
[Note: The release dates and album names were often different for British and American Beatles album releases. To minimize the confusion, we will only refer to the American releases.]

"Love Me Do"
written by John Lennon and Paul McCartney

"Love Me Do" was The Beatles first hit song. It was released in Britain in October of 1962 where it went to number four on the pop charts. "Love Me Do" was released in America on April 1964 and went to number one. Although listed as a Lennon/McCartney song, Paul mostly wrote it. The lyrics were very basic with most of the words containing only one syllable and the word *love* was repeated twenty-one times. The entire lyrical statement was essentially "I will love you forever so please love me in return." Most Beatles lyrics were analyzed to death for their obvious and (sometimes) hidden meaning. In an interview, McCartney said, "'Love Me Do' was our greatest philosophical song…for it to be simple, and true, means that it's incredibly simple." #1

On "Love Me Do," the gospel and blues influence of the band's vocals and Lennon's harmonica playing made the tune different from hundreds of other, then current love songs. John loved the harmonica playing of many blues artists and referred to gospel and rhythm and blues as some of his favorite music(s). John would go on to play harmonica on a number of other early Beatles' tracks. "Love Me Do" was included on The Beatles first extended record along with "Please Please Me,' "Thank You Girl," and " From Me to You."

In 1963, the first Beatles record to arrive in America, "Please Please Me." was released by the Chicago label, Vee Jay records. It did not make the pop charts. However that same year, the early phase of Beatlemania swept Britain with hits on EMI Records including; "Love Me Do," "Please Please Me," "From Me to You," and "She Loves You." The American affiliate of EMI, Capitol Records, released "I Want to Hold Your Hand" and its B side, "I Saw Her Standing There." They became the band's first official singles in America. They both received radio play by December and by the middle of January of 1964, "I Want to Hold Your Hand" went to number one on the pop charts. On January 20th, 1964, the album <u>Meet The Beatles!</u> was released by Capitol Records in America. By February 15th, it went to number one on Billboard's album charts and stayed there for eleven weeks.

What happened next on the pop charts was unprecedented. By March 21st, "I Want to Hold Your Hand," which had been on top of the charts since January 25th, was knocked out by The Beatles own "She Loves You." That single was number one until they again replaced it at number one with "Twist and Shout." A week later, they replaced "Twist and Shout" with another number one, "Can't Buy Me Love." With the exception of a brief takeover at number one by Louis Armstrong's "Hello Dolly," The Beatles captured the number one spot once more with "Love Me Do." On March 31st of that same year, The Beatles held *all five top chart positions*. Unprecedented!

On February 7th, 1964, The Beatles stepped off a plane in New York for the first time. They were met at the airport by approximately 5,000 fans and later by 4,000 fans in Miami for an *Ed Sullivan Show* appearance. Paul McCartney recalled the New York arrival saying, "I remember the great moment of getting into the limo and putting on the radio, and hearing a running commentary on us: They have just left the airport…It was like a dream. The greatest fantasy ever." #1 Their first press conference was watched carefully by many curious Americans as The Beatles charmed the masses with their quick wit and good manners.

Beatlemania

The first popular music explosion happened in America in 1955 and lasted until, more or less, 1957. That was until a major musical change was on the horizon. The 1964 pop explosion known as Beatlemania would invade America and last for approximately four years. The term Beatlemania was used as early as when The Beatles made a mini-tour of Scotland in October of 1963. From the day they landed at John F. Kennedy Airport in February of 1964, Beatlemania was a cultural phenomenon previously unseen in America. They quickly charmed an entire nation with their emotionally powerful songs and Fab Four personas. Their first tour of America was char-

Rock Hard Fact

The first Lennon and McCartney recording to reach the American charts was a cover of the song "From Me To You" by Del Shannon.

acterized by mass hysteria and mostly high-pitched screaming females, present at their every appearance.

The Beatles aired on the Ed Sullivan Show three times in one month and an estimated seventy-three million TV viewers tuned in for their February 9th appearance. They dominated newspaper headlines. The effect on America was unprecedented. In the nine days of that first visit, Americans bought more than two million Beatles records and spent more than two and a half million dollars on Beatles-related merchandise. It was everything Beatles: Beatles T-shirts, Beatles hats, Beatles pajamas, Beatles posters, even Beatles bubblebath, etc…

Beatlemania affected the feel and day-to-day life of many Americans. The Beatles created a presence. The culture of America was transformed by the Beatlemania pop explosion by the way people would dress, talk, create new personal heroes, and more. Beatlemania made America think about and sometimes alter their political beliefs, their sexual behavior, and social constructs of their personal relationships. The tremendous energy of Beatlemania became the redirected energy of adolescence frustration and repression. Thousands of individuals became attached to a group; that group being The Beatles themselves and more importantly, a unified generation of Americans.

The excitement of Beatlemania would eventually dissipate by late 1966. Constant touring, increased crowds, and never-ending demands by the press wore down The Beatles. The challenge of finding large enough concert venues created touring problems and the large stadiums made performing even more difficult; attributed to the deafening roar of thousands of screaming teenage girls.

The phenomenon of Beatlemania changed American culture forever.

> "We were driving through Colorado (in 1971) and we had the radio on and eight of the top ten songs were Beatles songs"
>
> – Bob Dylan

Moving forward, The Beatles released their first movie, *A Hard Day's Night* in the summer of 1964. They toured Holland, Scandinavia, Australia, and the Far East, thus extending their appeal worldwide. By August, they were back in America for their second tour which included twenty-three cities. Beatlemania reached new heights, as rabid fans were everywhere. The Beatles were forced to figure out exit strategies for their live appearances that included escape by armored trucks. By 1965, The Beatles had embraced the multimillion-dollar rock lifestyle. They bought big homes, luxury cars, and had an extended entourage. Besides the normal rock band use of alcohol, marijuana and pills, Lennon and Harrison were introduced to the mind-altering drug, LSD. This (only occasional) experimentation would later go on to influence their music and connect them to the psychedelic genre of rock, as seen in their sometimes ambiguous lyrics and experimental use of sound colors and instruments. Their second movie *Help!*, was released in 1965 and proved to be as successful as the first. A third American tour followed. It was marked by an outdoor concert at the enormous venue of Shea Stadium in New York. 55,000 screaming fans made the music inaudible. Ringo pointed out "I never felt people came to hear our show-I felt they came to *see us*." #2

In spite of all of the success, the band had grown tired of touring. They missed their families. They also hated having to escape concert venues and being unable to hear themselves on-stage. The Beatles generally had trouble reproducing their studio material live. But in spite of those issues, they were on top of the music business and their personas were larger than life. Most artists would be afraid to change a thing in fear of losing their audience and ticket to success. Not The Beatles.

There would be the dramatic shift in the direction of The Beatles' music. One example, was the mostly McCartney written tune "Yesterday." It contained an interesting chord progression not seen in many pop-rock songs. George Martin suggested that they add a string quartet arrangement, initially rejected by Paul. John contributed to the tune but was not a fan of soft love ballads with sentimental lyrics. The song went on to become one of The Beatles most covered songs and, of course, a number one hit in America. The song also showed two things. First, the musical personalities of John and Paul were growing in different directions. Paul was personally and musically more conservative, traditional, and sentimental (thus The Beatle love song) while John was more cynical, musically adventurous, and rebellious. Secondly, "Yesterday," later released on *Help!*, showed that The Beatles were capable of much more than relying on the simple pop tune formula that had previously made them superstars.

Going back to 1964, the musical direction of Lennon and McCartney began to expand. The music and lyrics of Bob Dylan hit them like a bombshell. Dylan's first three albums, including <u>The Freewheeling Bob Dylan</u> and <u>The Times They Are A Changin</u>, revealed to them the great potential within song lyrics to express a wide range of emotions. The Beatles felt free to experiment much more with lyrics of substance and the language of metaphor. John, especially inspired by Dylan, saw the potential to express his poetry and creative writing in a new songwriting approach. Examples of this included the Lennon/McCartney tunes "Help," "I'm A Loser," and "Norwegian Wood."

The Songwriting Genius of John Lennon and Paul McCartney

The Beatles recorded 208 songs, most of which were credited to John Lennon and Paul McCartney. Both benefited from a good high school education that included art and writing classes. They would eventually identify their creative approach as inspired by artists who worked in other fields, artists such as Dylan Thomas and Pablo Picasso. From this inspiration, John and Paul enhanced their craft of writing and recording rock songs. John Lennon remembered, "The person I actually picked as my partner…who I recognized had talent and I could get on with was Paul."

In the beginning, Lennon and McCartney both worked within the confines of the existing pop music market, writing in the styles of artists such as The Everly Brothers and Buddy Holly. Their early compositional approach grew out of their inspiration from other artist's songs, rather than serious events in the real world or from a deeper introspective place. Early on, John had written his personal observations of life in the form of poems and short stories. Some of these ideas were later published in two books titled Spaniard in the Works and In His Own Write and would be important sources for John's progression as a writer. The songwriting team admired most by John and Paul was Gerry Goffin and Carole King, one of the best of the New York Brill Building scene.

John Lennon and Paul McCartney had an uncanny ability to complement each other's musical ideas. Lennon explained, "The way we wrote a lot of the time; you'd write the good bit, the part that was easy like 'I read the news today' or whatever it was,

> "(George) Harrison's 'Something' is the greatest love song of the last fifty years"
>
> – Frank Sinatra

then when you got stuck or whenever it got hard, instead of carrying on, you just drop it, then we would meet each other and I would sing half and he would be inspired to write the next bit and vice versa…if he already thought it was a good song then sometimes we wouldn't allow any interference either." #3 A good example of their teamwork was the tune "Drive My Car" from Rubber Soul, where Paul wrote the melody and chords but got stuck on the storyline. Rather than forcing it, Paul had John come in to pull the song's lyrics together at the last minute.

John and Paul, both capable of writing at the piano or guitar, and both singing lead, were never restricted to the role of lyricist or melody writer. This way, either of them could contribute to any dimension of a song at any time. Also, both John and Paul seemed to have an innate sense of what the public wanted to hear. Each girl in the audience was made to feel that they were singing directly to them. This was reflected in the titles "From Me To You" and "Thank You Girl."

1964 marked a pivotal year in the Lennon/McCartney songwriting machine. They traveled extensively, mixing with artists and intellectuals in the London art world. More and more self-contained songs were written by each of them. By the time of the writing and recording of the album Rubber Soul, Lennon and McCartney were clearly moving in different songwriting directions. John's songwriting focused on rebellion, struggle, and sometimes anger. Paul wrote about different topics but still included love songs, now much more lyrically sophisticated than wanting to "hold your hand." Soon the divide widened even more on the album Revolver, with John and Paul growing further apart in their perceptions of themselves and their music. This was, in part; due to their contact was the emerging counter-culture and the effect of psychedelic drugs on their personal lives. Sometimes, Paul was motivated to write utilizing the sound of the words more than the content of the story itself. He was inspired by other artist's hit songs and continued to emulate styles such as the Motown sound with his "Got to Get You Into My Life," the first Beatles track to use brass instruments.

All the way to the recording of Abbey Road, Lennon and McCartney would still collaborate when it was necessary. They did whatever it took to arrive at the finished product. There has never been a duo throughout the history of rock that was as complete a package as the Lennon and McCartney songwriting machine. *Pure magic.*

The Beatles entered a whole new introspective and experimental period by the end of 1965. They released their tenth American album Rubber Soul, which revealed many changes. Gone were the simple, upbeat love songs about holding hands. Songs were now a more studio based constructive process with multi-step recording tape effects and complex mixes. Songs were built layer by layer with four-track recording that replaced the old two-track process. George Harrison had heard the Indian master, Ravi Shankar, play the sitar when The Beatles were on a tour of India. Shankar taught him some of the basics of the sitar including the microtonal shading capable of its very distinct sound that Harrison employed on "Norwegian Wood." Rubber Soul was different (including its distorted cover photo) in how each song flowed from one to the next. Now, whoever was singing the song was in charge even though all Beatles' songs without Harrison were still listed as Lennon/McCartney collaborations.

Rubber Soul also featured the hits; "Day Tripper," "We Can Work It Out," "Nowhere Man," "In My Life," and "Michelle."

"Norwegian Wood (This Bird Has Flown)"
written by John Lennon and Paul McCartney

Inspired by a new and musically powerful Bob Dylan influence, John Lennon moved away from the usual boy and girl innocent Beatles song to his eventual philosophy of love and its meaning in a deeper context. Dylan's use of imagery, symbolism, and metaphor, had a profound effect on Lennon and McCartney. It was felt here in Lennon's song "Norwegian Wood." The song's lyrics told the story of an affair John had experienced. It detailed a seduction scene at a woman's apartment. Lennon was stuck for ideas after coming up with the basic tune and the first verse of the lyrics. John asked Paul for help with the lyrics on the middle eight-bar phrase. Paul suggested that the story should be about a girl who leads men on and the story should end up with a man setting her apartment on fire as an act of revenge.

At this same time, George Harrison had become interested in the Indian instrument, the sitar. He first heard one while filming the movie *Help!*. The recording of "Norwegian Wood" became one of the first times a sitar was used on a rock record. "Norwegian Wood" represented a turning point in the folk-style rock ballad format. Lennon was developing the ability to quickly move from one lyrical image to another and leaving it to the listener's imagination to fill in the complete story. For the recording of "Norwegian Wood," The Beatles experimented with the arrangement by having Lennon overdub a lead vocal and then double track it at the end of each line in the verses. Harrison's sitar part worked well as an accompaniment with its mystical sounding drone effect. This employment of the sitar was to become a trend in **Indian rock** and psychedelic rock.

It now took longer for The Beatles to complete an album. Capitol Records released the album Yesterday and Today to give starving Beatles fans a new record while they worked on the next album, Revolver. The American release of Yesterday and Today featured tracks from their two most recent British albums (which had not yet been included on American albums), plus three tracks from their upcoming album to be released in England. This record contained the hits "Yesterday," "Nowhere Man," and " Day Tripper."

In March of 1966, The Beatles were in the middle of their greatest controversy. John Lennon had given an interview to a London reporter when he said, "Christianity will go. It will vanish and shrink. I needn't argue with that; I'm right and I will be proved right. We're more popular than Jesus now." #4 The public backlash was immediate and strong. There were radio record bans, protest marches, and record burning events. Eventually, John gave an apology and gradually things returned to normal.

In the summer of 1966 a new tour of America was coordinated with the release of Revolver. This would be The Beatles final tour of America. They again played Shea Stadium and gave their last public concert ever at San Francisco's Candlestick Park. They did play a spontaneous rooftop concert in London (seen in their film *Let It Be*). Revolver's cover was in black and white and showed sketches of the bands' faces. The album featured more experiments with tape effects of different speeds and backwards mixing. Lennon was writing songs with more cynical and sometimes surrealistic lyrics. Revolver

> **Rock Hard Fact**
>
> The Beatles tune "Helter Skelter" was a McCartney song written in response (to not be outdone) by Pete Townshend of The Who, who claimed to have written "the loudest, dirtiest rock and roll song ever."

> "We're (The Beatles) more popular than Jesus now"
>
> –John Lennon

featured lyrics that dealt with death, ocean adventures, sunshine, paying taxes, and psychedelic imagery. Revolver revealed The Beatles fascination with the growing counter-culture and the influence of avant-guard art. This would appeal to a new audience. None of Revolver's fourteen songs would ever be performed onstage. Revolver featured the hits "Paperback Writer," "Eleanor Rigby," "Yellow Submarine," and "Got To Get You Into My Life."

In 1967, The Beatles would move into their last musical phase. They began work on a record inspired by the concept album titled Pet Sounds by the Beach Boys. This would represent the height of their musical creativity and in the process, they revolutionized rock music. This period was also marked with tragedy. Brian Epstein died of a drug overdose. Feeling useless since The Beatles were no longer touring, Epstein's personal life had been in turmoil. Epstein became a victim of the Beatlemania he had helped to create.

Sgt. Pepper's Lonely Hearts Club Band was released June, 1967. The album started with the tune "Sgt. Pepper's Lonely Hearts Club Band" written by Paul. For many groups, there is a single identifying album that is considered to be their masterpiece. However, The Beatles were so prolific that the title of masterpiece could be bestowed on many of their albums. Still, this one was a game changer on many levels.

Groundbreaking album
Sgt. Pepper's Lonely Hearts Club Band

In the months preceding the release of Sgt. Pepper's Lonely Hearts Club Band, there were rumors circulating that The Beatles were working on a project that would amount to a historic musical landmark. The new album would take over seven hundred hours to record (as opposed to the twelve hours it took to record their first album). Rumors continued that it would include highly experimental recording techniques (sound shaping signal processing), hundred-voice choirs, and a huge orchestra. The anticipation was intense. An announcement was made when it would first receive airplay in England. Turns out, it was worth the wait.

Sgt. Pepper's Lonely Hearts Club Band was immediately recognized as a musical masterpiece. It was also a miniature pop explosion unto itself. Sgt. Pepper's Lonely Hearts Club Band was often referred to as a concept album held together by one unifying theme. The Beatles did not see it that way. John thought that only the title tune, its reprise and "A Day in the Life" were connected. The album was shaped around the idea of a fictional Sgt. Pepper Band. This alter ego group gave The Beatles the freedom to musically experiment. However, the Sergeant Pepper idea and song didn't appear until they were well along the way to completing the album. After considering the new album theme, Sgt. Pepper took on a life of its own.

On side one, the opening tune (and its reprise at the end of side two) did fit the definition of a concept album. Sgt. Pepper was presented in a psychedelic circus atmosphere in a series of acts. It started with crowd noises, then the music began, Sgt. Pepper's band was introduced, a brass band was heard, and then the crowd's reaction followed. George Martin and McCartney further denied that the songs had any connection to each other and that they were merely trying to create segues between the songs to support the flow of the record. The reprise at the end was George Martins' idea to help bring the work to a conclusion.

The first side then moved into "A Little Help From My Friends" and it was John who came up with the idea of starting each verse with a question such as "Do you believe in love at first sight?" The brilliant tune "Lucy in the Sky with Diamonds" followed. It has been interpreted to be about the drug LSD but John insisted it was inspired by his son Julian's drawing of his fourth grade friend Lucy. This was one of the first rock songs to shift back and forth between different meters going from 3/4 in the verses to 4/4 in the choruses and back. The first side continued with "Getting Better," "Fixing a Hole," "She's Leaving Home," and "Being for the Benefit of Mr. Kite."

Side two opened with "Within You Without You," then moved to "When I'm Sixty-Four," "Lovely Rita," and "Good Morning Good Morning." The album seemed to come to the end with a reprise of the opening tune but one of the classic Beatles songs, "A Day in the Life," finished side two and unified the album. It was a great success both with Beatles fans and critics. It revolutionized the music industry. It was seen as one of the first art rock albums and would help inspire a generation of progressive rock musicians. The album cover featured The Beatles in their Sgt. Pepper costumes and sixty celebrities and historical figures who were central to western culture. Actress Mae West first refused to allow her image on the cover of the album, but later changed her mind after receiving a personal letter from The Beatles. Sgt. Pepper's Lonely Hearts Club Band, considered by many to be one of the most important works of the twentieth century, has sold more than thirty-two million copies worldwide.

"A Day in the Life"
written by John Lennon and Paul McCartney

"A Day in the Life" was written in 1967 and marked an incredible feat of songwriting. A mostly complete Lennon tune was merged with a partially completed McCartney tune. The arranging and orchestration genius of George Martin was then utilized to make a coherent whole. John's song was about events he had read in the newspaper (he read the paper every day) including the line "I'd love to turn you on" that may have been about sex, drugs, or music. The line "He blew his mind out in a car" was about a man named Tara Browne, a friend of The Beatles, who had died in a car accident.

After an intense orchestral glissando (a full forty member orchestra was hired for the recording session), there was an abrupt segue into Paul's tune "Woke up, fell out of bed." Paul's section was about getting up in the morning and going to school on a typical day. He described going into a (perhaps marijuana-induced) dream and then transitioned to a return of the first section. Paul recounted, "It was just me remembering what it was like to run up the road to catch a bus to school, having a smoke and going into class…It was a reflection of my schooldays." #5 Paul's tune was then spliced between the second and third verses of John's song. It was remarkable how the two different songs worked together as Lennon, McCartney and Martin were able to bring it all together to create one of the defining Beatles songs. John ended the tune with a return to the line "I'd love to turn you on" and the intense wall of orchestral glissando returned, this time reaching a peak. A long silence ensued after a massive piano chord was held out. The added drama engaged

> "I'd Love to Turn You On"
>
> - John Lennon

the listener to reflect on the song and perhaps the whole album.

Moving forward from Sgt. Pepper, The Beatles recorded soundtracks for the films *Yellow Submarine* and *Magical Mystery Tour* in 1967. The songs "All You Need is Love," "Hello, Goodbye," "Lady Madonna," and "Hey Jude" were all on Magical Mystery Tour. This showed that there was no drop off in their prolific songwriting abilities. In Britain, Magical Mystery Tour went to number two and in America it reached the number one spot. Yellow Submarine was released in July of 1968 and it went to number three in Britain and number two in America.

In 1968, The Beatles released a double album that consisted of thirty tunes. It was simply called The Beatles but it became better known as The White Album since the cover was completely white and without names or graphics. The band was headed in different directions at this time and the eclectic nature of the songs would bare this out. The songs were in many ways a tribute to their many musical influences. The album was also influenced by their interest in the teaching of Indian guru, Maharishi Mahesh Yogi. They had all attended a ten-day course on Transcendental Mediation in North Wales and they visited the Maharishi in India in February of 1968. They were also still recovering from the death of Brian Epstein and this was a factor in seeking out the Maharishi. The trip to India helped to renew their friendships with one another. George Harrison was allowed to contribute four songs to the White Album including the classic "While My Guitar Gently Weeps." Harrison tried to stay out of the way of the growing divide between Lennon and McCartney. "While My Guitar Gently Weeps" was based on Harrisons'
reading of the *I Chang*, the Chinese book of changes. Harrison decided to apply these concepts of change to his songwriting. Both Lennon and McCartney were not very interested in his song so Harrison brought in Eric Clapton to play lead guitar and he played the rhythm guitar part. The White Album also contained an eclectic blend of songs including "Blackbird," "Birthday," "Helter Skelter," and "Revolution." The Beatles was released on The Beatles new label, part of their new company, Apple Corp Ltd.

1968 also saw the high profile weddings of Paul McCartney to Linda Eastman and John to Yoko Ono. In early 1969, The Beatles were realizing that they were becoming further detached both musically and socially. Paul suggested that they begin to play live again. The Beatles were legally committed to do a final movie for United Artists. They began filming and recording an 80 minute documentary of the group rehearsing in the studio and playing live on the roof of the Apple office building in London. This endeavor was intended to be a work about musical creativity, but the music and filming of *Let It Be* ended up more about musical disintegration. In order to get the album finished, McCartney took control as John and George became more and more indifferent about the process. Nevertheless, the album Let It Be contained some vintage Beatles songs such as "Get Back," "The Long and Winding Road," "The Ballad of John and Yoko," and, of course, "Let It Be." Let It Be was to become the last Beatles record released and it was often assumed that it was the last record they ever recorded. But even after the dysfunction that occurred in making Let It Be, The Beatles would go on to record Abbey Road.

The Beatles released Abbey Road in 1969. It had been seven years since their first recording at Abbey Road Studios, a time when they were intent on making their mark on the musical world. But by now, they were tired veterans of the music business and weighed down by power struggles over money and power. The songs on Abbey Road reflected their many issues. They were struggling with debt, getting ripped-off by everyone trying to take advantage of their success, fighting legal battles, and feeling the pressure of being The Beatles. Abbey Road would, however, go on to become their biggest selling album. George Martin has said many times that Abbey Road was his favorite Beatles album. He recalled that McCartney had asked him for help in returning to their earlier recording process; back when they had achieved a magical feeling. George Martin knew this was possible but he demanded that they give him their full co-operation.

The title "Abbey Road" referred to their EMI Abbey Road studio, where they had recorded for most of their career. Each Beatle contributed songs and they played as a group on almost every track. Harrison continued to emerge as a great songwriter with "Here Comes the Sun" and "Something." Lennon was being pulled in two different musical directions. On one hand, he was pursuing some avant-garde concepts with Yoko Ono and on the other, he was going back to old school rock with the song "Come Together."

Lennon's "I Want You," a hard rocking song with some electronic distortion, was nearly eight minutes long. The second side featured a collection of songs that Paul very skillfully unified into a suite. It began with Paul's "You Never Give Me Your Money" and culminated with "The End," the perfect song to end their illustrious Beatles career. "The End" was philosophical and very Beatles-like with Paul's line "the love you take is equal to the love you make." This was impressive to John and he declared it to be very cosmic, thus providing the final punctuation for The Beatles message of love.

George Martin
The fifth Beatle

George Martin (1925-2016) was thirty-six years old at the time he signed The Beatles to a recording contract. As a producer, his entire experience at the time consisted of working on some light classical recordings and producing a comedy show called The Gong Show. Martin remembered hearing The Beatles demo tape for the first time saying, "In defense of all those people who turned it down, it was a pretty lousy tape, recorded in a back room, very badly balanced, not very good songs, and a rather raw group…I liked them as people apart from anything else, and I was convinced that we had the makings of a hit group." #6. Often called the fifth Beatle, Martin was in charge of The Beatle's studio production throughout their entire career. The first thing Martin did was to take the raw original songs and shape and polish them. His ability to translate the groups' individual talents and convert all of the parts into a cohesive whole was extraordinary. He did all of this at a staff producer salary rate and he was never offered any royalties even when the albums sold into the millions. Only until later, did Martin make the kind of money he deserved when he formed his own production company called Associated Independent Recording (AIR).

George Martin was a gifted musician. He possessed perfect pitch and learned to play piano by age seventeen. He studied composition, conducting, theory, and orchestration at the London Guildhall School of Music. He also had a commanding personality that helped him to deal with The Beatles in the

---

Rock Hard Fact

The Vatican officially forgave The Beatles in 2010 for John's earlier comment that The Beatles were bigger than Jesus.

"From one generation to the next, The Beatles will remain the most important rock band of all time."

– Dave Grohl

Rock Hard Fact

The famous final chord in the tune "A Day in the Life" was simultaneously played by Lennon, McCartney, Starr, George Martin, and road manager, Mal Evans on three different pianos.

sometimes chaotic studio environment. Paul McCartney said, "He doesn't write the songs or play them-he doesn't fly the plane-but he is in charge. And that, tied in with his music, made him the perfect producer for The Beatles…He accommodated us. I think a lesser producer might not have done that." #7

George Martin transformed the recording studio into another instrument. He musically educated The Beatles on topics of orchestration and arranging. This in turn motivated them to experiment more in the studio and to compose more complicated songs. His strong musical influence was stamped on countless Beatles songs. For example, he wrote the string arrangement for the tune "Yesterday." On "Strawberry Fields Forever," he introduced backward tape recording and multi-layered musical effects. He contributed the addition of many instrumental sonorities such as French horn and harpsichord parts, the Mellotron, and string instruments. Martin played piano on most of The Beatles albums. George Martin's concept for "A Day in the Life" saw him hire an orchestra of forty musicians and record a glissando of chromatic notes four times, all on different starting points. Then, he combined all the versions to create a massive wall of sound that he used between sections and again at the end of the song. Incredible. That was George Martin, very fortuitous for The Beatles.

The Beatles and George Martin were long gone when American production icon Phil Spector was brought in to save the release of Let It Be. Paul was not happy with Spector's approach, as Spector added strings and multi-layers of sound to the basic tracks. Paul's objections were ignored and he announced his departure from The Beatles. This came as no surprise, since it was clearly over for the other Beatles as well. John Lennon and Yoko One had released the single "Give Peace a Chance" in the summer of 1969 and George was playing in Eric Clapton's band and preparing for his solo album, All Things Must Pass. Paul was leading his new band, Wings, and both he and Ringo Starr were preparing solo albums as well. Let It Be was premiered as a film in May 1970 and as a boxed album and book set. The album came out separately in November of 1970.

The collective achievements of The Beatles were musically and culturally groundbreaking. With mop-tops and Beatle boots, they came to represent a new version of the American dream. They infused a healthy lack of authority, central to connecting to their early fans and then repeatedly reinvented themselves and rock 'n' roll in the process. The Beatles just barely made it to 1970. No other band in rock music history made as big an impact and simultaneously morphed through such dramatic musical evolution. The Beatles created a musical and sociological revolution still felt today.

Discussion Question

Was the incredible early success of The Beatles due to them being in the right place at the right time or would they have been equally successful earlier or later in American history? Take a position and use specific musical and societal examples.

Rock Hard Fact

In the entire career of The Beatles (as a group and solo careers), there was only one song that was credited as being composed by McCartney, Lennon, and Starr. That song was "What Goes On" from Rubber Soul.

The Solo Beatles

When The Beatles broke up, the music didn't stop coming from any of the four musicians. All of The Beatles went on to have successful and prolific solo careers. It is unfair to compare any of their solo work to their collaborative work as the The Beatles. However, the comparisons were inevitable. As time passed, people (and musicians) matured, changed, and evolved. John, Paul, George, and Ringo were no different. However, because they were (obviously) still the same people, the personalities that they collectively brought to The Beatles continued in their solo careers. All of them continued to surround themselves with world-class musicians and impeccable producers. Their music and personalities continued to reach beyond the hits that they created as solo artists. The four musicians that were The Beatles (as well as George Martin, Billy Preston, Nicky Hopkins, and others) continued to create wonderful music that contributed to the musical and popular culture for decades to come.

John Lennon continued rebelling against society's proclivity for violence by writing meaningful music, cutting lyrics, and creating experimental music with his wife Yoko Ono. Paul McCartney continued to produce hit after hit and expanded the boundaries of pop music. He toured endlessly with talented working bands and collaborated with Michael Jackson, Elvis Costello, Stevie Wonder, Youth (from Killing Joke,) the three remaining members of Nirvana, and Kanye West. George Harrison fused his interests in Indian and pop music by creating larger than life, deeply spiritual solo recordings. He collaborated with Delaney and Bonnie, Ravi Shankar, Eric Clapton, The Traveling Wilbury's and his son Dhani Harrison. Ringo Starr's music has reached beyond the drums to create his many different All Starr Band tours, including the musicians; Levon Helm, Dr. John, Clarence Clemons, Todd Rundgren, Gregg Rollie, and Sheila E. Ringo even had a few hits such as "Photograph" and "It Don't Come Easy." And like Lennon, Ringo had devoted a great deal of his time to trying to ensure that the ideas of peace and love didn't become extinct. Ironically, despite the breakup, all of The Beatles continued to appear on each other's recordings. Both Lennon and Harrison appeared on several of Ringo's albums. Ringo guested on quite a few of Harrison's and Lennon's recordings. Ringo Starr even acted in McCartney's film *Give My Regards To Broadstreet*.

George Harrison (1943-2001) was the first Beatle to release solo recordings. They included Wonderwall Music, and Electronic Sound, although they weren't terribly popular. While still in The Beatles, George Harrison and Eric Clapton had struck up a friendship, which led to Harrison touring with the American band Delaney and Bonnie and Friends. This was an important occurrence, because it led to Harrison's third (and most popular) recording All Things Must Pass. This also led to Clapton forming the band Derek and the Dominos. On the tour, Harrison struck up a friendship with drummer Jim Gordon, bassist Carl Radle, and pianist Bobby Whitlock. They, along with Eric Clapton, Gary Brooker, Gary Wright, Dave Mason, Ringo Starr, and producer Phil Spector, would contribute heavily to Harrison's 1970 magnum opus All Things Must Pass. This album bore the hits "My Sweet Lord," "What is Life?" and "Isn't It a Pity." Interestingly, Harrison chose to include five extended instrumental jams on the original triple record set. These jam sessions became the first extended recordings of Clapton's Derek and the Dominos band.

In 1971, Harrison and longtime friend Ravi Shankar organized a concert and a recording called "The Concert For Bangladesh." Harrison and Shankar were working on the soundtrack for the film R*aga: A Film Journey into the Soul of India* when the idea was conceived for a benefit intended to draw attention and raise money for the people of Bangladesh. Next, the triple record set The Concert For Bangladesh, won a Grammy for Album of the Year. The relationship between Harrison and Shankar would culminate in the Harrison produced recording Ravi Shankar: Chants of India, released in 1997. The 2002 film *A Concert For George* also featured Shankar's daughter Anoushka Shankar performing some of Shankar's music.

In 1973, Harrison would follow with Living in the Material World. This album and its single, "Give Me Love (Give Me Peace on Earth)," quickly went to the top of the American charts. This recording featured many of the same musicians (with addition of tabla player Zakir Hussain) but without the big sound and production of Phil Spector. In 1974, Harrison recorded Dark Horse. Its subsequent tour was received badly. It featured several different bands but none of the grandiose arrangements or production. Harrison's next recordings were 1975's Extra Texture (Read All About It), 1976's Thirty-Three 1/3, 1979's self-titled and introspective George Harrison, and 1981's Somewhere In England, which reacted to the murder of John Lennon. In 1987, Harrison released Cloud Nine. In 1991, George Harrison borrowed Eric Clapton's band and went on tour for the first time since 1974. The record Live in Japan featured many of Harrison's hits as well as a few of his Beatles' era songs. While all of these recordings had their high points, it was his last recording, 2002's Brainwashed, that lived up to his Beatles roots and his early solo work. It combined his wry humor and sarcasm, with a deep spiritual subtext, Indian musical flavors, a soaring slide guitar, and a deep sense of groove.

While not necessarily a George Harrison solo project, Harrison as a last minute attempt to create a B-side to a single, created the band The Traveling Wilbury's (see chapter twelve) in 1988. All the members (Bob Dylan, Tom Petty, Roy Orbison, Jeff Lynne, and drummer Jim Keltner) of the band happened to be in LA, and all of them expressed the desire to be included in George's last minute super-band. George Harrison was inducted in the Rock and Roll Hall of Fame as a Beatle and as a solo artist in 2004.

"My Sweet Lord"
by George Harrison

In 1971 George Harrison's song "My Sweet Lord" from his recording All Things Must Pass became the best selling single of the year in the UK. It also topped the charts worldwide. It became the first number one single for any of the ex-Beatles, and remains popular today. These were not bad achievements for a songwriter who lived in the shadow of the songwriting team of Lennon and McCartney. By the end of The Beatles, it was clear that classics like "Taxman" and "While My Guitar Gently Weeps" showcased Harrison's more refined songwriting skills. "My Sweet Lord" blended both Christian and Hindu religious ideals, and was stamped with Phil Spector's Wall of Sound techniques.

Harrison had written the song while still in The Beatles, and intended to offer it popular gospel singer Edwin Hawkins. He instead offered it to Billy Preston (who was recording for The Beatles Apple Records label) who included it on his Encouraging Words record, which Harrison co-produced. There was controversy concerning the song's origin, as a 1970's lawsuit claimed that it plagiarized the Ronnie Mack song "He's So Fine," made popular by The Chiffons. Harrison instead insisted that the hymn "Oh Happy Day" was his inspiration for the song. In 1976, Harrison was found guilty, and claimed that he must have subconsciously plagiarized the song.

The song began with typical acoustic guitar rhythmic strumming, after which Harrison added his signature slide guitar part. The chant-like lyrics entered eventually alternating between Christian phrases and Hindu chants. After the lyrics repeated, the drums snuck in, along with a perfect tambourine groove. Together they created a light feel. Appropriately, all of these ingredients are made to sound much bigger by Spector's larger than life production. It was extraordinary that a song with such an overt religious message became as massively popular as Harrison's "My Sweet Lord," which harkened back to the days when gospel music ruled the airwaves.

In The Beatles, **John Lennon's** (1940-1980) lyrics commented on the world that he saw around him, but there was always the McCartney yin to Lennon's yang. What began as a perfect songwriting team evolved into Lennon's experimental music that was deeply emotional, reflective, often rebellious, stark, and frequently had a strong stream of consciousness feel to it. Upon the break-up of The Beatles, and Lennon's post Beatles recording career, nothing changed. He could be simultaneously raw and abrasive, and pretty and lyrical. The start of John Lennon's solo career started very quickly. In fact, it began while he was still "officially" in The Beatles. In 1969, Lennon released a single of the song "Give Peace a Chance." Next, in December of 1969, Lennon played a one off concert with his Plastic Ono Band (featuring Eric Clapton, Klaus Voorman, and Alan White) in Canada. Then, in February of 1970, after it was written and recorded in only 10 days, Lennon released the Phil Spector produced single "Instant Karma (We All Shine On)." This occurred simultaneously with The Beatles Let It Be release. After two singles, and one concert, Lennon's solo career was off and running. However, the second phase of Lennon's solo career didn't go as well. After the two earlier hit singles, Lennon and Ono released Unfinished Music Vol 1., Unfinished Music Vol 2., and The Wedding Album. These three recordings were all experimental and avant-garde in nature. They featured John and Yoko vocalizing over tape loops, electronic sounds, and with avant-garde jazz musicians. These recordings were panned and reviled by critics and listeners alike.

Lennon made a quick and abrupt turnaround with his 1970 release entitled John Lennon-Plastic Ono Band. Plastic Ono Band was universally accepted by critics and fans alike. With songs like "God," "Mother," "Working Class Hero" and (bonus track) "Power To The People," The Plastic Ono Band was one of Lennon's most personal recordings ever. The recording Imagine followed and included the title track which became the song that Lennon is most associated. Imagine was the most overtly commercial record that Lennon ever recorded. The schizophrenic Some Time In New York City featured collaborations with Frank Zappa, George Harrison, (the New York band) Elephant's Memory, Eric Clapton, and Keith Moon. This was a blatantly political record that had touches of musical experimentation and instrumental prowess. At the time of the recording, John Lennon was beginning to have issues with the U.S. government and with his wife Yoko Ono. Yoko began working on her record Feeling The Space, which included contributions from Lennon. Lennon liked Ono's studio band so much that he hired the same musicians for his Mind Games

> "[Lennon] said 'imagine,' that's all, just imagine it."
>
> – Ringo Starr

recording sessions. Like Harrison had done with Living In The Material World, Lennon chose to record Mind Games without Phil Spector. This record was the first in a while to offer some sounds from the past, including the rootsy rock 'n' roll of "Tight A$" and "Meat City." "Mind Games" was actually conceived while Lennon was still in The Beatles, and sounded like a strong Beatles track. The sessions also included a song called "Rock and Roll People" which Lennon gave to guitarist Johnny Winter to record. Mind Games was released to a mixed reaction, but was remembered fondly by fans.

Walls and Bridges was released in 1974, and used many of the same musicians from Mind Games. It included some sound experimentation and strong songwriting. Jim Keltner covered his drums with tea-towels on one track to simulate Ringo's drum sound. "Dream" was inspired by the George Harrison song "Living In The Material World." Lennon's next recording was simply entitled Rock and Roll. This was Lennon's tribute to the early rock 'n' roll of Gene Vincent, Chuck Berry, Fats Domino, and Sam Cooke. The record itself was an interesting study into the influence that early rock 'n' roll had on John Lennon.

The Impact of the Life of John Lennon

Certain tragic moments in American history were so profound that most people can recall where they were at the time and what they were doing. The John F. Kennedy assassination and the 911 attacks were two of the worst tragedies in American history. The murder of John Lennon was another low point in American history and was felt around the world. On December 8th, 1980, John Lennon was gunned down by a deranged man in front of his apartment building in New York City. Immediately, Lennon's death put an end to the wishes of anybody who held out hope for a Beatles reunion. The band had broken up a decade earlier, but for many, the death of Lennon marked much more than the start of the 1980's. Lennon was gone at age forty, and everyone who grew up as a Beatles fan (that would be almost everyone) was heartbroken. This marked the end of an innocent and happy time period when The Beatles brought a whole new musical style and culture to America. New music styles and the MTV era would soon come to dominate, but rock music was in a state of shock.

John Lennon assaulted rock music from multiple perspectives. Lennon held strong political and societal views reflected in the music he wrote and the conviction of his lifestyle. Lennon confronted the idea of war and believed that popular music should be utilized to do more to evoke political change. He approached songwriting with intelligence, great wit, and a belief in the good of humanity. There will never be a way to come to grips with the insanity and senselessness of his murder. But there are many ways to embrace the genius and range of John Lennon's music from early to late Beatles to his solo career. Paul McCartney remembered, "One of my great memories of John is from when we were having some argument. I was disagreeing and we were calling each others names. We let it settle for a second and then he lowered his glasses and he said: 'Its only me.' And then he put his glasses back on again. To me, that was John." John Lennon changed the face of rock 'n roll forever.

The Jack Douglas produced 1980 sessions created the music for the last two John Lennon records Double Fantasy and Milk and Honey. Both of these efforts were co-produced and included performances by Yoko Ono. These records included music written and performed by both Lennon and Ono. Double Fantasy marked the end of Lennon's long break from releasing music, and the music was very high quality. Unfortunately, the circumstances surrounding the release of records and Lennon's murder will always make the music bitter sweet. Ironically, Lennon's last public concert was a concert that was filmed for TV, and recorded (unfortunately for a posthumus release) called *Live In New York City*. Sadly it bookended a career that was cut short by the violence that Lennon rallied against. With such a strange and varied solo career, the collection titled Working Class Hero, The Definitive Lennon is an essential collection of his most important and groundbreaking work as a solo artist. John Lennon is inducted into the Rock and Roll Hall of Fame twice, as a member of The Beatles, and in 1994 as a solo artist.

"Imagine"
by John Lennon and Yoko Ono

In his book *Lennon Remembers*, Jan Wenner told how Yoko Ono had inspired John Lennon with a poem that she had written in 1964 called "Cloud Piece" (the poem was later reprinted on the sleeve to the record). Wenner continued to explain how civil rights activist Dick Gregory had also given Lennon an inspirational Christian prayer book. With these inspirations in mind, John Lennon sat at his piano in 1971 with Yoko close by, and in one sitting wrote a new song. Later in 1971, John Lennon, Yoko Ono, and producer Phil Spector walked into a studio. They were there to record a song for Lennon's upcoming record. They probably had no idea what was going to happen that day. The song they began to work on was a ballad and didn't have any grand harmonic twists, or surprises. Its form was nothing new. The other musicians that would play on the song were bassist Klaus Voorman, and drummer Alan White. There were no solos; there were no big musical crescendo's that demand your attention. Lennon, Voorman, and White did what musicians do, they set a groove, and they established a tone. Spector's signature wall of sound would only appear in a slight form and there was nothing initially big about this song. They recorded three takes, and the second take was chosen for release. Strings would be added later. Lennon had simplified all of his musical ideals and the musicians had stripped out all of the extra notes. What the music itself accomplished with its plaintive chords, haunting melody, and patient groove was simply brilliant.

The tongue in cheek lyrical sarcasm that Lennon employed with The Beatles was gone. In 1969, Lennon had demanded that we "Give Peace a Chance." In 1970 he had been both crafty with his emotional message of "Instant Karma," and brazen with "Working Class Hero." But this song would be different. Lennon was now asking a minor favor. He was asking us to… imagine. With his 22 lines of poetic magic, John Lennon created a beautiful, succinct, solemn, and prayer-like call for unity, brotherhood, and peace. President Jimmy Carter said, "In many countries around the world- you hear John Lennon's song "Imagine" used almost equally with national anthems." #8 George Martin called "Imagine" simply his favorite song of all. Everyone from Joan Baez to Madonna has covered "Imagine," and it has become one of the most covered songs of all time. John Lennon said, "The concept of positive prayer … If you can *imagine* a world at peace, with no denominations of religion—not without religion but without this my God-is-bigger-than-your-God thing—then it can be true…" #9 This title track from John Lennon's 1971 record Imagine became his signature song.

Rock Hard Fact

Paul McCartney was on an airplane in New York City and witnessed one of the planes crash into the Twin Towers on 9/11 … later he gave a charity concert for the victims and was made an honorary detective by the NYPD.

Despite being half of one of the greatest songwriting teams ever, **Paul McCartney** (1942-) had doubts about his musical future after leaving The Beatles. McCartney had two advantages; he was a world class multi-instrumentalist, and he had a supportive wife named Linda. After years of collaboration within a group of other fantastic musicians, McCartney could do everything by himself. In The Beatles, McCartney had played guitar, drums, and piano, aside from his traditional role of bassist and singer. On his chart-topping debut titled McCartney, aside from minor contributions from his wife Linda, Paul played and wrote everything! For his second solo recording Ram, McCartney brought in only drummer Denny Seiwell. Soon after, ex-Moody Blues guitarist Denny Laine joined McCartney and Seiwell to form the band **Wings**. Although their first two recordings, Wild Life and Red Rose Speedway, were viewed as being a little safe, McCartney did what his Beatles bandmates hadn't done. He immediately took his new band on the road. After the band found its traction with the James Bond theme song "Live and Let Die," and the 1973 record Band On The Run, that featured the song "Jet," more quality recordings followed. The band went through many personnel changes. McCartney then released Venus and Mars with the single "Listen to What the Man Said" and "Wings at the Speed of Sound." "Silly Love Songs" was a hit from the Wings at the Speed of Sound album. All of this led to the live record, Wings Over America, that spawned the single "Maybe I'm Amazed." It completed a run of five consecutive Wings records reaching number one on the US charts.

More personnel changes ensued and McCartney released 1978's London Town and 1979's Back To The Egg. McCartney assembled a huge all-star collection of musicians and recorded the song "Rockestra Theme," that included; John Paul Jones and John Bonham of Led Zeppelin, David Gilmour of Pink Floyd, and Pete Townshend of The Who, and many others. Wings did their final tour in 1979 and McCartney recorded his next solo record McCartney II, which signaled the end of the ten year run of the band Wings.

The 1980's would see McCartney collaborate with many top artists including Stevie Wonder on "Ebony and Ivory," Michael Jackson on "The Girl Is Mine" and "Say, Say, Say." Other collaborations included work with Elvis Costello on the record Flowers In The Dirt, and Eric Stewart (of 10cc) on the outstanding Press To Play. The latter included appearances from Pete Townshend, Phil Collins, and David Bowie collaborator Tony Visconti. Interestingly, like John Lennon's Rock and Roll release, McCartney then released a record of rootsy rock 'n' roll classics including; Eddie Cochran's "Twenty Flight Rock," Fats Domino "Ain't That a Shame," and the song that Elvis made famous "That's All Right Mama." The recording, called CHOBA B CCCP (translated: Back In The USSR), was originally only released in the USSR, but eventually made it to the rest of the world. The live recording Tripping The Live Fantastic was a fitting culmination of this period featuring a band that featured bassist Hamish Stuart from the Average White Band and keyboardist Paul "Wix" Wickens.

The 1990's would start with Paul McCartney venturing into classical music, and the beginning of a collaboration with Youth (from the band Killing Joke) that created a series of electronica records under the band name The Fireman. The duo began when Paul asked Youth to help mix and create some samples from the McCartney recording Off The Ground. The partnership progressed, and drew from the sound experimentation that began on the late Beatles records and integrated the influence of modern ambient and techno music. Paul McCartney, George Harrison, and Ringo Starr decided to devote the next four years to the creation of the massive Beatles Anthology project. This work was significant in setting the record straight about certain facets of The Beatles. The 1990's continued with The Beatles Anthology, inspiring McCartney's Flaming Pie recording. This new record found McCartney collaborating with ELO founder and Traveling Wilbury Jeff Lynne for the first time. George Martin and Ringo Starr were also there. Flaming Pie was the best-received McCartney solo record since Tug Of War and rekindled McCartney's interest in rock 'n' roll. He followed with a 1999 return to roots recording of rock 'n' roll classics featuring Ian Paice of Deep Purple and David Gilmour of Pink Floyd. This album, titled Run Devil Run once again included songs by Fats Domino, Gene Vincent, Elvis Presley, Carl Perkins, and Chuck Berry. The inspiration for this album came from his wife Linda who had died the year before.

The 2000's began by McCartney creating a new working band that included guitarists Rusty Anderson, Brain Ray, keyboardist Paul "Wix" Wickens, and drummer Abe Laboriel Jr. This top shelf band impeccably performed Beatles songs that had never been performed live, and created an outstanding studio record called Driving Rain. Continuing in the tradition of his first solo recording, McCartney followed with 2005's Chaos and Creation in the Backyard in which he played nearly all the instruments, and 2013's New. With New, McCartney continued his youth movement by employing four young producers. Mark Ronson, Ethan Johns, Paul Epworth, and Giles Martin, all helped accomplish the goal of creating a forward-looking modern pop masterpiece.

Finally, McCartney and his new band released a few notable live recordings. 2002's Back in the US is quite possibly the best live McCartney recording since Wings Over America. This was followed by 2009's Good Evening New York City. Paul was eager to point out that he has played with Anderson, Ray, Wickens, and Laboriel longer than he did with The Beatles or Wings. What made this band special was the fact that they were all supremely talented multi-instrumentalists who also sang. Their recreations of Beatle songs was so authentic that you felt jettisoned back in time to a 1960's Beatles performance. They were also creating vital new music with a composer whose lifeblood was inventing new sounds, ignoring barriers and labels, and utilizing new artistic approaches and structures. The present and the future has seen McCartney collaborate with the three surviving member of Nirvana; Dave Grohl, Krist Novoselic, and Pat Smear plus Kanye West, Rihanna, Paul Simon, and Alice Cooper. Longevity, creativity, and a fine tuned musical instinct has made Paul McCartney one of the most important musicians in modern rock and roll history. Paul McCartney has also been inducted into the Rock and Roll Hall of Fame twice, once as a member of The Beatles, and as a solo artist in 1999.

"Maybe I'm Amazed"
by Paul McCartney

"Maybe I'm Amazed" told the story of how McCartney's then wife, Linda who has since died, helped him through the tough times of leaving The Beatles, and moving on with his life and career. This version showed McCartney's prowess at playing guitar, drums, and piano, making him one of the greatest multi-instrumentalists ever. The piano and organ introduction (and the entire performance) was soulful, and even gospel infused. McCartney's vocals appeared with pleading and emotional intensity. The drums entered with sparse time keeping at first, but then evolved into a flowing tom groove that

> "I love to hear a choir. I love the humanity to see the faces of real people devoting themselves to a piece of music. I like the teamwork. It makes me feel optimistic about the human race when I see them cooperating like that."
>
> - Paul McCartney

included some uniquely spacious fills. Then, a melodic guitar solo fit perfectly into the texture of the song. Gospel piano breaks, alternated with drum breaks. There was an upbeat rhythm guitar part at the end that slightly implied a reggae feel and the propelling drum groove pushed to the end.

Lyrically, McCartney asked his wife for help, thanked her for her help, and "was amazed" at their strong relationship. The entire song found McCartney wondering aloud about his life situation at the time, and finding the strength to move forward in his career through his relationship and love for his wife. It was a touching love song. The original version captured an instrumental and vocal rawness. McCartney's band, Wings, performed the song on the Wings Over America record.

Ringo Starr's (1940-) Beatles career prepared him for a long and successful solo career. While in The Beatles, Ringo provided unique grooves that supported great songs and he often provided lead vocals on one song on each Beatle record. He brought his strong and personable personality to the forefront. Although there was only one song, "What Goes On" from Rubber Soul, that was credited to McCartney, Lennon, and Starr, Ringo learned how to write and co-write a song. Ringo also learned what the public wanted to hear.

While John Lennon and George Harrison released experimental recordings as their first forays into their solo careers, Ringo Starr choose to interpret classic and well-loved music. In 1970, Ringo enlisted some of music's best arrangers to record an entire record of jazz and popular standards entitled Sentimental Journey. Quincy Jones, who worked on Sentimental Journey, said of Ringo, "I can tell you first hand that his (Ringo's) keen instinct in choosing material, his ability to surround himself with individuals such as George Martin and an entourage of impeccable producers, musicians and writers, plus his terrific sense of humor in and out of the recording studio, has earned Ringo Starr iconic status and much love." 1970 also found Ringo recording the country flavored Beaucoups Of Blues which was recorded in Nashville.

In 1971, Ringo composed the tune "It Don't Come Easy" featuring the lyric, "Got to pay your dues if you want to sing the blues." This single was produced by George Harrison and reached number four on the U.S. pop charts. From his 1973 recording titled Ringo, Starr and Harrison composed the hit "Photograph" that reached number one on the U.S. pop charts. In 1972, Starr wrote and released the single "Back Off Boogaloo" which reached number one on the U.K. pop charts. Ringo was prolific throughout the 1970's. His solo career continued with 1973's Ringo, 1974's Goodnight Vienna, 1976's Ringo's Rotogravure, 1977's Ringo the 4th, and 1978's Bad Boy. These recordings featured collaborations with George Harrison, John Lennon, Steve Cropper, Harry Nilsson, Robbie Robertson, Elton John, and Peter Frampton. Ringo continued playing drums alongside session great Jim Keltner creating a unique eight-limbed percussive approach.

The 1980's brought Ringo's Stop and Smell The Roses, and the troubled Old Wave. The rest of the 1980's found him doing TV work and guesting at high profile concerts. 1989 saw Ringo embark on his long-standing tradition of touring All-Starr Bands. These band have continued to be very popular and have featured musicians such as; Joe Walsh, Rick Danko, Burton Cummings, Mark Farner, Jack Bruce, Howard Jones, Steve Lukather, and Rick Derringer. These groups and tours are annual musical events and have spawned ten recordings. In 1993, Ringo began working with producers Jeff Lynne (Traveling Wilbury's and ELO) and Don Was. Ringo spent a great deal of the 1990's working with fellow Beatles Paul McCartney and George Harrison on The Beatles Anthology set, touring with the All-Starr Band, and occasionally covering music written by his heroes, Carl Perkins and Buddy Holly. In 2015 Ringo Starr was inducted into the Rock and Roll Hall of Fame as a solo artist.

"Photograph"
by Richard Starkey and George Harrison

There have been only a few drummers throughout rock 'n' roll history who can boast of writing and singing a number one hit. Phil Collins, Don Henley, and Dave Grohl come to mind. Starr wrote "Photograph" while in Spain where George Harrison was teaching him how to play guitar chords. He released it in 1973 as part of the record titled Ringo. "Photograph" made it to number one the U.S. charts and number eight on the UK charts in October of that same year. Ringo said of the song, "I love the sentiment of 'Photograph.' When we did the *Concert For George*, I told the audience that 'Photograph' now has a different meaning, just because of the fact that George has left. But 'Photograph' is a song that fits into the universe." #10

The song started with a symphony of acoustic guitar strumming and drumset punctuations. Nicky Hopkins' piano part came in to support the catchy chorus before the first verse. A chorus of voices reinforced the sentiment of the song and supported Ringo's unmistakable lead vocals. Arranger Jack Nietzsche continued his wall of sound approach with great success. Bobby Keys provided a classic rock 'n' roll saxophone solo while Ringo's drum groove was augmented with Jim Keltner's big fills.

Discussion Question

Was it a necessary and natural evolution for each of the four Beatles to become solo artists or should they have resolved their musical and personal differences and remained as The Beatles? Discuss Harrison, Lennon, McCartney, and Starr as individual musicians and their artistic visions.

Chapter Five: The Beatles and The Solo Beatles

"The Beatles had gone through so much and for such a long time. They'd been incarcerated with each other for nearly a decade, and I was surprised that they had lasted as long as they did. I wasn't at all surprised that they'd split up because they all wanted to lead their own lives-and I did, too."

– George Martin

Chapter Six:
The British Invasion Continues and the American Answer

Besides the invasion of America by The Beatles, The Rolling Stones, and Led Zeppelin, there were a number of other influential British bands. The Kinks, Herman's Hermits, The Hollies, and The Who all made their mark on British and American audiences. British rock had become a fascination for Americans when the rockabilly era was over, now that Elvis was a movie star. The American answer to all of this came from an eclectic set of artists, none bigger than Jimi Hendrix and The Grateful Dead. It took the blues to go to England for it to come back and spark interest from the American public. Other artists like the Paul Butterfield Blues Band, Canned Heat, and Janis Joplin gained a new and wide audience. These artists and the genre of psychedelic rock will be covered in this chapter.

The Beatles had not only knocked on the American music door, they kicked it wide open for many groups from Liverpool and Manchester, England. Like The Beatles, most groups used the instrumentation of lead electric guitar, rhythm electric guitar, electric bass guitar, and drums. Buddy Holly, an influence big as rockabilly on many groups, was one of the first to use electric lead guitar. Fashion was also important. It became aligned with musical trends, seen in the British youth culture of the mods and the rockers. Some British kids liked the clean-cut image of the Dave Clark Five. These British youth were known as the mods (for modernists) and they wore trendy suits, had short hair, and rode motor scooters. The mods followed bands like The Who, The Kinks, and The Small Faces. The rockers were more blue-collar kids that loved the music of the rockabilly artists. Both groups developed an intense rivalry that Pete Townshend of The Who would later utilize for inspiration to compose his rock opera Quadrophenia.

Herman's Hermits (first called The Heartbeats) was formed in 1963 in Manchester, England. Former child actor Peter Noone joined the band in 1963 and they changed their name to Herman Hermits. They achieved strong commercial appeal with over fifteen top singles between 1964 to 1970. Their first hit was the Carole King and Gerry Goffin tune "I'm Into Something Good," released in 1964 on MGM Records. In 1965, they released "I'm Henry the VIII, I Am" (a tune intended to be funny) about a women who only married men named Henry. Herman's Hermits had a non-threatening innocent image matched by their bubble-gum simple pop melodies. Most of their American hits were aimed at a young audience and they were very popular.

The Hollies were formed in 1962 by guitarist/singer/composer Graham Nash and singer/songwriter Allan Clarke. In the 1960's, only The Beatles had more hits in Britain than The Hollies, although The Hollies didn't reach the top ten on the American pop charts until their 1966 song "Bus Stop." The Hollies derived their name from their love of Buddy Holly. They were one of the last British Invasion era bands to achieve success in America. The Hollies developed musical arrangements and innovative three-part harmonies to go along with psychedelic guitar timbres, thus giving them a unique sound. In 1968, some members of The Hollies wanted to record an album of Bob Dylan covers. This goal was not shared by Graham Nash, who decided to leave the band, especially when they refused to record his song "Marrakesh Express." The Hollies went on to release the album Words and

> "What disturbs me about The Who is the way they smashed through every door of rock and roll, leaving rubble and not much else for the rest of us to lay claim to."
>
> – Eddie Vedder

> "Ray Davies is almost indisputably rock's most literate, witty and insightful songwriter."
>
> - a Rock and Roll Hall of Fame staff writer

Rock Hard Fact

On their 1975 Another Night album, The Hollies covered the Bruce Springsteen tune "Fourth of July Asbury Park (Sandy)" before Bruce became a star.

Music of Bob Dylan in 1969. Even after he left the band, Nash was still proud of The Hollies' achievements. Another Hollies tune "Long Cool Women," was very popular and had a very Beatlesque quality. Over fifty years later, The Hollies are still together as a band and have produced an incredibly prolific output of over sixty-two albums and more than fifteen hundred songs.

"Bus Stop"
by Graham Gouldman

"Bus Stop" was written by British songwriter Graham Gouldman who also wrote tunes for The Yardbirds and Herman's Hermits. The song was The Hollies first hit in America, reaching number five on the charts. Gouldman actually wrote "Bus Stop" while riding on a bus traveling through Manchester, England. The song was about a couple that met at a bus stop on a rainy day. They shared an umbrella and that sparked their romance. The opening lyrics were the inventive and flowing line "Bus stop, wet day, she's there, I say please share my umbrella."

On "Bus Stop," The Hollies achieved a sound that would come to represent their trademark timbres of acoustic guitar mixed with psychedelic electric guitar solos. This helped to establish The Hollies as a big part of the Mersey beat sound, similar in some respects to early Beatles. "Bus Stop" has been covered many times by artists such as Herman's Hermits, Gene Pitney, and The Guess Who. Herman's Hermits would get the first crack at recording many of Gouldman's songs because their manager was married to Gouldman's sister.

The Kinks (1964-1996) started out as a band covering American Delta blues artists and performing Little Richards tunes. The band consisted of composer/singer Ray Davies, his brother guitarist Dave Davies, bassist Pete Quaife, and Mick Avory on drums. The Kinks were often considered one of the most under-rated bands in rock history. Never selling as many records as their music deserved, they were well respected by many accomplished musicians. From their start, Ray Davies was intent on developing a unique band sound, especially one that sounded British.

Ray Davies was a gifted lyricist whose topics ranged from personal relationships to attacks on people with self-interests and selfish lifestyles. He wrote about taboo subjects of the time such as a transgender in the tune "Lola." Davies felt that people developed lifestyles that lacked creative energy and were content to lead boring lives. The lyrics for The Kinks tune, "A Well Respected Man," highlight this viewpoint. The Kinks cultivated a fan base that understood their intention to reflect British lifestyles and culture. They released "You Really Got Me" which went to number one on the British charts and number ten on the American charts in October of 1964.

The Kinks were not comfortable with the idea of constant touring, especially in America where they needed to promote their albums. They were also victims of an American Federation of Musicians Ban that prevented them from touring America at the height of the British Invasion period. Never given a good reason for the ban, it was a four-year ban imposed on them supposedly due to their rowdy onstage performances. Ray Davies said " It cost us the top spot…by then people like Jimi Hendrix and The Who were coming back from the U.S. as megastars." #1 Another issue for The Kinks was the constant fighting between Ray and Dave Davies. This resulted in many band breakups, although they were able to regroup often over the years. They were fortunate to have session keyboardist Nicky Hopkins play on many of their studio recordings in the 1960's.

The Kinks pioneering guitarist Dave Davies

Dave Davies was one of the great innovators of the electric guitar. He grew up first playing skiffle music, similar a lot of other young British musicians. At the age of fifteen, Dave tried to connect a small amplifier into a bigger one resulting in a tremendous electrical shock that nearly killed him. He eventually experimented with slashing the speaker cone of his Elpico amp with a razor blade, thus giving his guitar a distorted and crackly tone. This later became popular as the effect called fuzztone.

The power chords Davies played on "You Really Got Me" were not the first ever played, but what was special was his display of raw power. This, aided by his use of distortion, would influence many who saw him as the first heavy metal guitar player. His influence reached many of his contemporaries including Pete Townshend and Robert Fripp. Dave Davies has helped to make famous the Gibson Flying V guitar that he started using in 1965. The Flying V became standard gear for Jimi Hendrix, Albert King, many other rock guitarists.

Dave Davies only occasionally wrote songs or sang lead vocals. Ray did most of the songwriting. But Dave was the sound of The Kinks. After the band officially broke up, Dave went on to have a fairly successful solo career. In 2014, Dave released a new album titled Rippin' It Up to celebrate the 50th anniversary of The Kinks. He appeared onstage with Ray to promote the record, marking the first time they appeared together in twenty years.

The Kinks had a hit with their satirical "Sunny Afternoon," which topped the British charts in the summer of 1966 and knocked The Beatles "Paperback Writer" out of the top spot. Another Kinks hit "Celluloid Heroes," referenced dead and fading Hollywood movie stars. Ray Davies lyrically commented on how great it would be if life were like a movie "because celluloid heroes never feel any pain… and celluloid heroes never really die." The band did have a resurgence and some commercial success between the years 1977 and 1986. The Kinks broke up in 1996 and an often-discussed reunion has never happened.

Ray Davies played a significant role in the development of early rock music. His songwriting skill and poignant social commentary brought a sophistication and wit to lyric writing that has stood the test of time. The Kinks placed five of their songs on the American Billboard charts and they are revered by many of their peers. The Kinks were inducted into the Rock and Roll Hall of Fame in 1990.

"You Really Got Me"
by Ray Davies

"You Really Got Me," written in 1964, began with one of the great guitar riffs in rock music. It continued throughout the tune. Each section followed an AABC phrasing format. In each section, the B phrase moved up a whole-step and the C phrase moved up a fourth from that point. This was unique for a rock song at the time. Ray Davies played around with different accents as he phrased the lyrics while Dave Davies produced an innovative guitar fuzztone sound by cutting the speaker cone of the amplifier.

Ray Davies had a focused approach to his songwriting process. Davies said, "I think the thought process is interesting. We didn't have tape recorders when I started writing songs. You couldn't tape ideas. I had to notate a lot of stuff. I've still got 'You Really Got Me' notated somewhere. Generally speaking, the good ideas stay in the head. I've got a couple of tunes going round my head and they won't leave me alone until they're finished. It's something I've built into my artillery. I use military words for songwriting: my artillery, my weaponry." #2 Ray Davies had claimed to be influenced by The Kingman's hit "Louie Louie" when he wrote the song. "You Really Got Me" influenced countless hard rock and heavy metal songwriters making it one of rock's most significant tunes.

The Who (1964-present) represent one of the defining British Invasion bands. The Who could have easily been placed in the punk rock genre as one of the first true punk bands. They exhibited punk characteristics of violence, aggressive behavior (on and off stage), attention to fashion trends, and a healthy disrespect for authority. Their early fans could be thought of as the first punk fans but without the mosh pits. Their fan base was made up of largely testosterone driven males ready to raise hell at every Who show. The Who would be the most unsightly group of individuals to emerge from the mod movement in London. Guitarist Pete Townshend was tall, awkward, and thin, and bassist John Entwistle was a huge stoic bear of a man. Keith Moon was a wild anarchist behind the drums and Roger Daltrey portrayed the tough guy definition of a thug. There wasn't a sex symbol in the band. Besides punk, they would also exert a big influence on hard rock and heavy metal bands.

Pete Townshend (1945-) was born in West London into a musical family where his father, Horace Townshend, was a composer and entertainer. Pete learned to play the harmonica, guitar, piano, and later the banjo. He learned the basics of dixieland jazz and the blues. Townshend formed a band, The Confederates, in the spring of 1958 with some school friends that included a trumpet player, John Entwistle (1946-2002). Soon, they worked as a duo. Townshend focused on electric guitar, adding an amplifier, while Entwistle made his own bass guitar after hearing the guitar sound of Duane Eddy. Entwistle had met singer and guitar player Roger Daltrey, who led a band called The Detours. Daltrey approached Townshend and asked if he was interested in joining The Detours, who were popular and had many gigs. The Detours played a whole gambit of styles from country to popular tunes, to Cliff Richard songs, and even "Hava Nagila." Townshend informed him that he was interested.

Both Townshend and Entwistle joined The Detours with Daltrey playing lead guitar. Soon, Daltrey fired the lead singer, Colin Dawson, and took over lead singing responsibilities. Along with their drummer Doug Sanden, The Detours played regularly at clubs all around London. Meanwhile, a hard-hitting drummer named Keith Moon was playing in the surf rock band, The Beachcombers; one of the premier working bands in Northwest London. The Detours and The Beachcombers shared some common musical ground since they both played rock 'n' roll classics and ballads. Both groups were keenly aware of the impact of important rock styles and the rising fame of The Beatles and other British Invasion bands. The Detours, however, began to move away from covering top hits, concentrated on rhythm and blues, and added more Delta influenced blues. They also rejected wearing suits and ties and soon adapted leather jackets and jeans.

Pete Townshend was bringing many musical influences to his emerging style (see Townshend profile). Like his London guitar contemporaries Keith Richards, Jeff Beck, Jimmy Page, and Eric Clapton; Townshend primarily focused on blues legends such as Jimmy Reed, John Lee Hooker, and Howlin' Wolf. By 1963, Townshend recorded his first song "It Was You," at a friend's home studio. This song was covered by a Mersey beat band, The Naturals. The fact that Townshend's song was recorded and published gave him the confidence he needed to further explore songwriting. It also allowed him to stand up to the very bossy leader of The Detours, Roger Daltrey. By the end of 1963, The Detours were set to open for The Rolling Stones. Townshend explained where he got one of his signature stage moves and said, "as Keith Richards waited for the curtain to open he limbered up by swinging his arm like a windmill. A few weeks later we supported them again at Glenlyn Ballroom, and when I noticed that Keith didn't use the windmill trick again I decided to adopt it." #3 After appearing on TV, The Detours changed their name to The Who because Entwistle had heard that another band was called The Detours. They knew their band deserved its own name.

The Who auditioned for Fontana Records in March 1964. Fontana liked their potential, except for drummer Doug Sandom. Keith Moon, when not working with The Beachcombers, would regularly attend The Detour's gigs. One such night Keith approached the band looking to sit in. Sandom had already left the band and a session drummer playing with The Who that night allowed Keith to play a few tunes. A bystander in the crowd remembered, "The whole kit was shaking as if it had been caught in a hurricane, this kid…was hitting the drums with so much venom it was as if he was holding them responsible for everything wrong in the world. By the time The Who thanked Keith, and asked the drummer to come back up to complete the set, the bass drum pedal was broken and at least one of the skins was torn. The hi-hat looked worse for wear as well…What was worse, the broken pedal ensured that the rest of the set sounded terrible, as if the session drummer wasn't half as good as the kid…Keith had not even joined The Who and already the band was paying for his damages (the session drummer charged them for the broken gear)." #4 Moon was excited about The Who, but was conflicted about leaving The Beachcombers. He loved his current band and he loved surf rock. After an inevitable conflict of multiple band bookings, Keith finally decided to leave The Beachcombers. The Who were now *complete*.

The Who had a manager, Helmut Gorden, who brought in publicist Pete Meaden to give the band an image makeover. Meaden was focused on linking The Who to the mod movement and its image of fashion, motor scooters, and lots of diet pills. Meaden dressed them in tailored white leather jackets, black pants, and French cut hairs. He booked them at the "in" mod clubs and began to build a strong following. Meaden then changed their name to The High Numbers (a number was a mod sub-group member who wore popular t-shirts with a numerical figure printed on the front). Meaden even wrote a few songs that he wanted the band to record. Shortly after, The High Numbers were approached by two young filmmakers looking to cast a band for a film project. Kit Lambert and Chris Stamp saw the band at the Railway Hotel, where they had taken up a residency and where Townshend had smashed a hole through the low ceiling of the club with his guitar. They made the film and cast the High Numbers. Then conflict ensued when Lambert and

Rock Hard Fact

Roger Daltrey made his first guitar, an imitation of a cherry red Stratocaster, by carving it out of a block of wood.

Rock Hard Fact

For all of the stories about the reckless and crazy escapades (many true) of Keith Moon, he never once drove a car into a swimming pool!

> "If we believed in anything, it was the power of music bringing people together. If we're touring for anything, that's a good enough reason for me."
>
> – Roger Daltrey

Rock Hard Fact

The Who's rock opera *Tommy* opened on Broadway at St. James Theatre on April, 22nd, 1993. It ran for a total of 899 performances.

Stamp offered to manage the band. Meaden eventually moved aside and Lambert and Stamp quickly returned the band name to The Who. They soon passed a BBC audition but then failed an audition for the record label EMI because they played too many R&B covers. The major labels were in search of bands that wrote their own tunes. Lambert and Stamp knew that Townshend could write and encouraged him to come up with some new material for the band. Townshend isolated himself and looked for inspiration in the music of Bob Dylan, Charlie Mingus, and John Lee Hooker. He also admired the Booker T. and the MG's tune, "Green Onions." Townshend recalled, "I tried to divine what it was I was actually feeling as a result of this musical immersion. One notion kept coming into my head: I can't explain. I can't explain. This would be the title of my second song, and I was already doing something I would often do in the future: writing songs about music." #5

"I Can't Explain"
by Pete Townshend

"I Can't Explain" was the first song Pete Townshend ever wrote for The Who (his second ever) and it was a major turning point for the band. After learning that the producer for The Kinks, Shel Talmy (who had a connection with Decca Records) agreed to hear the band, Pete scrambled to listen to The Kinks "You Really Got Me." That inspired him to write the music for "I Can't Explain" and compose the lyrics. Townshend has never denied that he borrowed the guitar riff from the tune "Louis, Louie" by the Kingsmen (later covered by The Kinks). Townshend essentially combined the influence of 'You Really Got Me" and "Louie, Louie" to write "I Can't Explain." Shel Talmy liked Townshend's new song and booked a session to make a recording. Talmy wasn't sure if Pete could solo, so he hired Jimmy Page, his favorite session guitarist. He also hired three male session singers called The Ivy League, because Talmy did not trust that The Who could sing the background vocals in the Beach Boys style he desired.

Roger Daltrey didn't like the tune and thought it was "soft." He wanted the material to be powerful and tough like the way The Who performed on stage. When The Who played "I Can't Explain" on *The Top of The Pops* radio show, it quickly went to number eight on the British charts. Townshend later said that the song was about some eighteen-year old boy who couldn't tell his girlfriend that he loved her because he had taken too many Dexedrine pills.

By now The Who was developing a reputation for their crazy stage shows. Since the days of smashing his guitar through the roof at the Railway Hotel, Townshend's guitar bashing had become a crowd favorite. With the crowd expecting no less, Keith Moon began to join in and trashing his drumset became standard performance art every night. Daltrey added to the fun by swinging his mic like a rodeo lasso overhead, running and assaulting the crowd and knocking over amplifiers. Entwistle preferred to just play great basslines and watch the mayhem. The Who were developing the most powerful and violent stage show in all of rock music.

During the summer of 1965, The Who toured Holland and Scandinavia (causing a serious street riot in Denmark). Townshend worked on the material for their first album, My Generation. The tune "My Generation" was inspired by the Mose Allison composition "Young Man Blues." Kit Lambert, as he often did, weighed in on the songwriting process and for "My Generation" suggested that they modulate to create some musical interest. Also, Daltrey had been experimenting with purposely stuttering when singing various songs and added that idea to "My Generation." The song was perfect for an American teen audience that felt alienated and disconnected from their future. The lyric of "hope I die before I get old" spoke directly to teen angst and rebellion.

One example of the constant volatility of life in The Who happened at a live performance in May of 1966 at the Ricky Tick Club in Newbury, England. Bruce Johnston, of the Beach Boys, was visiting Keith Moon and recalled in horror the events of the gig. Johnston said, "during the 'My Generation' finale, when Keith kicked over his drums, a cymbal hit Pete in the leg; in retaliation Pete went to swing his guitar into his speaker stack, and it caught Keith's head instead…all of a sudden they got in the biggest fight I've ever seen. Guitars are swinging, everybody's just in a frenzy." #6 It turned out that John and Keith had been late to the gig only to find Roger and Pete playing The Who's set with the previous act's drummer and bassist. Because of this, tensions were high throughout the night. As a result of the carnage, Moon quit the band. This was typical for the feuding Who. Moon was back in the drum chair by the next week.

A Quick One was the second Who album and was released in 1966. Pete wrote a collection of six songs and put them together into a "mini-opera." This song collection was a humorous story about an unnamed woman and "Ivor the engine driver." Each tune told an unfolding story of adultery and the six tunes helped The Who break through the three-minute song barrier. The album was released in time for Christmas in 1966 and went to number five in Britain. This was a significant period for the band since all members were now involved in the songwriting process. Said Townshend, "My reign set aside as an individual from the rest of the group was over and the group was becoming a group. It was only then that we started to work together musically." #7

The Who Sell Out was released in late 1967, almost too late for the Christmas market. The album didn't chart well, nor did it sell as well as the first two albums. However, the single "I Can See For Miles" had been previously released and did reach the top ten. The Who Sell Out was a concept album of songs that were commercials and jingles. It featured a spoof cover divided into four panels that showed each band member "selling" a product. Townshend did write another "mini-opera" with the song "Rael" on the second side but much of it was cut down to fit the album. The Who Sell Out was well received by music critics, especially the song "I Can See For Miles."

In 1967, The Who and Jimi Hendrix both performed at the Sunday night finale of the Monterey Pop Festival. Both performed an explosive and instrument smashing set. Monterey was a huge moment for The Who that would lead to a number of sold-out tours in America. Also in 1967, The Who appeared on *The Smothers Brothers Comedy Hour*. Moon had the idea to place tons of flash powder (dynamite) in his bass drum and at the end of "My Generation," he created a tremendous explosion sending cymbal shrapnel into his own leg. The explosion caused Townshend to sustain temporary hearing damage and suffer burns to his hair.

The Who followed many successful American tours with four groundbreaking albums from 1969 to 1973. The mini-opera concept was now a familiar direction for Townshend and he was inspired to expand his musical ideas, moving to a full-length rock opera in the form of a double album. 1969's Tommy proved to be an innovative and powerful vehicle for the concert stage (see the rock opera profile). The basic storyline was about a boy who became deaf, dumb, and blind due to traumatic events that occurred in his home life when he witnessed his father commit murder. Tommy's extraordinary talent for playing pinball proved to be a cathartic experience. Through his spiritual journal, he was healed and returned to a normal world of sight and sound. The critical success of Tommy gained the distinction of *fine art*. Tommy was first premiered by The Who in its entirety at Ronnie Scott's jazz club in England. In 1975, the film version of *Tommy*, directed by Ken Russell, brought it to a wider audience. In 1993, a new live version of *Tommy* debuted on the Broadway stage.

"Pinball Wizard"
by Pete Townshend

"Pinball Wizard" was released as a single and went to number four on the British charts. It eventually was a top twenty hit on the American charts. Townshend wrote "Pinball Wizard" in one day and cut a basic demo of the tune at his home studio. This included acoustic guitar and vocals on one track and electric guitar and backing vocals on another track. Townshend recalled, "It was relatively simple to interpolate 'pinball' into a couple of other places in the sequence of Tommy songs, and to redo the necessary vocal lines. I made a huge leap into the absurd when I decided that the hero would play pinball while still deaf, dumb, and blind. It was daft, flawed and muddled, but also insolent, liberated and adventurous. I had no doubt whatsoever that if I had failed to deliver The Who an operatic masterpiece that would change people's lives, with 'Pinball Wizard' I was giving them something almost as good: a hit." #8

"Pinball Wizard" did give The Who a song that could stand on its own outside of the whole Tommy storyline; thus allowing them to receive solid radio airplay. Pete Townshend's acoustic guitar rhythm throughout the tune was aggressive and flowing. It created a rhythmic bottom that allowed Moon's constant drumset flourishes and Townshend's own overdubbed power chords to embellish the feel. "Pinball Wizard" has been covered many times, most notably by Elton John (recorded for the *Tommy* movie), Alice Cooper, and Rod Stewart with The London Symphony Orchestra.

The Rock Opera

A rock opera can be defined as a large-scale work that utilizes character roles set in songs, all relating to a common storyline. The characters and theatrical stage production separates the rock opera from the concept album; although both the rock opera and concept album do allow composers to expand musical material. Sorrow by The Pretty Things, was acknowledged as the first rock opera when it was introduced in 1968. Another significant rock opera was Jesus Christ Superstar, which was introduced in 1970.

Pete Townshend had already dabbled with the mini-opera format when he expanded his compositional and literary vision to write Tommy. Tommy was many things; pure genius, spiritual message, brilliant melodies and orchestration, strong performances by each member of The Who, and a storyline that, at times, was somewhat silly. Townshend remembered what he was striving for when he said, "I knew that pop audiences would begin spiritual searching, as I had. I could write stories and clearly see theatrical dramas in my imagination. Whether I could realize them was still to be tested. But I began thinking about a project that I wouldn't allow anyone to divert." #9

It was at this time that Townshend met and began to follow the metaphysical beliefs of an Indian spiritual master, Meher Baba. Through Baba's teachings, Townshend set out to describe a disciple/master relationship and through reincarnation, a plan to connect the last seven lives of that disciple in an operatic drama that ended in spiritual perfection. Townshend further explained, "Each time the child/disciple Tommy is reborn, he returns with new inner wisdom, but still his life is full of struggle. Since the boy's ignorance of his spiritual growth is a kind of disability, I decided my deaf, dumb, and blind hero could be autistic. This way, when I wanted to demonstrate the glorious moment of his God-realization, I could simply restore to my hero the use of his senses. It was a good plan; the boy's sensory deprivation would work as a symbol of our own everyday spiritual isolation." #10

Townshend's next rock opera, Quadrophenia, although possessing a hard to follow storyline, did contain some strong compositions. This included the songs; "The Real Me," "5:15," and "Love Reign Over Me." Townshend wrote the story as a distorted dream view by Jimmy, the lead character, and this made it challenging to follow when he revealed his unhappy life. Quadrophenia also represented teenage rebellion and criticized the British economic and educational systems. Although Quadrophenia extended Townshend's credibility as a composer, it was a disaster to perform on stage. Ultimately, The Who infused the strongest of Quadrophenia's songs into their live performances.

Pete Townshend next turned his attention to an ambitious project called *Lifehouse*. Townshend looked to create a science fiction work that revealed visionary glimpses of the role that computers and synthesizers could play in futuristic music. The plot of *Lifehouse* was about a society that banned music and a government that controlled all aspects of society. *Lifehouse* was meant to reveal that music was the fundamental basis for human life. In it's storyline, every human had a specific musical melody that made him or her unique. When the complexity of the project failed to attract investors, the songs from *Lifehouse* formed the essence of what many feel was The Who's masterpiece, Who's Next. Not a weak song on the album, Who's Next featured "Baba O'Riley," "Bargain," "The Song is Over," "Behind Blue Eyes," " and the Who's anthem (and often live finale) "Won't Get Fooled Again." The album was recorded by Glyn Johns (Rock and Roll Hall of Fame 2000) who engineered tremendous recorded sounds from the band. He was able to get Keith Moon to play with more discipline when the music needed to settle into more of a groove. Many music critics have praised Who's Next as one of the greatest albums in rock history.

"Won't Get Fooled Again"
by Pete Townshend

"Won't Get Fooled Again" was at first intended to be the last song on Townshend's abandoned rock opera *Lifehouse*. Glyn Johns was able to skillfully re-use the synthesizer parts from Townshend's original demo recording. Keith Moon was able to lock in with the prerecorded synth parts, something he rarely had to do. Although this recording was only meant to serve as a demo, the band decided to use it as a final take. For the song's demo, Townshend played a Lowrey organ into an EMS VC3 filter. This was cutting edge at the time. Just

> "What I'm trying to do is find either existing properties...or angles or stories which will create music drama. It's my obsession."
>
> – Pete Townshend

listen for Townshend's power chords to *hear the power in power chords*. Entwistle's bassline seamlessly connected the guitar parts to Daltrey's vocal lines, a feature of his bass playing that was often overlooked. Released as a single, "Won't Get Fooled Again," went to number nine in Britain and number fifteen on the American charts.

Townshend's songwriting approach was influenced by the ineffective protest movements occurring around the world at the time. In order to express his spiritual connection to music, Townshend worked to transform the essence of human qualities into synthesizer parts for the song. Once introduced in live performance, Moon's brilliant drum fills led into Daltrey's famous scream toward the end of the song. This became a powerful part of every Who show and a legendary moment for rock music. Later, "Won't Get Fooled Again" was re-recorded for The Who's documentary *The Kids Are Alright*. It would be the last song Keith Moon ever played.

1973's Quadrophenia was The Who's second full-length rock opera. The storyline was about an English mod named Jimmy from the era of the mods vs rockers sub-culture. However, Quadrophenia was riddled with problems from the beginning. The storyline was hard to follow, especially for American audiences. Many synthesizer parts made it difficult to perform live and it was recorded under challenging circumstances. Still, Quadrophenia was an album of great historical significance. It successfully introduced a young generation to the past mod culture and the time of zoot suits, diet pills, and street-fighting weekends. Quadrophenia served to link The Who to their first fans from their early days when they worked the London clubs in the 1960's. Later, after the initial punk movement came and went, Quadrophenia served as a model for a full-scale mod revival in England.

The Influences and Songwriting of Pete Townshend

A songwriting genius of the caliber of Pete Townshend is very rare. His vast array of musical influences included; the dixieland and traditional jazz he heard from his father's band growing up, blues legends such as Lightnin' Hopkins, Howlin' Wolf, Little Walter, John Lee Hooker, Jimmy Reed, classical music, and more. He also heard Chuck Berry (only the pop-chart hits) and Bo Diddley. What gave Townshend more depth was his interest in rhythm and blues and jazz. He listened to Ella Fitzgerald, Frank Sinatra, Duke Ellington, Ray Charles, and Jimmy Smith. Pete remembered, "I didn't start to collect records and listen to guitar players properly until I went to art school, when I'd already been playing for five years. So my style was already formed, and that's why I think it's so unique." #11

Townshend revealed one of his striking musical influences recalling, "Kit Lambert had loaned me a record that changed my life as a composer. It was what I had played during my Scotch-fueled listening experiments-a Czech recording called Masters of the Baroque. It included the principal movements of Purcell's "Gordian Knot Untied," a Baroque chamber suite, the most powerful part of which was the Chaconne. The performance is passionate, tragic and deeply moving. I was struck by Purcell's unique, luxurious use of suspensions, a staple part of Baroque decoration at the harpsichord, but in Purcell's hands the suspensions were elongated into heartrending, tortuous musical modes, especially in the minor keys. I began to experiment, and the first time I used suspensions successfully, in 'The Kids Are Alright,' it was mostly to suggest a Baroque mood." #12

In the beginning, Pete Townshend faced the challenge of combining his evolving guitar sound, his musical influences, and ideas for song lyrics. For "I Can't Explain," Pete would listen to songs that inspired him and then develop guitar ideas. He quickly played them into his clunky old tape recorder to make simple demos. As his process became more refined, Townshend remembered, "A lot of the writing I do on tour. I do a lot on airplanes. At home, I write a lot, obviously. When I write a song, what I usually do is work the lyric out first from some basic idea that I had, and then I get an acoustic guitar and I sit by the tape recorder and I try to bang it out as it comes." #13 Townshend also became familiar with a standard music theory book called Orchestration. It contained the principles written by Walter Piston utilized by many classical composers.

After his initial success as a songwriter, Pete Townshend began to realize that he needed a bigger canvas to paint on. The simple three-minute pop song felt restricting. He still needed to write songs that could function as pop singles, but Townshend realized he needed to compose extended works that would develop the storyline for his rock opera Tommy. In preparation, Townshend recalled, "One of the important documents I referred to while writing Tommy was a diagram I had sketched of the beginning and end of seven journeys involving rebirth. I was attempting two ambitious stunts at once: to describe the disciple/master relationship and, in a Hermann Hesse-style saga of reincarnation, to connect the last seven lives of that disciple in an operatic drama that ended in spiritual perfection. In 'Deaf, Dumb, and Blind Boy' I borrowed from Meher Baba's teachings to underpin ideas I'd been playing with during the previous year of psychedelia." #14

Pete Townshend-compositional genius

The Who by Numbers was released in 1975 as The Who was struggling with personal issues and much public fighting. Townshend felt that the band was losing their relevance and were perceived, even by themselves, to be too old to play rock. The album took a long time to record and the lone hit was "Squeeze Box." The Who By Numbers did peak at number seven on the British charts and "Squeeze Box" was a hit in America. The Who's eighth studio album, Who Are You, was released in 1978. Who Are You continued Townshend's complex arrangements and use of multi-layered synthesizers. Some of the song themes were directly related to the *Lifehouse* project. The song "Who Are You," went to number fourteen on the American charts and featured keyboardist Rod Argent.

Who Are You would be the last album for rock drumming legend Keith Moon, who died on September 7th, 1978, only three weeks after the album's release. Moon's death was ruled accidental when he overdosed on Heminevrin, a drug used to treat alcohol withdrawal. The album cover of Who Are You showed an eerie picture of the band with Moon sitting in a chair with a sign that said "not to be taken away." The Who were devastated with the loss of Keith Moon and it looked like that could be the end of the band. Eventually, a replacement was found, Kenny Jones, formerly from The Faces.

Chapter Six: The British Invasion Continues and the American Answer

Drummer Keith Moon

Keith Moon played the drums like nobody else before or since. Listening to Keith Moon play is a whole lot easier than trying to play his drumset parts. He seemed to be reeking havoc, refusing to play time on his hi-hats (which he stopped using altogether at one point) or ride cymbal. He sounded more often than not like he was playing an endless drum solo over The Who's melodies, Daltrey's vocals, or Townshend's guitar solos. But he wasn't. Moon was listening carefully to the song and its arrangement and he heard tornado-like drumset flurries as a complement to the music. One of Moon's not so subtle tricks was to incorporate backbeats (accents on beats two and four) underneath his raging tom-tom assault. That, in turn, created the "illusion" of a time feel and not a solo. Everything he played had a reason; everything made musical sense. Pete Townshend was intrigued with Moon's approach to playing. Townshend said, "An eccentric player, Keith seemed to be showing off all the time, pointing his sticks up in the air and leaning over the drums, face thrust forward as if to be nearer the front of the stage. He was loud and strong. Slowly, too, we realized that his fluid style hid a real talent for listening and following, not just laying down a beat." #15

Moon found unorthodox ways to apply snare drum rudiments such as ruffs and ratamaques and then orchestrated them creatively around the drums. Moon's loose feel was similar in some respects to the loose feel that jazz great Elvin Jones achieved with jazz saxophone icon John Coltrane. Guitarist Jeff Beck said it best when he explained, "people underestimated him, he was the most incredible drummer. You can't even mimic him. Nobody's been able to do it! I've watched and stood beside him and just gone, Jesus! I could describe a car crash easier than I could describe his drumming." #16

Keith, sometimes called "Moon the Loon," discovered that fireworks were legal to buy in some American southern cities. Keith enlisted the help of John Entwistle to see what was possible with a few dozen inoffensive cherry bombs and a hotel room. Said Entwistle, "We tried one out in his suitcase. It blew a hole in the suitcase and a chair. So then we decided the hotel deserves to get fu**ed because we'd had so much trouble with room service…our idea was to put the cherry bomb down the toilet and flush it so we couldn't get blamed for it. Hopefully it would blow some pipes along the way. We crouched over, Keith lit it and I flushed and the cherry bomb just kept going round. The flush didn't work properly. We looked at it and went Aaaagh! and ran out. And as we slammed the door the explosion went off, and when we went back, there was just a hole in the floor where the toilet had been. The toilet was completely gone." #17
Keith Moon-Rock Legend

1981's Face Dances was the ninth studio album for The Who. On this record, Kenny Jones replaced the late Keith Moon. The song "You Better You Bet" became one of their featured live tunes on tour. Face Dances served as a successful comeback for the band after the loss of Keith Moon and the album went to number four on the American charts. 1982's It's Hard would be the last Who recording until 2006. It was also the last recording for John Entwistle. One day before a new tour of America in 2002, John Entwistle died from a heart attack at the Hard Rock Hotel and Casino in Las Vegas. Townshend and Daltrey released a statement "The Ox has left the building-we've lost another great friend. Thanks for your love and support."

Bassist John Entwistle "The Ox"

Rivaled by only bassist Jack Bruce, of Cream, John Entwistle defined the possibilities of what a rock bass player could possibly do. Entwistle had astounding bass guitar technique. His technique incorporated the use of a pick, fingerstyle picking, tapping, and the use of harmonics (finding pitches in the harmonic series of individual notes). Entwistle incorporated another concept, "typewriter technique," where he would position all four right hand fingers over his bass allowing himself to tap percussively on each string. This gave him the ability to play up to four strings at once, adding to his melodic and rhythmic approach.

John Entwistle realized that The Who needed more from the bass position than just typical rock basslines. As great a guitar player as Townshend was, he often played more rhythm guitar than lead. Entwistle responded by developing moving lines like a guitarist would play but often in the upper register of his bass. Frequently on stage, Entwistle and Townshend would essentially exchange roles, as the bass would take on the melodic line. Pete Townshend knew Entwistle was going where no rock bass player had gone before stating, " On the final demo of the tune 'My Generation' we also created space for an Entwistle bass solo. John was becoming the outstanding bass revolutionary of the day, and I wanted to provide him with a vehicle for his incredible playing." #18 While The Who were creating mayhem on stage by jumping, swinging microphones, and smashing drums and guitars, Entwistle always stood stoically in place. "The Ox" - bass legend

In the great void of time between later Who album releases, the 2000 Lifehouse Chronicles release was a box set of the material from the abandoned Lifehouse rock opera. Lifehouse Chronicles gave Townshend closure to this project that he wanted so badly to complete. It consisted of six CDs. 2006's Endless Wire was the first new recording by The Who in twenty-four years! A Townshend mini-opera, "Wire and Glass," was featured on the album. At this time, The Who consisted of Townshend, Daltrey, Pino Palladino on bass, Simon Townshend on guitar, John "Rabbit" Bundrick on keyboards, and Peter Huntington on drums (as regular drummer Zak Starkey-son of Ringo Starr was unavailable). Townshend and Daltrey were both very happy with Endless Wire and it energized The Who to continue touring the world.

The Who had a groundbreaking and prolific career; eleven studio albums, twelve live albums, twenty-five compilation albums, four EP's, fifty-eight singles, four soundtracks, three documentaries, and stage and film productions of the albums Tommy and Quadrophenia. No rock band has ever played with such unbridled energy and passion. The Who were inducted into the Rock and Roll Hall of Fame in 1990.

> "When the power of love overcomes the love of power, the world will know peace"
>
> – Jimi Hendrix

Rock Hard Fact

A band called the Psychedelic Rangers, including future Door's drummer John Densmore, formed in Los Angeles in 1965. This was the first known rock band to call themselves "psychedelic."

"Music is the timeless experience of constant change... You don't get adventure in music unless you're willing to take chances"

– Jerry Garcia

Rock Hard Fact

The Grateful Dead's album Aoxomoxoa (title is a meaningless palindrome) was one of the first rock recordings to utilize sixteen-track recording technology.

Discussion Question

After The Beatles and the rest of the British Invasion bands gained an audience in America, did American rock bands have new motivation to explore the blues? Be specific and give examples.

The American Answer and Psychedelic Rock

The **psychedelic rock** genre was a part of the American answer to the British invasion. The word psychedelic taken literately means to reveal the soul or the mind. Musically, this extended to an attempt to crossover the senses and to be able to hear sounds as colors. This was a core concept of psychedelic music and was, of course, aided by the help of hallucinogenic drugs such as LSD. Musicians experimented by altering sound with distortion, feedback, long drones, exotic scales, and instruments borrowed from Eastern music. Long, meandering improvisations fostered much musical experimentation that became a cooperative experience with some audience members in a state of psychedelic altered consciousness. Some psychedelic rock artists utilized elements of jazz improvisation, borrowing from 1940's to 1950's be-bop and the cool jazz era of the 1950's. Also, another influence was the Beat poetry writers such as Allen Ginsberg, Jack Kerouac, and their followers, known as Beatniks.

The psychedelic movement, although first initiated in New York City, soon influenced the thinking of a new generation in San Francisco. Another important part of the American answer included **The Doors** from nearby Los Angeles and the **Jimi Hendrix Experience**. No matter where it's geographic origin, all of these bands and artists had diverse musical roots. Emerging rock bands drew from blues, country and folk, and early rock 'n' roll. New approaches to composing looked to the exploration of experimental sounds in the studio and on stage and even borrowed from world music. This section will explore the continued development of American rock music at the time of the powerful import of British rock bands.

The San Francisco Scene

The first psychedelic rock band was **The Charlatans**, formed in the famed Haight-Ashbury section of San Francisco. Soon, a diverse mixture of other San Francisco bands started to appear on the scene. They included; **The Grateful Dead, Jefferson Airplane, Big Brother and the Holding Company** featuring **Janis Joplin, Country Joe** and **The Fish, Moby Grape, The Steve Miller Band, Santana,** and **The Quicksilver Messenger Service.**

This new music centered on a free, "hippie" lifestyle and it's associated drug culture. LSD, although not the only drug of choice, was freely experimented with by both musicians and audiences. The new "turn on and tune in" attitude was led by Dr. Timothy Leary and writer Ken Kesey. The new San Francisco sound of the mid 1960's was tied to political and social issues as seen in the protests of the Vietnam War and the Civil Rights Movement. The hippie counter-culture protested materialism and rebelled against conventional societal norms. The counter-culture also embraced communal living and non-conformist fashion and hairstyles. By 1965, this rebellious spirit and desire for change inspired local bands to create a new form of blues-based rock that was titled psychedelic music, or sometimes called "acid" rock.

The 1960's San Francisco music scene was different and exciting. It avoided the old rock 'n' roll sexual tension and macho rock image. It was hippies freely dancing to a happy psychedelic experience. When hundreds of amateur San Francisco garage bands popped up, some aspired to become more professional. Local bars and basements provided venues where the psychedelic bands could gain an audience. Concert promoter Bill Graham saw a lot of money to be made and rented the Fillmore Auditorium so that bands such as Jefferson Airplane and the Warlocks could develop their music and gain larger followings. Local bands were forced to improve or step aside. By 1967, the Haight-Ashbury lifestyle saw the number of psychedelic bands grow from around five hundred to over fifteen-hundred.

The core of the "San Francisco" sound was a healthy mix of the blues, country, and folk music. There was also a new fascination and emergence of the long concert jam when the concert experience itself became an important lifestyle component. This would later spark the jam band genre (see chapter twelve) in the following decades. A social component of psychedelic rock was the intense involvement of the audience, since the music provided an escape from reality or a "new" reality of its own. After gaining a national audience, the San Francisco scene would eventually fade away, but not before creating a new genre of rock music. Later, bands such as Santana added a new twist to the psychedelic sound by adding the influences of jazz and Afro-Cuban styles.

The Charlatans (1964-1969) were formed by a draftsman and designer named George Hunter, who didn't sing or play an instrument. They would become one of the first psychedelic bands on the San Francisco scene and their rebellious attitude and fashion statements would influence the summer of love in 1967. Hunter conceived of The Charlatans to be an artistic and visual answer to The Beatles. They played mostly folk music mixed with some ballads and **jug band tunes**. The venues they played were large dance clubs with an audience made up of mostly LSD experimenting hippies. The Charlatans could barely play their instruments and that, coupled with taking LSD prior to performing, produced some entertaining results.

The Charlatans had a very small recording output and didn't release their first recording, The Charlatans, until 1969. They were about fashion and wore boots, vests, string ties, and had long hair to create an image that was emulated by other emerging bands and the hippie counter-culture. The Charlatans were one of the first bands to utilize psychedelic poster art. They also helped to establish the club environment for the San Francisco music scene. In the end, their limited musicianship and desire to remain a drummer-less non-rock band spelled their early demise.

The Grateful Dead (1965-1995) were the most successful of the 1960's psychedelic era West Coast bands. Their longevity, seen in a thirty year period of endless touring, made them the face of the hippie-counter culture in America. The roots of The Grateful Dead began when guitarist/vocalist Jerry Garcia taught guitar by day and at night played in the clubs in Palo Alto, California. As early as 1961, Garcia was playing with organist/vocalist Ron "Pigpen" McKernan and Robert Hunter (a songwriter who would later become the main lyricist for The Grateful Dead). Garcia formed the band Mother McCree's Uptown Jug Champions with McKernan, and soon added guitarist/vocalist Bob Weir. Mother McCree played a mixture of folk, country, bluegrass, and jug-band music. In 1965, they added drummer Bill Kreutzmann and changed their name to The Warlocks. A few months later, a friend of Garcia's, bassist Phil Lesh, was asked to join The Warlocks. Lesh came with a background in classical and electronic music that complemented the increasingly loud and experimental Warlock improvisations.

The Warlocks continued to experiment with their sound and also began to experiment with LSD. Soon, writer Ken Kesey invited them to jam at his house and what was to be termed the first "acid test" (large events of public LSD parties) was born. Acid test parties would come to represent a component of the psychedelic collective consciousness of the hippie counter-culture. The Warlocks temporarily stopped playing conventional gigs and focused on playing acid test parties. They also changed their name at this time when Garcia opened a dictionary and randomly arrived at the term grateful dead, a folklore term meaning "deceased who must walk the earth performing good deeds." At that moment, The Grateful Dead were born.

By 1967, The Grateful Dead were major cult figures and were signed to Warner Brother Records. The Dead were developing a sound that virtually defied placing them in a rock genre. They integrated styles and different musical backgrounds from bluegrass to Garcia's folk repertoire to R&B to electronic music. The Dead played long improvised jams with a psychedelic flavor at loud rock 'n' roll volume. The strength of the band became their live performances where they would jam endlessly late into the night. The Dead often played for free at Golden Gate Park and became regulars at the Fillmore and Avalon Ballroom. They released their self-titled debut album The Grateful Dead in 1967. Their fans thought this was a solid debut when it peaked at number seventy-three on the American charts, but the band felt the album failed to capture their live sound. Also in 1967, drummer Mickey Hart and keyboardist Tom Constanten joined the band.

In 1968, The Dead released Anthem of the Sun, which contained both studio and live material. It peaked at number eighty-seven on the charts and featured long compositions and an interesting production approach. Drummer Bill Kreutzmann explained, "Jerry and Phil (Lesh) went into the studio with Dan Healy and, like mad scientists, they started splicing all the versions together, creating hybrids that contained the studio tracks and various live parts, stitched together from different shows, all in the same song-one rendition would dissolve into another and sometimes they were even stacked on top of each other…it was easily our most experimental record-groundbreaking in its time…a psychedelic listening experience to this day." #19

1969's Aoxomoxoa was the third Grateful Dead studio album. It reached number seventy-three on the American charts. This album achieved a new level in the band's experimental efforts. It appeared shortly before the Woodstock Festival and helping to capture the spirit of the times. Aoxomoxoa contained the song "St. Stephen," a solid representation of the Dead's experimental nature and one of the band's classics.

Live/Dead was released in 1970 and went to number sixty-four on the charts. Here in live performance, The Grateful Dead showcased their strong ability to improvise on psychedelic rock themes and blues-inspired ideas. Grateful Dead live shows could lead to onstage magic or become stale with overextended jams, but they were never predictable. Garcia had honed his extended guitar solos and Bob Weir proved to be a perfect complement to Garcia both vocally and in guitar interplay. Tom Constanten left in 1970, the same year they recorded two of their finest albums, Workingman's Dead, which peaked at number twenty-seven, and American Beauty, which peaked at number thirty. With Constanten gone, Pigpen went back to playing the Hammond B-3 organ and Keith Godchaux joined playing acoustic piano. On these records, The Dead returned to a more rootsy, acoustic sound. Influenced by Bob Dylan's John Wesley Harding, Crosby, Stills, and Nash, and The Band's first two albums, The Dead created some of their most enduring classics; "Truckin," "Casey Jones," and "Uncle John's Band."

"Uncle John's Band"
by Jerry Garcia and Robert Hunter

"Uncle John's Band" appeared on the Workingman's Dead album and along with "Casey Jones," were two singles that have endured, receiving classic rock radio play to this day. "Uncle John's Band" was written by Jerry Garcia on acoustic guitar and had a strong bluegrass influenced folk arrangement. The lyrics of Robert Hunter made references to the Americana nostalgia of Irving Berlin's "Alexander's Ragtime Band." Robert Hunter was also writing about what would become the hippie counter-culture's fate at the beginning of the 1970's. Who was Uncle John? Some theories state he was a reference to the biblical John the Baptist with the lyric "He's come to take his children home." Another reference may have been to blues musician Mississippi John Hurt (nicknamed Uncle John), since he was an early influence on the Grateful Dead. Maybe it's both.

Musically, "Uncle John's Band" contained a strong melody and was a crowd favorite that The Dead began playing live in 1969. The vocal arrangement featured close harmonies inspired by Crosby, Stills, and Nash (they later covered the song) and vocal timbres previously unheard on Grateful Dead recordings. "Uncle John's Band" peaked at number sixty-nine, their first single to make the charts. At first, the song was controversial and received limited radio play since it contained the word "Godda*m." Later, it was edited out.

Groundbreaking album
American Beauty
by The Grateful Dead

The Grateful Dead recorded American Beauty only a few months after recording Workingman's Dead. In the process, they expanded and improved on their bluegrass, folk, and psychedelic country explorations by producing some of their most enduring compositions. It was unusual for the Dead to go back in the studio so quickly but the results proved effective when American Beauty reaching number thirty on the U.S. charts, while the single "Truckin'" went to number sixty-four. This album saw the benefit of the prolific relationship between Jerry Garcia and lyricist Robert Hunter. At the same time, American Beauty resulted in more input from the rest of the band.

Side one opened with "Box of Rain," then "Friend of the Devil," "Sugar Magnolia," "Operator," and "Candyman." Phil Lesh and Robert Hunter collaborated on the Dead's classic "Box of Rain." Lesh dedicated the song to his dying father. He wrote the

> "The Grateful Dead weren't in the music business, they were in the transportation business."
>
> – Grateful Dead drummer Mickey Hart

Rock Hard Fact

As a touring band, The Grateful Dead performed over twenty-three hundred shows. That's the equivalent to touring and performing every day for more than seven straight years!

music, recorded it, and gave it to Hunter who quickly added the lyrics. Lesh then rushed to the hospital and sang it to his father before he passed. "Box of Rain" was also the last song the Grateful Dead ever performed live (July 9th, 1995 at Soldier Field in Chicago). "Friend of the Devil" was written by Jerry Garcia and John Dawson of New Riders of the Purple Sage. Robert Hunter wrote the original lyrics that stated, "I set out running but I take my time/It looks like water but it tastes like wine/If I get home before daylight/I just might get some sleep tonight." But the part of "It looks like water but it tastes like wine" just didn't work. John Dawson replaced the line with "a friend of the devil is a friend of mine." Now the verse and song title were complete. "Friend of the Devil" evolved over time, with Garcia stating that the version the Dead played in later years was inspired by Kenny Loggins' version of the song.

Another classic was "Sugar Magnolia," a creation of Bob Weir and Robert Hunter. "Sugar Magnolia" became a staple at Grateful Dead shows, often utilized by the Dead to end a performance. It's a perfect blend of the Dead's ability to blend country and blues influences and rock out on demand. This very popular song was basically divided into two parts, with the second part (the coda) frequently turning into an intense Grateful Dead extended jam, complete with Garcia's burning guitar solos. "Sugar Magnolia" featured the line "jump like a Willys in four wheel drive," that referred to a model of jeep manufactured by Willys-Overland Motors. The song was also known for the simple phrase "Sunshine Daydream," and the ensuing coda that took on a life of its own in live performance. Duane Allman recorded a version of "Sugar Magnolia" on his box set Skydog, the Duane Allman Retrospective. Duane frequently sat-in with the Dead and played on "Sugar Magnolia" where he traded solo phrases with Jerry Garcia. "Operator" was Ron "Pigpen" McKernan's only singing-songwriting effort on a Grateful Dead studio album.

Side two opened with "Ripple," then "Brokedown Palace," "Till the Morning Comes," "Attics of my Life," and "Truckin'." Jerry Garcia, Phil Lesh, Bob Weir, and Robert Hunter were all credited with writing "Truckin'," which created a great communal feeling between the band. Phil Lesh often said that the Dead took their experiences from the road and (with Robert Hunter) turned it into poetry. For many Deadheads, "Truckin'" was more than a great song. It became the soundtrack for their way of life. For the verse "What in the world ever became of sweet Jane/She lost her sparkle well you know she isn't the same/Living on reds, vitamin C and cocaine?/All a friends can say is ain't it a shame." The Dead were speaking about how drugs (somewhat ironic) can bring people into a deep depression. "Truckin'" displayed a lazy shuffle and a very catchy melody. It was their highest charting single until the surprise top-ten single "Touch of Gray" sixteen years later.

For American Beauty, the Dead added musicians; David Grisman on mandolin, David Nelson on guitar, Ned Lagin on piano, Dave Torbert on bass, and Howard Wales on organ and piano for various tracks. A semi-official 1972 Grateful Dead movie titled Sunshine Daydream took its title from the coda section of "Sugar Magnolia." In St. Louis, a number of popular stores also borrowed the name Sunshine Daydream. Usually the Grateful Dead shined brightest in live performance but American Beauty showed they could deliver timeless music in the studio.

The Grateful Dead saw change when Mickey Hart left the band in 1971 (later rejoining in 1974). Pigpen was having health issues and was hospitalized but was able to rejoin the band. Next, The Dead recorded two live albums, the second of which, Europe '72, was released that same year and peaked at number twenty-four. After the tour of Europe in 1972, Pigpen's health deteriorated and he was no longer able to continue with the band. Ron "Pigpen" McKernan died in 1973. Keyboardist Keith Godchaux's wife, vocalist Donna Godchaux, joined the band, toured, and recorded with the Dead on Europe '72. This recording was the first triple live album in rock history to be certified gold and later double platinum.

In 1973, The Grateful Dead formed their own record label, called Grateful Dead Records, and later that year released Wake of the Flood that peaked at number eighteen. On the heels of their chart success, The Dead recorded 1974's From the Mars Hotel which peaked at number sixteen. Feeling burnt out, The Grateful Dead decided to take some rare time off from touring. Just in time to record Blues for Allah, Mickey Hart rejoined the band in 1975. The Dead had stayed with a single drummer lineup in the time Mickey Hart was gone and Kreutzmann rose to the challenge, playing at a high level. Blues for Allah reached number twelve on the charts. On this album, The Dead took a different approach to recording. Instead of developing the songs onstage, Garcia wanted more individual band member input in the writing process and suggested they write the material for the album in the studio. Garcia was interested in experimenting with different music styles, including the use of Middle-Eastern themes. The band also explored odd meters and different instrumentation. Mickey Hart was now back with the Dead full time and he gradually brought in more world percussion instruments to enrich their sound. A double live album, Steal Your Face, was released in 1976 and it peaked at number fifty-six. It would be the last album recorded on the Grateful Dead record label.

The Grateful Dead signed to Arista Records and released Terrapin Station in 1977. It went to number twenty-eight on the charts. Much to the joy of their fans, they also returned to touring after a two-year hiatus. The songwriting collaboration of Garcia and Hunter continued to flow. They wrote the music and lyrics for "Terrapin Station Part 1" separately but skillfully put it together the next day. 1978's Shakedown Street followed and would be the last for Keith and Donna Godchaux. Lowell George, of the band Little Feat, was brought in to produce some of the songs. However, recording was interrupted when The Grateful Dead were given the opportunity to play three concerts in Egypt, in front of the Great Sphinx of Giza. This was a great experience for the band and gave them a chance to work on some of the unrecorded Shakedown Street songs before going back in the studio to finish the album. Shakedown Street was completed with the help of producer John Kahn, who also contributed some organ parts. The album reached number forty-one on the charts.

Go to Heaven was released in 1980 and would be The Dead's last studio album for the next seven years. It peaked at number twenty-three. Bob Weir played a bigger songwriting role than on previous albums and keyboardist Brent Mydland joined the band as a new member. The Dead next released two live albums, 1981's Reckoning, and Dead Set, that same year. In 1985, Jerry Garcia was experiencing many health issues. Besides struggling with drug addiction, Garcia was increasingly ill due to complications from diabetes. In 1986, he almost died when he went into a diabetic coma. Garcia's recovery was difficult. He had to relearn many basic daily living skills including how to play the guitar.

After a seven year recording drought, In the Dark was released 1987 and was surprisingly popular, peaking at number six. The single "Touch of Grey," became the band's only top forty hit and was in the MTV music video rotation. Dylan and the Dead, a collaborative live album from a tour featuring Bob Dylan and the Grateful Dead, followed in 1989. Although it reached number thirty-seven on the charts, it was largely received as a flop and was harshly reviewed by music critics. The album consisted of Dylan singing seven of his tunes backed by The Dead.

1989's Built to Last would be The Grateful Dead's last studio album. It was successful, rising to number twenty-seven on the charts. Brent Mydland's role in The Dead had increased and he was credited with writing about half of the album's songs. Mydland was a good vocalist and combined his tenor voice with Weir's and Garcia's to provide solid three-part harmonies. Tragedy struck in 1990 when Brent Mydland died. He was replaced by keyboardist/vocalist Vince Welnick, formerly of The Tubes. Without a Net, a 1990 compilation album of live performances, was released with material the Dead had taken from shows from 1989 to 1990. It reached number forty-three on the charts. Also at this time, keyboardist/vocalist Bruce Hornsby joined the band as a touring member from 1990 to 1992.

Jerry Garcia was sick again after returning from The Dead's 1992 summer tour. He received guidance in losing weight and embracing a healthy lifestyle. But by 1995, Garcia's physical and mental condition further declined. He stated using narcotics again and after a period of rehabilitation, died on August 9th, 1995 from a heart attack.

The Deadheads

The Grateful Dead were a unique rock group that cultivated an enormous network of fans starting with their very first concert. This fan base would develop into a recognized subculture in its own right. Since the late 1960's, Deadheads began to follow the band from show to show across America. Fans soon realized that The Dead never played the same show each night, making each performance a unique experience. The atmosphere at each Dead show quickly built a sense of community and a deep loyalty between the band and its audience. The Dead's relationship grew with its audience as The Dead themselves grew together as a band. Grateful Dead bassist Phil Lesh commented on The Grateful Dead's evolution when he said, "The unique organicity of our music reflects the fact that each of us consciously personalized his playing: to fit with what others were playing and to fit with who each man was as an individual, allowing us to meld our consciousness together in the unity of a group mind." #20 That group unity fueled their musical evolution, but most importantly, The Grateful Dead connected to it's audience, the collective consciousness of Deadheads everywhere.

When The Grateful Dead came to a town, it didn't matter if you couldn't get a ticket. Outside the concert venue, parking lots were transformed into small towns of their own. The atmosphere inside and outside the venue had "the vibe." Fellow Deadhead vendors sold tie-dyed shirts, food, and everything Grateful Dead. The code for a person looking for a concert ticket became "I need a miracle." Over the many years of The Dead's career, their fan base continued to evolve and change with the times. Much like any large community, Deadheads developed their own idioms and slang. Deadheads gained even more traction when a solicitation appeared inside the Grateful Dead's 1972 live double album cover (also known as Skulls and Roses). It read "Dead Freaks unite! Who are you? Where are you? How are you? Send us your name and address and we'll keep you informed." This Deadhead network, initially pushed a little by the band, took off into a bigger and more organized network that elevated Dead fandom into a full-blown lifestyle.

The Grateful Dead encouraged its fans to openly record bootlegs of its performances. It became customary for thousands of fans to exchange tapes of recorded performances. In 1971, a man named Les Kippel, started the First Free Underground Grateful Dead Tape Exchange. The purpose was to preserve the heritage of the Dead's live concert history. This began a new era in recording, collecting, and trading Grateful Dead tapes. One thing that never changed was that every Grateful Dead fan found an inner-connectedness to The Dead's music and the total experience of a Grateful Dead show. Many Deadheads often described a Grateful Dead show as a true spiritual experience. Jerry Garcia described the Deadhead mindset when he said, "It's an adventure you can still have in America…You can't hop a freight, but you can chase The Grateful Dead around." #21

The death of Jerry Garcia also marked the end of The Grateful Dead. Three year later, Phil Lesh, Bob Weir, and Mickey Hart formed a band called The Other Ones and released a live album. There have been many other spin-offs of The Grateful Dead that featured one or more of the core members of the band including; Dead and Company (see chapter twelve), Phil Lesh and Friends, RatDog, Furthur, and Billy and the Kids.

The Grateful Dead's recording output included; thirteen studio albums, eight compilation albums, ten video albums, twenty-seven singles, and six box sets. There have been over fifty retrospective live albums released. Bootleg tapes, by mostly Deadhead concept tapers, run into the hundreds of thousands, making them easily one of the most recorded bands in rock history. Jerry Garcia many times stated that recording was a necessary evil but that the spirit of The Dead was always best captured *live*. The Grateful Dead received a Grammy Lifetime Achievement Award in 2007 and were inducted into the Rock and Roll Hall of Fame in 1994. Jerry Garcia had always avoided being portrayed as The Dead's leader or spokesman. He wanted the group to be perceived as equal partners and contributors to the collective musical force known as The Grateful Dead.

Quicksilver Messenger Service (1964-present) was formed by guitarist John Cipollina, vocalist Jim Murray, and folk balladeer Dino Valenti. They derived their name from an astrological reference to their virgo-heavy band personnel. Their repertoire consisted of folk tunes, Chicago styled blues, some Rolling Stones tunes, and a few original compositions. The band was defined by Cipollina's clear vocal vibrato and clean guitar sound. Quicksilver added bassist/keyboardist David Freiberg, who like Cipollina, came from the folk music scene. The band was completed with the addition of drummer Greg Elmore and guitarist Gary Duncan. Similar in some respects to the Grateful Dead, the two bands often played shows together and often were billed as "The Quick and The Dead." Many roster changes limited their develop-

---

Rock Hard Fact

Jerry Garcia was a "shadow producer" on Surrealistic Pillow and was credited on the album as "spiritual advisor." He stated that the album sounded "as surrealistic as a pillow is soft," thus naming the album.

"If you don't own the stage, you shouldn't be in rock 'n' roll"

- Grace Slick

ment and Valenti was imprisoned for a few years on a drug charge. For a brief period, keyboard legend Nicky Hopkins joined the band.

Even though Quicksilver Messenger Service formed in 1964, they only started recording after a successful performance at the Monterey Pop Festival. They were signed by Capitol Records in 1967 and released their self-titled debut album Quicksilver Messenger Service in 1968. Their second album, 1969's Happy Trails, was a live recording and they also released Shady Grove in that same year. During 1970, Quicksilver made two albums, Just for Love and What About Me. Freiberg, Cipollina, and Hopkins all left, and the remaining trio of Valente, Duncan, and Elmore added personnel and released a few more albums before disbanding. A new album and tour was part of a reunion in 1975. In 1986, Duncan formed another version of Quicksilver and recorded more albums with Freiberg. Quicksilver Messenger Service was an important part of the early psychedelic movement and they continue to perform.

Jefferson Airplane/Starship (1965-present) was formed by an actor turned guitarist and vocalist, Marty Balin. His folk-rock group with guitarist Paul Kantner and vocalist Signe Toly, covered standards and electric versions of folk ballads in a Beatles influenced approach. Balin opened a club called The Matrix where his band experimented by combining the early psychedelic sound of the San Francisco scene with their current repertoire. They added some originals too. Joined by guitarist Jorma Kaukonen and bassist Jack Casady, they recruited Skip Spence (actually a guitarist) to play drums and became Jefferson Airplane. By signing with RCA in late 1965, Jefferson Airplane became the first San Francisco band to receive a major recording contract. They released their debut album, Takes Off, in 1965 and quickly gained a strong following in the Bay Area. Soon, Signe (Toly) Anderson left and a strong and confident vocalist, Grace Slick, joined the band. By the summer of 1967, Jefferson Airplane had two top ten singles, and their second album, Surrealistic Pillow, reached number three on the American charts. It was right behind The Beatles Sgt. Pepper's Lonely Hearts Cub Band in popularity. Jefferson Airplane became the image of the love generation, the Haight-Ashbury lifestyle, and the most visible band of "the summer of love." Their combination of folk-rock and psychedelia was original and complemented the pioneering efforts of other popular bands such as The Yardbirds, The Byrds, and The Beatles.

Grace Slick brought a strong songwriting background and her scathing sarcasm to her song "White Rabbit." She also did a hit version of "Somebody to Love," redefining the Airplane's direction and bringing the psychedelic sound to a national audience. Slick had a visual style and an attitude that she could deliver on stage. Slick and Balin sang folk-inspired harmonies, usually at the interval of a fifth, that contributed to The Airplane's unique sound. Even more, their collective sound of three guitars gave them a hard rocking edge. They would often musically stretch out in a blues and jazz direction.

"Somebody to Love"
by Darby Slick (sister-in-law of Grace Slick)

Guitarist Darby Slick wrote "Someone to Love" for her band The Great Society, a 1960's San Francisco rock band. Grace Slick was a member of The Great Society before replacing vocalist Signe Toly Anderson in Jefferson Airplane. Grace recorded the tune and changed the name to "Somebody to Love" in 1967. The lyrics of "Somebody to Love," with the lines "When the truth is found to be lies/And all the joy within you dies/Don't you want somebody to love?" took on much significance in late 1960's Americana. Jefferson Airplane was speaking about the Vietnam War, the John F. Kennedy assassination, and other frustrations felt by the youth culture in San Francisco and all across America. Jefferson Airplane understood its audience and was directing its message to them. They expressed multiple themes; the Airplane's love image, the culture of open drug experimentation, and commentary about the political climate of the times.

Specifically, "Somebody to Love" was about loyalty and being monogamous. Grace Slick was singing about finding a true love that would be supportive and get people through tough times. Musically, it had a driving four to the bar feel that gave it a relentless energy. Guitarists Kaukonen and Kantner created an effective guitar accompaniment where their solo lines surrounded Slick's vocal phrases. They also added psychedelic sounding guitar solos. The Jefferson Airplane version of "Somebody to Love" was much more aggressive that the original version by The Great Society.

Moving forward, Jefferson Airplane adopted a heavier sound and placed more emphasis on improvisation. They were influenced by the success of Jimi Hendrix and Cream. Jefferson Airplane made five more albums with the same lineup except for some changes in the drumset chair. In mid-1966, Skip Spence left the band and was replaced by drummer Spencer Dryden, who came from a jazz background. This string of recordings included; 1967's After Bathing at Baxter's and Crown of Creation, Volunteers in 1968, and Bark in 1971. On Crown of Creation and Volunteers, the band wrote about the hippie counter-culture and the need to become unified in social revolution. By this time, Kantner and Slick had established themselves as the main songwriters. Jefferson Airplane would receive national recognition after their appearance at the Monterey Pop Festival in 1967. This solidified them as ambassadors of flower-power music, goodwill, and love. Other major festivals followed. At Woodstock and Altamont, Jefferson Airplane was featured as one of rock's biggest acts. The Airplane was commercial with their short vocal songs and rock backbeats, but they continued to perform long, psychedelic improvisations like other San Francisco bands.

By 1970, Jefferson Airplane was done singing about love and now focused more on Kantner's political lyrics. 1972's Long John Silver, without Marty Balin (he left in 1971 following the 1970 fall tour), would be the last studio album for the original Jefferson Airplane. Long John Silver featured the fluid guitar and basslines of Jorma Kaukonen and Jack Casady.

In 1972, Jefferson Airplane fell apart. Kaukonen and Casady left to form a new band, **Hot Tuna**. Also working as a duo, Kaukonen and Casady played Jefferson Airplane material and standard covers of blues and country tunes. Hot Tuna went on to record over thirteen albums and are still performing today.

In 1974, Kantner and Slick remained and decided to reform the band naming it **Jefferson Starship**. In addition to Slick and Kantner, the new lineup included guitarist Craig Chaquico, violinist Papa John Creach, keyboardist David Freiberg (from Quicksilver Messenger Service), bassist Pete Sears, and John Barbata. Jefferson Starship released their debut album, Dragonfly, in 1974. Marty Balin would sing on one track and join the band full time moving forward. The album went to number eleven and featured the single "Ride the Tiger," that went to number eighty-four. 1975's Red Octopus would

> "Billie Holiday and Aretha Franklin. Now, they are so subtle, they can milk you with two notes"
>
> - Janis Joplin

become the most popular record of any Jefferson combination to date, reaching number one on the American charts. The hit single "Miracles" peaked at number three. Jefferson Starship now found a new commercial sound and a direction they would follow for future albums.

Jefferson Starship released Spitfire in 1976 and Earth in 1978, both finding commercial success. This would be the end of the 1970's lineup and there were several new members that joined the band including drummer Aynsley Dunbar. Grace Slick left and so did Marty Balin. 1979's Freedom at Point Zero, was their first album to feature vocalist Mickey Thomas. Grace Slick returned for 1981's Modern Times and Jefferson Starship was able to promote the album with MTV music video exposure. The band released Winds of Change in 1982. 1984's Nuclear Furniture would be the last recording for guitarist Paul Kantner.

In 1985, the Jefferson Airplane/Starship name was legally retired by all the former band members after Paul Kantner had everyone sign an agreement not to use the Jefferson name, unless all agreed. The remaining members continued to use the name **Starship**. Starship released three albums including; 1985's Knee Deep in the Hoopla, 1987's No Protection, and 1989's Love Among the Cannibals. Paul Kantner received legal permission by the former members to revive the Jefferson Airplane name.

In 1989, the classic lineup of Jefferson Airplane reunited (without drummer Spencer Dryden) for a tour and the self-titled album Jefferson Airplane. Besides this classic lineup, this album utilized first call Los Angeles studio musicians. The album, and its supporting tour, would be the last time Jefferson Airplane would perform until their 1996 induction into the Rock and Roll Hall of Fame. In 1999, Jefferson Starship released their first studio album, Windows of Heaven, since re-forming in 1989. Another ten-year period ensued before they released 2008's Jefferson's Tree of Liberty. A fourth album by Starship was released in 2013 titled Loveless Fascination. From the original Jefferson Airplane, to the classic lineup of Jefferson Airplane, to the many versions of Jefferson Starship and the (just called) Starship; Balin, Kantner, Slick, and company were pioneers in the development of psychedelic rock.

Big Brother and the Holding Company (1965-present) developed out of a series of public jam sessions held in the basement of a rooming house. Peter Albin, a country-blues guitarist, met rock guitarist Sam Andrew and formed Big Brother and the Holding Company when they met and jammed with another guitarist, James Gurley. After first playing with drummer Chuck Jones, they settled on drummer David Getz. Albin then switched to bass, and they played their first gig at the Trips Festival in early 1966. Big Brother soon became the house band at the Avalon Ballroom where they played a mostly psychedelic style of instrumental rock.

With the help of Chet Helms, a prominent promoter in the San Francisco scene, Big Brother recruited vocalist **Janis Joplin** (1943-1970) in mid-1966. Joplin had just arrived from her native Texas, and at first, the band did not exactly seem like a great fit for her. Joplin did not take control right away but shared lead vocals with other band members. Joplin needed to adapt to the band's loud and distorted guitar jamming and they had to adapt to her brand of folk and blues. It was soon clear that by embracing Janis Joplin's fiery passion, Big Brother could become a major force.

The 1967 Monterey Pop Festival was one of the first performances for Janis Joplin with Big Brother.

When she sang an inspired "Ball and Chain," it brought the band to national attention and later prompted Columbia Records to sign Big Brother (although they had to get out of a bad contract with a smaller label). Big Brother and the Holding Company released their debut album in 1967 and it went to number sixty on the American charts, a minor success. When they signed to Columbia, the album was re-released, this time with the words "featuring Janis Joplin" on the cover. The song "Down on Me" was a top forty hit from the album. Soon, Big Brother and Joplin did an American tour and people were taking notice of Joplin's strong, belting voice that seemed like a mix of Aretha Franklin and Bessie Smith.

Big Brother and the Holding Company released Cheap Thrills in 1968. It would be their second and last record with Janis Joplin. Cheap Thrills was a huge success when it went to number one on the charts and stayed there for eight consecutive weeks. Three very strong tunes from the record were "Ball and Chain," (by blues great Big Mama Thornton), "Piece of My Heart," and "Summertime" (by George and Ira Gershwin).

"Piece of My Heart"
by Jerry Ragovoy and Bert Berns

"Piece of My Heart" was a romantic love song that was originally recorded in 1967 by soul singer Erma Franklin. It was a much bigger hit when Janis Joplin and Big Brother and The Holding Company released the single in 1968. It peaked at number twelve on the American charts. The song was about a woman who was so in love with her man that she was willing to break off a piece of her heart and she pleads with him to take it. "Piece of My Heart" sounded like it was written specifically for Joplin and audiences could immediately relate to her powerful version.

This version of "Piece of My Heart" was arranged by guitarist Sam Andrew, who added three loud and distorted guitar solos, thus creating a distinctive psychedelic sound. Joplin sang the song with passion and a pleading sense of urgency. Her screams and shrieks were powerful and the emotion she brought to the song added to her unique legacy of singing the blues. "Piece of My Heart" has been covered and re-recorded many times. A partial list of artists included; Dusty Springfield, Faith Hill, Steven Tyler, Sammy Hagar, and a collaboration between Melissa Etheridge and Joss Stone in 2005. Janis Joplin also sang "Piece of My Heart" at the original Woodstock Festival as part of her encore.

Cheap Thrills helped to establish Big Brother and Janis as superstars, but this would prove to be short-lived. By the end of 1968, Janis Joplin had decided to leave Big Brother. She quickly formed a new group, The Kozmic Blues Band in 1969. The band featured keyboardist Stephen Ryder, saxophonist Cornelius Flowers, former Big Brother guitarist Sam Andrew, and bassist Brad Campbell. Their one and only record, I Got Dem Ol' Kozmic Blues Again Mama!, also added guitar great Mike Bloomfield on three of the songs. The single, "Kozmic Blues," went to number forty-one on the charts. Joplin then performed at Woodstock where she was billed as one of the main attractions. There, she performed adequately, although her drug and alcohol issues were getting out of control. After some time in Brazil, Janis formed a new band called The Full Tilt Boogie Band. Joplin was very happy with new band and toured in the spring of 1970. Joplin and The Full Tilt Boogie Band recorded at Sunset Sound Recorders what would be her last album, titled Pearl. Joplin arranged all nine tracks. Kris Krist-

> **Rock Hard Fact**
>
> Janis Joplin paid for the tombstone of her idol, blues great, Bessie Smith. It read "The Greatest Blues Singer in the World Will Never Stop Singing" -Bessie Smith 1895---1937

offerson and Fred Foster wrote the hit single "Me and Bobby McGee." Janis began working on another song, "Mercedes Benz," for the new album.

Tragically, on October 4th, 1970, Janis Joplin died of a drug overdose (this came only sixteen days after the also premature death of Jimi Hendrix). Pearl was posthumously released in 1971 and it would later peak at number one in America and number twenty in Britain. "Me and Bobby McGee" reached number one on the U.S. charts. Janis Joplin only recorded four albums in her way too short career. She went from being an unpopular high school student from Port Arthur, Texas to the queen of the Haight-Ashbury counter-culture scene. Big Brother and the Holding Company allowed Joplin to transition from an amateur to a professional musician. She was afraid they might hold her back, but some felt she could have brought them along with her; thus allowing Big Brother to transcend their limitations. Joplin did not write many songs, but she did interpret the songs of others and made them her own in a *powerful* way. This made her one of the most important women in the history of rock music. Janis Joplin was inducted into the Rock and Roll Hall of Fame in 1995.

When Janis Joplin left Big Brother, so did guitarist Sam Andrew. After disbanding in 1968 and re-forming in 1969, Big Brother and the Holding Company went on to experience many lineup changes. They recorded and released a number of studio, compilation, and live albums. Never able to achieve the popularity they did with Joplin, Big Brother and the Holding Company's current lineup includes founding members Albin and Getz, vocalist Darby Gould, guitarist Tom Finch, and guitarist Tommy Odetto.

Country Joe and the Fish (1965 -2006) began with Country Joe McDonald, a folksinger with roots in the jug band music style and the old protest folk song tradition. Joe McDonald was one of the only musicians of the San Francisco music scene to have served in the U.S. military. He spent the early 1960's serving in the U.S. Navy, in which he had enlisted at age eighteen. At first, McDonald worked solo gigs playing songs by folk legends Woodie Guthrie and Pete Seeger. However, he slowly began to mix in his own compositions. McDonald soon formed two bands; one called The Berkeley String Quartet and the other The Instant Action Jug Band.

McDonald transformed The Instant Action Band into Country Joe and the Fish when he added guitarist/vocalist Barry Melton, washtub player Carl Schrager, bassist Bill Steele, and vocalist Mike Beardslee. McDonald had previously self-produced an EP with an acoustic version of "I Feel like I'm Fixin' To Die," which became a hit. This allowed McDonald and The Fish to gain popularity and develop their group sound. At this time, the band explored LSD with their audience of hippies and political radicals. They frequently performed at political rallies where Country Joe wore flowers and protest buttons and became music's most visible anti-war campaigner. The Fish were an entertaining band that wore funny costumes and performed slapstick comedy in between their folkie melodies that were rooted in the jug band style.

The Fish transformed from playing the folk and jug band circuit to becoming a rock band by eventually changing their lineup to musicians who played electric instruments. McDonald and Melton recruited bassist Bruce Barthol, keyboardist David Cohen (moving from guitar), and drummer Gary "Chicken" Hirsh. In early 1967, Country Joe and The Fish released their debut album Electric Music for the Mind and Body. It was one of the first psychedelic albums to come out of the San Francisco music scene. They also experimented with psychedelic musical effects similar to early Jefferson Airplane. The band released their second album, I Feel Like I'm Fixin' To Die, that contained "The Fish Cheer" that became a staple at their concert performances. Their biggest opportunity came when they became a last minute addition to The Woodstock Festival. Country Joe and The Fish made four more studio albums before disbanding in 1970. A reunion album was released in 1977 and The Country Joe Band (a spin-off of The Fish) worked up until 2006. Some of the members occasionally still tour. Country Joe McDonald went on to a have a successful solo career that has spanned over thirty albums. He has remained an active anti-war campaigner.

Moby Grape (1966-present) formed when three members of a Seattle band, The Frantics, added original Jefferson Airplane drummer Skip Spence. They had a powerful sound led by the three guitars of Jerry Miller, Peter Lewis and Spence (who converted to guitar). By 1967, they quickly became very popular. Their debut album Moby Grape combined the excitement of a rock band with the psychedelic and folksy sensibility of the San Francisco scene. They achieved a tight sound and were known for commercializing the psychedelic blues. After a bidding war to sign them, Moby Grape committed to Columbia, where they were overhyped and had difficulty meeting the expectations of the label.
Moby Grape became one of the most popular bands in the San Francisco scene. They had a powerful sound and more flashy guitar solos than most of their contemporaries. Moby Grape were one of the only rock bands where every member of the band could and did sing lead vocals. They next released a series of four successful albums including: 1968's Wow/Grape Jam, 1969's Moby Grape '69 and Truly Fine Citizen, and 1971's 20 Granite Creek. Much later in 1984, they released Moby Grape '84.

Skip Spence encountered drug and personal problems but the band managed to move forward. He played with them on and off until his death in 1999. Moby Grape disbanded and re-formed with many lineup changes throughout the 1970's until 2001. In 2006 after many legal issues, Moby Grape won back the right to use their original name. Also in 2006, they reunited and played a Summer of Love Anniversary Celebration in San Francisco's Golden Gate Park. Moby Grape still performs today.

The Steve Miller Band (1966-present) was formed when vocalist/guitarist Steve Miller, from the Texas 1950's blues-rock scene, moved to Haight-Ashbury in 1966. Miller had a strong musical upbringing that included guidance from blues legend T. Bone Walker and guitar legend Les Paul. Miller first moved to Chicago to become immersed in the traditional blues scene. He worked with blues greats Muddy Waters, Howlin' Wolf, and The Paul Butterfield Blues Band. Next, Miller headed for the psychedelic San Francisco environment and quickly signed a lucrative recording contract with Capital Records. Soon, The Steve Miller Band was headlining the Avalon Ballroom giving the San Francisco scene some musical diversity via the blues.

The original Steve Miller Band featured Lonnie Turner on bass, Tim Davis on drums, and Miller's college friend and future solo artist, vocalist Boz Scaggs. Scaggs played guitar and sang on Miller's first two albums. Miller's voice was passionate and gutsy, while Scagg's sang in a smoother, more intimate style. The Steve Miller Band went through a number of personnel changes but went on to release over seventeen albums. From their 1968 debut

> "Added together, the message that we sought...was that life should be a sprawling unpredictable adventure leading either to a glorious early death, or to a wizardly serenity coupled with knowledge and power."
>
> – Darby Slick

Children of the Future to their 2011 release, Let Your Hair Down, Steve Miller has taken on the alter egos of *the joker* to *the space cowboy* to the *gangster of love*. One of Miller's most celebrated recordings was his self-produced 1973 release, The Joker, which went to number two on the American charts and the single "The Joker," that went to number one.

"The Joker"
by Steve Miller, Eddie Curtis and Ahmet Ertegun

"The Joker" was a single released from The Steve Miller Band's 1973 album The Joker. The song reached number one on the American charts. Sixteen years later, it went to number one on the British charts after it was featured in an advertisement for Levi's Jeans in 1990. For "The Joker," Steve Miller referenced a 1954 song by The Clovers titled "Lovey Dovey" when he sang "You're the cutest thing I ever did see/Really love your peaches, wanna shake your tree/Lovey dovey, lovey dovey, lovey dovey all the time." The "space cowboy" reference became an alternate persona for Steve Miller.

The musicians on the original recording were Steve Miller on guitar and lead vocals, Gerald Johnson on bass, Dick Thompson on organ, and John King on drums. The tune achieved a unique and funky feel. The bassline played a riff that functioned as part of the melody and Miller added supporting guitar rhythms. The parts locked in to arrive at a funky composite rhythm not very often achieved in rock music. "The Joker" has been covered numerous times and has been sampled many times as well. The song is still a staple on FM classic rock radio.

Santana (1966-present) was formed by guitarist and vocalist Carlos Santana in 1966. The son of a Mexican mariachi performer, Carlos moved with his family to San Francisco where he formed The Santana Bluesband. A strong lineup was soon established featuring keyboardist Greg Rolie, bassist David Brown, drummer Michael Shrieve, and percussionist Jose' "Chepito" Areas. Santana, although appearing on the psychedelic scene fairly late, provided a new slant by injecting major elements of **Afro-Cuban rhythms**, jazz, and fusion styles all with a cosmic, psychedelic vibe. The band rose in status quickly when promoter Bill Graham booked them as headliners at the Fillmore West and helped them to secure a record deal with the Columbia label.

Santana found success with their 1969 debut album Santana, but it was their second album, 1970's Abraxas, that established the Santana sound. The album contained "Black Magic Woman" and the Tito Puente classic "Oye Como Va," both of which brought a Latin music sensibility to rock music. Abraxas soared to number one in America and broke into the top ten in Britain.

"Black Magic Woman"
by Peter Green (covered by Santana)

"Black Magic Woman" was written by Peter Green of Fleetwood Mac in 1968. It first appeared as a single and then later on various Fleetwood Mac albums. In 1970, Carlos Santana and his band covered the song on their album Abraxas. Sung by Santana vocalist and keyboardist Greg Rolie, the song peaked at number four on the American charts. "Black Magic Woman" was a minor blues set to an Afro-Cuban son clave rhythm, giving it a very different character than the Fleetwood Mac version. Santana's version blended this Latin feel with a jazz and blues influence to create a hybrid Latin-rock feel that helped to define the Santana sound.

Carlos Santana was very influenced by Hungarian guitarist Gabor Szabo. Santana borrowed some guitar techniques and licks from Szabo's tune "Gypsy Queen" for the introduction to "Black Magic Woman." After the intro, the song moved to an eight-bar piano solo and two verses sung by Gregg Rolie. Santana's guitar solo followed and then a second section that utilized a modified version of the "Gypsy Queen." Carlos Santana added sustain and distortion to his guitar solo by manipulating the volume knob of his amplifier. Rolie sang with a relaxed sense of phrasing that gave "Black Magic Woman" a smooth and flowing quality.

1973's Santana III, also went to number one in America and saw the addition of guitarist Neal Schon and percussionist Coke Escoveco. Some tension existed in the band prompting Rolie and Schon to leave. They would find fame when they helped form the band Journey (see chapter eleven). Santana continued to release a steady stream of albums. Over his long career, Carlos Santana was also involved in more than fifty musical collaborations. A few included interaction with jazz and fusion greats such as guitarist John McLaughlin and the fusion band Weather Report. Santana created a jazz-fusion recording with the release of Caravanserai in 1992.

The release of Supernatural in 1999 was a blockbuster for Carlos Santana. It sold over twenty-six million copies and produced his biggest hit, "Smooth." Sung by Rob Thomas of the band Matchbox Twenty, "Smooth," rose to the top of the charts for twelve weeks and also earned Santana a Grammy for song of the year. Supernatural featured guitar legend Eric Clapton and vocalist Dave Matthews. In 2002, Santana continued his commercial success with the album Shaman. The followup was All That I Am, Santana's nineteenth studio album. It featured drumming great Dennis Chambers. In 2010, Santana released Guitar Heaven, a record with appearances by Joe Cocker, Scott Weiland (of Stone Temple Pilots), and Chris Cornell of Soundgarden. Over the years, Carlos Santana has had more than eighty sidemen appear on his albums. The Santana sound was, in part, created by some of the best Afro-Cuban percussionists in music. They included: conga and timbale virtuosos Jose' "Chepito" Areas, Michael Carabello. Pete Escovedo, Armando Peraza, Don Alias, and many others.

Santana has worked hard to have a very consistent and eclectic career. Aside from being a late addition to the psychedelic rock scene, he carved out a unique sound by blending Afro-Cuban rhythms with blues, jazz, and fusion, while simultaneously finding commercial success. He has sold more than one-hundred million records worldwide including; twenty-four studio albums, seven live albums, twenty-three compilation albums, sixty-one singles, and over a dozen collaboration albums. Carlos Santana and his band were inducted into the Rock and Roll Hall of Fame in 1998.

Other Answers (To the Invasion)

The Doors (1965-1973) formed in Los Angeles in 1965 and were just a bar band playing covers at clubs like the Whiskey A Go Go and The Strip. They became one of the biggest and most controversial rock bands in the 1960's, sparked by the lyrics and behavior of their leader, vocalist/poet Jim Morrison. Morrison was a film student at UCLA where he met keyboardist Ray Manzarek. Soon they joined forces to become The Doors with guitarist Robby Krieger and drummer John Densmore. The Doors never did add a bass player (only on some studio recordings), instead choosing to develop their sound around Krieger's guitar and Manzarek's organ and Fender Rhodes timbres. The Doors signed with Elektra Records in 1966 and released their 1967 debut self-titled The Doors. The record featured the hit single "Light My Fire," that went to number one on the American charts.

"Light My Fire"
written by The Doors

"Light My Fire" was mostly written by guitarist Robby Krieger but was credited to the whole band. Ray Manzarek played the bassline with his left hand on a Fender Rhodes and the other keyboard parts with his right hand on a Vox Continental keyboard. The producer for the session, Paul Rothchild, had Wrecking Crew L.A. session bassist Larry Knechtel add a bass part to double Manzarek's bassline. The song contained many of the classic "Doors-isms." Densmore, as he often did, infused a Latin feel into the tune. On "Light My Fire" he utilized a quazi-**bossa nova** feel. Krieger approached his guitar parts by blending blues with Eastern music tonalities. Along with Manzarek's musical organ solos, this defined The Doors sound and collectively, they achieved a psychedelic vibe that rivaled any of the San Francisco bands. Krieger was able to extend Manzarek's solo on "Light My Fire" and together, their solos transported the listener to a new place. Manzarek skillfully played a keyboard riff at the end of his solo that defined the tune and smoothly brought Morrison back for an explosive vocal ending.

"Light My Fire" proved to be a vehicle for some of Morrison's typical controversial moments. In one incident, after being asked to change the line "Girl, we couldn't get much higher," for an appearance on *The Ed Sullivan Show*; Jim Morrison agreed to change the word "higher" to "better." After having rehearsed the new TV friendly line, Morrison, of course, sang the original line on live TV. Sullivan refused to shake his hand coming off stage and Morrison "could care less" that they were banned from future *Ed Sullivan Show* appearances.

The Door's debut album would set a high bar the band struggled to match. However, their second album, 1967's Strange Days, did achieve commercial success. It reached number three on the American charts. The record yielded two top thirty singles "Love Me Two Times" and "People Are Strange." 1968's Waiting for the Sun, became The Door's first and only number one album in America while it peaked at number sixteen in Britain. It also featured their second number one single, "Hello, I Love You." The composition and recording process for this album proved to be difficult. Morrison had become depressed and the band struggled to create new material, having exhausted much of Morrison's earlier song ideas and poetry. Producer Paul Rothchild was frustrated and his perfectionist attitude became an issue with the band. Two of the songs, "Five to One" and "The Unknown Soldier" had militant themes. This was Morrison's reaction to the Vietnam War, especially "The Unknown Soldier." The track, "Waiting For the Sun," was left off of the album, but would later be added to the recording Morrison Hotel.

1969's The Soft Parade was The Doors' fourth studio album. It reached number six in America but was not nearly as successful in Britain. Once again, The Doors had some difficulty recording when Morrison was dealing with mounting personal issues. For this album, Robby Krieger assumed more of the songwriting process (drawing from his jazz influences). However, Morrison did continue to write some poetry that would fuel The Door's song lyrics. Rothchild also wanted to develop a full sound by incorporated string and brass arrangements. The result included three singles "Touch Me," "Wishful Sinful," and "Tell All the People." "Touch Me," written by Robby Krieger, went to number three on the charts.

In 1969, Morrison was arrested for indecent exposure at a concert in Miami, Florida. This single incident almost destroyed the band when many concert promoters became hesitant to book them. The Doors were able to rebound from their troubles with the release of 1970's Morrison Hotel. The record opened with "Roadhouse Blues" and the album went to number four in America achieving a hard rocking sound. Morrison also returned to more active songwriting. That same year, The Doors released their first live album, Absolutely Live. This material came from many live performances from The Door's 1970 tour. Paul Rothchild was trying to create the ultimate concert and recalled, "I couldn't get complete takes of a lot of songs, so sometimes I'd cut from Detroit to Philadelphia in mid-song. There must be 2,000 edits on that album." #22

The Doors continued to tour in the summer of 1970. The tour culminated at the Isle of Wright Festival when they performed alongside Jimi Hendrix, The Who, Miles Davis, Emerson, Lake and Palmer, and Joni Mitchell. The Doors last performance with Jim Morrison was on December 12th, 1970 in New Orleans. Morrison had a breakdown on stage and the band agreed that would be it for live performances. L.A. Woman, released in 1971, would prove to be Jim Morrison's final album. The tracks "L.A. Woman," "Love Her Madly," and "Riders of the Storm" would become classics and mainstays on FM classic rock radio stations.

Upon completion of L.A. Woman, Morrison went to Paris where he died of either a drug overdose or heart attack. The circumstances of his death remain unclear since the medical examiner claimed to have found no evidence of foul play and therefore, no autopsy was performed. Jim Morrison was buried at the Pere Lachaise cemetery in Paris, France. The three remaining Door's members first tried to carry on without him. The Doors released two albums, Other Voices in 1971, and Full Circle in 1972. Krieger and Manzarek shared the vocals on both recordings.

The Doors officially disbanded in 1973. Densmore and Krieger formed a band called The Butts Band that performed until 1975. Later, Manzarek and Krieger performed live as The Doors of the 21st Century with singer Ian Astbury of The Cult. In 1978, the three original members reunited to create the album An American Prayer. This was a complex project that had The Doors creating backing tracks set to previously recorded spoken word performances of Morrison reciting his poetry. Ray Manzarek died of cancer in 2013. In 2016, Krieger and Densmore reunited for a tribute to Manzarek at a benefit concert for Stand Up to Cancer.

Jim Morrison proved to be as big a star in the mid-1980's as he was in the 1960's and early 1970's. His legend has fascinated later generations of curious rock fans. Morrison was a complex individual, both an intellectual poet and troubled rebel. Musically, he was a gifted lyricist and dynamic performer. Electra Records sold many Doors' compilations and live albums while publishers have sold numerous Morrison and Doors biographies. In 1991, director Oliver Stone created the film, *The Doors,* about Jim Morrison with actor Val Kilmer starring as Morrison. The Doors were inducted into the Rock and Roll Hall of Fame in 1993.

Rock Hard Fact

The Doors tune "Break On Through" was the first ever music video. It happened because Elektra Records filmed The Doors to avoid paying for an expensive promo tour.

The "27 Club"
Prominent Members (partial list):

#1
Robert Johnson
Died 1938
poison (strychnine)
27 years, 100 days

#2
Brian Jones
Died 1969
drowned
27 years, 125 days

#3
Alan "Blind Owl" Wilson
Died 1970
Drug OD
27 years, 61 days

#4
Janis Joplin
Died 1970
Drug OD
27 years, 285 days

#5 Jimi Hendrix
Died 1970
Asphyxiation
27 years, 295 days

#6
Jim Morrison
Died 1971
Heart Failure
27, years, 207 days

#7
Ron "Pigpen" McKernan
Died 1973
Gastrointestinal Hemorrhage
27 years, 181 days

#8 Pete Ham
Died 1975
Suicide
27 years, 362 days

#9
Kurt Cobain
Died 1994
Suicide
27 years, 316 days

#10
Amy Winehouse
Died 2011
Alcohol poisoning
27 Years, 312 days

Rock 'n' roll is an art form that some have tried to link to the supernatural and even the occult. The blues and (later) rock music have often been portrayed as the "devil's music" for its bad influence on the young in terms of inciting rebelliousness and promoting raw sexuality. Not just musicians, but many artists in other creative fields have died way too soon. Over time, an uncanny list formed of rock musicians that died at the tender age of twenty-seven. It is mere statistical coincidence or is the infamous "27 Club" something more? The first membership to the club can be traced back to Delta blues great, Robert Johnson, whom the legend stated "made a deal with the devil." His genius helped spark the rock 'n' roll spirit of many great British blues-rock guitarists featured in this book from; Keith Richards to Eric Clapton to Jimmy Page and even another member of the "27 Club," ex-Rolling Stone Brian Jones.

Neil Young wrote, "It's better to burn out than fade away." That line was found in the suicide note left behind by Nirvana's Kurt Cobain. Some musician's in the "27 Club" died from health issues that took their lives. But most often, it was drugs and alcohol. The real cause of many of these deaths came from the pressures of too much fame, too much pressure to repeat earlier success, overly demanding tour and travel schedules, and too much money; all way too soon. Even the type of person drawn to the rock 'n' roll lifestyle has played a factor. Young creative artists tend to be emotional, rebellious, and inexperienced and confronted with sudden changes in their lifestyles. According to a study published in the British Medical Journal, musicians in their twenties and thirties were two to three times more likely to die prematurely than the general British population. #23

The deaths of many of the prominent musician's on this list have been sudden, controversial, and mysterious. For example, Brian Jones drowned in his swimming pool only weeks after being ousted by the Rolling Stones. Jim Morrison was found dead in a Paris, France bathtub, with details never made publicly clear. Janis Joplin died before she had the chance to really define her post-San Francisco psychedelic Big Brother legacy. Her tortured past put her on a path of self-destruction even though she had obtained superstar status. The speculation over the death of Kurt Cobain continues, and even now, the Seattle Police get inquires to reopen his case. Mere statistical coincidence or fate or conspiracy, the "27 Club" may be rock's greatest mystery. The tragedy is that everyone on this list was taken way too soon. That has been a great loss for rock music itself.

Jimi Hendrix (1942-1970) is considered one of the most influential rock musicians of the 20th century. His incredible rise to the top of the rock world occurred in the span of only four year. In that time, he created new possibilities for electric guitar and developed a unique musical vocabulary seen in his approach as a composer, bandleader and vocalist, and studio musician. Born in Seattle, Washington, and named Johnny Allen Hendrix, he was later renamed James Marshall Hendrix by Al Hendrix, his father. Hendrix took an early interest in acoustic guitar. He was self-taught and listened to every artist he could, especially the blues of Robert Johnson, Muddy Waters, and B.B. King. Buddy Holly was also a strong influence. Jimmy's first band was The Velvetones where he played acoustic guitar. But he soon left and joined The Rocking Kings, where he played his first electric guitar, a Supro Ozark model.

Jimmy joined the U.S. Army in 1961 and while stationed in Kentucky (where he heard lots of country music), formed the band the King Casuals with bassist Billy Cox. Hendrix was discharged from the Army due to an injury and soon found work as a session guitarist. He now used the name Jimmy James. By the end of 1965, Hendrix had performed and recorded with an impressive array of artists. They included; Little Richard, Sam

"His (Jimi Hendrix) artistic genius lay in how he created a sound all his own: Psychedelic Soul, or what I'd call Blues Impressionism"

- Pete Townshend

Cooke, The Isley Brothers, and Ike and Tina Turner. Making the move to fronting his own band, Hendrix formed Jimmy James and the Blue Flames. In late 1965, Hendrix moved to New York City and began playing many of the small cafes and clubs in Greenwich Village. The ex-Animals bassist and music businessman, Chas Chandler, heard Jimmy at a venue called Caf,Wha?. Chandler was impressed enough to sign Hendrix to a deal that would send him to London with the intention of forming a new band.

On his arrival to England, Jimmy changed the spelling of his name to Jimi and Chandler helped organize auditions for the new Jimi Hendrix Experience band. Powerful drummer Mitch Mitchell and bass virtuoso Noel Redding joined Hendrix to form what would become a superstar power trio. The Jimi Hendrix Experience signed a deal with Track Records, a new label formed by The Who's managers, Chris Stamp and Kit Lambert. The trio dressed in outlandish clothes and they all frizzed their hair to make a big fashion statement to mirror their musical statements. At first they played a repertoire of R&B tunes and some popular songs such as "Hey Joe" and Bob Dylan's "Like a Rolling Stone." Then, Hendrix originals began to appear. The Jimi Hendrix Experience collectively stunned both English musicians and audiences, setting the stage for their famous Monterey pop performance.

In 1967, Jimi Hendrix released the single "Hey Joe" and then his debut album Are You Experienced?. It would prove to be one of the most influential albums in rock history. Are You Experienced? reached number five on the American charts and number two in England. It featured the rock classics "Purple Haze," Hey Joe," "Foxy Lady," and "Fire."

"Fire"
by Jimi Hendrix

"Fire" was one of Jimi Hendrix's most exciting and popular tunes that he would feature in live performances. On "Fire," Mitch Mitchell developed one of the funkiest drumset feels ever recorded for a rock tune. The origin of the song goes back to when Jimi was visiting the home of bassist Noel Redding's family in England. Jimi asked Redding's mother if he could stand next to her fireplace to warm himself. Her dog was in the way so Jimi said, "Aw, move over, Rover, and let Jimi take over," which later became part of the lyrics. The lyrics also contained some sexual overtones. There are many live versions of "Fire" and Hendrix often took it significantly faster than the original tempo from his Are You Experienced? album. To cope with the increased tempo, Mitch Mitchell would play a James Brown rooted "fatback feel" changing the accents in a two bar phrase. This can be seen and heard on a 1970 live concert video from Toronto, Canada and from the Live From Winterland shows recorded in 1968. "Fire" was a showcase for some of Hendrix's most blistering guitar solos.

Noel Redding formed a bassline that created a sense of forward motion, something he often added to many of the trio's songs. "Fire" also provided Mitch Mitchell with a vehicle to display his incredible "hand/foot" drumset facility. Mitchell and Hendrix had a special musical relationship and it was never more evident than when they played with "Fire." "Fire" appeared on a number of Hendrix recordings including many live albums and compilations. "Fire" has been a challenge that many have dared to cover. Some of the best live covers of "Fire" have come from guitarist Steve Vai, Red Hot Chili Peppers, and Bruno Mars.

> **Rock Hard Fact**
>
> Jimi Hendrix eventually called his music the "electric church" because he believed music was his form of religion.

Jimi Hendrix reintroduced himself, along with Redding and Mitchell, to America when they played the Monterey Pop Festival in 1967. An electrifying performance following The Who brought a defining moment in rock history when Hendrix played a blistering version of "Wild Thing." Hendrix finished the song by pouring lighter fluid on his guitar, setting it on fire, and smashing it to pieces. Almost overnight, The Jimi Hendrix Experience became one of the most popular touring bands in the world.

Groundbreaking album
Are You Experienced?
by Jimi Hendrix

Are You Experienced? would establish new directions in psychedelic rock and help to define hard rock music moving forward. Jimi Hendrix took the musical world by storm with his original guitar sound, exciting soloing, and innovative songwriting. All of the songs on Are You Experienced? were written by Jimi Hendrix except "Hey Joe" which was written by Billy Roberts. The Breakaways, an English female vocal trio, sang background vocals on "Hey Joe." The album was produced by Chas Chandler and engineered by Eddie Kramer and Dave Siddle.

On this recording, Jimi's mastery of electric guitar was on full display and his arranging skills were equally formidable. Throughout the album, Mitch Michell played with a loose Elvin Jones like feel and together with Redding's active basslines, helped to create a multi-layered sound. This approach (along with Cream) defined the rock power trio. Each member of the Hendrix trio created full, musically interesting parts that fit together seamlessly to create an original and powerful sound.

On the American release, side one opened with "Purple Haze" and was followed with "Manic Depression," "Hey Joe," "Love or Confusion," "May This Be Love," and "I Don't Live Today." Side two opened with "The Wind Cries Mary" and moved to "Fire," "Third Stone from the Sun," and "Are You Experienced?" At times, Hendrix spoke with delicate lyrics that felt like poetry. "Third Stone from the Sun" showcased Hendrix's psychedelic guitar skills and his ability to harness distortion, feedback, and electronic effects.

Are You Experienced? wasn't the first power trio record of importance. It did however, redefine rock by stretching the limits of what a power trio could do. The album achieved compositional balance, musical interplay between all three players, strong lyrics, virtuosic instrumental skills, and most importantly, musical excitement.

Hendrix released his second album, Axis Bold As Love, in 1968. On this recording, Jimi took full charge of his musical direction and sound. He became laser focused on every aspect of the recording and production process. Axis Bold As Love fulfilled The Experience's contract with the Track Label. The album peaked at number five in Britain but its release in America was delayed due to fears that it would interfere with the sales of their debut album. Many of the tunes on Axis Bold As Love were composed with studio effects and were not usually performed live. However, the tunes "Little Wing" and "Spanish Castle Magic" were often in their live set list. "Spanish Castle Magic" was inspired by an experience from Jimi's youth when he had frequented a dance hall where he would jam with his band. On "Little

Wing," Jimi played his guitar through a Leslie speaker for the first time. Axis Bold As Love showed Hendrix's rapid growth as a songwriter, having composed all of the songs except Redding's "She's So Fine." Many critics thought this album was an overlooked masterpiece.

Jimi Hendrix set his sights on building his own recording studio, Electric Lady Studios in New York City. This building project became the basis for his next album, Electric Ladyland, a two record set. What would be Jimi's last recording with The Experience, Electric Ladyland brought the band's sound to new level. Engineer Eddie Kramer and Jimi experimented with echo effects, backward tape processing, experimental microphone recording techniques, chorusing, and more. The songs "Crosstown Traffic," "Voodoo Chile (Slight Return)," and Hendrix's interpretation of Bob Dylan's "All Along the Watchtower," were some of the classics on this recording. Again, Hendrix did most of the songwriting. Electric Ladyland went to number one in America, making it The Experience's most successful album. It went to number six in Britain. Many viewed this recording as Hendrix's best work. Due to other commitments by Noel Redding (he had formed a band called Fat Mattress), Hendrix had to play bass on many of the Electric Ladyland songs. Many prominent musicians guested on one or more tracks including; Al Kooper, Jack Casady, Steve Winwood, and Dave Mason.

Throughout 1968, the band recorded and toured at a frantic pace. In 1969, Hendrix disbanded The Experience. In the summer of that same year, Jimi gave his legendary performance at the Woodstock Festival. Leading an eclectic group called Gypsy Sun and Rainbows, it featured Mitch Mitchell, Billy Cox, and percussionists Juma Sultan and Jerry Velez. The Woodstock performance stunned everyone with Hendrix's version of "The Star Spangled Banner," that people talk about to this day. Later in 1969, Hendrix formed a new band, The Band of Gypsys, with drummer Buddy Miles and his old Army buddy, bassist Billy Cox. The Band of Gypsys gave a series of performances in New York City from January 31st, 1969 to January 1st, 1970. Material from these shows later appeared on compilation albums. Later in 1970, Jimi brought back drummer Mitch Mitchell, and along with Billy Cox, re-formed The Jimi Hendrix Experience. A few months later, Hendrix brought The Experience into the studio and recorded a few tracks for another two-album set, tentatively titled First Rays Of The New Rising Sun. A frantic tour schedule slowed down the recording process.

Tragically, on September 18th, 1970, Jimi Hendrix died from asphyxia while intoxicated with barbiturates and alcohol. Like so many of the rock elite that departed way too soon (see the "27" club profile), the musical world was in a state of shock. More than most other prominent musicians, Jimi Hendrix left behind numerous recorded material that was never released in his short lifetime.

The Four Musical Sides of Jimi Hendrix

Jimi Hendrix not only holds the title of Guitar God, but also was a multi-faceted musician. First of all, Hendrix would redefine the possibilities of what it meant to play rock guitar. His guitar approach started with him turning his Fender Stratocaster upside down to accommodate the fact that he was left handed. The Strat was his guitar of choice, but he would also use the Gibson SG, Flying V, and Les Paul. On rare occasions, Jimi played the Fender Duo-Sonic or the Fender Jazzmaster. To achieve distortion, Jimi utilized a Fuzz Face, a Univibe (to simulate a rotating speaker), and a wah-wah pedal. He was a master of creating feedback on a few of the guitar strings while playing lead on the other strings. This created the effect of sounding like two players at once. As for Jimi's electrifying stage presence, drummer Mitch Mitchell recalled his first time playing with him. Mitchell said, "It was on this first gig that we saw the whole other person, completely different from anything I'd seen before, even during rehearsals. I know he played really tasty guitar, but I didn't know about the showmanship that went with it. It was like, Whoosh! This man is really out-front. The showmanship-playing behind his head, with his teeth, was amazing. But even then it was obviously not just flashiness, he really did have the musicianship to go with it." #24

Secondly, Jimi Hendrix was a gifted composer and interpreter of other artist's songs. It started with his eclectic record collection. As far as the blues, Jimi had at least five Lightnin' Hopkins records, albums by Howlin' Wolf, Jimmy Reed, Albert King, etc. Perhaps his greatest influence was Bob Dylan, whom he has said inspired him to begin singing. Hendrix sought out albums of artists who covered Dylan such as The Byrds and Joan Baez. From the British scene he had albums by The Beatles, The Rolling Stones, The Animals, Eric Clapton, etc. His jazz collection featured Wes Montgomery, Jaki Byard, Charles Lloyd, and Roland Kirk. His soul collection included Otis Redding, The Temptations, and James Brown, etc. Rock recordings featured Elvis, Eddie Cochran, Little Richard, and Frank Zappa. He even loved Bill Cosby comedy albums.

From all of the above influences, Jimi just let them simmer in his mind without consciously trying to write in the style of any particular artist. Hendrix, when asked about where his songs came from, said "Just from me. It's like…where does it come from? I'm not sure…You see everything, experience everything, as you live….you see a lot of things if you have imagination…You go on into different moods, and when you write your mood comes through…The songs just come." #25

Thirdly, Jimi Hendrix was very effective as a singer and frontman. However, he was very insecure about the quality of his voice. Jimi frequently recorded his vocal parts while hidden behind screens set up in the studio. His vocals were not as virtuosic as his guitar playing, but they were personal and a big part of his unique sound design. Producer and manager Chas Chandler remembered, "We had a constant row in the studio about where his voice should be in the mix. He always wanted to have his voice buried and I always wanted to bring it forward. He was saying, 'I've got a terrible voice' but I'd say, "You may have a terrible voice, but you've got great rhythm in your voice." #26

Finally, Hendrix developed advanced concepts in his approach to recording and manipulating the studio to get the sounds that he heard in his head. Guitar great Joe Satriani weighed in on the recording of Hendrix's masterpiece Electric Ladyland saying, "It's definitely an experience to listen to. It was ahead of its time, and the production values were very much like The Beatles' Revolver album in the fact that they were really reaching, and there's an enthusiasm in their discoveries in the studio…All the whistles and noises that they did with tape speeds and stuff, and it doesn't sound like a Roland D-50 or a Fairlight synthesizer delivering something. It sounds kind of funky

"When I die, just keep playing the records."

– Jimi Hendrix

and unpredictable, and it's analog and it's complex."
#27 Also, Jimi Hendrix's studio perfectionism was legendary and at time frustrating. Mitch Mitchell and Hendrix recorded more than fifty takes of "Gypsy Eyes" over a period of three recording sessions before Jimi was happy.
Jimi Hendrix- Multi-faceted rock music legend

As a sideman, Hendrix contributed to nine albums and twenty-four singles by other artists. Among the albums Hendrix played on were; Don Covay and the Goodtimers in 1965, Get That Feeling by Curtis Knight in 1967, and Instant Groove by King Curtis in 1969. Just a few of the many singles Hendrix appeared on were; "Testify, Parts I and Part II" by The Isley Brothers, "Dancing All Around the World" in 1965 by Little Richard, and "Go Go Shoes" in 1965 by Lonnie Youngblood. The release of Valleys of Nepture (containing some unreleased tracks from 1967-1970) was often referred to as the lost studio album. A number of *authorized* compilation and live albums were released between 1968 and the time of Jimi's death. They included; the 1968 compilations Smash Hits and Electric Jimi Hendrix, the 1970 live albums Band of Gypsys and Woodstock: Music from the Original Soundtrack and More, and Historic Performances Recorded at the Monterey International Pop Festival. Many other authorized Hendrix *posthumous* compilations and live recording were also released. A few of these included; The Cry of Love, Rainbow Bridge, More Experience (a live album released in 1972 from the same live recordings from the Royal Albert Hall in London, February 1969), War Heroes (posthumous compilation of previously unused recordings released in 1972), Loose Ends in 1974, and many more. One album that showcased The Experience at their finest was Live at Winterland. It was recorded in 1968 over three nights of live shows at the Winterland Ballroom in San Francisco. This recording was released posthumously by Rykodisc in 1987. The complete posthumous discography of Jimi Hendrix (much of it archived material) included; 12 studio albums, 25 live albums, 27 compilation albums, 23 official bootlegs, and much more.

Jimi Hendrix was, without doubt, one of the greats in the history of rock music. He helped define the vocabulary of the electric guitar and was an electrifying performer and formidable songwriter. Hendrix synthesized the many genres of blues, American folk, R&B, jazz, 1950's rock 'n' roll, and more. His influence on guitar players can't be overstated. His overwhelming influence on the genres of hard rock, heavy metal, funk, and hip-hop are clear. Almost fifty years after his death, Hendrix remains as popular as ever! Jimi Hendrix and his music have received numerous awards since his death. They included: a star on the Hollywood Walk of Fame, a memorial stature in Seattle, a park named in his honor (also in Seattle), a United States postage stamp, and many Grammy awards, including a Lifetime Achievement Award in 1992. Jimi Hendrix and The Jimi Hendrix Experience were inducted into the Rock and Roll Hall of Fame in 1992.

The tradition of the blues didn't just influence the British rock musicians of the 1950's and 1960's. American musicians were also drawn to the rich blues traditions of the Mississippi Delta and Chicago. Most rock bands incorporated at least some traces of the blues while other artists were drawn to a more hardcore blues approach.

Canned Heat (1965-present) was a band started in Los Angeles with the singular purpose of playing the blues while adding a psychedelic element with lengthy guitar solos. This made them ideal for the popular and growing festival circuit in the 1960's. Initially formed by vocalist Bob Hite and guitarist Alan Wilson, Canned Heat added drummer Frank Cook, ex-Jerry Lee Lewis bassist Larry Taylor, and former Frank Zappa guitarist Henry Vestine. Drummer Adelfo "Fito" de la Parra replaced Cook on drums in 1967. The band took their name from an old blues tune "Canned Heat Blues" by blues guitarist Tommy Johnson. The term canned heat was a name for Sterno, a cooking fuel often consumed by alcoholics.

Canned Heat increased their fan base at an appearance at the Monterey Pop festival in 1967. Their debut album, Canned Heat, featured many obscure blues songs that were popular with blues purists. The band again raised its profile with a strong performance at the Woodstock Festival. Canned Heat's third album, Living the Blues, featured "Going Up the Country." It reached number eleven on the American charts. Today, it still receives frequent radio play on classic FM rock radio. In the 1970's, Canned Heat collaborated with blues greats John Lee Looker, Memphis Slim, and Clarence "Gatemouth" Brown. In 2009, Canned Heat played at the Heroes of Woodstock Tour that marked the fortieth anniversary of the festival. Canned Heat continues to tour with no members from the original lineup of 1965.

The Paul Butterfield Blues Band (1963-1987) was formed by blues vocalist/harmonica player Paul Butterfield in 1963. Butterfield had the advantage of being a native of Chicago where he met the legendary Muddy Waters, Howlin' Wolf, Little Walter, and other blues greats. They encouraged him and his band members by occasionally letting them sit in at their gigs. In the early 1960's, Butterfield met guitarist Elvin Bishop, bassist Jerome Arnold, and drummer Sam Lay (both Arnold and Lay from Howlin' Wolf's touring band). Soon, Butterfield added guitarist Mike Bloomfield to the band, giving him a powerful blues one-two punch. For their debut album by the same name, The Paul Butterfield Blues Band added organist Mark Naftalin. The album only went to number one hundred and twenty-three on the American charts. However, this was considered to be a success for a blues recording.

Butterfield's band became popular on the live concert and festival circuit with performances at the Fillmore West and East, The Monterey Pop Festival, and Woodstock. This was historically important because it gave rock musicians and their audiences a *pure connection to the blues*. Paul Butterfield proved that young white American musicians could play the blues authentically and not just replicate it. Butterfield and his band recorded several more successful albums and were very active until his death in 1987. Butterfield brought an original approach to his blues harp playing and as a band, they combined electric Chicago blues with a rock sensibility. Elvin Bishop and Mike Bloomfield went on to achieve great success as solo and session artists. The Paul Butterfield Blues Band was inducted into the Rock and Roll Hall of Fame in 2015.

Chapter Six: The British Invasion Continues and the American Answer

Discussion Question

How were 1960's and 1970's American rock bands and artists different than the British Invasion bands? Was it the social and political climate of America in the 1960's that defined American rock music? If so, how did this make the music different than British based rock music at the time?

"You have to get past the idea that music has to be one thing. To be alive in America is to hear all kinds of music constantly: radio, records, churches, cats on the street, everywhere music. And with records, the whole history of music is open to everyone who wants to hear it"

- Jerry Garcia

Part Two

Rock Finds New Directions

Chapter Seven:
Folk-Rock, Bob Dylan, and Singer/Songwriters

Before the first seeds of rock music generated legendary artists such as Chuck Berry, Little Richard, and Elvis Presley, the genre of folk music (see chapter one) was separate from rock in virtually every way possible. Folk music was created by (and for) purists who were generally not motivated by financial gain or commercial endeavors. Folk music was a language of and for the people. It represented a populist music genre and most folk songs came from a shared culture. They were not considered to be the property of composers who took ownership of their own songs. Some folk artists did want to take ownership of their original songs, but most folk music grew out of setting new lyrics to old (often really old) melodies. This well-established norm of folk music represented its own time period and different regions of the country.

The earliest rock music was a corporate phenomenon in the sense that someone, usually a professional songwriting team, wrote a song while someone else performed it. Record sales and live artist appearances enabled record companies, promoters, and managers to make a profit. Even in it's earliest stages, rock music was becoming a big, loud, and rebellious business. On the other hand, folk music represented more of a communal experience. Folk purists rejected rock and labeled it to be an unrefined product designed for mass appeal. Some rock fans viewed folk music to be dated, an ancient dinosaur, and a music genre from the past with no need for innovative instruments or even electricity.

The American folk singers of the 1940's and 1950's (see chapter one), including Woody Guthrie, Pete Seeger, and their shared band, The Almanac Singers, led a popular folk movement that revitalized the entire folk song tradition. They wrote new lyrics that stood up to labor-union issues and addressed civil rights injustice. This led to a rejuvenation of the folk music genre, which in turn motivated the folk artists of the early 1960's. In the 1960's, a new generation of college students were exposed to on-campus performances by **The Kingston Trio**, **The New Christy Minstrels**, **Peter, Paul, and Mary**, and **Bob Dylan**. Despite their folk sound, these artists, and others, were finding success on the pop charts. Folk music was now becoming both popular and profitable. A musical collision course was set for the creation of a new genre of music, **folk-rock**.

Bob Dylan would become an important musical catalyst, but not nearly the only one who evoked enormous musical change. Dylan and **The Byrds** both knocked down the door to pioneer the merger of folk and rock (Later, Dylan would do the same with country and rock). When the musical floodgates opened, many folk and rock artists had an epiphany. They could write meaningful lyrics, use rock rhythms, and continue composing with folk or rock harmonies and forms, to create exciting new music. Bob Dylan would quickly be recognized by The Beatles, Jimi Hendrix, the Rolling Stones, and countless others as the main pioneer in extending the lyrical boundaries of music. His lyrics inspired **The Lovin' Spoonful**, **Simon and Garfunkel**, **The Mamas and the Papas**, **Donovan**, **Buffalo Springfield**, and many more to create and provide messages that would hopefully change the world. By the end of the 1960's, **Crosby, Stills, Nash, and Young** would move folk-rock into the next decade. By that time, the folk-rock genre was so established within

"I like narrative story-telling as being part of a tradition, a folk tradition."

– Bruce Springsteen

popular music that almost no one would call it folk-rock anymore, it became part of rock's mainstream. Most importantly, Dylan pointed the way and led the movement that was responsible for elevating the intelligence and the meaningful lyrical content of rock music.

Bob Dylan (born Robert Zimmerman 1941-) grew up in the Mid-West in a small mining town in Minnesota. Importantly, he started out in a high school rock band and transitioned into an intense student of the folk tradition by listening to hundreds of folk artists. Additionally, some of Dylan's earliest influences were actor James Dean, country legend Hank Williams Sr., folksinger Odetta, and all of the rhythm and blues he could absorb from southern radio stations. In 1959, Dylan enrolled at the University of Minnesota, but spent most of his time in the local coffeehouses working out countless folksongs. At this time, he officially changed his name to Bob Dylan, after the poet Dylan Thomas. Dylan was inspired by the guitar playing and vocal phrasing of many blues musicians and soon added harmonica to accompany his songs by incorporating a harp rack worn around his neck. This allowed him to play guitar and harmonica simultaneously, and quickly switch between singing and playing harmonica. Dylan developed the persona of a rebel and a hobo, and his lyrics implied that he was looking at life as an outsider.

Dylan went to New York City in early 1961 to visit his hero Woody Guthrie, who was very sick and had been hospitalized. Guthrie was the perfect model for Dylan to imitate. Guthrie represented a skilled writer of Americana as he wrote his own lyrics for existing folk and country tunes, an approach Dylan would go on to utilize in developing his own songwriting career. The Greenwich Village folk music scene was a perfect fit for Dylan, although he struggled to adjust at first. Besides Guthrie, Dylan's strongest folk influences were Lead Belly and Pete Seeger. Dylan, much like Guthrie, Joan Baez, Peter, Paul, and Mary, and the Kingston Trio, sang about the issues that were facing American society at the time. David Dalton, an insightful Dylan biographer, noticed Guthrie's influence on Dylan when he said, "He is soon affecting an Okie accent. Bob begins honing his rusty barbed wire voice into a subtle and eccentric instrument and develops an aptitude for creating musical hybrids that synthesize American folk music-like singing spirituals to a hillbilly beat. In no time at all Dylan has *Woodyized* himself." #1

Dylan constantly reinvented his persona. He told journalists that he was an orphan (not true), and that he had travelled with a carnival since he was a little boy (also not true). This was all done in an effort to create a sense of mystery and intrigue. Bob Dylan also knew that his voice was limited, but at the same time, it possessed unique qualities that gave his songs an identity. Dylan explained, "What little voice I have-I don't really have a good voice. I do most of my stuff with phrasing. I think of myself as just having an edge when it comes to phrasing. I guess my voice sounds pretty close to a coyote or something." #2

Dylan continued to perform in the Village coffeehouses with a great sense of confidence. He impersonated many singers and characters and described himself as a song and dance man. Dylan was a continuation of American folklore itself as he delivered songs with the folk feel of the rural South. His repertoire at this time included some Woody Guthrie songs, some (country singer) Jimmy Rodgers songs, and a cross-section of American folk styles including country, blues, spirituals, and Appalachian ballads. When he tried to mix in with the Beatnik poets, he encountered many critics. One of those was not John Hammond, who saw his potential and signed him to a record deal at Columbia Records in 1961. This came shortly after Dylan had been turned down by all of the other folk record companies.

Dylan's 1962 debut album <u>Bob Dylan</u> featured traditional folk songs and two originals, one of which, "Song to Woody," was a tribute to Guthrie. The record did not sell very well, but Hammond had faith in Dylan and kept him signed to Columbia. The album revealed many of the classic Dylan qualities including his wide variety of regional music styles, his wit and humor, his intensity, and his personal style of phrasing and dialect.

Folk music is often associated with political and civil rights protest movements. Dylan continued that tradition. Dylan's second album, 1963's <u>The Freewheelin' Bob Dylan</u>, came out just as folk music was becoming involved with the volatile 1960's political movements. The album contained the anti-war song "Master's of War" and "A Hard Rain's a Gonna Fall," referring to nuclear weapons. The song "Blowin' in the Wind" would go on to become one of his most popular tunes and his most famous protest song. "Blowin in the Wind" was innovative in the sense that Dylan wrote a folk song in the dialect of pop music, thereby combining the two genres. He wasn't the first to do this (as seen in the success of groups like The Kingston Trio,) but this was a turning point in his musical direction. With a "hit" song, the often-reclusive Dylan was now becoming the charismatic performer-Bob Dylan.

"Blowin' in the Wind"
by Bob Dylan

"Blowin' in the Wind" was often revered as one of rock's all-time most influential songs and was an instant commercial success. Dylan originally composed the song in only a few minutes sitting in a café across the street from the Gaslight Club in Greenwich Village. He did not feel that it was anything special. Other folk artists agreed and were critical of the rhetorical lyrics. Dylan was soon performing a short two-verse version of the song in 1962, later adding a middle verse. Pete Seeger had identified the melody as similar to the old African-American spiritual "No More Auction Block." Seeger published "Blowin' in the Wind" in his magazine *Broadside*, a publication he founded that addressed political and social issues.

Critics felt there was no link between the relentless questions Dylan posed in the song. By the end of three verses, not one of the questions had been resolved, other than to say that the answer was blowing in the wind (an image so vague that it meant nothing). Others, like former Dylan business manager Roy Silver said, "'Blowin in the Wind' was the key to it all…that song made it all happen." #3 Dylan had discovered the power of deliberately being vague and found that a song like "Blowin' in the Wind" could be applied to almost any freedom issue. Like it or not, many folk musicians began to sing it and invent parodies of the lyrics.

The most commercially successful version of "Blowin' in the Wind" was not sung by Bob Dylan. Albert Grossman, who at the time managed both Dylan and Peter, Paul, and Mary, brought the tune to PP&M. The trio's version peaked at number two on the U.S. charts and sold more than 320,000 copies. "Blowin' in the Wind" represented a huge leap in Dylan's songwriting skill and some viewed it as the beginning of the end of Dylan's involvement with the folk movement.

Rock Hard Fact

Greenwich Village's Dave Van Ronk (aka "the Mayor of MacDougal Street") was an important folk musician, music store owner, and friend of Bob Dylan.

In 1963, Dylan added to his growing popularity by appearing onstage at the Monterey Folk Festival with Joan Baez. Dylan and Baez were also involved in a romantic relationship. That same year, Dylan was scheduled to appear on the *Ed Sullivan Show* but walked out when he was banned from performing his "Talkin' John Birch Paranoid Blues." Dylan was achieving mass popularity as his fame expanded from college crowds to pure folk audiences. With this success, Dylan became increasingly aware that many groups wanted to use him as spokesman for their cause, and he felt trapped and wary of organizations. He would never fully abandon folk music and fought to remain independent of other people's musical expectations and their political and societal agendas.

Folk lyrics began contributing a substance to rock music that had previously been based on simpler themes. Folk-rock still placed an emphasis on simple musical forms and harmonies, but the increased focus on meaningful lyrics would bring rock music to a new level of sophistication. As Dylan evolved as a songwriter and lyricist, he raised the level of lyrical expression in how outspoken, searching, truthful, and free a song could be. The whole world was taking notice of Dylan's messages about civil liberties and the human condition.

John Lennon had become profoundly aware of Dylan's song writing approach that centered on being a lyricist first, then picking up a guitar and letting the tune evolve. This changed the way many other prominent musicians approached rock songwriting. By 1965, John Lennon became tired of writing meaningless lyrics in the world's most famous pop-rock band. Dylan's influence was heard in Lennon's tune "Norwegian Wood" from The Beatles album Rubber Soul. Lennon wrote about an affair he had in his personal life. Lennon explained, "I was very careful and paranoid because I didn't want my wife Cyn, to know that there really was something going on. I was trying to be sophisticated in writing about an affair. But in such a smoke-screen way that you couldn't tell." #4

Dylan's third album, 1964's The Times They Are A Changin', focused on the important themes of civil rights and war protests. Dylan's ability to connect with the common person who has been victimized by society and those with greater wealth and power, was coming to the forefront. "The Lonesome Death of Hattie Carroll" told the story of a poor hotel barmaid who was killed by a wealthy man. Dylan made sure you knew that nobody seemed to care about her life. Dylan's fourth album, 1964's Another Side of Bob Dylan, contained love songs that focused on his personal life and relationships. Some of these tunes would soon be covered by The Byrds. However, with the release of his next recordings, Dylan was about to change rock music forever.

Released in 1965, Bringing it All Back Home was the beginning of a new genre of music, folk-rock. This and Dylan's next two records, Highway 61 Revisited and Blonde on Blonde, proved to be three of the most significant rock albums of all time. Bringing it All Back Home featured the new electric Dylan on side one while side two remained in the folk tradition, mostly solo and acoustic. Joan Baez remembered Dylan's songwriting for Bringing it All Back Home in the summer of 1964 in Woodstock when she said, "Most of the month or so that we were there, Bob stood at the typewriter in the corner of his room, drinking red wine and smoking and tapping away relentlessly for hours. And in the dead of night, he would wake up, grunt, grab a cigarette, and stumble over to the typewriter again." #5

Dating back to his high school days, Dylan's interest in rock was always there, but it was something he had put away as he immersed himself in the language of folk. He needed that time to develop all the different dimensions of his lyrical persona; the mystical geography of places and names, the cowboy and railroad references, his hillbilly jargon, and the fantasy of his extensive Americana obsession. Now, Dylan looked to transform folk music and his protest songs into full-blown electric tracks as he learned how to get the fusion of words and music to work together. Dylan's producer Tom Wilson helped in this process. Wilson first experimented by adding an electric backing track to Dylan's vocals and acoustic guitar parts on Dylan's acoustic recording of "House of the Risin' Sun" (much like Wilson did when he added electric instruments to Simon and Garfunkel's "Sound of Silence"). Meanwhile, The Byrds had great success combining folk and electric rock seamlessly when they recorded Dylan's "Mr. Tambourine Man."

Groundbreaking album Bringing it All Back Home
by Bob Dylan

Many rock critics and fans believe that Bringing it All Back Home was the most groundbreaking of all groundbreaking albums. After a Christmas break, Bob Dylan went in the studio in January 1965 with his producer Tom Wilson and a group of musicians. Their goal was to integrate rock 'n' roll with Dylan's storytelling abilities. Dylan chose the title Bringing it All Back Home because he wanted to bring rock music back to America where it all started in the 1950's with Elvis, Little Richard, and Chuck Berry. Dylan felt that rock music was American music that the British had borrowed. The Beatles had been pointing the way forward. However, in the summer of 1964, The Animals had a pop hit with the cover of the rhythm and blues tune "The House of the Risin Sun," which was a song they had learned from Dylan's debut album.

Dylan's musical transformation would see folk music's biggest star (Dylan himself) trade in his acoustic guitar for a solid body electric guitar. This was a sacrilegious act to many folk purists and Dylan's biggest fans. In the studio, Dylan would continue his habit (from his high school rock band) of not rehearsing, often not even discussing what he wanted to achieve. Kenny Rankin, one of the guitarists on the Bringing it All Back Home sessions said, "None of the songs that I played on were even counted off…he (Dylan) just started strummin' and we jumped in after about two or four bars. The resulting music was a joyous fusion of freeform verse and good-time rock 'n' roll. There's no overdubbing. There's no patching up. There's no splicing. What you heard is what we did." #6

The all-electric side one opened with "Subterranean Homesick Blues," then "She Belongs to Me," "Maggie's Farm," "Love Minus Zero/No Limit," "Outlaw Blues," "On the Road Again," concluding with "Bob Dylan's 115th Dream." The opener, "Subterranean Homesick Blues" was inspired by Chuck Berry's "Too Much Monkey Business." The song highlighted the growing difference between the establishment and growing counterculture of the 1960's. One of the song's most famous lyrics was "You don't need a weatherman to know which way the wind blows." This song became Dylan's first top forty hit. "Maggie's Farm" was a

> "I didn't listen to hard rock or heavy metal. I suppose I've always been influenced by folk music. I'm a big Bob Dylan fan."
>
> – Roger Glover of Deep Purple

declaration of Dylan's independence from the protest folk movement.

Dylan recorded side two with four long acoustic songs. Many thought this was a conciliatory gesture to his folk fans. It opened with "Mr. Tambourine Man," then "Gates of Eden," "It's Alright, Ma (I'm Only Bleeding)," and "It's All Over Now, Baby Blue." "Mr. Tambourine Man" was inspired by a tambourine owned by musician Bruce Langhorne. Dylan remembered that Langhorne had played a huge tambourine on a previous session and the image of him playing it stuck in his mind. On "Mr. Tambourine Man," Langhorne added a very musical countermelody guitar part. "Mr. Tambourine Man" would become one of Dylan's most influential and imitated songs.

Bob Dylan and his studio band proved that they had learned how to connect the lyrics and Dylan's messages to the energy of rock. The result was sometimes raw, but it had an urgency that made an instant impact on the rock world. When Bringing it All Back Home was released in March of 1965, it became Dylan's most successful record to date. It peaked at number six on the American charts and number one in England. While some folk purists were upset, many fans and music critics recognized Dylan's innovation. However, trouble was on the horizon when Dylan performed in the summer of 1965 at the Newport Folk Festival.

The Weekend that Rock Music Hi-jacked Folk Music

The Newport Folk Festival was one of the most potent symbols of the folk scene in America. Co-founded in the late 1960's by George Wein and Albert Grossman, the festival had been held in the seaside Rhode Island town of Newport since 1959. Dylan had gained new folk music fans when he first played the festival in 1963 with Joan Baez. However, after the March release of Bringing it All Back Home and just four days after recording "Like a Rolling Stone," Dylan took the stage on the night of July 25th to play his new electric music in front of the *folk music crowd.*

Tension had already mounted when earlier in the evening The Paul Butterfield Blues Band (with Dylan's new guitarist Mike Bloomfield) opened the night with a loud electric set. The folk festival sound system was not effective for projecting loud electric rock instruments to large crowds. Therefore, it was woefully ineffective for handling both Butterfield's and Dylan's bands. The headliner that evening (and for the whole festival) was Bob Dylan with his new backup band that featured Mike Bloomfield on guitar, Al Kooper on organ, Sam Lay on drums, Jerome Arnold on bass, and Barry Goldberg on piano. After getting their bearings onstage, Dylan and company blasted a blistering version of "Maggie's Farm," fresh from Dylan's electric side one of Bringing it All Back Home.

The legendary story was that Dylan and his band were both booed and cheered. Organist Al Kooper explained, "I had no idea why they were booing…. But whatever it was about, it wasn't about anything they were hearing." #7 Some of the booing was due to Dylan leaving the stage early, mostly because the festival director had cut the set short (this caused great animosity). Later in his career, Dylan would warn his backup band, The Hawks (later named The Band), to actually expect booing. Dylan's second song of the night, "Like a Rolling Stone" was followed by "It Takes a Lot to Laugh, It Takes a Train to Cry." After only fifteen minutes of music, the band's part of the performance was over. Dylan did go back on to perform a few acoustic songs including the popular "Mr. Tambourine Man," much to the delight of the folk crowd. However, after the performance was over, chaos ensued when fans were complaining that they could not hear Dylan clearly, due to the weak sound system. More chaos occurred backstage when some observers said that Pete Seeger wanted to cut the band's electrical power in protest, which he denied. Other observers said that the entire event evoked a mixed reaction due to Dylan's *abrupt change of musical direction.* One thing was clear. Dylan had made a musical statement and there would be no return.

Folk-rock was here to stay!

1965's Highway 61 Revisited was an allegory about American crimes. Dylan continued his great insight into American culture with songs about police brutality and shady characters who commit a host of crimes. This album featured a new producer, Bob Johnston, and Dylan was much more confident in the studio. Dylan had written "Like a Rolling Stone" (maybe his overall most popular song) after an exhausting tour of England. Disgusted with the music business and thinking about quitting, he wrote what he referred to as "twenty pages of vomit." Dylan pared it down to four verses and a chorus. His enthusiasm for creating music was restored.

"Like a Rolling Stone"
by Bob Dylan

"Like a Rolling Stone" was one of the most covered songs in rock music history having been played by The Rolling Stones (of course), David Bowie, Johnny Winter, Jimi Hendrix, The Grateful Dead, and My Chemical Romance, to name just a few.

The interpretation of "Like a Rolling Stone" is multi-faceted and complex. Dylan's lyrics were brilliant in the way they described the company that a young girl kept, and how those people seemed so enticing for an innocent girl. In analyzing the lyrics, the song was angry but the storyline revealed an element of sympathy for the girl. Dylan was genuinely concerned for how her new life was fulfilling her expectations. The line "when you got nothin', you got nothin' to lose" spoke to her new-found freedom. When Dylan sang, "You're invisible now, you got no secrets to conceal" it could be interpreted as a new beginning and not the end of the line for her.

The organ part, by guitarist/keyboardist/producer Al Kooper, was legendary because he wasn't supposed to be playing on the track at all. He just snuck in and played along with everyone and his gospel-like organ sound really added to the overall feeling of the tune. Kooper remembered, "If the other guy hadn't left the damn thing turned on, my career as an organ player would have ended right there. I figured out as best I could how to bluff my way through." #8 During the playback of the song, Dylan asked Tom Wilson to bring Kooper's organ part up in the mix.

In 1966, Dylan released a double album called Blonde on Blonde. Two of the most popular tunes were "Rainy Day Women #12 and #35" and "Just Like a Woman." Blonde on Blonde was a mix of rock 'n' roll, novelty songs, psychedelic country, Chicago blues, and ballads. Recorded in Nashville, Dylan hired some very good studio musicians for the sessions. Dylan was happy with the results and said, "The closest I ever got to the sound

---

Rock Hard Fact

Thirty-seven years after his infamous 1965 Newport Folk Festival performance, Bob Dylan returned to play the festival in 2002 wearing a wig and fake beard (in jest).

I hear in my mind was on individual bands in the Blonde on Blonde album. It's that thin, that wild mercury sound. It's metallic and bright gold, with whatever that conjures up. That's my particular sound." #9

The Bob Dylan library includes over 32 studio albums, 58 singles, 11 live albums, countless bootleg and reissue recordings, more that 30 compilation albums, 3 home videos, volumes of bibliographies, and a filmography all spanning more than a fifty-year career. No American musician has been the subject of more articles and books. The public fascination with the Dylan mystic and musical influence has never diminished. A creative and skilled poet, insightful social critic, torch-bearer of the American folk tradition, genius songwriter, and creator of both folk-rock and country-rock (see chapter nine), Bob Dylan may be the most significant figure in rock history and perhaps all of American music history! Bob Dylan was inducted into the Rock and Roll Hall of Fame in 1988.

Folk Rock

Peter, Paul, and Mary (1961-1970) (1978-2009) had a formidable career that spanned five decades. Their success dates back to the folk revival of the early 1960's and the influence of the Almanac Singers and The Weavers. The band formed when Mary Travers met Peter Yarrow and Paul Stookey. They developed an identifiable three-part vocal sound while rehearsing their early material. Peter, Paul, and Mary (PP&M) took that sound to the emerging folk scene in Greenwich Village and began to attract attention. Their 1962 self-titled debut album Peter, Paul, and Mary went to number one on the American charts. Their entire recording output included over thirty studio, compilation, and live albums. Their most popular song was "Leaving on a Jet Plane," and was written by John Denver. Also popular was "Puff, the Magic Dragon," and covers of "If I Had a Hammer," and "Blowin in the Wind."

By 1964, Peter, Paul, and Mary were directly competing with The Beatles and other British Invasion bands. The trio straddled the line between appealing to liberals and antiwar activists and also entertaining families with non-political songs. Their prolific songwriting was the key to their longevity, and they were one of the only folk-rock groups whose personnel remained intact throughout their career. However, by the early 1980's no major labels were interested in 1960's folk-rock groups. Therefore, PP&M self-produced and released a live reunion album titled Such Is Love on their own label. Finally, in 1992 Warner Brothers Records signed the trio and their comeback was underway. Their legacy was their unique blend of tenor (Peter), baritone (Paul), and alto (Mary) vocal harmonies. Peter, Paul, and Mary were important folk artists in their own right, but they also provided a significant bridge between the pure folk tradition and the evolving folk-rock genre of the 1960's.

The Byrds (1964-1973) (1989-1991) (2000) were a folk-rock group that achieved great popularity in the mid-1960's on a level close to The Beatles, The Rolling Stones, and The Beach Boys. Their founder, Jim McGuinn (he later changed his first name to Roger,) described The Byrds as "Bob Dylan meets The Beatles." They possessed a skillful combination of folk-rock elements that melded with psychedelic rock and (later) country-rock styles. The Byrds formed in 1964 in Los Angeles, California when folk circuit veteran vocalist/guitarist Roger McGuinn met ex-New Christy Minstrels vocalist/guitarist Gene Clark, and ex-Les Baxter's Balladeers vocalist/guitarist David Crosby. They added bluegrass influenced bassist Chris Hillman and drummer Michael Clarke. McGuinn had logged many coffeehouse folk gigs playing Beatles covers on acoustic guitar. However, when he discovered the twelve-string Rickenbacker electric guitar, he took a big step toward what would become The Byrds' unique sound.

Initially The Byrds argued about whether or not to record Bob Dylan's "Mr. Tambourine Man." But when they recorded their debut album in April of 1965, they ironically decided to call it Mr. Tambourine Man. Their version of Dylan's tune went to number one worldwide and helped to further unveil the emerging genre of folk-rock music. Dylan had released Bringing It All Back Home only one month earlier. Between the two of these recordings, folk-rock was born.

Groundbreaking album
Mr. Tambourine Man
by The Byrds

Bob Dylan provided the concept of *meaning* in rock lyrics but The Byrds provided the *sound* when they merged lyrics with the new psychedelic rock sound and a pop-rock sensibility. The music press first coined the term folk-rock when describing The Byrds album Mr. Tambourine Man. This recording featured four of Bob Dylan's songs and was generally recognized as a combination of folk material performed with a rock 'n' roll feeling.

Side one opened with "Mr. Tambourine Man," then "I'll Feel a Whole Lot Better," which served to define The Byrds' sound by combining McGuinn's twelve-string guitar and the distinctive vocal harmonies of the group. The album continued with "Spanish Harlem Incident," "You Won't Have to Cry," "Here Without You," and "The Bells of Rhymney." "Mr. Tambourine Man" created a wall of sound featuring smooth vocal harmonies that soared over biting guitar chords. The Byrds also added depth with the thick piano sound of Leon Russell. "Mr. Tambourine Man" (the song) had a quirky quality, very different than the original Dylan recording. The Byrds' characteristic San Francisco psychedelic sound connected the track to the strong 1960's counter-culture which became another dimension of the folk-rock genre.

Side two opened with "All I Really Want to Do," then "I Knew I'd Want You," "It's No Use," "Don't Doubt Yourself, Babe," "Chimes of Freedom," and "We'll Meet Again." The Byrds were reluctant to release another Dylan song but Columbia Records was insistent, smelling another hit. They brought in additional personnel for "Mr. Tambourine Man" and the Dylan penned "All I Really Want To Do" including drummer Hal Blaine, bassist Larry Knechtel, and guitarist Jerry Cole. Mr. Tambourine Man also introduced the songwriting skills of Gene Clark with his compositions' "Feel a Whole Lot Better" and "I Knew I'd Want You."

The Byrds Mr. Tambourine Man was a major step in defining folk-rock and psychedelic music. The Byrds' and Dylan's strong influence can be heard in the sound of numerous modern bands including; Wilco, REM, The Smiths, Tom Petty and The Heartbreakers, and recordings by Simon and Garfunkel, Jefferson Airplane, The Turtles, The Mamas and the Papas, and many others.

> "We (The Byrds) considered ourselves folk singers even when we strapped on electric instruments and dabbled in different things."
>
> – Roger McGuinn

1966's Turn! Turn! Turn! was less successful. However, The Byrds earned their second number one hit with the title track "Turn! Turn! Turn!" which was a cover of Pete Seeger's classic folk tune. By having two number one rock hits of folk tunes, The Byrds became even more established as the complete folk-rock band (considering Dylan to be a solo artist with a backup band). Pete Seeger had originally derived "Turn! Turn! Turn!" from a biblical verse, and now The Byrds had come along to interpret it as a rock song. Soon, trouble ensued when some members of The Byrds did not embrace Gene Clark's songs. Further complicating matters was Gene Clarke's fear of flying, which was necessary for the band to tour. These matters prompted Clark to quit the band. However, before Clark left, he did co-write another Byrds classic titled "Eight Miles High." Now a four-piece band, The Byrds continued by releasing 1966's Fifth Dimension that included "Eight Miles High." The album reached number twenty-four on the American charts and number twenty-seven in Britain. It showcased the characteristics of what would be called "psychedelic or acid rock," and did so without the help of any of Bob Dylan's songs.

"Eight Miles High"
by Gene Clark, Jim McGuinn, and David Crosby

"Eight Miles High" was one of rock's first tunes to be banned because it contained drug references. This came after it initially peaked at number fourteen on the U.S. charts. This success followed when many radio stations did not comply with the ban. Roger McGuinn's twelve-string guitar solo was influenced by the improvisational genius of jazz saxophonist John Coltrane, in particular his composition "India." McGuinn didn't actually play sitar on the song but you can hear the influence of a sitar drone. Chris Hillman added a strong and hypnotic bassline.

Equally influential to the compositional process and performance approach of McGuinn, was the Indian master sitarist Ravi Shankar. Although McGuinn denied it, "Eight Miles High" was responsible for helping to establish the subgenre of **raga rock**. However, David Crosby (like McGuinn) disliked the term raga rock. The experimental character of the song placed The Byrds at the center of the budding psychedelic movement. "Eight Miles High" was covered extensively, most notably by Crosby, Stills, Nash, and Young on their 2000 reunion tour. On their cover of the song, Neil Young performed a version of McGuinn's legendary guitar solo while CSN sang the song's three-part harmonies.

1967's Younger Than Yesterday opened with the song "So You Want to Be a Rock 'n' Roll Star." This song found The Byrds writing cynical lyrics addressing the hype of the suddenly famous band, The Monkees, and their hit TV show. This album also displayed bassist Chris Hillman and David Crosby's emergence as talented songwriters. However, it was clear that McGuinn was in charge. That created tension, resulting in Crosby being fired. 1968's The Notorious Byrd Brothers went to number eighty-nine on the American charts. The lead single was the Carole King and Gerry Goffin song "Goin Back." This album moved The Byrds further into experimental psychedelia by continuing to mix folk-rock, jazz, and some country music elements together. During the recording sessions for The Notorious Byrd Brothers, drummer Michael Clarke quite the band citing artistic differences. Session drumming greats Jim Gordon and Hal Blaine helped to complete the recording.

At this point, The Byrds were only a duo with just McGuinn and Hillman remaining. They recruited drummer Kevin Kelly and guitarist/vocalist Gram Parsons (although he was initially hired to play keyboards he soon went to guitar) who immediately sought to infuse his country music background in The Byrds' approach. Tensions arose quickly between McGuinn and Parsons but Parsons' brilliant musicianship led them to complete Sweetheart of the Rodeo in 1968. This new identity of The Byrds embraced country songs and ballads. It disappointed many Byrds fans, but McGuinn knew that their fan base was diminishing and decided to follow Parsons' lead. Although it was a radical departure for a Byrds' album, it was a profoundly influential country-rock album. By pre-dating Bob Dylan's Nashville Skyline by six months, Sweetheart of the Rodeo was *the first* country-rock album ever made. Returning to a successful formula, the album did feature two Dylan covers, "You Ain't Goin Nowhere" and "Nothing Was Delivered." This album also served as a blueprint for Parsons and Hillman to later form The Flying Burrito Brothers the following year (see chapter nine-country-rock).

After Gram Parsons left The Byrds, McGuinn and Hillman added session guitarist Clarence White, but Hillman soon left to join Parsons and The Flying Burrito Brothers. Kevin Kelly was replaced by drummer Gene Parsons (no relation to Gram) and this new Byrds' lineup recorded Dr. Byrds & Mr. Hyde and Ballad of Easy Rider in 1969. The Byrds continued with 1970's Untitled, and 1971's Byrdmaniax and Farther Along. However, these offerings did not chart well.

The original Byrds' lineup reunited hoping to recapture the old magic by recording the 1973 album Byrds. It yielded the marginally successful single "Full Circle" and a cover of Neil Young's "About To Rain." The Byrds officially called it quits in 1973. Individual members have since performed together and the band did reunite again for their inauguration into the Rock and Roll Hall of Fame in 1991. The music of The Byrds was innovative, intelligent, and inspirational. They were invaluable in the creation of the folk-rock genre while managing to contribute more innovations to the psychedelic and country-rock genres.

The Turtles (1965-1970) were an American folk-rock group that started as a surf-rock band called The Crossfires. They formed in Los Angeles when vocalists Mark Volman and Howard Kaylan added drummer Don Murray, guitarists Jim Tucker and Al Nichol, and bassist Chuck Portz. Out of Control was released in 1963 as the only Crossfires album. They soon changed their name to The Turtles and moved into the folk-rock genre.

1965's It Ain't Me Babe was The Turtles debut album. Like The Byrds, a Bob Dylan cover ("It Ain't Me Babe") became the title track for the record, and would become a hit, reaching number eight on the U.S. charts. In 1966, The Turtles recorded You Baby, which revealed their growth as songwriters. 1967's Happy Together became their most successful album, peaking at number twenty-five in America. Their signature hit "Happy Together," knocked The Beatles "Penny Lane" out of the top spot on the U.S. charts.

The Turtles released The Turtles Present the Battle of the Bands in 1968 and Turtle Soup in 1969. Their last recording was 1970's Wooden Head. The Turtles broke up in 1970 after making a significant contribution to the folk-rock genre in their short six-year career. After The Turtles called it quits, Volman and Kaylan joined Frank Zappa's Mothers of Invention. They took on the names of Flo & Eddie, recording with The Mothers, and appearing in Frank Zappa's 1971 film *200 Motels*. Later, Flo & Eddie recorded many albums on their own. From 2010 through 2015, The Turtles featuring Flo & Eddie, toured America as part of the Happy Together: 25th Anniversary Tour along with other "oldies" acts.

The Mamas & the Papas (1965-1968) grew out of the jug band The Mugwumps who had an unsuccessful career in the early 1960's New York folk scene. The Mugwumps moved to Los Angeles where two of the ex-members, vocalist Cass Elliot and singer/songwriter Dennis Doherty, joined forces with the couple John and Michelle Phillips to form The Mamas and the Papas. Phillips, Phillips and Doherty were all songwriters and the group's sound was based on their strong vocal harmonies arranged by John Phillips. The Mamas and the Papas recorded five studio albums and released seventeen singles over their short four-year career. Their 1966 debut album If You Can Believe Your Eyes and Ears was an instant success when it soared to number one on the U.S. charts. The album featured four singles, with "Monday, Monday" becoming the band's only number one hit.

"Monday, Monday"
by John Phillips

John Phillips was pressured by band member Denny Doherty to come up with some new material for the band. Overnight, he wrote "Monday, Monday" in a short fifteen-minutes. Doherty, who sang lead vocals on the tune, didn't think it would amount to much, but it soon went straight to the top of the charts. Phillips explained to the band that it was just a song about the working man and how people hated Monday since it's the beginning of the work week.

The Mamas and the Papas called on Lou Adler, who produced Carole King's Tapestry, to handle the production. Adler summoned the famous Los Angeles Wrecking Crew group of studio musicians to record "Monday, Monday." Larry Knechtel played keyboards, Joe Osborn added bass, and Hal Blaine played drums on the tune. P.F. Sloan (borrowed from The Grass Roots) added guitar and background vocals. Sloan's contributions were important. He gave Hal Blaine some ideas for the drum part, added a tremolo effect to his own guitar sound, and overdubbed multiple guitar parts.

1966's album, The Mamas & the Papas, reached number four on the U.S. charts, thus extending the band's success. However, internal personal issues resulted in the firing of Michelle Phillips. Vocalist Jill Gibson was hired to replace her (Gibson and Phillips both appeared on The Mamas and the Papas). Phillips was soon reinstated, and the band completed an East Coast tour. 1967's The Mamas & the Papas Deliver was released, but more infighting revealed tension between John Phillips and Cass Elliot. They reconciled and recorded 1968's The Papas & The Mamas. Elliot was featured on the tune "Dream a Little Dream of Me," but it was released against John Phillips wishes. By the end of 1968, it appeared the band was through. Elliot, John Phillips, and Doherty each focused on making solo records but The Mamas and the Papas were legally bound to record one more album. This resulted in 1971's People Like Us that achieved only marginal success and was the official end of the band. After a short, but successful career, Cass Elliot died of heart failure in 1974. John Phillips went on to release solo albums, but years of drug abuse led to his early death in 2001. Michelle Phillips went on to have a productive acting career and released one solo album. Michelle and John Phillips' daughter Chynna Phillips became part of the modern band Wilson Phillips (with Brian Wilson's daughters Carnie and Wendy consisting of the rest of the vocal trio). Denny Doherty, after a successful acting career, died in 2007. Having sold forty million albums worldwide, The Mamas and the Papas created unique vocal harmonies and many commercially appealing folk-rock songs. The Mamas and The Papas were inducted into the Rock and Roll Hall of Fame in 1998.

The Lovin' Spoonful (1965-1969) (1979) (1991-present) was formed by vocalist/guitarist/keyboardist John Sebastian, guitarist/vocalist Zale Yanovsky, bassist Steve Boone, and drummer Joe Butler. The band has its roots in the early 1960's folk-rock scene in Greenwich Village, New York. Sebastian and Yanovsky had been in The Mugwumps with vocalist Cass Elliot and singer/songwriter Denny Doherty (half of the future Mamas and The Papas).

The Lovin' Spoonful's 1965 debut album, Do You Believe in Magic, featured the top ten hits "Do You Believe in Magic" and "Did You Ever Have to Make Up Your Mind?" Many of the songs from Do You Believe in Magic were modern versions of lesser known blues songs. The Lovin' Spoonful was adamant about doing all of the playing on their records without the help of any studio musicians. They also incorporated many unusual instruments.

Over time, Sebastian became the band's main composer, drawing from many musical sources including the blues, folk music, and jug bands such as The Kweskin Jug Band. 1966's Daydream reached number ten in America on the heels of Sebastian's refined songwriting skills. The producers of the television show *The Monkees* planned to use The Lovin' Spoonful for the show, but the band was dropped over song publishing issues. 1966 was a busy year for the band yielding What's Up Tiger Lily?, a soundtrack for the Woody Allen movie of the same name. Also in 1966, Hums of the Lovin' Spoonful rose to number fourteen on the U.S. charts on the strength of four hit singles. This included "Summer in the City," a number one hit in America.

"Summer in the City"
by John Sebastian, Mark Sebastian, and Steve Boone

"Summer in the City" was written about the feeling of being in the inner-city when its hot and noisy. According to The Lovin' Spoonful, the noise and the heat made the city a sometimes less than desirable environment. However, it still remained the place to be, particularly at night. Given The Lovin' Spoonful's background, the song most likely referred to New York City. Considering the band's usual image of singing about good times, the edgy lyrics of "Summer in the City" were a little out of character. John Sebastian usually wrote most of the band's music. However, "Summer in the City" was a collaboration between himself, bassist Steve Boone, and Sebastian's brother (non-band member) Mark Sebastian.

Musically, "Summer in the City" began with an organ riff that progressed to verses in a minor key. Sebastian sang about images that described the relief of the setting sun when temperatures became more tolerable and the nighttime emerged. A catchy guitar riff with an organ background followed. Honking car horns and jackhammer sound effects created an aural image of the city. Cover versions of the song included a 1994 version by singer Joe Cocker and a 2000 version by singer Joe Jackson. "Summer in the City" achieved great success in-

> "The models for me were more the folk-rock singers of the 60's and 70's."
>
> – Carly Simon

ternationally, charting in the top ten in Australia, Canada, Norway, Britain, and other countries.

In 1967, Sebastian wrote an album of original music called You're A Big Boy Now, for the Francis Ford Coppola film of the same name. Yanovsky left the band after recording the soundtrack and was replaced by ex-Modern Folk Quartet keyboardist/arranger Jerry Yester. With their commercial appeal dwindling, The Lovin' Spoonful released their final studio album Revelation: Revolution '69 in 1969. The Lovin' Spoonful's contributions to folk-rock put a lighthearted spin on the entire genre. Their hit songs were about daydreams ("Daydream"), the raw power of rock 'n' roll ("Do You Believe in Magic"), and light subject matters such as "Rain on the Roof." The current lineup of The Lovin' Spoonful features Butler, Boone, and Yester. John Sebastian went on to have a successful solo career and often appears with the eclectic rock band NRBQ and The J-Band. The Lovin' Spoonful was inducted into the Rock and Roll Hall of Fame in 2000.

The Grass Roots (1965-present) are an American folk-rock band that began as a project by Los Angeles songwriters P.F. Sloan and Steve Barri. Together they wrote and recorded the song "Where Were You When I Needed You," with members of The Wrecking Crew, and sent it to a radio station that gave it airplay. The problem was that they had no band and no name, so they added vocalist Willie Fulton and became The Grass Roots. They recorded their debut album Where Were You When I Needed You in 1966. For 1967's Let's Live for Today, vocalist/bassist Rob Grill, keyboardist/guitarist Warren Entner, drummer Rick Coonce, and vocalist/guitarist Creed Bratton were brought in to complete the band. Sloan and Barri continued to write songs for the band and handled production duties. In 1968, The Grass Roots released Feelings and Golden Grass, which yielded their biggest hit, "Midnight Confessions." Over the years, they have endured numerous lineup changes but have gone on to record fourteen more studio albums, many of which produced hit songs. The Grass Roots are still active today.

Fairport Convention (1967-1979) (1985-present) is an English folk-rock band that formed in 1967. They began when bassist Ashley Hutchings, guitarists Richard Thompson and Simon Nicol, drummer Martin Lamble, and vocalist Julie Dyble became regulars on the London club scene. Vocalist Iain Matthews joined for their debut Fairport Convention album in 1968. The album faired poorly, and Dyble left and vocalist Sandy Denny joined for their What We Did on Our Holidays album. Denny contributed a distinctive voice (she also sang the duet "The Battle of Evermore," with Robert Plant on Led Zepellin IV). After 1969's Unhalfbricking, tragedy struck when drummer Martin Lamble was killed when the band's tour bus crashed. The band's future became uncertain.

In 1969, Fairport Convention regrouped with drummer Dave Mattacks and violinist Dave Swarbrick to release their influential album Liege & Lief. This record was a major catalyst in starting the English folk-rock movement in the late 1960's and would provide a distinctive English sound in the emerging folk-rock movement. Fairport Convention's musical approach integrated a great deal of traditional **English folk music**. They often created complex compositions that were versions of Irish reels and English jigs, both traditional folk-dance styles. Fairport Convention's music was very different from American folk rock. They relied heavily on Thompson's folk songwriting approach while the band utilized electric instruments.

Fairport's influence can be heard in bands like Jethro Tull, Steeleye Span, and Pentangle. Original member Richard Thompson has gone on to become a legendary singer and songwriter, original bassist Ashley Hutchings went on to create Steeleye Span. Later, bassist David Pegg became a member of Jethro Tull. Fairport Convention has released a formidable twenty-eight studio albums and have employed over twenty-five band members over a period of six decades. Their latest, 2017's 50:50@50, featured the lineup of bassist David Pegg, violinist/keyboardist Ric Sanders, violinist/vocalist Chris Leslie, drummer Gerry Conway, and original member, lead vocalist/guitarist Simon Nicol.

Simon and Garfunkel (1957-1970) (reunions from 1975 to 2010) are the most successful folk-rock duo in American music history. The two met when they were eleven year-old elementary schoolmates in Queens, New York. When they were both fifteen-years old, they landed a recording contract with Sid Prosen's independent label, Big Records. In 1957, Simon and Garfunkel, under the name Tom and Jerry, learned to harmonize and compose original material together. They achieved some minor success with "Hey Schoolgirl," a song that imitated their idols, The Everly Brothers. "Hey Schoolgirl" cost fifteen dollars to record and sold around 150,000 copies. Simon briefly wrote songs with Carole King before she teamed up with Gerry Goffin. After high school, Simon attended Queens College, earning a degree in English literature. Meanwhile, Garfunkel majored in architecture at Columbia University and joined the all-male a cappella group on campus, the Columbia Kingsmen.

After graduating in 1963, Simon joined Garfunkel (still at Columbia) to perform again as a duo. They performed three new originals "He Was My Brother," "Sparrow," and "The Sounds of Silence." That song quickly received the attention of Columbia Records producer Tom Wilson, who had worked with Bob Dylan. Simon convinced Wilson to record "The Sounds of Silence," and the duo was soon signed to Columbia.

In 1964, they recorded Wednesday Morning, 3 A.M., a soft and traditional folk-rock album that included their first major hit which was an acoustic version of "The Sounds of Silence." The album flopped, and a depressed Simon left to travel in Europe. While in England, Simon discovered the folk music of Martin Carthy and his version of "Scarborough Fair." Simon and Garfunkel would later adapt and record the song for the album Parsley, Sage, Rosemary and Thyme. Meanwhile, with Paul Simon in England, producer Tom Wilson transformed "The Sounds of Silence" into "The Sound of Silence" by overdubbing electric guitar, bass, and drums. These additions made "The Sound of Silence" into a number one hit on the U.S. charts.

"The Sound of Silence"
by Paul Simon

The history of "The Sound of Silence" is confusing, since the song started as the original acoustic version on Wednesday Morning 3 A.M. and later (as mentioned above) was transformed from "The Sounds of Silence" to become a number one hit with full band accompaniment called "The Sound of Silence." Both Simon and Garfunkel were not informed of its ambitious remixing until after its release. Normally, this would create major issues with recording artists, but when the song went to number one, a successful career was launched. The duo was sitting in Simon's car when a radio DJ came on the air and announced that the song had gone to number one! Simon and Garfunkel were in disbelief.

Some speculated that "The Sound of Silence" was about the John F. Kennedy assassination, since it was released only three months after his death. But Simon has stated many times that he wrote the song prior to the tragic event. Simon explained, "I was able to sit by myself and play (acoustic guitar) and dream. And I was always happy doing that. I used to go off in the bathroom, because the bathroom had tiles, so it was a slight echo chamber. I'd turn on the faucet so that water would run (I like that sound, it's very soothing to me) and I'd play. In the dark. 'Hello darkness, my old friend/I've come to talk with you again'." #10 Garfunkel has said the song represented people's inability to communicate with each other, especially emotionally.

With a number one hit under their belt, and Simon back in New York, the duo re-formed under the name Simon and Garfunkel. They quickly recorded their second album, 1966's Sounds of Silence. Almost all of the album's songs were written by Simon while he was in London, including the song "I Am a Rock." Sounds of Silence would go on to reach number twenty-one in America and number thirteen in Britain. The influence of Bob Dylan was clear in Simon's early songwriting. Simon seemed to feel competitive with Dylan for much of his career. For 1966's Parsley, Sage, Rosemary, and Thyme, the perfectionist duo spent three months in the studio creating a layered, and highly produced album. The single "Scarborough Fair/Canticle" (a traditional English ballad) went to number nine in England and number eleven in the U.S.

In 1967, the Mike Nichols's film *The Graduate* featured four Simon and Garfunkel songs (including "Mrs. Robinson"), and four more from the Parsley, Sage, Rosemary, and Thyme album. 1968's Bookends followed and reached number one on both sides of the Atlantic. The Wrecking Crew, including session drummer Hal Blaine, bassist Joe Osborn, and keyboardist Larry Knechtel, were called on to provide the rhythm section tracks.

Bookends and The Graduate soundtrack catapulted Simon and Garfunkel to stardom making them the biggest rock duo in the industry. However, both musicians aggressively pursued other music and acting projects and there were signs of growing tension between them. 1970's Bridge over Troubled Water would be their fifth and final studio album. It shot to number one in virtually every country worldwide and was often considered to be their crown jewel.

Groundbreaking album
Bridge over Troubled Water
by Simon and Garfunkel

Bridge over Troubled Water was a unified musical statement that fused gospel, R&B, rock, pop, jazz, and even some world music sensibilities. Side one opened with "Bridge over Troubled Water," then "El Condor Pasa (If I Could)," "Cecilia," "Keep the Customer Satisfied," and "So Long, Frank Lloyd Wright." On the title track, Simon asked session piano player Larry Knechtel to create a gospel sound while Simon added another verse of lyrics because the song seemed to be too short. Although the track sounded a little like The Beatles "Let It Be," it was actually more inspired by the vocal style that Phil Spector achieved with The Righteous Brothers recording of "Old Man River."

Side two opened with "The Boxer," then "Baby Driver," "The Only Living Boy in New York," "Why Don't You Write Me," "Bye, Bye Love," and "Song for the Asking." "The Boxer" was difficult to record, taking over one hundred hours of studio time. It was recorded at multiple locations including Columbia studios in Nashville and at St. Paul's Chapel in New York City. The song's lyrics spoke from the point of view of a singer who was describing his struggle to overcome poverty and loneliness in New York City. The final verse shifted the viewpoint to the third-person perspective of a boxer. "The Boxer" was released as the lead single from the album and reached number seven on the U.S. charts.

Bridge over Troubled Water was one of the most culturally relevant albums in American music history. The album embodied musical styles and rhythms that were unique to FM radio and pop music. It served to close out the 1960's in America. The album won multiple Grammy Awards including: Album of the Year and Best Engineered Recording. The title track won Song of the Year and Instrumental Arrangement of the Year as well.

After the recording of Bridge over Troubled Water, Simon and Garfunkel officially disbanded and headed in different directions. Garfunkel pursued an acting role in the Mike Nichols film, *Carnal Knowledge* and Simon studied music theory and songwriting at a one-week course at New York University. However, over the next thirty years, they would not lead completely separate lives. During this time they performed together on various occasions. Their first reunion was a benefit concert in 1972. In 1974 and 1975, they were present at John Lennon and Harry Nilsson recording sessions. Of special note, they reunited to play a free concert on the Great Lawn in Central Park, New York on September 19th, 1981 which was documented on their seminal 1982 release, The Concert in Central Park.

Fans have always held onto hope for a more permanent reunion, but Simon and Garfunkel have only reunited sporadically and usually only for special musical events. However, their 2003 reunion was captured on a DVD titled Old Friends that featured performances of many of the songs discussed here. Amid the various reunions, both have gone on to have successful solo careers (see singer/songwriter section in this chapter). Over their five-album duo career, Simon and Garfunkel matured both lyrically and musically to redefine the folk-rock genre. Simon and Garfunkel were inducted into the Rock and Roll Hall of Fame in 1990.

Buffalo Springfield (1966-1968) (2010-2012) began in 1966 when ex-Mynah Birds vocalist/guitarist Neil Young and bassist Bruce Palmer moved from Canada to Los Angeles. They were in search of Young's friend, ex-The Company vocalist/guitarist Stephen Stills. Musical fate intervened when, while stuck in a traffic jam, Stills (who had just failed an audition to join The Monkees) was driving with guitarist/vocalist Richie Furay. They spotted Young and Palmer driving a hearse with Ontario license plates down L.A.'s Sunset Boulevard. The four got together and soon added drummer Dewey Martin and Buffalo Springfield was formed. Their 1966 self-titled Buffalo Springfield featured the hit "For What It's Worth."

> **Rock Hard Fact**
>
> At the time, Simon and Garfunkel's free concert in Central Park was one the largest crowds to ever attend a live concert with an estimated 500,000 people.

"For What It's Worth (Stop, Hey What's That Sound)"
by Stephen Stills

Stephen Stills was inspired to write this protest anthem when counter-culture tensions erupted in Los Angeles in the mid-1960's. The result of this social unrest was referred to as the Sunset Strip (or The Hippie) Riots. Los Angeles residents became angry when crowds of club goers gathered late at night after attending music venues along the Sunset Strip. These complaints inspired the Sunset Strip curfews to be put in place. Those curfews incited demonstrations, which resulted in the subsequent riots. Among the hundreds of protesters were future actors Peter Fonda and Jack Nicholson.

After recording "For What It's Worth," Stills presented the song to Atlantic Records head Ahmet Ertegun, who signed Buffalo Springfield to a deal. The song's title emanated from Stills telling Ertegun that "I have this song here, for what it's worth, if you want it." The title was shortened to "For What It's Worth" and the subtitle of "Stop, Hey What's That Sound" was added from the lyric line. "For What It's Worth" has been covered and sampled many times. Public Enemy has sampled the tune for their 1998 song "He Got Game," that also featured Stephen Stills. "For What It's Worth" reached number seven on the U.S. charts.

___

Trouble ensued for Buffalo Springfield in 1969 when bassist Bruce Palmer was deported to Canada and Neil Young briefly quit the band. David Crosby of the Byrds filled in for Young at a Buffalo Springfield appearance at the 1967 Monterey Pop festival. 1967's Buffalo Springfield Again, often considered their best work, was more of a collection of solo compositions rather than a unified band album. Young contributed "Broken Arrow" and "Expecting to Fly," while Stills wrote "Rock 'n' Roll Woman" and "Bluebird." Buffalo Springfield's third strong songwriter, Richie Furay, contributed "A Child's Claim to Fame" and "Good Time Boy."

Bruce Palmer was replaced by vocalist/bassist Jim Messina. 1968's Last Time Around would be Buffalo Springfield's last recording. It included the Neil Young song "I Am a Child." In the spring of 1968, Buffalo Springfield disbanded. They reunited for six concerts in Oakland, California in 2011 and more concert dates followed. This version of the band included Young, Stills, Furay, and multi-instrumentalist Joe Vitale. While they were together for only a few years, Buffalo Springfield was an important folk-rock band that also pioneered country rock and led the way for bands such as Poco and The Eagles. Buffalo Springfield was inducted into the Rock and Roll Hall of Fame in 1997.

Crosby, Stills, Nash, and Young (1968-1970) (1973-1974) (1976-2016) were formed by David Crosby of The Byrds, ex-Buffalo Springfield Stephen Stills, and ex-Hollies Graham Nash. By the time they formed CS&N, they were all experienced and successful songwriters having honed their songs in the Laurel Canyon hills of Southern California. Crosby, Stills, and Nash had an immediate and recognizable sound with strong three-part harmonies and advanced acoustic guitar interplay. But the "supergroup" had some problems getting signed to a record deal. Surprisingly, CS&N was rejected by Apple Records before they were signed to Atlantic Records. Atlantic released their debut album Crosby, Stills, and Nash in 1969. CS&N catapulted to fame when the album shot to number six on the U.S. charts. It was loaded with intelligent and radio-friendly tunes like Crosby's "Guinnevere," Nash's "Marrakesh Express," and Stills' "Suite: Judy Blue Eyes." CS&N added the sublime drummer Dallas Taylor, and eventually (after their second record) added bassist Greg Reeves to the band.

With the addition of Neil Young, CSN&Y would create one of folk-rock's great vocal sounds. Neil Young brought emotional depth and a rock 'n' roll credibility to the band. Amazingly, in just their second show as CSN&Y, they performed at Woodstock in the summer of 1969. When Neil Young joined CS&N, the terms of their contract allowed Young to maintain his musical relationship with his band, Crazy Horse. The first CSN&Y album was the highly anticipated Déjà Vu, released in 1970. It did not disappoint and soared to the top of the American charts. The album cover featured CSN&Y and bassist Greg Reeves and Dallas Taylor all dressed in Civil War attire.

Groundbreaking album Déjà Vu
by Crosby, Stills, Nash, and Young

For Déjà Vu, the world-class songwriting of CSN&Y was on full display. Crosby wrote the rollicking "Almost Cut My Hair" and the title track, while Stills wrote "Carry On" and "4 + 20." Nash contributed the popular "Teach Your Children" and "Our House," while Young composed "Helpless" and "Country Girl: Whiskey Boot Hill/Down, Down, Down/Country Girl." Stills and Young co-wrote "Everybody I Love You." They also covered the Joni Mitchell classic "Woodstock." To complete the masterpiece, notable guest Jerry Garcia added pedal steel guitar on "Teach Your Children" and John Sebastian contributed harmonica to "Déjà Vu."

Stephen Stills has said that Déjà Vu took a long time to record with each individual track receiving painstaking attention to detail. Most of the tracks were recorded in individual sessions. Each member recorded their compositions and added whatever was needed at the time, from rhythm section tracks to four-part harmonies. The songs "Woodstock" and "Carry On" represented CSN&Y as a group while all of the other tracks showcased each member of the band.

Déjà Vu was famous for its musically superior harmonies, guitar accompaniments, and solos that provided exciting musical moments. "Carry On" demonstrated a strong and funky rhythm section interplay between Taylor and Reeves that drove Stills' scorching electric guitar solos. Contrast that with their rich vocal harmonies and signature acoustic guitar backdrop. The result was the rich, musical complexity of the CSN&Y sound. The sensitive folk and blistering rock direction of Déjà Vu hit the listener hard with a range of moods. It captured the folk-rock hippie counter-culture perfectly.

Even though Neil Young's composition "Helpless" provided a quality country influenced ballad to Déjà Vu, Young seemed detached from the band. Neil Young would continue his associations with both CSN&Y and Crazy Horse, but would refuse to commit entirely to either one. Shortly before CSN&Y's second tour, bassist Greg Reeves was replaced by Calvin "Fuzzy" Samuels and Taylor was replaced by drummer John Barbata. Neil Young then organized a one-day recording session and CSN&Y recorded his song "Ohio."

"The connection with our generation was profound, and we (CSN&Y) could feel it...we were all friends, experiencing a phenomenon together."

- Neil Young

Rock Hard Fact

Crosby, Stills, Nash, and Young are the only group to top the charts with three consecutive albums where one was a studio album (Déjà Vu), one was a live album (4 Way Street), and one was a greatest hits album (So Far).

"Ohio"
by Neil Young

"Ohio" was a protest song that defined the great frustration of an entire generation of counter-culture youth that were protesting the American involvement in the Vietnam War. Neil Young wrote this anthem in reaction to the Kent State shootings that occurred on May 4th, 1970. Twenty-nine Ohio National Guard members fired over sixty bullets that killed four students and wounded nine others. Young had seen photos of the incident in *Life Magazine* and soon CSN&Y, with new members Calvin Samuels and John Barbata, recorded the song live in only a few takes. Some radio stations banned the song because it called out the Nixon Administration, although most FM stations entered the song into their rotation.

The lyrics of "Ohio" painted a chilling effect that represented the horror and outrage felt by most Americans about the Kent State shootings. The line "Tin soldiers and Nixon coming" referred to Young's placing blame on then President Nixon and Ohio Governor Jim Rhodes. "Ohio" was released as a single along with Stephen Still's "Find the Cost of Freedom." "Ohio" went to number fourteen in America and there have been numerous covers of the song including versions by The Isley Brothers, Devo, and Tori Amos.

The band toured in 1970 although internal tensions arose again. Steven Stills was fired, but quickly reinstated to finish the tour. Nash produced the live double album 4 Way Street from the tour. It went to number one on the U.S. charts. CSN&Y became inactive, but from late 1970 to the spring of 1971, each of the four members recorded and released successful solo albums. In 1972, Nash and Crosby toured and released a duo album titled Graham Nash David Crosby. It did well and yielded Nash's hit "Immigration Man." In the summer of 1973, CSN&Y reconvened to record a new album, but infighting resurfaced resulting in the band going their separate ways.

In 1974, CSN&Y regrouped for a thirty-one date stadium tour. More tension ensued when Young tried to assert his dominance in preventing any new music from being recorded. By 1977, the foursome had become three again and released CSN which went to number two on the U.S. charts. At this point, Crosby and Nash had recorded three albums together, while Stills and Young had each released solo albums and were involved in other projects. The CSN album featured the versatile Joe Vitale (who had worked with Buffalo Springfield) on drums, organ, and percussion. Many other studio musicians played on the recording. More tours followed in 1977 and 1978. 1982's Daylight Again continued the trio's success with the hits "Wasted on the Way" and "Southern Cross." By the 1980's, David Crosby had gone through many personal issues, thus curtailing any further CS&N musical activity. Neil Young stepped in to help Crosby with his rehabilitation. In 1988, CNS&Y was back in business, releasing their ninth studio album, American Dream. It reached number sixteen on the U.S. charts. While Young did not participate in a tour to support the album, CSN&Y did come together for promoter Bill Graham's memorial concert in 1991.

In the 1990's, CS&N's popularity waned resulting in the poorly selling Live It Up, and After the Storm. CS&N was soon left without a recording contract but in 1999, CSN&Y was back and recording. Neil Young had saved the day by convincing his record label, Reprise Records, to record and release the CSN&Y album Looking Forward. Looking Forward was better received that the two previous albums and prompted 2000 and 2002 tours for CSN&Y.

For all the dysfunction of CSN&Y, Neil Young has always maintained great respect for his bandmates. Young said, "Crosby was forever the catalyst, always intense, driving us further and further. Just looking in those eyes made me want to deliver from the heart. He so believed in what we were doing. Graham was the consummate professional, always there with his parts, cheering us on as we jammed, and writing songs we became best known for. Stephen, my brother, always the soulful, conflicted one, was battling unseen demons, and many-colored beasts through the days and night, contributing an edge that was unmistakable." #11 The twenty-first century has produced very little new CSN&Y music, although their live performances have been impressive. Touring in 2006, CSN&Y were able to include Young's anti-Iraq War sentiments (from Young's Living with War album) into their live set. CSN&Y performed an acoustic set for a benefit in 2013. In 2015, Graham Nash publicly stated that CSN&Y would never record again. However, in 2016 Neil Young left open the possibility of a future reunion.

Amidst all the chaos, Crosby, Stills, Nash, and sometimes Young created their own legendary brand of folk-rock music. CSN&Y effectively blended folk elements with country rock while bringing the folk-rock ballad and four-part harmonies to a new musical level. CSN&Y inspired an entire roster of singer-songwriters from the Laurel Canyon, California area. These artists included; Linda Ronstadt, Joni Mitchell, Laura Nyro, Jackson Browne, and the Eagles. Crosby, Stills, and Nash were inducted into the Rock and Roll Hall of Fame in 1997.

Discussion Question

Do you believe that folk-rock would have happened without the influence and musical statements of Bob Dylan? Take a position and give musical examples of artists other than Bob Dylan. Explain if these artists made a significant impact on the new genre of folk-rock music.

Singer-Songwriters

Beginning in the early 1900's there were many songwriters who were known for writing popular songs and Broadway musicals. However, very few of these songwriters were actually performers. This tradition continued with many of the early rock 'n' roll and popular music songwriters. But like those before them, many of the Brill Building songwriters were not performers (or singers) either. There was also a long-standing tradition of legendary singers who wrote very few (often none) of their songs including Frank Sinatra, Joe Cocker, and others.

The modern folk and blues tradition popularized the idea of writing *and* singing your own songs with artists such as Bob Dylan. Then, beginning in the late 1960's, the culture of the pop **singer/songwriter** emerged. This occurred when songwriters began to express their experiences about their lives and personal relationships in their songs. But unlike before, many of these songwriters also happened to be very good singers. Many singer/songwriters did continue to write about the topics of social and political issues of the day. But the shift to

> "All I needed to do was sing with conviction, speaking my truth from the heart, honestly and straightforwardly"
>
> - Carole King

writing more personalized songs tied the songwriter's musical expression to the artists (singer's) performance. The idea of the songwriter who sang his or her own songs was popularized, and the term singer/songwriter was born. Today the term singer/songwriter has become a generic term for a soft rock solo artist. But that's not how the term originated.

Many of the original singer/songwriters still wrote for other artists, but now a whole new generation of artists emerged that wrote and performed their own material. Prototypical singer/songwriters were artists such as; **Laura Nyro**, **Leon Russell**, **Joni Mitchell** (featured in chapter eighteen), **Leonard Cohen**, **Randy Newman**, **J.J. Cale**, **Carole King, Richard Marx**, and **Bruno Mars**. Some of the singer/songwriters of the late 1960's and 1970's found record company support from David Geffen's Asylum records, and Warner Brothers producer/executive Lenny Waronker. Geffen admits that he began his label Asylum to create an artistic asylum for the great singer/songwriters who failed to find a home elsewhere.

Carole King (1942) is one of the most profound singer/songwriters of all time. King personifies the definition of a true singer/songwriter's ability to focus on the craft of composing melodies, harmonies, and lyrics. Long before her own hugely successful career as a solo artist, King (and often writing partner Gerry Goffin) wrote dozens of hit songs for other major artists. She was a prominent songwriter at the famous Brill Building in New York (see chapter three profile) and eventually cultivated her own solo career when she moved to Los Angeles.

Carole King was a child prodigy. At the age of three, she was already making up her own songs and developing her ear by singing intervals and improvising both melodies and words. Her parents would spend hours with her at the family piano. Growing up in New York City provided her with the ideal musical environment. Her mother exposed her to Broadway plays and musicals at the age of five. As a young teenage, King began to listen to DJ Alan Freed's nightly rock 'n' roll broadcasts on WINS radio. In 1955, she attended Alan Freed's *Easter Jubilee*, a musical review at the Brooklyn Paramount Theater. There, she experienced rhythm and blues artists such as The Moonglows, The Clovers, Lavern Baker, and blues great B.B. King. King was mesmerized by their performances and remembered "at that moment I knew I wanted to mean something to these people. I didn't want to *be* one of them. I just wanted them to know who I was and consider me worthy of respect." #12

In 1957, Carole King went to *Alan Freed's Labor Day Revue*. When the legendary Little Richard took the stage, she was very moved by how he played piano and sang with unbelievable energy. King said, "Though I knew nothing about the Gospel music that informed him, Little Richard's powerful presence was a remarkable experience." #13 In high school, King wrote and arranged songs for her school's musicals and choral classes. She also wrote some four-part harmonies for street-corner vocal groups. King remembered, "I've always loved wrapping layers around a melody. When arranging for voices with a band, usually I begin with a foundation consisting of melody, lyrics, and the chords and rhythm coming from my piano. Then I bring in the rhythm section…a drumbeat…a bassline that's pretty close to my left hand… then I add vocal harmonies. And if I'm lucky enough to have the use of an orchestra, I add a final layer of orchestral instruments." #14

At age fifteen, Carole King was able to play her songs for Alan Freed. He helped her to connect with Atlantic Records and she (still age fifteen) walked into Atlantic's office one day unannounced and asked to have her songs heard. Before she knew it, Atlantic owner Ahmet Ertegun escorted her to the piano and listened with interest as she played each of her songs. He was impressed and told her to return when she had written more original songs. Encouraged by this encounter, King next visited ABC-Paramount Records and shortly after playing her songs for A&R head Don Costa, was offered a recording contract on the spot. King next attended Queens College in 1958. There, she met and began to collaborate with her future husband, Gerry Goffin. Their writing chemistry was almost instant, and they completed their first song together in less than an hour.

Carole King soon met composer/vocalist Neil Sedaka, and he suggested she meet with Don Kirshner and Al Nivens from the Aldon Music Company. After playing a few compositions for them, King and Goffin were signed to a three-year contract by Aldon Publishing. King and Goffin became prolific songwriters composing for a long list of artists that included; Bobby Vee, The Chiffons, The Drifters, The Righteous Brothers, Tony Orlando, The Everly Brothers, Herman Hermits, The Monkees, Aretha Franklin, and many more.

By 1967, Jerry Wexler offered to sign Carole King to Atlantic as a recording artist. Her marriage to Gerry Goffin was in disarray and he moved to California. Soon, King also decided to move to Los Angeles (so their daughters could stay close to their father). It was now time for Carole King to emerge as a solo artist. She moved to Laurel Canyon where she met Joni Mitchell and James Taylor (with whom she would develop a strong musical relationship). King was signed to Ode Records and in 1970 released her debut album Writer. It met with marginal success, reaching number eighty-four on the U.S. charts. On the album, James Taylor played acoustic guitar and provided backup vocals.

1971's Tapestry would be her masterpiece and would reach number one in America and number four in Britain. It would go on to become one of the most successful albums in music history, selling over twenty-five million copies worldwide.

Groundbreaking album Tapestry
by Carole King

Tapestry represented the long overdue fruition of years of King honing her songwriting skills, and the fact that her voice was meant to express Carole King songs.
Tapestry was also inspired by her musical relationship with James Taylor. He strongly encouraged King to sing her own songs and essentially transition from being a behind the scenes songwriter to a full-fledged singer/songwriter. She wrote or co-wrote all of the songs on the album, but some of them had already been successful. "(You Make Me Feel Like) A Natural Woman" had been a hit for Aretha Franklin, and "Will You Love Me Tomorrow" was a success for The Shirelles. "You've Got a Friend" would soon become one of James Taylor's signature tunes. He was recording it at the same time as King and was even sharing some of the same studio musicians. Taylor also provided acoustic guitar and vocals while Joni Mitchell sang background vocals on the record. Despite all of her incredible songs and world-class musical support, King had no idea that Tapestry would become one of the most influential and popular albums in rock-pop history.

Side one opened with "I Feel the Earth Move," then "So Far Away," "It's Too Late," "Home

Again," "Beautiful," and "Way Over Yonder." King explained her mindset at the time she recorded Tapestry when she said, "I was simply doing what I'd always done-record songs that I had written or co-written…I knew how to convey the mood and emotion of a song with an honest straight-from-the-heart interpretation." #15

Side two opened with "You've Got a Friend," then "Where You Lead," "Will You Love Me Tomorrow," "Smackwater Jack," "Tapestry," and "(You Make Me Feel Like) A Natural Woman." Tapestry featured a long list of top studio musicians including; guitarist Danny "Kootch" Kortchmar, drummer Russ Kunkel, electric pianist Ralph Schuckett, and many others. Many of these backing studio musicians became known as "The Mellow Mafia" because of their contributions to the many singer/songwriter records by Carole King, James Taylor, Jackson Browne, and Joni Mitchell. Kunkel and Kortchmar even had a band (with bassist Leland Sklar and pianist Craig Doerge) called The Section who released three albums of their own.

While King recorded Tapestry, other significant albums were being recorded in studios nearby. The Carpenters and James Taylor were recording a few blocks away and at the same studio King was recording Tapestry, Joni Mitchell was working on her album Blue. King remembered the magic achieved when recording Tapestry when she said, "I liked that I could set a mood in (studio) B with the lights. And I always put the players where everyone could see each other." #16 Tapestry was wildly successful because of its quality of songs, excellent production by Lou Adler, and aggressive promotion. It represented an album of great personal intimacy and skillful musicianship.

"I Feel the Earth Move"
by Carole King

"I Feel the Earth Move" reached number one on the U.S. charts and number six in England. King's voice on this track is musically varied. At times she sounded bluesy and harsh, while at other times her voice displayed a "soothing" quality. The song achieved strong radio airplay until it was surpassed by another Tapestry hit, "It's Too Late." On the day of recording "I Feel the Earth," Carole King remembered that she and her band felt no sense of urgency in starting the session. That was until the studio manager told them that Joni Mitchell had booked the same studio in three hours from then. King recalled, "We scrambled to our places in the studio and rehearsed 'I Feel the Earth Move'… I usually sang during rehearsals but didn't sing while we were recording a basic track, so I could focus on the interplay between my piano and the other instruments. It took no more than three takes for us to get the rhythm track for 'I Feel the Earth'." #17

This song revealed King's great mastery of combining lyrics to music. For example, when King sang the words "tumbling down," she accented the end of the word "tumbling" rather than the beginning. This created a syncopated musical equivalent of a tumble. "I Feel the Earth Move" revealed King's tremendous piano feel. This marked a difference from the guitar-based singer/songwriter approach she took on her previous album, Writer. For the ending of "I Feel the Earth Move" King remembered, "To suggest an earthquake, I concluded with a continuous cluster of notes on the piano cascading rapidly downward in pitch until the band and I ended the run together on a final C bass note." #18 It was later decided to leave out "the earthquake" ending.

King was now a major recording artist, releasing successful albums at the incredible rate of a one per year in the 1970's. 1971's Music featured the hits "It's Going to Take Some Time" and "Sweet Seasons." King followed with 1972's Rhymes & Reasons, 1973's Fantasy, 1974's Wrap Around Joy, and 1975's Really Rosie. For 1976's Thoroughbred, King reunited with Gerry Goffin to write four of the songs and collaborated with James Taylor, David Crosby, Graham Nash, and Wadi Wachtel. For 1977's Simple Things, King collaborated with songwriter Rick Evers. They were married but he died suddenly of a drug overdose the following year. In 1978, King released Welcome Home, and Touch the Sky in 1979.

In 1980, King and Goffin collaborated to co-write all of the songs for Pearls: Songs of Goffin and King. She followed with 1982's One to One, and 1983's Speeding Time, which was her first album not to chart. King didn't record again for six years until she released 1989's City Streets. It achieved limited success on the U.S. charts. The title track featured a guitar solo by Eric Clapton. King recorded only one album in the 1990's, releasing Colour of Your Dreams in 1993. However, King was busy writing hits for Mariah Carey, Soraya, and Celine Dion. The 1990's also saw many of her songs covered by a number of prominent artists.

Carole King had occasionally appeared in acting roles and TV ads. Some of her performances included; the title character in *Really Rosie* (an animated TV special), *The Mary Tyler Moore Show*, *The Trials of Rosie O'Neill*, and *The Gilmore Girls*. In 2001, King released Love Makes the World with her usual lineup of top studio musicians. In 2010, King reunited with James Taylor (with Kortchmar, Sklar, and Kunkel) for their Troubadour Reunion Tour. In 2011, King released her seventeenth studio album, A Holiday Carole that went to number fifty-two in America.

Carole King retired from the music business in 2012. Throughout her career, she *embodied what it meant to be a songwriter* with her rare gift of musical and lyrical innovation. Her equally successful career as a solo recording artist is seen in her body of work that displayed great originality and emotional appeal. King's songwriting output (including co-written tunes) included over one hundred hits that found their way to pop charts over a span of over 45 years. Carole King was inducted into the Rock and Roll Hall of Fame in 1990.

Leonard Cohen (1934-2016) was a Canadian singer/songwriter. At first, he worked as a poet and novelist from the 1950's to early 1960's, before beginning his music career. His 1967 debut album, The Songs of Leonard Cohen was followed by three more folk albums; 1969's Songs from a Room, 1971's Songs of Love and Hate, and 1974's New Skin for the Old Ceremony. In 1976, Cohen toured Europe and his 1977 release, Death of a Ladies' Man, was modeled after the Phil Spector "wall of sound" approach. 1979's Recent Songs followed and 1984's Various Positions included the release of one of his most memorable songs, "Hallelujah."

"Hallelujah"
by Leonard Cohen

Leonard Cohen wrote over eighty draft verses of his song "Hallelujah." The song was about a love that has diminished and gone stale. The version that Cohen recorded for Various Positions contained biblical references to stories about Samson and Delilah and King David. Cohen explained that "Hallelujah" literally meant "glory to God" and that many kinds of Hallelujahs exist.

Rock Hard Fact

The popular 1960's folk singer Judy Collins was the inspiration for the Crosby, Stills, and Nash tune "Suite: Judy Blue Eyes."

"When it all started, record companies- and there were many of them… were run by people who loved records, people like Ahmet Ertegun, who ran Atlantic Records, who were record collectors. They got in it because they loved music."

- David Crosby

"Hallelujah," in Cohen's original version was in a 12/8 blend of early gospel and rock 'n' roll feels.

"Hallelujah" has been covered by many prominent artists including John Cale and Jeff Buckley. Buckley's version was played at The Boston Red Sox's Fenway Park to honor the victims of the 2013 Boston Marathon bombings. Leonard Cohen once showed the tune to Bob Dylan and later in 1988, Dylan performed it at two of his own concerts.

After 1988's I'm Your Man, Leonard Cohen went on to record six more studio albums, culminating with 2016's You Want It Darker. Leonard Cohen cultivated a strong audience over a six-decade career. He was one of the twentieth century's most personal and creative lyricists influencing generations of singer/songwriters. Leonard Cohen was inducted into the Rock and Roll Hall of Fame in 2008.

J.J. Cale (1938-2013) was an American singer/songwriter and guitarist who was one of the original musicians associated with the "Tulsa sound" (drawing on country, blues, rockabilly, and jazz elements). Beginning with his 1972 debut album Naturally, Cale released a total of fourteen studio albums over a thirty-seven year period. J.J. Cale has written and recorded numerous songs that have been covered by many prominent artists. They included; "Cocaine" and "After Midnight" recorded by Eric Clapton and "Call Me the Breeze" recorded by Lynyrd Skynyrd. Other artists that have performed his compositions included; Johnny Cash, John Mayer, Jerry Garcia, and Chet Atkins.

Judy Collins (1939-) is an American singer/songwriter who, early in her career, became interested in the folk music and lyrics of traditional folk singers such as Woody Guthrie and Pete Seeger. Collins performed traditional folk and protest songs and recorded versions of Dylan's "Mr. Tambourine Man" and Seeger's "Turn!, Turn!, Turn!." From her 1967 debut Hard Lovin' Loser to her last studio album, 1990's Fires of Eden, Judy Collins had a great influence on future generations of singer/songwriters. Like many other folk singers from her generation, Judy Collins utilized her musical voice to express her political and social views.

David Crosby (1941-) has had a prolific career. Along with his tenure with The Byrds from 1964 to 1973, (see The Byrds in this chapter) to his longtime association with Crosby, Stills, Nash and Young from 1968 to 2016 (see CSN&Y in this chapter), Crosby has simultaneously cultivated a solo career. He released his first album If I Could Only Remember My Name in 1971. He has also sung backup vocals for many other artists including; Paul Kantner and Grace Slick, Phil Collins, and David Gilmour. In 1996, Crosby formed the band CPR with pianist James Raymond (Crosby's son), and a session guitarist, Jeff Pevar. CPR released two studio albums and two live albums. In 2014, Crosby released Coz, his first studio album in twenty years. In 2016, he released another solo album, Lighthouse. Additionally, as a duo, Crosby and Graham Nash have recorded four studio albums and two live albums.

David Crosby's artistry grew out of his ability to synthesize his folk music roots with jazz and even Indian music influences. His melodic songwriting and rich voice helped to shape the innovative harmonies of CSN&Y. His longtime personal issues have sometimes deflected attention from his brilliant career but his passion for music is undeniable. David Crosby was inducted into the Rock and Roll Hall of Fame twice, first with The Byrds and then with Crosby, Stills, and Nash in 1997.

Graham Nash (1942-) is an English singer/songwriter who came to prominence with the English rock band The Hollies (see chapter six) and then with Crosby, Stills, and Nash (see CN&S in this chapter). Nash's solo debut album, Songs for Beginners was released in 1971. As a post-release to CSN&Y's masterpiece Déjà Vu album, Nash's debut album still managed to reach number fifteen on the U.S. charts with an impressive roster of supporting artists including; Dave Mason, Jerry Garcia, Phil Lesh, Rita Coolidge, David Crosby, and Neil Young. From 1974 to 2016, Graham Nash released five more studio albums including 2016's This Path Tonight.

Graham Nash was initially introduced to Stephen Stills and David Crosby while on tour with The Hollies in 1966. After moving to America, Nash became politically active, which he utilized for songwriting motivation. He composed "Marrakesh Express," one of CS&N's great early successes, and "Teach Your Children" (first rejected by The Hollies). Graham Nash's distinct tenor vocal range (he sang a lot of the high parts) added a light and airy timbre to CSN&Y's unique four-part harmonies. Nash's voice could also contribute a distinctive "twang-like" quality to the group's unique sound. Graham Nash has been inducted into the Rock and Roll Hall of Fame twice, first in 1997 with Crosby, Stills, and Nash and then as a member of The Hollies in 2010.

"Marrakesh Express"
by Graham Nash

Graham Nash actually wrote "Marrakesh Express" while still a member of The Hollies. Initially, Nash was inspired to write the tune when he was on vacation in 1966. He traveled by train from Casablanca to Marrakesh, Morocco. On the train, Nash moved about the railcars and was intrigued by the other passengers, some of which were ducks, pigs, and chickens! However, the band rejected "Marrakesh Express" as not being commercial enough. Nash eventually introduced it to his new bandmates, David Crosby and Stephen Stills.

When recording "Marrakesh Express," Nash delivered a vocal performance that resembled North African and Middle Eastern vocal qualities. He was also musically inspired by the flow of his Marrakesh train ride. Stephen Stills overdubbed two guitars to try to simulate an Indian sitar timbre. To thicken the sound, Stills also overdubbed Hammond B3 organ, piano, and bass parts. Session great drummer Jim Gordon played on this recording as well. The first public performance of "Marrakesh Express" was at the Woodstock Festival in 1969 between three and four in the morning. Nash announced the song as "a medley of our hit" to the crowd, since it was only CSN&Y's second gig ever.

Stephen Stills (1945-) is an American singer/songwriter who started his career with Buffalo Springfield (see Buffalo Springfield in this chapter) and then with Crosby, Stills, and Nash (also in this chapter). Stills released his debut album Stephen Stills in 1970 to great critical and commercial appeal. It peaked at number three on the U.S. charts. The album featured a stellar lineup of guest musicians that included; Eric Clapton, Jim Hendrix, John Sebastian, Booker T. Jones, Ringo Starr, Cass Elliott, Rita Coolidge, and Stills' bandmates Crosby and Nash. Besides his vocal parts, Stills overdubbed multiple guitars, piano, organ, steel drums, percussion, and horn and string arrangements. The album contained the hit "Love the One You're With."

"Love the One You're With"
by Stephen Stills

"Love the One You're With" was an instant hit, reaching number fourteen on the American charts and number thirty-seven in England. The song title and lyrics were inspired by keyboard great Billy Preston whom Stills overheard saying "If you can't be with the one you love, then love the one you're with." On this track, Stills came up with an infectious uptempo acoustic guitar riff with a Caribbean flavor. Cass Elliot, of The Mamas and The Papas, combined her rich voice with Stills' bandmates Crosby and Nash to provide great harmonic support. Peter Tork (of The Monkees) also sang backup on the song.

Stills added a conga part by Jeff Whittaker to thicken the rhythmic feel but also to keep the rhythmic feel light (by not including a full drumset). "Love the One You're With" has been covered by the British pop group Bucks Fizz, The Isley Brothers, Luther Vandross, The O'Jays and the legendary Aretha Franklin. A live version of the song appeared on the CS&N compilation recording Demos.

———

In 1971, Stills formed the band Manassas with ex-Byrd guitarist/bassist Chris Hillman. They produced two albums, 1972's Manassas and 1973's Down the Road, before dissolving in 1973. Stephen Stills went on to release eight more solo albums from 1971's Stephen Stills 2 to 2007's Just Roll Tape. Stills has very eclectic music influences drawing from blues, country, gospel, rock 'n' roll, and of course, the folk music genre. In addition to his prolific songwriting, Stills is an accomplished multi-instrumentalist who plays virtually everything from; guitar, banjo, keyboards, bass, percussion, drums, and clarinet. He is known for experimenting with alternate guitar tunings and possesses excellent fingerstyle acoustic guitar technique. Stephen Stills was the first artist to be inducted into the Rock and Roll Hall of Fame twice in the same night, with Buffalo Springfield and Crosby, Stills, and Nash.

Leon Russell (1942-2016) was a pianist, bandleader, singer/songwriter, producer who enjoyed a successful 60-year career in music. That career began in the nightclubs of Tulsa, Oklahoma (with fellow "Tulsa sound" musicians J.J. Cale and Chuck Blackwell). Upon moving to Los Angeles, he quickly rose to become an in-demand Wrecking Crew session musician. Russell brought his funky, gospel-infused southern boogie, blues and country flavored piano style to recordings by a long list of artists including; Phil Spector, The Byrds, Jan and Dean, The Beach Boys, The Ronettes, and Ike & Tina Turner.

However, Leon Russell was much more than a faceless session musician. He led successful bands, performed on very successful tours, and released popular records. His skills as an arranger and a multi-instrumentalist led him to become a popular sideman working with Joe Cocker, Delaney and Bonnie, and George Harrison. Russell was also more than a musician. He started the labels Shelter Records, and later Paradise Records, and finally Leon Russell Records. He owned and ran his own Church Studio in Tulsa, Skyhill Studio in Los Angeles, and Paradise Studio in Tennessee. He also produced records for Bob Dylan and Bruce Hornsby. But most of all, Leon Russell was a masterful songwriter.

Leon Russell's first commercial success as a songwriter came in 1969 when Joe Cocker recorded his song "Delta Lady." Helen Reddy later had a hit with Russell's tune "Bluebird." The Rolling Stones turned Russell's song "Get a Line on You" into "Shine A Light" from their Exile on Main Street album. The Carpenters had a hit with his song "Superstar." Gary Lewis and the Playboys had one of their biggest hits with Russell's "She's Just My Style." Leon Russell's classic "A Song for You" was recorded by everyone from Ray Charles, to Donny Hathaway to Whitney Houston to Amy Winehouse. Even jazz guitarist George Benson had a hit with Leon Russell's song "This Masquerade." All in all, in his lifetime Leon Russell composed over 400 songs. Some of music's best songwriters including Elton John and Elvis Costello call Russell's songs and songwriting style a major inspiration. Russell's touring career started when influential musicians Delaney and Bonnie hired him to play piano in their touring band. They introduced Russell to George Harrison and Eric Clapton, both of whom he would work with throughout his career.

Upon Russell's success in Delaney and Bonnie's band, Joe Cocker called on him to participate in his Mad Dogs and Englishmen tour and record. Cocker's band was a large group (involving three drummers, a horn section, and a choir) that featured many of the same musicians from the Delaney & Bonnie tour. Cocker's band was a successful endeavor that had a lot to do with his recording of Russell's song "Delta Lady." Russell had recorded "Delta Lady" on his own 1970 debut album Leon Russell, when he was joined by Eric Clapton, George Harrison, and Ringo Starr. Leon Russell went on to perform on dozens of albums as a leader and sideman. He collaborated with Bob Dylan, blues legend Freddie King, Elton John, Barbara Streisand, Willie Nelson, and Dave Mason.

"Delta Lady"
by Leon Russell

Leon Russell wrote "Delta Lady" in 1969 about singer Rita Coolidge, who he met and dated in 1967. Russell was playing piano, writing arrangements, and co-leading Joe Cocker's Mad Dogs and Englishmen at the time. Russell recorded "Delta Lady" on his own debut album and Cocker also recorded it at Russell's studio in Los Angeles. Rita Coolidge sang backup on the tune not knowing it would later become the title of her own autobiography, *Delta Lady*.

"Delta Lady" has racy lyrics that referred to the Delta Lady as "wet and naked in the garden" and how he (the singer) thinks about the times he is away from her and longs for her touch. He is obsessed with her wherever he goes. Leon Russell and Rita Coolidge both joined Joe Cocker on his Mad Dogs and Englishmen tour, where they performed the song. "Delta Lady" showcased Leon Russell's ability to synthesize his songwriting with his unique vocal and piano abilities.

Leon Russell and Elton John (a longtime admirer of Russell) released a Grammy nominated duet record in 2010 called The Union. Filled with masterful songs, lush arrangements, and talented guests, *Rolling Stone Magazine* called The Union one of the 30 best records of the year. Leon Russell was inducted into the Rock and Roll Hall of Fame and the Songwriters Hall of Fame in 2011.

———

> "Songwriting is too mysterious and uncontrolled a process for me to direct it towards any one thing."
>
> – James Taylor

The Tulsa Sound

The American city of Tulsa, Oklahoma is a unique musical city. It seems to lie in the middle of everything and nothing. It lies almost exactly halfway between New York and Los Angeles and its music reflects that. It has absorbed the many musical traditions of Texas and North Texas, the blues of the deep South, the soul of Memphis, and the twang of Nashville. If this unique fusion of music sounds like the recipe for rock 'n' roll, you would partially correct. The music that comes out of Tulsa is a unique brand of rock known as The Tulsa sound.

In 1969 Bonnie and Delaney Bramlett started a band called Delaney and Bonnie. The band melded country, blues, rock 'n' roll, and soul music in a unique fusion of styles. The band always had a revolving cast of musicians including; Duane and Gregg Allman, Leon Russell, Eric Clapton, George Harrison, Gram Parsons, Dave Mason, Carl Radle, King Curtis, and drummers Chuck Blackwell, Jim Gordon, and Jim Keltner.

The band made their recording debut with Home. This record included a large band of musicians that were mostly associated with the Memphis Stax record label including the influential Booker T and The MG's. However, the record failed to find success. Accept No Substitute, Motel Shot, and Delaney and Bonnie and Friends On Tour with Eric Clapton followed. With these recordings and their tours, bandleaders began to establish a core of musicians. Ironically, many of these musicians hailed from Tulsa, Oklahoma. They included drummer Jim Keltner, bassist Carl Radle, and Leon Russell.

However, those weren't the only musicians who hailed from Tulsa that were finding popularity. Guitarists Elvin Bishop and Dwight Twilley, guitarist/songwriter JJ Cale, drummer Jamie Oldaker, and drummer/producer Chuck Blackwell all came from Tulsa. All of them were beginning to have great success. Together, they were building on the Tulsa tradition of combining all of the southern musical styles (rockabilly, country, western swing, and blues) with rock and soul. In time, these musicians and their music would become known as The Tulsa sound.

After experiencing the Tulsa sound through his tours with Delaney and Bonnie, Eric Clapton used most of the Delaney and Bonnie band for his first record, then he used some of them for his Derek and the Dominoes band. Later Clapton hired other Tulsa musicians including Carl Radle, Jim Keltner, and Jamie Oldaker for his solo career. Clapton established a lifelong working relationship with Tulsa songwriter JJ Cale as well. In 1970, English singer Joe Cocker found himself booked for a tour, and without a band. He brought in Leon Russell with the task of assembling a band. Russell in turn brought in most of the Delaney and Bonnie band. This band of 20 plus musicians became The Mad Dogs and Englishmen, and a movie and successful double record of the same name followed.

Many of the Tulsa musicians moved to Los Angeles to become notable and influential session musicians including Leon Russell, Jim Keltner, and Carl Radle. Producers Chuck Blackwell and Bill Maxwell have all brought the influence of the Tulsa Sound to the thousands of projects between them. The Tulsa Sound, and the musical importance of Tulsa, Oklahoma belongs in the same league as Nashville, Memphis, Chicago, New York, and Los Angeles. From the creator of Texas Swing, Bob Wills and the Texas Playboy's, (a band who called Tulsa it's home), through Leon Russell to even country great Garth Brooks, the Tulsa sound has contributed a great deal to the history of rock music.

James Taylor (1948-) is an American singer/songwriter and guitarist originally from Boston, Massachusetts. He developed a personal, understated, and soothing vocal sound that he phrased over his simple acoustic guitar accompaniments. His father, a physician, moved their family to North Carolina where Taylor learned to play cello as a child. Influenced by the music of Woody Guthrie, he developed a finger-picking guitar style while playing duo with future session great Danny Kortchmar, whom he met while on vacation in Martha'a Vineyard. Soon, the duo was playing folk and blues songs at various coffeehouses, billing themselves as "Jamie and Kootch." With college admission looming, Taylor had slipped into depression and was in and out of a treatment center. Taylor and Kortchmar both moved to New York City and formed a band called The Flying Machine. When Taylor developed a severe drug addiction, his father rescued him and brought him back to North Carolina where he recovered.

In late 1967, James Taylor moved to London, England where he connected with Peter Asher, head of A&R for The Beatles' newly formed Apple Records label. Taylor was signed to Apple and in 1968, released his debut album James Taylor. The album was recorded while The Beatles were recording their White album. Paul McCartney, by now a big fan of Taylor's, brought in arranger Richard Hewson to add orchestrations to a few of Taylor's songs. A moderate hit from the album, "Carolina in My Mind," has been referred to as the unofficial state anthem for the state of North Carolina. It was also frequently played at the University of North Carolina (in Chapel Hill) at athletic events and graduation commencement ceremonies. On the track, Paul McCartney and (an uncredited) George Harrison guest on bass and background vocals.

1968 and 1970 were difficult years for James Taylor. More personal problems and drug issues plus a serious motorcycle accident temporarily derailed his career. In 1969, Taylor signed a new recording contract with Warner Bros. Records and released what many consider to be his masterpiece, 1970's Sweet Baby James. The album, and its breakout single "Fire and Rain," both reached number three on the U.S. charts. The album eventually sold over three million copies in America alone. Taylor's popularity was quickly growing, even prompting a 1971 *Time Magazine* cover story crowning him as "the face of new rock," and the founder of the new singer-songwriter trend in America.

Groundbreaking album
Sweet Baby James
by James Taylor

Taylor was far from recovered at the time of recording Sweet Baby James. Staying at producer Peter Asher's house and crashing on Danny Kortchmar's couch, Taylor drew strength from his rehabilitation process to record one of folk-rock's most recognized works. The personnel for the recording included; longtime collaborator guitarist Danny Kortchmar, the legendary Carole King on piano and vocals, and session drummer Russ Kunkel. Also appearing was bassist and founding member of The Eagles and Poco, Randy Meisner.

Rock Hard Fact

Stephen Stills' 1970 debut album Stephen Stills marked the only time Eric Clapton and Jimi Hendrix appeared together on an album.

Side one opened with "Sweet Baby James," then "Lo and Behold," "Sunny Skies," "Steamroller Blues," "Country Road," and "Oh, Susanna." Although, "Sweet Baby James" was not a hit at the time, this classic was considered by Taylor to be his best song. "Sweet Baby James" was somewhere between a 3/4 waltz and a lullaby that Taylor wrote while on the way to meeting his infant nephew for the first time. The song drew from the cowboy song tradition of Roy Rogers and Gene Autry, only now with the modern folk-rock approach of James Taylor. The instrumentation for "Sweet Baby James" was pedal steel guitar, acoustic piano, acoustic guitar, a very subtle bass part, and brushes on the drums. Taylor also covered a Stephen Foster classic, "Oh, Susanna," at the time when most folk-singers were more interested in heading straight for Bob Dylan covers.

Side two opened with "Fire and Rain," then "Blossom," "Anywhere Like Heaven," "Oh, Baby, Don't You Loose Your Lip on Me," and "Suite for 20 G." The hit "Fire and Rain" became one of Taylor's signature tunes. It was inspired by both Taylor's recovery from drug addiction and the tragic suicide of Suzanne Schnerr, a childhood friend of his. Taylor was thinking about Schnerr when he wrote the lyric "Suzanne the plans they made put an end to you." James Taylor also made reference to the musical journey he made from his days with The Flying Machine and his experiences with Paul McCartney and Apple Records.

Sweet Baby James was an important record that helped to usher in a new generation of singer/songwriters. James Taylor offered a soothing, calm, and gentle voice that led folk-rock away from the volatile and noisy protest years of the 1960's. The songwriter himself now became the focus.

1971's Mud Slide Slim and the Blue Horizon continued Taylors' success when the album peaked at number two on the American charts. Hits from the album included "You Can Close Your Eyes" and "You've Got a Friend," the later going to number one on the U.S. charts. Taylor's fourth album, 1972's One Man Dog, was a concept album recorded mostly in his home studio. It was less successful than his previous two recording, but still reached the top ten on the U.S. charts.

You've Got a Friend"
by Carole King

James Taylor's association with Carole King had been one of the great musical relationships in folk-rock history. Carole King wrote "You've Got a Friend" for her own Tapestry album and for James Taylor's Mud Slide Slim and the Blue Horizon album. Part of King's inspiration for "You've Got a Friend" was a line in the refrain of Taylor's classic "Fire and Rain" that stated, "I've seen lonely times when I could not find a friend." King had stated that her song practically wrote itself and she felt pure inspiration in its conception.

During the recording of Mud Slide Slim and the Blue Horizon, Taylor had some time remaining after finishing his recording sessions from the previous two days. Producer Peter Asher suggested that Taylor and his band should record the Carole King song "You've Got a Friend." Knowing they had a great track, Taylor called King and asked her permission to release his version of the song. On James Taylor's version, Russ Kunkel's brush feel and Danny Kortchmar's congas combined to create a smooth rhythmic feel that locked in with Taylor's acoustic guitar. Kortchmar also added another acoustic guitar part to Taylor's primary guitar part.

Based on their past experience and success, producer Peter Asher thought about how he might complement Taylor's unique and gentle voice. So, he brought in Joni Mitchell to sing background harmonies on the track. Taylor remembered, "Joni was singing a parallel fifth harmony that kinda makes the chord into a major ninth. It feels like it frames the music in an interesting way to have her coming off at such an unusual note. Her voice is so pure and so perfectly in tune and confident, that it works immediately no matter what she does." #19

In 1974, James Taylor married singer Carly Simon. During their marriage they would guest on each other's albums and have two hit singles as duet partners. 1974's Walking Man did not fare well but 1975's Gorilla, with a star-studded lineup of backup musicians, returned Taylor to the top five on the American charts. After 1976's In the Pocket, James Taylor signed to Columbia Records for his Greatest Hits album that would sell twenty million copies worldwide. Taylor would release JT in 1977 and go on to record nine more studio albums. Following a very successful tour with Carole King, Taylor and King released a concert CD/DVD set titled Live at the Troubadour in 2010. Taylor's recording career culminated with 2015's Before This World, his first number one album on the U.S. charts (forty-seven years after his debut album). James Taylor's unique and soothing voice, intelligent lyrics, introspective songwriting, and strong musicianship have placed his innovative stamp on the folk-rock genre. James Taylor was inducted into the Rock and Roll Hall of Fame in 2000.

Art Garfunkel (1941-) is best known as half of Simon and Garfunkel (see folk-rock section in this chapter). After the duo broke up in 1970, Garfunkel acted in two Mike Nichols films, 1970's *Catch-22* and 1971's *Carnal Knowledge*. In late 1972, Simon and Garfunkel released their Greatest Hits album and briefly reunited for a benefit concert. Garfunkel then launched his solo career with his 1973 release, Angel Clare. The album reached number five in America and was recorded in Los Angeles with members of the Wrecking Crew. The album also featured Garfunkel's cover of the Jimmy Webb tune "All I Know" that peaked at number nine on the U.S. charts. For his 1975 album Breakaway, Garfunkel enlisted the help of Paul Simon for the hit "My Little Town."

In 1976, Garfunkel recorded vocal duets with James Taylor, Stephen Bishop, and J.D. Southier. 1977's Watermark and 1979's Fate for Breakfast received only marginal success. Tragedy struck in late 1979 when Garfunkel's longtime girlfriend committed suicide, which rendered him depressed for much of the 1980's. After 1981's, Scissors Cut (that also sold poorly), Garfunkel reunited with Simon for their 1982 The Concert in Central Park and a world tour. In 1986, Garfunkel released a Christmas album that featured vocalist Amy Grant titled The Animals' Christmas. Then in 1988, he released his seventh studio album, Lefty.

In the next decade Garfunkel starred in more acting roles and finally in 1997 released his eighth studio album, Songs from a Parent to a Child. This recording was a concept album of children's songs and featured guest appearances by James Taylor and Paul Simon. Five years later in 2002, Garfunkel released Everything Waits to Be Noticed. In 2007, after another five years, he released Some Enchanted Evening.

Art Garfunkel has had a long professional relationship with director Mike Nichols, working with him not only in movies, but also on the Broadway stage. Beginning in 1982, Garfunkel was a featured singer for Mrs. Robinson in the revue *Rock 'N' Roll! The first 5,000 Years*. In 1992, he performed in *Together Again on Broadway*. In 2002, he starred in the stage adaptation of *The Graduate*, featuring songs by Simon and Garfunkel not used in the original film (including "Bridge Over Troubled Water)." Art Garfunkel, with his distinctive tenor voice, (usually singing the higher parts of Simon and Garfunkel harmonies) has had an impressive acting and solo music career.

Paul Simon (1941-) placed himself on the musical map during his teenage years with his then musical partner, Art Garfunkel (see Simon and Garfunkel section in this chapter.) From an early age, Simon developed an interest in many styles of music including black gospel, rhythm and blues, and **world music**. This would help to plant the seeds for his brilliant and innovative solo career. Simon recorded his first solo album, 1965's The Paul Simon Songbook when he was twenty-four years old, and five years before his official 1970 breakup with Garfunkel. He objected to the album's release by Columbia, feeling that when he wrote and recorded this record, it was a transitional period for him. However, it did contain some of his great songs such as "The Sound of Silence" and "I Am a Rock." In what he considered his real first solo album, Simon released Paul Simon in 1972. It contained his first inclusion of world music with "Mother and Child Reunion," which was recorded in Jamaica and became one of the first American reggae hit songs. The album peaked at number four in America and also featured the hit "Me and Julio Down by the Schoolyard." 1973's There Goes Rhymin' Simon showcased "Kodachrome," a number two hit on the U.S. charts. Another number two, "Loves Me Like a Rock," delved deeply into a gospel feel with background accompaniment by the famous gospel group, The Dixie Hummingbirds. 1975's Still Crazy After All These Years set a darker mood, reflected in his state of mind over his divorce. This album enlisted a who's who of first-call studio musicians and soared to number one in America and number six in Britain. It contained four U.S. top forty hits including "50 Ways to Leave Your Lover," "Gone at Last," "My Little Town," and the title track.

"Fifty Ways to Leave Your Lover"
by Paul Simon

This song was Paul Simon's first number one hit since his split with Art Garfunkel five years earlier. Simon awoke one morning hearing the lyric "The problem is all inside your head, she said to me." With the help of a drum machine, he began to complete the verses telling the story of his divorce. This was at the time he was completing the songs for his Still Crazy After All These Years album. When playing a rhyming game with his three-year old son Harper, Simon composed (for the song's choruses) a number of possible exits out of a relationship. For example, he wrote "Slip out the *back, Jack*/Make a new *plan, Stan*," you don't need to be *coy, Roy* and so forth.

The stellar musicians on the track were John Tropea and Joe Beck on electric guitars, Jen Asher on organ, Tony Levin on bass, and Steve Gadd on drums. Equally impressive were Patti Austin, Valerie Simpson, and Phoebe Snow on backup vocals. Steve Gadd came up with the legendary drumset pattern for the song's verses when improvising in the studio between takes. Gadd commented on the groove when he said "'Fifty Ways' was just a result of sitting at the drums and playing the hi-hat with my left hand. When playing be-bop (jazz), sometimes the hi-hat will play in four, or in different places…so 'Fifty Ways' was a result of using the hi-hat in different places and using the left hand on the hi-hat." #20

One-Trick Pony was a 1980 movie that Paul Simon wrote, directed, and assumed an acting role. This was his first project under a new contract at Warner Brothers Records. In the movie, Simon played the character of a musician whose marriage falls apart and whose music is going out of style. The movie was a commercial failure, but the soundtrack produced the song "Late in the Evening." Simon's historic free concert in Central Park followed with his (long awaited by many) reunion with Art Garfunkel. Although a successful reunion tour followed, their relationship was never fully repaired and Simon resumed his solo career. 1983's Hearts and Bones was ultimately seen as a quality album, but it achieved only moderate commercial success.

In 1984, a friend of Simon's played him a cassette of Gumboots: Accordion Jive Hits Volume II, a collection of the South African musical style called **township jive**, (aka mbaqanga- the street music of South Africa). Simon was intrigued that it reminded him of early 1950's rock 'n' roll. It was happy, upbeat music with accordion, bass, drums, and electric guitars. Simon soon got in touch with Hilton Rosenthal, a record producer who had worked in Johannesburg, South Africa. Rosenthal sent Simon some albums that covered an array of South African traditional and funky styles. These influences proved inspirational for the album that became a Paul Simon masterpiece, 1986's Graceland. Simon's mixture of musical styles including; rock, pop, New Orleans zydeco, and South African mbaqanga and isicathamiya was a stunning aural experience. Graceland achieved great worldwide popularity, selling over fifteen million copies.

Groundbreaking album Graceland
by Paul Simon

Paul Simon flew with recording engineer Roy Halee to Johannesburg to record with three groups that he had heard on the Gumboots: Accordion Jive Hits album. The groups were Eao Ea Matsekha, General M.D. Shirinda and the Gaza Sisters, and the Boyoyo Boys Band. Three months after the recording sessions in South Africa, Simon brought the rhythm sections of Ray Phiri, Bakiti Kamalo, and Isaac Mtshali to New York to continue working on his album.

The direct exposure to South African music led Simon to a deeper understanding of South Africa's languages and cultures. On Graceland, Simon skillfully employed isicathamiya, an a-cappella vocal style that originated from the South Africa Zulu ethnic group. It was a very soft singing style that literally translated to walking softly. Isicathamiya focused on achieving a blend of all-male vocal harmonies. For Graceland, Paul Simon enlisted the efforts of one of the most famous South African singing groups, Ladysmith Black Mambazo and their leader Joseph Shabalala. The South African style of mbaqanga also had Zulu roots and literally meant everyday cornmeal porridge. Mbaqanga developed in the 1960's, mixing jazz, western instrumentation, and South African vocal styles. It grew in popularity in the 1970's because of the influence of western pop, disco, and soul music that was performed in South Africa.

Side one opened with "The Boy in the Bubble," then "Graceland," "I Know What I Know," "Gumboots," and "Diamonds on the Soles of Her

> "One of the things that has always motivated me to write is the desire to get it out and look at it in an objective way, so that it doesn't cause me any serious pain by staying inside."
>
> – Carly Simon

Shoes." Simon said that "The music for 'I Know What I Know' comes from an album by General M.C. Shirinda and the Gaza Sisters, a Shangaan group from Gazankulu, a small town near Petersburg in northern South Africa…An unusual style of guitar playing and the distinctive sound of the women's voices were what attracted me to this group in the first place." #21 "Diamonds on the Soles of Her Shoes" featured a collaboration with Ladysmith Black Mambazo fused with a township jive beat.

Side two opened with "You Can Call Me Al," then "Under African Skies," "Homeless," "Crazy Love, Vol. II," "That Was Your Mother," and "All Around the World or the Myth of Fingerprints." The composition "Homeless" was co-written with Ladysmith leader, Joseph Shabalala. Simon remembered, "Joseph Shabalala and I wrote in English and Zulu, starting the piece in the middle and working outward to the beginning and the end…I suggested that he make any changes in harmony or words that he wanted, and told him to feel free to continue the story in Zulu, adding whatever melodic changes he felt appropriate." #22

What makes Graceland even more remarkable was Paul Simon's concept of bridging the musical cultures of South Africa and the deep American South. On "That Was Your Mother," Simon brought the listener straight to Louisiana. Simon said "Searching for a musical connection close to home, I thought of accordion and saxophone music I'd heard in South Africa, and the Zydeco bands of Cajun Louisiana… Good Rockin' Dopsie and the Twister (a Zydeco band from New Orleans) I watched in a dance hall bar in Lafayette, Louisiana, and the next day we began our recording sessions in a small studio behind a music store." #23

Simon refined a new technique while composing Graceland where he improvised and then edited in a stream of consciousness lyric writing approach while listening to the rhythm tracks again and again. Gradually and very carefully, Simon developed long lines of pop poetry that floated lightly over the music. Besides the above mentioned South African musicians and his usual lineup of top studio musicians, Simon recorded with the band Los Lobos, Adrian Belew, The Everly Brothers, Linda Ronstadt, and African vocal legend Youssou N'Dour.

Along with Peter Gabriel's So album and The Talking Heads' Remain in Light album, Simon's Graceland had introduced African music to rock music and the western world. Graceland was a bridge between cultures, music styles, and continents of people. It served to liberate musicians whose popularity had been severely suppressed under South Africa's white apartheid rule.

Simon followed Graceland with a world tour featuring many of the album's performers, along with exiled South African stars Hugh Masekela and Miriam Makeba. For 1990's The Rhythm of the Saints, Simon built on his world music approach. Brazil became a new location for his musical focus. Simon recorded with Olodum, a large percussion ensemble that specialized in **samba-reggae**. The songs on Rhythm of the Saints described a primitive spiritual search rooted in tribal spirits and their relationship with drums. Not as popular as Graceland, the album did manage to sell two million copies.

A Simon and Garfunkel reunion took place in 1993 and Simon followed with 1997's Songs from the Capeman and You're the One in 2000. 2006's Surprise was inspired by the 9/11 terrorist attacks and the Iraq War. For the album, Simon brought in producer Brian Eno and recorded the song "Father and Daughter." Simon released So Beautiful or So What in 2011 and for 2016's Stranger to Stranger, he reunited with former collaborator and record producer Phil Ramone. Over the years, Simon has appeared in a few films besides 1980's One Trick Pony. He has also appeared on Scturday Night Live fourteen times as either the host or musical guest. Paul Simon, beginning as a young teenager, evolved into one of the worlds' great songwriters and bandleaders. He masterfully fused poetry with many music genres such as folk-rock and world music to create a unique and personal style. Paul Simon was inducted into the Rock and Rock Hall of Fame in 2001.

Carly Simon (1945-) (no relation to Paul) is an American singer/songwriter, musician, and author of children's books. She has enjoyed a long career as a performer and recording artist with twenty-three studio albums to her credit. Simon's musical career began when she formed a group, The Simon Sisters, with her sister Lucy. Early in her musical development she remembered being conflicted about her musical direction. Simon stated, "Listening to the popular vocal trio Lambert, Hendricks, and Ross, I'd become dependent on hearing jazz intervals. I imitated Annie Ross and tried to scat-sing the way Jon Hendricks did. I was so attracted to so many different styles of music, it was difficult to know which one to follow." #24 After making one album with The Simon Sisters, she recorded her 1971 debut album Carly Simon, which peaked at number thirty on the U.S. charts and yielded the top-ten hit "That's the Way I've Always Heard It Should Be." On her third album, 1972's No Secrets, she recorded her most successful song "You're So Vain."

"You're So Vain"
by Carly Simon

Over the years, there has been much speculation about who was the subject of Carly Simon's tune "You're So Vain." The song contained a critical description of a self-absorbed lover. In the lyrics, Simon sang "You're so vain, you probably think this song is about you." The subject of the song has long been a mystery, with Simon yet to fully reveal the answer. She has stated that it's actually about three different men, with actor Warren Beatty the most likely candidate. In 1983, Simon also stated that the song was not about Mick Jagger, who contributed uncredited background vocals to the song. Simon has also said that "You're So Vain" was not about James Taylor whom she was married to from 1972 to 1983.

On the track, Carly Simon played piano, while the very prominent bass introduction was played by Klaus Voormann. Simon composed the string arrangements and the orchestration was done by Paul Buckmaster. "You're So Vain" has been covered by many artists including; Liza Minnelli, Queens of the Stone Age, Marilyn Manson, and The Foo Fighters. In 2013, Simon performed the tune with Taylor Swift on her Red Tour.

Carly Simon had a string of hits in the 1970's including "Anticipation," "You Belong To Me," "Jesse," "Mockingbird," and "Nobody Does it Better," (from the James Bond film *The Spy Who Loved Me*). In addition to a prolific recording career, Carly Simon has been a great influence on many prominent artists ranging from Tori Amos to Taylor Swift to Celine Dion.

> "I respect bands that give me something of themselves that I can feel. It all has to do with a feeling I have about them. That is what music is to me, a feeling. It's similar with people too."
>
> – Neil Young

Harry Chapin (1942-1981) was a singer/songwriter who released nine studio albums (many more compilation albums) in his short lifetime, from his debut 1966 Chapin Music, to his last complete album, 1980's Sequel. Chapin died tragically in a car accident just shy of his fortieth birthday. He was known for his hits "Taxi" and "Cat's in the Cradle" that went to number one in 1974 and became a standard in folk-rock repertoire. **Jim Croce** (1943-1973) was an American singer/songwriter whom, between 1966 and 1973, released five studio albums. He had two number one hits on the U.S. charts, "Time in a Bottle" and "Bad Bad Leroy Brown." At the age of thirty, Jim Croce died in a plane accident shortly after a concert at Northwestern State University, thus prematurely ending the life and musical career of a great American folk talent. **Don McLean** (1945-) is an American singer/songwriter who released his first studio album, Tapestry (unrelated to Carole King's album) in 1969. McLean reached the top of the U.S. charts with 1970's American Pie. The title track peaked at number one in America and number two in England, becoming his signature song. "American Pie" referred to ("the day the music died") the 1959 plane crash that killed the legendary Buddy Holly, Ritchie Valens, and The Big Bopper. McLean has had a long career, releasing albums throughout the 1970's to 2006's Addicted to Black. **Al Stewart** (1945-) is an English singer/songwriter who achieved success as part of the British folk revival in the 1960's and 1970's. His debut album, 1967's Bedsitter Images, was followed by fifteen more studio albums to his most recent 2008 Sparks of Ancient Light. Stewart's 1976 album, Year of the Cat, was produced by Alan Parsons and yielded his signature tune "Year of the Cat." It went to number eight on the U.S. charts. Stewart's 1978 Time Passages produced a hit single by the same name. "Time Passages" went to number seven in America and served as a good example of the depth of his songwriting, evident over his forty-year career.

Van Morrison (1945-) is an Irish singer/songwriter, instrumentalist, and producer. In the 1950's, Morrison worked in a few Irish showbands playing keyboards, guitar, harmonica, and saxophone. In the mid-1960's, he was the lead singer for an Irish rhythm and blues band called Them. Morrison soon began a very prolific career as a songwriter and bandleader. From his 1967 debut album, Blowin' Your Mind, to 2017's Roll With the Punches, his studio album output stands at thirty-seven. 1970's "Moondance," the hit from the album of the same name, established him as a major artist. Many of his other hits were heavy rhythm and blues influenced including; "Brown Eyed Girl," "Domino," and "Wild Night."

"Brown Eyed Girl"
by Van Morrison

"Brown Eyed Girl" virtually launched Van Morrison's career shortly after he left his band called Them. The song shot to number ten on the American charts and is ranked high on many greatest rock song lists. The original lyrics were at first considered to sexually suggestive for radio play. A radio edit was made that removed the lyrics "making love in the green grass," and were replaced with "Laughin' and a-runnin, hey hey." Van Morrison has never received any royalties for writing or recording the song, and his recording contract (signed without the benefit of legal advice) made him liable for the recording expenses of the tune.

The producer for "Brown Eyed Girl" was Bert Berns, who assembled a three-guitarist lineup for the recording session. Veteran studio guitarist Eric Gale, Hugh McCracken, and Al Gorgoni, were joined by bassist Russ Savakus, pianist Paul Griffin, and drummer Gary Chester for the session. "Brown Eyed Girl" is a staple in popular culture having been utilized for the films, The Big Chill, Born on the Fourth of July, and others.

Van Morrison has a distinctive voice and characteristic growl that blends folk, blues, soul, gospel, jazz, and Celtic influences in a unique approach. He has composed hundreds of songs, including many that contained a recurring theme of nostalgic yearning for his youth in Belfast, Ireland. Morrison has inspired the genre of **Celtic rock** which has generated a vital scene since the early 1970's. Celtic rock is a hybrid of traditional Irish, Scottish, Breton, and Welsh musical traditions and fuses them with rock music. The centuries old styles of jigs, reels, and ballads blended traditional Celtic instruments such as bagpipes, fiddle, accordion, bodhran, Celtic harp, and tin whistle with standard rock instrumentation. Some key artists are Scotland's **Capercaillie** (1984-present) and the singer **Donovan** (1946-), Ireland's **Planxty** (1972-2005 with some inactive years), and **Clannad** (1970-present). Van Morrison was inducted into the Rock and Roll Hall of Fame in 1993.

Neil Young (1945-) is a Canadian singer/songwriter who has written some of the most beautiful and gentle of folk ballads. He also rocks with the primal brutality of the punkiest and grungiest of them. Neil Young has insisted upon the freedom to musically move from one extreme to another. He has always created with contempt for the career expectations imposed on him by his record companies and even some of his fan base. In 1960, Young began performing in a Winnipeg-based cover band called the Squires and then briefly, in 1966, played with the Toronto-based Mynah Birds (that included frontman Rick James). The Mynah Birds bassist Bruce Palmer, and Young left the band and bought a car (a hearse). They drove to Los Angeles where they would go on to help form Buffalo Springfield (see section on Buffalo Springfield) in 1966. Young never quite fit in with Buffalo Springfield but his eclectic compositions were important to the band's musical identity. It was clear the Young had a unique voice, one that could sound fragile and thin but with a deep range of emotion and effect. After recording three albums, the first version of Buffalo Springfield disbanded, and Young set out on his solo career.

Neil Young soon signed a record deal with Reprise Records and hired manager Elliot Roberts (still his manager to this day), who also managed Joni Mitchell. His 1968 debut album, Neil Young, showed promise but made little impact. It did foreshadow his future with its edgy guitar and traditional ballad style songs such as "The Last Trip to Tulsa." It also featured the excellent guitarist Ry Cooder and Wrecking Crew musicians' bassist Carole Kaye and drummer Earl Palmer. For 1969's Everybody Knows This Is Nowhere, Young began his association with the band Crazy Horse, featuring guitarist/vocalist Danny Whitten, bassist Billy Talbot, and drummer Ralph Molina. Neil Young with Crazy Horse displayed an aggressive

---

Rock Hard Fact

Neil Young acquired not one but two hearses to travel to gigs. The first, a 1948 Buick Roadmaster, he named Mortimer Hearseburg or "Mort" and the second was a 1953 Pontiac hearse he named "Mort II."

electric guitar approach with a folkish simplicity; a dichotomy that Young would himself bounce back and forth between for most of his career. Young knew he had something special when he said, "somewhere along the line I had suggested the name Crazy Horse after the great Indian Chief, and the guys liked it. Neil Young with (not "and") Crazy Horse. There was a distinction there. I am not sure why I did that, but I liked it being different. I liked that I was with them. Like we were together, not separate." #25 Everybody Knows This Is Nowhere peaked at number thirty-four on the U.S. charts and spawned the classics "Down By the River" and "Cinnamon Girl." The raw intensity of Crazy Horse would fire up Young in a way that more refined studio backing never could.

"Cinnamon Girl"
by Neil Young

For his song "Cinnamon Girl," Neil Young has never revealed whom the cinnamon girl was, thus preferring to leave it to the imagination of the listener. The lyrics revealed the singer daydreaming about a girl to love, singing that he waits between shows for his lover. The lyrics are soft and erotic while Young and Crazy Horse attack with a heavy and hard-rocking accompaniment. The guitar solo is essentially one repeating note that drips with emotion. Young recorded the song utilizing his (then) newly acquired Gibson Les Paul that he called "old black."

Neil Young was excited about recording with his new backing band Crazy Horse. He said, "I remember saying to the guys, when we were playing 'Cinnamon Girl,' describing the modal instrumental theme that introduces the song, 'It's like the Egyptians rolling stones up to a pyramid on logs. It's huge and it's moving. Unstoppable. Think Egyptians!'…It was massive. I was so freed by this music. I was happy as Hell." #26 Danny Whitten sang the high harmony part while Young sang the lower part. "Cinnamon Girl" has been covered by numerous artists including; John Entwistle of The Who, Phish, Radiohead, The Smashing Pumpkins, Foo Fighters, and more.

Young's emerging solo career was soon interrupted when his friend and former Buffalo Springfield co-star Stephen Stills recruited him to join Crosby, Stills, Nash, and Young (see section on CSN&Y). Neil Young released 1970's After the Goldrush, that brought in a new decade. He returned to a mostly acoustic sound. Although he utilized Crazy Horse on some tracks, Young featured Stephen Stills, multi-instrumentalist Nils Lofgren, and CSN&Y bassist Greg Reeves. The album reached number eight on the American charts with the hit singles "Only Love Can Break Your Heart," "When You Dance I Can Really Love," and "Southern Man." On After the Goldrush, Young rejected instrumental virtuosity and established his artistic identity with a primitive directness that was more than the typical label of electric, folk or rock 'n' roll.

Neil Young had a prolific 1970's decade, making nine more studio albums. 1972's Harvest was another classic and reached number one in America and England. This album was recorded mostly in Nashville with The Stray Gators (a band Young would have an on-off relationship with) and notable guests James Taylor, Linda Ronstadt, and his CSN bandmates. Two of the tracks also featured the London Symphony Orchestra. Songs on Harvest included "Heart of Gold," "Old Man," and "The Needle and the Damage Done."

1973's Time Fades Away and 1974's On the Beach followed, as did a tour with CSN&Y. Young reunited with Crazy Horse to record 1975's Tonight's the Night. Crazy Horse guitarist Danny Whitten and roadie Bruce Berry both died of drug overdoses in the months before the albums' songs were composed. This recording became a direct expression of Neil Young's grief. After 1975's Zuma, Young reunited with Stephen Stills and recorded Long May You Run in 1976. 1977's American Stars 'n Bars was another recording that presented the opposite aesthetics of folk roots with its full force electric rock.

1978's Comes a Time brought the fans of Harvest (who had all but abandoned hope of ever again hearing a primarily acoustic Young album like Harvest) a return to folk-country purity. Vocalist Nicolette Larson blended with Young and Crazy Horse added the rhythm tracks. The record went to number seven in America. 1979's Rust Never Sleeps would prove to be another classic, moving to number eight on the U.S. charts and number thirteen in Britain.

Groundbreaking album
Rust Never Sleeps
by Neil Young with Crazy Horse

It is difficult to single out Rust Never Sleeps when you have such classics as After the Gold Rush, Harvest, and others to choose from. Rust Never Sleeps is often referred to as Neil Young's punk album because it used punk as a source of inspiration. On the opening and closing tracks, Young relates to the story of the Sex Pistols' Johnny Rotten. Young states, "it's better to burn out than fade away," in what has become one of rock music's most philosophical phrases. Years later, Nirvana's Kurt Cobain would quote this line in his suicide note. Most of Young's folk and rock peers felt threatened and betrayed by the punk music genre. Instead, Neil Young embraced it, even echoing punk's reckless and raw emotion.

Side one opened with "My My, Hey Hey (Out of the Blue.)" then "Thrasher," "Ride My Llama," "Pocahontas," and "Sail Away." At this time, Crazy Horse was comprised of guitarist Frank "Poncho" Sampedro, bassist Billy Talbot, drummer Ralph Molina, and Nicolette Larson who sang on "Sail Away." Rust Never Sleeps provided an accurate portrayal of Neil Young's ability to effectively manage the dichotomy of his simple and pure melodies with complex and profound lyrics.

Side two opened with "Powderfinger," then "Welfare Mothers," "Sedan Delivery," and "Hey Hey, My My (Into the Black)." Rust Never Sleeps effectively represented the human condition within rock music. It rejected corporate rock and highlighted how Neil Young could juggle the extremes of delicate acoustic nuance with the most brutal of rock aggression. Rust Never Sleeps led to a tour with Crazy Horse and the 1979 live album, Live Rust.

The 1980's continued Young's prolific recording career with nine studio records. First came 1980's mostly acoustic Hawks and Doves then 1982's rocking Re-ac-tor. At this time, Young left Reprise Records and signed with Geffen Records, a mistake that resulted in massive legal issues (see folk rock

---

> "There are no limitations with a song. To me a song is a little piece of art. It can be whatever you like it to be. You can write the simplest song, and that's lovely, or you can just write a song that is abstract art."
>
> – Laura Nyro

> "Randy Newman is a national treasure…He's a songwriter's songwriter; a musician's musician. He's also probably the most misunderstood and under appreciated recording artist alive."
>
> – Don Henley

> "(Tim) Buckley had a unique voice, which could soar like a bird—my favorite singer of all time. He wrote about things I'd never done, but I thought I knew how he felt anyway. I knew exactly how he felt. A good singer can do that."
>
> – Chrissie Hynde of The Pretenders

controversy profile) over his adventurous 1982 album Trans. 1983's Everybody's Rockin, was an unexpected encounter with some rockabilly covers. 1985 saw Young's return to his country roots with Old Ways. He fulfilled his Geffen contract with 1986's Landing on Water and 1987's Life. Neil returned to Reprise for 1989's Freedom which offered a ten-year follow-up to Rust Never Sleeps and his hit "Rockin' in the Free World." If you mixed the Freedom era Neil Young with country, and added a taste of punk, you hear him foreshadowing the grunge movement.

The 1990's brought five studio albums to the Neil Young catalogue. 1992's Harvest Moon was an acoustic return to the 1970's and sold over four million albums worldwide. Young toured extensively in the 1990's appearing with Pearl Jam and Sonic Youth, confirming his rock credibility and legendary status. Seven studio albums were produced in the 2000's, including the reflective sound of 2005's Prairie Wind. Young next encountered some health issues when he suffered a brain aneurysm. Thankfully, he was able to recover. The 2006 album, Living with War, revealed Young's return to activism (about the Persian Gulf War) much like his earlier song "Ohio" that he made famous with CSN&Y in 1970.

The next decade spawned 2010's Le Noise and a Crazy Horse album of folk standards, 2012's Americana. Five more releases ensued including 2016's Peace Trail. Some critics and fans have hoped that Neil Young would be less erratic and would keep his musical messages more predictable. Young never felt obligated to have to tell his listeners what to think or how to feel. He has consistently challenged audiences to do their own thinking and feeling. Neil Young has fully committed himself to creating simple rock. Simultaneously, his music has remained focused on complex and expansive lyrics that move with the times. Neil Young was inducted into the Rock and Roll Hall of Fame in 1995 as a solo artist and in 1997 as a member of Buffalo Springfield.

Warren Zevon (1947-2003) was an American singer/songwriter best known for his hits "Werewolves of London" and "Lawyers, Guns, and Money" from his 1978 Excitable Boy album. As a child, Warren Zevon showed great musical talent and even studied briefly with twentieth-century composer Igor Stravinsky. Zevon began his professional career as a jingle composer and session musician. In the early 1970's, Zevon served as musical director for The Everly Brothers. By 1975, Zevon was living with future Fleetwood Mac members Stevie Nicks and Lindsey Buckingham. In 1976, he worked with musician Jackson Browne, who produced Zevon's debut album Wanted Dead or Alive.

Zevon went on to release thirteen more studio albums including Sentimental Hygiene, which had the members of REM backing him up. He followed with 2003's The Wind. This album was released just two weeks prior to his death from an inoperable form of lung cancer. The Wind had a star-studded lineup of musical guests who loved recording with Zevon including; Bruce Springsteen, Ry Cooder, Don Henley, Mick Fleetwood, Jackson Browne, Tom Petty, Emmylou Harris, Joe Walsh, and actor Billy Bob Thornton.

Throughout his career Zevon was a frequent guest on *Late Night with David Letterman* because he was one of Letterman's favorite musicians. Letterman would even appear on Zevon's song "Hit Somebody (The Hockey Song)" from the recording My Ride's Here. Zevon would on occasion, fill in for musical director Paul Shaffer on the show. Warren Zevon is remembered as a talented songwriter (many feel under appreciated as an artist) who utilized dark humor and sarcasm to express his political and social messages.

"Werewolves of London"
by Warren Zevon, LeRoy Marinell, and Waddy Wachtel

"Werewolves of London" was one of the most fun tunes that is still a staple on classic rock FM radio today. Warren Zevon co-wrote the song with guitarist Waddy Wachtel when Zevon was working for The Everly Brothers. Phil Everly had asked both Zevon and Wachtel to write a dance song for The Everly's and call it "Werewolves of London." Wachtel and Zevon were just strumming away on guitars when someone asked them what they were playing and Zevon replied, "Werewolves of London." Wachtel then began to howl and Zevon on the spot sang the line "I saw a werewolf with a Chinese menu in his hand." The rest of the song came quickly when the lyrics told a story of "a hairy-handed gent who ran amok in Kent." He's well dressed ("I'd like to meet his tailor"), well groomed ("His hair is perfect") and he was "preying on little old ladies." When playing the song live, Zevon would often replace the line "I'd like to meet his tailor" with "And he's looking for James Taylor."

The personnel on the recording is one half Fleetwood Mac. Drummer Mick Fleetwood and bassist John McVie accompanied Zevon's singing and piano part while Wachtel added his guitar part. The Chinese restaurant referred to in the song is the actual restaurant *Lee Ho Fook*, located on Gerrard Street in London's Chinatown district. The owner proudly displays Zevon's photo in the restaurant. This would be Zevon's only top forty hit as a singer.

Laura Nyro (1947-1997) was one of the original American singer/songwriters who fused rock, folk, soul, jazz, gospel, and show tune styles to create an original songwriting approach. Nyro's writing style was similar to many of the New York Brill Building songwriters, and she was a favorite of David Geffen. Nyro was a pianist whose songs became hits for many artists, especially between the years 1968 to 1971. Some of the artists that recorded Nyro's songs included; Barbra Streisand with "Stoney End" and "Time and Love," The 5th Dimension with "Wedding Bell Blues" and "Stoned Soul Picnic," Three Dog Night with "Eli's Comin," Blood Sweat and Tears with "And When I Die," and many more. She even considered becoming the lead singer for Blood, Sweat and Tears after Al Kooper's departure.

Laura Nyro's career as a solo artist began with her 1967 debut album More Than a New Discovery. 1968's Eli and the Thirteenth Confession was a legendary singer/songwriter recording that contained themes of love, romance, death and drugs. The album had complex string arrangements, Nyro's multi-tracked vocals, and a cast of first call studio musicians and jazz greats. 1969's New York Tendaberry recording was considered to be one of her greatest works, especially in terms of songwriting. 1993's Walk the Dog and Light the Light brought her back into the public eye, which seemed to make her very uncomfortable. Laura Nyro ran away from commercial success for the rest of her career and went on to release seven more studio albums culminating with 2001's Angel in the Dark. She died in 1997 from ovarian cancer, at the age of forty-nine (the same age and disease that took her mother's life). Laura Nyro was inducted into the Rock and Roll Hall of Fame in 2012.

Cat Stevens (1948-) is a British singer/songwriter who released eleven studio albums and then

Chapter Seven: Folk-Rock, Bob Dylan, and Singer/Songwriters

four more as Yusuf Islam (after converting to the Islam religion and changing his name.) His 1967 debut album, Matthew and Son, sold well and featured the accompaniment of bassist John Paul Jones (of Led Zeppelin fame) and session great pianist Nicky Hopkins. His 1970 album Tea for the Tillerman and 1971's Teaser and the Firecat were among his most popular. Teaser and the Firecat yielded hits with the traditional hymn "Morning Has Broken" and "Moonshadow." He was inducted into the Rock and Roll Hall of Fame under the name of Cat Stevens in 2014.

Dan Fogelberg (1951-2007) was an American singer/songwriter and multi-instrumentalist whose songs were diverse blends of rock, pop, folk, bluegrass, jazz, and classical influences. His 1972 debut album Home Free, had limited success but his second release, 1974's Souvenirs, peaked at number seventeen on the U.S. charts. On this recording, Fogelberg sang lead vocals and played an incredible array of instruments including; acoustic guitar, acoustic piano, organ, electric guitar, vibraphone, Moog synthesizer, zither, and various percussion instruments. Eagles guitarist Joe Walsh produced and played guitar on the album. Fogelberg was also joined by other Eagles members including vocalist Glen Frey and vocalist/drummer Don Henley.

Dan Fogelberg went on to make twelve more studio albums. His highest charting record was 1979's Phoenix that reached number three on the American charts. Some of Fogelberg's prominent hits were 1980's "Longer," 1981's "Leader of the Band," and "Same Old Lang Syne." He was an incredibly talented songwriter and musician. Dan Fogelberg's life was cut short when he died at age fifty-six of prostate cancer.

John Hiatt (1952-) is an American singer/songwriter who is also a skilled guitarist and pianist. Hiatt's career began with his 1974 debut album, Hangin' Around the Observatory. His song "Sure As I'm Sittin' Here," became a top twenty hit when it was covered that same year by Three Dog Night. Hiatt's first album to make the rock charts was 1987's Bring the Family, which featured the hits "Thing Called Love," "Have a Little Faith in Me," and "Thank You Girl." Hiatt's band from the recording Bring The Family featured Ry Cooder, Nick Lowe, and Jim Keltner. It became the short lived super group called Little Village and released one record. Hiatt's songs have been covered by a wide variety of artists that included: Bob Dylan, Chaka Khan, Joe Cocker, Willie Nelson, Paula Abdul, Iggy Pop, Eric Clapton, and many more. John Hiatt recorded twenty-two studio albums over a forty-three year career. John Hiatt's legacy is that of a master songwriter who was comfortable writing and performing in diverse music genres such as folk, rock, blues, country, and pop.

Randy Newman (1943-) is an American singer/songwriter, arranger, composer, and pianist. Newman's early songs were recorded by Petula Clark, Gene Pitney, the O'Jays, and others. His 1968 debut album, Randy Newman, sold poorly but his lyric writing revealed a quirky talent with an ability to satirize social conventions of American life. His 1970 recording 12 Songs, and 1972's Sail Away, fared better commercially. Newman's 1974 Good Old Boys, was a concept album about a southern character named Johnny Cutler. This recording achieved major commercial success reaching number thirty-six on the U.S. charts. Newman's 1977 release, Little Criminals, peaked at number nine in America and contained perhaps his best-known hit tune "Short People."

"Short People"
by Randy Newman

"Short People" was one of the most misunderstood songs of the 1970's. On the surface, Randy Newman seemed to be making fun of short people by singing that short people have "stubby little fingers" and "nasty little feet," but he really was chastising people who are short-tempered and are small-minded. Toward the end of the song, Newman sang "short people are just the same as you and I. All men are brothers until the day they die." Newman has composed other songs that actually mock bigotry such as "Half a Man" and "Rednecks." In 1978, a politician in Maryland attempted to make it illegal to play "Short People" on the radio. The politician lost his court case.

"Short People" was a number two hit on the U.S. charts and popular around the world. Newman's catchy pop piano part was enhanced by a small brass section and conga part that appeared in the song's mix. "Short People" utilized first call session musicians including; guitarist Waddy Wachtel, drummer Jim Keltner, and bassist Klaus Voormann. Newman enlisted Eagles guitarist/vocalist Glenn Frey, Tim Schmidt, and J.D. Southier for background vocals.

Since the 1980's, Randy Newman worked mainly as a film composer, creating film scores for movies such as; The Parents, Awakenings, Ragtime, Cold Turkey, Seabiscuit, Leatherheads, and many more. Newman also scored animated films for Disney-Pixar that included; Toy Story and Toy Story 2, Monsters Inc., A Bug's Life, and others. Additionally, many of Newman's songs have been adapted for musical theatre. Also of note, Newman's song "Louisiana 1927," (in the wake of 2005's Hurricane Katrina) became an anthem about the disaster and gained great popularity on radio and TV broadcasts. Newman went on to release six more studio albums including 2017's Dark Matter. Randy Newman was inducted into the Rock and Roll Hall of Fame in 2013.

Controversies surrounding two of the great singer/songwriters

The goal, as seen in folk music and later in folk-rock and singer/songwriters movements, has been to question authority and shed light on the social and political issues of the day. However, some controversies have occurred between artists and their record company, and between the artist and those with political motivation.

Perhaps the artist who best defined these controversies was Neil Young. His entire career has been built on evoking musical change and performing delicate acoustic folk music while simultaneously embracing hard rock. On his 1982 Trans album, Young took a controversial stylistic turn. Young responded to the musical culture of the time by incorporating synthesizers, electronic beats, and singing through a vocoder. His inspiration for Trans was the theme of utilizing technology to enhance communication with his son Ben, who was afflicted with severe cerebral palsy and could not speak. Seven months later, Young took another unforeseen turn by releasing the rockabilly inspired Everybody's Rockin.

On December 1st, 1983, David Geffen, the head of Young's label (Geffen Records), sued Young for making music (both albums Trans and Everybody's Rockin' that was "unrepresentative of himself." However, it seemed that it was the lack of

---

Rock Hard Fact

Nora Jones is the daughter of legendary Indian sitar player and composer Ravi Shankar.

"A lot of people who were writing when I came through originally as a singer-songwriter have disappeared."

– Van Morrison

commercial appeal (not making money) that was the real source of Geffen's anger. Trans was very much a Neil Young album (contrary to Geffen's lawsuit). It embodied simple songs that were folkish in their simplicity. The musical backing on Trans utilized computer technology that Young had embraced instead of his customary approach of acoustic and electric guitar. The lawsuit was eventually settled in favor of Young and Geffen apologized to Young.

Another source of upheaval occurred with Paul Simon's 1986 album, Graceland. Following the initial success of the album, Simon faced accusations levied by the organization Artist United Against Apartheid and the Ghanaian Ambassador to the United Nations, James Victor Gbeho. Both parties claimed that Simon had broken the cultural boycott imposed by many countries against the political regime in South Africa that supported apartheid. Simon replied that he would not ask for permission from individuals or organizations about whom he could collaborate with musically.

Supporters of Paul Simon, such as South African musician Hugh Masekela (an exiled opponent of apartheid), felt that Simon was responsible for launching the international careers of many musicians such as the vocal group Ladysmith Black Mambazo to global audiences. Simon has also helped to make South African music popular around the world. Was Simon taking advantage of these musicians? Many supporters of Simon argued that because he had already achieved international success before the South African collaboration, he was not taking advantage of anybody. He was merely helping them achieve well deserved exposure.

Both of these conflicts occurred because two of the most creative artists in music, Neil Young and Paul Simon, were searching to expand and stretch the boundaries of their art form. Young, with his foray into electronic music and return to rockabilly, and Simon, with his interest in world music, were extending their musical possibilities. Both artists were not content to limit themselves or be forced into folk-rock formulas, much like Bob Dylan's earlier refusal to stay confined to folk music.

Tim Buckley (1947-1975) was a singer/songwriter and guitarist whose musical foundation was in folk music. He evolved considerably through his career by experimenting with funk, soul, jazz, psychedelic, and even avant-garde styles of music. Buckley's 1966 self-titled debut album, Tim Buckley, revealed a personal style of country and jazz influences performed with his formidable five octave vocal range. Tim Buckley's recording output totaled eight more studio albums, including 1969's Happy Sad, when he reached the height of his popularity. The record peaked at number eighty-one on the U.S. charts. Happy Sad would also mark the beginning of his experimental period when he incorporated more jazz elements and utilized his voice as an instrument. At the end of his short career, Buckley released three rock albums. Tim Buckley died of a drug and alcohol overdose in 1975 at the age of twenty-eight.

Tom Waits (1949-) is an American singer/songwriter, a composer of film scores and musicals, and accomplished actor. Waits has a distinctive voice and is known for his ballads and clever lyrics that often paint aural pictures of seedy characters and places. Wait's 1973 debut album Closing Time was a jazz oriented piano album. His trademark raspy, gravelly voice lent a uniquely personal quality to the characters he created on many of his recordings. Waits' recordings' Closing Time and Small Change were depictions of nightlife and shady characters. Both albums achieved cult and critical success. Heartattack and Vine continued the theme of nightlife, but this time with a southern tilt. From the 1980's moving forward, Waits increasingly worked in the theatre both as an actor and composer. After a long absence from recording, Waits released his 1998 album Beautiful Maladies, a retrospective of his work for Island Records.

From the time of his debut album, to his 2011 Bad as Me, Waits recorded sixteen studio recordings. However, quite possibly his most popular contributions to rock music were his hit songs "Jersey Girl" (popularized by Bruce Springsteen), and "Downtown Train" (popularized by Rod Stewart). Tom Waits was inducted into the Rock and Roll Hall of Fame in 2011.

New generations of singer/songwriters born in the 1950's to the 1990's had reinvented and revitalized the folk-rock genre. **Joan Armatrading** (1950-) is an English singer/songwriter and guitarist. For more than forty-years, she sustained a career releasing eighteen studio albums. **Ricky Lee Jones** (1954-) is an American songwriter and vocalist whose career has spanned five decades. From her 1979 debut album Rickie Lee Jones that included the hit "Chuck E.'s In Love," to her 2015 The Other Side of Desire release, she has contributed significantly to the folk-rock genre. **Suzanne Vega** (1959-) is an American singer/songwriter who has released nine studio albums to date, including her latest, 2016's Lover, Beloved: Songs from an Evening with Carson McCullers. Two of Vega's songs (both from her 1987 Solitude Standing album), "Tom's Diner" and "Luka," were top ten hits on the U.S. charts. **Tracy Chapman** (1964-) is an American singer/songwriter who came to international attention with her 1987 debut album Tracy Chapman. She is known for her social and political activism and has released a total of eight studio albums.

Jeff Buckley (1966-1997) was a singer/songwriter/guitarist and the son of Tim Buckley. After working as a session guitarist in Los Angeles for ten years, Buckley signed a recording contract with Columbia Records. He formed a band and recorded what would be his only studio album, 1994's Grace. Although it initially sold poorly, Grace gradually gained critical acclaim. David Bowie considered it to be a masterpiece. Buckley recorded the Leonard Cohen classic "Hallelujah" on Grace. Buckley's version had a deep and sorrowful tone, peaking at number one on the British charts. In 1997, Jeff Buckley had moved to Memphis, Tennessee, to work on an album to be titled My Sweetheart the Drunk. He had a collection of previously recorded studio tracks and planned to finish the album by adding more material with his backing band. Tragically, Jeff Buckley died while swimming in the Mississippi river while awaiting the arrival of his band from New York to record My Sweetheart the Drunk. Jeff Buckley's guitar style was highly evolved with many dimensions to his approach. He could play percussively, play in a country style, and use slide guitar effectively.

A later generation of folk singers have achieved success in the decades of the 1990's to present times and kept the folk-rock tradition alive. **Billy Bragg** (1977-) is an English singer/songwriter who has released eleven studio albums, from his 1983 debut Life's a Riot with Spy Vs Spy, to his 2017 release Bridges Not Walls. Bragg has maintained a strong political voice and a commitment to various activist causes. **Norah Jones** (1979-) is an

American singer/songwriter and actress that has sold over fifty million albums worldwide. In 2020, she released her debut album Come Away with Me. Her most recent release was 2016's Day Breaks. **Bon Iver** (2006-present) is an American indie folk band that was founded by singer/songwriter Justin Vernon. They have released three studio albums including the 2016 release 22, A Million. Other prominent artists are **Conor Oberst** (1980-) who was named best songwriter in 2008 by *Rolling Stone Magazine*, and popular singer/songwriter, **Ed Sheeran.**

Ed Sheeran (1991-) is an English singer/songwriter, guitarist, and record producer. His career took off after appearing on Taylor Swift's album, Red. He originally started in 2005 as an indie artist selling his songs independently on his own label. Sheeran has released nine EP's that have steadily gained commercial and critical acclaim. Signed to Atlantic Records in 2011, his first single was one of his most successful songs to date, "The A Team." Sheeran's three albums thus far are titled + (Plus), x (Multiply), and Divide. Each has met with phenomenal success. As measured by 2017 standards, Ed Sheeran's song output has generated over seventeen million downloads in the U.S. alone. Ed Sheeran is an example of a modern artist that sings in the folk-rock tradition capturing an audience both young and old. He is living proof that the singer/songwriter continues to hold a vital and relevant place in rock and pop music today.

"The A Team"
by Ed Sheeran

One of Sheeran's most popular songs, "The A Team" was released as a digital download in 2011 and served as the lead single from his debut album. "The A Team" was a folk ballad that Sheeran wrote about a woman he met when visiting a homeless shelter. Sheeran was deeply moved when he listened to the many troubling stories he heard there. The lyrics described a prostitute addicted to crack cocaine, a class A drug. The song quickly became an international hit in Europe, Israel, New Zealand, and Japan.

"The A Team" contained a strong melody with intelligent lyrics. Sheeran's vocal quality has a soft and emotional touch that extended the folk-song tradition. It's contemporary subject matter hits home for many listeners. Sheeran shot a video for the song at an underground station in London. The video told the story of a girl who was addicted to drugs and lived on the streets of London. Sheeran has performed the song at many venues and as a duet with Elton John at the 2013 Grammy Awards.

Over the past fifty years, the definition of folk-rock has grown so wide and flexible that the term had become almost meaningless. For some, a singer/songwriter in the folk-rock tradition was anyone armed with an acoustic guitar vocalizing over a rock beat. Others defined a singer/songwriter to be more about the songwriting, with the singing as an afterthought (often better recorded and sung by someone else). Pioneers such as Bob Dylan, The Byrds, Carole King, Paul Simon, and many others, have clearly defined the folk-rock and singer/songwriter genres. Their inventive and intelligent lyrics, combined with creative rock music elements, have evolved to express highly personal and universally relevant messages. No matter how folk-rock and singer/songwriters are defined, the resulting music has proved to be timeless, like the pure folk music that preceded it.

Discussion Question

Is a song more genuine or does it express more meaning if it's sung or performed by the musician that composed it? Can a song effectively cross-over from its composer to another singer or performer? Take a position and give specific examples.

Chapter Eight: Art Rock and Glam Rock

Although many music historians use the terms **art rock** and progressive rock interchangeably, there is a clear distinction between the two. In the decade of the 1960's pop music experienced a new direction. Some rock artists moved away from making singles and more toward making complete albums. These works, some of which we have already examined, such as The Beach Boys Pet Sounds and The Beatles Sgt. Pepper's Lonely Hearts Club Band, spoke as a whole. They communicated a complete story and were aptly named concept albums. Some bands aspired to make artistic statements while often infusing new musical elements into a rock music context. In their historical context, art rock artists were not a big part of the psychedelic and hippie movements. Rather, art rock was greatly influenced by a modernist, avant-garde direction that sought to explore experimental concepts utilizing novel approaches to sound, instrumentation, and compositional techniques. This approach was at times similar to progressive rock. However, it generally did not demand the classically trained instrumental techniques required for the music of most progressive rock bands. Also, art rock didn't borrow much from classical music repertoire. Some of the earliest examples of art rock artists and albums included; **Pink Floyd** with Dark Side of the Moon, **Frank Zappa** (Zappa is featured in chapter eighteen) with Freak Out!, and **The Velvet Underground** with The Velvet Underground and Nico.

Glam rock, synonymous with glitter rock, became popular in Britain in the early 1970's. Initially, this genre was about simple bubblegum melodies and simple rock 'n' roll rhythms mixed with theatrical stage showmanship. Glam artists experimented with gender conventions and dressed in outrageous, androgynous costumes and makeup. Some glam artists, such as **Queen**, challenged the masculinity of rock music and played into the artists desire to use their sexuality to create an onstage presence. Many male glam artists dressed in feminine clothes and wore makeup onstage. **David Bowie** defined art rock but also was *the* leading glam rock artist. He forged a new, high level of composition and performance artistry by inventing a number of intriguing stage personas. In 1971, the **New York Dolls** were the most important glam artists in America with their androgynous-like wardrobe and trashy sound. **T. Rex** was also extremely popular and important. Glam rock would be in decline by 1975 when most artists were moving away from the style.

Pink Floyd (1965-2014) was one of the first rock bands to experiment with the avant-garde concepts of **minimalism** and systematic music. They organized minimal compositional source material into organized repetitious patterns for some of their songs. Twentieth-century composers, such as Steve Reich and Philip Glass, first introduced rock musicians to these composition techniques. Pink Floyd also utilized non-musical sounds in their early compositions. This was another concept that was heard in the works of significant twentieth century composers, including John Cage and Edgard Varese. Both of these composers wrote music employing "organized sounds" which utilized sounds ranging from sirens and sleigh bells to "prepared piano," which was a technique that altered the piano strings in various ways. For these reasons, as well as their extended psychedelic improvisations, Pink Floyd can be considered an art rock band (although they did display some progressive rock characteristics). They didn't play with, or re-create an orchestra. Nor did they pursue and involve themselves in technical and virtuosic instrumental showmanship. Pink Floyd experimented with rock by daring to conceptualize sound differently.

Pink Floyd began when bassist and vocalist Roger Waters met drummer Nick Mason at London's Regent Street Polytechnic School. They both joined a

> "Pink Floyd were, straight off the bat, a band that could deliver a catchy hit single but had this other urgent desire to experiment with kaleidoscopes of sound."
>
> – Ian Anderson of Jethro Tull

Rock History - the Musician's Perspective

rhythm and blues cover band called Sigma 6 that featured keyboardist and vocalist Richard Wright. Soon, guitarist and vocalist Syd Barrett and guitarist Bob Klose joined the band. Together, Waters, Mason, Wright, Barrett, and Klose changed the name of the band to The Tea Set and made their first demo tape. By 1965, they changed the name again, this time to The Pink Floyd Sound. The new name was a combination of inspirational blues players Pink Anderson and Floyd Council. By 1966, Bob Klose had left and The Pink Floyd Sound dropped the "sound" from their name. Their early repertoire consisted of blues and R&B tunes. However, instead of wailing blues guitar solos, Pink Floyd created a wall of noise and sustain. They became the sonic backdrop of London's underground psychedelic scene in the late 1960's. Wright and Barrett were using an Echoplex effect on their keyboards and guitar and were generally experimenting live with sonic timbres.

In 1967, Pink Floyd released their debut album titled The Piper at the Gates of Dawn, on the EMI label. It was a top ten hit in Britain. Barrett came up with the album title based on a children's novel titled *The Wind in the Willows* by Kenneth Grahame (Barrett loved its story of mysticism and adventure). Syd Barrett showed that he was a strong songwriter by writing most of the songs. Although "See Emily Play" emerged as a hit, Pink Floyd would soon become known as an album-oriented band and were given the freedom by EMI (their record label) to explore their music without the pressure of creating hit singles. The Piper at the Gates of Dawn lyrics spoke about scarecrows, fairy tales, and space, all set to their psychedelic instrumental sound. All the while, Syd Barrett was losing a grip on reality due to his use of LSD and the onset of mental illness. His bandmates had to move quickly to find a new guitar player. Their choice was David Gilmour (a friend of Barrett) who was known for his blues-oriented sound and ability to play with emotional intensity. In 1968, Syd Barrett would only compose one song titled "Jugband Blues," for the second Pink Floyd album release, A Saucerful of Secrets. This album continued to feature extended psychedelic improvisations and electronic sounds. Classical composers and British movie producers had become interested in the music of Pink Floyd. Moving forward, Roger Waters and Richard Wright would continue to write most of the band's repertoire.

The creative and troubled life of Pink Floyd's Syd Barrett (1946-2006)

Syd Barrett was a very talented guitar player, songwriter, lyricist, and painter. He was also very troubled with mental and personal issues. Barrett was credited with naming (The) Pink Floyd (Sound). In his formative years, Barrett was a big fan of both The Beatles and The Rolling Stones. He learned to play many Beatles songs, studied blues guitar, and learned to play the bass. When guitarist Bob Klose left the early version of Pink Floyd, Barrett was largely responsible for changing the direction of the band by drawing from jazz improvisation and the emerging psychedelic rock genre. Barrett was an avid reader of fantasy literature such as Tolkien's The Hobbit and Carlos Castaneda's The Teachings of Don Juan. This had a profound impact on his lyric writing.

During the recording of Pink Floyd's The Piper at the Gates of Dawn, Barrett was experimenting with the drug LSD with increasing frequency. At performances to promote the album, Barrett's mental health seemed to be rapidly deteriorating. This manifested itself in his ability to perform onstage (or in the studio). It was later determined that Barrett was suffering from schizophrenia and his erratic behavior, hallucinations, disorganized speech, memory lapses, and periods of catatonia could be attributed to that illness. Barrett's illness prompted Pink Floyd to look for another guitar player, with David Gilmour eventually replacing Barrett. The Pink Floyd members had hoped to keep Barrett in the band as a non-touring member (similar to Brian Wilson of The Beach Boys) but this proved to be impossible due to Syd's increasingly erratic behavior. In the spring of 1968, Pink Floyd announced that Syd Barrett was no longer in the band. Barrett disappeared from the public for a year.

After leaving Pink Floyd, Barrett was active musically from 1969 to 1972. In 1969, he reappeared to begin his brief solo career. Syd recorded two albums, 1970's The Madcap Laughs and Barrett, released later that same year. On the first solo record, David Gilmour and Roger Waters helped produce (along with three other producers) and on the second album, Gilmour produced and Richard Wright added keyboard parts.

In 1975, during the recording sessions for Pink Floyd's Wish You Were Here, Barrett showed up at the Abbey Road studio session and watched while the band was mixing the song "Shine On You Crazy Diamond." This was ironically a song and album that was dedicated to him. Initially, the band did not recognize Barrett since he had gained weight and shaved his head, including his eyebrows. They were also heartbroken because they cared deeply about him. Pink Floyd made sure Syd was taken care of by always getting his royalty checks to him. Barrett's work would show up periodically on Pink Floyd official and bootleg releases such as the 1994's Crazy Diamond box set.

In his later years, Barrett lived in his late mother's home in Cambridge, England and lived a reclusive life of painting and gardening. Syd Barrett died in 2006 at age sixty from pancreatic cancer. At the time of Barrett's death, Pink Floyd's David Gilmour remembered him to be a musical genius that made people smile with his wonderfully eccentric songs about bikes, gnomes and scarecrows. Gilmour was sad that Barrett's career was cut short, yet he realized that Syd Barrett touched the lives of many people. Barrett's musical output with Pink Floyd included composing most of their debut album and contributing to their second. In 1996, Syd Barrett was inducted into the Rock and Roll Hall of Fame as a member of Pink Floyd, but did not attend the induction ceremony.

After the departure of Syd Barrett, Pink Floyd focused on composing extended epic works with a sense of classical construction. They released the albums More (recorded as a movie soundtrack) and Ummagumma in 1969. More drew from jazz, world music, acoustic folk-rock ballads, and blues. Ummagumma, a top five hit in Britain, was a double album that featured live tracks and band collaborations, as well as solo spotlights. In 1970, Pink Floyd released Atom Heart Mother which contained an album side long orchestral and choir-based title track, written in collaboration with Ron Geesin, a conductor familiar with electronic music and film composition. Atom Heart Mother reached number one on the British charts and broke into the top sixty albums on the American charts. Pink Floyd had enjoyed some success but felt to

---

Rock Hard Fact

Clare Torry, the 22 old year vocalist on Pink Floyd's "Great Gig in the Sky"(from The Dark Side of the Moon) thought the band hated her recorded vocal part. Torry was surprised to find her name in the album credits when she saw the album in a record store.

be at a musical crossroads in terms of their future musical direction.

    In 1971, Pink Floyd released the album <u>Meddle</u>. It was here that the band found creative inspiration and new direction. Some tracks were built in small musical increments such as the opening "One of These Days." Other songs combined British folk, church, psychedelic, and Delta blues influences. The entire second side was the twenty-three minute "Echoes," a song about a futuristic world. "Echoes" utilized impressionistic sounds that continued Floyd's interest in sonic exploration. <u>Meddle</u> was also a key album in establishing Pink Floyd's mass popularity. It peaked at number seven in Britain and number seventy in America. <u>Meddle</u> marked the beginning of internal friction between some of the band members and a very strong-minded Roger Waters, who was trying to establish himself as the band's producer and main composer. Also in 1971, Pink Floyd released a career retrospective titled <u>Relics</u> that included two Syd Barrett early singles. 1972's <u>Obscured by Clouds</u>, served as a movie soundtrack for the French film *La Vallee* by Barbet Schroeder. <u>Obscured by Clouds</u> was largely overlooked in the Pink Floyd catalogue. However, Floyd was looking forward. The band had already begun work on the music that would become the epic <u>Dark Side of the Moon</u>.

    Often considered their masterpiece, Pink Floyd released <u>Dark Side of the Moon</u> in 1973. <u>Dark Side of the Moon</u> grew out of a song cycle titled "Eclipse" that Roger Waters had composed, and the band had performed live, in 1972. The post-Barrett version of Pink Floyd had hit its stride. <u>Dark Side of the Moon</u> was an immediate success and became one of the largest selling albums in rock history, selling over *forty-five million* copies worldwide. It remained on the Billboard charts for a staggering seven hundred and forty one weeks!

Groundbreaking album
Dark Side of the Moon

    Pink Floyd had been developing the material for <u>Dark Side of the Moon</u> for some time before recording it in 1972 and 1973. The themes for the album were complex and varied. They included; the modern day British psyche, common every day stresses in relation to that psyche, a descent into insanity, a movement toward materialism in society, and an examination of the temporal nature of time and space. <u>Dark Side</u> contained a larger theme that examined the contrast between the "eternal" sun (that represented birth and youth) and the pull of its lunar companion (the moon). Additionally, the album themes addressed aging, mental illness, and death. Waters initially had the idea to create a work that revealed the pressures of their rock musician lifestyles and having to deal with the mental issues they faced with former member Syd Barrett. Waters was able to transform Barrett's LSD-induced insights into the real-life emotions of fear, hope, love, dementia, isolation, and death. All four members of Pink Floyd actively participated in the writing and production. They all agreed that Water's unified album theme was a good idea. Waters did, however, create many demo tracks at his home studio. <u>Dark Side of the Moon</u> started and ended with a heartbeat with moments of insane screaming, muttering, and the demonic laughter of the story's protagonist. Side one opened with "Speak to Me," a Nick Mason instrumental, that featured a looped bass drum representing a heartbeat. Soon, random voices spoke about insanity and met the ticking of clocks and haunting laughter. Next, "Breathe (in the Air)" was a meditation about slowing down life to appreciate what one has. Another instrumental, "On the Run," led into "Time," with its ringing alarm clock that served as a sonic wake up call. "The Great Gig in the Sky" ended side one and vocalist Clare Torry delivered a legendary and agonized gospel-like performance. Her section sought to take the listener through a deathbed scene and confession, ending with a spirit rising.

    Side two opened with the classic 7/8 metered "Money," and the hymn-like "Us and Them," both released as singles from the album. "Us and Them," used themes of war and the mental armor people employ to distance themselves from others. The instrumental "Any Colour You Like" served as a bridge to "Brain Damage," a song that featured a gospel choir, guitar spatial effects, and maniacal laughter inspired by Syd Barrett. "Eclipse" ended the album and reminded the listener of their own awareness of life's experiences. The last sounds heard were the heartbeat that began the recording.

    On the recording sessions, advancements were made in the utilization of tape loops and multi-track recording technology. Engineer Alan Parsons made important contributions and brought in the incredible vocalist Clare Torry. The album's cover art, by George Hardie, showed a prism dispersing light into color. The album design represented the band's live light show, their lyrics, and Richard Wright's request to make the cover simple. <u>Dark Side of the Moon</u> credited; four backup vocalists, Dick Parry on saxophone, David Gilmour-vocals, guitars, VCS 3; Nick Mason-drums, percussion and tape effects; Richard Wright-keyboards, vocals, VCS 3; and Roger Waters-bass, vocals, VCS 3, and tape effects. Waters has said many times that <u>Dark Side of the Moon</u> was a positive message about life and the undeniable idea that death is final and we have just one chance to get it right.

"Money"
by Roger Waters

    "Money" began with Roger Water's classic bassline in 7/4 time and Mason's drum part entering and accenting beats two, four, and six to make a nice flowing pattern. For Gilmour's extended guitar solo section, the song moved to 4/4 time. "Money" was based on a blues form and Dick Parry's bluesy saxophone solo added a stylistic contrast to the repetitious nature of the 7/8 rhythmic pattern. After Perry's solo, David Gilmour essentially soloed in three parts. On the first section, Gilmour used a Fender Stratocaster that was double tracked with thick reverb and delay effects. During the second solo section (also with the Strat), he removed the reverb and effects to define a stark contrasting guitar sound. The third section was recorded with a Lewis guitar, on which Gilmour could reach notes spanning two octaves on the neck; thus allowing himself to play some very high notes. This very clever and drastic change of guitars and timbral effects served to extend the very musical solo section.

    One of the unique qualities of "Money" was the rhythmic sequences of sound effects that introduced the track. Although bands such as The Beatles had previously utilized tape loops, no artist had taken it to this level. Waters spliced together sampled recordings of clinking coins, a ringing cash register, a counting machine, and other sounds that formed a 7/4 loop. The band utilized this very long loop as a backing track (like a metronome) and engineer Alan Parsons gradually faded out the loop before the vocal part entered.

"Money" was about the evil things that money can bring. Ironically, Pink Floyd made a lot of it, with Dark Side of the Moon selling over forty-five million copies. When Gilmour sang "money, it's a gas," many fans misinterpreted it as an endorsement that money was a good thing. At live performances from 1972 to 1994, Pink Floyd often played "Money" for an encore. Later, both Gilmour and Waters included the song in their post-Pink Floyd live sets. One excellent cover of "Money" (and the whole Dark Side album) was a 2002 reggae version by The Easy Star All-Stars called The Dub Side of the Moon. The intro money sounds were replaced by the sounds of someone smoking marijuana through a bong.

Creating a follow up to Dark Side of the Moon would provide to be a huge challenge. Roger Waters had developed ideas for a new concept album that would be a tribute to his father, whom he lost in World War II. The new album would also pay homage to Syd Barrett. Pink Floyd released Wish You Were Here in 1975. Waters, never comfortable being a rock star, often wrote lyrics with sharp sarcasm, anger, and a bitterness for the same music industry that made him and his bandmates rich and famous. Waters said "The dream is that when you're successful, when you're a star, you'll be fine…That's the dream, and as everybody knows, it's an empty one." #1 The lyrical content of "Shine On You Crazy Diamond," in parts one through five (parts six through nine features Richard Wright in instrumental passages) focused on Barrett's mental state with a sense of sadness and detachment. It would be a biography of sorts about how the pressures of rock stardom had destroyed Barrett's grip on sanity. Wish You Were Here succeeded as a follow up to Dark Side of the Moon, selling fourteen million records worldwide.

The next three albums would become a vehicle for Roger Waters's repressed anger and unresolved childhood issues. 1977's Animals contained themes of human beings represented as animals. Songs such as "Pigs," "Sheep," and "Dogs," personified animals and became symbols for people in western societies that lived in a modern day caste system. Extravagant Pink Floyd live shows brought these animal themes to life with a fifty-foot inflatable pig, a giant octopus, and a state of the art light show. 1979's The Wall was another Waters' concept record. This time the main character was an emotionally detached rocker named Pink. Pink protected himself and became detached by building a barrier (the wall) between himself and the outside world. For the concept of The Wall, Waters revealed, "The idea started to occur to me that the individual bricks might be from different aspects of the history of my life and other people's lives." #2 The visual effect of The Wall became the inspiration for the 1982 semi-animated movie *Pink Floyd: The Wall.*

1983's The Final Cut was Roger Waters' orchestrally composed follow up to The Wall. It would be the last Floyd album with Roger Waters. Richard Wright had already left the band (fired for apathy) before the recording of The Final Cut, and tensions remained high between Waters and his remaining bandmates. They decided not to tour in support of the album which led to the release of a Roger Waters solo record, 1984's The Pros and Cons of Hitchhiking. By 1985, Waters had officially left the band. Gilmour and Mason decided to carry on without Waters and recruited Richard Wright to record the 1987 album, A Momentary Lapse of Reason. Legal battles ensued over branding rights. Wright remembered, "We fought during 'The Wall,' which was an album Waters wrote, based on his family story, we clashed long before that, during the period of the 'Dark Side' and 'Wish You Were Here.'

Actually we never got along." #3 In 1994, Pink Floyd released The Division Bell and then Pulse in 1995.

Waters and Gilmour resisted opportunities to work together again. However, they each became successful solo artists. Both released several high quality solo recordings. Pink Floyd finally did reunite to headline the 2005 Live8 show. Tragically, Richard Wright died in 2008. Gilmour and Mason released The Endless River in 2014, a tribute to Wright.

The Pink Floyd Sound was merely a cult band at first, then Pink Floyd became a global musical phenomenon and changed the face of art rock and progressive rock music. Pink Floyd was inducted into the Rock and Roll Hall of Fame in 1996.

The Velvet Underground (1964-1973) (1990,1992-1993,1996) was an art rock band formed in New York City in 1964 by vocalist/guitarist Lou Reed, multi-instrumentalist John Cale, guitarist Sterling Morrison, and drummer Angus MacLise. The foundation of the band began with Lou Reed, a classically trained pianist. Reed started to compose songs and began to record at age fourteen. After attending Syracuse University with literary aspirations, he pursued some duo gigs with Morrison. Reed also began working as a songwriter for Pickwick Records. In 1964, he met John Cale, who had moved from Wales to America to study classical music on a scholarship. Cale had worked with experimental composers Cornelius Cardew and La Monte Young (performing with Young's *Theatre of Eternal Music*). La Monte Young (see avant-garde profile) would be an important influence on many musicians including Cale. Reed and Cale formed a group called The Primitives, where they performed Reed's songs, some of which they would develop into early Velvet Underground material. Morrison and MacLise were recruited to join the short-lived band Primitives and Reed continued to sing and play guitar while Cale played viola, keyboards, and bass. They soon changed the band name to The Warlocks and then The Falling Spikes. Eventually their fourth band name, The Velvet Underground (the name coming from the title of a paperback book on sadomasochism found on the street) proved to be the charm. The early Velvet Underground performed at screenings of experimental films. It was there that Lou Reed extended his songwriting skills. Maureen Tucker soon replaced MacLise to become the Velvet's new drummer. Tucker brought an unusual and creative drum set approach to the band by playing standing up and incorporating garbage cans into her setup. She was also influenced by African drummer Babatunde Olatunji and by Bo Diddley rhythms.

Influential pop-art artist Andy Warhol saw The Velvet Underground perform at a club in Greenwich Village in 1965. Warhol recognized the originality and significance of the Velvet Underground's repertoire and soon became their manager. He was able to expose the band to his audience by booking them at art galleries, including his own called The Factory. Warhol took The Velvet Underground on tour with his *Exploding Plastic Inevitable Roadshow* for which the band composed music (incorporating minimalist elements such as drones) for each multimedia event. Warhol secured a recording contract for the band at Verve Records. Lou Reed benefited greatly from his exposure to Warhol's art studio. He observed and documented (through his songwriting) the circus-like environment of the celebrities, sexual adventurers, high-society socialites, and art patrons that congregated at Warhol's studio.

Andy Warhol introduced the Velvet Underground to German singer and model, Nico (real name

> "Our music (Pink Floyd) has depth, and attempts to have philosophical thought and meaning with discussions of infinity, eternity and mortality."
>
> - David Gilmour

Christa Paffgen). Warhol also mentored the band as their producer and recognized the strong potential of Reed's romantic ballad songwriting. For their debut album, 1967's The Velvet Underground and Nico, Warhol stayed out of the studio but lent his name to the now famous album cover of a yellow banana sticker with "peel slowly and see" printed near the tip (those that removed the banana skin found a pink, peeled banana underneath). The Velvet Underground experienced problems when their record label, Verve, who was lax in promoting the album by delaying the records' release by a year. When it was finally released, the album had to compete with The Beatles Sgt. Pepper's.

Groundbreaking album
The Velvet Underground and Nico

The Velvet Underground and Nico was a commercial failure that was completely ignored by music critics. The record was instantly banned from many record stores due to the cover art of the album. The edgy and controversial nature of many of the songs' subject matter was an even bigger issue. This resulted in numerous radio stations refusing to play any of the songs. However, The Velvet Underground and Nico is now widely considered as a defining album in the art rock genre.

German singer Nico performed occasionally with The Velvet Underground and sang on three of the album's tracks including "Femme Fatale," I'll Be Your Mirror," and "All Tomorrow's Parties." Initially, some of the band members balked at including Nico on the album, but she was added at the insistence of Andy Warhol. Although listed as the album's producer, Warhol stayed out of the musical process with John Cale handling most of the production decisions.

Side one opened with "Sunday Morning," then "I'm Waiting for the Man," "Femme Fatale," "Venus in Furs," "Run Run Run," and "All Tomorrow's Parties." This album showcased The Velvet Underground's overt descriptions of many themes yet unexplored in rock music at that time. Lou Reed, who wrote most of the album's lyrics, was a student of notable poets and authors such as William Burroughs, Allen Ginsberg, and Raymond Chandler. Reed felt that the content of many of these literary figures' works would translate easily to song lyrics. Reed's intention was not based on shock value but rather his inspiration to write about the human condition. The tune "I'm Waiting for the Man" described an individual's effort to obtain heroin while "Venus in Furs" explored the darker sexual themes of sadomasochism, bondage, and submission.

Side two opened with the song "Heroin," and progressed to "There She Goes Again," "The Black Angel's Death Song," and "European Son." Lou Reed had a gift for creating simple rock 'n' roll songs that meshed very well with John Cale's experimental sensibilities of alternative sonic design. Cale utilized his viola timbres on the songs "Venus in Furs" and "Black Angel's Death Song." These complex and varied parts of The Velvet Underground puzzle created some very unique musical compositions.

"Heroin"
by Lou Reed

The lyrics to "Heroin" blatantly depicted heroin use and it effects. "Heroin" didn't endorse the use of the drug but it did not discourage it either. Lou Reed wrote the song while he was an English major at Syracuse University in the early 1960's. The lyrics were told from the haunting perspective of a heroin user's confession with a menacing matter-of-factness. Reed kept the dark and serious subject matter of heroin use focused by providing an objective description of the topic without taking a moral stance. Reed became upset when Velvet Underground fans would approach him saying they were inspired to use the drug when they heard the song. He stated in many interviews that he was not condoning drug abuse.

Reed's vocal tone on the track was amplified by John Cale's dissonant and "fingernails on blackboard screeching" on his viola. "Heroin" started with Reed's quiet guitar melody, then added Sterling Morrison's constant rhythm guitar part and Tucker's drum set feel. Tension was built effectively by increasing the tempo and dynamics with Cale's viola drone. The frantic crescendo emulated the euphoric affect felt by the narrator after taking the drug. It was further exacerbated by Reed's and Morrison's aggressive guitar strumming.

Reed's relationship with Warhol soured and the band became disassociated from Warhol. Nico was forced out and soon started a solo career. The Velvets moved on without Warhol. Live, their sound became harsher and louder with extended improvisations. In 1967, The Velvet Underground released White Light/White Heat. This record was deliberately distorted with much electronic sound experimentation that in spots was a cacophony of white noise. Tension mounted between Reed and Cale due to creative differences. Internal frustration mounted when the band received little public recognition for their efforts. John Cale soon quit and was replaced by vocalist/multi-instrumentalist Doug Yule.

1969's self-titled The Velvet Underground embodied a renewed sense of melody and harmony, but lacked the avant-garde edge that John Cale had provided. Reed's songs were more subdued and he shared lead vocals with Yule. The Velvet Underground spent much of 1969 on tour reworking old songs and developing new material. 1970's Loaded was the last Velvet Underground recording for Lou Reed who wrote all of the songs on the album, including the hits "Sweet Jane" and "Rock & Roll." Loaded also contained some of Reed's most passionate ballads including "New Age" and "Oh! Sweet Nuthin'." Lou Reed quit the band even before the release of Loaded. He was upset with the unauthorized editing of his tunes, and disputes arose over the credits on the album. Sterling Morrison soon left to pursue a Ph.D. in Medieval literature.

With the departure of Lou Reed, now pursuing a solo career, The Velvet Underground toured America with the lineup of Morrison, Tucker, bassist Walter Powers, and Doug Yule who took over lead vocals and guitar. 1973's Squeeze would be the last Velvet Underground album. It featured no members from the Lou Reed-John Cale era except Doug Yule, who wrote most of the songs on the record. Yule played guitars, keyboards, bass, sang lead vocals, and produced the album. Also appearing was saxophonist Malcom Duncan and drummer Ian Paice (from Deep Purple.)

The strong legacy of The Velvet Underground can be heard in the art rock of Roxy Music, David Bowie, and other significant bands such as Sonic Youth and The Strokes. Many punk and post-punk bands that formed over the next two decades would owe The Velvet Underground credit for inspiring their musical direction. The Velvet Underground redefined avant-garde sonic explorations and pioneered new ground with their probing lyrical themes. Then, they applied them to rock music.

> "I can't do anything I want to. I mean, I can't have my own TV show. I can't have my own movie. But within my little world, nobody tells me what to put on the albums."
>
> – Lou Reed

The Velvet Underground was inducted into the Rock and Roll Hall of Fame in 1996.

After quitting The Velvet Underground, **Lou Reed** (1942-2013) worked briefly at his father's accounting firm before he signed a recording contract with RCA Records in 1971. Reed's 1972 debut album, Lou Reed contained some songs that were originally written for The Velvet Underground Loaded album. Although it included top London session musicians including Yes's Steve Howe and Rick Wakeman, it was largely overlooked.

1972's Transformer would be Reed's breakthrough recording. It was co-produced by David Bowie and Mick Ronson and introduced Reed to a wider audience. "Take a Walk on the Wild Side" became Reed's biggest hit and described the characters whom Reed observed hanging around Andy Warhol's studio. Other prominent tunes from Loaded were "Vicious," "Andy's Chest," and "I'm So Free." 1973's Berlin, was a concept album where Reed again explored the mature themes of drug addiction, domestic violence, adultery, suicide, and prostitution. Reed's 1973 tour band featured guitarists Steve Hunter and Dick Wagner. 1974's Sally Can't Dance was followed by Reed's biggest selling record, the 1974 live album, Rock 'n' Roll Animal. It contained live versions of The Velvet Underground songs "Heroin" and "Sweet Jane."

"Sweet Jane"
by Lou Reed

There were two distinct versions of "Sweet Jane," with the first coming from The Velvet Underground's Loaded. The version examined here was titled "Intro/Sweet Jane" from Lou Reed's live album Rock 'n' Roll Animal. This version featured the twin guitar approach of guitarists Dick Wagner and Steve Hunter. The live sound of this touring band was a different approach for Reed, one he later rejected when he fired Hunter and Wagner at the end of the tour. "Sweet Jane" featured one of the most melodic and infectious guitar riffs from the 1970's.

Lou Reed was a profound lyricist and wrote "Sweet Jane" as a surreal look at the life of a rock star. The song was a narrative about life, and how through the aging process people were forced to compromise their values and ideals. "Sweet Jane" contained three characters, the narrator (in a rock 'n' roll band), Jack and Jane (in a relationship), and Jim (who drives a race car). The lyric "Sweet Jane" was literally Jack's professed love for Jane, and also a general reference to finding your happiness. The song followed the characters through their lives. It began by describing fun-loving adventure and big dreams and then by revealing that they had to work (both Jack and Jane found jobs to make money) for a living. The lyrics went on to explain that other people chose to live out their dreams (the singer in the rock band). In the end, the message was that even though life can be hard, you might find love or your place in life. Mott the Hoople covered "Sweet Jane" on their All the Young Dudes album and Reed loved their version (even helping them with the recording session).

1975's double album Metal Machine Music was a renewed effort by Reed to explore electronic music within his songwriting framework through utilizing electronically generated audio feedback. It was initially deemed a commercial failure, although later applauded by critics. 1975's Coney Island Baby was a warm, melodic record that renewed Reed's stories of city characters and their street hustle lives. 1976's Rock and Roll Heart was recorded on Reed's new label, Arista. 1978's Street Hassle demonstrated a harder edge, reflecting the rise of the punk genre that Reed and his Velvet Underground bandmates had helped to inspire. Lou Reed throughout his career was generally very dismissive of punk rock and rejected any affiliation with the genre. In 1978, he released his third live album, Live: Take No Prisoners, a record he often referred to as one of his best works. Reed employed jazz trumpeter Don Cherry for his 1979 album, The Bells. Many of the musicians in this edition of Reed's band went on to form the jazz-fusion ensemble called The Everyman Band.

The 1980's saw Lou Reed release six studio albums beginning with 1980's Growing Up In Public and ending with 1989's New York. In the wake of Andy Warhol's death in 1987, Reed and John Cale collaborated on an album inspired by Warhol's memory titled, Songs for Drella (Warhol's nickname). In 1990 and 1993, The Velvet Underground reunited for benefit concerts and brief tours. Reed released two albums in the 1990's, 1992's Magic and Loss, and 1996's Set the Twilight Reeling. Also in the 1990's, Reed recorded with, and married musician Laurie Anderson.

Lou Reed released the album Ecstasy in 2000, The Raven in 2003, and Hudson River Wind Meditations in 2007. Reed's final recording was 2011's Lulu, a collaboration with the heavy metal band Metallica. Reed and Metallica felt a musical bond and Metallica respected Reed's musical vision and willingness to take chances. Between his powerful career with The Velvet Underground and his own brilliant solo career, Lou Reed influenced a long list of artists and bands. They included; Brian Eno, David Bowie, Ian Hunter, The Talking Heads, The Strokes, Sonic Youth, and many more.

The Avant-Garde Meets Rock Music

There were significant avant-garde composers and musicians that greatly influenced the evolution of rock music from the late 1950's to present times. These musicians brought the ideas of minimalism, the use of non-musical sounds to create music, and alternative sound design, to the palette of rock music.

John Cage (1912-1992) was an avant-garde composer who developed innovative musical concepts that had a profound impact on both rock and jazz musicians. Cage believed that any object could become a musical instrument and any sound or noise could itself be music. In 1939, Cage wrote the groundbreaking composition "Imaginary Landscape No. 1," a work that blended two turntables with acoustic instruments. All through the 1950's, Cage's "chance music" (aka aleatory music where some element of a composition is determined by its performers during the performance process) grew increasingly experimental. It inspired the Fluxus art movement that included composers La Monte Young and Brian Eno. John Cage believed that anyone could be an artist by cultivating his or her own creative spirit.

La Monte Young (1935-) is an experimental composer and saxophonist who was most active in the 1950's and early 1960's. Young embraced the Fluxus art movement (mentioned above) that represented forward thinking musicians, actors, and visual artists. Young experimented with long, sustained notes that created intricate drone and harmonic effects. In the 1960's, Young collaborated with minimalist composers John Cale and Tony Conrad on a project called The Theater of Eternal Music. They utilized alternate tuning systems, sustained drones, and artificial scales to produce cutting edge compositions. Cale and Conrad went on to help form The Velvet Underground where their hypnotic drones inspired Lou Reed to compose pop melodies and turn them into innovative art rock compositions.

Philip Glass (1937-) is another important influence on art rock music. Glass, a minimalist composer, founded The Philip Glass Ensemble that performed extensively in the New York City underground rock clubs beginning in the 1970's. Glass and other minimalists such as Terry Riley (who invented tape delay loops), and Steve Reich, created compositions that emphasized legato and trance-like moods. Glass had a major influence on many rock artists such as Brian Eno and The Talking Heads.

From a broad perspective, the avant-garde brought a freedom of sound design and expression that creative artists often blended with blues, psychedelic, and other music styles. This greatly expanded the boundaries of rock music.

Captain Beefheart (born 1941-2010) (and **His Magic Band** 1964-1982) was an American singer/songwriter who played harmonica, saxophone, and other wind instruments. Beefheart's real name was Don Van Vliet. He formed His Magic Band in 1964 with a rotating group of musician's with whom he released thirteen studio albums. Beefheart and band integrated rock, psychedelic music, blues, free jazz, and experimental avant-garde styles to create his unique version of art rock.

Van Vliet was an artistic prodigy from childhood. He spent his teen years sculpting, painting, and listening to blues and modern jazz. Van Vliet met Frank Zappa when they were both students at the same high school. Although their association was brief, the duo formed a group called The Sorts where Zappa played distorted guitar and Van Vliet utilized his blues influenced deep bass voice. In early 1965, Van Vliet formed Captain Beefheart and His Magic Band. They briefly signed with, and were then dropped by A&M records. The band added drummer John French and guitar prodigy Ry Cooder, who would skillfully arrange the band's new material. French also contributed to the band's success by helping to write lyrics and by transcribing Van Vliet's musical ideas and presenting them to the other band members.

1967's Safe as Milk, the band's debut recording, did not fare well in America. However, Safe As Milk impressed both Paul McCartney and John Lennon. After being dropped by the label Buddah Records for not being pop-oriented enough, Captain Beefheart was signed to Blue Thumb Records and released Strictly Personal in 1968. For this recording, Van Vliet shook up The Magic Band and a new lineup emerged with guitarists Alex St. Clair and Jeff Cotton, bassist Jerry Handley, Van Vliet, and French. This recording contained psychedelic blues with added studio effects such as echo, phasing, and reverse tape effects.

Faced again with no record label, Captain Beefheart and His Magic Band appealed to Van Vliet's old friend, Frank Zappa. Zappa produced their next album, 1969's Trout Mask Replica and released it on his Straight label. Trout Mask Replica, a double album, was considered to be Captain Beefheart's most significant work. It combined elements of simple rock, blues, free jazz, rhythm and blues, and avant-garde styles. The music on Trout Mask Replica also featured the use of polyrhythms, multi-octave vocal parts, atonal melodies, and harmonies. Trout Mask Replica showed just how bizarre (some considered the album a big practical joke) and musical the avant-garde influence could be on rock music. Van Vliet now assumed full control of the band and rehearsed them for hours on end to achieve his artistic vision. Frank Zappa appeared on the songs "Pena" and "The Blimp."

"Moonlight on Vermont"
by Don Van Vliet

"Moonlight On Vermont" (not to be confused with the jazz standard of the 1940's titled "Moonlight In Vermont") was one of the best examples of Captain Beefheart's use of lyrical symbolism. The storyline was based on the lunar effects on the population of Vermont. It contained overtones of 1950's horror films including a werewolf plot and an explanation of how the moon could affect everybody's behavior. Beefheart wrote about the topics of indecent exposure ("even lifebuoy floatin'/ with his l'il pistol showin'"), the controlling effects of the moon, and included overt references to traditional gospel hymns ("give me that old time religion").

"Moonlight On Vermont" was one of The Magic Band's staples in their live performances. The rhythm section played a funky groove with screeching psychedelic guitars that complemented Van Vliet's Howlin' Wolf-like raw blues sound. "Moonlight On Vermont" was an art rock meeting of pure blues and the late 1960's psychedelic movement. This was fun music and sonic chaos that assaulted the listener's ears.

1970's Lick My Decals Off, Baby earned the band their only top twenty album in England. Captain Beefheart and His Magic Band released six more albums in the 1970's with an ever-changing lineup. Van Vliet steered the group in an increasingly more accessible blues-oriented direction. 1980's Doc at the Radar Station saw the band move into a post-punk style that was designed to appeal to a younger audience. 1982's Ice Cream for Crow would be the final Beefheart album. Shortly after it's release, Don Van Vliet retired from music to become a full-time artist. He became an accomplished and financially successful abstract expressionist painter. Unfortunately, Van Vliet was afflicted with multiple sclerosis which kept him wheelchair-bound for the next two decades of his life. Don Van Vliet died in late 2010. In 2012, the thirteenth Captain Beefheart album, Bat Chain Puller, was released two years after Van Vliet's death. It was initially recorded in 1976. Following a lawsuit settled in 1982, Frank Zappa's family released the original Bat Chain Puller in its original form. Captain Beefheart and His Magic Band achieved little commercial success but nevertheless were innovators in the art rock tradition. They held a substantial influence on many punk, new wave, and alternative rock musicians.

The Tubes (1972-present) are a band that started as rockers who combined wild satires of consumerism, politics, and media (and even references to soft-core pornography). These subjects were all joined and performed with high-level musicianship and refined songwriting. In live performances, The Tubes combined catchy musical elements with outrageous performance art concepts to make harsh and telling statements about popular culture. The origin of The Tubes occurred in the late 1960's when guitarist Bill Spooner, keyboardist Vince Welnick, and bassist Rick Anderson formed a band called the Beans. The Beans relocated to San Francisco in 1972 and added guitarist Roger Steen and drummer Prairie Prince. Soon after, they added vocalist (and onetime roadie) Fee Waybill and keyboardist Michael Cotton and changed their name to The Tubes.

Rock Hard Fact

Captain Beefheart (Don Van Vliet) refused to wear headphones in the studio and synced his vocals with the band via the faint leakage he could hear from the playback through the thick plate glass doors of the control room.

Rock Hard Fact

The Tubes live performances featured one of America's most outrageous stage shows in the 1970's complete with partial nudity, dancing girls, roadies dressed as giant cigarettes; all while wearing provocative costumes such as leotards with painted on nipples.

The Tubes developed a devoted cult following built on the band's live shows. On stage, they featured Waybill's bizarre characters that included Dr. Strangekiss, country singer Hugh Heifer, a "crippled Nazi," and Quay Lewd, a drug abusing British rock star. In 1975, The Tubes released their self-titled debut album The Tubes, produced by Al Kooper. The record featured the tune "White Punks on Dope" that reached number twenty-eight on the British charts. In late 1975, The Tubes had developed a new live stage show with films displayed behind every song. It was as if Saturday Night Live had joined forces with art-rock. 1976's Young and Rich followed, but The Tubes had trouble getting their studio recordings to reflect their on-stage theatrical complexity.

1977's Now was a fluid mix of blues shuffles, funky rhythm section parts, and complex band arrangements. However, Now did not fair well commercially. The Tubes toured England where some of their shows were banned. This ironically and fortuitously helped to make The Tubes a media sensation. For 1979's Remote Control, they recruited producer/musician Todd Rundgren to make a concept album that examined the influence of television. It was poorly received and The Tubes were dropped from A&M Records.

The Tubes were signed to Capitol Records and in 1981 released The Completion Backward Principle. Hitmaker-producer David Foster produced this "pop" concept album which included songs that described a sales training instructional manual. The band also created a long form music video for the record. The Completion Backward Principle yielded two hits, "Talk To You Later" and "Don't Want to Wait Anymore," and both received significant radio airplay. David Foster returned for 1983's Outside Inside that was recorded utilizing members of the bands Toto and Chicago. A suggestive MTV video of the single "She's a Beauty" went to number ten on the American charts. The Tubes again employed Todd Rundgren to produce 1985's Love Bomb. Following the release of the album, The Tubes went their separate ways with keyboardist Vince Welnick and drummer Prairie Prince joining Rundgren's touring band. Meanwhile, Fee Waybill officially left the band in 1986 and the remaining Tubes endured many more lineup changes. Fee Waybill rejoined the band in 1993 with original members Anderson, Prince, Steen, and new member keyboardist Gary Cambra. They released the musically strong Genius of America in 1996. In 2009, The Tubes released Fuel, a collection of previously unreleased songs. The Tubes continued to tour from 2009 to 2015, mostly in England and Europe. In 2017, they toured England as a supporting act for their theatrical equal, Alice Cooper. The legacy of The Tubes is a band that began with stunning theatrics matched with cutting edge musical elements that eventually evolved into a mainstream art rock pop band.

Talking Heads (1975-1991) were one of the most innovative bands to emerge from the art rock and new wave music genres. Composer/vocalist/guitarist David Byrne, drummer Chris Franz, and bassist Tina Weymouth were all friends at The Rhode Island School of Design in the early 1970's. Byrne and Frantz were briefly in a band called The Artistics and Weymouth would transport them to various gigs. The trio moved to New York City in 1974 and after an unsuccessful search for a bass player, Weymouth was persuaded to learn the instrument. Their debut gig as Talking Heads was as the opening act for The Ramones at the infamous CBGB's club in the summer of 1975. After a few years of writing and cultivating their sound, The Talking Heads released the single "Love→Building on Fire" in 1977. They recruited ex-Jonathan Richmond and the Modern Lovers keyboardist Jerry Harrison to complete the band.

1977's debut album Talking Head: 77 featured the fairly successful "Psycho Killer" (number ninety-two on the U.S. charts). The Talking Heads had established a unique sound complete with funky rhythms under Byrne's quirky vocal style. Rather than write about the usual subjects of sex and drugs, Byrne choose to sing about food, buildings, and a character inspired by Norman Bates from the Hitchcock film *Psycho*.

"Psycho Killer"
by David Byrne, Tina Weymouth and Chris Franz

Listeners thought that "Psycho Killer" was about the Son of Sam 1976-77 serial killings. But David Byrne had composed a song with introspective lyrics about the mindset of a murderer four years earlier. He thought the song was kind of silly and never believed that "Psycho Killer" would become a hit. Byrne commented on his writing process and said, "When I started writing this…I imagined Alice Cooper doing a Randy Newman-type ballad. Both the Joker and Hannibal Lecter were much more fascinating than the good guys. Everybody sort of roots for the bad guys in movies." #4

Part of chorus and bridge of "Psycho Killer" were written in French. Some have interpreted this to mean that the narrator was purposely made to sound pretentious, as if he was trying to be clever. The French lyrics translated to "What I made, that evening/What she said, that evening/accomplishing my hope/Headlong I go towards the glory" The lyric of "Fa Fa Fa" came from an Otis Redding song called "Fa Fa Fa Fa Fa (Sad Song)", revealing the influence of soul singers on The Talking Heads. "Psycho Killer" utilized a driving rhythm and contained one of the great basslines in rock music.

On tour with The Ramones in 1977, Talking Heads met musician Brian Eno in London. This led to a three-year association resulting in Eno's production of the band's next three albums. Eno's (see chapter eighteen) innovative compositional and production approach blended well with the band's adventurous and diverse exploration of musical styles from punk and new wave to psychedelic funk to African music. 1978's More Songs About Buildings and Food transformed Talking Heads from a quirky CBGB's live act to a band that could make cutting edge intelligent pop-rock music. On this album, the band covered soul singer Al Green's "Take Me To The River." The album reached number twenty-nine on the American charts and number twenty-one in England. 1979's Fear of Music continued the Eno and Heads collaboration and peaked at number twenty-one in the U.S. and number thirty-three in Britain. The hit "Life During Wartime" produced the classic line "this ain't no party, this ain't no disco" paying tribute to CBGB's and The Mudd club, two popular New York City nightclubs. 1980's Remain in Light was the band's strongest collaboration with Brian Eno and achieved commercial success when it reached number nineteen in America and number twenty-one in England.

Groundbreaking album
Remain in Light
by Talking Heads

One of Talking Heads' goals for Remain in Light was to make an album that didn't make it seem like the band was merely backing up David Byrne.

"At times words can be a dangerous addition to music-they can pin it down. Words imply that the music is about what the words say, literally, and nothing more. If done poorly, they can destroy the pleasant ambiguity that constitutes much of the reason we love music."

-David Byrne

The album was innovative with Brian Eno and the band drawing from strong West African rhythms and electronic music experimentation. Session musicians such as guitarist Adrian Belew (from King Crimson and Frank Zappa), vocalist Nona Hendryx (Labelle), and trumpeter Jon Hassell (minimalist artist with La Monte Young, Terry Riley, and Peter Gabriel) made significant contributions. Eno played bass guitar, keyboards, percussion, and backing vocals. He also added vocal arrangements.

Remain in Light was recorded in the Bahamas and in Philadelphia (at Sigma Sound Studios) in the hope of achieving a rhythm and blues feeling. When Brian Eno first arrived in the Bahamas to begin work on the album, he was not very enthusiastic but changed his mind when he heard the instrumental demo songs. Eno and the band were both inspired by specific West African music where individual rhythmic parts were blended to create layers of polyrhythms. Fela Kuti's, 1973 recording Afrodisiac was an important afro-beat recording and became the main source of inspiration for Remain in Light.

David Byrne was struggling with a case of writer's block but embraced one of Eno's concepts where lyrics utilized specific words to phonetically imitate, resemble, or suggest the sound that they described. For example, words like "oink," "meow," "roar," or "chirp" resemble animal noises. Employing this technique, Byrne would listen to his own previously recorded instrumental tracks and "scat" sing his own made up words over them until he found the right sounds for the song. This was a good example of how Eno focused the musical attention away from the importance of lyrical meaning in music.

The hit from the album was "Once in a Lifetime." Written by all of the band members and produced by Eno, it was the band's introduction (via Eno) to the complexity of African rhythms. For "Once In a Lifetime," Eno utilized the concept of beat displacement where he asked the band to feel beat three as if it was beat one. Eno also overdubbed each band member's different musical ideas (that they had developed independently). This process created repetitive two-measure ensemble patterns that enabled Eno to build entire song structures. Remain in Light would prove to be the height of the David Byrne and Brian Eno collaborations (for more on this album and other Eno/Talking collaborations see chapter eighteen).

In 1980-81, Brian Eno again collaborated with David Byrne (without Talking Heads) on the album My Life in the Bush of Ghosts. The project sonically integrated sampled vocals, "found sounds" (sounds derived from objects or products not normally considered to be musical instruments), African and Middle Eastern rhythms, and electronic music techniques. This recording is considered to be an innovative, groundbreaking work as applied to the genres of ambient (see chapter eighteen), electronic, and world music. My Life in the Bush of Ghosts was, in part, based on radio broadcasts collected by Eno in the United States that he combined with sampled recordings of rhythms from Africa and The Middle East.

In 1982, Talking Heads released the double live album The Name of This Band Is Talking Heads. The album contained live versions of songs from their first four studio albums. Continuing without the services of Eno, 1983's Speaking in Tongues featured The Talking Heads' hit "Burning Down the House." It reached number nine on the U.S. charts on the heels of a heavy MTV rotation. Tensions had been mounting in band with Byrne and Eno on one side, and (husband and wife) Franz and Weymouth on the other. Harrison remained somewhere in the middle.

Stop Making Sense, a 1984 concert film of a live Talking Heads performance, came next. Three more albums followed, 1985's Little Creatures, 1986's True Stories, and 1988's Naked. Little Creatures featured the hits "And She Was" and "Road to Nowhere." Naked went in a different direction when the band explored the topics of sex, death, and politics. It also saw the return to the strong African influence heard on the Remain in Light album. Despite a lack of interest from David Byrne, Talking Heads reunited with Weymouth, Frantz, and Harrison for the 1996 one-off album No Talking, Just Head. Byrne's focus at that time was firmly rooted in pursuing his own successful solo career. Besides his 1981 My Life in the Bush of Ghosts, Byrne has released nine solo albums including 2012's Love This Giant. Byrne has also written numerous books and composed many film scores including the outstanding soundtrack to *The Catherine Wheel*. Chais Frantz and Tina Weymouth continued to record and perform with the band The Tom Tom Club (that they had formed back in 1981).

Talking Heads created a legacy of tremendous musical innovation from art rock experimentation to polyrhythmic world rhythms with melodic pop sensibilities. They have influenced countless artists including R.E.M., Living Color (who covered "Memories Can't Wait"), Primus, Radiohead, The Weeknd, and many others. Talking Heads were inducted into the Rock and Roll Hall of Fame in 2002.

Discussion Question

For many of the art rock bands and artists, the influence of avant-garde music was present. How did it affect their approach to rock songwriting and performance? Be specific and give musical examples.

Glam Rock

David Robert Jones aka **David Bowie** (1947-2016) was one of the most influential artists in rock music history. Bowie created new dimensions in popular music from the early 1970's to 2017, pioneering the rock genres of art and glam rock and adding innovations to punk, new wave, electronic, and pop-rock styles. David Jones was from Brixton, a southern borough of London. He was shy but participated in his school choir and the local scouting troop. Jones learned guitar and saxophone in his adolescent years, playing songs such as "The Inchworm." This was one of his favorite songs that would later be a template for many of his best and saddest songs including "Life on Mars?" and "Aladdin Sane." Bowie remembered, "You wouldn't believe the amount of my songs that have sort of spun off that one song "The Inchworm"…there's a child's nursery rhyme element in it. It kept bringing me back to the feelings of those pure thoughts of sadness that you have as a child, and how they're so identified even when you're an adult…it was that song that did it for me." #5 English TV was another constant in Jones's childhood years, especially a BBC broadcast of a science fiction series titled *The Quatermass Experiment*. This introduced him to the concept of outer space, a theme he later utilized in his songwriting and acting career. Another strong influence was Little

> "All these different personas that he (David Bowie) had, they really weren't about him. They were about us."
>
> – Laurie Brown, journalist

Richard, for whom a ten-year-old Davey Jones admired as an iconic figure.

By 1962, fifteen-year old Davey Jones was playing saxophone in a local band around London and calling himself Dave Jay. He wrote a few songs and did his first professional recording, singing backup on the Kon-Rad's song "I Never Dreamed." Next, Jones helped to form the rhythm and blues band The King Bee's. The band was signed to a minor deal by Decca Records. By 1964, the King Bee's broke up and Jones became the lead singer and tenor saxophonist for The Manish Boys. They were soon billed as Davie Jones and The Manish Boys. Jones again moved on to another band, The Lower Third, where he released a series of unsuccessful singles. Jones next joined his fifth band called The Buzz and released the unsuccessful single "Do Anything You Say."

Davie Jones was dissatisfied with his stage name because it was often confused with Davy Jones of The Monkees. Therefore, he changed his name to David Bowie, after the 19th century American Revolutionary James Bowie. David's first professional recording as David Bowie was a song called "Can't Help Thinking About Me," recorded with his backing band, The Buzz. At this time, Bowie was strongly influenced by the Velvet Underground's recording The Velvet Underground and Nico. From this album, Bowie learned the potential of rock lyrics to explore many human issues and he played every song from this album on his twelve-string guitar. The Velvet Underground would later spark Bowie's love for New York City.

Bowie released his self-titled debut album David Bowie in 1967. Many of the album's songs were previously recorded in 1966 at Decca's studio with house producer Mike Vernon. The song "Rubber Band" revealed Bowie's love of singer Anthony Newley's theatrical tunes. The album sold poorly and Bowie was soon dropped from his label, Deram Records. Bowie also began to audition for acting roles at this time. Soon, Tony Visconti, a producer and bassist from New York, traveled to England and began to collaborate with Bowie in the studio. Bowie also met Lindsay Kemp, a dancer and choreographer, who would help him develop his physical abilities. Kemp in particular exposed Bowie to the tradition of Japanese Kabuki Theater with its costuming aesthetics. Bowie revealed, "I began to think about costuming music, creating an alternate version of reality onstage. I wasn't quite sure what the balance would be, but I was always open to other people's ideas and always so influenced by something I found dramatic." #6 Yet another influence on Bowie was Marc Bolan of T. Rex.

In 1969, Bowie released a single, "Space Oddity" that would have a major impact on his career. It was Bowie's first single to make the charts in England and upon its reissue in 1973; it peaked at number fifteen on the U.S. charts.

"Space Oddity"
by David Bowie

"Space Oddity," was initially inspired by Stanley Kubrick's 1968 film *2001: A Space Odyssey*. The song was first released as a single and would later be re-recorded for the opening track of Bowie's second album David Bowie/Man of Words, Man of Music. The song centered on the space launch of Major Tom, a fictional astronaut, but was quickly associated with the first ever Apollo moon landing. Bowie sang about Major Tom's communication with Earth being cut off and his future of spending eternity floating around in his tin can. However, the BBC utilized the song to cover the real space event. David Bowie recorded multiple versions of "Space Oddity," including the original that was used for a thirty-minute promotional film about his songwriting and singing.

The recording for the second album would be at Trident Studios in London with producer Gus Dudgeon (after Tony Visconti first turned it down). Bowie employed Yes-keyboardist Rick Wakeman on Mellotron, bassist Herbie Flowers, guitarist Mick Wayne, and drummer Terry Cox. The production was as precise as an actual space mission with the arrangements mapped out on the studio bulletin board dictating where the strings and other instrumental parts entered. Rick Wakeman remembered, "Gus was a different class…he worked to get on tape what the artist wanted…David was light years ahead of how the industry thought. Simple as that. I didn't think it was a novelty song at all. I thought it was astonishing." #7 "Space Oddity" would become David Bowie's signature song, often the first tune on many of his best of compilations.

1969's David Bowie/Man of Words, Man of Music (reissued as Space Oddity) was Bowie's second studio album. It contained elements of folk, ballads, and even progressive rock. Opening with "Space Oddity," the album also featured the song "Cygnet Committee," a nine-minute track that revealed some of Bowie's future musical direction. It's a dystopian narrative about a man who helped revolutionaries establish a new society. For Bowie, this was a transitional album from his cabaret/avant-garde days to a new musical approach utilizing rock and folk music styles.

In 1970, Bowie formed a band called The Hype that was inspired by the glam rock scene in England. Each band member was given a fully costumed stage persona. The band consisted of guitarist Mick Ronson (pinstriped suit-Gangsterman), bassist/producer Tony Visconti (crime-fighting Superhero), drummer John Cambridge (Cowboy Man-with hat and fringe) and Bowie (Space Star-rainbow costume prism of rainbow colors). At first they were laughed at on stage but Bowie exuded a strong onstage confidence and presence that lent credibility to the band. Cambridge was replaced by drummer Mick "Woody" Woodmansey and this lineup recorded Bowie's third studio album, 1970's The Man Who Sold the World. This was a dark album about a man coming of age in a world that was increasingly depraved and barren. It was Bowie's first hard rock/heavy metal album. The subject matter ranged from assassins to insanity to war commentary. Mick Ronson was looking to create a heavy sound with a blues influence like that of the band Cream. Ronson became involved with the production, assisting Visconti, and worked tirelessly to create a musical and cohesive rhythm section. The Man Who Sold the World went to number twenty-four in England and made the U.S. charts at one hundred and five.

1971's Hunky Dory was regarded as one of Bowie's defining works. It brought together Mick Ronson on guitar, Mellotron, and vocals, Trevor Bolder on bass and trumpet, Mick Woodmansey on drums, and Rick Wakeman on piano. Most of these musicians would eventually become the lineup for Bowie's Spiders from Mars band. Hunky Dory was a piano-driven album yielding the hits "Life on Mars" and "Changes." "Changes" was about artistic reinvention and a look to the future. "Life on Mars," considered one of Bowie's greatest pop tunes, was about a sensitive young girl's reaction to the media. Bowie considered Hunky Dory one of his best, but ultimately it was a transition to completely new musical and artistic ground.

Chapter Eight: Art Rock and Glam Rock

Ziggy played....the Performance Arts

While on tour in America, Bowie began to conceptualize a character that would eventually become Ziggy Stardust. He melded together the personas of rock stars Iggy Pop and Lou Reed. Bowie wrote notes describing a crazed rock star named Ziggy (a spinoff of the name Iggy) that looked like he had landed from Mars. Bowie was also inspired by a tailor's shop called Ziggy's that he would often pass by while riding on a train. The stardust name was borrowed from a musician named Norman Carl Odom (Bowie knew him because both had been artists at Mercury Records) who created a character called "Legendary Stardust Cowboy." Therefore, Ziggy Stardust was really a combination of real and imaginary characters. Other influences factored into Ziggy Stardust as well. Bowie mixed in some parts of Stanley Kubrick's film 2001: A Space Odyssey, with its themes of existentialism, human evolution, artificial intelligence and extraterrestrial beings. Another Kubrick film, A Clockwork Orange, brought its themes of social conflicts and upheaval from a dystopian future England.

The red-headed Ziggy Stardust, a perfect character to represent glam rock, was also a great vehicle to portray themes of sexual exploration and social issues. Ziggy's message was about giving hope to humanity while delivering it with rock star excesses of wild sexual promiscuity and drug intake. Ziggy would ultimately be destroyed by his own consumptions. Combined with Bowie's real life media manufactured sexual ambiguity, the character of Ziggy Stardust and the album served to fuel great interest and controversy.

It wouldn't be long until Bowie became Ziggy! About Ziggy's creation, Bowie said, "It was about putting together all the things that fascinated me culturally. Everything from Kabuki Theater to Jacques Brel to drag acts. Everything about it was a hybrid of everything I liked." #8 Bowie envisioned Ziggy to be a character he could create and act out on stage and still remain himself, a rock superstar committed to his project, yet safe offstage. But like Dr. Frankenstein, Bowie greatly underestimated the power of his creation. Ziggy Stardust became, for better and at times worse, a larger-that-life character. Bowie's band morphed into the Spiders and musically supercharged the Ziggy character on stage. However off-stage, the Ziggy character became difficult to shake. No rock star had taken a persona this far before. Mick Jagger's "Jumpin Jack Flash" was left onstage after the show was over. Peter Gabriel would wear a fox's head on stage with Genesis, but once he removed it, he could move to the next character or go back to being Gabriel. Not in this case, Ziggy consumed Bowie.

Bowie eventually realized that like an actor that gets typecast into playing the same role over and over, he would have to destroy Ziggy. If not, he would have remained Ziggy for decades to come. But like a great character actor, Bowie became artistically restless, and recognized his need to push the boundaries in new directions. Although Bowie dismantled the Spiders from Mars, Ziggy's dyed red hair stayed on a little longer.

1972's The Rise and Fall of Ziggy Stardust and the Spiders from Mars catapulted David Bowie to international stardom. Ziggy Stardust was a concept album but yielded three breakout hits; "Starman," "Suffragette City," and "Rock 'n' Roll Suicide." The album rose to number five in England and number three in the U.S. A concert film of the same name was recorded in 1973, but not released until 1983.

Groundbreaking album
The Rise and Fall of Ziggy Stardust and the Spiders from Mars
by David Bowie

The Ziggy Stardust album would have made a legend out of Bowie even if he had never released another album. About half of the album was recorded before the Hunky Dory record was even released. The core Spiders band on the album consisted of Mick Ronson, bassist Trevor Bolder, and drummer Mick Woodmansey.

Side one opened with "Five Years," then "Soul Love," "Moonage Daydream," "Starman," and "It Ain't Easy." "Five Years" opened with a solo drumset beat and the narrator informed you that Earth had only five years left before its destruction. The tone was set when Bowie addressing the listener directly, something not usually found in rock lyrics. "Soul Love" followed with a pre-apocalypse sense of frustration. "Moonage Daydream" continued to tell the story of an alien Messiah and described the creation of Ziggy as a complex blend of religion, sexual freedom, rebellion, and romance that evolved into a rock star. "Starman," released as a single, described Ziggy's message of bringing hope to the youth on Earth through the radio. Ziggy was not the Starman, but instead was his Earthly messenger. Mick Ronson's string arrangements and Bowie's acoustic guitar brought timbral depth and a soothing pop-rock sensibility to the track. "It Ain't Easy" functioned as an interlude between side one and two.

Side two opened with "Lady Stardust," then "Star," "Hang On to Yourself," "Ziggy Stardust," "Suffragette City," and "Rock 'n' Roll Suicide." The song "Lady Star" was possibly about T. Rex's Marc Bolan. The autobiographical "Star" described rock 'n' roll ambition. "Hang On to Yourself" fused a pre-punk riff with an Eddie Cochran-like rockabilly feel. Ronson achieved a raunchy and distorted Les Paul guitar sound on the track. "Ziggy Stardust" featured a classic Mick Ronson guitar riff that was instantly recognizable. This title track revealed the great diversity of Bowie's many voices. From the first verse's "Ziggy played guitar" to verse two's "Ziggy really sang" to the chorus "So where were the Spiders?" Bowie sounded like three different singers, each bringing a different emotion to the words. "Suffragette City" featured a Little Richard-like piano riff and lyrical references to the film A Clockwork Orange. A sexual theme was also alluded to with the classic line "Wham bam thank you ma'am!"

The album closed with "Rock 'n' Roll Suicide," that started with acoustic guitar and vocals and then slowly built to full band with string and brass accompaniments. It detailed Ziggy's final demise as an old and washed-up rock star. It found Ziggy discredited and wandering the London streets. It also was used to end the live Ziggy Stardust show. After the album was recorded, the Spiders rehearsed the new material and prepped for their new identity as sexed up outer-space rebels. Drummer "Woody" Woodmansey said "At first we were very reticent about the outfits and the makeup…I think we were tricked into the makeup thing by being told the big theatrical lights we were using would wipe out the features of your face."

> "There is so little time for us all; I need to be able to say what I want quickly and to as many people as possible."
>
> – Marc Bolan

Rock Hard Fact

Gary Glitter at one time owned more than thirty glitter suits and fifty pairs of his trademark silver platform boots.

#9 Eventually, the Spiders embraced their new and groundbreaking roles.

1973's Aladdin Sane (a pun on "A Lad Insane") went straight to number one in Britain and number seventeen in America. The Spiders band remained with the addition of jazz pianist Mike Garson. Ken Scott was now in charge of production (with Bowie still very hands on), and Mick Ronson continued to provide the arrangements. Aladdin Sane was the outgrowth of Ziggy Stardust in appearance and persona, both on the record and subsequent live performances. Bowie felt the pressure to keep up with Ziggy when he said "Aladdin Sane, that's me having a go at trying to redefine Ziggy, and making him what people wanted…I knew when I was making Aladdin Sane that the bottom had just fallen out of the whole idea." #10 One of the notable hits to emerge from the album was "The Jean Genie." That same year, Bowie released Pin Ups, a collection of covers and one original. Bowie still employed Ronson, Garson, and Bolder but now brought in drummer Aynsley Dunbar.

In 1974, Bowie moved to America and released Diamond Dogs, now moving in a funk and soul music direction. Garson and Dunbar (for some tracks) remained, but the other Spiders band members were now gone, including longtime guitarist and arranger Mick Ronson (some of his arrangements were previously recorded for the album). Now, guitar playing was done by committee, including Bowie. Bassist Herbie Flowers and drummer Tony Newman were added to the band. Diamond Dogs, a number one in England and number five in America, saw the return of producer Tony Visconti. The album, complete with Bowie's red hair, marked an end to his glam period with one last glam hit "Rebel, Rebel." The Diamond Dogs band was funkier than the Spiders and the album contained Bowie's best studio sound to date. The ensuing tour involved a massive stage production with Bowie in full rock star mode.

In 1975, Bowie reinvented himself yet again when he strongly embraced soul and rhythm and blues styles. Inspired by the "Philly sound," Bowie took up residence at Sigma Sound Studios in Philadelphia to record 1975's Young Americans album. Visconti produced and Bowie utilized a soulful and funky new guitarist, Carlos Alomar, who would go on to play on more Bowie albums than any other guitar player. Young Americans produced the classic hits "Fame" and "Young Americans." Vocalist Luther Vandross, drummer Andy Newmark, and saxophonist David Sanborn played on the album. The legendary John Lennon also added vocals and guitar on "Fame" and "Across the Universe." Young Americans went to number two in England and number nine in America. 1976's Station to Station presented yet another Bowie persona, The Thin White Duke, a character Bowie developed for a 1976 film he starred in titled *The Man Who Fell to Earth*. The album featured the hits "Golden Years" and "Station to Station."

After a struggle with drug addiction and other personal issues, David Bowie moved to West Berlin Germany in 1977. There, he recorded a series of three albums (known as the Berlin Trilogy). Bowie co-produced these albums with Tony Visconti and collaborated with musician/producer Brian Eno. The first of these recordings, 1977's Low, featured a more electronic and avant-garde approach (influenced by the band Kraftwerk). Also recorded in 1977, "Heroes," continued Bowie's ambient music experiments with Eno and now added the services of guitar great Robert Fripp. The album Heroes went to number three in Britain and featured the hit "Heroes."

"Heroes"
by David Bowie and Brian Eno

"Heroes" was a result of Bowie's "Berlin" period and told a story about two lovers, one from East and one from West Berlin, Germany. It was a strong statement confirming the will of the human spirit to overcome great adversity. The title of the song was based on a tune titled "Hero" by the German band Neu! (admired by both Bowie and Eno). Tony Visconti had the idea that the two lovers would kiss "by the wall" (rumored to be Visconti himself and a woman he was having an affair with). Bowie's performance of "Heroes" on June 6th, 1987 at the German Reichstag in West Berlin became a catalyst for the real life eventual fall of the Berlin Wall.

Brian Eno achieved a "wall of sound" type approach to make the track sound grand and heroic. Eno had the word heroes in mind before Bowie even wrote the lyrics. Adding to the basic arrangement of piano, bass, rhythm guitar, and drums, Eno built a massive synthesizer and electronic soundscape. Eno added an EMS VCS3 synth part that contained a low-frequency drone with three oscillators producing a distinctive effect. King Crimson guitarist Robert Fripp had worked with Eno before and on short notice, flew from New York to Berlin to work on "Heroes." Fripp developed a unique guitar sound with feedback and altered pitches recorded in different parts of the room. Visconti accidentally played all three guitar takes together that Fripp had recorded and decided to use all three simultaneously on the record. The resulting "wall of guitar" was jaw-dropping and instantly became the song's intro. Visconti also experimented with gated microphone techniques to which Bowie added altered vocal dynamic levels.

"Heroes" showed a true collaboration between Bowie, Eno, and Visconti. It has been covered by many artists. As well as being a sonic masterpiece, it is one of Bowie's signature tunes and one of his most artistic efforts.

1979's Lodger was recorded in Switzerland and New York City. Lodger was highly experimental and featured guitarist Adrian Belew. It was pop-oriented, yet utilized world music and the creative recording techniques of Brian Eno.

Bowie recorded five solo albums in the 1980's including; 1980's Scary Monsters and Super Creeps, 1983's Let's Dance, 1984's Tonight, and 1987's Never Let Me Down. In 1989, he also formed a young and hard rocking band called Tin Machine. Major hits included "Ashes to Ashes" and "Fashion" (from Scary Monsters), "Under Pressure" (a collaboration with Queen), "Let's Dance," "China Girl," and "Modern Love" (from Let's Dance). The aforementioned Tin Machine band released the Tin Machine album in 1989 followed by Tin Machine II in 1991. This band came with controversy in the form of political lyrics. The album's singles failed to chart and Tin Machine was disbanded.

Five more albums followed in the 1990's including; 1993's Black Tie White Noise and The Buddha of Suburbia, 1995's Outside (reuniting with Brian Eno), 1997's Earthling, and 1999's Hours. In 1992, Bowie performed at the Freddie Mercury Tribute Concert. Black Tie White Noise would be Bowie's last number one album in England. It featured guitarist Mick Ronson, who died of cancer only twenty-four days after the album's release.

In 2002, Bowie released Heathen. Visconti was back in the producers chair (at the time Visconti called this Bowie's magnum opus), with appearances by Pete

Townshend, bassist Tony Levin, and Dave Grohl. 2003's Reality was followed by a ten-year hiatus and then 2013's The Next Day. David Bowie's last album was 2016's Blackstar. Deliberately attempting to avoid making another typical rock album, Bowie was inspired by (and enlisted the support of) some of New York City's best young jazz musician's including guitarist Ben Monder, keyboardist Jason Linder, drummer Mark Guiliana, saxophonist Donny McCaslin and bassist Tim Lefebvre. This remarkable record leaned upon the young musicians' grasp of a new combination of electronica and improvisation.

Two days after Blackstar's release, David Bowie died of liver cancer at the age of sixty-nine. The lyrics for Blackstar revealed Bowie's awareness of his illness and impending mortality. David Bowie's legacy revealed an artist that gained unique status as a rock music icon by bringing sophistication and intellectual depth to his musical compositions, stage and theatrical characters, and overall artistry. Bowie owned perhaps the strongest cult following in rock music history. He also achieved great mainstream popularity that he cultivated from his vast body of work. Bowie's recorded output was astounding with twenty-five studio albums (two more with Tin Machine), eight EP's, ten live albums, fifty-one compilation albums, one-hundred and twenty eight singles, four film soundtracks, fourteen video albums, and seventy-two videos.

David Bowie was inducted into the Rock and Roll Hall of Fame in 1996.

Mick Ronson (1946-1993) was a British guitarist, songwriter, arranger, and producer who achieved most of his critical and commercial success working with David Bowie (see Bowie section in this chapter). Ronson was also a session musician and worked with Steven Morrissey, Ian Hunter, Van Morrison, Mott the Hoople, John Mellencamp, and Bob Dylan. Ronson's debut solo album was 1974's Slaughter on 10th Avenue. It featured many of his fellow Bowie sidemen including Trevor Bolder, Mike Garson, and Aynsley Dunbar. 1975's Play Don't Worry, an album of mostly covers, was arranged and produced by Ronson. Over the next twenty years, Ronson was extremely busy recording with and producing a variety of prominent artists.

Mick Ronson died in 1993 of liver cancer at the age of forty-six. In 1994, his album Heaven and Hull was posthumously released with appearances from David Bowie, Chrissie Hynde, Ian Hunter, and others. Other posthumous Ronson albums included; 1999's Just Like This and Showtime (a live recording from two shows from 1976 and 1989), and 2001's Indian Summer (a movie soundtrack for a film that was never made). Mick Ronson's legacy revealed one of the most influential guitarists of the 1970's. He was the foil to David Bowie's Ziggy Stardust. But more than that, Mick Ronson was a gifted arranger and producer that brought to life a rich body of rock music from the 1970's to 1990's. A Mick Ronson Memorial Stage stands as a tribute to his memory in Queen's Gardens, Hull, England.

Gary Glitter (1944-) (career 1960-1997) aka Paul Francis Gadd is a British glam rock singer who, along with his backing band **The Glittermen** (1972-1973), achieved success in the 1970's and 1980's. Glitter cultivated an extreme glam image by wearing glitter suits, make-up and platform boots. Glitter began performing as Paul Raven in the 1960's and rose to fame with the chart hits "Rock and Roll, Parts 1 and 2," "Do You Want to Touch Me," and "Hello, Hello, I'm Back Again." Some of Gary Glitter's albums included his 1972 debut Glitter and 1973's Touch Me. Glitter went on to sell over twenty million records with twenty-one hit singles on the British charts. He made five more studio albums from 1975 to 2001. The Glittermen continued to back Gary Glitter in the early 1970's, but changed their name to **The Glitter Band** and began to work as a separate entity. The band released their debut album Hey in 1974 followed by 1975's Rock 'n' Roll Dudes, Listen to the Band, and Makes You Blind. Their final studio album was 1977's People Like You. The Glitter Band has endured numerous lineup changes over the years and is still active today.

Bay City Rollers (1966-1990) (1998-2015 with some years inactive) were a Scottish pop-rock glam band. They became overnight teen sensations in their hometown of Edinburgh, Scotland and then throughout Europe. For a brief period, The Bay City Rollers expanded their popularity to become worldwide teen idols with the song "Rollermania." Their classic lineup was singer Les McKeown, guitarists Stuart John Wood and Eric Faulkner, bassist Alan Longmuir, and drummer Derek Longmuir. The band's first hit was "Keep On Dancing," a cover of a 1965 hit by The Gentrys. A number of British chart hits followed and by early 1975, The Bay City Rollers were one of the biggest selling bands in England. Later that year, the band released their first full length album Bay City Rollers that went to number twenty on the U.S. charts. Another hit "Money Honey" peaked at number nine in America. 1975's Once Upon a Star went to number one in Britain. Their hit "Bye, Bye, Baby" from their 1975 album Once Upon a Star album was another hit. In 1976, a North American only release, Rock 'n' Roll Love Letter, reached number thirty-one on the U.S. charts. Fans of the band even had their own style of dress with calf-length tartan pants (a Scottish pattern of criss-crossed bands in multiple colors) and scarves. By the late 1970's, the popularity of The Bay City Rollers had waned. However, the band persevered through the 1980's and 1990's. In 2015, The Bay City Rollers re-formed and announced that a new record would be forthcoming.

Slade (1966-present) was formed in England by vocalist Noddy Holder, guitarist Dave Hill, bassist Jim Lea, and drummer Don Powell. Slade was a dominant force on the British charts in the early 1970's with twelve top five hits between 1971 and 1974, three of which went to number one. The band released fifteen studio albums from their 1970 debut Beginnings to their latest, 2002's Cum on Let's Party. Slade was the most consistent British glam band of the 1970's selling more singles in England than any other band. One of Slade's most notable singles "Cum On Feel the Noize," was a hit in England and would later be covered by Quiet Riot, becoming a number five hit for Quiet Riot in America. Slade benefited from the production and management skills of Chas Chandler (former bassist of The Animals and Jimi Hendrix manager). Slade is cited by many artists as a major influence including; The Ramones, Sex Pistols, The Clash, Kiss, Nirvana, and many others.

T. Rex (1967-1977) defined the emerging British glam rock scene of the early 1970's. The band started as Tyrannosaurus Rex in 1967 and was formed by guitarist/singer/songwriter Marc Bolan. Bolan was originally in the band Susie & the Hula Hoops and then the short-lived band, John's Children. Forming a duo with percussionist Steve Peregrin Took, Bolan wrote and sang acoustic material that included Indian music influences (Bolan listened to Indian musician Ravi Shankar). Now formally known as Tyrannosaurus Rex, Bolan and Took released their 1968 debut album, My People Were Fair and Had Sky in Their Hair…But Now They're Content to Wear Stars on Their Brows with Tony Visconti in charge of the production. This recording also featured a disc jockey, John Peel, who read a children's story written by Bolan over the composition "Frowning Atahullpa (My Inca Love)." This track also included a long Hare Krishna chant. Tyrannosaurus Rex was considered to be a psychedelic folk band. That same year, the band released Prophet, Seers & Sage: The Angels of the Ages. 1969's Unicorn and 1970's A Beard of Stars would be the last recording before Tyrannosaurus Rex would change their musical direction and name to T. Rex.

In 1970, T. Rex released their debut album T. Rex. Bolan sang and played guitar, bass, and organ while his new partner Mickey Finn (he had joined for the A Beard of Stars album) played drums, bass, Pixiphone, and vocals. Besides production, Tony Visconti added string arrangements and played piano. Howard Kaylan and Mark Volman (aka "Flo and Eddie") sang backup and would go on to sing on many of the T. Rex's subsequent albums. T. Rex's move to an electric approach was gradual along with their emerging new minimal rock sound. The band recorded "Ride a White Swan" during the T. Rex album sessions but released the single separately. It has been credited with helping to establish the glam rock movement. Bolan did not wear any of the characteristic glam-rock stage clothing until the promotion for the follow-up single "Hot Love" (another stand alone single) which reached the top of the British charts. By this time, T. Rex had added bassist/guitarist Steve Currie and drummer Bill Legend.

1971's Electric Warrior earned great commercial appeal for T. Rex. Electric Warrior included their hit "Get It On" that went to number one in England and number ten on the U.S. charts. The tune was retitled in America to "Bang a Gong (Get It On)" to avoid confusion with the song "Get It On" by the group Chase. Another motivation to change the song title in America was to make the tune more radio friendly and less offensive (with its sexual overtones).

> "I've always dug Marc Bolan and he knows it…I'd let him get away with murder because of what he's doing for rock 'n' roll."
>
> – Pete Townshend

"Get It On"
by Marc Bolan

On the classic hit "Get It On," Marc Bolan was inspired to compose a guitar riff based on his love of the Chuck Berry "Little Queenie" riff. Recorded at Trident Studio in London, keyboardists Rick Wakeman and Blue Weaver both played on the track with Wakeman adding only piano glissandos several times throughout the song. King Crimson's Ian McDonald added alto and baritone saxophone parts as well.

"Get It One" was clearly about sex but many listeners did not pick up on it because the imagery was vague. "Get It On" stayed at the top of the British charts for four straight weeks and became T. Rex's biggest hit in England and only hit in America. A notable cover of "Get It On" by The Power Station peaked at number nine on the U.S. charts featuring vocalist Robert Palmer with members of Duran Duran and Chic. New Wave band Blondie also recorded a version of the song for their 1978 live album, Parallel Lines. "Get it On" is still in heavy rotation on FM radio playlists.

Groundbreaking album Electric Warrior
by T. Rex

Electric Warrior is considered to be one of glam rock's first and most significant recordings. On Electric Warrior, Marc Bolan altered his musical direction and mindset by not taking himself so seriously. Bolan utilized silly wordplay and gave way to any pretense of making an artistic record, creating lyrics that were purposely absurd and lacking in substance. This was part of the essence of glam rock, to write simple songs that would contain irresistible hooks with an infectious attitude. Elaborate theatrics and stage costumes would bring the songs further to life. Bolan received a lot of criticism from his many fans of the Tyrannosaurus Rex period that labeled him a sell out. Fans of T. Rex felt that Electric Warrior, taken in the glam rock context, stood the test of time.

Side One opened with "Mambo Sun," then "Cosmic Dancer," "Jeepster," "Monolith," and "Lean Woman Blues." The song "Jeepster," contained elements similar to the Howlin' Wolf song "You'll Be Mine," that was written by Willie Dixon. The song was also featured in a Quentin Taranto film Death Proof in 2007.

Side two opened with "Get it On," then "Planet Queen," "Girl," "The Motivator," "Life's a Gas," and "Rip Off." Marc Bolan shed some light on his move in the glam rock direction when he said, "I mean, I am my own fantasy. I am the 'Cosmic Dancer' who dances his way out of the womb and into the tomb on Electric Warrior. I'm not frightened to get up there and groove about in front of six million people on TV because it doesn't look cool. That's the way I would do it at home." #11 Bolan felt strongly that working in the glam genre gave him the freedom to express himself. He further stated, "Electric Warrior might appear simple on the surface but it has a lot of little 'sneakies' in there if you want to dig deeper…It's probably the loosest album I've ever recorded." #12

1972's The Slider became T. Rex's most successful album in the U.S. and it reached the number four spot in England. The hits "Metal Guru" and "Telegram Sam" both went to number one in England. On 1973's Tanx, T. Rex added the instrumental sounds of a Mellotron and saxophone. Bolan stretched his musical interests to include funk and soul music. The album was successful, peaking at number three in Britain. By 1974's Zinc Alloy and the Hidden Riders of Tomorrow, there were major changes for the band. Now known as Marc Bolan and T. Rex, Bill Legend quit the band and was replaced by bassist Davey Lutton. Vocalist Gloria Jones also joined (she was Bolan's love interest and sang backup) the band. This album reverted back to the Tyrannosaurus Rex period with long song-titles and complex lyrics. The band extended their lineup to include guitarist Jack Green and pedal steel player BJ Cole. Soon after the album's release, Producer Tony Visconti moved on (now working for David Bowie) and Mickey Finn left the band.

1975's Bolan's Zip Gun was self-produced by Bolan. The press attacked Bolan saying he had copied David Bowie's The Rise and Fall of Ziggy Stardust and the Spiders From Mars. 1976's Futuristic Dragon revealed a wall of sound approach to nostalgic songs in the old T. Rex style. It was released only in England and merely reached the fiftieth spot on the charts. T. Rex's twelfth and final studio album, 1977's Dandy in the Underworld, was released six month's before Marc Bolan tragically died in a car accident. After the death of Marc Bolan, Mickey Finn and Bill Legend both used the T. Rex name to form other versions of the band. A series of T. Rex compilations followed, including a top five British album Best of the 20th Century Boy. T. Rex had a huge impact on the glam rock, punk, and Britpop music genres. T. Rex influenced a diverse group of artists that included; The Who, R.E.M., Oasis, My Chemical Romance, and The Ramones.

Mott the Hoople (1969-1980) (reunions: 2009, 2013) was a British glam rock band most popular from the early to mid-1970's. They released seven studio albums and a series of singles from 1972 to 1974. Their musical influence would come to outweigh their modest success. Mott the Hoople's original lineup featured guitarist Mick Ralphs, organist Verden Allen, bassist Overend Watts, drummer Dale Griffin, and singer/pianist Ian Hunter. Their 1969 self-titled debut Mott the Hoople, contained a mix of hard rock with "Rock and Roll Queen," the Dylanesque "Half Moon," and a cover of "At the Crossroads." 1970's Mad Shadows followed, but it was the band's live shows that built their reputation. 1971's Wildlife dabbled in country rock. 1971's Brain Capers did not fare well on the charts.

Mott the Hoople was on the verge of breaking up when a fan of the band, David Bowie, intervened and offered them his song "Suffragette City," which they declined. However, they did accept Bowie's next offering, "All the Young Dudes," that became their biggest hit. David Bowie then produced their album of the same name, 1972's All the Young Dudes. On the album, Bowie played saxophone and Mick Ronson added strings and brass arrangements. Additionally, a cover of Lou Reed's "Sweet Jane" and Ian Hunter's "One of the Boys" gave All the Young Dudes great depth and Mott the Hoople renewed confidence.

"All the Young Dudes"
by David Bowie (Mott the Hoople version)

"All the Young Dudes" was considered to be one of glam rock's anthem songs. David Bowie learned from Mott the Hoople's bassist Overend Watts that the band was about to dissolve. In an effort to keep Mott the Hoople together, Bowie wrote "All the Young Dudes" in a hotel room in London in the presence of Hoople's vocalist, Ian Hunter. Bowie had intended to use the tune for his own concept album, The Rise and Fall of Ziggy Stardust and the Spiders From Mars. The "all the young dudes carry the news" line referred to the fact that Ziggy Stardust did not have the use of electricity and the song was about spreading the news. Meanwhile, Mott the Hoople had alienated their record label, Island Records, and getting studio time proved difficult. Bowie, once again came to the rescue. He asked for a favor from his record label and got them studio time at Olympic Studios (in London) in the middle of the night.

Bowie's description of the song's storyline referenced the dark themes of an apocalypse. The lyrics appealed to the gay community with lyrics such as "Lucy looks sweet 'cause he dresses like a queen." This was consistent with a glam rock concept where singers performed in makeup and feminine clothes while playing extravagant rock songs. The lyric "Lucy's stealing clothes from unlocked cars" was originally written as "Lucy's stealing clothes from Marks and Sparks," which was a British store called Marks and Spencer. The BCC refused to play the song at first because it violated their policy that stated that a product or business could not be mentioned by name in a song. Ian Hunter flew from New York back to London to re-record the lyric, now saying "from unlocked cars." "All the Young Dudes" was Mott the Hoople's only top ten U.S. chart hit.

1973's Mott contained the hits "Honaloochie Boogie" and "All the Way from Memphis," both achieving moderate success on the charts. However, the band members were moving in different musical directions, which resulted in many lineup changes. In 1973, guitarist Mick Ralphs joined Bad Company, while Mott the Hoople toured America with Queen in 1974. 1974's The Hoople peaked at number eleven in England and number twenty-eight in America. Guitarist Mick Ronson joined the band briefly for a live album titled Live, but left with Ian Hunter to form a duo. Mott the Hoople re-tooled their lineup and changed their name to Mott for 1975's Drive On and 1976's Shouting and Pointing. In October of 2009, Mott the Hoople re-formed for a series of well-received performances at London's Hammersmith Apollo. This lineup included original members Watts, Griffin, Allen, Hunter, and Ralphs. The band also released the documentary The Ballad of Mott the Hoople in 2011. Although Mott the Hoople never fully broke into the rock mainstream, their fusion of glam rock, hard rock, and edgy lyrics inspired many British punk bands, most notably The Clash.

Roxy Music (1970-2011) with some inactive years) was a British art rock and glam band that was formed in 1971 by vocalist/songwriter Bryan Ferry. In 1970, Ferry failed an audition for King Crimson but did impress Robert Fripp enough that he helped him obtain a recording contract with E.G. Records. Bassist Graham Simpson and saxophonist/oboist Andy Mackay joined Ferry and they recruited avant-garde musician Brian Eno. Eno joined the band as a synthesizer player and technical adviser. Ferry had originally named the band Roxy as homage to dance halls and movie theaters but changed the name to Roxy Music after learning that an American band was also called Roxy. Roxy Music played some live gigs through 1971 and recorded a demo of a few early compositions. After a change in personnel, drummer Paul Thompson and guitarist Phil Manzanera joined Ferry, Simpson, Mackey, and Eno to complete Roxy Music. Together they blended 1950's rock 'n' roll with Ferry's and Eno's art school aesthetics.

Early Roxy Music evolved from the late-1960's art rock movement but added a fascination with fashion, glamour, pop art, cinema, and the avant-garde. They dressed in outlandish and stylish costumes, while their pop music sensibility created an experimental variation within the art rock approach. Their 1972 self-titled debut Roxy Music was a diverse and glam-driven collection that made it into the top ten on the British chart. A non-album single, "Virginia Plain" also made it onto the British top ten singles chart. The album Roxy Music launched their visual theme of having a glamorous model on each album cover. 1973's For Your Pleasure was successful in England (but not in America) and was recorded with a new bassist, John Porter, who would became another in a long list of Roxy bassists.

"Do the Strand"
by Bryan Ferry

"Do the Strand" was a song modeled in the mode of the early 1960's "dance craze." For example, 1960's songs like "The Twist" attempted to convince the

---

"(Brian) Eno was our hero because he taught us how to make interesting music on ordinary instruments. We couldn't afford synths in the early days"

– Andy McCluskey lead singer for the band Orchestral Manoeuvres in the Dark

"All those rappers, they're the only glamorous people working in music now. They dress up in these chains of gold, cars, girls, and this and that, and high-heeled shoes."

– Bryan Ferry

Rock Hard Fact

Queen did not want to release their song "Another One Bites the Dust" but when Michael Jackson first heard the song, he insisted they release it. It went on to sell over seven million copies.

---

listener to dance specifically in a song's dance style. "Do the Strand" drew from many other sources. It's lyrics contained references to legitimate art including; Picasso's *Guernica*, de Vinci's *Mona Lisa*, and the ancient Greek mythical creature *The Sphinx*. Bryan Ferry defined the idea for "Do the Strand" as the "dance of life" that combined divergent dance sources such as The Ballets Russes and jazz-age dance crazes (like the Charleston). Ferry never instructed the listener as to how The Strand should be danced.

Roxy Music played "Do the Strand" with the feel of a "straight four to the snare drum" driving punk-like pattern, while Ferry made lyrical references to many dances and musical styles including; the waltz, the Brazilian samba, the mashed potato, the tango, and the beguine. The song's harmony was noisy and dissonant, complete with screeching saxophone punctuations and drones that built and maintained strong tension. "Do the Strand" was a great foreshadowing of what was to come in the groundbreaking career of Brian Eno. This song provided a clear example of how Roxy Music could rock hard with a primitive and trashy quality while simultaneously tying together many divergent art and cultural elements.

The first two Roxy Music albums were driven by the creative tension between Ferry and Eno. Each pulled the band in different directions with Ferry calling on American soul music and Beatlesque art-pop while Eno was deconstructing rock and leaning toward the sound of The Velvet Underground. Although this version of Roxy Music only made two albums, they inspired many art rock and new wave groups of the 1970's. Brian Eno's desire to experiment and his creative friction with Ferry (Ferry refused to record Eno's songs) prompted Eno's departure. Eno immediately launched a successful career as a solo artist and producer (see chapter eighteen on Brian Eno).

With 1973's Stranded, Roxy Music was now led only by Ferry. Stranded yielded the hit "Street Life" and reached number nine on the British charts. Stranded was the first Roxy Music album to feature Eno's replacement, ex-Curved Air electric violinist/keyboardist Eddie Jobson. Bassist John Gustafson also joined Roxy Music for Stranded and their next two studio albums. With 1974's Country Life, Roxy Music was finally able to break into the American market with the hits "The Thrill of It All" and the up-tempo rocker "All I Want is You." The album reached number three in England and number thirty-seven in America.

1975's Siren continued to build Roxy Music's audience with the hit "Love Is the Drug," that peaked at number two on the British charts. Siren was a simple album without much synthesizer layers or sound effects but Ferry's lyrical imagery was focused. However, after the 1976 tour to support Siren, Roxy Music disbanded. During this time, Bryan Ferry recorded two solo albums with Roxy bandmates Manzanera and Thompson.

Ferry re-formed Roxy Music after a four-year recording hiatus and released 1979's Manifesto. Gone was Jobson. The revived lineup was Ferry, Manzanera, Mackay, and Thompson with added musicians, keyboardist Paul Carrack, bassists Alan Spenner and Gary Tibbs. Ferry brought in session greats Steve Ferrone and Rick Marotta to play most of the drum parts, along with Richard Tee on piano. Thompson soon left and was replaced by Andy Newmark (Sly and the Family Stone, John Lennon). Manifesto peaked at number seven in England and number twenty-three in America. Manifesto began a more radio-friendly version of Roxy Music that produced the hits "Dance Away" and "Angel Eyes." Now a trio with Ferry, Mackay, and Manzanera (with supporting musicians), Roxy released 1980's Flesh and Blood that contained a softer approach. 1982's Avalon became the band's most popular recording, providing the hits "More Than This" and "Avalon." A tribute cover of John Lennon's "Jealous Guy" (released soon after his death) also went to number one on the British charts.

After quite a bit of touring, Roxy Music split up again in 1983. Ferry, Mackay, and Thompson again re-formed in 2001 and returned to extensive touring. Another short tour followed in 2003. In 2006, Eno returned to record a few tracks that were meant for a Roxy Music release. However, those songs made their way onto the Bryan Ferry solo album Olympia, released in 2010. Bryan Ferry had a successful solo career recording fifteen solo albums. From his debut These Foolish Things (recorded while leading Roxy Music), to his 2014 Avonmore, Ferry developed his distinctive voice and persona. Roxy Music created and maintained an image where stage presentation, music videos, and album cover art merged with a musical sensibility that took risks with experimental soundscapes. Roxy Music mixed all of these elements with *hard-edged* glam, complete with oboe solos.

Queen (1971-present) are one of the most dramatic and successful rock acts of all time. They are a major classic rock band that lends themselves to a glam rock classification by virtue of the androgynous implications of their name. Lead vocalist Freddie Mercury (AKA Farrokh Bulsara), guitarist Brian May, bassist John Deacon, and drummer Roger Taylor were all working on college degrees in areas other than music when they met and decided to pursue rock 'n' roll. Queen played the typical club scene around London to build their popularity while working on their demo tracks and an elaborate stage show before they approached a record company. Signed to EMI, they released their self-titled debut album Queen in 1973. Queen's first record was a blend of hard rock and progressive rock mixed with lyrical subjects such as religion and folklore. Mercury and May shared the songwriting with some input by Taylor. The songs were progressive in the sense of their complex arrangements and production. With stunning four-part vocal harmonies and multiple overdubbed Brian May guitar parts, Queen quickly established their sound with their solid recording debut. 1974's Queen II charted well in England and they gained momentum with their first British hit "Seven Seas of Rhye."

1974's Shear Heart Attack saw the band move to more hard rocking tracks and away from their earlier progressive approach. The album peaked at number two on the British charts and number twelve in the U.S. The single "Killer Queen" became their first international hit and began their FM radio rock identity, especially with its vaudeville influenced sound. 1975's A Night at the Opera (the name was inspired by a Marx Brothers movie) is considered to be a musical and production masterpiece by many fans and critics. It charted very well internationally and reached number one in England and number four in America. On stage, designer Zandra Rhodes created a distinct image for Queen by dressing them in theatrical black or white.

Groundbreaking album
A Night at The Opera
by Queen

The eclectic nature of A Night at The Opera demonstrated that Queen was not willing to compromise their artistic vision just to sell records. They drew from Japanese folk music, 1920's Americana, and included a guitar only version of "God Save the Queen." But it was the hit "Bohemian Rhapsody" that fused a special blend of a rock ballad, opera, and a hard rocking feel that defined their signature musical style.

Side one of A Night at the Opera opened with "Death on Two Legs," then "Lazing on a Sunday Afternoon," "I'm In Love with My Car," "You're My Best Friend," "39," "Sweet Lady," and "Seaside Rendezvous." The lyrics for "Death on Two Legs" stemmed from Mercury's harsh criticism of the band's first manager. On the Roger Taylor song "I'm in Love with My Car," the revving sounds of the engine of Taylor's actual sports car (an Alfa Romeo) was recorded and added to the mix. "You're My Best Friend" was bassist John Deacon's song that he wrote about his wife. It became a top ten hit. "39" was a Brian May song about a group of space explorers who believed they had made a one year space trip, only to find out that they had been gone for one hundred years.

Side two opened with "The Prophet's Song," "Love of My Life," "Good Company," "Bohemian Rhapsody," and "God Save the Queen." "The Prophet's Song" utilized the musical device of a canon (a counterpoint-based compositional technique where a melody is imitated at different entry points-for example like "Row, Row, Row, Your Boat"). The song's musical phrases were layered to produce a full-choral effect.

At the time of it's recording, A Night at the Opera was the most expensive album ever made. Queen was never a band to take itself too seriously, and was therefore able to pull off some arrangements that were exaggerated and somewhat overblown. Queen was very deliberate with crafting this album's sound with acoustic piano, harp, a-cappella vocals, unusual effects, and no synthesizers. With a touch of progressive rock, this album was grandiose and ambitious crossing musical boundaries by combining a number of musical styles. Queen's ability to blend heavy metal and elements of opera with a theatrical sophistication was unique, even to the present day. This record helped define the career of engineer-producer Mike Stone, who continued to work with Queen, and went on to produce bands like Journey, Asia, Whitesnake, and Y&T. Queen embarked on a massive A Night at the Opera tour that stretched from 1975 to 1976 across Europe, America, Japan, and Australia.

"Bohemian Rhapsody"
by Freddie Mercury

"Bohemian Rhapsody" was conceived as a "mock" or mini opera. Mercury composed all of the piano, bass, and vocal arrangements while Brian May composed the first guitar solo of the song. Mercury had the band record their parts individually without letting them know how the final arrangement would work. The band referred to the song as "Freddie's thing." Mercury recalled, "I have no set rules for writing…if I knew we're going into the studio, I just get my thinking process going. I can write songs to order…some songs come faster than other, 'Bohemian Rhapsody,' I had to work at like crazy." #13 The famous operatic section ("Galileos") served to connect the ballad and the hard rocking sections.

"Bohemian Rhapsody" parodied many elements of opera with bombastic choruses, sarcastic recitative passages, and distorted Italian operatic phrases. The lyrics began by questioning if life is "real" or "just fantasy caught in a landslide" and then concluded that there was "no escape from reality." Soon, the narrator proclaimed himself to be "just a poor boy" not in need of sympathy. Later, the narrator revealed that he was beaten down and bids the world goodbye but admitted that he didn't want to die. Later, rival factions fought over the narrator's soul. The many music sections of the song functioned like it's own complete mini-opera with it's many dramatic sections.

"Bohemian Rhapsody" topped the British charts for nine weeks in 1976 and reached number one again in 1991. The single was accompanied by a promotional video that practically invented the concept of music video, a full seven years before the advent of MTV. "Bohemian Rhapsody" was the third most successful single of all time in England. "Bohemian Rhapsody" re-entered the U.S. charts after being featured in the movie *Wayne's World*.

1976's A Day at the Races (another title from a Marx Brothers movie) functioned as a sequel to A Night at the Opera. The record reached number one in Britain and number five in America. Queen explored the gospel style on the hit "Somebody to Love," with Mercury, Taylor, and May multi-tracking their voices to simulate a one hundred voice choir. The tune "Tie Your Mother Down" was a Brian May composition that became a staple in their live performances. Next, Queen headlined a huge show in England for 150,000 fans in London's Hyde Park. 1977's News of the World saw Queen pare back from the usual grandiosity with some more streamlined songs. It yielded the hits "We Will Rock You" and "We Are the Champions." Both became sports arena anthems around the world. The tour for News of the World was one of their grandest and most spectacular. 1978's Jazz followed with the hit singles "Fat Bottomed Girls" and "Bicycle Race." Queen released a live album titled Live Killers in 1979 and continued to tour. A surprising move to the rockabilly style surfaced with a single titled "Crazy Little Thing Called Love." It peaked at number one in America.

Queen kicked off the 1980's with The Game and another venture into rockabilly, now mixed with a touch of disco with the hit "Another One Bites the Dust." The result was another number one hit in America. Queen ventured into the realm of film with 1980's *Flash Gordon*. In 1981, Queen collaborated with superstar David Bowie on the hit single "Under Pressure" that went to number one on the British charts and number twenty-nine in the U.S.

"Under Pressure"
by David Bowie and Queen

David Bowie had been working with Queen in the studio on a Queen song titled "Cool Cat" but was unhappy with his own vocal performance. Queen and Bowie moved on and co-wrote "Under Pressure," which included vocals from both Bowie and Mercury. Freddie Mercury wrote most of the song's lyrics, which dealt with how pressure can destroy lives and how love can be the answer to life's problems. When Mercury and Bowie were recording their individual vocal parts, they did so in isolation without the other present. However, Bowie did sneak in to hear Freddie's vocal takes. Later, Freddie was impressed with how Bowie could so easily add to his previously recorded parts (without realizing that Bowie had eavesdropped). The scat singing that was featured throughout the song came from an extended improvisation that Bowie and Queen did in the studio. During the

> "I won't be a rock star. I will be a legend."
>
> – Freddie Mercury

recording process, Bowie and Mercury became good friends. However, their first encounter was over a decade earlier when in 1969, Mercury was working in a shoe store and fitted Bowie with a pair of boots.

"Under Pressure" was a perfect example of pure collaboration. On the recording, Bowie and Mercury's very distinctive voices blended to create a unique and magical sound. "Under Pressure" was performed live by Queen from 1981 until 1986. It appeared on their live albums Queen Rock Montreal and Live at Wembley '86. Bowie included the song on many of his collections including; 2002's Best of Bowie, 2005's The Platinum Collection, 2014's Nothing Has Changed, and 2016's Legacy.

1982's Hot Space moved Queen into a more dance, funk, and rhythm and blues direction. It would also be the last year that Freddie Mercury would tour North America. Queen changed record labels, signing with EMI/Capitol, and released The Works in 1984. The Works had a few successful singles, but the band's popularity had declined in America. At the Live Aid Festival in 1985, Queen performed a masterful set for the largest TV audience (1.9 billion people) of all time. This performance served to revitalize the band for their 1986 release, A Kind of Magic. Three years later, they followed with The Miracle. In 1988, rumors surfaced about Mercury's failing health, but Queen kept working on songs for their 1991 release, Innuendo. All of the songs from the album were credited to Queen, and not to individual members.

The death of Freddie Mercury shocked the world and hit his bandmates hard. Mercury announced on November 22nd, 1991 that he had contracted AIDS. He died two days later. He had been rock's most ambiguously gay star, always leaving some mystery to his sexual orientation. Mercury had known that the end was near. In the fall of 1991, Freddie told his bandmates, "Keep writing for me, let's keep recording stuff. Then you guys can finish it when I'm gone." #14 Brian May remembered, "When Freddie died, it was like losing a family member, and we all handled it in different ways. For a time, I really wanted to escape from Queen; I didn't want to know about it. I think that was my grieving process. But I'm very proud of what we did together. My God, we really did go on some interesting excursions! Mostly, it makes me feel good." #15

Queen's last album, titled Made in Heaven was released in 1995, four years after Freddie's death. It consisted of material from previous recording sessions and re-worked
material from solo albums by May, Taylor, and Deacon. Queen returned to the studio to record a tribute song to Freddie Mercury titled "No-One but You (Only the Good Die Young)." They included it on the Queen compilation album Queen Rocks. At this point, the band would only perform sporadically but was encouraged by Elton John and others to reunite.

In 2004, Queen decided to reunite and to tour with another of rock's strongest voices, Bad Company's Paul Rogers. They released 2008's The Cosmos Rocks, a record billed as Queen with Paul Rogers (to suggest that Rogers was not to be Freddie's replacement). In 2011, the band marked their fortieth anniversary with a number of re-issues. In 2014, Queen released a new album Queen Forever, a compilation of old material and three new tunes featuring vocals from archived Freddie Mercury vocal tracks. In 2016, Queen (without bassist John Deacon) brought in another robust voice, Adam Lambert, and toured Europe and Asia as Queen plus Adam Lambert. Queen announced in 2017 that they would be touring North America again with Lambert. Though many were skeptical, the pairing of Queen and Lambert has proven to be spectacular.

Queen amassed a staggering total of eighteen number one albums, eighteen number one singles, and ten number one DVDs worldwide. Having sold well over two hundred million records worldwide, Queen is one of the world's best-selling bands of all time. The legacy of Freddie Mercury is one of incredible talent and desire for greatness. Brian May was amazed at his development as a musician recalling, "I think the first time it struck me was in the studio, when Freddie was listening to his voice come back, going, 'No, that won't do', and just working and working. He was exceptional, and there was a very quick period, you could almost have blinked and missed it, where he learned to harness his technique." #16 Queen took rock and heavy metal to new places by blending the styles of gospel, opera, classical art songs, rockabilly, and R&B, into their music. At different times Queen embodied the genres of pop-rock, hard rock, heavy metal, symphonic rock, and art rock. Ultimately all of it became the musical style of Queen. Queen was inducted into the Rock and Roll Hall of Fame in 2001.

The New York Dolls (1971-1977) (2002-2011) were a glam rock and punk rock band formed in New York City in 1971. The original lineup included vocalist David Johansen, guitarist Johnny Thunders, guitarist/pianist Sylvain Sylvain, drummer Billy Murcia, and bassist Arthur "Killer" Kane. The New York Dolls dressed in androgynous exaggerated drag attire complete with wigs, make-up, high heels, and garters. Their sound was raw rock 'n' roll and very punky, while Johansen and Thunders created a parody of Mick Jagger and Keith Richards. Drummer Billy Murcia tragically died in early 1972 and was replaced by drummer Jerry Nolan to complete their permanent lineup. The New York Doll's 1973 debut album, New York Dolls, became one of the most popular cult records in rock. It was produced by Todd Rundgren, and although the album captured their live sound, the band was dissatisfied with his approach. Critics liked the album but it sold poorly. The band proved difficult to market outside of New York City due to their onstage cross-dressing and vulgarity. At the recommendation of the legendary songwriters Leiber and Stoller, the band enlisted the skills of Shadow Morton to produce 1974's Too Much Too Soon. Songs such as "Chatterbox" revealed Johansen's ability to add depth to the characters he sang about, and Thunders innovative guitar playing came to prominence.

After much internal tension and drug abuse issues, The New York Dolls dissolved in 1975. Thunders and Nolan formed the band Johnny Thunders and the Heartbreakers (to distinguish themselves from Tom Petty's band) with ex-Television vocalist/bassist Richard Hell. Thunders died in 1991 from a drug overdose and Nolan died in 1992 from a stroke. David Johansen achieved success under the pseudonym Buster Poindexter, accompanied by The Uptown Horns, and performed jazz and novelty songs. Johansen also formed an Americana-blues-folk band called The Harry Smiths which paid tribute to roots music historian Harry Everett Smith. Johansen also appeared in several films and television series including the HBO drama *Oz*. Johansen, Kane, and Sylvain re-formed The New York Dolls for a 2004 festival appearance in London. Only weeks after the reunion concert, bassist Arthur Kane died of cancer.

In 2006, The New York Dolls released the album One Day It Will Please Us to Remember Even This. This album featured keyboardist Brian Koonin, drummer Brian

> **Rock Hard Fact**
>
> Lady Gaga's name was inspired by the Queen song "Radio Gaga."

Delaney, bassist Sami Yaffa, and guitarist Steve Conte. In 2009, the band released Cause I Sez So, and returned to the days of their debut recording with production handled by Todd Rundgren. In 2011, The New York Dolls released their fifth and final studio album, Dancing Backward in High Heels. This lineup included new guitarist Frank Infante, bassist/producer Jason Hill, Johansen, Sylvain, and Delaney. Ex-David Bowie and John Lennon guitarist Earl Slick joined the band for a tour opening for Motley Crue and Poison. The trademark reckless and purposely unrefined sound of their first two records documented how The New York Dolls were simultaneously an American answer to the British glam scene, and a predecessor to the punk rock movement.

Marilyn Manson (1989-present) is an American glam, shock, and industrial rock band started by vocalist Marilyn Manson (Brian Hugh Warner) and guitarist Daisy Berkowitz. Originally called Marilyn Manson & the Spooky Kids, their name was derived by combining cultural figures Marilyn Monroe and Charles Manson. Like David Bowie and Alice Cooper, Manson's persona has provided tremendous shock value and created interest in the band. In 1993, Marilyn Manson was signed to Trent Reznor's record label, where Reznor produced their 1994 debut album, Portrait of an American Family. Marilyn Manson's reputation and cult following expanded when they toured with Nine Inch Nails. Success also came with their Eurhythmics cover and MTV video of "Sweet Dreams (Are Made of This")". 1996's Antichrist Superstar, co-produced by Resnor, made the band internationally famous as industrial metal artists. The record was a rock opera concept album based on the 1971 Andrew Lloyd Webber musical, *Jesus Christ Superstar*. The album's theme was based on a supernatural being that seized power in order to create an apocalyptic event. Despite the album's eventual success, internal group tension prompted founding member Daisy Berkowitz to quit the band half way through the recording process.

1998's Mechanical Animals moved away from the industrial and alternative metal styles to focus on 1970's styled glam rock. Inspired by David Bowie's Ziggy Stardust character, Manson portrayed two different roles on Mechanical Animals. First, he created a drug abusing glam rocker and gender ambiguous alien named Omega. Second, Manson created another character called Alpha, based on himself and his perception of certain individuals that he found lacking emotion. Manson thereby labeled those people to be "mechanical animals."

Marilyn Manson has gone on to release seven more studio albums, including 2017's Heaven Upside Down. Manson's lineup has often changed between album releases. The 2017 version of Manson's lineup consists of guitarists Paul Wiley and Tyler Bates, drummer Gil Sharone, bassist Twiggy Ramirez, and Manson (Brian Hugh Warner). Manson has also made film and television appearances and is a serious watercolor painter. Marilyn Manson is known for their outlandish outfits and shocking stage performances. Marilyn Manson became one of the leading examples of the **shock rock** genre. Behind the provocative stage theatrics and "out there" album storylines, Manson has supported a number of charitable causes. Marilyn Manson is an artist and band that continues to push the boundaries of modern rock music and American culture.

Stefani Joanne Angelina Germanotta (1986-), aka **Lady Gaga**, is an American singer/songwriter and one of the most popular pop-rock artists in music today. Gaga was initially drawn to electronic dance and avant-garde music, but was also inspired by the glam rock styles of Queen and David Bowie. Gaga began playing piano at age four and wrote her first song at thirteen. At age seventeen, she enrolled at New York University in the Collaborative Arts Project 21. There, she studied art, politics, and songwriting. In 2005, Gaga recorded two songs with hip-hop artist Grandmaster Melle Mel and formed the Stefani Germanotta Band. At a 2006 songwriter's showcase, Gaga met producer Rob Fusari who helped her compose songs (they had a personal relationship until 2007). Together, they formed the music company Team Lovechild, LLC. Gaga soon met the artist Lady Starlight, who helped her to develop a stage persona and a live show they titled "Lady Gaga and the Starlight Revue." Like Madonna, Lady Gaga incorporated fashion with constant costume changes and provocative visuals. The main themes in her music were sexuality, androgynous references, violence, and power.

In 2008, Lady Gaga released her debut album The Fame (reissued in 2009 as The Fame Monster). The hits "Just Dance" and "Poker Face" emerged with the later becoming the best-selling single worldwide in 2009 (nine and a half million copies sold that year). The Fame went to number two in the U.S. and topped the charts in many other countries worldwide. The album featured the sounds of synth-pop (aka techno-pop) made popular by artists like Kraftwerk in the 1970's.

"Poker Face"
by Stefani Germanotta and Nadir Khayat

"Poker Face" was a controversial song about bisexuality and featured specific sexual innuendos. It was also about gambling and a tribute to Lady Gaga's rock 'n' roll boyfriends. The lyrics contained some very suggestive phrases such as "bluffin' with my muffin." The song also referred to a man who must read a woman's "poker face" to understand what she was thinking about regarding her sexual intentions.

On the chorus of "Poker Face," Gaga's dark vocal sound was combined with a synthesized sound to create an auto-tuned effect. This helped to provide a strong dance-oriented track. Gaga was going for the sound of the downtown New York underground pop-dance scene. "Poker Face" quickly reached the top of the U.S. charts and gained even more popularity when Gaga released a "Poker Face" video in which she attended a wild party.

2011's Born This Way was a huge success and the single "Born This Way" sold more than one million copies in five days! "Born This Way" addressed the self-empowerment of minorities including the LGBT community as well as racial minorities.

Lady Gaga was now firmly established as one of the biggest pop-rock stars in the world. 2013's Artpop debuted at the top of the U.S. charts and yielded the hits "Do What U Want" and "Applause." In 2014, Gaga took an extreme artistic turn and collaborated with legendary jazz crooner Tony Bennett. Together they co-released a record of jazz standards entitled Cheek to Cheek. This recording revealed Lady Gaga's stylistic diversity and the depth of her voice. On Cheek to Cheek, she was featured on "Lush Life," "Every Time We Say Goodbye," and "Bang Bang (My Baby Shot Me Down)."

2016's Joanne went straight to number one in America and established Gaga as the first woman to have four U.S. number one albums in the 2010's. Among her other highlights were; a tribute performance to the late David Bowie at the 58th Grammy Awards in 2016, a performance at the 2017 Super Bowl halftime show, and an appearance with Metallica at the 2017 Grammy Awards. Lady Gaga's attention to fashion and her androgynous and provocative stage act has strong roots in the glam rock era of the 1970's. Gaga's various collaborations show her musical breadth. Lady Gaga has absorbed the sounds of 1980's pop, electronica, and strong musical hooks to clearly become a pop-rock superstar.

Discussion Question

Some glam bands and artists utilized the glam elements of makeup and extreme fashion in various degrees. Did this have an impact on the actual music they created? Select two bands/artists and take a position. Be specific and give examples.

Chapter Eight: Art Rock and Glam Rock

"If you feel safe in the area you're working in, you're not working in the right area. Always go a little further into the water than you feel you're capable of being in... when you don't feel that your feet are quite touching the bottom, you're just about in the right place to do something exciting."

– David Bowie

Chapter Nine: Country and Southern Rock

This chapter is divided into two sections, country rock and southern rock. We briefly explored the earliest of country roots in chapter one. **Country rock** is a challenging genre to define. Is it country music with a backbeat? Or rock with a country twang? Many people assume that country rock was born and raised primarily in Nashville, Tennessee. However, in the late 1960's, a Southern California based collection of young, long-haired musicians decided to add some country music to their brand of rock 'n' roll. Coming from many musical directions, these musicians either played country with a rock 'n' roll attitude, or injected a country feel into their rock approach, or even added rock elements to their own folk or bluegrass music. These musicians were just doing what they loved to do. It just so happened that they were inadvertently developing a whole new genre, country rock.

> "If you really want to go back to the roots of country rock...it was Elvis. I'm talking Elvis when he was at Sun Records...that was untouchable. That was country rock, and, of course, rockabilly, it's all the same thing."
>
> – Chris Hillman

Country rock received another shot in the arm when Bob Dylan once again expanded outside of his folk roots. In 1969, Dylan recorded the groundbreaking album <u>Nashville Skyline</u>. Dylan combined the instrumentation of acoustic and electric guitars (and some steel guitar), electric bass, honky-tonk piano, and drums. He made a strong country rock statement by combining his vocal style with Johnny Cash's approach. Country music has evolved into the enormous contemporary genre of country-pop (that we will not explore). The Byrds also contributed early on to country rock with their 1968 groundbreaking album <u>Sweetheart of the Rodeo</u>.

Southern rock became a genre that evolved in the southern region of America. It combined country and rock traits such as an aggressive guitar-oriented approach. Southern rock developed independently of other musical movements of the 1960's and contributed recurring themes of southern pride with anthems like "Sweet Home Alabama" by **Lynyrd Skynyrd** and "The Devil Went Down to Georgia" by **The Charlie Daniels Band**. **The Allman Brothers Band** defined early southern rock with their two-guitar and drumset lineup. They combined blues, country, soul, and rock to create music with innovative instrumental improvisation. They strongly influenced other southern rock guitar-oriented bands such as **The Outlaws** and **The Marshall Tucker Band**.

Country Rock

In chapter one that examined the roots of country music, we touched on the styles of western swing and bluegrass. We also acknowledged legends such as The Carter Family, Jimmy Rodgers, Hank Williams Sr., and Johnny Cash. They provided some of the strongest regional roots in American music, based deeply in the traditions of Nashville, Tennessee and The Grand Ole Opry. The music of the legendary **Willie Nelson** (1933-), **Kris Kristofferson** (1936-), **Waylon Jennings** (1937-2002), and **Merle Haggard** (1937-2016) emerged as **outlaw country**. This sub-genre grew out of the earlier subgenres of rockabilly (see chapter two) and honky tonk. This movement began as a reaction to the slick studio productions of mainstream Nashville county music. Willie Nelson and Waylon Jennings gained more artistic freedom by procuring their own recording rights. They also refused to conform to society, adopting the attitude we will later see in many other rock genres. The above-mentioned outlaw artists rejected the formulaic Nashville sound, stripped their music to its country core, and added a rock edge to their songs.

The country roots of rock 'n' roll were very apparent in the twang of Scotty Moore's guitar on Elvis Presley's early Sun recordings and Carl Perkins's rockabilly tune "Blue Suede Shoes." The Everly Brothers' sang with the influences of Kentucky bluegrass harmonies. Jerry Lee Lewis songs like "Crazy Arms" revealed a strong country swing embedded in his rockabilly style. Outside of the rock music mainstream, a faction of Southern California musicians found a home at The Troubadour and Palomino clubs. Musical unions and associations were formed that produced innovative artists such as **The Flying Burrito Brothers**, **The Nitty Gritty Dirt Band**, **The Dillards** (1963-present), **Rick Nelson** (1940-1985), **Gene Clark** (1944-1991), and **Poco**. **The Byrds** (see chapter seven) and **The Eagles** (see chapter eleven) were also rooted in the Southern California country rock movement, the former having success in the folk rock genre and the later as one of rock's most popular bands. But before these artists ever hit the stage, important country artists like **Chet Atkins** and **Buck Owens** shaped the future of country rock.

Chet Atkins (1924-2001) was an American guitarist/vocalist/songwriter and producer. Atkins also played the banjo, mandolin, fiddle, and ukulele. He was one of the fathers of "the Nashville sound." Atkins had a direct effect by combining country music elements with pop and rock styles. By the mid 1950's, Atkins was a major session player in Nashville and frequent performer at the Grand Ole Opry. From his 1953 debut album <u>Chet Atkins' Gallopin Guitar</u>, to his 2003 posthumous release <u>Solo Sessions</u>, Atkins released an incredible eighty-eight studio albums. He also released three live albums, fifty-three compilation albums, nineteen EP's, and one hundred and thirteen singles.

Atkins' signature guitar picking style was heard on countless recordings, beginning when he joined a version of the legendary Carter Family that featured June Carter. Atkins was put in charge of RCA Victor's Nashville division when country music record sales were in decline and rock was gaining in popularity. Atkins, and fellow songwriter/producer Bob Ferguson, developed "the Nashville sound" that eliminated fiddles and steel guitar. Together, they produced crossover hits and helped bring county music to mainstream success. Chet Atkins produced albums for Elvis Presley, Hank Snow, Dolly Parton, Perry Como, The Everly Brothers, Waylon Jennings, and many more. Chet Atkins was inducted into the Rock and Roll Hall of Fame in 2002.

Buck Owens (1929-2006) was an American singer/songwriter and guitarist from Sherman, Texas. Owens and his band, The Buckaroos, recorded twenty-one hits that placed on the country music charts. Owens pioneered "the Bakersfield sound," a reference to Bakersfield, California, where he called home beginning in 1951. Owens referred to his band as having a "freight train" sound, complete with heavy guitar and a driving drumset feel. Owens released a total of thirty-nine studio albums, including his 1966 live recording <u>Carnegie Hall Concert</u>. It achieved crossover success on the pop charts. That same year, Ray Charles recorded cover versions of Owens' pop hits "Crying Time" and "Together Again."

The country music establishment heavily criticized Owens when he expressed his love of The Beatles music. In return, The Beatles covered a few of Owens' songs including his song titled "Act Naturally." The growing community of young country rock musicians was drawn to Owens' performance and compositional approach. Owens took the honky-tonk tradition of Hank Williams Sr. and Lefty Frizzell and added a very twangy electric guitar sound. His *tougher* style took traditional country and added a rock 'n' roll attitude. Owens was not shy about embracing rock songs when he recorded Chuck Berry's "Memphis" and "Johnny B. Goode." Owens believed that "Johnny B. Goode" was essentially a country song. Owens often said that he slightly changed the melody and lyrics of existing songs and turned them into his own sound that people liked.

"Who's Gonna Mow Your Grass"
by Buck Owens

"Who's Gonna Mow Your Grass" was a Buck Owens song from the <u>House of 1000 Corpses</u> movie soundtrack. Written in 3/4 meter, Owens performed the song live on the country show *Hee Haw*. On the original recording, Owens' guitarist Don Rich introduced an aggressive fuzz-tone guitar solo, one of the first rocking guitar solos in country music. Rich (along with James Burton with Elvis Presley) utilized a Telecaster and achieved a twang that set a standard for country rock. The song was a number one hit on the country charts and stayed there for fourteen weeks.

The lyrics for "Who's Gonna Mow Your Grass" were about a man who hoped to regain favor with a fickle girlfriend by reminding her about all of the menial chores he was willing to perform for her. The song was an example that a well respected country star, like Buck Owens, was musically open minded and not afraid to buck the heavy restrictions that Nashville imposed on its musicians.

In the later 1960's, a small group of young, longhaired musicians migrated to Southern California and began to fuse some country into their approach to rock (or some rock into their country). There really was no blueprint to follow. However, what would emerge was an entirely new genre referred to as country-rock. These musicians found common interests and growing support that encouraged them to pursue their vision of uniting the unlikely genres of country and rock 'n' roll music. The audiences at Southern California clubs such as The Troubadour and Palomino were small but fostered important musical relationships. The first wave of many country rock careers was soon launched.

> **Rock Hard Fact**
>
> Chet Atkins (attempting to copy his hero guitarist Merle Travis) developed a unique three fingers and thumb pseudo-classical technique of guitar picking. His approach influenced countless country rock guitarists.

> "I think pure country music includes rock and roll...I've never been able to get into the label of country rock... how can you define something like that? - I say this: It's music. Either you like it or you don't."
>
> – Gram Parsons

Chapter Nine: Country and Southern Rock

Gram Parsons-country rock pioneer

Ingram Cecil Conner III (1946-1973), aka Gram Parsons, was an American singer/songwriter, guitarist, and pianist. He was quite possibly the most important musician in the development of the country rock genre. Parsons was born in Winter Haven, Florida and after high school, he sparked an interest in country music while attending Harvard University. He formed The International Submarine Band (1966-1968) with guitarist John Nuese, bassist Ian Dunlop, and drummer Mickey Gauvin. The Submarine Band released their 1968 album Safe at Home, where they cultivated an approach to combining country and rock. Parsons remembered the influence the Submarine Band had on his career when he said, "The guys in The Submarine Band were important; they always had their ears open, and they reintroduced me to country music after I'd forgotten about it for ten years. The country singers, like George Jones, Ray Price, and Merle Haggard, they're great performers, but I had to learn to dig them, and that taught me a lot." #1

Parsons later moved The Submarine Band to Los Angeles. However, when the group was gaining traction, Parsons left in 1968 to join The Byrds (see chapter seven). Parsons played a crucial role in recording the Byrds seminal Sweetheart of the Rodeo album. This was a surprising move into the country rock genre for The Byrds. Within weeks of joining the band, Parsons delved into his country catalog of songs. That created a power struggle with The Byrd's Roger McGuinn. Parsons' stay with The Byrds was short lived. Parsons and fellow Byrd Chris Hillman left in 1969 to form The Flying Burrito Brothers. After The Burrito's made one of country rock's great albums, The Gilded Palace of Sin, and it's follow up, Burrito Deluxe, Parson's was fired. The Burritos cited his lack of interest in the band and his growing substance abuse.

Parsons quickly started his solo career when he signed with A&M Records. However, he cancelled his debut release in 1971 and moved to France where he lived with Keith Richards of The Rolling Stones. He moved back to America and met Emmylou Harris, who accompanied him on his first solo album, 1973's GP. This record and its follow up, Grievous Angel, were both met with critical acclaim but demonstrated little commercial appeal. GP was contemporary country music. It was a complete statement about where country music was headed. On this recording, Parsons and Emmylou Harris performed duets in the style of George Jones and Tammy Wynette. GP possessed every nuance of the country music genre, from country shuffles to instrumental Dobro guitar picking, fiddling, and pedal steel guitar parts. GP was not quite rock, but it went beyond traditional country.

Gram Parsons died at the age of twenty-six from alcohol and substance abuse issues. The average music fan may not have known Gram Parsons' incredible talent but the people who made the music certainly did. Gram was an innovator, one of the few visionaries (including his bandmate-Chris Hillman) to see the redeeming qualities in country music and combine it with other genres, including rock 'n' roll. Keith Richards said, "He (Gram Parsons) redefined the possibilities of country for me. If he had lived he probably would have redefined it for everybody." #2

The Flying Burrito Brothers (1968-present with some inactive years) were first formed and named by ex-International Submarine Band members Ian Dunlop and Mickey Gauvin. This version of the band never got off the ground but Gram Parsons and Chris Hillman borrowed the name and officially founded the band in 1968 in Los Angeles, California. They soon added bassist/keyboardist Chris Ethridge (a former International Submarine Band member) and session drummer Eddie Hoh. Parsons had loved the pedal-steel guitar playing of "Sneaky" Pete Kleinow for some time and approached him with an offer to become a Burrito Brother. "Sneaky" Pete remembered, "Gram and Chris came into the Palomino while they were still with the Byrds…and asked if I'd like to be in a new band. I didn't say no to anything back then. It sounded really interesting to me because they already had a deal with A&M Records." #3

The 1969 debut album by The Flying Burrito Brothers was titled The Gilded Palace of Sin. This landmark recording, lead by Parsons and Hillman, fused the folk and country genres with gospel, soul, and psychedelic rock styles.

Groundbreaking album
The Gilded Palace of Sin
by The Flying Burrito Brothers

The Gilded Palace of Sin was a landmark recording that defined the emerging country rock genre. The album sold a mere 40,000 copies but cultivated a devoted fan base, including many prominent musicians such as Bob Dylan and The Rolling Stones. The album consisted mostly of originals co-composed by Parsons and Hillman from their intense songwriting sessions. Hillman and Parsons were essentially able to utilize traditional country music as their base and add contemporary lyrics and themes that appealed to a young audience.

Side one opened with "Christine's Tune," then "Sin City," "Do Right Woman," "Dark End of the Street," and "My Uncle." The opening track "Christine's Tune" set the album's tone with Hillman and Parsons' Everly Brothers styled harmony and "Sneaky" Pete's virtuoso pedal-steel guitar parts. On "Do Right Woman," Parsons brought a rhythm and blues feel to his country vocal phrasing. Chris Hillman's vocal harmonies blended effortlessly with Parsons' lead vocals. The Burrito's vocal process was revealed when Hillman stated, "Gram would sing harmonies to me, and we'd switch on the chorus, where I would sing the harmony and he would sing the lead." #4

Side two opened with "Wheels," then "Juanita," "Hot Burrito #1," "Hot Burrito #2," "Do You Know How it Feels," and "Hippie Boy." Both "Hot Burrito #1" and "Hot Burrito #2 blended the pain of classic country sad songs with a contemporary lyrical sense of jealousy, anger, and confusion. Gram Parsons and bassist Chris Ethridge wrote "Hot Burrito #1" about Parson's breakup with his girlfriend. Parsons couldn't stand the idea of her being with another man and wrote the lyric "I don't want no one but you to love me." "Hot Burrito #2," also written by Parsons and Ethridge, showed Parsons taking a harder line with the same breakup theme.

The Burritos were more than a backing band for Gram Parsons. "Sneaky" Pete Kleinow's fuzztone steel guitar perfectly bridged psychedelic rock and country music. "Sneaky" Pete remembered, "I had been piling up gadgets I could use with the steel guitar.

I started hanging outboard equipment on my steel way before then even when I was playing the clubs. I tried to be as innovative as possible. I always felt the steel guitar was an instrument that could be boring, so I wanted to get as much variety into the sound as possible." #5 The Parsons and Hillman songwriting partnership was on full display on this recording.

The making of The Gilded Palace of Sin was not without its problems. Drummer Eddie Hoh was fired after recording two songs. This prompted The Burritos to hire a variety of drummers that included ex-ISB Jon Corneal, Dr. Hook & the Medicine Show member Popeye Phillips, and Sam Goldstein to complete the eleven tracks. The Gilded Palace of Sin barely registered on the pop music scene in 1969. However, hundreds of bands (most notably The Eagles) would find inspiration and far greater success by borrowing The Burrito's approach. This album continues to influence the alternative country movement today and artists including; Wilco, Elvis Costello, Travis Tritt, Vince Gill, Clint Black, and many others.

"Sin City"
by Gram Parsons and Chris Hillman

Parsons and Hillman wrote "Sin City" about their adopted hometown Los Angeles, California. Both musicians could see that Los Angeles was not a city for the faint of heart. Although Las Vegas is usually referred to as "Sin City," the Burritos chose to write about Los Angeles and its share of vice and sleaze. "Sin City" represented an example of The Burrito's tongue-in-cheek lyrics within a traditional country arrangement. "Sin City's" lyrics stated, "This old town's filled with sin, it'll swallow you in." Another line went "This old earthquake's gonna leave me in the poor house." This was a reference to the San Andres Fault line, that ran through California.

Musically, "Sin City" featured a lazy country shuffle. The Burrito's vocal harmonies were very prominent with tasteful accompaniment from "Sneaky" Pete's pedal steel guitar. Chris Ethridge's solid bass playing laid down a strong foundation, thus lending a subtle rhythm and blues flavor to the song. "Sin City" was Hillman's and Parsons' take on Hollywood while simultaneously taking a shot at their former manager.

Before embarking on their first tour, The Burritos added original Byrd drummer Michael Clarke as a permanent member. He remained in the drumset chair until 1971. The Burritos declined an invitation to perform at the Woodstock Festival and an American tour ended in disaster due to drug and alcohol issues. Unhappy with the band's lack of commercial success, Chris Ethridge quit in the fall of 1969. A&M Records attempted to market the band as a straight country group and The Burritos recorded a few traditional country standards, including covers of Buck Owens and Merle Haggard. They also recorded some pop covers with a country approach including "I Shall Be Released," "Bony Moronie," and the Rolling Stones "Honky Tonk Women." However, this direction was abandoned for a second album that would feature all originals and the addition of singer/songwriter and multi-instrumentalist Bernie Leadon. Their sophomore recording, 1970's Burrito Deluxe, did not live up to the standards of The Burrito's debut. The sarcastic wit that embodied their previous lyrics was gone. Burrito Deluxe leaned more in a rock and commercial direction and "Sneaky" Pete was under-utilized. The brilliant Everly Brothers styled harmonies were also gone. Parsons was struggling with personal issues and showing little interest in the future of the band. Also, their label, A&M, was extending very limited support. Chris Hillman reached a breaking point and fired Gram Parsons in the spring of 1970.

1971's The Flying Burrito Bros release now saw the addition of singer/songwriter Rick Roberts. Chris Hillman and Bernie Leadon would share the vocal chair. Hillman recalled, "We had to learn the songs really quick…we didn't do much gigging after Parsons was gone. I had a sinking feeling that, as erratic as Gram was, he was the resident boy-genius, where the rest of us were much more plodding and steady." #6 By the time 1972's The Last of the Red Hot Burritos album was released, "Sneaky" Pete and Leadon were gone, leaving only Chris Hillman as the only original Burrito member. Next came 1975's Flying Again, 1976's Airborne, and 1977's Sierra, an album released under the band name Sierra, while they continued to perform as the Flying Burrito Brothers.

The early 1980's brought a period of commercial success to the band when they became known as simply The Burrito Brothers. 1981's Hearts on the Line, and 1982's Sunset Sundown featured top Nashville and Los Angeles session musicians. Additionally, the band performed with Tammy Wynette, Jerry Lee Lewis, and Emmylou Harris at London's Wembley Stadium. The 1990's brought a revamped Burrito lineup and the release of 1994's Eye of a Hurricane, 1997's California Jukebox, and 1999's Sons of the Golden West.

"Sneaky" Pete Kleinow soon formed a new band called Burrito Deluxe. They released four albums in the 2000's including 2007's Disciples of the Truth. Another version of the band called The Burritos emerged in 2011, releasing Sound as Ever. Yet another incarnation of the band surfaced in 2012 and began to perform as The Burrito Brothers. They released Still Going Strong in 2017. The Flying Burrito Brothers served to generate the blueprint for the country rock genre by melding rock energy with country instrumentation and lyric themes. Although their glory days were brief, The Flying Burrito Brothers left a small but potent body of work that set the stage for the evolution of the country rock genre.

Nitty Gritty Dirt Band (1966-present) is an American country rock band that formed in 1966 in Long Beach, California. Founded by two guitarist/singer-songwriters, Jeff Hanna and Bruce Kunkel, they added multi-instrumentalists Ralph Barr and Les Thompson, and guitarist/vocalist Jackson Browne. The Nitty Gritty Dirt Band was primarily a jug band that gradually adopted the emerging Southern California folk and country rock genres. Browne's stay in the band was brief and he soon left to begin his successful solo career. In 1967, they released their self-titled The Nitty Gritty Dirt Band debut album that contained the hit "Buy for Me the Rain." 1967's Ricochet was less successful and by 1968, the band adopted electric instruments and drumset. Over their career, they have released twenty-five studio albums and forty-one singles that included three number one hits. In 2005, The Nitty Gritty Dirt Band won a Grammy Award for Best Country Instrumental.

Poco (1968-present) is one of the first and longest-lasting country rock bands in American music history. The roots of Poco grew out of the last days of Buffalo Springfield. After Stephen Stills and Neil Young exited Springfield in 1968, guitarist Richie Furay and vocalist/guitarist Jim Messina remained to complete Buffalo Springfield's final recording. This included a guest appearance by steel guitarist Rusty Young. Furay, Messina, and Young soon added drummer George Grantham and

---

> **Rock Hard Fact**
>
> Gram Parsons referred to his mixture of country, blues, folk, and rock styles as "cosmic American music."

bassist Randy Meisner to form the lineup for a new band called Pogo. This name didn't last long. Walt Kelly, the creator of the comic strip Pogo, filed a lawsuit, and Pogo soon became Poco.

Many people were impressed with Poco's material and sound, including Columbia Records. However, Messina and Furay were still tied to Atlantic Records (Buffalo Springfield contract). In stepped David Geffen, who brokered a deal that involved David Crosby and Graham Nash going to Atlantic Records and Messina and Furay to Columbia. This led to the release of Poco's 1969 debut album, Pickin' Up the Pieces. After some internal friction, Randy Meisner left the band (the first of many Poco lineup changes). After a stint playing with Ricky Nelson's Stone Canyon Band, Meisner became a founding member of The Eagles.

Groundbreaking album
Pickin' Up the Pieces
by Poco

Pickin' Up the Pieces was considered one of the first great country rock albums. This first version of the Poco sound contained high, rich harmonies and their approach captured a special merging of country and rock. Richie Furay recalled, "We knew there was something fresh and creatively unique about what we were doing…To have the talent and ability in the band to be able to do the things we wanted, like Rusty and Jimmy playing their duets like Buck Owens, was exciting. Nobody in rock was doing that back then." #7

The tracks on Pickin' Up the Pieces were "Foreword," then "What A Day," "Nobody's Fool," "Calico," "First Love," "Make Me a Smile," "Short Changed," "Pickin' Up the Pieces," "Grand Junction," "Oh Yeah," "Just in Case It Happens", "Yes Indeed," "Tomorrow," "Consequently, So Long," and "Do You Feel It Too." The title track "Pickin' Up the Pieces," while commercially unsuccessful, contained a positive message about leaving one thing behind and embracing a new beginning (much like Poco did as a band following the end of Buffalo Springfield). "Pickin' Up the Pieces" featured a country shuffle and exciting interplay between Messina's guitar timbre and Rusty Young's pedal steel work.

The first of many lineup changes occurred immediately when bassist Randy Meisner was asked to leave the band shortly before the album's release. Meisner was angry that only Messina and Furay were allowed to mix the final playback of the album. Meisner's image was removed from a painting that appeared on the front cover (replaced by a dog) of Pickin' Up the Pieces. Meisner's bass parts and backing vocals were left in the mix, but his lead vocals were removed and replaced by drummer George Grantham. Additionally, Poco added pianist Bobby Doyle and percussionist Milt Holland for the recording.

Randy Meisner knew that the presence of pedal-steel guitar in Poco's country rock context set them apart from other rock bands. Meisner said, "Nobody else had one. And Rusty (Young) was a real showman. Everybody just loved watching him. Rusty didn't play it a lot like a steel. He made a whole different instrument out of it by playing it through a Leslie speaker. That was really unique. He could get a B-3 organ sound so we could get that R&B feel, and when we did strictly country stuff he could go back to that." #8

1970's Poco again resulted in poor sales. A live album, 1971's Deliverin' followed with Tim Schmit replacing Meisner (he would again replace Meisner later in The Eagles). The album Poco pushed the band's range and received better reviews. Yet it failed to generate any hits. Messina left the band when he felt that Furay was exerting too much control. Messina was replaced by vocalist/guitarist Paul Cotton. Poco brought in Booker T. & the M.G's guitarist Steve Cropper to produce1971's From the Inside. This resulted in a heavier and more soulful sound. Poco next recorded 1972's A Good Feelin' to Know, including the Richard Furay song of the same name. The band was still lacking commercial success and was becoming discouraged with the music industry.

1973's Crazy Eyes peaked at number thirty-eight on the U.S. charts and finally, a sign of increased popular appeal. However, Furay soon quit the band. 1974's Seven failed to replicate the success of Crazy Eyes but Poco's fan base remained solid. Also released in 1974, Cantamos offered virtuoso level playing and strong compositions, including the hard rocking track "High and Dry." Poco then moved to ABC records and released 1975's Head over Heels that climbed to number forty-eight on the U.S. charts with the hit "Keep on Tryin." The rest of the decade brought 1976's Rose of Cimarron, 1977's Indian Summer, and 1978's Legend, Poco's most commercially successful album with two top twenty hits, "Crazy Love" and "Heart of the Night"

"Crazy Love"
by Rusty Young

"Crazy Love" became the first Poco tune to make the top forty charts in America, reaching number seventeen. Rusty Young wrote the song while doing some work on his house. He was looking out over the valley in Los Angeles when the chorus of the song just popped into his head. Having a guitar close by, Young quickly wrote the song. Because it came so easily, he felt it truly was a gift. Young used the syllables "Ooh, ooh, ahhh haaa" as a stopgap to later be replaced by formal lyrics, but the band told him to leave it alone.

"Crazy Love" would become Poco's only really big hit. Young felt the song's success was ironic since he wrote it and said, "When the band started all I did was play steel guitar, banjo, and dobro and that kind of stuff. I was the instrumentalist in the band- I didn't sing and I didn't write… But I've always said that as people have left the band, it's left room for others to grow. I had great teachers: Richie Furay, Neil Young and Stephen Stills…I could listen to them writing songs, working on songs and how they did it. Jimmy Messina taught me really a lot about the whole recording process and writing poems." #9

Poco struggled in the 1980's with numerous lineup changes but managed to release five albums from 1980's Under the Gun to 1984's Inamorata. Then in 1989, in a strange twist of fate, Poco's original lineup from 1968 including Messina, Furay, Young, Meisner, and Grantham reunited. They decided to record and tour again. A comeback single, "Call It Love," made the top twenty, accompanied by 1989's Legacy. However, the reunion didn't last beyond a tour. Lineup changes ensued and Poco continued to tour relentlessly with new personnel. Thirteen years after recording Legacy, Poco released Running Horse in 2002. Poco continued to perform live and a decade later released 2013's All Fired Up. Often overlooked in the early development of the country rock

> "I think Poco started country rock and the Eagles legitimized it"
>
> – Randy Meisner

genre, Poco has a unique place in country rock history with their distinctive sound and consistent innovation.

The country rock movement featured two very prominent female artists that made their mark beginning in the 1970's. Country rock artist **Emmylou Harris** gained early recognition from her work with Gram Parsons and **Linda Ronstadt** became an extremely successful solo artist.

Emmylou Harris (1947-) is an American singer/songwriter and guitarist from Birmingham, Alabama. Emmylou dropped out of college to pursue her musical goals and moved to New York City during the 1960's folk music era. She released her debut album Gilding Bird in 1969, a collection that included five folk-influenced originals. Chris Hillman had considered asking Emmylou to join The Flying Burrito Brothers. Instead, he recommended her to Gram Parsons, who was looking for a female vocalist to collaborate with on his first solo album, GP. In 1973, Harris toured as a member of Parsons Fallen Angels Band where the two created very musical vocal harmonies and duets. She also recorded with Parsons on his Grievous Angel album that was released posthumously in 1974 after his untimely death.

Harris launched her solo career with 1975's Pieces of the Sky album. She has recorded several of Parsons' songs over the years in her dedication to preserving his legacy and strong country music roots. Emmylou's song "Boulder To Birmingham" was her tribute to Parsons as well as her The Ballad of Sally Rose concept album. In 1987, Emmylou teamed up with Dolly Parton and Linda Ronstadt for their album Trio. Also in 1987, she showed her stylistic versatility by recording Angel Band, an album that featured traditional gospel songs with guitarist Vince Gill.

"Every Grain of Sand"
by Bob Dylan

"Every Grain of Sand" was a Bob Dylan original song from his 1985 Biograph album. Dylan's lyrics were partly inspired by William Blake's *Auguries of Innocence* including the passage "To see a world in a grain of sand-and a heaven in a wild flower-Hold infinity in the palm of your hand-and eternity in an hour." Emmylou picked this song to cover because of its emotional message.

Emmylou employed noted rock producer Daniel Lanois for the recording of her album, Wrecking Ball, that included "Every Grain of Sand." This album received *almost no* country radio airplay but it did bring Harris to the attention of alternative rock fans. She also enlisted the services of U2 drummer Larry Mullen Jr. This helped her to achieve a modern and more aggressive sound. Together, Harris and Lanois's collaboration won a 1996 Grammy Award for Best Contemporary Folk Album. Emmylou's version of this Dylan classic showcased the beauty of her voice and her ability to draw out the emotion and anguish of Dylan's profound lyrics. Emmylou performed "Every Grain of Sand" at the funeral of Johnny Cash in 2003 in a duet format with Sheryl Crow.

Emmylou Harris has made a career of balancing both traditional country and country rock. Harris has guested with a number of significant artists including Linda Ronstadt, Neil Young, The Nitty Gritty Dirt Band, and Bob Dylan on his Desire album. Emmylou later moved to Nashville, where she served as president of the Country Music Association and as a member of the Grand Ole Opry. She again paid tribute to Gram Parsons' legacy with her 1999 Return Of the Grievous Angel album. Emmylou Harris has recorded twenty-six studio albums in her long career of skillfully blending different music styles. Harris has made innovative contributions to the country rock genre.

Linda Ronstadt (1946-) is an American country and pop music singer/songwriter from Tucson, Arizona. Ronstadt established her career in the mid-1960's in the emerging country rock movement of Southern California. She began as a member of The Stone Poneys, with guitarist/vocalist Bobby Kimmel and guitarist Kenny Edwards. They recorded Ronstadt's first hit, a Mike Nesmith song titled "Different Drum." Nesmith recalled, "I was hangin' out with John Herald, a member of the Greenbriar Boys. He taught it ("Different Drum") to his bluegrass band, and they sang it. Linda was really a country freak, an ethnic purist. She heard it on their record and used their arrangement." #10 The Stone Poneys released three albums in a period from 1967 to 1968. In 1969, Ronstadt recorded her debut solo album Hand Sown... Home Grown. It has been recognized as the first female alternative country record. Ronstadt's 1970 Silk Purse revealed her ability to balance the worlds of pop and country. Recorded mostly in Nashville, she utilized top country session players to record the aching "Long Long Time" and a cover of Goffin and King's "Will Your Love Me Tomorrow." Along with other cover songs, Ronstadt also covered Gene Clark and Bernie Leadon's "Life is Like a Mountain Railway."

Linda Ronstadt employed what would become the nucleus of The Eagles; Don Henley, Glenn Frey, Bernie Leadon, and Randy Meisner for a short tour in 1971. They played on her 1972 album Linda Ronstadt. 1973's Don't Cry Now began the packaging of Linda Ronstadt as a pop star. Her first album on the Geffen Asylum Label, Ronstadt recorded songs tailored for her by J.D. Souther. She also added covers of The Eagles and Neil Young and utilized the slick studio production of Peter Asher. This recording stripped away any folk or bluegrass elements, resulting in a pure country rock album. Ronstadt's transformation into a full blown AM radio star came with 1974's Heart Like a Wheel that featured the hits "When Will I Be Loved" and "You're No Good." These two Ronstadt hits set a precedent for her to remake classic rock songs with a unique stylistic approach.

"You're No Good"
by Clint Ballard Jr.

"You're No Good" was originally recorded by Dee Dee Warwick in 1963 and was produced by the famous duo Jerry Leiber and Mike Stoller. Another strong version of the song was recorded by Betty Everett, who like Ronstadt, had a very powerful voice. "You're No Good" proved to be a breakout hit for Ronstadt, whose chart success to this point was inconsistent. Yet another cover was by a British Mersey beat group The Swinging Blue Jeans, who had a number three hit with the song on the British charts. Ronstadt and producer Peter Asher selected "You're No Good" as a last minute song for the recording session. Linda Ronstadt's version reached number one on the U.S. charts in 1975. Van Halen followed suit by covering the song a few years later.

The "You're No Good" lyrics clearly stated that the lowdown guy in the song was simply "no good." However, in the second verse, Linda turned it around and revealed that she had done some bad things herself. She sang "I broke a heart that's gentle and true-well I broke a heart over someone like you-I'll beg his forgive-

> "In the Troubadour (the club) days, it was all those songwriters that I hung around with all the time...We all knew each other, and we just carried each other's words around."
>
> – Linda Ronstadt

ness on bended knee-I wouldn't blame him if he said to me-you're no good." By the third verse, she was back to bashing the guy by singing "I'm telling you now baby and I'm going my way-forget about you baby 'cause I'm leaving to stay." On the track, Ed Black played six-string guitar and pedal steel. Black's riff on his Les Paul was echoed in octaves by bassist Kenny Edwards.

Linda Ronstadt went on to release over eighteen more studio albums from the mid-1970's up until 2004's Hummin' to Myself. Included in her prolific output was her 1987 release Canciones de Mi Padre, an album of all-Mexican traditional **Mariachi music**. Ronstadt has cultural and musical roots in the rhythms of traditional Mexican music. She has incorporated **Ranchera** into her country rock and pop songs. Ranchera is a style similar to mariachi music. Ranchera's lyrics are about love, patriotism, or nature and draw on traditional Mexican folk culture. Also important were Ronstadt's chart topping albums, Heart Like a Wheel, Simple Dreams, and Living in the USA. They helped to propel her to become the first *female* "arena rock star." Ronstadt's rock image was as famous as her music, having appeared on the cover of *Rolling Stone Magazine* six times, and on the covers of *Time* and *Newsweek*. Linda Ronstadt was inducted into the Rock and Rock Hall of Fame in 2014.

Two important country rock bands from the late 1960's shared the same San Francisco geography. However, **Creedence Clearwater Revival** wrote lyrics about the Mississippi Bayou's while **The New Riders of the Purple Sage** emerged from the West Coast psychedelic scene. Some of their original members would go on to form The Grateful Dead.

Creedence Clearwater Revival (1967-1972) was an American rock band from El Cerrito, California. Vocalist/guitarist John Fogerty, bassist Stu Cook, and drummer Doug Clifford first met in high school. They formed The Blue Velvets, a trio that played instrumentals and "juke box standards." The Blue Velvets backed Fogerty's older brother Tom in the studio and at live gigs. Tom soon became a member of The Blue Velvets. They later performed and released singles under the name The Gollliwogs, until renaming themselves Creedence Clearwater Revival in 1967. CCR's self-titled 1968 debut album Creedence Clearwater Revival yielded the hit "Susie Q," a cover of a Dale Hawkins song. CCR went on a roll with three hit albums Bayou Country, Green River, and Willy and the Poor Boys, all released in 1969. A slew of hits from this productive period included "Proud Mary," "Bad Moon Rising," "Green River," "Down on the Corner," and "Fortunate Son." The album Green River reached number one on the U.S. charts and CCR quickly became one of the hottest country rock bands in the country.

"Proud Mary"
by John Fogerty

John Fogerty conceived "Proud Mary" to be the story of a woman who worked as a maid for rich people. Everyday she took the bus to work and then rode it back home. Bassist Stu Cook had the idea of including a riverboat aspect of the song when he watched an episode of the television show *Maverick*. John Fogerty created the phrase "rolling on a river" and combined it with the maid (proud Mary) and the riverboat to create the lyrics for "Proud Mary."

John Fogerty was given an honorable discharge from the Army in 1968. Elated by the news, he ran outside and did cartwheels on his lawn. Then he went inside, picked up his guitar and started strumming the strings until a chord progression emerged. The lyric "Left a good job in the city" also came to him. Over a minor chord, he added "Big wheel keep on turnin'-Proud Mary keep on burnin.'" When he added "rolling, rolling on the river," he knew he had written his best song. Fogerty has cited that the funky pronunciation of his lyrics can be attributed to his love of blues great Howlin' Wolf.

"Proud Mary" was the first of five singles by CCR that all went to number two on the U.S. charts. Fogerty has the distinction of having the most number two songs while never having a number one hit. "Proud Mary" was a number four hit for Ike and Tina Tuner in 1971. "Proud Mary" has been covered over one hundred times and was recorded thirty-five times in 1969 alone.

Even though Creedence Clearwater Revival were rock stars at this point, their roots were strong in country music. In their off hours Stu Cook remembered, "We were into country music. We even had a country band, The Shi*-Kicker Three, with John on pedal steel, Doug Clifford on a practice drum set, and me on guitar. Lots of Merle Haggard, Buck Owens, Jimmie Rodgers, and so on. We'd come back to the hotel after the (CCR) show and play country music and drink all night." #11

1970's Cosmo's Factory brought even more hits including "Travelin' Band," "Who'll Stop the Rain," and "Lookin' Out My Back Door." Their style was now referred to as **swamp rock**, a combination of New Orleans styled rhythm and blues, country, and rock. "Travelin' Band" was inspired by Little Richard. The publishing company that held the rights to Richard's "Good Golly, Miss Molly" successfully sued CCR due to the song's similarities. "Lookin' Out My Back Door" was a tribute to the Bakersfield sound of Buck Owens. John Fogerty assumed leadership of CCR by singing, producing, arranging and playing guitar on all of the band's recordings. However, during the Cosmo's Factory recording sessions, John Fogerty's rigid control led to his older brother Tom's exit from the band. They continued as a trio. CCR's final album, 1972 Mardi Gras, did not meet the standards of their previous work and internal tensions mounted. Creedence Clearwater Revival was finished.

In 1973, John Fogerty began a successful solo career by releasing The Blue Ridge Rangers, a one-man band collection of country and gospel songs, on which he played all the instruments. Since then, Fogerty has released a total of nine solo albums including his 2013 Wrote a Song for Everyone. The Creedence Clearwater Revival legacy reveals a stylistic synthesis of swamp rock, country, rhythm and blues, and rockabilly. The tight and punchy arrangements of John Fogerty's classic compositions are instantly recognizable with his down-home twang backed by CCR's brand of economical and powerful country rock.

New Riders of the Purple Sage (1969-1997) (2005-present) is an American country rock band from San Francisco, California. The path to The New Riders started when Grateful Dead guitarist/vocalist Jerry Garcia began to play some gigs with guitarist David Nelson. While Garcia was busy establishing The Grateful Dead, Nelson joined the New Delhi River Band. Singer/songwriter John Collins Dawson played a few spontaneous concerts with Garcia and Nelson. Collectively, this trio formed a new psychedelic country rock band, The New Riders of the Purple Sage in 1969. The New Riders soon

Rock Hard Fact

Various members of The Eagles were previously in many pioneering country rock bands including; The Flying Burrito Brothers, Hearts and Flowers, Poco, and Shiloh.

added bassist Bob Matthews and Grateful Dead drummer Mickey Hart. Grateful Dead bassist Phil Lesh also played sporadically with the band. Bassist Dave Torbert was then recruited to play full time with The New Riders. The most commercially successful version of the band would soon be Dawson, Torbert, Nelson, ex-Jefferson Airplane drummer Spencer Dryden, and pedal steel guitarist Buddy Cage (who replaced Garcia).

The band released their self-titled debut album, <u>New Riders of the Purple Sage</u>, in 1971. Garcia played pedal steel guitar and banjo. It would be his only full studio album with the band. The New Riders wanted to gain their independence from The Grateful Dead and Garcia needed to focus full time on The Dead. They followed with 1972's <u>Powerglide</u> and <u>Gypsy Cowboy</u>. However, Garcia and Grateful Dead drummer Bill Kreutzmann guested on <u>Powerglide</u> as well as legendary session pianist Nicky Hopkins. Buddy Cage's formidable pedal steel playing became a focal point for the band. When Jerry Garcia and Cage jammed together for the first time, Garcia just stopped and said to Cage, "Sorry, I can't keep up with you." #12

The New Riders opened for some Grateful Dead and Jerry Garcia Band shows in 1977 and 1978, and basically served as the alter ego of The Grateful Dead. The New Riders toured and released many albums throughout the late 1970's and early 1980's with minimal commercial success. From the mid-1980's until the late 1990's, John Collins Dawson continued to lead The New Riders and was joined by bluegrass multi-instrumentalist Rusty Gauthier. An almost two decade period saw a host of New Rider lineups. In 1997, The New Riders called it quits and Dawson retired from music. After the death of Spencer Dryden in 2005, The New Riders re-formed, led by Nelson and Cage, and began to tour and record again. John Collins Dawson died in 2009.

The New Riders of the Purple Sage had a country sound that fused elements of psychedelic rock and folk music. John Collins Dawson and Dave Torbert were strong songwriters and The New Riders established a country rock sound that was somewhat more country and twangy than The Grateful Dead. The New Riders have enjoyed a long career and have released fourteen studio albums and numerous live recordings.

The beginning of the 1970's saw many country rock pioneers survive into the new decade and begin to move more toward rock. Country rock's lack of commercial success had been a source of much frustration for artists such as The Flying Burrito Brothers and Poco, who released more commercially oriented rock albums. Out of this musical shift emerged the most commercially popular rock band with country roots, **The Eagles** (see chapter twelve). The early 1970's also saw the emergence of more country rock artists and bands that included; **The First National Band** (1970-1972), **Loggins and Messina** (1971-1976) (2005-present), **Rick Nelson** (1940-1985) **The Stone Canyon Band**, and **Pure Prairie League**.

"I'll never be Bob Dylan. He's the master"

- Neil Young

"Not Monkeying around" country rock great Mike Nesmith

Michael Nesmith (1942-) never set out to help create the country-rock genre. He was merely drawing from his strong Texas roots to write songs. Nesmith joined the United States Air Force in 1960 and later enrolled at San Antonio College where he collaborated with singer/songwriter John London. At the height of the folk boom in the early 1960's, he moved to Los Angeles to play his country-influenced folk music in the clubs and coffeehouses. Nesmith has said that he brought together early country influences, but not consciously trying to play country rock. He was just trying to play music. Nesmith grew up listening to the country & western songs of Hank Williams Sr. and conceived of them as being just music. Nesmith also heard the connection between country and blues styles when he said, "The blues scales that you hear, from Stevie Ray Vaughn to B.B. King playing on the guitar, really only works against three chords-the three-chord progression...and country music really only works against that same three-chord progression." #13

Nesmith auditioned for and won the job for a new television series, The Monkees, that aired from 1966 to 1968 (see chapter three). At the same time, Nesmith issued his first solo album, 1968's <u>The Wichita Train Whistle Sings</u>. When The Monkees popular series ended, Nesmith quit the group and formed the First National Band, one of the pioneering bands of the country rock genre. For the First National Band, Nesmith recruited his old friend John London and drummer John Ware from Linda Ronstadt's band. He also secured pedal-steel ace Red Rhodes. Their debut album, 1970's <u>Magnetic South</u>, was the first of three albums for Nesmith to breathe life into his long overdue catalogue of over fifty original compositions. The album yielded the hit "Joanne" that went to number twenty-one on the U.S. charts.

Mike Nesmith paid a price for his Monkees fame. Many people in the music industry thought of him as a TV actor, and not a serious musician. But he persevered to record another First National's album, 1970's <u>Loose Salute</u>. Their third and last would be 1971's <u>Nevada Fighter</u>. The making of <u>Nevada Fighter</u> proved difficult when the band fragmented during the recording sessions. Nesmith turned to Elvis Presley's band that included Ron Tutt, James Burton, Glen D. Hardin, Joe Osborn, and Max Bennett to finish the recording. On this album, Nesmith was able to realize his musical goal to connect his deep Texas sound to his original country rock compositional approach. Nesmith went on the form The Second National Band and release 1972's <u>Tantamount to Treason Vol. 1</u> that included an appearance by singer/songwriter Jose Feliciano on congas. The Second Nationals took an eclectic approach that allowed Nesmith to remain committed to country rock and also explore other music genres. They followed with 1972's <u>And the Hits Just Keep on Comin'</u>. Mike Nesmith later formed his own record label, Countryside Records, dedicated to recording unknown country artists. Nesmith moved into music video and film production and later reunited with The Monkees to record and tour. Mike Nesmith brought a pop sensibility to his strong Texas roots and in the process became a major contributor to the country rock movement.

Pure Prairie League (1970-present with some inactive years) is an American country rock band from Columbus, Ohio. After some early lineup changes, Pure Prairie League consisted of vocalist/guitarist Craig Fuller, guitarist Jim Caughlin, steel guitarist John David Call, and drummer Tom McGrail. Fuller and McGrail named the band after a fictional 19th century temperance union (a social movement against the consumption of alcohol) featured in an old Errol Flynn cowboy film called *Dodge City*. Fuller grew up listening to country music but was also inspired by The Byrds and The British Invasion bands. The self-titled 1972 debut, <u>Pure Prairie League</u>, established their sound and built a solid fan base after constant touring throughout the United States. 1972's Bustin' Out featured their song, "Amie," but it didn't become a hit until RCA re-released Bustin' Out (after first dropping the band and re-signing them). Fuller left the band after serving time on draft evasion charges (conscientious objector status could not be arranged).

"Amie"
by Craig Fuller

Although Bustin' Out was first released in 1972, "Amie" was not released as a single until 1973. It became enormously popular on college radio stations and its airplay prompted RCA Records to re-sign the band. The song received almost equal airplay on country and pop radio, making it one of the first true crossover songs. The acoustic guitar solo connected with a country audience with its implied bluegrass feel. For the Bustin' Out album, Pure Prairie League had enlisted the services of ex-David Bowie guitarist Mick Ronson and he provided lush string arrangements and an overall light, affable sound for the recording.

"Amie" has been covered by many artists including Travis Tritt, Counting Crows, and Garth Brooks. At the time that "Amie" was pumping new life into Pure Prairie League, Craig Fuller was doing alternate service working in a hospital in Kentucky as punishment for not reporting for military service. "Amie's" popularity opened the door for more Pure Prairie League hits such as "Let Me Love You Tonight" and "I'm Almost Ready." "Amie" will always be remembered for Fuller's sweet and "radio friendly" voice.

1975's Two Lane Highway featured guest appearances by Chet Atkins, Emmylou Harris, and Don Felder of The Eagles. This was the beginning of a string of five consecutive top forty hits. In spite of more lineup changes, 1976's If the Shoe Fits, Dance, and 1977's Takin' the Stage were all successful releases. In 1978, John David Call left the band before the release of Just Fly. Shortly after, Nashville favorite Vince Gill got his first big break when he joined the band for 1979's Can't Hold Back. The early 1980's saw Pure Prairie League release Firin' Up and Something in the Night. Their record label, Casablanca Records, was sold to Polygram Records who dropped the band from their roster. Vince Gill soon left to start his very successful solo career.

After more lineup changes and miles logged on the road, Pure Prairie League disbanded in 1988. A decade later, they were back with a new lineup led by founding member Craig Fuller. After eighteen years, the band released All in Good Time in 2005. A pivotal band in the development of country rock, Pure Prairie League still maintains a busy tour schedule.

Bob Dylan's musical legend was cemented when he became a legendary folk singer and then the most significant catalyst in developing the folk-rock genre (see chapter seven). But Dylan was not done yet. By 1966, Dylan had released seven studio albums, including 1966's Blonde on Blonde. In that same year, Bob Dylan was in a bad motorcycle accident. After he recovered, Dylan became more reclusive and made his own film called Eat This Document. In 1967, he recorded more than 160 songs with the members of his new backing band that later became The Band (see chapter eighteen). They released a massive work called The Basement Tapes. The Band members Rick Danko, Robbie Robertson, Garth Hudson, Levon Helm, and Richard Manuel helped Dylan reach new levels of ensemble interplay. He learned how to work with these highly skilled musicians that were able to seamlessly assimilate his unique voice and phrasing with a variety of musical styles. What followed was his 1967 release John Wesley Harding. The pivotal tune was "All Along the Watchtower." Jimi Hendrix would later go on to record his own classic cover version of this song. Somewhere between John Wesley Harding and the year 1968, Bob Dylan went country.

What attracted Bob Dylan to country music? Dylan had always viewed country music as the natural progression of rural folk music. He has cited the country gospel sound of the tune "Driftin Too Far From the Shore" as one of his earliest memories of hearing music. In addition, he always had respect for the music of Hank Williams Sr.. Dylan said "I used to sing his songs way back even before I played rock as a rock 'n' roll teenager." #14 Bob Dylan had been going to Nashville to record on and off for nearly three years and then later appeared at The Grand Ole Opry with his good friend and occasional musical partner Johnny Cash. Nevertheless, this was considered to be a dry period for Dylan. For him to tack on two country songs on the end of John Wesley Harding (an album of biblical, doom-laden songs) was considered to be a sign that he was having trouble coming up with new material. Dylan's producer at the time, Bob Johnston, thought a collaborative recording between Dylan and Johnny Cash would jump-start Dylan's creative juices. In one sense, Bob Dylan had come full circle. He had been called a hillbilly when he first appeared in the Greenwich Village coffeehouses, but what did that crowd know about hillbillies? Dylan showed up at the studio infatuated with country music but had written only four songs for a recording session.

Nashville Skyline was released in April of 1969 and it stunned a number of Dylan fans that had once again expected him to do more of the same (now folk-rock). The country Dylan approached these songs with a simple musical and lyrical vocabulary. For a songwriter as profound and lyrically complex as Dylan, 1969's Nashville Skyline went in a whole new direction. The album featured Dylan and Cash on only one duet, "Girl from the North Country." It also produced one of Dylan's most popular tunes, "Lay Lady Lay." Nashville Skyline would go on to be one of his best selling and influential albums.

Groundbreaking album
Nashville Skyline
by Bob Dylan

Johnny Cash was at the same studio as Dylan (in Nashville) working on a new record. Without any preparation, Cash and Dylan decided to record together. In February 1969, the first sessions took place for Dylan's Nashville Skyline, an album that would have a profound effect on a new genre, country rock. Bob Johnston recalled, "I had microphones set up and stools and tapes, and everything…They looked at each other…got their guitars and started playing." #15 They recorded around eighteen songs, mostly playing acoustic on their own, but also using members of Cash's band.

Side one opened with "Girl from the North Country," then "Nashville Skyline Rag," "To Be Alone with You," "I Threw it All Away," and "Peggy Day." "Girl from the North Country" was inspired by Dylan's exposure to traditional English ballads (from his first trip to England in 1962) and by his relationship with Suze Rotolo. Musically, "Girl from the North Country" was very similar to his composition "Boots of Spanish Leather," from his album The

> "Creativity is like a freight train going down the tracks. It's something that has to be caressed and treated with a great deal of respect…You've got to program your brain not to think too much."
>
> – Bob Dylan

> "Somehow you can tell the difference when a song is written just to get on the radio and when what someone does is their whole life. That comes through in Bob Dylan, Paul Simon, Willie Nelson. There is no separating their life from their music."
>
> - Lyle Lovett

Times They Are a-Changin'. Dylan had written "I Threw It All Away" and played the song for George Harrison (who learned it himself). It's about a love that was lost by being cruel and angry. Unlike some of Dylan's songs about relationships (ex. "It Ain't Me Babe"), Dylan assumed responsibility for the failed relationship he sang about in this song.

Side two opened with "Lay Lady Lay," then "One More Night," "Tell Me That It Isn't True," "Country Pie," and "Tonight I'll Be Staying Here with You." Dylan had been asked to contribute a song for the movie soundtrack of Midnight Cowboy. For it, Dylan wrote "Lay Lady Lay" but did not deliver the song in time to director John Schlesinger who instead used Fred Neil's song "Everybody's Talkin'." For "Tonight I'll Be Staying Here with You," Dylan's lyrics expressed his devotion to his lover and desire to stay with her. Train imagery runs throughout the song (a very country thing to do). The accompaniment included piano, bass, and the all-important pedal steel guitar.

The new Bob Dylan was not only making a country album, but he also wasn't expressing his usual cryptic, prophetic, or biblical messages. On Nashville Skyline he was actually crooning in a Bing Crosby-like voice. There were two possible explanations for this. First, he had given up smoking and second, he was no longer nervous in the recording studio and could now sing in a relaxed tone.

Nashville Skyline sounded like a broad country record to many people not from the South. However, by Nashville standards, it wasn't considered to be a country album. It wasn't really pop or R&B or rock. It also had somewhat of a folk feel to it. Nashville Skyline contained a new sound, one that The Flying Burrito Brothers, Poco, and many others were pursuing. Dylan joined the Southern California group of country rock pioneers that were able to open the minds of a counter-culture that previously had considered country music to be hick stuff. Important session musicians on Nashville Skyline were drummer Ken Buttrey and bassist/vocalist Charlie Daniels (later to lead his own successful band-see southern rock section). Nashville Skyline peaked at number three on the U.S. charts, helping to bring this new genre of country rock to mainstream America.

It has also weathered the test of time.

"Lay Lady Lay"
by Bob Dylan

When Bob Dylan wrote "Lay Lady Lay," he offered it to The Everly Brothers, who mistakenly thought it was a song about lesbians. They turned it down. However, Dylan sang the line "Stay, lady, stay, stay with your man awhile" with warmth and affection. The song revealed that the singer was asking his lover spend the night with him. These lyrics spoke of romance and sexual anticipation. Many radio stations refused to play the song because of the inclusion of the word "lay" in the title, assuming it was about sex. Dylan denied that the song was sexual in any way.

The main hook of "Lay Lady Lay" was a recurring four-note pedal steel guitar riff that was crucial in providing the song with a traditional country sound. The harmony, viewed from a guitar perspective (Dylan often wrote songs on the guitar), contained a chord progression that went from the I to iii chord in A major (A major chord to C# minor). This then repeated a whole step lower to form a sequence. The chords can be voiced to form the chromatically descending melody of A to G# to G natural to F#. It formed a natural and beautiful chord progression. According to Johnny Cash, Dylan played "Lay Lady Lay" at a singer-songwriter get together at Cash's house near Nashville. At that event, Joni Mitchell played her "Both Sides, Now," Graham Nash played his "Marrakesh Express," Kris Kristofferson played "Me and Bobby McGee," and Shel Silverstein played his "A Boy Named Sue."

Some house party!

Dylan returned to Nashville two months later in late April 1969 with a ton of new songs. This new material contained some country material and other styles. The result was a compilation of songs recorded in both Nashville and New York, utilizing dozens of musicians over an eleven month period. These sessions produced 1970's Self Portrait and New Morning. Many fans and critics simultaneously praised and criticized Dylan's country explorations in the 1970's for being unpredictable. Dylan still employed The Band as his touring group and later appeared at their farewell concert (The Last Waltz) in 1976 along with Eric Clapton, Muddy Watters, Joni Mitchell, and others. Bob Dylan would later became a born again Christian in the late 1970's and release two gospel influenced albums, 1979's Slow Train Coming and 1980's Saved. Bob Dylan continued his prolific and legendary recording and performance career.

The impact of all of the Southern California bands and Bob Dylan's new found country persona was a major influence on countless artists throughout the 1970's and 1980's. This long list includes; **Glen Campbell** (1958-2017), **Hank Williams Jr.** (1949-), **Commander Cody and His Lost Planet Airmen** (1967-1976) (1997-present), and **Kid Rock** (see chapter seventeen). A small sampling of the many prominent country rock bands and solo artists that enjoyed mainstream success throughout the 1980's into the 2000's included; **Alabama**, **The Kentucky Headhunters** (1968-1982) (1986-present), **Eric Church** (1977-), **Lyle Lovett**, and **Dwight Yoakam**.

Alabama (1969-present with some inactive years) is an American country rock band that formed in Fort Payne, Alabama in 1969. They were founded under the name Wildcountry by vocalist/guitarist Randy Owens, bassist Teddy Gentry, and guitarist/keyboardist/fiddle player Jeff Cook. Alabama's three-musician lead vocal front appealed to a younger country audience with their edgy crossover sound. Over the years they have employed numerous drummers, the longest tenured being Mark Herndon. Alabama's greatest success occurred in the 1980's with seven multi-platinum albums and numerous hits on the country and pop charts.

Their self-recorded debut album, 1976's Wild Country, and 1977's Deuces Wild, came after struggles with their record label. With minimal label support, Alabama toured tirelessly in the late 1970's to build a strong fan base. In 1979, they released Alabama Band No. 3. 1980's My Home's in Alabama yielded the hit "Tennessee River" and 1981's Feels So Right featured "Love in the First Degree." Alabama followed with six more albums in the 1980's that produced a slew of hits including; "Mountain Music," "Dixieland Delight," "If You're Gonna Play in Texas," and "Song of the South."

"Song of the South"
by Bob McDill

"Song of the South" told a story about a poor Southern cotton farm-family from the era of the great depression. The song's lyrics opened with a reference from President Franklin D. Roosevelt's New Deal, "The cotton was short and the weeds was tall, but Mr. Roosevelt's gonna save us all." The family lost their farm after the mother became sick. The family eventually sought a life in an urban location and prospered. Alabama told this story authentically, since many of their band members grew up in cotton country.

Alabama evoked a strong sense of patriotism with "Song of the South." Musically, the tune utilized the country instrumentation of banjo and country fiddle. It also featured a chorus that developed a traditional bluegrass double time feel. "Song of the South" was a hit single from Alabama's twelfth studio album, 1988's Southern Star. In addition to "Song of the South," this album was loaded with the hits "High Cotton," "If I Had You," and "Southern Star."

Alabama's popularity waned slightly in the 1990's but they still managed to produce more hit singles and multi-platinum albums. They disbanded in 2003 but re-formed in 2010. Alabama's blend of traditional country and southern rock mixed with elements of gospel and pop. This combination became their formula to build a very strong fan base. The band thought of themselves to be a country band first, but with a crossover appeal to reach a wider audience. Alabama has sold over seventy-five million albums worldwide including 2015's Southern Drawl. Alabama is a dominant country rock band that continues to record and tour.

Two other artists were notable in the 1980's for their crossover country rock success. **Lyle Lovett** (1957-) is an American country rock singer/songwriter from Houston, Texas. Lovett has released thirteen albums and twenty-five singles since he began his solo career with his 1986 self-titled debut album, Lyle Lovett. Lovett's style is a fusion of traditional country with folk, blues, jazz, and gospel elements. Those characteristics are found on his classic Joshua Judges Ruth album. His 1996 album The Road to Ensenada won a Grammy Award for Best Country Album. **Dwight Yoakam** (1956-) is an American singer/songwriter from Pikeville, Kentucky. He emerged in the early 1980's with a traditional honky-tonk approach that was not very popular in Nashville. He then moved to Los Angeles and performed his original compositions in rock and punk clubs with bands like The Dead Kennedys and The Butthole Surfers. Yoakam's debut recording was a self-financed EP titled Guitars, Cadillacs, Etc., Etc. which led to his debut album of the same name. Two hit singles emerged, "Honky Tonk Man" and "Guitar, Cadillacs." Yoakam often utilized a heavy backbeat and a revival of a rockabilly sound. He also combined traditional fiddle parts with a Buck Owens' influenced guitar approach. Dwight Yoakam went on to record fourteen more studio albums, including 2016's all-bluegrass styled Smimmin'Pools, Movie Stars (a reference to the Beverly Hillbillies TV theme song). Dwight Yoakam has helped extend country rock's popularity by touring with punk bands like Husker Du. He has covered rock songs such as The Clash's "Train in Vain" and Cheap Trick's "I Want You to Want Me." Johnny Cash once cited Yoakam as his favorite country singer.

Throughout the new millennium, more and more country influenced singers emerged not just in the South, but also throughout America. Today, country music and pop-rock are often thought of as one and the same. Still centered in Nashville, Tennessee, country-pop artists as diverse as **Travis Tritt** (1963-), **Keith Urban** (1967-), and **Lady Antebellum** (2006-present) continue to thrive in the American pop-rock music scene. Other country-pop artists include; **Tim McGraw** (1967-), **Darius Rucker** (1966-), **Faith Hill** (1967-), **Carrie Underwood** (1983-), and **Rascal Flatts** (1999-present) to name a few. Country music characteristics such as the use of steel guitars, two-beat bass patterns, southern vocal dialects, and lyrical themes of the country lifestyle are now combined with many elements of rock and pop music. A mixture of rock and country instrumentation, rhythms, and chord progressions has also contributed to this assimilation of styles. This has defined today's modern country pop-rock sound. The wide-ranging country-pop genre became very popular and deserves it's own examination. Space limits how many of the great country rock bands we can cover.

Alternative Country Rock

Originally, the attempt to merge punk and country was pioneered by **Jason & the Scorchers** (1981-2007) (2010-present). The later 1970's into the 1980's saw the subgenre of **cowpunk**, a merger of country and punk. In the 1990's, cowpunk developed into the **alternative country rock** genre and **roots rock** (folk, blues, and country mixed with rock elements). Alternative country referred to bands and artists that existed outside of the traditions of mainstream country music. The genre took its name from the web site alt.country, a cyber world for artists that were branded as outlaws for their ideological, political, and social concerns. Here, they found a forum for their music. In other terms, if you're not played on traditional country radio, you're alternative country. The alternative trend moved away from the stringent rules and slick studio production of the Nashville dominated recording industry. Instead, alternative country favored a less polished approach, often infused with strong rock and punk attributes. Alternative country incorporated virtually all rock genres and even embraced electronica, psychedelic rock, and rhythm and blues; hence the term alternative country rock. Alternative country rock lyrics addressed many social issues but without many of the typical clichés often utilized by mainstream country musicians. Alternative country rock has taken a more traditional view of American rural life. It's closer to Woody Guthrie than Garth Brooks and maintains a direct connection with the past.

A magazine called No Depression was created in 1995 to portray the alternative country genre and did so in direct opposition to mainstream country music. Alternative country rock, like punk rock, has appealed to a disaffected young audience while maintaining a direct connection with an American past such as the simple life along the Appalachian Trail. A long and diverse list of early alternative country rock artists include; **John Prine** (1946-), **Commander Cody and His Lost Planet Airmen** (1967-1976) (1997-present), and **Asleep at the Wheel** (1970-present). The later 1980's saw the emergence of more alternative country rock artists such as **The Bottle Rockets** (1992-present), **Cowboy Junkies** (1986-present), **The Dixie Chicks**, **Uncle Tupelo**, and

---

Rock Hard Fact

The Dixie Chicks derived their name from the title of the third studio album by the Southern rock band Little Feat.

"Even when I don't think I'm writing, I'm writing. There's some part of my brain geared toward making songs up, and I know when I get a moment to be by myself, that's when they come out."

- Jeff Tweedy

> "The people who play it and sing it are conditioned by the way they grew up. Southern lifestyle: it's in the ground they walk on, the grits they ate, and the water they drank."
>
> – Jerry Wexler, Atlantic Records

Wilco. These and other modern artists and bands have moved the alternative country rock genre forward.

The Dixie Chicks (1989-present) are an American alternative country rock band from Dallas, Texas that formed in 1989. Their early lineup consisted of guitarist Robin Lynn Macy, bassist Laura Lynch, and multi-instrumentalist sisters Martie and Emily Erwin (Martie and Emily married and changed their names to Martie Maguire and Emily Robinson). The Dixie Chicks originally played bluegrass and a mix of country standards. All four-band members sang while Maguire and Robinson performed most of the instrumental accompaniment. Lynch and Macy shared the lead vocals.

The Dixie Chicks 1990 debut album, Thank Heavens for Dale Evans, and 1992's Little Ol' Cowgirl produced no chart singles. Robin Lynn Macy left the band in late 1992. 1993's Shouldn't a Told You That was the last recording for Laura Lynch. After a five-year period, The Dixie Chicks added lead vocalist Natalie Maines and recorded their breakthrough album, 1998's Wide Open Spaces. This album won a Grammy Award for Best Country Album and yielded a slew of hits that included "There's Your Trouble" and "I Can Love You Better." 1999's Fly debuted at number one on the U.S. charts. This resulted in elevated star status for The Dixie Chicks.

2002's Home featured an acoustic bluegrass sound that was in contrast to their previous country pop albums. While promoting the album, Natalie Maines made controversial comments about President George W. Bush and his political agenda concerning the impending invasion of Iraq. Her comments led to a boycott of The Dixie Chicks music by many radio stations. 2006's Taking the Long Way again saw The Dixie Chicks debut at number one on the charts and their hit, "Not Ready to Make Nice." This was the band's reaction to being punished for stating their political views.

"Not Ready to Make Nice"
by Martie Maguire, Natalie Maines, Emily Robison, and Dan Wilson

"Not Ready to Make Nice" was the lead single from The Dixie Chicks seventh studio album, 2006's Taking The Long Way Home. It evolved from a controversy that erupted over a comment Natalie Maines made about then President George W. Bush. She was critical of the impending invasion of Iraq. Maines said that she didn't want this war and that we're (The Dixie Chicks) ashamed that the President was from Texas. The Dixie Chicks have stated that they did not regret their anti-Bush statement even though it cost them airplay on many radio stations. Despite the radio ban, the song reached number four on the U.S. charts.

Musically, "Not Ready to Make Nice" has a serious tone of a single voice with acoustic guitar accompaniment. It reflected the huge political statement made by the band. The mood was dark and the chorus featured strong vocal harmonies. The vocals gained intensity and a full arrangement of strings build to a climax and then returned to a single voice and guitar. Produced by Rick Rubin, "Not Ready to Make Nice" won three Grammy Awards in 2007 for Record of the Year, Song of the Year, and Best Country Performance by a Duo or Group with Vocal.

Of the twenty-five singles that the Dixie Chicks have released, six have reached number one on the country singles chart. Several of their singles have crossed over to the mainstream rock charts including; "Not Ready to Make Nice." They have carved out their brand of alternative country rock with a sound that developed from a classic cowgirl image that mixed with traditional country, folk, and bluegrass music. The Dixie Chicks' traditional three-part vocal harmonies and instrumental prowess evolved to include a pop sensibility with a polished contemporary rock attitude.

Uncle Tupelo (1987-1994) was an American alternative country band that formed in Belleville Illinois in 1987. The band was formed by songwriter and multi-instrumentalist Jay Farrar, vocalist/guitarist Jeff Tweedy, and drummer Mike Heidorn. This trio recorded three albums for Rockville Records; 1990's No Depression, 1991's Still Feel Gone, and 1992's March 16-20, 1992. In the beginning, Uncle Tupelo played covers of punk, rock, and country songs for their fellow high school students. The band leaned in a country-influenced direction and assimilated style traits of The Byrds, The Flying Burrito Brothers, The Band, and Neil Young. March 16-20, 1992 was an album that sounded of authentic country mixed with rock elements. The band also discovered a number of esoteric folk songs from the 1930's and 1940's and began to record them. Jay Farrar's father was from the Ozark Mountains and taught his son some of the railroad blue-collar songs from his upbringing.

In 1993, Uncle Tupelo signed with Sire Records, expanded to a five-piece, and released Anodyne. Drummer Mike Heidorn left and was replaced by Ken Coomer. Also, bassist John Stirratt and multi-instrumentalist Max Johnston joined the band. Uncle Tupelo fused seemingly disparate genres of country and punk into an exciting hybrid. This recording featured the band's folksy blend of roots music combined with the power of alternative rock. Adodyne was influential for many up and coming bands and in the process became a cornerstone of the alternative country movement. Farrar and Tweedy split acrimoniously after a tour in support of Adodyne. Tweedy formed Wilco with other members of Uncle Tupelo, while Farrar started the band Son Volt.

Wilco (1994-present) is an American alternative country rock band that rose from the ashes of Uncle Tupelo. Wilco's founding members were Jeff Tweedy and bassist John Stirratt. Wilco endured lineup charges frequently during their first decade and the current lineup is Tweedy, Stirratt, guitarist Nels Cline, multi-instrumentalist Pat Sansone, keyboardist Mikael Jorgensen, and drummer Glenn Kotche. The Wilco name came from a military and commercial aviation radio voice abbreviation for "will comply."

Wilco's music is difficult to categorize. They drew from alternative rock, alternative country and indie rock. Wilco was inspired by classic literature for their approach to lyric writing. The band has also employed a different concept for lyric writing called cadavre exquis (a French term for a compositional method) where each band member takes turns writing lines on a typewriter, but is only allowed to see the previously written line.

Wilco released three albums in the 1990's; their debut album A.M. in 1995, Being There in 1996, and Summerteeth in 1999. Tweedy became something like Bob Dylan demonstrating his ability to write elaborate, moody pop and rock songs. From 1994 until 2001, Jay Bennett became a key member of Wilco, providing the band with another composer, keyboardist, and guitarist. Each Wilco record gained wider exposure and contributed to their fan base. They established a stylistically diverse music catalogue that was part roots rock, part honky-tonk, and part melodic pop.

Chapter Nine: Country and Southern Rock

2001's Yankee Hotel Foxtrot had its share of controversy when (Wilco's then label) Warner Brothers refused to release the album citing it wasn't commercially appealing. Wilco fought through the rejection and signed with Nonesuch Records, who released Yankee Hotel Foxtrot to universal appeal. It became Wilco's most popular album to date and included the hit "War On War." Wilco went on the release six more studio albums including 2016's Schmilco. Wilco is one of the most significant bands that have moved the alternative country rock genre forward.

"War On War"
by Jeff Tweedy and Jay Bennett

"War On War" is about the need to experience and ultimately accept failure if one is to live life to it fullest. The line "You have to learn how to die, if you want to be alive" meant that you must grow from your life experiences. This song's lyrics were appropriate due to Wilco's fight with their previous record label and their ability to overcome obstacles to achieve their hard fought success.

Musically, "War On War" had a roots rock feel with a down home strummed acoustic guitar over a power pop bassline. Wilco's harmonies were tight and complemented the optimistic message of the lyrics. The end of the song featured drummer Glen Kotche with a solo built on top of his direct and powerful drumset feel. "War On War" also skillfully employed electronic keyboard sounds, and together with Kotche's drum part, reached a climax to end the song. "War On War" was an example of how country could mix effectively with rock and pop elements.

Discussion Question

As you have just read, the early foundation of the country rock genre developed largely in Southern California and not in the country capital of Nashville, Tennessee. Why did this happen? Be specific and give musical examples.

Southern Rock

The story of **southern rock** is both inspiring and full of tragedy due to the short history of the original Allman Brothers Band and Lynyrd Skynyrd. The southern rock genre refers to artists that were defined by their cultural and geographic orientation. Southern rock bands emerged from Jacksonville, Florida (The Allman Brothers and Lynyrd Skynyrd), Macon, Georgia (home of Capricorn Records), and Mississippi, Arkansas, and the Carolinas. When crossover styles were expanding the definition of rock music in the late 1960's and early 1970's, many young, poor musicians raised on the blues, gospel, and soul music created a genre that was fiercely loyal to their families and the South.

The mixture of country, folk, and rock music took on a regional dialect with advent of southern rock. Roots music in Southeastern America was dripping in the blues. Similar to the early white rockabilly stars of the 1950's, southern rock musicians counted on the great blues artists such as Elmore James, Muddy Waters, and B.B. King for inspiration. Southern rock lyrics were full of stories about hard luck, cheating spouses, and the down and out loner. Family associations were common for southern rock bands with The Allman Brothers siblings Duane and Greg Allman, brothers Toy and Tommy Caldwell of The Marshall Tucker Band, and Ronnie and Donnie Van Zant of Lynyrd Skynyrd. In addition to fraternal loyalty, southern rock musicians exhibited an intense regional pride. This was evident in some of the South's biggest hits including; The Charlie Daniels Band's "The South's Gonna Do It," The Atlanta Rhythm Section's "Doraville," and Lynyrd Skynyrd's megahit "Sweet Home Alabama" that turned out to be a direct rebuttal to Neil Young's unflattering lyrics in his song "Southern Man."

In the 1960's, some of the greatest bands in rock music history came to embody the southern rock genre. They included; **The Allman Brothers Band**, **Lynyrd Skynyrd**, **The Outlaws**, and **Little Feat**. The rock music community was immediately put on notice that southern rock was serious and the musicianship *level was high.*

The Allman Brothers Band (1969-1976) (1978-1982) (1989-2014) was formed in Macon, Georgia in 1969 by guitarist Duane Allman. If an all-star lineup was created to represent the southern rock genre, each member of The Allman Brothers original group could occupy a spot. They simply set the gold standard for the southern rock genre and proved to be one of the great bands in rock music history.

Duane Allman was born in Nashville, Tennessee in 1946 and his brother Gregg was born one year later. Their father, Willis Allman, was an Army lieutenant that was tragically murdered when the boys were only two and three years of age. Shortly after, their mother Geraldine moved the family to Daytona Beach, Florida. When a thirteen-year old Gregg acquired a guitar, Duane countered with a motorcycle. Duane would secretly slip into Gregg's room to play his guitar, resulting in fights between the boys. When Duane (rather prophetically) brought his Harley home in a bag of pieces, his mother got him his own guitar. Duane developed an instant obsession with the instrument and soon dropped out of the tenth grade to practice incessantly. Gregg began to focus on his own voice and was drawn to the sounds of black artists such as James Brown and B.B. King. While Gregg was contemplating college, Duane was confident that his own guitar skills would secure a future for himself and Gregg in the music business.

Duane and Gregg formed a duo and then developed a band called The Escorts. That band later evolved into the Allman Joys. They played versions of rhythm and blues and surf rock hits. Bill McEuen, the manager of The Nitty Gritty Dirt Band, heard The Allman Joys and helped them secure a deal with Liberty Records. In 1967, at the insistence of their label, they moved to Los Angeles, California and recorded two unsuccessful albums under the name The Hour Glass. Both Duane and Gregg became disillusioned by the psychedelic music direction imposed on them by Liberty Records. Duane fled Los Angeles (abandoning Gregg to finish the terms of their contract) for the legendary recording studio environment of Muscle Shoals, Alabama to become a session player. Duane just showed up at Muscle Shoals uninvited and said to the management "I understand you're cutting a lot of records. I'd like to be a studio picker." #16 When Duane was told they had all the guitar players they needed, he promptly set up a tent on their property and slept there for two weeks until they gave him a listen. Duane was invited to do a session with singer Clarence Carter and overheard

Rock Hard Fact

Of the many Duane Allman studio session recordings, one of the finest was his studio work on the album To Bonnie from Delaney. It paired Duane with Delaney and saxophonist King Curtis.

"I'd (The Allman Brothers Band) rather just be known as a progressive rock band from the South. I'm damned proud of who I am and where I'm from, but I hate the term Southern Rock."

– Dickey Betts

Wilson Pickett selecting tunes to record on his next record. Duane suggested that Pickett record The Beatles "Hey Jude." After being initially shot down, Pickett eventually liked the idea and chose Duane to record The Beatles classic with him. The track was sent to Jerry Wexler at Atlantic Records and Duane Allman was on the recording map. This led to sessions backing artists such as Aretha Franklin and Otis Rush and brought a high profile to Duane's incredible guitar skills.

Duane's work at Muscle Shoals came to the attention of Phil Walden, who had managed Percy Sledge, Sam and Dave, and the recently deceased Otis Redding. Walden was impressed with Duane's session work on Wilson Pickett's most recent recording. Walden and Wexler convinced Atlantic to fund the creation of a new studio and label, Capricorn Records. This was to become *the* southern rock label and Duane Allman was signed as their first artist.

The first member recruited for Duane's quest for a new band was drummer Jai Johanny "Jaimoe" Johanson. Jaimoe recalled the first time he played with Duane when he stated, "He (Duane) rolled that Fender Twin in, cranked that bad boy up, and that was it, man. As soon as we played together I forgot all about moving to New York City…we just played constantly. Then Berry came and joined us." #17 The Berry that Jaimoe referred to was bassist Berry Oakley, who was playing with guitarist Dickey Betts around Jacksonville, Florida in the band Second Coming. Duane and Jaimoe began to frequently sit in with Second Coming with the intent of stealing Oakley for their own power trio. The keyboardist for Second Coming, Reese Wynans remembered, "I had never heard anything like Duane Allman and his slide guitar. He played it like a violin or saxophone…It was the most unbelievable sound and his phrasing was impeccable and his ideas were over the top. When he sat in with us it lifted the whole thing up." #18

Both Duane and Gregg were familiar with Dickey Betts, having recorded a few demos with him. Duane had fantasized to Jaimoe about having two guitars and two drummers in his dream band and Dickey was soon added to the lineup. Duane was also pushing for the two-drummer lineup because James Brown and Otis Redding employed two drummers. For the next piece of the puzzle, Duane thought of his old friend, drummer Butch Trucks (who had previously recorded demos with Duane). Trucks had a big house, so with the addition of Trucks, the now five-piece band began to rehearse there. Dickey Betts saw the potential of The Allman Brothers twin drummer setup and recalled, "Jaimoe was a real good drummer, but more of a pocket guy…we needed Butch, who had that drive and strength, freight train, meat-and-potatoes thing. It set Jaimoe up perfectly." #19 Jaimoe embellished the feel and drew from his jazz concepts while Butch laid down the groove. They listened carefully to each other and learned how to stay out of each other's way.

Berry Oakley only agreed to join Duane's new band after he learned that Dickey was in. Oakley was conflicted about leaving Second Coming but after playing with Duane, he knew his path was set. Oakley would bring a psychedelic element to The Allman Brothers with his love for jamming and the influence of The Grateful Dead and Jefferson Airplane's music. Keyboardist Chuck Leavell (who would later join The Allman Brothers) described Oakley's approach when he said, "Rather than just holding down the bottom end, he was very adventurous and constantly listening to the other instruments and popping out with great melodies. If he heard Dickey or Duane-or me-go to a certain scale or range, he was always there to support that improvisation. I could feel Berry following me if I started a melody, and it was just fantastic. He was not afraid to experiment, roam around and be adventurous, but he knew when to do that and when to go back and hold down the foundation." #20

The Allman Brothers Band knew they had something special, yet they lacked a strong vocalist and top-notch songs. Both holes would be filled with a single phone call from brother to brother. Gregg was still in Los Angeles, having remained after the breakup of The Hourglass. Gregg recalled, "I was miserable out in L.A. So I was ready to jump when Duane called. He said, 'We got two drummers, a great bass player and a hell of a lead guitar player.' And I said, 'Well, what do you do?' and he said 'I'll show you when you get here'." #21 When Gregg arrived and heard the band he was both impressed and intimidated. Gregg remembered, "I got my brother aside and said, 'I don't know if I can cut this. I don't know if I'm good enough.' And he starts in on me, 'Oh, you little punk, I told these people all about you and you don't come in here letting me down.'…Then he handed me the words to a Muddy Waters tune…they counted me off and I did my damnedest…I shut my eyes and sang, and at the end of that there was just a long silence. At that moment, we *knew* what we had." #22

A week after Gregg's arrival, the fully formed Allman Brothers Band worked their first gig at the Jacksonville Beach Auditorium. A month later, they relocated to Macon, Georgia, the home of Duane's label, Capricorn Records. The band's first live date outside of the South was opening for The Velvet Underground in Boston. In the summer of 1969, The Allman Brothers Band went to New York to record their self-titled debut album <u>The Allman Brothers Band</u>. Duane's previous studio experience and their hundreds of hours of rehearsing yielded a mature album that featured the classics "Dreams" and "Whipping Post." When Gregg first returned from L.A., he showed the band twenty-two songs he had composed. Only "Dreams" and "It's Not My Cross to Bear" were deemed usable for their debut recording. Over a period of five days, Gregg came up with "Whipping Post," an Allman Brothers' signature song complete with an introduction in 11/8 time. On "Dreams," Duane played both guitar solos, the first straight and the second with a slide guitar bottleneck technique. <u>The Allman Brothers Band</u>, despite its musical strength, only sold thirty-five thousand copies. However, the band had no doubts about its future, knowing that they were already making groundbreaking music.

Duane and Dickey's revolutionary dual-lead guitars

The twin guitar combination of Duane Allman and Dickey Betts was one of the great collaborations in rock music history. Many bands before and since have had two guitar players, one playing a melody or solo and the other relegated to rhythm playing. But Duane and Dickey routinely formed intricate patterns that interlocked with each other and the highly melodic bass playing of Berry Oakley. Reese Wynans remembered, "Dickey was the hottest guitar player in the area, the guy that everyone looked up to and wanted to emulate…He (Duane) and Dickey complemented each other-they didn't try to outgun one another-and the chemistry was obvious right away. It was just amazing that the two best lead guitarists around were teaming up. They were both willing to take chances rather than returning to parts they knew they could nail, and everything they tried worked." #23

Rock Hard Fact

On July 28th, 1973, The Allman Brothers Band and The Grateful Dead co-headlined at Watkins Glen Speedway in New York to play for over 600,000 fans - the largest ever rock concert (to date).

Duane set a new standard with his slide guitar solos but was equally complemented by Dickey's strong melodic solos. Additionally, Allman and Betts developed extensive guitar harmonies utilizing complementary techniques. First, Dickey had an uncanny ability to play solos that extended a song's melody. Secondly, Duane's ear was so good that he could improvise very musical harmonic variations in the moment. This duo interaction created rhythmic and melodic counterpoint over the grooving bass and twin drumset parts. Betts recalled, "From our first time playing together, Duane started picking up on things I played and offering a harmony, and we'd build whole jams off of that. We worked stuff out naturally because we were both lead players. We got those ideas from both jazz horn players like Miles Davis and John Coltrane and fiddle lines from western swing music. I listened to a lot of country and bluegrass music growing up. I played mandolin, ukulele, and fiddle before I ever touched a guitar." #24

Duane and Dickey's interplay was built on their awareness of rhythm. Often, they each placed rhythmic ideas in different places within the measure and the other found different spots to place a chord or begin a rhythmic line. This would avoid cluttered parts. They utilized question and answer phrasing and built phrases on the anticipation created by the first part of a phrase and answered it with the second. Duane preferred a trebly sound and phrased with a more staccato attack while Dickey's sound was more of a rounded tone. Their individual timbres were distinctive, yet they were perfectly complementary. Many of the classic Allman Brothers tunes featured extended solos that felt like instrumental extensions of the vocal melodies.

Duane and Dickey had a healthy competition. They pushed each other, but no one lost and the music itself was the big winner. Dickey remembered that Duane told him, "This isn't a contest. We can make each other better and do something deep." #25 Duane was once asked to join some friends to go riding (his motorcycle) and he saw Dickey off in the corner practicing. He replied, "I think I'll just stay here and work on things with Dickey." #26

Duane Allman and Dickey Betts = pure guitar magic

1970's Idlewild South was named after Betts' farm in Atlanta Georgia. The band brought in Atlantic producer Tom Dowd for the recording. Dowd had worked with many blues and jazz greats and would prove to be a great asset. Dowd also worked with Gregg on his Hammond organ approach, which came to be a recognizable element of the band's sound. Classics on Idlewild South were the songs "Midnight Rider" and "In Memory of Elizabeth Reed." "Midnight Rider," written by Gregg and Robert Payne became one of the band's signature songs. Idlewild South, like their debut album, was not a big seller, but heavy touring set the stage for the band's future. Also at this time, Dowd introduced Duane to Eric Clapton, who invited him to contribute to a recording session with his new band, Derek and the Dominos. After completing the Layla sessions, Clapton offered Duane a spot in his band. Duane considered it, but decided he couldn't leave his *brothers*.

The Allman Brothers realized that they were at their best when playing live. Over a three-night period in March of 1971, they recorded what became one of the most revered live albums in music history, 1971's At Fillmore East. Upon its release, this double live recording rapidly climbed the charts to number thirteen and would bring the band to stardom.

Groundbreaking album
At Fillmore East
by The Allman Brothers

The Allman Brothers Band had made their first Fillmore East in late 1969, opening for Blood, Sweat, and Tears for three nights. A month later, they played the Fillmore West opening with Buddy Guy and B.B. King in support of The Grateful Dead. For the band, recording the live record at At Fillmore East was a logical direction to pursue, since they feed off the energy of their live audiences. Duane had hired horn players for the live shows but their sound was leaking into the microphones and producer Tom Dowd quickly convinced Duane to cut the horn players. Duane did not put up a fight.

At Fillmore East showed the band's great eclectic mixture of rock, blues, country and jazz influences. Tom Dowd recalled, "The Fillmore album captured the band in all their glory. The Allman's have always had a perpetual swing sensation that is unique in rock. They swing like they're playing jazz when they play things that are tangential to the blues, and even when they play heavy rock. They're never vertical but always going forward, and it's always a groove. Fusion is a term that came later, but if you wanted to look at a fusion album, it would be Fillmore East… They tore the place up." #27 They were a rock 'n' roll band playing authentic blues with a pure sense of jazz improvisation captured with tremendous energy.

Side one opened with "Statesboro Blues," then "Done Somebody Wrong," and "Stormy Monday." The first thing that hits the listener was this live version of "Statesboro Blues," that was written and originally recorded by Blind Willie McTell in 1928. This Allman classic featured Duane's electric slide playing that immediately established the Allman Brothers sound. Side two contained one song, "You Don't Love Me." This version of Willie Cobbs' rhythm and blues tune was recorded in 1960 and latter by Bo Diddley. It featured a guitar figure that appealed to Duane and became a staple of many of their live shows.

Side three opened with "Hot 'Lanta," and "In Memory of Elizabeth Reed." Dickey Betts wrote his instrumental masterpiece "In Memory of Elizabeth Reed" inspired by a peaceful spot he would visit in the Rose Hill Cemetery in Macon, Georgia. He named the song from the headstone of a woman he never knew because that spot gave him so much peace and inspiration. Betts remembered his approach to writing an instrumental and said, "An instrumental has to be real catchy and when you succeed it's very satisfying because you have transcended words and communicated with emotion." #28

Side four contained one song, "Whipping Post." For "Whipping Post" (from their debut album) Gregg had initially written the tune as a ballad that sounded like the blues classic "Stormy Monday." Now at a faster tempo, Oakley added a heavy bassline. The song's arrangement evolved even more via the standard Allman Brothers' jam band approach. "Whipping Post" served as a prime example of how Berry Oakley shaped the songwriting of many of the bands' compositions.

In 2004, Fillmore East was selected for preservation in the Library of Congress and deemed

> "The Allman Brothers became the people's band. They were Southerners living in the South playing Southern music."
>
> – Phil Walden-founder of Capricorn Records

culturally, historically, and aesthetically important by the National Recording Registry. Dickey Betts remembered, "It was just special. The band felt it and the crowd felt it and it lit all of us up. The Fillmore was the high-octane gig to play in New York-or anywhere, really." #29

With the success of Fillmore East, The Allman Brothers were established as stars and rock's finest live band. However one of rock's worst tragedies occurred when Duane Allman died in a motorcycle accident on October 29th, 1971. The band was devastated, especially Gregg and Barry Oakley. They decided to persevere but did not want to add another guitar player, so Dickey proceeded as their only guitarist. They released Eat a Peach in 1972, a double album that contained some tracks with and without Duane. It featured the songs "Ain't Wastin' Time No More," "Melissa," "Mountain Jam," "One Way Out," "Blue Sky," and "Little Martha" (the only song Duane ever wrote entirely on his own). The album reached number four on the U.S. charts and the band added keyboardist Chuck Leavell to their lineup, a great player and a way to avoid replacing Duane.

"Melissa"
by Gregg Allman

A teenage Gregg Allman spent years struggling to find his voice as a songwriter. He penned and rejected over three hundred of his own songs before bringing in anything for The Allman Brothers Band to record. Gregg wrote "Melissa" but never showed it to the band feeling that it might be too soft for an Allman Brothers' album. But he also knew it became Duane's favorite song. In 1967, Gregg was in a Florida hotel room when he grabbed Duane's guitar, which was tuned to an open E. Gregg recalled, "I just started strumming it and hit these beautiful chords. It was just open strings…This is a great example of the way different tunings can open up different roads to you as a songwriter. The music immediately made me feel good and the words just started coming to me. I started singing but stumbled on the name." #30 The name came a week later when Gregg was in a grocery store and heard a woman yell to her little girl "Melissa come back."

While they knew they had a great song, it lacked an instrumental component as compelling as its chords, lyrics, and vocal lines. Dickey Betts took the song home and created the entire lead guitar part in one night. He walked into the studio the next day and they cut the track. Gregg has called Betts's melodic lead line on "Melissa" his greatest work. Gregg Allman knew it was good but never knew the impact it would have when he said "I've met a lot of Melissa's named after the song." #31

The Allman Brothers had barely recovered from the devastation of Duane's death when Barry Oakley died in a motorcycle crash on November 11th, 1972. It occurred only three blocks away from Duane's crash site and almost one year to the day. Again the band was in shock and again they decided to carry on, now without two of their founding members. The band brought in bassist Lamar Williams to finish recording their 1973 release Brothers and Sisters. This album was loaded with Allman classics including "Wasted Words," "Ramblin Man," "Southbound," and "Jessica." Oakley had played on "Wasted Words" and "Ramblin' Man." Chuck Leavell was a much-needed boost to the band both personally and musically. Brothers and Sisters peaked at number two and represented The Allman Brothers commercial peak.

They followed with stadium and arena tours but internal friction and drug issues began to tear the band apart.

1975's Win, Lose or Draw reached number five on the U.S. charts but it would be the last album by what remained of the original members. It was inconsistent and lacked the previous Allman magic. Gregg was living in L.A. (having his tabloid relationship with pop star Cher) and recorded his vocal parts in a California studio. The Allman Brothers agreed to call it quits. Dickey Betts formed the band Great Southern, Allman started The Gregg Allman Band, and Leavell, Jaimoe, and Williams played in the jazz-fusion band Sea Level. In 1976, The Allman Brothers released Wipe the Windows, Check the Oil, Dollar Gas, a double live album of previously recorded material.

Some members vowed not to work with Gregg again, but the Allman Brothers Band re-formed in 1978 and released Enlightened Rogues in 1979. New members included guitarist Dan Toler and bassist David Goldflies. The album yielded the hit "Crazy Love." Jaimoe's last album with the band would be 1980's Reach for the Sky. Its followup, 1981's Brothers of the Road, added drummer David Toler. The Allman Brothers again disbanded because they were unhappy with their post-reunion albums and wished to keep their reputation in tact.

In 1989, The Allman Brothers again reunited with Allman, Betts, Jaimoe, and Trucks. They added guitarist Warren Haynes, bassist Allen Woody, and keyboardist Johnny Neel. They recorded 1990's Seven Turns that charted well and 1991's Shades of Two Worlds. More albums followed in the 1990's including; 1992's An Evening with the Allman Brothers Band: First Set, 1994's Where it All Begins, and 1995's An Evening with the Allman Brothers Band: 2nd Set. Haynes and Woody had started a band, Gov't Mule (see later in this chapter) in 1994 as a side project. They soon left The Allman Brothers, feeling that another Allman breakup was imminent. In 2000, The Allman Brothers released a live album, Peakin' at the Beacon. It featured Allman, Betts, Butch Trucks, and Jaimoe. New members included guitarist Derek Trucks (Butch's nephew), bassist Oteil Burbridge, and percussionist Marc Quinones. 2003's Hittin' the Note featured the return of Warren Haynes and the departure of Dickey Betts. 2004's One Way Out saw the return of Derek Trucks. He and Warren Haynes showed great respect for the legacy of Duane and Dickey.

Founding Allman Brothers members Butch Trucks and Gregg Allman both died in 2017. They and their fallen bandmates before them left an incredible legacy. The original Allman Brothers Band blueprint for greatness was set by taking a wide array of musical styles including blues, jazz, country, rock 'n' roll, and psychedelia and fusing them into one seamless whole. In doing so, they pulled off the rare feat of playing the blues in a wholly natural, non-copying manner and jamming mightily while avoiding spaced-out and meandering excess. The Allman Brothers Band also did what few rock bands could achieve; they found an original way to introduce jazz elements into their overall concept without sounding pretentious or ponderous. The Allman Brothers were a true brotherhood that transcended race and ego. They played for *each other* and *the music*. The Allman Brothers Band was inducted into the Rock and Roll Hall of Fame in 1995.

Lynyrd Skynyrd (1964-1977) (1979) (1987-present) began when vocalist Ronnie Van Zant, guitarists Allen Collins and Gary Rossington, drummer Bob Burns, and bassist Larry Junstrom played parties and clubs around Jacksonville, Florida. They worked under

---

Rock Hard Fact

Lynyrd Skynyrd took their name from Leonard Skinnerd, a physical education teacher from their high school. Many of the future Skynyrd members were routinely disciplined by Skinnerd for having long hair.

the names The Noble Five and then, One Percent. At a show in 1970, Van Zant introduced the band as Lynyrd Skynyrd to great applause and the name stuck. After years of countless one-nighters in Florida bars, the band was offered a deal by the premier southern rock label, Capricorn Records. They turned it down, refusing to play third fiddle to the labels' established stars The Allman Brothers and The Marshall Tucker Band. Capricorn's roster of southern rock bands were serving notice to the music industry, including noted musician and producer Al Kooper, who took an interest in the Skynyrd band. In 1972, Kooper founded the Sounds of the South Label (part of MCA Records) in Atlanta and soon signed Lynyrd Skynyrd. He then became their producer.

Skynyrds' sound evolved from a hard driving-bar room blues approach (with some slight British rock influences) to more melodic songs. Important lineup changes saw Skynyrd roadie Billy Powell join on keyboards while Larry Jungstrom (to later join 38 Special) was replaced by bassist Leon Wilkeson and then Ed King. Al Kooper and Van Zant butted heads frequently in the studio but 1973's Pronounced 'Leh-nerd 'Skin-nerd was a strong debut for Lynyrd Skynyrd. The album featured three of their classic hits "Simple Man," "Gimme Three Steps," and "Free Bird." Pronounced initially did not do well on the charts but the singles gained increased national radio play. After the album's release, Wilkeson returned to play bass and King moved to guitar, thus giving Skynyrd its classic "three guitar army" of Collins, Rossington, and King.

"Free Bird"
by Allen Collins and Ronnie Van Zant

"Free Bird" meant many things to many people. The lyrics revealed a man explaining to a woman why he couldn't settle down and make a commitment. The opening verse stated, "If I leave here tomorrow, would you still remember me?" and was inspired by Allen Collins' girlfriend Kathy who had asked him that very question during a fight between them. Skynyrd would frequently dedicate "Free Bird" to the memory of Duane Allman, who died a few years before the song was released. Since 1977, Skynyrd decided to only perform "Free Bird" as an instrumental, with Johnny Van Zant (Ronnie's little brother who would later join the band) preferring to let the crowd sing the lyrics in tribute to the victims of the Skynyrd plane crash.

Initially, Ronnie Van Zant thought the song had too many chords to match to lyrics. Later, Van Zant asked Allen Collins to play the chords and Van Zant was able to write the lyrics and match them to the harmony. The band has frequently described "Free Bird" as a simple love song about leaving town and moving on. Al Kooper utilized a heavy gospel organ part in the beginning of the song that created a soulful mood against the delayed slide guitar. Kooper also recorded the guitar solos twice and placed one on top of the other to achieve a slurring and echo-like effect.

"Free Bird" wasn't released as a single until a year after the album came out because the record company thought it was too long for radio play. The single version of the song was often edited down but the full version remained more popular. Although "Free Bird" is shouted out as a mock request at many rock shows, it has become one of rock music's great anthems.

Lynyrd Skynyrd's fan base greatly expanded in 1973 when they opened for The Who's Quadrophenia Tour. Their 1974 Second Helping was a breakthrough going to number twelve on the U.S. charts. It yielded their southern anthem "Sweet Home Alabama," a song of southern pride that reached number eight on the U.S. charts. Music critics and fans were drawn to Skynyrd's simple melodies and powerful three-guitar attack. The Lynyrd Skynyrd hard-drinking and rowdy persona brought them to mainstream national attention.

"Sweet Home Alabama"
by Ed King, Gary Rossington, and Ronnie Van Zant

Guitarist Gary Rossington came up with the concept for "Sweet Home Alabama," while Ed King wrote the introduction and Ronnie Van Zant wrote the lyrics. It came together quickly and naturally for the band. The lyrics partially gave tribute to The Swampers, an accomplished group of studio musicians in residence at Alabama's famed Muscle Shoals Studio. However, "Sweet Home Alabama" was mainly the Skynyrd response to Neil Young's "Alabama," in which Young berated the South for its racist past. Although the Skynyrd band respected Young's music and no Skynyrd member was from Alabama, they thought it was important to defend the state. Neil Young and Van Zant were actually good friends. Young even wrote the song "Powderfinger" for Skynyrd, although they never recorded it.

The guitar solo in "Sweet Home Alabama" was purposely recorded in a different key than the melody. Producer Al Kooper noticed that Ed King played the solo in the key of G instead of D, the first chord in the progression. King's passionate and melodic blues lines utilized an E minor pentatonic blues scale and that allowed him to take a different direction for his solo. The piano solo that ended the song contained a funky honky-tonk feel that gave "Sweet Home Alabama" its signature emotional and southern rock flavor.

Neil Young actually performed "Sweet Home Alabama" once at a memorial to the three members of Lynyrd Skynyrd that died in the 1977 plane crash. The southern pride evoked by the song was featured in the movie *Sweet Home Alabama*, where actress Reese Witherspoon starred as a woman who must decide between her ex-husband from Alabama and her fiancé from New York. The South won when she chose her ex-husband.

In 1975, drummer Bob Burns was replaced by Atrimus Pyle. Al Kooper produced 1975's Nuthin' Fancy. Ed King also left, midway through a tour. The album peaked at number nine on the U.S. charts and spawned the hit "Saturday Night Special," a social commentary on the topic of handguns. After the moderately successful 1976 release of Gimme Back My Bullets, Skynyrd added guitarist/vocalist Steve Gaines (his sister Cassie Gaines had already sang backup vocals with the band). This move restored Skynyrd to its signature three guitar sound. They were especially strong with Gaines' slide guitar approach and excellent lead vocals. 1977's Street Survivors kept the hits coming with "What's Your Name," "That Smell," and "You Got That Right."

On October 20th, 1977, just three days after the release of Street Survivors, and only five shows into a big headlining tour, a devastating tragedy struck. Lynyrd Skynyrd's chartered plane (nicknamed Free Bird) ran out of fuel just before they were due to arrive in Baton Rouge, Louisiana. Pilots attempted an emergency landing but the plane crashed in a Mississippi swamp, killing Ronnie Van Zant, Steve and Cassie Gaines, road manager Dean Kilpatrick, and pilots Walter McCreary and William Gray on impact. The other band members all suffered serious injuries. Lynyrd Skynyrd could not overcome the devastation and disbanded immediately. The band's demise left a hole in the hearts of the *entire* southern rock community.

Collins, Rossington, Wilkeson, and Powell formed The Rossington-Collins Band and released two albums in 1980 and 1981. In 1987, Lynyrd Skynyrd re-united for a tour with Rossington, Powell, Wilkeson, Pyle, and King. Johnny Van Zant, Ronnie's younger brother, took over as the new vocalist and chief songwriter. The band produced a live album, 1988's Southern by the Grace of God, as a tribute to their fallen band-mates.

The decade of the 1990's saw the release of Lynyrd Skynyrd 1991, the first with their new lineup including Johnny Van Zant and guitarist Randall Hall. Artimus Pyle left in 1991 and was replaced by a number of drummers. Skynyrd followed with 1993's The Last Rebel, 1994's Endangered Species, 1997's Twenty, and 1999's Edge of Forever. Michael Cartellone became the permanent and current drummer in 1999. An ever rotating cast of players would find work on the road and the band continued to record new material through the new millennium. Skynyrd has done well on the charts with 2000's Christmas Time Again, 2003's Vicious Cycle, and 2009's God & Guns. 2012's Last of a Dyin' Breed was their first top twenty offering since Street Survivors. The southern rock music community has been inspired by the spirit of Lynyrd Skynyrd's surviving post-tragedy members. Skynyrd is for many, the heart and soul of southern rock music.

Lynyrd Skynyrd was inducted into the Rock and Roll Hall of Fame in 2006.

The Outlaws (1967-1971) (2005-present) are a southern rock band that formed in Tampa, Florida in 1967. The band had a number of lineups in their early years and opened for many southern bands including Lynyrd Skynyrd (Ronnie Van Zant lobbied to get them signed to Arista Records). Their 1975 self-titled debut album Outlaws, featured the lineup of vocalist/guitarist Hughie Thomasson, vocalist/Guitarist Billy Jones, bassist Frank O'Keefe, vocalist/guitarist Henry Paul, and drummer Monte Yoho. The Outlaws established their dual lead guitar interplay and a mixture of country and rock elements. A strength of the band was their vocal harmonies influenced by The Byrds, Eagles, and Poco. Outlaws featured two of the band's biggest hits "There Goes Another Love Song" and "Green Grass and High Tides."

"Green Grass & High Tides"
by Hughie Thomasson

"Green Grass & High Tides" was written by Hughie Thomasson when he was at a cookout on a Florida beach. The song's lyrics came to him when he was feeling an ocean breeze. He imagined a rock show played exclusively for himself by fallen rock stars including Jim Morrison, Janis Joplin, and Jimi Hendrix. Some people interpreted the lyrics to be about marijuana, but Thomasson has denied it. Thomasson has described his lyrics to generally be just a collage of words that don't contain much meaning. For "Green Grass," the words just fit and sounded right.

Hughie Thomasson's guitar style on "Green Grass and High Tides" featured his distinctive Fender Stratocaster sound that blended both country and blues ideas. Thomasson soloed on the introduction and then played the first of the two long guitar solos on the track. After the introduction, the song moved to a double-time country rock shuffle and then a halftime-feel for the verses. The chorus was driven in a straight four feel for the first guitar solo. After a return to more half-time verses, the second solo moved to the original double-time feel for Thomasson's blistering second guitar solo. The Outlaws usually closed their live shows with this song, often at least twenty minutes in length.

1976's Lady in Waiting and 1977's Hurry Sundown combined to establish The Outlaws "classic era" where they were referred to as "the Florida guitar army" by their fans. 1978's Playin' to Win and 1979's In the Eye of the Storm followed. Both records did not fare as well as their first three efforts. 1980's Ghost Riders was the last Outlaws album in a pure southern rock style. It yielded a hit with the cover of Stan Jones' "(Ghost) Riders in the Sky: A Cowboy Legend." The Outlaws released three albums after 1980, and each moved away from their original southern rock sound. Thomasson left to join Lynyrd Skynyrd in 1996. This essentially sidelined The Outlaws since his distinctive voice and guitar style had defined the band.

In the spring of 2005, The Outlaws re-formed with Hughie Thomasson, Henry Paul, Monte Yoho, and David Dix from their early days. They added guitarist Chris Anderson, bassist Randy Threet, and keyboardist Dave Robbins (these three were from the country band Blackhawks). In 2007, Hughie Thomasson tragically died of a heart attack. The Outlaws then finished Once an Outlaw. In 2012, another version of The Outlaws released It's About Pride and in 2016, the band released a two-CD concert set titled Legacy Live. The Outlaws, behind their three "guitar army" attack and Hughie Thomasson's vocals and lightening fast guitar work, were among the leading bands that defined the southern rock genre.

Little Feat (1969-1979) (1987-present) began in Los Angeles, California when vocalist/guitarist Lowell George met keyboardist/vocalist Bill Payne. George had been playing with Frank Zappa and his Mothers of Invention. George and Payne recruited bassist Roy Estrada and drummer Richie Hayward from George's previous band, The Factory. The four musicians formed Little Feat in 1969. Lowell George had recorded a demo of his (then) signature song "Willin." It would become inspiration for the early Little Feat sound, featuring George's soulful vocals and slide guitar. With the help of Frank Zappa, Little Feat secured a record deal with Warner Brothers and recorded 1971's Little Feat and 1972's Sailin' Shoes, both critically acclaimed but poorly selling albums.

Estrada soon left to join Captain Beefheart's Magic Band and was replaced by bassist Kenny Gradney. Little Feat also added a second guitarist, Paul Barrere and percussionist Sam Clayton. This new lineup collectively added a New Orleans funk element heard in their 1973 release, Dixie Chicken. It was produced by Lowell George. The album captured the Little Feat sound with the songs "Dixie Chicken" and "Fat Man in the Bathtub." Little Feat was becoming well known for their impressive live performances, but Dixie Chicken fared no better on the charts than their first two offerings. With band morale running low, Bill Payne temporarily jumped ship to join The Doobie Brothers, only to return for 1974's Feats Don't Fail Me Now. This album gained traction on the charts with "Oh Atlanta" and "Feats Don't Fail Me Now."

1975's The Last Record Album and 1977's Time Loves a Hero brought a new level of success to the band with songs such as "Day or Night" and "Time Loves a Hero." However, George's songwriting contributions were minimal because he felt Payne and Barrere were moving in too much of a jazz-fusion direction. In August of 1977, Little Feat recorded a live album from shows played at the Rainbow Theatre in London and Lisner

---

> "A musician, an artist had to have the ability to think beyond people who chain him to a wall and say, 'Here's who you are'."
>
> – Bill Payne

Auditorium in Washington, DC. The result was 1978's Waiting for Columbus, their most successful album.

Groundbreaking album
Waiting for Columbus
by Little Feat

Waiting for Columbus was a double live album taken from seven live performances. The band was backed by the Tower of Power horn section, whom they had previously recorded with on studio sessions. Little Feat initially wanted to release a triple album but decided to pare it down to double album length. After recording all the shows, they took selected tracks to the studio to tweak a few of the parts. Bill Payne recalled, "We went in to redo the guitars, and we redid a few vocals here and there. But for the most part, it's a live album…Little Feat was never a band that adhered to rules all that easily…You can do whatever the hell you want. It's a recording. It's a picture of a place in time, but if you want to fix something, then go on and fix it! It's still you playing it!" #32

Side one opened with "Join the Band," then "Fat Man in the Bathtub," "All That You Dream," "Oh Atlanta," and "Old Folks' Boogie." Bill Payne remembered, "'Fat Man in the Bathtub.' It's amazing. The drum sounds on that are just incredible…this was a powerful, powerful record…we were always more of a live band." #33

Side two opened with "Time Loves a Hero," then "Day or Night," "Mercenary Territory," and "Spanish Moon." On "Time Loves a Hero" the band stretched out and found little nuances to explore, thus showing the strength of their improvisational approach. "Day or Night" revealed Little Feat's ability to create a funky sixteenth-note feel combined with Bill Payne's fusion inspired keyboard comping and soloing (reminiscent of Joe Zawinul's sound with the fusion band Weather Report).

Side three opened with "Dixie Chicken," then "Tripe Face Boogie," and "Rocket in My Pocket." On "Dixie Chicken," Payne's southern boogie piano feel blended well with Barrere's blues guitar. This complemented Lowell George's down-home dixie lyrics to create the classic Little Feat sound. Side four opened with "Willin'," then "Don't Bogart That Joint," "A Apolitical Blues," "Sailin' Shoes," and "Feats Don't Fail Me Now." "Don't Bogart that Joint," a crowd favorite at Little Feat shows, has an interesting background. The word "Bogart" referred to when the legendary actor Humphrey Bogart would let a cigarette dangle from the corner of his mouth. Not surprisingly, this song and its cannabis reference were also performed often by The Grateful Dead and the band Phish.

Three of the unused tracks from Waiting for Columbus were included on Little Feat's 1981 album Hoy-Hoy!. Waiting for Columbus proved that even in a state of rapid decline (internal tension), Little Feat was a force to hear in live performance with their ability to take their music in so many different directions. Waiting for Columbus ranks as one of the great live albums in rock music history.

Lowell George's health and interest in the band were rapidly declining and he walked out on the recording sessions for Little Feat's next album. George was particularly upset with Bill Payne's jazz/fusion approach. He was intent on re-forming Little Feat at a later date without Payne or Barrere. George went on to release a solo album, Thanks, I'll Eat It Here, in 1979. However, while on tour to support the album, Lowell George tragically died of a heart attack.

Little Feat went on to finish and release 1979's Down on the Farm before disbanding. A retrospective double album of rare outtakes and live tracks titled Hoy Hoy! was released in 1981. Little Feats' ex-members became popular session musicians with many artists vying for their services. Richie Hayward played on Robert Plant's 1985 Shaken 'n' Stirred, and Bill Payne played with a variety of artist that included; The Doobie Brothers, Pink Floyd, Emmylou Harris, James Taylor, and many more.

Little Feat re-formed with the surviving members adding ex-Pure Prairie League guitarist/vocalist Craig Fuller and guitarist Fred Tackett. They recorded the commercially successful Let It Roll in 1988. However, 1990's Representing the Mambo was too jazz-rock for Warner Brothers, who dropped them from the label. Craig Fuller left after 1991's Shake Me Up and was replaced by vocalist Shaun Murphy in 1993.

Southern rock lost a great drummer when Richie Hayward died in 2010. Little Feat went on to record six more studio albums including 2012's Rooster Rag. Little Feat was one of the most under-rated bands in rock music history. A wildly eclectic mix of styles from; southern boogie, swampy New Orleans funk, jazz, fusion, country, blues, R&B, and rock 'n' roll combined with Little Feat's highly melodic songwriting to provide their music with great depth. The fans that heard Little Feat perform live were consistently treated to their gifted musicianship and instrumental virtuosity. A long list of prominent musicians that continue to play their music includes; Jackson Browne, Bob Dylan, Carly Simon, Van Halen, Bob Weir, Phil Lesh, Gov't Mule, Bonnie Raitt, and many more. Little Feat continues to be a hugely popular fixture on the live jam band scene.

The decade of the 1970's saw the expansion of the southern rock genre with talented bands that included; **Black Oak Arkansas** (1963-present), **Wet Willie** (1970-present), **The Atlanta Rhythm Section** (1971-present), **38 Special** (1974-present), **Molly Hatchet** (1975-present), **The Marshall Tucker Band**, and **the Charlie Daniels Band.**

The Marshall Tucker Band (1972-present) is an American southern rock band that formed in Spartanburg, South Carolina in 1972. The original lineup was a merger of the bands Toy Factory and Pax Parachute. Marshall Tucker included vocalist/guitarist Toy Caldwell, his brother bassist Tommy Caldwell, guitarist George McCorkle, drummer Paul T. Riddle, vocalist Doug Gray, and keyboardist/saxophonist/flutist Jerry Eubanks. The Marshall Tucker Band expanded the definition of southern rock by mixing jazz, country, gospel, rhythm and blue, and rock styles. Eubanks, with his saxophone and flute timbres, helped the band develop a unique sound. 1973's self-titled debut, The Marshall Tucker Band, was released on the Capricorn label. The album slowly climbed to number twenty-nine on the U.S. charts while the band toured constantly. They performed up to three-hundred shows a year on the heels of their hit "Can't You See."

"Can't You See"
by Toy Caldwell

Lyrically, "Can't You See" was full of southern references and vocal slang with lines that said "I gonna buy me a ticket now, as far as I can-ain't a-never comin'

> "Make sure to be honest with yourself, about if that's really what you want to do with your life-to make music…It takes a commitment of being the first one to get there and the last one to leave, doing what you want to do even if you have to work twice as hard as anybody else ever did."
>
> – Charlie Daniels

back-Ride me a Southbound-all the way to Georgia now-Till the train run out of track." Toy Caldwell painted a picture of being the victim (he wanted to crawl in a hole and die) of a woman who was mean and left him without even saying goodbye. "Can't You See" began and ended with Jerry Eubank's flute line. His sound blended with acoustic guitar to immediately lend the track a unique sound. The song also contained a gospel piano accompaniment that subtly supported the vocal line. The middle of the tune moved to a breakdown section of just voice and guitar and built to a strong finish.

"Can't You See" became an anthem for The Marshall Tucker Band and was very popular on Album Oriented Radio (AOR). It continues to receive strong airplay on many classic rock stations. "Can't You See" has been acknowledged as one of southern rock's classics, along with Lynyrd Skynyrd's "Sweet Home Alabama" and The Allman Brothers' "Melissa." All of these songs captured the spirit of southern rock. Covers of "Can't You See" included versions by Kid Rock, Waylon Jennings, and The Zac Brown Band.

1974's A New Life featured a collaboration with Charlie Daniels, as well as Where We All Belong, released that same year. By 1975's Searchin' for a Rainbow, The Marshall Tucker Band was recognized to be one of rock's strongest acts. 1976's Long Hard Ride became the band's fifth straight gold record and its instrumental title track again featured Charlie Daniels on fiddle. The band's most successful release was 1977's Carolina Dreams that yielded the hit "Heard It in a Love Song." Two more releases from the 1970's were 1978's Together Forever (their last on the bankrupt Capricorn label) and 1979's Running Like the Wind.

Their aptly titled album Tenth, their tenth recording, was released in 1980. However, tragedy struck when co-founder and bassist Tommy Caldwell was killed in a car accident. He was replaced by Franklin Wilkie, but Marshall Tucker struggled to repeat their past success. 1981's Dedicated (dedicated to Tommy Caldwell) followed with many lineup changes. The Marshall Tucker Band continued to record and tour, releasing thirteen more studio albums, including 2007's The Next Adventure.

The Marshall Tucker Band is one of the cornerstones of southern rock. They have the ability to blend country with gospel elements while featuring the extended and rocking instrumental passages of guitarist Toy Caldwell.

Charlie Daniels (1936-) (Charlie Daniels Band-1972-present) is an American vocalist and multi-instrumentalist who has been a major figure in the development of the genres of country, bluegrass, and southern rock music. Before he formed the Charlie Daniels Band in 1973, Daniels co-wrote a song with producer Bob Johnston titled "It Hurts Me." This song found its way onto the 1964 B-side of Elvis Presley's "Kissin Cousins." Later, Charlie Daniels left North Carolina for Nashville to become a session musician, where he played guitar and electric bass on three Bob Dylan albums, including the country rock landmark Nashville Skyline (see earlier in this chapter). Daniels also performed on recordings by the legendary Leonard Cohen.

Daniels released his 1971 self-titled Charlie Daniels and 1972's Te John, Grease, & Wolfman to little popular appeal. He formed the Charlie Daniels Band in 1972 and drew from the southern rock influence of The Allman Brothers and The Marshall Tucker Band. They served as his blueprint. The Charlie Daniels Band consisted of Daniels, guitarist Barry Barnes, keyboardist Joe DiGregorio, bassist Charlie Hayward, and drummer James W. Marshall. They released 1973's Honey in the Rock that featured the hit "Uneasy Rider." This song was about a hippie who got stranded in a Mississippi bar and was forced to endure a tense redneck environment. Daniels felt some success when "Uneasy Rider" reached number nine on the U.S. charts. After 1974's Way Down Yonder, The Charlie Daniels Band released Fire On the Mountain that yielded the hits "Long Haired Country Boy" and "The South's Gonna Do It." Both of these songs displayed a "good-ol-boy" country southern theme. In "The South's Gonna Do It," Daniels championed his southern musician peers and bands, referring to them by name, thus marking their esteemed place in contemporary southern music.

Throughout this time period, Daniels frequently recorded with and jumped onstage with The Marshall Tucker Band, further adding to his legend. During a show in 1974, Daniels was joined by The Allman Brothers Band and The Marshall Tucker Band, giving rise to the annual *Volunteer Jam*. 1975's Nightrider featured guest appearances by Marshall Tucker's Toy Caldwell and The Allman Brothers' drummer Jai Johanny Johanson. 1976's Saddle Tramp yielded the top forty country hit "Saddle Tramp" and was followed by High Lonesome that same year. By the late 1970's, Charlie Daniels sensed that the audience for southern rock was shrinking, so he moved his band to a more straightforward country sound. 1977's Midnight Wind was released and followed by 1979's Million Mile Reflections. It yielded the song "Reflections," a tribute to Elvis Presley, Janis Joplin, and Ronnie Van Zant of Lynyrd Skynyrd. This album also featured Daniels' classic hit "The Devil Went Down to Georgia," that crossed over onto the rock charts where it landed at number three.

"The Devil Went Down to Georgia"
by The Charlie Daniels Band

"The Devil Went Down to Georgia" was an uptempo bluegrass song about the devil's unsuccessful attempt to steal the soul of a young man named Johnny by out-playing him in a fiddle-playing contest. The song's story was a derivative of the traditional crossroads deal with the devil motif. Daniels began the song by revealing that a disappointed devil arrived in Georgia, having stolen fewer souls than expected. He then encountered Johnny, a fiddle playing young man. In the song, Johnny played a hot fiddle solo and the devil offered Johnny a golden fiddle if he could outplay him. If the boy failed, the devil would get his soul in return.

Musically, the devil next fiddled over a contemporary rock feel. Then Johnny soloed and made reference to two traditional songs from Appalachia, "Fire on the Mountain" (the name of the Daniels' 1974 album) and "Granny Does Your Dog Bite?" He also referenced the country standard "Ida Red" and a traditional southern folk song titled "The House of the Rising Sun." In the end, Johnny played a blistering solo, thus keeping his soul from the devil by displaying his musical virtuosity while simultaneously performing those great traditional songs of the south. "The Devil Went Down to Georgia" was the ultimate celebration of southern pride and added to the legend of Charlie Daniels.

Daniels achieved some rock crossover popularity when 1980's Full Moon and 1982's Windows achieved chart success. The Charlie Daniels Band sold well throughout the 1980's but didn't see another big hit until

> "Warren (Haynes) and I dove into the Allman Brothers gig at different times...There was so much respect for the Duane parts, the Dickey parts, the whole history...That was a pretty big book that we absorbed, and we lived it for awhile."
>
> – Derek Trucks

1989's Simple Man. In the 1990's, the band's albums didn't chart well, but they continued to be a strong concert draw. In the first decade of the new millennium, The Charlie Daniels Band quietly transitioned from a major label act to independent label's, releasing albums on the Blue Hat and Audium labels. In 2003, Daniels released a pro-Iraq War anthem 'This Ain't No Rag, It's a Flag," a strong patriotic statement. Charlie Daniels has gone on to record over twenty more albums in his storied career as one country and southern rock's most influential and significant figures.

A new generation of southern rock bands emerged in the late 1990's and into the new millennium. A few of these bands included **Blackberry Smoke** (2000-present) and the **Zac Brown Band** (2002-present). Two other prominent southern rock bands had their roots in The Allman Brothers Band. They are **Gov't Mule** and the **Tedeschi Trucks Band**.

Gov't Mule (1994-present) is an American southern rock band that formed in 1994 as a side project of The Allman Brothers Band. Guitarist Warren Haynes and bassist Allen Woody were members of The Allman Brothers Band that re-formed in 1989. Haynes provided a good foil for Dickey Betts and Gregg Allman in The Allman Brothers. They continued to perform with the Allman Brothers but simultaneously formed Gov't Mule (known by many fans simply as Mule) in 1994. They added drummer Matt Abts from the Dickey Betts Band. In 1995, Gov't Mule released their self-titled debut album Gov't Mule. The album was mostly recorded live with notable songs including "Rocking' Horse" (co-written with Gregg Allman) and "Mule." Gov't Mule quickly became a staple at music festivals across America, featuring prominent musical guests from many blues and funk bands. 1996's Live from Roseland Ballroom consisted of a set opening for Blues Traveler (John Popper from Blues Traveler had played harmonica on Mule's debut album).

Haynes and Woody left The Allman Brothers in 1997 to focus full-time on Gov't Mule. Their 1998 release, Dose, featured the songs "Thelonius Beck" and "Birth of the Mule," both direct tributes to jazz legends Thelonious Monk and Miles Davis. For 1999's Live… With a Little Help from Our Friends, Gov't Mule was joined by members of The Allman Brothers, Parliament Funkadelic, The Black Crowes, and The Derek Trucks Band. This was a live recording from their 1998 New Year's Eve concert, recorded at The Roxy in Atlanta, Georgia.

The new millennium brought Gov't Mule's 2000 album Life Before Insanity. However, shortly after its release, Allan Woody died. This prompted Warren Haynes to return to The Allman Brothers in 2001 after Dickey Betts' left the band. Gov't Mule continued with Andy Hess assuming the bass chair. A three-year period of rotating bassists ensued that included Meters great George Porter Jr. and Les Claypool of Primus. Haynes now became one of the busiest musicians around when he split his time between Gov't Mule, The Allman Brothers, and Phil Lesh and Friends. Next, Gov't Mule recorded two tribute albums to Allan Woody, 2001's The Deep End, Volume 1 and 2002's The Deep End, Volume 2. These albums featured many of Woody's favorite bassists that included; Jack Bruce, John Entwistle, Flea, Chris Squire, and others.

Gov't Mule has gone on to release fifteen more albums, notably 2015's Sco-Mule, featuring John Scofield and 2017's Revolution Come…Revolution Go. They have carved out a unique musical place by balancing an Allman Brothers' influence with a psychedelic sound, displayed by their bluesy power trio feel. Gov't Mule continues to maintain a high profile on the jam band scene and are an important link to the legacy of southern rock.

Tedeschi Trucks Band (2010-present) was formed in 2010 in Jacksonville, Florida by vocalist/guitarist Susan Tedeschi and guitarist Derek Trucks. Tedeschi established the Susan Tedeschi Band in 1993 with their debut recording Better Days, and 1998's Just Won't Burn. Derek Trucks, nephew of Allman Brothers Band drummer Butch Trucks, formed The Derek Trucks Band in 1994. In 2001, Susan Tedeschi and Derek Trucks were married. They first toured under the name Soul Stew Revival that utilized members from both their Susan Tedeschi and Derek Trucks bands. In 2010, both bands went on hiatus leading to the formation of The Tedeschi Trucks Band. The Tedeschi Trucks Band drew from multiple sources including the blues, southern rock, gospel, jazz, R&B, funk, and afro-beat styles.

2011's Revelator was the debut recording of The Tedeschi Trucks Band and featured bassist Oteil Burbridge, keyboardist/flutist Kofi Burbridge, and drummers Tyler Greenwell and J.J. Johnson. Tedeschi's vocal style on Revelator has been described as a cross between Janis Joplin and Bonne Raitt. Her guitar approach was heavily influenced by Freddie King, Buddy Guy, and Stevie Ray Vaughan. Revelator was a roots record that employed funky grooves with a modern approach to blues and southern rock. The band also featured a three-piece horn section. On Revelator, Derek Trucks displayed his command of slide guitar. His influences run the gamut from early rock 'n' roll to blues to traditional jazz. Trucks has been equally inspired by blues masters and jazz greats such as Charlie Parker and John Coltrane.

2012's Everybody's Talkin' was a live album that showcased The Tedeschi Trucks Band with an expanded eleven-piece lineup. 2013's Made Up Mind brought the band some success, peaking at number eleven on the U.S. charts. 2016's Let Me Get By continued to build their popularity and went to number fifteen on the charts. It also added the bass talents of Tim Lefebvre. 2017's Live from the Fox Oakland was nominated for a Grammy Award for Best Contemporary Blues Album. The Tedeschi Trucks Band has successfully taken the southern rock genre forward with their unique blend of southern rock, blues, soul, jazz, and country music. They continue to record and tour at a nonstop pace.

Discussion Question

Many southern rock bands drew from a wealth of different music genres to develop their style including The Allman Brothers Band. However, does the geography of a band's origin influence its musical direction? Take a position and give examples of bands in and out of the southern rock genre.

Chapter Ten: Heavy Metal and Hard Rock

There is much confusion when it comes to the differences between **heavy metal** and **hard rock**. By the 1990's, the two terms were often used interchangeably. We will make some distinctions, however, there is more in common than different between the two. The blues influence of Cream, The Rolling Stones, and Led Zeppelin helped to define both the hard rock and heavy metal genres. By the early 1970's, heavy metal was evolving in Britain and America. For some bands, the stylistic line between hard rock and heavy metal blurred and for some it became more defined.

Generally speaking, **heavy metal** tended to draw on more neo-classical influences while hard rock tended to be a little more blues influenced. Metal guitar solos evolved with advanced techniques combining hammering, slurring, and virtuoso "shredding." Metal guitar sounds were generally heavier (often tuned very low) and more distorted than in hard rock. Metal lyrics tended to be about darker themes, sometimes about the occult (mainly a fear of the devil, not so much about devil worship-which worried parents), folklore, or just being a "baddas*." Heavy metal was generally faster, louder, and used more double bass drums, plus more screaming. Also, metal bands tended to avoid keyboards. Heavy metal morphed into many subgenres such as **thrash metal**, **doom metal**, **black metal**, **metalcore**, and many many more.

Again in general terms, **hard rock** drew from the above-mentioned blues and sometimes folk and even country influences. Hard rock lyrics tended to be about your standard sex, drugs, and rock 'n' roll. Partly because the lyrics were about human relationships, female singers sometimes fronted hard rock bands. Both hard rock and heavy metal made use of the power chord, where a strong root and fifth was played with heavy distortion and sustain to add depth and power to the sound. The riff, a short repeated musical idea stated in the bass or guitar, was used as the structural foundation for some hard rock tunes and quite extensively in heavy metal. Early examples of compositional riffs included; Cream's "Sunshine of Your Love", and Led Zeppelin's 'Heartbreaker."

"If heavy metal bands ruled the world, we'd be a lot better off."

- Bruce Dickinson of Iron Maiden

Early Heavy Metal

Heavy Metal became a new style that developed gradually in the mid-1960's to early 1970's in England and to a lesser extent in the late 1960's in America. It was formed from a need to rebel and turn heads, with a level of intensity not experienced in pop and other rock styles. Many feel that the first sounds of heavy metal were present in 1964 in The Kinks single "You Really Got Me" (see chapter three). Guitarist Dave Davies utilized repetitive, nasty power chord guitar riffs combined with a crude distortion that shocked listeners and musicians alike. With the advancement of better and louder amplifiers and new ways to achieve effects, like distortion, artists like Led Zeppelin, Jimi Hendrix, Blue Cheer, and Black Sabbath introduced just how heavy music could sound.

Scorpions (1965-present) are a German hard rock/heavy metal band formed in 1965. They didn't begin recording until their 1972 debut album <u>Lonesome Crow</u>. Scorpions endured many lineup charges over the years but their classic lineup, active from 1978 to 1992, included Scorpions founder guitarist Rudolf Schenker, vocalist Klaus Meine, guitarist Matthias Jabs, bassist Francis Buchholz, and drummer Herman Rarebell. A series of recordings in the 1970's, from 1974's <u>Fly to the Rainbow</u>, 1975's <u>In Trance</u>, and 1976's <u>Virgin Killer</u>, defined their hard rock sound. By their 1979's <u>Lovedrive</u>, the Scorpions had changed their approach to more of a heavy metal sound while still retaining the power ballads and melodic ideas that had defined their earlier style. The Scorpions achieved some commercial success at the start of the 1980's beginning with their release <u>Animal Magnetism</u>. Greater success came from their 1984 album, <u>Love at First Sting</u>, featuring the hit "Rock You Like a Hurricane." It went to number twenty-five in America and gained heavy rotation on MTV. It also became an anthem played at numerous sporting events around the world.

The Scorpions best selling record was 1990's <u>Crazy World</u> that reached number twenty-one on the U.S. charts and number one in their native Germany. <u>Crazy World</u> contained the single "Wind of Change," a hit single selling over fourteen million copies worldwide. More importantly, this tune served as a symbolic anthem addressing the political changes in Europe in the late 1980's that helped to document the historic fall of the Berlin Wall. The Scorpions have sold over one hundred million albums worldwide and have released eighteen studio albums and seventy-four singles. They were pioneers in the development of early heavy metal because they embraced metal elements when the style was in its infancy. But they also were extremely versatile, even experimenting with techno-pop melodies in the late 1990's. In 2015, Scorpions celebrated their fiftieth anniversary and are still active today.

Iron Butterfly (1966-present) with some years of inactivity) formed after vocalist/keyboardist Doug Ingle went through some different lineups before settling on guitarist Danny Weis, bassist Jerry Penrod, vocalist Darryl DeLoach, and drummer Ron Bushy. Their 1968 debut recording <u>Heavy</u>, made them one of America's first heavy metal groups, although you can hear other influences such as the psychedelic sounding Jefferson Airplane and The Doors. The band's lineup changed when Weis, DeLoach, and Penrod left and were replaced by bassist Lee Dorman and guitarist Eric Braunn. Iron Butterfly's 1968 <u>In-A-Gadda-Da-Vida</u> produced one of the late 1960's best-known hard rock tunes "In-A-Gadda-Da-Vida." The album reached number four on the American charts.

"In-A-Gadda-Da-Vida"
by Doug Ingle

"In-A-Gadda-Da-Vida," over seventeen minutes in length, composed the entire second side of the album of the same name. The lyrics, heard at the beginning and end, were supposed to be "in the Garden of Eden." However, Ingle was slurring his words after drinking too much red wine. In-a-gadda-da-vida is what came out and the lyrics just stuck. Most of Iron Butterfly's material was structured short songs, but the band decided to experiment with a long-extended jam. The electric organ was the main instrument on the tune, but distorted guitar was added, and its influence set the stage for hard rock and metal bands to come. Late in the song, a two-minute drum solo served as a bridge for an instrumental call and response section. Then the bass riff returned.

A very short edited version of the song (fourteen of seventeen minutes cut) was released as a single in the U.S. and it made its way into the top thirty on the charts. The album would become Atlantic Records biggest seller, until being knocked out by <u>Led Zeppelin IV</u>. "In-A-Gadda-Da-Vida" has been covered by many artists (including Slayer and rapper Nas) and has been utilized in movie soundtracks and TV shows.

For Iron Butterfly, 1969's <u>Ball</u> was successful but lineup changes ensued. 1970's <u>Metamorphosis</u> made it into the top twenty but shortly after its release, Ingle quit the band. A revised lineup of Braunn, Bushy, and keyboardist Phillip Taylor Kramer recorded both <u>Scorching Beauty</u> and <u>Sun and Steal</u> in 1975. "In-A-Gadda-Da-Vida" still continues to satisfy audiences. Iron Butterfly has endured over three dozen lineup changes and has not recorded a new record in more than forty years, yet they still remain active today.

Blue Cheer (1967-2009 with periods of inactivity) was an American rock band from San Francisco that began playing psychedelic blues and then became an early pioneer of heavy metal. They began with a small lineup of vocalist/bassist Dickie Peterson, guitarist Leigh Stephens, and drummer Paul Whaley. Blue Cheer's debut album in 1968, <u>Vincebus Eruptum</u>, landed at number eleven on the American charts and contained a heavy sounding version of Eddie Cochran's "Summertime Blues." Blue Cheer went on to record nine more albums between 1968 and 2007 with lineup changes that totaled over twenty-five different musicians. Their heavy sound at the height of the hippie scene in San Francisco (their name derived from a powerful strain of LSD) brought a new level of guitar distortion to the rock scene, thus pointing the way to harder rock and metal styles to come.

Harder edged rock sounds continued to develop on the California psychedelic scene and in the music of Jimi Hendrix. Bands in England and other parts of Europe were getting louder and feeding off political and social turmoil for inspiration. **UFO** (1969-1989) (1991-present) is an English hard rock/heavy metal band that served as a transition to the new wave of British heavy metal. Over a career of forty-eight years and over twenty-two studio recording, UFO provided another gateway to hard rock and heavy metal. **Accept** (1968-1989) (1992-present with some inactive years) is a German heavy metal band that was also an early pioneer of heavy metal, particularly the thrash subgenre. With a career that spanned close to fifty

---

Rock Hard Fact

Queen guitarist Brian May played lead guitar on the heavy and evil sounding Black Sabbath song "When Death Calls" from their 1989's <u>Headless Cross</u> album.

Chapter Ten: Heavy Metal and Hard Rock

years, Accept was one of the first bands (including Scorpions) outside of England and America that influenced the heavy metal genre.

Black Sabbath (1969-2017) formed in Birmingham, England when vocalist John "Ozzy" Osbourne and guitarist Tony Iommi joined forces with drummer Bill Ward and guitarist turned bassist Geezer Butler. Bill Ward had quit his band, The Rest, and answered an ad placed by Iommi, who was looking for a new band (Iommi and Geezer had left their band Rare Breed). Together, Ward and Iommi, saw another ad that was placed by Ozzy and invited him to come over to jam. Ozzy and Geezer knew each other and had previously played together. The four musicians then became The Polka Tulk Blues Band. They added a sax player and a slide guitar player but broke up after only one week. They re-formed again as a four-piece band called Earth. Iommi then briefly joined Jethro Tull in 1968 when leader Ian Anderson loved his heavy guitar approach. However, Iommi missed playing with Ozzy, Ward, and Geezer and quickly reunited with them. Iommi did learn how to be a professional musician from his brief Jethro Tull stay and remembered, "They (Jethro Tull) used to go in at nine o'clock in the morning and work all day until five like a regular nine-to-five job. And we realized that's the way you gotta do it. You can't just go to some pub and rehearse for an hour and then get drunk. You gotta really put your mind to it and take it seriously. That's what gave us the kick up the a** that we needed." #1

Earth was playing around Europe, particularly England. On one occasion they played to an audience that expected to hear a pop band named Earth. The audience was stunned to hear the *wrong Earth* playing very loud and aggressive music. Conveniently, a movie titled *Black Sabbath* (starring horror film actor Boris Karloff) was playing across the street from Earth's gig. The band knew they needed a new name and they had it, Black Sabbath. Ozzy commented on the new name and direction of Black Sabbath saying, "With a name like Black Sabbath, what do you expect? And the album cover wasn't exactly about a bunch of flowers…we decided to write scary music because we really didn't think life was all roses. So we decided to write horror music. Then we started to read books about the occult and we realized that it wasn't just *a thing* that movies were made from. It was real. There was a thing called the occult." #2 The band members never really embraced the occult but some of their fanatical fans did. Sabbath received many occult themed letters and was asked to play at black masses and other occult-driven ceremonies.

The early Sabbath sound was strong, mysterious, and even frightening. Iommi played blues-based solos mixed with simple power chords. Ozzy, hardly an accomplished singer, nevertheless had a unique vocal quality that could sound like a siren going off. The band played a wide range of tempos (with Iommi's doom-laden guitar tone) in hypnotically repetitious riffs. Black Sabbath had found *a new sound* for rock music.

The Sabbath guitar sound came about partially from an industrial accident that Tony Iommi had incurred years earlier. The tips of a few fingers of his fretting hand were cut off. Iommi was forced to play with makeshift prosthetic fingertips that he would make for himself before each Sabbath gig. This altered Iommi's guitar approach since he could not play the interval of fourths but would now play fifths due to the accident. The band was amazed at Iommi's unique guitar playing and musicianship. Ozzy recalled "I've always maintained one thing about Mr. Iommi. You will never find another soul who comes up with better hard rock riffs than him. When we'd be together I'd always be, like, there is no way he can top that riff. Then he'd beat it every time." #3 In 1970, Black Sabbath released their debut album Black Sabbath, an aggressive offering with lyrics about darkness, death, and the devil. All of the band members were survivors of their hometown war-ravaged Birmingham, England and a sense of doom and gloom became a factor in their music. Black Sabbath was initially hated by the critics while simultaneously loved by their fans. Their album Black Sabbath soared into the top ten on the British charts reaching number eight. It went to number twenty-three on the American charts and stayed there for over a year.

1970's Paranoid went to number one on the British charts. The title track, "Paranoid," reached number four on the same charts and was their only top twenty hit. The album peaked at number twelve in America selling four million copies, but initially received minimal radio airplay. It contained the songs "War Pigs," "Iron Man," and "Paranoid."

"Iron Man"
by Black Sabbath

"Iron Man" was originally named "Iron Bloke" by Ozzy Osbourne after he heard a massive guitar riff that Toni Iommi had composed. It has become one of rock's most recognized heavy metal riffs. Inspired by the riff, Ozzy imagined a big iron bloke walking around. Geezer Butler wrote the lyrics about a man who traveled in time to the future and saw the apocalypse. When attempting to return to the present time, he turned into a steel Iron Man and was rendered mute, making him incapable of verbally warning others of the impending destruction. He was ignored and mocked and became angry. Iron Man then sought revenge on humanity by causing massive destruction.

In the extended version of the tune (not cut down for radio play), Black Sabbath would go into an adventurous double time improvisational section. Ozzy was very skilled at verbally adapting Geezer's lyrics to fit Iommi's basic riff. Ward and Butler utilized the space around the riff to play fills and create motion. Iommi used a second riff, a unison idea, to launch the instrumental section. Iommi created more great riffs in the improvisational section to support his own guitar solos. Kanye West sampled "Iron Man" and used it in his song "Hell of a Life" for his album My Beautiful Dark Twisted Fantasy. VH1 ranked "Iron Man" as the number one heavy metal song of all time.

Groundbreaking album Paranoid
by Black Sabbath

Often cited as one of the most influential heavy metal albums of all time, Paranoid defined the sound and feel of heavy metal, perhaps more than any other album in rock history. Bands such as Metallica, Slipknot, and Nirvana (to name just a few) have often mentioned Ward and Geezer's massive grooves, Iommi's "take no prisoners" riffs, and Ozzy's haunting and agonizing delivery when defining the heavy metal genre.

Most of the songs on Paranoid developed from improvisational onstage jams. By the time the debut album Black Sabbath came out, most of the Paranoid material had been composed. Side one opened with "War Pigs," then "Paranoid," "Planet

> "We (Black Sabbath) went to Switzerland and Germany for six weeks, and we were literally playing for eight hours a day…it was good because we got really tight musically. We sort of knew what each other was going to play before we even played it."
>
> – Geezer Butler

Caravan," and "Iron Man." "War Pigs" was originally titled "Walpurgis," which was a reference to black magic weddings. Geezer explained the death and destruction lyrics for "Walpurgis" when he said "Sort of like the Satanic Christmas. I was writing Generals gathered in the masses because that's what Satan is. War was the big Satan, not somebody who lives in the clouds. I was making an analogy, and Warner Brothers didn't like the title because it was too Satanic, so we turned it into War Pigs, which is a better title anyway." #4

"Paranoid" reached number four on the British singles chart and was the first single that the band released after their debut album. Sabbath initially wrote the song as a filler because they didn't have enough material for the Paranoid album. The tune "Paranoid" was released as the break out track. "Paranoid" was recorded in two or three days after Iommi came up with the basic riff and Geezer quickly wrote the lyrics that Ozzy read during the recording session. "Planet Caravan" was a mellow stoner-jam song about floating through the universe with one's lover. Iommi played flute and Tom Allom guested on piano. Ozzy achieved a vibrato effect by singing through a Leslie speaker.

Side two opened with "Electric Funeral", then "Hand of Doom," "Rat Salad" (a showcase for a Ward drum solo), and "Fairies Wear Boots." Black Sabbath became studio savvy by utilizing the recording technique of reverse multi-tracking and re-forwarding the tape. They also mastered the album with stereo delay.

The band wanted the album to be called War Pigs, but the title was banned because of the word pigs. The record company pressured them to title the album Paranoid. Black Sabbath was very unhappy with the imposed album title. Ozzy said "What the f*** does a bloke dressed as a pig with a sword in his hand got to do with being paranoid, I don't know, but they decided to change the album title without changing the artwork." #5

The Paranoid album sparked a number of controversies. After an American nurse committed suicide, some blamed Black Sabbath when Paranoid was found playing on the turntable in her room. Also, people who represented the moral majority cited Black Sabbath for promoting devil worship. The band responded that many of their lyrics contained anti-war, anti-drug, and science fiction content. Many of Paranoid's songs have been covered by prominent metal bands such as Slayer, Megadeth, Pantera, and Faith No More.

Black Sabbath, now firmly established as *the* metal band, released Master of Reality in 1971, Vol. 4 in 1972, and Sabbath Bloody Sabbath in 1973. These albums all achieved great success in America and Europe. However, Sabbath was plagued with drug/alcohol and management issues. 1975's Sabotage, 1976's Technical Ecstasy, and 1978's Never Say Die! were solid recordings, but would mark the end of an era for Black Sabbath. Ozzy's personal issues, erratic behavior, and increasing musical differences with Tommy Iommi would spell the end for Osbourne. Ozzy was fired from Black Sabbath in 1979 (he would soon begin his solo career). Also, Geezer Butler quit the band (but quickly returned). Former Rainbow vocalist Ronnie James Dio joined for the 1980 release Heaven and Hell and Sabbath was back in business. However, more instability resulted when Bill Ward quit, also due to personal issues. He was replaced by drummer Vinnie Appice, who played on 1981's Mob Rules.

Even more turmoil ensued when Dio and Appice left to form a band and Iommi and Butler recruited former Deep Purple vocalist Ian Gillan. Ward then returned and a reborn Black Sabbath released the appropriately titled Born Again in 1983. Drummer Bev Bevan was brought in to replace Ward, who again was plagued with personal issues. After a tour to support Born Again, Sabbath went on a hiatus. They returned in 1986 with Seventh Star, a record that was first conceived as a Tony Iommi solo record and then reworked for Black Sabbath. A number of lineup changes occurred for a string of albums beginning with 1987's The Eternal Idol, 1989's Headless Cross, 1990's TYR, 1992's Dehumanizer, 1994's Cross Purposes, and 1995's Forbidden.

In the summer of 1997, Iommi, Geezer, and Ozzy reunited to co-headline the Ozzfest Festival tour along with Ozzy's solo band (Ozzfest is an annual festival tour of American venues and sometimes Europe, featuring heavy metal and hard rock bands-founded by Ozzie Osbourne and his wife Sharon). Filling in for Bill Ward was Ozzie's drummer Mike Bordin. Later that year, Ward appeared with the original Black Sabbath for live shows that were recorded and released as the 1998 double live album Reunion. The original band started recording a new album in 2001 but decided to stop. Remarked Iommi, "We didn't go any further, and it's a shame because the songs were really good." #6

In 2007 Iommi and Butler reunited with Ronnie James Dio and Vinny Appice to record Live From Radio City Music Hall and later in 2009, Bible Black. However, Ronnie James Dio became very ill and died in 2010. In 2011, the original Black Sabbath attempted to reunite to do a full album and tour, but Iommi was diagnosed with cancer. Additionally, Ward could not come to terms with a business contract with the band. In 2013, Sabbath released their nineteenth and final album, 13, with drummer Brad Wilk (of Rage Against the Machine). It was produced by Rick Rubin. On February 4th, 2016, Black Sabbath, with a healthy Toni Iommi, played what they called their final concert in Birmingham, England (their birthplace). On March 7th, 2017, Black Sabbath announced they had disbanded. Black Sabbath was inducted into the Rock and Roll Hall of Fame in 2006.

Judas Priest (1970-present) has always been considered a pure heavy metal band, maybe the first, since Black Sabbath had at least a little blues-rock flavor in their metal sound. In 1969, vocalist Al Atkins, bassist Ian Hill, guitarist Kenneth Downing, and drummer John Ellis formed Judas Priest. Their name came from a short-lived band led by Atkins in which their bassist, Brian Stapenhill took the Bob Dylan song "The Ballad of Frankie Lee and Judas Priest," and turned it into the Judas Priest name. With Downing in charge of the band's direction, they worked the club circuit around their native Birmingham, England. Judas Priest would undergo many lineup changes over the years; the first of significance was the departure of Atkins in 1973 with vocalist Rob Halford taking his place. Halford brought with him drummer John Hinch. The following year, Priest added another lead guitarist, Glenn Tipton, from the Flying Hat Band, giving them one of heavy metal's great guitar duos.

Judas Priest released their debut album Rocka Rolla in 1974. It flopped, selling only a few thousand copies and receiving negative press. This left the band in financial distress. Judas Priest recorded the album live in the studio and was not happy with the sound quality and later, drummer John Hinch was fired. 1976's Sad Wings

---

Rock Hard Fact

Judas Priest fans were upset when the band was referred to as a "death metal" band in an episode of *The Simpsons*. Bart Simpson was punished in the following episode by having to fill a chalkboard repeating the words: "Judas Priest is Not Death Metal."

of Destiny, with new drummer Alan Moore, saw the band develop their sound and image. It attracted more praise by the critics but also sold poorly. 1977's Sin After Sin was produced by Deep Purple bassist Roger Glover and featured the great session drummer Simon Phillips. Priest was defining their sound with heavy driven guitar riffs and Rob Halford's impressive vocal style and range. The band made a move to Columbia Records (a subsidiary of Sony Corporation) and received the support they needed. Glenn Tipton recalled, "In the States we did six weeks alone in clubs and bars…then we were offered two shows on the West Coast with Led Zeppelin…we stuck around and did these shows and that actually helped to establish us. We had a great reaction…America really welcomed Priest with open arms." #7

Stained Class was released in 1978 and featured all five band members as contributing songwriters. It would be the first of three albums for yet another new drummer, Les Binks. The album's lyrical themes were dark and Judas Priest derived their heaviest sound to date. Stained Class was well received in Britain, but barely made the top two hundred on the American charts.

1978's Killing Machine was retitled Hell Bent for Leather for its American release, due it its controversial title. It moved Judas Priest into a more commercial direction but was still filled with dark lyrical themes. Metal music was gaining more popularity on an international level and Judas Priest focused more on their own image. The band adapted a new rough and tough leather look. Halford explained, "For me it was the little biker (leather) jacket. I wore it to rehearsal and everybody went, 'f***, that looks really tough. That looks really strong…like the music sounds." #8 This was an important development for the heavy metal genre and Judas Priest was leading the way. They would go even farther to promote their self-identity and metal image. Halford remembered when after a gig he said, "Wouldn't it be great if we could bring an actual bike (motorcycle) onstage when we do 'Hell Bent for Leather'…I would literally come roaring out onstage on this borrowed bike and the crowd would think, 'What the f*** is this? This is crazy." #9

1980's British Steel (and its iconic British steel razor blade logo) yielded Priest great success when it peaked at number four in Britain and number thirty-four in America. "Living After Midnight" and "Breaking the Law" (with a video of the band holding up a bank with guitars) were hits from the record. Yet another new drummer, Dave Holland, joined the band for British Steel and their 1981 release, Point of Entry. Priest was now very popular and they continued to produce songs that were melodic and radio friendly. Screaming for Vengeance followed in 1982 with the hit "You've Got Another Thing Comin." They released Defenders of the Faith in 1984.

Groundbreaking album British Steel
by Judas Priest

Judas Priest recorded British Steel at Tittenhurst Park, the former home of John Lennon and Yoko Ono, and then later owned by Ringo Starr. It would be the first Priest record to feature drummer Dave Holland (who would play with Judas Priest from 1979 to 1989). Judas Priest felt inspired knowing that they were working in the former residency of John Lennon and Ringo Starr. Priest was also inspired by AC/DC, whose songs they had heard while touring with them in 1979. Rob Halford recalled " We were moving at the speed of light, making a record every year…we put together a very uncomplicated, uncluttered, very minimally produced bunch of songs that really got the music and the message across in a very quick forty-minute blast." #10

Side one opened with "Rapid Fire," then "Metal Gods," "Breaking the Law," "Grinder," and "United." Judas Priest (without the help of modern digital sampling) added special effects to the tune "Breaking the Law" by recording the sound of smashing milk bottles. The song "Untitled" was similar to their previous song, "Take On the World," from their Hell Bent for Leather album.

Side two opened with "You Don't Have to Be Old to Be Wise," then "Living After Midnight," "The Rage," and "Steeler." Songs like "Rapid Fire" and "Steeler" had an uptempo energy that foreshadowed the thrash metal bands of the future. British Steel came at a time when the people of England were feeling the negative effects of a recession and street riots. People could relate to songs like "Grinder" that were about rejecting the establishment and "United" that presented a message about staying together and getting through turbulent times. British Steel greatly expanded the possibilities for a heavy metal band to reach a wider audience and still play with an aggressive attitude. British Steel was right on schedule in allowing Judas Priest to project their metal sound onto the 1980's glory days of metal.

"Breaking the Law"
by Rob Halford, K.K. Downing, and Glenn Tipton

Recorded on the British Steel album, "Breaking the Law" became one of Judas Priest's staples in their live performances. The lyrics told a story of someone that had hit rock bottom because they were unemployed and felt frustrated with life. This led to the person not caring and wanting to break the law. In addition to the sound of smashing bottles, Priest added a police siren sound effect to reinforce the lyrics. The common person in England could *relate* to this storyline.

The song contained a simple guitar riff typical of the Judas Priest sound. The mostly instrumental bridge was a perfect vehicle that Downing could stretch into effective live guitar solos. On the chorus, Halford shouted, "You don't know what it's like" before the police siren took the listener back to the main riff. Judas Priest made a video for the song that has become a classic. In it, Halford was seen riding in a car toward a bank, singing the first verse. At the bank, he meets the rest of the band and they proceed to break into the bank vault and steal a gold record. The song was ranked on VH1's 40 greatest metal songs and was utilized in many TV commercials and other popular culture features.

1986's Turbo saw Judas Priest add keyboards and guitar synthesizer timbres to their sound in an effort to stay contemporary. They released a live album Priest… Live! from a tour of North America, Europe, and Japan. Next followed their 1988 studio album Ram it Down. The year 1990 was marked with controversy when Judas Priest was accused of backmasking lyrics that allegedly led to the suicide attempts of two teenagers (the law suit was later dismissed).

Judas Priest changed drummers again in 1990 by adding Scott Travis to the band when they recorded the album Painkiller. Rob Halford left the band after the Painkiller tour to join a thrash metal group called Fight. Priest recruited a new vocalist, Tim "Ripper" Owens who had worked in a Judas Priest tribute band. This new line-up released Jugulator in 1997 and Demolition in 2001. In 2005, after eleven years apart, Rob Halford reunited with

> "That album (British Steel) was huge for us. My brother (late Pantera guitarist) Dimebag Darrell Abbott wore the Judas Priest (British Steel) razor blade around his neck his whole life. It meant everything to him"
>
> – Pantera drummer Vinnie Paul Abbott

Rock Hard Fact

Motorhead's Lemmy got his nickname because he was always asking friends to lend him money, as in "Lemmy a fiver."

Judas Priest to record Angel of Retribution. The album was successful on the American charts peaking at number thirteen and number thirty-nine on the British charts. Nostradamus followed in 2008 with an accompanying world tour in 2008-09. Judas Priest also appeared on the Metal Masters Tour in 2008 with Motorhead, Heaven and Hell, and Testament to promote their Nostradamus album. Downing retired from the band in 2011 and was replaced by guitarist Richie Faulkner. In 2014, Priest released Redeemer of Souls and continues to record and tour. Judas Priest has proven to be one of the most significant heavy metal bands in rock history.

Motorhead (1975-2015) was an English heavy metal band formed by bassist/vocalist/songwriter Ian Fraser "Lemmy" Kilmister, guitarist Larry Wallis, and drummer Lucas Fox. They hold a unique place in terms of rock genres, exhibiting elements of metal, biker hard rock, and pure rock 'n' roll. Motorhead was a precursor to the new wave of British heavy metal and was an overwhelming influence on many later heavy metal and punk bands in both England and America. Lemmy first roadied for Jimi Hendrix and played in Hawkwind, a talented experimental English band that incorporated many styles including progressive, psychedelic rock, and an interest in science fiction themes. Motorhead's 1977 self-titled debut album Motorhead, was recorded with a new lineup (their classic lineup) of guitarist/vocalist "Fast" Eddie Clarke, drummer Phil "Philthy Animal" Taylor, and Kilmister. This version of Motorhead would record more well crafted albums including; 1979's Overkill and Bomber, 1980's Ace of Spades, 1981's live album No Sleep 'til Hammersmith, and 1982's Iron Fist. No Sleep 'til Hammersmith would be Motorhead's most successful album peaking at number one in Britain.

"Motorhead"
by Lemmy Kilmister

"Motorhead" was the last song written by Lemmy before leaving the band Hawkwind and forming Motorhead (which he named after the song title). On this track, Lemmy, Eddie Clarke, and Phil Taylor captured their evolving Motorhead sound of Lemmy's raspy vocals over a speeding musical ride of intertwined guitar, bass, and drums. The trio played with a relentless energy that appealed immediately to both metal and punk rock bands.

Motorhead had been playing the song "Motorhead" live for a year and within a few hours of studio time, they had all of the backing tracks recorded. After tracking the vocals and some more guitar, the song was recorded quickly with a simple approach that produced an exciting result. Motorhead achieved a great "live feel" from the studio track "Motorhead" and decided to include it on their live album, No Sleep 'Til Hammersmith. It contained live tracks from their Sharp Pain in the Neck Tour. The track reached number six on the British charts.

The Motorhead lineup changed again when ex-Thin Lizzy guitarist Brian Robertson and drummer Pete Gill joined the band. Lemmy continued to lead Motorhead through a series of successful albums in the 1980's, although the raw attitude of their earlier sound was missing. These records included 1983's Another Perfect Day, 1986's Orgasmatron, and 1991's Rock 'n' Roll. Monty Python's Michael Palin guested on Rock 'n' Roll (adding some spoken dialogue). This was considered to be a comeback album for Motorhead after they experienced difficult times in the 1980's with record companies, managers, and more lineup changes. The 1990's saw Motorhead release six albums and profit greatly by Lemmy's charismatic presence and relationship with the media.

The Motorhead lineup of Lemmy, guitarist Phil Campbell, and drummer Mikkey Dee remained steady from 1992 through 2015. In 2004, guitar virtuoso Steve Vai guested on their album Inferno while 2006's album Kiss of Death featured appearances by Poison guitarist CC DeVille and Alice in Chains bassist Mike Inez. More than *thirty* years since their formation, Motorhead was able to crack the top one hundred on the U.S. charts with 2008's Motorizer and 2010's The World is Yours. In 2013, Motorhead released their twenty-first studio album, Aftershock. It had the typical Motorhead edge and contained a blues influence that was present throughout their storied career. Aftershock continued Motorhead's late rise in popularity by peaking at number twenty-two on the American charts.

2015's Bad Magic would be the last Motorhead album. After a battle with cancer, Lemmy Kilmister died in late 2015 at the age of seventy. Countless heavy metal musicians have praised Motorhead, particularly their ability to not only play fast, but play well at breakneck tempos. Motorhead was one of the first bands to harness the raw energy of punk rock. Even though Lemmy always denied that Motorhead was a metal band (he stated they were simply a rock 'n' rock band), their impact on the heavy metal genre is undeniable.

By the late 1970's, the founding fathers of heavy metal were now well established. Giants such as Black Sabbath, Judas Priest, Motorhead, and others inspired new generations of young metal musicians. This new wave of a British heavy metal movement (aka **NWOBHM**) was beginning to redefine the scene. British groups such as **Iron Maiden** and **Def Leppard** were leading the way. The movement had a wide sweep with more European bands gaining popularity.

Iron Maiden (1975-present) started when songwriter/bassist Steve Harris persevered through a revolving door of vocalists, guitarists, and drummers to form Iron Maiden in 1975. Maiden became one of the chief architects of the new wave of British heavy metal by facing the challenge of maintaining metal as a vital genre throughout the 1980's. The lineup of vocalist Paul Di'Anno, guitarists Dennis Stratton and Dave Murray, drummer Clive Burr, and Harris released their self-titled debut album Iron Maiden in 1980. The debut made an immediate impact by peaking at number four on the British charts, establishing the band as leaders of the new metal movement.

Iron Maiden took the concept of the dueling two-guitar setup and built an image around themes of death and destruction. They derived their name from a Medieval execution and torture device and reinforced that image with an image of a corpse spitting blood. The band's founder, Steve Harris, recalling his early influences said, "Once I got going, I started trying to be a bit clever and learn stuff by (Yes bassist) Chris Squire. I was heavily influenced by progressive rock like Genesis, Jethro Tull, ELP, Yes, King Crimson…I used to love off-the-wall changes coming out of nowhere." #11 In addition, Iron Maiden was able to harness the energy from the already well established punk music scene. This was particularly evident in the vocal style of Paul Di'Anno.

1981's Killers saw the departure of Stratton and guitarist Adrian Smith joined the band. This album built their fan base and shot to number twelve on the British charts. Killers reflected a harsher metal sound and Di'Anno's vocals were punkier and more intense. Harris was developing as a songwriter, having written every song

---

> "Motorhead was so important to the development of thrash metal because they were so f***ing fast and heavy. When Anthrax started out, we listened to Motorhead nonstop."
>
> - Scott Ian of Anthrax

except the co-written (with Di'Anno) title track. Soon, a major change ensued when the band fired Di'Anno and hired the impressive ex-Samson vocalist Bruce Dickinson.

1982's The Number of the Beast was the breakthrough for Iron Maiden that catapulted them to a new level. The album reached number one in England and number thirty-three in the U.S., selling over five million records worldwide. The Number of the Beast caused much controversy, particularly in America, due to the album's satanic cover art. The cover depicted Maiden's horrific mascot, Eddie, a devil-like green puppet with red hair. While Eddie was symbolic of the Antichrist, the main theme of the lyrics was intended to be fear of the beast. Religious conservatives were convinced that Maiden was preaching satanism and they organized public burnings of Iron Maiden records. Protests were conducted at many concert sites of Maiden's 1982 Beast on the Road Tour. The beast (image of Eddie) took on a life of its own and later became an alternate name for Iron Maiden reflected in compilations and live releases, including 1996's Best of the Beast and 2003's Visions of the Beast.

"Run to the Hills"
by Steve Harris

"Run to the Hills" was a largely misunderstood song when it was released on The Number of the Beast. It contained lyrics about the struggles between Native Americans and the European settlers who invaded their territories at the time of colonization and westward expansion. The first verse was written from the Native Americans (The Cree Indians) perspective with the lyric "White man came across the sea, he brought us pain and misery." The rest of the songs' verses were told from the view of the colonists with the lyrics "Chasing the redskins back to their holes, fighting them at their own game."

"Run to the Hills" was released as a single five weeks before The Number of the Beast hit the charts. The song peaked at number seven in England and made a huge impact internationally. It would become Maiden's first top ten hit in the U.K. Harris was trying to find ways to get the feel of the song to represent the lyrics. To achieve this, Harris wanted a feeling of galloping horses. The song highlighted Bruce Dickinson's powerful voice and Dave Murray's wah-wah pedal flavored guitar solo.

In 1982, drummer Clive Burr was replaced by ex-Trust drummer Nicko McBrain. Next, Iron Maiden released Piece of Mind in 1983 and Powerslave in 1984. Both were in the tradition of Number of the Beast in terms of chart success and musical style. Massive and successful supporting tours followed. 1986's Somewhere in Time featured synthesized bass and guitar timbres to add more layers to the Iron Maiden sound. 1988's Seventh Son of a Seventh Son was a concept album, their first to include keyboards. It shot to number one in England and number twelve in America. Harris included the other band members more in the songwriting process, thus creating greater band cohesion.

1990's No Prayer for the Dying marked the addition of guitarist Janick Gers after the departure of Adrian Smith. The record continued Maiden's success, reaching number two in England and number seventeen in America. In the 1990's, Iron Maiden produced an album every three years with 1992's Fear of the Dark, 1995's The X Factor, and Virtual XI in 1998. Dickinson had left the band before The X Factor and vocalist Blaze Bayley replaced him. Many Iron Maiden fans felt their sound has stagnated and Harris's songwriting had grown complacent. Maiden received a shot in the arm when Adrian Smith and Bruce Dickinson returned for the 2000 Brave New World release. This gave Iron Maiden a three-guitar lineup which they continued to employ through the decade. In the 2000's, Iron Maiden remained prolific with 2003's Dance of Death, 2006's A Matter of Life and Death, and 2010's The Final Frontier. Their latest release, 2015's The Book of Souls, was their sixteenth studio album. Iron Maiden's style remained largely unchanged throughout their career with the exception of guitar synthesizers in the 1980's. The later recording did move in a slightly more progressive direction. The true legacy of Iron Maiden was their early metal sound that secured them as one of the founding fathers of the new wave of British heavy metal.

In the mid-1970's, four English bands (still active today) played an important role in the development of the new wave of British heavy metal. **Raven** (1975-present) was rooted in hard rock and progressive rock and was known for their high-energy live stage show. Raven dressed in sports gear on stage and emphasized speed and power, thus influencing the soon to be thrash/speed metal genre. **Diamond Head** (1976-1985) (1990-1994) (2000-present) also had a long career. They can be seen as a bridge between 1970's hard rock bands such as Deep Purple and Led Zeppelin, and the later metal bands, most notably, Metallica. Another influence on metal was **Saxon** (1977-present), who had eight albums reach the top forty on the British charts. During the 1980's, Saxon was one of Europe's biggest metal bands and has sold more than fifteen million albums worldwide. Another major band was **Def Leppard.**

Def Leppard (1977-present) emerged early out of the new wave of British heavy metal scene. The band disliked that label, feeling it was a convenient label slapped on them by the British music press. They have also been described as another glam metal band, especially when their MTV videos fit the hair metal look. However, Def Leppard can be defined by their intense metal sound that melded with strong pop melodic hooks. Def Leppard began in 1977 when vocalist Joe Elliott, guitarist Pete Willis, and drummer Tony Kenning first met. In 1978, guitarist Steve Clark joined the band and soon Rick Allen became the permanent drummer. Their 1980 debut, On Through the Night, went to number fifteen in Britain. But many early fans did not appreciate their attempt to appeal to American audiences by recording tunes like "Hello America." The British media made accusations that they had sold out to the American market.

In 1981, Leppard made a good decision to hire AC/DC producer Mutt Lange to shape their sound for High 'N' Dry, released that same year. A video for the power ballad "Bringin' On the Heartbreak" (from High and Dry) became one of the first metal videos played on MTV, thus raising the bands' U.S. profile. The following year, Phil Collen, former guitarist of the glam band Girl, replaced Willis. Fueled by the singles "Photograph," "Foolin," and "Rock of Ages," Def Leppard released Pyromania in 1983. This record shifted from heavy metal to a more radio-friendly glam and hard rock sound and image. With its melodic hooks and heavy MTV exposure, Pyromania shot to number two in the U.S. and number eighteen in England. The album would go on to sell more than ten million copies in the U.S. alone.

In 1984, tragedy struck when drummer Rick Allen was driving at a high rate of speed after a New Year's Eve party when he lost control of his Corvette and rolled his car. He severed his arm below the shoulder and his future as Def Leppard's drummer appeared to be over. After recovering, Allen worked with the Simmons Company to design a custom electronic drum set that would allow him to utilize his feet more to replicate the multi-limbed parts of the Leppard repertoire. At the 1986 Monsters of Rock festival in England, Joe Elliot led an emotional introduction for a fully functioning Rick Allen back to the stage.

1987's Hysteria became the band's most popular record to date, selling over twenty-five million copies. It spawned seven hit singles and reached number one on both sides of the Atlantic. "Pour Some Sugar on Me" became the band's signature tune.

"Pour Some Sugar on Me"
by Steve Clark, Phil Colleen, Joe Elliott, Mutt Lange, and Rick Savage

"Pour Some Sugar on Me" quickly reached number two on the American charts and number eighteen in the U.K. There were two versions of the song's introduction. The first was a studio version that opened with the lyric "Step inside, walk this way, you and me babe, hey hey!" which went straight to a guitar section. The second version was recorded for the singles release and started with "Love is like a bomb."

There were also two different music videos produced for the song. In the first, the band was playing inside a house in Ireland while a wrecking ball and female construction worker with a sledgehammer destroyed the house from the outside. Although, the band didn't like this version, the public did, thus making "Pour Some Sugar on Me" a mega hit in America. The second version was a basic video of Def Leppard simply performing the tune. "Pour Some Sugar on Me" has been utilized in popular culture numerous times in movies, TV shows, and video games.

More tragedy followed when guitarist Steve Clark died in 1991 from a drug and alcohol overdose. The band reacted by deciding to continue but to not replace him. For Def Leppard's 1992 Adrenalize, Phil Collen replicated Clark's style and overdubbed guitar parts. Again the band achieved number one chart status on both sides of the Atlantic. Leppard did eventually hire another guitar player, ex-Dio and Whitesnake guitarist Viv Campbell. After successful compilation albums 1993's Retro Active and 1995's Vault, Def Leppard released the uninspired Slang in 1996. The band returned to their signature sound and popularity with 1999's Euphoria.

In the 2000's, Def Leppard remained prolific releasing X in 2002, Yeah! in 2006, and Songs from the Sparkle Lounge in 2008. The classic lineup of Elliott, Collen, Campbell, Savage, and Allen released the self-titled album Def Leppard in 2015. Not many band's have a twelfth studio album reach number eleven in England and number two in America, forty years into their career. Def Leppard has shown the ability to blend pop and heavy metal sounds with multi-layered harmonies and melodic guitar riffs. Their approach has placed them in a unique position in hard rock and heavy metal history.

Ozzy Osbourne (1948-) (1979-present solo career) began his solo career after being fired from the enormously successful Black Sabbath. Ozzie had signed away all of his rights to Black Sabbath and hit rock bottom by continuing his drug and alcohol abuse. He then locked himself away in a hotel room in Los Angeles. Ozzy had the good fortune to connect with Sharon Arden, daughter of former Black Sabbath manager Don Arden. She helped Ozzy get back on his feet and they launched his solo career by first getting a new band together. With no financial backing, Sharon and Ozzy recruited ex-Rainbow bassist/lyricist Bob Daisley, ex-Uriah Heep drummer Lee Kerslake, keyboardist Don Airey (who played on Sabbath's Never Say Die), and the virtually unknown ex-Quiet Riot guitar wizard Randy Rhoads.

In 1980, Ozzy released the successful Blizzard of Oz that effectively put his career back on track. Blizzard of Oz peaked at number twenty-one on the U.S. charts and produced the hits "Crazy Train," "Mr. Crowley," and "I Don't Know." The follow up, 1981's Diary of a Madman, was again successful but Ozzy was still having personal issues including many well-documented stage antics.

The eccentric Mr. Osbourne

In 1981, Ozzy was at a meeting with record executives in Los Angeles to sign his first solo record deal. He had, on Sharon's advice, been told to go into the boardroom and throw two live doves in the air as a sign of peace. However, Ozzy, drunk and stoned at the time, threw one dove in the air and bite the head off of the other one. The story made headlines before the day was over and added to the ever-growing Ozzy Osbourne legend. Sharon Osbourne defended Ozzy by often pointing out that he did not have a normal upbringing and worked in a slaughterhouse as a teenager. Ozzy believed that much of his behavior was normal, while everyone else would wonder how could someone act that way?

In January 1982, while performing at the Veterans Memorial Auditorium in Des Moines, Iowa, Ozzy bit the head off a bat while performing onstage. He thought it was a rubber bat, when in fact it was real. A seventeen-year-old boy, Mark Neal, thought that the bat was dead when he threw it onto the stage. Ozzy later claimed that the bat had managed to bite him. The result was that Ozzy had to undergo painful rabies injections at a hospital after the show. Ozzy was quick to take responsibility for his behavior when he said "I do some crazy things, some stupid things. But what right does anyone have to say I've lived a demonic existence? I don't sleep upside down on rafters (a reference to bats). I don't burn the first-born child of the person in the next room. I'm not a bloody Satanist." #12

Ozzy had to deal with a number of lawsuits over the years. In 1984, a teenager named John McCollum committed suicide while listening to Osbourne's "Suicide Solution." The songs' lyrics referred to the dangers of alcohol abuse. The allegations against Osbourne stated that the song promoted suicide. The court ruled in Ozzy's favor, stating there was no connection between the song and the young man's suicide. In a similar case in 1991, Ozzy was again sued, but he was acquitted of any wrongdoing. Ozzy has seen the courtroom for many music business disputes, most notably against his old Black Sabbath bandmate, Tony Iommi, over ownership of the Black Sabbath trademark. Both Ozzy and Tony decided to drop the case and put their friendship first, stating that it was only business and never personal.

Ozzy gained even more celebrity status with his own TV reality show, The Osbournes, that premiered in 2002 and ran until 2005. The show revealed the "interesting" home life of the Osbourne family; Sharon, Ozzy, and their children, Jack and Kelly and occasionally son Louis (oldest daughter Aimee did not appear). Ozzy's legend extends to the video game

---

"To us, heavy metal had to sound like a machine. The guitar had to have a buzzsaw sound to it, the drums had to have an edge to it."

- Pantera drummer Vinnie Paul Abbott

world with Guitar Hero World Tour. In the game, Ozzy is a playable character that can be unlocked upon completing "Mr. Crowley" and "Crazy Train" in the vocalist career section.
Ozzy Osbourne-Rock Legend

Tragedy stuck in 1982 when the brilliant guitarist Randy Rhoads was killed in a plane crash just before the start of the tour to promote the Diary of a Madman album. Ozzy was devastated by the death of Rhoads and said, "I suppose when he died, part of me died with him…he was the first person that came into my life who gave me hope." #13 Ozzy persevered and released three more albums in the 1980's; 1983's Bark at the Moon, 1986's The Ultimate Sin, and 1988's No Rest for the Wicked. Though Rhoads was irreplaceable, Ozzy employed the accomplished guitar players Jake E. Lee and Zakk Wylde. The 1990's brought No More Tears in 1991, and Ozzmosis in 1995.

Ozzy's most successful music business venture was the Ozzfest concert festival shows he organized with Sharon and his son Jack. Ozzfest was a big hit with metal enthusiasts. Over five million fans have attended Ozzfest shows and it has collectively grossed over one hundred million dollars. Ozzy reunited with Black Sabbath at the 1997 Ozzfest. The venue has also provided many young upstart metal bands with great exposure.

Ozzy remained a force in the 2000's with 2001's Down to Earth, 2005's Under Cover, 2007's Black Rain, and 2010's Scream. As stated in the section on Black Sabbath, Ozzy reunited with Sabbath in 2013 for a successful final album and subsequent final tour. Ozzy released 2014's Memoirs of a Madman and a CD/DVD compilation that contained seventeen singles that span his entire career. Ozzy Osbourne was inducted into the Rock and Roll Hall of Fame in 2006 (as part of Black Sabbath) and remains an active solo artist today.

Two other bands from the early 1980's made important contributions to the developing metal scene. **Mercyful Fate** (1981-1985) (1992-present) is a Danish heavy metal band from Copenhagen, Denmark formed in 1981 by guitarist Hank Shermann and vocalist King Diamond. Mercyful Fate, whose lyrics were about satan and the occult, would go on to influence black metal musicians in the 1990's and beyond. **Armored Saint** (1982-1992) (1999-present) is an American heavy metal band that formed in Los Angeles, California in 1982. Although they achieved only moderate success on the charts, Armored Saint's early material was an important catalyst for a growing heavy metal audience that would soon embrace the harsher sound of the thrash metal movement.

The development of heavy metal morphed into multiple and evolving subgenres. **Thrash metal** (see thrash bands later in this chapter) is an extreme subgenre that emphasizes a harsh, aggressive sound and fast to extremely fast tempos. The term **speed metal** is sometimes used interchangeably with thrash metal but some would describe speed metal as generally less harsh and more melodic than thrash, but obviously with a focus on speed. It comes down to each band's decision on how fast and thrashy it wants to play. Other musical characteristics of thrash that evolved in the 1980's were the addition of a hardcore punk rock attitude, heavy and complex guitar styles (especially seen in the NWOBHM bands), and plenty of double bass drum beats and fills. Some of the essential bands that influenced and ushered in thrash metal were Iron Maiden, Judas Priest, Motorhead, Raven, Diamond Head, and Venom, to name a few.

Doom metal is another extreme style of heavy metal that characteristically utilizes a thick and heavy (sludgy) sound, low-tuned guitars, and typically slower tempos. Doom metal started with bands such as Black Sabbath and Pentagram. The most defining element of doom metal is the pessimistic and gloomy lyrics, often about depression, fear, suffering, and anger. Some doom metal bands wrote lyrics involving religious themes or the occult. Doom metal also focuses strongly on the guitar riff.

Glam metal is another metal subgenre, also popular in the 1980's. Glam metal bands were overall less aggressive and infused metal with more pop music sensibilities. Glam bands emphasized their looks and stage presence by wearing spandex and leather and adopted "big hair." The glam scene was centered in Los Angeles. The MTV video market was a perfect complement to glam bands that were all about the good looks, emphasis on beautiful women, and carefree party lifestyles. Critics of glam bands suggested that the glam image superseded musicianship.

Rather than splitting hairs as to where to place each and every band, we will place most of the metal bands by major subgenres (more subgenres to come). But remember that *most* metal bands display features of multiple subgenres, therefore, we will attempt to describe what makes each band unique.

Glam Metal

Slade (1966-present) is one of the earliest British glam rock bands to gain popularity in the early 1970's. They achieved seventeen consecutive top twenty hits that included six number one singles on the British charts (see chapter eight). Shortly after, **Twisted Sister** (1972-1989) (2003-2016) (reunions: 1997, 2001, 2002) would make an impact with their sense of humor and song themes that explored parent and teenage conflicts. Twisted Sister produced seven studio albums between 1982 and 2006 that included their hit "We're Not Gonna Take It."

Quiet Riot (1973-present) is another early American glam metal band. They were formed in 1973 by guitar legend Randy Rhoads and bassist Kelly Garni. Quiet Riot endured many lineup and name changes but eventually settled on the name Quiet Riot. Their established lineup featured guitarist Randy Rhoads, vocalist Kevin DuBrow, bassist Kelly Garni, and drummer Drew Forsyth. After two albums titled Quiet Riot and Quiet Riot II, the band fell apart. Randy Rhoads joined Ozzy Osbourne's band but sadly died in a plane crash while on tour with Ozzy.

Quiet Riot re-formed and DuBrow added guitarist Carlos Cavazo, bassist Rudy Sarzo, and drummer Frankie Banali to the new lineup. This version of the band found success with 1983's Metal Health, that went to number one on the American charts. It sold over six million copies and was considered a classic among early heavy metal albums. Metal Health was credited as the first heavy metal record to make the Billboard charts. Vocalist DuBrow often dressed in a straitjacket and metal face mask. In 2007, Kevin DuBrow died at the age of fifty-two. Many more lineups ensued for Quiet Riot. They recorded ten more studio albums, including the 2017 release Road Rage.

Ratt (1976-1992) (1996-present) began with a shuffling lineup that was once called Firedome, then Crystal Pystal, then Buster Cherry, then Mickey Ratt,

Rock Hard Fact

Most of the 1980's Los Angeles area clubs had a pay-to-play policy. Glam metal bands that sought major record deals were required to purchase hundreds of dollars' worth of tickets in advance for the right to play.

Rock History - the Musician's Perspective

> "You know, when you really connect with the instrument everything just comes out on an emotional level very naturally through your playing. That's, you know, a great night."
>
> – Slash from Guns N' Roses

Rock Hard Fact

Slash, of Guns 'N' Roses, first wanted to play the bass but was convinced by his bandmate, drummer Steven Adler, to switch to guitar when they would hang-out while playing hooky from their eighth-grade middle school.

and finally in 1981, shortened to Ratt. Eventually, their self-produced EP led to a record deal with Atlantic and their debut album Out of the Cellar in 1984. Ratt scored hits through radio airplay and MTV exposure with "Round and Round," "Wanted Man," and "Lack of Communication." The band has shared a friendly rivalry with Motley Crue over the years and more hits followed with "You're in Love" and "Dance." From 1992 to 1996, Ratt was on hiatus but the classic era members reunited in 1996. Ratt has made seven studio albums over their forty plus year career. After many legal issues, an extended hiatus, and lineup changes of over twenty-five different members, Ratt has persevered and currently is still active.

Whitesnake (1978-1990) (1994,1997) (2002-present) formed when ex-Deep Purple vocalist David Coverdale was working on a solo album with guitarist Micky Moody. Moody and Coverdale went on to recruit another ex-Deep Purple bandmate, keyboardist Jon Lord and then formed Whitesnake. The band added guitarist Bernie Marsden, bassist Neil Murray, and drummer Dave Dowie. Whitesnake released five albums from 1978 to 1983, building a small but faithful fan base. Coverdale reshuffled the lineup for 1984's Slide It In and Whitesnake briefly made it onto the charts. Slide It In was successful due to Whitesnake's approach of creating riffs and melodic hooks reminiscent of Deep Purple and Led Zeppelin.

Another overhaul of band members and the release of 1987's Whitesnake featured the songs "Crying in the Rain," "Still of the Night," and "Here I Go Again." This album sold ten million copies in less than a year (over twelve million to date) with the help of the band's MTV friendly image and sound. Guitar virtuoso Steve Vai joined the band for their 1989 Slip of the Tongue and although the album sold well, Whitesnake didn't record another studio album until 1997's Restless Heart. Coverdale then embarked on a solo project in 2000. Whitesnake continued in 2008 with Good to be Bad and 2011's Forevermore. Whitesnake has toured regularly to take advantage of its popularity in international markets. Interestingly, in 2015 Whitesnake recorded The Purple Album, a reworking of Coverdale era songs from his time with Deep Purple.

From the time period of the late 1970's to early 1980's, a number of other glam metal bands competed for an audience and MTV exposure. These bands included; **Dokken** (1979-1989) (1993-present), **Hanoi Rocks** (1979-1985) (2001-2009), **Vixen** (1980-present with some inactive years), **Motley Crue**, and **Poison**.

Motley Crue (1981-2015) formed when bassist Nikki Sixx recruited vocalist Vince Neil, guitarist Mick Mars, and drummer Tommy Lee. The band's early years were especially chaotic with an endless parade of drugs and groupies. However, their 1981 debut Too Fast for Love earned them a record deal with Elektra Records. 1983's Shout at the Devil pulled them into the customary satanic theme controversy that defined many metal bands. Shout at the Devil contained the hit "Looks That Kill," which Motley Crue turned into a video hit as well. By 1987, the band had solidified their bad boy reputation with their release of Girls, Girls, Girls. Its title track reflected Motley Crue's hedonistic lifestyle of riding Harley's, partying, and life on the Sunset Strip nightclubs. From 1984 to 1988, Motley Crue rose to international fame but their issues with the law and substance abuse problems forced the band to undergo rehabilitation.

By 1989, Motley Crue was back on track with a number one album on the U.S. charts titled Dr. Feelgood. Hits from the album included "Kickstart My Heart," and "Without You." After the band released the compilation album Decade of Decadence, Vince Neil left and was replaced by vocalist John Corabi. 1994's self-titled Motley Crue did reach number seven in America but Corabi soon left and Neil returned to the band. In 1999, Tommy Lee quit and was replaced by ex-Ozzy Osbourne drummer Randy Castillo. 2000's New Tattoo was followed by a tour, but when Castillo was diagnosed with cancer, ex-Hole drummer Samantha Maloney filled in. The band then went on a hiatus.

In 2004, Motley Crue did reunite to make the compilation album Red, White, and Crue that included three new songs. After some legal issues, the band released their ninth and final studio album, Saints of Los Angeles, with the band's original lineup of Neil, Mars, Sixx, and Lee. In 2015, Motley Crue played its last concert in Los Angeles.

Poison (1983-present) was first known as the band Paris from Harrisburg, Pennsylvania. The lineup featured vocalist Bret Michaels, bassist Bobby Dall, guitarist Matt Smith, and drummer Rikki Rocket. Smith dropped out after they moved to Los Angeles and they added guitarist C.C. DeVille. Their 1986 debut album Look What the Cat Dragged In was an instant success and Poison achieved exposure with heavy rotation on MTV. The band would go on to produce six more studio albums from 1988 to 2007. Poison wrote many songs with themes about partying, lost innocence, sex, and lost love. The band's most successful single, "Every Rose Has Its Thorn," was a power ballad from their second album, Open Up and Say…Ahh!. The song lyrics, written by Bret Michaels, told the story of a failed love affair with a Los Angeles striper. Poison was plagued with internal issues and Deville was fired in 1991. Guitarist Richie Kotzen was his replacement. The band persevered through the 1990's (briefly disappearing altogether) and 2000's. DeVille returned in 1996. Poison's rapid decline from the charts happened as quickly as their rise to fame, but they proved to be survivors when most glam metal bands were victims of the grunge dominated 1990's. Poison is still active and in 2017, celebrated its thirty-year anniversary with a tour co-headlining with Def Leppard.

A prominent glam metal band whose time in the spotlight was brief but shining was **Warrant** (1984-present). Warrant's peak period, from 1989 to 1994, saw them release five albums that sold over ten million copies worldwide. The glam metal scene became even more crowded when more bands flooded the market in the mid-1980's. A few that achieved success were; **L.A. Guns** (1983-present), **Cinderella** (1983-1995) (1997-present), **Skid Row** (1986-1996) (1999-present), and **Guns N' Roses**.

Guns 'N' Roses (1985-present) are, alongside Motley Crue, the real bad boys of glam metal and one of the few that survived the advent of the 1990's grunge movement. Guns 'N' Roses grew out of the brief musical partnership of vocalist Axl Rose and guitarist Tracii Guns and his band L.A. Guns. Tracii Guns was replaced by guitarist Saul Hudson, aka Slash, one of the most revered guitarists in all of rock. The band added bassist Duff McKagan, guitarist Izzy Stradlin, and drummer Steven Adler. Guns 'N' Roses built a steady following around Los Angeles and released an EP titled Live?!*@Like a Suicide and signed a record deal with Geffen Records. Their debut album, 1987's Appetite for Destruction, was one of the highest selling albums in rock history, eventually selling more than thirty million copies worldwide. It featured the hits "Paradise City," "Welcome to the Jungle," and "Sweet Child o' Mine," helping to make the album the eleventh best-selling album in U.S. history. The band toured extensively to support the album.

"Sweet Child o' Mine"
by Guns N' Roses

Released as the third single on Appetite for Destruction, "Sweet Child o' Mine" became the band's first and only number-one single in America. It reached number six on the British charts. Guitarist Slash wrote the song's main lick by simply playing around at a jam session with the band. Rhythm guitarist Izzy Stradlin added some simple chords and the rhythm section filled in the groove to create a five minute tune that would help catapult Guns 'N' Roses to fame. Producer Spencer Proffer suggested that they add a breakdown jam section before the end of the song.

For the highly successful MTV video for "Sweet Child o' Mine," Guns 'N' Roses were filmed rehearsing at a ballroom with all of their (current at the time) girlfriends shown in the video. Much to the distain of the band, Slash's guitar solo was shortened for radio and video play. Even the shortened Slash guitar solo displayed his ability to extend a song's melody with his inventive approach to soloing. Slash's introductory guitar riff is revered by many rock guitarists. "Sweet Child o' Mine" appeared in many movies and has been covered by Sheryl Crow and Billy Preston.

———

The band struggled through drug/alcohol and numerous personal issues through the 1980's and 1990's including Stephen Adler's removal from the band. He was replaced by drummer Matt Sorum in 1990. Another issue was a controversy over some of the band's song lyrics. One example was "Used to Love Her" that contained the lyrics "Used to love her, but had to kill her." This led to accusations of being violently misogynist (which the band denied). Guns 'N' Roses embarked on an almost two year tour that basically tore them apart. Between 1994 and 1996, the band was in disarray and Slash and Rose were not on the same musical or personal page. Slash was replaced by guitarist Robin Finck in 1997. By 1999, when Guns 'N' Roses released "Oh My God," for the film End of Days, Rose was the only original member still in place.

After many lineup changes, Guns 'N' Roses released Chinese Democracy in 2008. The band on this recording included Rose, Robin Finck, and a host of other musicians, but none of the original members except Rose. After years of fighting, Guns 'N' Roses reunited and the current lineup is Axl Rose, Slash, Duff McKagan, keyboardist Dizzy Reed, guitarist Richard Fortus, drummer Frank Ferrer, and keyboardist Melissa Reese. Currently, Guns 'N' Roses has retained their hard rock persona but also expanded to include electronic and industrial rock elements. In the late 1980's, they were one of the most popular bands in the world. Guns 'N' Roses was inducted into the Rock and Roll Hall of Fame in 2012.

Heavy metal vocalist/guitarist and solo artist, **Lita Ford** (1980-1995) (2008-present), first gained prominence as a member of the all-female metal band, The Runaways. Ford played lead guitar while vocalist Joan Jett played rhythm guitar. The band played their last concert in 1978 when disagreements over the musical direction of the band surfaced. Jett went in a punk rock and hard rock direction while Ford wanted to continue performing in a metal style. Lita Ford then focused on her solo career. Her debut solo album Out for Blood was released in 1983. With little commercial success from her debut effort, Ford continued with 1984's Dancin' on the Edge, which faired better. More albums followed, but Ford went on a long hiatus from 1996 to 2007 to raise her family. In 2008, Lita Ford regrouped and released three albums including the recent 2016 Time Capsule. Throughout her career, Ford developed a rebellious and fashionably bad girl image that complemented her pop-metal sound. Lita Ford's most successful solo album was her self-produced Lita in 1988. Her ballad "Close My Eyes Forever," a duet with Ozzy Osbourne, became her most successful song peaking at number eight on the U.S. charts.

Doom Metal Bands

Doom metal (as described earlier) was inspired by Black Sabbath and other British early metal bands. Lazy tempos, sludgier riffs, and psychedelic timbres helped define the subgenre. Bands sprung up all over Europe and many regions of the United States. A few of these Doom metal bands included; **Pentagram** (1971-2005) (2008-present), **Trouble** ((1979-present), **Candlemass** (1984-present with some inactive years), **Danzig** (1987-present), and **Type O Negative. Type O Negative** (1989-2010) was an American gothic metal band that formed in Brooklyn, New York. They drew from many influences including psychedelic rock, old school hard rock, metal bands, and hardcore groups such as Agnostic Front. Their lyrics focused on themes of depression, romance, and death. The band released seven studio recordings from 1991 to 2007 and their songs have appeared in many movie soundtracks and video games. Type O Negative's musical career was cut short when lead vocalist and main songwriter Peter Steele died from heart failure.

Thrash Metal Bands

The golden era of thrash metal was 1981 to 1991, but thrash is currently alive and well. Along with the speed and aggression came a new phenomenon, the mosh pit. Borrowed from hardcore punk, thrash audiences created mosh pits where members of the crowd collided with each other, often inflicting damage on anyone who dared to enter. Many thrash bands engaged in "stage diving" right into the pit themselves. A few thrash metal bands from North America that had an early impact on the scene included the Canadian band **Anvil** (1978-present), and the California band **Exodus** (1979-present with some inactive years).

The "big four" of thrash metal came from America and soon *dominated* the heavy metal genre on the international stage. Now we turn our attention to the early 1980's entrance of the "big four" of thrash; **Metallica, Anthrax, Slayer,** and **Megadeth**. Then we will explore some of the prominent metal bands that came after them.

Metallica (1981-present) is a San Francisco based band that became the biggest selling act in heavy metal since their rise to fame in the mid-1980's. Metallica was formed in the summer of 1981 in Los Angeles when Danish drummer Lars Ulrich met vocalist/guitarist James Hetfield. The pair had jammed a few times with various musicians and Ulrich was determined to put together a band. Hetfield was in the band Leather Charm and brought his roommate, bassist Ron McGovney to a session. Ulrich subjected Hetfield to the metal sounds of earlier British metal artists and together, they wrote

> "The music of Woody Guthrie, early Bob Dylan, Johnny Cash, Pete Seeger-could be as heavy as anything that comes through a Marshall stack. The combination of three chords and the right lyrical couplet can be as heavy as anything in the Metallica catalogue."
>
> - Tom Morello from Rage Against the Machine

Rock Hard Fact

In 2002, in the wake of the 911 tragedy, politicians were randomly receiving bio-terrorism threats of letters laced with deadly anthrax spores. The metal band Anthrax was pressured to change their name and refused hoping that no further negative events would happen and it wouldn't be necessary.

the song "Hit the Lights" for a compilation album titled Metal Massacre. They came up with the name Metallica from an English book titled *Encyclopedia Metallica*, an obscure book about British heavy metal bands.

Metallica had utilized session guitarist Lloyd Grant to record "Hit the Lights" but replaced him with guitarist Dave Mustaine to complete the first incarnation of the band. They soon recorded more demos; the most widely distributed was "Power Metal" in 1982. Metallica replaced McGovney with bassist Cliff Burton and moved to Burton's hometown of San Francisco. The band played various gigs but then moved to New York City where a record-store owner, Jonny Zazula, offered to help them secure a record deal. After failed attempts to generate record label interest, Zazula formed his own label, Megaforce Records. He then recorded Metallica's debut album, 1983's Kill 'Em All. Dave Mustaine was Metallica's most charismatic member and co-composer of four of the songs scheduled for Kill 'Em All. But Mustaine's erratic behavior and other personal issues prompted the band to replace him with ex-Exodus guitarist Kirk Hammett just prior to recording the record.

Groundbreaking album Kill 'Em All
by Metallica

Metallica initially wanted to name the album Metal Up You're A** with a hand holding a sword emerging from a toilet bowl. The cover and title had to be changed because Zazula feared distributors would not promote the album. Kill 'Em All (named after the distributors who forced the name change) was a mild success on the U.S. charts and some believed it represented the true birth of thrash metal. It was fast and heavy with a unique combination of a metal sound and punk attitude.

Bands such as Moorhead, Raven, and Anvil influenced Metallica's compositional and performance process for the recording of Kill 'Em All. Metallica took many of these artist's musical attributes and developed them to define early American thrash metal. Metallica didn't achieve great commercial success just yet, but Kill 'Em All broke down the door. "Dimebag" Darrell Abbott, guitarist for Pantera, said, "Kill 'Em All was the first really consistent thrash album where every song was just a razor blade and the whole record was one direction (not the boy band). James's f***ing rhythm playing is unbelievable, especially for his first record. They wrote fantabulous songs and it made me motivated. It made me want to tear something up." #14

Side one of Kill 'Em All opened with "Hit the Lights," then "The Four Horsemen," "Motorbreath," "Jump in the Fire," "Anesthesia-Pulling Teeth," and "Whiplash." The first tune, "Hit the Lights," celebrated the idea of heavy metal itself as a genre created through its lyrics. The song ended with long guitar solos by Hammett and set the stage for the whole album.

Side two opened with "Phantom Lord," then "No Remorse," "Seek & Destroy," and "Metal Militia." The first song recorded at the Kill 'Em All sessions was "Seek and Destroy." Its simple, one-line chorus became a staple in Metallica live performances. "Metal Militia," one of the faster songs on the album, was a Mustaine composed riff (even thought he told them not to use his ideas) that simulated a marching army. The song was about the heavy metal way of life and the idea of nonconformity.

1984's Ride the Lighting reached number one

hundred on the American charts and established Metallica as *the* heavy metal band. Metallica made it clear that they were not interested in the spandex and eye make-up of the glam metal scene. 1986's Master of Puppets went to number twenty-nine in the U.S. Metallica supported Ozzy Osbourne on an American tour, further solidifying their fan base. Master of Puppets was considered one of the band's strongest and most influential efforts. In 2016, it's cultural and aesthetic significance made it the first metal album ever to be registered with the Library of Congress.

"Master of Puppets"
by Metallica

"Master of Puppets," the second track on Master of Puppets, dealt with the subject of drug abuse. The lyrics highlighted how drugs can begin to control the abuser's behavior and life choices. Although not initially a commercial success, "Master of Puppets" had become a fan favorite and was included in many of the band's set lists. The lyrics constantly referred to "how I'm killing you" (meaning the effects of the drugs). The song utilized extensive downpicking and a long instrumental section, which became a signature feature of the band. "Master of Puppets" became Metallica's most performed song, having been played live over 1,500 times.

"Master of Puppets" began with a stop time guitar riff and proceeded with a fast and heavy feel that interjected frequent half-time and stop-time figures. This served as a contrast to the basic feel of the song. "Master of Puppets" moved into a floating instrumental guitar solo section that returned to the hard and heavy frantic verse section. Another guitar solo followed that borrowed from a progressive rock influence. James Hetfield commented, "It was more of a challenge to write a long song that didn't seem long. The riff for "Master of Puppets"...it works good live. People love to scream 'Master.'" #15

Tragedy struck while on tour in 1986, when Metallica was traveling from Stockholm to Copenhagen (in Sweden). Bassist Cliff Burton was killed when their tour bus overturned. The band was shaken but eventually recruited ex-Flotsam and Jetsam bassist Jason Newsted. In 1988, Metallica released ...And Justice For All, their most progressive album to date. The record peaked at number six in America. The band next released its debut music video, the song "One," which went into heavy rotation on MTV. 1991's Metallica, also known as the black album, became their most popular record selling over twenty-five million copies worldwide.

1996's Load went to number one on both sides of the Atlantic. It showed a hard rock side of the band but alienated some of their fan base that expected another thrash album. 1997's Reload also went to number one in the U.S. and number four in England. Metallica again showed their willingness to take chances by blending some southern rock and some blues-rock influence with their signature metal sound. 1998's Garage, Inc. was a covers album and 2003 saw them release St. Anger. Metallica changed bass players when Newsted left and former Ozzy Osbourne bassist Robert Truillo joined the band. Producer Bob Rock played bass on most of St.Anger and Truillo was added by the end of the recording sessions. St Anger sparked more success, reaching number one in America and number three in Britain.

2008's Death Magnetic, produced by Rick Rubin, featured more complex musical structures and long, technical guitar solos by Hetfield and Hammett. The band successfully returned to their thrash metal roots, much to the delight of many of their longtime fans. In 2010,

Metallica headlined a tour, as part of heavy metal's "big four." It was the first time Metallica, Slayer, Megadeth, and Anthrax all played in England on the same concert bill. Metallica's tenth studio (double) album, Hardwired…to Self Destruct, was their sixth consecutive studio album to debut at number one in America. Metallica has proven to be one of the most influential heavy metal bands of all time. They have sold over one hundred and ten million albums worldwide. Metallica has thrived for over thirty-five years and are one of the founding fathers of the thrash metal genre. Metallica was inducted into the Rock and Roll Hall of Fame in 2009.

    Anthrax (1981-present) formed in their native Queens, New York in mid-1981. The earliest lineup featured vocalist Neil Turbin, guitarist Scott Ian, bassist Dan Lilker, and drummer Greg D'Angelo. Anthrax was discovered and signed by Megaforce Records owner Jonny Zazula. By the time of their 1984 debut release Fistful of Metal, Anthrax fired Danny Lilker and further adjusted their lineup by adding guitarist Dan Spitz, drummer Charlie Benante, and (briefly) vocalist Matt Fallon. Anthrax was not an instant success, but with great determination, would eventually work their way into the big four of thrash metal. Fistful of Metal contained the song "Metal Thrashing Mad," one of the first times the term thrash metal was used by the music press. The band also recorded a cover of Alice Cooper's "I'm Eighteen." The record was well received by the critics but sold only marginally well. Anthrax's first big tour was in the summer of 1984 with Metallica. Then, they opened for the metal band Raven, further building their audience.

    After a search for a new singer, vocalist Joey Belladonna was introduced on the EP Armed and Dangerous and then on their second album, 1985's Spreading the Disease. The band also added bassist Frank Bello. Spreading the Disease worked its way onto the U.S. charts and Anthrax promoted it with a tour with Black Sabbath. While Anthrax had started around the same time as Metallica and Slayer, it took them a little more time to achieve commercial popularity. That era arrived in 1987, with Among the Living and its propulsive guitar riffs, sing-along vocals, and breakneck tempos. What made them different was their onstage skater shorts and sense of humor with songs like "Caught in A Mosh." This appealed to new fans that were also new to heavy metal. Among the Living sold over a million copies and also revealed Anthrax's signature comic book references. The song "Among the Living," was based on writer Stephen King's (big fan of Anthrax) novel *The Stand*.

    1988's State of Euphoria sent Anthrax into the top thirty on both the British and American charts. The single "Antisocial," (a cover of a tune by the French metal band Trust) was worked into MTV's rotation on their *Headbangers Ball* show. 1990's Persistence of Time turned to more serious lyrics. In 1991, Anthrax collaborated with rap artists Public Enemy, recording their song "Bring the Noise." This was included on the Anthrax compilation album Attack of the Killer B's and on Public Enemy's Apocalypse 91…The Enemy Strikes Black. This was one of the first rap metal songs in music history (although five years before Aerosmith and Run DMC had collaborated on "Walk This Way").

'Bring The Noise'
featuring Chuck D from Public Enemy
by Carl Ridenhour, Hank Shocklee, Eric "Vietnam" Sadler, James Broan and George Clinton

    Anthrax had already entered the rap world with their 1986 spoof of the song "I'm the Man," but this re-recording of the Public Enemy classic led to a joint tour by the two bands. Chuck D gained new respect for thrash metal when both bands would often end their collaborative concerts together by performing "Bring the Noise." Scott Ian recalled "Public Enemy was my favorite rap band…All I could think of was 'How the f*** can we work with these guys?'…I wrote this bass riff based around "Bring the Noise'…I called Chuck (D) and told him we wanted him and Flavor Flav to come in and do vocals." #16 Public Enemy and producer Rick Rubin thought it was redundant to redo the song but Anthrax send them a demo of their version and it changed their minds. That led to a four-month world tour.

    "Bring the Noise" brought together a combination of musical energies Samples of the legendary grooves of James Brown's "Funky Drummer" and "Get Up, Get into It, Get Involved," and Funkadelic's "Get Off Your A** and Jam," combined seamlessly with Anthrax's thrashy sound. Chuck D was familiar with Anthrax before this collaboration and was flattered that Scott Ian would wear Public Enemy shirts while onstage with Anthrax. The Anthrax version would reach number fourteen on the U.S. charts and inspire other cover versions of the tune, including the Limp Bizkit version on their Take a Bite Outta Rhyme: A Rock Tribute to Rap album.

    In 1993, Belladonna quit the band and was replaced by ex-Armored Saint vocalist John Bush. Sound of White Noise, released that same year, had a darker sound influenced by alternative rock. The record also included orchestration by composer Angelo Badalamenti. Shortly after its release, Dan Spitz left Anthrax and was replaced by his guitar tech, Paul Crook. 1995's Stomp 442 and 1998's Volume 8: The Threat is Real were enhanced by appearances by Pantera's guitarist Dimebag Darrell. In 2001, guitarist Rob Caggiano joined the band and Anthrax released 2003's We've Come for You All. In 2002, the classic lineup of Ian, Spitz, Benante, Bello, and Belladonna reunited for a tour. In 2007, ex-Devilsize vocalist Dan Nelson joined Anthrax. The band joined the other three iconic metal bands for a "big four" of thrash metal tour in 2010. The following year, Anthrax released Worship Music that peaked in America at number twelve. In 2017, Anthrax announced they would be releasing a live album and would begin work on their twelfth studio album. Anthrax was one of the primary bands responsible for the emergence of thrash metal. They also played a key role in defining the genres of rap-rock and nu metal (see chapter seventeen) in the early 1990's.

    Slayer (1981-present) began in Southern California when guitarists Jeff Hanneman and Kerry King joined vocalist/bassist Tom Araya and drummer Dave Lombardo. The band played covers of Iron Maiden and Judas Priest at local shows when Araya invested all of his money to finance their debut album Show No Mercy in 1983. Slayer toured extensively in all kinds of suspect venues to promote the record and their early use of satanic themes made the metal community take notice. Although a part of thrash metal's big four, Slayer was also defining the death metal genre. This was evident on 1985's Hell Awaits that soon brought them to the attention

> "From the heaviest of the heavy to classical to country, that's what I listen to, I listen to a variety and I enjoy good music, good songs…I try to incorporate melody. Even though I'm screaming, I still like to think I bring melody into screaming."
>
> – Tom Araya from Slayer

of Rick Rubin. He signed Slayer to his Def Jam label. Their first collaboration with Rubin showed how effective the producer/artist relationship could be on their 1986 Reign in Blood album. Rubin did away with the complex arrangements and longer songs from the Hell Awaits album.

Groundbreaking album Reign in Blood
by Slayer

Reign in Blood was intense, fast, lyrically full of venom and malice, and above all, controversial. Columbia Records, Def Jam's distributer, refused to release Reign in Blood due to the song "Angel of Death" that was about Nazi concentration camps and the horror of the human experiments implemented by Nazi doctor, Josef Mengele. In defense of the song, guitarist Jeff Hanneman stated, "We're not praising Mengle or terrorists or serial killers. We just write from their perspective." #17 Eventually, the album was distributed by Geffen Records in late 1986. It received almost no radio play, yet reached number ninety-four on the U.S. charts.

Slayer basically rejected their own satanic themes they displayed on their first albums for more thematic issues that outlined the human condition. In addition to writing about Nazi concentration camps, the themes on Reign in Blood addressed serial killers, torture, terrorism, war crimes, anti-religion, and insanity. Slayer was delighted to be working with Rick Rubin and was very aware of his success with hip-hop artists Run DMC and LL Cool J. Rubin was able to bring a clean and professional production environment to the band. Songs were stripped down and a hardcore punk influence emerged, mixed in with Slayer's metal approach. This innovative change in Slayer's sound soon changed their audience's perception of the band.

In many aspects, Reign in Blood helped to define thrash metal. The songs were well thought out and skillfully produced. The sound was very heavy from start to finish. Slayer's infectious guitar riffs, down-tuned guitars, graphically violent lyrics, and even the harsh and shocking cover artwork set a new standard for emerging thrash (especially death metal) bands. Slayer was often branded as bad guys. They would defend themselves by pointing out that they simply wrote about subjects other bands refused to approach. Many heavy metal fans have praised Reign in Blood for its intensity and impact on the thrash metal genre. Slayer has often performed the entire album in live performances.

"Angel of Death"
by Jeff Hanneman

Jeff Hanneman was inspired to write "Angel of Death" after reading some books about Josef Mengele during a Slayer tour. Hanneman believed that the song's lyrics were obvious in implying that Mengele was a bad person. His bandmate, Tom Araya concurred when he said, "We got accused of being neo-Nazis because of 'Angel of Death.' If you look at it, the song just tells a story. It doesn't glorify anything. Anyone who thinks we're Nazis isn't paying close attention." #18 The graphic song lyrics talked about inhumane experimental surgeries conducted by the Nazis. The controversy over the song's lyrics has also led to accusations of racism, which Slayer has repeatedly denied.

The Slayer two guitar lineup created some of the wild excitement that thrash is all about. At the start of the song, Araya entered with a shrieking and wordless scream. Lombardo played a manic drumset feel and he sounded comfortable at a blistering quarter note equals 210 per minute. Bands attempting to cover "Angel of Death" often are confused by what key it's in and even drummer Paul Bostaph (who replaced Lombardo for a while) initially had trouble understanding some of the song's sections. "Angel of Death" has been referred to as the pinnacle of speed metal. A half-time riff in the song was sampled by Public Enemy for their tune "She Watch Channel Zero?!"

1988's South of Heaven saw Slayer incorporate more melodic singing and slower tempos. Although it disappointed some fans, the album was a commercial success. 1990's Seasons in the Abyss was their first album released on Rick Rubin's new Def American label. It went to number forty in America and number eighteen in Britain. Seasons in the Abyss returned to some of the pounding speed of Slayers' earlier work.

In 1992, drummer Dave Lombardo quit the band and was replaced by ex-Forbidden drummer Paul Bostaph. 1994's Divine Intervention featured themes about serial killers, sex offenders, murder, and the evils of organized religion. After some high profile tours, Slayer released Undisputed Attitude in 1996, an album of punk rock covers. Bostaph soon left and a new drummer, ex-Testament drummer Jon Dette was hired. After appearing at the 1996 Ozzfest, Dette was fired and Bostaph returned.

1998's Diabolus in Musica went to number thirty-one on the U.S. charts and was criticized by some for displaying the characteristics of the nu metal style. Diabolus in Musica featured an emphasis on grooves and down tuned guitars. The song "Bitter Peace" utilized a tritone interval (referred to in the album title as the devil's interval-aka Diablous). Slayer released God Hates Us All in 2001. In 2006, drummer Dave Lombardo returned for 2006's Christ Illusion, and 2009's World Painted Blood.

In early 2011, Jeff Hanneman became ill and sadly, died in 2013. Slayer decided to continue and released the album Repentless in 2015, with ex-Exodus guitarist Gary Holt replacing Hanneman. When thrash and death metal became an accepted part of popular culture around the world, much of the uproar over Slayer's song themes had been forgiven. Even Grammy Award voters expressed their approval when they awarded Slayer the Best Metal Performers in 2006 and 2007. Slayer continues to record and tour in 2017.

Megadeth (1984-present) began when guitarist/vocalist/frontman Dave Mustaine was fired from his former band, Metallica. Mustaine would hold a very public grudge against his former band for years to come. He also had an idea for naming his new band before he even got the musicians together. Riding on a bus (after getting fired) back to California, Mustaine said "I was writing lyrics on the back of anything I could get my hands on, and one of the things I was writing on was the back of a handbill from Senator Alan Cranston that was talking about nuclear armament, and it said the arsenal of Megadeth can't be rid." #19 Mustaine soon added bassist David Ellefson, guitarist Chris Poland, and drummer Gar Samuelson to form Megadeth. Between late 1984 and January 1985, Megadeth recorded their debut album Killing is My Business…and Business is Good. Despite it shaky audio quality, it is regarded as an innovative technical thrash record. Tension between all four-band members

---

Rock Hard Fact

The title track of Megadeth's Countdown to Extinction album was awarded The Humane Society's Genesis Award in 1993 for raising awareness about animal rights.

"What I couldn't say verbally I was able to express physically through the guitar."

- Dave Mustaine from Megadeth

threatened to send Megadeth to an early demise but their 1986 Peace Sells…But Who's Buying? album was a commercial success. It peaked on the U.S. charts at number seventy-six. This album established Megadeth's position in the extreme metal genre (more abrasive, harsher, and faster brand of metal). Peace Sell…But Who's Buying? revealed a technical style with fast sections and fairly complex arrangements. Megadeth's public stock was raised when the title track from the album entered the regular rotation on MTV.

By 1987, internal fighting over drug issues led to the firing of Poland and Samuelson. Megadeth hired guitarist Jeff Young and drummer Chuck Behler. 1988's So Far, So Good…So What? peaked at number eighteen in England and number twenty-eight in America. The album featured the power hits "Set the World Afire," and "Mary Jane." Megadeth next set out on the Monsters of Rock world tour with Anthrax, KISS, and Iron Maiden. 1990's Rust in Peace saw a new lineup with drummer Nick Menza and guitarist Marty Friedman joining Mustaine and Ellefson. By the early 1990's, Megadeth felt that they did not have to compete with Metallica any more. Bassist Dave Ellefson said, "When Dave set out to start his band (Megadeth) after Metallica, there was a lot of pressure on him. It wasn't until the early nineties that we stepped out of that shadow. People had to get their mind around the idea that Metallica didn't have to fail in order for Megadeth to be successful. Once that happened, people embraced Megadeth and the competition stopped." #20

Before the grunge era would take over in the 1990's, thrash had one more dramatic fling. The first Clash of the Titans tour in Europe would feature Megadeth with Slayer, Testament, and Suicidal Tendencies. Then in 1991, the tour continued in North America with Anthrax replacing Testament and the upstart Alice in Chains replacing Suicidal Tendencies. 1992's Countdown to Extinction and 1994's Youthanasia brought more success to Megadeth. Then 1997's Cryptic Writings peaked at number ten in America and its single "Trust," was nominated for Best Metal Performance at the 1998 Grammy's. Risk, released in 1999, and 2001's The World Needs a Hero, were commercial and critical failures when the band switched to a (unthinkable) softer approach. Megadeth vowed to return to their real sound. But before that could happen, Mustaine suffered some health issues and disbanded Megadeth. In 2003, Mustaine started working on what was to be his first solo album. A feud over royalties saw a parting of ways between Mustaine and Ellefson. Mustaine moved forward on his solo project by hiring session great drummer Vinnie Colaiuta and bassist Jimmie Lee Sloas. The project was put on hold when Mustaine agreed to remix Megadeth's entire back catalog of material on Capitol Records.

In 2004, Mustaine finished recording his solo tracks but it soon turned into the Megadeth release titled The System Has Failed. The album shot to number eighteen on the U.S. charts. After more tours, Megadeth used a new lineup of guitarist Glen Drover, bassist James LoMenzo, and drummer Shawn Drover to record 2007's United Abominations. Another lineup change for 2009's Endgame brought guitarist Chris Broderick to the band. In 2010, Megadeth took their place as one of the "big four of thrash metal" on a tour initiated by Metallica. 2011's Thirt3en went to number eleven in America and marked the return of Dave Ellefson to the band. Super Collider, released in 2013, rose to number six on the U.S. charts. After more lineup changes and health issues for Mustaine, Megadeth released Dystopia in 2016 with guitarist Kiko Loureiro, drummer Chris Adler, Mustaine, and Ellefson. Megadeth has sold over fifty million albums worldwide.

They were one of the founding fathers of thrash metal with their technical virtuosity and strong influence on the death metal subgenre.

Simultaneous with the early 1980's dominance of "the big four," thrash metal had exploded in popularity around the world. The leaders in German thrash metal worked their way up from the underground to achieve an international audience. The "big four of Teutonic" German thrash metal is **Sodom** (1981-present), **Kreator** (1982-present), **Destruction** (1982-present), and **Tankard** (1982-present). A small sampling of the world's other major thrash bands are: Canada's **Annihilator** (1984-present) and **Razor** (1983-1992) (1997-present), Japan's **Outrage** (1982-present), Spain's **Angelus Apatrida** (2000-present), Switzerland's **Coroner** (1983-1996) (2010-present), and England's **Venom** (1979-present with some inactive years), to name just a few.

In America the "big four" have had a lot of company on the thrash metal scene. A few of these bands are: **Overkill** (1980-present), **Testament** (1983-present), **Havok** (2004-present), **Death Angel** (1982-1991) (2001-present), **Toxic Holocaust** (1999-present), and **Exodus** (1979-present with some inactive years).

Pantera (1981-2003) was formed in 1981 by two brothers from Arlington, Texas, guitarist Darrell "Diamond" Abbott and drummer Vinnie Paul Abbott. At first they were just another glam metal band that wore spandex, teased their hair, and recorded albums that sounded some parts Kiss, Van Halen, and Motley Crue. The band was originally called Gemini and then Eternity before settling on Pantera The Abbott brothers added guitarist Terry Glaze, vocalist Donnie Hart, and bassist Tommy Bradford. Hart soon quit the band, leaving Glaze to sing lead vocals and Darrell to take over both lead and rhythm guitar responsibilities. Bradford also left and was replaced by bassist Rex Brown (aka Rex Rocker). Pantera established a local audience and was soon supporting fellow glam metal bands Dokken, Stryper, and Quiet Riot.

By early 1983, Pantera became tired of doing covers and began to write some originals. This led to their 1983 debut album Metal Magic that was produced by the Abbott's father, Jerry Abbott. They further keep it in the family by releasing Metal Magic on their own record label. Pantera followed with 1984's Projects in the Jungle and 1985's I Am the Night, still in a glam style. However, their sound was shifting towards a heavier direction and the heavy metal press was beginning to take notice.

The mid-1980's metal climate was changing with groundbreaking albums released by all of the "big four" metal bands (previously discussed). Pantera knew this was the direction they wished to pursue and that they needed a new singer. Glaze was out and after a search, ex-Razor White vocalist Phil Anselmo joined Pantera. The band embraced thrash metal and Darrell Abbott was becoming a real force through his strong work ethic and by copying guitar greats like Randy Rhoads. Soon, record executives like Atco Records president Derek Shulman were scouting the band. Pantera embraced a whole new image with 1988's Power Metal, a mix of thrash metal and hard rock. The band was rid of the commercial metal approach, now laser focused on honing their own thrash sound. Also gone were the spandex and big hair. At this time, Abbott auditioned for Megadeth and was offered the gig. The offer was rejected when Megadeth said no to Darrell's demand that he and his brother Vinnie were a package deal.

1990's Cowboys from Hell and 1992's Vulgar Display of Power introduced the hard and heavy Pantera

> "With Pantera, we lived through so many trend-of-the-day situations. When grunge was huge, we were still a heavy metal band; When hip-hop started getting incorporated into metal, we stuck to our guns and remained a heavy metal band, very purposefully."
>
> – Phil Anselmo

Rock Hard Fact

In 2010, a religious group from Tempe, Arizona, put on a play named "Lamb of God" and then wondered why so many confused looking heavy metal fans turned up for the first show.

> "What I couldn't say verbally I was able to express physically through the guitar."
>
> – Dave Mustaine from Megadeth

to a new fan based impressed with songs like "A New Level" and "Walk." Pantera catapulted to a new level of fame with a world tour. They also showed off the growing legend of their guitar hero, "Dimebag" Darrell.

"Primal Concrete Sledge"
by Pantera

"Primal Concrete Sledge" was the last song that Pantera wrote for their critically acclaimed Cowboys from Hell album. While recording the record, the band was in between takes of a song and Vinnie Paul came up with a fast, thrashy drumset feel and "Dimebag" added a crazy riff around the beat. Anselmo started scribbling down some lyrics and they had the song in no time. This track represented the sound of the band discovering themselves and setting the stage for their musical development going forward. Pantera bassist Rex Brown recalled their studio approach when he said, "Me and Dime would sit there with Terry (their producer) and do what we'd call 'the microscope.' We'd turn everything else off on the tracks except for me (the bass part) and him (the guitar part) and a kick and a snare. That's the way we'd make sure every guitar and bass note was picked the way it should be. That's how we got that real tight sound." #21

"Primal Concrete Sledge" had a raw, relentless energy that would define Pantera's approach just when many other metal bands were going in a more commercial direction. It's fitting that this was the last tune written for Cowboys From Hell as Pantera would keep moving in a heavier direction. Rex's Brown's basslines were often so in sync with Dime's guitar parts that at times, the bass seemed to disappear. This would make the guitar seem like it was sounding in a lower frequency. With this kind of laser precision, Pantera was becoming a well-oiled machine.

In 1994, Pantera released Far Beyond Driven and in 1996 The Great Southern Trendkill. Far Beyond Driven was a pleasant surprise for the band when it went to number one on the American charts. However, Anselmo was having some personal issues and was distancing himself from the band. 2000's Reinventing the Steel debuted at number four in the U.S., but it would prove to be their last album. Anselmo and the Abbott brothers were not speaking and the band called it quits in 2003. Darrell and Vinnie formed a new band, Damageplan, with vocalist Pat Lachman and bassist Bob Zilla.

Tragedy struck in December 2004 when Damageplan was performing in Columbus, Ohio and a mentally disturbed fan shot and killed Darrell Abbott onstage (three others were also murdered). The metal community was *devastated*. Currently, Phil Anselmo and Vinnie Paul Abbott remain permanently estranged, with no hope of a Pantera reunion. The legacy of Pantera is that of pioneers of American heavy metal and their influence on Korn, Limp Bizkit, Slipknot, and many others can not be overstated. Eddie Van Halen, in an act of great respect, placed his rare Charvel electric guitar (aka the "Bumblebee") in "Dimebag" Darrell Abbott's casket at his funeral.

Hybrid metal is a term utilized sometimes to define and clarify the almost ridiculous amount of metal subgenres that kept popping up. We will address some the most significant subgenres that had the most impact on the ever-evolving metal landscape. The first wave of **black metal** (aka satanic metal) was an extreme subgenre of heavy metal that referred to bands from the 1980's that featured lyrics focused on satanic themes and the occult. Other style traits included shrieking vocals and fast tempos. Artists often dressed in corpse paint. During the early 1980's, some thrash and death metal bands set the stage for black metal. The first wave of black metal bands expanded this subgenre internationally and included; **Venom** (1979-present with some inactive years), **Hellhammer** (1981-1984) who disbanded and re-formed as **Celtic Frost** (1984-1993) (2001-2008), **Bathory** (1983-2004), **Sepultura** (1984-present), and **Vektor** (2002-present).

The extreme metal subgenre of **death metal** emerged in the mid-1980's from thrash and black metal influences. Bands such as Venom, Kreator, and Celtic Frost were important early influences on death metal. The early pioneers of the subgenre were the bands **Death** (1983-2001), **Possessed** (1983-present with some inactive periods), **Obituary** (1984-1997) (2003-present), **Autopsy** (1987-1995) (2008-present), and **Morbid Angel** (1984-present). Death metal lyric themes can involve occultism, mysticism, nature, mythology, even slasher film-stylized violence. The lyrics may describe extreme acts of torture, mutilation, rape, and necrophilia. The music utilizes low-tuned guitars, distortion, vocal screams and growls, and powerful double bass and blast beat drumset feels. More bands gained popularity in the 1990's, especially in Norway, when a second wave of death metal appeared with **Mayhem** (1984-1993), **Darkthrone** (1986-present), **Burzum** (1991-1999) (2009-present), and **Gorgoroth** (1999-present).

Crossover thrash is a subgenre of both punk and heavy metal. It evolved when both styles began to borrow musical and non-musical elements from each other. (This subgenre will be covered in chapter fourteen on punk rock.)

Another popular subgenre of extreme metal is **metalcore**. Metalcore evolved around 1993 through the 2000's and combined elements of hardcore punk, thrash, and death metal. Metalcore utilizes slower parts of songs (aka breakdowns) and generally revisits the heavy groove of 1990's metal hardcore. Metalcore also utilizes more non-aggressive vocals. A few of the prominent metalcore bands include; **Shadows Fall** (1995-present), **Unearth** (1998-present), **Bleeding Through** (1999-2014), **Avenged Sevenfold** (1999-present), **Killswitch Engage** (1999-present), **Trivium** (1999-present), **As I Lay Dying** (2000-2014) and **Lamb of God.**

Lamb of God (1994-present) was formed in Richmond, Virginia by vocalist Randy Blythe, bassist John Campbell, guitarists Willie Adler and Mark Morton, and drummer Chris Adler. Many of Lamb of God's fans see them as a groove metal band with some of the musical qualities of thrash metal but often playing tempos at moderate speeds. Lamb of God achieves a balance by combining post-Pantera metal with an old school ability to construct quality metal guitar riffs. Their metalcore sound gained more popularity from 2008 to 2010, when they toured as part of Metallica's World Magnetic Tour. To date they have released eight studio albums, one live album, and three DVD's.

An associated subgenre of metalcore is the hybrid metal subgenre of **deathcore**. It combines elements of death metal and metalcore and to some extent hardcore punk. It utilizes drumset blast beats (extremely fast eighth notes or sixteenth note patterns played on unison bass drum, snare drum and ride cymbal or hi-hat) and metalcore breakdowns. There are hundreds of deathcore bands and the style is particularly popular in Southern California and other parts of the Southwestern Unites States. Some notable deathcore bands are **Suicide Silence** (2002-present), **Whitechapel** (2006-present), **Chelsea**

Grin (2007-present), **Thy Art is Murder** (2006-present), and **Carnifex** (2005-present).

Another metal subgenre is **grindcore**, which gained popularity in the early to mid-1980's. Grindcore fuses hardcore punk with extreme metal, industrial, and noise rock. Its sound comes from overdriven bass, very fast tempos, blast beats, distorted and down-tunes guitars, and high-pitched or growling vocals. Two prominent grindcore bands active on the scene are the English band **Napalm Death** (1981-present), and **The Locust** (1994-present) from San Diego, California. Both create grindcore with the elements of hardcore punk and noise rock.

Industrial metal is yet another subgenre of metal. The word industrial can be utilized to envision the lyrics and music to represent the grind of an automotive factory, the noise of a sawmill, or even the dirty environment of an underground coalmine. The music would eventually evolve into industrial dance music. Industrial became more structured and when technology advanced, artists added samples, loops, and DJ techniques to the music. Industrial music, and its associated artists, is covered in chapter seventeen. **Nu metal** is a form of alternative metal that merges elements of metal with grunge, hip-hop and rap, alternative rock, and funk. A new process began when bands became inspired by collaborations between Aerosmith and Run-DMC with "Walk This Way" and Anthrax and Public Enemy with "Bring the Noise." It would be only a matter of time when bands like Korn, The Deftones, and Limp Bizkit would emerge to combine metal with other styles. The nu metal style is explored in chapter seventeen.

Progressive Metal Bands

Another of the never-ending subgenres of heavy metal is **progressive metal**, a fusion of metal characteristics with the complexity and (sometimes) influence of European classical music. Progressive rock (defined in detail in chapter thirteen) brought complex rhythmic concepts and odd times to the heavy metal genre. Keyboard and synthesizer sounds, plus other cutting edge music technology combined with the speed and power of heavy metal to inspire a new wave of bands in the 1980's. They included; **King's X** (1979-present), who are an American alternative/progressive metal band that drew from soul and funk; **Queensryche** (1981-present), an important and prolific progressive metal band from Bellevue, Washington; and **Flotsam and Jetsam** (1981-present), an American progressive metal band from Phoenix, Arizona. **Coroner** (1983-1996) (2010-present) is a popular Swiss thrash metal band that re-formed in 2010. They combined elements of progressive rock, jazz, classical, avant-garde, and industrial metal. They have been referred to as "the Rush of thrash metal." Still another important progressive metal band was **Opeth** (1989-present), a Swedish death metal band that mixed a myriad of styles including; progressive, folk, blues, classical, and jazz. Other significant metal bands with progressive elements are **Dream Theater** (see chapter thirteen), **Fates Warning** (1982-present), **Animals as Leaders** (2007-present), and **Meshuggah**.

Meshuggah (1987-present) was formed in the city of Umea, Sweden. Known for their extremely complex use of polyrhythms and polymeters combined with downtuned eight-string guitars, Meshuggah has forged a unique sound and style. The band came to international prominence with their second release, Destroy Erase Improve in 1995. This album presented a fusion of death and thrash metal combined with progressive and jazz-fusion elements. Meshuggah has released eight studio albums and eight music videos. Their most successful album to date was 2012's Koloss, reaching number seventeen on the American charts. Meshuggah is a growing force that blends equal parts of extreme, progressive, and even avant-garde metal subgenres. The Meshuggah current lineup is vocalist Jens Kidman, guitarist Fredrik Thordendal, guitarist Marten Hagstrom, bassist Dick Lovgren, and drummer Tomas Haake.

Heavy metal has always been rooted in nonconformity, musical intensity, and finding ways to escape. The many subgenres have consistently mutated over the past fifty plus years and metal has proved to be perhaps the most international of any rock music genre (like soccer is to the sporting world). Metal has sustained and continues to grow in popularity in Europe, Asia, South America, and virtually every continent. All over the world, there are metal fans from every ethnic group and social class imaginable. Soldiers often rely on the aggression of heavy metal to get them through life and death threatening situations. Metal has proven to help people combat depression, and overcome all types of adversity. It can be the soundtrack for rebellion (just like punk music), especially teens that feel disenfranchised and alienated from society. The increase in metal subgenres may create some confusion at times but it does serve to keep the music growing and morphing to fit the needs of its fans and musicians. The premature death of heavy metal and hard rock (covered later in this chapter) has been announced many times over the past forty years. Some thought that 1970's punk, 1980's new wave, or 1990's grunge would be the demise of metal. When other rock styles diminished in popularity, heavy metal hung in there. It gained strength from many fans and musicians that were dissatisfied with the lack of passion and musical substance in popular music. Until the human condition eradicates anger, angst, disenfranchisement, and depression, there will always be a place for heavy metal in its ever-evolving forms.

Discussion Question

After studying the many different subgenres of heavy metal, is each subgenre still heavy metal? What, if any, musical elements are in common between metal bands across the many subgenres of metal? Be specific with your answer and provide examples.

Hard Rock

As described in the chapter introduction, the term hard rock is often used interchangeably with heavy metal. Some of the following bands demonstrate metal qualities to various degrees but many were blues-based and void of the lyrical themes found in many heavy metal songs. Like many metal bands, hard rock bands frequently build their compositions around guitar riffs and power chords. Over a dozen of the most prominent hard rock bands are featured in this section.

Vanilla Fudge (1967-present with some inactive years) evolved from a band called The Pigeons that featured vocalist/keyboardist Mark Stein, bassist/vocalist

---

Rock Hard Fact

Swedish progressive metal band Meshuggah derived their name from the Yiddish word for "crazy."

Tim Bogert, guitarist Vince Martell, and drummer Carmine Appice. They changed their name to Vanilla Fudge when they were signed to Atlantic Records in 1967. Their 1967 debut album Vanilla Fudge would be their only top ten recording (it reached number six in America). But their nine studio albums, spanning a fifty-year career, made them one of the most enduring bands in rock history. Vanilla Fudge's most successful song was a cover of the Supremes "You Keep Me Hangin' On." Vanilla Fudge was a significant bridge between the psychedelic rock movement and hard rock.

Deep Purple (1968-1976) (1984-present) began as a progressive rock band with skillful musicianship and the ability to rock with intensity. The band was founded by guitarist Ritchie Blackmore, keyboardist Jon Lord, bassist Nick Simper, vocalist Rod Evans, and drummer Ian Pace. The early years for Deep Purple revealed a blend of Blackmore's psychedelic blues riffs and Lord's classically derived keyboard ideas. Their 1968 Shades of Deep Purple went to number twenty-four in the U.S. and produced a hit with the cover of Joe South's "Hush." Also in 1968, Deep Purple released The Book of Taliesyn which was less successful. 1969's Deep Purple contained mostly psychedelic and progressive rock originals but with a harder edge than their earlier work. Blackmore was growing as a songwriter but there were conflicts with Jon Lord's desire to integrate more classical influences into their approach.

Deep Purple replaced Evans and Simper to embrace a much harder rock sound. In addition, the band made a serious songwriting upgrade by bringing in vocalist Ian Gillan and bassist Roger Glover. Gillan said, "we spent a long time learning the craft of songwriting, Roger Glover and I, for a few years before we joined Deep Purple. You learn about the percussive value of words, and you learn about rhyme and meter. You learn that you can't transform a poem into a song lyric, mostly because the spoken shape of words is different than the sung shape of words." #22 Also at this time, keyboardist Jon Lord wrote a **rock concerto** (a concerto is a composition for orchestra and soloist). Deep Purple released this composition on the album Concerto for Group and Orchestra. The band performed it with the Royal Philharmonic Orchestra at London's Royal Albert Hall. Despite great critical acclaim for this change of direction, Deep Purple directed their efforts to the metal sounding Deep Purple in Rock, released in 1970. The album peaked at number four in England and featured the songs "Child in Time" and "Speed King." They focused on producing singles and found success with "Black Night" and "Strange Kind of Woman," both reaching the top ten in England. The Deep Purple heavy sound was complete with the classic lineup of Blackmore's metal riffs, Gillan's shrieking vocals, and the powerful rhythmic support of Pace, Glover, and Lord.

1991's Fireball followed and then 1972's Machine Head, which became a major influence in the development of heavy metal. It was Deep Purple's most successful album reaching number one in Britain and number seven in America. Two of the hits on Machine Head, "Highway Star," and "Smoke on the Water," defined the Deep Purple sound.

"Smoke on the Water"
by Deep Purple

"Smoke on the Water' contained one of the most recognizable guitar riffs in rock history. The song went to number four on the U.S. charts and number twenty-one in England. The simple riff, created by guitarist Richie Blackmore, was a four-note theme derived from a minor blues scale that was harmonized in parallel fourths. Jon Lord doubled this guitar part on a Hammond C3 organ that he ran through a Marshall amplifier with distortion.

Deep Purple was in Montreux, Switzerland in 1971 to record tracks for what would become their album Machine Head. They had rented a mobile recording unit from The Rolling Stones (referred to as the "Rolling Truck Stones thing' and "a mobile" in the songs lyrics). On the night before Deep Purple was scheduled to record, a Frank Zappa and The Mothers of Invention concert was held at the nearby Montreux casino. Deep Purple was to rent the casino's theatre the next day. During the Zappa concert, a fan in the audience fired a flare gun at the ceiling, resulting in a massive fire that burnt down the entire casino complex. The song title came to bassist Roger Glover in a dream he had about the incident. The smoke from the huge fire that spread over Lake Geneva was the inspiration for this classic rock song.

Deep Purple released the live double album Made in Japan in 1972. It became one of rock's highest selling live concert recordings. 1973's Who Do We Think We Are and its hit "Woman from Tokyo," made Deep Purple the largest grossing band of 1973. However, constant touring and internal tension over the band's future direction prompted Roger Glover and Ian Gillan to quit. They were replaced by vocalist David Coverdale and bassist Glenn Hughes. In 1974, Deep Purple recorded Burn and Stormbringer, resulting in continued success. But in 1975, Richie Blackmore left to form the band Rainbow. Vocalist Tommy Bolin replaced Blackmore, but 1975's Come Taste the Band would be the end of Deep Purple. Tommy Bolin died shortly after. Coverdale and Lord formed the band Whitesnake and later they were joined by Ian Paice. After a failed attempt to re-form Deep Purple, Gillan briefly played in Black Sabbath.

What became known as the "Mark II" lineup, Deep Purple re-formed in 1984 with Blackmore, Paice, Lord, Glover, and Gillan to record Perfect Strangers. 1987's The House of Blue Light followed but more internal struggles saw Gillan quit again. He was replaced by vocalist Joe Lynn Turner for their 1990's Slaves and Masters album. Gillan returned for 1993's The Battle Rages On… album. Blackmore again quit, this time during a tour. This prompted the band to bring in guitar virtuoso Joe Satriani to finish the concert series. Satriani could not commit to the band's future plans and another virtuoso, ex-Dixie Dregs guitarist Steve Morse, joined the band in time to record 1996's Perpendicular. This lineup of Gillian, Lord, Glover, Paice, and Morse released a live double album in 1997 and the studio recording Abandon in 1998.

The final lineup change occurred when Lord left in 2002 to pursue his longtime classical direction. Ex-Whitesnake keyboardist Don Airey joined Deep Purple for 2003's Bananas and 2005's Rapture of the Deep. They continued in a progressive hard rock direction with 2013's Now What?! and 2016's Infinite. Deep Purple, after many lineup changes and musical direction shifts, has emerged as one of Britain's great contributors to hard rock and heavy metal. Deep Purple was inducted into the Rock and Roll Hall of Fame in 2016.

Alice Cooper (1968-1974 the band) (1974-present solo artist) developed from a band titled Nazz, formed by vocalist Vincent Furnier in Phoenix, Arizona in 1968. Nazz featured guitarists Glen Buxton and Michael Bruce, bassist Dennis Dunaway, and drummer Neal Smith. Furnier decided to change the name of the band to Alice

---

> "When The Beatles walked into a room, everybody wanted to be near them. I always said, 'When Alice Cooper walks into a room, I want everyone to take a step backwards'"
>
> – Alice Cooper

Chapter Ten: Heavy Metal and Hard Rock

Cooper after using a Ouija board (to communicate with a seventeenth-century witch named Alice Cooper). Furnier would go on to legally change his own name to Alice Cooper in 1974. Early on, the band conceived of a highly theatrical stage show with unconventional routines, which included a fake onstage guillotine and electric chair executions, plus a live snake around Furnier's neck while he sang. Alice Cooper moved to Los Angeles and was signed to Frank Zappa's Straight Records label. Their 1969 Pretties for You and 1970's Easy Action were commercial failures.

With the help of Canadian producer Bob Ezrin, 1971's Love it to Death found success with the hits "I'm Eighteen" and "The Ballad of Dwight Fry." Another 1971 release, Killer reached number twenty-one on the U.S. charts and featured the band's teen-targeted lyrics of rebellion. 1972's School's Out brought more success peaking at number two in America. The single "School's Out" became Alice Cooper's most identifiable anthem.

"School's Out"
by Alice Cooper, Glen Buxton, Dennis Dunaway, and Neal Smith

"School's Out" was Alice Cooper's first major hit single, peaking at number seven on the U.S. charts and number one on the British charts. It's popularity gained respect for the band proving they were more than a novelty theatrical act. A few radio stations banned the song from their playlists when they feared that it gave students a green light to rebel against education. Parents, school principals, and teachers also fought to ban the song when they worried it would negatively influence students.

Alice Cooper (Vincent Furnier) had often said that he was inspired to write "School's Out" when he realized that the last three minutes of the last day of the school year was one of the greatest moments many students ever felt. The goal was to catch the feeling of that *moment* in a song. Cooper has stated that another source of inspiration for the tune was a warning often used in the Bowery Boys movies where one of the characters proclaimed to another, 'School is out,' meaning to "wise up." The album cover's design would ensure even more controversy. The album cover opened like a school desk and contained a pair of paper panties. The lyrics implied that not only was it the end of the school year, but the school itself had been blown up. The song ended with a school bell sound that faded out. "School's Out" has been utilized in numerous movies and TV shows and has been covered by many artists.

Alice Cooper enjoyed continued success with 1973's Million Dollar Babies. It topped the charts in the U.S. and England. But the group was beginning to fall apart due to drug and alcohol issues. Another 1973 release, Muscle of Love, would be the band's last record before Furnier would dissolve the band after a final tour of Brazil in 1974.

It was at this time that Vincent Furnier ventured out as a solo artist (and legally changed his name to Alice Cooper to avoid legal complications over ownership of the group name). He then released Welcome to My Nightmare in 1975, which sold three and a half million copies worldwide. Cooper borrowed some of his stage theatrics from horror movies and his popularity soured when he was featured in a 1975 TV special, *Alice Cooper-The Nightmare*. While Alice Cooper became a viable solo artist, he was also struggling with alcohol and sought treatment in a rehabilitation facility.

Cooper continued to release albums from 1977 to 1991. While he was absent from the recording studio in the early 1990's, he toured extensively throughout the later 1990's. From 2000 to 2005, Alice Cooper recorded a steady stream of studio albums. His most current recording was 2017's Paranormal. By overcoming his alcohol issues, Alice Cooper has become an inspiration to (and has counseled) other rock musicians with addiction problems. In 2017, the Alice Cooper band lineup included; guitarists Ryan Roxie, Tommy Henriksen, and Nita Strauss, bassist Chuck Garric, and drummer Glen Sobel. Alice Cooper was the originator of *shock rock* and had a profound influence on later metal bands around the world. The original Alice Cooper band and the solo career of Alice Cooper has yielded a prolific output of over twenty-five studio albums. Alice Cooper (the original group and Furnier) were inducted into the Rock and Roll Hall of Fame in 2011.

Mountain ((1969-2010 with some inactive years) was formed in Long Island, New York by guitarist/vocalist Leslie West, bassist/vocalist/producer Felix Pappalardi, keyboardist Steve Knight, and drummer N.D. Smart. Mountain was highly regarded among prominent musicians, especially by their 1969 performance at the Woodstock festival. Soon after the festival, drummer Corky Laing replaced Smart on drumset. Mountain was influential in the development of hard rock and heavy metal in the 1970's. Pappalardi had collaborated with Cream and was experienced in studio production, which proved to be a key component in the quality of Mountain's studio sound and output. Mountain's 1970 debut album, Climbing!, peaked at number seventeen on the American charts. It produced their best-known tune "Mississippi Queen."

"Mississippi Queen"
by Leslie West, Corky Laing, Felix Pappalardi, and David Rea

"Mississippi Queen" put Mountain on the map in America. Guitarist Leslie West had developed a few guitar ideas that he combined with drummer Corky Laing's lyrics. Laing, a big fan of The Band, was inspired by Levon Helm's drumset feel on their tune "Cripple Creek," and adopted it for "Mississippi Queen." Leslie West had worked out the main riff and then focused on fitting the lyrics over his guitar part. At the recording session for "Mississippi Queen," the incessant cowbell part was initially used to count off the tune. But Pappalardi liked the feel that the cowbell provided and decided to include it throughout the whole song.

The song's lyrics were about a seductive woman who showed the singer about the ways of love. The Mississippi city of Vicksburg was mentioned in the song because Laing asked David Rea (a friend of the band) if he knew of any towns in the state. Rea responded with Vicksburg, a small city on the Mississippi River, known as the site of a famous Civil War battle in 1863.

Tragically, Felix Pappalardi was shot and killed by his wife Gail Pappalardi in 1983. Two years later, West and Laing regrouped with bassist Mark Clarke and recorded 1985's Go For Your Life before dissolving the band. Eleven years later, Mountain again regrouped and added guitarist Eddie Black for 1996's Man's World. Mountain would go on to make two more studio recordings culminating in 2007's Masters of War. It consisted entirely of twelve Bob Dylan covers and a guest appearance by Ozzy Osbourne. Mountain's sound is reminiscent

---

> "We knew we had to move away from the New York Dolls thing. So we bought some black T-shirts and some glittery pants that circus performers wore. Then we went down to the West Village (NYC)... and bought leather items at a hardcore sex shop...there was something about the studs and the leather that seemed right to us."
>
> – Paul Stanley from Kiss

of Cream and they have had a direct impact on many prominent musicians including guitarists John McLaughlin and Martin Barr (of Jethro Tull fame).

Aerosmith (1970-present) began in Boston when vocalist/frontman Steven Tyler met guitarist Joe Perry, bassist Tom Hamilton, and drummer David Scott. Soon, Scott was replaced by drummer Joey Kramer (who also named the band). Aerosmith added a second guitarist, Ray Tabano, but he was soon replaced by guitarist Brad Whitford and by 1971, their lineup was set. Their self-titled 1973 debut Aerosmith was met with little fanfare, but did yield the classic rock power ballad "Dream On." This song worked its way onto the U.S. charts at number fifty-nine. The album Aerosmith also established their signature no-nonsense rock sound mixed with a strong blues influence. 1974's Get Your Wings fared a little better by reaching seventy-four on the American charts and featured the blues-rock classic "Train Kept A-Rollin." Aerosmith was inspired to play this song after hearing The Yardbirds' powerful version. Get Your Wings also showed Aerosmith's musical sophistication by adding tenor saxophonist Michael Brecker and trumpeter Randy Brecker on a few of the songs.

1975's Toys in the Attic brought the band into superstar status when it went to number eleven on the U.S. charts. The singles "Sweet Emotion" and "Walk This Way" were giant hits and the band was routinely compared to the hard edge and raw sexuality of The Rolling Stones and Led Zeppelin.

"Walk This Way"
by Steven Tyler and Joe Perry

"Walk This Way" began with a two-bar Joey Kramer drumset feel followed by a guitar riff by Joe Perry that has become one of the most famous in rock history. Perry claimed that he was inspired by the legendary New Orleans group The Meters (see chapter seventeen), and especially their classic funk tune "Cissy Strut." Perry created the iconic "Walk This Way" riff at a sound check. When Stephen Tyler first heard it, he immediately ran out to the microphone and sang some nonsense syllables just to get a feel for the song. Tyler wrote the lyrics that same night in his hotel room. Perry soon realized that Tyler's lyrics were very rhythmic and like a percussion instrument.

Ten years later in 1986, Stephen Tyler and Joe Perry collaborated on another version of "Walk This Way," when hip-hop group Run D.M.C. covered the tune on their album Raising Hell. Some of the Run D.M.C. members were not sold on collaborating with Tyler and Perry until their producer, Rick Rubin, convinced them to record with them. This version of "Walk This Way" became the first hip-hop song to break into the top ten on the Billboard Hot 100. It was credited with helping to introduce hip-hop to mainstream rock and pop music. This also marked a major comeback that served to revive the sagging (at the time) career of Aerosmith. On the Run D.M.C. cover version, a drum machine and turntable are added to reinforce the hip-hop vibe.

1976's Rocks was successful, yielding the hits "Back in the Saddle" and "Last Child." Rocks had a substantial influence on Gun's 'N' Roses, Metallica, and even Kurt Cobain of Nirvana. 1977's Draw the Line sold well and the band toured extensively but was suffering with drug issues. Although 1979's Night in the Ruts went to number fourteen in America, there was major turmoil in the band and Joe Perry quit about half way into recording the album. Shortly after he left, Perry formed his own band, The Joe Perry Project. Nights in the Ruts was completed with the help of guitarists Richie Supa and Jimmy Crespo. For 1982's Rock in a Hard Place, Aerosmith endured more chaos when guitarist Brad Whitford left the band and was replaced by guitarist Rick Dufay.

1985's Done with Mirrors marked the return of Perry and Whitford. This album was also the band's first recording on the Geffen label. 1986 saw the band reinvigorated with their collaboration with Run D.M.C. on "Walk This Way." 1987's Permanent Vacation (selling five million copies in the U.S.) and 1989's Pump returned Aerosmith to form and good health (now all band members were drug free). 1993's Get a Grip was the band's first album to debut at number one with the singles "Livin' on the Edge" and "Eat the Rich." Get a Grip also featured appearances by the Eagles Don Henley and Lenny Kravitz. Aerosmith went on to release Just Push Play in 2001. They returned to their rhythm and blues roots in 2004 with Honkin' on Bobo.

For the next few years, Aerosmith's relentless touring yielded the live Rockin the Joint, released in 2005. An unfinished album and health problems in the band left their future uncertain. Perry returned to the stage with The Joe Perry Project but assured everyone that he was not quitting Aerosmith again. But now Steven Tyler's future was unclear. In 2012, Aerosmith released the long awaited Music from Another Dimension (with Steven Tyler). Aerosmith has sold more records than any other American hard rock band, more than two-hundred million albums sold worldwide. They have inspired countless rock and metal bands with their signature blend of hard rocking riffs and ever present blues edge. In 1995, Tyler and Perry were asked by Jimmy Page to induct Led Zeppelin into the Rock and Roll Hall of Fame. Aerosmith was inducted into the Rock and Roll Hall of Fame in 2001.

Kiss (1972-present) became perhaps the greatest example of a corporate rock band. Their powerful and lucrative brand name sold officially sanctioned Kiss merchandise that included comic books, action figures, and even lunchboxes. Of course, they sold million of records and concert tickets too. Kiss formed after two New York natives, vocalist/guitarist Paul Stanley and vocalist/bassist Gene Simmons, played in a band called Wicked Lester. After their demo tape was rejected by Epic Records, Simmons and Stanley decided that they needed a flashier stage presentation and a new sound. They fired the other Wicked Lester band members and recruited drummer Peter Criss and guitarist/vocalist Ace Frehley and officially named the band Kiss. Their direction began to take shape after auditioning guitarist Ace Frehley. Simmons recalled, "Let's let this guy try out and get him out of here…We weren't expecting much. But we started playing and hit the solo part (of the tune 'Deuce')…and Ace blew us away. We could not believe it. We knew that was the sound of Kiss." #23

Kiss was drawn to makeup wearing glam artists like David Bowie and The New York Dolls. However, they quickly came to the conclusion that the androgynous glam look wasn't for them. They adapted an original look of black and white kabuki-style designs that masked each Kiss member as a separate character. Simmons was a fire-breathing, blood drinking *demon*; Stanley was a *starchild*; Criss was a *cat*; and Frehley was a *spaceman*. After more unsuccessful efforts to secure a record deal, Kiss somehow got studio master Eddie Kramer to produce a new demo and they were signed by Casablanca Records.

> **Rock Hard Fact**
>
> AC/DC got their name after Malcolm and Angus Young's sister, Margaret, spotted the electricity-related acronym for alternating current/direct current on her sewing machine.

Chapter Ten: Heavy Metal and Hard Rock

Their 1974 debut album Kiss was followed by Hotter Than Hell that same year. Both of these albums and 1975's Dressed to Kill were received with little fanfare. However, Kiss's outlandish stage show solidified their reputation as a strong opening act. Kiss knew that they were capable of headlining status. Their big break happened with a live album, 1975's Alive!. By the mid-1970's, Kiss was one of America's most popular rock bands. Alive! was a double album that reached number nine on the U.S. charts and spawned the hit "Rock and Roll All Nite."

"Rock and Roll All Nite"
by Paul Stanley and Gene Simoons

"Rock and Roll All Nite" would become a staple in Kiss's live performances and often served as their closing song. It reached number twelve on the American charts. The band was able to meet the challenge to come up with an anthem that provided a rallying cry for their fans. Stanley and Simmons were inspired by the Slade song "Cum on Feel the Noize." Musically, Paul Stanley wrote the chorus while Gene Simmons wrote the verses. Simmons borrowed parts of a song that he (himself) had previously written titled "Drive Me Wild." Stanley added the lyric "I want to rock and roll all night, and party every day."

Kiss performed "Rock and Roll All Night" at the half-time show of the Super Bowl in 1999 and had dancers dressed like the band. They also shot a video of the song with the cast members of *That '70's Show*. In addition, Kiss utilized "Rock and Roll All Night" for many TV shows in pop culture such as *Family Guy*, *The Fairly Odd Parents*, and the movie *Dazed and Confused*.

Kiss released a steady stream of successful albums throughout the rest of the 1970's. By 1978, they were at the peak of their popularity. They simultaneously released four solo albums by their individual members in 1978. Kiss's 1980 Unmasked album would be the last for drummer Peter Criss (until the band reunited in 1996). He was replaced by drummer Eric Carr after extensive auditions. Regarding his makeup, Carr settled on the appearance of a *fox*. Kiss made six studio recordings throughout the rest of the 1980's. In 1985, Ace Frehley would also quit the band (he would return in 1996). Guitarists Vinnie Vincent, Mark St. John, and Bruce Kulick would record or tour with the band. In 1991, drummer Eric Carr sadly died from cancer. Kiss continued with drummer Eric Singer in his place.

1992's Revenge and 1993's live album, Alive II, did well on the charts. But Kiss would struggle to remain a leading act when they had to compete with many of the new grunge era bands (that they had often inspired). In 1995, Stanley and Simmons got the classic band back together for a 1995 MTV *Unplugged* special. 1998's Psycho Circus was a success and peaked on the America charts at number three. Peter Criss once again quit and once again Eric Singer assumed the drumset chair. An orchestra-based recording, Kiss Symphony: Alive IV, was released in 2003. Peter Criss came back to Kiss, only to see Ace Frehley leave again. Kiss added guitarist Tommy Thayer for 2009's Sonic Boom. It went to number two on the U.S. charts.

Kiss went on to release Monster in 2012. The band toured in 2016 and remains active today. Kiss, with their commercial mix of anthem hard rock and shock rock costumes, was able to carve their own successful niche in rock history. Kiss's sound provided the groundwork for the arena rock and pop-oriented metal that dominated the late 1980's. Kiss was inducted into the Rock and Roll Hall of Fame in 2014.

AC/DC (1973-present) is an internationally successful Australian band that was sometimes referred to as a heavy metal group. They called themselves simply a rock 'n' roll band. Formed by two brothers, guitarists Malcolm and Angus Young, their early days were filled with a shifting lineup. They eventually added dynamic singer Ronald "Bon" Scott, drummer Phil Rudd, and bassist Mark Evans to record their debut album High Voltage (released in Australia only) in 1975. AC/DC became very popular at home in Australia and Angus Young raised the band's profile with his formidable guitar skills and unique school uniform stage look (he still wears it to this day). The AC/DC persona was good time rock 'n' roll, crunchy blues based riffs, Bon Scott's powerful growls, and a thunderous rhythm section. Their second album, 1975's T.N.T. (released in Australia and New Zealand) contained what would become one of rock's most famous anthems, "It's a Long Way to the Top."

In 1976, AC/DC was signed to Atlantic Records prompting their eventual rise to international fame. 1976's High Voltage was the second time they used the same album title but this time it was issued internationally. It contained tracks from the earlier High Voltage and T.N.T. albums. Another 1976 recording, Dirty Deeds Done Cheap, (first released in Australia and Europe) was later released in America and contributed to their popularity. It peaked at number three on the charts. This album contained the hits "Ride On," "Problem Child," and the title track. 1977's Let There Be Rock fared better in Britain, reaching number seventeen but received a lethargic reception in the U.S. It did however, contain the hit "Let There Be Rock." Bassist Mark Evans was fired at the end of 1977 and was replaced by Cliff Williams. 1978's Powerage was less successful than previous recordings but was praised by many musicians and critics.

In 1979, AC/DC made the great decision to hire producer Mutt Lange to revamp their sound. He refined their hard edge while retaining the energy of their live sound. 1980's Highway to Hell was AC/DC's breakthrough. The album shot to number seventeen in America and is considered a classic today. It would prove to be Bon Scott's last recording. Scott tragically died while working on AC/DC's album Back in Black. He lost his life the same way John Bohnam did, from pulmonary aspiration. AC/DC briefly contemplated retiring but was encouraged by Bon Scott's parents to continue. Various singers were considered before they chose vocalist Brian Johnson. Bon Scott had previously heard Johnson sing and thought he sang well in the style of Bon's favorite singer, Little Richard. 1980's Back in Black turned the band into superstars. It went straight to number one in England and number four in America.

Groundbreaking album Back in Black
by AC/DC

Back in Black is remarkable in the sense that most bands would have folded after loosing a dynamic and charismatic frontman of the caliber of Bon Scott. Brian Johnson effectively stepped in but did not try to replace or replicate the style of Scott. He provided a distinctive voice and his love of the blues and soul music was evident from his exciting performance style. He made an immediate contribution as a composer and lyricist. Again Mutt Lange was in charge of production and he demanded a high level of musicianship from the band.

"The Piano is a universal instrument. If you start there, learn your theory and how to read, you can go on to any other instrument."

– Eddie Van Halen

Side one opened with "Hells Bells," followed by "Shoot to Thrill," "What Do You Do for Money Honey," "Given the Dog a Bone," and "Let Me Put My Love into You." AC/DC was growing as songwriters, especially with the addition of Brian Johnson. Angus Young recalled, "At first, when you're young, a lot of temptation comes at you…There's that feeling of eternal youth going. That doesn't work for me. I think what's eternal is getting a good song. If you can span generations with that song, it becomes timeless." #24

Side two opened with "Back in Black," then "You Shook Me All Night Long," "Have a Drink on Me," "Shake a Leg," and "Rock and Roll Ain't Noise Pollution." The lyrics for "You Shook Me All Night Long" were borrowed from the classic Willie Dixon blues "You Shook Me." The all black album cover tied into the album name and also revealed the band paying their respects to their late singer Bon Scott. Back in Black was an enormous success, selling more than fifty million copies worldwide. This made it the second highest selling album in music history, second only to Michael Jackson's sixty-five million selling Thriller.

"Back in Black"
by Angus Young, Malcolm Young, and Brian Johnson

The lyrics for "Back in Black" were a tribute to their late singer Bon Scott. AC/DC asked Brian Johnson when he first joined the band to write sometime that would celebrate Bon's life. He responded with the lyric "Nine lives. Cats eyes. Abusing every one of them and running wild." With all due respect to Aerosmith's "Walk This Way," and Queen's "We Will Rock You," "Back in Black" is *the* rock 'n' roll groove. Malcolm Young had been playing around with the legendary guitar riff for years in sound checks. That guitar riff, and the basic (and yet so effective) drumset groove, are the definition of a tight and clean rhythmic rock feel.

"Back in Black" has been covered by a diverse array of artists that included; Kid Rock, Carlos Santana, The Backstreet Boys, Muse, The Red Hot Chili Peppers, and more. The song has also been a favorite rallying cry for many sports teams that include the Atlanta Falcons and Appalachian State University football teams. It was also the first song that Kurt Cobain ever learned to play on guitar. The Beastie Boys were denied by AC/DC when they asked permission to sample part of the song. AC/DC responded by telling them that it wasn't personal, but they did not support the sampling of their music.

1981's For Those About to Rock We Salute You yielded the band's first number one placement on the American charts. However, mounting tension between drummer Phil Rudd and Malcolm Young resulted in Rudd's firing. He was replaced by Simon Wright. 1983's Flick of the Switch and 1985's Fly on the Wall were both uninspired and commercially unsuccessful by AC/DC standards. In 1988, the band returned to form with Blow Up Your Video when they reunited with their earlier production team of George Young (the older brother of Angus and Malcolm) and Harry Vanda.

AC/DC released two studio albums in the 1990's. 1990's The Razors Edge was a comeback album that featured the hit "Thunderstruck." 1995's Ballbreaker saw the return of drummer Phil Rudd and was produced by Rick Rubin. In the 2000's, the gap between album releases had widened but the band remained popular. 2000's Stiff Upper Lip went to number twelve in the U.S. and number one in many countries including Sweden, Germany, Austria, and Finland. 2010's Black Ice achieved more international successful, reaching number one in twenty-nine countries.

AC/DC released Rock or Bust in 2014. Malcolm Young retired from the band in 2014 due to health issues and Phil Rudd was replaced by drummer Chris Slade that same year. Guitarist Steve Young, nephew of Malcolm Young, joined the band in 2014. In 2016, Brian Johnson also retired due to hearing loss issues and AC/DC announced that Guns N' Roses frontman Axl Rose would join the band for a world tour. In 2016, Rose would join AC/DC full time. Bassist Cliff Williams retired in 2016 citing the retirement of so many of the core members.

AC/DC brought a primal rock energy with addictive riffs and witty lyrics that connected to a large audience while avoiding musical gimmicks. The rock community, historically centered in America and England, was strengthen when AC/DC represented Australia as international rock stars. AC/DC was inducted into the Rock and Roll Hall of Fame in 2013.

Van Halen (1974-present) came out of the gate making a profound impact on the international rock scene. They formed in 1974 and their self-titled debut album Van Halen was released in 1978. It was an immediate sensation climbing to number nineteen on the U.S. charts and eventually selling over ten million copies in America alone. The classic lineup for Van Halen was guitarist Eddie Van Halen, drummer Alex Van Halen, vocalist David Lee Roth, and bassist Michael Anthony. Eddie would raise the bar for guitar virtuosity and the band developed an exciting stage show. In 1978, Van Halen was stealing the show opening for a Black Sabbath that was a little past their prime. It would be the end of an era and a glimpse into the future of hard rock and heavy metal, especially the era of guitar shedders (see chapter seventeen on guitar slingers).

Eddie was changing the very face of rock guitar, evoking instrumental excitement not seen since Jimi Hendrix. Meanwhile, Roth commanded the stage with acrobatic leaps and an "in your face" interaction with the audience. Roth was charismatic, and his personality brought a sense of fun to the Van Halen stage show.

Groundbreaking album Van Halen
by Van Halen

Right from the beginning of their debut Van Halen, Eddie Van Halen became a game changer on electric guitar. He rejected the traditional blues-based riff building approach of so many of the 1960's and 1970's British guitarists. Instead, Eddie took the classical piano training that both he and brother Alex received as youths, and applied it to his groundbreaking guitar technique. Eddie's amazing approach was a combination of hammering (hitting and pulling strings), artificial harmonics, two-hand high-speed fretboard tapping techniques, and more. Eddie took this advanced approach and applied it to a screaming overdriven amplifier. His solos were rapid-fire flurries of notes produced with classical precision.

Side one opened with "Runnin' with the Devil," then "Eruption," "You Really Got Me," "Ain't Talkin' 'bout Love," and "I'm the One." The guitar solo "Eruption" served as a musical link between "Runnin' with the Devil" and the cover of the Kinks tune "You Really Got Me." Here, Eddie started with a short intro accompanied by Alex's drums, then applied his classical technique of two-handed tapping with a repeated classical harmonic cadence. Eddie's

---

Rock Hard Fact

Van Halen was one of the first bands to demand a contract rider, now standard practice in the music industry. In their rider they specified that a bowl of M&M's, with the brown M&M's removed from the bowl, be placed in their dressing room. This was done to ensure the full rider had been read and executed.

innovative techniques influenced countless rock guitarists.

Side two opened with "Jamie's Cryin'," "Atomic Punk," "Feel Your Love Tonight," "Little Dreamer," "Ice Cream Man," and "On Fire." The album was mostly recorded live with some guitar overdubs. Roth usually sang live in an isolation booth at the same time the full band recorded the track together. This allowed the band to capture their live sound that reflected their onstage energy. Sometime in late 1977, Van Halen filmed three lip-synced videos for the album at the bar Whisky A GoGo to capture the dazzle of their live show.

1979's Van Halen II had similar success, reaching number six in America, and yielded the hits "Beautiful Girls," and "Dance the Night Away." In between 1980's Women and Children First and 1981's Fair Warning, Van Halen built their audience with successful tours. However, onstage rivalry emerged between Eddie and Roth. 1982's Diver Down came next and as a side project, Eddie and Alex contributed to the film score for the movie *The Wild Life*. 1984's 1984 would be the pinnacle of Van Halen's commercial success selling more that sixteen million copies worldwide. The album yielded many hits including; "Jump," "I'll Wait," "Panama," and "Hot for Teacher." 1984 featured the use of synthesizers, something Eddie could easily handle from his classical piano background.

"Jump"
by Van Halen

Eddie wrote the arrangement for "Jump" a few years before the 1984 recording. Roth was not crazy about the (now famous) synth riff because he felt that it diverted the band's sound away from Eddie's signature guitar approach. Eventually, he came to like the song. Roth was inspired to write the lyrics when he watched footage a man undecided about whether or not to jump off a tall building. The production of "Jump" was another source of tension for the band when Eddie built his own studio. It was there that he recorded the instrumental parts of the track away from the influence of Roth and producer Ted Templeman. Later, Roth and Templeman finished "Jump" at Eddie's studio, adding the vocal parts.

The song still featured a guitar solo by Eddie that was overdubbed from multiple takes. "Jump" shot to number one in America and placed high on charts around the world. "Jump" has been used by the Chicago Cubs baseball team, the soccer team A.C.Milan, and the Canadian hockey team the Winnipeg Jets. Also, a music video of "Jump" was directed by David Lee Roth.

Never without controversy, David Lee Roth would soon leave the band. For 1986's 5150, Van Halen added ex-Montrose vocalist Sammy Hagar. The album was a huge hit and went to number one in the U.S., with the hits "Why Can't This Be Love," "Dreams," and "Love Walks In." The next three albums, 1988's OUB12, 1991's For Unlawful Carnal Knowledge, and 1995's Balance all went to number one in America. Although Van Halen was a wealthy band, the grunge era would cut into their popularity. Sammy Hagar left the band after disputes over a planned compilation album. David Lee Roth returned to the band which helped take the compilation album to number one. Roth soon left again and ex-Extreme vocalist Gary Cherone joined in time to make 1998's Van Halen III. The album reached number four in America but tours with Cherone were not well attended.

Van Halen would go on hiatus from 1999 to 2003 and Cherone would leave on good terms. In 2003, Hagar returned for a new compilation album and summer tour. Hagar would again leave and a second reunion with Roth occurred from 2006 to 2008. Also in 2006, longtime bassist Michael Anthony left the band and was replaced by Eddie's son, Wolfgang Van Halen. For the next few years, Van Halen was not the most stable of bands. However, in 2012 they released their twelfth studio album, A Different Kind of Truth. It peaked at number two in the U.S. and number six in England with Roth and now, three Van Halen's: Eddie, Alex, and Wolfgang, in the band. This proved that the Van Halen magic was alive, still recording, and touring. Van Halen was inducted into the Rock and Roll Hall of Fame in 2007.

Rainbow (1975-1984) (1994-1997) (2015-present) started when guitarist Ritchie Blackmore became dissatisfied with the musical direction of his then current band, Deep Purple. This decision meant walking away from sold out stadiums and touring by way of private jet. But Blackmore held to his convictions and recruited ex-Elf member's vocalist Ronnie James Dio, bassist Craig Gruber, drummer Gary Driscoll, and keyboardist Mickey Lee. After Rainbow's 1975 debut release Richie Blackmore's Rainbow, Blackmore fired the whole band except Dio. The new lineup for 1976's Rising was keyboardist Tony Carey, bassist Jimmy Bain, drummer Cozy Powell, Dio, and Blackmore. Rainbow's emerging musical style was partly based on Blackmore's background as a cellist that exposed him to classical harmony and counterpoint. In addition, Ronnie James Dio and Blackmore were both interested in Medieval themes. Dio could sing in the harder rock style that Blackmore had honed in Deep Purple but was also capable of singing lighter ballads. These musical elements established Rainbow's different and unique sound. 1978's Long Live Rock 'n' Roll was the band's third studio album and it achieved success, especially in Britain.

However, the next few years saw more lineup changes. Dio exited for Black Sabbath after Blackmore wanted to move in a more commercial direction. Ex-Marbles vocalist/guitarist Graham Bonnet and ex-Deep Purple bassist Roger Glover joined Rainbow for 1979's Down to Earth. It yielded the hit "Since You Been Gone." 1981's Difficult to Cure and 1982's Straight Between the Eyes introduced yet another singer, Joe Lynn Turner. Rainbow's commercial success continued. 1983's Bent Out of Shape contained the hit "Street of Dreams."

In 1984, Blackmore disbanded Rainbow and then joined a re-formed Deep Purple (see Deep Purple earlier in this chapter). The reunion with Purple lasted until 1990. In 1994, Richie Blackmore re-formed Rainbow with a new lineup and released Stranger in Us All. That prompted a world tour. However, Blackmore put Rainbow on hold again to turn his attention to his longtime **Renaissance** and **Medieval music** passion. In 1997, Blackmore and vocalist/multi-instrumentalist Candice Night formed a traditional folk-rock duo (still active today) to pursue Renaissance music styles. In 2015, Blackmore once again re-formed Rainbow. The band continues to tour under the name Richie Blackmore's Rainbow.

Joan Jett and The Runaways (1975-1979) were an American hard rock band that was active in the mid to late 1970's. The Runaways were formed in 1975 by drummer Sandy West and vocalist/guitarist Joan Jett. They soon added vocalist/bassist Micki Steele and lead guitarist Lita Ford (see metal section for Ford's solo career) and were signed to Mercury Records. Their 1976 debut album, The Runaways, did not chart well but did yield the hit "Cherry Bomb." Disagreements over the band's musical direction led to the band's demise in 1979. Soon after, Joan Jett formed her own record label called Blackheart Records (one of the first labels started by a female recording artist), after being rejected by over twenty other labels. Before forming The Blackhearts, Jett released a solo album Bad Reputation in 1980. It contained the hits "You Don't Own Me" (a cover of a Lesley Gore song) and "Bad Reputation."

Jett's second studio album, 1981's I Love Rock 'n' Roll, introduced **Joan Jett and The Blackhearts** (1979-present). This was the first time Jett featured her backing band of guitarist Ricky Byrd, bassist Gary Ryan, and drummer Lee Crystal. The single "I Love Rock 'n' Roll" (written by Alan Merrill and Jake Hooker) shot to number one in the U.S. and was a big hit worldwide. Joan Jett and The Blackhearts would go on to record ten more studio albums from 1983 to 2013. In 2014, Jett sang with the remaining members of Nirvana for their induction into the Rock and Roll Hall of Fame. In 2015, Joan Jett and The Blackhearts opened for The Who's fiftieth anniversary tour. Jett sings with a hard-edged delivery in a pure and simple rock 'n' roll style. Joan Jett and the Blackhearts were inducted into the Rock and Roll Hall of Fame in 2015.

Some other prominent rock artists have made lasting and significant contributions to the hard rock genre. **Ted Nugent** (1948-) (solo career 1975-present) is a hard-rocking guitarist from Redford, Michigan who has released ten solo albums and has sold over thirty million records. His signature tune was "Cat Scratch Fever," from the album of the same name. Nugent has long been a controversial figure with his political positions, pro-gun law stance, and opposition to animal rights. **The Cult** (1983-1995) (1999-2002) (2006-present) is a British hard rock band that blended post-punk goth rock styles mixed with some heavy metal influences. The Cult entered mainstream rock with their 1985 album Love that spawned the hit "She Sells Sanctuary." Two other important artists/bands are **Lenny Kravitz** (see chapter seventeen), and **Queens of the Stone Age**.

Queens of the Stone Age (1997-present) was formed by vocalist/guitarist Josh Homme who came from Kyuss, a band that played in the desert rock style (from California) of heavy guitar riffs coupled with catchy melodies and hooks. The band lineup included guitarist/keyboardist Troy Van Leeuwen, bassist/keyboardist Michael Shuman, keyboardist/guitarist Dean Fertita, and drummer Jon Theodore. The band released their self-titled Queens of the Stone Age in 1998. For 2000's Rated R album, the band added bassist Nick Oliveri. Foo Fighters frontman Dave Grohl provided the drumset parts for their 2002 release Songs for the Deaf that also added strings, horns, accordion, and a theremin. The album obtained critical and commercial success with the singles "Go with the Flow" and "No One Knows." Both songs received exposure on MTV. Queens of the Stone Age released four more studio albums from 2005 to 2017. The band has always been musically adventurous by expanding the instrumentation on their recordings. They have also utilized many guest musicians in the studio. Queens of the Stone Age has maintained a basic rock 'n' roll approach while moving their unique sound forward with the influence of electronic trance music elements. Josh Homme has described their sound as "robot rock."

Discussion Question

Most metal bands rock hard but some hard rock bands aren't very metal-like. Of the non-metal influenced hard rock bands, what musical qualities do they possess that define their sound? Be specific. Name and describe at least three of these hard rock bands.

"At its primitive core, the way metal makes us feel touches us at the most basic, animalistic level. It's different from any other kind of music because of the power and influence it possesses."

- Jon Wiederhorn and Katherine Turman, authors of Louder Than Hell.

Chapter Ten: Heavy Metal and Hard Rock

"When Van Halen started out, there was no path to fame. We just played what we liked. Even today it always comes down to the simplicity of rock and roll"

— Eddie Van Halen

Chapter Eleven:
Classic Rock

The very definition of the word classic means that something has withstood the test of time. **Classic rock** became a label for the radio format used by album-oriented rock (AOR) radio stations. This started in the early 1980's. The music itself emerged from the late 1960's to the late 1980's and early 1990's. Classic rock was often heard as a blend of hard rock, rock songs with catchy melodic hooks, and maybe a few "softer" metal-oriented songs, usually in an approximately three minute (or so) time frame. This also included songs by a few alternative and grunge styled bands. For many, The Beatles marked the beginning of the classic rock era. A variety of bands and solo artists eventually made their way onto classic rock radio playlists, suggesting that longevity played a part in inclusion into the classic rock label. Key questions in determining what was considered a classic rock song included: When was the song recorded? And was it a big hit when it came out? Of course, much older music was not necessarily considered to be classic rock; it simply fits the definition of being an oldie. Is classic rock strictly a genre of music? No, because many classic rock stations play music from dissimilar genres. Even the location of classic rock stations influences which artists receive airplay. For example, you will hear Pearl Jam on the West Coast of the United States played much more than on the East Coast.

Classic rock is a moving, fluid category where the legacy of a band determines if its music remains popular and survives to receive continued radio play. No one doubts that Led Zeppelin is a classic rock but bands like The Talking Heads (see chapter eight) or The Foo Fighters (see chapter sixteen) are constantly added to classic rock radio playlists. Even a grunge band such as Nirvana is considered by some to be a classic rock band, as the baby on the Nevermind album cover is at least an adult that is well into his late twenty's by now. When bands continue to stand the test of time, the number of artists who fall under the label of classic rock will continue to grow. Remember that classic rock usually includes artists that were making album-orientated music and not only producing "get rich quick" hit singles.

We divided classic rock into two chapters. This chapter will focus on classic rock bands that may or may not have a defined leader. The next chapter will focus on classic rock bands that are built on the strong presence of a singer/leader whose songs and musical direction are the central focus. Sometimes the line between the two is thin. Most classic rocks bands were formed before 1980 and a surprising amount of them are still active.

Rock Hard Fact

Classic rock evolved from album-oriented rock (AOR) radio stations that promote a format featuring rock music generally from the late 1960's to late 1980's.

Classic Rock Bands

The Animals (1962-1969) (first mentioned in chapter four) could also easily fit into our British Invasion chapter. Formed in Newcastle, England in 1962 the original lineup consisted of Alan Price on keyboards, Hilton Valentine on guitar, Bryan "Chas" Chandler on bass, John Steel on drums, and vocalist/leader Eric Burdon. Their high energy stage presence led to their name, The Animals. They focused on American blues covers by artists like Jimmy Reed and John Lee Hooker and soon established themselves as a premier rhythm and blues band on the London scene. The Animals signed to EMI and produced a number of hits including 1964's "House of the Rising Sun" and 1965's "We Gotta Get Out of This Place." "House of the Rising Sun," featured Eric Burdon's rich and gravelly voice, and rose high on the charts in Britain and America.

The Animals continued to record hits including covers of Sam Cooke and Nina Simone songs but tension in the band over its musical direction led to Alan

Price's departure. Eric Burdon pursued a solo career and Chas Chandler soon left to become the manager for Jimi Hendrix. Burdon relocated from London to California and formed a new version of the band that was billed as Eric Burdon and The Animals. Looking to capitalize on the San Francisco scene in the late 1960's, Burdon pushed the band in the direction of the popular psychedelic sound. After a period of shifting band lineups, Burdon disbanded The Animals in 1969. The Animals were inducted into the Rock and Roll Hall of Fame in 1994.

"The House of the Rising Sun"
traditional folk song

"The House of the Rising Sun' was a traditional folk song that was sometimes referred to as the "Rising Sun Blues." Like many folk ballads, the tune's true composer was in question and musicologists generally think that it was based on the tradition of a broadside ballad dating back to sixteenth century Europe. The oldest known recording of the tune was by Clarence Ashley and Gwen Foster. In 1941, folk legend Woody Guthrie recorded another version of the song. This version by The Animals was about a person's poor life experiences in the city of New Orleans.

Eric Burdon first heard the song in England. The Animals were on tour with Chuck Berry and decided to record the song to give them some different material than what other bands were playing. Animals' guitarist Hilton Valentine began the song with an A minor arpeggio on his electric guitar while Alan Price played an organ part that filled out the band's sound. "House of the Rising Sun" was a hit, topping the British charts at number one and then reaching number one in America. The Animals were able to take an extremely old tune and make it relevant in the mid-1960's psychedelic rock environment. Many have asked the question; what is the house of the rising sun? Some thought it to be a brothel, although the lyrics never make that clear. Some believed it stood for a prison or maybe even a gambling hall.

The Spencer Davis Group (1963-1969) (1973-74) (2006-present) was started in 1963 in Birmingham, England by guitarist Spencer Davis, vocalist/keyboardist/bassist Steve Winwood (only fifteen years old), bassist Muff Winwood. and drummer Pete York. In 1964, they signed with Island Records. In 1965, The Spencer Davis Group recorded a hit, "Keep On Running," that peaked at number one on the British charts. By early 1967, the group found more success with "I'm a Man" and "Gimme Some Lovin" which brought them to the attention of American audiences with their hard driving pop-soul sound. "I'm a Man" has been covered many times, most notably by the horn band Chicago (see chapter seventeen). The Spencer Davis Group released numerous albums beginning with 1965's Their First LP, culminating with Living In a Back Street in 1974. Their First LP featured only three originals and was mostly covers of blues and rhythm and blues artists like John Lee Hooker, Little Walter, and Ike and Tina Turner.

Guitarist Spencer Davis drew from diverse musical influences including skiffle, jazz, blues, and rhythm and blues. Steve Winwood added his soul inspired vocals. The band kept developing a hard driving rhythm and blues influenced rock sound. By the time they were coming into their own, Steve Winwood left to form Traffic in 1967. His brother Muff, went on to be an A&R executive at Island Records. Spencer Davis regrouped in 1973 and again later in 2006.

"Gimme Some Lovin"
by Steve Winwood, Muff Winwood, and Spencer Davis

Chris Blackwell, from Island Records, asked The Spencer Davis Group to write a song that would became a hit with American audiences. They responded with "Gimme Some Lovin." The song peaked at number two in England and number seven in the U.S. Steve Winwood had heard a tune written by Homer Banks titled "Ain't That A Lot of Love" and borrowed the basic riff from their tune.

The song was put together quickly by Spencer Davis, Muff Winwood, and Steve Winwood when they began improvising with a bassline. The basic melodic riff soon followed with Winwood just singing the phrase "gimme, gimme some loving." The band knew they had a good song and did not hesitate to take it into the studio the following day. After recording "Gimme Some Lovin," they performed it that same night in a North London club and received a strong response from the audience. For the American release, producer Jimmy Miller added percussion and a female chorus to the track. Steve Winwood worked out the harmony on his Hammond B-3 organ which provided the perfect accompaniment to his soulful vocals. In 1980, the Blues Brothers cover of "Gimme Some Lovin" rejuvenated interest in the song when it went to number eighteen on the charts. It was also covered by The Grateful Dead.

Traffic (1967-1994) began after Steve Winwood left The Spencer Davis Group. He decided to explore psychedelia and a harder rocking sound to complement the soulful rhythm and blues of his past. Along with drummer Jim Capaldi, guitarist/vocalist/bassist Dave Mason, and keyboardist/woodwind player Chris Wood, Winwood formed Traffic in 1967. Traffic took the concept of a psychedelic band and added the instrumental timbres of the Mellotron, harpsichord, sitar, and various reed instruments. They also worked some elements of jazz improvisation into their compositions. Capaldi, Mason, and Wood had previously played together, thus making it a smooth transition when Steve Winwood joined them. In 1967, they released a single titled "Paper Sun" that went to number five in Britain and number seventy in America. Written by Capaldi and Winwood, it featured a sitar solo by Dave Mason. They followed with another hit, "Hole in My Shoe," that reached number two on the British charts.

Traffic was signed to Island Records and released their debut album Mr. Fantasy in 1967. Dave Mason would leave the band due to artistic differences before the release of Mr. Fantasy but would return briefly in 1968 to contribute to their second recording. Mr. Fantasy combined a "one-two punch" of Dave Mason's unique voice and Winwood's distinctive blues voice. Winwood brought the same authentic rhythm and blues feel that he displayed in The Spencer Davis Group, this time fusing it with Capaldi's skillful lyrics. Mason, Winwood, Capaldi, and Wood were all capable writers, giving Traffic strong composers to complement their instrumental abilities. Winwood said, "Living together is very important for writing. It wouldn't be important if we were like just getting other people's numbers together, we'd just have to meet at rehearsals, but writing is something almost completely different. A song, no matter who writes it, really has to come to all of us, and writing with us is really a slow process…if each of us wrote individually and each lived in different places, then I don't think that the songs that were written would be common to all three of us." #1 Mr. Fantasy peaked at number sixteen on the

British charts and number eighty-eight on the American charts. The British and American releases featured some different songs and were mixed differently (some tracks stereo and some mono).

1968's album Traffic went to number nine in Britain and number seventeen in America. Mason wrote and sang about half the songs on Traffic, including his hit "Feelin' Alright?" However, Mason was moving in more of a pop songwriting direction, which was at odds with the harder rocking blues approach of the other Traffic members. Mason left after Traffic was completed (he would return in 1971 for a tour and to honor the band's record contract). 1969's Last Exit was a collection of random songs put together by Island Records after a brief breakup of Traffic. The first half of Last Exit contained studio tracks and the second half was recorded Live at the Fillmore West. The album peaked at number nineteen on the American charts.

Steve Winwood started to do some jam sessions with Eric Clapton, drummer Ginger Baker, and bassist Ric Grech that soon turned into the short lived supergroup Blind Faith (see later in this chapter). Winwood then began work on a solo record and brought in Capaldi and Wood to work on the project. This soon grew into a new Traffic album, 1970's John Barleycorn Must Die. This became Traffic's highest charting American album at number five. Traffic expanded in 1971 with the addition of ex-Derek and the Dominos drummer Jim Gordon, Ghanaian percussionist Rebop Kwaku Baah, and bassist Ric Gretch. A live album ensued, 1971's Welcome to the Canteen, that also featured the return of Dave Mason (again back to fulfill the bands' contract) before leaving for good. The album ended with "Gimme Some Lovin," from Winwood's Spencer Davis Group days.

The Low Spark of the High Heeled Boys was released in 1971 and went to number seven on the American charts but failed to even chart in England. On this recording, particularly the eleven and a half minute title track, Traffic achieved a rare balance between commercial radio friendly melodies and adventurous improvisation. They were able to successfully draw from both soulful rhythm and blues and jazz and then make it stretch out and rock.

"The Low Spark of the High Heeled Boys"
by Steve Winwood and Jim Capaldi

"The Low Spark of the High Heeled Boys" was inspired by an interaction between Jim Capaldi and actor Michael J. Pollard. They were in Morocco and were planning to work on a film project that never materialized. Together, they were writing lyrics in the attempt to create a plot for their movie. The "low spark" came to symbolize a rebel attitude of somebody dressed in leather just standing on a street corner. Pollard just came up with the phrase "low spark of the high heeled (meaning cowboy boots) boys."

The track began with a fade-in and ended by fading out. At almost twelve minutes in length, its extended solos utilized a sense of jazz improvisation to explore many musical ideas. Harmonically, Traffic played in a minor key for the verses and modulated to a major key in the choruses to change the emotion within the tune. The verses had a relaxed and sparse rhythmic feel and the choruses moved into a double-time feel. A live version of the tune can be seen and heard on Traffic's only concert video. "The Low Spark of the High Heeled Boys" had been covered by former members of the Grateful Dead, Widespread Panic, and singer Rickie Lee Jones.

By late 1971, personnel problems again besieged Traffic when Winwood was suffering from health issues and both Gordon and Grech left the band. After making a successful solo record, Jim Capaldi invited Muscle Shoals Studio drummer Roger Hawkins and bassist David Hood to join Traffic. The band released three successful albums including; Shoot out at the Fantasy Factory in 1973, a live album titled On the Road in 1973, and When the Eagle Flies in 1974. Winwood left Traffic again and began doing sessions with ex-Beatle George Harrison. Winwood would go on to have a very productive solo career (see chapter twelve). Traffic was now done for now, but would resurface twenty years later.

In 1994, Capaldi recorded with Steve Winwood, leading to a renewed Traffic. With a new lineup, Traffic toured with The Grateful Dead and in that same year, released their eighth studio album, Far from Home. In 2005, Jim Capaldi died, thus ending the resurgence of Traffic. Traffic was inducted into the Rock and Roll Hall of Fame in 2004.

The Faces/The Small Faces (1965-present) were formed by bassist Ronnie Lane, guitarist Steve Marriott, drummer Kenny Jones, and keyboardist Jimmy Winston in 1965. They were initially a mod styled group that would go on to launch the solo career of singer Rod Stewart (see chapter twelve). Their first hit was "Whatcha Gonna Do About It." The Small Faces lineup changed when keyboardist Ian McLagan replaced Winston as their second hit, "Sha La La La Lee," and their debut album peaked at number three on the British charts. After more success, Marriott left to form Humble Pie (see later in this chapter). Meanwhile, both Rod Stewart and guitarist Ronnie Wood would leave The Jeff Beck Group to join The Small Faces. They soon dropped Small to become just The Faces.

The Faces' debut album, Long Player, was successful in both Britain and America. At the same time, The Faces backed Rod Stewart's solo career and were sometimes called Rod Stewart and The Faces, which didn't sit too well with some members of the band. Another hit for Rod Stewart and The Faces was "Stay With Me," from their successful album A Nod Is As Good As a Wink ... to a Blind Horse. Stewart became more focused on his solo career and The Faces disbanded in 1975, just in time for Ronnie Wood to join The Rolling Stones. Next, The Faces got back together but then Kenny Jones left to replace Keith Moon in The Who. Also, Rick Wills, their third bass player, left to join Foreigner. Various member of The Faces have played and supported Rod Stewart on and off for a number of years. In 2010, a new Faces band without Stewart re-grouped and continues to tour.

The Arrival of FM Rock Radio

The genre of classic rock was partially defined by the radio play that many rock bands received. But before rock artists could gain national exposure on the airwaves, things had to change with the entire format of national radio. To begin, much of the 1960's rock movement in America was anti-establishment. Therefore, it's hard to believe that the federal government (via the Federal Communications Commission or FCC), and not hippies or hard rock fans, was responsible for the advent of FM radio. Before the 1960's, very little rock music was played on commercial AM stations. These stations were supported by advertisers that required DJ's to play only top forty songs in the effort to reach a broad and large audi-

> "I'd give Steve (Winwood) a complete lyric, titled, written out with the verse, the bridge, the shape and rhyme and then Steve had to figure out how the meter of the words would fit musically."
>
> – Jim Capaldi

ence. AM stations had great reception range; thus the ability to reach a larger audience, while FM stations had better sound quality, but more limited range. Before the mid-1960's, few homes and almost no cars had FM receivers, which meant there was a very limited audience. Also, there was almost no original programming to help FM radio gain any ground by converting AM radio audiences. The FCC stepped in and put into law the ruling that FM stations had to carry at least fifty percent original programming instead of having to replay material from their AM affiliates. FM radio would now look to rock music as the source of this new material.

At first, FM stations were only funded to play classical music. However, a number of subscriber-supported stations were in business. More and more FM stations popped up and soon psychedelic rock and other non-pop "underground" music found a home that would grow their audience. The man largely credited with the advent of FM as a rock venue was DJ and promoter Tom Donahue, from San Francisco's KMPX radio station. Donahue played psychedelic rock songs and aired extended album cuts by new and noncommercial rock bands. Donahue also hired a staff of DJ's that were well informed about the current state of rock bands. Together, they promoted current rock bands without pop singles, jingles, or talk-overs. Eventually, Donahue resigned due to conflicts with management. However, he and his staff moved to another FM station, KSAN radio, where they became the first full-time FM rock station in the country. This led to the creation of FM rock stations all around America including; WNEW In New York, WABX in Detroit, KSHE in St. Louis, WASH in Washington, WMGK in Philadelphia, and many more. Now rock 'n' roll had a new nationwide delivery system for its bands and artists. This led to an enormous increase in rock album sales over the sales of singles. It would also be the end of the formulaic three-minute pop song.

The James Gang (1966-1977) (1996-2012) formed in 1966 in Cleveland, Ohio. The James Gang has released nine studio albums, one live album, and three compilation albums. Their original lineup consisted of Greg Grandillo and Ronnie Silverman on guitar, Tom Kriss on bass and vocals, Jimmy Fox on drums, and Phil Giallombardo on keyboards and vocals. After a few lineup changes on guitar, Joe Walsh (future member of The Eagles) joined the band in 1968 on guitar and vocals staying until 1971. This version of the band formed the "classic" James Gang lineup of Jim Fox, Dale Peters, and Joe Walsh that recorded James Gang Rides Again. Three of their most successful tunes were hits in the 1970's, "Funk #49," "Walk Away," and ""Must Be Love." The James Gang developed an original sound by combining Joe Walsh's creative guitar riffs and voice with elements of hard rock and blues. On the suite of songs "The Bomber/ Closet Queen/ Bolero/ Cast Your Fate to the Wind," they even incorporated Ravel's "Bolero" (and Vince Guaraldi's "Cast Your Fate to the Wind") into a hard rock 'n' roll anthem. They opened for many of the biggest rock bands in the world including; The Who, The Kinks, and Led Zeppelin. The James Gang reunited with Joe Walsh for a few appearances in the late 1990's and performed at the Rock and Roll Hall of Fame in 2001.

Fleetwood Mac (1967-present) (first mentioned in chapter four) was formed shortly after drummer Mick Fleetwood joined John Mayall's Bluesbreakers in 1967. Vocalist Peter Green was also in the Bluesbreakers (having replaced Eric Clapton in 1966), but only a month later, Mayall fired both Fleetwood and Green. They quickly formed Fleetwood Mac adding guitarist Jeremy Spencer, and bassist Bob Brunning. Bassist John McVie (also a fired Mayall alumni) soon replaced Brunning to complete the original Fleetwood Mac lineup. In 1968, they released their self-titled debut album Fleetwood Mac, a mixture of Green and Spencer originals and blues covers. The record barely made the American charts but did go to number four in England. At the time, the band released the Peter Green composition "Black Magic Woman" (later a hit for Santana). Fleetwood Mac now enjoyed a high profile in Britain behind Green's skillful blues songwriting and musicianship. 1969's Mr. Wonderful, another strong blues offering, added horns and ex-Chicken Shack keyboardist Christine Perfect (who would later marry John McVie to become Christine McVie). After the release of Mr. Wonderful, they added a third guitarist and prolific songwriter, Danny Kirwan. More blues followed with 1969's English Rose that contained new songs by Kirwan including a hit, "Albatross."

In 1969, Fleetwood Mac went to America to record at the legendary Chess Records Studio. There, they recorded with Otis Spann, Buddy Guy, and Willie Dixon. 1970's Then Play On would be the last album for Peter Green and Jeremy Spencer only played on one song. In the coming months, Peter Green (not in good health) announced his departure from the band. He later recorded occasional solo albums before joining the band, Splinter Group. Also released in 1970, Kiln House was the last album for Jeremy Spencer. Christine McVie contributed to the album but was not yet considered a full member of the band.

While on tour in early 1971, Jeremy Spencer told members of the band that he was going out to get a newspaper. He never returned. After a frantic search, it was discovered that he had joined a religious cult, The Child of God. Peter Green was able to finish the tour in Spencer's place. 1971's Future Games was the debut for new Fleetwood Mac guitarist Bob Welch (and now full-time member Christine McVie). The band continued to tour with more lineup changes and then released Bare Trees in 1972. Two more albums emerged in 1973, Penguin, and Mystery to Me, but the band was in disarray due to internal stress and interpersonal issues.

1974 saw the bizarre emergence of a "fake" Fleetwood Mac band that was assembled by their manager Clifford Davis. A successful lawsuit followed and stopped the fraud but it put the real Fleetwood Mac temporarily out of commission. In spite of the chaos, Heroes are Hard to Find was released in 1974 and did well at number thirty-four on the U.S. charts. Bob Welch announced he was leaving the band and now the depleted core of Mick Fleetwood, John McVie, and Christine McVie were firmly based in Los Angeles. They needed to regroup. The band heard a demo tape by guitarist Lindsey Buckingham and singer/songwriter Stevie Nicks and a new Fleetwood Mac was born.

1975's Fleetwood Mac was released as their second self-titled album. This sent a message that this would be a new band and musical direction. Fleetwood Mac took some time to gain momentum but it eventually went to number one in America. The hits included "Over My Head," "Say You Love Me," and "Rhiannon (Will You Ever Win)." The band was exploding but so were their interpersonal relationships. However, they would persevere with their good fortune of having three good songwriters and three distinctive voices to sing their songs. Christine McVie brought a soft rock sound, Nicks had a haunting voice that complemented her own supernatural song

Chapter Eleven: Classic Rock

lyrics, and Buckingham became a formidable vocalist and guitar player.

"Rhiannon (Will You Ever Win)"
by Stevie Nicks

Stevie Nicks wrote "Rhiannon" after reading the book *Triad* by Mary Leader. The plot of the book involved a woman who thought she was possessed by the spirit of a woman name Rhiannon. This theme came from mythology where Rhiannon was a Welsh goddess. The myth stated that Rhiannon, a goddess of fertility, rejected a god and married a mortal man. The god frames her for the murder of her own son, and she was forced to tell everyone that she murdered her own child. Stevie Nicks learned the mythic story after she wrote "Rhiannon" but then felt it fit her own song. In concert, Nicks explained that Rhiannon was a "good" witch.

"Rhiannon" reached number eleven in America and number forty-six in Britain. Stevie Nicks did enlist the help of Lindsey Buckingham when she wrote the song at the piano. Her working (and romantic) relationship with Buckingham became a strong presence when they both joined Fleetwood Mac. Nicks would sing "Rhiannon" with great passion live in concert and at one time considered making the story of Rhiannon into a film project.

The romantic tension in the band continued and was reflected in some of the song lyrics. This prompted Fleetwood Mac to title their 1977 album, Rumours. It soared to number one, spending thirty-one weeks at the top, until it was knocked out by Michael Jackson's Thriller. This Grammy Award Album of the Year yielded the four hits; "Don't Stop," "Dreams," "You Make Loving Fun," and "Go Your Own Way." Fleetwood Mac had become one of rock's biggest acts.

1979's Tusk was an American number four and British number one double album. It featured Buckingham's more experimental approach. The title track and "Sara," were both hits. Increasingly obsessed with keeping Fleetwood Mac's sound relevant in a post-punk and new wave world, Buckingham utilized more streamlined arrangements. Soon, side project albums were recorded by Nicks, Buckingham, and Fleetwood. The band returned for 1982's Mirage that went to number one in the U.S. with a radio-friendly soft rock sound. More solo albums ensued as Fleetwood Mac went on hiatus.

With Stevie Nicks solo career taking off, Fleetwood Mac did not regroup until late 1985. They released the moderately successful Tango in the Night in 1987. Buckingham abruptly left the band before a tour scheduled for later that year and Fleetwood Mac responded by adding two new guitar players, Billy Burnette and Rick Vito. From their 1975-1988 era, a Greatest Hits album followed and then 1990's Behind the Mask album. In 1991, both Stevie Nicks and guitarist Rick Vito announced they were leaving the band. At the request of then President Bill Clinton, the combination of Nicks/Buckingham/McVie/McVie/Fleetwood performed at Clinton's first Inaugural Ball in 1993. With more personnel changes in place, Fleetwood Mac recorded Time in 1995. The new lineup featured vocalist/guitarist Dave Mason, vocalist Bekka Bramlett, Billy Burnette, Christine and John McVie, and Mick Fleetwood. The album reached number forty-seven in England but failed to chart in America.

Fleetwood Mac broke up in 1995 and reunited two years later. The full Rumours lineup recorded the live album, The Dance, in 1997. In 1998, Christine McVie quit the band, leaving Nicks and Buckingham to sing all of the lead vocals for Fleetwood Mac's 2003 album Say You Will. More tours followed and an EP, titled Extended Play, was recorded in 2013. Christine McVie returned in 2014 to re-form the classic lineup of Fleetwood, McVie, McVie, Buckingham, and Nicks. Fleetwood Mac continues to be a superstar group of soft rock in spite of their internal tensions. They have created an enduring body of work that spanned from 1974 to current times. Fleetwood Mac was inducted into the Rock and Roll Hall of Fame in 1998.

Steppenwolf (1967-present) was formed in 1967 when Toronto based vocalist John Kay, drummer Jerry Edmonton, and keyboardist Goldy McJohn from the band Sparrow, moved to California. They soon added guitarist Michael Monarch to form the band Steppenwolf. The last addition was bassist Rushton Moreve in 1967 to complete the band. Their name was inspired by the Herman Hesse novel of the same name. Their success came rapidly as two hits "The Pusher" and "Born To Be Wild" came from their first album, 1968's Steppenwolf. These songs were also featured in the classic movie *Easy Rider* in 1969. Steppenwolf went to number eight on the American charts and the single "Born To Be Wild" went to number two on the American pop charts.

Steppenwolf continued their early success when their second album, The Second, went to number three on the charts. From that record, another major hit (the very funky), "Magic Carpet Ride," peaked at number three on the charts. Steppenwolf was becoming a major force in rock music. However, internal friction was creating instability in the band. Moreve and Monarch left and were soon replaced. Steppenwolf's 1969 release, At Your Birthday Party, went top ten on the charts. By 1971, Steppenwolf had released more studio and live albums. In the early 1970's they began to lose popularity and by 1972, Steppenwolf broke up. Re-formed in 1974, they recorded three more albums and again called it quits in 1976. Since then, Steppenwolf members have fought over the rights to the band's name as various members toured under the Steppenwolf name until 1980. John Kay eventually won that battle and has released more Steppenwolf albums in the 1980's and 1990's. They continue to tour to this day and have sold over twenty-five million albums worldwide.

"Born To Be Wild"
written by Mars Bonfire

"Born To Be Wild," was written by Mars Bonfire who was a member of a band (that predated Steppenwolf) called Sparrow. The tune featured one of rock's most imitated and enduring riffs. "Born To Be Wild" was the band's third single from their 1968 debut album. Considered one of rock music's great anthems of freedom and rebellion, it stood as a Vietnam War protest song. "Born To Be Wild" had an edgy, driving rock feel that projected the energy of youth at the time when late 1960's counter-culture often turned to more mellow sounds. The song has inspired many hard rock and metal bands and is often played on FM classic rock radio.

"Born To Be Wild" had the sounds of roaring motorcycles added to it for the soundtrack of the popular counter-culture movie *Easy Rider*. "Born To Be Wild" has been featured in a great number of movies, commercials, and TV shows. It was Steppenwolf's most popular tune and went to number two on the American pop charts. "Born To Be Wild" has been covered by a wide range of artists including; Bruce Springsteen, Blue Oyster Cult,

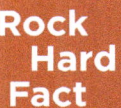

Rock Hard Fact

Steppenwolf's "Born To Be Wild" marked the first time the words "Heavy Metal" were used in a rock song. The second verse contained the lyric "heavy metal thunder."

"If you wanted to learn the lesson of how to perform live, Humble Pie was the band to see."

– Chad Smith- drummer for The Red Hot Chili Peppers

Ozzy Osborne, INXS, Slayer, and even rhythm and blues great Wilson Pickett.

The J. Geils Band (1967-present) became one of Boston's most popular rhythm and blues bands in the late 1960's. First, guitarist John "J" Geils, harmonica player Richard "Magic Dick" Salwitz, and bassist Danny "Dr. Funk" Klein formed a blues trio. They soon added singer Peter Wolf and drummer Stephen Bladd to become The J. Geils Band Blues Band. Next, they were signed to Atlantic Records and added keyboard player Seth Justman. At this point, the band decided to drop the Blues from their name. After a series of successful albums, The J. Geils Band moved in more of a rock direction and left Atlantic Records. They signed with EMI in the late 1970's and released both Sanctuary and Love Stinks. In 1981, the band had tremendous success on the charts with Freeze Frame, which brought them to new levels of popularity. Freeze Frame went to number one on the charts in America and number three in Britain in 1982, spawning the hit "Centerfold." In 1983, Peter Wolf left the band after a tour of England (in support of The Rolling Stones). While Wolf went on to a solo career, Bladd and Justman shared the vocal responsibilities. The J. Geils Band made one more album, You're Getting Even While I'm Getting Odd. The band reunited with Peter Wolf in 1999 for an American tour and has played together on and off ever since.

Blue Oyster Cult (1967-present) was formed in New York by vocalist Les Braunstein, Donald "Buck Dharma" Roeser on guitar, keyboardist Allen Lanier, bassist Andrew Winters, and drummer Albert Bouchard. The classic lineup solidified when Joe Bouchard replaced Winters on bass and Eric Bloom replaced Braunstein on vocals. They developed a sound that bordered on heavy metal and featured creative lyrics. Their 1972 debut Blue Oyster Cult was a critical success, as well as their next three albums. The band's strongest commercial success happened with their 1976 Agents of Fortune. It yielded their biggest tune "Don't Fear The Reaper."

"Don't Fear the Reaper"
by Donald Roeser

Before recording their fourth album, Agents of Fortune, Blue Oyster Cult was a cult band with a logo that represented the Greek god Chronos. "Don't Fear the Reaper" came to Roeser when he was thinking about his own mortality. It's a story about a love affair that transcended death. The song's popularity was extended by the lyrics of the second verse. Roseser utilized the word "Valentine" as a metaphor for mortal love and "Romeo and Juliet" stood for a couple who had the faith to take their love to another world (transcending death-hence the reaper). Their story unfolded with the reality that their freedom to love on this Earth would not be permitted. The suicide part of their story created controversy and some radio station managers were hesitant at first to play the song.

Roeser wrote a catchy psychedelic sounding guitar riff and utilized the studio to experiment with the extended solo section. The song made Blue Oyster Cult instantly identifiable within the psychedelic rock genre. The tune featured a repetitious cowbell part that ordinarily would not work for most songs, but it helped bring the track together. First released as a single, "Don't Fear the Reaper" went to number twelve in the U.S. and has been covered by numerous bands and used in movie soundtracks. In 2000, comedian Will Ferrell performed the "More Cowbell" sketch on *Saturday Night Live* with actor Christopher Walken, mocking an overzealous cowbell player in the studio.

In 1977, Blue Oyster Cult's album Spectres featured another hit, "Godzilla." Subsequent albums went in a more pop direction but the band returned to their harder edge with Cultosaurus Erectus in 1980. 1981 brought the successful Fire of Unknown Origin, and the hit "Burnin' For You." Blue Oyster Cult has always been at their strongest when performing live. This was evidenced by their recording, Extra Terrestrial Live. Blue Oyster Cult has endured numerous lineup changes while continuing to record and tour today.

REO Speedwagon (1967-present) was formed by two University of Illinois students, keyboardist Neal Doughty and drummer Alan Gratzer. They soon added guitarist Gary Richrath, bassist Gregg Philbin, and vocalist Terry Luttrell. Speedwagon's self-titled debut album sold poorly but the band built a following by relentlessly touring the American Mid-West. Luttrell soon left and was replaced by new frontman Kevin Cronin, who played on their second release R.E.O. T.W.O. Once again, Speedwagon changed vocalists and for their 1974 release Ridin' the Storm Out, they added Mike Murphy. This record was mildly successful only reaching one hundred seventy-one on the charts, but Murphy added a strong voice to their evolving sound.

Speedwagon released 1974's Lost in a Dream and the following year, This Time We Mean It. Murphy then left and Kevin Cronin returned for a series of successful albums that included 1977's R.E.O. and 1978's You Can Tune a Piano, But You Can't Tuna Fish. REO Speedwagon found commercial appeal by focusing on power ballads geared to teenage girls and catchy tunes targeted for FM radio. The band's greatest fame came with 1980's Hi Infidelity. It became one of 1981's biggest selling albums and produced three hits, the power ballad "Keep On Loving You," "Don't Let Him Go," and "Take it on the Run." Hi Infidelity brought Speedwagon to arena size popularity, selling more than nine million copies. REO Speedwagon went on to record numerous studio, live, and compilation albums and continues to tour today.

Humble Pie (1968-2002) formed in England at the end of 1968 with ex-Small Faces frontman vocalist/ guitarist Steve Marriott, ex-Herd guitarist/vocalist Peter Frampton, and ex-Spooky Tooth bassist Greg Ridley. They added ex-mod band Apostolic Intervention drummer Jerry Shirley. Humble Pie had three capable lead vocalists that fueled their hard-edged blues-rock sound. In 1969, Humble Pie had a top five hit on the British charts with "Natural Born Bugie." They followed with their 1969 debut album As Safe as Yesterday Is. Their second album, Town and Country, had no promotion due to their record label going bankrupt. The band carried on and Steve Marriott, with his bluesy and strong voice, was asked to exert control of the band's heavier rock direction. Peter Frampton remembered, "We'd all been writing songs on the acoustic so when we first got together that was the direction. But it evolved from there. When we first got together, Steve didn't want to be the front man…we all bowed down to Steve as being one of the all-time blues rock voices in history. He wanted us all to take the lead." #2 By 1971, Humble Pie was gaining a strong reputation in America as a great live band. This was realized with the album Performance Rockin' the Fillmore. It peaked at number twenty-one on the American charts.

Shortly after, Peter Frampton left Humble Pie and would go on to have a successful solo career. Guitarist Clem Clempson replaced Frampton and Humble Pie moved towards an even harder sound. 1972's Smokin' became the bands' most successful album, reaching number six on the American charts. Marriott looked to change the musical direction of Humble Pie to include more rhythm and blues influence and followed with three albums; Eat It in 1973, Thunderbox in 1974, and Street Rats in 1975. Humble Pie then disbanded. In 1979, Marriott and Shirley regrouped with a new lineup and released two albums in the early 1980's, On To Victory and Go for the Throat. But once again, Humble Pie called it quits. In 1988, Jerry Shirley obtained the rights to the name Humble Pie and re-formed the band. They appeared at the 1989 Woodstock Festival's Twentieth Anniversary concert. A final version of Humble Pie released the album Back on Track in 2002. Humble Pie made seven live albums, six singles that charted in America, and numerous compilations. Their long career saw them achieve success with large audiences in both England and America.

Free (1968-1973) got their name from British blues master Alexis Korner when he introduced bassist Andy Fraser to vocalist Paul Rodgers, guitarist Paul Kassoff and drummer Simon Kirke, all under the age of nineteen. Formed in 1968, Free's early records did not sell well, but their album Fire and Water contained the tune "All Right Now" which still receives constant FM radio airplay. "All Right Now" went to number two on the British pop charts and number four on the American charts.

By the early 1970's, Free had established itself as one of England's major blues-rock bands. In 1971, Free released their fourth studio album, Highway, but it did not fare well on the charts. The band called it quits in 1971, due to internal conflicts and drug issues. However, their record company quickly released a live album, Free Live!. The band re-formed in 1972 and soon released Free at Last, in the same year. Andy Fraser then left the band and was replaced by Tetsu Yamauchi and studio keyboardist John "Rabbit" Bundrick. Free's sixth and last album, Heartbreaker, was released in late 1972 and there were more lineup changes. In 1973, Free broke up for good and all of the band members went on to different groups. Paul Rodgers and Simon Kirke formed the very successful band, Bad Company (see later in this chapter).

"All Right Now"
by Andy Fraser and Paul Rodgers

Free knew that their early repertoire contained too many slow and medium tempo blues tunes and that they needed more musical excitement, especially to close their live performances. Therefore, bassist Andy Fraser sat down right in the dressing room, after a less than inspired show, and started to write "All Right Now." Fraser was only sixteen years old when he co-wrote the tune with Paul Rodgers. Fraser would go on to write songs for Robert Palmer, Rod Stewart, and Chaka Khan. Paul Rodgers wrote the song lyrics for "All Right Now" about a guy trying to pick up a girl. "All Right Now" had one of the most recognizable guitar riffs in rock history that has inspired many rock songwriters. The bass part that served as a lead-in to Paul Kossoff's guitar solo was very melodic and smoothly sets up the solo section. Simon Kirke's drum part possessed a great feel and a sense of space that locked in rhythmically with the guitar riff and bassline.

Paul Rodgers vocal performance on "All Right Now" would establish him as one of England's great blues-rock singers. In addition to forming Bad Company, Rodgers has gone on to work with Jimmy Page in The Firm and he replaced Freddie Mercury in Queen (where he did perform "All Right Now" as part of Queen's live set). As for the legacy of the band Free, "All Right Now" proved to be bittersweet. The song's great popularity worldwide would elevate them to star status, but they were never able to follow "All Right Now" with another blockbuster hit.

Delaney and Bonnie (1967-1972) were a duo of singer/songwriters that formed a rock and soul music inspired band in 1967. The band always featured star-studded lineups and musical "friends." This included, at various times; Eric Clapton, Dave Mason, Leon Russell, George Harrison, Greg Allman, Duane Allman, Bobby Whitlock, King Curtis, Rita Coolidge, and more. In 1967, Delaney Bramlett married Bonnie Lynn O'Farrell when they met in Los Angeles. They released their 1969 debut album, Home, and later that year, The Original Delaney & Bonnie & Friends (Accept No Substitute). George Harrison brought Delaney and Bonnie to the attention of Eric Clapton, who made them the opening act for his band, Blind Faith. Clapton began to join Delaney and Bonnie onstage, leading to his musical association with them.

Delaney and Bonnie's third release, a live album titled On Tour with Eric Clapton, reached number twenty-nine in America and number thirty-nine in Britain. This version of the band featured most of the members of Clapton's Derek and the Dominos, as well as Dave Mason. Many of the Delaney and Bonnie members worked with George Harrison on his celebrated All Things Must Pass album. Delaney and Bonnie continued to produce strong records over the rest of their relatively short career. They ended as a band in 1972 and were divorced in 1973. Both continued to work as professional musicians. Delaney Bramlett died in 2008.

Blind Faith (1969-1969) was an instant supergroup that formed when Cream's Eric Clapton and Ginger Baker joined forces with Traffic's multi-instrumentalist Steve Winwood and Family's bassist Ric Grech. When Clapton left Cream he remembered, "I had been thinking a lot about Steve Winwood, who I heard had left Traffic…I called him and started going over there (Steve's cottage)…we'd drink and smoke and talk a lot, and play our guitars." #3 Winwood persuaded Clapton to bring in Ginger Baker (who just showed up one day) and Ric Grech left his band in mid-tour to complete the band. They started their career with a free concert in London's Hyde Park in 1969, but they had very little material and needed to play Traffic and Cream tunes (which bothered Clapton). 1969's Blind Faith topped the charts in America, England, and Canada. The album yielded two hits, Winwood's "Can't Find My Way Home," and Clapton's "Presence of the Lord." This was followed by a short tour of Scandinavia and a successful American tour.

Groundbreaking album Blind Faith
by Blind Faith

Easily one of the greatest "one hit wonders" in rock album history, Blind Faith reached number one in America and England. A buzz was building about Blind Faith even before they recorded the album. Many critics and fans knew this new band contained two Cream members. Clapton, when asked, said that he was just going in the studio to make a record on his own with Steve Winwood. The recording of the album was interrupted by a tour of Scandinavia

> "I was an evil person back then. I think Eric Clapton just wanted to get away from me (in Blind Faith)."
>
> – Ginger Baker

and America. Blind Faith returned to the studio to quickly finish the album.

Side one opened with "Had to Cry Today," then "Can't Find My Way Home," "Well … All Right," (written by Buddy Holly,) and "Presence of the Lord." Winwood's composition "Can't Find My Way Home," brought an acoustic folk element that combined with Clapton's ever-present blues firepower. This gave Blind Faith a remarkable range of styles and the musical freedom to explore many directions. Clapton's tune "In the Presence of the Lord" was one of the first great songs he ever composed. It projected a very soulful message, blending Winwood's voice and acoustic piano with the passion of Clapton's musicianship.

Side two contained only two compositions "Sea of Joy" and "Do What You Like." Ric Grech added a violin part to "Sea of Joy," a song that revealed Winwood's growth as a lyricist. The song spoke of escapism and the rapidly approaching end of the 1960's. It utilized the metaphor of sailing away from the reality of everyday life. "Do What You Like," was written by Ginger Baker and featured a jazz and blues psychedelic groove. It started with a minor key vamp followed by an extended Winwood organ solo and then Clapton's guitar solo. Next, the tune moved into a riff section, drum solo, and finally back to the opening vocal section.

The original album cover art was not without controversy. It showed a topless pubescent girl holding a hood ornament of a car. To many, this suggested a phallic symbol. The American version of the album replaced the girl with a picture of the band. Musicians, critics, and fans held Blind Faith in high regard and this album revealed the unquestionable musical potential of the band Blind Faith.

Clapton began to spend a lot of time with one of the opening acts on the Blind Faith tour, Delaney and Bonnie. Clapton later appeared on Delaney and Bonnie's albums and also had them and their band play on (and mix) his 1970 debut solo album, Eric Clapton. Meanwhile, Winwood was showing little interest in continuing as Blind Faith. Winwood and Grech briefly joined Baker's new band, Ginger Baker's Air Force. This group was short lived because Winwood and Grech left to start work on a new recording with a reunited Traffic. In 2007, Eric Clapton and Steve Winwood reunited as a duo and performed at the Crossroads Guitar Festival in Illinois where they played Blind Faith songs. This prompted more performances in 2008 and in 2009 when Winwood and Clapton did an American tour. They followed this with more tours, first in Europe in 2010 and then in London and Japan in 2011. An outstanding DVD of this reunion was filmed at Madison Square Garden.

Uriah Heep (1969-present) was another British band that has survived a number of lineup changes along the way. They have released more than fifty studio, live and compilation albums over an almost fifty year career. Their peak years were from 1971 to 1975. Uriah Heep began when British 1960's band The Stalkers split up and some of the members combined to form a new band, Spice. This band later went on to become Uriah Heep. The band had found its most success in the countries of Germany and Norway, where they still continue to be popular. Their most requested tune was "Lady in Black." Uriah Heep first became popular in 1971 with their album, Look at Yourself, which made the top one hundred in America. Uriah Heep had elements of progressive rock mixed with a somewhat hard rock edge. Some have even called them a mix of progressive rock, blues, and heavy metal. Their next three albums all went gold in America. In 1975, Uriah Heep achieved their strongest popularity in England with their top ten album Return to Fantasy. They also have the distinction of being the first western band to tour in the Soviet Union. Uriah Heep has sold over four million albums in America and some of their most popular songs were "Sweet Lorraine," and "Easy Livin." They have sold over forty million albums worldwide.

Thin Lizzy (1969-1984) (1996-present) began in Dublin, Ireland in 1969 when vocalist/bassist/composer Phil Lynott and drummer Brian Downey met as schoolboys. Beginning in 1974, they became one of rock's first bands to employ two lead guitars. Similar approaches had been taken by Wishbone Ash, Peter Green's Fleetwood Mac, The Allman Brothers, and Lynyrd Skynyrd. Thin Lizzy added lead and twelve-string guitarist Eric Bell to record their debut album 1971's Thin Lizzy. Lynott, the band's main creative force, was an articulate lyricist who wrote about working-class issues while mixing in Irish literary traditions. Also, as a black musician, Lynott overcame racial issues when he felt like an outsider in the mostly white world of hard rock. He became a skilled lyricist from the perspective of an artist outside the normal rock 'n' roll world. From 1972 to 1977, Thin Lizzy pumped out a studio album per year.

1975's Fighting saw a lineup change that added guitarists Brian Robertson and Scott Gorman. Thin Lizzy's big break occurred with their album, Jailbreak, that yielded their signature hit "The Boys Are Back in Town," and "Jailbreak." Their music had evolved to fuse the musical influences of blues, psychedelic rock, soul, and even some traditional Irish folk music, all with a hard rocking sound. Through the years, there would be many lineup changes, especially the lead guitar chair becoming a revolving door. Thin Lizzy hired unsung great guitarist Gary Moore for recordings in 1974 and again in 1977. The band experienced some internal musical tension and personal issues but continued to release a series of albums including; Johnny the Fox in 1976, Bad Reputation in 1977, Black Rose: A Rock Legend in 1979, and Chinatown in 1980.

"The Boys are Back in Town"
by Phil Lynott

"The Boys are Back in Town" was inspired after Thin Lizzy observed that many of their fans were working class guys who just wanted to have some drinks and have fun. The immediate popularity of the tune gave the band a worldwide audience outside of their native Ireland. Thin Lizzy was taken back when the tune became a hit because they initially didn't even want to include it on their Jailbreak album. The band recorded fifteen songs and chose ten for the album. "The Boys" was not one of them until they were convinced otherwise. The lyric that referred to *Dino's Bar and Grill* was inspired by a real bar in Dublin, Ireland owned by a friend of Phil Lynott named Dino.

One of the defining features of the song was the twin guitar lead by Scott Gorham and Brian Robertson. Gorham and Robertson both joined Thin Lizzy at the same time and were crucial to the band's thick guitar sound and background vocals. Robertson often collaborated with Lynott as a songwriter. He was also one of the first guitar players to utilize a wah-wah pedal in his solos rather than only for pure rhythmic effect. Later, Brian

---

Rock Hard Fact

In 1984, Billy Gibbons and Dusty Hill turned down one million dollars offered to them to shave their beards for a TV commercial by the Gillette razor company.

Robertson joined the metal band Motorhead in 1982. Gorham co-founded another band called Black Star Riders in 2012. "The Boys are Back in Town" went to number twelve on the U.S. charts and number eight in England.

Phil Lynott recorded a solo album, Solo in Soho, in early 1980. That same year, he began working on a second solo album, while simultaneously working on the next Thin Lizzy recording. 1981's Renegade, saw Thin Lizzy lose popularity and experience more personal problems. 1983's Thunder and Lightning added ex-Whitesnake guitarist John Sykes to what would be their last album before disbanding. Phil Lynott would go on to form a new band, Grand Slam, but became increasingly ill. Unfortunately, in 1986 Phil Lynott died. Ten years later in 1996, guitarist/vocalist John Sykes decided to re-form Thin Lizzy as a tribute to Lynott and his musical legacy. This version of the band would tour until 2010. Thin Lizzy veteran guitarist Scott Gorham formed yet another version of the band that same year. This lineup included original drummer Brian Downey, bringing the band full circle. Thin Lizzy has produced over twelve-studio recordings and continues to perform to this day.

ZZ Top (1969-present) is a blues-rock trio whose longevity has spanned almost fifty years. Vocalist/guitarist Billy Gibbons first played with organist Lanier Greig and drummer Dan Mitchell. After playing with ex-Stevie Ray Vaughan bassist Billy Ethridge, Gibbons met vocalist/bassist/keyboardist Dusty Hill, and drummer Frank Beard. The trio formed ZZ Top in 1969 in Houston, Texas. Gibbons soon emerged as the band's leader, lyricist and arranger. He is also one of the most under-rated guitarists in rock and roll. Gibbons had explained that the band's name emanated from their admiration for the great B.B. King. He interpreted the last name "King" as meaning the "top." Then, he figured that since B.B. had used the beginning of the alphabet with the initials "BB," they would use the end of the alphabet with the initials "ZZ." When the two were combined, the name ZZ Top was born.

Starting with their first show in 1977, ZZ Top began touring incessantly. In the beginning, their tours focused primarily in the Texas, Mississippi, and Louisiana areas where they built a steady following. 1971's ZZ Top's First Album and 1972's Rio Grande Mud, both recorded on London Records, were not very successful outside of Texas. In early 1973, ZZ Top opened some shows for The Rolling Stones and later that year released Tres Hombres, their first top ten showing on the U.S. charts. The album produced the hit "La Grange" that utilized a classic guitar riff inspired by their love of blues great John Lee Hooker. In 1974, they created Fandango!, a set of live songs from an American tour mixed with studio tracks. 1976's Tejas was not as successful and ZZ Top, burnt out from touring, decided to take a two-year break. It was during this time that Gibbons and Hill grew their famous super long trademark beards.

"La Grange"
by Billy Gibbons, Dusty Hill, and Frank Beard

"La Grange" is a good example of a traditional boogie blues rhythm that ZZ Top successfully utilized in many of their compositions. This feel, more than any other, helped to capture the ZZ Top sound. The band borrowed the boogie blues rhythm from the artist John Lee Hooker," who employed it on "Boogie Chillen," and from Slim Harpo, who also used in for his "Shake Your Hips." In "La Grange," the lyric of "a-how-how-how-how" was quoted from a John Lee Hooker song titled "Boom Boom."

"La Grange" was inspired by the Chicken Ranch, a well-known bordello in La Grange, Texas. This same "house of ill-repute" was also the subject of the 1982 movie *The Best Little Whorehouse in Texas*, starring Bert Reynolds and Dolly Parton. For years, La Grange city officials never welcomed ZZ Top to play the song in their town. Gibbons recalled "For four decades one of our popular numbers, being 'La Grange,' had yet to see the band perform in La Grange." #4 That all changed when town officials finally invited them to perform in La Grange, which they were happy to do.

1979's Deguello featured the hit "Cheap Sunglasses" and a Sam and Dave cover "I Thank You." In 1981, more hits followed including "Tube Snake Boogie," and "Pearl Necklace," from the album El Loco. ZZ Top's greatest critical and commercial success occurred with 1983's Eliminator. It went to number three in the U.S. and number nine in Britain. It's many hits included; "Gimmie All Your Lovin," "Got Me Under Pressure," "Legs," and "Sharp Dressed Man." Commercially, Eliminator fused ZZ Top's old-school boogie with sequenced drum beats and the addition of synthesizers to their sound. Although these changes were a major departure for the band, the album placed a few songs in MTV's heavy rotation and received some MTV Video awards.

1985's Afterburner went to number four in America. ZZ Top continued to dress up their Texas blues sound with futuristic synthesizers. This approach satisfied some of their listeners but not the hard-core blues fans. 1990's Recycler did return somewhat to a more blues-based material but still with a synth and pop sensibility (ironically some critics felt Recycler did recycle an earlier formula of hit making).

After signing a new contract with RCA Records, ZZ Top released a series of albums; 1994's Antenna, 1996's Rhythmeen, 1999's XXX, and 2003's Mescalero. Along the way, album sales declined but the band experimented with the styles of country and Tex-Mex music. ZZ Top slowed down a little from their rigorous tour schedule but almost a decade later, released La Futura in 2012. ZZ Top created a unique image for themselves but most importantly created a *unique sound* that stayed true to the Texas blues, yet with a melodic and hard-driving edge. ZZ Top was inducted into the Rock and Roll Hall of Fame in 2004.

Discussion Question

Are there general differences between classic rock bands that got their start in the 1960's compared to bands that began in the 1970's? Did the changing social climate in America from 1960 to 1980 play any role in how different bands evolved? Be specific and give examples.

Derek and the Dominos (1970-1971) were formed in 1970 by guitarist/vocalist Eric Clapton, keyboardist/singer Bobby Whitlock, drummer Jim Gordon, and bassist Carl Radle. Bobby Whitlock partnered with Clapton to write songs and they soon decided to form a band by adding Radle and Gordon. This group of musicians had already established a sound while performing together backing Delaney and Bonnie, and while working on George Harrison's All Things Must Pass. In fact, Harrison's record featured many extended "jams" between these core musicians that really helped create their sound. Under-rated musician Bobby Whitlock recalled the great rhythm section of Derek and the Dominos when he said, "Jim (Gordon), Carl (Radle), and I were such a tight unit…Jim and Carl were so experienced and there was me playing by the seat of my pants! But the thing I had was feel, my gospel and R&B background was a product of living my whole life absorbing southern soul." #5 The beginning of the sessions for their 1970 double album Layla and Other Assorted Love Songs were uneventful, but a chance meeting between Clapton and guitar great Duane Allman, led to Allman's inclusion on most of the tracks. With this strong band lineup, compositional chemistry between Clapton/Whitlock, and the Allman/Clapton partnership; Derek and the Dominos was on the short list for one of the greatest bands that was only briefly meant to be. The album reached number sixteen in America but failed to chart in England, although it was highly regarded by music critics. Layla and Other Assorted Love Songs included some cover songs of blues standards and the Jimi Hendrix's classic "Little Wing." "Layla" and "Bell Bottom Blues" remain as two of Clapton's most enduring songs.

"Layla"
by Eric Clapton and Jim Gordon

Layla and Majnun was a love story that took place in 7th century Arabia. The Persian poet Nizami Ganjavi wrote a popular poem praising this love story in the 10th century. Ganjavi's poem inspired Eric Clapton and he projected the story on his own love for Pattie Boyd, then wife of ex-Beatle George Harrison. Clapton later married Boyd after her divorce from Harrison.

Clapton initially wrote the first section of "Layla" as a ballad but the song soon changed when guitar legend Duane Allman came up with the tune's signature rocking riff. The recording of this first section consisted of sixteen tracks, six of which were overdubbed riffs and solos by Clapton and Allman. Afterwards, Clapton heard drummer Jim Gordon playing an original composition on piano (taken from a melodic idea composed by Gordon's girlfriend, singer/songwriter Rita Coolidge). Clapton asked Gordon if he could use it for the second part of "Layla" and he agreed. On the recording session, Gordon played the piano part and Clapton added acoustic and slide guitar. Duane Allman contributed electric and bottleneck slide guitar. Additionally, keyboardist Bobby Whitlock and bassist Carl Radle performed on this classic rock song. Its unusual to have a two-part rock song (think classics "Stairway to Heaven" and "Free Bird") where the second part is *slower* than the first but "Layla" is no *usual song*.

Derek and the Dominos toured and did some memorable TV appearances. But eventually Duane returned to The Allman Brothers and the band was scaled down to a four piece. This version of the band recorded an outstanding set of music in 1970 that has been released as (first) In Concert, and more recently Live at the Fillmore. These concerts (and the recording) featured the band playing the material from their debut record, and several blues standards. Although Allman is missed, these recordings created a fantastic document of one of rock 'n' roll's greatest (and most short lived) bands.

The Doobie Brothers (1970-present) started when drummer John Hartman moved to California with the goal of re-forming the band Moby Grape. Instead, he formed a power trio with guitarist Tom Johnston, and bassist Gregg Murphy. Dave Shogren soon replaced Murphy and they added vocalist/guitarist Patrick Simmons in 1970 to become The Doobie Brothers. In their early days, The Doobie Brothers employed a post-hippie boogie sound with acoustic guitars and some country music influences. They played all around Northern California attracting a following of Hells Angels bikers. Their debut album, 1971's The Doobie Brothers, did not fare too well, but producer Ted Templeman was honing their musical direction. The band added a second drummer, Michael Hossack, and a new bassist, Tiran Porter. 1972's Toulouse Street featured the breakout hit "Listen to the Music," that peaked at number eleven in the U.S., and the hit "Jesus is Just Alright."

Templeman created his own version of the "wall of sound" for their next record, 1973's The Captain and Me. The Doobie's utilized interlocking guitar parts, power double drumming, and strong vocals to produce an album of well played and produced tracks. The addition of guest pedal steel guitarist Jeff "Skunk" Baxter on the tunes "Dark Eyed Cajun Woman" and "Without You" served to refine the Doobie Brothers' sound.

1974's What Were Once Vices Are Now Habits saw the addition of vocalist/drummer Keith Knudson and their hit "Black Water," a country rock song, that received national airplay. By now, Jeff "Skunk" Baxter joined the band permanently when he learned that his current band, Steely Dan, was retiring to work exclusively in the studio. The western themed Stampede followed in 1975, featuring the Johnston hit cover of "Take Me in Your Arms." Knudsen now had replaced Michael Hossack to become the second drummer alongside Hartman.

A new phase for the Doobie Brothers was introduced when Tom Johnston began to suffer from severe health issues. The band brought in vocalist/keyboardist Michael McDonald. 1976's Takin' It To the Streets introduced a new Doobie Brothers sound of less guitar based rock and more soft rock and soul influences. The distinctive voice and songwriting skills of McDonald would come to redefine the bands' sound. Takin' It To the Streets rose to number eight on the American charts and spawned the hit singles "Takin' It To the Streets" and "It Keeps You Running."

"Takin' It To The Streets"
by Michael McDonald

"Takin' It To The Streets" was the first Doobie Brothers tune with McDonald singing lead vocals. It marked a shift in the Doobie's musical direction with McDonald's more soulful and aggressive voice from their previous more mellow approach. Michael McDonald was inspired by a letter his sister had written with the words "take this message to my brother," which he used for the lyrics of the song. "Takin' It To The Streets" opened with a half-time feel and gained momentum at each chorus with strong backbeats. McDonald showed his gospel music influence by the way he vocally improvised around the lyric "Takin' It To The Streets," sung by the background vocalists throughout each of the choruses.

Before joining The Doobie Brothers, Michael McDonald was a member of Steely Dan's touring group (see chapter eighteen). He appeared on their classic Katy Lied, The Royal Scam, Aja, and Gaucho albums. In 2006, McDonald again played in Steely Dan's touring band and doubled as their opening act. He also appeared with The Doobie Brothers to re-record "Takin' It To The Streets" with the Nashville duo of Love & Theft for their Southbound album. "Takin It To The Streets" was a hit in the U.S. peaking at number thirteen on the charts.

1977's Livin' on the Fault Line was successful reaching number ten on the U.S. charts, but did not yield any hits (except for "You Belong to Me" that later was a hit for co-writer Carly Simon). Founding member Tom Johnston left the band during the sessions (he would soon start a solo career). Still under the guidance of producer Ted Templeman, the McDonald-led Doobie Brothers were refining a blend of soul and R&B mixed with a polished pop-rock sensibility. 1978's Minute by Minute rose to the top of the American charts but oddly did not chart in England. "What a Fool Believes," co-written by McDonald and Kenny Loggins, was a number one hit in America. The Doobie Brothers were flying high but the pressures of touring and yearly album releases resulted in the near collapse of the band. Hartman and Baxter decided to leave.

The remaining Doobie Brothers lineup of McDonald, Simmons, Knudsen, and Porter restructured by adding drummer Chet McCracken and multi-instrumentalist John McFee. 1980's One Step Closer saw the return of percussionist Bobby LaKind (added previously in 1974) and the band had another hit with "Real Love." The band seemed now to be merely Michael McDonald's backup band. This prompted the Doobie Brothers to call it quits after the release of their Farewell Tour live record. The Doobie Brothers reunited after five years in 1987 when Keith Knudson asked eleven past Doobie Brothers members to support him in a concert to support Vietnam Veterans. A comeback album, Cycles, was released in 1989 with the return of a Tom Johnston led-band without McDonald.

With different lineups, the Doobie Brothers continued to record, producing Brotherhood in 1991. In 1996, The Doobie Brothers played a benefit concert for the Wildlife Conservation Society. That show yielded the double live album Rockin' Down the Highway. It marked the first time that Tom Johnston, Patrick Simmons, and Michael McDonald all performed together. More records ensued with Sibling Rivalry in 2000, World Gone Crazy in 2010, and Southbound in 2014. Michael McDonald went on to have a successful solo career and continued to appear with the band at various times. The Doobie Brothers crafted enduring pop melodies, blending soul and R&B with the unique vocal abilities of Tom Johnston and Michael McDonald. The Doobie Brothers continue to tour and in 2017 headlined music festivals alongside Fleetwood Mac and Steely Dan.

Electric Light Orchestra (1970-present) grew out of a band called The Move, led by vocalist/keyboardist Roy Wood. He joined forces with vocalist/bassist/string player Jeff Lynne and drummer Bev Bevan to form ELO in 1970. Their 1971 self-titled debut album, The Electric Light Orchestra, contained cellos, violins, and horns all overdubbed by Wood. Early ELO was a progressive rock band but took the unique approach of consistently hiring full orchestras for their recording sessions. Their initial sound was a combination of a Beatles pop sensibility set to classical arrangements. For their second album, 1973's ELO 2, The Electric Light Orchestra added the diverse instrumentation of a French horn player, a violinist, and three cellists. These musicians included Hugh McDowell, Will Gibson, Mike Edwards, Kelly Groucutt, and Mik Kaminski. They created a unique sound for a rock band format. ELO also added classically trained keyboardist Richard Tandy and bassist Mike de Albuquerque. ELO 2 went to number thirty-five on the British charts and number sixty-two on the American charts. The album featured an interesting cover of the Chuck Berry classic "Roll Over Beethoven." This hybrid version melded long, symphonic passages woven into Berry's rock anthem. It soon gained a steady rotation on American classic rock FM radio.

1973's On the Third Day moved to shorter songs. ELO continued the implementation of classical instruments and added a Moog synthesizer that provided a blend of traditional sound and new technology. This again served to define the ELO sound. British audiences rejected the album but On the Third Day peaked on the American charts at number fifty-two. The band dropped The from their name and Electric Light Orchestra moved on to record Eldorado: A Symphony by Electric Light Orchestra in 1974. Jeff Lynne hired arranger Louis Clark to direct a twenty-piece orchestra for this recording. The hit single "Can't Get it Out of My Head" soared to number nine in America and increased the band's popularity.

1975's Face the Music outsold Eldorado and most importantly, marked a transition for ELO to more pop-disco songs and away from the progressive and orchestral approach. Face the Music continued to gain an American market when it reached number thirteen but again did not chart in England (later it would be part of a 1978 ELO box set). "Evil Woman" went to number ten on both sides of the Atlantic and another hit, "Strange Magic," featured Lynne's high-pitched falsetto voice that drew comparisons to The Bee Gees. 1976's A New World Record firmly established ELO as the international symphonic pop band. It included the hit "Do Ya." Never to do anything small, ELO's next release was a double studio album. 1977's Out of the Blue sold over fifteen million copies and yielded four international hits, including "Mr. Blue Sky." The band did a supporting world tour and was now at their commercial and creative zenith.

"Evil Woman"
by Jeff Lynne

Jeff Lynne wrote "Evil Woman" very quickly and it became ELO's first major hit. Toward the end of the recording sessions for their Face the Music album, ELO needed one more song and Lynne sat at the piano where the opening gospel-like piano riff came to him. Later, the band came in and recorded the backing track. The very next day, the lyrics were written and recorded. A string arrangement and female choir parts were soon added at a different recording studio.

There was an instrumental break in the tune with a synthesizer part that occurred just before a return to the vocal choir section. "Evil Woman" presented a good example of how Electric Light Orchestra was able to skillfully integrate synthesizer sounds, orchestral strings, choirs, and lead and background vocal parts; all within a rock band setting. ELO was able (in this song and many others) to replace typical rock guitar sonorities with string instrument sounds. This helped to create the "ELO sound." "Evil Woman" reached number ten on both the U.S. and British charts.

With Discovery in 1979, ELO now topped the British charts and for the first time, abandoned strings with the hit, "Don't Bring Me Down." In 1980, ELO worked with Olivia Newton-John on the soundtrack for the film *Xanadu*. Then in 1981, ELO moved away from a commercial direction with their record titled Time. It was a concept album about a time traveler from the 1980's who was stuck a century into the future. ELO lost some of their worldwide popularity with the waning sales of Secret Messages in 1983. Amid conflicts with their record

"Joni Mitchell became a huge influence on us (Ann and Nancy Wilson). But it wasn't till after the initial Beatles explosion that you started seeing women come forward as their own songwriters."

- Nancy Wilson from Heart

company and drummer Bev Bevan's desire to play with Black Sabbath, ELO recorded Balance of Power in 1986. This would be ELO's last album before disbanding (then re-forming in 2000). Jeff Lynne would go on to become a well-respected producer and join George Harrison and the Traveling Wilburys, featuring Tom Petty, Roy Orbison, and Bob Dylan.

2001 marked an Electric Light Orchestra comeback with their album Zoom. Though released as an ELO record, only Lynne and Tandy returned. Lynne continues to lead ELO today. Although ELO was initially criticized as wanna-be Beatles, they carved out their own space as a symphonic rock-pop band with strong hit-making appeal. Electric Light Orchestra was inducted into the Rock and Roll Hall of Fame in 2017.

Supertramp (1970-present) started as a progressive band fusing instrumental arrangements with a few catchy pop melodies. They were privately funded by Dutch millionaire Stanley Miesegaes who offered his support to put together a dream band. Over the 1970's and 1980's, they became one of most popular groups to emerge from Britain. Supertramp was formed in 1969 by ex-The Joint vocalist/pianist Rick Davies. He soon added guitarist Richard Palmer, percussionist Robert Miller, and vocalist/bassist Roger Hodgson. Their debut album, 1970's Supertramp, did not fare well and prompted a lineup change. Richard Palmer and Robert Miller left the band while Hodgson moved from bass to guitar. Supertramp added bassist Frank Farrell, percussionist Kevin Currie, and Dave Winthrop on saxophone and flute. After 1971's unsuccessful Indelibly Stamped, major lineup changes saw the addition of bassist Dougie Thomson, drummer Bob Siebenberg, and saxophonist John Helliwell. Supertramp moved away from a progressive rock direction to more pop melodies and irresistible hooks. This resulted in 1974's Crime of the Century, that rose to number four in Britain and yielded the hits "Dreamer," and "Bloody Well Right."

Supertramp now had a solid audience for Hodgson's unique falsetto vocals and electric piano sound. 1975's Crisis? What Crisis? followed and Even in the Quietest Moments in 1977. The later featured the hit "Give a Little Bit," that moved Supertramp into the top twenty on the U.S. charts. The band moved to America and worked meticulously on their next record, 1979's Breakfast in America. This album shot to number one in America and yielded four hits including; "The Logical Song," "Goodbye Stranger," "Take the Long Way Home," and the title track. At the peak of their popularity, tension was brewing in the band. After the release of 1982's "...famous last words...", Hodgson left to begin a solo career.

1985's Brother Where You Bound found some success with the added guitar sound of Thin Lizzy's Scott Gorham and Pink Floyd's David Gilmour. After Free as a Bird in 1987, Supertramp disbanded in 1988. Eight years later, Rick Davies re-formed the band with Helliwell and Siebenberg and added bassist Cliff Hugo, guitarist Carl Verheyen, keyboardist/guitarist Mark Hart, and brass player Lee Thornburg. This resulted in the recording of 1997's Some Things Never Change. Slow Motion was released in 2002, followed by a tour. In 2010, Supertramp regrouped again for a world tour to mark their 40th anniversary. Rick Davies and Roger Hodgson have issued statements to the effect that they most likely would never work together again. In 2015, Supertramp cancelled a tentative world tour due to the health problems of Rick Davies. While Supertramp started with progressive rock ambitions, they gained great commercial success with their FM radio friendly pop-rock songs.

Heart (1970-present) grew out of a band called White Heart, led by guitarist Roger Fisher that eventually turned into Heart. The early lineup included Fisher, keyboardist David Belzer, drummer Jeff Johnson, and guitarist James Cirrello. When vocalist Ann Wilson joined in 1972, the band was renamed Hocus Pocus. Nancy Wilson, Ann's sister, joined in 1974 and the band played numerous shows around their home base of Vancouver, Canada. Heart would have many lineup changes over their four-decade career, but the Wilson sisters remained at the core. Ann Wilson's role in Heart was as lead singer/songwriter/electric guitarist while Nancy was a songwriter/acoustic guitarist/background vocalist. Ann and Nancy fronted the band together, giving Heart a unique appearance that they promoted on the cover of *Rolling Stone Magazine*.

For their 1976 debut Dreamboat Annie, Heart recorded with the lineup of Fisher, Ann and Nancy Wilson, keyboardist Howard Leese, drummer Michael DeRosier, bassist Steve Fossen, and numerous additional musicians. It was released on a Canadian independent label. Dreamboat Annie was an instant hit in America, charting at number seven. It went to number thirty-six in England. This album spawned three hits "Crazy on You," "Magic Man," and "Dreamboat Annie." Ann Wilson was the principle songwriter but Nancy collaborated on three of the tracks. 1977's Magazine saw controversy when its release was unauthorized by the group, due to conflicts with their record label. That same year, Heart released Little Queen featuring the hits "Barracuda," "Little Queen," and "Kick it Out."

"Barracuda"
by Ann Wilson, Nancy Wilson, Michael DeRosier, and Roger Fisher

"Barracuda" was a song written out of the anger and hostility felt by Ann Wilson toward Heart's record company, Mushroom Records. The label wanted to portray the Wilson sisters in a fictitious and incestuous relationship to gain media attention. Ann wrote the lyrics in her hotel room and was later joined by Nancy to write the song's melody. Heart left Mushroom records immediately to sign with Portrait Records. Musically, "Barracuda" was Heart's very successful attempt to create a song with a hard rocking metal feel. Roger Fisher's classic guitar riffs, power chords, and use of distortion (comparable to a Jimmy Page-like Led Zeppelin vibe), have been emulated by many guitar players. The middle instrumental section made use of more Zeppelin inspired ideas including a dotted quarter-note drumset figure that complemented the guitar part and created a temporary feeling of suspending the time feel.

"Barracuda" peaked at number eleven in America and charted in many countries around the world. It has been covered by numerous artists from; Alice in Chains, Fergie, The Bad Plus, indie rock band The Dismemberment Club, and more. In popular culture, the song was featured in many movies and in the video games *Guitar Hero III* and *Grand Theft Auto*.

Commercial success followed with 1978's Dog and Butterfly and 1980's Bebe le Strange. Heart also released a double album Greatest Hits/Live in 1980 that peaked at number twelve on the U.S. charts. From 1981 to 1984, Heart experienced a decline in popularity with 1982's Private Audition and 1983's Passionworks. The band changed labels to Capitol Records and bounced back strong with 1985's Heart. There were some changes with the lineup, now featuring the Wilson sisters, keyboardist/guitarist Howard Leese, bassist Mark Andes, and drummer Denny Carmassi. Heart shot to number one in America and number nineteen in Britain with five hits. "These Dreams" went to number one and "What About Love" peaked at number ten. 1987's Bad Animals and 1990's Brigade produced more hits. The Wilson sisters next put together an acoustic group called The Lovemongers to do some side projects. In 1998, Ann Wilson decided to tour with Heart without Nancy. More lineup changes ensued.

Heart returned in 1993 with Desire Walks On and then Nancy Wilson decided to focus on raising a family. The Lovemongers made the album Heart Presents a Lovemongers' Christmas in 2001 that was eventually released as a Heart album. In 2002, Ann and Nancy returned to tour as Heart with another new lineup. 2004's Jupiters Darling was their first studio recording since 1993. Another studio album, Red Velvet Car appeared in 2010 followed by 2012's Fanatic. Also, in that same year, the Wilson sisters performed a version of Led Zeppelin's "Stairway to Heaven" at the annual Kennedy Center Honors with Jason Bonham. 2016's Beautiful Broken went to number nine on the American charts and featured Metallica's James Hetfield. In 2017, both Ann and Nancy were leading separate bands but announced that Heart was on hiatus and had not permanently disbanded.

Selling over thirty-five million records worldwide, Heart helped to define the MTV power rock ballad. They created their own unique sound with a hard rocking edge. Additionally, Heart was more than capable of combining their hard rock attitude with a softer acoustic sensibility. Heart was inducted into the Rock and Roll Hall of Fame in 2013.

Foghat (1971-1984) (1986-present) began in England when vocalist/guitarist Dave Peverett, bassist Tony Stevens, and drummer Roger Earl left their British blues band Savoy Brown and joined forces with guitarist Rod Price. They all moved to America where Foghat was signed to Bearsville Records. 1972's self-titled Foghat was produced by Dave Edmunds. Their Willie Dixon cover "I Just Want to Make Love To You" became a hit on FM radio. Their next record, 1973's (also called) Foghat, continued to build their audience. Throughout the 1970's, Foghat produced seven more records. 1975's Fool for the City yielded their biggest hit, "Slowride." Their 1977 live album titled Live, would become their most popular, peaking at number eleven on the American charts.

In the mid-1980's, guitarist Erik Cartwright replaced Rod Price who left the band to pursue a more new wave and pop direction. In the late 1970's, record sales dropped off and Foghat disbanded in 1984 when Peverett quit and moved back to England. In the early 1990's, Foghat re-formed and continued to record and tour. Peverett returned to the United States in 1990 and formed his own version of the band called Lonesome Dave's Foghat. In 1993, the original lineup reunited to record a studio album titled Return of the Boogie Men. After six more years together, Price retired from touring. Dave Peverett died in 2000 and Rod Price died in 2005. The current lineup of Foghat is original member drummer Roger Earl, supplemented by bassist Craig MacGregor, guitarist Bryan Bassett, and lead vocalist/guitarist Charlie Huhn. Foghat started with a basic, hard rocking blues based sound. They developed a strong audience, particularly in America, where they headlined sold out concerts until the punk and disco movements cut into their popularity.

One of classic rock's greatest and most enduring bands was part of the groundwork that created the genre of country rock (see chapter nine). **The Eagles** (1971-present) came to embody country rock combined with a California-based rock sound. Along the way, they became the highest selling American band in rock history (the sheer volume of incredible hits is impressive). They are credited with selling over one hundred and fifty million records (one hundred million in America alone), including five number one singles. The Eagles started in 1971 as a backup band for singer Linda Ronstadt. They consisted of vocalist/drummer Don Henley, vocalist/guitarist Glenn Frey, former Poco founder bassist/vocalist Randy Meisner, and ex-Flying Burrito Brothers veteran guitarist Bernie Leadon. The Eagles played on Ronstadt's debut album in 1971. Signed to David Geffen's Asylum label, The Eagles recorded their debut album Eagles in London in 1971. Legendary producer Glyn Johns guided the band to a perfect mix of rock and country styles. It soared to number twenty-two on the American charts. Although The Eagles created their own California sound, their two principle singer/songwriters, Henley and Frey, were from opposite parts of the country. Frey came from urban Detroit while Henley grew up in a small town in Texas.

Eagles yielded the hits "Take it Easy" (number twelve on the charts), "Witchy Woman" (number nine), and "Peaceful Easy Feeling" (number twenty-two). Glyn Johns was not initially impressed with the band because he thought they were conflicted about their musical direction. However, David Geffen convinced him to listen again and when he heard them harmonize Johns said, "There it was, the sound. Extraordinary blend of voices, wonderful harmony sound, just stunning." #6 For the album, Henley and Frey wanted a strong rock 'n' roll approach but Johns encouraged them not to abandon their country roots by utilizing Bernie Leadon's banjo playing. The common denominator proved to be the excellent Crosby, Stills, Nash, and Young-ish harmonies.

1973's Desperado digressed to number forty-one on the charts but contained the hits "Desperado" and "Tequila Sunrise." Desperado was a concept album with song themes that depicted life in a rock band while simultaneously living the lifestyle of the "old west" Dalton outlaw gang. Henley felt that the band was being stereotyped in the country category and therefore, The Eagles added guitarist Don Felder to bring a harder rock edge. 1974's On the Border placed in the top twenty albums in America and the hit "Best of My Love" reached number one.

What happened next was extraordinary in rock history. The Eagles produced *four* consecutive number one albums! 1975's One of These Nights delivered the hits "Lyin' Eyes," "Take it to the Limit," and the title track. However, there was some tension in the band that resulted in Leadon leaving and being replaced by guitarist/vocalist Joe Walsh (formerly of The James Gang). This move enabled The Eagles to move in a harder rock direction and include some of Walsh's ballads with lush harmonies.

1976's Hotel California went immediately to number one in America and number two in England. "New Kid in Town" went to number one, "Hotel California" was also a number one, and ""Life in the Fast Lane" went to number eleven. This album ranks high on many "greatest rock album lists" and showcased The Eagles at their creative and commercial peak.

Rock Hard Fact

The Eagles are among the highest selling artists in the world with more than 150 million albums sold but they have never signed an endorsement deal or let their music be used for commercial use.

"While the band did break up in 1980, our music continued without us…It was becoming increasingly apparent to me that, no matter where I went or what I did, for the rest of my life I would always be an Eagle."

– Glenn Frey

Groundbreaking album
Hotel California
by The Eagles

One of rock's most legendary albums, Hotel California, was full of mystery, intrigue, and classic hits. It took the band eight months in the studio to record the album. Their first recording without the country influences of Bernie Leadon, and the first with the hard rocking guitarist Joe Walsh, this record was the band's pivot to a harder edge. At the same time, Don Henley emerged as the band's most dominant vocalist and lyricist. Henley wrote six of the record's compositions and basically composed a concept album that portrayed the state of California as a metaphor for a world of superficial motivations and a lifestyle of excess.

Side one opened with "Hotel California," then "New Kid in Town," "Life in the Fast Lane," and "Wasted Time." Bassist Randy Meisner and drummer Don Henley locked-in with the best grooves that the band had yet experienced. Plus, The Eagles now had the one-two punch of guitarists Felder and Walsh. "New Kid in Town" featured Glenn Frey singing lead vocals and Henley singing the main harmony parts. This variety of lead vocal timbres gave the Eagles great diversity. "Life in the Fast Lane" grew rapidly out of a guitar riff that Joe Walsh was playing around with while warming up in a rehearsal. The band told him to keep it because it could become a great song. While The Eagles were recording at Criteria Studios (in Miami, Florida), Black Sabbath was next door, also recording an album. The Eagles had to stop more than once when Sabbath's massive sound kept coming through the wall.

Side two opened with "Wasted Time (Reprise)," then "Victim of Love," "Pretty Maids All in a Row," "Try and Love Again," and "The Last Resort." Again, The Eagles showcased their incredible vocal versatility when Henley, Walsh, and Meisner all sang lead on songs on side two. Hotel California marked what felt like a whole new band, one that just made one of the best selling records in rock history. The Eagles now became both a large draw as an arena rock band and an enduing classic rock band. Worldwide, Hotel California has sold more than seventeen million copies.

"Hotel California"
by Don Henley, Glenn Frey, and Don Felder

"Hotel California" was about a person who took a luxury hotel visit on a trip to the dark side. "Hotel California" also functioned as an allegory for the hedonistic and carefree lifestyle that many musicians exhibited throughout the 1970's. Don Henley has pointed out many times that The Eagles band members were all middle-class working guys from the Mid-West. "Hotel California" would become their interpretation of the movie stars, beaches, bikinis, and *everything* California. Glenn Frey said "this album was the zenith of The Eagles in that what we had to say came together with our learning of how to make records…all of our songs were cinematic…we decided to create something strange, just to see if we could do it. And then a lot was read into it-a lot more than probably exists." #7

"Hotel California" was a long and intricate rock ballad with an exciting, dueling guitar coda. Henley and Frey wrote the lyrics while Don Felder wrote most of the music on his home studio four track recorder. The band thought the song was a weird mixture of musical influences and gave it a working title of "Mexican Reggae." It took many days to record the closing guitar riffs that trade back and forth and many attempts to find the perfect drum fills. They also had to keep changing the song's key to find the right range for Don Henley's vocal part.

In 1976, The Eagles released Their Greatest Hits, a collection of hits from their first four albums. Not only did it go to number one, it became America's best selling record in the 20th century, until it was surpassed by Michael Jackson's Thriller. After three long years of difficult recording sessions, The Eagles delivered The Long Run, another number one. The hits continued with "Heartache Tonight," "I Can't Tell You Why," and the title track. Their long run had come to an end when on tour in 1980, The Eagles decided to call it quits (after being seen openly arguing). The former members then pursued solo careers, with Don Henley achieving the most success.

In 1982, The Eagles compiled Greatest Hits Vol 2 and it proved to be popular. After a twelve-year period, The Eagles were involved in an Eagles country tribute album titled Common Thread: The Songs of the Eagles. A tour ensued and a live album titled Hell Freezes Over (named for Henley's previous statements about when the band would get back together). Don Felder sued the band after he was fired in 2001. The band continued to tour in 2001 with some lineup changes, including the addition of guitarist Steuart Smith. By 2007, The Eagles consisted of Walsh, Frey, Henley, and bassist Timothy B. Schmit. 2007 also saw the release of Long Road Out of Eden, their first studio recording since 1979. It produced another number one album and a new legion of fans. More tours followed, and in 2013, the band made a career-spanning documentary.

In early 2016, Glenn Frey died at the age of sixty-seven. The current Eagles lineup added Glenn Frey's son, Deacon Frey, and the band continues to perform. In the end, The Eagles broke up because they were no longer having any fun. They were tired of the pressure of having to outdo themselves from record to record. They realized there was nowhere to go after reaching number one on the charts so many times. The Eagles had it all; skillfully crafted songwriting, strong harmonies, high level musicianship, burning guitar solos, and the unique vocals of Henley, Frey, and later Walsh. No band better defined a post-1960's American rock sound than this superstar California based band. From the early country sounding Eagles to their rise to stardom, they never totally abandoned their country roots. The Eagles clearly evolved to define classic rock. The Eagles were inducted into the Rock and Roll Hall of Fame in 1998.

Styx (1970-present) was formed in Chicago, Illinois by twin brother's drummer John Panozzo and bassist Chuck Panozzo. They added pianist Dennis DeYoung, guitarist John Curulewski, and guitarist James "J.Y." Young. Styx signed with the Wooden Nickel label and recorded four records including; 1972's Styx, 1973's Styx II and The Serpent is Rising, and Man of Miracles in 1974. The band's early approach combined a progressive rock and art-rock sound but without complex meters. They toured Mid-West America and built a steady following. The power ballad "Lady" (from Styx II) began to sell well. Styx moved to the major label A&M and released Equinox in 1975. It featured the song "Suite Madame Blue" that earned them more FM radio exposure. John Curulewski was replaced by guitarist Tommy Shaw and Styx hit their stride with a series of popular albums.

1977's Grand Illusion shot to number six on the American charts and spawned the hits "Come Sail Away" and "Fooling Yourself." Styx was solidifying a style of songwriting that portrayed fantasy themes that functioned as allegories and commentaries about American lifestyles. 1978's Pieces of Eight again rose to number six on the charts and yielded the hits "Sing for the Day," "Blue Collar Man," and "Renegade." Cornerstone followed in 1979 and went to number two in America. The band charted for the first time in England. The hit "Babe" went to number one in America. Next, Styx released a fourth consecutive triple-platinum album with 1981's Paradise Theatre, their only number one album. The hit "Too Much Time on My Hands" went to number nine and "The Best of Times" went to number three.

By 1983, Styx experienced creative differences surrounding their record Kilroy Was Here. They broke up after recording their first live album, Caught in the Act. Dennis DeYoung and Tommy Shaw pursued solo careers before the band reunited in 1990. The reunion was short lived and by 1992 they called it quits again. By 1995, Styx once again re-formed, and would go to record four more studio albums including the 2017 release, The Mission. This album returned them to their progressive rock roots.

Bad Company (1973-present) was formed in 1973 when the band Free split up. Paul Rodgers and Simon Kirke joined forces with former Mott The Hoople guitarist Mick Ralphs and ex-King Crimson bassist Boz Burrell. They were managed by Led Zeppelin manager Peter Grant until 1982 (Grant stepped down when he was devastated by the death of Led Zeppelin's John Bonham). Bad Company became a supergroup as they obtained great success throughout the 1970's. Their first three albums, 1974's Bad Company, 1975's Straight Shooter, and 1976's Run With The Pack, all reached the top five on the British and American pop charts. Instant success came as the first album contained "Ready For Love," and "Can't Get Enough of Your Love." The second album, Straight Shooter, keep the hits coming with "Feel Like Makin Love," "Shooting Star," and "Good Lovin' Gone Bad."

Bad Company toured heavily and released more albums. However, they called it quits in 1982 when Rodgers left to form The Firm with (by then) ex-Led Zeppelin icon Jimmy Page. By 1986, Mick Ralphs and Simon Kirke decided to re-form Bad Company, now with vocalist Brian Howe. A new release in 1986, Fame and Fortune, had little commercial success but their next album, 1988's Dangerous Age, fared much better. Many lineup changes ensued. Bad Company was successful but inconsistent through the late 1980's and into the early 1990's. In an unexpected turn of events, the original Bad Company reunited in 1998 and lasted until 2002. Paul Rodgers was asked to join the supergroup Queen, where he stayed from 2004 until 2009. Once again Bad Company re-formed and they still continue to tour.

"Shooting Star"
by Paul Rodgers

Initially not even released as a single from Straight Shooter ("Good Lovin' Gone Bad" and "Feel Like Makin' Love" were the singles), "Shooting Star" proved to be one of Bad Company's most enduring tunes. The song was inspired lyrically by the tragic alcohol and drug related deaths of Jim Morrison, Janis Joplin, and Jimi Hendrix. It told the story of a young guitar player, Johnny, who grows up to become a rock star, but falls victim to the rock star lifestyle and dies of an overdose. Paul Rodgers wrote the song to serve as a warning.

"Shooting Star" highlighted the Bad Company sound that successfully blended acoustic rhythm guitar with electric guitar power chords and solos. The shooting star analogy was an excellent use of symbolism. In the song, Johnny was a big rock star and then went away via an overdose. It was very comparable to how a shooting star burns brightly and then fades away. Paul Rodgers brought a strong ability to improvise on "Shooting Star." At the end of the recording, his vocals alternated effectively with the burning lines of guitarist Mick Ralphs (perhaps one of the most under-rated guitar players in rock history). "Shooting Star," like Johnny's legacy, is a timeless rock classic.

Bachman Turner Overdrive (1973-present) is a Canadian band that started when guitarist Randy Bachman and ex-Guess Who singer Chad Allan added Bachman brother Robbie Bachman on drums and bassist Fred Turner to form the band Brave Belt. After a few failed albums, Allen left and they added another Bachman brother, guitarist Tim Bachman. They changed the band name to Bachman-Turner Overdrive. Their self-titled debut album did not produce any hits but did establish a solid fan base. BTO's second album featured the hit "Let it Ride" which eventually went to number twenty-three on the American charts. It also featured "Takin' Care of Business" that went to number twelve and became their most popular tune. Next, Tim Bachman left to become a full-time producer. They replaced him with guitarist Blair Thornton.

BTO went on the release four albums from 1974 to 1977, including the classic and under-rated Not Fragile, which included their only number one hit on the American charts, "You Ain't Seen Nothing Yet." Multiple lineup changes followed and the band had less commercial success. After a 2005 hiatus, BTO reunited in 2009 to record a new album and to tour. The band has sold thirty million records worldwide and their hits continue to receive consistent radio airplay on classic rock stations.

Journey (1973-present) began as a San Francisco based all-star band. In Journey's over forty year existence, they have gone through personnel changes, an exciting musical evolution, and eventual worldwide popularity. They have sold over forty eight million records in America, and ninety million worldwide. These figures make Journey one of the world's best selling bands of all time. But that's not how they began. In 1973, two members of Santana, guitarist Neal Schon and organist/vocalist Gregg Rolie, left a successful career in Santana to form a band with ex-Steve Miller Band bassist Ross Valory. They also added rhythm guitarist George Tickner and (briefly) drummer Prairie Prince (who went on to join The Tubes). Prince was replaced by popular English drummer Anysley Dunbar (formerly of John Mayall, Frank Zappa, David Bowie, and others), who brought with him an impressive reputation and resume.

Journey relied on music business veteran Herbie Herbert as their manager. Herbert knew Schon and Rolie through Santana, and Valory and Tickner from the San Francisco psychedelic band Frumious Bandersnatch. He guided the quintet through their self-titled 1975 debut Journey. But Journey was paired down to a quartet for the next two recordings, Look Into the Future and Next. With Schon, Rolie, Valory, and Dunbar, a super-group was born, but big success still proved to be elusive. At first, Journey was an adventurous jazz-rock band rather than the hit-makers they would become. Although Rolie's

> "A lot of people don't even know there was a Journey before Steve Perry."
>
> – Jonathan Cain

lead vocals (that graced many of Santana's early hits) were more than capable, Herbert felt that the band needed a soaring voice that would stand next to the chart topping bands of the day such as Boston and Foreigner. Journey's first singer/frontman was Robert Fleischman, but he didn't last long. Herbert suggested Steve Perry, a hybrid of the vocal styles of Robert Plant and Sam Cooke.

Perry's strong falsetto voice, combined with the soulful songs written by Rolie, Schon, and Perry, turned into hits. Journey released 1978's Infinity that yielded the hits "Wheel In The Sky" and "Lights." The band's popularity and touring schedule grew consistently. In 1979, Dunbar left (to join Jefferson Starship) and was replaced by jazz-rock drummer Steve Smith who Journey had heard playing with Ronnie Montrose (on a tour that also featured Van Halen as a supporting act). This version of the band recorded 1979's Evolution, and 1980's Departure that included the hits "Lovin' Touchin' Squeezin'," and "Anyway You Want It." The live record Captured featured the last recordings of this lineup of the band. In 1981, The Babys' keyboardist Jonathan Cain replaced Rolie. Cain brought with him a highly refined style of pop songwriting skills that melded perfectly with Perry's voice, and the "classic" lineup of Journey was formed. With this lineup, the band created the albums Escape, Frontiers, (parts of) Raised on Radio, and Trial By Fire. These recordings produced multi-platinum sales and numerous top ten hits including "Don't Stop Believin," "Separate Ways," "Be Good To Yourself," and "When You Love A Woman."

"Don't Stop Believin"
by Steve Perry, Jonathan Cain, and Neal Schon

"Don't Stop Believin" was written for Journey's seventh studio album Escape in 1981. The song contained an interesting musical structure since the full chorus didn't occur until the very end of the tune. After the second and third verses, a "pre-chorus" entered. Jonathan Cain began the song with a very soulful and identifiable keyboard riff and Steve Perry was able to fully demonstrate his wide and powerful vocal range. Drummer Steve Smith was inspired by Terry Bozo's drumming in the band Group 87 to develop a unique drum part that skillfully integrated the sound of the toms and the bell of the ride cymbal throughout the tune.

The title of "Don't Stop Believin" came from the advice and inspiration received by keyboardist Jonathan Cain from his father. He told his son to "don't stop believing in yourself" when Jonathan was feeling discouraged about the difficulties of trying to make it in the competitive Los Angeles music scene. This song has been an inspiration for many sports teams including The Chicago White Sox baseball team, The Los Angeles Dodgers baseball team, and The Detroit Red Wings hockey team. "Don't Stop Believin" has sold more digital copies than any song in the twentieth century.

After a period of uncertainty, Steve Perry was replaced by a series of singers including Jeff Scott Soto, Steve Augeri, and Arnel Pineda. Veteran drummer Deen Castronovo (who Schon and Cain had worked with in the bands Bad English and Hardline) replaced Steve Smith who left to continue his career as a successful bandleader with his jazz-rock band Vital Information. Since the departure of Perry, Journey has recorded four formidable albums including Arrival, Generations, Revelation, and Eclipse. In 2016, Steve Smith returned to tour with the band replacing Castronovo, while Arnel Pineda's (who has now been in Journey longer than any other singer) vocals continued to soar through Journey's hits. Today, this powerhouse that established itself during the 1970's continues to tour extensively. They provide fans with shows of non-stop sing-along hits and musical virtuosity that spans generations and decades. In 2017, Journey was inducted into the Rock and Roll Hall of Fame.

The Babys (1974-1981) (2013-present) are a British rock band formed in 1974 that released five studio albums from 1977 to 1980. They generated tremendous hype when they formed with the expectation that they might become a great band in the future. The core lineup was keyboardist/guitarist Michael Corby, bassist/vocalist John Waite, guitarist Wally Stocker, and drummer Tony Brock. The band signed a lucrative contract in 1977 and in that same year released The Babys and Broken Heart. "Isn't It Time" was a hit from Broken Heart. Jonathan Cain (who later joined Journey) replaced Corby and bassist Ricky Phillips was added in 1978. The band focused on the American market after the punk and new wave movement first gained strength in England. 1979's Head First achieved their strongest success reaching number twenty-two on the American charts. Their biggest hit "Every Time I Think of You," came from the Head First record. They recorded I'll Have Some of That in 1980. The Babys broke up in 1981 but reformed in 2013 with a new lineup.

Foreigner (1976-present) evolved from the early career of multi-instrumentalist/composer Mick Jones, who was a veteran of the bands Spooky Tooth and Nero and the Gladiators. Jones added ex-King Crimson multi-instrumentalist Ian McDonald, vocalist Lou Gramm, bassist Ed Gagliardi, keyboardist Al Greenwood, and drummer Dennis Elliot to form Foreigner. The band made a fast start with their 1977 self-titled debut album that produced three hits and reached number four on the American charts. It sold over four million copies. The single "Feels Like the First Time" went to number four, "Cold as Ice" went to number six, and "Long, Long Way From Home" peaked at number twenty. Foreigner was an instant success playing arenas and venues worldwide. Lou Gramm proved to be a powerful frontman and Jones wrote melodic hooks with great skill.

"Feels Like the First Time"
by Mick Jones

Guitarist Mick Jones was in the process of writing "Feels Like the First Time" and also auditioning around fifty singers for Foreigner when he heard a demo tape of vocalist Lou Gramm. Jones knew he was the right guy to sing "Feels Like the First Time." The tune and the addition of Gramm were both catalysts to getting Foreigner off the ground. The song also helped them to secure their first record deal when record executive, John Kalodner, liked the song and signed them to Atlantic Records.

"Feels Like the First Time" proved that Foreigner could craft a well-conceived rock song. Mick Jones knew that a slow tempo would allow his opening guitar riff to create a great rock feel to support Gramm's vocal lines. "Feels Like the First Time" moved to an interlude section in a half time feel where a synthesizer-based arpeggio figure repeated, adding a great contrast to the opening guitar dominated verses. Toward the end of the song, Jones and Ian McDonald doubled a guitar riff to create a thick sound. The drum part was reduced to state only beats two and four. This section set up a return to the tune's chorus which then led to a fade out.

> "The studio work is the nasty, tedious, hard and nerve-wracking part, interrupted by moments of exhilaration. Playing live is the chance to actually have some fun and get on a stage."
>
> – Tom Scholz

Chapter Eleven: Classic Rock

1978's Double Vision continued Foreigner's popularity, selling over five million copies in America. It yielded the hits "Hot Blooded" and the title track "Double Vision." 1979's Head Games continued to showcase more hits with "Dirty White Boy" and "Head Games." The band saw changes when Greenwood and McDonald were fired due to Mick Jones' desire to move the band in a different musical direction. In 1981, Foreigner released the album 4 that went to number one on the American charts. "Waiting for a Girl Like You" reached number two and became their first top ten hit in Britain. Foreigner made some lineup changes and continued to tour in 1981-82.

Foreigner achieved more success with 1984's Agent Provocateur and its power ballad "I Want to Know What Love Is." 1987's Inside Information followed. By the late 1980's, Lou Gramm became interested in developing a solo career and left Foreigner by 1990. Mick Jones was determined to carry on and enlisted vocalist Johnny Edwards for their 1991 album Unusual Heat, which was met with little success. Gramm returned in 1992, but Foreigner's chart days were behind them. They continued to tour at smaller venues through the rest of the decade. In addition to leading Foreigner, Mick Jones established himself as a producer working with Van Halen on their breakout album, 1986's 5150.

With more lineup changes, 1994's Mr. Moonlight fared poorly but the band continued to perform live. Gramm left again in 2003 and the band responded by adding vocalist Kelly Hansen, drummer Jason Bonham (John Bonham's son), and other musicians to record Can't Slow Down in 2009. This was Foreigner's first studio album in fifteen years, returning them to the American and British charts.

Boston (1976-present) was formed in Boston, Massachusetts in 1976 by guitarist and composer Tom Scholz. Joined by vocalist/guitarist Brad Delp, guitarist Barry Gourdreau, bassist Fran Sheehan, and drummer Sib Hashian, Boston made an immediate impact with the highest selling debut album in rock history. The album Boston went to number three on the American charts and number eleven on the British charts, selling over seventeen million copies worldwide. Its success was based on the hits "More Than a Feeling," "Rock and Roll Band," and "Foreplay/Long Time." Their second album, 1978's Don't Look Back, was also successful although issues with their record company slowed the band down in terms of touring and recording.

After some lineup changes and an eight-year gap, Boston released 1986's Third Stage. Tom Scholz, a bit of a perfectionist, was happier with the band's studio sound and production. The album sold well and featured the hits "We're Ready," and "Cool the Engines." Eight-years later and more lineup changes saw Boston release 1994's Walk On and of course, after another eight-years, in 2002 they released Corporate America. After an even longer gap, Boston released only their sixth album in 2013, Life, Love and Hope.

Tom Scholz is one of the few guitarists who has an immediately recognizable guitar tone. Scholz had invented the Rockman portable guitar amplifier and his own line of guitar effects utilizing his master's degree from MIT. His guitar sound is unique and very clean as he combines guitar technology with superior production. Many guitar players, including studio great Steve Lukather, credited Scholtz with being the first to create a perfect wall of power chords. Scholtz commented, "I grew up listening to classical music, so on a song like 'More Than a Feeling,' when it breaks into that chorus part, that's what I wanted to hear-that symphonic power, that impact.

I discovered that what I needed to do was have stereo guitars for rhythm parts, split up on the sides. I'd usually track two separate guitars on each side, purposely detuning each pair at least 10 cents apart in pitch, sometimes including a center track." #8 At times, Scholz's guitar sound even achieved a violin-like quality that helped to *define* Boston's sound. Boston is a band that has achieved great success while working at their own pace.

Dire Straits (1977-1988) (1991-1995) began when the multi-talented Scottish singer/songwriter, guitarist, vocalist, film score composer, and record producer Mark Knopfler joined his younger brother, Dave Knopfler, to form a band. Dave is a singer/songwriter, guitarist, pianist, record producer, poet and author. In 1977, the brothers added bassist John Illsley and drummer Pick Withers to complete Dire Straits. The bands' sound drew from the many musical influences of blues, jazz, country, folk, and Mersey beat (Liverpool sound) all within a rock 'n' roll context. Dire Straits' sound developed into a stripped down minimalism that grew out of the pub rock environment around London.

Their 1978 debut album, Dire Straits, was an immediate international success peaking at number two in America and number five in Britain. "Sultans of Swing" was a hit single that was released before the debut album was recorded. It received very positive radio play and generated much record company interest, thus earning Dire Straits a record contract at Phonogram Records.

"The Sultans of Swing"
by Mark Knopfler

Mark Knopfler wrote "The Sultans of Swing" about people who go to clubs after work to have a good time and hear bands play live music. The lyrics stated that these club patrons were not impressed by a band's image but rather, were only interested in their music. Knopfler was inspired to write the song's lyrics after watching a poor quality band perform in a club. Knopfler noticed that the bar crowd was pretty drunk and when the band finished their last set, they announced to the crowd that they (themselves) were "the sultans of swing." Knopfler was stunned at their arrogance.

Despite the title, "The Sultans of Swing" does not have a swing feel. Knopfler was able to deftly combine his signature guitar picking style with a great mix of blues and country ideas. This can be heard in the interplay of his guitar comping ideas and the originality of his solo guitar lines. The lyric of "The band was playing dixie double four time," referred to a style (dixie double) popularized by Django Reinhradt and Les Paul where the guitar and bass play technical and fast ideas together. The characters of "Guitar George" and "Harry" referred to George Young and Harry Vander, both guitarists in the band The Easybeats. Mark Knopfler has stated that he was sick of playing the tune, having done so thousands of time. "The Sultans of Swing" peaked at number four in the U.S. and charted well internationally.

1979's Communique was quickly recorded and was very similar to their debut album. It did well, selling three million copies worldwide. During the recording of their third album, 1980's Making Moves, Dave Knopfler left the band to pursue a solo career. His replacement was guitarist Hal Lindes and the band added keyboardist Alan Clark. The record gained popularity on the strength of radio and MTV hits "Skateaway" and "Romeo and Juliet." Dire Straits followed with 1982's Love Over Gold that contained long experimental passages (and mallet

> **Rock Hard Fact**
>
> In 1985, The Philips Music Corporation used the Dire Straits' Brothers In Arms album to launch the compact disc format worldwide.

player Mike Mainieri on two tracks). It went to number one in England and number nineteen in America. Shortly after recording Love Over Gold, Pick Withers left the band and was replaced by ex-Rockpile drummer Terry Williams. Also during this time, Mark Knopfler produced Bob Dylan's album Infidels. 1985 Brothers in Arms was an international breakthrough album for the band. However, there were lineup changes before the recording sessions for the album. Another keyboardist, Guy Fletcher was added, guitarist Jack Sonni replaced Hal Lindes, and drummer Omar Hakim recorded many of the drum parts. The result produced the largest selling album in England in the 1980's and it went to number one worldwide! The hit "Money for Nothing" peaked at number one in America and was the first video played on MTV in England.

Groundbreaking album
Brothers in Arms
by Dire Straits

Brothers in Arms was one of the best selling albums in rock history having sold more than thirty million copies worldwide. What makes the album special is the tremendous musicianship on display and the great attention to detail that Dire Straits made in recording the album. Mark Knopfler hired producer Neil Dorfsman for his production skills (having produced jazz vibraphonist Mike Mainieri's excellent recording titled Wanderlust). Knopfler had written all of the songs and rehearsed them with the band before going into the studio. This allowed them to focus on getting a great sound. This also proved to be a challenge since the studio they utilized had limited space to separate the instruments and allow for optimum microphone placement. Side one opened with "So Far Away," then "Money for Nothing," "Walk of Life," "Your Latest Trick," and "Why Worry."

When the recorded drum parts proved to be inadequate for the album, fusion drumming great Omar Hakim was brought in to re-record the drum parts over a two-day period. Side two opened with "Ride Across the River," then "The Man's Too Strong," "One World," and "Brothers in Arms." Mark Knopfler gave insight into the song "Brothers in Arms" when he said, "it is sung by a soldier who is dying on the battlefield. You can't just write off the top of your head; you have to dig deep to get those things. You have to experience, if a thing is really going to be realistic, if you're gonna try and get whatever you feel across. So, in a sense you're an outsider, but you're also digging inside to do it properly…If you stay outside of these experiences, they're just not going to translate to people." #9 The single "Money For Nothing" gained much exposure on MTV. Also, Sting was given co-writing credit for the tune. In 1986, Brothers in Arms won two Grammy Awards and has been consistently praised by many musicians for its sound quality and high-level of musicianship.

After Brothers in Arms, Mark Knopfler took a break from Dire Straits and focused on solo projects. The band regrouped for Nelson Mandela's 70th Birthday Tribute concert in 1988 but there would be no permanent reunion at that time. Knopfler formed a new band called The Notting Hillbillies that played in a country music style. In 1991, Mark Knopfler re-formed Dire Straits and they recorded their final studio album On Every Street that same year. Knopfler then disbanded Dire Straits again in 1995 to pursue his solo career full time.

Toto (1977-2008) (2010-present) started when keyboardist David Paich (son of arranger/musician Marty Paich) met drummer Jeff Porcaro (son of session percussionist Joe Porcaro) when they were both in high school. They formed the band Rural Still Life. They soon added bassist David Hungate, guitarist Steve Lukather, and keyboardist Steve Porcaro (Jeff's brother) to the band. The last addition was ex-S.S. Fools vocalist Bobby Kimball. Most of the band members had extensive experience doing session work (see the session work of Toto profile). The band was signed to Columbia Records in 1977 and started to work on their debut album with Paich doing much of the composing. In order to keep their demo tapes separate from other session tapes the band would play on, Jeff Porcaro wrote "Toto" on them. When asked in interviews, the band members would say Toto took its name from the dog in *The Wizard of Oz* movie.

Their debut album Toto was released in 1978 and immediately spawned three hits that broke into the top fifty on the charts. "I'll Supply the Love," "Georgy Porgy," and "Hold the Line," shot the album to number nine in America and number thirty-seven in Britain. "Hold the Line" went to number five with its heavy guitar licks and strong triplet feel. The band members were thrilled to hear their original songs on the radio even though they could be heard as hired guns on hundreds of other artists' recordings. Critical review for Toto was mixed with some saying the band failed in attempting to transition from career session work to a working band. Other critics, prominent musicians, and their fans, felt differently as demonstrated by their success. However, 1979's Hydra and 1981's Turn Back did not sell as well and Toto felt the pressure from their record company to match the success of their debut record.

1982's Toto IV delivered one of the decades most commercially successful records. It produced three top ten hits; "Africa," "I Won't Hold You Back," and "Rosanna." The band gained exposure to a worldwide audience when they toured to support the record. In that same time period, Steve Porcaro co-wrote Michael Jackson's "Human Nature," and Lukather and Jeff Porcaro played on Jackson's Thriller album. David Paich has always viewed Toto as a collective songwriting team. Paich said, "It's a collaborative effort you know, I always tried to pattern ourselves after The Beatles and Fleetwood Mac. I thought it would be better to have more talent and more songwriters. But it comes down to we have to be objective with the material and pick the best songs …I learned a lot from Quincy Jones making Thriller." #10

"Rosanna"
by David Paich

"Rosanna" was the opening track on the album Toto IV and went to number two in the U.S. and number twelve in England. A misconception was that the song was named after actress Rosanna Arquette, who was dating Steve Porcaro at the time, but the band denied this rumor. Composer David Paich claimed the song was inspired by a girl that he had dated in high school.

When the song's verses transitioned from key to key, the lead vocal parts moved from Steve Lukather to Bobby Kimball. Drummer Jeff Porcaro revealed that the now legendary drumset part was a combination of (also legendary) Bernard Purdie's half-time shuffle and the (again legendary) Bo Diddley beat. The buzz surrounding the release of the song was so strong that prominent musicians were *waiting in their cars* the day of its release to hear its first radio play. The song ended with a jam when

Paich played a honky-tonk piano feel while the band rocked-out full throttle.

There was an accompanying video for "Rosanna" with actress and dancer Cynthia Rhodes starring as Rosanna. Actor Patrick Swayze also appeared in the video. When the song's lyrics stated "Not quite a year since she went away," there was a finger snapping part added to the mix that was inspired by a scene in the musical West Side Story.

Bassist David Hungate left Toto before the 1984 release of Isolation. Another Porcaro brother, Mike Porcaro, replaced him. Next, Bobby Kimball was fired from the band. 1986's Fahrenheit returned Toto to more of a pop-rock direction. Vocalist Joseph Williams (son of composer John Williams) joined the band as well as vocalist Barbara Ruick. Guest musicians including; Doobie Brothers' Michael McDonald, Eagles' Don Henley, and jazz great Miles Davis also appeared on Fahrenheit. This recording produced two hit singles; "I'll Be Over You" and "Without Your Love." 1988's The Seventh One featured the singles "Pamela" and "Stop Loving You," with Jon Anderson of Yes singing background vocals on the latter. Toto released a greatest hits album in 1990 but endured instability at the lead vocal position when temporary new singer Jean-Michel Byron was fired. For 1992's Kingdom of Desire album, Steve Lukather assumed the lead vocalist chair and became the band's new frontman.

Tragedy struck when drummer Jeff Porcaro died suddenly from a heart attack. The band (and the entire L.A. recording industry) was devastated. Toto nearly broke up but Porcaro's family insisted that they continue. Toto enlisted British drumming great Simon Phillips because Jeff respected him highly and Phillips had worked previously with Lukather. In 1993, Toto released a live album dedicated to Jeff's Memory. In 1992, a tribute concert was held in Jeff's memory with many luminaries from the music business in attendance performing Toto songs with the remaining Toto members.

1995's Tambu was their first album with Simon Phillips. A successful tour followed with drummer Gregg Bissonette filling in for Phillips, who was sidelined with back issues. 1998's Toto XX celebrated the band's twentieth anniversary and 1999's Mindfields saw the return of vocalist Bobby Kimball. In 2002, Toto made an album of covers titled Through the Looking Glass. They recorded tunes by Elton John, George Harrison, Bob Marley, and Steely Dan. A live album and DVD to promote their twenty-fifth anniversary was then released in 2003. David Paich took a temporary leave of absence in 2003 and session great Greg Phillinganes filled in for him.

2006's Falling in Between would be Toto's first album of new compositions since 1999. In 2008, Steve Lukather disbanded Toto, but two years later he reunited the band for a short tour of Europe to help ailing bassist Mike Porcaro (who had developed the debilitating disease ALS). The band again went on hiatus until they decided to tour in 2011 and 2012. Some lineup changes occurred when drummer Simon Phillips left and was replaced briefly by Steely Dan drummer Keith Carlock, then Nashville session drummer Shannon Forest. In 2014, Toto co-headlined a tour with Michael McDonald and released their fourteenth studio album Toto XIV the following year. Sadly, bassist Mike Porcaro died in 2015 due to complications from his battle with ALS (Lou Gehrig's disease.) Current Toto members include; Lukather, Paich, Steve Porcaro, Shannon Forest and Joseph Williams. In 2018, Toto released 40 Trips Around the Sun, a greatest hits album with three previously unreleased tracks. Toto continues to tour worldwide.

The Studio World of Toto

Many of the greatest musicians in rock history had initially worked as studio musicians (aka session players) before forming their own band or joining a major group. The list is long and it includes; Led Zeppelin's Jimmy Page and John Paul Jones, Jimi Hendrix, and keyboardist Nicky Hopkins. Also, complete bands like The Hawks (later The Band) backed stars such as Bob Dylan and the Stax Records' session band, led by Booker T., went on to form the band Booker T and the MG's. But the original members of Toto, originally Los Angeles first-call studio musicians, played with perhaps the most incredible list of artists ranging from Steely Dan to Boz Scaggs to Michael Jackson to George Benson. This gave them an advantage over many bands whose musicians had minimal or no studio experience when it came to recording albums. The core Toto members came to the table with a wealth of musical experience, having played a wide variety of pop and rock styles. All of them possessed excellent time and feel, and the ability to get a great sound on their respective instruments.

Guitarist Steve Lukather recorded for a wide variety of artists that included; Barbara Streisand, Boz Scaggs, Cher, The Pointer Sisters, Cheap Trick, Elton John, Herb Alpert, Chicago, Neil Diamond, Joni Mitchell, Michael Jackson, and countless others. Lukather talked about what it took to be successful as a studio musician when he recalled, "You had to be on the game. Like, the first take was like…you were supposed to nail it in one take. They didn't have multi-track-when I started out, there was one 24-track machine before they figured out how to sync them all up. So you had to bring it. There was no second chance. So you had to be good…you do it all the time, you get better at it and more confident with more experience, the amount of sessions you do. …Next thing you know, you're doing 25 sessions a week." #11

David Paich had an equally formidable studio resume that included work on numerous soundtracks and albums by artists including; Aretha Franklin, Diana Ross, The Doobie Brothers, Elton John, Rod Stewart, Randy Newman, Steely Dan, and countless others. David Paich remembered the circumstances of working on Michael Jackson's Thriller when he said, "Michael first of all is probably one of the most talented persons who ever lived. Out of everybody I have ever seen. He could dance, sing, do it all, and write. And then you put Quincy Jones with him and you have a magical team-like to me that's the equivalent to George Martin working with Paul McCartney. And I ended up working with Paul McCartney because I was co-arranger on "The Girl is Mine." So we had Quincy Jones, Paul McCartney - all these people and it was a unique project." #12

Drummer Jeff Porcaro was another Toto member that was a first-call studio icon. His credits included; Paul McCartney, Pink Floyd, Donna Summer, Eric Clapton, Bruce Springsteen, Seals and Crofts, Dire Straits, Al Jarreau, Boz Scaggs, Herbie Hancock, Paul Simon, Stan Getz, and countless others. Jeff remembered one challenging session making a direct-to-disc recording for James Newton Howard & Friends. Jeff said, "Those are very high-pressure records because you can't screw up. Say, if you have five songs on one side and you mess up song five, then you have to start all over again. And there's no rest in between tunes. If the first tune is a burner in 7/8, then you've got the amount of time between songs on an

---

Rock Hard Fact

The members of Kansas were interviewed for a VH1 *Behind The Music* special, but the show was never produced because their off-stage personal lives were too boring.

album to A; change your music if you're reading, and B; just get yourself psyched up for the next tune which is a waltz with brushes. You know what it's like when you're playing real hard to make a quick switch to a slower tempo? —your hands are still shaking from the intensity from the track before. It's tough." #13
Many of the other Toto musicians, original and later additions, had deep studio experience.

The beauty of Toto was that they could have exclusively continued to have great careers as first call session players, but they wanted to experience the unity and special musical relationships that only a composite band of their quality could provide. Toto is, the Musician's Band!

Kansas (1973-1984) (1985-present) began as a melding of bands from the Topeka, Kansas area. In 1969, guitarist/keyboardist/songwriter Kerry Livgren was in the band called The Reasons Why. They changed their name to Saratoga over the next year and Livgren was able to hone his original compositions. In 1970, Saratoga changed their name to Kansas and merged with a rival band, White Clover. The first version of Kansas added ex-White Clover bassist Dave Hope and drummer Phil Ehart. More early lineup changes ensued until the group was set with Livgren, Ehart, Hope, vocalist/keyboardist Steve Walsh, violinist Robby Steinhardt, and guitarist Rich Williams. They released their self-titled debut album, Kansas, in 1974. The band's approach was a blend of progressive rock with odd meters and complex arrangements with some elements of the boogie rock style. Steinhardt's violin timbres added to the bands' sound. Kansas did make the American charts and they gradually built their mostly Mid-Western audience with 1975's Song for America and Masque (both still progressive rock oriented). On the later, Walsh and Livgren playing a host of instruments including; Moog synthesizer, clavinet, ARP synthesizers, organ, piano, acoustic guitar, and more.

Kansas found their way into mainstream rock with their fourth record, 1976's Leftoverture, that peaked in America at number five and produced the hit "Carry On Wayward Son." The song went to number eleven in the U.S. and number fifty-one in England. 1977's Point of Know Return yielded similar results and the fatalistic ballad "Dust in the Wind" went to number six. It also contained the hit "Point of Know Return," another hit. Kansas was now recognized as an arena rock band that could be heard regularly on classic rock radio stations.

After the moderately successful Monolith in 1979, Audio-Visions followed in 1980. Kansas members felt some creative and personal differences and became interested in other side projects. Steve Walsh, the voice of Kansas, left to form a new band and other lineup changes ensued. Vocalist/keyboardist John Elefante joined for 1982's Vinyl Confessions. The band went in a new direction and began to focus on religion in their lyrics. Drastic Measures found moderate success in 1983. Kansas modified their lineup with bassist Billy Greer and the formidable ex-Dixie Dreg guitarist Steve Morse. The band received a boost with 1986's Power that included the single "All I Wanted." This gave Kansas a necessary shot in the arm by peaking at number nineteen on the American charts and receiving airplay on MTV.

The next two albums were 1988's In the Spirit of Things, 1995's Freaks of Nature. 1998's Always Never the Same hinted at their earlier progressive rock roots. The year 2000 saw Kansas return to their classic lineup for Somewhere to Elsewhere, with all songs written by Livgren. Kansas continued to tour into the next decade and in 2014, Steve Walsh announced his retirement.

In 2015, Kansas signed with a new label and released 2016's The Prelude Implicit, a mixture of hard rock and progressive rock elements. Early Kansas was one of America's true answers to the dominance of British progressive rock. Their ability to write interesting and catchy melodies moved them from a progressive to a classic rock direction, ultimately giving them two fan bases.

"Carry On Wayward Son"
by Kerry Livgren

"Carry On Wayward Son" was a prime example of how Kansas was able to combine a pop-tune melody within a fairly complex progressive rock arrangement. The song was written by Kerry Livgren as a sequel to the final song "The Pinnacle," from their previous album, Masque. Livgren has expressed that the song explored a spiritual searching but was not religious in nature. Livgren was an Evangelical Christian and often wrote songs that referenced his own search and desire to "Carry On." He viewed himself as the "Wayward Son," who was alienated from reality but continued to strive to know that same reality.

Musically, the a cappella vocals in the beginning of this song gave it a very distinctive introduction. After the lyrics stated Livgrens' above mentioned struggles, the instrumental section took the listener on a musical journey. The song revealed a complex progressive arrangement to a classic rock audience, many of whom had limited exposure to progressive rock music. "Carry On Wayward Son" was not only the band's biggest hit, it gave Kansas the staying power that it needed to be a force for years to come.

Discussion Question

In addition to receiving widespread FM radio airplay, are there specific musical attributes that categorize a band as "classic" rock? If yes, describe the musical attributes of a few bands that you believe fit the classic rock genre. If not, are there bands labeled as "classic" rock simple because they have longevity? Do they fit other rock genres?

Chapter Eleven: Classic Rock

"Classic Rock radio gave us our longevity...the reason it has lasted thirty years is for one reason and one reason only: Classic Rock radio"

- George Thorogood

Chapter Twelve: Classic Rock Singer-Led Bands

This chapter continues with the evolution of classic rock but now our focus shifts to artists that were strong songwriters and utilized a band format to realize their artistic vision. Many classic rock bands (reviewed in the previous chapter) with a dynamic front man or woman received crucial contributions by their other band members, both live and in the studio. The bands in this chapter, however, were typically built around the performance style and the musical requirements of an individual artist. Record companies marketed the persona of the solo artist and often band members were viewed as being interchangeable. That's not to say there weren't, for example, strong musical relationships between band leaders such as Bruce Springsteen and his saxophonist Clarence Clemons, or Dave Matthews and drummer Carter Beauford. A fine line often existed when we placed classic rock bands and classic solo artists in these chapters.

A number of post-psychedelic groups better known as **jam bands** evolved in the 1980's and 1990's, including Phish and Dave Matthews Band. The musical and cultural phenomenon known as the jam band scene was directly related to the legacy of The Grateful Dead. Influential jam bands (although most are unique) generally drew from the genres of psychedelia, rock, blues, folk, country, and jazz to create extended instrumental improvisations, mostly in live settings. After the death of the legendary Jerry Garcia in 1995, the Grateful Dead continued in various permutations (see The Dead and Company in this chapter). The Grateful Dead's legacy cultivated a jam ethos,characterized by the The Dead's infamous approach to three or four hour jam-inspired concerts. Even though Phish started in the early 1980's, the jam band scene really didn't take off until a decade later in the early 1990's. We will explore the jam band world later in this chapter.

> "Tom Petty's music and songs are timeless. He was a wonderful writer, musician, and singer. Irreplaceable and unique."
>
> – Elton John

The 1970's produced many talented singers that led very successful classic rock bands in America and England. Among these many popular artists were **Joe Cocker, Elton John, Jackson Browne, Huey Lewis and the News** (1967-present), **Billy Joel, Eddie Money** (1949-), **Meat Loaf** (1967-present), **Bob Seger, Bruce Springsteen, Eric Clapton, Peter Frampton, John Mellencamp, Tom Petty, Rod Stewart, Steve Winwood, Tori Amos** (1979-present), and many more.

Joe Cocker (1944-2014) was born in Sheffield, England in 1944. Cocker sang with a gravely, soulful voice and delivered strong emotional performances. His biggest influences growing up were skiffle artist Lonnie Donegan and Ray Charles. Cocker began his career struggling under the stage name Vance Arnold. He honed his performance skills working the pubs of England, singing both rock and soul songs with a strong backup band. His 1969 debut recording, <u>With a Little Help from My Friends</u>, hit number one on the British charts. Cocker's version of The Beatles classic of the same name brought him to international fame when he performed it at the Woodstock Festival in 1969. On the heels of his Woodstock performance, Cocker released <u>Joe Cocker!</u> in1969 and once again went to The Beatles songbook to record "She Came in Through the Bathroom Window" and "Something."

Joe Cocker next put together a stellar group of more than twenty musicians, calling them Mad Dogs & Englishman. This band featured pianist/bandleader Leon Russell, three drummers (including Jim Gordon, Jim Keltner, and

Chuck Blackwell), and backup singers Rita Coolidge and Claudia Lennear. This led to a 1970 tour and the live recording Mad Dogs and Englishmen. Drawing from rock and soul influences, this album also featured a three-piece horn section. 1974's I Can Stand a Little Rain yielded the emotional romantic ballad "You Are So Beautiful," a chart topping hit.

"You Are So Beautiful"
by Billy Preston and Bruce Fisher

"You Are So Beautiful" was considered to be one of Joe Cocker's most impassioned vocal performances. The song appeared on the album I Can Stand a Little Rain and contained a who's who of studio musicians. It featured guitarists Cornell Dupree and Jay Graydon, bassist Chuck Rainey, drummers Bernard Purdie and Jeff Porcaro, keyboardists Nicky Hopkins, David Paich, Richard Tee, and Randy Newman, and many other session musicians.

"You Are So Beautiful" was written by Billy Preston and Bruce Fisher. However, Dennis Wilson (of The Beach Boys) contributed to the song but remained uncredited. The song was first recorded by it's co-composer, Billy Preston, before Cocker. It did not chart in England but became very popular in America. "You Are So Beautiful" was featured in the 1981 film *Modern Romance* and 1993's *Carlito's Way*. Joe Cocker sang this ballad with a great sense of sincerity and musical expression.

Joe Cocker went on to have a long and prolific career, recording seventeen more studio albums from 1975's Jamaica Say You Will to 2012's Fire It Up. Cocker also released the Live at Woodstock album in 2009. He was a unique artist that successfully fused rock music with soul elements with his fiery and emotionally charged vocal style. Joe Cocker sang with a hard-edged gritty voice and was known for his expressive and often spasmodic body movements onstage.

Elton John (1947-) was born Reginald Kenneth Dwight in 1947 in Middlesex, England. He would go on to become the biggest-selling rock-pop artist of the 1970's and sell more albums on each side of the Atlantic than any other British male artist. Elvis and Frank Sinatra were the only solo male artists that bettered Elton John's transatlantic chart success. In 1973 and 1974, John recorded four consecutive number one albums in England and America.

Dwight began playing the piano at age four and won a scholarship to the Royal Academy of Music at age eleven. After six years of study, he formed the group The Corvettes and then joined the band Bluesology. By 1965, Bluesology became the backup band for touring American R&B musicians such as Patti LaBelle and The Isley Brothers. A year later, Bluesology came to the attention of the artist Long John Baldry and became his supporting band. At this time, Dwight tried out for two of the biggest progressive rock bands, Gentle Giant and King Crimson. He failed both auditions to become their lead vocalist. He then failed an audition with Liberty Records. However, they gave him some lyric sheets left to them by a writer named Bernie Taupin. Dwight began to match music to Taupin's lyrics and corresponded with him through the mail. They met six months later, only now Dwight went by his new stage name, Elton John. He derived the name by combining the first names of Bluesology saxophonist Elton Dean with John Baldry. Elton John remembered, "Some guy at Liberty told me to go to Dick James Music and do some demos. I was receiving Bernie's lyrics and writing the songs and doing demos before I even met Bernie. One day I was doing a session and noticed him in the corner. I said, 'Oh are you the lyrics writer, and he said yeah, and we went around the corner for a cup of coffee and that was it, really'." #1

John and Taupin became house songwriters for DJM Records in 1968. They wrote at lightening speed, Taupin writing often at the clip of a song per hour and Elton matching his lyrics at the same rate. Bernie Taupin reflected on the special approach that he and Elton shared. Taupin said, "You can write one or two 'classics,' that will last and be covered again in a few years time, but I think a majority of good pop songs nowadays are disposable...I think that's healthy in a way. You should always have fresh material coming along...The reason we've (Taupin and Elton) survived and will continue to survive for a good long time is because we've got the upper hand on everybody else and can turn our ideas into anything, any sort of music. We can do things like just playing rock & roll, country material, blues...I mean, we've done every type of music." #2 This prolific duo continued to develop their chemistry by writing songs for pop singers Lulu and Roger Cook. Additionally, John recorded some cover versions of current hits.

By the summer of 1968, Elton John was recording and releasing his own original songs. DJM released his debut album Empty Sky in 1969 to little fanfare. His 1970 follow-up, Elton John, employed many musicians and had a top ten single, "Your Song." Eventually, a steady band emerged with guitarist Caleb Quaye, bassist Dee Murray, drummer Nigel Olsson, and percussionist Ray Cooper (a revolving door of dozens of rhythm section players and backup singers would be heard on Elton John's thirty studio albums). In 1970, he gave his first American concert at the Troubadour in Los Angeles. Elton soon came to the attention of Quincy Jones and Leon Russell. (Empty Sky was not released in America until 1975, well after Elton John established himself as a rock artist.)

The decade of the 1970's saw Elton record eleven studio albums. 1970's Tumbleweed Connection made the top ten in America with heavy FM radio airplay. 1971's Madman Across the Water built his fan base but 1972's Honky Chateau became the first of seven consecutive number one albums with the mega hits "Honky Cat" and "Rocket Man." This brought Elton to super stardom. Next followed 1973's Don't Shoot Me I'm Only the Piano Player. The John/Taupin hit machine was unstoppable with sixteen top twenty hits in a row! This included "Crocodile Rock," "Daniel," "The Bitchis Back," "Philadelphia Freedom," and "Saturday Night's Alright for Fighting."

"Rocket Man"
by Elton John and Bernie Taupin

"Rocket Man," from Elton John's Honky Chateau, was released around the time of the Apollo sixteen space mission. Bernie Taupin took his inspiration for the "RocketMan" lyrics from the short story *The Rocket Man*, written by Ray Bradbury. The book told the story from the perspective of a child, whose astronaut father had mixed emotions about leaving his family to pursue the danger of space travel. Bradbury's story was the basis of a previously recorded song also titled "Rocket Man," by the folk group Pearls Before Swine. This song gave Taupin his motivation to write his own "Rocket Man."

Musically, "Rocket Man" showcased Elton John's mastery of the rock ballad. He deftly merged gos-

---

> "I think visuals are very important to me, not in the sense of an act like Alice Cooper who's got it down to a fine art, but in the sense of high camp and just very, very tongue-in-cheek."
>
> – Elton John

Rock Hard Fact

Elton John is referred to as Sir Elton Hercules John, CBE. The CBE stands for Commander of the Order of the British Empire. This is the third highest rank in Britain's Order of Chivalry.

pel styled piano with acoustic guitar to create the songs' unique feel. Davey Johnstone's guitar part added some very clever sliding effects to highlight Elton's vocal punctuations when he sang the words "Rocket Man." On live versions, Elton often improvised elements that effectively mixed blues and gospel styles in his piano solo. Vocalist Kate Bush covered "Rocket Man" on the 1991 Elton John tribute album titled Two Rooms.

    1973's Goodbye Yellow Brick Road shot straight to the top of the charts in Britain and America. It temporarily identified Elton as a glam rock star with his elaborate costumes and flamboyant stage personality. Goodbye Yellow Brick Road sold over thirty million copies worldwide. It also featured at least five hits including the title track and "Bennie and the Jets," the latter going to number one on the charts.

Groundbreaking album
Goodbye Yellow Brick Road
by Elton John

    Goodbye Yellow Brick Road was initially intended to be recorded in Jamaica. However, poor studio conditions prompted the location to be moved to Chateau d'Herouville in France. Elton John was inspired by the (then) recent Rolling Stones album Goats Head Soup that had recently been recorded there. This change of scenery provided Elton and his band with much creative inspiration. When the sessions produced a number of quality tracks, Elton decided to include seventeen of the recorded songs on this double album. By utilizing cinematic metaphors, Goodbye Yellow Brick Road was inspired by memories of a childhood left in the past. Taupin was motivated to write many of the songs' lyrics from his memories of nights he spent at the market Rasen Pub, where he frequented in his youth.

    Side one opened with "Funeral for a Friend/Love Lies Bleeding," then "Candle in the Wind," and "Bennie and the Jets." The song "Candle in the Wind" was originally written as a tribute to Marilyn Monroe, who had died eleven years earlier. It later became the second largest selling single (after John re-wrote it in memory of Princess Diana) in music history behind Bing Crosby's "White Christmas." In "Bennie and the Jets," the narrator sang about a fictional band. Taupin has described the lyrics as a satire on the 1970's music business. In live performance, Elton frequently played the middle section piano solo with many variations, often extended with elaborate improvisations.

    Side two opened with "Goodbye Yellow Brick Road," then "This Song Has No Title," "Grey Seal," "Jamaica Jerk-Off," and "I've Seen That Movie Too." The title track was inspired by an image from the movie *The Wizard of Oz*. Taupin's lyrics, often about Elton, were about giving up a life of opulence for one of simplicity in a rural setting. This song was a great example of Elton's ability to sing with great emotion and sense of nostalgia.

    Side three opened with "Sweet Painted Lady," then "The Ballad of Danny Bailey(1909-34)," "Dirty Little Girl," and "All the Girls Love Alice." Side four opened with "Your Sister Can't Twist (But She Can Rock 'n Roll)," "Saturday Night's Alright for Fighting," "Roy Rogers," "Social Disease," and "Harmony." "Saturday Night's Alright for Fighting" became one of the most rocking songs in Elton's catalogue. It's a throwback to early rock 'n roll with a glam rock feeling. Elton played "Saturday Night" with the fire of Jerry Lee Lewis. The band recorded the rhythm tracks first and Elton later overdubbed his intense piano part. The guitar chords added great power to the feel. Taupin was inspired to write about a ten-year period when he attended British dance clubs where fights would routinely break out. Elton John recorded the vocals standing up and leaping around, not his usual seated approach. Goodbye Yellow Brick Road, one of classic rock's classics.

    1974's Caribou and Greatest Hits, 1975's Captain Fantastic and the Brown Dirt Cowboy and Rock of the Westies all went platinum. Elton John next founded his own record label, Rocket (distributed by MCA), that enabled him to sign Kiki Dee and Neil Sedaka. Elton remained with MCA for a record-breaking eight million dollar contract in 1974. That same year, Elton appeared on John Lennon's comeback single "Whatever Gets You Through the Night." Also at this time, Pete Townshend of The Who asked John to play a character called the "Local Lad" and perform the song "Pinball Wizard" in the film version of the rock opera *Tommy*. After 1976, Elton cut his performance schedule due to exhaustion and retired from live performance in 1977. John's relationship with Taupin became strained following the release of 1976's double album Blue Moves. 1978's A Single Man yielded no top twenty hits but John did return to live performing. 1979's Victim of Love did not fare well but did produce the hit "Mama Can't Buy You Love."

    The 1980's were a productive period when Elton John recorded nine studio albums. Elton reunited with Bernie Taupin for 1980's 21 at 33, featuring the hit "Little Jeannie." He followed with 1981's The Fox and 1982's Jump Up!. 1983's Too Low for Zero yielded two hits, "I'm Still Standing" and "I Guess That's Why They Call It the Blues." These songs began another streak of hit singles. The rest of the decade saw Elton John release 1984's Breaking Hearts, 1985's Ice on Fire, 1986's Leather Jackets, 1988's Reg Strikes Back, and 1989's Sleeping with the Past.

    Elton John went on to record eight more studio albums, from 1992's The One to 2016's Wonderful Crazy Night. However, the late 1980's and early 1990's were a difficult time for Elton John. He struggled with personal and health issues. By 1991, he was again healthy and founded the Elton John AIDS Foundation. John announced that he would donate his royalties from his single sales to AIDS research. To date, he has raised over $200 million dollars to fight the disease. Elton John was active in the 2010's including the release of 2017's Diamonds, a compilation that marked the fiftieth anniversary of his songwriting partnership with Bernie Taupin.

    2018 found Elton John announcing the beginning of a lengthy farewell tour that was inspired by his desire to spend more time with his children. He has stated that he will continue to compose and record, and hasn't ruled out occasional live appearances. However, he has said that his touring days are over.

    Elton John was the biggest pop-rock star of the 1970's (he could make a claim as "king of pop" at least for that decade). His flamboyant stage attire and outspoken persona only added to his star status. In a remarkable career that kept him on the charts for over twenty-five years, Elton John adeptly changed with the times. Elton's musical relationship with Bernie Taupin has rivaled the legendary partnerships of Lennon and McCartney and Tin Pan Alley's Rogers and Hart. Elton John crafted Beatlesque catchy pop and rock songs that infused soul, disco, pop ballads, and country styles. His great versatility, combined with uncanny melodic skill, puts him in a classic rock league of his own. Elton John was inducted into the Rock and Roll Hall of Fame in 1994.

Jackson Browne (1948-) is an American vocalist and singer/songwriter from Los Angeles, California (born in Heidelberg, Germany). Browne began his music career by joining the Nitty Gritty Dirt Band in 1966. His tenure with The Dirt Band was brief and he moved to New York City and became a staff writer for the Elektra Records publishing company. A few of his early songs were recorded by The Nitty Gritty Dirt Band, Nico, Gregg Allman, The Eagles, The Byrds, and others. Browne moved back to L.A. in 1968 and formed a folk band. His debut album, 1972's Jackson Browne, contained the hit "Doctor My Eyes." Shortly after, "Take it Easy," a song he co-wrote with Glenn Frey, became a hit for The Eagles. 1973's For Everyman did not fare well but 1974's Late for the Sky went to number fourteen on the U.S. charts. In 1976, Jackson Browne released his breakthrough album, The Pretender that contained the hit of the same name. 1977's Running on Empty achieved even greater success, reaching number three on the American charts, yielding the hits "Stay/Load-Out" and "Running on Empty."

"Running On Empty"
by Jackson Browne

"Running On Empty" reached number eleven on the U.S. charts. Jackson Browne wrote the song while he was driving with his gas tank on empty. He only had to drive a few blocks from where he lived to get to the recording studio and was not afraid of running out of gas. Figuratively, "Running On Empty" was a reflection of the singers' past and where he was headed at various stages of his life.

Musically, "Running On Empty" featured a musical pedal steel guitar solo by David Lindley that lent the track a country-rock feeling. Craig Doerge's piano accompaniment added a gospel feel that added to the songs' eclectic approach. Additionally, vocalists Doug Haywood and Rosemary Butler provided excellent backup vocal harmonies. The Running On Empty album became a part of American culture, reflected by its appearance on the TV sitcom *Mork & Mindy* (starring Robin Williams). A framed copy of the album cover hung on the wall in Mindy's apartment.

In the decade of the 1980's, Browne's popularity went to another level on the strength of his 1980 release, Hold Out, his only number one album. Browne spent much time pursuing social and political causes, especially protesting the use of nuclear energy. Jackson Browne went on to record eight more studio albums, from 1983's Lawyers in Love to 2014's Standing in the Breach. Jackson Browne has represented the prototype of the California singer/songwriter of the early 1970's. His literate and introspective lyrics combined with his ability to compose catchy melodic hooks and fueled the eighteen million albums he sold in America alone. Browne's political consciousness lent purpose to his prolific songwriting career. Jackson Browne was inducted into the Rock and Roll Hall of Fame in 2004.

Billy Joel (1949-) is an American vocalist/pianist that was born in Hicksville, Long Island New York in 1949. In his youth, he pursued two passions, playing the piano and street fighting. By 1964, Joel joined The Echoes, a band that covered British Invasion tunes. In 1965, at the age of sixteen (after some amateur boxing matches), Joel was hired as a session musician and played on The Shangri-Las' song, "Leader of the Pack." In 1967, Billy joined The Hassles. They released two unsuccessful albums and four singles. By 1969 he formed Attila, a duo ensemble, with drummer Jon Small. In this setting, Joel played the organ through a variety of effect pedals to create a heavy psychedelic rock sound void of guitars. Epic Records released Attila's one and only album in 1970. It was a commercial and critical failure. With the quick demise of Attila, Joel went to work as a music journalist and was hired to record commercial jingles, including one for singer Chubby Checker. However, Joel was experiencing severe depression, prompting him to receive treatment.

Billy Joel signed a bad recording contract with Family Productions in 1971, a deal that would haunt him for years. The label released his 1971 solo debut, Cold Spring Harbor, to little fanfare and Joel was unhappy with the production of the album. Furthermore, Family Productions had major legal difficulties that prevented Joel from recording an immediate follow-up to the album. Joel moved to Los Angeles in early 1972. He began a residency performing as a solo pianist nightly at the Executive Room. A local radio station began playing a live version of Joel's "Captain Jack." This created great interest and Joel signed with Columbia Records. The legal ramifications of the Family Productions' contract forced Joel to pay them royalties on every record he would sell for many years. 1973's Piano Man put Billy Joel on the map by reaching number twenty-seven on the U.S. charts. His career was gaining momentum and the title track became a top ten hit.

"The Piano Man"
by Billy Joel

"The Piano Man" is a melancholy song inspired by the nightly experiences Billy Joel acquired while performing at the Executive Room lounge in Los Angeles. The song drew from the real life characters Billy encountered from night to night. The "waitress practicing politics" was Elizabeth Weber, who married Billy in 1973 (and divorced him in 1982). Joel worked the Executive Room under the name Bill Martin (Martin is Billy Joel's middle name). That explained why the patrons in the song called him Bill. Joel played these gigs for six months to pay his rent.

Musically, "The Piano Man" is a 3/4 waltz, uncommon for a pop tune. Joel utilized accordion (played by Michael Omartian) and harmonica (inspired by Bob Dylan) to create a nostalgic feeling to accompany his clever lyrics. Elton John made reference to a piano man in his song "Tiny Dancer." John and Joel are friends and have toured together. Billy Joel was surprised to learn that "The Piano Man" appealed to a younger generation, something he learned when performing at the Bonnaroo festival in 2015.

Soon, Joel put together a touring band and opened for The Doobie Brothers and The J. Geils Band. He followed with 1974's Street Life Serenade, that peaked at number thirty-five and produced the hit "The Entertainer," one of Joel's signature songs. The albums' minimal success was compounded by Joel's tense relationship with some music critics. For the recording, Joel utilized a number of session players including his touring band of guitarist Don Evans, bassist Patrick McDonald, saxophonist Johnny Almond, and drummer Rhys Clark. In late 1975, Billy played piano and organ on a few tracks for Bo Diddley's The 20th Anniversary of Rock 'n' Roll album. 1976's Turnstiles did poorly on the charts but it

> "Don't be afraid of mistakes, because the only original thing we ever do is make mistakes."
>
> - Billy Joel

still yielded two of Joel's greatest songs, "New York State of Mind" and "Say Goodbye to Hollywood." Hard hitting drummer Liberty DeVitto and bassist Doug Stegmeyer cut the albums' basic tracks with Joel. Soon, guitarists Russell Javors and Howie Emerson, and saxophonist Richie Cannata were added to complete the more permanent Billy Joel Band.

Producer Phil Ramone was hired to produce Joel's breakout album, 1977's The Stranger. It was a great commercial success, spawning four top twenty-five hits including; "Movin Out," "Only the Good Die Young," "She's Always a Woman," and "Just the Way You Are." Another important track, "Scenes from an Italian Restaurant," became a staple in his songbook. Joel said, "That ('Scenes') ended up becoming a very important recording in my career. Towards the end of the night, that's one of the big finale songs. I don't think I could do a show without performing that song...Its basically the story of Brenda and Eddie told through a meeting at an Italian restaurant during a dinner. It's something that a lot of Long Islanders do-kind of reminisce over Italian food. And everybody's got their Italian restaurant." #3

Groundbreaking album The Stranger
by Billy Joel

Billy Joel, after writing many of the songs for The Stranger, was excited to record them with his touring band. He also met with Beatles producer, George Martin, who showed interest in producing the album. Martin didn't want to use Joel's touring band (but he did like the band's live energy) and he backed out. Joel next approached producer Phil Ramone, who agreed to work on the album.

Side one opened with "Movin' Out (Anthony's Song)," then "The Stranger," "Just the Way You Are," and "Scenes from an Italian Restaurant." For the opening track, Joel wrote about the lower-middle class that was obsessed with increasing their social status by gaining more material possessions. For "The Stranger," Billy whistled the song's theme for producer Phil Ramone. Joel then told Ramone that he couldn't figure out what instrument to use to play the theme. Ramone told Joel that he already found the right instrument, his whistling. "Scenes from an Italian Restaurant," started out as a short song to be titled "The Ballad of Brenda and Eddie," but it ended up being the third section of the over seven-minute epic song. Billy Joel was inspired by the suite of songs on The Beatles' Abbey Road album. He then skillfully wrote the music and added interesting tempo changes, a variety of instruments (including a clarinet solo), intricate piano passages, and complex section changes.

Side two opened with "Vienna," then "Only the Good Die Young," "She's Always a Woman," "Get It Right the First Time," and "Everybody Has a Dream." Before settling on a shuffle feel, "Only the Good Die Young," was first treated with a reggae feel. The song's lyrics created controversy when some church officials criticized its storyline of a guy's attempt to seduce a Catholic girl. One Catholic University even banned "Only the Good Die Young" from being played on their college radio station. Upon hearing that news, that university's students came out in large numbers to buy the album. The stellar personnel on The Stranger was Joel's regular lineup of bassist Doug Stegmeyer, drummer Liberty DeVitto, and saxophonist Richie Cannata. Additionally, Joel employed the high level musicianship of acclaimed guitarists Steve Khan and Hiram Bullock, jazz saxophonist Phil Woods, organist Richard Tee, vocalist Patti Austin, and percussionist Ralph MacDonald. Patrick Williams handled the orchestrations. The Stranger spent six weeks at the number two spot on the U.S. charts and number twenty four in England.

1978's 52nd Street went to number one in America, selling over two million copies in its first month. It won a Grammy for Album of the Year on the strength of the hits "Big Shot," "My Life," and "Honesty." Joel was a big star but still at odds with many music critics and was openly vocal about their criticism. 1980's Glass Houses again hit the number one spot and this was Joel's harder-edged response to the popular punk/new wave movement. Its hits included "You May Be Right" and "It's Still Rock 'n' Roll To Me." He followed with a live album, 1982's The Nylon Curtain. Joel was sidelined with a severe hand injury from a motorcycle accident in 1982. He bounced back with 1983's An Innocent Man, that yielded the hits "Uptown Girl and "Tell Her About It." This album has sold over seven million copies. During 1983-84, Billy Joel became one of the first 1970's stars to receive significant video rotation on MTV. He also married model Christie Brinkley at this time.

1985 saw Joel release a double-compilation album titled Greatest Hits that eventually sold over ten million copies. 1986's The Bridge followed and reached number seven with the hits "A Matter of Trust" and "This Is the Time." Billy Joel toured Russia in 1987. Later that year, he released a double live album from the tour titled Kohuept (meaning concert in Russian). After some managerial and legal issues, Joel released 1989's Storm Front. It contained the hit "We Didn't Start the Fire." Joel spent the next few years quietly, but returned with 1993's River of Dreams. It entered the charts at number one and produced a top ten hit, "River of Dreams."

In a complete surprise to many of his fans, Billy Joel released Fantasies & Delusions in 2001, an album of his own classical compositions. In 2006, Billy released a four CD/DVD career retrospective titled My Life. Also that year, Joel released 12 Gardens Live, a 32 track two CD set. In 2007, Joel released the ballad "All My Life," followed by a song "Christmas in Fallujah," sung by Cass Dillon. In 2013, Billy Joel toured England and began a regular residency performing at Madison Square Garden, performing twenty-one shows in 2014.

Billy Joel became one of the most popular performers of the late 1970's into the 1980's. Billy Joel reflected on how he developed his original sound when he said, "We are all a culmination of all our influences. Nobody grows up in a test tube. A lot of times you get accused of being a derivative. Well, of course you sound like people you admire! Eventually you practice it in your own way and it becomes original." #4 Billy Joel has an ability to combine Beatlesque melodies with a traditional **Broadway show tune** approach and a penchant for Tin Pan Alley influenced songs. His great piano virtuosity is often overlooked, understandably by those focused on his prolific songwriting output. Billy Joel was inducted into the Rock and Roll Hall of Fame in 1999.

Bob Seger and the Silver Bullet Band (1968-present) was formed by vocalist/guitarist/keyboardist Bob Seger in Detroit, Michigan in 1968. Seger was initially inspired in his formative years by Elvis Presley and Little Richard. Seger formed a trio in 1961 called The Decibels with guitarist Pete Stanger and drummer H.B. Hunter. After playing with another band, Doug Brown & The Omens, he formed Bob Seger and The Last Heard in 1966. The band released a series of singles under the

Rock Hard Fact

In June 1976, Bob Seger played for 50 fans in a Chicago bar. Three days later, he played in front of 76,000 devoted fans in the Pontiac Silverdome outside of Detroit.

Cameo-Parkway Label. Seger then signed a major record deal with Capitol Records and changed the band's name to The Bob Seger System. The band climbed onto the U.S. charts with the single "Ramblin' Gamblin' Man" that reached number seventeen. Seger's album debut was 1969's Ramblin' Gamblin' Man. The lineup at this time was Seger, bassist Dan Honaker, organist Bob Schultz, and drummer Pep Perrine. Also released in 1969, his album Noah featured the Seger classic song of the same name. Vocalist/multi-instrumentalist Tom Neme was also added to the band lineup.

The next decade saw the release of 1970's Mongrel and 1971's Brand New Morning, a solo album with Seger singing and accompanying himself on guitar and piano. This was followed by 1972's Smokin' O.P. and 1973's Back in '72 that featured a cover of The Allman Brothers' "Midnight Rider." 1974's Seven was Seger's first to involve The Silver Bullet Band, which he would employ for the rest of his career. The personnel was Seger, guitarist Drew Abbott, keyboardist Robyn Robins, bassist Chis Campbell, saxophonist Tom Cartmell, and drummer Charlie Allen Martin. Seger moved back to Capitol for 1975's Beautiful Loser. Seger would tour extensively with the Silver Bullet Band even before they had yet to make a hit album. Through touring, they increased their popularity and cultivated a widespread grassroots fan base across the country.

1976's Live Bullet was a double live breakout album for Seger and the Silver Bullet Band. They recorded it live at Detroit's Cobo Hall in front of their passionatehometown fans. The material drew from his Beautiful Loser album and was delivered with great musical intensity. Live Bullet spent three year on the U.S. charts and eventually sold over four million copies. 1976's Night Moves brought the band into the U.S. top ten. Seger recorded half of the tracks with the famous Muscle Shoals (legendary Alabama recording studio) rhythm section. Night Moves generated the hits "Mainstreet," "Rock & Roll Never Forgets," and "Night Moves."

"Night Moves"
by Bob Seger

Bob Seger was inspired to compose "Night Moves" from his personal experiences. Seger attempted to recapture the freedom he recalled from his teenage years. The song also described Seger's socializing with a rough crowd of kids and a romantic relationship that he pursued with a girl, whose boyfriend was away in the military. The boyfriend returned and they married, which broke Seger's heart. Seger was also inspired by the movie *American Graffiti*. He thought that nobody had ever told a story about how it was to grow up in his neck of the woods. The descriptive imagery Seger used in the song was inspired by "Me and Bobby McGee," a tune by Kris Kristofferson.

"Night Moves" revealed Seger's ability to combine musical styles that began with a gospel inspired mixture of piano and organ. Seger's raw emotional delivery also showcased his strong blues and soulful vocal inflections. "Night Moves" was composed in sections and the challenge was that Seger needed to connect its two distinct bridges.After hearing Bruce Springsteen's "Jungleland," he employed tempo changes to fuse the sections together. "Night Moves" has a timeless quality that captured the nostalgic feeling found in many of Seger's classic songs.

1978's Stranger in Town continued Seger's success and featured the hits "Still the Same," "Hollywood Nights," and "Old Time Rock & Roll." The decade of the 1980's brought Seger and The Bullet Band their first number one album in America, with 1980's Against the Wind. All of its hits, "Fire Lake," "Against the Wind," and "You'll Accomp'ny Me" were ballads. 1982's The Distance followed and 1986's Like a Rock featured Don Henley and Timothy B. Schmidt. Bob Seger went on to record five more studio albums from 1991's The Fire Inside to 2017's I Knew You When that was dedicated to the recently deceased Glenn Frey. Bob Seger is one of the most successful heartland rock artists over the last forty-plus years. Through his dedication to a hard edged R&B and soul sound, he crafted his distinctively American sound. Bob Seger was inducted into the Rock and Roll Hall of Fame in 2012.

Bruce Springsteen and the E Street Band (1971-present) evolved with the emergence of vocalist/guitarist Bruce Springsteen and his long time association with the E Street Band. Springsteen (aka The Boss) was born in Freehold, New Jersey to a working class family in 1949. Bruce acquired a guitar after seeing Elvis on *The Ed Sullivan Show* in 1956 but didn't take music seriously until 1963. His first band was The Beatles-influenced Castiles. After high school, Bruce frequented clubs in Asbury Park, New Jersey and joined a hard rock-styled band called Earth. His next band, Child (soon renamed Steel Mill), featured future E Street members keyboardist Danny Federici, drummer Vini Lopez, and guitarist Steve Van Zandt (who joined on bass). After Steel Mill's demise, Bruce formed a short lived big band, Dr. Zoom & the Cosmic Boom. This quickly became The Bruce Springsteen Band. This group added pianist David Sancious and bassist Garry Tallent to the existing members of Springsteen, Federici, Lopez, and Van Zandt (who switched to guitar). They also assembled a horn section that eventually was reduced to a single saxophonist named Clarence Clemons. The band was all there, but there wasn't many performance opportunities, so Springsteen worked solo in the clubs in New York City. Bruce soon acquired a manager, Mike Appel, who introduced him to John Hammond, of Columbia Records. Hammond (who previously signed Bob Dylan over a decade ago), signed Springsteen to Columbia in 1972.

Bruce Springsteen released his 1973 debut album, Greetings from Asbury Park, N.J. to little fan fare. However, the opening track, "Blinded By the Light," would later be a number one hit for Manfred Mann's Earth Band. For the album, Bruce added jazz bassist Richard Davis on "The Angel" and pianist Harold Wheeler on "Blinded By the Light" and the classic "Spirit in The Night." Van Zant was mostly unavailable (out on tour with The Dovells). Greetings From Asbury Park ranked as one of the all-time great debut records by a rock artist. Bruce's songwriting showcased his ability to compose meaningful lyrics with accessible melodies and elaborate arrangements. When Springsteen gave Columbia the completed album, they wanted to promote him as an artist from New York City. Springsteen pushed back by naming the album after the town its songs were actually written about. Springsteen recalled, "The main reason I put it (the name Greetings from Asbury Park) on that first album was because Columbia was pushing for this big New York thing...I said, 'wait, you guys are nuts or something. I'm from Asbury Park, New Jersey. Can you dig it? NEW JERSEY. I want this on the album cover.' They fought and fought, but we finally got it put on. And it's a part of my thing, it's like-I'm from New Jersey! It's important for people to get a clear picture of me." #5 Other standout tracks from the album included "Growin'

> "I saw rock and roll's future-and its name is Bruce Springsteen."
>
> – rock critic Jon Landau

Up" and "It's Hard to be a Saint in the City." 1973's <u>The Wild, the Innocent & the E Street Shuffle</u> was another early masterpiece that was initially ignored by the public. This work departed from Bruce's earlier folk influences and moved toward a fusion of nostalgic rock mixed with soulful R&B. It's romanticized and diverse compositions included "The E Street Shuffle," "Kitty's Back," and "Rosalita (Come Out Tonight)."

"Rosalita (Come Out Tonight)"
by Bruce Springsteen

"Rosalita" can be viewed as Springsteen's musical autobiography. After years of working the Jersey shore bars and fighting to get a record deal, this song documented his struggles. It was his message to everyone that believed he had no future in music. It also proved that a love song (Bruce felt "Rosalita" was his best love song) didn't have to be slow or sappy. "Rosalita" was a story about forbidden love between a man and a girl named Rosalita, whose parents were disapproving of his lifestyle in a rock 'n' roll band. In live performances, audiences loved when The Boss sang the line "The record company, Rosie, just gave me a big advance." Springsteen did receive a $25,000 advance, thus proving himself to his doubters.

Musically, "Rosalita" featured the hard-driving R&B saxophone sound of Clarence Clemons. The track built to a climax and skillfully brought the listener to a musical interlude ("I know your Mama don't like me cause I play in a rock 'n' roll band and-your Papa don't dig me but he never did understand"). Although it was never officially released as a single, "Rosalita" was acknowledged as a rock classic that still receives substantial airplay on classic rock radio. Springsteen often closed his concert sets with "Rosalita," often extended to incorporate band member introductions. After appearing on the covers of *Time* and *Newsweek*, Springsteen sometimes changed the words to "Tell your papa I ain't no freak, cause I got my picture on the cover of Time and *Newsweek*" when he performed it live.

Large scale commercial success finally arrived with 1975's <u>Born to Run</u>. It produced the anthemic title track and many classics including "Thunder Road," "Tenth Avenue Freeze-Out," and "Jungleland." <u>Born to Run</u> reached number three on the U.S. charts and began a nearly two decade run of staggering prosperity. Almost everything Springsteen would touch going forward went multiple platinum on a worldwide scale!

Groundbreaking album Born to Run
by Bruce Springsteen and The E Street Band

On <u>Born to Run</u>, Bruce Springsteen made fewer references to New Jersey, with the purpose of reaching a wider audience than his previous works. It would contain a maturation in his storylines and the end of his adolescent themes of love and freedom. The album was not easy to make, taking fourteen months to record, with "Born to Run" itself demanding six months of effort. Having composed all of the songs on piano, Springsteen opted to develop introductions for each song in order to set a distinct mood for each. While Bruce was looking for a "Roy Orbison sings Bob Dylan approach," he also went for a Phil Spector-like "wall of sound." The E Street Band now added drummer Max Weinberg to its roster and he played on all of the tracks except "Born to Run" which featured drummer Ernest "Boom" Carter. Keyboardist/vocalist Roy "the Professor" Bittan also joined the band. Additionally, <u>Born to Run</u> utilized many top session musicians including Michael and Randy Brecker, and David Sanborn.

Side one opened with "Thunder Road," "Tenth Avenue Freeze-Out," "Night," and "Backstreets." The opener "Thunder Road," was conceived to be an introduction to the whole album. Springsteen was setting the stage to view a larger experience that the rest of the album would bear out with its sense of personal exploration. "Tenth AvenueFreeze-Out" had a distinctive R&B feel with a 1950's rock 'n' roll triplet accompaniment and horn arrangement. Tenth Avenue was a street that ran through E Street in Belmar, New Jersey where the band used to rehearse. Springsteen has said that he had no idea what a Tenth Avenue freeze-out was.

Side two opened with "Born to Run," "She's the One," "Meeting Across the River," and "Jungleland." The title track "Born to Run" was recorded four times at a low-budget studio where Bruce had done his first two albums. He moved to a better studio to finish the song, refusing to settle until it was just right. Springsteen has said that the phrase "born to run" just came to him. He liked it because it suggested a cinematic drama that he thought would work with the music he was hearing in his mind. "Born to Run" went on a musical journey and conceptualized a romantic ideal where the singer and his girl act on their destiny because like the line said, "tramps like us-baby we were born to run." "Jungleland" has been compared to Dylan's song "Desolation Row." "Jungleland" was a song about life on the streets that moved through a series of abstract images and introduced a number of characters, including Magic Rat and Barefoot Girl. Bruce and The E Street Band played this song live for a year before taking it into the studio to record. <u>Born to Run</u> has sold over eleven million copies worldwide. It is also listed in the Library of Congress' National Recording Registry of historic recordings.

Due to some legal issues, Springsteen was prevented from recording until 1977. He also hired a new manager and producer, Jon Landau. 1978's <u>Darkness on the Edge of Town</u> served to fortify his career and helped him weather the punk/new wave storm. <u>Darkness on the Edge of Town</u> went to the top ten and the single "Prove It All Night"made the top forty. Springsteen became more serious with songs like "Factory" that revealed a new affinity for the working man. In 1979, Springsteen ramped up his political efforts by headlining two shows to benefit Musicians United for Safe Energy (MUSE), that raised funds for anti-nuclear groups following the Three Mile Island accident.

1980's <u>The River</u> was a double album that sold over five million copies and yielded the hits "Hungry Heart" and "Fade Away." 1982's <u>Nebraska</u> was a one-man show full of introspective songs. Springsteen played guitar, mandolin, harmonica, glockenspiel, organ, synthesizer, and tambourine. The Boss even produced it. <u>Nebraska</u> was full of songs that dealt with ordinary people, often down-on their-luck-blue collar characters who faced life's hardships. These songs were initially intended to be demos for The E Street Band, however Springsteen decided to it release the raw demos. At this time, Van Zandt amicably left to start a solo career and was replaced by guitarist Nils Lofgren.

1984 saw the release of <u>Born in the U.S.A</u>, a blockbuster number one album. It spearheaded a two-

> **Rock Hard Fact**
>
> Bruce Springsteen's E Street Band got their name when they first rehearsed at keyboardist David Sancious' mother's house on E Street in Belmar, New Jersey.

year international tour and spawned seven top ten hits including "Glory Days," "My Hometown," and "Born In The U.S.A." By selling over thirty million copies, Born In The U.S.A. put The Boss in the rare company of Michael Jackson's Thriller and Prince's Purple Rain. At this point, Bruce and The E Street Band were as big as you could get! 1987's Tunnel of Love was a more introverted work and Springsteen retreated from the public eye. During this time, he was divorced from his first wife, Julianne Phillips. He then married Patti Scialfa, who had joined The E Street Band as a backup vocalist in 1984. Bruce also broke up The E Street Band in 1989.

Springsteen returned to action with a new back-up band to record 1992's Human Touch and Lucky Town that went to number two and three on the charts. In early 1995, Springsteen re-formed the E Street Band to record some new tracks for his 1995 Greatest Hits album that sold over ten million copies. A full on reunion was halted with another mellow and almost all-acoustic album, 1995's The Ghost of Tom Joad. Bruce next went into his catalogue of unreleased songs to assemble the four-CD-box set titled Tracks in 1998. A fully reunited E Street Band was present at Springsteen's induction into the Rock and Roll Hall of Fame in 1999. All of the 1974 to 1989 versions of Springsteen's band returned for the induction. With both Van Zandt and Lofgren playing guitar, Bruce and The E Street Band next did a world tour that resulted in the Live in New York City album.

In the new millennium, Bruce Springsteen released 2002's The Rising, a number one album that addressed the 9/11 tragedy. Then, after another long tour with The E Street Band, Bruce released 2005's Devils & Dust, another introspective effort. 2006's We Shall Overcome: The Seeger Sessions, featured arrangements from Pete Seeger's catalogue of folk songs. It reached the top ten on the U.S. charts and won the Grammy for Best Traditional Folk Album. Springsteen recorded a new rock record titled Magic in 2007 and Working on a Dream in 2009. Unfortunately, longtime E Street Band keyboardist Danny Federici died in 2008. Bruce and The E Street Band next performed live at the Super Bowl XLIII half-time show. By 2009, Springsteen ranked fourth among all touring acts (in concert ticket sales) of the first decade of the 21st century, behind only The Rolling Stones, U2, and Madonna. Tragically, another key member of The E Street Band, Clarence Clemons, died in 2011. He had last appeared on the track "Land of Hope and Dreams," that would later appear on Wrecking Ball. In 2012, Springsteen and The E Street Band embarked on a 26 country tour to promote Wrecking Ball. 2014's High Hopes was a collection of covers and reworked songs from their library. It went to number one in America. Another box set was released in 2015, titled The Ties That Bind: The River Collection. Bruce then released his memoir titled Born to Run, accompanied by a career-spanning collection titled Chapter & Verses.

Bruce Springsteen achieved worldwide superstar popularity and became an American icon, and all while maintaining a high level of musical integrity with his vast catalogue of albums and songs. Springsteen suffered a few rough patches along the way. However, his almost unbroken string of critical and commercial successes often served to challenge himself and his listeners. Occasionally, The Boss veered off in some unexpected musical directions where he altered the sound of his music. Springsteen consistently found creative approaches to build musical arrangements with The E Street Band. He also professed lyrical messages that were at times overtly political. All of these attributes kept his music fresh. Springsteen has always found a way to return to one of his great strengths, providing his native country with his standard three-hour plus live performances that came to define American rock 'n' roll. Bruce Springsteen was inducted into the Rock and Roll Hall of Fame in 1999. The E Street Band was inducted into the Rock and Roll Hall of Fame in 2014.

Eric Clapton (1945-) was already a rock superstar by the time he embarked on his solo career. His long resume of prominent groups included; The Yardbirds (see chapter four), John Mayall's Bluesbreakers (see chapter four), Cream (see chapter four), and Blind Faith (see chapter eleven). This pedigree established Clapton as one of the very best guitarists of his generation. Before Clapton would release his debut solo album, he formed Derek and the Dominos (see chapter eleven) to record the classic album Layla and Other Assorted Love Songs with Duane Allman. Clapton's 1970 debut, Eric Clapton, produced a top forty hit "After Midnight," written by J.J. Cale (who would have a long association with Clapton). This album featured the classic "Let It Rain," a song Clapton wrote with Delaney and Bonnie. The next few years were difficult for Eric Clapton while he struggled with substance abuse. However, he was back to perform a concert at the Rainbow Theatre in London in early 1973. This resulted in the live album, Eric Clapton's Rainbow Concert, with an all-star band that included Steve Winwood.

"Let it Rain"
by Eric Clapton, Bonnie Bramlett, and Delaney Bramlett

Eric Clapton wrote "Let It Rain" with the help of Bonnie and Delaney Bramlett while they were touring together in 1969. Clapton was with Blind Faith and Bonnie and Delaney were opening for them. Organist Bobby Whitlock, bassist Carl Radle, and drummer Jim Gordon played on this track and went on to form Derek and the Dominos with Clapton. Jerry Allison and Sonny Curtis, former members of Buddy Holly's Crickets, sang background vocals on the track. Also singing background vocal parts were Rita Coolidge and Bonnie Bramlett.

"Let it Rain" contained a strong guitar riff while the melody blended with the folk-like chord changes of the song. The lyrics were creative in how they utilized the words "rain" and "reign" to describe the power of love. The guitar solo in the middle of the composition was performed by guest musician Stephen Stills. Toward the end of the song, Clapton was soloing on his favorite Fender Strat (he called Brownie) as Stills continued to solo. A nineteen minute version of "Let It Rain" appeared on Derek and the Domino's Live at the Fillmore album. It featured an extended instrumental jam, including a very musical Jim Gordon drum solo.

1974's 461 Ocean Boulevard was the beginning of Clapton's sustained solo career. This album yielded the number one hit "I Shot the Sheriff," a brilliant cover of Bob Marley's classic song. Clapton's next three efforts; 1975's There's One in Every Crowd, the 1975 live E.C. Was Here, and 1976's No Reason to Cry (with an appearance by The Band) were less popular. It was 1977's Slowhand (Eric Clapton's nickname) that took his solo career to new heights when it peaked at number two on the U.S. charts. Slowhand produced the hits "Lay Down Sally," "Cocaine," and "Wonderful Tonight."

> "There is always something to listen to, to aspire to, with the guitar. It is still the most flexible instrument. You can improvise on it. You have such freedom. I don't think there is a limit to it."
>
> – Eric Clapton

Groundbreaking album Slowhand
by Eric Clapton

Slowhand featured Clapton's band of guitarist George Terry, keyboardist Dick Sims, bassist Carl Radle, drummer Jamie Oldaker, saxophonist Mel Collins, and background singers Yvonne Elliman and Marcy Levy. The band showed a grasp of musical genres by alternating between authentic blues, mainstream rock, and country styles. This ensemble was confident and never flashy. Clapton also enlisted the production expertise of Glyn Johns, who brought a very professional work ethic to the studio sessions.

Side one opened with "Cocaine," then "Wonderful Tonight," "Lay Down Sally,""Next Time You See Her," and "We're All the Way." The opener "Cocaine" was originally written and recorded by blues guitarist J.J. Cale, who Clapton would later team up with to record the album The Road To Escondido. The song featured one of the all-time great blues-rock guitar riffs. The lyrics were about drug addiction, something Clapton was all too familiar with. Clapton often said that he could sing objectively about a drug, even when it was hurting him. When Clapton became sober, he became active with helping others get through their addictions. The ballad "Wonderful Tonight" was written while Clapton was waiting for his girlfriend (Nell) to get ready to go out to dinner. Clapton remembered, "It was the classic domestic situation; I was ready and she wasn't. I went back downstairs to my guitar, and the words of the song just came out very quickly. They were written in about ten minutes, and actually written in anger and frustration. I wasn't that enamored with it as a song...I could have just as easily have thrown it away." #6 For "Lay Down Sally," Clapton's lyrics have the singer attempting to convince a girl to hang out with him instead of leaving. This song was a good example of Clapton's stylistic versatility by venturing into a country feel "train beat" and some authentic county guitar picking.

Side two opened with "The Core," then "May You Never," "Mean Old Frisco," and "Peaches and Diesel." "The Core" was based on a Clapton repeating guitar riff and was originally titled "The Riff," then "Burning Hot Core," and finally "The Core." Clapton alternated singing verses with Marcy Levy (she also sings on "Lay Down Sally"). Drummer Jamie Oldaker played a funky off-beat cymbal ostinato and Mel Collins added a saxophone solo, which was the first time Clapton utilized a horn since his debut album. The album was titled after Clapton's nickname, "Slowhand," which Clapton realized was popular with his friends. In later live performances, Clapton began to sing "that dirty cocaine" while performing the song "Cocaine" to reinforce his anti-drug message to the audience.

1978's Backless featured a top ten hit "Promises." Then, Clapton released another live record, Just One Night in 1981. That same year, he released Another Ticket that contained the hit "I Can't Stand It." The rest of the 1980's saw a dip in Clapton's popularity with 1983's Money and Cigarettes, 1985's Behind the Sun, and 1986's August. However the 1980's also found Clapton honing his songwriting skills. For the rest of his career, Clapton would create some very fine pop songs that differed from the blues-based music that he had written in the past. A retrospective four disc box set titled Crossroads was released in 1988 and served to revitalize his career. It spanned Clapton's entire career from The Yardbirds to his early 1980's solo recordings. 1989's Journeyman went to number one on the U.S. charts with the hit "Pretending," a song written by Jerry Lynn Williams. This song contained a great guitar hook and featured drummer Steve Ferrone's heavy groove. Clapton also covered the songs "Hound Dog" by Leiber and Stoller and "Run So Far" by George Harrison.

Tragedy struck in 1991 when Eric Clapton's four-year-old son died in a fall. While he mourned the loss, Clapton recorded an epic live album called 24 Nights. Clapton next recorded the 1992 movie soundtrack Rush. It featured the huge hit "Tears in Heaven," written about his son. In the spring of 1992, Clapton recorded an MTV Unplugged concert that became his biggest-selling record ever. He followed in 1994 with the successful From the Cradle. Both of these recordings found Clapton revisiting his love for the blues by performing many blues songs written by Robert Johnson, Bo Diddley, and Muddy Waters. Another box set was released in 1996 titled Crossroads, Vol. 2: Live in the Seventies. 1998's Pilgrim debuted at number four on the strength of the pop-styled "My Father's Eyes."

The decade of the 2000's began with 2001's Reptile and a 2004 collection of songs honoring the legendary bluesman Robert Johnson, titled Me and Mr. Johnson. He soon followed with another volume, Sessions for Robert J. Earlier in 2000, Clapton had teamed up with another blues legend, B.B. King to record blues standards. Riding with the King showed Eric Clapton's continued commitment to the blues as a pure art form (see the blues profile in this chapter). In 2005, Clapton released Back Home, his fourteenth album of original songs. Also that same year, Clapton reunited with Ginger Baker and Jack Bruce for a Cream reunion series of concerts.

In 2008, Eric Clapton began playing again with his old Blind Faith bandmate, Steve Winwood, for a series of gigs. Their interaction was recorded on the 2009 double live album Live from Madison Square Garden. 2010's self-titled Clapton debuted at number seven in England and number six in America. The songs "Rocking Chair" and"When Somebody Thinks You're Wonderful" became staples in his live performances. 2013's Old Sock contained two new Clapton compositions, "Gotta Get Over" and "Every Little Thing." A number of prominent guests appeared on Old Socks including Paul McCartney, Taj Mahal, J.J. Cale, Chaka Khan, and Steve Winwood. The album also featured many session musicians including; bassist Willie Weeks, and drummers Matt Chamberlain, Abe Laboriel Jr. Jim Keltner, and Steve Gadd (Clapton's regular touring drummer). In 2014, Clapton recorded The Breeze: An Appreciation of JJ Cale, followed by 2015's Forever Man, a compilation album. 2016's I Still Do found Clapton reuniting with Slowhand producer Glyn Johns. This album debuted at number six on the U.S.charts.

Eric Clapton has enjoyed one of the most remarkable careers in rock music history. He was a central figure in the continuing evolution of both blues and rock guitar. Clapton grew as a songwriter and vocalist with a distinct, soulful voice. No rock guitar player has greater mastery of the blues or has been a greater champion of the blues genre. Along the way, he has championed many lesser-known guitarists by featuring them in his bands, including them on his albums, and by inviting them to perform on his Crossroads concert series. Eric Clapton is the only three-time inductee into the Rock and Roll Hall of Fame, as a solo artist, as a member of The Yardbirds, and as a member of Cream.

Rock Hard Fact

Eric Clapton received the nickname "Slowhand" when he constantly broke guitar strings playing fast runs and bending notes. He would go backstage to change strings and the audience would begin a "slow hand" clap until he returned.

The Blues Will Never Die

The importance of the blues has been documented throughout this book and countless other rock history sources. Although it took a trip to England (see chapter four) to force a blues merger with rock, the American answer saw the strong presence of the blues in innovators such as Jimi Hendrix, Janis Joplin, The Allman Brothers Band, and many others. Blues-rock artists emerged from many regional areas. The hard touring *George Thorogood and The Delaware Destroyers* (1974-present) have been on the road for over forty years. While keeping that schedule they have managed to produce hits such as "Move It on Over," "Who Do You Love?" and "Bad To the Bone." They have helped keep the bar room blues alive by consistently breathing new life into songs by Hank Williams, Bo Diddley, and John Lee Hooker. Texas' *Stevie Ray Vaughan* (1954-1990) gave the music world a well-needed shot in the arm of blues during the 1980's. Vaughn and the band Double Trouble had a take no prisoners style of performing that turned heads on every stage that they played. They found popular success with hits such as "Love Struck Baby" and "Pride and Joy." Stevie Ray was inspired by blues guitarists Albert King, Freddie King, Otis Rush, and Lonnie Mack, but the Hendrix comparisons were inevitable. Vaughn fused the fire of the electric blues with popular songwriting approaches. He also had a soulful vocal style that got him noticed by Jackson Browne, who offered him the use of his studio, and David Bowie, who hired him to play guitar on his Let's Dance recording and subsequent tour (which Vaughn turned down). Vaughn (and four other people) died in a helicopter crash departing from a gig in 1990. Stevie Ray Vaughn was inducted into the Rock and Roll Hall of Fame in 2015.

As decades passed, many artists and bands drew from multiple rock genres and styles while retaining a strong sense of the blues. Detroit born *Jack White* (1975-) combined blues with garage rock and a post-punk aesthetic with his band The White Stripes (1997-2011). The White Stripes popularized the garage rock revival with the release of White Blood Cells and Elephant. Their song "Seven Nation Army" has become a rock anthem. They brought a sense of romance and mystery to the indie underground movement with their 2005 release Get Behind Me Satan. White went on to co-lead the bands The Raconteurs and The Dead Weather. However, it is his solo career that showed his deeply rooted and gritty brand of blues infused rock. His recordings Blunderbuss, Lazaretto, and 2018's Boarding House Reach simultaneously look forward and backward. In his career he has worked with Loretta Lynn, Bob Dylan, The Rolling Stones, Elton John, and Beyonce.

The Atlanta, Georgia based *Black Crows* (1989-2002) (2005-2015) effectively combined classic rock with blues and a southern rock jam band mentality. *Blues Traveler* (1987-present) was formed in Princeton, New Jersey by vocalist/harmonica player John Popper. They combined blues with psychedelic rock elements to create their extended improvisational style. Other bands such as *The Black Keys* (2001-present) formed in Ohio and emerged from a second wave of garage and indie rock bands. The Black Keys skillfully combined a raw blues sound that drew from the tradition of Robert Johnson and Howlin Wolf. Another important blues-rock artist was *Joe Bonamassa* (1977-) from New Hartford, New York. Bonamassa has extensive performance credits playing with Eric Clapton, Steve Winwood, Buddy Guy, Warren Haynes, and others. Bonamassa works to promote the blues genre by running a nonprofit organization called The Keeping the Blues Alive Foundation, whose mission is to provide music scholarships and educational resources to schools in need.

The greatest modern ambassador for the blues is the legendary Eric Clapton. For so many, he embodies the definition of the blues by linking its past with the present. Clapton founded the Crossroads Guitar Festival, an ongoing series of music festivals and benefit concerts that funds the Crossroads Centre (a drug treatment center-also founded by Clapton). The first Crossroads concert was held at Madison Square Garden in New York in 1999. A 2004 three-day Crossroads Festival was held at the Cotton Bowl in Dallas Texas. An incredible list of guitar greats that performed at this festival included; Robert Cray, Larry Carlton, Vince Gill, Buddy Guy, Eric Johnson, B.B. King, Robert Lockwood Jr., John Mayer, John McLaughlin, Carlos Santana, Derek Trucks, Steve Vai, Joe Walsh, and of course Eric Clapton, and many others. Other Crossroads Festivals were held in 2007 and 2010 in Illinois and 2013 at Madison Square Garden. Each of these events were documented on DVD. Many of the artists that appeared on The Crossroads Festivals excel in a variety of music genres but the overwhelming spirit of the blues is what galvanized these experiences. Nobody in rock music history better represents the meaning and emotion that the blues brought to rock 'n' roll than Eric Clapton.

Peter Frampton (born 1950-) got his start in music as a member of the band The Little Ravens. Both he and David Bowie were schoolmates at a technical school in England. Frampton became a member of The Herd in 1966 and soon joined Humble Pie (see chapter eleven) in 1968. While in Humble Pie, Frampton did some side project recording sessions with Harry Nilsson, John Entwistle (of The Who), and Jerry Lee Lewis. After completing four studio albums with Humble Pie, Peter Frampton left to pursue a solo career in 1971. His solo debut album, Wind of Change, was released in 1972 and featured guest artists Billy Preston and Ringo Starr. Frampton followed with 1973's Frampton's Camel, 1974's Somethin's Happening, and Frampton in 1975. These were not well received but his 1976 live double album, Frampton Comes Alive!, was a breakout success. It featured the hits "Show Me the Way," "Baby, I Love Your Way," and "Do You Feel Like We Do."

"Do You Feel Like We Do"
by Peter Frampton, Mick Gallagher,
Rick Wills, and John Siomos

"Do You Feel like We Do" originally appeared on Frampton's Camel, a much shorter version than the live recording. The live track was over fourteen-minutes long, with a quiet bridge that included a keyboard solo by Bob Mayo and Frampton's guitar solo that featured his signature talk box skills. The talk box involved Frampton's employment of an effect pedal that redirected the guitar signal through a tube coming out of Frampton's mouth. This allowed the guitar to mimic human speech, similar to an instrument called a vocoder. The song was built on an infectious melodic riff that Frampton utilized to build his solo lines.

"Do You Feel Like We Do" was a song about experiencing a hangover. The lyrics described that the singer woke up one morning with a wine glass by his bed

---

"Songwriting is work. It's hard work. Most people don't want to put that kind of work into it. And that's one difference between now and, say, the Sixties or early Seventies. People really wrote songs."

- Tom Petty

and he wondered how it got there stating, "Whose wine? What wine? Where the hell did I dine?" Peter Frampton has noted the communal nature of the song and viewed it as a crowd participation event. Played live, the crowd would often take over the vocals and pick upon Frampton's stage gestures when he would point to emphasize the "you" in the songs' title.

After the success of Frampton Comes Alive!, Peter Frampton became one of the biggest arena rock stars of the 1970's. 1977's I'm in You was a quick follow-up that went to number two on the U.S. charts. After a near fatal car accident in 1978, Frampton released the moderately successful Where I Should Be in 1979. In the 1980's, Frampton recorded five studio albums with diminishing commercial results including 1989's When All the Pieces Fit. Frampton next played with his old schoolmate, David Bowie on Bowie's Never Let Me Down album. Peter Frampton went on to record seven more studio albums, from 1994's Peter Frampton to 2016's Acoustic Classics. Peter Frampton's became a breakthrough star to worldwide audiences on the strength of his live performances. His contributions to other artists as a session guitarist is often overlooked.

John J Mellencamp (1951-) (aka John Cougar Mellencamp) is an American vocalist/guitarist from Seymour, Indiana. Mellencamp began his career under the stage name Johnny Cougar. He developed a mixture of folk-rock and rock styles. His style of heartland rock coincided with his interest in social issues, which he has frequently championed. Mellencamp signed a recording deal with MCA and released his debut album Chestnut Street Incident in 1976. This album did not fare well and MCA dropped him from their label. Two years later, he signed with Riva Records and released 1978's A Biography. It yielded "I Need a Lover" that was a hit in Australia. The song reappeared on his 1979 release, John Cougar, and went to number twenty-eight on the U.S. charts. Although 1980's Nothin' Matters and What If It Did, was only moderately successful, it saw Mellencamp continue to build his fan base. 1982's American Fool would be his commercial breakthrough album with the hits "Hurts So Good" and "Jack and Diane."

"Jack & Diane"
by John Mellencamp

"Jack and Diane" was Mellencamp's tribute to the people of rural working class America. He was inspired by his hometown of Seymour, Indiana, a small town of only 13,000 people. "Jack and Diane" was about a typical boy-girl relationship. The lyrics told the story of the young high school couple (Jack was a former football star) that fell in love and struggled to make their relationship work. The story resonated with Mid-West audiences and the simple characters easily allowed them to identify with the song. It was Mellencamp's most popular tune and only single to rise to number one the U.S. charts.

Musically, "Jack and Diane" successfully integrated an acoustic guitar accompaniment to Mellencamp's vocal narrative. Its power chords and a heavy drumset fill served as a transition between sections of the tune. Guitarist and producer Mick Ronson worked with Mellencamp on American Fool, including "Jack and Diane." Ronson brought a powerful rock feel to the song that balanced perfectly with Mellencamp's acoustic storytelling ability.

1983's The Kid Inside was previously recorded for MCA but when they dropped Mellencamp, this album was shelved until Main Man Records decided to release it. 1985's Uh-Huh was the first album that Mellencamp used his real last name. It went to number nine on the U.S. charts. Mellencamp went on to record sixteen more studio albums including 2017's Sad Clowns & Hillbillies. John Mellencamp has incorporated a variety of country and folk instruments into his rock style including the autoharp, dulcimer, accordion, and fiddle. This has helped to establish his roots rock approach. Some of Mellencamp's other hits were "Crumblin Down," "Pink Houses," and "Small Town." John Cougar Mellencamp was inducted into the Rock and Roll Hall of Fame in 2008.

Tom Petty (1950-2017) (**and The Heartbreakers** 1976-2017) was a singer/songwriter, multi-instrumentalist, record producer, and actor from Gainesville, Florida born in 1950. Petty began playing music in high school and formed a band called the Sundowners, who later became The Epics. By 1971, that band evolved into Mudcrutch, featuring (future Heartbreakers) guitarist Mike Campbell and keyboardist Benmont Tench. Mudcrutch moved to Los Angeles but called it quits after struggling to make an impact. Petty continued to promote his songs and landed a record deal with Leon Russell's Shelter Records. In 1976, Petty called on Campbell and Tench and added bassist Ron Blair and drummer Stan Lynch to form Tom Petty and The Heartbreakers.

In 1976, they released their self-titled debut album Tom Petty and The Heartbreakers. It yielded the singles "American Girl," "Breakdown," and "Anything That's Rock 'N' Roll." The album went to number fifty-five in England, establishing Petty and The Heartbreakers' sound as distinct, yet with the clear influence of bands such as The Beatles and The Byrds. 1978's You're Gonna Get It! rose to number twenty-three on the U.S. charts and produced the hits "I Need to Know" and "Listen to Her Heart."

"American Girl"
by Tom Petty

"American Girl" was never a big hit for Tom Petty and The Heartbreakers but it became one of their most enduring songs. Petty wrote the song about an urban myth that was set in his hometown of Gainesville, Florida. The story went that a prototypical all-American blond female student from The University of Florida took hallucinogens in her dorm room. She thought that she could fly and dove out of her dorm room window to her death. This song represented the end of innocence that was felt by baby-boomers during the 1970's.

Musically, "American Girl" saw Petty and The Heartbreakers create a rock shuffle feel built around a melodic bass line. The guitar parts contained very raw and rhythmic guitar comping that complemented the driving drumset feel. Played live, "American Girl" was always a showcase for the band's exciting guitar solos. Petty was told the song sounded like something The Byrds would write. He responded that "'American Girl' doesn't really sound like The Byrds; it evokes The Byrds. People are usually influenced by more that one thing, so your music becomes a mixture. There's nothing really new, but always new ways to combine things. We tried to play as good as whoever we admired but never could. #7 Tom Petty performed "American Girl" at The Hollywood Bowl on September 25th, 2017 to close his set. It was the last song that he ever performed before his death one week later.

In 1979, Tom Petty and The Heartbreakers released a masterpiece, Damn the Torpedoes. It was produced by Petty and recording guru Jimmy Iovine. It featured the huge hits "Refugee," "Don't Do Me Like That," and "Here Comes My Girl."

Groundbreaking album
Damn the Torpedoes
by Tom Petty and The Heartbreakers

Damn the Torpedoes was the first top ten album for Tom Petty and The Heartbreakers and it went to number two on the U.S. charts. This success came out of conflict. Not long after Petty's label, Shelter Records, was sold to MCA, he struggled to become free from the major label. This led to serious financial trouble for Petty. Eventually, Petty settled with MCA, pulled out some old Mudcrutch songs, and wrote some new ones. The sound on Damn the Torpedoes featured the polished and clean production of Jimmy Iovine. The Heartbreakers had evolved into a powerful and tight unit that was reminiscent of the Rolling Stones. Their musicality and strong ensemble play brought out the distinctive voice of Petty.

Side one opened with "Refugee," then "Here Comes My Girl," "Even the Losers." "Shadow of a Doubt (A Complex Kid)," and "Century City." For "Refugee," Tom Petty wrote about the pressures of the music business. Petty was (rightfully) angry with the whole music business and this was reflected in the entire tone and mood of the album. Guitarist Mike Campbell wrote the music for "Refugee" on a four-track machine and Petty added the lyrics. The band did as many as one-hundred takes to capture the "right feel" of the song. The lyrics for "Here Comes My Girl" described a girl that kept rejecting the singer but he kept going back to her. Petty came up with a unique approach to half-speaking and half-singing the verses, where he kept reminding himself that he can't keep this (the relationship) up. On the choruses, Petty sang with an excited tone when the girl came by to see him.

Side two opened with "Don't Do Me Like That," then "You Tell Me," "What Are You Doin in My Life," and "Louisiana Rain." "Don't Do Me Like That" featured a 1950's rock piano eighth-note comping feel. The band incorporated a gospel-inspired organ sound and blues guitar comping lines that answered Petty's vocal phrases. The lyrics for "Don't Do Me Like That" were about the singer pleading with a girl not to dump him and that he had a friend who recently had his heart broken. The mixture of styles on Damn the Torpedoes revealed how subtly Tom Petty and The Heartbreakers derived their unique roots rock approach. Very few mainstream rock albums from the late 1970's and early 1980's were as powerful as Damn the Torpedoes.

In 1981, Tom Petty and The Heartbreakers released Hard Promises, a top ten record that spawned the hit "The Waiting" and a duet with Stevie Nicks titled "Insider." Petty recorded another duet with Nicks, "Stop Draggin' My Heart Around," that went to number three on the U.S. charts. Shortly after, bassist Ron Blair quit the band and was replaced by Howie Epstein (who added significant vocal parts). 1982's Long After Dark followed and contained the hits with "Change of Heart" and "You Got Lucky." In 1985, the band played at Live Aid at Philadelphia's JFK Stadium. That same year, Petty and The Heartbreakers recorded Southern Accents, an album that saw Petty stretch his songwriting collaborations with musicians outside of the Heartbreakers. He wrote songs with Dave Stewart of The Eurythmics and Robbie Robertson of The Band. The moody "Don't Come Around Here No More" provided Petty with his biggest British hit to date. In 1986, Petty and The Heartbreakers joined Bob Dylan for a world tour called the True Confessions Tour. Petty and Dylan composed the song "Jammin' Me," a top twenty hit. This song opened Petty and The Heartbreakers' next release, 1987's Let Me Up (I've Had Enough). This also led to the formation of The Traveling Wilburys (see Traveling Wilburys profile).

The Traveling Wilburys
Old School Supergroup

The "dream band" formation of The Traveling Wilburys was, for many rock fans, the second coming of the Million Dollar Quartet with Elvis Presley. In 1988, Tom Petty and Bob Dylan joined forces with former Beatle George Harrison, ELO's Jeff Lynne, and the legendary Roy Orbison to create this supergroup. Jeff Lynne had produced George Harrison's solo album Cloud Nine. Harrison introduced the idea to Lynne that the two should start a band together. Harrison and Lynne became friendly with Tom Petty in the fall of 1987 when Petty and The Heartbreakers toured Europe as Bob Dylan's backing band. Lynne began collaborating with Petty on Petty's Full Moon Fever album. Tom Petty had been writing songs with Roy Orbison for the album, which then led to all five members getting together.

The Traveling Wilburys recorded the single "Handle with Care" as the "B" side to the George Harrison single "This Is Love." The Wilburys next decided to record a full length album. 1988's Traveling Wilburys Vol. 1 immediately found its way onto Rolling Stone Magazine's Top 100 Albums of All Time list. A video for "Handle with Care" was set in a recording studio and it focused on each of the legendary members and their collaborative performance. It reminded viewers that no matter what the current rock trends were about, these guys were going to show you what rock 'n' roll was all about. The album and video also served to revitalize the solo careers of Harrison, Lynne, and even Orbison.

During the recording of Vol. I, Harrison approached Dylan and told him that they were all in awe of him but would try to treat him like anyone else. Dylan responded he was in awe of all of them as well. Petty later described George Harrison as the leader of The Wilburys. Harrison and Lynne ran the recording sessions while Harrison was left with the task of figuring out which member should sing a particular lead vocal part. They all bonded on their shared love for the comedy of Monty Python. Harrison had worked with the members of Monty Python previously.

The tragic and sudden death (a heart attack) of Roy Orbison on December 6th, 1988 would end the supergroups' short reign. However, in 1990 ex-Byrd Roger McGuinn substituted for Orbison on the band's second and final release. Confusingly, they mis-numbered the album on purpose calling it Traveling Wilburys Vol 3. In a tribute to Roy Orbison, The Traveling Wilburys recorded a video for their single "End of the Line," and placed Orbison's guitar rocking in a chair as the rest of the band performed. The Traveling Wilburys were the ultimate supergroup that represented four distinct eras of rock music history. They

> "I think a lot of people came into rock 'n' roll to try to change the world. I came into rock 'n' roll to make music."
>
> – Steve Winwood

never acted with an air of self-importance. Rather, they just made some great rock 'n' roll music.

In 1989, Petty released Full Moon Fever, his first solo album. Produced by Jeff Lynne, it was met with great critical praise and commercial success but without the full musical assistance from The Heartbreakers. This album would prove to be Tom Petty's commercial peak, selling over five million copies worldwide and reaching number three on the U.S. charts. Three monster hits were released including "I Won't Back Down," "Runnin' Down a Dream," and "Free Fallin." Recorded in the relaxed environment of Heartbreaker Mike Campbell's garage studio, Petty received recording contributions from all of the Traveling Wilbury members except Bob Dylan. Jeff Lynne helped shape the record by adding layers of keyboards and backing vocals, making it somewhat Beatlesque.

Tom Petty teamed up with the full Heartbreakers band for 1991's Into the Great Wide Open, yielding the singles "King's Highway," and "Learning To Fly." Petty also hired keyboardist/guitarist Scott Thurston to boost the band's sound. Drummer Stan Lynch was fired from the band and for a brief period, Dave Grohl joined the band (before starting the Foo Fighters). Soon, drummer Steve Ferrone was hired as the permanent replacement. Tom Petty released his second solo album, Wildflowers, in 1994. This started a great relationship with producer Rick Rubin that would lead to their collaboration on a movie soundtrack, 1996's She's the One. 1999's Echo reached the American top ten and was again produced by Rick Rubin.

In the new millennium, Tom Petty and The Heartbreakers recorded 2002's The Last DJ, an album-length critique with songs about the practices within the music industry. It reached number nine on the U.S. charts. For this recording, bassist Ron Blair returned following the tragic death of Howie Epstein from substance abuse. In 2006, Petty released his third solo album, Highway Companion. He also revived the pre-Heartbreakers Mudcrutch band to tour and release a single (they recorded fourteen songs for an iTunes 2008 release). On February 3rd, 2008, Tom Petty and The Heartbreakers performed live at the Super Bowl XLII half-time show. 2010's Mojo featured a bluesy approach and went to number two on the American charts. The band's last recording would be 2014's Hypnotic Eye. It debuted at number one on the U.S. charts, their first ever to top the charts.

Sadly, Tom Petty died from cardiac arrest on October 2nd, 2017. Tom Petty was a prolific musical artist that developed many interesting musical projects and collaborative efforts. Petty was a champion for the rights of artists to maintain their artistic control and freedom. He always remained true to his rock 'n' roll roots. Petty demonstrated a strong sense of artistic integrity with great consistency over a forty-year career. He combined elements of British Invasion rock, American garage rock, and a Bob Dylan-like singer/songwriter sensibility to create his distinctively American hybrid style. Petty's uniquely nasal and slurred voice was comparable to none. Tom Petty and The Heartbreakers were inducted into the Rock and Roll Hall of Fame in 2001.

Rod Stewart (1945-) began his career singing with various bands in the early 1960's including folk singer Wizz Jones. He joined the R&B band Jimmy Powell and the Five Dimensions and then The Hoochie Coochie Men. They evolved into Steampacket and supported The Rolling Stones on a tour in 1965. In early 1966, Stewart joined the blues-rock band Shotgun Express and then by the end of the year, was recruited to sing with The Jeff Beck Group.

After two successful albums, Stewart and guitarist/bassist Ron Wood joined The Small Faces. Simultaneously, Stewart signed a solo recording contract. He then released his 1969 solo debut album An Old Raincoat Won't Ever Let You Down. The Faces next released their album, First Step in early 1970. Later that fall, Stewart released his second solo record, Gasoline Alley. Meanwhile, The Faces (with Stewart) released a second album, Long Player. Rod continued doing double duty, still recording with The Small Faces but his third solo album was the charm. 1971's Every Picture Tells a Story would prove to be his breakout recording with a number one hit on both sides of the Atlantic titled "Maggie May."

"Maggie May"
by Rod Stewart and Martin Quittenton

Rod Stewart's record company didn't think "Maggie May" would be a hit so they released it on the B-side to his single "Reason To Believe." A few disc jockeys liked "Maggie May" better so they played that as the single instead. The song was autobiographical, about Stewart's first sexual encounter. Instead of using the real name of his partner in the song, he borrowed the name Maggie May from the title of a folk song about a prostitute.

Musically, "Maggie May" began with an acoustic classical guitar introduction that launched into the song after a brief pause. The musicians on this track (and the entire Every Picture Tells a Story album) were guitarist Martin Quittenton, bassist (and Faces' bandmate) Ronnie Wood, and drummer Mickey Waller. Quittenton came up with the introduction and harmony for the song. Session player Ray Jackson added the very musical mandolin part that was improvised on the spot. "Maggie May" became one of Stewart's signature songs that helped to define his career.

After a spring tour with The Faces, tensions grew in the band while Rod Stewarts' solo career gained momentum. Stewarts' 1972's Never a Dull Moment was almost as successful as Every Picture Tells a Story. After The Faces released their final album, 1973's Ooh La La, Stewart countered with 1974's Smiler. Rod Stewart went on to record twenty-five more studio albums. With 1981s Tonight I'm Yours, Stewart incorporated some new wave and synth-pop sounds into his musical approach. Rod Stewart also reunited with Ron Wood (now a Rolling Stone) to film an MTV Unplugged concert in 1993. In addition to his prolific recording career, Rod Stewart has made a number of cover albums referred to as his Great American Songbook series. In 2015, he released Another Country that featured the single "Love Is." In 2017, Stewart collaborated on a remix of one of his most popular hits, "Do Ya Think I'm Sexy?" with vocalist Joe Jonas and DNCE. Rod Stewart is a talented musician with a distinctly warm vocal presence that elevated him to become one of Britain's most enduring rock artists. Rod Stewart was inducted into the Rock and Roll Hall of Fame in 1994.

Steve Winwood (1948-) is a British vocalist/multi-instrumentalist that was born in Handsworth, Birmingham, England in 1948. After establishing stardom with The Spencer Davis Group, Traffic, and the super-group Blind Faith (see chapter eleven), Winwood was ready to embark on his solo career. He recorded his

---

Rock Hard Fact

Stevie Nicks' Soldier's Angel Foundation benefited wounded soldiers who fought in Iraq and Afghanistan by providing them with iPods pre-loaded with music.

self-titled debut album Steve Winwood in 1977 to little fanfare. His second effort, 1980's Arc of a Diver, was a breakthrough album that featured his first hit, "While You See a Chance." It peaked at number three on the U.S. charts. Winwood was able to establish a solo persona after years doing recording sessions and being part of the above mentioned high-profile rock bands. 1982's Talking Back to the Night was less successful but did yield a minor hit, "Valerie."

Winwood took his time to craft the slick, sophisticated pop-rock Back in the High Life in 1986. It received great critical and commercial acclaim, selling over three million copies. This album contained Winwood's first number one single, "Higher Love," that won a Grammy for Record of the Year in 1987.

"Higher Love"
by Steve Winwood and Will Jennings

Will Jennings had collaborated with Steve Winwood on the Arc of a Diver and Talking Back to the Night albums. Jennings has described "Higher Love's" lyrics as inspired by the beautiful old hymns he heard in his Arkansas church while growing up. The line "Bring me a higher love" meant that there must be higher love on a deep spiritual level.

"Higher Love" embodied a funky rhythm section feel with skillful horn arrangements and innovative percussion parts. The drum machine programming by Jimmy Bralower and drumming of John "JR" Robinson were clear examples of how studio technology could be combined with real musicians to develop a danceable and funky groove. Winwood brought in the great R&B vocalist Chaka Khan to lend the track a distinct gospel flavor. "Higher Love" also featured guitarist Nile Rodgers (of the band Chic and David Bowie) playing a funky rhythm guitar part.

Winwood next moved from Island Records to Virgin Records and released Roll with It in 1988. This album and its single, "Roll with It," (also co-written by Will Jennings) both went to number one. 1990's Refugees of the Heart was less successful but the lead single, "One and Only Man," was a strong collaboration with ex-Traffic bandmate Jim Capaldi. After a few years of inactivity, Steve Winwood reappeared in 1994 for a Traffic reunion with Capaldi. Next came a return to his own solo career with 1997's Junction Seven. The following year, Winwood started a new project called Latin Crossings. It was a Latin-jazz group that featured legendary Cuban musicians that included percussionist Tito Puente and trumpeter Arturo Sandoval. Unfortunately, this ensemble never recorded. After more time off, Winwood released 2003's Latin influenced About Time and five years later, 2008's Nine Lives.

2008 brought a reunion between Steve Winwood and Eric Clapton for a series of concerts at Madison Square Garden. The result was documented on 2009's Live fromMadison Square Garden. Winwood's session work over the next decade included an appearance on Miranda Lambert's 2011 For the Record and Gov't Mule's 2013 album Shout! (see chapter nine). In 2017, Winwood released his first solo live album, Greatest Hits Live.

Steve Winwood has had a remarkable career spanning over fifty years. His strong musicianship, great keyboard skill, and excellent guitar work made him an in-demand musician for numerous recording sessions. His membership in The Spencer Davis Group, Traffic, and Blind Faith made him a rock legend. He has fused jazz, R&B, blues-rock, and elements of psychedelic rock with his powerful and soulful voice. Winwood capped this off with a stellar solo career. Steve Winwood was inducted into the Rock and Roll Hall of Fame in 2004 as a member of Traffic.

From the 1980's to current times, many significant singer-led classic bands have continued to produce enduring rock music. Many of these artists have drawn from a number of diverse rock genres. A few of these artists include; **Pat Benatar** (1953-), **Stevie Nicks, Sheryl Crow** (1962-), **Jon Bon Jovi, Alanis Morrisette** (1974-) **Fiona Apple** (1977-), **Sting, Amy Winehouse** (2003-2011), and **John Mayer**.

Stevie Nicks (1948) has led a successful career as a key member of Fleetwood Mac (see chapter eleven). Nicks and Lindsey Buckingham co-led the release of 1973's Buckingham Nicks. From there, they both joined Fleetwood Mac, and enjoyed great commercial and critical acclaim. Nicks' vocals were the focal point of Fleetwood Mac with major hits such as"Dreams" and "Rhiannon." Stevie took some time off from the group to record her 1981 solo debut album, Bella Donna. It proved very popular, going to number one on the U.S. charts on the strength of three hits, "Stop Draggin' My Heart Around" (a duet with Tom Petty), "Leather and Lace" (a duet with Don Henley), and "Edge of Seventeen."

"Edge of Seventeen"
by Stevie Nicks

"Edge of Seventeen (Just Like the White Winged Dove)" just missed the top ten on the U.S. charts going to number eleven. Nicks was first inspired to write the songwhen Tom Petty's wife told her that she and Tom had met "at the age of seventeen." However, Stevie thought she said "edge of seventeen." Nicks ended up utilizing this phrase for the title for a new song in which she wrote about both the death of her uncle Jonathan and the murder of John Lennon. These two sad events occurred in the same week in December of 1980. The lyrics of "Edge of Seventeen" utilized the metaphor of a white winged dove that represented the spirit leaving the body upon death. When the backup singers sang "ooh baby ooh" it was meant to simulate a dove singing.

Musically, "Edge of Seventeen" utilized a 16th note guitar riff played by session great guitarist Waddy Wachtel. Wachtel was inspired to come up with the riff when he heard Andy Summer's guitar part on The Police's "Bring on the Night." Nicks often ended her live performances with "Edge of Seventeen," citing it as a highly personal moment that connected her to her audience. "Edge of Seventeen" was an example of Stevie Nicks'great ability to express her personal emotions in her songs.

Stevie Nicks had only twelve weeks to tour in support of Bella Donna before she had to return to work with Fleetwood Mac. In 1983, Nicks recorded her solo followup, The Wild Heart. It contained the hit "Stand Back." Then two years later, she released 1985's Rock a Little. After a long hiatus, Fleetwood Mac reunited to record the album Tango in the Night. Nicks countered with her 1989 release The Other Side of the Mirror. After Fleetwood Mac suffered a series of lineup changes and lower album sales, Stevie Nicks left the band in 1993. A year later, Nicks released Street Angel. In 1997, she reunited with Fleetwood Mac to tour and record.

In 2001, Nicks recorded Trouble in Shangri-La with guests Sarah McLachlan, Sheryl Crow, Macy Gray,

> "Great music is as much about the space in between the notes as it is about the notes themselves."
>
> - Sting

and Dixie Chicks member Natalie Maines. Nicks again recorded with Fleetwood Mac in 2003. She next released the 2007 CD/DVD recording titled Crystal Visions: The Very Best of Stevie Nicks. 2011's In Your Dreams saw Nicks expand her musical horizons to sing a mix of Bob Dylan-inspired folk songs and Italian love ballads. This album debuted at number six on the U.S. charts. Nicks again rejoined Fleetwood Mac in 2013 to record and tour. In 2014, she released the album 24 Karat Gold: Songs from the Vault. Stevie Nicks developed her vocal style by emulating Janis Joplin and Grace Slick. She has a very expressive, yet gruff and distinctive voice in the range of a contralto (very low for a female voice). Stevie Nicks has inspired many vocalists and songwriters including Sheryl Crow, Vanessa Carlton, Beyonce, and Mary J. Blige.

Stevie Nicks was inducted into the Rock and Roll Hall of Fame in 1998 as a member of Fleetwood Mac.

Jon Bon Jovi (1962-) (aka John Bongiovi, Jr.) is an American singer/songwriter and producer born in Perth Amboy, New Jersey in 1962. Bon Jovi first played in local rock bands in New Jersey with keyboardist David Bryan. They worked under the names John Bongiovi & The Wilds Ones, The Lechers, and The Rest. Bon Jovi and Bryan cut a demo song, "Runaway," that became a hit on New Jersey radio stations.They soon added bassist Alec John Such, guitarist Dave "The Snake" Sabo, and drummer Tico Torres to form the Bon Jovi Band. The success of "Runaway" led to a recording contract with Polygram/Mercury. Before going in to record, Bon Jovi replaced Sabo with guitarist Richie Sambora.

Bon Jovi released his 1984 self-titled debut album Bon Jovi that yielded a top forty hit with the original version of "Runaway." The following year, Bon Jovi released 7800 Fahrenheit. Then, 1986's Slippery When Wet became the largest selling album of the year. With the help of songwriter Desmond Child, this album produced two number one hits, "You Give Love a Bad Name" and "Livin' on a Prayer." Slippery When Wet went on to sell over twenty-six million albums worldwide.

"You Give Love a Bad Name"
by Jon Bon Jovi, Richie Sambora, and Desmond Child

"You Give Love a Bad Name" was written in the basement of Richie Sambora's mother's house in New Jersey. Legendary hit-maker Desmond Child came up with the name and Bon Jovi added the first line of "Shot Through the Heart." Next, they put the rest of the song together. "You Give Love a Bad Name" was a simple story about a guy whose relationship with his girlfriend yielded negative consequences. Desmond Child would later co-write many more songs with Bon Jovi and Richie Sambora. Child has also written for Aerosmith, Cher, and Ricky Martin.

"You Give Love a Bad Name" was one of the biggest arena anthem rock songs of the 1980's. In live performance, Richie Sambora played the song's signature guitar riff and then a blistering solo. This was followed in the song's arrangement by a breakdown of just vocals accompanied by Tico Torres' powerful drum groove. "You Give Love a Bad Name" was the quintessential hair metal power tune of the 1980's.

1988's New Jersey rocketed straight to number one on the U.S. charts and yielded two number one hits, "Bad Medicine" and "I'll Be There for You." After a year and a half on tour, Bon Jovi took a hiatus. In the fall of 1992, the band released Keep the Faith.They followed with a greatest hits album titled Cross Road and then 1995's These Days that featured the ballad "Always." In the new millennium, Bon Jovi recorded seven more studio albums, including 2007's country album Lost Highway. In 2016, he released This House Is Not for Sale that debuted at number one on the U.S. charts. Bon Jovi's slew of hits helped to bring in the era of pop-rock mixed with heavy metal elements. He then transcended "big hair" metal in the late 1980's to lead one of the biggest selling rock bands in American history, selling over 130 million albums worldwide. Over time, Bon Jovi and his band moved away from arena rock to occasionally embrace country music while staying true to their rock roots. Jon Bon Jovi was inducted into the Rock and Roll Fall of Fame in 2018.

Sting (1951-) (aka Gordon Sumner) began to cultivate his solo career even before The Police (see chapter sixteen) officially broke up. Despite the great success of The Police, Sting was anxious to expand his musical boundaries and establish himself as a serious songwriter on his own terms. In late 1984, Sting assembled some of the jazz worlds' finest musicians including; saxophonist Branford Marsalis, pianist Kenny Kirkland, bassist Daryl Jones, drummer Omar Hakim, and himself on lead vocals and guitar. They soon recorded his first solo project, 1985's The Dream of the Blue Turtles. It was met with mixed critical reviews, although it reached number two on the U.S. charts and number three in England. The single "If You Love Somebody Set Them Free" contained a heavy jazz influence and has remained one of Sting's concert favorites. Another single, "Fortress Around Your Heart," was inspired by a divorce Sting was going through.

Sting's move to a jazz and fusion oriented lineup wasn't all that shocking since he had played with numerous jazz and progressive bands prior to forming The Police. After an extensive tour, Sting filmed the band for a 1986 documentary titled *Bring on the Night* and released a live double album of the same name. Also in 1986, Sting briefly reunited with The Police, which yielded a re-recorded version of their classic "Don't Stand So Close to Me."

1987's ...Nothing Like the Sun built on his jazz explorations and expanded to include reggae, funk, and dance-rock styles. For this double album, Sting retained the services of Branford Marsalis and Kenny Kirkland but added drummer Manu Katche, replacing Omar Hakim. Many prominent musicians guested including; Eric Clapton, guitarists Mark Knopfler, Hiram Bullock and his ex-bandmate Andy Summers. ...Nothing Like the Sun showed substantial growth in Sting's songwriting and his imaginative arrangements. The single "Be Still My Beating Heart" was nominated for a Grammy Song of the Year. At this time, Sting became more socially involved by campaigning for Amnesty International and helping to establish the Rainforest Foundation.

After an unsuccessful revival of *The Threepenny Opera* in 1989, Sting recorded 1991's The Soul Cages. This was a concept album dedicated to the life of Sting's father, who had recently died. Many of the songs contained Sting's reflections about his relationship with his father. Previously, Sting had developed a writer's block in his attempt to come up with new material for what was to be The Soul Cages. After writing "Why Should I Cry for You," (the first song on the album), Sting was able to compose the rest of The Soul Cages with relative ease.

"All This Time"
by Sting

The composition "All This Time" was part of a group of songs that Sting wrote for The Soul Cages. The album's opener "Island of Souls," told the story of Billy, the first son in a family of riveters. Billy would watch the ships sail that his father helped to build and he would dream of escaping to sea with his father. His dreams continued when his father was injured and told he had only three weeks to live. This was where the song"All This Time" entered in the flow of a series of songs for the album. It's the story of Billy's desire to bury his father at sea upon his death, despite the objections of two priests. Sting was really writing about the death of his own father. Sting gained solace from the idea that when someones' life ended, a river continued to flow, symbolizing that those left behind had to carry on with their own lives.

The lyrics were understandably very dark but Sting has pointed out that they were contrasted by the upbeat sound of the musical accompaniment of the song. Musically, "All This Time" (and the entire The Soul Cages album) was the first to feature Sting's longtime guitarist, Dominic Miller. Miller played a very melodic guitar accompaniment on "All This Time" that echoed Sting's vocal lines on the choruses. Midway through the song, the band modulated keys and went to a driving four to the bar groove. Sting, who often received inspiration from sources outside of rock music, was inspired by a cello suite from the Baroque master composer J.S. Bach.

In 1993, Sting released Ten Summoner's Tales, an album of extraordinary compositions and musicianship. It has sold over ten million copies worldwide and contained two hits, "If I Ever Lose My Faith in You" and "Fields of Gold."

Groundbreaking album
Ten Summoner's Tales
by Sting

Ten Summoner's Tales was recorded at Lake House, Wiltshire and mixed at The Townhouse Studio in London. A long form performance video was filmed utilizing three tracks from the album, in addition to versions of the other songs. Visually, the band pretended to record the tracks at Sting's Lake House property. The video won a Grammy Award for Best Long Form Video in 1994. The album's title came from a combination of Sting's family name, Sumner, and the summoner character from Chaucer's The Canterbury Tales. For the album, Sting explored the themes of love and morality with musically adventurous arrangements that tested the limits of the pop-rock format.

Ten Summoner's Tales contained the songs "If I Ever Lose My Faith in You,"then "Love is Stronger Than Justice (The Magnificent Seven)," "Fields of Gold," "Heavy Cloud No Rain," "She's Too Good for Me," "Seven Days," "Saint Augustine in Hell," "It's Probably Me," "Everybody Laughed but You," "Shape of My Heart," "Something the Boy Said," and "Nothing Bout Me." The opening track and biggest hit from the album, "If I Ever Lose My Faith in You," peaked at number seventeen on the U.S. charts and remains one of Stings' signature songs.

Ten Summoner's Tales is a tremendous study in how complex odd meters can be employed both compositionally and in performance to make enduring music. Traditionally, rock music has been composed with an even number of (primary in groups of four pulses to the bar) pulses in every measure. Sting broke away from this tradition. The compositions "Love Is Stronger Than Justice" (in 7/4), "Seven Days" (in 5/4), and "Saint Augustine In Hell" (in 7/8) are all prime examples. Drummer Vinnie Colaiuta has explained his approach to creating odd time feels on this album. For the 5/4 "Seven Days" Colaiuta said, "I phrased it by playing over the barline, so the hi-hat pattern resolves every two bars. #8 For the 7/8 "Saint Augustine in Hell" Colaiuta said," These patterns in seven are very similar...his (Sting) idea is to have the listeners locked into the seven as easily as they would be in four. For the most part, people aren't used to hearing songs in seven...when I play odd times, I like to smooth them out." #9

Ten Summoner's Tales and its odd meter feel helped to push the creative boundaries of pop-rock music. Ten Summoner's Tales was nominated for six Grammy awards and won for Best Engineered Album and Best Male Pop Vocal Performance for "If I Ever Lose My Faith in You." The album has sold over ten million copies worldwide.

1996's Mercury Falling was Sting's first recording in three years. Although failing to achieve the commercial success of Ten Summoner's Tales, this album featured melodic compositions that explored more odd meters and again contained highly musical multi-layered arrangements. 1999's Brand New Day went to number nine on the U.S. charts. It sold close to four million copied in America on the strength of the hits "Desert Rose" and "Brand New Day." Brand New Day had a lighter feel that contained love songs with no overt political messages. Sting continued to utilize a stellar lineup of musicians that included; guitarist Dominic Miller, drummers Vinnie Colaiuta and Manu Katche, keyboardist/programmer Kipper (aka Mark Eldridge) and pianist Jason Rebello. Prominent musicians Stevie Wonder, James Taylor, Chris Botti, and Branford Marsalis also guested on the record. Sting followed with 2003's Sacred Love. He then released 2006's Songs from the Labyrinth, a collaboration with Bosnian musician Edin Karamazov, that featured the music of 16th century composer John Dowland.

Sting agreed to a brief reunion and sporadic tours with The Police before releasing If on a Winter's Night... in 2009. The following year, Sting did a tour alongside The Royal Philharmonic Concert Orchestra, who added symphonic arrangements to his songs. An album documenting this achievement was released in 2010, titled Symphonicities. Three years later, Sting completed the musical *The Last Ship* and it's 2013 album of the same name. *The Last Ship* made its Broadway debut in 2014. After two years of touring, sometimes co-headlining with Paul Simon and sometimes with Peter Gabriel, Sting released 2016's 57th & 9th. This album featured longtime Sting band members Dominic Miller and Vinnie Colaiuta, supplemented by drummer Josh Freese and guitarist Lyle Workman.

Sting disbanded The Police at the height of their commercial appeal in 1984 to establish a brilliant career as a viable solo artist. He has remained a serious and dedicated songwriter. On the subject of composing, Sting said, "People aren't really used to songs being articulate anymore...they're just kind of meaningless. They have the semblance of meaning, but it's not connected. I don't like that. I like songs that actually mean something." #10 Sting's obvious ambition was to expand the boundaries of pop-rock music by mixing elements of jazz, classical, and even world beat styles into his music. He has remained at the forefront of composing intelligent pop-rock songs

---

Rock Hard Fact

John Mayer once worked as a gas station attendant for seven dollars an hour to earn enough money to buy a 1996 Stevie Ray Vaughn Model Stratocaster guitar.

with musical and ambitious ensemble interplay. Sting, long under-rated as a bassist, has remained one of the premiere musical talents of the twenty-first century. Sting was inducted into the Rock and Roll Hall of Fame in 2003 as a member of The Police.

John Mayer (1977-) is a vocalist/guitarist/songwriter from Bridgeport, Connecticut born in 1977. In his youth, Mayer developed a love for the blues and enrolled at the Berklee College of Music in 1997. He moved to Atlanta, Georgia after a year in school and performed original songs that he co-wrote with songwriter Clay Cook (Mayer's former classmate) in local coffeehouses. Cook went on to join The Marshall Tucker Band and The Zac Brown Band. Mayer recorded several of the duo's songs, along with some of his own for his 1999 self-released EP Inside Wants Out. Mayer received a recording contract with Aware Records and expanded his (mostly acoustic) early approach to release 2001's Room for Squares. This full-album debut shot to number nine on the U.S. charts on the strength of the hits "No Such Thing" and "Your Body Is a Wonderland." Room for Squares was produced and engineered by John Alagia, who played a number of instruments on the album.

"Your Body Is a Wonderland"
by John Mayer

This song was written by John Mayer at the of age fourteen and titled "Strawberry Wonderland." It was about his first girlfriend. He changed the title to "Your Body is a Wonderland," after moving to Atlanta. The song's subject was clearly about sex. Mayer came up with the opening guitar part that he would play for hours. "Your Body Is a Wonderland" won a Grammy for Best Male Pop Vocal Performance in 2003. Mayer beat out some stiff competition to win this Grammy including Elton John, Sting, and James Taylor. This was one of the reasons John Mayer made a big impact on the music world in a very short time.

Musically, "Wonderland" has a simple and infectious groove played by drummer Nir Z and bassist David LaBruyere. Together, they built an off-beat comping pattern that contrasted well with the straight forward part of the drumset feel. John Alagia and Mayer skillfully added very subtle supporting timbres such as organ pads, piano, toy piano, synthesizer, electric piano, and percussion to the track. The song moved to a middle section interlude that highlighted the groove before returning to the chorus. "Your Body is a Wonderland" introduced Mayer's fans to his soft, soulful, and very expressive voice.

2003's Heavier Things was successful and produced the soulful ballad "Daughters." Mayer's interest in the blues led to his forming The John Mayer Trio with two formidable musicians, drummer Steve Jordan and bassist Pino Palladino. Their musical chemistry led to a live record titled Try!. This album moved away from acoustic pop-rock to covering blues songs. It was a distinct change of direction and a bold move for Mayer's career. On Try!, Mayer, Jordan, and Palladino recorded strong rhythmic versions of Jimi Hendrix's "Wait Until Tomorrow" and Ray Charles' "I Got a Woman." The band also performed two songs from Heavier Things and previewed two songs from Mayer's forthcoming album, Continuum. During this time, Mayer also collaborated with a host of blues and jazz legends that included; B.B.King, Buddy Guy, Herbie Hancock, and John Scofield.

2006's Continuum debuted at number two on the U.S. charts and saw Mayer return to more pop-rock songs, only now with the influence of blues and soul elements. Pino Palladino, Steve Jordan, and a host of top jazz musicians guested on many of the tracks. Continuum spawned the hit "Gravity," and Steve Jordan co-produced the album with Mayer. 2009's Battle Studies sold well and 2012's Born and Raised reached number one on the charts. Mayer hired producer Don Was to help him record 2013's Paradise Valley, an album with Americana flavored songs.

In 2014, John Mayer was hired by Bob Weir, Bill Kreutzmann, and Mickey Hart to tour with the spin-off Grateful Dead band called The Dead & Company (see jam bands section of this chapter). They toured in 2016 and 2017, while Mayer also released The Search for Everything in 2017. John Mayer is a versatile artist who has fully assimilated the blues, rock, and soul genres with his distinct vocal style. John Mayer has become one the most significant musicians of the past two decades.

Discussion Question

Some of the band leaders profiled in the chapter control almost every aspect of their band's creative process from the songwriting to recording to live performance. Other leaders find success with a more democratic group process. Give an example of a singer-led classic rock band where the leader encourages his or her band to have creative input in a variety of ways. Give specific examples.

Jam Bands

The initial wave of jam bands played a loose type of melodic rock that easily adopted lengthy improvisational passages. Many **jam bands** borrowed from The Grateful Dead's idea of allowing their fans to tape live bootleg recordings of their shows. The majority of jam bands have failed to sell many records. One reason was the lack of wide-spread commercial appeal through radio or MTV. Many jam bands have pursued greater visibility through word of mouth, extended touring, and internet distribution. Jam band albums were often recorded on independent labels. Album sales became secondary to *touring and merchandise sales*, which for the most part, has kept bands in business.

Over the years, a number of festivals have been organized to promote jam band artists. The H.O.R.D.E. Festival (The Horizons of Rock Developing Everywhere tour) surfaced in 1992 as a showcase for bands that excelled in live jam band performance. This was conceived of by Blues Traveler frontman John Popper and his colleague David Frey. The H.O.R.D.E. Festival was very successful and ran every summer from 1992 through 1998. Popper (through this festival) encouraged band members to sit in with other bands, lending the festival a spirit of cross pollination of musical sounds and styles. Early arrivals on the jam band scene included; **Phish**, **Widespread Panic** (1986-present), **Spin Doctors** (see chapter seventeen), **Big Head Todd and the Monsters** (1986-present), and **Aquarium Rescue Unit** (1988-1997) (2004-2007) (2015).

> "Every piece has its own identity which we (Phish) develop by the rule 'We know no limits.' We follow the inspiration of the moment and don't worry if what we're playing is alternative, progressive or fusion rock."
>
> – Page McConnell of Phish

Rock Hard Fact

Dave Matthews was born in South Africa and his family moved to Virginia (when he was two years old) and back to South Africa when he was thirteen. This gave him a unique perspective about politics and social issues such as racism.

Phish (1983-2000) (2002-2004) (2009-present) is an American jam band that formed in 1983 by three students attending The University of Vermont. They would emerge as the heirs to the Grateful Dead's jam band legacy. Vocalist/guitarist Trey Anastasio, guitarist Jeff Holdsworth (until 1986), and drummer Jon Fishman started the band by jamming in their dorm rooms. They soon recruited bassist Mike Gordon and keyboardist Page McConnell to complete the group. The current lineup is the same without Holdsworth. Phish is an eclectic band that incorporates elements of jazz, folk, country, and pop-rock with a loose approach that values free-form improvisation. Phish has cultivated a large and devoted fan base developed by word of mouth and the exchange of bootleg Phish recordings. In 1986, Phish recorded their debut Phish, also known as The White Tapes (which they released on cassette). A number of musicians guested on the album. Phish served as a collection of original material that the band successfully utilized for promotion purposes.

1989's Junta established the improvisational nature of Phish. At first, Phish sold the album only on cassettes at local shows. After years of traveling through Southeast America, Phish recorded 1990's Lawn Boy. They followed with 1992's A Picture of Nectar on their new label, Elektra. This album featured improvisatory jams, strong songwriting, and a more polished production that began to reach a wider audience. The rest of the 1990's saw the release of 1993's Rift, 1994's Hoist, 1996's Billy Breathes, 1998's The Story of the Ghost, and 1999's The Siket Disc. Phish's popularity grew considerably in the latter half of the 1990's when their incessant touring made them a top concert draw. However, by the release of 2000's Farmhouse and a mainstream single, "Heavy Things," Phish announced a temporary hiatus. Phish became more ingrained in American culture when they made an appearance on the TV show, *The Simpsons*, before releasing a massive set of live albums during the spring of 2002.

After each member recorded side projects, Phish returned with 2002's Round Room. This was in anticipation of their 2002 New Year's Eve reunion concert at Madison Square Garden. The band followed with 2004's Undermind, 2009's Joy, 2014's Fuego, and 2016's Big Boat.

"Joy"
by Trey Anastasio and Tom Marshall

"Joy" was written by guitarist Trey Anastasio and Tom Marshall, who has been the band's primary lyricist for their whole career. Marshall has contributed lyrics to over ninety Phish songs. His role was similar to that of The Grateful Dead's lyricist, Robert Hunter. Marshall's reflective lyrics for "Joy" were nostalgic and created an atmosphere for the album. Well respected producer Steve Lillywhite, had previously produced the Phish album Billy Breathes. After he supervised the recording of the song "Joy," Lillywhite went to his first live Phish performance. When he heard how inspired the band performed live, Lillywhite demanded that they re-record "Joy." Lillywhite encouraged Phish to approach the studio with the looseness and excitement of their live performances.

Anastasio's inspired guitar solo on "Joy" served as a short and effective melodic interlude that connected the songs' verses. The vibe on "Joy" conveyed a sense of introspection and real emotion. "Joy" represented Phish's sense of joyful music making over their long and prolific career. All ten songs from Joy, including the title track, were performed live during the band's 2009 summer tour.

Phish, much like The Grateful Dead, are true representatives of the jam band movement. They have remained grounded in live performances (always different) that featured extended and experimental improvisations. Phish has sold over eight million albums and DVDs and has led the jam band movement in America for over thirty years.

While the commercial rock of the 1990's was more a product of the studio environment, the jam band movement was fueled by cerebral, talented, and often musically educated musicians that developed before a live audience. Gradually more bands formed and found their inspiration from a wider palette of music genres. This added significantly to the music's diversity. The 1990's saw the jam band scene gain more momentum with bands that included; **Dave Matthews Band, String Cheese Incident** (1993-2007) (2009-present), **Medeski Martin and Wood, Galactic** (1994-present), **Umphrey's McGee** (1997-present), **Jazz is Dead** (1998-2006) (2015 to present), **Garaj Mahal** (2000-2011), **Grace Potter and the Nocturnals** (2002-present), **John Scofield** (1951-), **The Dead and Company,** and many others.

Dave Matthews Band (1991-present) was formed in the early 1990's by South African vocalist/guitarist Dave Matthews. Matthews was living in Charlottesville, Virginia and recruited drummer Carter Beauford, bassist Stefan Lessard, saxophonist Leroi Moore, and keyboardist Peter Griesar to complete the Dave Matthews Band lineup. The group initially secured a regular spot at a popular Charlottesville nightclub and then hit the college tour circuit. This led to their 1993 independently released Remember Two Things. Later that year, DMB released a live EP titled Recently. Based on these releases and a growing cult following, DMB was signed by RCA Records. They next released 1994's Under the Table and Dreaming. It took a little while, but this album sold over four million copies in the U.S. on the strength of the hits "Ants Marching," "Satellite," and "What Would You Say."

"What Would You Say"
by David J. Matthews

"What Would You Say" was one of the first compositions Dave Matthews Band composed and performed live. This song also helped to build their large following through constant touring, particularly the college circuit. Like many of the band's songs, "What Would You Say" contained a complex arrangement that featured an array of instruments. It began with Matthews strumming an acoustic guitar and then included flute, alto and tenor saxophones, and the harmonica skills of Blues Traveler's John Popper. The band became known for extending their solos (including Boyd Tinsley's violin solos) at their exciting live shows.

The lyrics for "What Would You Say" were basically nonsensical with lines like "The bear ate his head, though it was a candy." Even though the band had been playing the song live for years, "What Would You Say" eventually reached a radio audience in 1995. This cultivated a casual fan base to add to their core followers. A huge fan of the band was the great artist Michael McDonald, who added background vocals to the track. "What Would You Say" saw DMB fuse a folky acoustic approach with elements of funk and fusion to achieve their unique sound.

1996's Crash debuted at number two on the U.S. charts and the band spent most of 1996 touring in support of the album. It yielded the hits "So Much To Say," "Crash Into Me," and "Too Much." Crash further emphasized DMB's formidable instrumental and improvisational skills. At this time, Dave Matthews launched an attack on bootleggers in conjunction with the federal government, targeting stores that were selling unauthorized CD's of the band's live performances. To support this fight, Dave Matthews Band released an official double live record, Live at Red Rocks that debuted on the charts at number three. It unexpectedly sold a million copies within six months. This would lead the way for a number of future concert recordings. 1998's Before These Crowded Streets saw the band reach new levels of musicianship. They augmented their sound with more complex rhythms, Middle Eastern sounds, and the string arrangements of The Kronos Quartet (on two of the tracks).

In the new millennium, the band first recorded 2001's Everyday, the first time DMB utilized an electric guitar. 2002's Busted Stuff surfaced from sessions with producer Steve Lillywhite and spawned the hit "Where Are You Going." That same year, the band released Live at Folsom Field. Dave Matthews Band next performed for 100,000 fans in New York's Central Park and at Philadelphia's Live8 concert for a global audience of millions of fans. Dave Matthews recorded a solo album in 2003 titled Some Devil and a single, "Gravedigger," that won a Grammy for Best Male Rock Vocal Performance. Violinist Boyd Tinsley also released a solo album at this time. 2005's Stand Up went to number one on the U.S. charts, providing DMB with their fourth straight number one album (a feat accomplished by only U2 and Metallica). The band followed with the Live Weekend on the Rocks and the two CD compilation, The Best of What's Around, Vol. 1. More live recording would follow until 2009's studio album, BigWhisky & the GooGrux King. It would warrant two Grammy nominations. Again, DMB made more live recordings until their studio album, Away from the World, was released in 2012.

Dave Matthews Band developed into the most musically complex and adventurous jam band on the scene. They infused virtually every conceivable style into their approach, from jazz, blues, pop-rock, folk, funk, roots rock, and world music. DMB didn't yield to the conventions of electric guitar (not present on the majority of their recordings). They composed and performed with a vast array of instruments and sound combinations, further setting them apart from other rock bands. They have sold well over thirty million records in the U.S. alone and their total records sales are in the company of bands such as Queen, The Who, and The Beach Boys. Dave Matthews Band plays with the skill of a virtuosic fusion band mixed with a live jam band mentality. Add in their ability to create interesting melodies presented by the distinctive vocal style of Dave Matthews. The result yields one of the most innovative and influential bands of modern rock music.

Medeski Martin and Wood (1991-present) is an American jazz-funk jam band that consists of keyboardist John Medeski, drummer Billy Martin, and bassist ChrisWood. They first met when jazz drummer Bob Moses (who had performed with Medeski and Wood) introduced his student, Billy Martin, to Medeski and Wood. Their debut album, Notes from the Underground, was released in 1992. Initially the band was an acoustic jazz trio, however Medeski added a Hammond organ, Mellotron, clavinet, and melodica to their sound. MMW received a boost when they performed with Phish in 1995, which helped them make inroads into the jam band scene. 1993's It's a Jungle in Here, featured versions of Thelonious Monk's "Bemsha Swing" and Bob Marley's "Lively Up Yourself." They followed with 1995's Friday Afternoon in the Universe, considered to be their breakthrough album. Martin and Wood's grooves were funky and Medeski's solos were soulful. By the time of 1996's Shack-Man, MMW were firmly established in the jam band scene by their relentless touring and continued association with the band Phish.

1997's Farmer's Reserve and 1998's Combustication, (their first release on the Blue Note label) further extended their popularity. MMW also collaborated with DJ Logic and guitarist John Scofield. MMW recorded many more studio albums from 2000's Tonic to 2008-2009's The Radiolarian Series (a three album project). MMW recorded the 2014 album Juice, their third collaboration with John Scofield. This was an album of original compositions, inspired by Brazilian and Caribbean influenced music, with a Medeski, Martin, and Wood jam band twist.

The Dead & Company (2015 to present) is an American band that consists of former members of the Grateful Dead that include vocalist/guitarist Bob Weir and drummers Bill Kreutzmann and Mickey Hart. After the death of Jerry Garcia, The Grateful Dead decided not to try and replace him. In 2015, the four core surviving members marked The Grateful Dead's 50th anniversary in a series of concerts presented as their final performances together. However, over the years a number of spin-off bands have featured one or more of The Dead's core members. The spin-off bands included; Furthur, The Rhythm Devils, Phil Lesh & Friends, RatDog, Billy & the Kids, and The Dead & Company.

The Dead & Company was founded when vocalist/guitarist John Mayer was guest hosting *The Late Late Show* and asked Bob Weir to join him in a studio performance. The above mentioned ex-Grateful Dead members had been preparing for their 50th anniversary tour and Mayer began to learn some of the Grateful Dead's extensive catalog of music. Weir, Kreutzmann, and Hart then invited Mayer to join The Dead & Company. Phil Lesh, the original Grateful Dead bassist, declined an invitation to join the band. The Dead & Company's lineup was completed with the addition of bassist Oteil Burbridge (who had toured with The Allman Brothers for many years) and keyboardist Jeff Chimenti. Although Jerry Garcia is clearly irreplaceable, John Mayer brings a unique and soulful voice to The Dead & Company that complements the vocal style of Bob Weir. Mayer also comes from a strong blues tradition that he effectively blends with The Dead & Company's live versions of timeless and classic Grateful Dead songs. The Dead & Company have not recorded any studio recordings to date (but are considering a studio recording). Recordings from all of the concerts from their 2016 and 2017 tours have been digitally released. The Dead & Company continue to tour and create their own legacy.

Discussion Question

How could a jam band approach of extended live improvisation help to shape the music of an original rock band? If you think it can, then be specific when describing the music of a specific band. If not, then explain why you think live improvisation is ineffective.

> "Since Jerry (Garcia) checked out, he hasn't departed in the least... I can hear the crackle of his harmonic content, where he would live in a song... It's wonderful to see these songs reinvigorated-regenerated with new life."
>
> – Bob Weir of The Dead & Company

Chapter Thirteen: Progressive Rock

Demographically, **progressive rock** was a music born in southeast England and created by middle and upper class British boys. Many progressive bands rehearsed and developed in the pastoral and suburban countryside environment of rural England. Progressive rock flourished in the mid to late 1960's and then later gained popularity in the United States throughout the 1970's. The genre was often packaged as a unified work of art that combined music, visual arts (cover and sleeve art), and stage production. In England, the music found a loyal audience and surprisingly, a strong audience in America as well. Progressive rock was well-received in the American Northeast (not so much in the South) between the late 1960's until the mid to late 1970's. Fans were typically middle-class students who attempted to identify with English musicians as their cult-figure heroes. Many American (and some British) music critics were highly critical of progressive rock on the grounds that it lacked a political stance (not Jethro Tull) and that it was over reliant on high culture and an elite audience. Progressive rock utilized a diverse recipe that also drew from American blues and rhythm and blues as well as the 1960's psychedelic movement. It was also influenced by the **classical music** traditions of Bach, Mozart, Wagner, and Stravinsky. Even more music factored in where a fusion of jazz, folk, and world music, such as Indian and **Gamelan** styles, occasionally came to play a role.

Some think that psychedelic music belonged exclusively to mid-1960's America. However, England also had a psychedelic scene in addition to strong folk roots and The Beatles. A number of clubs opened in London in 1966 and 1967 where a close relationship developed between artists and audiences. Record companies started to give unprecedented *creative control* of the music to experimental bands. The underground press and underground radio also emerged, further providing vehicles for musical expression. These factors encouraged the development of early British psychedelic bands such as The Moody Blues, Procol Harum, The Nice, and Pink Floyd between the years 1966 to 1970. This laid the foundation for progressive rock.

Most progressive rock bands sounded unique but shared common musical ground. Many artists became interested in keyboard technology and the traditions of European classical music. Essential progressive bands to emerge were **King Crimson, Emerson, Lake, and Palmer, Yes, Genesis, Van der Graaf Generator, Jethro Tull, Gentle Giant,** and **Curved Air.** All of them English. Some music historians utilized the term art rock (see chapter eight) interchangeably with progressive rock. This book does not. Also, another term that described progressive rock was Canterbury rock.

"I like to think of it (progressive rock) as an expansion of rock...breaking out of the two guitars, bass, and drums format"

– Ian McDonald (co-founder of King Crimson)

The Roots of Progressive Rock

By the year 1967, there were four recordings that launched progressive rock. **The Moody Blues** released Days of Future Passed, Pink Floyd (see chapter eight) released their debut The Piper at the Gates of Dawn, and **Procol Harum** released the single "A Whiter Shade of Pale." But the strongest single album to influence progressive rock was The Beatles Sergeant Pepper's Lonely Heart's Club Band. This album showed that a concept album format could have commercial credibility and that the studio could become the sonic playground for creative future artists. As discussed in chapter five, Sgt. Pepper's (and The Beach Boy's Pet Sounds) were blueprints for how musicians could create complete unified musical statements. Sgt. Pepper's achieved unity by tying a series of songs together with a recurring melodic theme, all done with avant-garde experimentation, including George Martin's brilliant tape effects. Concept albums inspired artists such as Ian Anderson of Jethro Tull to compose the forty-minute composition Thick as a Brick (an entire album in length).

Progressive rock bands drew from many diverse sources. Many artists referenced classical themes while others created large multi-movement reductions of complete symphonic works. Some progressive bands utilized jazz and fusion musical elements, as well as a broad range of cultural and ethnic music influences. Still other artists drew from avant-garde sources and were inspired to experiment in the studio. The fantasy world created in the studio was brought to the concert stage with elaborate stage costumes and light shows. Progressive rock artists often utilized instrumentation outside of typical rock including; flutes, string instruments, and percussion. The most striking change in sound design was the popular use of synthesizers, especially the Mellotron, Moog, and Taurus bass pedals. This continued all the way into the 1980's when Frank Zappa (see chapter eighteen) composed with, the then state of the art, synclavier. The Mellotron, often doubled with a Hammond B3 sound, was brought back in the mid-1990's and has continued to enhance the sound of some later neo-progressive bands.

Progressive rock lyrics avoided the typical rock subject matter of love, teen rebellion, and partying. Artists now wrote themes about folklore, fantasy worlds, and social situations. For example, Peter Gabriel wrote surreal stories with many esoteric characters woven into a storyline. Stage theatrics became elaborate, some even outrageous. Again, Peter Gabriel wore strange costumes onstage and acted out the parts for his characters. The use of lasers and light shows provided a mystical atmosphere for live performers. Album cover art became an important tool to market bands and help create a band's identity. Artist Roger Dean developed album covers and a stage design that gave the band Yes a powerful image.

Musical Characteristics of Progressive Rock

European art music that impacted progressive rock included; symphonic music, smaller chamber ensembles, classical piano and guitar etudes, Renaissance and Baroque sacred music, and Medieval music. These traditions mixed with jazz improvisation and avant-garde concepts. Rock borrowed from many enduring musical structures and forms, harmonic approaches, instrumental virtuosity, and expanded instrumentation. Simultaneously, new instruments and combinations of sound came to define progressive rock innovation.

The Keyboard Sounds of Progressive Rock

The early 1960's saw the emergence of the Hammond organ with circuits, oscillators, and phonic wheels. The Hammond organ and The Leslie cabinet were soon utilized by blues, jazz, and rock musicians from Jimmy Smith to Steve Winwood. Soon, an American engineer, Robert Moog, began to design synthesizers and by 1964 he had found new ways to manipulate sound with ring modulation and oscillator circuitry. Robert Moog rejected the idea of a polyphonic keyboard because it was too much like an organ. The Moog synthesizer was modular and monophonic and inspired keyboard players to redefine the role of keyboard parts in music. The new Moog synthesizer was first used by keyboardist Walter Carlos in 1966 on the Switched on Bach album. On the progressive rock scene, Keith Emerson was among the first to use the new Moog synthesizer. Around the same time, Frank Zappa also began to explore synthesizer sounds and tape manipulation techniques.

The Mellotron was the next major innovation in keyboard technology. The Mellotron worked like a modern day sampler, only it generated its sound by audio tape. When a Mellotron key was pressed, a tape that was connected to it pushed against a playback head, much like a tape recorder. By pulling a section of magnetic tape across a head, different portions of the tape could access different sounds. The Mellotron achieved great orchestral sounds and combined different combinations of strings and brass. The first notable musician to record with a Mellotron was Graham Bond in 1965. The Beatles were also among the first to utilize one on their single "Strawberry Fields Forever." King Crimson purchased two Mellotrons in 1969 after first hearing Mike Pinder use one on the Moody Blues album Days of Future Passed. Tony Banks employed a Mellotron on the Genesis composition "The Fountain Of Salmacis" from their Nursery Cryme album. Banks also used it on the massive introduction to the Genesis composition "Watcher of the Skies," in 1972. Countless others have used the Mellotron including more recent progressive bands such as Porcupine Tree and Spock's Beard.

By the mid 1970's, design advancements allowed for polyphonic synthesizers such as the sequential circuits Prophet-5. This instrument was the first to use a microprocessor as a controller. Later, musical instrumental digital interface (MIDI) set a new standard for digital code transmission by allowing electronic keyboards to connect to computers and other devices for input and programming. Today's manufactures such as Roland, Yamaha, and Kurzweil continue to lead the way in keyboard technology. From the first Hammond organ, Moog, and Mellotron, progressive rock has utilized innovative keyboard technology to help define the entire genre.

Progressive rock composers often utilized the classical forms of the symphonic poem and the programmatic multi-movement suite. **The symphonic poem** consisted of separate interlocking sections while longer programmatic forms were often instrumental music that

---

Rock Hard Fact

Before forming Emerson, Lake, and Palmer, keyboardist Keith Emerson played on the album Music from Free Creek with Eric Clapton, Jeff Beck and Mitch Mitchell.

conveyed ideas or storylines depicting visual images or landscapes. Each movement often consisted of one or more melodic ideas that were developed throughout the work. Skilled composers created musical interest through the use of complex rhythms and meters, textures, and advanced harmonic progressions. Progressive rock compositions avoided the verse-chorus-bridge forms. Form was often extended with longer sections and interludes. Long instrumental passages were part of the musical landscape. Extended instrumental improvisations were borrowed from jazz and fusion genres, and then set to complex arrangements that challenged the musicianship of the performers.

Melodies were often modal and long, sophisticated lines that unfolded over extended phrases rather than shorter pop-rock hooks. This was a deliberate move away from blues-based melodies and harmonies. Some progressive rock compositions made allusions to classical themes or even utilized direct classical thematic quotes. Aggressive and more passive sections were often alternated to provide musical contrast. Dynamics were also crucial. Tony Banks, composer/keyboardist for Genesis, wrote the compositions "The Musical Box" and "Supper's Ready" employing many of these concepts.

Much progressive rock drew from advanced rhythmic and metric concepts such as 7/8, 5/4, and other odd meters. Artists wrote and played what they heard, even if it meant expressing some quirky, weird phrases. Many tempo changes were written into arrangements that created a sense of unpredictability in the music. The progressive genre utilized non-traditional chords where harmony was often altered and expanded with chords that added extensions of 6th, 7th, 9ths, etc… Many composers experimented with frequent change of keys, increased use of dissonance, and even some atonal passages. The role of the bass player also became an important part of the compositional process. In various extended passages, it was common to incorporate a "pedal tone," or the same repeated root note, played by the bass player under a series of moving chords. Additionally, some melodic passages utilized the bass playing a 3rd or 5th note of a triad, usually under a major chord, rather than the usual common root. Many progressive rock groups of the 1960's and 1970's benefited greatly from record labels that allowed their artists to exercise more creative control in the studio without demanding hit singles for radio play.

The role of guitarists, drummers, and bassists changed significantly as progressive rock evolved. Most progressive rock bands used one guitar player and eliminated rhythm guitar. Guitar players emphasized single melodic lines, ostinato figures, and arpeggios rather than strumming chords (unless on acoustic guitar). Guitarists like Robert Fripp of King Crimson and Steve Hackett of Genesis played melodic lines that were important to the structure of the composition rather than just for extended solos. Drummers had to become adept at odd time signatures, how to play complex ensemble rhythmic figures, and learn how to complement a wide variety of instrument timbres. Many drummers expanded their abilities by learning orchestral percussion instruments such as timpani and mallet instruments. The function of the bass was expanded by virtuosos such as Chris Squire of Yes who stated, "The bass is just as much a solo and melodic instrument as the guitar or even organ." #1 Bassist Geddy Lee of the progressive band Rush said, " For us to be in seven is the most natural thing in the world. It's probably as natural to us as it is for Bill Bruford to play in five. He can make it seem so smooth." #2

Progressive rock placed many demands on vocalists. Many singers learned to alternate between singing and speech-like passages. Mostly male singers (females included Sonja Kristina of Curved Air and Annie Haslam of Renaissance) were often tenors, often with the ability to hit high notes. A band's material largely affected the musical approach of their vocalist but on the other hand, highly individual vocal qualities helped define the best progressive rock. Some bands featured one singer; some had two, but The Moody Blues had four, making them one of the first to experiment with choral effects. Progressive rock redirected the tradition of classical music virtuosity when complex solos could come from any instrumentalist, not just a guitar player. It was common to hear grandiose vocal harmonies as well as contrapuntal vocal lines that moved against each other. Bands like Gentle Giant and later, Spock's Beard, were inspired by classical choral pieces.

The First Wave of Progressive Rock Bands

The Moody Blues (1964-present) were at first a rhythm and blues band in the mid-1960's, hence the blues in their name. The original lineup was guitarist Denny Laine, vocalist/flautist Ray Thomas, keyboardist Mike Pinder, bassist Clint Warwick, and drummer Graeme Edge. They toured behind Chuck Berry and The Beatles but split briefly in 1965 only to re-form with vocalist/guitarist Justin Hayward and vocalist/bassist John Lodge replacing Warwick and Laine. The band moved to Belgium and worked for almost a year on their groundbreaking 1967 album Days of Future Passed. On this recording, The Moody Blues successfully fused symphonic music with rock. This was a conceptual album based on a metaphorical theme that referred to someone's entire life-span. It went to number twenty-seven on the British charts and number three in America. John Lodge looked back at their new direction and stated, "We became part of the progressive rock avalanche…at the time we thought we were writing and recording our very own personal music with no regard for anyone else. We were always looking for new avenues to explore." #3

The Moody Blues benefited greatly from the production skills of producer Tony Clarke (often called "the sixth Moody"). On Days of Future Passed, Clarke developed what he referred to as a "cinematic feel" by cross-fading one song into another, which gave the illusion of one continuous work. The Moody Blues sound combined studio experimentation with the woodwind sounds of Ray Thomas, mixed with lush string passages. Vocally, they combined a smooth delivery of the lyrics with sometimes-deep spoken word poetry and layered harmonies. The Moody Blues were one of the first bands to use the Mellotron. It added great depth and another sonic dimension to their music.

"Nights in White Satin"
written by Justin Hayward

"Forever Afternoon (Tuesday)" and "Nights in White Satin" were top twenty hits in Britain. "Nights in White Satin" was originally released in 1967. It went to number nineteen in Britain. However, it only reached one-hundred and three in America where it was difficult to get radio play for six-minute songs. Only later in 1972,

> "Stewart Copeland and I agree that drumming is the hardest job, but singing is the worst job"
>
> – Neil Peart of Rush

did "Nights in White Satin" crack the top ten on the American charts.

Hayward titled the song after his girlfriend gave him some satin bedsheets. The lyrics were about a man yearning for love and Hayward felt it was a very personal song that had great meaning to him. The Moody Blues utilized The London Symphony Orchestra for the introduction accompaniment, the last chorus, and the final section of the tune. Keyboardist Mike Pinder experimented with a Mellotron to find an orchestral sound for the main section of the song, thus helping to define the Moody Blues sound. Hayward created a powerful emotional song with "Nights in White Satin" that has stood the test of time and is a frequently heard composition on classic rock radio.

―――

From 1968 to 1978, The Moody Blues released seven more studio albums where they honed their sound and expanded their fan base, including In Search of the Lost Chord. The band broke up in 1974 but re-formed in 1978. Mike Pinder left the band but was replaced by former Yes keyboardist Patrick Moraz. The Moody Blues went on to experience more commercial and critical success and failures. After many lineup changes, the 2000's saw the remaining members of Hayward, Lodge, and Edge continue to write, record, and tour.

The Nice (1967-1970) was the first successful band for keyboardist Keith Emerson. They were formed in 1967 by Emerson, bassist Keith "Lee" Jackson, drummer Ian Hague, and guitarist David O'List. At first, the band played a weird mix of classical themed songs and Bob Dylan songs. They achieved a little commercial success with an instrumental arrangement of Leonard Bernstein's "America," from his *West Side Story* musical. The Nice had its first break when they played at The National Jazz and Blues Festival in Windsor in 1967. Their 1967 debut album, The Thoughts of Emerlist Davjack (incorporating the band member's names), featured an arrangement of Dave Brubeck's "Blue Rondo a la Turk." The Nice were unknown to progressive rock fans, but all the ingredients were there. They had Emerson's spacey Hammond organ sound, guitar feedback that imitated Mellotron strings, innovative classical music arrangements, and good production techniques.

The Nice downsized to a three-piece band after firing O'List. Emerson continued fronting the band from the keyboard position. Without having a guitar out front, Keith Emerson began to redefine the role of keyboard players in a rock setting. Their second album, Ars Longa Vita Brevis, featured an arrangement of J.S. Bach's "Brandenburg Concerto No. Three" and Jean Sibelius's "Intermezzo" from the Karelia Suite. The Nice's third album, As Nice As Mother Makes It, again presented their arrangements of classical compositions.

The Nice were an exciting and unpredictable live band. Emerson would trash his Hammond L-100 organ by tipping it over and stabbing it with knives. He was inspired by Jimi Hendrix and even Jerry Lee Lewis with his stage antics. In 1969, Emerson was unhappy with the band's progress and direction. He approached bassists Jack Bruce and Yes's Chris Squire about forming a new band, but both rejected his offer. In 1970, The Nice collaborated with the Los Angeles Philharmonic Orchestra, conducted by Zubin Mehta. Soon after, Keith Emerson would go on to form Emerson, Lake, and Palmer.

Procol Harum (1967-1977) was a progressive rock band that formed in 1967 by singer/songwriter Gary Brooker, organist Matthew Fisher, guitarist Ray Royer, bassist David Knights, and poet Keith Reid. They recorded "A Whiter Shade of Pale" and a follow up hit titled "Homburg," added guitarist Robin Trower. Their debut album, titled Procol Harum, featured most of the songs written by Gary Brooker and Keith Reid. Their second album, Shine On Brightly, moved the band in more of a progressive rock direction.

1969's Salty Dog featured the title track "A Salty Dog," written by Brooker and Reid. It marked the first time the band had recorded with an orchestra. On this recording, Procol Harum expanded The Beatles use of acoustic instruments that were not previously associated with rock albums. They utilized the timbres of the celesta, bells, recorder, marimba, and various orchestral and ethnic percussion instruments. Salty Dog gained more popularity and the band expanded their fan base. Many different lineup changes ensued. However, Procol Harum continued to develop their symphonic rock sound. In 1972, they recorded with a live orchestra on their Procol Harum Live: In Concert with the Edmonton Symphony Orchestra. After more lineup changes, Procol Harum disbanded in 1977. The band re-formed in 1991 with Brooker, Trower, Fisher, and Reid to release The Prodigal Stranger.

"A Whiter Shade of Pale"
by Gary Brooker, Keith Reid and Matthew Fisher

"A Whiter Shade of Pale" went to number one on the British charts and number five on the American charts. The Hammond organ was utilized as a substitute for a grand pipe organ to create a huge cathedral-like sound that was heard in many other Procol Harum songs. "A Whiter Shade of Pale" incorporated elements of J.S. Bach's Suite No. three in D major. This classically inspired organ timbre by Gary Brooker combined with guitarist Robin Trower's blues lines to create the Procol Harum sound. Procol Harum keyboardist Matthew Fisher explained, "I was interested in some of the far more serious music of Bach, B Minor Mass, and things like that. I was never that stuck on James Brown…It was within the two that there was nevertheless a large area of overlap in our musical tastes." #4

―――

Procol Harum's lyricist Keith Reid revealed that "A Whiter Shade of Pale" was about a relationship between two people on a journey. When Gary Brooker saw Reid's lyrics, he became motivated to compose a song that expressed an atmosphere and the feeling of leaving. Brooker wanted to get the soul of those lyrics across vocally and make people experience the sense of sadness felt by the characters. When Brooker first heard the written lines of the song, he was sitting at a piano and found the chords that fit the storyline. "A Whiter Shade of Pale" helped define the Procol Harum soulful sound of Hammond organ, piano, and blues guitar.

The Second Wave of Progressive Rock Bands

The second wave of progressive rock saw the emergence of Emerson, Lake and Palmer, King Crimson, Van der Graaf Generator, Genesis, Yes, Jethro Tull, Gentle Giant, Curved Air, and Soft Machine. This would become the "classic age" of progressive rock. Progressive

---

Rock Hard Fact

Procol Harum's 1969 album, A Salty Dog, utilized a sea journey as a metaphor for a spiritual quest.

rock would soon develop into some of the world's most challenging and intricate music for listeners, composers, and performers.

Van der Graaf Generator (1967-present) was formed in 1967 when singer/songwriters Chris Judge Smith and Peter Hammill met at Manchester University, England. In the 1970's, the band achieved some early popularity, mostly in Italy. They chose the band's name from a mechanical device that produced static electricity with lightning-like flashes. They soon added organist Nick Pearne, bassist Keith Ellis, and drummer Guy Evans. Van der Graaf Generator released their 1979 debut album, The Aerosol Grey Machine, to little commercial success. The band then changed lineups by adding multi-instrumentalist David Jackson and Nic Potter replaced Ellis on bass. They also added keyboardist and Mellotron player Hugh Banton. 1970's The Least We Can Do is Wave to Each Other followed. In the same year, the band released H to He Who Am the Only One with Robert Fripp guesting on guitar. They later added violinist Graham Smith to the lineup.

Van der Graaf Generator developed a dark sound with complex lyrical themes that often dealt with the subject of mortality and science fiction. The band's musical style evolved from the early acoustic guitar of Peter Hammill to more complex instrumentation, odd meters, and group arrangements. Their experimental and adventurous style has been compared to King Crimson. Van der Graaf Generator followed with ten more studio albums, some of which were reissues of previous material. The band has been cited as an influence on some of the goth bands of the 1980's and neo-progressive bands such as Marillion. They have broken up and restructured over the years. The most recent version of Van der Graaf Generator re-formed in 2005 and continues to perform.

King Crimson (1969-present) has defined and redefined progressive rock throughout their long career. They were pioneers of symphonic rock and fused the improvisation of jazz with avant-garde musical concepts. In spite of numerous lineup changes, King Crimson was able to establish a musical identity based on constantly changing their musical direction. Before there was Crimson, guitarist/composer/keyboardist Robert Fripp, bassist Peter Giles, and his brother, drummer Michael Giles formed a trio in 1968. They soon recorded an album titled The Cheerful Insanity of Giles, Giles and Fripp. Next, they added vocalist Judy Dyble and multi-instrumentalist Ian McDonald. This group of musicians recorded The Brondesbury Tapes, material that they would use on future albums. Next, Dyble left and they added vocalist/bassist Greg Lake (bassist Peter Giles was asked to step down). They also added lyricist Peter Sinfield. The King Crimson original lineup was now in place.

Understanding King Crimson means trying to understand Robert Fripp. Fripp learned some of the basics of American blues based electric guitar. But, he also drew from European classical and folk traditions. Fripp was an avid reader, which would influence many of his ongoing musical decisions. Steve Wilson (of the band Porcupine Tree) said, "Robert has a reputation of being quite prickly, but that reputation comes from the music press-and he's prickly with the music press, because he sees them as rather irrelevant to what he does." #5 King Crimson played their first live show in London in 1969. The musical chemistry was strong between them and they performed with great power and intensity. People were stunned at their level of musicianship and ensemble sensibilities. Steve Hackett, before he joined Genesis, was one such onlooker that was amazed at what King Crimson was playing. Said band member Ian McDonald, "You could play almost anything that came to mind and know that the other players would be with you, hearing and supporting it." #6 King Crimson's 1969 debut album, In the Court of the Crimson King, was a stunning album that instantly brought the band to prominence.

Groundbreaking album
In the Court of the Crimson King
by King Crimson

The 1969 release of King Crimson's debut album In the Court of the Crimson King was a risky project that was self-financed and self-produced. It might be the most important recording in the history of progressive rock. In the Court of the Crimson King signified the emergence of the mature progressive rock style that reached its creative and commercial height between the years 1970 to 1975. This album achieved the sound of melancholy with minor-key passages and Mellotron sonorities together with the timbre of the acoustic guitar. This was contrasted by nasty, fuzz tone guitar mixed with jazz influenced alto saxophone improvisation.

Side one opened with "21st Century Schizoid Man," then "I Talk to the Wind," and "Epitaph." The compositions "Epitaph" and "21st Century Schizoid Man" both revealed apocalyptic themes. "21st Century" contained verses with disconnected phrases that presented a series of images. The song also referenced the Vietnam War with the lyric "Politician' funeral pyre/innocence raped with napalm fire." The song featured Greg Lake's heavily distorted vocals and an adventurous instrumental middle section called "Mirrors."

Side two opened with "Moonchild," then "The Court of the Crimson King." "Moonchild" consisted of two parts, "The Dream," and "The Illusion." "The Court of the Crimson King" consisted of "The Return of the Fire Witch," and "The Dance of the Puppets." "The Court" featured a strong riff played on a Mellotron. The song utilized four verses that evoked imagery of a queen, a funeral march, and a fire witch in a Medieval royal court. The storyline of "The Court" was broken up by an instrumental section called "The Return of the Fire Witch."

The multi-faceted influence of this landmark record inspired many young progressive bands to explore their own unique voices as the progressive rock genre gained traction. Never before had the Medieval images of puppets, a purple piper, a pilgrim's door, a keeper of the city keys, a black queen, etc… been combined with equal musical imagination. In the Court of the Crimson King went to number five on the British charts and made the top thirty on the U.S. charts.

"Twenty-First Century Schizoid Man"
by King Crimson

This composition utilized Medieval imagery and mystical undertones to create its own musical environment. All three verses followed a set pattern and each presented its own image. "Schizoid Man" has a very percussive and singable melodic line. By using the text "Twenty-first century," it implied a modern environment but with a dark edge. King Crimson phrased the alto saxophone, guitar, bass, and drums in unison to create a tight sound. The song went back and forth from 4/4 to 6/8 but the end of the song was free of meter. Michael Giles

---

"We thought we were hot stuff until Crimson came along... they we so much better than us that we said, 'We have to rehearse a lot more'"

-original Yes guitarist Peter Banks

Rock Hard Fact

Many thought that Ahmet Ertegun (owner of Atlantic Records) would hate In the Court of the Crimson King, but he loved it and released it in America.

navigated through the middle section called "Mirrors" with a jazz drumset feel and comping ideas.
Peter Sinfield wrote the lyrics for "Twenty-First Century Schizoid Man" as a political statement of the times, especially the Vietnam war. Each song on the album was about the generation gap and how people in power control other people's lives. Sinfield was writing about the divide between the elites and common people in the world. It's an observation by King Crimson.

> "Crimson has to keep reinventing itself"
>
> - Adrian Belew

Things were going very well for King Crimson but soon the bottom would drop out. Towards the end of an American tour in 1969, Giles and McDonald quit to pursue their own project. The 1970 revamped lineup of Fripp, Lake, and Sinfield added Mel Collins on woodwinds. Also, a return of Peter Giles on bass and Keith Tippett on piano marked a new Crimson lineup. The second album, In the Wake of Poseidon, was another hit on both sides of the Atlantic. However, Greg Lake decided to leave to join Keith Emerson in The Nice. King Crimson was reduced to a studio band when they next recorded their third album, Lizard. It was basically Fripp and Sinfield with many studio musicians coming in and out of the lineup. Lizard's timbres were very dark and horn-driven. 1972's Earthbound followed with slight lineup changes.

King Crimson broke up again and Sinfield was out. But Fripp reorganized the band in 1972. A new super lineup consisted of bassist John Wetten, former Yes drummer Bill Bruford, David Cross on violin, Jamie Muir on percussion, and lyricist Richard Palmer-James (a founding member of Supertramp). 1973's Lark's Tongues in Aspic achieved a new and more improvisational direction. This period saw the band incorporate world music influences from Middle Eastern to West African sounds and rhythms. Fripp expanded his musical vision by experimenting with European classical ideals with direct quotes from Igor Stravinsky's "The Rite of Spring." Drummer Bill Bruford commented that "In King Crimson, we did outrageous things with the rhythmic intensity and with what the instruments were supposed to do, or not supposed to do." #7

By 1974 King Crimson was performing at a high level but Robert Fripp was going through a spiritual transformation. When Fripp reconnected with the band, they recorded Red, and he really found his voice as a guitar player. The record was loud, aggressive, and heavy metal-like. Just as the band was on the verge of gaining a very large popular audience, Fripp pulled the plug on King Crimson again. From 1975 to 1980, Fripp collaborated on many studio sessions with producer Brian Eno (see chapter eighteen). Together they experimented with analog tape loop effects and created what they titled Frippertronics. John Wetten worked with Roxy Music, Uriah Heep, U.K., and Asia. Bruford worked with Gong, Genesis, his own rock/fusion band, and U.K.

After a long lapse of time, Fripp and Bruford re-formed King Crimson again, now with ex-Frank Zappa guitarist Adrian Belew, and Peter Gabriel bassist Tony Levin. They recorded three quality albums, 1981's Discipline, 1982's Beat, and 1984's Three of a Perfect Pair. These recordings assimilated rock and jazz elements while Bruford experimented with MIDI electronic drums and percussion. Belew treated his guitar like a keyboardist by using a Roland guitar synthesizer and tons of effects to create new timbres. Also, Tony Levin utilized the Chapman Stick. Some of the older Crimson fans did not like the new musical direction or sound combinations. Then, of course, this version of King Crimson disbanded. For ten years.

In 1994, King Crimson reunited and went to a "double trio" lineup with two guitarists-Fripp and Belew, two drummers-Bruford and Pat Mastelotto, and two bassists- Levin and Trey Gunn. They recorded 1994's Vroom, and Thrak and B'Boom, both in 1995. After Tony Levin and Bruford left, the band made The ConstruKction of Light in 2000 and The Power to Believe in 2003. Throughout all of these later King Crimson recordings, the band continued to explore the outer limits of musical possibilities. The lasting influence of King Crimson is enormous. The very heavy riffs in songs like "21st Century Schizoid Man" and "Lark's Tongues Pt.1 and 2," eventually led to the sub-genre of progressive metal. After another hiatus in 2009, King Crimson was at it again in 2014 to present.

Emerson, Lake, and Palmer (1970-2010) Keyboardist/composer Keith Emerson of The Nice met vocalist/bassist Greg Lake of King Crimson when both were sharing a tour of America. They soon met drummer/percussionist Carl Palmer, who had previously played with Atomic Rooster, and formed Emerson, Lake, and Palmer in 1970. On only their second live performance, ELP played at the Isle of Wright Festival for six hundred thousand fans and quickly gained popularity. They performed a twenty-minute version of Mussorgsky's "Pictures at an Exhibition" that included Emerson stabbing his keyboard with a knife and real cannons firing. Emerson was the first musician to play live with a Moog synthesizer when ELP employed the latest technologies both live and in the studio. Carl Palmer utilized a full battery of percussion instruments and constructed long drum solos for every tour. Greg Lake had a versatile, refined voice and he was able to simultaneously cover the bass parts.

Emerson, Lake, and Palmer's self-titled debut album was released in 1970. It quickly went to number four in Britain and number eighteen in America. Emerson used the huge Festival Hall organ in London while producer Eddie Offord created innovative sound structures through the techniques of overdubbing, phasing, and other multi-tracking concepts. Emerson was not very drawn to the sound of the Mellotron that had become standard gear for most progressive rock keyboardists. On their debut record, ELP recorded an arrangement of composer Bela Bartok's piano piece "Allegro Barbaro." They also recorded Emerson's composition "The Three Fates," that has sections in 7/8 time and a Baroque influence. Greg Lake's ballad, "Lucky Man," was a hit single that stills receives FM classic rock radio play.

"Lucky Man"
by Greg Lake

"Lucky Man" was lucky to make it onto Emerson, Lake, and Palmer's debut album. On their last day of recording their debut, they realized that they didn't have enough material to complete the album. Greg Lake volunteered a folk-like ballad he had written when he was only twelve years old. A disinterested Keith Emerson told Lake and Palmer to record it themselves and that he was going down to a local pub. Lake added bass and some guitar overdubs, including an electric guitar solo. Emerson returned and after listening to the track, was impressed. He had just received a new toy, a Moog synthesizer and wondered if their was a sound on the new gadget that would work for the song. Emerson then added one of the most famous Moog synth solos in rock history. The first four chords Lake ever learned on guitar were the four chords in "Lucky Man," a D triad, A minor, E minor, and a G triad.

Lyrically, "Lucky Man" had a sad ending. It was a story about a "lucky man" that achieved great wealth and acclaim and then decided to fight for his country. He gets shot in battle and died. Green Lake has said that many people identified the song with the Vietnam War and that whole time period in general. By ELP standards, "Lucky Man" was a very basic song, which provided a nice balance to their complex instrumental repertoire. "Lucky Man" had evolved from a simple, little folk song to a featured major jam at ELP shows.

For 1971's Tarkus, ELP saw great success when the record went to number one on the UK charts and number nine in America. The first side of Tarkus, written by Emerson and Lake, was a collection of seven interwoven pieces collectively titled "Tarkus." At first, Greg Lake did not like the direction of the title piece and Emerson threatened to quit the band. Eventually, Lake came to understand the composition and added another piece titled "Battlefield." For Tarkus, Emerson said that he was attempting to create "a vast sheet of sound that defies conventional structures… and had a free-floating sense of time signature and key." #8 In one section of Tarkus, the band played fluidly in 10/8 time as Emerson created unusual and complex harmonies with jazz-based chords and a Baroque styled ground bass ostinato. The cover art for Tarkus was unique and gave ELP an identity with a half-tank and half-armadillo creature, complete with tire treads and a long barrel gun. The compositions contained on Tarkus alternated between vocal and full instrumental pieces.

Emerson, Lake, and Palmer released a live album, Pictures at an Exhibition, in 1971. It consisted of the band's arrangement of "Pictures at an Exhibition" by composer Modest Mussorgsky. Pictures went to number two on the British charts and number ten in America. The suite used four of Mussorgsky's original ten pieces and ELP performed it live as one continuous piece. It was an adventurous work that revealed how skilled ELP was in reducing a full orchestral piece to a three-piece band. However, it was not without its critics. Greg Lake commented that "The moment you start applying lyrics and vocals to classical music, you are almost condemned to becoming crass." #9

More success came to Emerson, Lake, and Palmer with 1973's Brain Salad Surgery and they toured constantly. ELP's stage show featured a massive sound system with over thirty tons of equipment, including Palmer's revolving drum kit. They followed in 1974 with the only triple album to get to number ten on the U.S. charts with Welcome Back My Friends to the Show That Never Ends…Ladies and Gentlemen, Emerson, Lake, and Palmer. From there, ELP released a two-record set titled Works Volume I and then took a two-year break.

Subsequent albums sold poorly and ELP went on hiatus for the next twelve years. Carl Palmer joined Steve Howe (of Yes) in 1981 to form a new supergroup, Asia. Emerson and Lake regrouped by adding drummer Cozy Powell to form Emerson, Lake, and Powell in 1985. This trio was successful and received strong radio airplay. They also found their way onto MTV video rotation with the song, "Touch and Go."

Emerson, Lake, and Palmer reunited in 1992. However, their last recording, In the Hot Seat, sold poorly and ELP played one last show at London's Victoria Park in 2010. Emerson, Lake, and Palmer made significant contributions to the progressive rock genre with their creative reductions of symphonic music and Keith Emerson's great keyboard virtuosity. In live performance, Emerson, Lake, and Palmer was one of progressive rock's most exciting live bands with their aggressive showmanship and Greg Lake's feathery soft voice. Sadly, Keith Emerson and Greg Lake both died in 2016.

Gentle Giant (1970-1980) was formed in 1970 by three brothers, Derek, Ray, and Phil Shulman, all born in Scotland and raised in England. Before forming Gentle Giant, the Shulman brothers played in the soul and R&B band Simon Dupree. They were a hits-oriented band (Elton John had auditioned and was rejected) but the Shulman brothers wanted to compose and perform more serious music. The band's name was inspired by the name of Francois Rabelais's sixteenth-century work *Gargantua and Pantagruel*. Gentle Giant soon added composer/keyboardist/percussionist Kerry Minnear, guitarist Gary Green, and drummer Martin Smith. Ray played bass and violin, Derek was the lead vocalist and saxophonist, and Phil played saxophone, recorder, trumpet, and sang some lead. The members of Gentle Giant were multi-instrumentalists influenced by a variety of musical sources including jazz, folk, classical, and early fusion. They also drew from European Renaissance and Medieval music.

Gentle Giants' self-titled debut album was released in 1970 and featured the songs "Giant," "Alucard," and "Nothing At All." These tracks displayed the bands' diverse musical timbres including synthesizers mixed with blues guitar, church organ, Mellotron, vibraphone, cello, and multiple saxophone and trumpet sounds. 1971's Acquiring the Taste revealed their musical growth on a grand level. They employed Renaissance hymns in the style of Palestrina and Holst, orchestral percussion mixed in with the drumset parts, vocal lines with contrapuntal structure, Medieval ballads, complex tempos and time signatures, and blues guitar riffs. The brothers all shared in the production of the album and often wrote melodic ideas and arrangements together.

1972's Three Friends saw a change of drummers with the addition of Malcolm Mortimore, who was more advanced technically and better able to handle the increasingly difficult demands of the music. As Gentle Giant was set to make their American tour debut, Mortimore was hurt in a motorcycle accident and was soon replaced by drummer John Weathers. Weathers could also handle more complex ideas but was also adept at holding the music together with simpler drumset parts. Gentle Giant's 1973 Octopus would be the last for Phil Shulman who decided to leave the band during a tour of Italy. Even without Phil, Gentle Giant created one of their most musical records, 1973's In a Glass House.

Gentle Giant slowly built a following in America to complement their growing popularity in Europe. However, they were never able to achieve the popularity of progressive bands such as Yes, Genesis, or Jethro Tull. Derek Shulman commented on the bands' struggle to achieve more success when he said, "We saw bands like Genesis and Yes and even Kansas, having hit singles on album-oriented rock radio. We were playing shows with them supporting us as special guests and we watched them leapfrog over us, scoring hits. I wanted my share, but changing our approach just didn't work for us." #10

Gentle Giant evolved over time. From 1970 to 1980, they represented what progressive rock was all about in terms of their musical influences and complex, dense compositions. After In a Glass House, Gentle Giant went on to record over eight more studio albums. Even though they had many artistic disagreements, over the years the lineup remained stable with Derek and Ray Shulman, Minnear, Green and Weathers. Derek Shulman had also developed a career as a record executive working for PolyGram, Atco, Mercury and Roadrunner

Rock Hard Fact

Before forming ELP, Keith Emerson and Greg Lake were considering drummer Mitch Mitchell and at the suggestion of Mitchell, adding Jimi Hendrix to their lineup. Instead, they went with drummer Carl Palmer.

> "Back in the 60's and 70's there wasn't a thing called Prog music, there were only bands...I mean Pink Floyd are not like Gentle Giant, who are not like King Crimson, who are nothing like Genesis, who are nothing like Curved Air."
>
> – Sonja Kristina of Curved Air

Rock Hard Fact

The first Genesis album From Genesis to Revelation initially sold only 650 copies, partly because record stores thought it was a religious album and placed it accordingly.

Records. Shulman was instrumental in bringing the metal and progressive metal movement of the late 1980's and early 1990's to the forefront by signing bands like Dream Theater and Pantera. Full reunion attempts for Gentle Giant have failed. However, in 2009 Minnear, Green, and Mortimore formed the band Three Friends and continue to perform today.

One part of the British progressive rock movement was known as the Canterbury scene. Canterbury, England was a major religious center and the home of the Church of England. The music scene it represented in the early to mid-1960's saw a combination of British jazz, psychedelic influences, and elements of the emerging progressive rock style. An early Canterbury band called The Wilde Flowers gave rise to bands such as **Soft Machine** and **Caravan** and later to **Gong** (1967-present), **Camel**, and **Matching Mole** (1971-1973).

Soft Machine (1966-present) combined rock and jazz elements to become one of the most important early progressive bands to emerge from the Canterbury scene in England. Named after the 1961 William Burroughs novel *The Soft Machine*, the band was formed in 1966 by ex-Wilde Flowers drummer/vocalist Robert Wyatt, bassist/vocalist Kevin Ayers, and keyboardist Mike Ratledge. Their 1968 debut album, Soft Machine, featured a sound built on organ and horn timbres as they deliberately avoided guitar. Soft Machine looked to create a mix of psychedelic experimentation with jazz improvisation. It wasn't until their seventh band lineup, that they added guitar great Allen Holdsworth to record 1975's Bundles. More lineup changes ensued as Soft Machine recorded more than thirteen albums. They continue to perform today.

Another Canterbury band, **Caravan** (1968-present with some inactive years), also grew out of the band The Wilde Flowers. Caravan's debut album Caravan was released in 1969. The original members were vocalist/bassist Richard Sinclair, vocalist/guitarist Pye Hastings, keyboardist David Sinclair, and drummer Richard Coughlan. Caravan effectively mixed jazz harmonies, folk music, and odd meters. In addition, they blended classical influences with psychedelic elements to create their own progressive rock approach. Caravan endured many lineup changes and some years of musical inactivity. They have recorded over fourteen records and the latest version of the band assembled in 1995 and continues to perform.

Camel (1971-present) started when guitarist Andrew Latimer, bassist Doug Ferguson, and drummer Andy Ward were working in England as the band, The Brew. They added keyboardist Peter Bardens to complete the original Camel lineup. In 1972, they released their self-titled debut album Camel. The Camel progressive sound focused on long instrumental compositions. They employed jazz improvisation and used a variety of Latin based rhythms. Camel had many lineup changes and evolved into adept studio musicians. They have utilized acclaimed drummers Phil Collins and Simon Phillips on their albums and have recorded with The London Symphony Orchestra. Camel recorded fourteen studio albums, fourteen singles, and many compilation and live records. In 2017, Camel released a live DVD of a performance in Tokyo. Camel still actively performs.

Curved Air (1970-present) evolved out of the band Sisyphus when violinist/keyboardist Darryl Way was looking to form a new band in 1970. The original Curved Air lineup was lead vocalist Sonja Kristina, multi-instrumentalist Francis Monkman, bassist Robert Martin, drummer Florian Pilkington-Miksa and Darryl Way. Curved Air found their own sound by becoming one of the first progressive bands to feature the violin as a solo instrument. They combined folk, classical, fusion, electronic, and rock sounds to achieve an original sound. Curved Air released a total of eight studio albums. Their one hit single, "Back Street Luv," went to number four on the British charts in 1971. The band has employed many prominent musicians over the years including drummer Stewart Copeland. Copeland joined the band in 1975 and stayed through 1976, recording two albums. He then left to form The Police. Copeland later married Sonja Kristina in 1982 (divorced in 1991). Curved Air was inactive from 1991 to 2007. They re-formed in 2008 and are still performing today.

Genesis (1967-1997) was formed in 1967 when schoolboys from England's prestigious Charterhouse boarding school merged two competing band's, The Anon and The Garden Wall. The first lineup that would become Genesis consisted of vocalist/flutist Peter Gabriel, keyboardist/pianist Tony Banks, guitarist/bassist Michael Rutherford, and guitarist Anthony Phillips. Not overly concerned with working as a band, they were most interested in songwriting and creating a unique acoustic sound with twelve-string guitars, piano, and flute mixed with Gabriel's multi-dimensional voice. They fashioned their own musical atmosphere, isolated from the rest of the musical world, although they felt the influences of The Bee Gees and Crosby, Stills, and Nash. Soon, their demo "She Is Beautiful," grabbed the attention of producer Jonathan King. He loved Gabriel's voice and began to mentor them. He also named them Genesis.

From Genesis To Revelation was Genesis's 1969 debut album. Jonathan King next secured them a record deal with Decca Records. For the album, Genesis added drummer John Silver to the lineup but would soon replace him with John Mayhew. From Genesis To Revelation, was a concept album based on stories and figures from the Bible. The public was not excited about the record. However, Genesis was persistent and continued to write new material and build a small audience. The early days for Genesis were difficult as Peter Gabriel recalled, "there was definitely one gig up north when there were more people on the stage than there was in the audience. It was suggested that we should stop and buy them a drink. It seemed a better way to entertain them." #11 Their relationship with Jonathan King was soon over but new manager Tony Stratton-Smith signed them to his Famous Chrisma label.

1970's Trespass saw Genesis refine their twelve-string guitar, flute, and organ sound with their most ambitious track to date, a nine-minute composition titled "The Knife." Other songs included "Looking for Someone," and "White Mountain." These were examples of a developing Genesis sound that assimilated European folk influences with English nineteenth-century Renaissance music. Mixed in with some twentieth-century art music and some American gospel, (with a rock edge), Genesis began to embody a unique blend of instrumental sonorities that merged seamlessly with Gabriel's vocal timbres. Trespass also featured the cover art of illustrator Paul Whitehead, who would collaborate on many Genesis album covers. Trespass did not chart well in England or America and many believed Genesis was doomed to fail. Fortunately, Stratton-Smith felt strongly about their music as a vital art form and continued to support and encourage them financially through his record label.

Some members of the band felt that the drumset chair needed an upgrade. Meanwhile, drummer Phil

Collins was becoming a well-known drummer, touring with artists in Central and Eastern Europe. Soon, Collins auditioned for Genesis and became their next drummer. Another lineup change for the band would be far more difficult. Anthony Phillips had great anxiety about touring and left the band abruptly. Genesis was shaken and felt that his strong musical personality and friendship would be difficult to replace. Without Phillips, the band played live as a four-piece for some shows and Tony Banks played guitar lines on a keyboard using a fuzz box amplifier in addition to his usual keyboard parts. After answering an ad in the music magazine *Melody Maker*, Genesis welcomed guitarist Steve Hackett into the band. Hackett brought a unique concept to Genesis. He utilized many guitar effects and pedals but more importantly contributed clean melodic guitar lines that were a perfect complement to Bank's organ, piano, and Mellotron parts. Hackett also employed a Rose Morris MXR Phase 90 pedal to achieve one of his unique guitar sonorities. The new members, Collins and Hackett, joined in time for a 1970-71 tour in support of Trespass.

Next, Genesis worked on new material that moved from a more folk-oriented approach to incorporate more aggressive electric guitar and keyboard timbres. They released their third studio album, 1971's Nursery Cryme. The album cover revealed a girl, Cynthia, holding a croquet mallet, and a few human heads lying on the ground as croquet balls. Illustrator Paul Whitehead remembered, "The cover was obviously Alice in Wonderland inspired, an old English Victorian story, set on a croquet field…but instead of croquet balls, we'd use rolling heads." #12 The album went to number thirty-nine on the British charts. Nursery Cryme featured the complex and demanding compositions "The Musical Box" and "The Return of the Giant Hogweed." On "Hogweed," Hackett utilized a guitar tapping technique that essentially turned the guitar fretboard into a keyboard. The technique was later made popular by guitarist Eddie Van Halen.

Genesis had developed their writing process when Gabriel often wrote the lyrics the night before a session. The band would then match them to music or they sometimes worked from the music first and then moved to the lyrics.

"The Musical Box"
written by Genesis

"The Musical Box" was initially composed by Anthony Phillips as an instrumental composition. The lyrics, written by Gabriel, were a Victorian style fairy tale about two children that lived in a country house. A girl, Cynthia, killed a boy, Henry, by chopping off his head with a croquet mallet. She then found Henry's musical box. She opened it and the song "Old King Cole" played. Henry's spirit returned but aged very quickly. He experienced a lifetime of sexual desire in a few moments and tried to seduce Cynthia. The noise alerted his nurse and she threw the musical box at them, killing them both. "The Musical Box" featured added guitar parts by guitarist Mick Barnard (Barnard had a brief tenure with the band before the arrival of Hackett). In addition to his own part, Hackett kept the guitar parts that were recorded by Phillips and Barnard. Gabriel added an oboe part during the "Old King Cole" section.

On Nursery Cryme, skilled producer John Anthony worked closely with Tony Banks to create huge Mellotron chords combined with voices that would appear in different parts of the mix. Referring to "The Musical Box," Banks said, "The part I was most happy with on that particular song was the final section, where Mike had this little chord sequence and I started playing these very simple major chords on top of it so that it became almost like a fugue, quite quietly, before developing into something that was really, really exciting." #13 The album's sound had depth and gave strong support and perspective to Gabriel's lyrics. In live performances, Peter Gabriel wore an old man mask and would unzip the front of his black jumpsuit for the final verse.

Tony Banks

Tony Banks played a major role in developing the intricate musical sound combinations of Genesis. Banks had an uncanny ability to develop solos that were highly melodic adventures. This became a key ingredient in developing the extended compositions that separated Genesis from most other progressive rock bands. Banks composed elaborate arrangements and performed virtuoso keyboard solos on the instrumental sections of "Watcher of the Skies," "The Cinema Show," and "Supper's Ready." These examples provided some of the most musical and dramatic moments in progressive rock history. For the introduction to "Firth of Firth," on Selling England by the Pound, Banks played the grand piano in a classical style weaving his phrases through a rhythmically complex section containing measures of 13/16 and 15/16 that alternated with 2/4 measures.

Besides his great acoustic piano skills, Banks assimilated many keyboards into his setup throughout his tenure with Genesis. His arsenal included; the Arp Pro Soloist synthesizer, the Yamaha CP-70, the Hammond T-102, a Roland RS-202 string and brass synth, a NED Synclavier II, and the Mellotron. The band had bought a Mellotron from King Crimson to record the Foxtrot record. Banks used it to build a massive sound for the intro section of "Watchers of the Skies." Banks said, "It was an extraordinary sound. On the old Mellotron Mark 2 there were these two chords that sounded really good on that instrument. There are some chords you can't play on that instrument because they'd be so out of tune. These chords created an incredible atmosphere. That's why it's just an incredible intro number. It never sounded so good on the later Mellotron." #14 Banks also utilized a pianet, a type of electro-mechanical piano that contained steel spring reeds whose vibrations were converted to an electrical signal by a pick-up. The pianet was built by the Hohner Company.

Banks has always incorporated new sounds and technology into his keyboard setups. While the piano was at the core of his compositional approach, he pioneered many unique keyboard and synthesizer sounds throughout his career. The evolving use of sampling pushed him to acquire an array of rack mounted synth modules including; the Korg Wavestation, Roland A-90, E-mu Proteus I and II, and E-mu EIV.

Tony Banks also played twelve-string guitar. This gave him another approach to songwriting and allowed him to get to new chord progressions in an unpredictable manner. This led to his unique chordal sequence for the opening section of "Supper's Ready." Banks reflected on the compositional and performance approach of Genesis when he said, "everything we did then was very structured…people would complain, 'You always play the same thing every night' and I'd say, 'But don't you understand that when people improvise, they tend to play the same things every night but just in a different order.'" #15

> "I was always afraid that the guys would start arguing about any of the visual costumes bits that I was trying to do, so I would smuggle it in as late as possible when they were so preoccupied with getting everything else sorted."
>
> – Peter Gabriel

Classical music was at the core of Tony Banks' earliest musical influences. At a young age, his repertoire grew when he learned the piano music of Sergei Rachmaninoff and Maurice Ravel. Banks cited the works of Erik Satie, Dmitri Shostakovich, Jean Sibelius, and Gustav Mahler as strong influences. In 2004, Banks released a classical album titled <u>Seven: A Suite for Orchestra</u>, performed by The London Philharmonic Orchestra. In March of 2012, Banks released another classical album titled <u>Six Pieces for Orchestra</u>, performed by the City of Prague Philharmonic orchestra.

Tony Banks- composer and keyboard instrumental virtuoso.

Genesis released their fourth studio album, <u>Foxtrot</u>, in 1972. The band began to work with a new producer, John Burns, whom they utilized on their next three records. <u>Foxtrot</u> featured the demanding "Watcher of the Skies," a tune with complex ensemble rhythms in 6/4 meter, sometimes set against other rhythms in 4/4. This created an interesting polyrhythmic effect. These rhythms built dynamically with great intensity over a Mellotron chorus of strings. Genesis often opened live performances with this composition. Side two featured the epic "Supper's Ready," a twenty-three-minute composition written by the whole band. It's considered one of their masterpieces. It's divided into seven sections with a number of melodic and lyrical themes recycled throughout the work in a pseudo-sonata form. The "Apocalypse in 9/8" section was a particularly challenging passage that Phil Collins has mentioned as one of his favorite Genesis compositions. Gabriel has described "Supper's Ready" as "a personal journey which ends up walking through scenes from Revelation in the Bible." #16 Gabriel has also said that the song was influenced by an experience his wife had when sleeping in a purple room (and the nightmares that ensued). <u>Foxtrot</u> reached number twelve on the British charts, a milestone for Genesis in terms of their popularity at the time.

1973's <u>Genesis Live</u> was their first live recording. The tracks were taken from various shows during the band's tour supporting <u>Foxtrot</u>. It reached number nine on the British charts and went to one hundred and five in America. The album helped establish Genesis as a great live band and captured their power and mysticism. It also showed that Genesis was capable of performing complex and long compositions in a live setting.

<u>Selling England by the Pound</u> was also released in 1973. This very British centric album continued Genesis' quest to make music outside of the mainstream. <u>Selling England by the Pound</u> delivered Genesis's first hit, "I Know What I Like (in Your Wardrobe)." The band had been developing innovative stage shows with Peter Gabriel wearing bizarre costumes such as a fox's head, bat wings, and a giant sunflower to portray the many fantasy characters in the music. Now, as their audience grew, their theatrics were helping to create an identity with the public.

Groundbreaking album
<u>Selling England by the Pound</u>
by Genesis

Considered by many to be Genesis's greatest work, it showcased the band at its creative peak, in terms of composition, instrumental virtuosity, and ensemble interplay. <u>Selling England by the Pound</u> saw Genesis return to their English eccentricity from their first album while simultaneously taking the listener on a storybook ride with many overt literary allusions. This work functioned as a collection of short stories, fables, and fairy tales, while rocking hard in strategic places. Gabriel chose the album's title as a message to the British music press informing them that Genesis would not "sell out" to the American music industry. On the album, Genesis dealt with serious subjects such as war and the mythical Grail but at the same time, wrote music with a sense of humor and lightness.

Side one opened with "Dancing with the Moonlit Knight," then "I Know What I Like (In Your Wardrobe)," "Firth of Fifth," and "More Fool Me." "I Know What I Like" was the band's first single to reach the British charts at number twenty-one. "Firth of Fifth" began with a classical piano introduction and progressed to a rhythmically complex section with measures of 13/16 and 15/16 alternating with measures of 2/4 time. The song later featured a flute melody played by Gabriel, followed by a synthesizer-led instrumental section that restated the opening piano theme. Hackett's guitar playing was very compositional. He treated the instrument more as a single line voice that stated and often continued the melodic material introduced by Banks and Gabriel.

Side two opened with "The Battle of Epping Forest," then "After the Ordeal," "The Cinema Show," and "Aisle of Plenty." On "The Battle of Epping Forest," Gabriel's voice covered different British accents. The band strived to avoid settling for a commercialized American approach. "The Cinema Show" and "Firth of Fifth" (written mostly by Banks) were extended works that are considered two of their best compositions. Both compositions were part of the band's live repertoire for many years. Also, Banks had upgraded to a newer version of the Mellotron for the album.

<u>Selling England by the Pound</u> went to number three on the British charts and number seventy in America. Steve Hackett has stated that this was his favorite Genesis album and said, "There were moments in <u>Selling England by the Pound</u> that would have given the Mahavishnu Orchestra a run for their money: little bits of what I called guitar tapping, furious drums, great ensemble playing. And that's just the first number." #17

"The Cinema Show"
by Genesis

The storyline of "The Cinema Show," (referring to Shakespeare's Romeo and Juliet) described the principal characters that were preparing for a date at a cinema show. Romeo was hoping for a sexual conquest that evening. On another level, the lyrics revealed a contrast in the lack of depth felt by a pair of modern lovers to the spiritual fullness experienced by the mythological figure Tiresias (who was both male and female). The role of Tiresias symbolized the combination of both matriarchal and patriarchal values. The lyrics were written by Rutherford and Banks and were inspired by the T.S. Eliot poem *The Waste Land*.

"The Cinema Show" was composed in two sections with all the classic Genesis-isms on display. The first section functioned as a complete composition that captured the Genesis acoustic twelve-string guitar sound, Gabriel and Collins' vocal harmonies, and Gabriel's flute and oboe passages. The second part was a four and a half minute instrumental journey that extended and complemented the first section. The ensemble played challenging melodic lines in 7/8 featuring Banks on the ARP Pro

Soloist keyboard. This section developed a life of its own. Banks repeated melodic material, only this time augmented by the Mellotron. Banks, Collins, and Rutherford all developed complex phrasing in the 7/8 feel. Banks composed most of the complex melodic and harmonic material, which Genesis turned into brilliant ensemble interplay. After ending the extended musical journal, brief acoustic sections with vocals reprised the storyline and returned to the fantasy world of the introduction.

The Lamb Lies Down on Broadway was released in 1974 and would be the final recording for Peter Gabriel. The Lamb was a concept double album, a first for Genesis as it both inspired some listeners and confused others. Genesis found many unique sounds for the record and musician Brian Eno was employed to manipulate Gabriel's voice with a VCS-3 synthesizer. The storyline for The Lamb was based on religious metaphors and revealed a strange dreamlike plot. Peter Gabriel explained, "It tells of how a large black cloud descends into Times Square, straddles out across Forty-Second Street, turns into wool, and sucks in Manhattan Island. Our hero, named Rael, crawls out of the subways of New York and is sucked into the wool to regain consciousness underground. This is the story of Rael." #18 On the supporting tour (to be Gabriel's last), audiences were confused because Genesis performed the entire double album before it's official release. This meant that the audience was hearing it for the first time. By the end of the American tour for The Lamb, Gabriel had announced that he was leaving the band. Many in the public had assumed Gabriel was the main creative force in Genesis, and therefore, the band would not survive his departure. They would turn out to be wrong.

Phil Collins
"Not just a great singer
Not just a great drummer"

Phil Collins was a child drumming prodigy, who started playing at the age of five. He was in show business from an early age acting in theatre productions and he had a small part in The Beatles' *A Hard Day's Night* (his scene was actually cut from the film). Collins was a member of the pop-rock band Flaming Youth before auditioning for Genesis. At his Genesis audition, he arrived early at the house of Peter Gabriel's parents and was asked to wait outside. While waiting, he heard the mistakes other drummers were making and then auditioned, winning the job. Peter Gabriel remembered Collins audition "I was convinced from the first moment. I knew when Phil sat down on the kit, before he'd played a note, that this was a guy who really was in command of what he was doing…so confident." #19

One thing that separated Phil Collins from other progressive rock drummers was his ability to create and sustain a groove much like the many great rhythm and blues drummers. And that included his ability to do so in odd time signatures. Collins' drumming concepts were jazz and fusion based, his toms were tuned high to achieve a melodic sound, and his playing was highly interactive and detailed. Chester Thompson, brought in later to play drums on Genesis tours, described playing with Collins and stated, "I don't think I've ever locked with someone as quickly… we found that we had listened to a lot of the same players growing up, the heavy jazz players: Tony Williams especially…Phil knew these guys and their styles…he was much better versed than I was on the English rock drummers like John Bonham and Keith Moon." #20 Phil's side project to Genesis, the band Brand X, gave him an outlet to explore high level fusion music that he utilized to help shape his approach to Genesis' more demanding musical passages and songs.

Phil Collins shocked the progressive rock world when he assumed lead vocal duties in Genesis. Having sung background parts on many Genesis tracks and lead vocals on a few, Collins took over as the Genesis frontman when more than three-hundred audition tapes yielded no suitable replacement for Peter Gabriel. Collins sang most of repertoire that Gabriel had sung, only without the costumes and masks. He was able to make the characters his own and the new material took on his own persona. Later, Collins developed into one of the world's premiere pop singers (with Genesis moving in that direction also) with his commercially successful career as a solo artist.

1976's A Trick of the Tail would be Genesis's ninth studio album. The band wanted to prove the critics wrong who said that they couldn't carry on without Peter Gabriel. Phil Collins eventually emerged as the new frontman and would continue to play drums on the studio recordings. Critics and fans were impressed with the new material with songs like "Dance On a Volcano," "Squonk," and "Robbery, Assault, and Battery." New producer David Hentschel achieved an improved sound quality to their previous albums. For the supporting tour, Collins decided to invite ex-Yes and King Crimson drummer Bill Bruford to join the band. On the instrumental passages, Collins continued to play drums and developed an exciting drumset duet with Bruford. A Trick of the Tail went to number three on the British charts and number thirty-one in America, helping Genesis accomplish more commercial success.

1976's Wind and Wuthering followed and would be Steve Hackett's last album before leaving to pursue a solo career. Although written and recorded without the post-Gabriel confusion, there was some internal friction as Hackett felt some of his material was rejected in favor of songs that Banks had written (Hackett did later cite the album as one of his favorites). Many believe that Wind and Wuthering was Genesis's most focused and highest-level recording. The band continued to evolve as their strong musicianship could be heard in precise and complex ensemble interplay. Banks contributed the songs "One for the Vine," "All in a Mouses's Night," and "Afterglow." Rutherford wrote the only single, "Your Own Special Way," which became a hit in Britain and America. Both A Trick of the Tail and Wind and Wuthering were certainly very progressive albums, yet they both planted the seeds of the future Genesis more commercial approach. On the supporting tour, drummer Chester Thompson (ex-Frank Zappa and Weather Report) was added to the lineup when Bruford left after the previous tour. The addition of Chester allowed Genesis to expand the popularization of the live double-drumset solo. In 1977, Genesis released a live double album, Seconds Out. It was during the mixing of this album that Hackett decided to leave.

And Then There Were Three was Genesis's appropriately titled 1978 album with now only Banks, Rutherford, and Collins remaining. This marked a new era for Genesis, as they became one of the biggest pop bands in the world selling millions of albums. Phil Collins simultaneously pursued a solo career, often with a similar sound to the 1980's Genesis. Genesis added guitarist Dar-

> "Aqualung was a difficult and very tense album to record…while I was playing the solo, Jimmy Page walked into the control room and started waving, I thought, should I wave back and mess up the solo or should I just grin and carry on? I just grinned."
>
> – Martin Barre

yl Stuermer for their tours and continued to employ drummer Chester Thompson. Extremely successful albums followed with; Duke in 1980, Abacab in 1981, Three Sides Live in 1982, Genesis in 1983, Invisible Touch in 1986, We Can't Dance in 1991, The Way We Walk: The Shorts in 1992 (live recording with pop material from the 1980's), and The Way We Walk: The Longs in 1993 (also live recording with more extended material). Phil Collins left Genesis in 1996 to focus exclusively on his solo career. Genesis made one more record, now with singer Ray Wilson. They released 1997's Calling All Stations and decided not to tour, thus ending their storied career.

Jethro Tull (1967-present) began in 1967 when drummer (later keyboardist) John Evan, bassist Jeffrey Hammond, guitarist Michael Stephens, and vocalist/flutist Ian Anderson formed the band The Blades. Ian Anderson began his music career by learning blues guitar but realized that he could stand out from other musicians when he switched to flute. He would study (by ear) classical pieces by J.S. Bach and the improvisational style of jazz artist Rahsaan Roland Kirk. Continuing to play their version of British blues, The Blades re-formed to become The Smash when Anderson's friend, blues guitarist Mick Abrahams joined the band along with bassist Glenn Cornick. The Smash booked gigs under many names, including The John Evan Blues Band. Their management stumbled on the name of a nineteenth-century agriculturalist and musician, Jethro Tull, who had invented the seed drill (it planted seeds in a row). To this day, many people mistakenly believe that Ian Anderson is Jethro Tull.

Jethro Tull would be complete with Anderson, Abrahams, Cornick, and a new drummer, Clive Bunker. The band's 1968 debut album, This Was, went to number ten on the British charts. It had modest success in America reaching number sixty-eight. This Was utilized blues and folk elements when both Anderson and Abrahams wrote separately for the band. Eventually, Abrahams wanted to pursue an exclusive blues-rock focus and left to join the successful band, Blodwyn Pig. Anderson wanted to move in a much more eclectic direction.

Soon after, guitarist Martin Barre joined the band. Anderson now wrote inventive compositions that included instruments such as the bouzouki and mandolin. He also listened to many styles and musical eras for inspiration. 1969's Stand Up, showed Anderson's jazz-inspired flute sound and his eccentric and musically powerful personality. Anderson now established full control of the band's music and lyrics. The Jethro Tull sound began to reveal an amalgamation of Renaissance and Baroque instrumental music combined with rhythm and blues and English/Scottish folk music. It blended well with the powerful blues-rock guitar style of Martin Barre. Stand Up quickly went to number one on the British charts and a single, "Living in the Past," (not on the record) went to number three.

Jethro Tull followed with their third album Benefit in 1970. John Evan returned to the band, this time on piano/keyboards adding new timbres to their increasingly denser sound. Benefit very skillfully combined folk, blues, jazz, and hard rock elements. It included the songs "Teacher," "Nothing to Say," and Andersons' increasing move away from the blues. 1970's Aqualung was their breakout album and all-time best selling record. At this time, Jeffrey Hammond rejoined the band on bass. With the song "Aqualung," Anderson was able to make a personal and political statement that successfully raised public consciousness about the subject of homelessness. Aqualung yielded two hit singles, "Hymn 43" and "Locomotive Breath." By this time, Ian Anderson had fully developed his stage presence, often displaying a fixed stare as he stood on one leg and wore a checkered coat, lace-up boots, elegant tights and frizzy hair. This persona was perfect for transforming into the aqualung character seen on the album cover. Aqualung was a heavy rock record but what came next drastically changed the direction of Jethro Tull.

Thick as a Brick saw a change in drummers as Barrimore Barlow joined the band (having played with Ian Anderson in The Blades). Barlow was a great fit for the increasingly difficult arrangements and complex odd time signatures that would become common for Jethro Tull's approach (John Bonham called Barlow the greatest rock drummer to ever come out of England). Thick as a Brick was Jethro Tull's first complete progressive rock album. Also, keyboardist and composer David Palmer became a full-time member and added skillful orchestral arrangements.

Groundbreaking album
Thick as a Brick
by Jethro Tull

1972's Thick as a Brick was Jethro Tull's defining progressive rock concept album. It contained a "tongue in cheek" story that was part Monthy Python humor and part cynical and sarcastic commentary about rock music's pretentiousness and its critics. The original album cover design replicated a local newspaper; The St. Cleve Chronicle. Ian Anderson, Jeffrey Hammond, and John Evan wrote the twelve-page newspaper. It took more time to write than the actual music for the album. The paper featured many inside jokes and puns, a review of the Thick as a Brick album, and much British humor, including an adult themed connect the dots children's activity.

The paper was complete with an award-winning epic poem (the album's entire lyrics) by the fictional child literary genius, the eight-year old Gerald Bostock. This storyline was set to music by a band (Jethro Tull, of course). The front page stated that due to the disturbing nature of the poem, Bostock was stripped of the award given to him by the Society for Literary Advancement and Gestation. The poem, and album lyrics, expressed Ian Anderson's views on young men coming of age in British society. Anderson commented about governmental manipulation and stated his opinion about organized religion.

Thick as a Brick was one continuous song in eight sections, taking up both sides of the recording and weighing in at forty-two minutes. The parts were: 1. Really Don't Mind/See There a Son is Born 2. The Poet and the Painter 3. What Do You Do When the Old Man's Gone?/From the Upper Class 4. You Curl Your Toes in Fun/Childhood Heroes/Stabs Instrumental 5. See There a Man is Born/Clear White Circles 6. Legends and Believe in the Day 7. Tales of Your Life 8. Childhood Heroes Reprise

Musically, Thick as a Brick was an incredible mixture of musical influences. Eastern European and Middle Eastern scales were combined with Celtic modes and set to Baroque, Medieval and Classical influenced themes. In addition, many odd meters, military marches, and symphonic orchestration combined with heavy rock guitar passages. Anderson layered flute, saxophone, trumpet, and violin in addition to his dense vocals. Ian Anderson was legendary for his demands on the band and rehearsed them endlessly for each recording and tour. It showed in how incredibly tight the ensemble passages sounded. Thick as a

---

Rock Hard Fact

For Jethro Tull's twenty-fifth anniversary tour, the band would select a member of the audience and seat them on a sofa onstage to watch the show.

Brick contained many recurring themes that made it a prime example of a progressive rock concept record. The album went to number one on the American charts and number five on the British charts. Thick as a Brick saw Jethro Tull at the top of their creative peak with Anderson, Barre, Hammond, Evan, Barlow, and David Palmer.

1973's A Passion Play was Jethro Tull's sixth studio recording. Another concept album, A Passion Play featured songs arranged into one continuous piece, split by two sides on the original vinyl. The theme of the record was the life of a man, Ronnie Pilgrim, and his spiritual journey in the afterlife. To support the album tour, Jethro Tull utilized three videos to enhance their live stage production. A Passion Play went to number one on the American charts but only number thirteen in England. Again, full of complex arrangements, a demanding storyline, and odd meters, Jethro Tull was pushing the boundaries of progressive rock musicianship. The album also received many negative reviews from critics who found it representative of the excesses and self-indulgence of progressive rock.

Jethro Tull followed up with War Child in 1974, Minstrel in the Gallery in 1975 and Too Old to Rock 'n' Roll: Too Young to Die! in 1976. Each was musically demanding and featured the complex arrangements of David Palmer. The band had a strong following but was beginning to sell less and less recordings. Their release of 1977's Songs From the Wood achieved a musical balance unlike previous recordings. Songs From the Wood fused traditional folk music with the counterpoint of the Renaissance composer Palestrina. It also combined Baroque and Renaissance dance tunes with strong drums and electric blues-rock guitar. This album worked as a virtual history of British popular music from the previous thousand years. The musical brilliance of Ian Anderson (armed again with a strong band) was a powerful force when combined with the sophisticated orchestrations and arrangements of David Palmer.

In 1978, Jethro Tull released Heavy Horses, another complex album. The punk movement was gaining momentum and this was not a good answer. Jethro Tull was losing popularity and they were being labeled as a folk-progressive band. Next, they released a double album, Bursting Out: Jethro Tull Live, a strong blend of previous material. It sold fairly well. A series of lineup changes ensued and Ian Anderson explored some new directions, both in a solo career and under the Jethro Tull name. 1987's Crest of a Knave won a Grammy, ironically for best heavy metal album. In 2012, Ian Anderson went on tour to perform Thick as a Brick and its sequel, which he credited to himself. Ian Anderson was modest when asked about his great musical ability. Anderson said, "I play only by ear: I don't read music…I don't have any formal musical training whatsoever. I learned from David Palmer some things that I couldn't quite put my finger on." #21

Yes (1968-present) is one of the most popular and lasting progressive bands in rock history. Bassist Chris Squire and vocalist Jon Anderson formed the band in 1968 after meeting in a club in London. They wrote some songs together and added drummer Bill Bruford, guitarist Peter Banks, and organist Tony Kaye to form the first lineup of Yes. Anderson and Squire were both influenced by The Beatles and Simon and Garfunkel while Bruford listened to jazz drummers Max Roach and Art Blakey. Peter Banks was self-taught and had played in Mabel Greer's Toyshop. All of the Yes musicians had been working in bands for roughly ten years, so they all were somewhat seasoned. Yes focused on finding a different approach by experimenting with three part harmonies and writing aggressive bass and guitar lines. Tony Kaye also explored the timbral limits of the Hammond B3 organ. The result was the creation of sophisticated harmonies and intricate arrangements, which they utilized to record and perform many covers and a few originals.

Yes's 1969 self-titled debut album, Yes, was released on Atlantic Records. It was in the psychedelic pop-rock vein featuring the songs "Beyond and Before," "Harold Lang," and a cover of the Byrds "I See You." This inspired them to develop their own progressive rock approach. Their second album, Time and a Word, was critically acclaimed but sold as poorly as their first album. Jon Anderson decided to incorporate an orchestra on Time and a Word. This element expanded Yes's sonic palette. Yes was also crafting their signature sound with the song, "Astral Traveller." However, the band moved to replace Peter Banks when they felt his improvisations weren't working within the musical context.

Yes took another step closer to their classic sound when guitarist Steve Howe was asked to join. Howe was very experienced having worked with The Syndicat, Bodast, The In Crowd, and others. Yes knew that their next record would be their last chance on Atlantic Records when they released The Yes Album in 1971. It sold much better and reached number seven on the British charts. Yes next toured America to build a fan base. The band now had an established sound, but still felt the need to pursue another direction. Progressive bands King Crimson, Emerson, Lake, and Palmer, and Jethro Tull had established their audiences and Yes was feeling the pressure to compete. They also battled Emerson, Lake, and Palmer for the services of engineer/producer Eddie Offord, who was working with both bands at the time (eventually Offord committed to Yes). The impact of Steve Howe was immediate. On "Yours Is No Disgrace," Howe played complex guitar lines with a twangy, yet metallic tone that became a big part of the Yes sound. Howe added a fingerpicking style of acoustic guitar technique that further helped to define the band. "Yours Is No Disgrace" featured sounds of the Moog synthesizer and Anderson's signature high-pitched vocals. On "Starship Trooper," the lyrics captured Anderson's fantasies about space travel and UFO imagery.

Yes was a band of composers and virtuoso soloists. The competition within the band for writing credits helped to push them to greatness. They were able to balance their egos and were encouraged to experiment with extended compositions. Yes was also developing musically by incorporating advanced recording techniques. Even though Tony Kaye used a Moog on The Yes Album, he was not driven (in a progressive rock mindset) to explore new technology. Tensions rose and Yes decided to replace Kaye (and his organ sound) with the flashy, cutting edge synthesizer player Rick Wakeman, who had played with David Bowie and The Strawbs. This completed the classic Yes lineup.

The 1971 album Fragile brought Yes to their mature sound with five individuals that drew from varied musical styles and influences. Yes had become one of progressive rocks' dominant groups. Fragile managed to produce a commercial hit with "Roundabout," that went to number thirteen on the American charts. "Roundabout" featured interwoven individual parts that managed to support the melody and Anderson's lyrics. Steve Howe said, "When I moved to acoustic guitars with Yes on 'Roundabout,' I proved to myself that I wasn't going to

Rock Hard Fact

Jon Anderson of Yes sang one song on the King Crimson 1991 album Lizard.

"'Close to the Edge' is the album where we first attempted to do the extra-long-form piece of music, having one song taking up the whole side of a piece of vinyl…we actually had played it from beginning to end before we recorded it in the studio."

– Chris Squire

be pinned down as a guitarist…I knew I wasn't going to be a blues guitarist and nothing else." #22 Fragile also showcased Rick Wakeman on a multi-keyboard excerpt that interpreted the third movement of Brahms's Symphony No. Four. Additionally, Chris Squire wrote and recorded a groundbreaking bass composition, "The Fish." Bruford and Anderson were also featured with individual musical passages.

Yes hired artist Roger Dean to do the cover illustrations for the Fragile album and many later albums. Dean also helped design the Yes logo for their live performances. Dean's cover art gave the band a visual branding; images that also helped to define progressive rock itself. Through Dean's artwork, Yes was able to visually define their complex storylines that were mythical and often about spiritual journeys of enlightenment.

For many, 1972's Close to the Edge was Yes's masterpiece. Close to the Edge was their fifth studio album and would be their last with Bill Bruford. It went to number three on the American charts and number four in England. Once the recording was completed, Bruford left the band to join King Crimson. He was soon replaced by drummer Alan White of The Plastic Ono Band. Shortly after, Yes went on their biggest world tour to date in 1972-73 to support the album.

Groundbreaking album
Close To The Edge
by Yes

Close to the Edge was based on German author Hermann Hesse's book *Siddhartha*. It's about a spiritual awakening of the main character in his development toward becoming the supreme Buddha and founder of Buddhism. Close to the Edge consisted of only three tracks: "Close to the Edge" on side one and "And You and I" and "Siberian Khatru" on side two. The recording sessions, led by producer and sound engineer Eddie Offord, took many grueling twelve-hour days, which proved very frustrating for drummer Bill Bruford. Disagreements about the direction of the album, including sound mixing and other production issues, were evident in the growing tension between band members. Offord explained that "from Bill's point of view, (the music was) over overdubbed and had too much going on that you lost the original basis of the band." #23 Nevertheless, the result was a landmark recording for progressive rock music.

"And You and I" originated as a folk-oriented song that Anderson developed with Howe. Anderson has described that the song was similar to a hymn. "Siberian Khatru" featured complex time signatures and was divided into multiple sections, alternating between vocal and instrumental passages. The song began with an introductory guitar riff, followed by the main instrumental keyboard theme. The main theme was phrased using mixed meters consisting of three measures of 4/4 followed by a 3/4 measure. The song progressed through various sections with solos by Howe and Wakeman. A polymetric section followed, featuring Howe playing in 12/8 while the bass and drums overlapped a pattern in 4/4. This created a sense of rhythmic tension and interest.

The composition "Close to the Edge" weighed in at almost nineteen minutes and followed the general format of classical sonata form, which is in three-parts consisting of an exposition, a development, and a recapitulation. The music and lyrics were credited to Jon Anderson and Steve Howe. It's in four movements that described different stages of a spiritual quest: I. "The Solid Time of Change" II. "Total Mass Retain" III. "I Get Up, I Get Down" IV. "Seasons of Man." The lyrical content of Close to the Edge focused on surrealistic imagery and a stream-of-consciousness flow.

The movement "The Solid Time of Change" revealed that the singer, the story's protagonist, was spiritually broken and sought a greater spiritual awakening. The subsequent movements musically and lyrically described his spiritual journey. The lyrics worked through an entry into a ritual world and then an encounter with new realities. The protagonist assimilated those realities where a return to the "normal world" ensued with new perceptions and identities (all pretty deep stuff). The final movement began with a massive instrumental crescendo heard on Wakeman's pipe organ and Moog synthesizer.

"Close to the Edge" set a new standard for how a progressive rock composition could begin and end in different keys. It contained more than one tonal center and explored advanced harmonic structures. Yes was now at their creative peak.

In 1973, Yes released the double album Tales from Topographic Oceans. It went to number one in Britain and number six in America. The album broke musical barriers in many ways and Yes worked on it for months, seven days a week. It was a concept album based on Jon Anderson's ideas and dreams about the four bodies of Hindu texts, known as the Shastras. Tales from Topographic Oceans featured four long tracks, each between eighteen and twenty-two minutes. Anderson wrote the lyrics with Howe while the music was credited to the whole band. The album received mixed critical reaction while one negative response claimed that listeners were disinterested in the lengthy songs and detailed storylines. Rick Wakeman believed that the band was moving in a jazz-rock direction and left after the Topographic tour. He was replaced by keyboardist Patrick Moraz.

Yes's seventh studio album Relayer was released in 1974. It went to number four on the British charts and number five in America. The band had moved into a jazz-fusion direction, especially with the influence of Patrick Moraz. Yes's sound became more adventurous and musically daring. This kept Yes at the forefront of cutting edge progressive rock. Again, long compositions were the format while side one consisted of "The Gates of Delirium" and side two featured "Sound Chaser" and "To Be the One." Even though Rick Wakeman left, he had already made a name for himself with his successful all-instrumental concept record, The Six Wives of Henry VIII.

After Relayer, some members of Yes recorded solo albums. When Yes decided to begin work on a new record, they fired Moraz because he wanted to go too far in a jazz direction. This set the stage for Wakeman's return on 1977's Going for the One. It did very well at number one in Britain and placed in the top ten in America. But, punk was gaining popularity and Yes began to lose ground, seen in the mixed results of their 1978 release, Tormato. Jon Anderson and Wakemen soon left and were replaced by Trevor Horn and Geoff Downes from the pop group, The Buggles. The 1980 album Drama saw Trevor Horn sing lead vocals. However, Yes temporarily disbanded in 1981. For 1983's 90125, singer Jon Anderson returned to join Squire and White. Yes would have a top ten hit on the American charts with "Owner of a Lonely Heart," that moved the band consistently in a more pop direction. Yes added guitarist/keyboardist Trevor Rabin

---

Rock Hard Fact

Before Jon Anderson rejoined Yes for the recording of 90125, Chris Squire, Alan White, Tony Kaye, and newcomer Trevor Rabin had formed a new group called Cinema. This lineup was also known by Yes fans as Yes West, due to their time spent recording in Los Angeles, California.

"Pete Townsend for me was a huge influence. Because essentially they were a three-piece band and the way he structured his chords and took up a lot of space musically in the songs was really important to the way Rush developed."

– Alex Lifeson

and they brought back original keyboardist, Tony Kaye. The band continued to move in a more pop-oriented direction for the next few albums. More lineup changes ensued.

In the early 1990's, Yes began to return to their progressive roots. 1994's Talk featured a three-part epic song titled "Endless Dream," that really brought Yes back to their original progressive form. Despite continued lineup changes involving old and new members, later Yes albums have generally fallen into the progressive category with longer songs and more technical compositions. The 2001 album Magnification, featured a full symphonic work. The Yes catalogue totals twenty-studio albums and many live recordings. Their legacy places them among one of progressive rock's greatest and most experimental bands. Yes was inducted into the Rock and Roll Hall of Fame in 2017.

Discussion Question

Music critics for the most part hated progressive rock. Do some research to find out why. Were at least some of the criticisms by rock music journalists valid? Explain and give specific examples.

Rush (1968-present) formed in 1968 when guitarist Alex Lifeson met bassist/vocalist/keyboardist Geddy Lee and drummer John Rutsey. Inspired by Cream, Led Zeppelin, and The Jimi Hendrix Experience, Rush was manufactured in the "power trio" mold. The band spent their first five years playing blues-rock covers and a few originals in the bar scene in Toronto, Canada. With no early interest from any major record labels, Rush recorded and released their self-titled debut album Rush in 1974. A single from the album, "Working Man," received local radio airplay and Rush was signed to Mercury Records. Before recording their second album, Rutsey left the band and Neil Peart auditioned and won the drumset chair.

1975's Fly by Night saw the band move in a progressive rock direction. It was decided that Lifeson and Lee would do the songwriting. Peart would handle the lyrics, a good move considering that he was a writer and an avid reader of science fiction. Fly By Night featured the tune "Anthem." It demonstrated the band's ability to move easily from 4/4 to 7/8 passages that would become a trademark for Rush. 1975's Caress of Steel saw Rush moving to longer compositions and lyrics about sword and sorcery images. The new punk era was ending the careers of many progressive rock bands, but Rush was able to survive. The Rush sound was powerful with Lifeson's guitar distortion and shredding solos combined with heavy metal power, all displayed with a progressive rock sensibility. Rush released a more commercial album, 1976's 2112. It helped to build a wider audience. It also sparked the genre of progressive metal (see chapter ten). 1977's A Farewell to Kings yielded the Rush classics "Closer to the Heart," and "Xanadu." A strong progressive record on many levels, A Farewell to Kings gave Rush the balance of commercial success while maintaining their musical sense of adventure. 1978's Hemispheres was their most ambitious work to date, yielding even more popular appeal. On this album, the complex composition "Cygnus X-1" took an entire album side and challenged the listener both musically and lyrically. Hemispheres was so complex that it literally exhausted Rush.

The 1980's were a decade of change for Rush. Most progressive rock bands were either finished or focused on surviving in a world dominated by FM rock radio. Rush managed to create strong progressive material and achieve more commercial success. 1980's Permanent Waves featured the hits "The Spirit of Radio" and "Freewill." The band felt they needed to get back to a more focused songwriting format, a process that yielded the success of Permanent Waves. This would be a transition period for Rush, still very progressive but now moving in a somewhat more "radio friendly" direction.

"The Spirit of Radio"
by Geddy Lee, Neil Peart, and Alex Lifeson

"The Spirit of Radio" was a hit for Rush when it went to number thirteen on the British charts and number fifty-one on the American charts. The song was a statement of how the band thought radio was moving to a more rigid format and away from a time when the radio provided a free forum for music. Neil Peart wrote lyrics for "The Spirit of Radio" that parodied the Simon and Garfunkel lyrics from their classic "The Sound of Silence." The original line from Simon and Garfunkel's classic was "For the words of the prophets were written on the subway walls, and tenement halls…and echo with the sound of silence." Peart's version was "For the words of the prophets are written on the studio wall, and concert halls…and echo with the sound…of salesman."

Musically, Lifeson wanted the opening guitar riff to support the lyrics and give it a sense of radio waves bouncing around. Lifeson displayed his formidable guitar chops while his guitar lines filled a lot of space, making Rush sound much fuller than most power trios. In a section inspired by the band The Police, Rush moved to a light reggae feel that provided a nice contrast to the heavy and aggressive feel of the tune. When the song returned to the main riff, the band imitated the sound of turning the dial of an analog radio, where one can briefly hear multiple stations at once for a moment before fully tuning into a station. There is also a strong sequencer part under the guitar riff that built another layer of the collective band sound. Played live, Rush would use Moog Taurus pedals that allowed Lee and Lifeson to play synthesizer parts with a tap of the foot while continuing to play either guitar or bass. Rush often-performed "The Spirit of Radio" to open their live shows.

1981's Moving Pictures became Rush's most popular album, reaching number four on the U.S. charts. It featured the hits "Tom Sawyer," "YYZ," and "Fly By Night." "Tom Sawyer" was an example of Rush's move to synth parts mixed with Lifeson's metal guitar riffs. The whole middle synthesizer part in 7/8 time started out as one of Geddy's sound check keyboard riffs during the Permanent Waves tour. Geddy Lee's distinctly high vocal sonorities further defined the Rush sound. Also, as recording technology kept improving, Rush was able to take advantage of increased multi-tracking, having access to forty-eight tracks (using ten tracks for the drums alone). All of a sudden, Rush was everywhere, on the radio and MTV, when Moving Pictures went to number three on the British charts and sold almost seven million copies.

Rock Hard Fact

Neil Peart is more than just a drummer and Rush's primary lyricist. He is also an author with six books to his credit that have chronicled his travels as a touring musician and motorcyclist.

"YYZ"
by Geddy Lee and Neil Peart

"YYZ" was first released on Moving Pictures and then shortly after on the live Rush album Exit…Stage Left. "YYZ" became one of Rush's signature instrumental compositions and a showcase for Neil Peart's exciting live drum solos. YYZ is literally the IATA airport transmitter identification code for the Toronto Pearson International Airport, where the members of Rush live nearby. Every airport is assigned a specific three-letter code, and that code is transmitted so pilots can tell where they are and verify that their navigational radios are properly tuned. A VHF system at the airport broadcasts the YYZ identifier code in Morse code. Neil Peart heard the rhythms of the code and in the songs' introduction, Rush played in the meter of 10/8, repeatedly *replicating* Y-Y-Z in Morse Code in their musical arrangement.

"YYZ" was a tour de force that was considered one of progressive rock's première instrumental adventures. Alex Lifeson developed an intricate guitar part that featured bizarre-sounding harmonics heard before his solo. He achieved the sound by playing off of a pick and placing his thumb on the guitar string. By holding the pick so that his thumb could mute the string, it allowed the harmonic to ring. The crashing noise heard between the breaks of the guitar solo was the sound of wind chimes tied to a 2X4 (piece of wood) that was slapped against a wood table. On "YYZ," Geddy Lee recorded one of the defining bass parts in progressive rock history. In 1982, "YYZ" was nominated (and lost to The Police's "Behind my Camel") for a Grammy Award for Best Rock Instrumental.

Signals was released in 1982 and some fans were confused by Rush's shift to a more keyboard dominated sound. Despite the move to more keyboards, the song "Subdivisions" and "New World Man" were hits and the popularity of Signals keep Rush selling albums. 1984's Grace Under Pressure, 1985's Power Windows, and the (slightly) less popular 1987 release, Hold Your Fire, extended the band's popularity. Even though Rush continued to produce hits, Alex Lifeson was becoming uncomfortable with the band's direction and sound. Lifeson eventually influenced his bandmates to turn back to a heavier, guitar trio-oriented approach. More albums followed in the late 1980's and early 1990's.

Neil Peart is a great drummer of extreme precision. Peart has worked out his drumset time feels, fills, and solos in great detail. Longtime Rush producer Terry Brown in describing Peart's great work ethic and attention to detail said, "he would continue to prepare himself in the studio for hours on a fill that was giving him a particularly hard time. He would work on that fill and play a verse and a chorus going into a fill and keep going over the sections of material constantly until he was totally comfortable with it." #24 Peart has added numerous percussion parts to many Rush compositions, especially orchestra bell parts, which he incorporated live on a mallet kat. Neil is also the band's main lyricist, which has connected him intimately to the bands' overall musical philosophy. Peart is an avid reader (sometimes reading three books a day). This has served to inform his lyric writing and he has become an author of various books of his own in the past decade. Providing the lyrics for Rush has also taught Peart to phrase his drumset parts to simultaneously *connect the words to the music.*

In the 1990's America saw an explosion of indie, alternative, and grunge bands. Rush never forgot that *they were* once an indie band having recorded on their own independent label Moon Records, before Mercury signed them. Motivated by the grunge energy, Rush released Counterparts in 1993 and received FM radio play alongside alternative and grunge bands with songs like "Cold Fire," and "Stick It Out." Rush was now reinvigorated and their approach was appreciated by many rock bands of the 1990's. After a tour following their 1996 Test for Echo album, Rush went on a five-year hiatus when Neil Peart suffered personal tragedies when both his wife and daughter died.

Rush returned with 2002's Vapor Trails, Feedback in 2004, Snakes and Arrows in 2007, and Clockwork Angels in 2012. Rush has always been a powerful and exciting live act. Over their storied career, Rush has also released a number of live albums including 1976's All The World's a Stage, 1981's Exit…Stage Left, and 2011's Time Machine, and more.

Rush has retired from touring recently. Peart was the one to call it quits but Lifeson and Lee have agreed to an extended hiatus with no real answer to their fate as yet. Geddy Lee reflected on the Rush legacy when he stated, "Some people say we never left progressive rock, and some people lament the fact that we don't write any more twenty-minute songs…it's hard to look backward, but if we find ourselves at a point where we think it is appropriate to do a twenty-minute song again, I certainly wouldn't discount it." #25 The legacy of Rush looms large as they continued to evolve throughout the 1970's to the new millennium by incorporating blues-based rock, earlier progressive rock elements, new wave, reggae, and pop-rock. They were innovative with their extensive use of synthesizers, sequencers, and electronic percussion combined with irregular and shifting time signatures. Rush created a vast repertoire utilizing fantasy and science fiction-themed lyrics, earning them the status of one of progressive rock's greatest bands. Rush provided a progressive rock bridge from the Genesis, Yes, and Jethro Tull era to the third wave of the progressive rock genre. Rush was inducted into the Rock and Roll Hall of Fame in 2013.

The Third Wave of Progressive Rock Bands

The early 1980's saw three trends in the progression of progressive rock. First, the movement as a whole fell into rapid decline while many of the major progressive bands labored to continue or revive their earlier careers. Second, King Crimson launched a post-progressive approach, with their 1981 release Discipline. This introduced a new movement that included ethnic music and minimalism in their compositions and performances. Third, a neo-progressive movement gained traction as younger progressive bands, such as Marillion, began to build on the past. Kansas and Styx both started as progressive rock bands but moved into more commercial material (see chapter eleven). Some of the neo-progressive bands utilized many of the compositional approaches and musical devices first introduced by the progressive bands of the late 1960's and 1970's. Neo-progressive bands such as **Marillion, Dream Theater,** and **Porcupine Tree** began to incorporate the styles of heavy metal and hard rock, punk, and even funk.

Rock Hard Fact

Dream Theater began when John Petrucci, John Myung and Mike Portnoy began covering Rush and Iron Maiden songs in the rehearsal rooms at Berklee College of Music.

Marillion (1979-present) was founded by drummer Mick Pointer and bassist Doug Irving. The band was first called Silmarillion, named after the J.R.R. Tolkien novel of the same name. Soon the band changed its name to Marillion and was completed with the addition of guitarist Steve Rothery and keyboardist Brian Jelliman. In 1981, bassist Diz Minnitt replaced Irving and vocalist Derek William Dick (aka Fish) became the outspoken leader of the band. More lineup changes followed with Mark Kelly replacing Jelliman on keyboards while Pete Trewavas replaced Minnitt on bass.

Marillion drew comparisons to Genesis with their use of odd meters, extended songs, and the Peter Gabriel-like (or even Phil Collins) vocals of Fish. The band released their first album, Script for a Jester's Tear, in 1983 and Fugazi in 1984. They achieved considerable commercial success, which was difficult to do in the era of Duran Duran and Boy George. Drummer Ian Mosley replaced Mick Pointer in 1984 and Marillion released 1985's Misplaced Childhood. This album yielded the hits "Lavender," and "Kayleigh," both of which featured infectious melodies. "Kayleigh" was in heavy rotation in America on MTV. Misplaced Childhood reached number forty-seven on the American charts and went to number one in England, quite a feat for a progressive based band. It was regarded as one of the most popular concept records in the genre and has influenced many bands to compose concept albums in a similar fashion.

Fish's vision for their next album was not shared by the rest of the band. He was also having difficulty with Marillion's demanding tour schedule and soon left. With the future of Marillion in question, the band found a strong replacement in vocalist Steve Hogarth. The first post-Fish album, 1989's Seasons End, yielded three hit singles and a successful transition into Hogarth's vocal style and strong songwriting ability. Hogarth was a good fit for the band's musical identity. However, in the mid-1990's, Marillion struggled to maintain their following and was dropped by their longtime label, EMI. Meanwhile, Fish went on to have a successful solo career.

In 1996, Marillion made new and innovative connections with its fans by becoming one of the first bands to build an audience through the use of the Internet. This approach worked well for their 1999 album that they aptly titled Marillion.com. Since that time, Marillion has functioned as one of the first completely independent bands to issue studio and live albums on their own label. They have also effectively self-promoted and self-managed themselves by raising funds from their internet audience to pay for recording costs. Marillion played a significant role in the next evolution of progressive rock. Their musical experimentation fused world music influences, complex arrangements, and diverse instrumentation.

Dream Theater (1985-present) formed in 1985 when guitarist John Petrucci, drummer Mike Portnoy, and bassist John Myung met at the Berklee College of Music and began to play under the name Majesty. Soon, they changed their name to Dream Theater and added vocalist Charlie Dominici. Dream Theater's 1989 debut album, When Dream and Day Unite, was met with little fanfare. Their lineup changed when they added vocalist/songwriter James LaBrie. Keyboardist Kevin Moore played on the first three albums and Derek Sherenian played on their fourth album, Falling into Infinity. Keyboardist Jordan Rudess joined Dream Theater for their next recording, Scenes From a Memory, and then became a permanent member on the band's later recordings.

Dream Theater is one of the most accomplished progressive metal bands and has sold over twelve million records worldwide. Known for their instrumental virtuosity, they combined the influence of Yes and Rush with heavy metal bands such as Judas Priest and Iron Maiden. Mix speed metal influences, distorted guitar, and some attention to melodic writing (with the influences of Journey, Metallica, and Peter Gabriel), and you get Dream Theater. Their most successful record commercially was 1992's Images and Words, which peaked at number sixty-one on the American charts. Another important Dream Theater album was Scenes From a Memory, a story-oriented concept album.

In 2011, Dream Theater released their eleventh studio album, A Dramatic Turn of Events, after drummer Mick Portnoy had left the band. After auditioning some very talented drummers, Mike Mangini emerged and played on A Dramatic Turn of Events. For the album, the band underwent some musical changes and moved to lyrical themes that focused on historical events. In 2013, Dream Theater was nominated for a Grammy Award in the Best Hard Rock/Metal performance category for their single "On the Backs of Angels." Their 2013 self-titled twelfth studio album was also nominated for a Grammy with a single titled "The Enemy Inside."

Porcupine Tree (1987-2010) was a neo-progressive rock band from England formed by guitarist/vocalist/songwriter Steve Wilson in 1987. Porcupine Tree started as a solo project for Wilson and he added keyboardist Richard Barbieri, bassist Colin Dewin, and drummer Chris Maitland. In 2001, drummer Gavin Harrison replaced Maitland. Porcupine Tree has progressive sensibilities with elements of experimental and ambient soundscapes. Wilson's experience as a producer and studio technician included extensive work with King Crimson, Yes, Jethro Tull, Roxy Music, and Tears for Fears. This provided Porcupine Tree with a unique musical perspective. Porcupine Tree has released ten studio albums, from their 1992 debut On the Sunday of Life, to their last album, 2009's The Incident Over the years, Steve Wilson has disliked the notion that Porcupine Tree was labeled a progressive rock band. He now sees the term in a broader sense and wants the band to be viewed as its own entity, void of comparison to other bands of any genre.

The resurgence of progressive rock in the late 1990's and 2000's was built on a number of divergent forces. This included a healthy progressive rock festival circuit, the growth of independent record labels, and the widespread use of the Internet that provided worldwide exposure to many up and coming artists. Another factor was the musicians themselves, many of whom were inspired by the great progressive bands of the past. Some bands showed elements of "progressivity," from the electronic experimentation of Radiohead and Pink Floyd to the half-hour jams of bands like **Mars Volta**. Many other bands such as **Tool, Big Big Train, Spock's Beard, Symphony X** (1994-2017), **The Flower Kings** (1994-present), **Coheed and Cambria** (1995-present), and **The Dillinger Escape Plan** fused rock and metal with other diverse musical styles to create new strains of progressive rock.

Tool (1990-present) formed in 2009 in Los Angeles, California. Tool's lineup includes vocalist Maynard James Keenan, guitarist Adam Jones, bassist Justine Chancellor, and drummer Danny Carey. Tool's 1993 debut album Undertow, effectively mixed heavy metal with a progressive rock approach. Their sound incorporated elements of art rock and added the influence of works of art into their live performances, music videos, and

"In 1977 my brother came home with Genesis's Selling England By the Pound. He'd play it extremely loud...I was 12 and the minute I heard it-it hit home as something unusual and beautiful, I've never forgotten that."

- Greg Spawton

album covers. Undertow spawned the Tool song "Sober," which gained the band a lot of attention. Undertow also contained the single "Prison Sex," a song that sparked controversy over its graphic and potentially offensive nature, as Tool became the target of censorship issues. The video for the song was removed from MTV rotation due to its symbolism depicting the subject of child abuse. Other Tool albums followed with 1996's popular release AEnima, 2001's Lateralus and 2006's 10,000 Days. Tool's style is cerebral with the use of many complex time signatures and polyrhythms. They embody musical contradictions by pivoting from a melodic approach to an abrasive sound. Tool continues to perform and tour today and are known for their unorthodox stage shows and video displays. Their 10,000 Days album won a Grammy for Best Recording Package in 2006.

Big Big Train (1990-present) is a British progressive rock band that formed in Bournemouth, England in 1990. The current lineup is guitarist Dave Gregory, violinist/vocalist Rachel Hall, vocalist/multi-instrumentalist David Longdon, keyboardist/bassist Danny Manners, drummer Nick D'Virgilio, keyboardist/guitarist Rikard Sjoblom, guitarist/bassist/keyboardist Gregory Spawton, and guitarist/bassist/keyboardist Andy Poole. From their inception until 2009, Big Big Train was primarily a studio project band led by Poole and Spawton with numerous interchangeable lineups and guest musicians. Poole and Spawton were first inspired by progressive bands Genesis and Van der Graaf Generator.

Big Big Train's 1994 debut album Goodbye to the Age of Steam featured intelligent and melodic progressive elements. 1997's English Boy Wonders received little acclaim and minimal record company support. Big Big Train's future was in question. After three years where Poole and Spawton remained the creative core, the band recorded 2002's Bard. 2004's Gathering Speed, did just that, and built a fan base and moved the band in a strong progressive rock direction. 2007's The Difference Machine brought some important guest appearances from future full-time members drummer Nick D'Virgilio and bassist Dave Meros (both from Spock's Beard). Big Big Train released The Underfall Yard in 2009, their sixth studio recording.

The decade of 2010 saw Big Big Train reach new heights in the progressive genre. In the fall of 2012, the band released the first part of a double album, English Electric Part One. The second part, English Electric Part Two, was released in the spring of 2013. This earned the band the accolade of the breakthrough award at the 2013 Progressive Music Awards.

"The First Rebreather"
by Greg Spawton

"The First Rebreather," from English Electric Part One, was a showcase for many of the musical attributes that made Big Big Train one of the leading progressive bands in the 2000's. David Longdon achieved a vocal sound that was reminiscent of Phil Collins and Peter Gabriel's strong vocal harmonizations. "The First Rebreather" literally explored an orchestra full of sonic timbres. With the help of seventeen guest musicians, Big Big Train experimented with dozens of instrumental timbres and combinations including; violins, viola, cello, cornet, trumpet, trombone, tuba, recorders, banjo, accordion, melodica, mandolin, flute, vibes, Mellotron, Moog and standard rock instruments.

"The First Rebreather" began by recalling the Genesis (the band) pastoral acoustic sound of acoustic guitar and flute. When the song gathered momentum, the meter shifted back and forth from 7/8 to 4/4 followed by a gentle acoustic interlude. The track paused, propelled by a string passage, and led into a clean melodic guitar solo. Longdon's powerful vocals were followed by an emotional instrumental adventure (featuring a very old school Mellotron solo section) that brought the track to a climax. "The First Rebreather" highlighted the band's capability of constructing an extended story both lyrically and musically.

Big Big Train released 2016's Folklore and then Grimspound and The Second Brightest Star in 2017. These albums continued to show the band's ability to take listeners on extended trips, exploring fantasy worlds and landscapes. It is impossible not to connect attributes of Big Big Train to the early and mature era progressive approach of Genesis. However, Big Big Train does extend modern progressive rock. They developed a sophisticated approach by composing unique melodies, endless instrumental combinations, extended storylines, and a passion for musical adventure.

Spock's Beard (1992-present) is an American progressive rock band that formed in Los Angeles, California in 1992. Two brothers, vocalist/keyboardist Neal Morse and vocalist/guitarist Alan Morse, joined forces with bassist John Ballard (eventually replaced by bassist Dave Meros) and drummer Nick D'Virgilio to create the first version of the band. Spock's Beard draws from the great progressive traditions of Yes, Genesis, and Gentle Giant. Their approach also displays a pop sensibility with intricate, multi-part vocal harmonies. The band took their name from an episode of the TV series *Star Trek*. In the episode titled "Mirror, Mirror," Mr. Spock sports a beard when he's in a parallel universe.

The Morse brothers were greatly inspired after seeing and hearings a performance by the band Yes in 1972. Neal Morse recalled, "It was the Fragile tour, and I'm not exaggerating when I say that it changed my life. Yes had this magic." #26 Alan Morse was at the same show and said "I saw Steve Howe with a pedal steel and knew it wasn't exactly country music, but that rock music could have this whole other sonic palette. That was an event that opened up a whole lot of things." #27 In 1995, Spock's Beard released their debut album, The Light. The eight-part title track is considered to be their signature song. 1996's Beware of Darkness saw the addition of keyboardist Ryo Okumoto to the group. The title track was a cover of George Harrison's song, "Beware of Darkness." Momentum gradually built, especially in Europe, where the band played in many venues.

"The Light"
by Neal Morse and Alan Morse

After Spock's Beard performed the music from The Light at 1995's San Francisco Progfest, their career began to gain traction. Thomas Waber, of the InsideOut record label, signed them to a deal and The Light was released in Europe. The thing people quickly noticed about Spock's Beard was their long and intricate arrangements that also contained catchy pop melodies. The songwriting was highly evolved, even at this early juncture of their career.

Spock's Beard displayed a mixture of many styles on "The Light" including; flamenco guitar, European art songs, jazz ballads, and classical piano excerpts. Their precise and intricate ensemble passages sound equal parts Yes, Genesis, King Crimson, and of course, them-

> "I'm not really interested in music. Music is just a means of creating a magical state."
>
> – Robert Fripp

selves. Alan Morse achieved a very pure guitar sound reminiscent of Steve Hackett of Genesis. After a vocal and piano introduction, "The Light" quickly went on a musical journey complete with a blistering rock guitar solo in an adventurous and syncopated ensemble passage.

1998's The Kindness of Strangers and 1999's Day for Night built an even stronger fan base. 2000's V featured the band's longest composition to date, the twenty-seven minute Neal Morse composition "The Great Nothing." 2002's Snow was the last for Neal Morse, who left immediately after the release of the album. Drummer Nick D'Virgilio moved into the lead singer spot and drummer Jimmy Keegan was hired for live performances. In 2011, Nick D'Virgilio left the band and later joined the progressive band Big Big Train. Spock's Beard released six more studio albums, including 2015's The Oblivion Particle. As of March 2017, Nick D'Virgilio agreed to play on Spock's Beard's upcoming thirteenth album. Now a devout born-again Christian, Neal Morse has gone on to have a very successful solo career in the progressive music world. Morse's solo material has gone on to shape the subgenre of **Christian progressive rock** with efforts like 2003's Testimony. Spock's Beard is a prime example of a new generation of talented musicians that continued to explore the possibilities of the progressive rock genre. It is clear that Spock's Beard listened to the past masters of progressive rock and in the process, found their own unique voice.

The Dillinger Escape Plan (1997-present) is an American progressive metal band from Morris Plains, New Jersey that formed in 1997. The band's current lineup is guitarist/programmer Ben Weinman, vocalist/guitarist Greg Puciato, bassist Liam Wilson, drummer Billy Rymer, and guitarist Kevin Antreassian. They are considered to be pioneers of **mathcore**, a dissonant mixture of heavy metal, hardcore punk, and math rock that utilizes complex time signatures and rhythmic experimentation. Dillinger features dissonant guitar lines and a willingness to explore avant-garde musical concepts.

Dillinger's 1999 debut album Calculating Infinity, was a tour de force of unpredictable shifts of tempos and unusual song structures. Dillinger prided itself on breaking many musical rules including harmonizing a melody with intervals of seconds and adding episodes of white noise. Calculating Infinity sounded angry with its ultra-aggressive and extremely technical approach. The intricate drumset parts were played by original drummer Chris Pennie. In 2002, Dillinger Escape Plan released an EP with guest vocalist Mike Patton. 2004's Miss Machine was more accessible due to less musical complexity and the use of slower tempos, increased use of vocals, and simpler song structures. 2007's Ire Works was recorded with new drummer Gil Sharone when Chris Pennie left the band.

In 2009, Billy Rymer became the new permanent drummer after Sharone exited (to join Marilyn Manson). Dillinger raised their international profile when they joined Nine Inch Nails onstage at the Soundwave festival in Australia. The Dillinger Escape Plan went on to release 2010's Option Paralysis, 2013's One of Us Is the Killer, and 2016's Dissociation. The Dillinger Escape Plan legacy is that of a progressive metal band that created intense, hardcore punk and metal compositions. They also drew from the progressive approach of precision musicianship with meticulously worked-out rhythms and song structures.

Mars Volta (2000-2014) was a progressive band drawing from a wide variety of musical influences. They were inspired by King Crimson, Led Zeppelin, world music icon Fela Kuti, and the heavy punk energy of Black Flag. Mars Volta had many band members over their career but the last lineup included; vocalist Cedric Bixler-Zavala, bassist Juan Alderee, keyboardist Marcel Rodriquez-Lopez, and drummer Deantoni Parks. The band's name came from a Federico Fellini book about his films (a new movie scene was referred to as a *Volta*) and the Mars part came from Bixler-Zavala's interest in science fiction. Their albums included 2003's De-Loused in the Comatorium and 2008's The Bedlam in Goliath. Most of the band's music was composed by Rodriguez-Lopez while the lyrics and vocal melodies were written by Bixler-Zavala. In 2009, Mars Volta won a Grammy Award in the best hard rock performance category for the song "Wax Simulacra."

At its core, progressive rock as a genre challenged both the listener and the musician to extend the boundaries for musical expression. The genre embraced many musical influences never heard before in rock music. The real goal of the progressive movement was to expand the possibilities for rock through the use of more complex musical components and to conceptually explore new worlds of lyrical expression. To that end, progressive rock got it done.

Discussion Question

In the past thirty years, a lot of innovation has occurred in the music world that wasn't present at the time of the early classic progressive rock bands of the 1970's. Did the compositional direction of progressive rock bands like Marillion and Spock's Beard benefit from these musical developments? Take a position and give specific musical examples.

> "Prog didn't really go away. Just took a catnap in the late Seventies. A new generation of fans discovered it, and a whole new array of bands and solo artists took it into the new millennium."
>
> – Ian Anderson

Part Three
Rock Gets Angry and Evolves

Chapter Fourteen: Punk Rock and New Wave

The Punk Rock Movement

The **punk rock** movement was an exception to rock music's predictable mainstream actions and politics. The exact time frame and birthplace of punk rock is debatable. It began in the late 1960's to early 1970's in New York City and in the early to mid-1970's in London. The New York scene had the biggest impact on punk's musical style while the British scene provided more of the fashion, political, and sociological attitudes. Some music historians felt that the punk movement was over by 1980, while others (including us) believe it is alive and well, even today.

The punk rock movement consisted mainly of underprivileged working class white youths that felt anger, frustration, and alienation over their poor social and financial conditions. Unemployment and poor social conditions affected American, British, and other European youth leading to expression through a new music medium. Life, as punk rockers saw it, was meaningless and hopeless as they expressed rage at society and anyone who conformed to the system. Punks questioned conformity not only by sounding and looking different, but also by questioning the prevailing modes of thought. Punks came to question things other people in mainstream society took for granted such as norms involving work, race, sex, and the overall quality of life. Punks lost respect for authority in general. By acting as anti-authoritarian nonconformists, punks were not treated well by those people whose commands to conform they rejected. Authorities usually reacted to punks with distain and further alienated anyone connected to the movement. American and British societies viewed punks as rebels, deviants, and trouble-makers by their defiance to the status quo.

Young people are traditionally known to go through a phase of rebellion that manifests itself against parents, school, and authority in general. Young girls were warned not to watch or listen to Elvis. Punk has been incorrectly labeled as one of those phases where the rebellious teen tried to show that he or she was different from their peers. Yes, punk was designed to be shocking to the mainstream public, but it wasn't an appearance-oriented movement. What it was, was an effort to consciously become one's own self. Many committed punks, achieving the realization of their own non-conformity, came to the realization that society was not set up to accommodate a civilization of individuals.

Early punks utilized many of the same revolutionary tactics employed by members of avant-garde art movements. Punk bands demonstrated this through the utilization of unusual fashion, intentional provocation of their audiences, the use of untrained amateur performers, and a drastic reorganization of accepted performance styles and practices. The punk dress code was about creating shock. Punks took their message to the streets wearing outrageous clothes, piercings, and makeup (especially the punks of Kings Road in London). The punk policy of provocation saw actions that included performers spitting at the audience (while they spat back) and performers displaying wounds that were the result of self-mutilation.

Punk sparked a DIY (do it yourself) movement. It's helpful to compare punk rock to the big business world. Rock fans don't run the music business. Businessmen run the music business. Early punk was never regulated or allowed itself to be manipulated by commercial managers, agents, producers, or stockholders. If musicians went into punk to make lots of money, they eventually came away poor.

> "I don't think punk ever really dies, because punk rock attitude can never die."
>
> – Billy Idol

Rock Hard Fact

Punk bands were mandated to only perform original material at the infamous New York punk venue CBGB's because the owner couldn't afford to pay ASCAP royalties for cover songs.

Thousands of bands, promoters, fanzine writers, and even small independent record labels enjoyed the music and its basic concepts and philosophies. In the mid-1970's, the punk movement strongly appealed to its respective audience. The energy of punk was great but the themes of non-conformity and violence would never attract a large audience. So the punk movement was a youth movement focused on rebellion and change. It was also a formidable voice of opposition that created its own music, own lifestyle, and own culture.

Music critic Dave Marsh was the first to coin the term punk rock when in a 1971 issue of the magazine *Creem*, he described a 1960's garage rock band as giving a "landmark exposition of punk rock." Writer Greg Shaw also wrote in his 1971 fanzine that he was now calling some white teenage hard rock groups "punk rock" bands. By 1972, the term punk rock was in wide circulation in articles in *The New Yorker, The Los Angeles Times,* and *Rolling Stone Magazine.*

Musical Characteristics of Punk Rock

Progressive rock music fans were passionate about their favorite artists and bands but the music was too complex for many listeners. Punks firmly rejected intricate music and instrumental virtuosity. Early punk was, to some extent, inspired by British Invasion bands such as The Who (maybe the first real punk band), The Kinks, and even the early Rolling Stones. A late 1960's influence on punk came from the dark sound and decadent subject matter of The Velvet Underground. The brash glam rock of T-Rex, Mott the Hoople, and David Bowie, plus the arty decadence of Roxy Music were other influences on punk. Perhaps the most immediate predecessor of punk was The New York Dolls with their provocative music and image.

Punk was about loud and fast. The truest punk bands were small, streamlined bands that played only basic, fundamental chords. Solos were minimal or non-existent. Fast and faster tempos were the norm. Most songs were very short and structurally simple. It was rock stripped down to its very basic components, usually guitars, bass and drums with maybe a keyboard here or there. The common form was often a few verses and a chorus, delivered with simple harmonies and high energy. From this simplicity, came music with incredible raw power, which later mixed effectively with heavy metal since the two genres shared some of these same characteristics.

Early punk rockers felt that rock 'n' roll had moved away from its core musical values. They believed that the teenaged music of the 1950's did express the feelings and concern of youth but current mainstream rock did not. Old rock lyrics had dealt with confusion, alienation, and most importantly, a sense of rebellion-all emotional elements of adolescence. Punk lyrics were in a sense a modern version of past rock lyrics. Punk lyrical subject matter generally matched punk music with frequently terse expressions of angry and negative feelings. American punk bands tended to write songs with personal and social themes, while political expression was more common to British bands. Most punk bands shouted aggressively making declamations, accusations, and rants with their lyrics. Songs like "Anarchy in the U.K." by the Sex Pistols and "Blitzkrieg Bop" by The Ramones conveyed a sense of shock and outrage.

Some of the later punk bands eventually broadened their stylistic influences. They would make music that was more accomplished and complex by adding ethnic styles and greater rhythmic diversity. Punk would also merge with metal to create crossover-hardcore and with pop elements to create punk-pop. First we will explore the origins of punk rock in America (and its regionalization) and England and then the more recent punk subgenres.

The Origins of Early American Punk

The origins of punk rock began with a New York City scene that goes back to the late 1960's and an early 1970's underground rock movement centered in Greenwich Village. By 1974, a new scene was developing at a lower Manhattan club called CBGB. An alternative band called **Television** was an early fixture on the CBGB circuit. Television was influenced by The Velvet Underground (see chapter eight), avant-garde jazz, and early 1960's rock. The band's bassist/singer, **Richard Hell**, created a fashion look of ragged hair, ripped T-shirts, and black leather jackets that would go on to influence the punk rock fashion style. Singer **Patti Smith** would often see Television perform and quickly developed her own concept of an intellectual and feminist approach to rock music. Smith recorded a cover of the single "Hey Joe," that featured Television guitarist Tom Verlaine. This single was acclaimed as the first punk rock record and sparked a do it yourself (DIY) ethic for a new generation of musicians. Soon, Patti Smith and Television shared a two month residency at CBGB's, thus raising the club's profile and creating a home for the emerging NYC punk rock movement. Richard Hell left Television and formed the **Heartbreakers** (1975-1978 with later reunion years) with ex-New York Dolls Johnny Thunders and Jerry Nolan. Shortly after, a summer festival at CBGB's featured over thirty new bands and in the process, brought the scene significant media coverage. Many bands became regulars at CBGB's including **Mink DeVille** (1974-1986) and The Talking Heads (see chapter eight). In the spring of 1976, **The Ramones** had released their self-titled debut album and Richard Hell had left the Heartbreakers to form a new group, **The Voidoids**. Another prominent New York punk band was **The Dictators** (1973-2008). The word punk became an umbrella term for the whole scene in general but soon came to signify the musical style as well.

Television (1973-1978) (1991-1993) (2001-present) originated in New York City in the early 1970's as The Neon Boys. This short-lived trio featured vocalist/guitarist Tom Verlaine, bassist Richard Hell, and drummer Billy Ficca. They released two independent singles but never performed live. By the end of 1973, they morphed into the band Television, adding guitarist Richard Lloyd. Television persuaded Hilly Kristal, the owner of the club CBGB, to let them play there. Songwriting responsibilities were shared between Verlaine and Hell, but internal tension occurred when Hell's punky onstage presence and limited musicianship ran counter to the band's growing musical sophistication. In 1975, Hell was replaced by bassist Fred Smith. Malcolm McLaren would later credit Hell's appearance of spiky hair and torn clothes as his inspiration for his presentation of The Sex Pistols.

One year later, Television released the single "Little Johnny Jewel (Parts One and Two)," an influential song about the burgeoning New York scene. Although Television recorded a demo when Hell was still in the band (produced by Brian Eno), they didn't release an album until the well acclaimed Marquee Moon in 1977. A

"Eliminate the unnecessary and focus on the substance."

– Tommy Ramone

Rock Hard Fact

Joey Ramone of The Ramones has a street sign named in his honor at the corner of Bowery and East Second Street in New York. It has been stolen four times since 2003.

single, "Marquee Moon," made little impact in America but was hailed as an instant classic in England where it was a commercial success.

"Marquee Moon (Part 1)"
by Tom Verlaine

"Marquee Moon" was first released in Britain in 1977 and it's first pressing was limited to 25,000 copies. First as a twelve inch single in stereo on side one and mono on the other side. Later pressings were in the format of a seven-inch single, with the track split into two over the A-side and B-side. When performed live, Television often extended the tune to over fifteen minutes.

Each of "Marquee Moon's" three verses began with a guitar introduction before Billy Ficca's drums entered. After the second chorus, Richard Lloyd played a brief guitar solo. Tom Verlaine took a very long solo after the third chorus, based on a mixolydian scale. The lyrics in the third verse referred to entering graveyards in Cadillacs, suggesting the relationship between the drug abuse and the death of rock stars. "Marquee Moon" was a showcase for Verlaine and Lloyd's skillfully interlocking guitar parts.

In 1978, Television released Adventure and broke up later that year. Verlaine went on to have a successful solo career, releasing popular albums throughout the 1980's. Television re-formed and released Television in 1992. More albums followed with Live at the Academy, 1992 and Live at the Old Waldord, both released in 2003. Television was admired by their fans and peers for their musical vision and their fundamental role in the development of punk rock.

The Ramones (1974-1996) formed in 1974 when vocalist Jeffrey Hyman (aka Joey Ramone), guitarist John Cummings (aka Johnny Ramone), bassist Douglas Colvin (aka Dee Dee Ramone), and drummer Thomas Erdelyi (aka Tommy Ramone) first played together. These four friends from an upper middle class neighborhood in Queens, New York took their brotherly surname from a pseudonym that Paul McCartney used on occasion. The Ramones became the embodiment of punk rock with their stripped-down sound, terse songs, fast tempo delivery, and teenage apparel of T-shirts, tight jeans, sneakers, and black leather jackets. Their look was topped off with their bowl haircuts.

The Ramones won a recording deal with Sire Records who recorded their 1976 self-titled debut album Ramones for only $6,400. With their musical concision and energy, Joey's distinct vocals, and an album cover that made the band look like a teenage gang, Ramones came to represent the punk genre.

Groundbreaking album Ramones
by The Ramones

The Ramones, on their album Ramones, took rock music back to the basics with simple stripped down songs, using only guitar, bass, drums, and voice. The subject matter was somewhat dark at times but the band also brought you right into their basement with cartoonish fun and a high-energy brand of rock 'n' roll. The album's fourteen-songs rushed by in twenty-eight minutes and mashed together in a surge of buzz-saw guitars. Most of the songs on Ramones were written by Dee Dee Ramone about his personal experiences including "Blitzkrieg Bop" (with its cry of "Hey! Ho! Let's go!"), "Now I Wanna Sniff Some Glue," and "Judy is a Punk." Punk fanzine publisher Mark Perry said. "Once I got it (the album Ramones) home…I was completely converted. It was such a breath of fresh air, so exciting. It was like rock taken down to a level it should be at, real street level. Because rock by that time had become terribly overblown, people doing long guitar solos…but The Ramones were like saying, 'Enough of that. Let's take rock back.' It was almost like year zero again! Get rid of all that rubbish." #1.

Side one opened with "Blitzkrieg Bop," then "Beat on the Brat," "Judy is a Punk," "I Wanna Be Your Boyfriend," "Chain Saw," "Now I Wanna Sniff Some Glue," and "I Don't Wanna Go Down to the Basement." The song "Blitzkrieg Bop" became a popular song at sports events often shouted as a rallying cry. The song's title came from a German World War II tactic that meant lightning war. The simple musical approach of bar chords and chord roots played by bassist Dee Dee Ramone created the song's simple rock feel. At their last ever show, The Ramones played the already fast (quarter note equals 177 bpm) song at a blistering tempo well over 200 bpm.

Side two opened with "Loudmouth," then "Havana Affair," "Listen to My Heart," "53 & 3rd," "Let's Dance," "I Don't Wanna Walk Around with You," and "Today Your Love, Tomorrow the World." The song "53 & 3rd" referenced a well-known location for male prostitution in New York City. Dee Dee's lyrics spoke to a seedy image of a teenage hustler who confused being purchased with being attractive. "I Don't Want to Walk Around You" consisted of two lyric lines and three major chords. It faded into "Today Your Love, Tomorrow the World," a song that referred to a Hitler Youth member.

Ramones ignited the punk rock era with it's speed, melodic hooks, simplicity, and sense of purposeful stupidity. Ramones successfully disconnected from the mainstream rock tradition and this recording was the start of The Ramones influence on many genres of rock music.

The Ramones were the first of the New York punk bands to play in London. Their show at the Roundhouse Theater, on July 4th 1976 (ironically the American bicentennial) was inspirational in fueling the burgeoning British punk scene. 1977's Leave Home included "Pinhead" that immortalized the band's "gabba, gabba, hey!" catchphrase. That same year, the band released Rocket to Russia with "Rockaway Beach" (their biggest hit) and "Teenage Lobotomy." In 1978, Tommy Ramone, tired of touring, became The Ramone's producer. His successor, drummer Marc Steven Bell (aka Marky Ramone) debuted on 1978's Road to Ruin that featured Joey's "I Wanna Be Sedated."

The Ramones recorded seven studio albums in the 1980's. 1980's End of the Century defied punk conventions with "Do You Remember Rock 'n' Roll Radio" with production by the legendary Phil Spector. The album also featured guest musicians that included guitarists Dan and Dave Kessel and drummer Jim Keltner. After 1981's Pleasant Dreams and 1983's Subterranean Jungle, drummer Marky Ramone was fired for alcohol-related issues. Richard Reinhardt (aka Richie Ramone) joined for 1984's Too Tough to Die. This recording, with Tommy producing, leaned toward hardcore punk and heavy metal rather than the pop-oriented focus of their previous few albums. 1986's Animal Boy featured Dee Dee writing and singing amid a considerable amount of conflict between band members. 1987's Halfway to Sanity was the last

> **Rock Hard Fact**
>
> The Ramones were effectively the house band at CBGB's where their first show was attended by only the bartender and his dog.

> "Punk rock really came out of New York as a philosophy before the groups were ever recorded. I had a kind-of-intellectual interest in the idea of creating a new scene that could be a grassroots thing."
>
> - Greg Ginn of Black Flag

album for Richie Ramone. This recording contained a wide range of styles from hard rock to crossover thrash and songs with a bubblegum pop feel. Marky Ramone returned for 1989's Brain Drain.

In the 1990's, The Ramones released 1992's Mondo Bizarro, 1993's Acid Eaters, and 1995's Adios Amigos! before retiring in 1996. The Ramones became the *first true* punk band and in doing so, sparked the British punk scene. They turned musical limitations into strengths and influenced everyone from The Sex Pistols (who attended The Ramones' first British tour in 1976) to Bruce Springsteen, who wrote "Hungry Heart" for them before deciding to keep it for himself. They left a legacy of twenty-one studio and live albums.
The Ramones were inducted into the Rock and Roll Hall of Fame in 2002.

Patti Smith (1946-) started her music career in the early 1970's after previously attending Glassboro State College in Southern New Jersey and then heading to New York City. She digested a range of influences from Stax-Volt recordings to girl groups to Jimi Hendrix and The Rolling Stones. Smith began by performing poetry readings around Manhattan in 1971. She then enlisted guitarist Lenny Kaye and pianist Richard Sohl to accompany her. Gradually, Smith started singing her own compositions along with rock covers, alongside her poetry. By the mid-1970's her performances were drawing crowds and her song, "Piss Factory," was released by a small label. Patti Smith soon signed to the Arista label and rounded out her band by adding bassist/guitarist Ivan Kral and drummer Jay Dee Daugherty. Smith's 1975 debut album, Horses, was produced by ex-Velvet Underground vocalist John Cale. This album combined all the musical elements that had inspired her to play rock 'n' roll. Its lyrics were a surreal mixture of ambiguous sexuality, biblical references, and Symbolist-influenced poetry. Smith's androgynous persona and jarring vocal mannerisms added to the album's impact. Onstage (often at CBGB's), she gave provocative and radical monologues, which she referred to as "babelogues."

1976's Radio Ethiopia was more dense and less accessible than her debut. Populist political tirades combined with eerie sounds and noises to punctuate her songs. In concert, Smith was intense. In a performance in Florida, she accidentally fell offstage, breaking her neck. Her career was sidelined for over a year with an intensive period of physical therapy. In 1978, Patti Smith was back with Easter, an album that brought her commercial success by breaking the top twenty on the U.S. and British charts. It featured her biggest hit, "Because the Night," co-written with Bruce Springsteen.

"Because the Night"
by Patti Smith and Bruce Springsteen

"Because the Night" was a song that Bruce Springsteen partially wrote and gave to Patti Smith because he knew it suited her voice. Springsteen was recording his Darkness on the Edge of Town album and Smith was in an adjacent studio working on her Easter album when he had producer Jimmy Iovine gave Smith a tape of the song. Springsteen had the music, including the chorus, but not the verses. Patti Smith wrote the lyrics in one night. Springsteen later recorded it and released it on his box set Live 1975-1985.

Patti Smith's version made the song more of a passionate lust story, with a pre-chorus of "touch me now" at the end of the verse. In Springsteen's version, his lyrics were more comforting to the girl when he took the persona of a working man by singing "I work all day out in the hot sun." He further tempered her fears with his love by telling her, "they can't hurt you now." Smith and Springsteen's versions revealed the contrasting perspectives of the couple depicted in the song. Springsteen joined Patti Smith on stage in 1976 and 1977 to perform "Because the Night."

After releasing 1979's Wave, Patti Smith retreated from the music scene and married ex-MC5 guitarist Fred Smith, with whom she would have two sons. She remained out of the limelight until the release of 1988's Dream of Life, a strong collaboration with her husband. This album gave proof that her artistic vision was still focused. In the next two decades, Patti Smith released six more studio recordings including 2012's Banga.

Patti Smith was a poet, singer/songwriter, and provocative musician who was both a seminal and iconic figure in the punk rock movement. Smith was the first artist to release an independent single and major-label album that tied punk to New York's literary and artistic undergrounds. She pioneered a new image for female rockers that embraced androgyny and glamour. Her work helped to enable punk to gain credibility while she simultaneously brought punk into the mainstream with her top twenty hit "Because the Night."
Patti Smith was inducted into the Rock and Roll Hall of Fame in 2007.

Richard Hell and The Voidoids (1976-1979) (1982-1984) (1990) was formed after Hell worked for only a few months with The Heartbreakers, the band he joined after leaving Television (see earlier in this chapter) in 1975. Hell's real name was Richard Mayers. His stage name was inspired by a poem titled *A Season in Hell*, written by French poet Arthur Rimbaud. For a new band he would name The Voidoids, Hell recruited guitarists Ivan Julian and Robert Quine and drummer Marc Bell. In 1977, The Voidoids released their debut album, Blank Generation. The title track became a definitive punk anthem (The Sex Pistols drew from it to compose their song "Pretty Vacant"). Hell and the Voidoids drew their inspiration from various sources that included; The Beatles, Bob Dylan, the proto-punk band The Stooges, and The Velvet Underground. The Voidoids released Destiny Street in 1982 and a live record, 1989's Funhunt. The band broke up in 1984 and briefly reunited in 1990. Richard Hell went on to establish himself as a published poet as well as an actor.

The Misfits (1977-1983) (1995-present) were founded in Lodi, New Jersey by singer/songwriter and multi-instrumentalist Glenn Danzig, bassist Jerry Only, and drummer Manny Martinez. Danzig and Only were the only consistent band members during their first six years. The Misfits were known as the progenitors of the **horror punk** subgenre, blending punk with horror film imagery and themes. Their 1982 debut Walk Among Us and 1983's Earth A.D/Wolfs Blood were considered landmark recordings of the early 1980's hardcore punk movement. The Misfits disbanded in 1983 and Glenn Danzig formed the band Samhain and then Danzig.

In 1995, a new version of The Misfits formed. It was led by vocalist Michale Graves and Jerry Only. The band released 1996's Static Age, an album they had previously recorded in 1978. They next released 1997's American Psycho and 1999's Famous Monsters. For 2003's Project 1950, Jerry Only took over as lead vocalist and the band added ex-Ramone's drummer Marky Ramone. In 2011, The Misfits released The Devil's Rain. In 2016,

---

Rock Hard Fact

Richard Hell and The Voidoids first pioneered the "punk look" that later became popular with The Sex Pistols.

Danzig and Only reunited to headline shows at the Riot Fest in Chicago and Denver. Each version of The Misfits utilized horror film and science fiction film-inspired imagery and themes. They successfully drew from punk, heavy metal, and even 1950's rock and rockabilly styles to lead the subgenre of horror punk music.

The Origins of British Punk

Punk started in New York City, but it had its greatest impact on British youth culture. England was ripe for such a phenomenon to arrive. Postwar British youth culture had previously embraced subcultures that linked to music. The 1960's Mods and the Rockers identified with specific modes of dress and set their own rules. Television, national radio, daily newspapers, and four weekly national music papers all covered the shock and awe of the punk movement.

Traditional English culture bred a strong oppositional character that appeared in the nation's punk band movement. This meant that the *outrage* of punk music and punk culture were far bigger news *than* in America. Also, the lyrical messages of English punk rock were far more *political* in nature. Punk occurred in a turbulent era of British national discontent. The strong ideology of British punk was much more intense than that displayed by American punk bands.

The Sex Pistols took punk rock musical and cultural ideas to their most shocking and vulgar pinnacle in their very brief blaze of twisted rebellious glory. **The Clash** further defined the punk genre and then expanded it to create powerful and multifaceted songs that included worldwide chart hits and albums that sold into the millions. A swarm of other British bands rose under the punk banner and by the late 1970's, had seized control of the punk rock movement. The Sex Pistols and The Clash led the way but **The Jam**, **Public Image Ltd**, **The Slits** (1976-1982) (2005-2010), **X-Ray Spex** (1976-1979) (1991) (1995-1996) (2008), **Buzzcocks**, **The Damned**, **Generation X** and **Billy Idol**, **The Damage Manual** (2002-2004), and many others all made significant contributions.

The Jam (1972-1982) was an English punk rock band that formed in Woking, Surrey in 1972. While they played fast tempos and shared the angry attitude of their punk rock contemporaries, The Jam also embraced more recent rock genres that other punk bands rejected. They fused a number of 1960's rock and r&b influences, from Motown to The Who. These influences and their smartly tailored suits (not ripped clothes and piercings) set them apart from their punk peers. The Jam's lineup consisted of vocalist/guitarist Paul Weller, bassist Bruce Foxton, and drummer Rick Buckler.

The Jam released a single, "In the City," followed by the album In the City in 1977. It featured loud and fast paced songs with politically charged lyrics condemning police brutality and made critical statements about the declining British Empire. That was followed by 1977's This is the Modern World, 1978's All Mod Cons, and 1979's Setting Sons, that included their first top ten British single, "The Eton Rifles." 1980's Sound Affects featured "Start!" that went to number one on the British charts. This song borrowed heavily from The Beatles song "Taxman." 1982's The Gift would be the band's final recording and crowning achievement, reaching number one on the British charts. The Jam was at the forefront of the mod revival movement, yet still added their presence to the early English punk movement.

The Sex Pistols (1975-1978) (1996-2008 with some inactive years) initially lasted only two and a half years, releasing a mere four singles and one studio album. But their impact on the English and the international scene was *profound*. Guitarist Steve Jones, a working class boy with a love of rock 'n' roll, left home at age fifteen and lived with the family of his schoolmate, drummer Paul Cook. They formed a band in 1972 called The Strand with a revolving cast of musicians, including guitarist Wally Nightingale. They also hung out at a clothing shop called SEX, a trendy shop run by Malcolm McLaren and Vivienne Westwood. By early 1974, Steve Jones convinced McLaren to manage The Strand (he had briefly managed The New York Dolls). McLaren allowed The Strand, who had recently recruited bassist Glen Matlock, to rehearse at his clothing store. McLaren had been talking to New York Dolls Sylvain Sylvain about coming to London to front the band, but that never materialized.

In late August 1975, a nineteen-year old John Lydon wearing a Pink Floyd T-shirt with the words "I hate" handwritten above the band's name (and holes scratched through the eyes in the band's logo) was spotted near the clothing store SEX. McLaren had renamed the band The Sex Pistols, a name that promoted his clothing shop. He also suggested that The Sex Pistols audition John Lydon to sing lead vocals for the band. After Lydon sang along to Alice Cooper's "I'm Eighteen" playing from the shop's jukebox, McLaren convinced the band to begin rehearsing with Lydon. Lydon recalled, "The Sex Pistols, when they spotted me on the Kings Road with my I Hate Pink Floyd' T-shirt on, thought, 'Oh, he'll do.' I don't think they knew what they were getting hold of. What they really wanted was a kind of upmarket pub band because **pub rock** (a back-to-basics movement to small intimate music venues) was very fashionable at that time. Eddie and the Hot Rods, bands like that." #2 Days later, Lydon was renamed **Johnny Rotten** (for the poor state of his teeth and his attitude) and began to rehearse with the band. By October, The Sex Pistols were writing their own songs, including "Pretty Vacant" and "Seventeen" to add to their covers of The Small Faces and The Who.

The Sex Pistols
Baddest of the Bad Boys

Until this point, The Rolling Stones were known as the official bad boys of rock. The Sex Pistols rewrote the book on truly bad attitude and behavior. In November of 1975, the band played its first show at St. Martin's College. By this time Johnny Rotten was living up to his onstage name with his demeanor and confrontational attitude with audiences. Sex Pistols' shows were almost always marked by Rotten's riotous and often violent behavior. This only fueled their rapidly growing fan base. In February of 1976, The Sex Pistols opened for Eddie and The Hot Rods at London's Marquee Club. Johnny Rotten was now really pushing the boundaries of performance, walking off stage, sitting in the audience, throwing chairs and people around, and even smashing the headlining band's gear. A review in a local London paper warned with the headline "Don't Look Over Your Shoulder But The Sex Pistols Are Coming."

In December of 1977, the band appeared on London's evening show *Today* and shouted profanities

> "Actually we're (The Sex Pistols) not into music. We're into chaos."
>
> –Steve Jones

at the host. It made front-page news and thrust the band into the British national spotlight. As a result, the band cancelled a number of performance dates and EMI dropped them. However, A&M Records signed them only to drop them when The Pistols trashed the company's offices after celebrating their own signing.

Another incident saw The Pistols playing at The 100 Club Festival as the punk movement was quickly gaining traction. They appeared with The Damned, The Buzzcocks, and The Clash (the Clash's first major gig). Newcomer Sid Vicious threw a glass at the stage, hitting a beam and shattering glass over people and hitting a girl in the eye with a splinter of glass. Sid was arrested, beaten up, and served jail time. These were just a few of the almost nightly incidents that got them banned from most British venues.

The Sex Pistols played their last ever gig at the San Francisco Winterland in 1978. There, Rotten asked the audience "did you ever get the feeling you've been cheated?" When asked what he meant, Rotten stated "I felt I had been personally cheated and the band too and the audience! By the jealous shenanigans of band management, we were allowed to resent each other, and left up to our own devices, which unfortunately turned to spite. But we were young, and too young for the adults all around us who while we were not looking, put themselves in the driving seats." #3 The Sex Pistols broke rock 'n' roll in half because they turned it back on itself. They exposed rock's easy answers to false questions and made it necessary to consider all popular culture with suspicion. They made it necessary to ask what really counts as rock 'n' roll.

Many fans and musicians had sensed that the music scene in London was in a rapid state of change. Mick Jones (of The Clash) remembered, "Everyone had been waiting for a band like the Pistols to happen…You knew straight away that was it, and this was what it was going to be like from now on. It was a new scene, new values-so different from what had happened before. A bit dangerous." #4 The Sex Pistols were having a similar effect on another future member of The Clash. In the spring of 1976, The Pistols made their debut at the other major London pub rock venue, The Nashville, supporting the band The 101ers who were fronted by Joe Strummer. After seeing The Pistols live, Strummer promptly quit The 101ers, although they were rising fast on the London pub circuit. As exciting as a Sex Pistols set could be, Rotten's musicianship was called into question. Glen Matlock remembered, "It could be chaotic at times. John would be singing the words to the song perfectly but they may not have been the song that the rest of us were playing at the time!" #5

The Sex Pistols signed to the major label EMI Records in October of 1977 and released the single "Anarchy in the U.K." During this time, Matlock was fired and replaced by Lydon's friend, John Ritchie (aka Sid Vicious). The band's bad reputation made it almost impossible to secure any gigs, but Virgin Records stepped in to offer them another contract. The release of their *royalty* insulting "God Save the Queen" was timed to coincide with a celebration of Queen Elizabeth's twenty-fifth year on the throne. Some record plants refused to press the record, but it still became a big seller. In the fall of 1977, The Sex Pistols finally released their debut album Never Mind the Bollocks, Here's the Sex Pistols. Many British records stores refused to stock it, but it still sold well enough to go to number one on the U.K. charts.

Rock Hard Fact

Bassist/songwriter Glen Matlock of The Sex Pistols was a lover of pop songs, particularly by the band ABBA. He mangled the guitar riff of their song, "S.O.S," into the Pistols' song "Pretty Vacant."

Groundbreaking album Never Mind the Bollocks, Here's the Sex Pistols
by The Sex Pistols

The Sex Pistols only released one true studio album in their brief and volatile career. They managed to offend many people, even with the album title (bollocks means testicles). Many record stores refused to stock the album and even some record charts refused to list the album, instead just showing a blank space in its place. There were, of course, problems recording the album. New bassist Sid Vicious only performed on "Bodies," since his bass skills were deemed inadequate. Glen Matlock agreed to come back (after being fired) to record on the condition he was paid in advance. When that didn't happen, Matlock refused to show up and Steve Jones played the bass parts (besides his normal guitar parts).

Never Mind the Bollocks was effective in articulating the rage, frustration, and general dissatisfaction of the British working class with the establishment. The Sex Pistols, although lacking great musical skills, were able to translate these feelings and attitude in harsh rock music terms. The tracks on Never Mind the Bollocks were "Holidays in the Sun," then "Liar," "No Feelings," "God Save the Queen," "Problems," "Seventeen," "Anarchy in the U.K.," "Bodies," "Pretty Vacant," "New York," and "E.M.I."

"God Save the Queen" was assumed by the general public to be an attack on Queen Elizabeth II and her monarchy. The title was taken from the national anthem of England. Rotten's goal was to create sympathy for the British working class and provide a general resentment toward the monarchy. Rotten explained, "I wrote the song 'God Save the Queen' as a laugh. It's a giggle, it's vaudeville, it's burlesque. It's not a rampant anti-royal statement. Far from it…If you really listen, it's not structured in any normal way at all, as indeed is any Sex Pistols song…We break every rule in the book." #6

"Anarchy in the U.K." contained inflammatory venomous lyrics wrapped in musical brute force. Rotten was endorsing a violent concept of anarchy that reflected a sense of anger, confusion, social alienation, and economic frustration that was felt by an entire generation of disenfranchised youth in the mid-1970's. Musically, Steve Jones' guitar parts were multi-tracked to create a wall of sound. Jones felt that when recording this song, The Sex Pistols hit their musical stride, grooving hard on the basic guitar riff. Jones avoided the typical "me first" guitar solo, instead staying within the nasty feel of Rotten's vocal lines. The band captured a rawness and driving energy on the track.

Never Mind the Bollocks opened the door for countless other punk bands and artists in other rock genres to make similar rebellious statements. Rotten's furious rants jump-started a musical and cultural revolution that has stood the test of time. His bitterly sarcastic attacks were political statements about the status quo that questioned the very foundation of British society.

In January of 1978, The Sex Pistols went on a chaotic twelve-day tour of America. The tour ended with a performance at San Francisco's Winterland Ballroom, after which Johnny Rotten quit the band. He soon formed the band Public Image Ltd (see below). Sid Vicious struggled with substance abuse and went to New York with his girlfriend, Nancy Spungen. On October 12th, 1978, Spungen was stabbed to death in the couple's room at the Chelsea Hotel, and Vicious was charged with the crime. After a court hearing, Vicious died of a drug overdose.

Almost twenty years since releasing "Anarchy in the UK," Lydon, Jones, Cook, and Matlock reunited for a tour. A fiery live album, 1996's Filthy Lucre Live, was released from a date they played at London's Finsbury Park. Other recordings of the Sex Pistols include; a 1977 release of a bootleg demo album titled Spunk, the 1979 soundtrack album The Great Rock 'n' Roll Swindle that included performances by other artists, 1979's interview album Some Product: Carri on Sex Pistols, and the 1980 compilation albums Flogging a Dead Horse and Sex Pack. More compilation and live albums followed including 2008's Live & Filthy. Although they created far more controversy than they did actual music, The Sex Pistols conveyed a threat to the music establishment. They also challenged British social and political mores. With their blasting guitar sound and Rotten's angry voice that screamed of defiance and anarchy, The Sex Pistols affected just about everybody and everything.

Public Image Ltd (1978-1992) (2009-present) is a post-punk band formed in 1978 by vocalist John Lydon following the wreckage of the Sex Pistols. Lydon recruited ex-Clash guitarist Keith Levene, bassist Jah Wobble, and drummer Jim Walker for their 1978 debut Public Image: First Issue. This album featured the hit "Public Image," about Lydon's feeling of being exploited in The Sex Pistols by Malcolm McLaren and the press. It peaked at number nine on the British charts. First Issue explored elements of noise, dub, and progressive rock. Walker soon left and the drum chair became a revolving door. 1979's Metal Box pushed the band in a more avant-garde direction and is regarded as an important post-punk album including their hit "Death Disco."

"Death Disco"
by Public Image Ltd

First released as a single, "Death Disco" climbed to number twenty on the British charts. It was then released in an alternate version as "Swan Lake" on Metal Box. Lydon wrote the song for his mother, who had died from cancer. She had asked him to write a disco song for her funeral. Guitarist Keith Levene recalled, "The person he (Lydon) was singing about, 'Seeing in your eyes,' was his mother, who was going through the process of dying from cancer. That's what John was singing about-very passionately, I might add…I was just trying to do something with the music." #7

The Public Image Ltd hit "Death Disco" combined elements of dub and disco and even a musical quote heard in Keith Levine's guitar part from Tchaikovsky's "Swan Lake." Johnny Lydon's musical maturity was evident on this song with the successful inclusion of dub, funk, disco, and avant-garde styles in a Captain Beefheart-like new direction for the punk genre. "Death Disco" featured Lydon's sardonic poetry at its best, propelled by Jah Wobble's dub-styled rhythmic basslines and Keith Levene's abrasive and metallic guitar sound.

Bassist Jah Wobble left before 1981's The Flowers of Romance. 1984's This Is What You Want…This Is What You Get came after Keith Levene's departure. The latter album spawned Public Image's biggest commercial hit, "This Is Not a Love Song." After many lineup changes, Lydon assumed full control and Public Image recorded 1986's Album, 1987's Happy?, 1989's 9, and 1992's That What Is Not. After a long hiatus, Lydon re-formed Public Image Ltd and released 2012's This Is PiL, and 2015's What the World Needs Now….

The Clash (1976-1986) were punk rock's fulfillment of the promise made by the early demise of The Sex Pistols. From basic punk beginnings, The Clash matured into an expansive musical band whose artistic direction embraced reggae, rockabilly, and even rap music. Their early punk polemics grew into radical and worldwide left-wing political statements. It took some time, but the band eventually achieved great success in America and became one the biggest bands of the early 1980's. Even though the punk credo embodied a DIY mindset, The Clash knew how to play their instruments.

The Clash formed in London in 1976. Vocalist/guitarist Joe Strummer (aka John Mellor) had left his pub-rock band, The 101ers, after seeing The Sex Pistols perform. A manager by the name of Bernie Rhodes introduced Strummer to vocalist Mick Jones and bassist Paul Simonon of the band London SS. Rhodes next set up a series of auditions for potential band members. Mick Jones recalled "We advertised in the *Melody Maker* every week: 'Anybody who's into the New York Dolls, Stooges, MC5'. And that was enough because if you had heard of those people you would be right. We met all the people interested-everyone who was around." #8 Bernie Rhodes also asked Jones to teach Simonon to play bass. Guitarist Keith Levene (later of Public Image Ltd) and drummer Terry Chimes soon completed the lineup. Rhodes, not only helped to put The Clash together, but became one of the key figures in punk rock. His abrasive personality was perfect for the times and he was crucial in shaping The Clash, especially with his pop culture awareness and political views.

The band played their first show on July 4th, 1976, opening for The Sex Pistols. After playing a couple of shows that were *not canceled* on the Sex Pistols' Anarchy tour, The Clash were signed by CBS Records in early 1977. Chimes quit, disgusted by the punk habits of bottle throwing and spitting, and was replaced by drummer Rob Harper (although Chimes did appear on their first album). Soon, drummer Nicky "Topper" Headon took over the drumset chair. The Clash had cultivated an image and were gaining songwriting traction. Mick Jones said, "There was never a planned look. It was much more of a natural thing. Bernie gave us the right outlook…Bernie had his hand in everything. Not the lyrics-he didn't help with the lyrics. He didn't tell us not to write love songs, as the myth goes…He told us to write about what we knew." #9

In 1977, The Clash released their self-titled debut The Clash to great acclaim in England. It contained the songs "Janie Jones," "White Riot," and ""I'm So Bored with the U.S.A." This album wasn't released in America (later with some different tracks) until after their second album due to fears that it lacked radio-friendly songs. With "White Riot," The Clash wrote about riots that occurred at the Notting Hill Carnival the previous year when black youths had clashed with police. Strummer expressed his feelings that white people should vent their outrage over oppressive government just like the black youth, through direct action. This, and other songs, found The Clash to be flag-wavers of the new punk rock consciousness. They were able to effectively connect with the everyday street lives of their audience. 1978's Give 'Em Enough Rope went to number two on the British charts but barely made a dent on the American charts. Their first U.K. single, "Tommy Gun," peaked at number nineteen. In support of the album, The Clash toured En-

> "When you listen to The Clash, you're facing up to life, and at the same time being given strength to deal with it."
>
> –Pete Townshend

gland supported by The Slits and The Innocents. Then the band made its first (largely successful) tour of America in early 1979.

1979's double album, London Calling, was their breakout release in America, and is considered to be their strongest artistic statement. London Calling went to number nine in England and number twenty-seven in America.

Groundbreaking album
London Calling
by The Clash

London Calling saw The Clash fuse a vast array of musical styles including; reggae, rockabilly, ska, r&b, pop, jazz, hard rock, and of course punk. The lyrical content on this nineteen song double album dealt with racial conflict, social displacement, unemployment, drug abuse, and the responsibilities of being an adult. The band had recently separated from their manager and guru, Bernie Rhodes, and moved from their rehearsal studio in Camden Town to Vanilla Studios. The Clash's principal songwriters, Jones and Strummer, hadn't written a new song in over a year. They rehearsed in a very disciplined manner and worked extensively on cover songs from a variety of music genres. This open approach to diverse styles eventually influenced their songwriting, thus providing a whole new world of musical possibilities. Jones composed and arranged most of the new songs while Strummer generally wrote the lyrics. Overall, The Clash had moved away from a pure punk approach as far back as Give 'Em Enough Rope. Now, a fascination with early rock 'n' roll and r&b were evident in their new material.

Side one opened with "London Calling," then "Brand New Cadillac," "Jimmy Jazz," "Hateful," and "Rudie Can't Fail." The band's anthem, "London Calling," was an apocalyptic song, detailing many ways the world could end. It effectively addressed a number of social issues including; the 1979 nuclear reactor incident at Three Mile Island in Pennsylvania, rising unemployment, racial conflict, and drug abuse in England. Musically, "London Calling" had a simple, direct quarter note feel and Mick Jones strummed simple chords. The words London Calling were constantly utilized for question and answer lyrical phrasing. Side two opened with "Spanish Bombs," then "The Right Profile," "Lost in the Supermarket," "Clampdown," and "The Guns of Brixton." "The Guns of Brixton" was the first Paul Simonon composition that the band recorded and the first to have him sing lead.

Side three opened with "Wrong 'Em Boyo," then "Death or Glory," "Koka Kola," and "The Card Cheat." On "Death or Glory," Strummer examined his own life in retrospect and acknowledged the difficulties of life as an adult. Side four opened with "Lover's Rock," then "Four Horseman," "I'm Not Down," "Revolution Rock," and "Train in Vain." The final song, "Train in Vain," was meant to be given away through a promotion, but was added to the album at the last minute.

London Calling celebrated the romance of rock 'n' roll rebellion and captured The Clash's primal energy. It sounded more purposeful than most double albums and opened the door to post-punk musical explorations. This album established The Clash as much more than a simple punk band without compromising the bands' original dynamism and immediacy.

1980's Sandinista! was a more diffuse and experimental recording than previous Clash albums. It was a triple album that continued to mix styles, now with more Latin and Jamaican dub-step influences. The Clash continued to sharpen their global political message and social observations. 1982's Combat Rock was The Clash's most successful album reaching number eight in America with the hit "Rock the Casbah" and "Should I Stay or Should I Go." However, years of constant touring began to take its toll. Headon was fired in the spring of 1982 due to substance abuse issues and drummer Terry Chimes returned.

"Rock the Casbah"
by The Clash

The sad irony about "Rock the Casbah" was that drummer Topper Headon wrote The Clash's most popular song and shortly after was fired because of drug problems. For "Rock the Casbah," Headon also recorded the piano, bass, and percussion parts. In the MTV music video for the song, Clash original drummer Terry Chimes was seen behind the drums. Headon's original lyrics were about how much he missed his girlfriend.

Joe Strummer decided to take Headon's lyrics in a new direction. Strummer re-wrote the lyrics to be about the cultural discrimination that had occurred in Iran. If someone owned a disco album in Iran, the Arab ruler Shareef would physically punish them. This served as the inspiration for Strummer's lyrics and the title "Rock the Casbah." The song's lyrics also featured many Arabic, Hebrew, Turkish, and Sanskrit words. When the band performed "Rock the Casbah" live, they had no piano player to play the very identifiable part, so the song was played with a heavier, rocked out guitar approach.

After Combat Rock, tension between Jones and Strummer steadily rose. Jones left the band in 1983 and formed Big Audio Dynamite. Chimes quit for the final time and Strummer and Simonon recruited drummer Pete Howard, and guitarists Nick Sheppard and Vince White. 1985's Cut the Crap would be The Clash's final studio album. After a tour to support the new album, The Clash disbanded in 1986. The Clash was a fiery and idealistic band, charged with political and social righteousness. They were the most musically adventurous punk band with two exceptional songwriters in Strummer and Jones, each with a distinctive voice and style. The Clash were extremely effective in lashing out against injustice and rebelling against the establishment, pretty much what punk rock was all about. The Clash were inducted into the Rock and Roll Hall of Fame in 2003. Joe Strummer died in 2002.

The Damned (1976-present) are an English punk rock band from London, England that formed in 1976. The original lineup consisted of vocalist Dave Vanian, guitarist Brian James, bassist Captain Sensible, and drummer Rat Scabies. The Damned were the first U.K. punk band to release a *full-length* album, 1977's Damned Damned Damned. This recording also contained the first ever British punk single "New Rose."

"New Rose"
by Brian James

"New Rose" began with vocalist Dave Vanian's line "Is she really going out with him?" a parody of

---

"Punk rock should mean freedom, liking and accepting anything that you like. Playing whatever you want. As sloppy as you want. As long as it's good and it has passion."

– Kurt Cobain

Rock Hard Fact

The Clash's double album London Calling and their triple album Sandinista! both cost only the price of a single LP, in their effort to be fan-friendly.

the 1964 Shangri-Las song "Leader of the Pack." Punk sarcasm was born. Brian James wrote the song in fifteen minutes and the band recorded it in only one day. Producer Nick Lowe also mixed the song in one day. The B-side to "New Rose" was a cover of The Beatles "Help!"

Bassist Captain Sensible remembered "People, when they heard 'New Rose,' said we must have speeded the tapes up, which is ridiculous. People honestly thought we were cheating, and they came to see us live and saw we played the songs twice as fast again!" #10 Also, "New Rose" quickly showed that punk rock could have a melodic element. Drummer Rat Scabies recalled "Captain is a great bass player, even though he hates playing bass-he wanted to be a guitarist…the bass carried the melody-it's kind of because the Captain hated the bass that it was played like that." #11

1977's Music for Pleasure did not fare well but The Damned quickly reorganized without Brian James for 1979's Machine Gun Etiquette. In the 1980's, they recorded four studio albums, 1980's The Black Album, 1982's Strawberries, 1985's Phantasmagoria, and 1986's Anything. The latter two albums did not include Captain Sensible, who had left the band in 1984. After more line-up changes, James and Sensible rejoined The Damned to play what was meant to be their last live show. The band then re-formed for a tour in 1991. The Damned didn't release another studio album until 1995's Not of This Earth, which was Scabies's last recording with the band. This was followed by 2001's Grave Disorder and 2008's So, Who's Paranoid?. The Damned exerted great influence on later hardcore bands with their energy and penchant for fast tempos. They also influenced gothic rock with vocalist Dave Vanian's vampire themed costumes and dark lyrical themes. The Damned, often referred to as Britain's first punk band, were central to the development of the English punk movement.

Buzzcocks (1976-1981) (1989-present) are an English punk rock band from Bolton, England that formed in 1976. They were formed by vocalist/guitarist Pete Shelly and vocalist/guitarist/keyboardist Howard Devoto after traveling to London to see The Sex Pistols perform. They added bassist Garth Davies and drummer Mick Singleton to make an EP titled Spiral Scratch. The Buzzcocks scored a major label hit with the song "Orgasm Addict," a bold examination of compulsive sexuality. Devoto made a quick exit from the band and Shelly shuffled the band lineup to eventually settle on bassist Steve Garvey, guitarist Steve Diggle, and drummer John Maher. In 1978, The Buzzcocks recorded their debut album, Another Music in a Different Kitchen. This recording featured songs about relationship issues with song titles often posing questions. 1978's Love Bites followed, then 1979's A Different Kind of Tension.

After recording demos for a fourth album, The Buzzcocks decided to disband in 1981. The band has re-formed several times since 1989 with the Shelley, Diggle, Garvey and Maher lineup. However, after a fifteen year period, they released 1993's Trade Test Transmissions with bassist Tony Barber and drummer Phil Barker joining Shelly and Diggle. The Buzzcocks went on to record five more studio albums including 2014's The Way. The Buzzcocks, initially inspired by The Sex Pistols, brought an intense punk energy to the three-minute pop song format. They later influenced many punk-pop bands such as Husker Du and grunge icon Kurt Cobain.

Generation X (1976-1981) (1993) was best known as a starting point for the solo career of Billy Idol. Idol had played briefly in the punk rock band Chelsea that he left in 1975. Generation X started when guitarist William Broad (aka Billy Idol) met drummer John Towe. Idol and Towe soon added bassist Tony James and vocalist Gene October to form the band Generation X. The band took their name from the term representing the demographic of people born between the mid-1960's to early 1980's. A lineup shift saw Billy Idol move to lead vocals. Then, they added guitarist Bob Andrews and Mark Laff (James stayed as the bassist) for their 1978 Generation X UK. The album was a success, yielding the hit "Ready Steady Go," that peaked at number forty-seven on the British charts. 1979's Valley of the Dolls continued to churn out hits with "King Rocker," "Friday's Angels," and the title track. By the time of 1981's Kiss Me Deadly, Billy Idol and Tony James had broken up Generation X and rebranded the band as Gen X. This new name fit the emerging British **new romantic pop** cultural movement of the early 1980's. New romantic music, (quick to come and go) was a reaction to punk and was heavily influenced by former glam rock stars of the 1970's. Idol and James soon parted ways and James formed the rockabilly band Sigue Sigue. Idol moved to New York to begin his solo career. Gen X later released Sweet Revenge in 1998, an album originally recorded in 1979.

Billy Idol (1955-) remixed and re-released the single "Dancing with Myself, a Gen X tune from their Kiss Me Deadly album. Idol then released his 1982 self-titled solo debut Billy Idol. It contained the hits "Hot in the City," and "White Wedding." His second release, 1983's Rebel Yell, was a major commercial breakthrough with the hit "Rebel Yell" that reached number six on the American charts.

"Rebel Yell"
by Billy Idol and Steve Stevens

The introduction to "Rebel Yell," performed alone on guitar by co-writer Steve Stevens, sounded like a combination of electric guitar and electronic keyboard. Stevens stated that he was inspired by the acoustic guitar style of guitarist Leo Kottke. Stevens created a ray-gun effect on his solo utilizing a Lexicon PCM 41 digital delay processor. However, he later figured out how to get a more distinctive sound by using an *actual* ray-gun. By tweaking a toy ray-gun, he held it to his pickup and generated the strange sounds on the recording. Stevens' "ray gun guitar" became a popular moment in many Billy Idol concerts. Idol achieved an intense vocal sound by blending his harsh, aggressive attack with a strong melodic sensibility.

Billy Idol named "Rebel Yell" after attending an event where Keith Richards, Mick Jagger, and Ron Wood of The Rolling Stones were taking swigs from a bottle of "Rebel Yell" whiskey. The song was about a passionate one-night stand with a woman who wanted "more more more." "Rebel Yell" has been included in the film *The Legend of Billie Jean* and a documentary by Warren Miller titled *Impact*. The "Rebel Yell" video gained heavy rotation on MTV, greatly aiding Idol's popular appeal.

Billy Idol followed with six more studio recordings including; 1986's Whiplash Smile, 1990's Charmed Life, 1993's Cyberpunk, 2005's Devil's Playground, 2006's Happy Holidays, and 2014's Kings & Queens of the Underground. Billy Idol rocketed to stardom with his album Rebel Yell. He established himself as an artist that could harness the raw energy of punk combined with catchy pop melodies. Billy Idol further created a unique

> "From the start, The Bad Brains were really constructive. They were encouraging, they were inspirational, and their music was undeniable. They made you want to do something"
>
> – Ian MacKaye

Rock Hard Fact

Before forming The Bad Brains, several of their members were part of a group called Mind Power, which focused on the fusion music of The Mahavishnu Orchestra and Chick Corea's Return to Forever.

musical persona with a pair of eye-catching videos for the tracks "White Wedding" and "Dancing with Myself," again scoring major airplay on MTV. This solidified his punky rock star image.

The Regionalization of American Punk

Washington/Baltimore Punk

Commonly referred to as DC **hardcore**, the punk scene in Washington, D.C. gained traction in the late 1970's. The Georgetown University radio station, WGTB, (run with little supervision from the university administration) soon became a vehicle for the emerging punk movement. A number of punk clubs opened as well as recording studios that catered to punk bands. Important early punk bands were **Bad Brains, Minor Threat, Government Issue** (1980-1989), **The Velvet Monkeys** (1981-present), **Void** (1980-1983), **Youth Brigade** (1980-1981), **The Faith** (1981-1983), and later **Embrace** (1985-1986), and **Fugazi** (1987-2003).

Bad Brains (1977-present with some inactive years) are an American hardcore punk band from Washington, D.C. that formed in 1977. With early roots in fusion music, the band first worked under the name Mind Power. They developed a fast and intense hardcore style that incorporated complex rhythms and elements of funk, reggae, metal, and hip-hop. The band broke up and re-formed several times with different singers and drummers. The Bad Brains classic lineup since 1994 has been vocalist Paul D. Hudson (aka H.R. for Human Rights), his brother drummer Earl Hudson, bassist Darryl Jenifer, and guitarist Dr. Know (aka Gary Miller). H.R. had a vision for the band. He said, "What we wanted to do was an amplification of the inner thoughts of people's hearts and their minds so they could work on their motor skills and find themselves a little creative immortality and focus on the supernaturalistic gifts that God has offered them in the fine arts impulses." #12 Bad Brains has released nine studio albums, from their 1982 self-titled debut Bad Brains to 2017's Mind Power. Bad Brains helped to shape hardcore punk with their strong musicianship and infusion of many music styles.

Minor Threat (1980-1983) was a hardcore punk band from Washington, D.C. that formed in 1980. Vocalist Ian MacKaye and drummer Jeff Nelson had played in the punk band Teen Idles. They recruited guitarist Lyle Preslar and bassist Brian Baker to form Minor Threat. MacKaye and Nelson were strong believers in the DIY mentality. Their 1981 EP Minor Threat contained the song "Straight Edge" that helped to launch the punk straight edge movement across the East Coast up to Boston. The message was simple; you don't have to smoke, drink, or do drugs to have a good time. Minor Threat had the courage to stick to their personal convictions.

"Straight Edge"
by Ian MacKaye

"Straight Edge" inspired the entire punk straight edge subculture. An anti-inebriation movement had developed in punk prior to this song, and it would be a catalyst in giving the scene a name. "Straight Edge" was an unusually short song, clocking in at only forty-six seconds. The track had a strong cultural impact with its anthemic, pulse pounding message. Ian MacKaye summed up the straight edge philosophy with the opening lyrics "I'm a person just like you-but I've got better things to do-than sit around and f*** my head-hang out with the living dead."

Musically, the song was fast and aggressive with a dissonant guitar riff that matched MacKaye's screaming vocal intensity. Minor Threat played this song with a take no prisoners mentality that added to the seriousness of their message. Punk band NOFX covered "Straight Edge" with a jazz approach sung with a raspy Louis Armstrong styled vocal sound.

1981's second EP In My Eyes, featured the song "Out of Step," which was another straight edge movement message song. 1983's Out of Step reworked the title song from their previous release and influenced many other D.C. area hardcore bands. Minor Threat broke up in 1983 over their musical direction. In 1985, Minor Threat released the EP Salad Days, two years after their breakup. After Minor Threat disbanded, Ian MacKaye played with the hardcore band Embrace. In 1987, he then formed the influential hardcore band, Fugazi who were known for their DIY ethic and contempt for the music industry.

Midwestern American Punk

Not many think of Midwestern America as a source for punk music. But the great states of Michigan, Ohio, and Illinois produced some of the most important **proto-punk** (garage bands from 1960-1970's that pre-date punk) and punk bands from America. These bands included; **MC5, Iggy Pop and The Stooges, The Dead Boys** (1976-2017 with many inactive years), **Husker Du** (1979-1988), and more recently, **Rise Against** (1999-present).

MC5 (1964-1972) (1992) (2003-2012) was a proto-punk band from Lincoln Park, Michigan that formed in 1964. Their original lineup was vocalist Rob Tyner, guitarists Wayne Kramer and Fred "Sonic" Smith, bassist Michael Davis, and drummer Dennis Thompson. MC5 were innovators of the punk movement in America with their leftist political ties and anti-establishment lyrics. MC5's name was in homage to their Detroit roots (short for Motor City Five). MC5 built a reputation as a great live band, touring to enormous responses. Their 1969 debut, Kick Out the Jams, reached number thirty on the U.S. charts and spawned the hit "Kick Out the Jams." MC5 next released 1970's Back in the USA and 1971's High Time, both to limited popular appeal. Atlantic Records dropped MC5 and they disbanded in 1972. The band reunited briefly in 1992 and then re-formed with a new lineup in 2003 and toured until permanently disbanding in 2012. MC5 had an enormous influence on the emerging punk movement of the 1970's as well as a variety of artists in many rock genres.

"Kick Out the Jams"
by MC5

"Kick Out the Jams" was part funky groove meets psychedelic guitar, with an energy that was a foreshadowing of the soon to emerge punk movement. MC5 achieved a very Hendrix-like feel on this song. The initial pressing of the song contained the words "Kick out the jams, motherfu**ers." Later pressings featured the revised line "Kick out the jams, brothers and sisters."

Rock Hard Fact

When Jim Morrison died in 1971, The Doors asked Iggy Pop to join the band. He declined the offer.

This song also foreshadowed the punk attitude when MC5 was dropped from their record label. This was due to a popular chain of record stores in the Detroit area who refused to stock the album because of the infamous opening line. Rage Against The Machine covered "Kick Out the Jams" on their album Renegades. "Kick Out the Jams" came to be known as a slogan of the 1960's ethos of revolution and liberation in America. In many ways, MC5 were a band ahead of their time.

The Stooges (1967-1971) (1972-1974) (2003-2016) were a proto-punk band that formed in Ann Arbor, Michigan in 1967. The band consisted of vocalist Iggy Pop (aka James Osterberg Jr), guitarist Ron Asheton, bassist Dave Alexander, and drummer Scott Asheton. They released their 1969 self-titled debut The Stooges and 1970's Fun House to little commercial appeal. Fun House did begin to generate a strong cult following when fans recognized the unique avant-garde rock sound of their music. The Stooges disbanded briefly and re-formed with a different lineup to release 1973's Raw Power. Raw Power was considered to be a forerunner of the punk rock movement with its high quality songwriting and chaotic sound quality. In early 1972, Iggy Pop befriended David Bowie at the height of his Ziggy Stardust popularity. Being a big Stooges fan, Bowie was happy to help resuscitate the careers of Iggy and The Stooges, as the band was now billed. However, the Stooges called it quits again in 1974, due to limited performance opportunities and Pop's escalating drug issues and erratic off-stage behavior.

Iggy Pop and the Asheton brothers reunited in 2003 and toured extensively until 2008. They also released some re-mastered versions of their first two albums. In 2007, The Stooges released The Weirdness, their first new studio album in thirty-four years. Founding member guitarist Ron Asheton died in 2009. In 2013, The Stooges released their final album, Ready to Die. A year later, founding member drummer Scott Asheton also died. The Stooges were pioneers of the proto-punk style that was both simple and vicious and was a clear precursor of the punk rock movement. The Stooges were inducted into the Rock and Roll Hall of Fame in 2010.

Iggy Pop (1960-present) carries the distinction and label of *The Godfather of Punk* for his work with The Stooges and his solo career. Pop's solo debut was 1977's The Idiot and was a musical departure from his hard rocking Stooge efforts. On The Idiot, Pop collaborated heavily with David Bowie on the writing and recording process. Pop achieved an introspective feeling and utilized electronic sounds comparable to Bowie's "Berlin Trilogy" albums. The Idiot was important to the later development of industrial and gothic rock artists. Pop's 1997 Lust for Life would become one of his most successful albums reaching number twenty-eight on the British charts. It was less experimental, more rock 'n' roll, and less Bowie influenced that The Idiot. David Bowie played keyboards and sang background vocals on the album. Lust for Life yielded the hits "Success" and "Lust for Life."

"Lust for Life"
by Iggy Pop and David Bowie

"Lust for Life" was co-written by David Bowie (he wrote the music on a ukulele) and Iggy Pop wrote the lyrics. Drummer Hunt Sales' rhythmic approach was inspired by the groove from The Supremes tune "You Can't Hurry Love." The overall rhythm section feel was an energetic throwback to the 1950's and later, the Motown sound.

"Lust for Life" was about Iggy Pop's lifestyle as a hard-living heroin addict. The title was taken from the 1956 film *Lust for Life*. The lyrics for "Lust for Life" also contained references to Johnny Yen, a character from a William S Burroughs' novel. Since the chorus of the song can be interpreted as a message to live life to its fullest, the song was often used in commercials, including one for Royal Caribbean Cruises. The cruise line was reaching out to a younger demographic and Pop's upbeat style was perfect for their advertisements. There have been numerous cover versions of "Lust for Life" by artists including; Motley Crue, The Smithereens, Noel Gallagher, and Tom Jones.

Iggy Pop next released 1979's New Values, his first solo album without any involvement from David Bowie. Although critically well received, it was not a commercial success. Iggy Pop recorded five studio albums in the 1980's, from 1980's Soldier to the heavily pop-oriented Instinct. Iggy Pop collaborated with many artists to release nine more studio recordings including 2016's Post Pop Depression. Just about every punk band from the past to present has been influenced directly or indirectly by Iggy Pop. From his shocking performances in the late 1960's with The Stooges, to his seminal collaborations with David Bowie, to his prolific output of punk meets pop albums; Iggy Pop is "The Godfather of Punk."

Northwest American Punk

The punk scene in Northwest America has always taken a backseat historically to the well-publicized grunge scene of the 1990's. However, many of these punk bands heavily inspired later grunge movement bands. Early Northwestern bands were **Melvins, Green River** (see chapter sixteen), **The Fartz** (1981-1983) (1999-2003), **Fitz of Depression** (1987-1997) (2002-present), and the **riot grrrl movement** (see women of punk rock profile) that included **Bikini Kill** and many other punk bands.

Melvins (1983-present) are a band from Montesano, Washington that formed in 1983. The Melvins have performed mostly as a trio beginning with vocalist/guitarist Buzz Osborne, drummer Dale Crover, and bassist Matt Lukin. Their current lineup is Osborne, Crover, and vocalist/bassist Steven Shane McDonald. Initially, Melvins started as a hardcore punk band but they eventually explored a variety of different styles throughout their career. The punk band Black Flag was an early influence on their approach but noise rock, avant-garde, and jazz-rock styles helped to shape their music. Their debut self-titled EP, Melvins, was released in 1986 and their first full-length album, Gluey Porch Treatments, followed in 1987.

Dale Crover played drums with Nirvana when they recorded a ten-song demo that later became part of Nirvana's Bleach album. When grunge hit the mainstream, Melvins were able to capitalize on the success of Nirvana. They were later signed to Atlantic Records and released 1993's Houdini, their first major label release. Melvins have recorded twenty-five studio albums and three EP's. Their ability to combine punk with a heavy Black Sabbath tradition had an impact on grunge, alternative metal, and doom metal artists.

Bikini Kill (1990-1997) was a punk rock band that formed in Olympia, Washington in 1990. They consisted of vocalist Kathleen Hanna, guitarist Billy Karren, bassist Kathi Wilcox, and drummer Tobi Vail. Bikini Kill was the pioneering band of the riot grrrl movement and was known for their exciting live performances and radical feminist lyrics. Hanna published a fanzine called Bikini Kill to help promote the band's first tour in 1991. The band encouraged females to come to the front of the stage and handed out lyric sheets to their songs for them to sing. Hanna would "crowd surf" to seek out male hecklers. However, in addition to raising the profile of their female fans, Bikini Kill did reach a male audience as well. In 1991, Bikini Kill released an independent demo cassette titled Revolution Girl Styles Now!. They followed with their EP, Bikini Kill. Their 1993 debut album Pussy Whipped included the single "Rebel Girl." Bikini Kill endured unfair misrepresentation from the media and felt vilified during much of the 1990's. 1996's Reject All American would be their final album and Bikini Kill disbanded later that year. A compilation of their singles recorded between 1993 and 1995 was released in 1998 titled, The Singles. In 2017, Hanna, Wilcox, and Vail reunited to play one song at a book-release concert.

"Rebel Girl"
by Bikini Kill

"Rebel Girl" was released in three different recorded versions in 1993; an EP, album, and seven-inch single. The single version was produced by Joan Jett and featured Jett on guitar and background vocals. Although the band collectively wrote "Rebel Girl," Hanna was credited with writing the lyrics. Hanna cited feminist artist Juliana Luecking as inspiration for the song. The lyrics were an ode to feminist solidarity. Specifically, it gave a voice to an unconcealed lesbian perspective. It was an explicit and bold love song from a woman to a woman.

Musically, "Rebel Girl" featured a hard-driving four to the snare feel. Billy Karren achieved a raw and raunchy guitar sound that was both punk and sludgy. The short and sparse guitar solo was more about attitude than instrumental virtuosity. "Rebel Girl" was considered both a classic punk genre song and an anthem of the riot grrrl movement of the 1990's. Bikini Kill were passionate both musically and in stating their message.

Women Take Their Rightful Place in Punk Rock

Punk rock and heavy metal have been portrayed as a male dominated aggressive and often violent subculture. However, many talented and passionate women have helped to liberate women both musically and in society. Patti Smith came onto the scene and showed that her androgyny and rock-star prowess could play the same game as men. The Los Angeles band, The Runaways, proved that women could play guitar, bass, and drums at a high level. Joan Jett and Lita Ford's post-Runaways long-term success showed that woman can rock as hard as any man.

In England, *Siouxsie Sioux* (aka Susan Dallion) was one of the original Sex Pistol fans that was inspired by a global DIY ethos. Siouxsie's wild makeup, hairstyles, and sharp vocal attacks turned traditional female rock imagery inside out. Also, Marion Elliot and Susan Whitby started *X-Ray Spex*. Their single "Oh Bondage, Up Yours," announced that sexually outrageous themes were no longer just the province of male rock stars. The British punk scene also produced all-female bands such as The Slits and The Raincoats that were the direct antecedents of the 1990's riot grrrl movement.

The *riot grrl movement* had its origins in Washington state in the early 1990's led by Bikini Kill (see this chapter), Sleater-Kenny, Bratmobile, Heavens to Betsy, Huggy Bear, and others. Riot grrl bands addressed significant issues such as domestic abuse, sexuality, rape, racism, and female empowerment. The riot grrl movement became a subculture that advocated for political action, activism, and a DIY ethic that said that women could do anything. The riot girl movement spread quickly through grassroots organizations. Its members and proponents worked tirelessly to end sexism and physical and emotional violence against women and girls.

Punk rock catapulted women beyond the domain of being a novelty act or backup singers for a male dominated band. It signaled that females could play, sing, and write anything in the rock genre that men could, and bring it all with a liberated female perspective. The all-boy's club was over.

Los Angeles/West Coast Punk

Los Angeles was home to the early 1970's glam rock scene and the beginning of the country rock genre. However, there was still room for more musical innovation. Following the examples set by bands such as The Ramones, The Sex Pistols, and The Clash, Southern California was ready to add to the continued regional growth of punk music. By 1976, many new punk bands were emerging from Los Angeles and the Orange County areas. These bands included; **Black Flag, The Dead Kennedys, Social Distortion** (1978-1985) (1986-present), **Bad Religion** (1979-present), **Circle Jerks** (1979-1990) (1994-1995) (2001-2010), **MDC** (1979-1995) (2000-present), **X** (1977-present), **NOFX** (1983-present), and many more.

Black Flag (1976-1986) (2003) (2013-present) was formed in Hermosa Beach, California by guitarist/songwriter Greg Ginn. Black Flag developed a sound based on the raw attitude of The Ramones with an anti-authoritarian and nonconformist message. Henry Rollins joined the band in 1981 and Black Flag continued to evolve by mixing punk and heavy metal with elements of free jazz and breakbeat music. Black Flag's 1981 debut album, Damaged, featured Ginn, Rollins, guitarist Dez Cadena, bassist Chuck Dukowski, and drummer Robo (aka Julio Valencia). While Damaged was initially received poorly, the songs "Six Pack" and "TV Party" were later cited as important hardcore punk recordings with their violent guitar riffs and Rollins's aggressive screams. Kurt Cobain credited it as one of his favorite recordings.

"TV Party"
by Greg Ginn

"TV Party" was first released on the EP titled TV Party after the release of their album Damaged. The song was a satire about drinking, boredom, and the American obsession with watching television. "TV Party" was a parody about people that take themselves too seriously. To promote the EP, Black Flag made a "TV Party" video featuring band members and their friends drinking beer and calling out their favorite television shows in front of a TV set.

Musically, "TV Party" was fueled by Chuck Dukowski's bassline and featured Henry Rollins distinctive vocals. The band chanted "TV Party Tonight" four times to begin the song over the bassline. After citing various TV shows by name, the band further chanted "we have nothing better to do" and "watch TV and have a couple

---

Rock Hard Fact

Henry Rollins of Black Flag is a humanitarian and political activist. He has organized many charity events and has visited Afghanistan and Burma to document the effects of poverty and war.

"I was a much older and a more mellow person than Johnny Rotten or Sid Vicious, but I could relate to that anti-establishment feeling. The energy and aggression-hatred!"

– Sting

of brews." "TV Party" went to number thirty on the UK indie charts. The song also appeared in the underground punk film Repo Man, that was organized by executive producer Michael Nesmith (The Monkees).

Black Flag released four more studio albums in the 1980s including 1984's My War and 1985's In My Head. The band broke up in 1986, citing growing tensions due to their relentless touring schedule and infighting. After their breakup, Henry Rollins formed his own band and worked as a spoken-word artist, book publisher, and actor. In 2013, Ginn and vocalist Ron Reyes re-formed Black Flag and released 2013's What The…. Black Flag was known as one of the pioneering hardcore punk bands. They successfully experimented by infusing punk with sludge metal, jazz, blues, spoken work, and other music genres.

The Dead Kennedys (1978-1986) (2001-present) are a punk band that formed in San Francisco, California in 1978. After a number of lineup changes, the current members are guitarist East Bay Ray (aka Raymond John Pepperell), bassist Klaus Flouride, drummer D.H. Peligro, and vocalist Ron Greer. As their name implies The Dead Kennedys were a provocative and political punk band. Started by vocalist Jello Biafra, The Dead Kennedys debuted in 1978 with a hit single, "California Uber Alles." The band released their debut album Fresh Fruit for Rotting Vegetables in 1980. Shortly after, Biafra started his own label, Alternative Tentacles, to release music by The Dead Kennedys and other bands. The band released the 1981 EP In God We Trust, Inc., 1982's Plastic Surgery Disasters, 1985's Frankenchrist, and 1986's Bedtime for Democracy. Controversy often followed the band, especially due to Biafra's political profile as a free speech activist. The Dead Kennedy's re-formed in 2001 with vocalist Ron Greer replacing Biafra. The Dead Kennedys were one of the first American hardcore bands to have a significant impact in England. They were known for their harsh lyrics that expressed a staunch left-wing view of contemporary America.

Crossover-Hardcore Meets Thrash

In the early to mid-1980's thrash metal and hardcore punk fans, who had at one time been fierce rivals, realized that their music and lifestyles had much in common. We can define **Crossover-Hardcore-Thrash** as a subgenre of both punk and heavy metal. Crossover occurred when both styles took musical and non-musical elements from each other to form a hybrid style of music. Due to the fact that they weren't easily accepted by the mainstream rock community (or society in general), crossover artists and their fans formed their own culture. The crossover scene in New York City yielded a number of bands throughout the 1980's. They included: **Agnostic Front** (1980-1992) (1997-present), **Cro-Mags, Carnivore** (1982-present with some inactive years), **Stormtroopers of Death** (1985-2007 with some inactive years), and **Biohazard**.

Cro-Mags (1981-present) are a crossover band from New York City that went from strictly hardcore punk to adding more metal riffs and a heavier sound. They have built a strong cult following on the strength of their first album, 1986's The Age of Quarrel. This album utilized many fast tempos. However, songs like "Malfunction" and "Seekers of the Truth" were more heavy metal, foreshadowing the crossover hardcore *thrash* style of their later albums. The original lineup featured vocalist John Joseph, guitarist Parris Mitchell Mayhew, guitarist Doug Holland, bassist Harley Flanagan, and drummer Mackie Jayson. The band knew the tough life of the New York streets and it showed in their music. Joseph recalled, "I was raised on the streets when it was really f***ing dangerous. The band was an outlet to express what I was feeling from being on the streets, and it was cool because we had this spiritual message about looking for meaning in life. But we were unlike bands who delivered their message with a flower. Cro-Mags delivered it with a baseball bat." #13 The Age of Quarrel became a model for the East Coast hardcore movement with the songs "World Peace," "Street Justice," and "We Gotta Know."

"We Gotta Know"
by John Joseph, Harley Flanagan and Parris Mitchell Mayhew

"We Gotta Know" featured a slow introduction with a powerful Black Sabbath-like guitar riff. Cro-Mags utilized this riff to alternate with manic fast punk vocal verses. A short shredding metal solo moved to another fast instrumental section. The Cro-Mags played with a drive and energy that made the fusion of punk and metal flow easily.

"We Gotta Know" received airplay on MTV's *Headbangers Ball* broadcast. It combined the speed of Motorhead with the attitude of The Sex Pistols. Many musicians such as Karl Buechner of the metalcore band Earth Crisis have stated that the video for "We Gotta Know" was their motivation to enter the hardcore crossover scene.

By 1989's Best Wishes, lineup changes saw Joseph and Jayson leave the band while bassist Harley Flanagan moved to lead vocals and Pete Hines took over the drumset chair. The Best Wishes album cover revealed the band's interest in the Hare Krishna religion. This would ultimately result in the demise of the band when a faith of pacifism stood in contradiction to the violence of the band's music. Unable to coexist, Joseph and Flanagan bounced in and out of the band between hiatuses. The band released three more studio albums including; 1992's Alpha Omega, 1993's Near Death Experience, and 2002's Revenge. The Cro-Mags endured many more lineup changes and Flanagan and Joseph have simultaneously led separate versions of the band. The Cro-Mags were one of the first to combine heavy metal and hardcore. They continue to perform.

Biohazard (1987-2006) (2008-present) is a crossover band that formed in Brooklyn, New York in 1987. They are one of the first bands to fuse hardcore punk with heavy metal. However, they added a twist of hip hop. Their early lineup consisted of vocalist/bassist Evan Seinfeld, guitarist Bobby Hambel, and drummer Anthony Meo. Guitarist/vocalist Billy Graziadei would soon join, thus making the band a four-piece. Biohazard released their self-titled debut Biohazard in 1990 to little fanfare due to poor promotion. The album addressed street issues such as gang-wars, drugs, and violence but struggled to find an audience. Graziadei remembered, "We didn't exactly fit in anywhere. When we played with bands like Exodus and Slayer, we got the vibe we weren't metal enough. Then we would play with hardcore bands and we were too metal. We were outcasts. So we just did our own thing and created our own style, which eventu-

Rock Hard Fact

After their 1983 debut album release, Suicidal Tendencies was banned from playing in Los Angeles due to the band's supposed connection to "gang relations and violence." The ban was lifted in 1989.

ally became popular." #14 Biohazard has released eight more studio albums including 2012's Reborn in Defiance. Biohazard has achieved success by mixing syncopated beats, crushing metal riffs, and blistering solos with hip-hop influenced vocals.

In the early 1980's, the crossover scene was thriving all across America. Bands were formed from Washington D.C to North Carolina to Texas to Southern California, and everywhere in between. Some crossover shows in bigger cities were booked at established rock venues. However, in regions where bands weren't as popular, gigs were held in gyms, VFW halls, old warehouses, or community centers. A few of these crossover bands included **Void** (1980-1983), **The Faith** (1981-1983), and **Suicidal Tendencies**.

Suicidal Tendencies (1980-1995) (1997-present) is a crossover thrash band formed in Venice, California in 1980. The band was started by vocalist Mike Muir and the current lineup is Muir, guitarist Dean Pleasants and Jeff Pogan, bassist Ra Diaz, and drummer Dave Lombardo. The crossover pioneering Suicidal Tendencies became the "go to group" for metal-loving gangster types on the West Coast. While the band members weren't in a gang, they certainly looked the part and didn't discourage violence at their live shows. Their 1983 self-titled debut album, Suicidal Tendencies, was one of the punk genre's best sellers featuring the song "Institutionalized," that was included in the 1984 cult film *Repo Man*. That same year, Suicidal Tendencies added guitar shredder Rocky George, who remained in the band for eleven years and whose hard riffing style was imitated by many crossover guitarists.

"Institutionalized"
by Mike Muir and Louiche Mayorga

"Institutionalized" was written mostly by bassist Louiche Mayorga and was about a teenage boy that went through a series of social conflicts with his parents and friends. The boy's friends noticed his behavior but he refused their help when they wanted to talk. The boys' parents insisted he was on drugs and needed help. The boy retaliated and denied there was a problem. Rather than sing the vocals, Mike Muir spoke the lyrics in a run-on sentence style.

The guitar part complemented the lyrics, which were subdued at the beginning of the verses, but gained intensity and became more powerful when the lyrics highlighted the boy's emotional outbursts. The drumset part in the verses was a heavy metal-like shuffle groove. On the choruses, Suicidal Tendencies captured a chaotic musical feeling that matched the conflict portrayed in the lyrics. A video for "Institutionalized" was first shown on MTV in 1984. The song appeared in the films *Iron Man*, *Repo Man*, and *The Brady Bunch Movie*.

Mike Muir felt the band was always being judged when he said, "We've always been the outsiders. There are certain people that try to be outsiders. We never did. We just were outside. We realized that, and everywhere we went there were people watching us warily. Even when we were in a room, the people there were afraid we were going to trash the place." #15 Suicidal Tendencies went on to record twelve more studio albums including 2016's World Gone Mad. Mike Muir is the only original member left in the band amid numerous lineup changes over the years. Suicidal Tendencies combined heavy metal with thrash, funk, punk, and alternative elements to establish their crossover style. They have influenced countless metal, punk, and hard rock bands in other genres.

Two more 1980's crossover bands outside of New York and Los Angeles were **D.R.I. (Dirty Rotten Imbeciles)**, and **Corrosion of Conformity**. Both of these bands went from strictly being hardcore to adding more metal riffs and achieving an even heavier sound. They also both came from scenes far removed from the major crossover action and had no choice but to adopt a strong DIY mentality.

D.R.I. (Dirty Rotten Imbeciles) (1982-present) is a crossover thrash band that formed in Houston, Texas in 1982. Since 2015, the lineup has consisted of drummer Walter Ryan, bassist Harald Oimoen, and founding members vocalist Kurt Brecht and guitarist Spike Cassidy. D.R.I. released their 1983 debut album Dirty Rotten LP. Known for their very short compositions, the full length CD contained forty-five songs that weighted in at just over fifty minutes in length. D.R.I. released six more studio albums from 1985's Dealing with It! to 1995's Full Speed Ahead. Starting as a speed driven straight ahead punk band, D.R.I. gradually blended metal elements into their approach. Their songs became longer and contained a variety of tempos. Their crossover sound appealed to metal, hardcore, and skate-punk fan bases.

Corrosion of Conformity (C.O.C.) (1982-2006) (2010-present) are from North Carolina. They started as hardcore punk and moved to a heavy metal sound with slower and blues influenced elements. Beginning with their 1984 Eye for an Eye, the band has released nine studio albums, four EPs, one compilation, and one live album. Their current lineup of vocalist/guitarist Mike Dean, guitarist Woody Weatherman, drummer Reed Mullin, and vocalist/guitarist/bassist Pepper Keenan appeared on their 2014 album IX. Mullin recalled how the band evolved when he said, "The three of us (me, Mike Dean, Woody Weatherman) all learned how to play our instruments together. We had a common interest in bands like Black Sabbath, Deep Purple. Bands who had different time signatures, etc... and for whatever reason, we morphed into Corrosion of Conformity. It's been about thirty years now." #16 C.O.C. became known for their aggressive sound combined with intelligent political lyrics. Corrosion of Conformity successfully broke away from both metal and hardcore conventions and later shifted to a more stripped-down Black Sabbath meets the deep South to create their unique crossover approach.

Punk-Pop Bands

Pop-influenced punk rock originated in the mid to late 1970's with some similarities to power pop. Until the 1990's, the punk rock movement never really took hold in any large-scale commercial way. Many rock and pop musicians didn't buy into the uncompromising sound, aggressive attitude, and DIY mentality that punk rock brought to the table. Major recording labels and mainstream radio also stayed clear of punk rock. That was until **Green Day** and a wave of neo-punk bands arrived. **Punk-pop** musically merged upbeat pop melodies with catchy hooks and simple harmonies with fast punk tempos and loud, distorted guitars. The trick was to make radio friendly songs that retained the speed and (somewhat) raw attitude of punk. Lyrical content of punk-pop focused on love, lust, and adolescence.

> "Punk wasn't like it is now where everyone's listening to Green Day and you can buy the latest punk fashions in Hot Topic."
>
> - Billy Graziadel from Biohazard

Punk rock did remain the bedrock of underground and alternative rock throughout the 1980's. However, it wasn't until the early 1990's that the corporate music industry because interested in the commercial appeal of punk-pop. This was partially realized by the success of Nirvana. Then, many bands became encouraged by the possibilities of alternative music in general. With the door slightly open, a few neo-punk bands demonstrated different motives than the original punk bands. The musical world didn't really experience a punk revival (punk didn't need reviving). However, a commercial compromise was reached by many punk-pop bands that emerged in the mid-to late 1980's and well into the 1990's. Some of these bands included; **The Offspring, Green Day, Rancid** (1991-present), **Less Than Jake** (1992-present), **Sum 41** (1996-present), and **Blink-182**.

The Offspring (1983-present) are a punk-pop band that formed in 1984 in Garden City, California. The Offspring was one of the first bands to bring punk rock into the mainstream in the 1990's. The original lineup featured vocalist/guitarist Bryan "Dexter" Holland, bassist Greg K (aka Greg Kriesel), guitarist Kevin "Noodles" Wasserman, and drummer James Lilja. Their longest (of five) tenured drummers was Ron Welty, who replaced Lilja in 1987 and stayed until 2003. Welty was replaced by Atom Willard in 2003 and he was later replaced with current drummer Pete Parada in 2007.

The Offspring have released nine studio albums, from their 1989 self-titled debut The Offspring, to 2012's Days Go By. The band catapulted into the mainstream market with their third album, 1994's Smash. It sold over twelve million copies worldwide, making it the biggest selling independent label album of all time. Along with Green Day's Dookie, Smash paved the way for punk-pop with the hits "Come Out and Play," "Gotta Get Away," and "Self Esteem." The Offspring developed a hard-driving sound that produced a number of anthemic punk-pop singles in the 1990s. Their Smash album inspired many bands and opened the door for punk bands to achieve mainstream success.

"Come Out and Play"
by Dexter Holland

"Come Out and Play" was The Offspring's breakout hit and it received widespread radio play. The song was about gang and gun violence in schools. The lyric of "Gottta keep 'em separated" came when Dexter was in medical school and was experimenting with bacteria in a science laboratory. He was cooling down the bacteria with Erlenmeyer flasks (a lab flask with a flat bottom and conical body) and came up with the song's lyric about separating two different samples.

"Come Out and Play" was written after a trip made by Dexter to the Middle East. Having heard Arabic scales, Dexter wrote the songs' guitar riff inspired by Middle Eastern music. The Offspring were able to mix the catchy melody with a hard punky edge. "Come Out and Play" was basically a social commentary. The video for the song received strong MTV rotation and was shot almost entirely in black and white. It featured The Offspring performing the song in the garage of a house with tinfoil covering the walls.

Green Day (1987-present) is a punk-pop band that formed in East Bay, California in 1987. The band, first called Sweet Children, was originally part of the DIY punk scene in Berkeley, California. They changed their name to Green Day and released their 1990 debut release 39/Smooth. They followed with 1991's Kerplunk on the independent record label, Lookout Records. Their first major label release, 1994's Dookie, was a huge success producing the hits "Longview," "Basket Case," and "When I Come Around." The videos for all three of these hits received extensive MTV airplay. Green Day had started as a hobby for guitarist Billie Joe Armstrong and bassist Mike Dirnt. Original drummer John Kiffmeyer (aka Al Sobrante) was replaced by longtime current drummer Tre Cool (aka Frank Edwin Wright III) in 1990 prior to the recording of Kerplunk. Guitarist Jason White (who had toured with the band since 1999) was a member of the band from 2012 to 2016.

Groundbreaking album Dookie
by Green Day

Dookie was a worldwide commercial launching pad for the career of Green Day. It initially peaked at number two in America and charted in seven countries. Although "Longview," "Basket Case," and "When I Come Around" were instant hits, "Welcome to Paradise" and "She" were also big hits. The album won a Grammy Award for Best Alternative Music Album in 1995, and has sold over twenty million copies worldwide to date.

The songs on Dookie were "Burnout," then "Having a Blast," "Chump," "Longview," "Welcome to Paradise," "Pulling Teeth," "Basket Case," "She," "Sassafras Roots," "When I Come Around," "Coming Clean," "Emenius Sleepus," "In the End," and "F.O.D." Most of the songs were written by Billie Joe Armstrong, except for "Emenius Sleepus," written by Mike Dirnt. A hidden track, "All by Myself," was composed by drummer Tre Cool. The subject matter of Dookie focused on the band's various experiences with subjects such as anxiety, boredom, sexual orientation, divorce, mass murder, ex-girlfriends, and masturbation.

"Basket Case" was a song about anxiety attacks and was both personal and cathartic for Armstrong, who suffered from panic attacks while growing up. "Longview" was about the negative feelings of being a loner and bored. Again, Armstrong was writing from the difficult times he had experienced in his youth. For "When I Come Around," Armstrong wrote about being away from his girlfriend when Green Day was out on tour. While performing "When I Come Around" at the 1994 Woodstock show, Green Day got into a mud throwing fight causing bassist Mike Dirnt to sustain some injuries that occurred onstage. Dookie gave Green Day a blockbuster album that was almost as revolutionary as Nirvana's Nevermind, thus setting the stage for big-label punk-pop music.

2004's American Idiot, a rock opera, rocketed to number one in America and England. It yielded five hits including "Boulevard of Broken Dreams" and "Wake Me Up When September Ends." In 2009, Green Day did it again with 21st Century Breakdown, their fifth Grammy winner. This solidified Green Day's place as punk-pop icons. Green Day were punk revivalists who recharged the punk mindset with speed and catchy three-chord hit songs. They brought the sound of late 1970's punk to a new, younger generation. Green Day was inducted into the Rock and Roll Hall of Fame in 2015.

Blink-182 (1992-2005) (2009-present) is a punk-pop band that formed in Poway, California in 1992. Since 2015, Blink's lineup featured vocalist/bassist Mark

> "I always expect there to be a new counter-culture coming up, something that would make punk look as ridiculous as punk made the hippies look."
>
> – Grant Hart of Husker Du

Hoppus, guitarist/vocalist Tom DeLonge, and drummer Travis Barker, who replaced original drummer Scott Raynor in 1997. Matt Skiba replaced DeLonge in 2015. Their 1995 debut, Cheshire Cat, brought the band success, especially within the San Diego skate punk scene. Blink-182 released six more studio albums including 2016's California. Blink combined pop melodies and fast tempos with a radio-friendly sensibility. At a time when teen pop and nu-metal were gaining popularity, Blink-182 produced a string of hits, often presented with humorous, tongue-in-cheek music videos that were popular in the waning days of MTV. In 2016, Blink-182 released a career-spanning vinyl anthology titled Box Set that contained all six of the band's studio albums prior to their album California.

The punk subgenre of **emo** was originally an artsy outgrowth of hardcore punk. Some emo moved toward a progressive side with a complex guitar approach, unorthodox song structures, and wide dynamic shifts. Other emo bands embraced a more intricate punk-pop direction with deeply personal lyrics or even free-associative poetry. Either way, emo bands were less macho but still held the punk ideals of preoccupation with authenticity and anti-commercialism. Emo also grew out of the conviction that commercially oriented music was artificial and too calculated, void of genuine emotion. Some of the significant emo bands included; **Rites of Spring** (1984-1986), **The All-American Rejects** (1999-present), **Panic! At the Disco** (2004-present), **My Chemical Romance**, and **Fall Out Boy**.

My Chemical Romance (2001-2013) was an emo post-punk band that formed in Newark, New Jersey in 2001. Their classic lineup was vocalist Gerard Way, guitarists Ray Toro and Frank Iero, bassist Mikey Way, and drummer Bob Bryar. My Chemical Romance embodied a number of punk subgenres such as punk-pop, post-hardcore, and emo. Their 2002 debut, I Brought You My Bullets, You Brought Me Your Love, was considered to be an emo album with its raw guitar riffs and screaming vocals drawn from hardcore punk. 2004's Three Cheers for Sweet Revenge was instrumental in launching the emo style into mainstream rock. My Chemical Romance followed with 2006's popular The Black Parade and 2010's Danger Days: The True Lives of the Fabulous Killjoys. After the band broke up in 2013, they released 2014's May Death Never Stop You, a greatest hits album.

Fall Out Boy (2001-2009) (2013-present) was an emo post-punk band that formed in Chicago, Illinois in 2001. The band had its roots in the Chicago hardcore punk scene. The classic lineup was vocalist/guitarist Patrick Stump, guitarist Joe Trohman, bassist Pete Wentz, and drummer Andy Hurley. Fall Out Boy's 2002 debut, Take This to Your Grave, was an underground success and Grave's songs "Grand Theft Autumn/Where Is Your Boy" and "Saturday" laid the groundwork for 2005's From Under the Cork Tree. This album reached the top ten on the U.S. charts with the single "Dance, Dance" and "Sugar, We're Goin Down."

"Sugar, We're Goin Down"
by Pete Wentz and Patrick Stump

For "Sugar, We're Goin Down," Patrick Stump wrote the music and Pete Wentz wrote the lyrics. Wentz deliberately slurred the lyrics and was going for a punk feeling. The song was about a boy who pursued a girl. However, he meant nothing to her as heard in the line "I'm just a notch in your bedpost but you're just a line in a song." The song further expressed how their relationship wasn't working. In the chorus, the lyric of "I'll be your number one with a bullet, a loaded God complex cock it and pull it" meant that she might as well be killing him since he was feeling so much emotional pain.

Musically, "Sugar, We're Goin Down" featured grungy guitars and a brief interlude between verses with a driving four to the bar drumset feel. Initially, Fall Out Boy's label mistakenly doubted the song's commercial potential. "Sugar, We're Goin Down" went on to sell over five million copies and may be the most popular emo song of all time.

Fall Out Boy rose to the forefront of emo punk-pop in the mid-2000's selling over four million albums. Their underground status, driven by Pete Wentz's extroverted personality, brought the band to star status. Fall Out Boy released their sixth studio album, American Beauty/American Psycho in 2015. It combined their core emo sound with elements of electronica, r&b, and hip-hop, debuting at number one in America. Fall Out Boy continues to tour and released Mania in 2018.

Discussion Question

Can a band (punk or otherwise) keep a radical, uncompromising political stance while working for a major record label whose mission it is to sell records to a mass audience? Be specific and use examples of the success or failure of at least two bands/artists.

New Wave

In the 1970's punk rock startled the rock music industry out of its complacency. However, punk's aggression and raw sound was too confrontational for mainstream radio. To the major record labels, punk appeared practically unmarketable. In America and England, the genre of new wave soon developed when bands combined more mainstream rock characteristics with punk-like energy, less angry guitar sounds, and less "I want to kill you" lyrics. **New wave** music brought back to rock music a direct, danceable energy that had largely been abandoned. New Wave artists like the B-52's returned rock audiences to the dance floor. Songs like Cheap Trick's "I Want You To Want Me," Devo's "Whip It," and Blondie's "Heart of Glass" suffused the new wave style.

New wave bands emphasized smooth bass lines, keyboard or electronic sounds, and a focus on a modern stylistic approach with catchy melodies. The synthesizer came to represent a new wave timbre with less emphasis on virtuosity (as heard in progressive rock music). Some bands utilized the synthesizer to blur the lines between "man" and "machine." Many new wave bands such as Devo, sang with a detached vocal style and a common theme of the de-humanization of the current culture. A British new wave movement would be built on bands that returned to the pubs and bars to create musical experiences. Many new wave artists from America and England rose to prominence in the early to mid-1970's. Some of these important artists included; **Elvis Costello**, **Joe Jackson** (1954-), **Oingo Boingo** (1972-1995), **The Jam** (1972-1982), **Devo, Cheap Trick, Blondie, Squeeze** (1974-present with some inactive years), **B-52s** (1976-present), and **The Cars**.

Rock Hard Fact

Declan MacManus (aka Elvis Costello) took his fake first name from, of course, Elvis Presley. His fake last name is a tribute to his father's fake stage name, D.P. Costello.

Elvis Costello (1954-) (aka Declan Patrick MacManus) is a British musician/singer/producer from London, England. Costello formed a pub rock (defined earlier in the chapter) band called Flip City. He developed his songwriting craft and was signed to a solo recording deal with Stiff Records in 1977. At the height of the British punk movement, Costello released his 1977 debut My Aim is True. This record shared some of punk's energy and anger, although its lyrical stance and musical styling set it apart. Costello was backed by an American West Coast band called Clover, some of whom would go on to play with Huey Lewis and The News. Two of the notable hits from My Aim is True were "Alison" and "Watching the Detectives."

"Watching the Detectives"
by Elvis Costello

"Watching the Detectives" was Elvis Costello''s first hit single and it reached number fifteen on the British charts. The single was produced by Nick Lowe and the backing band included bassist Andrew Bodnar and drummer Steve Goulding, both from Graham Parker's band, The Rumour. Keyboard parts were later added by Steve Nieve. The song featured an authentic half-time reggae feel over which Costello was very comfortable phrasing his vocal lines.

Elvis Costello wrote the song after an all-night session of listening to The Clash's debut album The Clash. He drank an entire jar of instant coffee and stayed awake for thirty-six hours. Costello considered "Watching the Detectives" to be his favorite from the first five years of his career. He later performed it as a big band arrangement. "Watching the Detectives" was covered by the band Toto and Duran Duran.

In 1977, Costello formed a new backing band called The Attractions with pianist Steve Nieve, bassist Bruce Thomas, and drummer Pete Thomas. Costello and The Attractions appeared on an episode of *Saturday Night Live* (replacing The Sex Pistols). They performed their song "Radio Radio" that criticized the commercialization of the airwaves, which NBC and Lorne Michaels had forbidden them to play. Costello was subsequently banned from the show and he received much attention when (from his performance) the media portrayed him to be an angry British rocker (the ban was lifted in 1989).

1978's This Year's Model featured the hit "Pump it Up." 1979's Armed Forces brought Costello to the top ten in America with "Oliver's Army" and "Accidents will Happen." The 1980's saw Costello release nine albums including 1980s Get Happy! and 1981's Trust. From the 1990's until the release of 2010's National Ransom, Elvis Costello remained a prolific recording artist. During that time, he collaborated with songwriter Bert Bacharach, jazz musicians Alan Toussaint and Marian McPartland, and The London Symphony Orchestra. Elvis Costello has fused many genres from country, reggae, Tin Pan Alley, to pop and new wave styles. His lyrics of biting cynicism and anger are smart and literate. Elvis Costello is one of new wave's great songwriters and vocal artists.

Devo (1973-1991) (1996-present) is a new wave band that formed in Kent and Akron, Ohio in 1973. The classic lineup consisted of two sets of brothers. They are vocalist/multi-instrumentalist Mark Mothersbaugh, vocalist/guitarist Bob Mothersbaugh, vocalist/multi-instrumentalist Gerald Casale and multi-instrumentalist Bob Casale. The band also included drummer Alan Myers (aka the human metronome). In 1970, Gerald Casale met Mark Mothersbaugh at Kent State University, which led to the formation of Devo. The name came from the word "de-evolution," a concept that proposed that instead of continuing to evolve, mankind began to regress, as seen by the dysfunction and herd mentality of American society. Devo performed with different configurations creating songs and making short films. They got their break when they were recommended by David Bowie and Iggy Pop to Warner Bros. Records who signed them in 1978. This led to their 1978 debut Q: Are We Not Men? A: We Are Devo!, produced by Brian Eno (see chapter eighteen). After receiving great exposure from an appearance on *Saturday Night Live*, Devo released Duty Now for the Future and Freedom of Choice in 1980. Freedom of Choice, contained their biggest hit, "Whip It," and moved the band to an almost all electronic sound while keeping acoustic drums and guitar.

"Whip It"
by Mark Mothersbaugh and Gerald Casale

"Whip It" contained lyrics written by Gerald Casale that intended to satirize American society with a nonsensical theme revolving around the idea of solving ones problems by "whipping it." Casale was inspired by a historical novel by author Thomas Pynchon. Mark Mothersbaugh created the "Whip It" distinctive riff by twisting Roy Orbison's song "Oh, Pretty Woman" in a new direction. Devo recorded many ideas for the song, and every day the band would rehearse everybody's snippets of ideas. The "Whip It" drum beat emerged and they built the bassline around it.

Mark Mothersbaugh believed the songs' great popularity resulted from people assuming the lyrics were about sadomasochism. The accompanying music video took that sexual theme and featured Mothersbaugh whipping the clothes off a woman on a dude ranch. The video was very successful on MTV and received strong rotation. "Whip It" was one of the first new wave hits to feature a synthesizer as the lead instrument. Devo, through their song "Whip It," created their own version of *shock rock*.

Devo released 1981's New Traditionalists, 1982's Oh, No! It's Devo, and 1984's Shout, before going on hiatus. They re-formed for 1988's Total Devo with new drummer David Kendrick, replacing Myers. 1990's Smooth Noodle Maps was not well received and the band broke up in 1991. Many years later, Devo released Something for Everybody in 2010. Alan Myers died in 2013 and Bob Casale died in 2014. Devo was one of new wave's most innovative and misunderstood bands. Their music portrayed a view of American society as repressive, mechanical, and rigid. They expressed this perspective with music effects of jerky, robotic rhythms with an obsession for technology and electronics. Devo was also very cutting edge with their use of atonal melodies and unusual chord progressions. All of this filtered through the image of geeky misfits. Devo was a cult sensation that briefly broke through the mainstream. To call them a one hit wonder (with "Whip It") would be unfair to their musicianship and intellect.

Cheap Trick (1973-present) is a new wave band that formed in Rockford, Illinois in 1974. Their lineup consisted of vocalist Robin Zander, guitarist Rick Nielsen, bassist Tom Petersson, and drummer Bun E. Carlos. Drummer Daxx Nielsen later replaced Carlos in 2010. Cheap Trick produced songs with a hard rock sound and a new wave punkish attitude. In 1977, they released their

> "We didn't share the sensibilities of punk. We knew what we were angry about, and we knew who we were angry at."
>
> - Mark Mothersbaugh of Devo

self-titled debut album Cheap Trick, and In Color, that same year. Both albums found early success in Japan. 1978's Heaven Tonight contained the hit "Surrender." But it was 1978's live album Cheap Trick at Budokan, recorded in front of screaming Japanese fans, that gave them their breakthrough. It reached number four on the U.S. charts, and yielded a live single of "I Want You to Want Me" that went to number seven on the charts.

"I Want You To Want Me"
by Rick Nielsen

"I Want You To Want Me" was written by Rick Nielsen somewhat as a joke, because of all the pop music he heard on the radio at the time. Nielsen pictured an over the top ABBA-like heavy metal pop song. By 1978, Cheap Trick had dropped the song from their set list, but restored it when they toured Japan later that same year. The live version was faster than the original studio version from their In Color album. Bun E. Carlos gave the song character by beginning with a punk-like shuffle feel on his snare drum. The live version also contained two guitar solos, while a less aggressive studio version had a piano fill in the second instrumental section.

The famous At Budokan version was inspired by a French cover version (titled "J'attend Toutes les Nuits) by an obscure French synth-pop artist named Niko Flynn, who sped up the tempo. Many early Cheap Trick songs written by Rick Nielsen were from the perspective of a character who was a little unhinged. The band played that up with their eccentric fashions and accessories. The man portrayed in the lyrics to "I Want You To Love Me" was desperate and delusional, figuring that a shoeshine and new shirt would make the girl fall in love with him.

1979's Dream Police was another successful release with the hits "Dream Police" and "Voices." By 1980's All Shook Up, Cheap Trick was headlining arenas all over the world. However, Tom Petersson left the band that same year. Cheap Trick replaced him with bassist Pete Comita and then with Jon Brant. The band wasn't able to repeat the success with their next few albums, 1982's One on One and 1983's Next Position Please. Cheap Trick kept working hard with 1985's Standing on the Edge and 1986's The Doctor. By 1988's Lap of Luxury, Petersson had returned and they produced a number one hit, "The Flame," from that record. The band went on to record nine more studio albums including 2017's We're All Right and Christmas Christmas. Cheap Trick combined strong pop songwriting and crunchy guitar power chords with a penchant for the absurd and sarcastic. They provided a significant link between 1960's pop with (then current) elements of new wave and metal. Cheap Trick was inducted into the Rock and Roll Hall of Fame in 2016.

Blondie (1974-1982) (1997-present) is a new wave band that formed in New York City in 1974. Guitarist Chris Stein met vocalist Debbie Harry and added drummer Clem Burke and bassist Gary Valentine to complete the band. Blondie worked often at New York clubs Max's Kansas City and CBGB, and by 1975 had added keyboardist Jimmy Destri to make a demo recording. The band signed with Private Stock Records to record their 1976 self-titled debut album Blondie. This record contained the song "X Offender," originally titled "Sex Offender" but radio stations would not play a song with such a provocative title. Blondie's first commercial success happened in Australia in 1977 when their video, "In the Flesh," was mistakenly aired. Debbie Harry knew how to use her sexuality to sell the band. She remembered, "We started making music videos in 1976, maybe a little earlier. A lot of times we couldn't go to England to promote a single, and they used a lot of video on TV there. We had a big following in Australia as well, and traveling to Australia every time you released a song was out of the question. Our videos were stunning, and so ahead of their time. They have an innocent flavor to them. My nipples are showing in "Heart of Glass.' Maybe that's why people liked the video so much." #17

1978's Plastic Letters had moderate success but that same year Blondie released their breakout album, Parallel Lines. It went to number one in England and number six in America on the strength of the aggressive new wave hit "One Way or Another" and the disco-inspired "Heart of Glass." Parallel Lines would go on to sell over twenty million albums worldwide.

"Heart of Glass"
by Debbie Harry and Chris Stein

"Heart of Glass" was originally called "Once I Had a Love" which Harry and Stein wrote four years prior to recording it for Parallel Lines. The band would refer to the song as "the disco song." It was inspired by The Hues Corporations' hit disco song "Rock the Boat." Harry has stated that they experimented with the feel of "Heart of Glass" by playing it as a ballad and with a reggae groove but had no luck until they applied a disco feel.

When Blondie recorded the song they incorporated the electronic sounds of European disco with the electronic approach taken by the German band Kraftwerk. While the tune was recorded with a standard 4/4 disco feel, the instrumental interlude went to a 7/4 meter. "Heart of Glass" was a pioneering example of a Bee Gees styled disco feel that met the new wave genre.

Blondie's next albums were 1979's Eat to the Beat and 1980's Autoamerican, featuring the hit "The Tide is High." Blondie recorded six more studio albums including 2017's Pollinator. Blondie embraced a broad range of music including; garage rock, reggae, Latin styles, British Invasion rock, hip-hop, and punk. They were the most commercially successful band to emerge from the New York new wave community of the late 1970's. Blondie was inducted into the Rock and Roll Hall of Fame in 2006.

The Cars (1976-1988) (2010-present) are a new wave band that formed in Boston, Massachusetts in 1976. Vocalist/guitarist Ric Ocasek and bassist/vocalist Benjamin Orr had previously worked together in Columbus, Ohio. They added guitarist Elliot Easton, keyboardist Greg Hawkes, and drummer David Robinson to complete The Cars. Robinson suggested the name and due to its simplicity, it stuck. Live gigs showcased The Cars to be a well-oiled machine. A demo tape of their "Just What I Needed" received heavy airplay and they were soon signed to Elektra Records. Roy Thomas Baker was hired for production and the band recorded their 1997 self-titled The Cars. The result was one of the greatest debut albums in rock history. The album yielded multiple hits and stayed on the Billboard charts for almost three straight years.

Groundbreaking album The Cars
by The Cars

All of the songs on The Cars were written by Ric Ocasek except "Moving in Stereo" which was

---

"I've always been a fan of poetry. I grew up with Lawrence Ferlinghetti and the Beat poets. I really followed that stuff for a while. I just love the way people threw words around like they were painting."

- Ric Ocasek

co-written by Greg Hawkes and Ocasek. The Cars, with all nine tracks becoming rock classics, was a genuine new wave masterpiece. The Cars often referred to the album as their greatest hits package. The production, by ex-Queens producer Roy Thomas Baker, was polished and highly professional.

Side one opened with "Good Times Roll," then "My Best Friend's Girl," "Just What I Needed," "I'm in Touch with Your World," and "Don't Cha Stop." The lead off song "Good Times Roll," was Ocasek's sarcastic commentary about the supposed good times to be had in rock music. "My Best Friend's Girl" was about a man's frustration with a woman who was dating his best friend after their relationship ended. "Just What I Needed" was key to getting The Cars on the map when the band took a two-track demo to a popular rock station in Boston. It quickly became the station's most requested song.

Side two opened with "You're All I've Got Tonight," then "Bye Bye Love," "Moving in Stereo," and "All Mixed Up." "You're All I've Got Tonight" featured a clever arrangement with a thumping tom-tom groove and fuzzed-out guitar power chords that captured the classic Cars' sound. "Bye Bye Love," as sung by Benjamin Orr, was one of The Cars oldest songs dating back to his group Cap'n Swing, that featured Ocasek, Orr, and Elliot Easton in a pre-Cars band.

The Cars debut was brilliant on many levels. Elliot Easton may be one of the most underrated guitarist of the new wave era. This album merged new wave elements with Ric Ocasek's pop sensibilities and a band that played with great ensemble precision. All nine of these classic tracks are still in classic rock radio rotation.

1979's Candy-O proved to be a strong follow-up with the hits "Let's Go," "Dangerous Type," and "It's All I Can Do." The Cars were perfectly suited to deliver Ocasek's musical vision, from catchy pop to dark and skewed moods. 1980's Panorama was somewhat more experimental and 1981's Shake It Up began to reveal the strain of The Car's success. Both Ocasek and Hawkes released solo albums at this time. 1984's Heartbeat City produced the hits "You Might Think," "It's Not the Night," and "Hello Again." The Cars remained visible with their videos in heavy rotation on MTV. In 1985, The Cars released The Cars Greatest Hits, an album that sold over eight million copies. 1987's Door to Door would be their last recording before calling it quits in 1988.

Sadly, in 2010 Benjamin Orr died. That same year, the four surviving members reunited to record 2011's Move Like This that featured the songs "Sad Song" and "Blue Tip." The Cars were able to combine the contemporary musical trends of their time including punk, minimalism, and synthesizer driven-pop. To that they added the 1950's element of rockabilly and elements of art rock. The Cars blended all of these influences with a highly evolved melodic power-pop sensibility that resulted in the creation of cutting edge new wave music.

By the mid to late 1970's, new wave music had established a decidedly different musical approach from early 1970's mainstream rock. Some of the prominent new wave artists included; **Thomas Dolby** (1958-), **Gary Numan** (1958-), **Adam and the Ants** (1977-1982), **Graham Parker & the Rumour** (1976-1982) (2011-2015), **Simple Minds** (1977-present), **The Human League** (1977-present), **Thompson Twins** (1977-1993), **Men at Work** (1978-1986) (1996-2002), **Echo & the Bunnymen** (1978-1993) (1996-present), **The Knack, The Pretenders,** and **Duran Duran.**

The Knack (1978-1982) (1986-1992) (1994) (1996-2010) was a new wave band from Los Angeles that formed in 1978. The band consisted of vocalist Doug Fieger, guitarist/keyboardist Berton Averre, drummer Bruce Gary, and bassist Prescott Niles. Their 1979 debut Get the Knack was one of the most successful debuts in music history, selling over one million copies in less that two months. It spawned the hits "Good Girls Don't" and the blockbuster "My Sharona" that went to number one on the U.S. charts.

"My Sharona"
by Doug Fieger and Berton Averre

The inspiration for the song was Sharona Alperin, a high school girl that Doug Fieger met at a clothing store. He was eight years older than her but he was immediately love-struck. "My Sharona" contained an instantly recognizable guitar riff that was created by Berton Averre years before he joined The Knack. Doug Fieger loved the riff and promised to utilize it in a song, although he had no ideas for the lyrics yet. Fieger has acknowledged that the drumset tom-tom rhythm was a version of the Smokey Robinson and the Miracles song "Going to a Go-Go." Drummer Bruce Gary created a full sound by applying a surfer-beat energy to the song.

"My Sharona" has been referred to as an anthem of the new wave era. The song was meant to be fun and full of a teen-like energy. Run-D.M.C. utilized the guitar riff for their song "It's Tricky." "My Sharona" has been featured in the film *Rocketman* and for a trailer for *Charlie's Angels: Full Throttle*. Sharona Alperin appeared on the cover of the Get the Knack album.

The Knack quickly recorded a follow-up album, 1980's …But the Little Girls Understand. It reached number fifteen on the American charts on the strength of the hits "Baby Talks Dirty" and "Can't Put a Price on Love." The Knack went on to release six more studio albums including 2012's Rock & Roll Is Good for You: The Fieger/Averre Demos. This album included early demo recording made by Fieger and Averre that would later be made into some of The Knack's hit songs. Doug Fieger died in 2010 and The Knack called it quits. The Knack regenerated a power pop scene but with a new wave pop sensibility that was neither punk nor hard rock. "My Sharona" was one of new wave's classic anthems.

The Pretenders (1978-1987) (1990-2012) (2016-present) are an American-British new wave band that formed in Hereford, England in 1978. At their core, The Pretenders are one of the most punk of the new wave bands. That happened because vocalist/guitarist/songwriter Chrissie Hynde, originally from Akron, Ohio, moved to London in 1973. There, she worked at the UK music magazine *NME* and met rock journalist Nick Kent. She next worked at the SEX clothing store for Malcolm McLaren (of Sex Pistol's fame). Hynde then played and sung in a number of musical ventures with Mick Jones (of the Clash) and Tony James (of The Damned). Mick Jones remembered, "I played with Chrissie Hynde for a bit. Me and Chrissie were playing songs in my bedroom and we sang together: 'Something's Got a Hold On Me' and Aretha Franklin's 'Every Little Bit Hurts.' I was still a kid and she was quite exotic to me, being from America." #18 Before Chrissie would put together her own band, she embraced the emerging London punk scene and even

> "What punk was about was non-discrimination. And that's why I started trying to get a band together, because I knew that it wouldn't be a novelty that I was a chick. It was like, 'Oh you can play the guitar, let's get together.'"
>
> – Chrissie Hynde

tried to teach Johnny Rotten how to play the guitar (much to the distain of Malcolm McLaren). Chrissie recalled, "In 1976, I went to every (London) club every night, with my guitar. I just walked around the streets looking for someone to get a band together. I was desperate and determined…and I knew when I found my guys that we were going to be right." #19 At one point, Hynde asked Johnny Rotten to marry her just to get a work permit to stay in England.

Hynde next played in a few up and coming punk bands including Master of the Backside, which later became The Damned. In 1978, Hynde organized the band that she would name The Pretenders after the Platters song "The Great Pretender." The original Pretender's lineup was Chrissie Hynde, guitarist/keyboardist James Honeyman-Scott, bassist Pete Farndon, and drummer Martin Chambers. The band's greatest work would be their 1980 self-titled debut album Pretenders. The album shot right to number one on the British charts and made the top ten in America with the hits "Stop Your Sobbing," "Kid," and "Brass In Pocket."

Groundbreaking album Pretenders
by The Pretenders

The album Pretenders has more great songs on it that initially were not hits, but later became rock classics. Many of them still receive major radio airplay today. Nick Lowe had produced The Pretenders first single, "Stop Your Sobbing," but did not want to produce the album because he thought the band was going nowhere.

Side one opened with "Precious," then "The Phone Call," "Up the Neck," "Tattooed Love Boys," "Space Invader," "The Wait," and "Stop Your Sobbing." The opening song "Precious" showcased Hynde's unique vocal style of a steady stream of syllables mixed with jive talk, punk scat, vocal tics, and stabbing aggression. The song became angrier and the climax of her vocal rant was the line "But not me, baby, I'm too precious/F*** off!" "Tattooed Love Boys" represented the most punk of all The Pretenders songs. It was dripping with punk attitude. "Stop Your Sobbing," written by The Kinks Ray Davies (who Hynde later married), was a catchy pop song with a 1950's throwback feel.

Side two opened with "Kid," then "Private Life," "Brass in Pocket," "Lovers of Today," and "Mystery Achievement." One of The Pretenders signature songs "Brass in Pocket" came after Hynde asked someone backstage whose trousers were sprawled over the back of a chair. Someone replied that she would take them "if there's any brass in the pockets." Chrissie didn't know that brass was slang for money and fell in love with the expression. In the video for "Brass in Pocket," Hynde appeared as a waitress, implying the brass was the change she got from tips. Hynde had worked as a waitress in Ohio before moving to London. "Brass in Pocket" had a catchy hook and equally melodic bassline with a relaxed drumset "in the pocket" feel.

Pretenders was a sleek and stylish fusion of new wave pop, aggressive punk attitude, mixed with Rolling Stones-ish rock 'n' roll. Chrissie Hynde didn't fit any female stereotype, nor did her songs. Pretenders delivered many infectious melodies with sheer energy and force, and in the process helped to define the new wave genre. The Pretenders were a premiere band that appeared on the scene fully mature, not just a backup to Chrissie Hynde's powerful songwriting and stage presence.

This very musical Pretenders lineup only managed to record one more record, 1981's Pretenders II, before self-destructing. Farndon was fired for substance abuse in 1982 and shortly after, Honeyman-Scott died from substance abuse. Frandon died the following year, drugs again. 1981's Pretenders II was another strong album with the hits "Talk of the Town" and "Message of Love." 1984's Learning to Crawl featured more lineup changes but the hits kept coming with "Middle of the Road" and "Back on the Chain Gang."

"Back on the Chain Gang"
by Chrissie Hynde

"Back on the Chain Gang" was recorded shortly after Pete Frandon was fired and James Honeyman-Scott died. With only Hynde and drummer Martin Chambers left, The Pretenders brought in guitarist Billy Bremner of Rockpile, guitarist Robbie McIntosh, and bassist Tony Butler to record the track. Most of the song was recorded live in the studio, with Chambers up on a drum riser. Hynde, as she often preferred, went back in to record the vocals by herself, including the overdubs. Later, Chambers and Butler added a chain-gang vocal chant. The sound of clanging hammers was made by banging various metal pieces together.

The lyric of "I found a picture of you" was about a picture Chrissie found in her wallet of Ray Davies. She later dedicated "Back on the Chain Gang" to the memory of Honeyman-Scott. This was an emotional song for Hynde to sing and she would sometime tear up when performing it live. The song went to number four on the U.S. charts and number seventeen in Britain.

For 1986's Get Close, Hynde was still in peak form with number one hits "Don't Get Me Wrong" and ""My Baby." Martin Chambers had left the band, replaced by Blair Cunningham. P-Funk keyboardist Bernie Worrell also appeared on the album. In the 1990's, The Pretenders released three studio albums with Chambers returning for 1994's Last of the Independents. The Pretenders went on to record 2002's Loose Screw, 2008's Break Up the Concrete, and 2016's Alone. In addition to her work with The Pretenders, Chrissie Hynde has appeared with a number of artists, most notably with Frank Sinatra on his 1994 Duets II album.

The Pretenders were the vehicle for Chrissie Hynde's skillful songwriting. But The Pretenders also crossed the bridge between punk and a new-wave. They became a hits producing machine more that any other band since The Cars. A huge part of The Pretenders sound was guitarist James Honeyman-Scott's sonic palette that contained suspended chords and syncopated rhythms with tons of effect pedals. Their string of melodic singles were immediately accessible while Hynde broke through the traditional male dominated role of punk and rock 'n' roll superstars. The Pretenders were inducted into the Rock and Roll Hall of Fame in 2005.

Duran Duran (1978-present) is a new wave band that formed in Birmingham, England in 1978. Although there were numerous lineup changes, the classic lineup was keyboardist Nick Rhodes, bassist John Taylor, vocalist Simon LeBon, guitarist Andy Taylor, and drummer Roger Taylor. Duran Duran released their self-titled debut Duran Duran in 1981. Although initially unsuccessful in America, the album peaked at number

---

Rock Hard Fact

Annie Lenox performed The Queen/David Bowie song "Under Pressure" with David Bowie and the surviving members of Queen at the 1992 Freddie Mercury Tribute Concert at London's Wembley stadium.

three on the British charts with the hit "Girls on Film" and "Planet Earth." The video age catapulted Duran Duran into mainstream popularity when many of their videos received substantial airplay on MTV. 1982's Rio went to number three in England, although it did not initially do well in America. Rio was later released and promoted as a dance-oriented album later that year and climbed the American charts quickly. It featured the hits "Rio" and "Hungry Like the Wolf." Duran Duran went on to record twelve more studio albums including 2015's Paper Gods. Duran Duran's quick rise to stardom was more than just the good looks of a boy band. They built a strong commercial brand and infused synth-pop elements into their new wave style.

"Hungry Like the Wolf"
by Duran Duran

Keyboardist Nick Rhodes began writing what became "Hungry Like the Wolf" with a sequencer one morning in a London studio. Throughout the day, each Duran Duran member arrived at the studio and contributed to the song. The lyrics were inspired by the classic story of *Little Red Riding Hood*. Andy Taylor developed the guitar part from his love of Marc Bolan (of T. Rex). The bass and drums were added next and the track was completed by the end of the day.

Duran Duran travelled to Sri Lanka to shoot the video for "Hungry Like the Wolf." In the video, Simon Le Bon chased a beautiful "tiger-like" woman from an open market in a city through obstacles in the jungle. The video was soon in heavy rotation on MTV, played four times a day. The release of "Hungry Like the Wolf" as a single helped their album Rio reach number three on the British charts.

A second wave of new wave bands started in the early 1980's. By this time, new wave had established a unifying theme of modern freshness and daring musical ideas. New wave had successfully separated from rock's mainstream conventions. The label of new wave could now be applied to a wide swath of disparate musical styles and sounds. Some of the second generation of new wave bands from the 1980's included; **XTC** (1975-2006,) **Missing Persons** (1980-1986) (2001-2003) (2011-present), **A Flock of Seagulls** (1980-1986) (1988-present), **Depeche Mode** (1980-present), **Level 42** (1980-1994) (2001-present), **Pet Shop Boys** (1981-present), **The Bangles** (1981-1989) (1998-present), **Eurythmics**, and **Culture Club**.

Eurythmics (1980-1990) (1999-2005) were the music duo of vocalist/songwriter Annie Lennox and multi-instrumentalist/songwriter David A. Stewart. They met in 1976 and began a musical and personal relationship while playing in a pop band, The Catch, and then with The Tourists. Lennox and Stewart ended their personal relationship when The Tourist disbanded and in 1980, formed The Eurythmics. Their 1981 debut album, In the Garden, received little fanfare but established their signature sound of electronic synthesizer pop songs driven by robotic beats. Soon after, The Eurythmics did achieve global success with their 1983 release Sweet Dreams (Are Made of This), which yielded the hit of the same name.

"Sweet Dreams (Are Made of This)"
by Annie Lennox and David A. Stewart

"Sweet Dreams" was The Eurythmics breakthrough hit and established the duo as a worldwide force. This song showcased the duo's move to electronic music. They acquired new synthesizers and Stewart wrote the main riff on a synth while Lennox added more parts on another synth. This resulted in an innovative interaction where the two musicians performed a dueling synthesizer section.

Annie Lennox was unhappy at the time of the breakup of The Tourists and felt that she was in a dream world. Her line "Sweet dreams are made of this" was her commenting on how they were not going to be able to achieve their dreams. However, Stewart thought the lyrics were too depressing and added the lyric "hold your head up," to express at least a little hope for the future. Lennox multi-tracked the vocal harmony parts. An accompanying video for "Sweet Dreams" received heavy airplay on MTV. "Sweet Dreams" has also been covered by Marilyn Manson.

1983's Touch went to number one in England and featured the ballad "Here Comes the Rain Again," "Right By Your Side," and "Who's That Girl." The latter had an accompanying video that depicted Lennox as both a blonde chanteuse and as a gender-bending Elvis Presley clone. After 1984's 1984 (For the Love of Big Brother), the duo's next recording was 1985's Be Yourself Tonight. It contained a stronger r&b influence, string arrangements, duets with Lennox and Aretha Franklin and Elvis Costello, and a guest appearance by Stevie Wonder on harmonica. 1986's Revenge continued with an r&b flavor. In 1985-86, Stewart produced a number of superstar artists including Mick Jagger, and Tom Petty. Eurythmics reconvened in 1987 to record Savage and then 1989's We Too Are One. The duo quietly went on hiatus in 1990. Lennox began a solo career in 1992 while Stewart continued producing records and writing film soundtracks. Eurythmics reunited to release the album Peace in 1999. Another reunion occurred in 2005, when Lennox and Stewart recorded two new songs, "I've Got a Life" and "Was It Just Another Love Affair?" The Eurythmics were a talented duo that brought British new wave synth-pop music to a new level of creativity and musicianship.

Culture Club (1981-present with some inactive years) is a British new wave band that formed in 1981. Vocalist Boy George (aka George Alan O'Dowd) sang with the band Blitz Club and the group Bow Wow Wow under the stage name Lieutenant Lush. George soon recruited bassist Mikey Craig, guitarist Roy Hay, and drummer Jon Moss to form Culture Club. Realizing they were multi-racial and from different countries, the name Culture Club was perfect. The band released a series of singles and their 1982 debut album, Kissing to Be Clever, featured the hits "I'll Tumble 4 Ya" and "Do You Really Want to Hurt Me."

"Do You Really Want to Hurt Me"
by Culture Club

"Do You Really Want to Hurt Me" reached number one on the British charts and held the number two spot on the U.S. charts behind Michael Jackson's "Billie Jean." Culture Club's popularity rose further after the group appeared on *Top of the Pops* (a British music chart television show) making newspaper headlines when Boy

---

> "Music is an extraordinary vehicle for expressing emotion- very powerful emotions. That's what draws millions of people towards it."
>
> - Annie Lennox

George's androgynous style of dress and sexual ambiguity drew great attention.

The song featured a soft reggae-styled pop feel. Also, bassist Mikey Craig brought a Caribbean influence to the band that would be heard in many of their songs. Boy George later revealed that the song was about a relationship he had with the band's drummer, Jon Moss. They had an affair for about six years that was kept hidden from the public. In America, "Do You Really Want to Hurt Me" crossed over to Adult Contemporary Radio.

1983's <u>Colour by Numbers</u> contained another big hit, "Karma Chameleon," that launched the band into international fame. They followed with 1984's <u>Waking Up with the House on Fire</u> and 1986's <u>From Luxury to Heartache</u>. However, internal tensions within the band and George's struggles with substance abuse forced Culture Club to break up in 1986. After an unsuccessful attempt to reunite in 1989, Culture Club did reunite in 1998. However, their new efforts found only moderate success with their 1999 release, <u>Don't Mind If I Do</u>. After a tour in 2002, the band went on hiatus. In 2014, Culture Club again re-formed and currently continues to tour and record.

Culture Club successfully combined a British new wave sound with American soul and Jamaican reggae styles. They also brought other styles such as country, salsa, and calypso to their approach. Boy George sought to create a bridge between rock and soul. He represented many ethnic groups through his solo work and Culture Club's music. Boy George's musical approach was often classified as a cross between r&b and reggae.

Discussion Question

If The Beatles were currently an up and coming band, what rock genres do you think would influence their songwriting and musical style? Would grunge, punk, or new wave be a factor? Be specific with your response.

Chapter Fourteen: Punk Rock and New Wave

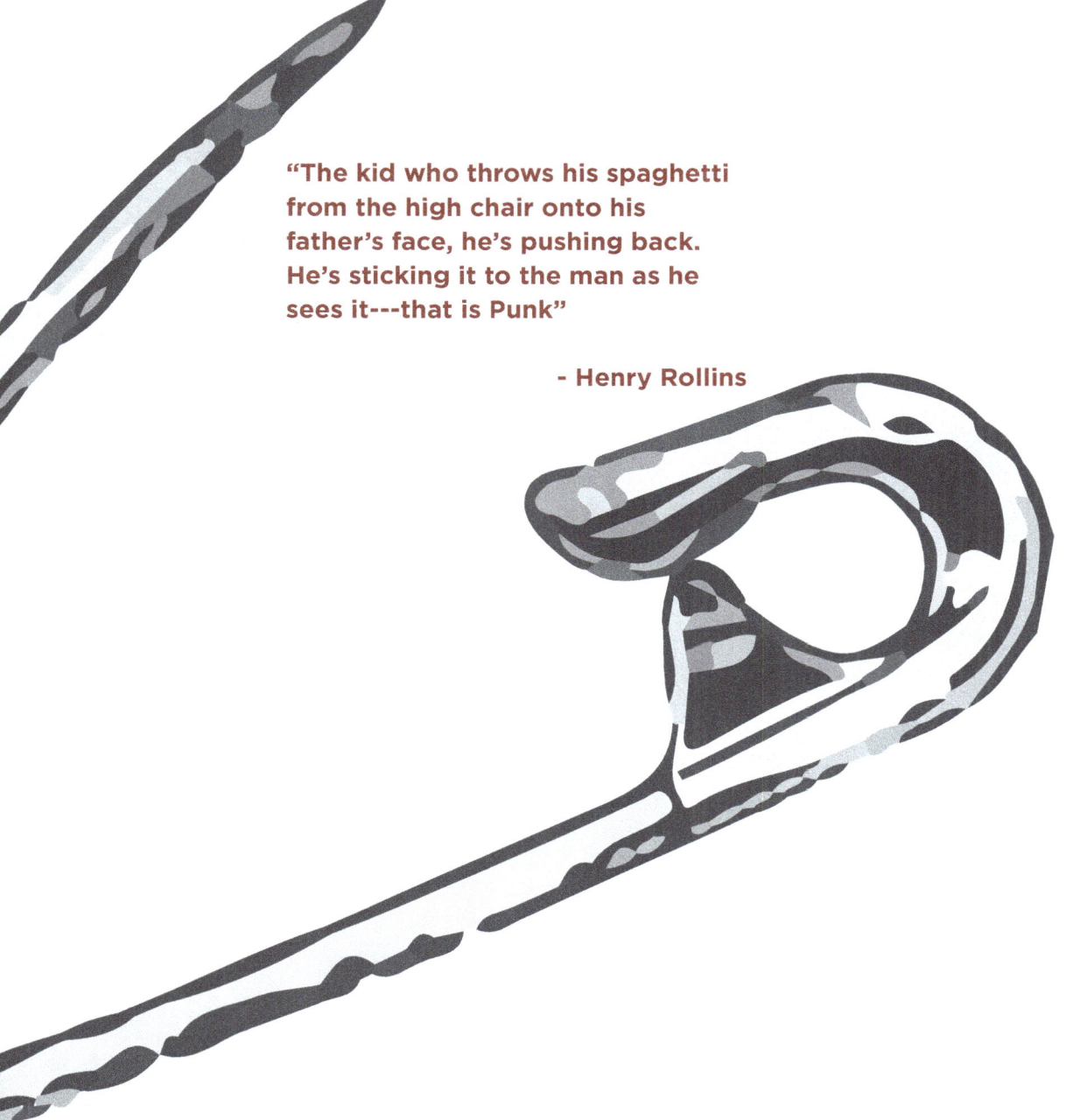

"The kid who throws his spaghetti from the high chair onto his father's face, he's pushing back. He's sticking it to the man as he sees it---that is Punk"

- Henry Rollins

Chapter Fifteen: Pop-Rock

Popular music in America dates back to before the first great songwriter, Stephen Foster of the mid-1850's. The influence of Elvis Presley, rockabilly, and the early rock 'n' roll of the 1950's produced the genre of **pop-rock**. It emerged as the public showed an appetite for a softer, and smoother sound. By the 1960's, a singles market (not albums) developed with the emphasis on songwriting and studio production. The Brill Building songwriters and teen idols (see chapter three) of the 1950's to early 1960's accounted for the foundation of mid-1960's pop to the present day. *1970's FM radio pop-rock* soon followed. Some of these artists included; The Bee Gees, Abba, Gino Vanelli, and The Jackson Five. When *1980's pop-rock* music evolved, it contained a little more of a rock edge. These artists included; Robert Palmer, Cyndi Lauper, Hall and Oates, Paul Young, and Bryan Adams. There were many bands (some successful and some that failed to find wide ranging success) that exemplified and further advanced the aesthetic of pop-rock music. From The Beatles and The Beach Boys to bands such as Tears For Fears, Crowded House, and Level 42; many bands brought high levels of songwriting, production, and arranging skills into the modern era. Space precludes an analysis of many pop-rock bands and artists that exhibited a softer pop style with a softer pop-rock style. That vast list would include; The Carpenters, The Captain & Tennille, Sonny and Cher, Neil Diamond, and many more. Eventually, pop-rock became more powerful. This led to powerful pop bands such as Dave Edmunds and Nick Lowe's band Rockpile, The Romantics, and Weezer. Emerging from its history, pop-rock as a genre was defined by three towering artists; **Michael Jackson, Madonna,** and **Prince**. However, there was another artist that had an important hand in the formation of some of the most important pop music ever created.

Quincy Jones (1933-) is a musician, producer, arranger, and giant in the entertainment business. He drew early inspiration from Ray Charles and worked with jazz musicians Lionel Hampton, Count Basie, and Dizzy Gillespie early in his career. He wrote music for films and television, was the vice president of Mercury records, and worked with Frank Sinatra for 40 years wearing many different musical hats.

Jones brought his vast musical knowledge, and his appreciation for all musical approaches to the pop-rock world when he began producing hit records such as "It's My Party," "You Don't Own Me," and "Look of Love," in the 1960's for singer Lesley Gore. Jones recorded 1969's Waking in Space and 1971's Smackwater Jack, when he developed a musical identity outside of jazz. His new musical palette included utilizing the talents of various jazz musicians as studio talent to create pop music under his leadership. In 1978, he produced the soundtrack for The Wiz starring Diana Ross and Michael Jackson. In 1981, Quincy Jones' released The Dude. This album allowed him to continue to fine tune his pop music production sensibilities. Quincy Jones was inducted into the Rock and Roll Hall of Fame in 2013.

> "When we worked together on Bad, I was in awe of his (Michael Jackson) absolute mastery of movement on the one hand, and of the music on the other."
>
> – Martin Scorsese, film director

Groundbreaking album The Dude
by Quincy Jones

The Dude brought Jones and Michael Jackson together again. It also established Quincy Jones as a certified hit maker and helped to forge musical relationships with many of the musicians and songwriters that he would later recruit to contribute to the Michael Jackson recordings Off The Wall, Thriller, and Bad.

The Dude yielded three top forty hits including; "Just Once," "One Hundred Ways," and "Razzmatazz." It was nominated for twelve Grammy Awards while winning three. It introduced the musical world to vocalist James Ingram and producer David Foster. Additionally, it united Jones and legendary songwriter Rod Temperton for the first time, and firmly established the hit-making team of producer Quincy Jones and engineer Bruce Swedien.

Quincy Jones' *genius* was his arranging and conducting skills, his ear for recognizing when a musical idea was (or wasn't) working, his ability to recognize (and sculpt) a hit song, and his penchant for procuring the best musical talent for the job at hand. Simply put, like George Martin did years before with The Beatles, Quincy Jones was defining the job of the modern music producer. This process began with his records Walking in Space and Smackwater Jack. It was further crystalized on his hit record, The Dude. It would be perfected by the dream-team of songwriter Rod Temperton, engineer Bruce Swedien, producer Quincy Jones, and songwriter/singer Michael Jackson.

Michael Joseph Jackson (1958-2009) was an American singer/composer/dancer and the undisputed "King of Pop." Michael was the seventh of nine children born to Katherine and Joseph Jackson from Gary, Indiana. Michael was a child music prodigy. He had already achieved iconic status in the 1960's and early 1970's when he became the frontman and lead voice for the extremely successful pop group, The Jackson 5 (along with his brothers Jackie, Tito, Jermaine, and Marlon). Michael emerged as a solo artist in the early 1970's. At age thirteen, he began releasing solo albums on the Motown label starting with 1972's Got to Be There and Ben. 1973's Music and Me and 1975's Forever, Michael followed. The title tracks from the first two albums, "Got to Be There" and "Ben" were hits, along with a cover of Bobby Day's "Rockin' Robin." In spite of all this early success, Michael was never able to enjoy a normal childhood like peers his age. Jackson recalled "I would do my schooling which was three hours with a tutor and right after that I would go to the recording studio and…I'd record for hours and hours until it's time to go to sleep. I remember going to the recording studio and there was a park across the street and I'd see all the children playing and I would cry because it would make me sad that I would have to work instead." #1

In 1975, The Jackson 5 signed with Epic Records and renamed themselves The Jacksons. Younger brother Randy joined while Jermaine stayed at Motown to pursue a solo career. Between 1976 and 1984, The Jacksons released six albums and continued to tour internationally. Michael honed his songwriting skills and wrote many of the group's hits including; "Shake Your Body (Down to the Ground)," "This Place Hotel," and "Can You Feel It." In 1978, Michael played the scarecrow in the film *The Wiz*, co-starring with Diana Ross. It was there that he met musician/arranger Quincy Jones, who would go on to help Michael make music history.

1979's Off the Wall was Michael's breakout solo album, yielding four top ten hits and to date has sold over twenty million copies worldwide. Off the Wall began Jackson's longtime association with Epic Records, where he would remain throughout his entire career. Two number one hits emerged from this record, "Rock with You" and "Don't Stop Until You Get Enough." This was an important transition period for Jackson in the sense that his lyrical themes now addressed loneliness, escapism, romance, and liberation. Off the Wall would begin Jackson's three-album association with producer Quincy Jones, who produced all of the tracks on the album. Looking for creative freedom and a move away from the Jacksons' sound, Michael began to combine more musical styles such as soft rock, funk, disco, jazz, Broadway tunes, and pop ballads. Jackson and Jones utilized a wealth of studio musicians that included ex-Rufus and Chaka Kahn drummer John "JR" Robinson, keyboardists Greg Phillinganes and George Duke, vocalist Patti Austin, and many others. Michael also collaborated with Stevie Wonder on the song "I Can't Help It" and Paul McCartney on "Girlfriend." Off the Wall, considered by some to be a masterpiece for its musicality and dance floor longevity, is sometimes eclipsed by what was soon to follow.

1982's Thriller would forever change pop music and create the blueprint for the pop-rock genre. Thriller is the best selling album (of any music genre) in music history with sales to date exceeding sixty-six million copies worldwide! It won a record-breaking eight Grammy Awards in 1984, including Album of the Year. Thriller remained in the number one position on the American charts for thirty-seven weeks. The album featured seven top ten hits, including two number one hits, "Beat It" and "Billie Jean."

Michael Jackson embraced MTV, and MTV embraced him. He made videos for many of his hits, and most featured his signature dance moves and choreography. Video budgets were growing, and their influence and importance were growing as well. At the time of Michaels's Thriller video (see chapter sixteen), Jackson's career was already well established, and it was inconceivable that there could be a hit song of his that didn't have a video on MTV. The "Thriller" video only broadened his and MTV's growing legend and importance. Rarely had a video overshadowed, or become more popular than the song. Jackson was a legendary musician, but he was a performer that had to be seen. In 1983, Jackson took the stage on the nationally televised Motown 25th anniversary show. Dressed in a black mock military-styled suit, white socks, black loafers, and a single white-sequined glove (that would became his trademark), he performed his famous moonwalk that created a televised musical moment that would join The Beatles appearance on the *Ed Sullivan Show* as a cultural phenomenon.

Groundbreaking album Thriller
by Michael Jackson

Upon it's release, Thriller initially yielded a number two hit, the duet with Paul McCartney titled "The Girl is Mine." From there, Thriller went on a roll of unparalleled success drawing comparisons of Michael to iconic figures such as Elvis Presley and The Beatles. Producer Quincy Jones and Michael worked on about thirty songs for the album, eventually pairing it down to nine. Michael wrote four of the songs for Thriller utilizing his standard approach of initially singing a melody and lyrics into a tape recorder instead of notating the songs on paper. Jones enlisted members of Toto to play on the record includ-

---

"With Thriller, I don't think any of us were ready for it…you have to leave space for God to walk into the room, and man did he/she ever. With it, Michael had successfully transcended from the world of 'bubble-gum' pop and planted his flag on top of the 80's music mountain."

- Quincy Jones

ing; pianist David Paich, guitarist Steve Lukather, synthesizer player Steve Porcaro, and drummer Jeff Porcaro. Bassist Louis Johnson, keyboard player Greg Phillinganes (who had both also appeared on Off The Wall), and well established session musicians drummer Ndugu Chancler and guitarist Dean Parks also played on this landmark recording. Quincy Jones chose to include songs written by Rod Temperton, James Ingram, and Steve Porcaro to augment the songs that Jackson had written.

Side one opened with "Wanna Be Startin' Somethin'," then "Baby Be Mine," "The Girl is Mine," and "Thriller." "Wanna Be Startin' Somethin'" was written by Jackson and had a complex, infectious rhythm and horn arrangement. The lyrics dealt with a stranger who spread rumors to initiate an argument for no apparent reason. For the duet with Paul McCartney, "The Girl is Mine," Quincy Jones requested that Michael write a song about two guys fighting over a girl. Michael woke up one night and sang the song into a recorder complete with melody, ideas for the keyboard parts, and even the string arrangements. Jackson had often said that "The Girl is Mine" was one of his most memorable moments in the studio. "Thriller" (the song) utilized sound effects like a creaking door, thunder, feet walking on wooden planks, howling dogs, and more. "Thriller" composer Rod Temperton (a legendary songwriter who had written songs for George Benson, Patti Austin, and James Ingram) recruited actor Vincent Price to add his legendary horror film voice at the end of the song.

Quincy Jones lent his perspective to what made Thriller so special recalling, "With 'Thriller,' every song works together to create one album that gives the listener a dramatic experience in nine scenes. You also need to give the ear six choices of things to listen to on each song so that every time they listen, they hear something new. That way, they have to listen to a song multiple times to get the full experience of it… people were buying three and four copies of the record because they would wear them out playing them over and over again." #2

Side two continued the string of hits. Beginning with "Beat It," then "Billie Jean," "Human Nature," "P.Y.T. (Pretty Young Thing)," and "The Lady in My Life" (see tune inserts for "Beat It" and "Human Nature"). "Billie Jean's" lyrics have been the subject of multiple interpretation. For example, some believe the song was about a female fan of Jackson's who claimed that Michael had fathered her twins. Michael explained that "Billie Jean" was based on various groupies that he had encountered. "Billie Jean" was one of the best selling singles in music history with its infectious bassline by Louis Johnson and drumset feel by Ndugu Chancler. Michael later reworked "Billie Jean" for a commercial jingle and called it "Pepsi Generation." "P.Y.T. (Pretty Young Thing)," was written by James Ingram and Quincy Jones. Michael had his sisters Janet and La Toya sing backup vocals. Ironically, Michael Jackson never performed "P.Y.T." live.

Thriller has a legacy all on its own. Its exploration of pop, post-disco, funk, and ballads helped give it an iconic musical definition.

"Beat It"
by Michael Jackson

"Beat It," co-produced by Quincy Jones and Jackson, was the third single released from Thriller. Michael also released a Beat It video in which he brought together two rival gangs through the power of his music and dancing. Quincy Jones convinced Michael that he should include a hard rock tune on the album. "Beat It" started with a Tom Bahler synthesizer intro and a programmed drum beat. A rhythm section track provided by Toto member's drummer Jeff Porcaro, keyboardist Steve Porcaro, and guitarist Steve Lukather was added to the programmed drums to make the tune come alive.

"Beat It" was built in rhythmic layers that arrived at an unexpected climax provided by a surprise guest. When Eddie Van Halen was first contacted by Quincy Jones about overdubbing a guitar solo for the song, he thought it was a prank phone call. Initially, Eddie had turned down the session, but later agreed to do it on three conditions: 1. He would never be credited (so his Van Halen bandmates would not know-due to their agreement never to do any side projects). 2. He didn't need to get paid-just a case of beer would suffice. 3. Eddie would have Michael teach him how to dance someday. Eddie Van Halen played one of the most blistering rock guitar solos ever recorded on any rock album, much less a pop record. Michael gave Eddie full control of the song and Eddie re-arranged "Beat It" to fit his concept for an intense guitar solo. Michael loved it. However, Steve Lukather (later in the mix) toned down Eddie's guitar distortion. An unconfirmed rumor was that Eddie's monitor speaker burst into flames during the recording of the solo. The groundbreaking and hard rocking inclusion of Eddie Van Halen (and guitarist Steve Lukather) on "Beat It" was one of the great crossover musical moments that added a new ingredient to pop-rock music.

"Human Nature"
by Steve Porcaro and John Bettis

Often regarded as the most significant ballad on Thriller, "Human Nature" contained moody and introspective lyrics. Steve Porcaro wrote the song after his first grade daughter came home from school crying after a boy pushed her off of a slide. Porcaro explained to his daughter that it was just *human nature* for the boy to behave that way. Initially, Quincy Jones did not feel that the song was right for Michael, but when he heard a rough demo and at the end the dummy lyric 'why, why, dah dah da-dum dah dah, why, why,' he knew this was a special song with a magical melody and feeling. Composer John Bettis took the concept for the song and worked up the lyrics in two days.

Steve Porcaro co-wrote "Human Nature" and many Toto band members played on, and arranging the song. It felt like a Toto record with Michael singing and Quincy producing. Guitarist Steve Lukather, who had previously worked on Quincy Jones's The Dude, recalled, "I came up with a lot of parts for that (The Dude). I'd get a chord sheet and come up with these quirky little muted parts. So Quincy knew I did that, and he called me and said, 'Look, this ("Human Nature") is a great pop song, but it's not funky. I need you to funk it up." #3 "Human Nature" became a model for future soul and pop ballads. It's slower than the other Thriller songs and served to give the album more of a balance. The lyrics resonated with Michael Jackson's constant yearning to become free from his frequent isolation from society and his fans. "Human Nature" became the fifth hit from Thriller. It has been widely covered by many notable artists including John Mayer and Stevie Wonder. Perhaps the greatest cover of "Human Nature" was by the legendary jazz musician, Miles Davis.

> "I would love to have some sort of 'Back To The Future' Delorean time machine travel device so I could go back to 1981 to see that very first Jackson 5 concert I went to, back when I was a kid."
>
> – Questlove

> "I'm never pleased with anything. I'm a perfectionist, it's part of who I am."
>
> – Michael Jackson

Rock Hard Fact

In addition to her legendary music career, Madonna has acted in twenty-two Hollywood movies, including Evita that earned her a Golden Globe Award.

In 1984, The Jacksons released their last album, Victory. It was recorded with Michael doing all of the lead vocals. Victory peaked at number four on the U.S. charts and sold over seven million copies worldwide. Also in the early 1980's, Michael collaborated with Queen's Freddie Mercury and Mick Jagger on the song "State of Shock," featured on the Victory album. Shortly after the Victory tour, Michael and Marlon quit the Jacksons, leaving Jermaine, Tito, Randy, and Jackie Jackson to continue. The Jacksons would go one to release one more studio album, 1989's 2300 Jackson Street (Michael sang on the title track).

1987's Bad was the five-year follow up to Thriller and sold a *very* respectable thirty-five million copies worldwide. Jackson wanted it to sell one hundred million copies. Bad was the final collaboration between Michael and Quincy Jones. Five of the album's singles went to number one and a sixth made the top ten. The title track, "Bad," was written by Jackson and was originally intended to be a duet between him and Prince, but it never came to be. "Bad" was edgier than previous songs and gave Jackson an image change (heard in his trash talking lyrics) of direction. The song was about a kid originally from a rough neighborhood who came back from private school and got into a conflict with jealous kids. Michael made an eighteen-minute music video for Bad that was directed by legendary film-maker Martin Scorsese.

From 1986 to 1990, Michael Jackson weathered a storm of controversy from reports of plastic surgeries to skin bleaching to his becoming more detached from reality. Jackson built the Neverland Ranch in California at a cost of seventeen million dollars, complete with carnival rides, movie theaters, and a zoo. In 1991, Jackson renewed his recording contract with Sony for a record-breaking sixty-five million dollars. 1991's Dangerous was his eighth studio album and was produced by Jackson and Teddy Riley. Again a top seller (thirty-two million copies sold worldwide), Dangerous yielded four top ten hits including the number one hit "Black or White." Lyrical themes for Dangerous focused on racism, the welfare of children, poverty, and romance. The title track for the album proved to be one of Jackson's most danceable and harder rocking songs. As usual, Michael Jackson employed many of L.A.'s greatest session players and on two tracks, Guns N' Roses guitarist Slash.

By the time of 1995's double album release titled HIStory: Past, Present and Future, Book I, Jackson had been through many personal issues, including sexual abuse allegations and a short marriage to Lisa Marie Presley. HIStory: Past, Present and Future contained greatest hits and some new songs. It sold over twenty million copies. During the HIStory World Tour, Michael married his longtime friend Deborah Jeanne Rowe. They had two children, Michael Jackson Jr (known as Prince) and Paris-Michael Katherine Jackson. They were divorced in 1999 with Jackson retaining full custody of the children. In 1997, Jackson released Blood on the Dance Floor: HIStory in the Mix, a collection of remixes of hit singles from HIStory and five new songs.

2001's Invincible was the most expensive album ever made (in music history) and cost over thirty million dollars to record. It went to number two in America and number one in thirteen countries around the world. More than eighty musicians participated in the recording, not including numerous engineers and arrangers. Notable musicians included rapper Notorious B.I.G. and guitarist Carlos Santana. At this time, Michael endured more personal issues including the closure of Neverland and other legal battles. In September of 2007, Jackson began working on his next album that would never be completed. In March of 2009, Michael announced a comeback world tour called This Is It.

Three weeks prior to the start of the tour, scheduled to open in London, Michael Jackson died from cardiac arrest. His death received a global outpouring of shock and grief. Media coverage was unprecedented and tickets for his memorial were distributed by a lottery. Over thirty-one million viewers watched a stream of the memorial service. Jackson's staggering popularity was seen in the thirty-five million copies of his albums sold within the year following his death.

In 2010, the posthumous album Michael was released. It contained all new material and four hit singles: "Hold My Hand," "Behind the Mask," "Hollywood Tonight," and "I Like The Way You Love Me." Notable guest musicians included rapper Curtis "50 Cent" Jackson, Lenny Kravitz, and drummer Dave Grohl. 2014's Xscape was another posthumous release of all new material and featured eight tracks that were recorded between 1983 and 1999. Two hits from the record were "Love Never Felt So Good" and "A Place with No Name."

The legacy of Michael Jackson makes him the true "King Of Pop" with his unprecedented musical success and worldwide cultural influence. Jackson's highly evolved musical style was molded by a vast array of influences that included; Jackie Wilson, Little Richard, Diana Ross, Fred Astaire, James Brown, and many others. Michael Jackson's influence on other artists included practically *everyone*. His recording output included; twelve studio albums, seventy two compilations albums, six EPs, one live album, three soundtracks, seven remix albums, and (so far) two albums have been released posthumously. Jackson summed up his own legacy when he said, "I think being humble and believing in yourself and having true love in your heart for the world and really trying to help people through lyrics and the love of music and dance is important. I truly do love people very much." #4

Jackson's brand of pop included ingredients from the genres of rhythm and blues, soul, funk, disco, pop, rap, hard rock, and jazz. These diverse influences gave him stylistic freedom to explore the genius of his own creative musical vision. Michael Jackson elevated the pop-rock genre and then set the bar. *High.*

Madonna Louise Ciccone (1958-) is an American singer/songwriter and actress often referred to as the "Queen of Pop." Madonna's rise to pop-rock stardom was built on questioning the roles of women in society and exploring the issues of race, gender, and sexuality. Madonna dealt with tragedy at the age five when her mother died from breast cancer. Deeply affected, she felt powerless while at the same time she developed a strong work ethic in an attempt to fill the void in her life. Madonna became a dancer in high school and won a dance scholarship to the University of Michigan in 1976. Two years later, she moved to New York City and occasionally worked as a model and dancer. She decided to pursue singing after her friends told her that her voice wasn't bad. Before she developed her vocal talents, Madonna first learned to play drumset and guitar.

Madonna was aware of the history of female rock and pop singers that came before her. She knew that female artist Joan Jett displayed a sense of independence and that Ann and Nancy Wilson commanded respect leading their band, Heart. Madonna also admired Blondie's Debbie Harry, who was a leading figure in new wave music. Inspired by these female artists, Madonna built her image by flaunting her sex appeal and by making bold musical statements. Madonna drew from various influences including Nancy Sinatra, Karen Carpenter, Chrissie Hynde, The Supremes, and Led Zeppelin. She also reached back to the music from the Baroque and Classical eras. Madonna further drew inspiration from great actresses including; Rita Hayworth, Judy Holliday, Marilyn Monroe, and Bette Davis.

Madonna possesses a mezzo-soprano vocal range. She's been keenly aware of the quality of her voice and has often compared it to Ella Fitzgerald, Chaka Khan, and Prince, who she considers to be her idols. Madonna's vocal (and musical) style is always evolving. She blends both rock and pop vocal qualities by combining an aggressive approach contrasted by occasional soft and sensitive vocal timbres. She took vocal lessons to increase her range and learned to incorporate many idiosyncrasies in her vocal phrasing.

In 1982, Madonna lived in New York and played drums in a New York band called The Breakfast Club. She signed as a solo artist with Sire Records in 1982. Despite battling with record producer Reggie Lucas, Madonna released her self-titled debut album, Madonna, in 1983. It reached number eight on the U.S. charts and number six in England. Five singles emerged from the album, including "Borderline," "Lucky Star," and the previously released "Everybody." The sound of Madonna utilized the new technology of the Linn drum machine and Moog bass. It also featured the sounds of the OB-X synthesizer that she employed to create upbeat synthetic sounds. Madonna's approach quickly dominated nightclub dance floors and spawned a new style of dance-pop. Another song from Madonna, "Holiday," became an international hit and was especially popular in many European countries. By this time, Madonna had also developed a strong sense of fashion that featured bleached hair, lace tops, and crucifix jewelry. Madonna's look created one of the dominant female fashion styles of the 1980's, and similar to her music, evolved throughout her career.

1984's Like a Virgin was the defining album of Madonna's skyrocketing career. For the recording, she employed former Chic guitarist and producer Nile Rodgers, known for his work with Sister Sledge, Diana Ross, and David Bowie. Rodgers utilized many of the band members from Chic to play on the record. For Like a Virgin, Madonna took a decidedly hands on approach and was involved in all of the recording sessions. Together, Madonna and Rodgers created a record whose songs and sound would help define a musical decade. Like a Virgin went to number one in America and reached the top of the charts in England, Germany, Italy, and many other countries. It has sold over twenty-one million copies worldwide.

Groundbreaking album Like a Virgin
by Madonna

Like a Virgin raised Madonna to superstar status. The tracks on Like a Virgin were "Material Girl," then "Angel," "Like a Virgin," "Over and Over," "Love Don't Live Here Anymore," "Dress You Up," "Shoo-Bee-Doo," "Pretender," and "Stay." Madonna and Nile Rodgers utilized synth arrangements, layered vocal harmonies, and thick rhythm section dance grooves to make the album extremely "dance floor friendly." "Material Girl" was a definitive statement that identified with the concept of materialism. Lyrically, the song's narrator asked for a rich lifestyle rather than romance and a relationship. Madonna was writing about the possessions that money can buy and that *wealth* could last longer than personal emotion. A music video for "Material Girl" was inspired by Marilyn Monroe's 1953 performance in the film *Gentlemen Prefer Blondes*.

"Like a Virgin" was written by Tom Kelly and Billy Steinberg. The lyrics were intentionally ambiguous in that for virgins, the song encouraged them to remain sexually cautious. For those who were no longer virgins, it meant that they could relive the feelings of their first sexual encounter all over again. Madonna performed "Like a Virgin" on the 1984 *MTV Video Awards Show*. During the choreographed dance sequence, she performed sexually provocative movements that gained much public scrutiny. The song and video brought even more controversy when some believed it promoted sex without marriage and undermined family values, thus labeling Madonna sexually promiscuous.

Like a Virgin revealed Madonna's uncanny pop-rock instincts and ability to create a new type of female pop icon. She asserted her sexuality in ways that only male rock stars had previously achieved. This made some people uncomfortable, but Madonna took a strong stance. A female artist in full control of her sexuality and career, Madonna had created a new phenomenon in popular music and culture.

In 1985, Madonna expanded her career by acting in the film *Desperately Seeking Susan*. Also in 1985, Madonna married actor Sean Penn. 1986's True Blue was an immediate global success and sold over twenty-five million copies. The album featured themes of love, freedom, and social issues like teenage pregnancy, seen in the song "Papa Don't Preach." Madonna was clearly growing as a songwriter. She also expanded her musical sources to include Classical and Cuban music elements on this recording. A powerful track from True Blue was "Live to Tell."

"Live to Tell"
by Madonna and Patrick Leonard

"Live to Tell" was originally composed by Patrick Leonard (who with Kevin Gilbert led the band Toy Matinee) for the film score to the movie *Fire with Fire*. An instrumental track was given to Madonna and she then wrote lyrics and offered the song to (then husband) Sean Penn for his film, *At Close Range*. The lyrics dealt with mistrust, deceit, and painful childhood memories (Madonna thought about her relationship with her own parents). She saw the beauty of the melody and was inspired to move in a different musical direction. Madonna said, "'Live to Tell' is a very sad song…about being very young and having to grow up quickly because you've seen certain things that force you to be a grown-up ahead of your time." #5 Madonna also came up with the melody for the bridge of the tune.

Patrick Leonard created a basic structure for "Live to Tell" on piano and later added the background synthesizer parts and drum machine programming. "Live to Tell" spoke with a haunting and dark mood. Madonna sang it was a sense of mystery and conviction that created a pop song with great depth of expression. Madonna premiered "Live to Tell" at Madison Square Garden in New York for an AIDS research benefit concert. "Live to Tell" has been covered by many artists, including one notable version by jazz guitarist Bill Frisell on his Have a Little Faith album.

> "I'm always looking for something new: a new inspiration, a new philosophy, a new way to look at something."
>
> – Madonna

Rock History - the Musician's Perspective

1989's Like a Prayer continued Madonna's success by reaching number one on the U.S. charts and selling fifteen million copies worldwide. On Like a Prayer, Madonna added funk and gospel styles along with references from her Catholic upbringing. This was seen in the title track "Like a Prayer," that was about a young girl and her emotions tied to her religious beliefs. Madonna was able to successfully combine a pop song with strong, conflicting emotions. Also at this time, Madonna and Sean Penn divorced. The successful 1991 concert tour documentary *Truth or Dare* and the 1992 film, *A League of Their Own* followed. 1992's Erotica was a concept album about sex and romance while 1994's Bedtime Stories was inspired by modern rhythm and blues with lyrical themes of love and romance (less about sex). Madonna finished the 1990's with 1998's Ray of Light, an album based on ambient and electronic dance music. It was produced by William Orbit (Blur, U2, Pink, Queen).

In the 2000's, Madonna released more studio albums including 2000's Music, 2003's American Life, 2005's Confessions on a Dance Floor, and 2008's Hard Candy. The album Music uniquely combined William Orbit's brand of dance-pop and electronica timbres with elements of country and folk music. For this album, Madonna reinvented her image to be a cowgirl. It reached number one on the U.S. charts, returning Madonna to the top of the charts for the first time since Like a Prayer. Confessions on a Dance Floor was musically constructed like a DJ's live set. The songs were sequenced and segued together without any gaps in between tracks. The lead single, "Hung Up," was considered by many to be her best dance track to date. "Hung Up" became one of the best selling singles of all-time with over nine million copies sold worldwide. On 2008's Hard Candy, Madonna collaborated with singers Justin Timberlake, Pharrell Williams, and rapper/DJ Timbaland.

The next decade saw the release of 2012's MDNA and 2015's Rebel Heart. MDNA was a pop and EDM (electronic dance music) effort. Madonna explored themes such as infatuation, partying, love of music, heartbreak, and separation. MDNA received strong promotion when Madonna appeared at the Super Bowl XLVI halftime show. Her MDNA Tour became one of the highest-grossing tours of all time. However, the MDNA Tour was not without controversy. Madonna made strong statements about human rights, violence, and politics. She also utilized fake firearms onstage. Madonna's 2015 release, Rebel Heart, represented her rebellious and romantic sides. It went to number two on the American charts. On this recording, she combined the musical styles of 1990's house and reggae and employed a gospel choir.

Through her many successes and occasional failures, Madonna has remained a sustainable pop-rock artist, cultural phenomenon, and supporter of many social causes. Her assertive and sometimes shocking persona has influenced the careers of countless artists, particularly female. Madonna is the best selling female recording artist of all time, having sold more than three hundred million records worldwide. She is one of the highest-grossing solo touring artists of all-time, earning more than $1.3 billion dollars from her concert ticket sales since 1990. Her legacy is that of a performance artist who has pushed the boundaries of lyrical content in mainsteam pop-rock. The visual imagery of her music videos and stage shows has been both cutting edge and controversial. Like artists that push the boundaries in many fields, Madonna became a lightening rod for the cultural definitions of sex, race, gender, and religious subject matters. Madonna was inducted into the Rock and Roll Hall of Fame in 2008.

Rock Hard Fact

In 1984, Prince accomplished something only The Beatles had done before him: he simultaneously topped the charts with an album (*Purple Rain*), a film (*Purple Rain*), and a single ("When Doves Cry").

Prince Roger Nelson (1958-2016) was an American singer/songwriter/multi-instrumentalist/record producer from Minneapolis, Minnesota who created a unequaled body of work that crossed stylistic boundaries. He also created countless hits. Very few artists were as prolific and varied in stylistic approach as Prince.

Named after his father's jazz band, The Prince Roger Trio (his mother was often their featured vocalist), Prince began playing music early in his life. However, his future became clear when he saw the legendary James Brown in concert at the age of ten. By the time he entered high school, Prince was an accomplished guitarist and pianist. He soon joined his cousin's band, Grand Central. Within a year (his cousin left the band), Prince became the bandleader and changed their name to Champagne.

In 1977, at age nineteen, Prince signed a recording contract with Warner Brothers Records and became the youngest producer in the label's history. Prince recorded an unbelievable thirty-nine studio albums in his career (only a small sampling of them covered here). In 1978, he recorded his debut album, For You. Throughout his career, it became common to look at his album credits and read the words composed, arranged, performed, and produced by Prince. Other important artists had created entire records by playing and singing all of the parts including; Stevie Wonder, Steve Winwood, Paul McCartney, Lenny Kravitz, and Dave Grohl. However, for a young untested artist such as Prince making his recording debut, this was very uncommon.

The lead single on For You, "Soft and Wet," went to number ninety-two on the U.S. charts. This served to establish Prince as a new popular artist on the pop music scene. 1979's album Prince built momentum with his fan base and sold three million copies. Prince's music evolved to become more musically accomplished when he ventured into urban rhythm and blues with his classics "I Wanna Be Your Lover" and "Why You Wanna Treat Me So Bad?" The song "I Feel for You" was a precursor to Prince's adventurous and sexualized signature sound, that was all held together with a strong melody.

1980's Dirty Mind was a defining album for Prince. It was a one-man explosion of raw sexuality and swagger. The music exhibited hooky Beatlesque melodies, sweet ballads, and rocking guitar solos. Recorded at Prince's home studio, Dirty Mind contained an exciting stylistic blend of pop, funk, rhythm and blues, and even new wave influences; all presented with sexual references that provided shock value. "When You Were Mine," a popular song from Dirty Mind, was considered one of Prince's strongest early compositions. It became a staple of his live performances and was later covered by Cyndi Lauper. 1981's Controversy and 1982's 1999 continued Prince's rise to pop-rock stardom. 1999 was an ambitious double album that crossed over between the pop and r&b charts, thus building a wider audience. With videos for "1999" and "Little Red Corvette" in MTV rotation, Prince became one of the first African-American musicians featured on MTV. His popularity even rivaled Michael Jackson. "Little Red Corvette" peaked at number six on the U.S. charts.

"Little Red Corvette"
by Prince

The concept for "Little Red Corvette" came to Prince after falling asleep in the back of his backup singer's 1964 Mercury Montclair car after an all-night recording session. The song lyrics came to him in bits and pieces. "Little Red Corvette" was his first song to reach the top ten in America. The song was about sex and was just ambiguous enough to not offend most listeners or radio DJ's. The lyrics told a story about the narrator having a one-night stand with a beautiful and promiscuous woman. He told her to find a love that would last before she regretted her actions. Prince utilized an automobile metaphor by comparing the narrator and the woman's sexual encounter to that of a limousine ride. The song also explored the human element about being vulnerable and having a fear of casual sex. The vocal line "she had a pocket full of horses, Trojans..." referred to condoms. The "Jockeys" Prince sang about represented men who have previously slept with the girl. This was not the first, and would not be the last *double entendre* found in Prince's lyrics.

The accompanying video to "Little Red Corvette" received substantial MTV airplay. "Little Red Corvette" came right after Michael Jackson was able to break the pop-rock race barrier with his Billie Jean MTV video. In Prince's video, and at concerts, Prince would perform exciting James Brown-styled dancing with an array of splits and spin moves on songs such as "Little Red Corvette."

Prince made a strong impact on other Minneapolis-based pop-rock bands, specifically the groups Vanity 6 and The Time. Prince was supportive (often behind the scenes) and influenced the musical direction of both bands. The Time released four albums between 1981 and 1990, with Prince writing and performing many of the instrumental parts and backing vocals, while Morris Day handled the lead vocals.

In the early 1980's, Prince named his band The Revolution. He then secured a contract to create and star in a major motion picture in which The Revolution would also have an important role. The result was the 1984 film *Purple Rain*, a rock music drama where Prince played "The Kid," a semi-autobiographical character. The plot showed "The Kid" to be a talented but troubled frontman of a Minneapolis-based band, The Revolution. He escaped the verbal and physical abuse of his father and rehearsed to compete with a rival band fronted by Morris Day and his group, The Time. A love interest, Apollonia Kotero, thickened the plot and "The Kid" triumphed musically and romantically in the end. 1984's Purple Rain was the accompanying soundtrack to the movie. Considered by many to be Prince's greatest work, Purple Rain has sold over twenty-five million copies worldwide. It is the third best selling movie soundtrack of all time.

Groundbreaking album Purple Rain by Prince

Acknowledged as one of pop-rock's greatest albums of the 1980's (along with Thriller), Purple Rain validated Prince to superstar status in the league of Michael Jackson and Madonna. With his band, The Revolution, Prince refined his funk and rhythm and blues approach on Purple Rain and added hard rock and psychedelic elements. No longer working as a one-man band, Prince built multiple layers of synthesizers, guitars, and drum machines with The Revolution. Purple Rain enabled Prince to fuse all of his musical influences from James Brown to Jimi Hendrix to Chic, and express a variety of emotions to create truly legendary music.

Side one opened with "Let's Go Crazy," then "Take Me with U," "The Beautiful Ones," "Computer Blue," and "Darling Nikki." On "Take Me with U," Prince sang a duet with Apollonia Kotero. This track was originally intended for her Apollonia 6 album but instead was included on Purple Rain. "Darling Nikki" was controversial for its explicitly sexual lyrics. It was a catalyst for much social and political debate and the future inclusion of parental advisory stickers on many artists' album covers. "Darling Nikki" told the story about a "sex fiend" named Nikki who seduced the singer. In the *Purple Rain* film, this song was directed toward Apollonia Kotero's character when she began working with Prince's rival character, played by Morris Day.

Side two opened with "When Doves Cry," then "I Would Die 4 U," "Baby I'm a Star," and "Purple Rain." Prince reached the top of the U.S. charts with "When Doves Cry," a song he composed after all of the Purple Rain tracks were complete. "When Doves Cry" was different than most pop songs in that it didn't contain a bass line. The song ended with a classically inspired keyboard section accompanied by a layered synthesizer solo. "When Doves Cry" became one of Prince's signature tunes. "Purple Rain" was a power ballad that combined pop-rock, rhythm and blues, gospel, and orchestral styles. Prince explained the meaning of "Purple Rain" when he stated, "When there's blood in the sky red and blue = purple…purple rain pertains to the end of the world and being with the one you love and letting your faith/God guide you through the purple rain." #6

Prince was afraid that "Purple Rain" sounded too much like Journey's "Faithfully" so he asked (Faithfully's composer) Jonathan Cain what he thought. Cain replied that it was fine because the two songs only shared a few of the same chords. Purple Rain earned Prince two Grammy Awards and an Academy Award for Best Original Score.

Prince went on to record thirty-three more studio albums in his career! The 1980's saw five of these releases after Purple Rain including the 1985 follow-up Around the World in a Day. This was Prince's first album produced on his Paisley Park record label. This album moved in a psychedelic direction with some simple, yet brilliant melodies. In 1986, Prince announced his retirement from live performance, only to later change his mind for a promotional tour for his 1986 release of Parade. A hit from the album, "Kiss," went to number one in America. At the end of the Parade Tour, Prince disbanded The Revolution and went solo for a while. He returned in 1987 with new musicians and another strong recording, the double album 1987's Sign o' the Times. This album contained many styles that again revealed Prince's wide range of musical expression.

Prince released an unheard of eleven albums in the 1990's! He began with his 1990's soundtrack album Graffiti Bridge, recorded with his new backing band, The New Power Generation. Diamonds and Pearls and 1992's Love Symbol album (the symbol on the cover represented Prince's new stage name) are outstanding funk pop masterpieces. 1994's Come and The Black Album were more raw. Next came 1995's successful The Gold Experience, and 1996's Chaos and Disorder and Emancipation. Prince battled with his record company over control and ownership of his music. However, he managed to release four more albums in the 1990's including 1998's Crystal Ball, a four-disc set of bootlegs recordings and new material.

In the 2000's, Prince was more prolific than ever, releasing a staggering sixteen albums! 3121 was an inspired recording where Prince reconnected to his past with some uplifting funky grooves. His last studio recordings were 2015's HITnRUN Phase One and HITnRUN

> "I feel like my peers now are artists like Madonna and the Stones, Michael Jackson and Prince. These are people who were able to take their careers beyond the normal here-today-gone-tomorrow life span."
>
> – LL Cool J

> "My listening changed when I heard music from Stax, Atlantic, Motown...I had to find my own rock 'n' roll... and I found it in African-American soul music."
>
> - Robert Palmer

Phase Two. On these albums, Prince established a soulful and streamlined approach with less concern for electronics or flashy guitar solos. Both albums achieved moderate success on the charts.

Many of Prince's songs were covered and made even more popular by other artists. They included "I Feel For You," which became Chaka Khan's biggest hit, and "Nothing Compares 2 U," a number one hit for Sinead O'Connor. Prince wrote The Bangles first hit, "Manic Monday," and Cyndi Lauper recorded his "When U Were Mine." Prince also wrote Sheila E's hit "The Glamorous Life." Additionally, Prince helped produce records for Madonna, No Doubt, and others.

Sadly, Prince died of an accidental drug overdose on April 21st, 2016. His legacy is that of America's first *"everything"* pop-rock star who defied categorization of musical genres. He was an American icon known for his androgynous sexuality and defiance of racial stereotypes. His lasting influence on the music business was one that foreshadowed the controversies surrounding the ownership of intellectual property, copyright infringement, artistic control, and music distribution. Prince was a daring and relentlessly experimental musician, a true artist. He connected with his audience while simultaneously progressing through remarkable musical growth and stylistic diversity. The list of artists that influenced him is as long as the list of those that *he* influenced. Prince was inducted into the Rock and Roll Hall of Fame in 2004.

Discussion Question

Very few artists rival the musical and cultural impact of Michael Jackson in music history. Compare and contrast Jackson's musical and performance innovations to another groundbreaking artist or band from an earlier or later era. Be specific with your musical examples.

The genre of pop-rock enjoyed unprecedented popularity around the world from the 1980's to this present day. We have seen how superstars such as Michael Jackson, Madonna, and Prince broke new ground and paved the way for each generation of pop-rock artists to find their own voice and audience. In the 1980's, MTV (see chapter sixteen) expanded global audiences and pop-rock artists took advantage of an ever-changing musical climate that has led to the current digital music environment. The following artists and bands have made substantial contributions to the pop-rock genre.

Robert Palmer (1949-2003) (1964-2003 band) was a British vocalist, singer/songwriter, and producer. Palmer had a successful solo career and was a member of the band, The Power Station. His voice was soulful and his earlier work effectively combined r&b, rock, and reggae styles. Palmer cultivated a suave and handsome image by dressing in sharp suits. Palmer's career began at age nineteen when he joined a band called The Alan Bown Set. He moved on to the band Dada, a twelve-piece soul group, and they changed their name to Vinegar Joe. Three albums later, Robert Palmer released his 1974 debut album, Sneakin' Sally Through the Alley. On this recording, Palmer made the great decision to utilize The Meters, Lowell George (of the band Little Feat), and drummer Simon Phillips as his backing band for a funky and soulful sound. On 1975's Pressure Drop, Palmer employed the entire Little Feat band, and once again, the album was funky. Lowell George's slide guitar, combined with keyboardist Bill Payne and the Muscle Shoals Horns, gave Palmer great musical support. However, the album had only moderate success on the U.S. charts. By the late 1970's, Robert Palmer was beginning to find more commercial appeal starting with his 1979 album Secrets and the single "Bad Case of Loving You (Doctor, Doctor)." It gave Palmer his first chart hit, which peaked at number fourteen.

When the band Duran Duran went on a hiatus, their guitarist Andy Taylor and bassist John Taylor joined forces with former Chic drummer Tony Thompson and Palmer to form the band Power Station. Their debut album, The Power Station, yielded two hits "Some Like it Hot" and a cover of T. Rex's "Get It On (Bang a Gong)." Palmer soon left but recruited Thompson and Andy Taylor to play on his 1985 breakout album Riptide. This recording went to number eight in America and number five in England on the heels of the hit, "Addicted to Love."

"Addicted to Love"
by Robert Palmer

"Addicted to Love" was originally intended to be a duet with vocal great Chaka Khan. This didn't happen due to the fact that her record company would not allow her to work on Palmer's label, Island Records. Khan was still credited with the vocal arrangements on the record. "Addicted to Love" started with a massive drumset groove aided by synthesizer parts that contributed heavily to the overall funky ensemble rhythm. Palmer had grown into a vocalist with a keen sense of rhythmic phrasing, an aspect of his musicianship that was often overshadowed by the pop image he was creating for himself. "Addicted to Love" went straight to the top of the charts in the U.S.

Even though the melodic hook and it's *addicting* groove made it a pop-rock hit, it was the music video for "Addicted to Love" that made it a true classic. Palmer was a prime example of an already established artist whose profile was raised considerably by MTV. The video featured Palmer fronting a band of female models, all with pale skin, heavy makeup, dark hair, and seductive mannequin-like facial expressions. Palmer's goal was to have the models act and look like animated showroom mannequins gazing out with blank stares. The five models were all "mock playing" their instruments (they never learned to mimic real instrumental techniques). Palmer would later utilize the visual imagery of the models for other songs such as "Simply Irresistible."

1988's Heavy Nova (named for Palmer's love of heavy metal and bossa nova rhythms) continued to build Palmer's popularity with the hit single "Simply Irresistible." In the 1990's, Palmer released four albums including; 1990's Don't Explain, 1992's Ridin' High, 1994's Honey, and 1999's Rhythm & Blues. His final studio recording was 2003's Drive, a blues album inspired by an invitation he received to participate in a Robert Johnson tribute. It also provided the chance to record the soundtrack for a film set in the deep South in the 1940's. The material for this recording contained many covers such as Little Willie John's "I Need Your Love So Bad," ZZ Top's "TV Dinners," and Keb' Mo's "Am I Wrong?" Palmer filtered these blues and others through his modern pop sensibilities to put his stamp on the blues, one of the styles where he first began.

Robert Palmer tragically died in 2003 from a heart attack at age fifty-four. Robert Palmer released fourteen studio albums, three live albums, and eleven compilation albums.

Janet Jackson (1966-) is an American singer/songwriter/dancer/actress who was the youngest of the famous Jackson family siblings. Janet Jackson has sold over one hundred million albums worldwide, making her one of the best-selling artists in pop-rock history. Her 1982 debut album, Janet Jackson, and 1984's Dream Street achieved only moderate success. However, it was her third album, 1986's Control, that went to number one on the U.S. charts with its five singles. Jackson filmed "MTV ready" videos for many of her singles from Control and they all highlighted her dancing ability. She closed the 1980's with her 1989 release, Janet Jackson's Rhythm Nation 1814. Jackson had previously worked with producers Jimmy Jam and Terry Lewis. They contributed strongly to the overwhelming success of Rhythm Nation. Jimmy Jam and Lewis continued to work with Janet throughout the 1990's and 2000's. Their collaborations included; Janet, The Velvet Rope, All For You, and Unbreakable, all achieving great popular success.

2001's All for You peaked at number one in America and showed a refined dance-oriented pop sound that fused disco, funk, rock and some soft rock elements. It's lyrical content focused on romance, passion, themes of betrayal and deceit, and sex. Some of the lyrics were controversial with the media due to their sexually explicit nature. The lead single, "All For You," earned her the title "Queen of Radio" by MTV when it gained great popularity on pop and urban radio stations.

"All For You"
by Janet Jackson, Jimmy Jam and Terry Lewis

"All For You" had instant worldwide success and soared to number one on the U.S. charts, where it stayed on top for seven consecutive weeks. The song was a throwback to the disco era while adding elements of rhythm and blues. The lyrics explored Janet's view on dating. The song's storyline was set in a nightclub where she flirted with a man that seemed to be intimidated by her celebrity. In an erotic and suggestive tone, she assured him that her celebrity status was not a factor and then continued her flirtatious behavior.

Musically, "All For You" ignored the current trends in top forty-radio by combining a soulful feel with Jackson's ability to deliver a strong melodic hook. The MTV video for the song opened with Jackson admiring a man she met while riding the subway. Jackson and her dancers performed a high-energy choreography all through the video, which featured creative dance breaks. The video ended with Janet spotting the man close to a nightclub. He smiles at her and she waved at him before leaving the scene.

Janet Jackson recorded three more studio albums in the 2000's and her album Unbreakable was released in 2015. Janet successfully distanced her professional career from her brother Michael's and the rest of the Jackson family. From the start of her career, Janet acted like she had something to prove. Her unique and creative songs and videos established her as a leader in contemporary pop and rhythm and blues. Her music was intelligent with lyrical content that simultaneously explored socially conscious issues and sexuality. Janet Jackson, along with Madonna, has shaped pop-rock music and led the way for many female stars such as Lady Gaga and Beyonce.

Hall and Oates (1970-present) are an American pop-rock duo that have sold over forty million albums worldwide. In the process, they became the third best selling music duo of all time. Both from Philadelphia, vocalist Daryl Hall and guitarist/vocalist John Oates met when they both attended Temple University. In 1966, Hall recorded a single with Kenny Gamble and the Romeos (a group that would help create the Philly soul sound.) In 1967, Hall began performing with Oates, who was leading his own soul band called The Masters. The duo recorded some songs on the Elektra label but Hall focused more on recording backup vocals with The Stylistics, The Intruders, and The Delfonics. In 1969, Oates returned from an extended stay in Europe and the duo focused on their songwriting partnership. They released their debut album Whole Oats in 1972. On 1973's Abandoned Luncheonette, Hall and Oates cultivated their soulful approach and yielded a hit, "She's Gone." 1974's War Babies moved in a more rock-oriented direction, but none of these first three albums were very successful.

1975's Daryl Hall & John Oates, their first album on Atlantic Records, presented them (in appearance only) as a glam rock duo. The album produced their first top ten hit "Sara Smile," peaking at number four on the U.S. charts. 1976's Bigger Than Both of Us brought them their first number one hit, "Rich Girl." However, in the late 1970's, disco was gaining popularity and the duo's Beauty on a Back Street and Along the Red Ledge albums achieved only moderate success. On the later, George Harrison played on the track "The Last Time." Their next album, 1979's X-Static, combined rock and dance music. It also faired poorly with the exception of a top twenty hit, "Wait for Me."

The 1980's were a very different story for Hall and Oates. Moving from Los Angeles to New York City and recording at Electric Lady Studio pushed them in a new direction. 1980's Voices reached number seventeen on the U.S. charts with four top-forty hits. 1981's Private Eyes brought Hall and Oates to a new level of popularity with two number one hits, "Private Eyes," and "I Can't Go for That (No Can Do)." On Private Eyes, they perfected their combination of soul roots and doo-wop vocals with new wave and edgy rock elements. 1982's H2O, was a slick studio album adorned with walls of synthesizers. It brought their biggest success and the biggest hit of their career, "Maneater." Both Hall and Oates sang lead vocals and the backing vocal parts. They also added keyboards, guitars, and synthesizers.

"Maneater"
by Sara Allen, Daryl Hall, and John Oates

You might think that "Maneater" was about a woman, but Hall and Oates revealed that the song was written about being in New York City in the 1980's. The lyrics used the metaphor of a woman described as alluring but an ominous warning presented in the chorus said "Oh-oh, here she comes/watch out boy she'll chew you up, oh-oh, here she comes/She's a Maneater." The call and response chorus added an infectious melodic hook with a reggae-like rhythm guitar part.

A two-beat shuffle feel, surrounded by polished keyboards and synthesizer accompaniment, created a strong and distinctive feel. Hall performed one of his most passionate r&b styled vocal performances on this track. The studio production of "Maneater" was skillful and polished. It was further enhanced by the soulful Charlie DeChant's saxophone solo. "Maneater" defined the Hall and Oates pioneering pop and soul sound (also

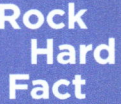

Rock Hard Fact

Because of their incredible chart success, Billboard magazine named Hall and Oates the most successful duo of the rock era, surpassing The Everly Brothers.

referred to as "Blue Eyed Soul") that carved out a unique space for them in the pop-rock genre. "Maneater" was also the biggest American hit of the 1980's to feature a saxophone solo.

By late 1983, Hall and Oates were one of the biggest pop-rock groups in America. Their greatest hits album, <u>Rock 'n Roll Soul part 1</u>, reached number seven. "Say It Isn't So," went to number two, competing with Michael Jackson's <u>Thriller</u>. Hall and Oates went on to release seven more studio albums including the big 1980's production of <u>Big Bam Boom</u>. Their 1985 recording, <u>Live at the Apollo</u>, featured the Temptations Eddie Kendricks and Eddie Ruffin singing a medley of Temptations' hits with Hall and Oates and their band. In 2007, Daryl Hall began a series called *Live From Daryl's House* where he performed with high profile musical guests. During the 2010's, the duo was very active continuing to tour and release compilation albums. Daryl Hall and John Oates have placed thirty-four hits on the U.S. charts (surpassing The Everly Brothers) and have recorded six number one hits in their prolific careers. They created well-crafted songs with strong melodic hooks that stayed true to the soul music tradition while simultaneously incorporating rock and new wave styles. Daryl Hall and John Oates were inducted into the Rock and Roll Hall of Fame in 2014.

Cyndi Lauper (1953-) (1977-present band) has secured her place as a pop-rock star having sold over fifty million albums and twenty million singles worldwide. Her 1983 debut album, <u>She's So Unusual</u>, was produced by Philadelphia's Rick Chertoff, and was one of the best selling records of the 1980's. It featured four songs that Lauper wrote or co-wrote, and songs written by several Philadelphia songwriters such as Robert Hazard, and Rob Hyman and Eric Bazilian. Lauper interpreted many of the songs in a new wave synth-pop style. The record featured her first worldwide hit "Girls Just Want to Have Fun." This album also yielded the hit "Time After Time," which was her first number one hit on the U.S. charts.

"Time After Time"
by Cyndi Lauper and Rob Hyman

Cyndi Lauper co-wrote "Time After Time" with Rob Hyman of the band The Hooters. Hyman also contributed backing vocals on the track. Lauper and Hyman were separately experiencing conflict in their individual personal relationships. Inspired by her troubled relationship, Lauper sang a love song of devotion. In the song's storyline, the narrator believed that she was unworthy of love, thus causing her to run away. The lyrics further revealed that the boyfriend loved her unconditionally and reached out to help her. The listener learned that the couple had a deep and intimate relationship and gave each other support. Lauper named the song after a science fiction film titled *Time After Time*.

Musically, "Time After Time" was built around simple chords on a keyboard synthesizer and a drum machine part. One of pop-rock's most emotional ballads, it's a haunting melody that interacted musically with the bassline and guitar parts. Lauper and Hyman wrote the chorus to *extend* the melody as the phrases connect seamlessly to one another. "Time After Time" was covered by many artists, most notably by jazz great Miles Davis who covered it on his 1985 album <u>You're Under Arrest</u>. Davis was a great interpreter of the ballad form and he constantly re-invented the melody by dissecting it and then building phrase *after* phrase.

Cyndi Lauper released ten more studio albums from the mid-1980's to her 2016 album <u>Detour</u>. Her "Girls Just Want to Have Fun" established her as a feminist and role model for many female vocalists in a variety of rock genres. Some of her other hits included; "She Bop," "True Colors," and "Change of Heart." She was able to mold punk and new wave influences with elements of synth-pop to create her distinctive sound. In 2013, Cyndi Lauper won a Tony Award for Best Original Score for composing the Broadway musical *Kinky Boots*.

Bryan Adams (1959-) is a Canadian singer/songwriter and guitarist. Adams' self-titled 1980 debut <u>Bryan Adams</u> was the first of his fourteen studio albums. His career has spanned over three decades including 2015's <u>Get Up</u>. Known as a master of the power ballad, Adams achieved his greatest success with his fourth studio album, 1984's <u>Reckless</u>. His hit "Run To You" and the power ballad "Heaven" were two of the featured songs on <u>Reckless</u> and served to help define his career.

Debbie Gibson (1970-) is an American singer/songwriter who released her debut album <u>Out of the Blue</u> in 1987. It reached number seven on the U.S. charts. Gibson became a pop phenomenon in the late 1980's, releasing a string of hit singles when she was only seventeen years old. "Lost in Your Eyes," from her second album titled <u>Electric Youth</u>, was her biggest hit. It reached number one on the American charts. Gibson sang catchy dance oriented pop-rock in the style of Madonna and was versatile enough to sing ballads. Gibson's time at the top of the charts was brief, yet it yielded five top ten singles. She released eight more studio albums, culminating with 2010's <u>Ms. Vocalist</u>. Debbie Gibson went on to star on Broadway playing the characters Eponine in *Les Miserables* and Sandy in *Grease*.

The pop-rock genre was not limited to America and England. Its international appeal began in the early 1960's with the Australian band **The Bee Gees**. The Swedish pop-rock group **Abba** (1972-1982) (reunions in 1986, 2008, 2016) was another extremely successful commercial band in the early 1970's, selling well over one hundred and forty million albums worldwide. They released eight studio albums that included the hits "Dancin Queen" and "Mamma Mia." Abba was inducted into the Rock and Roll Hall of Fame in 2010. Australia re-entered the world stage in the late 1970's with the pop-rock band **Men at Work** (1978-1986) (1996-2002). They released three studio albums and reached number one on the U.S. charts with their hits "Down Under" and "Who Can It Be Now?" The 1980's produced another Australian successful pop-rock band, **Crowded House** (1985-1996) (2006-2011) (2016). Their self-titled debut album, <u>Crowded House</u>, reached number twelve on the American charts. It yielded the band's most successful international single, "Don't Dream It's Over."

The Bee Gees (1958-2003) (2009-2012) are one of the most popular pop-rock groups of all-time having sold over two hundred and twenty million albums worldwide. Founded by the Gibb brothers Barry, Robin, and Maurice; few bands have matched their endurance and ability to abruptly switch genres and career direction. Originally from a small island off the West Coast of Britain, the Gibb family later moved to Brisbane, Australia. In 1960, the brothers formed The Bee Gees and released a number of singles. In 1966, their eleventh single titled "Spick and Specks," became a chart hit in Australia. They soon moved to England, signed a record deal with Leedon

---

"It's that anonymous person who meanders through the streets and feels what's happening there, feels the pulse of the people, who's able to create."

- Cyndi Lauper

Records, and recruited drummer Collin Petersen and guitarist Vince Melouney.

From the mid to late 1960's, The Bee Gees recorded six albums starting with their 1965 debut The Bee Gees Sing and Play 14 Barry Gibb Songs. In the early 1970's, The Bee Gees, with their strong Beatles influenced sound, worked hard to built a fan base. There was a lot of international touring, television appearances, and some very good recordings. This included the progressive approach of their album Odessa. Odessa was regarded as the Bee Gees Sgt. Pepper's or Pet Sounds in it's scope and grandeur. The direction and ambition of this recording was not reflected in critical or mass acceptance.

In 1975, the Bee Gees made an important career move and moved to Miami, Florida. There, they joined forces with American soul music producer Arif Mardin and turned to the **disco** style. They signed a five-year deal with Robert Stigwood, who would manage the band to unimagined heights. Under Stigwood's guidance, The Bee Gees recorded the American and British chart topping double album soundtrack to the film *Saturday Night Fever*. This album became pop-rock's largest selling album until the arrival of Michael Jackson's Thriller. The disco mega hits "Jive Talkin," and "You Should Be Dancing" made them international stars. The Gibb brother's songwriting yielded five U.S. number one hits in 1978 including; "Stayin Alive," "How Deep is Your Love," and "Night Fever." In 1978 alone, the Gibb brothers wrote and performed thirteen singles that made the U.S. charts.

"Staying Alive"
by Barry Gibb, Robin Gibb, and Maurice Gibb

A pop-rock disco song written for the soundtrack to the movie *Saturday Night Fever*, "Staying Alive" became one of The Bee Gees' signature songs. It was recorded in France; due to The Bee Gees tax exile issues (problematic for many artists at the time). While recording the soundtrack, their drummer Dennis Bryon, left the band after the death of his mother. Instead of hiring another drummer, The Bee Gees *unsuccessfully* tried using a drum machine to record the drumset part for the track. They ended up utilizing a *sample* of a two-bar phrase from their previous song, "Night Fever."

The lyrics for "Staying Alive" were serious and spoke directly about people trying to survive on the streets of New York City. The song's storyline described that everyone struggled against the world and how people had to fight against the many things that could drag you down. The lyrics proclaimed that surviving was a victory in and of itself. The music video for the song was different from the *Saturday Night Fever* movie concept. The video presented the band singing the song on an abandoned subway terminal set at MGM studios.

The Bee Gee's found more popularity in 1987 with the hit "You Win Again." 2001's This is Where I Came In would be the last Bee Gees album. Maurice Gibb died in 2003 from cardiac arrest and Robin Gibb died in 2012 from cancer. The Bee Gees enormous success yielded fifty U.S. and British chart singles, eleven of them reaching number one. Few artists in any music genre rivaled their songwriting skills. Their signature three-part vocal harmonies featured Robin's distinctive vibrato lead vocals and Barry's falsetto. This combined with catchy melodic hooks and elaborate production to define The Bee Gee's sound. They influenced countless future artists in the pop-rock genre. The Bee Gees were inducted into the Rock and Roll Hall of Fame in 1997.

The Disco Movement - Stayin Alive with Rock's Unlikely Cousin

Disco first emerged in the early 1970's out of a subculture of excess in America. It would dominate the pop music world for several years before evolving into the culture of the Big 1980's. During its brief reign, disco would restore the dance groove and bring a new energy to popular music. Dance clubs (including New York's studio 54) featured DJ's with their turntables who soon became a large part of urban dance parties. Rather than placing an emphasis on singers and musicians, early disco focused on dancers, whose sense of fashion and ability to dance garnered the spotlight.

The soft rock, country rock, progressive rock, heavy metal, and even the oldies of the first half of the 1970's were based on *listening*. Disco was all about the *moving*. Disco became an international craze with the massive success of the movie *Saturday Night Fever*, and it's soundtrack (performed by the Bee Gees) became the biggest selling album in pop-music history (at the time). New disco artists such as The Village People and Gloria Gaynor emerged. Already established artists such as Diana Ross looked to revitalize their careers through the popularity of disco. Hit disco songs included Donna Summer's "Love To Love You Baby" and Kool and The Gang's "Ladies Night." Guitarist Nile Rodgers and bassist Bernard Edwards founded the disco super-group Chic and created hits like "Le Freak," "Good Times," and "Dance, Dance Dance." Rodgers' production and guitar playing became a key ingredient in the sound of disco. Chic became the studio band for many of disco's biggest hits including; Diana Ross' "Upside Down," and "I'm Coming Out," and Sister Sledge's "We Are Family." Rodgers would go on to have continued success outside of disco with artists like David Bowie, Madonna, The B-52's, Daft Punk, Jeff Beck, and Mick Jagger. In 2017, Nile Rodgers was inducted into the Rock and Roll Hall of Fame.

Rock answered the disco movement when Frank Zappa's "Dancin Fool," from his 1979 album Sheik Yerbouti, mocked disco. In the song, Zappa portrayed a character that sang that he *just had* to dance, despite how awful a dancer he was. In the song, he referred to his own dancing as "social suicide" and sang the lyric "The beat goes on and I'm so wrong." On the other hand, The Rolling Stones *embraced* disco with their song "Miss You" from their 1978 album Some Girls. Mick Jagger and Charlie Watts would often go to trendy disco clubs in Europe and New York City. Jagger and keyboardist Billy Preston came up with the bassline for "Miss You" and the Stones released an extended dance mix of the song. Vocalist Rod Stewart offered his answer to disco with his song "Do Ya Think I'm Sexy?" which was co-written by Vanilla Fudge drummer Carmine Appice.

"Disco sucks" was a popular movement embraced by many rock fans and the rock press in the late 1970's and early 1980's. The "disco sucks" era softened when it became clear that disco was never really a threat to rock music. Rock music was on solid ground coming from a deep and rich tradition. Disco and rock moved in parallel universes and in the end, disco was good for rock by contributing new musical dimensions, thus giving rock a slightly new direction.

The British pop-rock genre rose to prominence in the 1980's with a number of successful artists

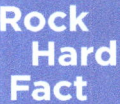

Rock Hard Fact

Tears for Fears derived their name from a form of trauma-based psychotherapy called primal therapy. This "tears for fears" therapy was developed by an American psychologist named Arthur Janov, whose famous clients included Beatles legend John Lennon.

> "To see a lot of the smaller labels disappear or get gobbled up by the bigger labels, that's a shame. It was a bit of a shock at first to see the demise of the record stores."
>
> – Phil Collins

and bands. Collectively, they laid the groundwork for the Britpop movement of the 1990's and beyond. **Boy George** (1961-) is an English singer/songwriter that achieved fame with **Culture Club** (1981-1986) (1998-2002) (2011-present) in the 1980's. At the height of their fame, Culture Club (see chapter fourteen) released the international hits "Do You Really Want to Hurt Me," and "Karma Chameleon." Boy George blended soul and reggae, all with a glam rock sensibility. **Wang Chung** (1980-1990) (1997 present) was another popular British band in the 1980's. They built a strong fan base in the U.S. and enjoyed five top forty hits between the years 1983 and 1987. Some of their hits were 1984's "Dance Hall Days," 1986's "Everybody Have Fun Tonight," and 1987's "Let's Go!" **George Michael** (1963-2016) was a British singer/songwriter who has sold more than one hundred and fifteen million albums worldwide. George Michael first rose to fame in 1981 as part of the duo **Wham!** (1981-1986) (reunions 1988,1991) with his musical partner Andrew Ridgeley. Wham! sold more than twenty-eight million records between 1982 and 1986 including the hits "Wake Me Up Before You Go-Go" and "Last Christmas." Other British pop-rock artists that gained popularity in the mid-1980's were **XTC** (1972-2006) **Howard Jones** (1955-), **The Thompson Twins** (1977-1993), and **Tears for Fears**.

Tears for Fears (1981-present) are an English pop-rock duo formed in 1981 by singer/songwriter, guitarist and keyboardist Roland Orzabal and vocalist/songwriter, keyboardist/bassist and guitarist Curt Smith. In the early 1980's, Tears for Fears initially developed a new wave sound that utilized synthesizers. By the mid-1980's, they moved to a more pop-rock approach that led to international chart success. 1983's debut album, The Hurting, went to number one on the British charts and included their first chart hit, "Mad World." 1985's Songs from the Big Chair peaked at number one in America and number two in England. Their most popular album to date, it featured five hits including; "Mothers Talk," "Shout," "Everybody Wants to Rule the World," "Head Over Heels," and "I Believe."

"Everybody Wants to Rule the World"
by Roland Orzabal, Ian Stanley, and Chris Hughes

"Everybody Wants to Rule the World" launched Tears for Fears to international fame. The lyrics were first written as "Everybody Wants to Go To War" but Roland Orzabal thought that title didn't adequately capture the song's meaning. He wanted the song to express that many individuals seek power and control and how that power can lead to unfortunate consequences. Early in their career, Tears For Fears had established a synth-pop approach but wanted to move to a bigger and more powerful sound. "Everybody Wants to Rule the World" was first built around two simple chords that Orzabal played on an acoustic guitar. To make it more powerful, the band added two hard rocking guitar solos, a big fully processed sound, and an infectious groove.

"Everybody Wants to Rule the World" reached number one on the U.S. charts and won best single at the 1986 Brit Awards. A promotional clip for the song was filmed in 1985 with Curt Smith driving an antique Austin-Healey 3000 sports car around numerous locations in Southern California. This clip was mixed in with episodes of Tears For Fears performing the song in a London studio.

Tears for Fears went on to release four more studio albums including 1989's The Seeds of Love, 1993's Elemental, 1995's Raoul and the Kings of Spain, and 2004's Everybody Loves a Happy Ending. They remain one of the most creative and influential pop-rock bands to emerge from the British 1980's pop-rock scene.

Phil Collins (1951-) is a drummer, vocalist, and songwriter who began his career as the drummer and then lead singer of the progressive rock band Genesis (see chapter thirteen). Collins never imagined that he would take over the lead vocalist chair in Genesis when Peter Gabriel left to begin a solo career. Tony Banks remembered, "Since people knew we (Genesis) were looking for a new singer, we had been receiving tapes from all over the place. We used to see two or three people a day (eventually almost three hundred total)…and as we auditioned them, Phil would often sing the melody to teach it to them, and he actually sang a lot better than these guys." #7 Phil Collins had a very pure, almost choirboy-like vocal quality. His experience fronting Genesis provided him with the challenge and opportunity to develop his range and power that he would so effectively use to launch his solo career. Collins subsequently developed an incredibly successful solo career and released eight studio albums.

Phil Collins' recording output has yielded over thirty three million album sales in America and over one hundred and fifty million worldwide! However, it began quite innocently. In December of 1978, Genesis went on hiatus and Collins went to Canada to be with his family. He returned to England in 1979 to find that Banks and Rutherford (of Genesis) were working on solo albums. This provided Collins with the time to record and tour with the fusion band Brand X. At the same time, Collins also began writing material for his debut solo album. Soon after, Banks and Rutherford joined Collins to start working on the Genesis album, Duke.

In 1981, Collins released his debut solo album Face Value to international acclaim. It reached number one in seven countries and number seven in America. On this debut (and his subsequent releases), Collins would help to define the sound of 1980's pop-rock.

Groundbreaking album Face Value
by Phil Collins

On Face Value, Phil Collins wrote music and lyrics about his troubled personal life. Many of the songs reflected his emotional state from going through a divorce. While writing the material, Collins stayed in the house for weeks that he had long shared with his wife and kids. Some of the songs Collins wrote at this time would end up on the 1980 Genesis album Duke. For Face Value, Collins decided to incorporate the Phenix Horns, the horn section for the funk band Earth, Wind, and Fire. Although Phil is renowned as one of the rock's greatest drummers, he was inspired to utilize drum machine parts on Face Value. This inspiration came from his former Genesis bandmate, Peter Gabriel, who had recently composed drum machine parts for one of his recordings.

Face Value opened with the epic "In the Air Tonight," and proceeded with "This Must Be Love," "Behind the Lines," "The Roof is Leaking," "Droned," and "Hand in Hand." For "The Roof is Leaking," Collins approached the lyrics as if he were writing a novel. Collins stated, "You use inflection and psychological warfare with the audience to bring them into the story." #8 The vocals clearly showed the emotional pain he was feeling about the breakup of his marriage.

The new-aged sounding "Droned" was influenced by Collins' previous association with Brian Eno.

Side two of the LP opened with "I Missed Again," then "You Know What I Mean," "Thunder and Lightning," "I'm Not Moving," "If Leaving Me is Easy," "Tomorrow Never Knows," and the hidden track "Over the Rainbow." The fragile ballad, "If Leaving Me is Easy," served again to revisit Collins' depressed state of mind. However, "I'm Not Moving," combined a catchy melody with forceful lyrics to show his rising ability as a hitmaker.

The production on Face Value was a big part of the 1980's sound of pop-rock music. The combination of fretless bass, lush synth pads, and huge gated drums set a standard for the 1980's pop-rock sound. Ironically, Collins helped to popularize the drum machine (again, he was one of rock drumming's finest), and especially the cheesy, thin sound of the Roland CR-78. On Face Value, Collins also utilized a Roland VP-330 vocoder, a Prophet-5 synth, a Fender Rhodes piano, and percussion including; congas, marimba and handclaps. Guest musicians included; Eric Clapton, violinist Shankar, bassist Alphonso Johnson, vocalist Stephen Bishop, and Genesis touring guitarist Daryl Stuermer. Arif Mardin added some of the string arrangements.

"In the Air Tonight"
by Phil Collins

Around the three-minute mark of the song "In the Air Tonight," you hear a Sequential Circuits Prophet-5 analog synthesizer, a Roland CR-78 drum machine, and an electric guitar build in intensity. Collins is singing the line, with the aid of a Vocoder, "The hurt doesn't show, but pain still grows-it's no stranger to you and me." At this point Phil Collins entered with one of the most intense and memorable drum fills in rock music history. Collins remembered, "There were different stages for that song. When we had Eric Clapton and some of his guys come up to the studio, we played 'In the Air Tonight' for them. When the drums came in, everybody said, 'F***ING HELL! What the f*** is that?' Nobody had ever heard anything like that. Frankly, drums were never that loud. But it was *my* album, and it worked!" #9

Hugh Padgham co-produced "In the Air Tonight" and would produce many of Collins future projects. The song was an instant hit on the British charts at number two and an accompanying music video received strong MTV airplay. In 1985, Collins performed the song twice on the *same day* (taking a Concorde turbo jet) at the double-venue Live Aid benefit concert in *London* and *Philadelphia*. "In the Air Tonight" has been covered and sampled by many artists including; Nas, Tupac Shakur, Lil' Kim, and even basketball great Shaquille O'Neal in his song "Edge of Night."

1982's Hello I Must Be Going sent nine of its ten songs to multiple charts around the world. The album included a cover of the Supremes' "You Can't Hurry Love," and revealed Collins' long time love for rhythm and blues. 1985's No Jacket Required contained four top ten hits including "Sussudio." Peter Gabriel and Sting both made guest appearances. 1989's ...But Seriously became the best selling album of 1990 in England and reached number one in America. It was followed by 1993's Both Sides, and for this effort, Collins made the entire album on his own by playing all of the instruments and handling the production.

Up to this point, Collins had been juggling his solo career and his commitment to Genesis. In 1996, he left Genesis permanently (under amiable conditions). Collins went on to release 1996's Dance into the Light, 2002's Testify, and 2010's Going Back. Although these three albums were less successful, Going Back completed his long time goal of performing an entire album covering classic Motown songs.

Phil Collins' later career as a successful movie soundtrack balladeer and Disney music composer has created a significant amount of media-driven criticism, and he has often fought back. However, commercial success should never force an artist to endure undue criticism. Through his songwriting and career as a solo artist, Phil Collins has proven to be an iconic figure in American popular music. Collins has even influenced urban artists such as Kanye West, Beyonce, and Alicia Keys. Many hip-hop artists have sampled his grooves including Wu-Tang Clan and Lil'Kim. In 2009, Collins revealed that he could no longer play drums or piano due to complications from neck surgery. He announced his retirement from music in 2011 due to these and other health issues. However, in 2015 Collins came out of retirement and signed a deal with Warner Music Group. Plans included touring and writing a new album. In 2017, Collins launched his Not Dead Yet Tour. Phil Collins was inducted into the Rock and Roll Hall of Fame in 2010 as a member of Genesis.

The 1990's brought a new era of American pop-rock artists. The advent of *American Idol* and other similar reality-based television shows has provided a new route for the dream of rock stardom. There have been many high quality rock and pop talents to come out of this process like **Adam Lambert**, **Jennifer Hudson** (1981-), **Taylor Hicks** (1976-), **Jordin Sparks** (1989-), and **Kelly Clarkson**. The rock band in the pop-rock tradition is alive and well. A few of these prominent artists include; **Train** (1993-present), **Maroon 5** (1994-present), **Fall Out Boy** (2001-2009) (2013-present) and more recently, **OneRepublic** (2002-present) and **Imagine Dragons**.

Kelly Clarkson (1982-) is an American singer/songwriter who rose to fame in 2002 after winning the inaugural season of the television show *American Idol*. Her 2003 debut album, Thankful, went to number one on the U.S. charts. Her second release, 2004's Breakaway, saw her move to a more pop-rock oriented sound. Five singles from Breakaway became worldwide hits and established Clarkson as an international star.

Those singles included; "Since U Been Gone," "Breakway," and "Because of You." Clarkson has recorded six more studio albums, including 2017's Meaning of Life. She has sold over twenty five million albums worldwide with her powerful and versatile voice.

"Since U Been Gone"
by Max Martin and Lukasz Gottwald

"Since U Been Gone" was an uptempo pop-rock song that alternated between soft pop passages and contrasting loud, aggressive sections. Max Martin originally wrote the song for the singer Pink, but she rejected it. Hilary Duff also turned the song down when she realized she could not reach the high notes. At first, Clarkson was not sold on the song because it didn't have any lyrics yet and a raw version of the melody had only been recorded. However, she was able to see its potential by adding guitar and drumset.

Rock Hard Fact

In addition to receiving honorary doctorates in music from Fairleigh Dickinson University and Berklee College of Music, Phil Collins also holds an honorary doctorate of history from McMurry University for his research and collection of Texas Revolution artifacts and documents.

The music video for the song showed a girl that completely destroyed her ex-boyfriend's house. Clarkson had been labeled as a ballad singer and "Since U Been Gone" was really a breakout track for her. It showed that she could rock hard and balance her sound between dance-pop and more rock-oriented material. "Since U Been Gone" was a worldwide success, reaching the top ten in many European countries and Australia.

Adam Lambert (1982-) took the experience that he gained in the theater when he appeared in early productions of *Hello Dolly, Grease,* and *The Music Man,* to the bigger stage when he appeared in *Hair, Brigadoon,* and *The Ten Commandments.* This training helped him become the runner-up in the eighth season of *American Idol*. On the show, he successfully channeled different aspects of his own "idols" that included; Freddie Mercury, David Bowie, and Robert Plant in memorable performances week after week. His *American Idol* exposure catapulted him to record For Your Entertainment, Trespassing, and The Original High. Beginning in 2012, Lambert began appearing as a front-man with Queen (following Paul Rogers who originally stepped in for Freddie Mercury), and has excelled in that situation. It is not only Lambert's voice that has created a vocal continuum for the band, but his on-stage presence and charisma has provided a sense of re-birth for the resurging Queen.

Imagine Dragons (2008-present) is an American pop-rock band from Las Vegas, Nevada. The band consists of vocalist Dan Reynolds, guitarist Wayne Sermon, bassist/keyboardist Ben McKee, and drummer Dan Platzman. Imagine Dragons developed a sound that fused pop-rock with elements of alternative and new wave styles. Their 2012 debut album, Night Visions, found immediate success by reaching number two on the U.S. charts. Two singles from the album, "Radioactive" and "Dragons" stayed on the charts for more than sixty consecutive weeks, giving Imagine Dragons the distinction of the first band to accomplish that achievement. The band's sound relied heavily on the fact that all of it's members play more than one instrument (sometimes on the same song). This versatility gave the band the ability to create many different musical approaches and timbres within the same song, resulting in a huge sound.

In 2015, Imagine Dragons released Smoke + Mirrors and their latest release was 2017's Evolve. The former went to number one and the later peaked at number two on the U.S. charts, catapulting Imagine Dragons to worldwide popularity. Imagine Dragons have proven that they can craft radio-friendly hits and power anthems that successfully combine alternative and indie rock in a pop-rock format.

"Radioactive"
by Imagine Dragons, Alexander Grant, and Josh Mosser

"Radioactive" combined the stylistic elements of pop, alternative rock, and the subgenre of dubstep. The drums were powerful and the strong electronics made it stand out from most pop-rock songs. The lyrics spoke of an apocalyptic end of the world. The revolutionist themes revealed in the lines "I'm waking up to ash and dust" and "This is it, the apocalypse" created clear imagery for the song. "Radioactive" was about someone having a great awakening by seeing the world in a new way. The heavy subject matter was not the norm for most pop-rock songs.

"Radioactive" was the best selling pop-rock song in American digital history. It went straight to number one on the U.S. singles chart. The song has been utilized in media venues such as the video game *Assassin's Creed* III and to promote numerous TV shows. The music video for "Radioactive" showed a mysterious female drifter on a mission to save her friends (Imagine Dragons) from an evil, underground puppet-fighting ring.

Britpop

The term **Britpop** was first coined around 1994 when the media began to use the "Brit" prefix to describe the success of British fashion designers and films. However, the Britpop label referred to a new marketing term for a new musical movement. Britpop emerged in England in the later 1980's after an interest in club culture and rave music (breakbeat and techno music played at rave parties) developed. Simultaneously, electronic dance music (EDM) was dominating the underground dance clubs in England. In America, the dark and moody grunge movement of the early 1990's was growing in popularity. Britpop music began as a musical reaction to these occurrences and provided another example of the evolution of rock 'n' roll. Young British musicians found themselves looking for their *own* sound, and became inspired by many of the early British mod and glam bands. Consequently, Britpop signified a return to guitar-oriented rock, but with an updated pop sensibility. Britpop bands created catchy pop melodies with positive themes. And they rocked hard. America's independent music scene and grunge movement inspired this new emerging English music scene. Suddenly, British indie record labels and bands such as **The Smiths** were developing just as independent bands had in America.

The Smiths (1982-1987) were a British rock band that formed in 1982. The lineup consisted of vocalist Morrissey, guitarist Johnny Marr, bassist Andy Rourke, and drummer Mike Joyce. Some might call The Smiths a British version of the band R.E.M. The Smiths everyday sense of fashion (consisting of blue jeans and black t-shirts) didn't set them apart, but their independent style of music did. The Smiths combined the musical style of the New York Dolls with the rawness of Patty Smith and Neil Young and the energy of The Who. They took the songwriting styles of The Cult and The Pretenders and combined it with the melodicism of The Byrds. The Smiths only recorded four records including; 1984's The Smiths, 1985's Meat is Murder, 1986's The Queen is Dead, and 1987's Strangeways, Here We Come. However, their influence was huge.

In their relatively short career, The Smiths inspired the bands; **Happy Mondays** (1980-present with some inactive years), **The Stone Roses** (1983-1996) (2011-2017), **Charlatans UK** (1989-present) (they added the UK to avoid confusion with the American psychedelic band The Charlatans), **Pulp** (1979-2002) (2011-2013), and **Suede** (1989-2003) (2010-present). All of these bands created a new musical scene, which the media dubbed "Britpop." And like the term "grunge" in the U.S., this term was largely media driven. Britpop was the next step in the evolution of British rock 'n' roll.

That next step came to fruition with the arrival of two "competing" bands, **Blur** and **Oasis**. Similar to the earlier media driven competition between The Beatles and The Rolling Stones; there weren't winners and losers, just great music.

> **Rock Hard Fact**
>
> Damon Albarn in his post-Blur career has recorded an album of all African music, composed Chinese operas, and produced albums of soul singers.

Blur (1988-2003) (2008-present) is a British pop-rock band formed in London in 1988. Their lineup consists of singer/guitarist Damon Albarn, singer/guitarist Graham Coxon, drummer Dave Rowntree, and bassist Alex James. Their 1991 debut album, Leisure, sold well with its mixture of alternative rock, 1960's pop, and psychedelic influences. In the early to mid 1990's, Blur released 1993's Modern Life is Rubbish, 1994's Parklife, and 1995's The Great Escape. These three albums established them as one of the leading bands of the Britpop movement. Blur had a big hit, "Country House" in 1985. Their Britpop rival, the band Oasis, simultaneously issued their own hit titled "Roll With It." This fueled a chart battle that made the national news in England.

"Country House"
by Blur

"Country House" was a simple pop tune with a catchy melody. Blur skillfully created background vocal harmonies that functioned as a counter melody. Throughout the tune, they utilized a horn section for backgrounds and then featured the horns to eventually play a section at the end of the song. "Country House" had a very *British* feel, from the vocal inflections to the lyrical content. The song reached number one on the British charts.

"Country House" was about a wealthy man who led a very boring life in a country mansion. He had a very cynical attitude about his job and moved to the country to escape the rat race. The song was based on the life of one of the owners of Blur's record label, Food Records. The band used a picture of a castle in Bavaria, Germany on the album cover to depict the mansion. The song received a lot of media attention when Blur's label moved the release date of "Country House" to coincide with the release date of their rival Oasis's song, "Roll With It."

1997's album Blur saw the band change their musical direction by moving to a more indie rock sound. Their single, "Song 2," raised their profile in America. Their next album, 13, moved in an electronic and gospel direction with very personal lyrics. Coxon quit the band while recording 2003's Think Tank but returned for a series of concerts in 2009. Blur's first major release in twelve years, 2015's The Magic Whip, brought them back to the top of the British charts. Over their career, Blur has retained their core musical identity while simultaneously embracing different musical ideas and styles.

Oasis (1991-2009) was a British pop-rock band that formed in Manchester, England in 1991. The band's lineup included vocalist Liam Gallagher, guitarist Paul Arthurs, bassist Paul McGuigan, and drummer Tony McCarroll. Later, Liam's brother Noel Gallagher joined on vocals and lead guitar. Their 1994 debut release Definitely Maybe, made them instant peers of the already established Britpop supergroup, Blur. Definitely Maybe went straight to number one in England, the fastest album to get to the top in British music history. Noel Gallagher focused his writing on optimistic themes (in reaction to the American grunge movement) with hit songs like "Live Forever" and "Supersonic."

In 1995, drummer Tony McCarroll was replaced by Alan White for Oasis's 1995 album (What's the Story) Morning Glory?. It would become England's fifth best-selling album of all-time and solidified the group's place as a leading Britpop band. The Gallagher brothers were often featured in the British tabloid newspapers for their wild lifestyles and sibling arguments. A single from (What's the Story) Morning Glory? titled "Roll with It," went to number two on the British charts in a battle with Blur's "Country House."

"Roll with It"
by Noel Gallagher

"Roll with It" spoke to the importance of trying to be yourself and stop complaining about life. This was a standard lyrical theme that ran through many Oasis songs. The composition immediately reminded the listener of early Beatles, however, it contained a gritty guitar timbre that defined the streamlined Oasis sound. "Roll with It" provided a strong example of how Oasis wrote lyrics and played with a blue-collar attitude. This would connect them first to their British audience, and then the rest of the world.

"Roll with It" was the first track that Oasis recorded with their new drummer Alan White (not the drummer of the same name that recorded with John Lennon and joined Yes). White gave them a hard rocking approach. Their rival, Blur, won the "*battle* of Britpop" race to the number one spot on the British singles chart with "Country House." However, Oasis eventually won the war when (What's the Story) Morning Glory? sold over sixteen million copies worldwide. This established their superstar status.

Oasis confirmed their status as one of rock's top acts with two big shows at Britain's Knebworth Park in 1996. 1997's Be Here Now went to number one in England and number two in America. By the time Oasis released 2000's Standing on the Shoulder of Giants, only Liam and Noel Gallagher remained from the original lineup. This album had a psychedelic sound with the addition of drum loops, samples, synthesizers, and a Mellotron. Oasis released three more albums in the 2000's before calling it a career in 2009, amid internal conflict between the Gallagher brothers. Oasis rose from obscurity to stardom in the mid-1990's and became one of the world's most popular bands. They were a major force on the Britpop scene with their Beatlesque melodic hooks, punk-like rebelliousness, and massive guitar sound. More than any other band, Oasis legitimized the Britpop movement throughout the world.

In the mid-to late 1990's established bands such as **Radiohead** (see chapter sixteen) and **The Verve** were beginning to gain more popularity, having been previously overshadowed by the Britpop movement. Later, the post-Britpop band **Coldplay** achieved an even wider international audience.

The Verve (1990-1997) (2007-2009) was a British rock band formed in 1990 by vocalist Richard Ashcroft, guitarist Nick McCabe, drummer Peter Salisbury, and bassist Simon Jones. They soon added a fifth member, keyboardist/guitarist Simon Tong. Their 1993 debut recording, A Storm in Heaven, had moderate commercial success reaching number twenty-seven on the British charts. The Verve distanced themselves from the Britpop movement while still creating a pop oriented sound. They effectively incorporated elements of psychedelia, Classical, an affinity for The Beatles, and an ability to cultivate material through extended jam sessions. 1995's A Northern Soul focused on an alternative rock sound and produced the fairly successful "This is Music" that went to number thirty five on the British charts. However, internal tension in the band led to Ashcroft's departure and a temporary end of The Verve.

> "For people who write songs, it's a gift you're given. You become good at the craft, but you're given the gift."
>
> – Chris Martin of Coldplay

> "I was lucky enough to grow up in an era when radio was less formatted... You could hear a jazz song then a pop song then a show tune.... Whatever the DJ felt like playing...He was educating you and exposing you to things you would never hear otherwise."
>
> - Todd Rundgren

Ashcroft re-formed the band in 2007 and they released Urban Hymns, an impressive recording that yielded their first big hit, "Unfinished Symphony." It went to number two on the British charts. Although The Verve received legal permission to sample four bars of The Rolling Stones tune "The Last Time," they released the single without explicit permission from the administrator of the song's rights. Therefore, The Verve was forced to give one hundred percent of the royalties for "Unfinished Symphony" to Mick Jagger and Keith Richards. Urban Hymn also produced "The Drugs Don't Work," giving the band its first British number one hit and catapulting the album to number one (knocking out Oasis' Be Here Now out of the top spot).

"The Drugs Don't Work"
by Richard Ashcroft

"The Drugs Don't Work" was a very dark tune and sought to capture the mood and internal struggle of lead singer Richard Ashcroft. It's about his emotional state when he recalled (at age eleven) the hardship of watching his father dying of cancer. Ashcroft stated in the lyric, "The drugs don't work, they just make me worse, and I know I'll see your face again." This was a poignant, yet depressing ballad. When it was released on September 7th, 1997, it also captured the somber mood of the nation following the tragic death of Princess Diana of Wales, that occurred one week earlier.

"The Drugs Don't Work" featured an acoustic guitar introduction supplemented by a string ensemble to support the vocal entrance. Electric guitar figures answered the vocal lines, adding another rhythmic layer to the song. The track built more momentum when the drums entered, raising the intensity and emotion of the lyrics.

Ashcroft launched a successful solo career, releasing three consecutive British top three albums. However, the original Verve members reunited in 2007 for a comeback tour that sold out arenas in only twenty minutes. In 2008, The Verve released their final album, Forth. It went to number one in England and number twenty-three in America. By 2009, some members of The Verve were no longer on speaking terms and the band broke up for good.

Coldplay (1996-present) is a very successful (post-Britpop) band that formed in 1996. Their lineup consists of vocalist/keyboardist Chris Martin, guitarist Jonny Buckland, bassist Guy Berryman, and drummer Will Champion. They first released an EP, Brothers and Sisters, and then signed to Parlophone Records. They next released another EP, The Blue Room. This laid the groundwork for their 2000 debut album Parachutes and their hit single, "Yellow." Parachutes went to number one in England and number fifty-one in America. The album had an alternative rock sound with a moody and "atmospheric" soundscape. This brought Coldplay comparisons to the band Radiohead (see chapter sixteen). 2002's A Rush of Blood to the Head increased Coldplay's audience with its increased use of electric guitar and piano-driven ballads. This album went straight to the top in Britain and has sold over twenty-two million copies worldwide. 2005's X&Y topped their previous success by becoming the best-selling album worldwide that same year! This album yielded the hits "Fix You," "Speed of Sound," "Talk," and "The Hardest Part."

"Fix You"
by Coldplay

"Fix You" was a song that spoke about true love, helping someone in their time of need, and learning from your mistakes. Chris Martin used a keyboard that his late father-in-law, Bruce Paltrow, gave to his actress daughter Gwyneth (Martin was married to Gwyneth Paltrow). Martin was inspired by the sound of this keyboard and also by the Jimmy Cliff song "Many Rivers to Cross." "Fix You" was built around a slow tempo and Martin's falsetto vocals. Its feel was enhanced by the addition of acoustic guitar, piano, and a string section. At the bridge, the song transitioned to a sing-a-long anthem-like section with the addition of a synthesizer. "Fix You" ended with a return to the opening chorus, a slow and melancholic piano part heard in the background.

The track reached number eighteen on the U.S. charts and number four in England. "Fix You" has been covered and sampled by numerous artists. It's guitar solo is utilized at the beginning of the National Hockey League's Montreal Canadians' home games and was played live at the Steve Jobs memorial celebration in 2011.

For 2008's Viva La Vida or Death and All His Friends, Coldplay enlisted the help of super-producer Brian Eno. Even though the band was already immensely successful, under Eno's direction they took some musical chances by extending songs and writing lyrics that were much more abstract than on previous albums. Chris Martin experimented vocally by transitioning from his trademark falsetto to a lower vocal register. Eno challenged Coldplay to embrace sounds outside of their comfort zone, including the influences of tribal music and Afropop. The title track, "Viva La Vida," went to number one on both sides of the Atlantic and won Grammy song of the Year. 2011's Mylo Xyloto was another Eno collaboration and extended their stylistic explorations by including a duet with rhythm and blues artist Rihanna. A single from the album, "Every Teardrop Is a Waterfall," peaked at number six on the British charts. 2014's Ghost Stories was a spiritually driven album that utilized the themes of unconditional love and one's accountability for their past actions. In 2015, Coldplay released their seventh studio album, A Head Full of Dreams. This album has sold over five million copies worldwide, adding to Coldplay's reign as one of pop-rock's most successful bands.

Power Pop

The **power pop** genre gained mainstream success in the late 1970's and early 1980's when artists combined strong melodies, simple arrangements, clear vocals, and catchy guitar riffs. Two of the early power pop founders were the bands **The Raspberries** (1970-1975) (2004-2009), and **Big Star** (1971-1974) (1993-2010). Other early power pop bands that played prominent roles in the late 1960's and 1970's were **Nazz, Badfinger, Rockpile,** and **The Romantics**.

Nazz (1967-1970) (2006-present) was formed in Philadelphia, Pennsylvania by singer/songwriter/guitarist/producer **Todd Rundgren** (1948-) and bassist Carson Van Osten. They soon added drummer Thom Mooney and keyboardist/vocalist Robert Antoni. Nazz was first marketed by their manager, Michael Freeman, as a teeny-bopper styled band similar to The Monkees. Their 1968 debut album Nazz did not fair well on the charts but did produce one of Rundgren's signature songs, "Hello It's Me." The Nazz sound was a combination of psychedelic rock and power-pop.

"Hello It's Me"
by Todd Rundgren

"Hello It's Me" enjoyed mild U.S. chart success in 1970 but was remade in 1972 for Rundgren's solo album Something/Anything?. The new version was much more successful and became Rundgren's only top ten pop hit, peaking at number five on the American charts. Rundgren was influenced by jazz organist Jimmy Smith's version of the standard "When Johnny Comes Marching Home" for its block chords. He utilized this harmonic progression for the song's introduction. Rundgren would also draw from these chords changes to inspire the melody and lyrics. On Rundgren's solo version, he employed the great Randy Brecker on trumpet and legendary Michael Brecker on tenor saxophone.

This was the first song that Todd Rundgren ever composed. It's about the end of a young couples relationship. The lyrics narrated a phone call that revealed the details of their breakup. The listener heard only one side of the phone call that started with a familiar greeting that stated they have been together for a while. Then, they had the breakup "talk," where he explained why they couldn't be together and that she should have her freedom. He asked her to think of him once in a while. Rundgren was inspired to write "Hello, It's Me" by a personal relationship he had in high school.

1969's Nazz Nazz was an experimental, piano oriented album based on Todd Rundgren material. Rundgren was heavily influenced by singer/songwriter Laura Nyro at the time. Antoni and Mooney both wanted to move in a Yardbirds and Cream direction prompting Rundgren to leave the band to begin his solo career. Van Osten quit soon after. Nazz recruited guitarist Craig Bolyn and bassist Greg Sempler and continued to tour in 1970. They released the final Nazz album, Nazz III in 1971. Rundgren went on to have a successful solo career with the band Utopia and as a producer. In 2006, Antoni re-formed Nazz with an all-new lineup.

Badfinger (1970-1975) (1978-1984) was an English pop-rock band that evolved from the band The Iveys. The Iveys were the first band to be signed by The Beatles' Apple label in 1968. They were renamed in 1969 to Badfinger and over the next five years recorded five albums for the Apple label before the label dissolved in the chaos of The Beatles break-up. After many lineup changes, the core lineup of Badfinger became vocalist/guitarist/keyboardist Pete Ham, drummer/vocalist Mike Gibbins, guitarist/bassist/vocalist Tom Evans, and guitarist/keyboardist/vocalist Joey Molland.

Badfinger's first album was recorded *under the name* The Iveys. They recorded three songs for a movie soundtrack called Magic Christian Music and added some of their previously recorded Ivey's tracks. One of the songs on the soundtrack, "Come and Get It," was written by Paul McCartney. All of the tracks were then released as *Badfinger's* first album that coincided with the name change from The Iveys.

"Come and Get It"
by Paul McCartney

"Come and Get It" was offered to The Iveys to record (before they became Badfinger) when Paul McCartney signed a contract to supply three songs for the movie The Magic Christian. McCartney told the band to play "Come and Get It" exactly like the demo he (McCartney) had recorded in 1969, at a Beatles recording session for the Abbey Road album. On the demo, McCartney played all of the instruments and sang the lead vocal part. When McCartney met with The Iveys in the studio, he auditioned each of the four members to sing the lead vocal part. He ultimately picked Tom Evans.

"Come and Get It" was used for the opening theme for The Magic Christian that starred Peter Sellers and Ringo Starr. The song contained a straight forward eighth-note piano accompaniment and simple drum and bass parts. "Come and Get It" embodied a not so surprising Beatles-like quality. Badfinger did what they were told to do by McCartney and "Come and Get It" did become the hit McCartney predicted it would be.

1970's No Dice and 1971's Straight Up saw Badfinger struggle with their label regarding the production of their songs. George Harrison and Todd Rundgren were both brought in to produce the band. Although the hits "Without You," "Day After Day," and "Baby Blue" emerged, the Apple label was falling apart. Badfinger's last Apple recording was 1973's Ass. After signing with Warner Bros. Records in 1974, the band released Badfinger and Wish You Were Here, both achieving only moderate success. Wish You Were Here was withdrawn from the market because of legal issues and this severely hurt Badfinger's ability to build an audience. Keyboardist Robert Jackson joined the band for the recording of their next album, Head First. Again, legal problems halted its release until many years later. Warner Bros. was ready to drop them from their label and Badfinger was a band in financial and personal turmoil. Molland and Ham both quit the band. Still more legal issues over production and distribution soon led to the end of Badfinger.

Pete Hamm tragically took his own life in April of 1975. In 1978, Badfinger regrouped and signed a new deal with Elektra Records. They released 1979's Airwaves and Say No More in 1981. However, more legal battles ensued over the use of the band's name, again ending Badfinger. In 1983, Tom Evans sadly took his own life. In 1984, Gibbins, Mollard, and Jackson reunited for a tour. All four Badfinger albums on Apple were re-released in 1975 and Head First was finally released in 2000. Badfinger endured about as much personal tragedy and legal problems as any band in rock history. Yet, former member Joey Molland still continues to tour under the name Joey Molland's Badfinger.

Rockpile (1976-1981) was an English power pop band that formed in the mid-1970's. The lineup consisted of vocalist/guitarist Dave Edmunds, vocalist/bassist Nick Lowe, vocalist/guitarist Billy Bremner, and drummer Terry Williams. Rockpile fused a number of styles, including rockabilly with a pop sensibility. Dave Edmunds had recorded a 1970 solo album titled Rockpile and billed his band Dave Edmunds and Rockpile. However, the band broke up when Edmunds returned to do studio work. Edmunds also worked as a producer and one artist he worked with was Nick Lowe. Soon, Lowe began doing session work with Edmunds that led to the formation of Rockpile. Rockpile went on to record four studio albums, although only one, 1980's Seconds of Pleasure, was released under the Rockpile name. Two albums, 1978's Tracks on Wax 4 and 1979's Repeat When Necessary, were released as Dave Edmunds' solo albums. 1979's Labour of Lust was released as a Nick Lowe solo album. The Rockpile lineup remained the same for all

---

Rock Hard Fact

Pop music all started with Stephen Foster (1826-1864), recognized as the first great American popular songwriter. He composed over two hundred of America's best-known songs. Foster was one of the first composers to negotiate royalties for his published songs (often two to five cents a written copy).

four recordings with the addition of Huey Lewis and Elvis Costello on Labour of Lust. This album also contained the hit "Cruel to Be Kind." Dave Edmunds and Nick Lowe made Rockpile a formidable power pop band in the late 1970's. Rockpile would go on to influence many new wave bands in the 1980's.

"Cruel to Be Kind"
by Nick Lowe and Ian Gomm

"Cruel to Be Kind" reached number twelve on the American and British charts in 1979. Nick Lowe described the original demo for the song as very soulful, similar to the sound of Harold Melvin and The Blue Notes. The lyrics told the story about the attitude of the narrator toward his lover. Musically, "Cruel to Be Kind" utilized a continuous strumming acoustic guitar and the melody has a simple and effective hook.

A video for the song was made using actual footage of Nick Lowe's real wedding. Lowe and his wife Carlene Carter (the daughter of country music legend June Carter) were married in 1979 right after a Rockpile tour. Lowe and Carter toured together in 1982, opening for The Cars, with both singers utilizing the same band. Rockpile co-leader, Dave Edmunds played a chauffeur in the video. "Cruel to be Kind" was featured in the 1999 film 10 *Things I Hate About You* and was one of two hundred and six videos that were first broadcasted on MTV.

The Romantics (1977-present) are an American power-pop band from Detroit, Michigan that formed in 1977. They formed on Valentine's Day and were inspired to take their name from that day. Their original lineup consisted of vocalist/guitarist Wally Palmer, vocalist/guitarist Mike Skill, bassist Rich Cole, and vocalist/drummer Jimmy Marinos. The Romantics 1980 self-titled debut album The Romantics included one of the band's best-known hits, "What I Like About You." That same year, they released National Breakout to only moderate success. 1981's Strictly Personal and 1983's In Heat followed. In Heat was their most popular recording with the hit "Talking in Your Sleep" that reached number three on the U.S. charts. The Romantics released Rhythm Romance in 1985 and 61/49 in 2003. Despite not having a studio issue in fourteen years, The Romantics still continue to tour.

"What I Like About You"
by Wally Palmer, Mike Skill, and Jimmy Marinos

"What I Like About You" attracted little attention and was only a minor hit from The Romantics debut album. It found a new audience later when it was utilized for an advertising jingle for Budweiser beer. Since then, "What I Like About You" has became an anthem for parties, celebrations, and sporting events.

The song had a raw and simple rock 'n' roll feel that represented The Romantics energetic approach to rock. A short harmonica solo entered on the solo chorus, thus lending the song a slight blues influence. The Romantics added effective vocal harmonies that became their signature sound. "What I Like About You" was a throwback to a 1950's rock 'n' roll feel. Often compared to the band The Knack, The Romantics split their lead vocals between guitarist Wally Palmer and drummer Jimmy Marinos. It was Marinos singing lead vocals on "What I Like About You."

A few of the many current American power pop rock bands that have achieved success include: **Dwight Twilley Band** (1974-present), **Gin Blossoms** (1987-1997) (2002-present), **Jimmy Eat World** (1993-present), **Ben Folds Five** (1993-2013 with some inactive years), **Paramore** (2004-present), **Jonas Brothers** (2005-2013), **R5** (2009-present), and **Weezer**.

Weezer (1992-present) is an American pop-rock band that formed in Los Angeles in 1992. The lineup consists of vocalist/guitarist Rivers Cuomo, guitarist/keyboardist Brian Bell, bassist Scott Shriner, and drummer Patrick Wilson. Weezer has released eleven studio albums beginning with their 1994 self-titled debut Weezer (the blue album). The single "Beverly Hills," from their 2005 album Make Believe, became their first single to reach the top ten on the U.S. charts. Vocalist Rivers Cuomo has cited The Beach Boys as a major influence. Weezer effectively combines elements of alternative and indie rock with their distinctive power pop sound.

Music and cultural icons Michael Jackson, Madonna, and Prince clearly defined the pop-rock format. However, all of the artists and bands examined in this chapter have collectively demonstrated the great variety, longevity, and depth of creativity that is the pop-rock genre.

Discussion Question

This book constantly refers to the chart success of an artist or a band's albums or singles. What is it specifically about the lyrics or musical elements that make a song popular on an international level? Can you think of any songs that have spoken directly to you either musically or lyrically that have not achieved popular success? Be specific.

Chapter Fifteen: Pop-Rock

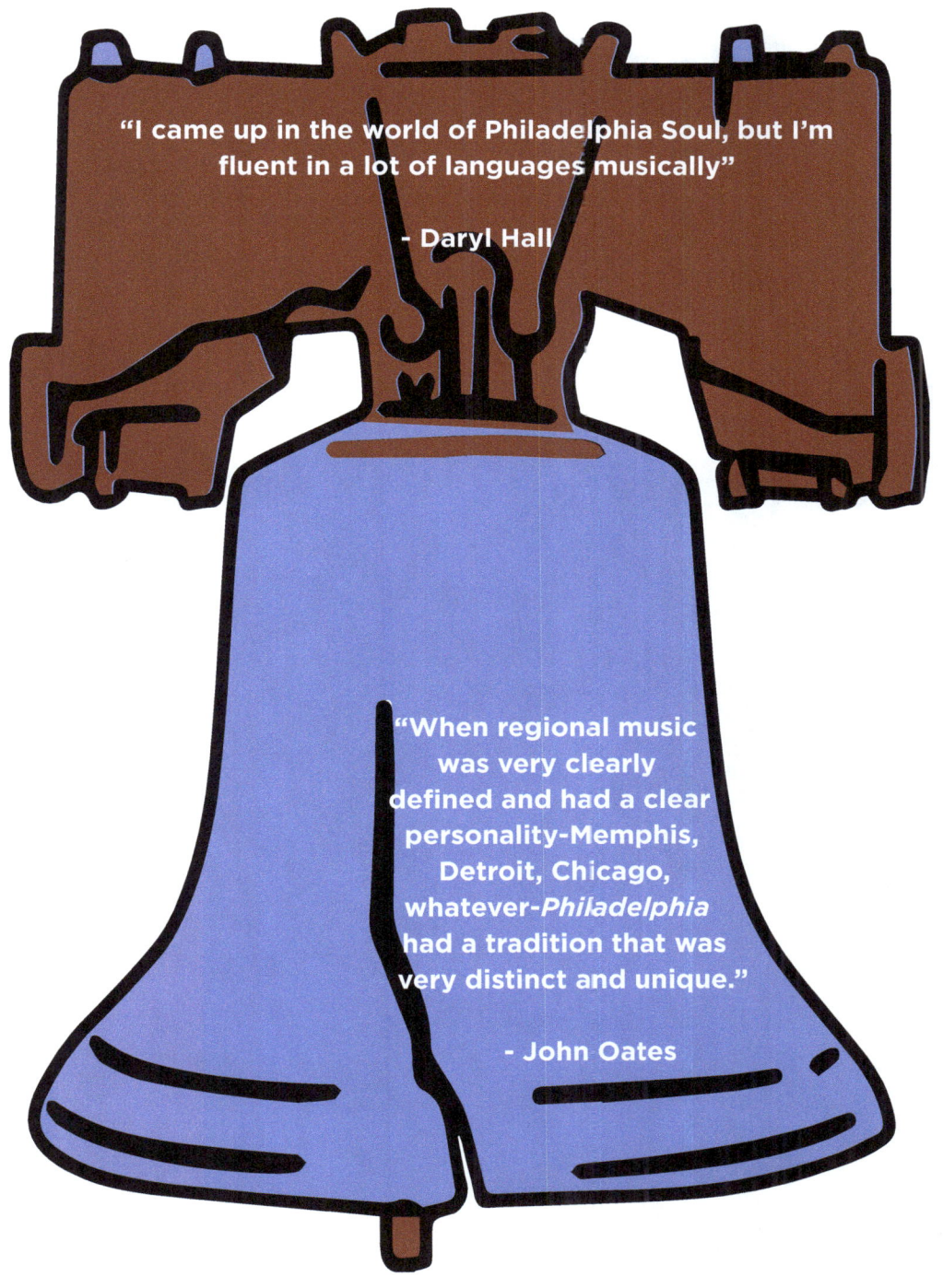

"I came up in the world of Philadelphia Soul, but I'm fluent in a lot of languages musically"

- Daryl Hall

"When regional music was very clearly defined and had a clear personality-Memphis, Detroit, Chicago, whatever-*Philadelphia* had a tradition that was very distinct and unique."

- John Oates

Chapter Sixteen:
The Big Eighties, Grungy Nineties and the Alternative

The decade of the 1980's began with the tragic murder of John Lennon. It also saw great diversity and much change in the music industry. "Big" hair metal bands and "big" arena rock shows dominated as well as "big" and expanded methods for delivering rock music. The compact disc replaced vinyl records and the invention of music television-**MTV** revolutionized the public's perception of various music genres in the 1980's. Many musical styles competed for an audience when rap, new wave, subgenres of heavy metal, techno-pop, and country-rock all strived to build their fan base. The advent of digital recording utilized synthesizers and drum machines (especially Simmons Drums and The Linn Drum Machine), thus helping to facilitate the many new studio enhanced subgenres of techno and house music. By reaching mainsteam success, late 1980's alternative rock was another popular music genre.

Television had first introduced America to Elvis Presley and The Beatles in the 1950's and 1960's. Shows like *American Bandstand* broadcast music with dance and established a visual connection between the two. "I want my MTV" soon became a common slogan soon after MTV first aired on August 1st, 1981. Capitalizing on the visual and production possibilities of MTV were pop-rock superstars **Michael Jackson**, **Madonna**, and **Prince**. MTV was central to the careers of dozens of performers including Peter Gabriel, Cyndi Lauper, and the Stray Cats' revitalization of rockabilly. MTV dramatically changed the method of music delivery and promoted, even saved many music careers.

In addition to MTV's reshaping of the 1980's musical landscape, **U2** would become one of rock's biggest bands by embracing values that many other artists would consider taboo. U2's fans supported their (U2's) desire to speak the truth without worrying if it would impede their success. U2 emerged as an important international band that would help set a standard for an indie post-punk alternative movement. Their strong moral and political views were right on schedule for a decade ripe for change. **R.E.M.'s** rise from an obscure indie band (heard most often on college radio) to mainstream popularity became a blueprint for 1980's rock bands. Another groundbreaking band, **The Police**, was able to assimilate many styles such as punk, new wave, and reggae with their strong melodies. They brought their music to a worldwide audience.

Nirvana *re-invented* rock by becoming the defining band of the new **grunge** movement of the 1990's. Grunge got its name from nasty, loud and often down-tuned guitar sounds. With plenty of mid-range and feedback, grunge riffs made use of distortion, not expensive rack mounted effects. Influenced by punk, grunge lyrics were often topics of anger, frustration, and depression. Basically, grunge expressed cynical and negative outlooks on life. The look of grunge was torn jeans, ratty t-shirts and lots of flannel. Not the look of big rock stars. In the late 1980's, early grunge bands such as Mudhoney and Green River set the stage for Soundgarden, Pearl Jam, Alice in Chains, Stone Temple Pilots, and of course Nirvana. The Seattle independent record label Sub-Pop released many of the core grunge recordings. By the early 1990's, grunge had expanded to California and many other areas across the country.

With the release of <u>Nevermind</u> in 1991, Nirvana and leader Kurt Cobain, brought grunge to the mainstream. Their song "Smells Like Teen Spirit" helped

> "MTV sort of bridges the whole country (America) together almost like the BBC does in England. It's opened up everything so wide that it's possible for everyone to have different ideas."
>
> – Joey Ramone

make grunge not only a movement in rock, but also a lifestyle and gave worldwide exposure to a subculture. Cobain's suicide in 1994 brought an end to Nirvana. Grunge was already in decline as the commercialization of this music by corporations ran counter to the objectives of the grunge movement itself, that being a do-it-yourself attitude of non-conformity. **Post-grunge** is currently still popular with bands such as Matchbox Twenty and Pearl Jam. Alternative rock bands such as Smashing Pumpkins continue to be relevant.

The term **alternative rock** is often misunderstood. Alternative is a *broad* term for rock music that represented the independent music underground in the late 1980's. It became confusing when the term was used to mean *every* underground rock or punk band that gained mainstream success. Alternative rock radio differed from mainstream rock radio in terms of its sound, social context, and even its regional location. Initially a movement based on word of mouth and college radio airplay, alternative rock bands often experienced very little commercial success. Mainstream radio play and large record deals remained out of reach. Underground bands such as The Pixies and The Violent Femmes were a few of the artists that influenced the early alternative rock movement. Also, the punk music of the 1970's helped to create the foundation of alternative rock. Specific subgenres such as indie rock, indie pop, alternative hip-hop, noise pop, emo, gothic rock, and of course, grunge gained popularity in the 1990's.

Three Big Rock Bands of the "Big 80's"

The Police (1977-1986) (2008) were a "perfect storm" of incredible musicianship, strongly defined personalities, and diverse musical styles that ignited what would become (for a short while) the most popular rock band in the world. Vocalist/bassist Sting (aka Gordon Sumner) was working at a number of English music venues with a jazz-rock combo called Last Exit. Sting had earlier secured a songwriting contract with Virgin Records but not a record deal. He soon met drummer Stewart Copeland of the progressive rock band Curved Air (see chapter thirteen). Copeland dropped in on a Last Exit gig and was impressed with Sting's musicianship. The two agreed to jam in the near future. After playing for over an hour, Sting recalled, "Even at this very early moment of our relationship, it is clear that there is something going on, some chemistry, some understanding, some recognition, a rapport and a tension between the amphetamine pulse of his kick drum and the shifting, rolling ground of the bass…I realize very quickly that this guy is the most exciting drummer I've ever worked with, almost too exciting." #1

The musical environment in mid to late 1970's London was an eclectic bag of styles. The impact of the Sex Pistols and the punk movement was well under way while progressive rock was rapidly losing steam (including Curved Air). Late 1970's London also was home to many reggae and ska bands while blues and jazz styles were still present. These genres would all play a factor in the original sound of The Police.

Stewart Copeland had been thinking about forming a new band (he already had the name The Police in mind) and fresh off his session with Sting, he looked for a guitarist. He came up with Henri Padovani. The three rehearsed a few times and recorded the first Police single, the energetic punk inspired "Fall Out," a Copeland composition. In the spring of 1977, "Fall Out" was released. Copeland recalled, "It was a heartfelt lyric, all about a personal disinclination to follow the styles of my peers…We recorded it in a tiny studio and it was one of the rare instances in which I got to play the guitar (Padovani played the solo while Stewart played the main guitar parts). #2 "Fall Out" was one of the first Copeland compositions that Sting would hear. What it had lacked in musical sophistication, it made up for in raw power and energy.

Sting was still unsure if he wanted to commit to joining The Police and playing punk music in general. Sting said, "I don't want to sing tuneless, disaffected rants. I sing tender love songs. This is what I'm good at. But I also realize that there's an opportunity in the chaos, and that I am perfectly able to morph, adapting what I do to suit the current climate without necessarily compromising the integrity of my songs." #3 Meanwhile, Stewart's brother, Miles Copeland, had started a record label and booking agency. He offered Stewart, Sting, and Padovani an opportunity to play in a band with the artist Cherry Vanilla and an opening spot for The Police on her British tour. The Police were now developing their sound with their short ten-song set. What would be fortuitous for the future of The Police, in the spring of 1977, Sting was invited to play a one-off gig with a band called Strontium 90 in Paris. Copeland was also invited to perform when their drummer bailed out. At a brief Strontium rehearsal, Sting and Copeland were introduced to Strontium's guitar player, Andy Summers. Sting's immediate impression of Summers was "Andy blows us all away. He is clearly a fine musician, a master of many musical styles and techniques, from classical to jazz and everything in between. This is the kind of musician I could write for, the kind of musician I could entrust with my songs, who could inspire me, who could realize the music in my head… this is exactly the kind of musician that The Police need. I can tell that Stewart is impressed too." #4 It wasn't long before Henri Padovani was out and a *new breed* of power trio barely known as The Police were ready to make their move.

The Police, with financial help from Miles Copeland, went into Surrey Sound Studio in 1978 to record their debut album. Once Miles heard the just recorded track "Roxanne," he immediately sold it as a one-off single to A&M Records. He then booked The Police on a tour to open for the band Spirit.

"Roxanne"
by Sting

While recording their debut album, Miles Copeland would often stop by the studio to hear how the sessions were proceeding. Miles was not sold on the inclusion of Andy Summers in the band because he feared it would undermine the Police's punk rock credibility. After his initial listen to "Roxanne," Sting looked at Miles and thought "I brace myself for the worst of his anger and derision…he draws a long breath, shaking his head. Miles said 'It's a godda*n classic, it's f***ing smash'." #5 Miles was less enthusiastic about some of the other tracks, but "Roxanne" was issued as a single in 1978 while the rest of the debut album was still being recorded. "Roxanne" received critical praise but because of the controversial subject matter dealing with prostitution, it did not get much radio play.

Musically, "Roxanne" was first conceived of as a jazz-tinged bossa nova rhythm. The song evolved into a hybrid-like reggae meets heavy tango feel with Copeland's stressing beat two (along with Sting's bass) on the bass drum. These mixtures of musical styles and rhythmic ideas forced Sting to re-think the original melody, thus making it more angular and unpredictable. During the re-

---

> "I see songs not as a commodity used up when the album goes off the charts, which is often the case with pop songs. I see them as a body of work. Life should be breathed into them."
>
> - Sting

Rock Hard Fact

Sting received a part in a Wrigley's chewing gum advertisement and persuaded the director to use Andy Summers and Stewart Copeland. Part of the deal was that they had to all dye their hair blond.

cording, Sting accidentally sat down on a piano keyboard, resulting in an atonal piano cluster and the laughter at doing so was recorded and preserved in the final mix of the song.

In 1978, The Police's debut album Outlandos d'Amour was released along with the singles "So Lonely" and "Can't Stand Losing You." Introduced by the lead single "Roxanne," the album went to number six in England and was their "foot in the door" to the American market, reaching number twenty-three. Miles Copeland at first wanted to name the album Police Brutality but changed his mind when he envisioned a more romantic image for the band. That prompted him to choose the name Outlandos d'Amour, which loosely translated in French meant "Outlaws of Love."

Groundbreaking album Outlandos d'Amour
by The Police

Outlandos d'Amour linked The Police to punk and to their future. Side one opened with "Next to You," then "So Lonely," "Roxanne," "Hole in My Life," and "Peanuts." "Next to You" sounded of pure punk aggression and was a simple three-chord harmonic progression. Stewart and Andy wanted to make it more aggressive so they wrote the line "I'm going to take a gun to you," but Sting refused to sing it. He wanted it to be a love song and a compromise was agreed upon as long as the love lyrics were shouted aggressively. Sting was inspired by reggae legend Bob Marley's "No Woman, No Cry" when he composed "So Lonely." The verse lyrics were borrowed from one of Sting's Last Exit songs titled "Fool in Love." Sting realized the irony of singing a song about misery ("So Lonely") in such a joyous fashion.

`"Roxanne" was a sign to The Police that punk sensibilities were loosening and many punk fans were embracing the more popular new wave genre. "Roxanne's" co-mingling of rock and reggae was unique and would go on to define much of The Police's sound. It was very clear on Outlandos d'Amour that The Police had the musicianship to fuse reggae's complex rhythmic counterpoint with rock, and even the frenetic force of the punk genre. Sting recalled, "The predominance of the bass in the music, allowed Stewart and me to explore subtle areas of interplay that were rarely touched on by less experienced outfits. To create a hybrid using the drag-race horsepower of rock and roll and welding it seamlessly to the rolling stock of reggae music would make for an interesting journey, especially now that the post-punk landscape was beginning to look like a war zone…that war zone looked like nothing less than an opportunity to us." #6

Side two opened with "Can't Stand Losing You," then "Truth Hits Everybody," "Born in the '50's," "Be My Girl-Sally," and "Masoko Tanga." The lyrics to "Can't Stand Losing You" were about a young lover being driven to suicide following a breakup. It became the groups' first single to make the charts, reaching number twenty-seven in Britain. While Outlandos d'Amour initially received low exposure, the album went on to become one of the greatest debut albums by any rock band in any rock genre. The Police were able to quickly define their own subgenre of *reggae-punk-new wave* rock with Outlandos d'Amour.

1979's Reggatta de Blanc featured the band's first two British number one hits, "Message in a Bottle" and "Walking on the Moon." Andy Summers remembered "Message in a Bottle" when he said, "It was always my favorite song to play live, the best track we recorded and probably the fans' favorite before 'Every Breath You Take.' It had all the trademarks. There was something joyous about it." #7 The album went to number one in England and number twenty-five on the U.S. charts. Reggatta de Blanc proved more difficult to make than Outlandos because they simply didn't have enough songs. Besides the above mentioned two hits, they only had Sting's "The Bed's Too Big Without You" when they went into the studio to record. Copeland filled in the gaps with his compositions ""On Any Other Day," "Contact," and "Does Everyone Stare." Sting recycled much of the lyrics for "Bring On the Night" from another of his Last Exit tunes titled "Carrion Prince O Ye of Little Hope." The instrumental "Reggatta de Blanc" became one of the Police's only collaborative group compositions. It came from a long instrumental section from a live performances of "Can't Stand Losing You."

The Police had interrupted the Regatta de Blanc recording sessions to embark on a second American tour in April 1979. In March of 1980, after the Regatta de Blanc release, the band went on a twelve-month non-stop world tour. They visited countries that rarely hosted foreign performers including; India, Taiwan, Hong Kong, Greece, Egypt, and Mexico. The hits "De Do Do Do, De Da Da Da" and "Don't Stand So Close To Me" came from their 1980 release Zenyatta Mondatta. The trendy "Voices Inside My Head" became a NYC disco scene favorite and Summer's "Behind My Camel" received a Grammy award (although Sting and Copeland hated the song). Zenyatta Mondatta was written in one month during their world tour and the band felt that they were rushed into recording the album. Sting's "Driven To Tears" was another hit and contained political overtones. It would be the beginning of a political activism that would later be found in much of Sting's and The Police's future recordings. Zenyatta peaked at number one in Britain and number five in America.

The Police were desperately in need of some rest and took some time off to compose some new material. 1981's Ghost in the Machine proved to be a big change of musical direction. The album featured layered soundscapes (all three members added keyboard parts on different tracks), expanded vocal timbres, and saxophone parts. Ghost in the Machine made a big impact worldwide and went to number one in England and number two on the U.S. charts. Recorded mostly at George Martin's studio in Montserrat, a Caribbean flavor was present on the chart-topping hit "Every Little Thing She Does is Magic." The album title came from Sting's inspiration from reading philosopher Arthur Koestler works'. Ghost in the Machine opened with "Spirits in the Material World," and featured keyboards dubbed over Summers' reggae-inspired guitar parts. Summers was not happy with the band's direction on this album, feeling that their raw-trio approach was lost with the new emphasis of synthesizer and horns parts. The Police were not strangers to internal conflict (mostly due to their strong individual musical wills) and Sting would often arrive with high-quality demos that left little opportunity for Copeland and Summers to contribute as they had done on earlier albums. A video for the song "Invisible Sun" was banned by the BBC due to its footage of the conflict in Northern Ireland.

Numerous side projects included Copeland's composition of a film score for Francis Ford Coppola's

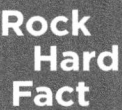

Rock Hard Fact

The Police did a video shoot at the Kennedy Space Center, in Houston, Texas for their "Walking on the Moon" single.

Rumble Fish and Sting's first big budget acting role in the movie *Dune*. This proved to be detrimental to the already deteriorating relationship between Sting and Copeland. Additionally, both Sting's and Summers' marriages failed. 1983's Synchronicity was a musical and *physical* struggle to create when Copeland and Sting had to be pulled apart during the recording process. This would prove to be their last studio album. At the same time, many considered them to be the biggest rock band in the world. "Every Breath You Take" was number one practically everywhere and the band set out on The Synchronicity Tour in the summer of 1983. On this tour, The Police played before 70,000 fans at Shea Stadium in New York where Sting announced to the fans "We'd like to thank The Beatles for lending us their stadium." After the tour, The Police went on hiatus and Sting recorded his solo jazz influenced debut album Dream of the Blue Turtles. Synchronicity was nominated for the Grammy Album of the Year, but lost to Michael Jackson's Thriller.

The Police played three concerts for the Amnesty International-A Conspiracy of Hope Tour in 1986. After a tense and very brief reunion in the studio, "Don't Stand So Close to Me '86" was released in October of 1986. It would be their last single and marked that The Police were through. Sting, Copeland, and Summers would go on to focus on their solo careers. Sting recorded many strong albums (see chapter twelve) and toured with great success. Copeland produced movies, TV soundtracks, and recorded and toured with the bands Animal Logic and Oysterhead. Stewart Copeland also released a solo album titled The Rhythmatist, in which he wrote, produced, and recorded most of the instruments himself and then went on to tour with a group of the same name. Summers recorded solo jazz albums and played on Sting's 1987 album Nothing Like the Sun. Andy Summers, like Sting, has done a fair amount of acting as well.

In 1995, A&M released a double live Police album titled Live! It was produced by Andy Summers and contained tracks from a 1979 show in Boston and a 1983 performance in Atlanta, Georgia from the Synchronicity Tour. The Police reunited for a tour in 2007-2008 to mark their thirtieth anniversary, over twenty years since their breakup. In 2008, The Police released Certifiable: Live in Buenos Aires, a Blu-ray DVD, and CD set of two performances in Buenos Aires, Argentina from the 2007 tour.

The Police released five studio albums, two live albums, seven-compilation albums, twelve video albums, four soundtrack albums, and twenty-six singles. They have sold over one hundred million albums worldwide. Concerning the final demise of The Police, Sting stated "The songs I had written in the obscurity of our basement flat would become some of the most celebrated songs of the decade…confirmed and reinforced by endless concert tours in massive sports stadiums, and all the attendant hoopla and hype of a traveling circus. That the band would break up at the pinnacle of its career when our position seemed virtually unassailable surprised everyone but me. I saw my own future very clearly outside of the band, because I wanted more freedom. I couldn't have played with two better musicians than Stewart and Andy but I wanted to make music that wasn't tied to the limitations of a three piece band." #8 The Police were inducted into the Rock and Roll Hall of Fame in 2003.

The seeds of **U2** (1978-present) began in 1976 when Irish drummer Larry Mullen Jr., then only fourteen years old, decided to form a band. He recruited his Dublin Schoolmates guitarist David "The Edge" Evans, bassist Adam Clayton, and vocalist Paul "Bono" Hewson. Their original lineup, known as Feedback, also included Edge's brother Dik Evans, Peter Martin, and Ivan McCormick. Soon, McCormick and Martin left and the band became known as The Hype but when Dik Evans left, they became the rock band U2. In 1978, U2 won a talent contest that landed them a demo session. This led to a three-year recording contract with CBS Records. They released their first recording, a three-song project titled U2-3, and a new deal with Island Records that included an extensive promotional tour.

U2's debut album, Boy, was released in 1980 to some critical acclaim. Even then, U2 wrote songs with focused commentary about global issues. This soon attracted a fan base devoted to humanitarian causes and their music. 1981's October was spiritual and more mellow. It produced a popular single, "Gloria." Both Boy and October were aided by the expertise of producer Steve Lillywhite. 1983's War brought the band into the big leagues and was regarded as their first blatantly political record. This was, in part, because of Bono's (and the rest of the band's) perception of a world dominated by war. War focused on the physical realities of war but also on the devastating emotional and psychological damage inflicted on humanity. Musically, War sounded harsher than their first two albums and they expanded their sound with brass instruments and electric violin. War peaked at number twelve in the U.S. and number one in England. The album produced the hits "New Year's Day" and "Sunday Bloody Sunday," a protest song whose lyrics described the horror of a deadly encounter between British troops and Irish citizens.

"New Year's Day"
by U2

"New Year's Day" became U2's first international hit. It was a political song written about the Polish Solidarity movement. Initially, the lyrics were from a love song Bono had written for his wife. Adam Clayton played a melodic bassline that provided a powerful bottom for the song's haunting melody. The Edge began the song on piano before moving to the song's signature guitar riff. "New Year's Day" revealed the Edge's great musical versatility, highlighted by his highly melodic guitar solo that constantly changed timbres. "New Year's Day" was a strong example of U2's ability to create an effective melody with only a few notes. Mullen's drum part, especially the intro, became a very recognized hook for the song.

When U2 performed "New Year's Day" live, the Edge switched back and forth between piano and guitar. The video for "New Year's Day" was U2's first to receive heavy rotation on MTV. The video featured four people riding on horseback that appeared to be the four U2 members (in reality they were four Swedish teenage girls disguised in winter clothes as U2). The video also showed World War II footage of Soviet troops advancing in the wintertime.

In 1983, U2 recorded Live at Red Rocks: Under a Blood Red Sky that added to their growing popularity in America. For 1984's The Unforgettable Fire, U2 reached out to Brian Eno and Daniel Lanois to produce and help cultivate a more ambient sound within an abstract musical environment. Bono had feared that they might be in danger of falling into a formula of stale arena rock songs. The Unforgettable Fire reached number one in England and number twelve in America. The title track and "Pride (In the Name of Love)" were two hits from the record. U2 stayed with basic rhythms and chords and their most experimental songs still possessed a rock 'n' roll simplicity that remained accessible to their wide fan base. U2 per-

---

"Feelings are much stronger that thoughts. We are all led by instinct, and our intellect catches up later."

- Bono

Rock Hard Fact

Bono has received numerous humanitarian awards including: an honorary Knighthood from the Queen of England (2007), *Time Magazine*'s Person of the Year (2005), and France's Legion d'honneur-presented by President Jacques Chirac (2003).

formed at the Live Aid concert for Ethiopian famine relief at Wembley Stadium in July 1985. This very successful performance further raised the band's international profile while they continued to headline large stadium venues, headlining the Amnesty International's Conspiracy of Hope Tour.

In 1987, U2 released what many believed to be their masterpiece, The Joshua Tree. The album catapulted them to superstar status when it went to number one in over twenty countries. In America it stayed at number one for nine consecutive weeks. It became the band's greatest selling album with twenty-five million copies sold worldwide. The hits included "With or Without You," "I Still Haven't Found What I'm Looking For," and "Where the Streets Have No Name" (the first two both becoming number one singles in the U.S.).

Groundbreaking album
The Joshua Tree
by U2

The Joshua Tree focused on U2's interest in America's foreign policies and the American ideals of freedom and democracy. The music had a sense of location and the lyrics drew on the imagery created by American authors. The lyrics for all of the tracks were written by Bono and the music was written collectively by U2. The Joshua Tree opened with "Where the Streets Have No Name," then "I Still Haven't Found What I'm Looking For," "With or Without You," "Bullet the Blue Sky," "Running to Stand Still," "Red Hill Mining Town," "In God's Country," "Trip Through Your Wires," "One Tree Hill," "Exit," and "Mothers of the Disappeared."

"I Still Haven't Found What I'm Looking For" (much like the whole record) was inspired by U2's fascination with America and American music. In this song, the band drew from gospel music and choir-influenced backing vocals sung by Edge and producers Brian Eno and Daniel Lanois. A music video for the song was filmed in Las Vegas, Nevada. It showed Edge on Fremont Street playing an acoustic guitar while the other band members were wandering around the street.

"With or Without You" is a dark love song that reflected Bono's conflicted feelings about his life as a musician and that of being an ordinary man. Edge created a unique sound utilizing the Infinite Guitar. Edge allowed a single note to sustain indefinitely while other individual notes were treated to create new sounds. Edge commented on how U2 approached music as a band when he said, "The band is a family. Everyone looks after everyone else and no individual ego is bared to the public. There's a band ego, there's a band ambition. There's a band arrogance as well, sometimes. And there's also a belief that contemporary music can be more than just a soundtrack. It can be worthwhile and lasting, with a timeless quality when it's really working. It should transcend any barriers of time or location, so anyone can find something in it, so that it doesn't exclude people by being too fixed in its context." #9

U2 continued to utilize the great musicianship, production skills, and overall musical vision of Brian Eno (see chapter eighteen) and Daniel Lanois from their previous work on The Unforgettable Fire album. On The Joshua Tree, Eno played keyboards, DX7 programming, and backing vocals while Lanois added an Omnichord (an electronic instrument with preset rhythms), rhythm guitar, tambourine, and backing vocals. Drummer Larry Mullen Jr. really felt that Lanois, in particular, took great interest in the rhythmic aspects of the songs. "Where the Streets Have No Name" and "In God's Country," conveyed a deep-seated yearning felt through Edge's screaming guitar.

1988's double album Rattle and Hum, intended as a tribute to American music, featured guests Bob Dylan, blues great B.B. King, Tom Petty keyboardist Benmont Tench, and the Memphis Horns from Stax records. Rattle and Hum was another number one album. However, 1991's Achtung Baby saw a U2 musical transformation. The band wrestled with their musical approach when Bono and the Edge wanted to move in an industrial and electronic dance musical direction. U2 employed and still had great faith in Eno and Lanois' production approach. Thematically, Achtung Baby was a personal and introspective record that served as a pivot point in the band's career. It also met with great commercial success and reached number one in America and number two in Britain. It sold eighteen million copies worldwide. Achtung Baby also produced five hits including "The Fly" and "Mysterious Ways." Bono now featured a new look with wraparound sunglasses and skintight leather. He also ramped up his worldwide activism and became a spokesman on an international level outside of the band. 1993's Zooropa, completed U2's transformation and utilized samples and loops in their effort to explore electronic music. On Zooropa the legendary Johnny Cash guested on the song "The Wanderer."

U2 took some musical risks by recording an experimental record titled Original Soundtracks 1. Brian Eno contributed compositions and performances to the album. To keep it separate from a U2 album, the band released it under the band name Passengers. Mullen was out of service with back surgery and the band enlisted the help of programmer Howie B. 1997's Pop was U2's further adventure in electronic music, this time with even more of a focus on nightclub-like dance rhythms. The record initially did well, but quickly dropped off of most charts. 2000's All That You Can't Leave Behind returned U2 to a back to basics approach. Again employing Eno and Lanois, the album sold over twelve million copies worldwide and yielded the hits "Beautiful Day," "Walk On," and "Elevation." "Beautiful Day" reached number twelve in the U.S. and was a number one in many other countries. In 2002, U2 was featured at the halftime show of Super Bowl XXXVI, performing a tribute to the victims of the 9/11 tragedy.

U2 released the hard-hitting How to Dismantle an Atomic Bomb in 2004, No Line of the Horizon in 2009, and Songs of Innocence in 2014. The No Line of the Horizon Tour was one of the highest grossing in rock history. Songs of Innocence was met with some controversy when the band made it free as a download on iTunes. The problem was that it was automatically added to customers' music libraries without asking their permission. Bono apologized for the intrusion.

In 2017, U2 embarked on a tour to celebrate the thirty-year anniversary of The Joshua Tree. Bono commented on his approach to singing songs written decades ago when he said, "Part of the fun of doing these shows is I'm changing the lyrics when I want to and I'm sticking to the arrangements on the albums. But I was in a band early on in the 1980's (U2) where the lyrics were not really the priority, strangely It was, 'What's the song about? What's the tune? What's the beat?' And you had people like Brian Eno who was against the concept of the old-school lyric. He was saying, 'Just look at these

> "Half of me says 'I know I can't change the world' and there's another half of me that, everytime I write a song, I want it to change the world."
>
> - Bono

beautiful sonic paintings you're doing with your voice. Why do you need words?'" #10

U2 is a band that fully assimilated the musical traditions of the 1960's and 1970's. They did this while simultaneously transforming rock into a medium for self-realization and spiritual growth for multi-generations of their fans. U2 projected innocence, passion, political courage, and an unwavering commitment to humanitarian values. U2 has made thirteen studio albums and sold more than one hundred and seventy million records worldwide. They have accumulated twenty-two Grammy Awards (more than any other band or artist). U2 was inducted into the Rock and Roll Hall of Fame in 2005.

R.E.M. (1980-2011) was an American rock band that formed in Athens, Georgia in 1980. The lineup consisted of vocalist Michael Stipe, guitarist Peter Buck, bassist Mike Mills, and drummer Bill Berry. In the early 1980's, when "hair" metal, power ballads, and pop-rock dominated the charts and the radio, R.E.M. really was the alternative. They were a pivotal bridge that stood in contrast to the popular post-punk and new wave genres that preceded them. R.E.M. brought guitar pop and Stipe's purposely-mumbled vocals to an underground audience in a unique approach that simultaneously sounded traditional and modern. R.E.M. drew from the guitar style of the Byrds and folk-styled vocalists of the 1960's. They formed a musical identity through their relentless D.I.Y. work ethic. In 1981, the band toured the South and (that summer) recorded their first single, "Radio Free Europe." The single became a hit on college radio stations and soon they were signed to I.R.S. Records. R.E.M. then released their 1982 debut EP, Chronic Town. This recording established the folk and garage rock elements that became the band's signature sound.

1983's debut Murmur would not be R.E.M.'s greatest selling album, but it would inspire and influence hundreds of alternative rock bands. R.E.M.'s sound featured understated production and was noticeably different with its haunting and subdued quality. *Rolling Stone Magazine* named it the best album of 1983 (beating out Michael Jackson's Thriller and The Police's Synchronicity).

Groundbreaking album Murmur
by R.E.M.

On Murmur, R.E.M. created a sound that characterized the soft and introverted approach that represented the first wave of the alternative rock movement in America. R.E.M.'s sound was new and innovative with bright, ringing guitar timbres and the punchy sound of Mike Mills' Rickenbacker bass. Mills was a very melodic bassist, something often overlooked about the R.E.M. approach. Michael Stipe sang with a distant and obscure lyrical quality that lent depth and mystery to the R.E.M. sound.

Side one opened with "Radio Free Europe," then "Pilgrimage," "Laughing," "Talk About the Passion," "Moral Kiosk," and "Perfect Circle." The opener, "Radio Free Europe," created a blueprint for indie rock recordings. It broke through the college radio format in the face of mainstream radio's general indifference to alternative bands. These songs worked as a collection to subvert the typical folk and pop music conventions. Peter Buck developed a style of unpredictable twists and turns with his melodic and measured guitar riffs.

Side two opened with "Catapult," "Sitting Still," "9-9," "Shaking Through," "We Walk," and "West of the Fields." Stipe has referred to his lyrics on the chorus of "Sitting Still" as nonsense syllables. After writing lyrics with a conventional approach, Stipe began to write in a *non-linear manner*, purposely placing very little emphasis on any clear enunciation. Some songs, contained no real words at all, just Stipe's vocalization of his feelings. Through this approach, Stipe redefined the voice (his voice) as a viable instrument.

Murmur was rooted in the American folk-rock and post-punk genres. Through their sophisticated songwriting and atmospheric production, R.E.M. delivered a detached sense of mystery. R.E.M.'s sound flourished when Peter Buck de-emphasized guitar solos, choosing to play in an economical, arpeggiated, and poetic style. Mike Mills focused on melody rather than playing power bass. Not many bands could so effectively utilize folkish and punkish elements to specifically create a distinctive and collective voice such as R.E.M.'s.

1984's Reckoning featured a rough edged sound and the college radio hit "So. Central Rain (I'm Sorry)." By this time, the band had become well known on the American underground scene. They continued to tour constantly while avoiding the cliché of making 1980's ready for TV videos. Scores of bands began to imitate Stipe's detached stage presence and Buck's jangling guitar sound. 1985's Fables of the Reconstruction was recorded in London and focused on the mythology of the American deep South with songs like "Old Man Kensey" and Buck's banjo led "Wendell Gee." The material on Fables of the Reconstruction drew from R.E.M.'s own experiences traveling through the American countryside. 1986's Lifes Rich Pageant moved in a more pop-rock direction and 1987's Document brought the band more mainstream success with it's strong rock riffs. R.E.M. was moving from reflections on personal relationships to politically charged fiery statements like "Exhuming McCarthy," that examined American exceptionalism during the Reagan era. Document would become R.E.M.'s breakout album and their first single "The One I Love," charted in the U.S. top-twenty.

1988's Green was R.E.M.'s debut on Warner Bros. Records. This recording continued to explore political issues while the band expanded their composite sound by adding accordion, mandolin, pedal steel guitar, and cello. R.E.M. next released 1991's Out of Time featuring the hit "Losing My Religion." This song would become one of R.E.M.'s most popular when it gained great exposure on MTV's *Unplugged*. 1992's Automatic for the People reached number two on the U.S. charts. Some of the songs contained string arrangements by John Paul Jones and was considered one of the best alternative albums of the 1990's. The hit "Everybody Hurts" peaked at number twenty-nine on the American charts and became one of R.E.M.'s signature songs.

"Everybody Hurts"
by R.E.M.

Mostly written by drummer Bill Berry, "Everybody Hurts" was originally a short country song without a chorus or a bridge. Berry was strumming a guitar and finally settled on an Otis Redding-like Stax Records feeling to finish writing the song. Berry programmed a drum machine rather than adding real drums and John

---

Rock Hard Fact

R.E.M.'s song "Man in the Moon" became the signature track of the 1999 movie *Man in the Moon*. Both the song and the movie were about the late comedian Andy Kaufman.

"I don't know how the band (R.E.M.) does what they do. God, they're the greatest. They've dealt with their success like saints, and they keep delivering great music."

– Kurt Cobain

Paul Jones, of Led Zeppelin fame, added a very musical string arrangement.

Berry was aiming the lyrics at the typical teenager that had a difficult time in high school. Specifically, it was about suicide and reaching out to people that felt they had no hope. On many R.E.M. songs, Stipe purposefully sang indecipherably, but was very articulate on "Everybody Hurts" because he didn't want the message to get lost. A very emotional mix of "Everybody Hurts" was produced with sound bites from the 9-11 tragedy. In 2010, a charity cover of "Everybody Hurts" was recorded for a fundraiser to help the victims of the devastating earthquake that ravaged the country of Haiti.

1994's Monster was a change of pace from the band's preceding albums of loud, distorted guitar chords and simple arrangements. Monster was also a monster on the charts, going to number one on both sides of the Atlantic. It's many hits included "What's the Frequency, Kenneth?" and "Crush with Eyeliner." However, just when things were going very well, Bill Berry collapsed on stage from a brain aneurysm and would leave the band following the recording of 1996's New Adventures in Hi-Fi. 1998's Up did not sell as well as typical R.E.M. albums and the band's commercial base was shifting from America to England.

R.E.M. went on to record four more albums; 2001's Reveal, 2004's Around the Sun, 2008's Accelerate, and 2011's Collapse into Now. Accelerate provided their seventh British chart-topper and restored R.E.M. to the top of the British charts and number three on the U.S. charts. R.E.M.'s early breakout success inspired countless alternative bands including; Sonic Youth, Radiohead, and Nirvana. Kurt Cobain, before his death in 1994, had planned to collaborate with Michael Stipe on a musical project. R.E.M.'s legacy was that of an underground, punk-inspired group that stayed true to their artistic vision while managing to sell over thirty million albums between 1991 and 1994. Spanning their entire career, R.E.M. sold in excess of eighty-five million albums worldwide. They created songs with abstract visions that revealed great imagery of a new landscape for America. R.E.M. was inducted into the Rock and Roll Hall of Fame in 2007.

The Arrival of MTV

It was stated in this chapter's introduction that music television began much earlier than the advent of **MTV**. One of the first to be televised was Elvis Presley with his choreographed scene with prison inmates in his 1957 film *Jailhouse Rock*. Also, The Beatles received great exposure with their 1964 film *A Hard Days Night*. TV shows such as *Don Kirshner's Rock Concert* were also groundbreaking. But when MTV first aired on August 1st 1981, rock music and television would never be the same. MTV's first hours featured music videos by The Pretenders, The Who, Styx, Rod Stewart, Pat Benatar, and others. However, MTV made a statement right out of the gate with *their very first* music video, Video Killed the Radio Star by a British group, **The Buggles**. MTV also introduced their hosts, called video jockeys or VJs. Over fifteen hundred applicants auditioned from all over America. Also, within only six months of its introduction, MTV signed up over two million subscribers. They were poised to become a significant influence on American culture and then, the world.

MTV opened new and creative approaches for artists to express their musical, social, and political ideas.

MTV was exclusively a video and music related medium for its first few years. The rapid growth of MTV in its golden age from 1981 to 1992 had a profound effect on American popular culture. The MTV aesthetic of youth culture radically changed the concepts of advertising, film, art, fashion, teen sexuality, race relations, and even politics. A new audience was catered to that had been largely ignored in the past. Previous TV markets had cartoons for kids and evening news for adults but not much for an audience of young adults. In fact, *teens* were an untapped audience, a great invisible force. Later, with the introduction of *Yo! MTV Raps*, young adults were given what they wanted and they made MTV their cultural "home-base."

MTV aired its debut program on that fateful August, 1981 evening. At first transmission came from Long Island and New Jersey. Then with the expansion of cable television, MTV became available to most of America by the mid-1980's. Before MTV, the record companies and radio were joined at the hip. TV had not been effectively utilized as a primary vehicle for the exposure of rock 'n' roll. However, popular TV shows such as the *Ed Sullivan Show*, *the Smothers Brothers*, *American Bandstand*, and *Hullabaloo* did help to introduce some bands to the public. In spite of these early groundbreaking TV shows, radio remained the primary source for rock record sales and promotion.

During the 1970's, the advent of FM radio (see chapter eleven) allowed for newer and narrower music formats. By the 1980's, radio stations began to cater even more to the specific interests of their audiences. More and more stations now focused on only a single music genre such as classical, jazz, or the specific rock genres of classic, new wave, heavy metal, or pop-rock. At first, MTV functioned in a similar manner like its radio counterparts. VJs presented the same upbeat between-songs dialogue that their TV viewers could associate with, similar to radio DJs. In typical television fashion, commercials were interspersed with music videos. TV interviews with artists enhanced the video-chatter format, while news of artists' tours and soon-to-be-released albums served to promote the record industry as a whole. Record companies raced to provide MTV with promotional rock music videos for airplay. Now, artists and their record companies sought to create a *visual* message to sell songs. Many times, the video would have little or nothing to do with a song's lyrics or meaning.

At first, MTV played mostly mainstream album-oriented rock with occasional diversions into the punk and new wave genres. The channel broadcast continuous programming, rather than individual shows. The "Big M" MTV logo brought with it a somewhat anti-establishment "rule-breaking" attitude that was consistent with the aesthetics of rebellious rock 'n' roll. MTV executives worked to get the support of major rock stars in order to give their new format credibility. MTV executive Jack Schneider recalled that "(Mick) Jagger saying 'I want my MTV'- I don't think we ever thanked him enough. It legitimized us. People called their cable companies and said to the poor operators, in these lousy imitations of Mick Jagger, 'I want my MTV." #11

MTV took almost everyone by surprise. Billy Gibbons of ZZ Top remembered "One night I got a phone call from Frank Beard, our drummer. He said, 'Hey, there's a good concert on TV Check it out.' So a couple of hours went by while I watched TV, and I called him back and said, 'How long does this concert last?' He said, 'I don't know.' Twelve hours later, we were still glued to the TV. Finally somebody said, 'No, it's this twenty-four

---

"When 'Video Killed the Radio Star' came out, we took it with a grain of salt. We thought, Well, video's not gonna kill the radio star. It did. The song was prophetic."

– Stevie Nicks

Rock Hard Fact

Originally, MTV's station tag was going to be astronaut Neil Armstrong's "One small step for man, one giant leap for mankind," but after trouble obtaining the rights to the quote, MTV used "Ladies and gentlemen, rock and roll!"

hour music channel.' I said, '*Whaaaat?*' MTV appeared suddenly-unheralded, unannounced, un-anything." #12

MTV made careers happen. Young directors, producers, executives, film makers, Playboy playmates, choreographers, dancers, mimes, pyro-technicians, hair-dressers, dry-ice vendors, and of course, recording artists all benefited from this new phenomenon. Established stars were made into even bigger stars (Michael Jackson and Madonna to name the obvious) but music videos created overnight celebrities as well. For many young rockers, MTV opened the door to their imagination. Dave Grohl remembered "It seemed like a transmission from some magical place. Me and all my friends spent a lot of our time at the record store or staring at album covers. With music videos, there was a deeper dimension to everything. On Friday nights, you'd go to a friend's house to get f***ed up before going out to a party, and you'd have MTV on." #13 If an artist's peak years were during the MTV golden age, they might be one of the enduring musical acts that could still sell out arenas and stadiums. Many early MTV viewers are now parents and relive their youth by attending previous MTV artists' concerts such as Madonna, Bon Jovi, Bruce Springsteen, or Janet Jackson.

Three Groundbreaking MTV Videos

There were many career-defining videos that were broadcast on MTV. Some of them raised the profile of this new music media while simultaneously skyrocketing the careers of certain rock artists. Here's three.

#1 Video: Video Killed the Radio Star
by The Buggles

The song "Video Killed the Radio Star," was written in 1978 by Trevor Horn, Geoff Downes, and Bruce Woolley. It was recorded by Bruce Woolley and The Camera Club and later by the British group, The Buggles. The song's music video was written, directed, and edited by Russell Mulcahy and was the first video shown on MTV in America. The video was shot in London in only one day. Director Mulcahy recruited his friend, model Virginia Hey. The theme of the song was nostalgia, with the lyrics referring to a period of technological change in the 1960's.

Some of the MTV executives were afraid to launch MTV with a video based on a song that wasn't a hit. However, its symbolism was strong and was meant to send a message that visual music was the way of the future. MTV's second video, Pat Benatar's You Better Run, contained another message and was aimed at the major record labels. Trevor Horn of the Buggles said "We wrote 'Video Killed the Radio Star' in 1979. It came from this idea that technology was on the verge of changing everything. Video recorders had just come along, which changed people's lives. We'd seen people starting to make videos as well, and we were excited by that. It felt like radio was the past and video was the future. There was a shift coming." #14 The video for Video Killed the Radio Star began with a girl sitting in front of a radio. It moved to a black and white shot of Trevor Horn singing into a radio-era microphone. The radio blows up during the first chorus of the song and then in the second verse, the girl was seen transported into the future. There, she met Horn and a woman in a silver jumpsuit in a clear plastic tube.

#2 Video: Thriller
by Michael Jackson

It's hard to say if MTV helped the album Thriller's record sales more, or did Michael Jackson's (see chapter fifteen) heavily promoted Thriller video solicit more subscribers for the MTV channel? MTV enhanced Jackson's record-breaking album sales and Jackson enabled MTV to almost double its subscriber base from just over nine million views to over sixteen million. The video (more like a short movie) was known independently as "Michael Jackson's" Thriller (first aired December 2nd, 1983) and was directed by John Landis. It took music video to a new artistic level. Inspired by the 1950's horror film *Night of the Living Dead*, Thriller featured the story of a teenaged Michael who ran out of gas while driving with his girl-friend (played by former playboy model Ola Ray). He gave her a ring and under a full moon, he transformed into a werewolf. The scene cut to a movie theater where Michael and his girlfriend were watching a horror movie. She ran out of the theatre and passed a graveyard where Zombies appeared and broke out into an elaborate song and dance number. The video was released in late 1983 and was considered to be the most successful and influential pop-rock video of all time, selling over nine million copies. The Thriller video had a profound effect on pop culture and was historic in the sense of its unprecedented merger of film and music. In 2009, it became the first music video to ever receive the honor of being inducted into the National Film Registry by the Library of Congress.

On the Thriller video, Michael Jackson displayed his already famous moonwalk with funky, urban choreography and a sleek Fred Astaire-like dance style. It was highly effective in capturing a large TV audience. Thriller's sophisticated dance sequences became popular with millions of viewers and were often imitated by high school kids who tried to mimic the intricately staged movements. Thriller's longevity can be seen in the 2004 film *13 Going on 30*, in which a grown-up corporate executive (played by actress Jennifer Garner), livens up a dull cocktail party by getting the thirty-something guests to participate in a spontaneous reprise of Thriller's ghoulish dance routine.

Michael Jackson's Thriller video-one of a kind.

#3 Video: Vogue
by Madonna

Throughout the 1980's, Madonna (see chapter fifteen) was at the center of a number of controversies. One example was her spontaneous and sexually suggestive movements performed in a wedding dress to her hit, "Like a Virgin," at the 1984 MTV awards. Another example was a homage to film legend Marilyn Monroe in her Material Girl video. The subject of unwed motherhood in her Papa Don't Preach video provided another example.

Vogue, a stylish black and white video, again served to connect the visual images of Madonna to film legends of an earlier era. The video looked back at the films and photography from the golden age of Hollywood. Many of the scenes in Vogue were recreations of photographs taken by photographer Horst P. Horst.

Vogue featured the dancers from Madonna's then-upcoming Blond Ambition Tour. The video premiered worldwide on MTV in 1990 and on the

> "I told them basically if they were really going to want to bring back heavy metal to a program on MTV (*Headbangers Ball*), then they are really going to have to get in touch with what real heavy metal is."
>
> – Phil Anselmo of Pantera

BET network that same year. In the video, Madonna wore a controversial sheer lace dress. Some of the scenes showed Madonna in different outfits creating imitations of golden-era Hollywood stars. Vogue raised some eyebrows when Madonna wore her iconic "cone-bra." MTV wanted to make some edits but Madonna refused, thus Vogue aired with all the original costumes. With Vogue, Madonna took a major step forward in gaining control of her own artistic license. This empowered woman artists in all of the arts.

Controversy and Criticism of MTV

The first two years of MTV broadcasts featured mainly white rock artists. MTV executives received strong criticism. They countered saying that there were very few promotional videos available from black or minority artists. This prompted a significant change when MTV began to broadcast videos from Michael Jackson's album Thriller. Initially, MTV hesitated to air the Billie Jean video. Since they were under fire with accusations of racism, MTV soon jumped on the opportunity to play Billie Jean. It worked as a test case for them. It didn't take long for the videos, Billie Jean (first aired March 10th, 1983) and Beat It (first aired March 30th, 1983), to become the most popular videos of all time.

This was followed by the historic airing of Jackson's fourteen-minute mini-film Thriller. The director of Thriller, John Landis recalled, "One of the reasons people liked Thriller so much is because it's a little movie…The song was five minutes long, and I needed it to be twelve minutes long for the video… Quincy Jones would not let me have the master tracks. So Michael and I went to the recording studio at three in the morning. We walked past the guard…put the tracks in a big suitcase and walked out with them… duped them and put them back…I cut it up and changed things." #15 When it seemed that the album Thriller's run was over, Michael Jackson released the Thriller video just before the Christmas buying season. Jackson had spent one million dollars making the mini-film. It would become the most elaborate video ever made and now MTV was fully supportive. This would clearly bring MTV to a more racially diverse audience and pave the way for later spin-off channels such as the BET network.

MTV also faced criticism as being sexist toward women. An example occurred when MTV aired the J. Geils Band's video for their song "Centerfold." It featured Victoria's Secret-attired women dancing suggestively to lead singer Peter Wolf's high school fantasy memory. This angered many feminists and female rock artists who feared MTV would set women's rights back to a pre-rock 'n' roll era. Some MTV executives felt that the failure or refusal of women artists to create sexy images would hurt record sales and MTV ratings. Could a punky Patti Smith image or a cool, detached Chrissie Hynde compete with Madonna's raw sexuality or Whitney Houston's seductive look? Eventually, MTV aired a wide range of female artist-led videos. This empowered female musicians to express their diverse artistic goals.

Another issue for suddenly powerful MTV executives (just like the radio DJ's of early rock radio) concerned which artists would receive substantial (or any) MTV video rotation. Criticism over airtime came from the record industry, prominent musicians, and most importantly, music fans. This issue raised ongoing questions and underscored the great power and influence that embodied the MTV platform.

Early MTV Objectives

In its earliest days, MTV championed three music movements/genres: The New Wave of British Heavy Metal (see chapter ten), New Wave (chapter fourteen). and many "one hit wonders." MTV was instrumental in giving many NWOBHM bards a ton of exposure. Some of the beneficiaries were Judas Priest, Iron Maiden, Saxon, Motorhead, AC/DC, and Def Leppard. Normally, a TV channel like this would cater to the pop world, yet these heavier bands were exposed in the same light as pop artists and bands. Secondly, the electronic instruments that dominated pop music at the time were now seen when MTV showcased new wave bands including: Duran Duran, Devo, Culture Club, The Eurythmics, and then later: Erasure, The Pet Shop Boys, Depeche Mode, and New Order. These were all electronically-driven bands that dominated the charts. Thirdly, many "one hit" wonders were given a new way to introduce their "hit single." The idea was that an artist or band's individual song could be promoted hard, resulting in a mega-hit with no follow-up singles to rank as high. Some of these artists and songs included: Kajagoogoo's "Toc Shy," Bow Wow Wow's "I Want Candy," Frankie Goes to Hollywood's "Relax," Gary Newman's "Car," and Tony Basil's "Mickey."

The Expansion and Pop Culture Influence of MTV

MTV answered its critics by developing new projects and shows that responded to its detractors. The MTV platform addressed current issues and interests in rock music and American culture. Within six month of first broadcasting, MTV aired its first concert with REO Speedwagon. By late 1981, the network had contests for a lucky winner to "spend a night" with major rock bands such as The Rolling Stones and Journey. In direct competition with Dick Clark's *New Years Rockin' Eve*, MTV launched its first annual *New Years Eve Rock and Roll Ball*. This was a difficult task, but MTV's younger VJs offered an alternative to the legendary Dick Clark New Year's tradition. In the summer of 1985, MTV revealed its social conscience when it broadcast a seventeen-hour live telecast of the *Live Aid Concert*. Transmitting from two continents simultaneously was previously unheard of and by doing so, MTV stressed the importance of global awareness and the plight of famine victims in Ethiopia. *Live Aid's* broadcast was a real world event and gathered artists from around the world to provide famine relief. This was a high moment in the history of MTV. Also, *The MTV Awards' Show* was also launched in 1984.

In 1987, MTV launched *Headbangers Ball,* a program that consisted of heavy metal music videos. The show was broadcast late at night and offered a stark contrast to the pop-music oriented videos that were shown mostly in the daytime hours. *Headbangers Ball* proved to be one of the most popular shows to ever air on MTV. It ran for almost eight years and primarily showed videos from the more mainstream friendly "hair metal" genre of the 1980's.

When "hair metal" lost popularity, *Headbangers Ball* moved to feature the more aggressive metal bands of the late 1980's and 1990's. Later, the show expanded again to include grunge-influenced bands like Soundgarden and Alice in Chains. It opened the door for other significant metal bands like Pantera, Megadeth, and Anthrax. It even exposed the thrash metal of Slayer to a mass audience. Also (for a short period of time right before the advent of grunge), a few progressive bands made their way to the MTV platform. They included:

> **Rock Hard Fact**
>
> R.E.M. performed on MTV's *Unplugged* in 1991, helping to make them the first independent group to break through to a large, mainstream audience.

King's X, Dream Theater, Queensryche, Fates Warning, and Jellyfish.

In early 1990, MTV delivered what would become one of its signature shows, *MTV Unplugged*. The first broadcast featured acoustic performances by Squeeze, Syd Straw, and Elliot Easton of The Cars. The show became a hit and later featured superstars such as Eric Clapton and Nirvana. From 1988 to 1995, MTV aired the program *Yo! MTV Raps*. It was the first hip-hop based show on the network and featured a mix of rap videos, interviews with rap stars, and live in studio performances. The Run DMC/Aerosmith version of "Walk This Way" and the Public Enemy/Anthrax version of "Bring the Noise" helped cross cultures and turn a new audience on to rap music. There was also a Brazilian version of the show that was broadcast from 1990 to 2005. After *Yo!* began to air, the MTV audience embraced artists such as Eric B & Rakim, Public Enemy, The Geto Boys, and LL Cool J. *Yo! MTV Raps* revealed the diversity of hip-hop.

For many, the MTV phenomenon opened up new musical possibilities through its innovative format. However, some critics and fans viewed it as a threat that would compromise rock 'n' roll's musical integrity. Despite a range of public opinions, it was clear that the MTV format created a new kind of music star. Suddenly, video image became almost as important as musical quality. MTV had a major impact on popular culture starting in the 1980's. It influenced everything from clothing to hairstyles and gave exposure to the subculture lifestyles of neglected ethnic groups. In a short time frame, technology saw consumers move from vinyl albums to cassette-friendly Walkmans to the compact disc. In that time, MTV became a proactive agent that inspired and even forced cultural change. MTV challenged its viewers to embrace new musical and television programming. Rock music was now exposed to a new generation of ears and now, eyes.

Discussion Question

The MTV video format was used extensively to promote many rock bands throughout the 1980's and beyond. Does the addition of a visual component enhance all rock music or are there some bands that are better off utilizing only an audio format to express their music? Use musical examples to support your position.

The Grungy Nineties

Like Chicago and Minneapolis, the city of Olympia, Washington was home for an independent music scene. However, Olympia didn't possess the music culture displayed by the slick major-label bands from those other cities. An early 1980's band from Olympia called **Beat Happening** (1982-present) and their leader Calvin Johnson, ignited an Olympia pop music scene that became ground zero for DIY music. This movement is still alive today. Olympia musicians stood in direct opposition to the accepted norms of rock music. They rejected a slick and professional product, opting instead for a rawer sound and an unschooled punk ethic, only less angry.

Neighboring Seattle, Washington was an even earlier home to the sounds of do-it-yourself **garage rock**. Seattle bands such as **The Sonics** (1960-present) and **The Kingsmen** (1959-present) (best known for their cover of Richard Berry's "Louie, Louie") defined loud, distorted *garage-rock* before it became a socially acceptable form of rock music. Another Seattle native, Jimi Hendrix (see chapter six), went on to leave his loud and legendary mark on rock. A style later coined as "**grunge**," with its brash and distorted guitar sound, would eventually emerge from this tradition of uncompromising rock sensibilities. Many musicians, who would come to represent the first wave of grunge bands, grew up listening to indigenous Seattle garage rock and the sounds of punk and metal styles. The earliest grunge bands would all share reckless musical abandonment and a refusal to conform to traditional music standards. In general terms, grunge would be defined by its often-unskilled musicianship (much like early punk), yet with a sense of urgency and raw energy that provided its songs with emotional power.

In the early 1980's, a fanzine (a non-professional magazine produced by enthusiasts of a particular cultural genre such as grunge) was started by musician Bruce Pavitt. It was called *Subterranean Pop USA*. In it, Pavitt provided commentary about music, culture, and politics. Pavitt and his business partner, Jonathan Poneman, started a small rock label called Sub Pop that would go on to sign and help develop the careers of many grunge bands. Sub Pop's earliest band roster included; Green River, Soundgarden, Blood Circus, and Swallow. By the early 1980's, Seattle music audiences had become disillusioned by the affluence of many individuals and corporations in society. Often called "slackers" or "generation X-ers," many of these youth had a jaded attitude about politics, social issues, and other elements of popular culture. For them, punk rock, "hair metal," and synth-pop had run its course and never really quenched their musical appetite. This youth culture was ready for a change, both musically and culturally.

By the mid 1980's, change was on the way. New bands formed such as **The Wipers** (1977-1989) (1993-1999), **Malfunkshun** (1980-1988) (2006-present), **The Melvins** (1983-present) (see chapter fourteen), **The Screaming Trees** (1985-2000), **Skin Yard** (1985-1993), **Green River, Mudhoney**, and **Soundgarden**. All of these Pacific Northwest bands shared a new musical vision that resulted in the musical revolution called grunge.

Green River (1984-1988) (2008-2009) was an American rock band that formed in Seattle, Washington in 1984. They gained very little commercial appeal but did have a profound impact on the grunge movement. Green River consisted of vocalist/guitarist Mark Arm, guitarist Steve Turner, bassist Jeff Ament, and drummer Alex Vincent. Later, guitarist Stone Gossard joined the band to free Mark Arm to concentrate on vocals. Green River became the first band signed to the Sub Pop label and they released their 1984 debut EP, Come On Down. The main guitar riff of the title song exhibited a raw sound that would help to define the grunge style. A 1986 compilation album titled Deep Six on the label C?Z Records contained the Green River songs "10,000 Things" and "Your Own Best Friend." This compilation showcased the new grungy "Seattle sound" and was considered to be the *first* grunge album. Two years later, Green River released their first full-length album, 1988's Rehab Doll. Tension over the band's musical direction caused them to breakup. However, Green River's sludgy mix of hard rock, metal, and punk would influence many up and coming grunge and post-grunge artists.

> **Rock Hard Fact**
>
> Mark Arm was the first to coin the term "grunge" when he wrote about a new music genre in an early 1980's Seattle fanzine publication.

> "I felt like it was necessary for Soundgarden- as it was for all of these Seattle bands- to prove that we deserved to be on an international stage, and we weren't just part of a fad that was based on geography." - Chris Cornell

Mudhoney (1988-present) is an American grunge band that grew out of the demise of the band Green River. Mudhoney consisted of ex-Green River vocalist/guitarist Mark Arm and guitarist Steve Turner. They added bassist Matt Lukin and drummer Dan Peters. Mudhoney's 1988 debut single on the Sub Pop label was "Touch Me I'm Sick." Along with their 1988 debut EP, Superfuzz Bigmuff, Mudhoney strongly influenced the early Seattle grunge scene. Their sound was grounded in highly distorted and dirty guitar timbres. The New York band Sonic Youth were fans of Mudhoney and invited them to tour England with them in 1989. Superfuzz Bigmuff made it onto the British indie charts and earned the band international recognition. Kurt Cobain often cited Superfuzz Bigmuff as one of the albums that influenced Nirvana's sound. 1989's Mudhoney was their debut full-length album. Mudhoney's reputation spread rapidly and college radio stations quickly embraced the new Seattle sound. Mudhoney would go on to release eight more studio albums including 2013's Vanishing Point (still on the independent label Sub Pop).

The Seattle scene was gaining strong momentum and the "anybody can be in a band" attitude was cranking out hundreds of bands without the pretense of becoming big rock stars. This was seen in the stage attire of flannel shirts and ripped jeans-the same clothes music fans wore to their day jobs. This down to earth attitude closed the gap between performer and audience, instantly making rock music more accessible. Fans responded. Other Sup Pop artists such as **Tad** (1988-1999), **The Fluid** (1984-1993) (from Colorado), **Soundgarden**, and **Nirvana** soon became visible on the indie club circuit and the college radio format.

Soundgarden (1984-1997) (2010-present) is an American rock band that was formed in 1984 in Seattle by vocalist/guitarist Chris Cornell, guitarist Kim Thayll, drummer Scott Sundquist, and bassist Hiro Yamamoto. Drummer Matt Cameron replaced Sundquist in 1986. Shortly after, Yamamoto left and Ben Shepherd became the permanent bassist in 1990. Soundgarden named themselves after a metal pipe sculpture in Seattle's Point Park. The sculpture made howling and weird sounds when the wind blew through the park.

The band's first recording was a three-song contribution to the 1986 compilation album Deep Six. Soundgarden next recorded two EP's, 1987's Screaming Life and 1988's Fopp on the Sub Pop label. In 1988, Soundgarden signed with the independent label SST Records and released their 1988 debut album, Ultramega OK. Soundgarden's sound was evolving with a health mix of heavy metal, psychedelic rock, some hardcore punk, and even a hint of progressive rock. The band's goal was to refine their sound, yet keep a harder edge by mixing punk and metal elements.

In late 1988, Soundgarden became the first grunge band to sign with a major label, A&M Records. This was an important step for the grunge genre as a whole. 1989's Louder Than Love only grazed the U.S. charts at number one hundred and eight. The band was moving to a more metal direction which upset some of their earlier punk rock fans. 1991's Badmotorfinger (unfortunately released concurrently with Nirvana's Nevermind), eventually found a more mainstream rock audience. This happened when Soundgarden toured with Guns N' Roses on their Use Your Illusion Tour and brought their sound to a whole new audience. Badmotorfinger revealed Soundgarden's evolution of cerebral lyrics, alternative guitar tunings, and odd time signatures. 1994's Superunknown was Soundgarden's breakout album, debuting at number one on the U.S. charts. Five singles, including the Grammy winning "Spoonman" and "Black Hole Sun," drove the album.

Groundbreaking album Superunknown
by Soundgarden

Soundgarden began working on Superunknown after they appeared on the 1992 Lollapalooza Tour. The band gave each other greater freedom as far as individual input was concerned and they spent more time devoted to the recording process than on previous recordings. With the help of new producer, Michael Beinhorn, Soundgarden thickened their sound by layering more parts and experimented with different guitar and drum timbres. Beinhorn brought a more sophisticated approach to sound design by moving the band away from their previous penchant for brute force.

The innovation of Superunknown was Soundgarden's ability to meld their signature metal sound with an effective blend of pop and psychedelic influences. Lyrically, the album was dark and mysterious. It addressed issues like suicide, depression, and substance abuse. Recurring themes included; fear, loss, revenge, and overall annihilation. Chris Cornell was inspired by the writings of Sylvia Plath. In addition, the band utilized a Middle Eastern flavor on the song "Half" and a Beatlesque influence can be heard on "Head Down" and "Black Hole Sun."

Superunknown contained fifteen tracks. Five of them were released as singles including "Spoonman," "The Day I Tried to Live," "Black Hole Sun," "My Wave," and "Fell on Black Days." The song "Spoonman" utilized a riff written in 7/4 time and was originally written for the movie soundtrack Singles. "The Day I Tried to Live" also utilized odd time; now in a cycle of one measure of 7/4 then two measures of 4/4. "Fell on Black Days" was a very grungy Chris Cornell song that spoke to a fear that your life was going well and then all of a sudden you're unhappy without any particular event that caused your perspective to change.

Superunknown sold over nine million copies worldwide and remained Soundgarden's most popular recording. The album pushed beyond any previous boundaries while still replicating the heavy riffs Soundgarden had always borrowed from Black Sabbath and Led Zeppelin. The band embraced elements of a psychedelic sound, thus providing a wider sonic palette. The melodic content of the songs, especially "Black Hole Sun," combined masterfully with dissonance and odd time signatures to give Soundgarden their own unique musical voice.

"Black Hole Sun"
by Soundgarden

Chris Cornell wrote "Black Hole Sun" in about fifteen minutes. He didn't think the band would like it, nor did he imagine it would become Soundgarden's biggest hit. Cornell had described the song as a surreal dreamscape and that he was really just going for a words for words sake type of approach. Just playing around with the lyrics, he was not trying to get any particular idea across to the listener. However, in an interview in 1995, Cornell revealed that "Black Hole Sun" was a sad song and that it addressed the idea that "It's really difficult for

---

Rock Hard Fact

The week after Christmas (in 1991) Nirvana bounced to the top of the charts after Tower Records had experienced an incredible number of kids returning the CD's that their parents had bought for them. They exchanged them a copy for Nevermind.

a person to create their own life and their own freedom. It's going to become more and more difficult, and it's going to create more and more disillusioned people who become dishonest and angry and are willing to f*** the next guy to get what they want." #16

Producer Michael Beinhorn asked Cornell to listen to recordings of the legendary Frank Sinatra before recording the vocal part to "Black Hole Sun." The song had a very Beatlesque feel with its Lennon-like melody and George Harrison styled guitar sound. A music video for "Black Hole Sun" showed the band performing in an open field while people were swallowed up when the Sun suddenly turned into a black hole. The video featured the stunning computer-generated visual effect of a black hole.

1996's Down on the Upside was a move away from Soundgarden's heavy guitar riff grunge sound. Chris Cornell and Kim Thayil clashed over the band's direction when Cornell wanted to experiment with a more acoustic group sound. Down on the Upside received favorable reviews but did not sell as well as Superunknown. After a 1996 Lollapalooza tour with Metallica and a worldwide tour, Soundgarden decided to disband in 1997. After numerous projects by many of its band members, Soundgarden re-formed in 2010 after a twelve-year hiatus that included Cornell's membership in the supergroup Audioslave and Matt Cameron's tenure in Pearl Jam. In 2012, Soundgarden released King Animal, their sixth and final studio album. It contained some similar songs to Down on the Upside and the band appeared to pick up where they left off in the late 1990's. Soundgarden continued to tour and former Pearl Jam drummer Matt Chamberlain replaced Cameron for live shows in Europe and South America in 2014.

In the spring of 2017, Chris Cornell tragically took his own life. Currently, the band's future remains uncertain. Soundgarden was one of the pioneering bands of the grunge genre. They effectively mixed punk rock and metal elements. Along with noisy and down-tuned guitars, they created an original sound with Cornell's wide vocal range and his dark, existentialist lyrics. At its core, the Soundgarden sound was a Black Sabbath meets psychedelic rock approach, yet they were able to expand their musical direction with their later releases.

Nirvana (1987-1994), along with Elvis Presley and The Beatles, were among the few acts in rock music history to evoke sweeping cultural and musical change. Nirvana effectively changed what people listened to, what clothes they wore, and even how music impacted their lives. Vocalist/guitarist Kurt Cobain and bassist Krist Novoselic formed Nirvana in 1987. Like other musicians with a grunge sound, they were both well grounded in the punk style and the 1980's DIY rock movement of Northwest America that would pre-date the grunge movement.

Kurt Cobain (1967-1994) was born in Aberdeen, Washington in 1967. He experienced a very unsettled upbringing (see Cobain profile). Kurt managed to discover musical influences that ranged from The Beatles, Led Zeppelin, and Black Sabbath to The Pixies and The Velvet Underground. By the summer of 1983, Cobain discovered punk rock and his musical world would gain a new focus when he saw and befriended the punk meets metal band, The Melvins (see Chapter Fourteen). After seeing The Melvins for the first time, Cobain wrote in his journal "They played faster than I ever imagined music could be played and with more energy than my Iron Maiden records could provide. This was what I was looking for." #17 Kurt and Krist Novoselic had met while both attended Aberdeen High School, although they never connected while in school. The two became friends while hanging out at the practice space of The Melvins. Kurt gave Krist a demo tape of his band, Fecal Matter, and later Krist suggested that they form a band. Cobain was already writing songs at a fast pace, listening to vast amounts of music, and attending live shows. Cobain simultaneously formed three or four bands (sometimes only in his mind) including one band with himself on guitar, Krist on bass, and a drummer. Another band featured Kurt on drums and Krist on guitar. They formed a band named The Sellouts that only rehearsed Creedence Clearwater Revival songs, and yet another band called the Stiff Woodies that played for high school kids.

Beginning in early 1987, Kurt and Krist jammed with a drummer, Aaron Burckhard. This would become the early seeds of Nirvana. At this time, Cobain began to move away from the sound of The Melvins and embraced elements of pop-music in his songwriting. While his friends were content to experience music for fun, Kurt would endlessly practice guitar riffs. He became obsessed with songwriting. Cobain, Novoselic, and Burckhard's unnamed band practiced every night. They worked their first gig about an hour south of Aberdeen, at a house party in Raymond, Washington. Cobain biographer Charles Cross revealed, "They began with 'Downer,' one of the first songs Kurt ever wrote. It listed classic Cobain laments on the pitiful state of human existence with lyrics like, 'Hand out lobotomies/To save little families.' The dark lyrics were completely lost on the Raymond crowd, who could hear nothing more than the chunky guitar and bass riffs...their very first public show, it was all there, every bit of the Nirvana that would conquer the world in the years to come: the tone, the attitude, the frenzy, the slightly-off kilter rhythms, the remarkably melodic guitar chords, the driving bass lines that guaranteed to move your body, and most important, the hypnotizing focus of Kurt...all the raw, essential building blocks were in place. He was worth watching, if only because he seemed so intense." #18

By late 1987, Cobain's musical aesthetic was an eclectic mix of punk and heavy metal, supplemented with The Beatles and obscure alternative bands. On a daily basis, Kurt wrote in his journal in a therapeutic-like obsessive-compulsive ritual where he expressed his innermost thoughts. His writing, both imaginative and disturbing, was often obsessed with human bodily functions ranging from sexuality, birth, urination and defecation. At this time, Kurt began to cover a tune called "Love Buzz" by a Dutch band called The Shocking Blue. "Love Buzz" became Kurt's signature tune.

Kurt and Krist next moved to Tacoma and lost contact with Burckhard. They began to practice with The Melvin's drummer, Dale Crover. In January of 1988, they decided to record a demo from their growing repertoire of dozens of songs. They recorded ten songs in one day at Reciprocal studio, where Mudhoney, Soundgarden, and Mother Love Bone had all recorded. Even before settling on a permanent name, Kurt was convinced that a video on MTV was their ticket to success. He convinced the band to play at the Aberdeen RadioShack and had the gig filmed on a low-rent video camera. After watching the performance, Kurt noticed that they looked more like amateurs pretending to be rock stars rather than seasoned professionals. Kurt also realized that punk rock, despite being a liberating genre of rock music, came with its own social and style conventions. This would eventually lead to a new concept of style and dress that would be adapted by grunge musicians everywhere.

Rock Hard Fact

While Nirvana was established and on the rise, Kurt Cobain and Krist Novoselic started an unsuccessful office cleaning business called Pine Tree Janitorial.

Crover soon left to rejoin The Melvins but he recommended drummer Dave Foster for the band. At Kurt's house, Foster saw a poster advertising a gig for the band Nirvana. When he asked Kurt who Nirvana was, Kurt informed him that it was their new name and that it meant the attainment of perfection. Kurt now considered himself to be a Buddhist, though his only experience with the religion was having watched a TV show on the topic. By the fall of 1988, Nirvana was a working band but had only performed two-dozen shows during their brief history.

Nirvana was able to get their demo tape to various Seattle disc jockeys and to Jonathan Poneman, co-owner of Sub Pop Records. Although not initially impressed, Sub Pop agreed to record four songs including their cover of "Love Buzz." Kurt admitted that "Love Buzz" was Nirvana's strongest live tune. However, he lobbied to record one of his original songs for their debut release. Sub Pop won the argument and "Love Buzz" would be recorded and promoted. Kurt was not thrilled with the sound quality of "Love Buzz." The band wanted a more raw and raunchy sound (this would be a consistent theme throughout Nirvana's recording career). Nothing Nirvana would ever do in the studio or onstage would ever match what Kurt was hearing in his head. He was always in pursuit of perfection. Initially, Aaron Burckhard was brought back for the recording and to rejoin the band, but soon went to jail on a DUI charge. After advertising for a new drummer, Chad Channing joined Nirvana. In October of 1988, Nirvana played their first big gig, opening for The Butthole Surfers. "Love Buzz" was also breaking big on college radio stations.

Between December 1988 and January 1989, Nirvana recorded their debut album Bleach. The album was well received by critics but failed to make the U.S. charts. It would later be re-released by Geffen Records in 1992 (following the success of Nevermind). Bleach debuted at number eighty-nine in America. Typical for Kurt, he'd written the melodies, but only a few of the lyrics before the first Bleach recording session. He had stayed up most of the night before the session frantically working on the lyrics. The recording yielded ten songs, however Kurt didn't like his vocal takes. The lyrics of the song "Blew" made no sense, but Kurt was able to combine the melody and lyrics to effectively express the emotions of hopelessness and despair. These were consistent themes heard in many Nirvana songs.

In the spring of 1989, Nirvana added Jason Everman as a second guitarist, making them a quartet for the first time. Everman was listed in the credits of Bleach, although he did not play on the recording. Cobain liked the idea of adding a second guitarist because it freed him up to focus more on singing. In June of 1989, following the release of Bleach, Nirvana embarked on their first tour, a West Coast swing that included San Francisco. On the heels of only 1000 pressed copies of "Love Buzz," many of their shows attracted only a half dozen people or were cancelled altogether. This depressed Kurt and the band greatly. Nirvana was much more popular in Seattle where their frenzied sound was perfect for crowds that engaged in slam-dancing (a swirling mass of fans slamming off of one another in front of the stage) and stage-diving (fans jumping onstage and diving back into the crowd). Cobain loved these fan behaviors and how his music could be utilized to create chaos. Also in the summer of 1989, Nirvana played Sub Pop's Lamefest opening for the label's two biggest bands, Mudhoney and Tad. Kurt saw fans lineup up to buy Bleach.

Bleach separated Nirvana from their musical peers. In a positive way, the album was inconsistent by mixing old Cobain songs with recent songs like "About a Girl." On sludgy songs such as "Sifting," the chords were heavy and crude while the lyrics were clever. Bleach showed how Nirvana combined elements of garage grunge with alternative noise and hell-raising thrashy metal without fully committing to any one of these genres. The lyrics were contradictions of sincere opinions while providing both sarcastic and funny rebuttals towards clichés. Nirvana's dualism gave them enough different-sounding songs that radio stations could play multiple Nirvana songs without wearing out the band to their listeners. Bleach slowly caught on with college radio stations around the country.

"About a Girl"
by Kurt Cobain

Kurt Cobain wrote "About a Girl" about his girlfriend at the time, Tracy Marander. He had rehearsed and played the song in front of her, never revealing that she was the song's subject. This was an example of Kurt's failure to make a commitment in his own personal relationships. When Kurt played the song for the band, drummer Chad Channing asked him what it was about. He simply replied, "It's about a girl," which instantly became the title. "About a Girl" was a significant step in Cobain's songwriting since it was his first love song, even though the lyrics were twisted (in typical Cobain style).

"About a Girl" was so melodic that audiences often mistook it for a Beatles' cover. Cobain had said that he listened to Meet The Beatles for three straight hours before writing the song. At the same time, "About a Girl" captured the rage and hurt of the broken and failing relationship of Kurt and Tracy. The song captured the balance that would come to define Nirvana's ability to express a simple pop sentiment on top of a heavy grunge sound. On Nirvana's MTV Unplugged special, Cobain said to the audience "This is off our first record, most people don't own it." Six months after the death of Kurt Cobain, "About a Girl" reached number twenty-two in America.

While still on tour in 1989, Kurt was suffering from serious stomach issues and finally began to see doctors about the condition. At the end of the tour, the band decided to cut ties with Everman and return to being a trio. In August, Nirvana recorded an EP to promote an upcoming tour of Europe. They tracked five Cobain songs including; "Stain," "Been a Son," "Even in His Youth," "Polly (later on Nevermind)," and "Token Eastern Song." Nirvana songs were moving more and more in a pop direction while addressing conflict in relationships and other emotional issues.

In the spring of 1990, the band began their follow up to Bleach by working with producer Butch Vig at Smart Studios in Wisconsin. During the recording sessions, Kurt and Krist became dissatisfied with Channing's drumming. Channing was unhappy at being left out of the songwriting process. Nevertheless, Nirvana cut eight songs, many of which would later be redone for Nevermind. The tracks included "In Bloom," "Immodium" (later renamed "Breed"), "Pay to Play" (later renamed "Stay Away") and "Dive." The resulting demos (under Vig's excellent production) were circulated to major labels. At this time, Channing left the band. Soon after, Nirvana recorded a single, "Silver," with Mudhoney drummer Dan Peters. That August, Nirvana hired drummer Dale Crover and embarked on a short American West Coast tour, playing opposite of Sonic Youth.

> "The kid (Kurt Cobain) has heart"
>
> – Bob Dylan after hearing "Polly" live at a Nirvana show

In September of 1990, Buzz Osborne of the Melvins introduced Kurt and Krist to ex-Scream (hardcore-punk band) drummer Dave Grohl. After Grohl auditioned for Nirvana, Cobain and Novoselic knew they found their missing piece. Grohl then joined Nirvana on a short tour of England to promote "Silver." Unhappy with Sub Pop, Nirvana began shopping for a major record label (since no small indie label could afford to buy out the group's contract). Nirvana then signed to David Geffin's label, DGC Records, in late 1990. They also retained Butch Vig as their producer, and began work on their landmark album, Nevermind. Nevermind would go on to sell over thirty million copies worldwide, making it one the most popular albums in music history. It would, in part, become a major catalyst in redefining alternative rock and bring grunge to a mainstream audience.

Groundbreaking album Nevermind
by Nirvana

Between May and June of 1991, Nirvana recorded their second full album Nevermind. To earn enough gas money to get to Los Angeles, Nirvana played a show where they debuted "Smells Like Teen Spirit." They were given a budget of a mere $65,000 to record Nevermind. Nirvana sent Butch Vig rehearsal tapes of songs they had previously recorded with him at Smart Studios, along with demos of "Smells Like Teen Spirit" and "Come as You Are."

Kurt initially wanted the album to feature a *"boy side"* and a *"girl side,"* with a track titled "Something in the Way" to close the recording. Cobain also wanted Nevermind to sound like The Knack and the Bay City Rollers meet Black Sabbath and Black Flag. The band had rehearsed the material so much that the drum and bass tracks were done very quickly. Cobain, on the other hand, spent hours on guitar overdubs, the vocal parts, and writing the lyrics (still often done only a few minutes before recording). Cobain's vocal phrasing was so consistent that Vig was able to mix takes together to create overdubs.

Nevermind opened with "Smells Like Teen Spirit," then "In Bloom," "Come as You Are," "Breed," "Lithium," "Polly," "Territorial Pissings," "Drain You," "Lounge Act," "Stay Away," "On a Plain," and "Something in the Way."

Specifically, "Smells Like Teen Spirit" was influenced by many issues in Cobain's life including his anger at his parents, boredom, cynicism, and his relationship with ex-girlfriend Tobi Vail (of the band Bikini Kill). "Teen Spirit" contained the lines "She's over-bored and self-assured" and "Who will be the king and queen of the outcast teens?" The song title of "Smells Like Teen Spirit" came from a line of graffiti that read "Kurt Smells like Teen Spirit," that Kathleen Hanna (of Bikini Kill) spray-painted on Cobain's apartment wall. Tobi Vail used a teenager deodorant and Kathleen taunted Kurt implying that he was marked with his girlfriend's (Tobi's) scent.

Cobain described the lyrics to "Come As You Are" as contradictory and that the song was about the expectation of how people are supposed to act. The line "Take your time, hurry up, choice is yours, don't be late," are all cliché phrases about what people are supposed to do. The line "I swear that I don't have a gun" takes on an eerie quality in light of Cobain's eventual suicide. "Come As You Are" began with Cobain playing an unaccompanied guitar riff. He was joined by the band on the first verse with a moody and subdued feel. Kurt's guitar solo, one of his longest on record, was a musical complement to the song's melody.

"In Bloom" focused on people outside of the underground music scene who failed to understand the band's message. At first, "In Bloom" was very punk rock until Cobain added elements of a pop song. "In Bloom" saw Butch Vig trick Kurt in double-tracking his vocals (he hated to do it) by telling him that was what John Lennon had done. Grohl added background vocals and recorded an additional track of backing harmonies. "Lithium" was about a man who, after the death of his girlfriend, turned to religion instead of suicide. The band had trouble staying in time as they were constantly rushing the tempo. Vig made them play to a click track and simplify their parts. Cobain became frustrated at the slow progress when recording "Lithium" and instead went into an instrumental jam that the band had been working on. Vig recorded the jam and they called it "Endless, Nameless" and used it as a ghosted track at the end of the album.

Many of Cobain's early tunes were one-dimensional rants about the problems of society. For "Polly," (originally called "Hitchhiker"), Kurt was motivated by a newspaper article he had read about a horrible real-life incident that occurred in 1987. A young girl had been kidnapped, raped, and tortured with a blowtorch. Kurt wrote the song from the perspective of the perpetrator and captured the horror of the incident. The lyrics were in contrast to the song's sweet melody.

Nirvana was not satisfied with the album's mix and brought in Andy Wallace (the band loved his work with metal band Slayer). Wallace ran the songs through special effects boxes and modified the drumset sounds. However, Nirvana was still unhappy with the sound of the final mix, claiming that it was too polished and not as raw and punk-like as they desired. Cobain later expressed that the clarity of his vocals (often criticized as difficult to understand) were not important and that journalists often came up with "second rate" Freudian evaluation of his lyrics.

The famous Nevermind album cover featured a naked baby boy, alone underwater with a dollar bill on a fishhook just out of his reach. Cobain thought of the cover while watching a TV show with Dave Grohl about water births. The lead single "Smells Like Teen Spirit" was soon followed by another huge hit "Come As You Are." Nevermind replaced Michael Jackson at the top of the U.S. charts. By that time, Nevermind was selling 300,000 copies a week. Two more singles, "Lithium" and "In Bloom" followed and reached number eleven and twenty-eight in England.

Nevermind was breaking sales records weekly and Nirvana went on tour in Europe. Kurt was uneasy with his and the band's quick rise to fame. He had also developed a relationship with Courtney Love from the band Hole. At this time, Kurt began using hard drugs and his stomach issues persisted. This resulted in cancelled tour dates in Scandinavia. However, Nirvana appeared on *Saturday Night Live* in early 1992. Later that year, Cobain sought to reorganize the group's songwriting royalties to receive a larger percentage, since he was the chief songwriter (this caused a rift in the band that was never fully resolved). In February of 1992, Cobain and Love were married on a tour stop in Hawaii. Their daughter, Frances Bean Cobain, was born in August that same year.

In 1992, Nirvana released Incesticide, a joint venture between DGC and Sub Pop. It was a compilation of rare Nirvana recordings. It was intended to replace the poor quality bootleg versions of the songs that ardent fans of the band desired. In early 1993, with the aid of producer Steve Albini, Nirvana started recording songs for their next album. They traveled to Pachyderm Studios in Minnesota. Again unhappy with the sound of many of the tracks, they brought in longtime R.E.M. producer Scott Litt to remix some of the songs. Meanwhile, Cobain was slipping deeper into drug addiction.

In September of 1993, Nirvana released their third and final studio album, In Utero. It debuted at number one on the U.S. and British charts. Cobain wanted to title the album "I hate myself and I want to die" but Courtney Love talked him out of that title. The subject matter of In Utero's songs was Kurt's obsession with birth, death, disease, and addiction, all cultivated from his dreams. This album was recorded in only twelve days but Kurt took more time to compose the song lyrics than ever before. Many feel that In Utero, despite the mega-success of Nevermind, was their crowning achievement. This album contained uptempo rockers with lyrical depth such as "Very Ape" and "Radio Friendly Unit Shifter." "Milk It" was punk inspired and done in one take while "Dumb" was about a decent into drug addiction. "Heart Shaped Box" was Kurt's love song to Courtney Love.
In October of 1993, Nirvana added guitarist Pat Smear of the punk band Smear for a tour of the United States. In November, Nirvana recorded a performance for MTV's *Unplugged* series. Augmented by Smear, cellist Lori Goldston, and Cris and Curt Kirkwood of the Meat Puppets, the band wasn't exactly unplugged; just more like turned down and mellowed *without* electric guitars. Nirvana began a six-week European tour in February of 1994, but it was canceled after Cobain suffered a drug overdose in Rome.

After numerous interventions and drug rehabilitation stints, Kurt Cobain committed suicide in April of 1994 as the result of a self-inflicted gunshot wound. Nirvana dissolved immediately. Dave Grohl went on to form the extremely successful Foo Fighters (see this chapter) and Krist Novoselic focused on political activism and other musical projects. The album *MTV Unplugged in New York* was released in late 1994 and debuted at number one on the U.S. charts.

The musical ingredients of Nirvana were many. Kurt Cobain always believed that music came first and only then should the lyrics follow. Key to Nirvana's unique sound was their utilization of power chords that combined pop hooks with massive guitar dissonance. Nirvana spent hours of rehearsal time experimenting with shifting dynamics where a song would change from quite verses to loud and nasty choruses. Cobain used a number of different guitars including a Fender Mustang, a Fender Jaguar, and the Fender Stratocaster. His guitar sound featured crunchy distortion and multiple effects pedals. Novoselic often tuned down his bass guitar a half-step or whole step to achieve a "fat sound." Grohl was, by far, the hardest hitting of what seemed to be a never-ending parade of Nirvana drummers. Nirvana was unique in that they never catered to a mainstream audience or the indie rock fans that first supported their debut album, Bleach. Nirvana, more than any other 1990's band, helped to create a generational shift in music similar to the rock 'n' roll revolution of 1950's Elvis and the 1960's Beatles. This was consonant-sounding Beatles meets the dissonance of Arnold Schoenberg. Nirvana and their groundbreaking Nevermind, showed that the new alternative wasn't just something off to the side. Rather, it became the new reality.

The Tortured Genius of Kurt Cobain

The focus of this textbook has been on rock music itself and not the distractions of the personal lives of the hundreds of rock musicians throughout its history. However, the life of Kurt Cobain was so compelling that to ignore it would mean to not come even close to understanding Nirvana. The study of Kurt Cobain's life could consume a psychiatrist's life work.

Don and Wendy Cobain decided to get divorced when Kurt was nine years old and Kurt thought it was his fault. It would have a traumatic effect that would shape Kurt's personality and everything he trusted in, from his ideals of family and security to his own lifestyle and personal maintenance. Kurt spent much of his youth bouncing back and forth between parents. He was eventually homeless or staying with friends and families that would take him in for brief periods of time. By the age of fourteen, Kurt would talk indifferently about the concept of suicide. Conflicts with his parents heightened. A seventeen-year old Kurt was a junior in high school when he left home for good, quit high school, and was living on the streets. Seven years later, he would write the song "Something in the Way," an important song about a singer that lived under a bridge. It would be autobiographical in nature. Throughout this period, Kurt would experiment with drugs and have a few run-ins with the law.

From an early age, Kurt Cobain envisioned himself as an artist. He would keep notebooks that he used to document his thoughts. Kurt utilized sketchbooks where he would draw images, many very disturbing in nature. Kurt could not afford canvases to paint on nor quality paper, so his art backgrounds were often the back of game boards he found at thrift stores. His artistic creations were his vehicle to present his feelings and his perception of the world was usually morbid, dark, and twisted. Kurt's sketchbooks displayed aliens and exploding guitars. He acquired dolls and other collectables that he deconstructed and then reconstructed with parts juxtaposed in explicit and graphically disfigured ways.

Kurt Cobain's art and music were often cathartic expressions of his very depressed emotional state. After a childhood of rejection and emotional pain, Kurt Cobain longed to be loved. His motivation was never about fame and fortune. The 1992 birth of his and Courtney Love's daughter, Frances Bean Cobain, was to be the beginning of the stable family that he never had as a teenager. The rapid fame and fortune gained from the pandemonium of Nevermind was intense pressure that Kurt was unable to handle. His slip into severe heroin addiction was something that he first rationalized to gain relief from his terrible stomach pain (that numerous doctors could never properly diagnose). When Kurt spoke about his hopes for his daughter's life he said, "We (he and Courtney) have lacked love all our lives, and we need it so much that if there's any goal that we have, it's to give Frances as much love as we can, as much support as we can." #19 Kurt Cobain died at the age of twenty-seven, another member of the worse club in rock history.

Alice in Chains (1987-2002) (2005-present) is an American heavy metal grunge band that formed in Seattle in 1987. The original lineup included vocalist/guitarist Jerry Cantrell, drummer Sean Kinney, bassist Mike Starr (replaced by Mike Inez in 1993), and lead vocalist Layne Staley. Alice in Chains released their debut album,

> "I was looking for something a lot heavier, yet melodic at the same time. Something different from heavy metal, a different attitude."
>
> – Kurt Cobain

Facelift, in 1990 and rose to fame as part of the grunge movement. 1992's Dirt reached number six on the U.S. charts and 1994's acoustic based EP, Jar of Flies, became the first EP to top the U.S. charts.

"Them Bones"
by Jerry Cantrell

"Them Bones" was the opening track from Alice in Chains second and most acclaimed album, Dirt. The lyrics were about human mortality and that when everyone dies, all the beautiful experiences and knowledge acquired will end when you are gone. The subject matter was as much about loneliness as it was about the afterlife. Jerry Cantrell wrote the song with a sense of sarcasm and believed everyone should enjoy the time that they have on Earth.

"Them Bones" was built on a very sludgy metal guitar riff. The verses were in 7/8 time and the chorus was in 4/4. Alice in Chains often utilized odd time signatures knowing that they added an effective element to their compositions. "Them Bones" peaked at number twenty-four in America and number thirty in Britain. The music video for the song was featured in an episode of *Beavis and Butt-head*, where Butt-head claimed that "Them Bone" was the coolest video he had ever seen.

For much of 1994 to 1995, Alice in Chains was inactive. Vocalist Layne Staley left the band and was replaced by vocalist William DuVall. The band released 1995's Alice in Chains and it peaked at number one in America. It's singles included "Grind" and "Again." Alice in Chains encountered some band issues and soon dissolved. Sadly, Layne Stalye died of a drug overdose in 2002. Cantrell, Kinney, and Inez reunited in 2005. Alice in Chains released 2009's Black Gives Way to Blue and their latest release was The Devil Put Dinosaurs Here in 2013. The band has sold over twenty million albums worldwide. Alice in Chains has a Beatlesque harmonic sense with an interesting combination of a very heavy sound mixed with melodic vocal harmonies. Alice in Chains developed an approach built on heavy riffs that mixed a sludgy metal sound with elements of the grunge style.

Stone Temple Pilots (1989-2002) (2008-present) are an American rock band from San Diego, California. The band's classic lineup featured vocalist Scott Weiland, drummer Eric Kretz, guitarist Dean DeLeo, and bassist Robert DeLeo (brothers). First forming as the band Mighty Joe Young, they signed with Atlantic Records and changed their name to the Stone Temple Pilots. Their 1992 debut album, Core, was one of the most successful albums of the 1990's. The Pilot's sound was grunge influenced yet with a metal approach that utilized power chords. With Core, the band was attempting to revive the album-oriented format of the 1970's. 1994's Purple debuted at number one on the U.S. charts and yielded the hits "Vasoline" and "Interstate Love Song." Another single from the album, "Big Empty," was featured on a Stone Temple Pilots' 1993 *MTV Unplugged* acoustic performance.

"Plush"
by Robert DeLeo, Scott Weiland, and Eric Kretz

The lyrics for "Plush" were inspired by a horrible news story about a missing young woman who was found murdered in San Diego (the hometown of the Stone Temple Pilots). Vocalist Scott Weiland had described the song as a metaphor for an obsessive relationship that ended in tragedy. "Plush's" dark lyrics were very common for dozens of grunge bands at the time. It would be the Stone Temple Pilot's breakout hit from their major label debut album Core. The band's songwriting process was very collaborative for the songs on this recording.

Bassist Robert DeLeo composed the basic riff for "Plush" in the back of a U-Haul truck the band was renting for a local tour. DeLeo has said the chord progression for "Plush" was inspired by his love of ragtime music. In America, "Plush" was not available for purchase as a single. This was due to the band's label, Atlantic Records, interest in only selling the full album Core, and not a $2 dollar single. A video for "Plush" was released in 1993 and entered heavy rotation on MTV.

In 1995, problems ensued when Weiland struggled with addiction issues. However, he was able to contribute to 1996's Tiny Music…Songs from the Vatican Gift Shop. Temporality disbanding in 1997, Kretz and the DeLeo brothers formed a band titled Talk Show and Weiland released a solo album, 12 Bar Blues. Both flopped. Stone Temple Pilots re-formed in 1998 and released 1999's hard rocking No. 4. This album put the band in competition with a new generation of alternative metal bands. 2001's bossa nova-infused Shangri-La Dee Da was not successful and marketing support from their label was minimal. Tension mounted in the band and they called it quits in 2002.

Scott Weiland formed a new band with members of Guns N' Roses and the DeLeo brothers formed the band Army of Anyone. However, in 2008 the Stone Temple Pilots re-formed again and toured North America in 2009. Their 2010 self-titled Stone Temple Pilots prompted a world tour in 2011. In 2013, Scott Weiland was fired from the band and lawsuits ensued over usage of the band's name (the DeLeo brothers and Kretz retained rights to the name). In 2013, Stone Temple Pilots, along with Linkin Park singer Chester Bennington, released a five song EP titled High Rise.

Sadly, Scott Weiland died in 2015. Stone Temple Pilots were working on material for a new album and searching for a permanent vocalist in 2017. While initially rising to fame as a grunge band from the early 1990's, Stone Temple Pilots fused grunge with psychedelic rock, classic rock, and even Brazilian bossa nova. They successfully blended 1980's and 1990's alternative rock with the previous hard rock of the 1970's.

Hole (1989-2002) (2010-2012) was an American grunge and alternative band that formed in Los Angeles, California in 1989. The band started when vocalist/guitarist Courtney Love and guitarist Eric Erlandson joined forces and worked with a revolving lineup of drummers and bassists. Drummer Patty Schemel and bassist Kristen Pfaff completed the group. From their 1991 debut album Pretty on the Inside to 1994's Live Through This, Hole made a name as one of the most successful bands to discuss feminist issues in their songs. Love's aggressive and violent lyrical content addressed themes of sexual exploitation, body image, and abuse.

Courtney Love married Kurt Cobain in 1992 and had a daughter, Frances Bean Cobain, in 1992. After the death of Cobain, Love was thrust into the media spotlight and at times displayed erratic behavior. But Hole continued to record and perform. Love also took on some acting roles (she had acted before forming Hole). 1998's Celebrity Skin saw a musical change away from Hole's previous grunge and punk influences. Celebrity Skin was a very popular record, with Billy Corgan (from Smashing

> **Rock Hard Fact**
>
> In the years 2000 and 2001, Pearl Jam recorded and released 72 live albums from their 2000 Binaural Tour.

Pumpkins) exerting a considerable influence on Love. Hole now changed their musical direction by embracing a power-pop sound. The band made some lineup changes when bassist Melissa Auf der Maur replaced Pfaff and session drummer Dean Castronovo replaced Patty Schemel.

Hole disbanded in 2002 and Love formed a new punk band called **Bastard**. Love also revived her acting career with supporting roles in several TV series. Courtney Love re-formed Hole in 2010 with a new lineup and released 2010's Nobody's Daughter. Hole had a significant impact on female-led alternative bands from the 1990's to present. Their early approach was an aggressive mixture of punk and grunge elements and even experimental sounds. Hole later moved into a more pop-oriented direction. Love's lyrics were important for her views on the topic of feminism, although she was never associated with the riot grrrl movement.

Pearl Jam (1990-present) is an American rock band from Seattle, Washington that formed in 1990. The current members are vocalist Eddie Vedder, guitarist Mike McCready, guitarist Stone Gossard, bassist Jeff Ament, and drummer Matt Cameron. Gossard and Ament were previously members of the grunge-pioneering band Green River. They both joined another Seattle band, Mother Love Bone but when it dissolved they added McCready, Vedder, and drummer Dave Krusen to form the band Mookie Blaylock (a reference to ex-NBA basketball star Mookie Blaylock). In 1991, they changed their name to Pearl Jam and signed a record deal with Epic Records.

Pearl Jam debuted with 1991's Ten. It was not an immediate success but by late 1992, it went to number two on the U.S. charts. Pearl Jam has often been accused of jumping on the grunge bandwagon but Ten was actually recorded before the release of Nirvana's Nevermind. Ten was considered a very strong debut album that helped to define the grunge and alternative music movement of the early 1990's.

Groundbreaking album Ten
by Pearl Jam

On Ten, Pearl Jam attacked with a heavy guitar sound that reminded the listener of Led Zeppelin. Vedder's very deep and strong voice gave the band an instantly recognizable sound. Pearl Jam managed to fuse the gritty anger of 1980's post-punk with a classic rock stadium feel. Many of the songs on Ten began as long instrumental jams to which Eddie Vedder added impressionistic lyrics about homelessness, depression, suicide, and abuse. Many of Ten's songs were introspective and charged with a powerful emotional appeal. These musical characteristics, when combined with their driving bass and drums, defined the Pearl Jam sound.

Ten opened with "Once," then "Even Flow," "Alive," "Why Go," "Black," "Jeremy," "Oceans," "Porch," "Garden," "Deep," and "Release." All of the lyrics for Ten were written by Vedder (except the song "I've Got a Feeling" by John Lennon and Paul McCartney that was a bonus track on the Japanese release of Ten). Three of the tracks became hits including; "Alive," "Even Flow," and "Jeremy." When recording Ten, Pearl Jam was very efficient in the studio, nailing most of the songs in only a few takes. However, "Even Flow" proved to be the exception, requiring at least fifty takes. Pearl Jam made accompanying videos for each of the hit songs.

Critics of Ten accused the band of selling out commercially and that it was not a true alternative album. Others were jealous of their success. However, many Pearl Jam members had labored for years in obscure Northwestern grunge and alternative bands. Ten sold slowly upon is release, but it became a breakthrough success in the second half of 1992. Pearl Jam managed to stay true to their vision and still simultaneously clicked with a large audience. Ten had great longevity by spending a total of 261 weeks on the U.S. charts. It has sold over ten million copies in America.

"Alive"
by Stone Gassard and Eddie Vedder

Stone Gossard, Mike McCready, and Jeff Ament made a three-song demo tape that included the music for a song written by guitarist Stone Gossard called "Alive." The demo was called Stone Gossard demos '91 and featured Soundgarden drummer Matt Cameron. San Diego musician Eddie Vedder got his hands on the demo and added lyrics and vocals to the songs, including "Alive." Gossard and Ament heard the Vedder enhanced demo and flew him out to Seattle for an audition. Vedder was hired and their band, Mookie Blaylock, was soon signed to Epic Records and changed their name to Pearl Jam.

The lyrics for "Alive" were Eddie Vedder's semi-autobiographical story about a son that discovered his father was actually his stepfather (his real father had died).
The lyrics of "Alive" were complicated and twisted. They detailed the sexual abuse of the boy by his own mother, because she claimed that he resembled the biological father. In real life, Vedder was raised by his stepfather without knowing it and later met his real father without realizing they were related. The chorus of "I'm Still Alive" was meant to be a positive affirmation of life. When Pearl Jam went to record "Alive," they had trouble capturing the feel of the demo. So, they decided to record the lyrics over the actual demo, adding Vedder's vocal and an additional guitar solo by McCready at the end of the song.

Shortly after the recording sessions for Ten were complete, Dave Krusen left Pearl Jam due to personal issues. Drummer Matt Chamberlain joined briefly but was reluctant to tour and was replaced by Dave Abbruzzese. Aided by the explosive rise of Nirvana, Pearl Jam quickly expanded their fan base. 1993's Vs. was their first recording with producer Brendan O'Brien. It went straight to the top of the U.S. charts, remaining there for five weeks. Vs. featured a rawer and looser sound than Ten. Pearl Jam decided not to record a music video for any of the album's singles and they wanted to slow down their commercial success in general. For 1994's Vitalogy, Vedder took more control of the band and Jack Irons replaced Abbruzzese on drums. Also, Pearl Jam became angry with Ticketmaster when they learned that service charges were added to tickets from a charity concert the band had played.

1996's No Code debuted at number one in America but quickly fell down the charts. This album contained a wide range of emotions and the lyrical themes were introspective and dealt with issues of self-examination. 1998's Yield utilized a straightforward rock approach with structured songs that Pearl Jam spent much time composing and rehearsing. Later in 1998, Pearl Jam once again changed drummers with the addition of former Soundgarden drummer Matt Cameron (at first on a temporary basis).

> "The word 'grunge' became a household term, and fashion runways were filled with flannel shirts and long underwear... Every now and then when I'm feeling a little nostalgic, I put on my 'grunge tuxedo'-flannel shirt, long shorts with long underwear underneath them, and a pair of Doc Martens."
>
> – Dave Grohl

Pearl Jam released five albums in the 2000's with the addition of keyboardist Boom Gaspar. 2013's Lightning Bolt was their tenth studio album and they released a live album and 2017 concert film, *Let's Play Two*. Pearl Jam, when compared with other grunge bands from the early 1990's, was less heavy and displayed a classic rock sound reminiscent of The Who and Led Zeppelin. They successfully expanded their musical approach by experimenting with elements of garage rock, punk, and worldbeat rhythms. Pearl Jam was inducted into the Rock and Roll Hall of Fame in 2017.

Post Grunge Bands into the Alternative

The death of Kurt Cobain marked the end of the first-wave of grunge bands. Record labels were left with many second-rate imitators who lacked the dynamism and edginess of the original grunge artists. Many radio stations and retail music outlets failed to distinguish the imitators from the originals. Some bands, a few very good, were nevertheless vilified for taking advantage of the grunge trend whose hero (Kurt Cobain) had so recently taken his own life. The public reaction only confirmed that grunge had become an American rock cliché. Despite some commercial viability, grunge was fading quickly.

Grunge served as a pivot point for rock moving forward. Grunge, like it's predecessor punk, dismissed the indulgent rock styles of the past. Grunge's breakthrough launched the rapid rise of alternative rock. Radio formats were destroyed, thus proving that underground music could succeed in mainstream markets. Nirvana and their peers opened the rock playing field to all comers. Now, any rock genre or subgenre could be a commercial possibility. New bands realized that the old code of rock protocols were gone. Bands could make their own rules, play their own music, and express their own views without record industry repercussions. The major labels *had* to listen to the musical direction of young musicians. This was similar to the way these same big companies had to recognize the psychedelic bands of the late 1960's hippie era. The 1990's would see musical barriers come down. Popular music culture was fractured and age barriers disappeared while different generations borrowed each other's music styles and sounds. This can be heard in the music of **post-grunge** to alternative bands. Some of the prominent post-grunge bands were **Candlebox** (1990-2000) (2006-present), **Nickelback**, **Matchbox Twenty**, **Hoobastank** (1994-present), **Creed** (1993-2004) (2009-2012), **Staind** (1995-2012) (2014) (2017), and **The Foo Fighters**.

Nickelback (1995-present) is a Canadian rock band that formed in Alberta, Canada in 1995. After some early lineup changes, their current lineup is vocalist/guitarist Chad Kroeger, his brother and bassist Mike Kroeger, guitarist/keyboardist Ryan Peake, and drummer Daniel Adair. Their first full-length album was 1996's The Curb, which achieved only moderate success. In 1999, Nickelback signed with Roadrunner Records and re-released their once-independent album, The State. This record faired better as the band moved from a grunge style to a more pop-radio friendly sound. Two hits from the album, "Leader of Men" went to number eight on the U.S. charts, and "Breathe" went to number ten. 2001's Silver Side Up featured a number of hits but "How You Remind Me" became the most played song on U.S. radio stations in the 2000's (played over 1.2 million times).

Nickelback has recorded six more studio albums including 2017's Feed the Machine. Their sound has evolved from their early grunge days to include elements of pop-rock and nu metal. This has given them longevity and continued popularity.

"How You Remind Me"
by Nickelback

Chad Kroeger wrote "How You Remind Me" just before Nickelback recorded their Silver Side Up album. The band finished the song in less than fifteen minutes and knew that they had a hit. The album was released on September 11th, 2001 and has long been associated with remembrances of the tragedies of that day. Kroeger wrote the song about his old girlfriend and their dysfunctional relationship. Kroeger purposely kept the lyrics ambiguous in order to allow as many people as possible to relate to an ex-girlfriend or ex-boyfriend. The lyrics told the story of his ex-girlfriend who pointed out all of his faults, which resulted in great heartbreak. Near the end of the song, the band dropped out and Kroeger sang, "for handing you a heart worth breaking!"

"How You Remind Me" hits with a hard and heavy guitar edge for a rock ballad. Nickelback was able to take Chad Kroeger's raw vocal sound and fuse it with grungy guitars. This made his pleading lyrics come to life. "How You Remind Me" combined the intensity of early 1990's grunge with a radio-friendly melodic hook. Rick Parashar, who had previously worked with Pearl Jam and Alice in Chains, produced the song. "How You Remind Me" was only the second time a song by a Canadian band hit number one on the U.S. Charts.

Matchbox Twenty (1995-present with some inactive years) is an American rock band that formed in Orlando, Florida in 1995. The original lineup was vocalist/guitarist/keyboardist Rob Thomas, guitarist Kyle Cook, bassist Brian Yale, and drummer/guitarist Paul Doucette. The band (first spelled their name Matchbox 20) rocketed to international acclaim when their 1996 debut album Yourself or Someone like You went to number five on the U.S. charts. This recording established the band's post-grunge and traditional rock sound while featuring lyrical themes of loneliness, depression, anger, and alcoholism. Hits such as "Push" and "3 AM." pushed the album to over fifteen million sales worldwide. 2000's Mad Season reached number three on the U.S. charts and moved the band to a more pop-oriented sound. Meanwhile, Rob Thomas co-composed the hit "Smooth" with Itaal Shur for Carlos Santana and recorded it on Santana's album titled Supernatural. "Smooth" was the hit that basically set up Rob Thomas' solo career outside of Matchbox Twenty.

2002's More Than You Think You Are brought Matchbox Twenty more success. In addition, Thomas collaborated with Mick Jagger to write the hit "Disease." Matchbox Twenty went on hiatus in 2004 after the departure of guitarist Adam Gaynor. When the band reunited in 2007, Paul Doucette took over the rhythm guitar spot and drummer Ryan MacMillan joined Matchbox Twenty. A compilation album, Exile on Mainstream, followed in 2007 and showcased six new songs. After a world tour, the band took another hiatus while Thomas focused on his solo career. Matchbox Twenty released North in 2012. It debuted at number one in America and number fourteen in Britain. Matchbox Twenty has successfully harnessed the grit and energy of grunge while developing quality radio-friendly material.

> **Rock Hard Fact**
>
> Nickelback derived their name when bassist Mike Kroeger worked at Starbucks and when giving change back to customers routinely said, "Here's a nickel back sir."

> "The first Foo Fighters record was not meant to be an album, it was an experiment and for fun. I was just f***ing around. Some of the lyrics weren't even real words."
>
> - Dave Grohl

The Foo Fighters (1994-present) are an American band from Seattle (now an L.A. band) that was formed by ex-Nirvana drummer Dave Grohl (see chapter eighteen) in 1994. The Foo Fighters almost didn't happen because Grohl had considered joining Pearl Jam and then almost joined Tom Petty and the Heartbreakers. Grohl had written countless songs during his tenure with Nirvana but suppressed his urge to record them while in awe of his then bandleader, Kurt Cobain. As the only official member, Grohl formed The Foo Fighters and released the 1995 self-titled Foo Fighters. Besides the guitar part on the song "X-Static" (played by Greg Dulli of the band Afghan Whigs), Grohl wrote all of the songs, played every instrument, and sang all of the vocals on every track on Foo Fighters. Next, he needed to form a real band to support the album. Initially, Grohl approached former Nirvana bandmate Krist Novoselic about joining, but they both decided against it, fearing too much comparison to Nirvana. Instead, Grohl recruited ex-Sunny Day Real Estate bassist Nate Mendel and drummer William Goldsmith. He also added guitarist Pat Smear, who had briefly toured with Nirvana after their In Utero album. Grohl licensed Foo Fighters to Capitol Records, and then released it on his new record label, Roswell Records. The album was a smash hit, peaking at number three in England and number twenty-three in America. A number of hits emerged from the album including "This Is a Call" and "I'll Stick Around."

1997's The Colour and the Shape was the first Foo Fighters group album. The lineup became guitarist Pat Smear, bassist Nate Mendel, and Grohl singing lead, also adding rhythm guitar and playing some of the drum parts. William Goldsmith had originally recorded the drum tracks, but Grohl was unhappy and re-recorded most of them himself. Eventually, Grohl and producer Gil Norton decided to keep Goldsmith's parts for "Doll" and "Up in Arms." Just as the album was near completion, drummer Taylor Hawkins was hired as the new permanent Foo Fighter's drummer. Hawkins added drum parts to "Requiem" and "Drive Me Wild." The Colour and the Shape made the top ten in America and number three in Britain.

Groundbreaking album
The Colour and the Shape
by The Foo Fighters

The extremely talented Dave Grohl was able to record a debut album virtually all on his own utilizing his musicianship as a composer, drummer, guitarist, and singer. But The Foo Fighters sparked ensemble magic with their The Colour and the Shape recording. By bringing in producer Gil Norton to obtain a pop sensibility, plus Pat Smear and Nate Mendel to provide some hard rocking tracks, The Foo Fighters became a band that would ultimately *define* the post-grunge genre.

The album opened with "Doll," then "Monkey Wrench," "Hey, Johnny Park!" "My Poor Brain," "Wind Up," "Un in Arms," My Hero," "See You," "Enough Space," "February Stars," "Everlong," "Walking After You," and "New Way Home." The songwriting for all of the tracks were collaborative band efforts, with the exception of "Enough Space" and "Walking After You" that were exclusively written by Grohl. "Wind Up" was a song about the press and musicians that do nothing but complain. It was motivated by Grohl's gratitude for being in a position to make music for a living.

For The Colour and the Shape, Grohl gained confidence in his vocal abilities and his lyric writing. This was reflected in his new found desire to explore topics that meant something to him. "Monkey Wrench" was about understanding that you might be the source of problems in a relationship. "My Hero," was thought to be about Kurt Cobain, but Dave Grohl said, "That's my way of saying that when I was young, I didn't have big rock heroes, I didn't want to grow up and be some big sporting hero. My heroes were ordinary people and the people that I have a lot of respect for are just solid everyday people-people you can rely on." #20

The Colour and the Shape highlighted Dave Grohl's strong sense of melody and his ability to grind out three chord simple harmonies with big hooks. Grohl's drumming gave the tracks the raw feel and power that he brought to Nirvana (and Taylor Hawkins would later deliver). Most of the album's tracks displayed an aggression that when combined with Gil Norton's slick production, produced the sound that defined post-grunge. This album revealed how elements of punk and mainstream rock could be effectively blended. The Colour and the Shape helped to set new directions in rock.

The Foo Fighters next recorded 1999's There is Nothing Left to Lose as a three piece after Pat Smear left (he would return in 2006) the band. This album made the top ten in the U.S. and yielded the hit "Learn to Fly." After completing There is Nothing Left to Lose, guitarist Chris Shiflett joined as the lead guitarist. The band next released 2002's One by One. 2005's In Your Honor saw a different approach with one disk of hard rock tracks and a second of all acoustic material. A duet with vocalist Norah Jones on "Virginia Moon" showcased more of The Foo Fighters' versatility.

"Learn to Fly"
by Dave Grohl, Nate Mendel, and Taylor Hawkins

"Learn to Fly" was a song about inspiration. Dave Grohl's lyrics were about looking to the sky and looking for the things that make you feel alive, no matter if they were good or bad. Grohl also wrote about looking for signs of life and that he needed help to get through his own life. But it was still a positive and uplifting song that captured the Foo Fighters ability to create a strong melodic hook over crunchy power-chords.

"Learn to Fly" was one of the Foo Fighter's most successful tunes and was released as two different singles in England in 1999. A music video for the song took place on a commercial airplane, parodying the movie Airplane!. In the video, the band avoided being served coffee, instead choosing liquor. They were then forced to land the plane by themselves. In the video, each Foo Fighter band-member portrayed themselves. The video also featured The Foo Fighters (and others) playing different roles including an FBI agent who arrested two airline mechanics (played by Jack Black and Kyle Gass from Tenacious D).

In the summer of 2005, The Foo Fighters headlined for 85,000 fans in London's Hyde Park with support from The Strokes and Motorhead. After a two-year hiatus, the band released 2007's Echoes, Silence, Patience & Grace that contained the hit "The Pretender," a rock anthem that went to number eight in England. The Foo Fighters were now "stadium rock star" big and demonstrated this when they played Wembley Stadium, London

---

Rock Hard Fact

During World War II, Allied aircraft pilots referred to UFOs and other aerial phenomena as "foo fighters."

"Every now and again, the alternative culture is cherished by the mainstream for what it is, rather than how it should be, like the mainstream popular music."

– Thurston Moore of Sonic Youth

in the summer of 2008. At that performance, Grohl (on drums) and Hawkins (on vocals) were joined onstage by Jimmy Page and John Paul Jones for a version of Zeppelin's "Rock and Roll."

2011's Wasting Light proved to be a classic Foo Fighter's album. Pat Smear returned to the band full-time and Nevermind's producer Butch Vig recorded this album in Grohl's basement studio utilizing only analog recording equipment. Cameo appearances by Krist Novoselic and Husker Du's Bob Mould helped make the album a success. It reached number one in eleven countries and won a Grammy for Best Rock Album. 2014's Sonic Highways featured contributions from many guest musicians with ties to the unique music of different American cities. The process was filmed for a television series titled, *Foo Fighters: Sonic Highways*, and was broadcast on HBO TV. This was a groundbreaking concept for a music project. It put the Foo Fighters in an innovative position that made them "Ambassadors of American rock music."

2017's Concrete and Gold was the latest Foo Fighter's studio album. It featured appearances from Justin Timberlake and Paul McCartney playing drums on the song "Sunday Rain." The Foo Fighters are seasoned songwriters and their songwriting process has evolved over the years. Guitarist Chris Shiflett explained "We usually do kind of a similar thing where Dave has a bunch of song ideas and he'll usually demo them first, just himself. Then he sends us all the songs, and we'll all get together and jam on them…that's usually the method of this band, we just demo and demo and demo and do them over and over and tweak them along the way…Back in the old days, the first few records I did with this band we'd record all the drums, then all the bass, and all the guitars…But for Wasting Light there was a change where we just started doing one song at a time." #21

The Foo Fighters were often compared to Grohl's previous band, Nirvana. Grohl has recognized Kurt Cobain's strong influence on his own songwriting. Grohl's great sense of rhythm serves to musically inform his guitar playing and his overall songwriting style. The Foo Fighters possess a great love for diverse music from The Beatles to Queen to punk rock and heavy metal. They consistently rock very hard while expressing simple melodies and acoustic timbres. The Foo Fighters personified post-grunge but continue to play rock with a vision to the future.

Alternative Rock

Initially, alternative rock was a very broad term for a diverse collection of underground rock bands and artists who chose to play music considered to be outside of mainstream music. Nirvana, Soundgarden, and Pearl Jam all crossed over into the mainstream with their overwhelming commercial success. Suddenly, the alternative took on a redefined definition of bands that embraced elements of many different rock genres. An alternative band could be part post-punk, post-grunge, old school or new metal hybrids, or even pop-rock influenced. Alternative rock grew out of the indie underground bands that were all on independent labels with their music played mostly on college radio stations and for less commercial-oriented listeners. Many alternative bands avoided trends while managing to attract an audience that found their unique combination of styles to be original and exciting.

From the mid-to late 1970's, alternative bands formed all over the world. Among them were the British bands **The Cure** and **Siouxsie and the Banshees** (1976-1996) (2002), Scottish band **Simple Minds** (1977-present), and Australian band **INXS**.

The Cure (1976-present) is an English rock band that formed in 1976. The current lineup is vocalist/guitarist/keyboardist and songwriter Robert Smith, bassist/keyboardist Simon Gallup, keyboardist Roger O'Donnell, drummer Jason Cooper, and guitarist/bassist Reeves Gabrels. The Cure started out as the Easy Cure (then dropped the Easy from their name) and released a single "Killing an Arab." Their 1979 debut album, Three Imaginary Boys, was punk influenced but lacked a musical direction. Robert Smith expanded his musical palette finding inspiration in the music of Jimi Hendrix and David Bowie. 1980's Seventeen Seconds was released after The Cure toured in support of Siouxsie and the Banshees. Smith's new songs were considered to be examples of gothic rock with darker themes and introspective, romantic lyrics. Seventeen Seconds reached number twenty on the British charts. 1981's Faith and 1982's Pornography continued to refine The Cure's dark sound and Robert Smith had developed an onstage goth image with his towering black hair and red lipstick.

The Cure grew in international stature with each new release. Their seventh studio recording, 1987's double album Kiss Me, Kiss Me, Kiss Me, spawned a U.S. top forty hit, "Just Like Heaven." 1989's Disintegration continued to build an international reputation. 1992's Wish catapulted The Cure to chart topping status in England and Australia. The Cure have released a total of thirteen studio albums, ten EPs, and over thirty singles. They helped to define the gothic rock movement but emerged with an original approach that featured acoustic guitar mixed with six-string bass and Smith's unique voice. The Cure increasingly utilized layers of guitars and synthesizers to further develop their sound. This solidified their status as one of rock's earliest alternative bands.

INXS (1977-2012) was an Australian rock band that formed initially as The Farriss Brothers in Sydney, Australia in 1977. Three brothers, guitarist Tim Farriss, drummer Jon Farriss, and keyboardist Andrew Farriss, joined forces with guitarist Kirk Pengilly, bassist Garry Bears, and vocalist Michael Hutchence. INXS began with a focus on new wave and pop styles and then began to add more funk to their approach. In 1980, they released their self-titled debut album, INXS, in their native Australia to moderate success. It wasn't until their fourth album, 1984's The Swing, and its breakout single "Original Sin," that they had an international hit.

1987's The Kick went to number three on the U.S. charts and number nine in England. It yielded four top ten hits on the U.S. charts including "New Sensation" and the sensuous ballad "Never Tear Us Apart. " The later described an instant connection between two people who formed a lifelong bond. Kick was INXS's most popular album and established them as international stars. Sadly, lead singer Michael Hutchence died in 1997. The band did not perform for nearly a year but regrouped with vocalist Jon Stevens. INXS developed a hard-edged alternative sound while maintaining sleek pop grooves that earned them international popularity. INXS retired in 2012.

The 1980's saw an explosion of prominent alternative bands that included: **Violent Femmes** (1980-present with some inactive years), **Soul Asylum** (1981-present), 10,000 Maniacs (1981-present), **The Flaming Lips** (1983-present), **Stones Roses** (1983-1996) (2011-present), **The Jesus and Mary Chain** (1983-1999)

(2007-present), **The Pixies** (1986-1993) (2004-present), **Better Than Ezra** (1988-present), and **Pavement** (1989-2010). Four of the most influential were **Meat Puppets, Sonic Youth, The Butthole Surfers,** and **Radiohead**.

Meat Puppets (1980-present with some inactive years) are an American band that began as a punk band but established their own unique approach. From their 1982 self-titled debut album, Meat Puppets, to their 2013 release Rat Farm, the Meat Puppets released a total of fifteen studio albums. The band's profile was raised when Meat Puppet members Cris and Curt Kirkwood appeared as guests on Nirvana's *MTV Unplugged* performance in 1993. The Meat Puppets successfully mixed country music with elements of psychedelic rock with strong vocal harmonies. They have influenced many bands including Nirvana, Soundgarden, and Pavement.

Sonic Youth (1981-2011) was an American rock band formed in New York City in 1981. They helped to pioneer the genre of **noise rock.** Noise rock, which spun off from punk rock, utilized extreme levels of guitar distortion and to some extent, electronic instrumentation to create abrasive droning timbres. Sonic Youth combined this with post-punk and new wave elements. The Sonic Youth core lineup was vocalist/guitarist Thurston Moore, vocalist/bassist/guitarist Kim Gordon, guitarist Lee Renaldo, and drummer Steve Shelley (after a series of short-term drummers). From their self-titled debut EP Sonic Youth, to their 2009 The Eternal, Sonic Youth released a total fifteen studio albums. A key aspect of the Sonic Youth sound can be heard in the diversity of their influences from Joni Mitchell to 1980's hardcore bands such as Minor Threat. Sonic Youth utilized alternative guitar tunings and formed musical relationships with avant-garde artists that included John Cage and Henry Cowell.

Sonic Youth never achieved great commercial success. However, their 1994 release Experimental Jet Set, Trash and No Star did reach number thirty-four on the U.S. charts. It spawned the hit "Bull In the Heather" and was considered by many to be a classic indie rock anthem.

"Bull in the Heather"
by Sonic Youth

"Bull in the Heather" was the name of an actual racehorse. Bob Nastovich, from the band Pavement, was a horse racing fan and gave Kim Gordon and Thurston Moore a bumper sticker with the horse's name on it. In the song, the horse was really a metaphor for sex and prostitution. Gordon's vocal tone had a sensual quality delivered with a punk aloofness that highlighted how the narrator craved attention. Gordon had said that the song was about a woman who refused to participate in a male-dominated culture and reacted by becoming passive. The lyrics compared the long odds of winning a horse race to someone's expectations of unrealistic sexual fantasies.

Musically, "Bull in the Heather" created an effective background of avant-garde ambient noise blended with a funky drumset groove. Sonic Youth, much like their predecessors The Velvet Underground, developed a unique alternative sound while still expressing a pop sensibility. "Bull in the Heather" had a catchy punk-inspired melody where Gordon deliberately sang "wrong" pitches and other "out of tune" notes. Gordon somehow took these dissonance sounds and created an effective melodic hook. A video for the song featured a scene with singer Kathleen Hanna (of the band Bikini Kill) dancing.

Sonic Youth were considered to be one of the pioneering alternative bands. Although signed by David Geffen to his DGC label, Sonic Youth remained largely an underground band that built a loyal following over many years. They did headline the Lollapalooza festive in 1995. Many punk, new wave, and alternative bands, including Nirvana, considered Sonic Youth to be a major influence on their musical approach.

Butthole Surfers (1981-present) are an American rock band that formed in San Antonio, Texas in 1981. The band has undergone many personal changes but the current lineup is vocalist Gibby Haynes, guitarist Paul Leary, drummer King Coffey, and bassist Jeff Pinkus. Their approach was rooted in the 1980's hardcore punk scene but their sound expanded to include elements of psychedelic rock, noise rock and electronica.

In 1983, the Butthole Surfers released a self-titled EP, Butthole Surfers, and in 1984 they released their debut album titled Psychic…Powerless…Another Man's Sac. The band built a steady and loyal audience and recorded three more studio albums in the 1980's. 1991's piouhgd moved the band in a more electronic direction and did not fare well commercially. 1993's Independent Worm Saloon yielded a minor hit with "Who Was in My Room Last Night?" Bassist Jeff Pinkus left in 1994 (he returned in 2008) and the band released a compilation album in 1995 titled The Hole Truth…and Nothing Butt. 1996's Electriclarryland brought some success, reaching number thirty-one on the U.S. charts on the strength of their hit, "Pepper." 2001's Weird Revolution was their most electronic inspired record to date. Known for their chaotic and disturbing live shows, The Butthole Surfers are well respected by their peers and have cultivated a strong fan base. Their punk rock and art rock background combined with electronic music and violent (sometimes even disturbing) live performances to give them a unique musical identity. The Butthole Surfers are a significant pioneering alternative band that has sustained their popularity for over thirty-five years.

Radiohead (1985-present) is a British rock band that formed in Abingdon, Oxfordshire, England in 1985. The band has been remarkably stable and consists of vocalist/guitarist/keyboardist Thom Yorke, guitarist/keyboardist Jonny Greenwood, guitarist Ed O'Brien, bassist Colin Greenwood, and drummer Phil Selway. Radiohead has worked with the same producer, Nigel Godrich, since 1994. Their debut single, 1992's "Creep," became a worldwide hit. "Creep" forged a sound between a grunge and emo approach and contained intensely self-deprecating lyrics. The band's debut album, 1993's Pablo Honey, was led by Yorke and featured Radiohead's three-guitar attack. Their 1995 follow-up, The Bends, raised their profile significantly in England. It explored topics such as paranoia, alienation, and politics through Yorke's intelligent and revealing lyrics. 1997's OK Computer catapulted Radiohead to international fame. It eventually sold over six million copies worldwide while going straight to number one on the British charts and number twenty-one in America. OK Computer was a work of remarkable depth that displayed ambient soundscapes and a palette of electronic sounds.

Groundbreaking album OK Computer
by Radiohead

Often cited as Radiohead's masterpiece, OK Computer removed the band from any link to the Britpop movement. OK Computer established Radio-

> "I think the most important thing about music is the sense of escape."
>
> - Thom Yorke of Radiohead

Rock Hard Fact

The voices for the characters (seen traveling to the moon) in the Smashing Pumpkins' video Tonight, Tonight were recorded by Tom Kenny and Jill Talley. They are also the voices of SpongeBob and Plankton.

head as a defining alternative rock band that delivered a melancholy and atmospheric style that would lead the way into the next decade. Thom Yorke described the album as a cross between British skiffle music with musical characteristics of Pink Floyd and Queen. OK Computer addressed fears about the approaching new millennium.

OK Computer featured twelve tracks all composed as a collaborative effort by all of the band members. It opened with "Airbag," then "Paranoid Android," "Subterranean Homesick Alien," "Exit Music (For a Film)," "Let Down," "Karma Police," "Fitter Happier," "Electioneering," "Climbing Up the Walls," "No Surprises," "Lucky," and "The Tourist." Five of the thirteen tracks were released as promotional singles. Yorke has said that the starting point for OK Computer was the 1970 avant-garde jazz-fusion music of the legendary Miles Davis. Radiohead drew further inspiration from film composer Ennio Morricone. The band also expanded their concept of instrumentation by recording tracks utilizing a Mellotron, cello and other strings, a glockenspiel, and various electronic effects.

The album's opening track "Airbag," was inspired by the music of DJ Shadow and featured a digitally sampled electronic drum track. "Airbag" referred to car accidents (the idea of fatal car crashes) and the concept of reincarnation. "Paranoid Android" utilized an unconventional structure and was inspired by The Beatles ("Happiness is a Warm Gun") and Queen. "Subterranean Homesick Alien" borrowed from the Bob Dylan classic "Subterranean Homesick Blues" and utilized more electronic timbres. "Climbing Up the Walls" was inspired by 20th century composer Krzysztof Penderecki and his composition "Threnody to the Victims of Hiroshima."
OK Computer was a groundbreaking album that received great popular and critical acclaim. It's futuristic vision, both reflected it its musical and lyrical content, created a new direction for Radiohead and alternative music moving forward.

2000's Kid A saw Radiohead move away from a rock sound by utilizing synthesizers, drum machines, and string and brass instrumentation. Although no singles were released from the album, it still went to number one on the British charts. Thom Yorke became concerned that other bands were imitating Radiohead. He also suffered from a case of writer's block. Keyboardist Jonny Greenwood became more involved in the compositional process of the band. Greenwood had contacted Princeton University music professor Paul Lansky to ask permission to borrow segments from one of his computer-based compositions titled "mild und leise." Greenwood eventually used a sample from "mild and leise" for the Radiohead song "Idioteque." Lansky recalled, "My first reaction on listening to 'Idioteque' was that I felt as if I had participated in a musical time warp. I had recorded my part in the early 1970's…Radiohead had woven a song around my chord sequence, using it repeatedly as the harmonic underpinning of 'Idioteque.'"…I had never heard anything like it…Its profile was strange: sections were repeated many times…the textures were extremely unusual…It took a number of hearings to begin to understand it…I was fascinated by what Radiohead had done and how they had done it." #22

2001's Amnesiac was similar to Kid A and drew from electronic music and 20th century compositional techniques. The 2000's brought three more albums including 2003's Hail to the Thief, 2007's In Rainbows, and 2011's The King of Limbs. Radiohead's latest release, 2016's A Moon Shaped Pool, topped the charts in several countries and became their sixth number one album in England. Radiohead has proved to be one of the most innovative and creative bands in the alternative rock genre. They have effectively utilized an amalgamation of musical styles to create their unique voice.

Some alternative bands borrowed heavily from heavy metal, progressive rock, and even funk genres. They included **Faith No More, Primus, Smashing Pumpkins,** and **Jane's Addiction**.

Faith No More (1979-1998) (2009-present) is an American rock band that formed in San Francisco, California in 1982. Started by bassist Billy Gould and drummer Mike Bordin, Faith No More went through many personnel changes. The current lineup consists of Gould, Bordin, guitarist Jon Hudson, keyboardist Roddy Bottum, and ex-Mr. Bungle and Dillinger Escape Plan vocalist Mike Patton. Their 1985 debut, We Care a Lot, was released on an independent label and featured the single "We Care a Lot" that saw minor success on MTV. 1978's Introduce Yourself was released on the major label Slash Records and featured a re-recorded "We Care a Lot." The song achieved a metal sound with a sarcastic lyrical parody of modern culture and the pomposity of the Live Aid generation.

1989's The Real Thing featured their single titled "Epic," that would be their breakout and only top ten U.S. chart hit. The song blended funk, rap, and heavy metal and was credited to have inspired a few prominent rap-rock artists (see chapter seventeen). Faith No More released three more albums in the 1990's including; 1992's Angel Dust, 1995's King for a Day…Fool for a Lifetime, and 1997's Album of the Year. Faith No More decided to call it quits in 1998 to pursue other individual music projects. After eleven years, they reunited for 2015's Sol Invictus album. Faith No More has a unique sound that combined elements of alternative rock and experimental funk metal. They were influential in the evolution of nu metal bands such as Deftones and Korn.

Primus (1984-present with some inactive years) is an American rock band that formed in San Francisco, California in 1984. The band went through a number of lineup changes. The current members are vocalist/bassist Les Claypool, guitarist Larry LaLonde, and drummer Tim "Herb" Alexander. Primus began as a metal band with strong elements of progressive rock and Frank Zappa-like humor before building an underground following. They released their 1990 album, Frizzle Fry, that included a minor hit "John the Fisherman." This attracted enough attention to be signed to major label Interscope Records where they recorded 1991's Sailing the Seas of Cheese. The single "Jerry Was a Race Car Driver" was a big hit on *Headbangers Ball* and eventually brought them wider appeal. On this recording, Les Claypool performed innovative basslines within Primus's riff-driven progressive rock and metal grooves. The band went on to record seven more studio albums, from 1993's Pork Soda to 2017's The Desaturating Seven. Primus, by defying stylistic categorization, is an alternative band in the true sense of the word.

Smashing Pumpkins (1988-2000) (2006-present) are an American rock band from Chicago, Illinois that formed in 1988. The Smashing Pumpkins began when vocalist/guitarist Billy Corgan met guitarist James Iha and they soon added bassist D'Arcy Wretzky and drummer Jimmy Chamberlin. The band has undergone many lineup changes but the current personnel includes Corgan and guitarist/keyboardist Jeff Schroeder. Presently, Chamberlin and multi-instrumentalists Katie Cole and Sierra Swan tour with the band.

The Smashing Pumpkins created their alternative sound void of punk roots, instead relying on densely layered guitar sounds and elements of heavy metal, pop, gothic, progressive, and psychedelic influences. Corgan is the primary songwriter and his cathartic lyrics and strong melodies have brought mainstream success. Their 1991 debut album Gish was produced by Butch Vig (Nirvana producer) and Corgan played most of the instrumental parts. With the breakout popularity of grunge, The Smashing Pumpkins (to the irritation of the band), became associated with the suddenly popular movement. 1993's Siamese Dream peaked at number ten on the U.S. charts, despite Corgan's bout with depression and Chamberlin's battle with drug addiction.

1995 was a prolific songwriting period for Corgan who wrote fifty-six songs that year. His work resulted in the 1995 double album Mellon Collie and the Infinite Sadness. It debuted at number one in America, sold over ten million copies, and yielded six singles including "Bullet with Butterfly Wings" and "Tonight, Tonight."

"Tonight, Tonight"
by Billy Corgan

In composing "Tonight, Tonight," Billy Corgan was inspired by the band Cheap Trick. The lyrics delved into dark comedy with Corgan writing about his own past and his escape from an abusive childhood. The song packed an emotional punch and instantly become an enduring rock anthem for the band's fan base.

Corgan changed the key of "Tonight, Tonight" from C to G when he had trouble recording in the original key. A full thirty-piece string section from the Chicago Symphony Orchestra was employed for the recording session. Corgan described the rich timbre as "one of the most exciting recording experiences I have ever had." #23 A music video for "Tonight, Tonight" was inspired by Georges Melies's silent film titled *A Trip to the Moon*. It was filmed in the style of a turn of the century silent movie with theater-styled backdrops and primitive special effects.

The Smashing Pumpkins finished the 1990's with many difficult internal issues. Their 1998 release Adore saw a significant change in style when the band moved in an electronic direction. After the release of 2000's Machina/The Machines of God and Machina II/The Friends & Enemies of Modern Music, the Smashing Pumpkins disbanded. After a number of other musical projects by Corgan and Chamberlin, the band announced plans to revive The Smashing Pumpkins. Corgan and Chamberlin revamped the Pumpkins' lineup for 2007's Zeitgeist, 2009-2014's Teargarden by Kaleidyscope, and 2012's Oceania recordings. Corgan signed a new record deal with BMG in 2014 and the band released Monuments to an Elegy that same year. Like many alternative and Nirvana-inspired bands, The Smashing Pumpkins effectively utilized shifts in dynamics, moving from loud to quiet passages within songs. They have been at the forefront of artistic and creative music video production (rather than merely using the format to obtain commercial success). The Smashing Pumpkins drew inspiration from a wild array of rock genres to create an uncompromising alternative sound all their own.

Jane's Addiction (1985-present with some inactive years) is an American rock band that formed in Los Angeles in 1985. Their current lineup is vocalist Perry Farrell, guitarist Dave Navarro, drummer Stephen Perkins, and bassist Chris Chaney. The 1987 self-titled debut album Jane's Addiction contained covers of The Velvet Underground and The Rolling Stones. However, it failed to chart. 1988's Nothing's Shocking grazed the charts at number one hundred and three, but word of mouth was strong and the band gained a steady and devoted following. 1990's Ritual de lo Habitual sold over four million copies and the band reached number nineteen on the American charts with hits such as "Stop!" and "Been Caught Stealing." Unfortunately, drug issues plagued Jane's Addiction and in late 1991, they promptly disbanded.

In 1994, guitarist Dave Navarro joined the Red Hot Chili Peppers. Then, along with bassist Flea, Navarro joined Porno for Pyros in 1997. That same year, Farrell, Perkins, Navarro, and Flea re-formed Jane's Addiction for a tour they called their "Relapse" tour. Flea soon returned to the Chili Peppers. Jane's Addiction reunited again for 2003's Strays, which fared well internationally. The band splintered again in late 2003 but returned eight years later in 2011 with The Great Escape Artist. This album featured David Andrew Sitek on bass. Shortly after, bassist Chris Chaney rejoined Jane's Addiction on a permanent basis (Chaney had played on Strays). Jane's Addiction was a pioneering alternative metal band with elements of funk and progressive rock. They have influenced many alternative and metal bands that included; The Smashing Pumpkins, Tool, Limp Bizkit, and Korn.

The 1990's into the 2000's was a successful period of time for alternative bands that could adapt and infuse different combinations of rock subgenres. 1990's prominent bands included; **Soul Coughing** (1992-2000), **Modest Mouse** (1992-present), and **Muse**. The 2000's featured significant bands such as; **The Killers**, **Artic Monkeys** (2002-present), and **Cage the Elephant** (2006-present).

Muse (1994-present) is a British rock band that formed in 1994. The lineup is vocalist Matt Bellamy, bassist/keyboardist Chris Wolstenholme, and drummer Dominic Howard. Muse spent their first few years rehearsing, honing their live show, and releasing two EP's. Their 1999 debut album, Showbiz, featured Bellamy's falsetto voice and the band's alternative sound. It reached number twenty-nine on the British charts. 2001's Origin of Symmetry revealed expanded instrumentation and some classical music influences. It made its way to number three in England. Muse followed with 2003's Absolution and 2006's Black Holes and Revelations. They continued to build their audience with punchy, dramatic songs while incorporating electronic timbres.

2009's The Resistance and 2012's The 2nd Law helped Muse to solidify their place as a worldwide stadium act. The Resistance yielded Muse a Grammy for Best Rock Album in 2011. 2015's Drones saw the band return to a harder rocking style by moving away from their signature orchestral and electronic sound. It was a concept album about drone warfare.

"Resistance"
by Matthew Bellamy

Matt Bellamy was heavily influenced by George Orwell's prophetic novel *1984* and its theme of a future repressive totalitarian regime. Bellamy had read the book

> "We (No Doubt) were making music that was the opposite of grunge and what was popular on the radio, and we were fine with that."
>
> – Gwen Stefani

when he was a student. He was first drawn to the political aspect of the work. Upon a second reading, he was moved by the romance side of the book and felt that the concept of love contained a sense of freedom from the oppression of society. The lyrics for "Resistance" were further guided by his belief that love can be a political act, especially when the state can't invade your privacy. Therefore, the song was really a love story.

Musically, "Resistance" utilized layers of synthesizers and a driving sixteenth-note feel. Bellamy multi-tracked his vocal parts, creating stacks of harmonies with his emotional voice. Bellamy is a powerful musical force, heard in his creative guitar and piano parts. Muse's strong orchestral timbres were combined with electronic sounds to continue some of the musical experimentation first pioneered by many British progressive rock bands. "Resistance" went to number three on the British charts, two places above another Muse hit, "Uprising."

The Killers (2001-present) are an American rock band that formed in Las Vegas, Nevada in 2001. The current lineup is vocalist/keyboardist Brandon Flowers, guitarist Dave Keuning, bassist/guitarist Mark Stoermer, and drummer Ronnie Vannucci, Jr. The Killers have recorded five successful albums including; 2004's Hot Fuss, 2006's Sam's Town, 2008's Day & Age, 2012's Battle Born, and 2017's Wonderful Wonderful. The later went to number one in both America and England. The band created an alternative style that combined indie rock, new wave and punk elements. The Killers are known for exciting concert performances. This was evident in their 2009 release, Live at the Royal Albert Hall. They have also headlined huge shows at London's Hyde Park in 2009 and 2011.

"Wonderful Wonderful"
by Brandon Flowers, Mark Stoermer, Ron Vannucci, and Jacknife Lee

"Wonderful Wonderful" revealed The Killers to be moving into darker territory than previously ventured. The Killers frontman, Brandon Flowers, wrote the song about his wife Tana's childhood trauma that she suffered as a result of PTSD (post-traumatic stress disorder). The song referenced Tana as a "motherless child" being rescued by the Mormon couple's faith. Flowers stated that the song served to bond he and his wife and deepen his compassion for her condition.

Musically, "Wonderful Wonderful" began with a haunting bass line in a minor key that created a dark mood. The drums added a pounding rhythm on tom-tom drums to capture a primal feel. The guitar and synth lines established an eerie mood that enabled the lyrics to paint a brooding soundscape. "Wonderful Wonderful" captured a gothic and post-punk feel with its menacing bassline and screechy and glitchy electronic effects. Flowers remembered that he was inspired to create the dark mood when he was in the desert and saw a storm approaching.

Mid-1980s to Present Alternative Pop Bands

Beginning in the mid-1980's, many alternative bands with a pop-rock sensibility had achieved commercial success. By utilizing elements of grunge, metal, punk, new wave, folk music, and even country music, these bands developed a unique voice that appealed to a larger pop audience. Some prominent **alternative pop** bands were **No Doubt, Crowed House** (1985-1996) (2006-2011) (2016), **Goo Goo Dolls** (1985-present), **Hootie and the Blowfish, and Barenaked Ladies** (1988-present).

No Doubt (1986-2004) (2009-present) is an American rock band that formed in Anaheim, California in 1986. The band consists of vocalist Gwen Stefani, bassist/multi-instrumentalist Tony Kanal, guitarist/multi-instrumentalist Tom Dumont, and drummer Adrian Young. Their 1992 self-titled debut album, No Doubt, featured a ska, grunge, and punk rock sound but met only limited success. Their 1995 The Beacon Street Collection and Tragic Kingdom saw No Doubt build their fan base and climb up the charts with their hit "Just a Girl." The band released Return of Saturn in 2000 and Rock Steady in 2001. However, Gwen Stafani decided to focus on her solo career in 2003. After a 2004 tour with Blink-182, No Doubt went on a hiatus. After a ten-year gap, the band released 2012's Push and Shove, completing a successful comeback. In the course of their career, No Doubt created a unique alternative rock approach. They skillfully mixed ska, punk, new wave, and Jamaican rocksteady styles with radio-friendly pop-rock melodies.

Hootie and the Blowfish (1986-2008) (currently on hiatus) is an American rock band that formed in Columbia, South Carolina in 1986. The current lineup is vocalist/guitarist Darius Rucker, guitarist/pianist Mark Bryan, bassist/pianist Dean Felber, and drummer Jim Sonefeld. Their five studio albums included; 1994's Cracked Rear View, 1996's Fairweather Johnson, 1998's Musical Chairs, 2003's Hootie & the Blowfish, and 2005's Looking for Lucky. Hootie and the Blowfish achieved a pop-rock sound that added blues-rock and jam band elements. Their Cracked Rear View was one of the best selling debut albums in rock history and yielded a series of hits including; "Hold My Hand," "Only Wanna Be with You," and "Let Her Cry." Hootie and the Blowfish went on hiatus in 2008 while Darius Rucker pursued a solo career as a country music artist.

"Only Wanna Be with You"
by Mark Bryan, Dean Felber, Darius Rucker, Jim Sonefeld, and Bob Dylan

"Only Wanna be with You" was a tribute to Bob Dylan. Dylan's response to the song was to successfully sue Hootie and the Blowfish for referencing three of his songs from his Blood on the Tracks album. Some of the lyrics came directly from Dylan's "Idiot Wind" song. Dylan received a large out of court settlement in 1995.

The video for "Only Wanna Be with You" featured the band interacting with former pro quarterback Dan Marino, former pro golfer Fred Couples, and some of the ESPN sports anchors. The song contained a catchy pop hook stated over a strumming acoustic guitar while electric guitar lines complemented the melody. The song suggested a country feel, foreshadowing Rucker's later move to a country music direction.

The 1990's into the 2000's saw more alternative pop bands emerge. The trend of mixing a variety of rock subgenres with commercial popular appeal continued. Some of these bands included; **Counting Crows, Creed** (1993-2004) (2009-2012), **3 Doors Down** (1996-present), **Death Cab for Cutie** (1997-present), **The All-American**

Rock Hard Fact

The Kings of Leon have used Wolfgang Amadeus Mozart's "Requiem in D Minor" for their "pre-show" music as they walk on stage.

Rejects (1999-present), **Kings of Leon**, and Arcade Fire (2001-present).

Counting Crows (1991-present) is an American rock band from Berkeley, California that formed in 1991. The band endured a few personnel changes but the current lineup is vocalist/pianist Adam Duritz, guitarist David Bryson, multi-instrumentalist Charlie Gillingham, bassist Millard Powers, multi-instrumentalist David Immergluck, guitarist Dan Vickrey, and drummer Jim Bogios. Adam Duritz began playing duo gigs with David Bryson around San Francisco in 1991. They formed Counting Crows and released their 1993 debut album August and Everything After. It sold over ten million copies worldwide (their most popular album to date).

"Round Here"
by The Himalayans and Counting Crows

Adam Duritz revealed that "Round Here" was autobiographical in nature and was about a guy who left his woman and other people in his life. The more he left behind, the more he began to feel he had left himself behind as well. By the end of the song, the central character was resentful about the good things that he was told would happen (they didn't happen) if he was well behaved as a child.

Musically, "Round Here" began with a simple electric guitar riff with Duritz singing about his childhood. A half-time drumset feel entered and the track built with support from the bass, guitar and an organ part. It later moved to a funky section before a breakdown section. "Round Here" dated back to Duritz's days in a band called the Himalayans. That band wrote most of "Round Here" and Duritz completed a new final version of it with Counting Crows. Both bands are credited with writing the song.

Counting Crows released six more studio albums from 1996's Recovering the Satellites to 2014's Somewhere Under Wonderland. Duritz is a master songwriter and the band is known for their ability to play covers from a wide array of artists. Since 2010, Duritz, Vickrey, and Bogios have been involved in a number of side projects. Counting Crows are an angst-filled hybrid of genres with influences from R.E.M. to Van Morrison to The Band. They have successfully blended an upbeat rock sound with mellow alternative country flavored songs to carve out their place in alternative rock.

Kings of Leon (1999-present) is an American rock band that formed in Nashville, Tennessee in 1999. The band consists of three brothers; vocalist/guitarist Calab Followill, bassist Jared Followill, drummer Nathan Followill, and their cousin guitarist Mathew Followill. Kings of Leon's style exhibited the early roots of blues and country rock but expanded to incorporate more alternative rock elements. The band initially found success in England where their 2003 debut album, Youth & Young Manhood, went to number three on the charts. 2004's Aha Shake Heartbreak broadened their fan base and 2007's darker and more expansive Because of the Times brought major success. It debuted at number one in Britain and number twenty-five in America. 2008's Only by the Night entered the British charts at number one and finally placed the Kings high on the American charts at number four. The singles "Sex on Fire" and "Use Somebody" were hits from the album.

"Sex on Fire"
by Kings of Leon

Lyrics about sex were not a typical songwriting focus for Kings of Leon. However, "Sex on Fire" was about what it sounds like, hot sex. Caleb Followill has said the lyrics were about a great sexual relationship that you would remember. Followill always felt that there was an element of sexuality in Kings of Leon's music and that this song would serve to sum it all up.

"Sex on Fire" had an aggressive hard rocking feel that began with a grungy guitar hook. The main guitar riff was played high up on the neck of the guitar. The additional layers of rhythm guitar parts created constant motion that helped to propel the vocal lines forward. "Sex on Fire" won a Grammy Award for best rock vocal performance by a duo or group. A remix of the song was utilized for the runway soundtrack for the 2009 *Victoria's Secret Fashion Show*.

After 2010's Come Around Sundown and a subsequent tour, the band released Mechanical Bull in 2013. 2016's WALLS was Kings of Leon's first number one album in America. Adding to their fan base, the band headlined a concert in London's Hyde Park in the summer of 2017. Kings of Leon have carved out their own unique brand of alternative rock. The Kings started with country and blues influences mixed with a garage band mentality. Over time, The Kings of Leon morphed into a more experimental alternative band.

Discussion Question

How does the genre of grunge music relate to punk rock both musically and culturally as seen in specific societal issues? Be specific and give examples.

"I'm Happy for those guys (Kings of Leon)... When I hear live drums and real guitars and people singing on the radio, it makes me feel that there's still hope for this world."

- Dave Grohl

Chapter Seventeen: Important Musical Styles That Mixed with Rock

Many artists have integrated multiple musical styles to achieve their unique direction in rock music. This chapter addresses some of these important musical styles and approaches including; **funk, rap, horn-rock bands, electronica, new innovations in metal,** and **guitar "slingers."** We also briefly explore the beginning of the **fusion music** genre.

Funk and Funk-Rock

The genre of **funk** has exerted a strong influence on rock music. Beginning in the 1960's, the legendary **James Brown** almost singlehandedly created funk out of the soul, gospel, rhythm and blues, and doo-wop styles of the 1950's and 1960's. Funk soon evolved from a number of different sources, from the New Orleans based **The Meters** to the commercially appealing **Sly and the Family Stone** (1966-1983) and **Parliament-Funkadelic** (1968-present). **Herbie Hancock and The Headhunters** (1973-2011 with some inactive years) added their groundbreaking funky approach coming from a jazz improvisation perspective.

James Brown (1933-2006) was an American singer/songwriter/producer and bandleader from Toccoa, Georgia. Brown began as a gospel vocalist with the Gospel Starlighters. He gained national attention in the late 1950's with rhythm and blues ballads "Please, Please, Please" and "Try Me." James Brown built a reputation as a relentless live performer (often called "the hardest working man in show business") next with The Famous Flames and then as the James Brown Orchestra. His career continued to develop through the 1960's with the album Live at the Apollo and more hits including "Papa's Got a Brand New Bag" and "It's a Man's Man's Man's World."

It was songs such as 1967's "Cold Sweat," 1968's "I Got the Feelin," and 1969's "Funky Drummer" that James Brown revolutionized music and created the genre of funk. Brown had an uncanny ability to conceptualize syncopated rhythms and express them to his rhythm section players. The interlocking parts of displaced drumset patterns, percussive guitar riffs, and melodic basslines were innovative in Brown's ensemble grooves. With the help of his brilliant saxophonist Maceo Parker, Brown's horn section added another funky and interlocking element to the sound. Nobody had ever heard this new style of funk before and his innovative approach would change music forever.

> "The essence of the funk is being loyal to the funk. Living by it 24 hours a day. It's the true universal language."
>
> – Flea

"Cold Sweat"
by James Brown and Pee Wee Ellis

"Cold Sweat" was recorded in May of 1967. It peaked at number seven on the pop singles chart and was a number one hit on the rhythm and blues charts. In the lyrics, Brown described how his woman's affections just make him "break out in a cold sweat." Like many of Brown's compositions, "Cold Sweat" evolved out of an earlier song. It came from the blues "I Don't Care," recorded five years prior. The groove, however, was a futuristic sonic and emotional adventure that Brown was only beginning to investigate. "Cold Sweat" would be the first of many great James Brown modal songs that reduced the significance of pitch and elevated the status of rhythm.

James Brown heard the parts for "Cold Sweat" in his musical mind and sang the bassline to his saxophonist Pee Wee Ellis. Meanwhile, Ellis was listening to a lot of Mile Davis at the time, including his composition "So What." Inspired by the "So What" horn line, Ellis arranged horn section parts for the song. Brown's guitarists, Jimmy Nolen and Alfonzo "Country" Kellum created highly percussive and interlocking guitar parts. "Cold Sweat" was built on a single chord with an emphasis on its hypnotic repetition. The true genius of the song was the drum part of Clyde Stubblefield that utilized the rhythmic technique of beat displacement over the bar line of a two-measure phrase. Barnard Odum's bassline created harmonic ambiguity over the dorian horn vamp by sustaining dissonant bass notes to develop movement and tension in the song. "Cold Sweat" was quite possibly the first true funk song. Initially, musicians were confused but ultimately inspired by the truly innovative "Cold Sweat."

James Brown endured a lot of drama and controversy in his lifetime but musically, he demanded precision and discipline from every version of his legendary band. He strove for perfection on every recording and live performance. James Brown had a staggering recording output that included; 63 studio albums, 15 live albums, 49 compilation albums, 7 video albums, 10 music videos, 2 soundtrack albums, and 144 singles. James Brown is revered as one of the most significant musicians of the 20th century. He received numerous awards and honors throughout his lifetime and after his death. James Brown was inducted into the Rock and Roll Hall of Fame in 1983.

The Meters (1965-1977) (1989-present) are an American funk band formed in New Orleans, Louisiana in 1965. The original lineup was vocalist/organist Art Neville, guitarist Leo Nocentelli, bassist George Porter Jr., and Joseph "Zigaboo" Modeliste. Later they added percussionist/vocalist Cyril Neville. After James Brown, The Meters are considered one of the originators of funk music. The Meter's sound is a brand of funk that evolved from their New Orleans heritage of highly syncopated "second-line" rhythms. They developed a unique ability to create sparse, interlocking guitar and organ riffs that meshed with Porter's basslines and Zigaboo's melodic approach of creating funky drumset parts.

The Meters began as the house band for Allen Toussaint and his record label, Sansu Enterprises. Their 1969 debut album, The Meters, yielded two rhythm and blues hits "Sophisticated Cissy" and Cissy Strut." That same year Look-Ka Py Py was released with the classics "Look-Ka Py Py," "Pungee," "Funky Miracle," and "Yeah, You're Right." Many of these songs were created when the band jammed on one of their signature grooves and tweaked it with a new instrumental vamp. The Meters often just improvised until they liked what they heard. Art Neville explained, "The Meters did a lot of free stuff, what I call organized freedom, but it was some special music. The Meters never did rehearse or practice-we just played."#1

> **Rock Hard Fact**
>
> James Brown was dismissed from school for not having sufficient clothes. He found work doing everything from shining shoes to janitorial work. By the end of the 1960's, Brown owned a publishing company; three radio stations, and a Learjet.

"Cissy Strut"
by The Meters

"Cissy Strut" was released as a single from The Meters debut album and reached number four on the r&b charts and number twenty-three on the pop charts. It became The Meters signature song and one of the defining songs in the history of the funk genre. The simple and catchy hook of the A section moved to an equally catchy hook in the B section. Art Neville played a short solo that emphasized the groove in a soulful way without looking to demonstrate instrumental virtuosity. "Cissy Strut," with its stripped down and sleek approach, showed what was possible when a band left space and let the music breathe.

Originally, the musicians that became The Meters frequently performed at a club on Bourbon Street where they were called Art Neville and the Neville Sounds. The band moved to another club called the Ivanhoe where they developed "Cissy Strut." George Porter explained, "We used to play 'Cissy Strut' as a break song at the Ivanhoe all the time. It was like the last thing you played in the set, and Art would have time to talk over it. I really don't know who played the lick first, me or Leo, because on a lot of the early stuff we were playing the same line, but it was done basically off a drum groove. Zig set up the lick, and we just played in between the spaces." #2

In the 1970's, The Meters released six more studio albums including; 1970's Struttin', 1972's Cabbage Alley, 1974's Rejuvenation, 1975's Fire on the Bayou, 1976's Trick Bag, and 1977's New Directions. By 1972, The Meters had worked for Dr. John, Paul McCartney, Robert Palmer, and others. Struttin' was their first record to feature vocal performances by Art Neville on three of the tracks. Rejuvenation was a high point for funk music with a fully mature Meters' sound fusing Mardi Gras, gospel, r&b, and country influences. Classic tracks included "People Say," "Just Kissed My Baby," "Hey Pocky A-Way," and "Africa." Guitarist Leo Nocentelli remarked, "Rejuvenation was my favorite out of all the albums that we've done. It showed the versatility in the musicians more than any of the traditional albums we did." #3

When Mick Jagger heard The Meters, he invited them to open for the Rolling Stones on their 1975 American tour and their 1976 tour of Europe. In many ways, The Meters were New Orleans to the core. Their approach defined funk with sparse interlocking parts but with a down home earthy quality. Despite their devoted cult following and enormous respect from high level musicians, The Meters never broke into the mainstream. Their sound, best heard live in a hot, sweaty New Orleans club, provided the basis for funk and hip-hop in the 1980's moving forward. The Meters (like James Brown) have been sampled by numerous rap artists including LL Cool J, Public Enemy, A Tribe Called Quest, Cypress Hill, and more. The Meters were nominated for induction into the Rock and Roll Hall of Fame in 2017.

By the early 1980's, a few innovative rock bands such as **Red Hot Chili Peppers** and **Living Colour** were inspired by the great funk masters of the past. The funk elements of displaced drumset feels, syncopated basslines, and hypnotic-like guitar ostinato patterns blended well with rock's aggressive attitude of loud and distorted guitars.

Red Hot Chili Peppers (1983-present) are an American **funk rock** band formed in Los Angeles, California in 1983. The current lineup is vocalist/guitarist Anthony Kiedis, bassist Flea, guitarist Josh Klinghoffer, and drummer Chad Smith. The Chili Peppers went through a number of lineup changes while developing their unique style of funk rock with the influences of punk, psychedelic, and jam band music. They sold over eighty million records worldwide making them one of the most popular bands in rock music history.

Red Hot Chili Peppers released their self-titled debut album The Red Hot Chili Peppers in 1984 and Freaky Styley in 1985. Both of these early efforts established the band's idiosyncratic funk-punk sound, fueled by Anthony Kiedis's semi rap-sung vocal approach. The debut album received airplay on college radio stations. However, exposure on MTV greatly added to their fan base. To get an authentic funk sound, The Chili Peppers enlisted funk legend George Clinton to produce Freaky Styley. James Brown sidemen Maceo Parker and Fred Wesley contributed to some of the album's tracks.

1987's The Uplift Mofo Party Plan was the band's last studio album to feature the four founding members including guitarist Hillel Slovak, drummer Jack Irons, Flea, and Kiedis. The album brought more success than their previous efforts, reaching gold status with its reggae and heavy metal influences. Shortly after its release, Slovak died of a drug overdose and Irons quit the band. For 1989's Mother's Milk, the band regrouped with the addition of guitarist John Frusciante and drummer Chad Smith. This recording transformed The Chili Peppers from limited underground notoriety to mainstream success with the hits "Knock Me Down" and a cover of Stevie Wonder's "Higher Ground."

1991's Blood Sugar Sex Magik launched Red Hot Chili Peppers into international stardom. The album has sold over twelve million copies and featured the hits "Give It Away" and "Under the Bridge."

Groundbreaking album
Blood Sugar Sex Magik
by Red Hot Chili Peppers

The second time proved to be the charm when super-producer Rick Rubin (who had previously turned the band down) agreed to produce Blood Sugar Sex Magik. Rubin was very involved with shaping the album's drumset feels, guitar melodies, and even the lyrics. The Chili Peppers wanted to record the album in an unconventional setting in the hope of enhancing their creative process. So they set up a recording studio in the house that magician Harry Houdini had once occupied. The band documented the creative process of recording the album and had Flea's brother-in-law film the sessions. They later released the film, which they titled *Funky Monks*.

The seventeen tracks on the album were "The Power of Equality," then "If You Have to Ask," "Breaking the Girl," "Funky Monks," "Suck My Kiss," "I Could Have Lied," "Mellowship Slinky in B Major," "The Righteous & the Wicked," "Give It Away," "Blood Sugar Sex Magik," "Under the Bridge," "Naked in the Rain," "Apache Rose Peacock," "The Greeting Song," "My Lovely Man," "Sir Psycho Sexy," and "They're Red Hot."

The first single, "Give It Away," contained a The Chili Peppers' funky guitar riff that was repeated throughout the verse while Flea added a complex bassline. Kiedis's lyrics were about being selfless and generous with your possessions. On other songs, including "Suck My Kiss" and "Sir Psycho Sexy," Kiedis focused on sexual references and strong innuendos.

"Under the Bridge," the second single from the album, featured a superbly crafted melody that would become one of the band's defining songs in the 1990's.

On Blood Sugar Sex Magik, Flea moved away from his well-known slapping technique in favor of more melodic basslines. The band also utilized less jamming and focused on developing songs with more structure. John Frusciante's guitar parts were clean and dry, adding to a noticeably more focused overall band sound. The composite effect of blending soul, funk, blues, and even acid-rock styles redefined The Chili Peppers approach. This recording brought the Red Hot Chili Peppers sound to a new level moving forward. Blood Sugar Sex Magik became a cornerstone of the funk rock genre.

1995's One Hot Minute was recorded with guitarist and founding member of Jane's Addiction, Dave Navarro. The album yielded three hits but failed to match the commercial sales expectations of Blood Sugar Sex Magik. Navarro introduced more heavy metal riffs into the Chili Peppers approach but was ultimately fired in 1998 due to creative differences. With the band on the brink of a breakup, Frusciante returned to The Chili Peppers to help record 1999's Californication. This became the band's most successful recording (to date) selling over sixteen million copies worldwide. The album was less rap-driven and contained the hits "Scar Tissue," "Otherside," and "Californication."

"Californication"
by Kiedis, Smith, Flea, and Frusciante

"Californication" was a song about the deterioration of society and how the world was becoming a very superficial environment, much like the movie industry in California. The song also made references to pornography, moon landing conspiracy theories, and even some pop culture references including mention of Kurt Cobain and David Bowie. After Kiedis had written the lyrics, The Chili Peppers had difficulty deciding how the song should sound musically.

Frusciante and Flea both contributed sparse combinations of guitar and bass notes for the song's main riff. In support of the dark lyrics, the song began in A minor and after the second chorus; Frusciante modulated to A major and played a sixteen-bar guitar solo before returning to A minor. Kiedis in describing "Californication" said, "I love very much the guitar solo in the middle of 'Californication,' because it seems like just the perfect amount of notes to tell a story during that song. When I listen to that guitar solo, it speaks to me in kind of a non-verbal language." #4

Since the early 2000's, The Chili Peppers established themselves as a stadium filling force, especially in England and the rest of Europe. The Chili Peppers released By the Way in 2002. 2006's Stadium Arcadium reached number one in England and America with Rick Rubin once again in charge of production. After their 2006-2007 Stadium Arcadium World Tour, the band went on hiatus. By 2009, Frusciante left again to pursue his solo career and guitarist Josh Klinghoffer joined The Chili Peppers. 2011's I'm with You, and most recently, 2016's The Gataway, have extended the longevity of the band.

The Chili Peppers have reached a musical maturity that came from years of musical exploration. Flea remarked, "As I learn more about music, I become less and less interested in doing anything fancy. Sometimes

> "I think there is always going to be inspired music. There are always going to be inspired listeners and there is always going to be an inspired method of getting it from A to B."
>
> – Anthony Kiedis

the simplest, boring little thing will make the song sound the best. I've become more about just serving the song, and less about 'Hey, I can play some really amazing, trippy bass lines that will blow your mind." #5 Red Hot Chili Peppers broke musical barriers in the 1980's by creating an intoxicating hybrid of funk and punk and expressed it in their explosive live performances. Red Hot Chili Peppers were inducted into the Rock and Roll Hall of Fame in 2012.

Living Colour (1984-1995) (2000-present) formed in New York City, New York in 1984. After a number of different members, the permanent lineup became vocalist/guitarist Vernon Reid, vocalist/guitarist Corey Glover, bassist/guitarist and programmer Doug Wimbish, and drummer/keyboardist Will Calhoun. Living Colour creates a unique fusion of funk, hard rock, heavy metal, hip-hop, jazz, country, and alternative rock styles. Their 1988 debut album, Vivid, shot to number six on the U.S. charts and contained a few hits including "Cult of Personality." On the heels of their debut album, Living Colour was named Best New Artist at the 1989 MTV *Video Music Awards*.

"Cult of Personality"
by Corey Glover, Vernon Reid, Muzz Skillings, and Will Calhoun

"Cult of Personality" contained a highly political statement that began with an edited speech by Malcolm X. His words appeared in the song as "And during the few moments that we have left…We want to talk right down to earth in a language that everybody here can easily understand." Later in the song, a line from John F. Kennedy's inaugural address is heard "Ask not what your country can do for you." The lyrics also referred to Frank D. Roosevelt, Benito Mussolini, Joseph Stalin, and Mahatma Gandhi.

Musically, the "Cult of Personality" was written in a single rehearsal session by the entire band. Living Colour stumbled onto a funky riff that also drew from heavy metal. The band skillfully extended the riff to answer the vocal phrases throughout the song. Drummer Will Calhoun brought a funky, yet no nonsense hard rocking drumset feel to the song. Vernon Rein took a blistering wah-wah guitar solo and nailed it on the first take. "Cult of Personality" won a Grammy Award for Best Hard Rock Performance in 1990.

1990's Time's Up also won a Grammy and featured songs that drew from jazz, fusion, punk rock, blues, hip-hop, thrash metal, and funk. Guests included Maceo Parker and the legendary Little Richard. The album peaked at number thirteen on the U.S. charts. After 1992's Stain, Living Colour disbanded citing a lack of common musical goals and the desire to pursue solo efforts. The band re-formed in late 2000 and has released three more studio albums including 2017's Shade. Living Colour broke down racial barriers in the 1980's that largely excluded ethnically diverse bands. This led, in part, to a racially more open minded musical landscape that would later open doors for bands such as Rage Against the Machine.

Spin Doctors (1988-1999) (2001-present) are a rock band from New York City that formed in 1988. The current lineup is vocalist Chris Barron, guitarist/vocalist Eric Schenkman, bassist Mark White, and drummer Aaron Comess. The origin of Spin Doctors dates back to the late 1980's, when the band was called Trucking Company with vocalist John Popper. He left to play full time with Blues Traveler and along with a name change to Spin Doctors, the band added Comess and White.

Their 1991 debut album, Pocket Full of Kryptonite, featured the hits, "Two Princes" and "Little Miss Can't Be Wrong." This album established Spin Doctors sound to be both funky and pseudo-hippie in a jam band oriented style. Pocket Full of Kryptonite was well received, selling millions of albums worldwide. Spin Doctors built a steady fan base with more releases in the 1990's including 1994's Turn It Upside Down, 1996's You've Got to Believe in Something, and 1999's Here Comes the Bride. In the early 2000's, the band was inactive until they made some sporadic live performances beginning in 2002. Spin Doctors released Nice Talking to Me in 2005 and If the River Was Whiskey in 2013.

"Two Princes"
by Spin Doctors

For the song "Two Princes," vocalist Chris Barron was inspired by literature such as *The Lord of the Rings, The Hobbit*, and *Sir Gagain and the Green Knight*. As a child, Barron was intrigued by wizards, kings and queens, and princess and princesses. This allowed him to gravitate toward the kind of imagery experienced in those time periods. In "Two Princes," Barron sang from the perspective of a poor prince who tried to convince a girl that she should marry him instead of another man who was wealthy.

Musically, "Two Princes" featured a hypnotic and funky drumset feel by Aaron Comess. Spin Doctors slowed down the original tempo at the time they recorded it which helped to establish the right feel for the lyrics. Barron's vocal lines, over a combined Comess drumset feel and Schenkman rhythm guitar part, fueled one of the funkiest tunes to ever hit classic rock radio. Spin Doctors performed a parody of "Two Princes" on *Sesame Street* where Elmo and Telly were portrayed as two princes that ask for a play date. This song was also featured in the Sarah Silverman episode, *Maid to Border*, as the only song her friend and neighbor had on his iPod.

Lenny Kravitz (1964-) is an American singer/songwriter, actor, and producer. His musical style has been referred to as "retro," meaning he fused rock, blues, soul, jazz, pop, folk, r&b, and funk elements. Kravitz's 1989 debut album, Let Love Rule, successfully combined rock and funk with a 1960's sound. It reached number sixty-one on the U.S. charts. His 1991 album, Mama Said, yielded the hit "It Ain't Over 'til It's Over." Kravitz cemented his star status by producing Madonna's "Justify My Love," writing a song for Aerosmith called "Line Up," and by appearing on a Mick Jagger solo album. However, it was his 1993 release, Are You Gonna Go My Way, that became his first top twenty album in America. Other Kravitz hits included "Fly Away" and a cover version of The Guess Who's "American Woman." From 1995 to 2017, Lenny Kravitz recorded nine more studio albums and has appeared in a number of movies, including the first two *Hunger Games* films.

"Are You Gonna Go My Way"
by Lenny Kravitz and Craig Ross

"Are You Gonna Go My Way" was a song Lenny Kravitz wrote about Jesus Christ, who he referred to "the ultimate rock star." The lyrics referred to how God gave choices to man about where to turn to in life. Kravitz has said that he and guitarist Craig Ross wrote the song while jamming in the studio. It was done in five minutes and Kravitz later wrote the lyrics on a brown paper bag. A diverse mix of artists including Metallica, The Spice Girls, and Adam Lambert have covered the song.

"Are You Gonna Go My Way" frequently drew comparisons to Jimi Hendrix for its guitar distortion and driving feel that was reminiscent of Hendrix's "Purple Haze." Kravitz performed the song on *Saturday Night Live* in 1993 and two months later, it reached number one on the American charts. Kravitz's guitar sound on "Are You Gonna Go My Way" also won a MTV Video Award for Best Male Video in which Kravitz appeared with dreadlocks and high-heeled platform boots.

Rap-Rock

Out of the cultural, social, and political unrest of the 1970's, the styles of **hip-hop** and **rap** saw the rise of innovative artists such as **Grandmaster Flash** and the **Sugarhill Gang's** 1980 megahit "Rapper's Delight." Rap began to connect to rock music with the music of **Afrika Bambaataa**, whose style was influenced by the German band Kraftwerk's electronic rhythms. Bambaataa teamed up with Soulsonic Force to create early 1980's hip-hop songs including the hit "Planet Rock." Hip-hop continued to break new ground in the 1980's. **Run-D.M.C.** burst onto the rap scene in 1984 and their 1986 album Raising Hell combined with rappers **2 Live Crew**, whose album As Nasty as They Wanna Be, took rap in new directions. By the late 1980's, artists such as **Public Enemy** and **N.W.A.** were developing a politically charged style of rap music.

The hybrid style of **rap-rock** was born when rock artists were inspired to rap their vocals rather than sing them. In addition, the rhythms of rap-rock drew from both hip-hop and funk styles. Many rap artists including; LL Cool J, Public Enemy, Eminem, Ice-T, Vanilla Ice, and The Fat Boys soon utilized samples derived from *rock songs*. **The Beastie Boys,** and **Cypress Hill** were among the first to be described as alternative hip-hop artists and rap-rock artists. Run-D.M.C. and Aerosmith's (see chapter eleven) 1986 remix of "Walk This Way," was a pioneering cross-style collaboration. The success of this remix brought a hip-hop audience together with a mainstream rock audience. Red Hot Chili Peppers had featured Anthony Kiedis rapping on the band's 1984 self-titled debut album. In 1991, thrash metal band Anthrax (see chapter ten) collaborated with hip-hop artists Public Enemy on a version of the latter's "Bring the Noise." On this innovative track, Anthrax's Scott Ian and Public Enemy's Chuck D shared the rapping vocals over a heavy guitar and bass riff. Public Enemy was at it again with their song "She Watch Channel Zero?!" and featured Chuck D rapping over a riff from the Slayer tune "Angel of Death."

The Beastie Boys (1981-2012) were originally a hardcore punk band called the Young Aborigines. After a few lineup changes, vocalist/bassist Adam "MCA" Yauch, vocalist/drummer Michael "Mike D" Diamond, and vocalist/guitarist Adam "Ad-Rock" Horovitz formed The Beastie Boys in 1981. The Beastie Boys achieved some success in 1983 with a single "Cooky Puss." After opening for Madonna on a 1985 tour, they released their debut album Licensed to Ill, in 1986. A single from the album titled "(You Gotta) Fight for Your Right (to Party)" reached number seven on the U.S. charts and became one of their defining songs. They went on to release seven more studio albums. The Beastie Boys were pioneers in the rap rock genre. They crossed racial barriers as a white band that gained respect in the African-American urban music genre of hip-hop. The Beasties went on to achieve great success by selling over fifty million albums worldwide. The Beastie Boys were inducted into the Rock and Roll Hall of Fame in 2012.

"(You Gotta) Fight for Your Right (to Party)"
by The Beastie Boys, Rick Rubin, and Tom Cushman

"You Gotta Fight" began as a parody of dumb rock songs. The Beastie Boys first recorded the song as a joke, but the video they made presented a drunken party boy image that launched them to superstardom. Legendary producer Rick Rubin exposed the Beasties to hard rock bands like AC/DC. Rubin also directed The Beastie Boys to add a big drum and guitar sound to the rapping lyrics. The Beasties and Rubin captured an overwhelming power where hard rock and punk met rap head on.

The song became a radio hit before the now famous video (for the song) ever hit the TV market. MTV knew it would appeal to their base audience of young males, so they put the video in heavy rotation as soon as production on it was finished. When the video was first aired, the song surged in popularity. "Fight for Your Right" became a party anthem and revealed The Beastie Boys as transcendent to race, gender, and social economic divisions. In the video, modeled after a scene from the 1963 movie *Breakfast at Tiffany's*, the band members crashed a party for nerds and geeks. They trashed the place and escaped with beer and beautiful girls. The video resulted in a great mixture of humor, satire, and The Beastie's hard driving rap lyrics.

Cypress Hill (1988-present) is an American hip-hop group from California that formed in 1988. The band was started by Senen Reyes (AKA Sen Dog), his brother Ulpiano Sergio Reyes (AKA Mellow Man Ace), Lawrence Muggerud (AKA DJ Muggs), and Louis Freese (AKA B-Real). Together, they formed the hip-hop group DVX (Devastating Vocal Excellence). Mellow Man Ace soon left to pursue a solo career. They soon changed their name to Cypress Hill and went on to represent West Coast rap and achieve great popularity, selling over eighteen million albums worldwide. Cypress Hill mixed their rap style with rock rhythms and a heavier sound on their fifth album, 2000's Skull and Bones. This recording featured Chino Moreno of the Deftones and Brad Wilk of Rage Against the Machine. The band continued their fusion of rap with rock on their 2001 album Stoned Raiders. One of Cypress Hill's defining musical characteristics was B-Real's high-pitched nasal vocal sound. In addition, both B-Real and Sen Dog wrote lyrics in Spanish and English. Some of Cypress Hill's songs moved in a rap metal direction and others exhibited a hardcore rap style with an angry and aggressive style. Cypress Hill has released a total of nine studio albums.

Rap rock continued to enter the rock mainstream throughout the 1990's and into the 2000's. The rock artists **Hed PE** (1994-present), **Kid Rock, Rage Against the Machine,** and **Faith No More** (see chapter sixteen) fused hip-hop and rock. **Limp Bizkit** and **Linkin Park** followed them in the mid-1990's. Two spin-off bands of Rage Against the Machine were **Audioslave**, who took an alternative metal approach, and **Prophets of Rage**, who continued in the rap-rock tradition.

Kid Rock (1971-) (AKA Robert James Ritchie) is an American vocalist/rapper and songwriter from

> "The younger generation is supposed to rage against the machine, not for it. They're supposed to question authority, not question those who question authority."
>
> – Bill Maher, comedian/political commentator

Detroit, Michigan. His first five albums, including his 1990 debut, Grits Sandwiches for Breakfast, were rap and hip-hop based. In 1999, Kid Rock embarked on his first major tour, opening for Limp Bizkit. His rock style began to draw more from a wider range of musical genres including; rap-rock, metal, country, hip-hop, and even nu metal. Rock's 2001 Cocky was his first album to feature the blues and country genres. 2007's Rock 'n' Roll Jesus became his first number one album on the U.S. charts with the lead single "So Hott," reaching number two. In 2015, Kid Rock released his first all country record titled First Kiss. He has released a total of eleven studio albums including his latest, 2017's Sweet Southern Sugar. A Sheryl Crow/Kid Rock duet, titled "Picture," initialized Kid Rock's transformation from a rap-rocker to a country musician. This has put him in the unique position of being an innovator in the hybrid style of rap-country. Prominent country musicians who have occasionally borrowed from Kid Rock's rap-country influence are Toby Keith, Trace Adkins, and Blake Shelton.

Rage Against the Machine (1991-2000) (2007-2011) (hiatus) is an American rap-rock band from Los Angeles, California that formed in 1991. The lineup is rapper/vocalist Zack de la Rocha, guitarist Tom Morello, bassist Tim Commerford, and drummer Brad Wilk. Rage became known for their ground breaking rap-rock style and political activism. The band derived their name from a song that de la Rocha had written for his former hardcore punk band, Inside Out. Tom Morello came to the band after honing his hard-hitting guitar style in his former band, Lock Up.

Rage's self-titled 1992 Rage Against the Machine was both innovative and uncompromising. This album described Rage's view of the modern world to be media-driven and governed by a callous military-industrial complex. Rage reached a generation of fans in much the same way that Nirvana spoke to their generation. Anthrax's Scott Ian recognized the innovation of Rage when he said, "Rage Against the Machine were the ones who created the whole rap-metal genre. 'Bring the Noise' was collaboration between a metal band and a rap band. It wasn't one band creating something new. Whereas, when Rage came out, they weren't like anybody else. They took something organic and they made the Rage Against the Machine sound. We might have opened the door, but they drove the f***ing truck through it." #6

Groundbreaking album
Rage Against the Machine
by Rage Against the Machine

Rage's debut album was one of the first albums to successfully merge the vocal qualities of rap with the overwhelming force of heavy metal. The subject matter was delivered with undeniable conviction and an uncompromising political consciousness. The album cover featured a photo of the self-immolation of Thich Quang Durc, a Vietnamese Buddhist monk in Saigon in 1963. This album cover was representative of how each song on the album contained political messages.

Rage Against the Machine opened with "Bombtrack," then "Killing in the Name," "Take the Power Back," "Settle for Nothing," "Bullet in the Head," "Know Your Enemy," "Wake Up," "Fistful of Steel," "Township Rebellion," and "Freedom." The song "Bullet in the Head" referred to Rage's belief that the American government used media to control the population. This song featured one of Tom Morello's best-known riffs along with his innovative guitar techniques including the use of the Digitech whammy pitch shifter and wah-wah pedal effects. "Bombtrack" focused on social inequality. "Freedom" had an accompanying video that revealed the case of Leonard Peltier (a leader of the American Indian Movement) who was convicted for the murder of FBI agents in a controversial 1975 conflict on the Pine Ridge Indian Reservation. "Know Your Enemy" featured Tool vocalist Maynard James Keenan and percussion by Stephen Perkins. Rage Against the Machine made a statement in the album sleeve notes stating that no samples, keyboards, or synthesizers were used in the making of the record.

The creative relationship of Tom Morello's hard-hitting riffs and Zack de la Rocha's vocal delivery of meaningful rhymes with emotionally charged conviction found an undeniable chemistry. Rage's approach would later inspire many nu metal bands. Morello took the venomous "Wake Up" and created a Jimmy Page like riff that exploded with sheer power. The album Rage Against the Machine sent at least four songs to regular rotation on MTV and mainstream radio. This was a remarkable achievement given the graphic language and blistering anger heard in these compositions.

"Killing in The Name"
by Rage Against the Machine

"Killing in The Name" was about institutional racism and police brutality. It became known as the band's signature song and for its profanity laced lyrics. The lyrics were an expletive-driven tirade against what was wrong with American society. The song built with intensity when Zack de La Rocha chanted "F*** you, I won't do what you tell me" seventeen times. The song also alleged that some American policemen were members of the Ku Klux Klan. This reflected the growing racial tension that existed in America. British DJ Bruno Brookes accidentally played the uncensored version of the song on the BBC Radio 1 Top-40 Chart show.

Musically, "Killing in The Name" featured a guitar riff that Tom Morello found while teaching a student to play a drop D tuning (where the lowest guitar string was tuned down from the usual E note to a D note). He then recorded the idea on his Fender Telecaster. Brad Wilk's heavy and funky drumset feel, along with Tim Commerford's forceful bassline, gave "Killing in The Name" a dose of brute force. This song introduced Rage's melding of hard rock and punk with the hip-hop influence of Dr. Dre and Public Enemy styled vocals.

Despite rumors of an eminent breakup, Rage Against the Machine recorded Evil Empire in 1996. It debuted on the American charts at number one. 1999's The Battle of Los Angeles also went straight to number one. Rage released a collection of covers on 2000's Renegades that included Cypress Hill rappers Sen Dog and B-Real. However, Rage was feeling internal tension and called it quits in September of 2000. After the breakup, Morello, Wilk, and Commerford reorganized and added (then former Soundgarden frontman) Chris Cornell to form Audioslave (see Audioslave in this section). Meanwhile, de la Rocha worked on developing his solo career.

Rage Against the Machine reunited in 2007 and toured the United States, Japan, New Zealand, and Australia. In late 2009, two Rage fans named Jon and Tracy Morter (husband and wife), launched a plea on the social media site Facebook. They encouraged fans to

---

"Emotionally, I was affected a lot by Rage Against the Machine, not specifically the literal intention of the words or what it was about, but the feel, the sound, those phrases that got me."

– Fred Durst

buy "Killing in the Name" to prevent the winner of the *X Factor* TV show from achieving the Christmas number one slot in Britain for a fifth consecutive year. Rage took the top chart spot and in June of 2010, they performed a free 'thank you' concert for 40,000 fans in Finsbury Park, a public park in London. The profits from the sale of "Killing in The Name" were donated to the charity Just Giving.

Rage Against the Machine released a 20th anniversary box set in 2012. In 2014, drummer Brad Wilk announced that a previous show from 2011 might have been their last performance ever. In May of 2016, a new supergroup, Prophets of Rage (see in this section), had formed including; Morello, Wilk, Commerford, Chuck D of Public Enemy, and B-Real of Cypress Hill. Rage Against the Machine represented a new music recipe that blended; one part funk, one part heavy metal and punk, and one part Hendrix/Led Zeppelin. Rage's political stance was an aggressive, unrelenting attack of leftist rants against corporate America, cultural imperialism, and government oppression. Their innovative sound was combined with politically charged messages and delivered with brute force. Rage Against the Machine was the *defining* rap-rock band.

Limp Bizkit (1994-2006) (2009-present) is an American rap-rock band from Jacksonville, Florida that began in 1994. After playing with a number of bands in the Jacksonville area, vocalist Fred Durst combined his two passions of metal and hip-hop to form Limp Bizkit. The initial lineup was Durst, bassist Sam Rivers, drummer John Otto, guitarist Wes Borland, and turntablist DJ Lethal. Programmer/sampler Franko Carino also works with the band. Limp Bizkit's 1997 debut, Three Dollar Bill, Y'all$, revealed their intentionally angry, abrasive sound and found an enthusiastic fan base. 1999's Significant Other debuted on the U.S. charts at number one. The accompanying video for their song "Nookie" made them superstars. Controversy followed when Limp Bizkit performed at the Woodstock '99 Festival, where riots unfortunately occurred. Durst was criticized for inciting an already rowdy crowd. Durst also became an outspoken advocate for online music trading when Napster faced online pirating accusations in 2000.

2000's Chocolate Starfish and the Hot Dog Flavored Water brought more mainstream success to Limp Bizkit. Wes Borland left in 2001 (he returned in 2005). He was replaced by guitarist Mike Smith for 2003's Results May Vary and subsequent tours. After 2005's The Unquestionable Truth (Part 1), Limp Bizkit went on a hiatus. The band returned for a comeback album, 2011's Gold Cobra, which restored them to the U.S. top twenty. Limp Bizkit is currently working on a new album to be called Stampede of the Disco Elephants. Limp Bizkit has managed to infuse their rap-rock musical base with nu metal and even neo-psychedelic elements. Drummer John Otto has contributed Brazilian and Afro-Cuban rhythms as well as funky grooves to the band's collective sound. Various controversies and Fred Durst's outspoken viewpoints have raised the band's profile. Limp Bizkit was an important catalyst for bringing rap-rock from the 1999's to the 2000's.

Linkin Park (1996-present) is an American band from Agoura Hills, California. The band lineup consists of vocalist/guitarist Mike Shinoda, vocalist Chester Bennington, guitarist Brad Delson, bassist Phoenix Farrell, drummer Rob Bourdon, and programmer/keyboardist Joe Hahn. Linkin Park fused rap-metal with nu metal in a radio-friendly approach that brought them instant success. Their 2000 debut Hybrid Theory peaked at number two on the U.S. charts, sold over eleven million copies worldwide, and became the best-selling album of the year 2000.

"In the End"
by Linkin Park

"In the End" was about a fifteen-year old boy, Charles Andrew Williams, who in March of 2001, shot and killed two of his classmates at his high school in Santee, California. In the attempt to explain his feelings, Williams wrote in a note "I tried so hard and got so far, but in the end, it doesn't really matter." Linkin Park used this line in the song's lyrics. The song was originally about feeling that there was no point to living. A haunting piano melody opened the track (and ended it) and moved to a rapping background vocal. The track built momentum with a funky drumset feel and distorted guitars.

The music video for "In the End" was shot at various points along Linkin Park's appearances at the 2001 Ozzfest tour. Although the video's background was filmed on location in a California desert, the band filmed their performance on a studio stage in Los Angeles. This allowed Joe Hahn and director Nathan Cox to set off water pipes above the stage to drench the band. The video was ultimately viewed in a positive light, beginning with a very bleak and depressing desert scene. However, the mood of the video changed when the rain came and there were flowers and rivers.

A relentless tour schedule confirmed Linkin Park's international status and 2003's Meteora sold over twenty-seven million copies worldwide. Meteora contained nu metal and rap metal styles with innovative effects and lyrics about depression, anger, and loneliness. For 2007's Minutes to Midnight, Linkin Park brought in production master Rick Rubin. 2010's A Thousand Suns extended the band's defiance of commercial trends. 2017's One More Light featured a pop music focus and was self-produced. Critics accused the band of selling out but many Linkin Park fans have praised their effort to branch out in new directions. Long after the peak of the nu metal genre, Linkin Park has retained their international popularity.

The Fight Over the Censorship of Rock Lyrics

Rock music has captured the attention and respect of young people since the earliest appearances of Elvis Presley, Chuck Berry, and The Beatles. Many young fans have been passionately devoted to and influenced by their favorite rock artists and their songs. Therefore, the lyrical content of rock music is invariable contentious. Many people have placed the blame for juvenile delinquency, promotion of casual sex, drug abuse, and even suicide on uncensored rock lyrics. The issue of censorship has centered on the conflict between artists who challenged the boundaries of free expression and the establishment that strove to enforce those boundaries. Proponents of uncensored lyrics cited the first amendment of the United States Constitution that protects the right to freedom of speech and free press. Specifically, the First Amendment decrees that "Congress shall make no law" abridging these rights. In that strict sense, only government suppression or punishment of protected speech qualifies as censorship. Examples of this are the obscenity and indecency rules in broadcasting that is enforced by the Federal Communications Com-

---

> "Rap music is the only vital form of music introduced since punk rock."
>
> - Kurt Cobain

Rock Hard Fact

Linkin Park was rejected forty-four times by record companies before finally getting signed by Warner Brothers Records, who had previously turned them down three times. Later, Linkin Park became the first rock band to achieve over one billion hits on YouTube.

mission (FCC). The blacklisting of artists concerning censorship has stretched back to early folk singers. Pete Seeger and The Weavers were targeted amid the anti-Communist fervor of the 1950's.

The advent of rock 'n' roll, with its sweeping stereotype of sexually stimulating, morally degrading, and obscene lyrics caused a number of radio stations to drop rock as an acceptable format. Elvis was permitted to be filmed from only the waist up. At some of his live shows, police threatened to arrest Elvis on obscenity charges if he kept gyrating his hips. In the 1960's, suggestive songs, such as the Rolling Stones "(I Can't Get No) Satisfaction," and provocative stage shows by artists from Little Richard to Jim Morrison, were strictly criticized by members of the moral establishment. As rock evolved in the 1970's and 1980's, stars like Ozzy Osbourne, Madonna, and Prince were extremely controversial with their live performances and lyrical content. From the punk styled Sex Pistols' "God Save the Queen" to Madonna's pop song "Like a Prayer," rock received tremendous criticism.

In 1985, activist Tipper Gore (and others) formed the Parents Music Resource Center (PMRC) to screen their children's musical selections for objectionable content. In Senate hearings, Gore and other PMRC representatives proposed a rating system for popular music similar to that applied to the movie industry. Representing the right for free expression was Frank Zappa and other well-known musicians. They were adamant that the proposal would constitute illegal censorship. No legislation resulted from the hearings, but a deal was made between the PMRC and the Recording Industry Association of America (RIAA). The industry agreed to attach warning stickers to albums with explicit content to identify strong language or references to sex, drugs, and violence. This has evoked an ongoing censorship fight between artists, their record labels, and the public.

The focus of the controversy over explicit lyrics and warning labels began to move from the mostly white musical genres of rock, punk, and heavy metal to the emerging African-American genres of hip-hop and rap. Many rap artists brought lyrical profanity to a new level and some "gangsta rap" encouraged violence and misogyny. For example, the group N.W.A. released its 1988 debut album Straight Outta Compton, with the song "F*** Tha Police" (protesting racial profiling). The FBI contacted N.W.A. and its record label to express disapproval for the derogatory portrayal of police officers. Many artists continue to exercise their right to free speech from 2 Live Crew to Rage Against the Machine and others. The battle for uncensored expression in rock music (and all of the arts) remains a relevant issue.

Audioslave (2001-2007) (2017) combined Rage Against the Machine former members Tom Morello, Brad Wilk, and Tim Commerford with former Soundgarden vocalist Chris Cornell. Audioslave was in a position to reach for a new musical direction moving from the rap-rock of Rage supplemented by the unique voice of Cornell. Audioslave moved in a 1970's hard rock meets 1990's alternative metal direction. 2002's Audioslave sold over three million copies in the U.S. and featured the hit "Cochise." The album was compared to a style reminiscent of 1970's Black Sabbath. 2005's Out of Exile went to number one on the U.S. charts and was nominated for a Grammy Award for Best Hard Rock Performance in 2006. Audioslave released their third and final album, Revelations in 2006. Audioslave effectively explored different musical territory, especially by composing slower and more melodic material. Audioslave was the beneficiary of the masterful production skills of Rick Rubin on their first two recordings.

Chris Cornell left the band with personal issues shortly after Revelations was released. Audioslave then went on hiatus. Cornell decided to delay an Audioslave tour until 2007 and concentrate on his second solo album. Audioslave disbanded in 2007 and Cornell eventually reunited with Soundgarden in 2010. Rage Against the Machine reunited in 2007 with all four of the original members. Audioslave did a reunion concert in 2017, just four months before the tragic death of Chris Cornell.

Prophets of Rage (2016-present) is *the* supergroup of rap-rock that formed in 2016 with personnel from three major bands. The Prophets' lineup includes former Rage Against the Machine and Audioslave members guitarist Tom Morello, bassist Tim Commerford, and drummer Brad Wilk. Add in rapper Chuck D and DJ Lord from the legendary hip-hop group Public Enemy, and rapper B-Real, from the rap-rock band Cypress Hill. Prophets exhibit the socially conscious and political stance of Rage, the fearlessness of Public Enemy, and the threatening persona of Cypress Hill. Prophets of Rage made their performance debut in the spring of 2016 in Los Angeles performing Rage Against the Machine hits mixed with a few Public Enemy songs and a Cypress Hill medley. The band's debut EP, The Party's Over, was released in the summer of 2016. Prophets of Rage released their self-titled debut Prophets of Rage in 2017. It reached number six in Britain and number sixteen in America. Guitarist Tom Morello has stated that the intent of Prophets of Rage was to work as a group of revolutionary musicians determined to confront the current political establishment.

Discussion Question

Should the issue of censorship in rock and rap lyrics be a legal issue for the courts to handle? Or should the issue be about societal values and cultural morality? Or should lyrics not be subject to any censorship? Take a position and provide specific examples.

Jazz Rock and the Horn-Rock Bands

Beginning in the 1940's and 1950's, jazz and rock had spent years evolving separately. Early blues, New Orleans and dixieland music merged into swing and eventually big band jazz. Bebop came out of the big band tradition while cool jazz and hard bop followed. Early Delta blues evolved into electric blues, soul music and r&b. Both jazz and rock have similar and deep roots in the blues. While jazz and rock spent years growing apart; it was inevitable that they eventually reconnected. But who combined jazz and rock? Louis Jordan was an early figure that fused r&b and jazz. Later, organists Wild Bill Davis, Jimmy Smith, and trumpeter Lee Morgan began to combine jazz and r&b as well. Trumpeter and Rock and Roll Hall of Famer, Miles Davis began moving towards **jazz-rock** (and fusion). He began with subtle musical allusions on 1968's Miles In the Sky and more forcefully on Filles de Kilimanjaro. In 1969, the creation of jazz-rock became more clear with Davis's recordings In a Silent Way, and in 1970 with his groundbreaking recording, Bitches Brew. Miles refined the sound and the process of melding jazz and rock music.

Simultaneously, rock-jazz further evolved with the horn-rock bands of the 1960's and 1970's. They included; **The Buckinghams, Chicago, Blood, Sweat and Tears, The Electric Flag,** and **Tower of Power.** Some of the musicians playing in this new style of rock music were inspired by a very popular musical source. In 1966, The Beatles recorded "Got To Get You Into My Life" on their classic recording Revolver. The horn parts from this song inspired some young musicians from the Chicago area to bring a more focused jazz influence to their new band.

Chicago (1967-present) originally called Chicago Transit Authority, utilized horn arrangements as a defining musical element of their sound. The members of Chicago had grown up hearing the hard driving r&b music with horns that had already been emanating from the Chicago music scene. Chicago wrote memorable songs and performed them with a rock 'n' roll flash combined with a jazz flair. Chicago built their own powerful sound and emerged as the most popular **horn-rock band**.

Although the inclusion of horns into the Chicago sound was important, it wasn't only about the horns. Chicago integrated other musical ingredients into their music. Terry Kath's soulful and screaming guitar work was the early heart and soul of the band and was lauded by none other than Jimi Hendrix as being "better than me." Danny Seraphine's drumming seamlessly traversed the odd time signatures that had been heard years earlier in the music of The Don Ellis Big Band.

Trombonist and founding member James Pankow brought a strong jazz influence to the band while bassist Peter Cetera had a rock 'n' roll sound. Guitarist Terry Kath was influenced by r&b, and trumpeter Lee Loughlane had jazz and show band experience. Saxophonist Walter Paradizer brought a classical influence, and keyboardist/vocalist Robert Lamm brought a wild combination of Moby Grape and Mose Allison. Drummer Danny Seraphine tied all of these ingredients together.

Chicago's recordings made an impression not only for their musical precision, songwriting, and second to none musicianship, but for the fact that their first three records were released as double albums. This was followed by a fourth release, a four record live set recorded at the prestigious Carnegie Hall in New York City. Most of Chicago's records carried a Roman numeral as a title. Chicago's albums are known as Chicago I through Chicago XXXVI.

Throughout the years, the band had its share of lineup changes and tragedy. Terry Kath died from an accidental gunshot in 1978. Danny Seraphine left the band in 1990 when conflicts arose between himself, the band, and producer David Foster. Singer and bassist Peter Cetera left in 1985 to pursue a solo career. Seraphine's replacement, drummer Tris Imboden, also left in 2018. The band has had over twenty different members throughout its long career. Chicago has sold over 100 million records worldwide. Chicago was inducted into the Rock and Roll Hall of Fame in 2016.

Groundbreaking album Chicago (sometimes called Chicago II)
by Chicago

Chicago's second album was one of the defining recordings of the horn rock genre. On this double record set, Chicago established their ability to take seemingly divergent musical styles and create some of the most effective pop-rock music of the 1970's. Side one opened with "Movin In," then "The Road," "Poem for the People," and "In the Country." Side two opened with "Wake Up Sunshine," then the audacious seven part suite "Ballet for a Girl in Buchannon." This was a thirteen-minute suite, composed by trombonist James Pankow that produced two top ten hits, "Make Me Smile" and "Colour My World." Both songs were sung by guitarist Terry Kath.

Side three opened with "Fancy Colours," then the hit "25 or 6 to 4," and concluded with the suite "Memories of Love." Side four opened with "It Better End Soon," 1. "1st Movement" 2. "2nd Movement" 3. "3rd Movement" 4. "4th Movement," and "Where Do We Go from Here?"

Robert Lamm's high energy "25 or 6 to 4" was built on a catchy guitar riff and a driving quarter-note drumset foundation. The song became a showcase for Chicago's horn section. Terry Kath's guitar solo utilized a distorted, wah-wah pedal that balanced the song's rock and jazz influences. Chicago often played "25 or 6 to 4" as the last song at their live shows. On a tour with Earth, Wind, and Fire, the song provided a great showcase for both band's horn sections, who would combine forces. Lamm has stated that the title of "25 or 6 to 4" was him trying to write a song about the various times of the day.

New York's **Blood, Sweat, and Tears** (1967-1981) (1984-present) are another horn rock band that was important in the creation of horn-rock. BS&T's original members of leader Al Kooper, guitarist/vocalist Steve Katz, and drummer Bobby Columby began assembling a band influenced by James Brown, Otis Redding, The Beatles, and others. In early 1968, BS&T released their debut recording, Child Is Father To The Man. It included the simmering boogaloo "Refugee From Yuhupitz" that was strongly influenced by Lee Morgan's composition "The Sidewinder." Blood, Sweat and Tears' second album, the self-titled Blood, Sweat, and Tears featured their biggest hits "You Make Me So Very Happy" and "Spinning Wheel." This recording included a unique rendering of the jazz standard "God Bless The Child" and an Aaron Copeland meets Johnny Cash styled song called "And When I Die." Perhaps the best representation of Blood, Sweat, and Tears' prowess was their song "Smiling Phases," that featured shifting time signatures, funky grooves, jazz soloing, and strong vocals.

Throughout Blood, Sweat and Tears' existence many important jazz-oriented musicians joined the band including: Mike Stern, Larry Willis, and Joe Henderson. Trumpeter Randy Brecker played on the first BS&T recording and would reappear in many jazz-rock groups (including his own band The Brecker Brothers). Blood, Sweat, and Tears had a strong horn section that played intricate arrangements and a jazz-based drummer in Bobby Columby.

Both Chicago and Blood, Sweat and Tears were inspired by an earlier horn-rock band from Chicago called **The Buckinghams** (1966-1970) (1980-present). BS&T's original members of Kooper, Katz, and Columby, and members of Chicago were musically inspired by The Buckinghams. The band was formed by singers George LeGros and Dennis Tufano, guitarists Nick Fortuna and Carl Giammarese, keyboardist Dennis Miccolis, and drummer John Poulis. Their early singles were covers of Beatles and James Brown songs. Their first number one single, "Kind of a Drag," featured a horn section arranged by Frank Tesinsky. Chicago, Blood, Sweat and Tears, and The Buckinghams were all preceded by another Chicago rooted and San Francisco based band that featured their own horn section.

The Electric Flag (1967-1969 (1974) (2007 reunion) had already played The 1967 Monterey Pop festival by the time both Chicago and BS&T had released their debut recordings. The Black Flag lineup consisted of guitarist Mike Bloomfield, vocalist Nick Gravenites, bassist Harvey Brooks, keyboardist Barry Goldberg, and drummer Buddy Miles. Paving the way for the above mentioned bands, The Electric Flag incorporated a full horn section. They featured a strong blues-based approach. This was seen in their debut recording with their cover of the Howlin' Wolf blues standard "Killing Floor." The Electric Flag also featured drummer-vocalist Buddy Miles, who would go on to record with guitarists Jimi Hendrix, John McLaughlin, and Carlos Santana. The Electric Flag recorded the soundtrack for the 1968 psychedelic film, *The Trip*. Before Michael Bloomfield formed The Electric Flag, he was a member of the Paul Butterfield Blues Band.

On the West Coast, saxophonists Emilio Castillo and Stephen "Doc" Kupka met in 1968 and decided to form a band called The Motowns. The band quickly evolved into a horn-rock band and found a fan in promoter Bill Graham (who would soon produce their first record). Trumpeters Mic Gillette and Greg Adams were added along with saxophonist Skip Mesquite. Together they would become the legendary and awe-inspiring horn section that fronted the band **Tower of Power** (1968-present).

Tower of Power featured a spectacular horn section. They were anchored by a funky rhythm section consisting of guitarist Willie Fulton, organist Chester Thompson, bassist Francis Rocco Prestia, and drummer David Garibaldi. Together, they would create slippery grooves matched with soulful lyrics and intertwined horn section parts to classic T.O.P. (as they were sometimes called) songs that included "Soul Vaccination" and "What is Hip?" While the clever lyrics, and strong melodies were memorable, T.O.P. was a different sort of band. This renowned horn section created a band within a band and took the place of the typical rock 'n' roll guitar led-group. The tight rhythm section created an intricate sound that thrived on rhythmic surprise. T.O.P. was a band of musical virtuosos that earned a loyal following through tireless touring, a reputation for high quality musicianship, and legendary live performances (including the live recordings Live and in Living Color and Hipper Than Hip).

Tower of Power took everything to a new level when they recorded one of their most memorable and popular songs called "Soul Vaccination." The band had already begun to establish themselves as a powerful band that toured constantly, making people dance from coast to coast.

> **Rock Hard Fact**
>
> The Tower of Power horn section played on albums by Little Feat in the 1970's, Huey Lewis in the 1980's, Elton John in the 1990's, and Aerosmith in the 2000's.

"Soul Vaccination"
by Emilio Castillo and Stephen "Doc" Kupk

The song began with a deceptively innocent David Garibaldi drum intro that led into a unison horn section line that immediately put the listener on notice. The drums and Rocco Prestia's bass entered with a groove that disguised the rhythmic pulse of the song. However, this disguise didn't hide the songs' dance-ability or the infectious groove. The horn line and the groove quickly became one to create a hook before a word was ever sung. When the vocals of Lenny Williams entered, the horns exited. Williams sang about how Tower of Power was giving the nation a well-needed soul vaccination. However, in the horns absence, the horn players were heard singing the title of the song. Bruce Conte's rhythm guitar could have easily appeared in one of many James Brown songs, it's that funky. The rhythm guitar was the glue that held everything together. It wove around the busy drums, bass, and horns. After a verse and a chorus, Garibaldi played a surprising drum break that offered a rhythmic yin to the yang of his groove in the rest of the song.

For most of the song, the horn section was playing call and response with themselves, singing "Soul Vaccination," and playing a horn response to their own vocals. The eight-bar bridge featured the horn section playing a highly syncopated line which led to a soulful tenor saxophone solo. This led to some unique interplay between the soloist and the horn section. In many cases, the Tower of Power horn section played with an advanced rhythmic (as opposed to a melodic) sense. The song moved to a rhythmic breakdown where the baritone sax created the sounds once heard in an old-time r&b juke joint. All of this rhythmic interplay built great musical tension. Drummers have turned this song into a benchmark in which other grooves and drummers are judged. This was a musical conversation you could dance to!

In 2011, Tower of Power celebrated its 40th year together with the live recording 40th Anniversary Live. T.O.P. has released more than twenty albums (both studio and live). Throughout their long career, many singers and musicians have passed through the band including; singers Lenny Williams, Michael Jeffries, Rick Stevens, and Hubert Tubbs. Horn players have included; Lenny Pickett, Greg Adams, Mark Russo, Norbert Stachel, and Lee Thornburg who have all contributed to the legendary Tower of Power horn section. To date, over fifty different musicians have passed through T.O.P.. After recordings such as East Bay Grease, Back To Oakland, In the Slot, and Oakland Zone, Tower of Power stands as a soulful musical institution of power, virtuosity, and groove.

By 1972, funk bands had been incorporating horn sections for a long time. Some of these bands included; **The Average White Band**, **Earth Wind and Fire** (1969-present), **Parliament Funkadelic** (1968-present), **WAR** (1969-present), **Charles Wright** and **the Watts 103rd Street Rhythm Band** (1962-present), and of course, **James Brown** (see earlier in this chapter).

The Average White Band (1972-1983) (1989-present) debuted in 1973 with their recording Show Your Hand. The record was poorly received, but they did manage to play some opening shows for Eric Clapton. The recording AWB was released in 1974 with the number one hit and Grammy nominated "Pick Up The Pieces." AWB also included the popular song "Person To Person." They recorded their second album, Cut The

Cake, that featured the title track and the cover song "If I Ever Lose This Heaven."

The Average White Band recorded many popular albums including 1976's Soul Searching and the 1976 live double record Person To Person. AWB's classic grooves have been sampled by rap groups TLC, Beastie Boys, and A Tribe Called Quest. Drummer Steve Ferrone went on to become a first call session musician, tour with Eric Clapton, and became a member of Tom Petty and the Heartbreakers. Original AWB guitarist/vocalist/composer Hamish Stuart joined Paul McCartney's band for several recordings and tours. Currently, original members Alan Gorrie and Onnie McIntyre still lead the band. They have released nearly twenty records in a forty-year career. The Average White Band continues to tour and record.

"Pick Up the Pieces"
by The Average White Band

While "Pick Up The Pieces" wasn't the first single off of the AWB record (that was "Nothing You Can Do") it was the biggest, reaching number one on the pop charts, and number five on the r&b charts. It was a deeply funky track that thrived in its simplicity. The song was based almost exclusively on one chord. Hamish Stuart's rhythm guitar part was similar to Jimmy Nolan's approach featured on many James Brown recordings. The famous horn line was influenced by the legendary sounds of Sam and Dave and Otis Redding. Also, Robbie McIntosh's drum groove and breaks were in the styles of legendary drummers Bernard Purdie and James Gadson.

Founding member and saxophonist Roger Ball wrote out the horn part while Hamish Stuart wrote the guitar riff. They put them together and shoved in the words 'pick up the pieces' on the song's breakdown because they had a strong percussive effect. The lyric of "Pick up the pieces" was about picking yourself up when your life wasn't going very well. The band was frustrated because they weren't making much money at the time. "Pick Up the Pieces" was produced by Arif Mardin.

The groundbreaking musicianship of seminal guitar-oriented rock bands such as The Jimi Hendrix Experience, The Allman Brothers, and Cream all played a significant role in the establishment of the **fusion music** genre. Had Jimi Hendrix (see chapter six) lived longer, his planned collaboration with **Miles Davis** (and Gil Evans) would have been a real musical game changer. A significant early fusion music catalyst was musician composer/arranger **Gil Evans**. He recorded important albums from 1969 to 1975 that included; Blues In Orbit, Svengali, There Comes a Time, and The Gil Evans Orchestra Plays The Music Of Jimi Hendrix. These were important transitional recordings that were influenced by George Russell, Miles Davis, Jimi Hendrix and others. Another important milestone was the 1971 collaboration that featured jazz flautist Herbie Mann and guitarist Duane Allman. Mann's 1971 recording Push Push featured some of Allman's best early work, and some of his only excursions into fusion. Allman's southern roots were a strong presence on this recording and brought a different ingredient to fusion. This approach was expanded through The Allman Brothers' improvisational skills and the Allman's offshoot band **Sea Level**, founded by Chuck Leavell and Allman Brothers' drummer Jai Johanny Johanson. Sea Level established a southern style of fusion that influenced another band, **The Dixie Dregs**. This musical approach of fusion with a "southern flavor" still exists today in the culture of the many popular jam bands.

Ex-Cream (see chapter four) bassist **Jack Bruce** had an impressive body of work as a leader. Bruce released 1969's Songs For a Tailor, 1970's Harmony Row, and 1971's Things We Like. Bruce's recordings included many fusion innovators such as John McLaughlin, who would go on to form the seminal fusion band, **The Mahavishnu Orchestra** (1971-1976) (1984-1987). Fusion music was further built on the groundbreaking work of legendary bands that included, **Weather Report** (1970-1986), **Herbie Hancock's Headhunters** (1973-2003), and **Chick Corea's Return To Forever** (1972-1977) (1983) (2008) (2010-present), among others.

Discussion Question:

Why would a relatively simple song like "Pick Up The Pieces" become so popular, while a more complex piece of music like "Soul Vaccination" remained relatively unknown to the masses. Do people relate more to simplicity? Or do they become turned off by complexity? Be specific with your answer.

Electronica to Electronic Dance Music (EDM)

Electronica is a broad term that includes electronic-based genres such as techno, ambient, house, jungle, **drum and bass**, and industrial dance music. In the late 1990's, the mainstream music industry used the term electronica to describe the above-mentioned genres. Electronica was first used to describe the emergence of electronic music that targeted a listening audience rather than dancers. The term was also utilized in the title of a series of album compilations that spotlighted Detroit techno artists such as **Juan Atkins** (1980-present) and **Underground Resistance** (1989-present) as well as various European artists. By the late 2000's, the music industry replaced the term electronica in favor of **electronic dance music** (EDM). EDM also came to represent post-rave electro house and dubstep music. The term electronica is still in use today, especially in England, where it refers to non-dance-oriented music. This includes the experimental style of downtempo electronic music (similar to ambient music with greater emphasis on rhythm). Electronica is based on the rapid advancements of music technology. Electronic musical instruments such as synthesizers, drum machines, music sequencers, and digital audio workstations have swept the music industry at a blinding pace. Individual musicians began to utilize computers to create samples and digital loops for the source material of their electronic music compositions.

Electronica was central to the pioneering work of artists such as **Kraftwerk** in the early 1970's and **Moby** (1978-present) in the later part of the decade. The 1980's brought new innovations in electronica with artists such as **New Order** (1980-2001 with some inactive years), **Aphex Twin, The Sugarcubes** (1986-1992) (2006), and **The Chemical Brothers**.

Kraftwerk (1969-present) began when German classical music students Florian Schneider and Ralf Hutter formed an experimental rock band called Organ-

> "Computers and electronic music are not the opposite of the warm human music. It's exactly the same."
>
> – Bill Laswell, bassist and producer

> **Rock Hard Fact**
>
> In addition to his work with Nine Inch Nails, Trent Reznor produced the soundtrack for the film Natural Born Killers (directed by Oliver Stone) and he also produced the soundtrack for David Lynch's film Lost Highway.

> "Nine Inch Nails Pretty Hate Machine birthed the first real mainstream breakthrough for industrial rock."
>
> – David Bowie

isation. After one album, Schneider and Hutter formed Kraftwerk (from the German word for "power station"). Kraftwerk's 1970 debut album Kraftwerk featured all-instrumental music that displayed electronic effects and sudden tempo changes. Many lineup changes ensued in the band's early years. 1972's Kraftwerk 2 was another all-instrumental album which they recorded utilizing a drum machine. 1973's Ralf and Florian featured more synthesizers. On the track "Ananas Symphonie," Kraftwerk created the first use of electronically treated vocals.

1974's Autobahn yielded Kraftwerk's mainstream breakthrough with a twenty-two minute title track that was both shocking and soothing. Autobahn reached number eleven in Britain and number twenty-five on the U.S. charts. It was the pioneering record that displayed ambient, electro-funk, and synth pop styles. This genre became known as electro-pop.

"Autobahn"
by Florian Schneider, Ralf Hutter, and Emil Schult

"Autobahn" contained swooping synthesized sounds that evoked both the momentum and the monotony of driving on a motorway. Ralf Hutter recorded the passing cars that were heard in the background of the recording by dangling a microphone out of his Volkswagen window as it traveled down an autobahn. However, the resulting recording was deemed inferior and the car sounds were instead recreated utilizing synthesizers. This was Kraftwerk's first song to use lyrics. The words were in German and the line "Wir fahren fahren fahren auf der Autobahn" translated into English was "We drive drive drive on the Autobahn. Some people mistakenly thought the phrase was a reference to the Beach Boys song "Fun, Fun, Fun."

The instrumentation for the innovative track utilized; electronic percussion, Moog bass to play the bassline (voiced in octaves with analogue echo), a vocoder to process some of the vocals, and a drum machine. The Moog was also used to reproduce the sound of a car. Additionally, the song contained acoustic guitar and flute. Kraftwerk has performed "Autobahn" throughout their career and the live arrangements have continuously evolved, especially with the addition of new technology. "Autobahn" was edited down to a pop-length format and became the groups' only hit in America.

Kraftwerk recorded Radio-Activity in 1975 and used vocoders and ominous electronic tones. The album exhibited themes that addressed the subjects of radiation and radio broadcasting. 1977's Trans-Europe Express and 1978's The Man-Machine developed a style referred to as "Robot Pop," that combined electronic music with pop melodies and repetitive rhythms. 1981's Computer World focused on the impact of information technology. The next Kraftwerk album, 1986's Electric Café, was delayed when Hutter was hurt in an accident. The band released two more albums, 1991's The Mix and 2003's Tour de France Soundtracks. Kraftwerk's music has impacted virtually every new development in contemporary pop music in the late 20th century. Their musical style has also influenced other genres such as hip-hop, house, and drum and bass. Kraftwerk are regarded as the pioneers of the electronica music genre.

Aphex Twin (1985-present) is the recording alias name of Richard David James (1971-). James is an English musician known for his pioneering work in **ambient techno** and intelligent dance music (IDM) in the 1990's. He was also the co-founder of Rephlex Records. Aphex Twin established commercial popularity with their 1997 EP Come to Daddy and a hit single, 1999's "Windowlicker." Aphex Twin has released six studio albums, from 1992's Selected Ambient Works 85-92 to 2014's Syro. James utilized a huge array of keyboards, synthesizers, and samplers on these recordings. His command of midi and recording software included; Pro Tools, Cubase, Reason, Logic Pro, and much more. James has been referred to as one of the most inventive and influential musicians in contemporary music.

The Chemical Brothers (1989-present), aka Tom Rowlands and Ed Simons, made their name first as party DJs in England. When The Chemical Brothers ran out of enough rock records to play at these parties, they set their sights on remixing classics and writing their own songs. The Chemical Brothers use of rap-rock and dance-electronic mixtures were the first of its kind to be heard at large venues. Their song collections were full of percussive breakdowns and numerous effects. They are considered pioneers in the style of big beat, which is electronic music created with heavy breakbeats and synth generated loops (also common in acid house and techno music). The Chemical Brothers have released eight studio albums from 1995's Exit Planet Dust to 2015's Born in the Echoes.

Electronica music elements can be found in a wide array of other prominent artists such as **Bjork** and **Godfrapp** (1999-present). Pop-rock superstar **Madonna** was also involved in electronica's move into mainstream rock and dance music. In the 1990's, artists such as **The Prodigy** (1990-present), and **The Crystal Method** (1993-present) made a continued impact on the electronica genre.

Bjork (1993-present solo career) Guomundsdottir is an Icelandic singer/songwriter, record producer, and DJ. She initially was the lead singer for the alternative rock band The Sugarcubes. In 1977, Bjork released her first studio album, Bjork, at the age of eleven. Her solo career continued with the 1993's Debut. Bjork was successful in mixing electronic, house, and jazz on this album, and therefore was one of the first musicians to introduce electronic music into the pop mainstream. Bjork is a soprano with great vocal range and ability to scat sing. She released a total of eight more studio albums, from 1995's influential Post to 2017's Utopia. Bjork incorporated the diverse genres of electronic music, jazz, alternative rock, and even contemporary classical styles.

"Human Behaviour"
by Bjork and Nellee Hooper

"Human Behaviour" was Bjork's first international hit. The song was co-written and produced by Bjork's longtime collaborator, Nellee Hooper. "Human Behaviour" contained lyrics that explored the subjects of human nature and emotion from an animal's point of view. The song was inspired by the documentaries of naturalist David Attenborough and his perspective on the relationship between humans and animals. When Bjork composed the song, she was also influenced by her childhood walks in nature settings.

Producer Nellee Hooper sampled a bossa nova rhythm from Brazilian master musician Antonio Carlos Jobim. This provided the song with a smooth and natural feel that combined with a constant melodic bassline played on tympani drums. Bjork and Hooper together created a mood that was dark and ominous. The song successfully fused techno and orchestral elements. "Human Behaviour" was a hit on the British singles chart.

Another form of electronic music emerged in the early 1990's called **intelligent dance music** (IDM). It consisted of abstract or "cerebral" sound that focused on listening rather than dancing. Yet another offshoot of electronica was **ambient house** music that fused house music with ambient sound. Some contemporary IDM artists include; **Autechre** (1987-present), **Team Doyobi** (1991-present), and **Himuro Yoshiteru** (1997-present).

New Innovations in Metal

Industrial Metal (briefly defined in chapter ten) is a subgenre of metal that began in the late 1970's. Industrial metal is represented by lyrics and sounds that portray the sound of factory machinery, the buzz and grind of automotive factories, or the harsh noise of a sawmill. The industrial metal term came from the record label, Industrial Records. The British band **Throbbing Gristle** (1976-1981) (2004-2010) was an early pioneering band on the Industrial label. Industrial metal eventually evolved into industrial dance music and became more structured. Technology also evolved when artists added samples, loops, and DJ techniques.

Industrial bands continued to emulate the sounds of industrial machinery by combining performance art with analog samples and electronic drum beats. Other early industrial bands included **Cabaret Voltaire** (1973-1994) (2014-present), and **SPK** (1978-1988). In 1980, the West German band **Einstruzende Neubauten** (1980-present) took a literal approach to industrial music by combining the actual machinery of chainsaws and jackhammers with harsh German vocal sounds. More industrial bands soon followed including; **Skinny Puppy** (1982-1995) (2003-present), the German band **KMFDM** (1984-1999) (2002-present), **Front Line Assemble** (1986-present), and **Ministry**.

Ministry (1981-2008) (2011-present) is an industrial band from Chicago, Illinois. The band has seen many lineup changes but key musicians that have joined Ministry are vocalist/guitarist/programmer Al Jourgensen, keyboardist John Bechdel, guitarist Sin Quirin, guitarist Cesar Soto, bassist Jason Christopher, and drummer Derek Abrams. Ministry began as a synth pop dance band. Their first record, 1983's Sympathy, was lightweight pop music with syrupy vocals. By 1986, Ministry evolved into a hard-edged industrial band with their guitar-less and keyboard heavy album titled Twitch. By 1988's The Land of Rape and Honey, Ministry added caustic metal riffs and digital samples to their electronic mix. This served as a model for groups such as Nine Inch Nails and Rammstein. Ministry went on to record eleven more studio albums including 2018's AmeriKKKant.

In the late 1980's, more industrial bands emerged that won over metal fans. New York City's **Prong** (1986-1997) (2002-present) started out with a strong hardcore approach and then perfected a mid-paced, staccato thrash sound with serrated riffs and sing-along choruses. A band from Birmingham, England called **Godflesh** (1988-2002) (2010-present) was also deeply rooted in industrial music. Godflesh displayed crushing, repetitive riffs that were accompanied by relentless drum machine rhythms. Also of significance, **Marilyn Manson** (see chapter eight) displayed some industrial rock characteristics and became the first act signed to Trent Reznor's Nothing Records label. A 1980's trend started when more and more bands combined electronic music with alternative rock and metal elements.

Industrial metal reached its commercial zenith in the early to mid-1990's. The offbeat, psychedelic noise rock of **White Zombie** (1985-1998) launched the industrial metal solo career of filmmaker-musician **Rob Zombie** (1997-present band) A popular industrial band that grew out of thrash metal was **Skrew** (1990-1998) (2009-present) from Austin, Texas. However, the peak of industrial metal was seen in the rise to superstardom of **Nine Inch Nails**.

Nine Inch Nails (1988-present) is an American industrial band from Cleveland, Ohio. NIN was founded in 1988 by singer/songwriter, instrumentalist, and producer Trent Reznor. He has been the only constant member and main creative force throughout the band's history, although British musician Atticus Ross was later introduced as a permanent member. Reznor developed a very specific process for creating the music of NIN. He utilized a large number of guest musicians on many of their studio recordings. Reznor usually edited and processed many of the recorded parts until they were unrecognizable, even by the musicians that played them.

In 1988, Reznor assembled a live band for the first NIN tour that included drummer Ron Musarra and keyboardist Chris Vrenna. Both musicians appeared on NIN's 1989 synth-pop debut Pretty Hate Machine, which peaked at number seventy-five on the U.S. charts. Working as a nighttime janitor at the Right Track studio in Cleveland, Trent Reznor utilized the studio to record and develop his own songs. For the demo of Pretty Hate Machine, Reznor played most of the guitars, keyboards, samplers, and drum machine parts. The album's computerized synthesizer riffs and processed-sounds featured an aggressive industrial approach and elements of techno-pop dance music. Unlike most of NIN's industrial band contemporaries, Pretty Hate Machine contained catchy riffs and verse-chorus song structures rather than repetitive electronic beats. Reznor was aware of NIN's identity when he said, "I don't mind the term industrial applied to us, but I think the reason people cringe is what it connotes-Throbbing Gristle, Test Department-bands Nine Inch Nails have very little in common with. What is industrial, then? I'd basically define it as dance music that's a bit harder, a bit tougher, definitely with a drum machine and maybe some distorted vocals." #7 NIN followed their debut with the 1992 EP's Broken and Fixed.

1994's The Downward Spiral entered the U.S. charts at number two and has sold over five million copies worldwide. The Downward Spiral contained many moods and timbres that highlighted the mental progression of a central character that appeared throughout the album.

Groundbreaking album
The Downward Spiral
by Nine Inch Nails

In contrast to their debut album, The Downward Spiral, NIN moved their musical direction into a blend of heavy metal, techno, and industrial rock. The album contained abrasive lyrics and dark themes that focused on the destruction of a man. The songs on The Downward Spiral were open to much lyrical interpretation due to their many layers of metaphors. Thought to be somewhat autobiographical, Reznor wrote a complete storyline for the album that followed

> "In my life, I was always floating around the edge of the dark side and saying- what if I take it a little bit too far, and who says you have to stop there, and what's behind the next door. Maybe you gain a wisdom from examining those things."
>
> – Trent Reznor

the protagonist's "downward spiral" with interwoven themes of self-abuse. Reznor referred to issues of violence, dehumanization, religion, disease, drugs, sex, and suicide. On the recording, the protagonist strips himself of everything until there is nothing left. This was a dark concept album about literal self-destruction that resulted in an attempted suicide.

The tracks on the album were "Mr. Self Destruct," then "Piggy," "Hersey," "March of the Pigs," "Closer," "Ruiner," The Becoming," "I Do Not Want This," "Big Man with a Gun," "A Warm Place," "Eraser," "Reptile," "The Downward Spiral," and "Hurt." Trent Reznor frequently utilized dissonance, chromatic harmonies, and angular melodies throughout the album. "Mr. Self Destruct" revealed lyrics that told the story of a person in a position of power. The lyrics were sung against the background sounds of an industrial roar and a digital loop of automated machinery. "The Becoming" addressed the state of *being dead* and the protagonist's transformation into a non-human organism. Released as a single, "Closer," contained sexually explicit lyrics that reflected on the theme of self-hatred. On "Piggy," another single from the album, Reznor played frantic, intense "live" drums on the studio recording.

Reznor reflected on the concept of The Downward Spiral when he stated, "The safest I could have done was make another Broken (EP) that was tough and mean and would show everybody how many great metal riffs I can write. It would have been the least artistically challenging thing, so I wasn't going to do that. I started The Downward Spiral on guitar but ended up using a lot of computer instead of guitar to write because it was a lot more inspiring to me. I was also trying to make a record that was fairly broad in its scope musically, rather than everything being really hard and fast." #8

"Hurt" referred to self-harm and drug addiction and is open to further lyric interpretation. "Hurt" utilized the constant move back and forth from whispers to screams to create musical drama. Reznor harmonized the song with highly dissonant tritones played on guitar at the verses. "Hurt" was covered by country legend Johnny Cash (see chapter one) who loved Reznor's ability to express emotional pain throughout the song.

The Downward Spiral has been critically acclaimed to be one of the most important albums of the 1990's. This work established Trent Reznor as industrial music's version of Phil Spector by painting complex and layered soundscapes with a wide range of timbres. The album featured shifting arrangements, expanded song structures, and odd time signatures that came from the influence of progressive rock. Reznor had also cited the influences of Pink Floyd's The Wall and David Bowie's Low albums for their moods and song structures. The Downward Spiral was produced by Reznor and Flood (aka Mark Ellis).

1999's The Fragile utilized the skills of producer Bob Ezrin, new drummer Jerome Dillon, and NIN's largest supporting cast. Reznor and NIN then went on hiatus from 2000 to 2003. 2005's With Teeth was written throughout 2004 when Reznor was battling substance issues. From 2007's Year Zero to 2013's Hesitation Marks, Nine Inch Nails released four more studio albums. Trent Reznor went on to record with his wife Mariqueen Maandig. At this time, Reznor also made (previously mentioned) Atticus Ross a full-time member of NIN. In 2016, Nine Inch Nails released an EP titled Not the Actual Events and another EP, 2017's Add Violence. Nine Inch Nails took the industrial genre in a melodic direction where Reznor's pop instincts tamed the harsh electronic beats that had previously dominated the music. Reznor has placed his personal identity on a genre that was built on impersonal machines.

Two other important industrial bands were Los Angeles based **Fear Factory** and the German band **Rammstein**. The former was one of the first hardcore metal bands to experiment with electronics and samples and the later burst onto the scene adding a new level of theatrics to industrial metal.

Fear Factory (1989-present with some inactive years) is an American band that has embraced many metal subgenres from industrial, thrash, death, and nu metal. The band has undergone many lineup changes but currently features vocalist Burton C. Bell, guitarist Dino Cazares, bassist Tony Campos, and drummer Mike Heller.

Fear Factory debuted with Soul of a New Machine in 1992. The album exhibited an industrial metal sound with Bell's harsh, yet still melodic vocals. Fear Factory integrated industrial samples and down-tuned guitars with death metal riffs. They would later move away from a death metal approach to more accessible songs. Burton Bell recalled, "I have been told a few times that the whole metalcore vocal style is all my fault. When we started out, it definitely took people aback." #9 Fear Factory's commercial peak came with 1998's Obsolete, a well-crafted and aggressive metal album laced with catchy melodies. The band has also emphasized lyrics focused on science fiction set in a concept album format. Fear Factory obtained some popular success with their collaboration with musician Gary Numan on his 1979 hit, "Cars." Hoping to repeat that success, Fear Factory added a hip-hop element to their 2001 album Digimortal. It featured a collaboration with Cypress Hill's B-Real on the song "Linchpin." Fear Factory has released a total of nine-studio albums including their latest, 2015's Genexus.

Rammstein (1993-present) is a German industrial metal band that formed in 1993. In 1995, the music press in Europe called them "Neue Deutsche Harte" which translated to "New German Hardness." Rammstein's lineup has always been vocalist Till Lindemann, guitarist Richard Z. Kruspe, guitarist Paul H. Landers, bassist Oliver Riedel, keyboardist Christian Lorenz, and drummer Christoph Schneider. Rammstein has a crossover style that combines groove metal with industrial and techno elements. They play brutally intense hard rock with lyrics sung in German in a deep, forceful male voice. Rammstein has performed songs entirely or partially in English, Spanish, French, and Russian.

Rammstein's roots were in a four-piece East Berlin punk band called Feeling B. Expanding to their current six-piece lineup, they quickly established a reputation for powerful and theatrical live performances. Their 1995 debut, Herzeleid, immediately struck a chord with a German youth audience. It featured the Rammstein sound of heavy drums and bass, waves of feedback, clipped electronic beats, and over-enunciated vocals.

Guitarist Richard Kruspe described the band's start and recalled, "when we formed in 1993, the music scene in East Germany was divided. One part was the professional, educated type of musician, and the other was the so-called amateur, and the amateur was not allowed to play onstage without having another job to get money. We had to play in front of a jury to get a docu-

---

"I always enjoy rhythms and melodies, but I always use my voice as more of an instrument and less of a soapbox for me to say or to preach."

- Chino Moreno

ment that allowed us to have concert for a certain amount of money. Even then, no one wanted to let us play." #10

German bands singing in their native tongue have rarely broken into the international music scene. But by 1996, Rammstein was performing in London as part of MTV's *Hanging Out* series. Then, Trent Reznor selected two Rammstein songs from Herzeleid for David Lynch's movie titled *Lost Highway*. 1997's Sehnsucht hit the German charts at number one. The band toured America with Korn and Limp Bizkit, giving them international visibility. Sehnsucht went to number forty-five on the U.S. charts and earned Rammstein a Grammy nomination.

"Du Hast"
by Rammstein

The German phrase "Du hast" does not translate to English but it can be interpreted to have two possible meanings. It can mean "to have" or "you hate." The phrase "Du hast" was also about marriage and could mean "you hate me but still want to marry me," or "you want to marry me but I don't want to." The whole song was a play on German wedding vows. The singer was talking to his girlfriend and she was questioning him about his love for her.

Musically, "Du Hast" contained an almost disco-like driving four to the floor bass drum pattern and techno synth lines over a heavy guitar riff. The sludgy rhythmic feel, fused with a pop sensibility, made this song accessible to a large audience. "Du Hast" featured multiple breakdown sections with just drums and vocals. Rammstein effectively added synthesizer layers to build momentum as the song progressed. "Du Hast" was featured in the movie soundtrack for *The Matrix: Music from the Motion Picture* and the music video games *Guitar Hero 5* and *Rock Band 3*.

Rammstein released four more albums in the 2000's, including 2009's Liebe ist fur alle da. Rammstein's dominating industrial metal output of six studio albums featured militaristic guitar riffs and melodic keyboards. Their operatic vocals express lyrics about control, submission, and sex. Rammstein is also known for their exciting live performances with shocking pyrotechnics, flame-throwing muzzles, and even exploding babies.

Nu Metal (first described in chapter ten) is a form of alternative metal that merged elements of metal with grunge, hip-hop, alternative rock, and funk. From the late 1980's through the mid-1990's, prominent nu metal bands emerged that included; **The Deftones**, **Incubus**, **P.O.D.** (1992-present), **Papa Roach** (1993-present), **Korn**, and many others. Nu Metal would dominate the commercial metal landscape from the mid-1990's until around 2001.

Deftones (1988-present) are an American alternative metal band from Sacramento, California that formed in 1988. The current lineup is vocalist/guitarist Chino Moreno, guitarist Stephen Carpenter, drummer Abe Cunningham, bassist Sergio Vega, and turntablist/keyboardist Frank Delgado. Initially rooted in thrash metal, Deftones have drawn from the diverse genres of punk, pop, and psychedelia. Deftones started earlier than most nu metal bands but didn't attract much attention until after their 1995's debut album, Adrenaline. Slowly, they built a fan base. They followed with their second release, 1997's Around the Fur. A few high-profile tours with Ozzy Osbourne and Korn pushed them to the forefront of the nu metal movement. 2000's White Pony debuted at number three on the U.S. charts and yielded their most popular song to date, "Change (In the House of Flies)." This album saw an experimental incorporation of new wave elements and trip hop (a fusion of hip hop and electronica styles).

"Change in the House of Flies"
by Deftones

"Change in the House of Flies" featured both a very dark and haunting melody and a storyline to match. Lead singer Chino Moreno has referred to the song as metaphorical, but it could be interpreted in a literal sense of watching someone turn into a fly and then taking them home and pulling off their wings. Another interpretation of the song revealed an innocent and naïve female who was introduced to hard drugs and changed in a negative way.

Deftones wrote the song together with every band member contributing what they wanted in a very free setting. The song began with a dissonant guitar riff with an eerie keyboard sound. The drums and bass entered with a slow funky feel and Chino's vocal lines were stated with a soft, almost spoken quality. The chorus attacked with powerful guitar chords and Chino raged through the powerful line "I watched you change in you-it's like you never had wings-now you feel it's like you feel so alive." Deftones filmed a video for the song at Moreno's house to capture a true sense of who they were.

Since 2003, Deftones have released five more studio albums, including 2016's Gore. Deftones continued their fusion of genres on Gore with a gospel influence and an electronically based atmosphere. They have grown to consistently push the boundaries of metal while managing to remain popular and relevant. Deftones have been compared favorably to a cross between Radiohead and heavy metal.

Incubus (1991-present) is an American rock band from Calabasas, California that formed in 1991. The current lineup is vocalist Brandon Boyd, guitarist Mike Einzinger, drummer Jose Pasillas, bassist Ben Kenney, and turntablist Chris Kilmore. Incubus drew from a myriad of styles including funk, art rock, thrash and rap metal, techno, and post-grunge to create their alternative nu metal sound. The band has also utilized many non-traditional instruments on their recordings including; the sitar, didgeridoo, African djembes, and Afro-Cuban percussion. Incubus has released seven studio albums, including their 1995 debut Fungus Amongus to 2011's If Not Now, When?." To promote the release of If Not Now, When?, Incubus shot a real-time documentary called *Incubus HQ Live*. This allowed for unprecedented fan access and interaction with the band. Incubus has pointed out that what separated them from other nu metal artists was their positive lyrics (not the often-typical nu metal misogynist lyrics). Their musical versatility provided a unique identity that was not based on any particular genre. Incubus, although a part of the nu metal and alternative movements of the 1990's, have redefined what it means to be *the alternative*.

Korn (1993-present) is an American nu metal band that started in Bakersfield, California in 1993. Korn formed when three former members of the funk metal band L.A.P.D., bassist Reginald "Fieldy" Arvizu, drummer David Silveria, and guitarist James "Munky" Shaffer, decided to start a new band. They combined forces with vocalist Jonathan Davis and guitarist Brian

> **Rock Hard Fact**
>
> In 1998, a boy at a Zeeland, Michigan high school was suspended for wearing a Korn T-shirt when the principal claimed their music was obscene. Korn responded by handing out free T-shirts in front of the school.

> **Rock Hard Fact**
>
> System of a Down's name was inspired by a Daron Malakian poem called "Victims of a Down" but they went with 'system' partly because their albums could sit closer to Slayer's in record store bins.

"Head" Welch. The band developed a raw and aggressive approach built on manic guitars that drew from grunge and metal influences. Davis' lyrics were controversial and covered taboo subjects such as sexual abuse, child abuse, and childhood bullying with a stream-of-consciousness delivery. Korn's ability to separate from the metal mainstream made them one of the first and most innovative nu metal bands.

Korn's 1994 self-titled debut album, Korn, was well received and sold over five million copies. The album's cover art was a disturbing picture that featured a young girl on a swing in front of the shadow of a menacing and towering figure. The girl's shadow appears hanging by her neck from the "K" of the group's (Korn) logo.

Korn built their fan base by relentlessly touring with Danzig, Megadeth and Ozzy Osbourne. 1996's Life is Peachy shot to number three on the U.S. charts with the singles "No Place to Hide" and "Good God." 1998's Follow the Leader and 1999's Issues both debuted at number one in America. Korn was clearly the dominant nu metal band of the late 1990's. They also launched the Family Values Tour with similarly controversial artists such as Ice Cube, Limp Bizkit, and Rammstein.

Groundbreaking album
Follow the Leader
by Korn

Follow the Leader is often credited with launching the nu metal genre. The album featured twenty-five tracks with twelve that were each five seconds of silence. This combined first minute of silence (and later the track "Justin") was included in respect for a Korn fan named Justin, who was dying of cancer. This album shaped elements of rap, metal, and punk with a brutal and aggressive edge. Korn created anthems of thunderous beats and shouts of gut-wrenching rage for fans that felt alienated from society. Jonathan Davis provided Korn with vocals that portrayed a dark and disturbing world. The victim of a broken home, Davis sang about going insane with an angst-ridden paranoia in what he believed was a world gone wrong. These songs were about extreme dysfunction and connected well with a large audience of similarly disaffected youth.

Follow the Leader opened with "It's On," then "Got the Life," "Dead Bodies Everywhere," "Children of the Korn," "B.B.K.," "Pretty," "All in the Family," "Reclaim My Place," "Justin," "Seed," "Cameltosis," and "My Gift to You." The song "Got the Life" achieved great success. The music video for the track became the most requested video on MTV's *Total Request Live* television series. "Freak On a Leash" was an example of the Korn sound with Davis' angry vocals against the backdrop of aggressive guitar distortion and dissonance. "Freak on a Leash" received a Grammy Award in 2000 for Best Short Form Music Video. It was nominated for an incredible nine MTV Video Music Awards.

On Follow the Leader, Korn guitarist James "Munky" Shaffer achieved a unique sound. Munky said "I started using a seven-string guitar to make the music really dark and different-sounding and lower. A Korn guitar tone has gotta be heavy, but with clarity. When we record, sometimes we layer three or four different tracks to get the right sound- a clean tone, a really dirty tone underneath, and then something between the two. Then we use lots of sound effects to make it sound even weirder. But I don't know how to play a standard six-string guitar anymore. It feels like I'm missing a finger when I try." #11 Follow the Leader also featured guest performances by Ice T and Limp Bizkit's Fred Durst.

By 2001, the genre of nu metal had reached its commercial peak. However, Korn's prolific output would continue. From 2002's Untouchables to 2016's The Serenity of Suffering, Korn released eight more studio albums. Korn's consistency and longevity became the envy of their nu metal peers. Their brazen approach opened the door for many like-minded metal bands to come. Korn has sold over thirty-five million albums worldwide and twelve of their releases have reached the top ten on the U.S. charts.

By the mid-1990's a new wave of bands joined the explosively popular nu metal movement. They represented regions from all over America including; New York's **Helmet** (1989-1998) (2004-present), Massachusetts's **Godsmack** (1995-present) and **Staind** (1995-2012) (2014) (2017), California's **System of a Down** and **Queens of the Stone Age** (1996-present) (see chapter ten), Illinois' **Mudvayne** (1996-2010), Chicago's **Disturbed** (1996-2011) (2015-present), and Iowa's **Slipknot**.

System of a Down (1994-2006) (2010-present) is an American-Armenian band from Glendale, California that formed in 1994. The current lineup is vocalist/keyboardist Serj Tankian, vocalist/guitarist Daron Malakian, bassist Shavo Odadjian, and drummer John Dolmayan. Legendary producer Rick Rubin heard the band and quickly signed them to his American-Columbia Record label. Their 1998 self-titled debut album, System of a Down, sold well and yielded two singles "Sugar" and "Spiders."

System of a Down drew from an interesting combination of musical styles and genres. With clear thrash metal and progressive metal influences, the band incorporated avant-garde and **Middle Eastern rhythms**. System incorporated a wide range of instruments such as ouds, sitars, electric mandolin, and twelve string guitars. Malakian often wrote songs with an E flat tuning, sometimes changing to a drop C tuning. 2001's Toxicity was a breakout album for System with the hits "Aerials," "Toxicity," and "Chop Suey!" System of a Down's lyrics was often Dadaist (often rejecting logic, reason, and the values of a modern capitalist society) and referred to a range of topics from politics, religion, drug abuse, and sex.

"Chop Suey!"
by System of a Down

"Chop Suey!" dealt was the topic of death and how people are judged on how they die. The song was originally titled "Suicide" but the band changed it when they realized that it wasn't very radio friendly. The album, Toxicity, was number one at the time of the September 11th, 2001 attacks. Therefore, the song was controversial for some people, especially the lyric "I don't think you trust in my self-righteous suicide." Many radio stations pulled the song in the effort to be as sensitive as possible after the tragedy.

Musically, "Chop Suey!" had drastically contrasting verses that ranged from hardcore punk to soft acoustic choruses. The song was broken up and featured a big, full chorus that was highly emotional. "Chop Suey" contained a passage paraphrased from the Bible, specifically Luke 23:46 when Jesus Christ said, "Why have you forsaken me?" Avril Lavigne did a cover of "Chop Suey"

> "The guitar is a small orchestra. It is polyphonic. Every string is a different color, a different voice. Lean your body forward slightly to support the guitar against your chest, for the poetry of the music should resound in your heart."
>
> - Andres Segovia, virtuoso classical guitarist

that was largely panned by many System of a Down's fan base.

2002's Steal This Album! did not fare as well on the charts. However, 2005's Mezmerize and Hypnotize both debuted at number one in America. System of a Down went on hiatus but reunited in 2011 for a string of European festival concert dates. The band announced that they were working on material for a follow-up to the Mezmerize and Hypnotize albums. System of a Down effectively created their own style out of wildly diverse influences. They have been inspired by The Dead Kennedys, Black Sabbath, Frank Zappa, and their Middle Eastern and **Armenian music** heritage.

Slipknot (1995-present) is an American nu metal band that formed in Des Moines, Iowa in 1995. Founded by drummer Joey Jordison and percussionist Shawn Crahan, Slipknot went through numerous lineup changes before settling on nine band members. The current lineup is Crahan, programmer Craig Jones, guitarist Mick Thomson, vocalist Corey Taylor, turntablist Sid Wilson, percussionist Chris Fehn, guitarist Jim Root, bassist Alessandro Venturella, and drummer Jay Weinberg. Slipknot is known for their individual facemasks and matching uniforms (usually jumpsuits) and each member is assigned and referred to by a number based on their role in the band (#0 through #8). The band claimed that the masks were not attention seeking but rather a way to divert attention from themselves and onto the music.

Slipknot released their 1999 self-titled debut album, Slipknot, and found success with the singles "Surfacing," "Wait and Bleed," and "Spit it Out." Three tours on the Ozzfest circuit built their already rabid fan base while 2001's Iowa went to number one in England and number three in America. Slipknot attempted to distance themselves from the nu metal movement stating that nu metal and their career merely happened at the same time. Musically, they utilized samples, a big percussion section, down-tuned guitars, and turntables. Recently, Slipknot began to experiment with acoustic guitars and a more melodic vocal style in addition to their well-known growling and screaming vocals. After a 2002 hiatus and DVD release that same year, Slipknot released 2003's Vol. #3: (The Subliminal Verses).

"Before I Forget"
by Paul Gray and Corey Taylor

The guitar riffs heard in "Before I Forget" came from an early Slipknot song called "Carve" that was featured on Slipknot's unreleased album Crowz. Vocalist Corey Taylor's lyrics were open to interpretation. The song dealt with the concept of evolution and the nature of man. Musically, the groove was fast and relentless in a very heavy thrash metal style. The vocals were aggressive and there were episodes of DJ voiced over phrases. A loop entered at the end of the song that came from a section of a verse. A beeping sound at the end of the song was Morse code, which spelled out the word Slipknot.

"Before I Forget" won a Grammy Award for Best Metal Performance in 2006. Slipknot was nominated for the award six years running until finally winning. Slipknot has rarely appeared without their signature masks, but then did so in the video for the song. The video made use of strategic camera techniques where the members' faces were never totally shown. Their masks were shown next to themselves while they performed.

Slipknot released a live record in 2005 titled 9.0: Live. Then in 2008, their All Hope is Gone went to number one on the U.S. charts. In 2010, Slipknot founding member Paul Gray tragically died. Bassist Alessandro Venturella replaced Gray and drummer Joey Jordison left the band in 2013, soon replaced by Jay Weinberg. Their latest release was 2014's .5: The Gray Chapter. Slipknot has created a mix of explosive metal with creative samples, turntables, and dark, nihilistic lyrics. Their Marilyn Manson-esque shock rock live performances, complete with masks and jumpsuits, gave them a unique identity and an image that resonated with a strong fan base.

Guitar "Slingers"

Throughout the years they have been called many things: guitar soloists, guitar slingers, virtuosos, shredders... Whatever name is chosen, they are the guitarists who have completely absorbed musical styles like jazz, country, blues, and classical into their own brand of over the top rock 'n' roll. They have augmented their guitar-centric music with new sounds and techniques. However, they haven't relied on musical instrument companies to create their new sounds and instruments. Since Les Paul first put six strings on a solid block of wood, there has been a tradition of guitarist-inventors who have created (or helped create) pieces of guitar equipment that would aid the musician in finding a definitive sound. This tradition emerged again in the surf era (see chapter three) when guitarists created instrumental hits and helped invent different guitar tones and sounds that were integral to that style of rock music. Boston's Tom Scholz continued the tradition with his Rockman products in the 1980's. In the 1990's, Steve Vai became inspired to re-investigate the seven-string guitar, which had been introduced by the gypsy guitarists of the 1800's. With six or seven strings, outboard effects, technique to spare, and boundless creative imagination, modern virtuoso rock guitarists have continued to raise the bar for the modern rock guitar approach. These musician's jaw-dropping solos have inspired generations of guitarists and have pushed the boundaries of the instrument. Sometimes their solos were about speed, but they were often about new sounds. No matter how much equipment was employed, it all started with the guitarist's hands. Those two hands that started it all belonged to guitarist Les Paul.

Les Paul (1915-2009) was not only a pioneer of guitar technique, but he was also an innovative guitar builder and pioneer in multi-track recording. He is the only person to be inducted into the Rock and Roll Hall of Fame and the National Inventors Hall of Fame. Paul's first recording was released in 1936, and his many recordings blurred the lines between jazz, country, and rock. His early musical innovations and inventions were the inspiration for the solid body Les Paul model electric guitar. Paul also invented the harmonica holder that strapped around ones' neck and enabled a musician to play guitar and harmonica simultaneously, as popularized by Bob Dylan.

Les Paul was an innovator in the field of multi-track recording and overdubbing. This began in 1949 when he modified an early reel-to-reel audio tape recorder called the Ampex Model 200. He then invented a process called Sound on Sound recording. This technique enabled a musician (or group of musicians) to play along with a previously recorded track, creating a recorded performance that could subsequently be bounced to another track to create a multi-track recording. This technique

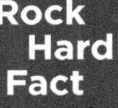

Rock Hard Fact

The legendary Les Paul is the godfather to another rock legend, guitarist/vocalist Steve Miller.

now called *multi-tracking*, would be used throughout the history of rock music, and is still used today.

In 1951, Les Paul utilized his musical inventions to create the hit recording "How High The Moon." This song was already a jazz standard recorded by Nat King Cole and (most popularly) Ella Fitzgerald. But Les Paul and singer (his then wife) Mary Ford's version would set the music world on its ears. Their version would feature a multi-tracked Mary Ford harmonizing with herself, creating a sound similar to the Andrews Sisters, while Les Paul's multiple guitar parts created a unique musical accompaniment. Their recording of "How High the Moon" has been named by The Rock and Roll Hall of Fame as one of the songs that shaped rock. It was inducted in the Grammy Hall of Fame in 1979. Jeff Beck and singer Imelda May paid tribute to Les Paul and Mary Ford's recording by performing this song at the 2010 Grammy Awards. Les Paul was inducted into the Rock and Roll Hall of Fame in 1988.

Jeff Beck (1944–) has been omnipresent since the beginning of the rock era. He burst onto the scene when he replaced Eric Clapton in The Yardbirds in 1965. He announced his arrival as a solo artist in 1967 with the release of a single, "Beck's Bolero" (see chapter four), that became an instrumental hit in the mid-1960s. He led The Jeff Beck Group from 1967 to 1972, and featured Rod Stewart on vocals. From 1972 until present, he has released solo records that utilized elements of hard rock, r&b, electronica, blues, early rock and roll, fusion, and large group orchestral works. Beck's early love of the blues of B.B. King and Willie Dixon evolved into an early hard rock sound that predated Led Zeppelin. After producing a hard-edge approach heard on recordings such as Truth and Beck-Ola, Beck recorded at Motown and hired Stax guitarist Steve Cropper as his producer.

Along with his position as a true guitar innovator, Jeff Beck has always been a musical sponge. He has recorded Stevie Wonder songs "Superstition," "Cause We've Ended As Lovers," Elvis Songs' "All Shook Up," and "Jailhouse Rock," and a Bob Dylan song, "Tonight I'll Be Staying Here With You." On his Rough and Ready album, Beck wrote six original songs. By 1972, the formally titled Jeff Beck Group had run its course. This led Beck to form the super-group, Beck, Bogert & Appice. They recorded and toured from 1972 to 1974.

From 1975 through 1980, Jeff Beck recorded a trio of solo instrumental records that introduced him to the jazz-rock world. The innovative album Blow By Blow, became his best-selling record and benefited from collaborations with producer George Martin, Stevie Wonder, and the keyboardist Max Middleton. The exciting album, Wired, further cemented Beck's legendary instrumental rock reputation. After a tour opening for The Mahavishnu Orchestra, Beck hired Mahavishnu members Jan Hammer and Narada Michael Walden to appear on Wired. He also recorded the Charles Mingus composition "Goodbye Pork Pie Hat." Jeff Beck toured with Jan Hammer's group and released a live album, which led to his next record, There & Back, a continuation of the musical relationship established between Beck and Hammer. Beck then took a five-year break. He returned with Flash (produced by Nile Rogers), an album that yielded a hit with a cover of Curtis Mayfield's "People Get Ready," and a Grammy award for the song "Escape."

Rock Hard Fact

According to drummer Nick Mason, when Syd Barrett left the band, the other members of Pink Floyd wanted Jeff Beck to join the band. Later, when The Rolling Stones guitarist Brian Jones died, Beck was asked to join The Stones.

Rock Hard Fact

Guitarist Steve Vai transcribed the music for Frank Zappa's "Inca Roads" guitar solo completely from memory (with complex time signatures) while riding on a bus.

Groundbreaking album
Blow by Blow
by Jeff Beck

Blow by Blow was an all-instrumental album that reached number four on the U.S. charts. Released in 1975, it was Beck's fifth effort as a leader and marked a significant change from his earlier rock-based works. Considered by many to be one of the greatest albums in the fusion genre, Beck brilliantly created an instrumental work that flowed like a rock concept album. Drummer Richard Bailey exhibited incredible musicianship by orchestrating and complementing the melodies and complex arrangements. Beck effectively mixed sensitive ballads, funk, and jazz.

For Blow by Blow, Jeff Beck hired legendary Beatles producer George Martin to handle the production. Beck had previously worked with keyboardist Max Middleton (his earlier Jeff Beck Group) and hired him to play Fender Rhodes, clavinet, and analog synthesizers. Beck also solicited the help of the legendary Stevie Wonder who gave Beck his songs "Thelonius" and "Cause We've Ended as Lover." Wonder played clavinet on "Thelonius" but was uncredited. Beck also decided to cover The Beatles song "She's a Woman" and the song "Diamond Dust," by Bernie Holland from the group Hummingbird. The other five songs were Jeff Beck originals with help from Middleton.

Side one opened with "You Know What I Mean," followed by "She's a Woman," "Constipated Duck," "Air Blower," and "Scatterbrain." The last track on both sides of the album featured string arrangements by George Martin. On "You Know What I Mean," Beck played a blistering blues-based solo with angular lines. "Air Blower" featured elaborate layers of rhythm and segued into "Scatterbrain" with twin keyboard and guitar solos.

Side two opened with "Cause We've Ended as Lovers," which preceded "Thelonius," "Freeway Jam," and "Diamond Dust." Beck dedicated "Cause We've Ended as Lovers" to guitarist Roy Buchanan. This song also highlighted Beck's great ability to express his emotions in a ballad setting. Jeff Beck achieved a new creative peak on Blow by Blow. This album ranked as one of the premiere examples of high-level collaboration, compositional skill, and virtuoso performance in the instrumental rock genre.

1989's Guitar Shop became an instant classic, pairing Beck with drummer Terry Bozzio (Frank Zappa, Missing Persons) and past collaborator keyboardist Tony Hymas. It was the beginning of Beck's finger-style guitar approach (no use of a guitar pick). Jeff Beck returned in 1993 with The Big Town Playboys, a tribute to Gene Vincent and his Blue Caps. On 1999's Who Else, the musically restless Beck found a new collaborator in guitarist Jennifer Batten. Beck absorbed Batten's influence and blended it with Tony Hymas' compositional approach to create (yet another) musical approach for his guitar genius. After 2003's Jeff, Beck assembled a touring band with drummer Vinnie Colaiuta and keyboardist Jason Rebello and headlined his own tours for several years. He followed with a blistering live DVD entitled Live At Ronnie Scott's. 2016's Loud Hailer saw Beck return to a smaller group sound.

Jeff Beck displayed an early talent for mimicking the styles and sounds of guitarists such as Les Paul, Buddy Holly, and Roy Buchanan. He appeared as a ses-

Chapter Seventeen: Important Musical Styles That Mixed with Rock

sion guitarist on early records by the Fitz and Startz, and later appeared on a record by Upp. Later, he would appear as a guest on recordings by Mick Jagger, Stevie Wonder, Cyndi Lauper, and Jon Bon Jovi. Jeff Beck was part of the all-star The Honeydrippers project that also featured Robert Plant, Jimmy Page, and Nile Rogers in 1984. Beck broke musical barriers and raised the bar for guitarists around the world. Jeff Beck was inducted into the Rock and Roll Hall of Fame twice: in 1992 as a member of The Yardbirds and in 2009 as a solo artist.

Many other prominent guitar "shredders" soon made a name for themselves including; **Albert Lee** (1943-), **Rick Derringer** (1947-), **Ronnie Montrose** (1947-2012), **Pat Travers** (1954-), **Johnny Winter, Joe Satriani, Steve Vai,** and **Yngwie Malmsteen.**

Johnny Winter (1944-2014,) and his brother Edgar, were from the fertile Texas music scene. After sitting in with Mike Bloomfield in 1968, Johnny Winter was offered a recording contract with Columbia records. He was one of the first guitarists to use a finger-picking technique combined with a thumb-pick. Winter covered songs by "Sonny Boy" Williamson, B.B. King, Chuck Berry, The Rolling Stones, and Bob Dylan. Winter hired fellow guitarist Rick Derringer, and together they formed the band called Johnny Winter And. They released the classic live recording Live Johnny Winter And. The band's biggest hit was the Derringer penned "Rock and Roll Hoochie Koo." Winter would go on to be an integral member of Muddy Waters band producing four classic recordings. Winter brought an over the top style of blues-rock guitar to the big stage. Johnny Winter released over 25 solo albums over his career.

Joe Satriani (1956-) is the biggest selling instrumental guitarist in music history. He is an influential soloist, bandleader, songwriter, teacher, and sideman. His ex-students include Steve Vai, Kirk Hammett (Metallica), and Larry LaLonde (Primus). Satriani has released over 15 albums, and he has been nominated for 15 Grammy's.

Satriani self-financed his first album titled Not Of This Earth. He followed with his breakthrough recording, Surfing With The Alien. Satriani put together a powerful trio with bassist Stu Hamm and drummer Jonathan Mover, and toured relentlessly to promote that recording. This album featured the Grammy nominated song "Always with Me, Always with You." It received strong MTV video airplay. In 1988, Mick Jagger asked Satriani to tour (replacing Jeff Beck who played on Jagger's She's The Boss). In 1992, Satriani released his most successful recording titled The Extremist, featuring the popular songs "Summer Song," "Friends,' and "Cryin.'" In 1993, he was asked to join Deep Purple, but he declined. Many of Satriani's solo releases featured science fictional titles and themes, including his 1998 release Engines of Creation that delved into the electronica and techno genres.

In 1996, Joe Satriani founded the G3 tour, which is a yearly tour that features virtuoso guitarists fronting their own bands. It exposes audiences to guitar-centric music not normally found on the big stage. In 2008, Satriani began co-leading the super-group Chickenfoot, with Sammy Hagar, Michael Anthony, and Chad Smith. Satriani has also guested on recordings by Dream Theater, Alice Cooper, The Yardbirds, and Blue Oyster Cult. Following in Les Paul's footsteps, Joe Satriani has developed many guitar equipment inventions working with amplifier manufacturers Marshall and Peavey, Dimarzio pickups, Vox effects, and Ibanez Guitars.

"Always with Me, Always with You"
by Joe Satriani

From Joe Satriani's Surfing with the Alien record, "Always with Me, Always with You" was a tender-hearted instrumental ballad. The song was a unique combination of an instrumental ballad played with a distorted rock guitar sound. "Always with Me" contained a simple one bar electronic percussion part. Satriani's guitar entered with a four-bar staccato rhythm guitar part, accompanied by a sparse and loping bassline. The constant melody led to a guitar improvisation that was supported by an occasional and distant sitar strumming sound. Satriani restated the melody and then improvised using a signature tapping technique. It's a beautifully simplistic song that was supported by a memorable melody, some new guitar sounds and techniques, and a sense of melancholy that was reflected in the songs' title.

"Always with Me, Always with You" was nominated for the Best Pop Instrumental Performance Grammy in 1989. It was also made into a conceptual video that was in regular rotation on MTV. The mere appearance of an instrumental song on MTV or on popular radio made this song a great success and a true musical enigma.

Steve Vai (1960-) is the premier guitarist, or as Frank Zappa described him, "stunt guitarist" of his generation. Vai coaxes sounds out of the guitar that no one else can create. He is a musical instrument inventor, composer, arranger, educator, bandleader, and sideman. Vai was inspired by jazz, fusion, rock, blues, classical, and broadway show music. After an early obsession with the guitar styles of Jimmy Page, Jeff Beck, Jimi Hendrix, and Brian May, Vai discovered the music and guitar playing of Frank Zappa. Steve's extreme interest in Zappa's music led him to transcribe a great deal of his recorded solos and performances. In 1980, Zappa auditioned Vai to be a guitarist in his band. As a protégé to Zappa, Vai's musical world and concepts erupted. During his tenure with Zappa, Vai released 1984's Flex-able. Vai's reputation grew quickly. He remained with Zappa through 1983

In 1985, David Lee Roth debuted his new band that included; Steve Vai, bassist Billy Sheehan (from the band Talas), and fusion drummer Gregg Bissonette. After two recordings; Roth's debut, Eat' Em and Smile, and the poppier Skyscraper, Vai left the Roth band in 1989 to further his musical horizons. Vai next recorded one of the most influential guitar records, 1990's Passion & Warfare. Vai's career would progress with his evolving musical and guitar approach on his albums that included; 1993's Sex & Religion, 1996's Flex-Able Leftovers, 1999's The Ultra Zone, 2005's Real Illusions: Reflections, 2012's The Story of Light, and 2016's Modern Primitive. Vai has composed many soundtracks and released several live DVD's. He even played a satanic guitarist in an unforgettable scene from the movie *Crossroads*. Steve Vai has also contributed to the legacy of the guitar by inventing several products including his Ibanez Jem guitars.

By the mid-1980's, Joe Satriani and Steve Vai had shaken the guitar world with their innovative recordings. Another brilliant guitar talent, **Yngwie Malmsteen** (1963-) made his stunning musical entrance. His work with the bands Steeler and Alcatrazz was the beginning of his solo career. Between these three guitarists, *shredding* guitar was fully defined. In 1983, Yngwie Malmsteen made his recording debut with the heavy metal band Steeler (who broke up after the recording). Malmsteen joined the band Alcatrazz and released two albums, No

> "Here's the secret about the guitar-It's defiant. It will never let you conquer it. The more you get involved with it, the more you realize how little you know."
>
> – Les Paul

Parole From Rock 'n' Roll and Live Sentence. Malmsteen's neo-classical guitar approach was a hyper-driven progression from the style of Ritchie Blackmore, while his vocabulary emanated from classical composers J.S. Bach and Niccolo Paganini. His solo debut titled Rising Force featured drummer Barrimore Barlow from Jethro Tull and keyboardist Anders Johansson. It was nominated for a Grammy and named by Guitar World as one of the great guitar shred albums. Rising Force included Malmsteen's two most popular and requested songs, "Black Star" and "Far Beyond the Sun."

In 1996, Malmsteen recorded a covers record titled Inspiration. It found him playing songs by Kansas, Deep Purple, Jimi Hendrix, UK, Rainbow, and Rush. 1997's Facing the Animal, included the legendary drummer Cozy Powell (Jeff Beck, Rainbow, Whitesnake). After several more solo recordings, Malmsteen recorded his masterpiece in 1998 titled Concerto for Electric Guitar and Orchestra in E Flat Minor Op. 1. In 2003, Malmsteen joined Satriani and Vai on the G3 tour, resulting in a DVD. In 2014, Malmsteen created the Guitar Gods 2014 Tour that featured guitarists Bumblefoot and Gary Hoey. In 2016, Steve Vai called on Malmsteen to join his all-star heavy metal band and tour called Generation Axe. Yngwie Malmsteen has released over 20 solo records.

There have been many popular guitar shredders besides Satriani, Vai, and Malmsteen. They have all brought different musical characteristics to the table. Some of these artists included: **Tony MacAlpine** (1960-), **Shawn Lane** (1963-2003), and **Paul Gilbert** (1966-). Other influential guitar "slingers" included; **Richie Kotzen** (1970-), **Greg Howe** (1963-), **Guthrie Govan** (1971-), **Eric Johnson** (1954-), and **Buckethead.**

Buckethead (1969) is a very popular underground musician. He has an enormous cult following of fans and musicians alike. He has collaborated with bassist Bootsy Collins, bassist-producer Bill Laswell, avant-garde jazz musician John Zorn, Primus's Les Claypool, and Iggy Pop. Buckethead was in Guns 'N Roses for four years appearing on their Chinese Democracy recording and has released over 30 solo recordings. For most of his career, he has performed with a "Freddy styled Halloween" (horror movie) white mask over his face, and an upside down bucket on his head, thus keeping his true identity unknown. He came to prominence through his appearance on the super-group Praxis' record Transmutation. Some of Buckhead's most accessible work was his collaboration with bassist Jonas Hellborg and Santana drummer Michael Shrieve on the recording Octave of the Holy Innocents. His style ranges from avant-garde walls of guitar sound to blistering heavy metal, to minimal acoustic soundscapes.

Discussion Question

Which of the styles discussed in this chapter had the most impact on rock music? Does this style, mixed with other rock elements, provide the potential for the further evolution of rock music going forward? Be specific and give musical examples.

Chapter Seventeen: Important Musical Styles That Mixed with Rock

Rock Hard Fact

Termites eat through wood two times faster when listening to rock music.

"Real Fact" #33,
Snapple Ice Tea Bottle Cap

Chapter Eighteen:
Rock Music Visionaries

The definition of a visionary is multi-faceted. It could denote a person with original ideas about the future, a person with the ability to "see," or for our purposes, "to hear" the future. A visionary is someone who thinks about the future or makes advancements in a creative and imaginative way. A visionary is also a person who is ahead of their time and who has a powerful plan for change in the future. These definitions are often used to describe the blueprint for the perfect CEO of a corporation, someone that can take risks, yet communicate effectively with the employees in their company and other leaders in the outside world.

This final chapter isn't a "save the very best for last" chapter. Previously profiled artists such as David Bowie, Jimi Hendrix, and bands like The Who and Led Zeppelin exhibited musicianship at the highest of levels. Still, the artists and bands highlighted in this chapter *do* represent some of the highest levels of musicianship in rock music history. They also defy simple genre categorization. In the former golden age of record stores, how easy was it to place Steely Dan or The Band in a bin in the *rock section*? Not easily done. Some of the artists and bands discussed in this book straddled the line between rock and other music genres. Some bands possessed musical elements of both punk and metal, some were both country and hard rock, while others were progressive and pop-oriented.

Some artists and bands created entirely new genres of rock music while others combined genres in completely unique ways with stunning and unpredictable results. This chapter examines four solo artists and two bands that have demonstrated extraordinary musical vision and have redefined rock music in a variety of ways. These music visionaries are **Frank Zappa**, **The Band**, **Joni Mitchell**, **Steely Dan**, **Brian Eno**, and **Peter Gabriel**.

Frank Zappa (1940-1993) was an American vocalist/guitarist/composer, activist and filmmaker born in Baltimore, Maryland in 1940. Frank's father, Francis Zappa, worked for the U.S. Government and defense industry, resulting in many geographical moves for the Zappa family. In late 1951, The Zappa family moved to California where Frank took his first steps to becoming a musician by joining the school band and playing the snare drum. Zappa developed a love for rhythm and blues and doo-wop music. By 1955, he joined a band as their drummer. Unusual for a young R&B drummer, Frank Zappa also developed an interest in avant-garde classical music, especially the works of Edgard Varese and Igor Stravinsky (see Zappa classical profile). After graduating from high school, Zappa took harmony and arranging courses at a few local colleges and switched from drumset to the guitar.

Zappa married Kathryn Sherman in 1960 (got divorced in 1964). He continued to play in a variety of rock and R&B bands and began to compose film scores for low budget B-movies. While working on the score for the film *The Worlds Greatest Sinner*, Zappa worked at the Pal Recording Studio with Paul Buff. They formed a partnership and began composing and recording pop songs together. Next, Zappa moved to Los Angeles and joined an R&B band called The Soul Giants. Along with vocalist Ray Collins, bassist Roy Estrada, and drummer Jimmy Carl Black, they played Zappa's original tunes and changed their name to The Mothers. Zappa's multiple music interests made him different from other R&B artists. Besides his evolving rock and film scoring career, Zappa continued to explore the works of contemporary classical composers.

Zappa secured a recording contract with MGM to create five albums over a two year period (they were forced to change the band name so they went with The Mothers of Invention). Their 1966 debut double album, Freak Out!, slowly climbed the U.S. charts to a respectable number twenty-three. Freak Out! pushed the limits of how close a rock album could get without being classified as an avant-garde recording. Recognized as one of rock's first concept albums, Freak Out! focused

> "I live my daydreams in music. I see my life in terms of music...I get the most joy in life out of music."
>
> - Albert Einstein

> "There's just something about it. The earliest, most primitive rhythm and blues. All different styles from Delta stuff to Doo Wop vocal groups. I just loved it because of what was in it... because of the sound of it, and because of the feelings that the performers had in that music at that time. It really said something to me."
>
> – Frank Zappa

on the tumultuous 1960's culture of America with songs like "Trouble Every Day" that addressed the Watts' riots and other events in 1965 Los Angeles. After going East to tour in New York and Montreal, The Mothers of Invention endured some lineup changes and recorded Absolutely Free in 1967. Innovative like Freak Out!, this album continued with Zappa's extended compositions, abrupt meter changes, and brilliant lyrics. Later that same year, Zappa recorded his first solo album, Lumpy Gravy, having signed with Capital Records (after a conflict with the band's deal with MGM). The Mothers of Invention added keyboardist/composer Ian Underwood and recorded 1968's We're Only In It for the Money. This recording was an elaborate parody of The Beatles' Sgt. Pepper's Lonely Hearts Club Band. By this point, The Mothers of Invention had established their approach to writing complex songs that parodied American culture utilizing blues, jazz, R&B, early rock 'n' roll, and doo-wop vocals. Zappa's love of avant-garde compositional techniques and electronic sounds was on full display.

In 1968, Zappa and The Mothers of Invention recorded Cruising with Ruben & the Jets, an authentic collection of R&B and doo-wop songs (vocalist/guitarist Lowell George joined at this time). 1969's double album, Uncle Meat, reached the U.S. charts top fifty (a home video release of Uncle Meat was issued in 1989). 1969 also saw Zappa and his new business associate, Herb Cohen, form a new record label, Bizarre Records. Zappa then released a compilation titled Mothermania. Zappa soon began work on his second solo album and announced that he was breaking up the band, although he would continue to use the Mothers of Invention name (also Lowell George and Roy Estrada left to form Little Feat). In the fall of 1969, Zappa released his solo album, Hot Rats. It would become one of his most popular recordings and spawned the classic instrumental composition "Peaches en Regalia." Zappa also archived an extensive collection of songs that were previously recorded with The Mothers of Invention. He would later release this material.

"Peaches en Regalia"
by Frank Zappa

If there is such a thing as a jazz-fusion standard, then "Peaches en Regalia" certainly qualifies. "Peaches en Regalia" contained one of Frank Zappa's most enduring melodies. The song's introductory drum fill, recorded by drummer Ron Selico, has become an instantly recognizable announcement of the tune. On the studio recording, Zappa played a short solo on an instrument known as an "octave-bass." Ian Underwood overdubbed numerous instruments on this track including; saxophone, clarinet, flute, and keyboard parts. Zappa recorded "Peaches" on three albums but the Hot Rats version was the strongest. A second arrangement included wordless vocals by Howard Kaylan and Mark Volman and was recorded live on Zappa's Fillmore East-June 1971 album.

Beginning in 1971, "Peaches en Regalia" was an important part of Zappa's live performances all the way up until his 1988 tour. "Peaches" was often a show opener (especially with the above mentioned opening drum fill) and Zappa also utilized it as an encore in later live performances. Zappa commented on the appeal of "Peaches" when he said, "It's the only thing I've never heard anybody say they didn't like (about his songs)." #1 1981's Tinseltown Rebellion release contained another version titled "Peaches III." This version featured keyboardist Tommy Mars' signature synthesizer sound and an altered bridge section.

The 1970's saw Frank Zappa release over twenty studio albums, a dizzying pace by any standards. A new lineup, now simple called The Mothers, was formed in 1970 with vocalists Mark "Flo" Volman and Howard "Eddie" Kaylan (from the pop group The Turtles). Zappa also added keyboardist George Duke and drummer Aynsley Dunbar. This theatrical lineup was known for their provocative epics about life on the road. They lasted until the end of 1971. 1970's Burnt Weeny Sandwich, Weasels Ripped My Flesh, and Chunga's Revenge mixed Zappa's archived Mothers of Invention tracks with more recent recordings of the current band. 1971's Fillmore East-June 1971 showcased guest appearances by John Lennon and Yoko Ono and had some commercial success. At a live 1971 performance in London, Zappa was pushed off the stage by an audience member causing him to break his ankle and sustain other injuries. In 1972, Zappa and The Mothers released a live show, Just Another Band from L.A., that charted in the top 100.

While recovering from his injuries, Zappa organized a big band in L.A. to play jazz-fusion and called it The Grand Wazoo Orchestra. They made two albums in 1972, Waka/Jawaka and The Grand Wazoo. By 1973, Zappa had fully recovered and put together a new band still called The Mothers that included; vocalist/saxophonist Napoleon Murphy Brock, drummer Chester Thompson, and percussionist Ruth Underwood. This unit made numerous recordings and toured until disbanding in 1974. Their recording output included 1973's Over-Nite Sensation, and 1974's Apostrophe (') that featured ex-Cream bassist Jack Bruce. Apostrophe (') became the highest charting (to date) Zappa album, peaking at number ten on the U.S. charts with the hit "Don't Eat the Yellow Snow." 1974's Roxy & Elsewhere was live double album that was credited to Zappa/Mothers.

1975's One Size Fits All followed with a collaboration by Zappa and his old pal, Don Vliet (Captain Beefheart). It was titled Bongo Fury and released in 1975. After 1976's rock-oriented Zoot Allures, Zappa wanted to release a four-album set to be titled Lather. However, the Warner Bros. label refused, so Zappa separately released Zappa in New York and Studio Tan in 1978 and Sleep Dirt and Orchestral Favorites in 1979. Zappa established another record label in 1979 and released his highest charting album in five years with Sheik Yerbouti. This album marked some Zappa milestones. With clever and smutty lyrics, parodies, and creative compositions, Sheik Yerbouti reached number twenty-one on the U.S. charts and the hit, "Dancin' Fool," went to number twenty-three. This would lead to Zappa's ambitious rock opera that he released in two volumes, 1979's Joe's Garage Act I and Joe's Garage Acts II & III.

Groundbreaking album Joe's Garage Act I
by Frank Zappa

In Joe's Garage Act I, Frank Zappa continued to explore his interest with road stories, ethnic stereotypes ("Catholic Girls"), and crude subjects such as venereal disease ("Why Does It Hurt When I Pee?"). Zappa reflected on his approach when he said, "It started out to be just a bunch of songs, but together, they looked like they had continuity. So I went home one night midway through recording, wrote the story and changed it into an opera. It's probably the first opera that you can really tap your feet to and get a couple of good laughs along the way." #2

Rock Hard Fact

In 1968, Frank Zappa appeared on The Monkees TV show dressed as guitarist Mike Nesmith. Later in the episode, Zappa was seen "playing" a car by striking it like a drum.

Chapter Eighteen: Rock Music Visionaries

<u>Joe's Garage Act I</u>, and its sequel, <u>Joe's Garage Acts II & III</u>, comprised a three-part rock opera that told Frank Zappa's semiautobiographical story about a musician in a society who regarded music as a social ill. This album series explored themes of censorship, free will, individualism, and human sexuality, all while satirizing Catholicism and Scientology. Zappa also used these works as a platform to criticize government. The liner notes explained that "JOE'S GARAGE is a stupid story about how the government is going to try to do away with music. (a prime cause of unwanted mass behavior)...If the plot of the story seems just a little bit preposterous, and if the idea of The Central Scrutinizer enforcing laws that haven't been passed yet makes you giggle, just be glad you don't live in one of the cheerful little countries where, at this very moment, music is either severely restricted...or, as it is in Iran, totally illegal." #3

Side one opened with "The Central Scrutinizer," then "Joe's Garage," "Catholic Girls," and "Crew Slut." "The Central Scrutinizer" was Frank Zappa speaking through a small plastic megaphone and delivering a funny and sarcastic commentary about the environment of Los Angeles. "Catholic Girls" was an attack on the culture of how teenaged school girls are groomed for society. The story progressed into the track "Crew Slut," about one of Zappa'a favorite subjects, groupies.

Side two opened with "Wet T-Shirt Nite," then "Toad-O Line," "Why Does It Hurt When I Pee?," and "Lucille Has Messed My Mind Up." <u>Joe's Garage</u> was one of Zappa's works that involved extensive use of metric shifts. Also, most of the guitar solos were taken from live shows and pasted into the studio tracks. Zappa would check to see what key a particular live solo was in and then attempt to match it to one of <u>Joe's Garage</u>'s studio tracks.

Frank Zappa had many talented versions of his band over the years. The lineup for <u>Joe's Garage</u> was one of his most impressive. They were; Zappa, guitarists/vocalists Warren Cuccurullo and Danny Walley, vocalist Ike Willis, keyboardists Peter Wolf and Tommy Mars, bassist Arthur Barrow, percussionist Ed Mann, drummer Vinnie Colaiuta, and others. At the end of <u>Joe's Garage</u>, Zappa professed his credo of "Information is not knowledge. Knowledge is not wisdom. Wisdom is not truth. Truth is not beauty. Beauty is not love. Love is not music. Music is the best."

Frank Zappa became very frustrated with the constant censorship of his music and the artists that he championed. He made newspaper headlines in the mid-1980's when he battled the Parents Music Resource Center (PMRC), a politically powerful interest group (see chapter seventeen) that lobbied to have warning labels printed on albums that they found obscene. Zappa began to issue a warning label on his own albums that illustrated his combination of witty satire and serious social activism.

The decade of 1980's was even more prolific for Zappa (than the 1970's), recording and releasing over twenty-five studio recordings! 1981's double album, <u>Tinsel Town Rebellion</u>, was the first release on Zappa's new Barking Pumpkin Label. The title track "Tinsel Town Rebellion," provided a good example of Zappa's lyrical wit and cynical attitude toward the music industry. Zappa described a bands' fate in an excerpt of the song's lyrics: *If they're lucky they'll get famous for a week or two perhaps/They'll buy some ugly clothes to wear and hope the business don't collapse/Before some stupid magazine decides they're really good'/They're a Tinsel Town Rebellion Band from downtown Hollywood."*

In 1981, Zappa simultaneously released three instrumental albums via mail order including; <u>Shut Up 'n Play Yer Guitar</u>, <u>Shut Up 'n Play Yer Guitar Some More</u>, and <u>Return of the Son of Shut Up 'n Play Yer Guitar</u>. Zappa also made available the incredible transcribed parts of his guitar solos as well as the drum parts of Vinnie Colaiuta and Terry Bozzio.

1981's <u>You Are What You Is</u> showcased former Mothers' drummer Jimmy Carl Black and 1982's <u>Ship Arriving Too Late to Save a Drowning Witch</u> featured Zappa's daughter, Moon Unit, on vocals. The later yielded Zappa's biggest chart hit, "Valley Girl." In 1983, he followed with the rock album <u>The Man from Utopia</u> and then <u>Baby Snakes</u>.

The Orchestral Music of Frank Zappa

When Frank Zappa was only a teenager, he understandably fell in love with R&B music. However, his interest in the classical avant-garde music of Edgard Varese seemed to come out of nowhere. Zappa first learned about Varese from a magazine article which stated that Sam Goody (and his record store) could sell any music, even the dissonant composition "Ionisation" by Edgard Varese. An interested Frank Zappa acquired this work and listened to it endlessly. Later, Zappa would correspond with Varese by mail but never did get to meet him. Zappa equally loved R&B bands and composers such as Varese and Igor Stravinsky. He remembered, "what appealed to me in the Varese album was that the writing was so direct. It was like, here is a guy who's writing dissonant music and he's not f***ing around." #4

Zappa took every theory and composition class he could in high school and later in junior college. He read H.A. Clarke's book titled *Counterpoint: Strict and Free* and Walter Piston's *Harmony*. Zappa was introduced to *serial music* (while in high school) and the works of Arnold Schoenberg and many post-Wagner avant-garde composers. He soon began to compose *film scores*. In 1961 (at the age of twenty-one), Zappa was able to get his score for "The World's Greatest Sinner" performed by the fifty-two piece Pomona Valley Symphony Orchestra. Zappa's first solo album, 1967's <u>Lumpy Gravy</u>, announced his double life as a serious orchestral composer. It contained collaged bits of orchestral music, spoken word passages, and occasional pop-influenced material. The music was loosely tied together with bits of dialogue. Zappa employed the fifty member Abnuceals Emuukha Electric Symphony Orchestra for the project. Next, an invitation by Los Angeles Philharmonic Orchestra conductor Zubin Mehta prompted Zappa to assemble a new group of rock musicians and write a work titled <u>200 Motels</u>. Zappa and his new band, now called The Mothers, performed this work at UCLA in the spring of 1970. A movie version of *200 Motels* was made with The Royal Philharmonic and featured guest appearances by Ringo Star and Keith Moon.

In 1979, Zappa recorded <u>Orchestral Favorites</u>, an instrumental album that consisted of five pieces that were recorded live, again with the Abnuceals Emuukha Electric Orchestra at Royce Hall, UCLA. This was Zappa's third album to utilize a full orchestra. In the winter of 1983, The London Symphony Orchestra, under the direction of conductor Kent Na-

Rock Hard Fact

Scientists from various fields have honored Frank Zappa by naming new discoveries after him. Belgian biologists Bosmans and Bosselaers discovered a type of spider in Cameroon and named it Pachygnatha Zappa.

349

gano, performed compositions by Frank Zappa. This was in preparation for three days of recording sessions that produced 1983's London Symphony Orchestra, Vol. I followed by London Symphony Orchestra, Vol. II in 1987. The Ensemble InterContemporain (a 16 piece ensemble), under the direction of Pierre Boulez, recorded and released some of Zappa's smaller chamber works on Boulez Conducts Zappa; The Perfect Stranger in 1984. On this same album, Zappa released four tracks that he recorded on the Synclavier, an advanced synthesizer. The Synclavier would open new possibilities for composition and orchestration by freeing Zappa from the technical limitations of live classical musicians (even highly skilled). Zappa was fascinated with the possibilities of replicating orchestral arrangements on the Synclavier and moving forward, he turned to it increasingly.

Zappa also discovered the manuscripts of music composed in the 18th century by an ancestor of his, Francesco Zappa. He recorded an album of these reworked compositions on the Synclavier in March of 1984 and released the results, 1984's Francesco Zappa. This was particularly ironic, given the frothy relationship Frank had with his own father. Zappa's last orchestral work, The Yellow Shark, was released only weeks before he succumbed to cancer. This album of orchestral music consisted of string quartets and ensemble works, from challenging contemporary classical pieces to old Zappa favorites. It included the Synclavier compositions "The Girl in the Magnesium Dress" and "G-Spot Tornado," transcribed for orchestra. The CD also included the compositions "Outrage at Valdez," "Welcome to the United States," and a piano duet, "Ruth Is Sleeping." This grand finale brought to full circle the strong influence that a one-time teenage Frank Zappa felt for the music of Edgard Varese and Igor Stravinsky. It also firmly placed Frank Zappa in that company.

The mid-1980's saw Zappa record 1984's Them or Us, Thing-Fish, and The Old Master, Box I. In 1985, he released Frank Zappa Meets the Mothers of Prevention, and then 1986's Does Humor Belong in Music?, The Old Master, Box II, and Jazz from Hell. The latter was an instrumental album of mostly Synclavier compositions that delivered Zappa's first Grammy win for Best Rock Instrumental Performance. The track "Jazz from Hell" earned a nomination for Best Instrumental Composition. Zappa followed with 1987's The Old Masters, Box III. In 1988, he released the first of a six volume series titled You Can't Do That on Stage Anymore Vol.1 (that culminated with You Can't Do That on Stage Anymore, Vol. 6 in 1992). Also in 1988, Zappa recorded Broadway the Hard Way featuring Sting.

Although ill at the time, Zappa managed to tour in Czechoslovakia and Hungary in June of 1991. In the fall of that year, Zappa was to appear in New York at a performance called "Zappa's Universe," a concert by Zappa band alumni. However, his children had to publicly explain that he couldn't attend due to his suffering from prostate cancer. Zappa next released the 1991 album, Make a Jazz Noise Here, that resulted from his Czechoslovakia visit. Zappa went to Germany in the summer of 1992 to work with the Ensemble Modern on a piece titled "The Yellow Shark" (they had commissioned this work for Zappa to compose). Zappa next released 1993's Ahead of Their Time, an album previously recorded in 1968 by Zappa and The Mothers of Invention at the Royal Festival Hall in London. In October of 1993, Zappa released Playground Psychotics, an archival album of previously unreleased material from the 1970-1971 era of The Mothers. The Yellow Shark was released in November of 1993.

Sadly, Frank Zappa died at age fifty-two from prostate cancer on December 4th, 1993. Frank Zappa released a staggering sixty-two albums during his lifetime. Since 1994, The Zappa family trust has released forty-eight posthumous albums. After Zappa's death, his widow Gail Zappa sold his existing catalog to Rykodisc. However, Zappa had accumulated a vast archive of studio and live recordings that Gail Zappa released posthumously for still hungry Zappa fans. The first of those recordings was 1994's Civilization Phaze III, an album Zappa was working on at the time of his death. Many more albums of both studio recordings and live concerts have been released. Also, expanded versions of previously released albums such as Zappa's debut, Freak Out!, were posthumously released. Frank Zappa's son, Dweezil Zappa, has kept his father's music alive with his own touring band, Zappa Plays Zappa. They debuted in 2006.

Among Zappa's favorite compositions from his own catalogue were; "Oh No" (the theme from Lumpy Gravy), "Uncle Meat," "Brown Shoes Don't Make It," "Dinah-Moe Humm," "Peaches en Regalia," and others. Zappa essentially gave up playing guitar around 1988 to focus on keyboard composition utilizing the Synclavier. It's interesting to speculate how Zappa would have utilized the rapidly evolving music and computer technology had he lived longer. Around the time of his death, Zappa was also starting to explore world music.

Frank Zappa cultivated his rare musical genius by drawing from an enormous variety of musical sources to form a prolific and creative body of work. His impact on twentieth-century music was formidable in many different ways. Zappa's compositions ranged from simple doo-wop vocals to jagged atonality and complex harmonic structures. This created a musical crossover never before seen. Frank Zappa's guitar playing was daring and provided the melodic basis for many of his unique compositions. He was a real 1960's guitar hero in the company of Beck, Page, and Hendrix. As a bandleader, Zappa steered rock music in new directions. He wrote compositions that showcased the individual talents of some of rock musics' best musicians. His works were extremely challenging to perform and taxed the skills and imagination of his sidemen. A few of these prodigious musicians included; guitarists Steve Vai, Adrian Belew, and Warren Cuccurullo, keyboardists George Duke, Tommy Mars, and Eddie Jobson, vocalists Ray Collins and Ike Willis, and drummers Aynsley Dunbar, Chester Thompson, Terry Bozzio, and Vinnie Colaiuta.

A great amount of Zappa's work was journalistic in nature. He wrote from a writers perspective, rather than a musician's. He was an iconoclast in the American tradition of Ken Kesey, Lenny Bruce, Allen Ginsberg, and William S. Burroughs. Zappa operated as an informed insider in the tradition of a late arriving beat poet. His views on politics and the broader social condition were difficult to separate from his music. Frank Zappa never bought into the lifestyle and ideals of the counter-culture. In fact, he relentlessly satirized it as much as he did mainstream culture and the establishment. Part of Zappa's great legacy was his live performances that mixed theatrical improvisation with high level ensemble interplay. Zappa looked back on his brilliant approach and said, "I never had any intention of writing rock music. I always wanted to compose more serious music and have it performed in concert halls, but I knew no one would play it. So I figured that if anyone was ever going to hear anything I

"He's the guy that showed me how to fit any random number of beats inside a bar of music. That's sort of where math and science and music all come together. He opened up rock 'n roll, making something so 'out' actually groove. People are finally starting to scratch the surface and understand what Zappa was all about."

- Gary Lucas, guitarist for Captain Beefheart's band

composed, I'd have to get a band together and play rock music. That's how I got started." #5

Frank Zappa's extreme contrast of influences alone make him unique, but it was his extraordinary musical vision that allowed him to synthesize it all; complete with sarcastic and humorous lyrics that revealed biting social commentary. Zappa was a champion for freedom of expression, evidenced by his stance against the censorship of rock lyrics. No American artist or band has so brilliantly and successfully manipulated rock music to evoke such meaningful social commentary. Zappa never employed the overt sexual underpinnings of glam rock or the pretentious nature of progressive rock. Rather, he invented a dramatic and unique approach to rock music as theater that functioned as a powerful vehicle to express poignant social commentary. Similar to some of the ideals of the punk movement, Zappa was a determined and ruthless adversary of conformity. His sometimes bizarre (and often misunderstood) music and simultaneous image of a madman made him a "larger than life" figure. Denigrated as a freak, castigated as a troublemaker, honored as a patriot, but most of all lauded as a musical genius, Frank Zappa was a true music visionary.

Frank Zappa was posthumously inducted into the Rock and Roll Hall of Fame in 1995 and given a Grammy Lifetime Achievement Award.

The Band (1968-1977) (1983-1999), from 1968 through the mid-1970's, became one of the most influential and popular (more with music critics than mainstream rock fans) bands in rock music history. Their progression from Ronnie Hawkin's backup band to performing that same role for Bob Dylan, allowed them to evolve and build a unique musical rapport. The Band retired from touring after their historic The Last Waltz concert in 1976 but they did re-form in 1983 and worked as solo artists as well.

In 1957, vocalist Ronnie Hawkins, a rockabilly musician and ambitious bandleader from Arkansas, assembled a backup band he named **The Hawks** (1957-1963). Drummer **Levon Helm** (who also played guitar and sang) was the first to join the Hawks in early 1960. Levon spent his youth soaking in the rich blues tradition of the Mississippi Delta and music scene in West Helena, Arkansas. Levon at first played guitar and sang before becoming a drummer. He eventually got up the nerve to sit in with the great Conway Twitty. Helm recalled, "I got up and probably did one of Sonny Boy Williamson's things, and that might have been my debut as a singer in front of a band. I can't tell you what a feeling it gave me to be up on that stage. I was in *high cotton!* #6

Hawkins and his Hawks, with Levon on drums, gigged all over the American South and played in Ontario, Canada, where they made more money than at home. Hawkins was looking to fill some holes in his group and first encountered guitarist **Robbie Robertson** (only fifteen years old), who would initially play bass in The Hawks. Robertson, like Helm, was another musical sponge and had very good ears. He also wrote songs and worked very hard on his guitar skills. Hawkins liked Robertson, but was at first reluctant to hire him due to his young age. Plus, he didn't need another guitar player. However, Hawkins did need a bass player and said to Robertson, "Son, can you play any bass? (Robertson lied and said yes). Hawkins replied, start practicing. I'll call you next week." #7 Hawkins didn't call but Robertson persisted and begged his way into the band. Hawkins would not be sorry, since Robertson progressed at an astonishing rate. Robertson developed a Steve Cropper-like rhythmic guitar feel and possessed tremendous ensemble listening skills.

By the summer of 1961, bassist **Rick Danko** joined the band and Robertson moved to rhythm guitar behind Fred Carter's (and for a short time, Roy Buchanan's) lead guitar playing. Danko, like Robertson, was a raw talent who worked hard on his bass skills. Helm had his doubts about Danko but Hawkins saw his potential. Hawkins said, "The boy's (Rick Danko) a *hell* of a talent. Take my word for it. He's gonna play bass when Rebel (bassist Rebel Paine) goes home." #8 Next, Pianist **Richard Manuel** was added in the fall of 1961. Manuel was in a band called The Rebels when the Hawks first heard him sing. Helm, immediately impressed, said, "Richard Manuel was a whole show unto himself. He was hot. He was about the best singer I'd ever heard; most people said he reminded them of Ray Charles. He'd do those ballads, and the ladies would swoon. To me that became the highlight of our show." #9

The last to join was piano/organist/saxophonist **Garth Hudson.** Hudson, a classically trained pianist, was well versed in music theory and many thought he'd rather play Bach than rock. He was easily considered the best musician on the club circuit where The Hawks performed. Hawkins had tried to hire him as early as 1959, but Hudson showed no interest. Finally, Hudson only agreed to join The Hawks if he was paid more and gave lessons to the other band members. One by one, the future members of The Band were now in place as The Hawks. This was like adding special ingredients to a recipe that you didn't even know you were preparing to cook. The taste would later produce some of the greatest music in American music history and become the bedrock of a music genre called **Americana**.

Ronnie Hawkins & The Hawks were a rock 'n' roll force in the early 1960's. They were Toronto, Canada's rockabilly answer to Elvis Presley, with a sound that was high energy and R&B based. Their approach was influenced by the blues of artists from Chess Records mixed with the R&B of artists from Sun Records. They also had that Bo Diddley beat. The Hawks were a tight unit that played with precision. They were at their best performing for crowds that wanted to dance and have a good time. Rick Danko saw the musical potential and remembered, "I knew that Richard and I sounded great singing together. He brought a lot of power and strength to the group. He brought in gospel music from his church upbringing. Plus, he loved to play and just come up with new things. It was like having a force of nature in the band." #10

The group was developing real chemistry but Hawkins was a task-master of a leader. The new Canadian members of Danko, Manuel, and Hudson, whom had replaced Hawkins' southerners, were ready to do their own thing. Hawkins soon lost control of The Hawks. In the summer of 1963, Ronnie Hawkins and his backup Hawks parted ways. The group had outgrown their leader's overbearing personality. Levon Helm recalled, "It was a combination of a lot of things that led us to leave the Hawk late in 1963. But the band really split up because of age as much as anything else. We were younger, and everyone wanted that independence that youth craves. Ronnie had a set of rules, and he'd fine you if you broke em. He played the kind of music he was interested in, and we wanted a band where everyone played and had a voice. #11

The Hawks continued both as the Levon Helm Sextet (sometimes still referred to as The Hawks) and The Canadian Squires, recording albums under both names. Soon, Helm's band met John Hammond Jr. and did a series of recording sessions in New York. This led to their introduction to Bob Dylan. The timing was right since

---

Rock Hard Fact

The Band were a big influence on Eric Clapton, who was in Cream when Music From Big Pink was released. The Band played on Clapton's 1976 No Reason to Cry album.

"The Band is probably the ultimate example of people taking all kinds of music, from gospel to fife-and-drum blues from Southern Mississippi to shape-note singing to mountain music to folk music to on and on and putting them all in this big pot and mixing up a new gumbo."

- Robbie Robertson.

Dylan was in need of a backup band for some upcoming concert dates. Helm and Robertson backed Dylan at a 1965 Forest Hills concert in New York and afterwards, Dylan heard the complete Hawks. He decided to employ the whole band. At first, Helm and The Hawks didn't even know how popular Dylan had become. They were excited to play with Dylan but it did come at a price. The Hawks had previously met and played with the legendary blues man Sonny Boy Williamson II (remember Helm was from Helena, Arkansas). They were ready to record with him. By the time they could return to the South to collaborate with him, Sonny Boy had died.

Dylan played a series of concerts from September 1965 to May 1966, billed as Bob Dylan and The Band (still officially The Hawks). Backing up Bob Dylan presented many challenges for Helm and The Hawks. Dylan was looking to play electric adaptations of folk music, with lots of guitar strumming. But Helm and The Hawks possessed the excitement of Chuck Berry, Bo Diddley, and Jerry Lee Lewis all rolled into one. This approach would be shelved, at least for now. Another issue was Dylan's relationship with his audience. Many of their concerts were met with unhappy and heckling audiences that still contained folk music purists. Dylan was performing for crowds that often rejected him on principle. Helm was affected by the negativity and left after a little more than a month. He went home to work on an oil rig in the Gulf of Mexico and missed their world tour in 1966. Also, Dylan was not big on rehearsing which resulted in performances that were freewheeling, since he made spontaneous musical changes along the way. In a positive sense, this would later make The Band a more flexible live unit with their quick ears and an ability to musically adjust on the fly.

On July 29th, 1966, while on break from the tour, Dylan was badly injured in a motorcycle accident. He isolated himself by moving to Woodstock, New York. Briefly, The Hawks (still not called The Band) returned to the barroom circuit, often backing up other singers. Dylan wanted The Hawks to join him in Woodstock in February 1967. The four remaining members of The Hawks, on the advice of Dylan's manager, Albert Grossman (who would later manage The Band), joined Dylan in Woodstock. They did recording sessions that would later become the 1968 double album, <u>The Basement Tapes</u>. Hudson, Manuel, and Danko rented a large pink house in West Saugerties, New York (famously known now as Big Pink). At first, Dylan and The Hawks recorded some rough demos at Dylan's' house in Woodstock (initially without Helm) and then moved the sessions to Big Pink. Levon Helm soon returned for the ongoing sessions.

Part of Dylan's involvement with The Hawks was his intention to continue to move his music forward from his innovative folk-rock albums <u>Bringing it All Back Home</u>, <u>Highway 61 Revisited</u>, and <u>Blonde on Blonde</u> (Robertson played on <u>Blonde on Blonde</u>). However, those recordings were made up of session players and Dylan hadn't worked with a steady band since high school (usually choosing to perform solo). Touring and rehearsing new material with The Hawks had reacquainted Dylan with the feelings and demands of being part of a collective unit. A really good one. Dylan's camaraderie and shared musical interests with The Hawks led to a relaxed working relationship. This allowed for time (no studio meter running) to musically experiment with song ideas and mixtures of styles. Dylan reawakened The Hawk's interest in country music. In turn, The Hawks passion for early rock 'n' roll influenced Dylan's own musical development. <u>The Basement Tapes</u> contained old folk songs mixed with country and blues elements. Dylan and The Hawks fostered a sense of youthful fun with the occasional Elvis or doo-wop cover. What emerged was the collective sound of Dylan with five strong individual voices that mixed folk, gospel, blues, R&B, classical, and rock 'n' roll. All rolled into one. <u>The Basement Tapes</u> was a transcendent work that foreshadowed the unique sound that would characterize the future Americana style of The Band. Aside from The Hawks standard instrumentation, a new sound emerged from <u>The Basement Tapes</u> with the inclusion of mandolin (played by three band members), accordion, and clavinet.

The sessions with Dylan were over by October 1967. The Hawks composed new songs at Big Pink and now pursued the goal of producing an album that sounded totally unique. This would now be their music, developed in isolation from contemporary music trends and the radio. They felt liberated from their past background of the club circuit and the environment (often hostile) of Bob Dylan tours. Levon Helm explained, "We'd grown up with Ronnie Hawkins, playing that quicker tempo of tunes. Now we cut our tempo, or pulse, right in half. The sense of teamwork and collaboration was incredible. Robbie was writing stuff that evoked simple pictures of American life. Richard was writing beautiful songs like 'In a Station' and 'Lonesome Suzie.' Garth took a great song like 'Chest Fever' and composed an organ prelude. Rick's playing and singing were amazing, and that blend of the three voices-Richard, Rick, and me-sounded really rich." #12 Helm was eluding to an ensemble vocal technique The Hawks referred to as "stacking" (voices on top of each other). They collectively learned this by listening to many gospel and soul artists such as The Staple Singers and The Impressions.

When the soon to be former Hawks went into the studio to record their new music, they realized that they didn't have an official name. They soon picked the name Dylan used when referring to them as his backing musicians, The Band. In 1968, The Band released their landmark debut album, <u>Music from Big Pink</u>. Widely acclaimed, the album included three songs written or co-written by Bob Dylan including; "This Wheel's on Fire," "Tears of Rage," and "I Shall Be Released."

Groundbreaking album
Music from Big Pink
by The Band

<u>Music from Big Pink</u> was recorded at A&R studios in New York under the direction of producer Phil Ramone. They recorded in the barn-shaped seventh-floor studio built on top of the building, a room that had very good live acoustics. Helm recalled, "I'd set up in the middle of the room. There was a soundbooth against the wall, which is where Garth placed some of his speakers, so it would be a little muffled... The piano'd be there, and Rick and Robbie would sit on folding chairs, with their amps beside them...There were sound-baffles around the drums, and John (Simon-who engineered the recordings) would lean over them to discuss different drum ideas and strategies... That was the way it worked." #13

Side one opened with "Tears of Rage," then "To Kingdom Come," "In a Station," "Caledonia Mission," and "The Weight." "Tears of Rage" was a slow song about rebellion. With so many psychedelic albums out with burning guitar solos and long jams, The Band deliberately went against the grain. Manuel gave a great vocal performance and Helm created a drumset part where you can hear the drum notes bend

---

"For me, Richard (Manuel) was the true light of The Band. The other guys were fantastic talents, of course, but there was something of the holy madman about Richard. He was raw. When he sang in that high falsetto the hair on my neck would stand on end. Not many people can do that."

- Eric Clapton

down in pitch. "In a Station" was Manuel's song about Overlook Mountain and the peace that The Band now felt after living on the road for so many years. "The Weight," one of The Band's classics, was a song about some of their favorite characters. Real people, such as "Crazy" Chester, were referenced throughout the song. Levon, Rick, and Richard would sing different verses of the song and they all sang the chorus of "put the load right on me!" "The Weight" represented the impossibility of sainthood.

Side two opened with "We Can Talk," then "Long Black Veil," "Chest Fever," "Lonesome Suzie," "This Wheels On Fire," and "I Shall Be Released." Manuel's "We Can Talk" captured the way they all communicated with each other. Manuel, while sitting at the piano, played with a gospel feel and came up with the line "But I'd rather be burned up in Canada/Than to freeze down in the South." "Chest Fever" contained improvised lyrics that Robertson put together in rehearsal but never finished writing. Hudson added an introduction, inspired by J.S. Bach's "Toccata and Fugue," while the bridge had a funny, tuneless Salvation Army band-like feel. Rick Danko played violin, John Simon added baritone horn, and Hudson played tenor saxophone. "Long Black Veil" sounded like an old southern ballad. "This Wheels on Fire" contained Bob Dylan's lyrics that Danko put to music. Hudson added a weird sound by running a telegraph key through a Roxochord toy organ. The album closer, "I Shall Be Released," was the third song Dylan had written for them. The drum sound featured Helm playing the snares of an upside-down drum with his fingers.

Music from Big Pink was an album that would come to define the genre of Americana. The Band found themselves in the process of making this recording. Helm said, "This is what's so important about The Band: Everybody played something that was meaningful and that meshed. There were hardly any solos, and nothing was gratuitous." #14

Music from Big Pink -The Band had arrived!

The Band moved to California to work on their second album and get away from the long winter and temptations of the Woodstock lifestyle. 1969's The Band, dominated by Robertson's writing, was as good as Big Pink. Their climb out of the Bob Dylan shadow was complete and two songs in particular, "The Night They Drove Ol' Dixie Down" and "Up on Cripple Creek" further defined them. Other classic songs were "Across the Great Divide" and "Rag Mama Rag," a full group collaboration.

"Up On Cripple Creek"
by Robbie Robertson

"Up on Cripple Creek" told the story of a mountain man and girl named Bessie. The lyrics talked about a trip to the horse races, listening to Spike Jones, and how the singer was really happy when she "dipped her doughnut in his tea." Levon Helm sang the lead vocals with a very country, folksy feeling. The song was a good example of how Robertson often wrote about curious characters with quirky personalities. "Up on Cripple Creek" became one of The Band's best known tunes. Recorded two or three times in California, most group members didn't like it, so they re-recorded it at The Hit Factory Studios in New York.

On the final studio version, The Band added a few parts to the chorus with new harmonies to complete the song. Garth Hudson found a very funky sound with a Hohner Clavinet D6 played through a Vox Wah Wah pedal. This song is vintage The Band, a unique blend of styles like no other group of musicians could quite imagine. The Band fused funk, country, folk, gospel and rock 'n' roll into a seamless whole. The song was released as a single and eventually peaked at number nine on the U.S. charts. In the fall of 1969, "Up on Cripple Creek" was a hit record and led to The Band's appearance on The *Ed Sullivan Show*. Robertson was listed as the sole songwriter of this tune, although his bandmates disputed that, claiming they co-wrote it. Songwriting credits going to Robertson would become a great source of friction in The Band.

By the time of 1970' Stage Fright, things were changing within the group. The pressures of touring and repeating their earlier successes became a strain. The songs on Stage Fright were more personal and featured denser arrangements. Some of the songs acted as metaphors for the trouble the group was encountering. This was heard in the song, "The Shape I'm In." 1971's Cahoots was released when the group was having problems honoring all of their commitments, including touring and composing new material. 1973's Moondog Matinee was a collection of studio versions of material that The Band had performed onstage, mixed with some old Hawks' tunes. The Band did play a major show that year, a concert at Watkins Glen, New York, before the largest rock crowd (to date) ever assembled. At this venue, The Band took their place in the rock pantheon alongside The Allman Brothers Band and The Grateful Dead.

In 1974, The Band recorded Planet Waves with Bob Dylan and prepared to do a huge national tour with him. It would be more about money than producing any great new music, as heard on a live album recorded from the tour titled Before the Flood. By the end of 1974, The Band members were struggling with a variety of issues. But, they received a boost with the *official* 1975 release of The Basement Tapes (recorded back in 1968). It was first heard as a bootleg release titled The Great White Wonder. This late The Basement Tapes release reminded everyone that The Band and Dylan could evoke musical magic. Also in 1975, The Band's Northern Lights-Southern Cross served as a mild comeback, even with an element of synthesizers slapped onto their writing and production. One last album, 1977's Islands, fulfilled the groups' recording contract.

The Band knew they were finished and marked their end with a historic film documentary, directed by Martin Scorsese, called *The Last Waltz*. This was a live concert performed and filmed on Thanksgiving Day, November 25th, 1976 at the Winterland Ballroom in San Francisco. It was a star-studded affair with guest appearances by Neil Young, Eric Clapton, Muddy Waters, Van Morrison, more than a dozen other music luminaries, and of course, Ronnie Hawkins. 1978's The Last Waltz was a triple live album soundtrack to *The Last Waltz* film.

The Band reunited in 1983 and resumed touring, now without Robbie Robertson, who decided not to return to the group. They recruited some of the old members of The Hawks for the tour. After a performance in Florida in March of 1986, Richard Manuel tragically committed suicide. After some time off, The Band appeared at Bob Dylan's 30th anniversary concert in 1992 and began working on a new album. They recorded Jericho, The Band's first new album in sixteen years. They followed with 1996's High on the Hog and 1998's Jubilation, that included a guest appearance by Eric Clapton. Some of the surviving members of The Band went on to record solo

---

Rock Hard Fact

First looking to call themselves The Crackers or The Honkies (shot down by their record company), Robbie Robertson said "everyone calls us Bob Dylan and The Band," so without Dylan they simply became The Band

---

"As with all Joni Mitchell songs, the musical content supports the lyrics in such a profound way that the entire effect is deepened. It's eerie. Joni has a deep, rich, elaborate, and finely tuned ear for harmony and its effects."

– jazz trumpeter Dave Douglas

albums and pursue acting careers. Sadly, Rick Danko died in 1999 and Levon Helm died in 2012.

The legacy of The Band puts them on a par with The Beatles and Elvis Presley. When they were initially assembled as members of The Hawks, each musician brought extraordinary musicianship and the most eclectic of musical influences that could be imagined. The time that they served to make Ronnie Hawkins' and Bob Dylan's music come to life was only their musical apprenticeship. This was crucial time spent in learning how to make somebody else sound great! It was as if they were a top of the line live studio band. The Band represented what it meant to collaborate and surrender your heart and soul to the collective ensemble. Then, when it came time for Music From Big Pink, The Band created their own genre of music that became known as Americana. And they did it with soul, feeling, and musicianship of the highest caliber. The Band was inducted into the Rock and Roll Hall of Fame in 1994.

Joni Mitchell (1943-) is a Canadian musician and painter born in Saskatoon, Canada in 1943. Her birth name was Roberta Joan Anderson. Joni, at a young age, loved music. She fell in love with the songs of Chuck Berry, Ray Charles (especially What'd I Say"), Elvis Presley, and The Everly Brothers. When she heard Rachmaninoff's "Rhapsody on a Theme of Paganini," Joni new that she wanted to be a musician.

Somewhat of a rebel and a little bit anti-intellectual, Joni loved to paint and dance. She would go on to become a world class painter, near the level of her astounding musicianship and songwriting abilities. In high school, Joni immersed herself in creative writing and was influenced by her writing teacher Arthur Kratzmann. Aware of Joni's art works, Kratzmann told her "if you can paint with a brush, you can paint with music." #15 Joni would later title one of her televised concerts *Painting with Words and Music*. In 1953, at age ten, Joni contracted polio and was initially paralyzed (Jonas Salk's polo vaccine not available until 1955). She fought the disease by dancing and singing. Joni acquired a ukulele and discovered the folk music of The Kingston Trio. She practiced daily and began to listen to jazz musicians like Duke Ellington and Miles Davis. Joni began to believe that her destiny was to deflect all of her loneliness and struggles into music and to make other people feel that they weren't alone. After high school, Joni enrolled in the Alberta College of Art and Design. She also taught herself guitar with the help of a Pete Seeger instructional record. By the fall of 1964, Joni was gigging at nearby folk clubs and performing traditional folk songs such as "When Johnny Comes Marching Home" and "Reuben James."

By 1965, there were major changes in Joni's personal life. Joni moved to Toronto and had a baby that she gave up for adoption. Feeling desperate and alone, she met a musician, Chuck Mitchell, and soon married him and moved to Detroit. Together, they started a publishing company and moved to New York City. Joni Mitchell performed in the NYC folk clubs, but soon began to move away from her folk repertoire, developing her own approach to songwriting. Mitchell frequently experimented with open guitar tunings which influenced her harmonic approach, but also her sense of melodic construction. Joni's earliest compositions were unlike anyone else's. Her songwriting quickly evolved with compositions such as "Born to Take the Highway" and "Urge for Going."

In the fall of 1965, Joni appeared twice on the folk music TV show *Let's Sing Out*, hosted by Oscar Brand. Her first appearance on the show was as the folk singer Joni Anderson. The second was as the transformed Joni Mitchell, with her own music clearly not in the folk tradition. Joni's life was to again change quickly. She divorced Chuck Mitchell and began to attract a lot of attention as an emerging artist. Joni wrote a song titled "Both Sides, Now," that was heard by the legendary musician and producer Al Kooper. Soon, singer Judy Collins became another fan of Joni's and recorded "Both Sides, Now." Joni didn't like Collin's version but knew the exposure would help her (Joni's) career.

"Both Sides, Now"
by Joni Mitchell

"Both Sides, Now" was one of Join Mitchell's early compositions that helped to launch her career. Joni had read Saul Bellow's *Henderson the Rain King* while riding on an airplane. The book referred to seeing clouds while looking out of a plane and that's just what Joni did. She thought about what a privilege it was to be able to see clouds from both sides. Affected by this experience, she had a dream and visualized looking down at the clouds and then up at them. She then wrote "Both Sides Now."

Joni wrote the line "I've looked at life that way" accompanied by a blues riff on her guitar that she repeated on every turnaround. The lyrics expressed a figurative verbal idea that she developed throughout the song. Joni sang, "I've looked at clouds from both sides now" then later sang, "I've looked at love from both sides now." Joni returned to this phrase a little differently each time and with more depth. "Both Sides, Now" demonstrated a strong aspect of her songwriting; the ability to take a four-minute melodic structure and refuse to let the chorus be merely a catchy refrain. Joni Mitchell chiseled away at the song structure and lyrical ideas until something more powerful was revealed. Joni's music and lyrics had become a laboratory that she utilized to probe, explore, and ask questions. The result was only the beginning of her highly creative and unique songwriting.

Joni soon met another legend, Leonard Cohen. They had a brief romantic relationship and he became another fan of her great talent. Cohen remembered, "Joni was some kind of musical monster, her gift somehow put her in another category from the other folksingers. There was a certain ferocity associated with her gift...she is a formidable presence." #16 Joni next met musician David Crosby, another instant fan of her music. He took her to Los Angeles, introduced her to the music community, and asked to produce her debut album. This would be the first of Mitchell's nineteen innovative studio albums that would define her brilliant career.

In 1968, Joni Mitchell released her debut, Song to a Seagull. She was unhappy with the overall sound achieved by David Crosby's production techniques. Nevertheless, the album was a powerful debut. From Joni's now formidable songbook, a few of the songs on Seagull included "Cactus Tree" and "Night in the City." 1969's Clouds featured Joni's daring expression of emotions such as sorrow and enchantment, combined with complex and musically adventurous harmonies. It finally included her own version of "Both Sides, Now" and "Chelsea Morning." Mitchell was now composing at a fast pace and these songs revealed a fantasy world that took the listener on emotional journeys. 1970's Ladies of the Canyon followed with three masterpiece songs, "Big Yellow Taxi" (with the famous line "They paved paradise, put up a parking lot"), "Woodstock," and "The Circle Game." Half of the tracks were stripped down by featuring just Joni's voice and her own instrumental accompaniment.

"That's the music I play at home all the time, Joni Mitchell...she's able to look at something that's happened to her, draw back and crystallize the whole situation, then write about it. She bring tears to my eyes."

- Jimmy Page

Mitchell's fourth album, 1971's Blue, featured recurring themes of love, loss, escape, and a quest for spiritual truth. Blue would become the landmark recording that confessional singer/songwriters would be measured by. This album firmly established Joni Mitchell as a star. On Blue, Mitchell was able to reconcile her life by composing music that focused on her search for personal contentment. Blue was simultaneously sad, poetic, funny, and revelatory. Some of the standout tracks were "River" and "The Last Time I Saw Richard."

Joni felt like it was time for personal change and moved to Vancouver, Canada. She remembered, "Fame made me really nervous and uncomfortable. So I isolated myself and I made my attempt to get back to the garden. I lived with kerosene, stayed without electricity for about a year...I read nearly every psychology book I could get my hands on and threw them all against the wall...depression can be the sand that makes the pearl." #17 Her next album, 1972's For the Roses, was a transitional record. For the Roses represented Joni's shift away from personal exposes' while she moved toward impressionistic vignettes. Joni was now equally inspired by Bob Dylan and some writings about classical music great Ludwig Von Beethoven. This inspired Joni's composition titled "Judgement Of the Moon and Stars" (Ludwig's Tune). For the Roses contained three songs, "Lesson in Survival," "Let The Wind Carry Me," and "Women of Heart and Mind," that were among the best in her vast catalogue.

1972's Court and Spark was Joni Mitchell's most successful album commercially. It peaked at number two in America, number one in Canada, and reached the top twenty in England. It's difficult to pick one breakthrough album from Joni Mitchell's catalogue. Most of her albums revealed her rapid and constant musical growth. Court and Spark was brilliant on many levels.

Groundbreaking album
Court and Spark
by Joni Mitchell

Court and Spark began Mitchell's embrace of jazz and her interaction with world class jazz musicians. Joni, along with her producer, Henry Lewy, heard saxophonist Tom Scott and The L.A. Express one night at the L.A. club, The Baked Potato. Scott had previously added woodwinds and reeds to Joni's For the Roses. However, this time Mitchell brought the entire L.A. Express lineup into the studio to built the arrangements for her new songs. From the L.A. Express band, Joni employed; Tom Scott, keyboardist Joe Sample, guitarist Larry Carlton, bassist Max Bennett, and drummer John Guerin. This new approach wasn't seamless. Joni recalled, "the group didn't really know how heavy to play, and I was used to being the whole orchestra. Many nights I would be very discouraged...but we suddenly overcame the obstacles." #18 Mitchell needed to learn how to not dominate all of the musical space and the band had to play lighter and not view Mitchell as just a folk singer. They soon realized the complexity and richness of her compositions.

Joni Mitchell's unique harmonic sense and innovative guitar playing was on full display on Court and Spark. Her left hand, weakened by childhood polio, could only spare a single finger to run up and down the guitar's neck. But she built polychords with her innovative open tunings. This would be the basis of her complex chromatic harmonies. Session great Larry Carlton remembered, "When we went into the studio with Joni, my job was to help make those songs as great as I thought I could...to help arrange behind her so that she could present those great chords on her songs. Let's take a C major seventh chord and you put a G major chord on top of it. Now you have a C major ninth sharp eleventh chord. Joni would instinctively hear those kinds of sounds." #19

The first side opened with "Court and Spark," then "Help Me," "Free Man in Paris," "Peoples Parties," and "Same Situation." "On Court and Spark," Mitchell began at the piano before the band moved into view behind the song's first verse. Each section built the song emotionally as Mitchell's lyrics explored the topic of love versus freedom. "Help Me," was Joni's only top ten single as a recording artist. It explored various moments from the inside of a personal relationship and was mulit-faceted in its understanding of the topic of love.

The second side opened with "Car on a Hill," then "Down to You," "Just Like This Train," "Raised on Robbery," "Trouble Child," and "Twisted." The song "Down to You" was about looking for love and finding lust instead. The lyrics found the singer reflecting on meaningless relationships. The closing song, "Twisted," after much lyrical soul bearing, ending the album with the line "Instead of one head-I got-two-and you know two heads are better than one."

Court and Spark was a romantic record, in the musical sense and in the way that Joni's songs were about seductions, follies, and illusions of eros. Her musical ideas really were about courting and sparking and flirting with the listener. While it was Joni's biggest seller, Court and Spark was also important because it featured a world of brilliant studio and jazz musicians. Mitchell immediately proved that she was at least their equal and it marked the beginning of her most experimental phase. Other exceptional guest musicians that appeared on Court and Spark included; Robbie Robertson, Jose Feliciano and Joni's old pals, David Crosby and Graham Nash. Cheech Marin and Tommy Chong also added background vocals to "Twisted."

1975's The Hissing of Summer Lawns was an album about Joni Mitchell's view of western society. She continued to utilize many of the best studio and jazz musicians and added the new instrumentation of the Moog and Arp synthesizer. Standout songs included "Edith and the Kingpin" and "In France They Kiss on Main Street." 1976's Hejira contained some of Joni's most expansive writing. Each song, such as "Coyote," was filled with unanswered questions about the definition and contradiction of fulfillment. The great Jaco Pastorius played bass and Neil Young added harmonica parts.

1977's Don Juan's Reckless Daughter was a double album that continued to show the potency of Joni's vision and her ability to extend her musical boundaries. This album immersed deeply into jazz and featured many prominent musicians including; saxophonist Wayne Shorter, Jaco Pastorius, and world percussionists Alex Acuna, Manolo Badrena, and Airto Moreira. 1979's Mingus, her tribute to the legendary jazz bassist Charles Mingus, was not well received by rock or jazz radio stations, but was critically acclaimed.

Joni Mitchell made three studio albums in the 1980's. 1980's Wild Things Run Fast was a sleeker, more contemporary approach that featured bassist Larry Klein, guitarists Michael Landau and Steve Lukather, and drummer Vinnie Colaiuta. A host of other prominent musicians including; Wayne Shorter, Larry Carlton, and Victor Feldman also contributed. 1985's Dog Eat Dog followed

> "I'm more prolific with melodies than with words, but quite often I write poems and then set them to music. I guess I'm primarily an artist; what I like best is making new music. It's like going into a trance; I sit down with a melody and reminisce. I find it easier to think about my feelings in retrospect."
>
> – Joni Mitchell

and then 1988's Chalk Mark in a Rain Storm, with guest appearances by Tom Petty, Peter Gabriel, Willie Nelson, and Billy Idol.

The 1990's yielded three more Joni Mitchell recordings. 1991's Night Ride Home, 1994's Turbulent Indigo, and 1998's Taming the Tiger saw Mitchell's melodic invention and intelligent lyricism still on display. On Taming the Tiger, Joni discovered the possibilities of the Roland VG8 "virtual guitar." This new toy (the VG8) allowed her to expand her sonic explorations with the sound of a muted steel drum on "Harlem in Havana." This album also featured drummer Brian Blade, Wayne Shorter, Larry Klein, Michael Landau, and trumpeter Mark Isham.

The new millennium brought the release of 2000's Both Sides Now. This recording was an orchestral concept album that included covers of the songs "At Last," "A Case of You," and "Stormy Weather." To bring things full circle, Joni recorded a new version of her landmark song "Both Sides, Now." Joni Mitchell had said that 2002's Travelogue would be her last recording. At this point in her life, Joni placed more focus on her great painting skills, something she had done at a high level her whole life (as seen on many of her album covers). In 2007, on the same day that Joni released her final album titled Shine, jazz master Herbie Hancock released his tribute to Joni and her work. It was titled River: The Joni Letters.

Joni Mitchell has suffered from serious health issues that included a brain aneurysm. As of 2017, she had recovered. Joni Mitchell's songwriting and musicianship has placed her in rare company as one of the most revered musicians of the twenty-first century. Her uncanny ability to combine substantive lyrics, creative melodies, and inventive harmonies (heard in her open tunings and poly-chordal approach), has produced a personal style that defies categorization. She is a true music visionary and unequalled talent. Joni Mitchell was inducted into the Rock and Roll Hall of Fame in 1997.

Steely Dan (1972-1981) (1993-present) was founded by guitarist/vocalist/composer **Walter Becker** (1950-2017) and vocalist/keyboardist/composer **Donald Fagen** (1948-). In 1965, Donald Fagen enrolled at Bard College in New York to study English Literature. He remembered, "I studied some orchestration and composition and definitely knew I was going for a career in music of some kind, even though I ended up with a degree in literature. #20 Two years later, Fagen heard Walter Becker playing guitar in a Bard practice room. They soon shared their different musical influences with each other. Becker was immersed in the blues of Howlin' Wolf and B.B. King while Fagen was focused on jazz greats such as Miles Davis, Charlie Parker, and Duke Ellington. Fagen and Becker were writing songs within days of first meeting. Fagen recalled, "We had both been jazz fans since we were nine or ten years old, listened to the same jazz shows and radio and we both got into soul and pop in the mid-sixties." #21 Although the duo started to work together in different musical configurations, they had no future plans, other than the shared desire to one day receive a recording contract. Fagen and Becker started to play some gigs with another Bard student, composer/vocalist Terence Boylan, who secured a recording deal with MGM. Boylan brought Fagen and Becker in to help him arrange his original compositions. This would be Fagen and Becker's first exposure to a big time recording studio (The Hit Factory in New York) that would later become the domain of Steely Dan. Boylan toured to promote his album with Fagen and Becker, but soon the duo left his band to return to school. Fagen graduated from Bard while Becker failed out after three semesters. The duo next relocated to New York City (Fagen moved to Brooklyn while Becker moved to Queens) where they focused on writing songs together.

Unable to afford the recording costs of a demo tape, Fagen and Becker aggressively pursued their songwriting ambitions by approaching anybody who would care to listen to their compositions. After many rejections, they walked into the famous Brill Building in New York City and knocked on the door of JATA Enterprises. JATA was the acronym for Jay and The Americans, a popular vocal group from Brooklyn who had connected with the famous songwriting team of Leiber and Stoller (see chapter three) in the early 1960's. JATA producer Kenny Vance listened to the duo's compositions and was impressed by the originality of the material. He offered to produce a demo for Fagen and Becker and quickly recorded some of their earliest compositions including; "Parker's Band," "Charlie Freak," and "The Roaring of the Lamb." Vance set out to take this demo to all of his contacts in the business. However, he encountered the same negative reaction that Fagen and Becker had experienced. Some people were shocked, some bemused, but all showed no interest.

Fagen and Becker remained undeterred from their main goal, to form a band. They answered an ad in the Village Voice looking for a bassist and keyboardist that were into jazz. The ad had been placed by (later Steely Dan member) Denny Dias, who played guitar in a band called Demian. Fagen and Becker soon joined his band. It wasn't long until they took control of Demian and brought in Vance for consultation. After spending more time marketing the previously recorded demos (with minimal success), Vance realized the duo needed to work and invited them to join Jay and the Americans on a tour. While the duo gained valuable experience backing JATA, they were bored with the music and the whole routine of being on the road (this would later surface in Steely Dan). The duo also arranged horn and string parts for Jay and the Americans and composed songs for JATA's publishing company for $50 per tune.

At this same time, a young producer named Gary Katz met Fagen and Becker at the JATA office. The duo next worked on some projects that included writing and recording material for a soundtrack for a movie titled *You Gotta Walk It Like You Talk It* (recorded with guitarist Denny Dias). They also recorded music for vocalist Linda Hoover. Katz introduced Fagen and Becker to guitarist Jeff "Skunk" Baxter, who they met at a gig in Boston. Shortly after, the duo gave Jay and the Americans notice that they were leaving to concentrate on their own songwriting. In a key career move, Gary Katz brought Fagen and Becker to ABC Records in Los Angeles to become staff songwriters for the label. When Fagan and Becker left New York, Denny Dias still remained in their future plans.

Fagen and Becker were determined to manipulate ABC into allowing them to form their own L.A. band and then release their own records on the label. They knew that moving out West was a familiar career move for many rock bands looking to make an impact in the early 1970's. Meanwhile, the ABC roster was full of artists that didn't write their own material, therefore ABC was in need of a constant flow of original songs. Fagen and Becker wrote compositions for ABC on a daily basis including "Tell Me a Lie" for The Grass Roots (that was never recorded). However, their real focus was writing for themselves and cultivating their band. Fagen and Becker utilized the ABC facilities to write and rehearse their new

---

"Blues is the most important ingredient of pop music. That's what really gives it the soul and the forward motion. Just starting with a regular blues structure is the way a lot if our songs were written... expanding it either harmonically or changing the structure."

- Donald Fagen

Rock Hard Fact

Jimmy Page once said that Elliot Randall's solo on "Reelin' In the Years" was his favorite guitar solo of all time.

songs for a debut album with Denny Dias, guitarist Jeff "Skunk" Baxter (who they invited from New York), and drummer Jim Hodder (who they had previously met).

The management at ABC was impressed with the Fagen/Becker original song "Dirty Work," and thought it would work well for either the Grass Roots or Three Dog Night. ABC also saw the potential of Fagen and Becker's original band dream and put some resources (and expectations) into funding them. The duo signed a contract with ABC (heavily in ABC's favor) and continued to rehearse their new band in the summer of 1972. Gary Katz was chosen to produce their debut record. Donald Fagen was never comfortable or confident with his own lead vocal abilities, particularly singing in public. Katz wanted Fagen to sing all of the lead vocals but Fagen and ABC thought it would be best to bring in another singer. At the suggestion of drummer Jim Hodder, vocalist David Palmer was brought in to add a pop sensibility to some of their songs. Fagen and Becker now had the songs and the band in place. But they still needed a band name. They chose Steely Dan, the name for a sex toy referred to in novelist William Burroughs' book, *Naked Lunch*.

Steely Dan released their debut album Can't Buy a Thrill in 1972. It yielded the surprise hits "Do it Again" that went to number six on the U.S. charts and "Reelin' in the Years" that made it to number eleven (Fagen sang lead vocals on both). On the strength of the hits, Can't Buy a Thrill was a critical and commercial success. However, the supporting tour was a disaster, including an under-rehearsed band and unappreciative audiences. On Can't Buy a Thrill, Fagan sang lead vocals on four songs, Palmer sang lead on two, and Fagen and Palmer shared lead on three (Becker helped on one as well). ABC requested that Steely Dan edit the almost six-minute "Do It Again" to a more radio-friendly length, which they grudgingly did. Steely Dan also employed the highly skilled engineer Roger Nichols, who along with Katz would be central to the great sound of their future recordings.

ABC Records pushed Steely Dan out on the road to promote Can't Buy a Thrill. In late 1972, they opened for The Kinks. Later, they would open for a number of artists including; Elton John, The Beach Boys, Uriah Heep, The James Gang, The Guess Who, and others. Life on the road never suited Fagen and Becker. They hated hotel rooms, rental cars, and most of all, the inconsistency of sound systems and the sound quality at different venues. It also became apparent to Fagen that he was best suited to sing his own material because no one else could accurately deliver the nuances of his lyrics. By April of 1973, Palmer was out of the band. Fagen explained, "If we had known about David Palmer earlier, we could have incorporated him more fully into the Steely Dan sound... He was a good singer for us early on but he didn't really have the attitude to put the songs over. So I started doing it myself, much to my chagrin. It seems to have worked out." #22

"Reelin' in the Years"
by Walter Becker and Donald Fagen

"Reelin' in the Years" was about a guy remembering his past relationship with his girlfriend and his breakup with her. Fagen and Becker never really liked the tune but realized that it was commercially effective. Both Fagen and Becker saw that both Skunk Baxter and Becker (himself) were not right for the guitar solo on "Reeling in the Years." Guitarist Elliot Randall had been invited by Skunk Baxter to come to the studio to say hi to the guys. Baxter was struggling with the guitar solo and asked Randall to give it a try. Within a few takes, Randall performed a blistering guitar intro and (what became) a legendary solo on the track.

Fagen and Becker developed the musical ideas for "Reelin' In the Years" first and then added the lyrics later. For as much as Fagen detested his own singing voice, he sang the difficult verses with relative ease. Drummer Jim Hodder played an effective shuffle feel while both Denny Dias and Jeff Baxter created supporting rhythm guitar parts. Walter Becker would sometimes play bass on specific tracks and he did so here. The day after Elliot Randall's solo was in the can, Fagen and Becker asked Randall to join Steely Dan but he declined because he knew that they were rigidly controlling the band. He also didn't want to live in Los Angeles. "Reelin' in the Years" barely missed the top ten on the U.S. charts.

1973's Countdown to Ecstasy was a critical success but did not fare as well commercially, failing to generate any hit singles. The tracks included; "Bodhisattva," "The Boston Rag," "Your Gold Teeth," "Show Biz Kids," and "My Old School." Countdown was another step in the Fagen/Becker songwriting evolution. Similar to Can't Buy a Thrill, Countdown to Ecstasy featured four to five minute rock songs with a strong jazz influence. Fagen and Becker created the structural framework for the compositions and left room for improvisation. After Palmer was fired from the band, Fagen sang all of the lead vocal parts on the album. The track "Show Biz Kids" featured the strong slide guitar lines of Rick Derringer. "My Old School" referred to drug busts from their Bard College days. It contained aggressive piano riffs and an interesting horn arrangement. The album's lyrical themes explored the excesses of the Hollywood lifestyle, class envy, and drug abuse. The album title mocked the attempt by some people who rationalized a genuine (but really false) sense of spirituality. The opening "Bodhisattva" was a parody of the concept of ridding oneself of life's possessions in order to obtain spiritual enlightenment. Fagen and Becker were living in California but writing about life in New York.

On Countdown, Steely Dan was beginning their process of utilizing top studio musicians. Guest musicians included; percussionist/pianist Victor Feldman, saxophonist Ernie Watts (six saxophone players on the album), and guitarist Rick Derringer. Fagen stressed the fact that the whole band was collaborating to create their sophisticated arrangements. The band's choice of "Show Biz Kids" as the lead single was a poor one, going to only sixty-nine on the charts. "My Old School" also failed as a single. Steely Dan begrudgingly felt that they needed to increase their visibility by touring. For a band that hated to tour, they performed well live. In September of 1973, Steely Dan played their first show as a headliner. They added both vocalist Royce Jones to help with the lead vocals and two female backup singers. Steely Dan was feeling (and resenting) the record company pressure to match the success of their debut album.

Pretzel Logic was released in 1974 and reached number eight on the American charts. It would be the final Steely Dan album to feature the lineup of Becker, Fagen, Dias, Baxter, and Hodder. The sessions for Pretzel Logic were not as experimental as the first two records. Now, Fagen and Becker worked out the songs more before presenting them to the band in the recording studio. Katz helped to hire the "right" studio musicians. Many first call L.A. session players contributed including; guitarist Dean Parks, drummers Jim Gordon and Jeff Porcaro, keyboardists Michael Omartian and David Paich, and bassist Chuck Rainey. By employing Gordon and Porcaro, Steely Dan now widened the possibilities for creative and highly

> "Aja (the song and album) will go down in history as one of the greatest recordings of organized music and it would not be so without the genius of Donald Fagen and Walter Becker."
>
> - Chuck Rainey

skilled drumset contributions. Jeff Porcaro would become the bands' live drummer (now replacing Hodder) and vocalist/keyboardist Michael McDonald joined as well.

"Rikki Don't Lose That Number," reached new chart heights going to number four. "Rikki's" very Horace Silver-like (prominent jazz musician) piano riff emphasized the band's strong jazz influences. Rikki had been a real student at Bard College that left an impression on Fagen and Becker. Also on this album was "East St. Louis Toodle-oo," a quirky rendition of a Duke Ellington song. This would be the last cover song that Steely Dan would record. Dias and Baxter shared the guitar part for "Any Major Dude," with Dias playing without vibrato and Baxter playing with vibrato. Roger Nichols spliced the two parts together (something that would become routine). "Any Major Dude" was a delicate song about insecurity and madness.

By the end of a tour in 1974, Steely Dan stopped touring all together. Tension had grown when Hodder and Baxter wanted to continue to tour. Becker recalled, "It was unfair for us to spend eight months writing when Jeff Baxter and the others wanted to tour…We weren't making very much money and everybody wanted to be touring a lot. We (himself and Fagen) didn't. That was that." #23 Fagen and Becker were still receiving salaries from ABC. However, they were trying to break their record company's financial grip that required them to work in a repetitive cycle of recording an album and then having to tour for promotion purposes. The duo schemed that the only way out was to dismantle the band. Without a group, touring would not be possible.

Fagen and Becker would become free to *embrace* the studio. They could now utilize the "best of the best" studio musicians to create high level music as they chased perfection. Their combination of jazz, blues, pop, gospel, old R&B, and rock styles fused with their incredible arranging skills. Steely Dan had the necessary ingredients to arrive at new musical places. Within a few months, Fagen and Becker had six new songs ready to record. The duo felt that a strict set band lineup was limiting and now they could continue with Dias and anybody they decided to hire for any *specific track or musical idea they might imagine.*

1975's Katy Lied reached number thirteen on the U.S. charts. The single, "Black Friday," was a story about a crooked speculator who made a lot of money and escaped to Australia. It went to number thirty-seven. "Black Friday" also featured pianist Michael Omartian who would appear on many future Steely Dan recordings. Omartian often acted as an intermediary between Fagen and Becker and the band by writing out many of their musical ideas. Other songs included the classic Steely Dan tracks "Bad Sneakers," "Doctor Wu," and "Your Gold Teeth II." Fagen and Becker were perfecting their songwriting and approach to recording. Fagen stated, "we'll set up a framework, no matter how bizarre it may be, and proceed to write a song on that basis. I'll come up with an idea and he'll (Becker) come up with a scenario, and we'll decide what we think the song is about and which part of the exposition is happening in each verse and get a title together, and no matter how strange the idea may be, we just go along and hope we can finish the song." #24 Drummer Jeff Porcaro played on all the Katy Lied tracks except "Any World (That I'm Welcome To)" that featured drummer Hal Blaine. This album marked the first appearance by guitarist Larry Carlton and a number of other first call L.A. studio musicians that made significant contributions to the album. Also, Michael McDonald again added vocal parts.

Steely Dan finally acted on their distain for touring and at this point became a *strictly* studio-based group. Jeff Baxter and Jim Hodder both moved on to other musical projects while McDonald went on the join The Doobie Brothers. The Royal Scam, released in 1976, showcased the fluid jazz-blues based lines of guitarist Larry Carlton. The Royal Scam became know as the Steely Dan "guitar album" with so many prominent guitar greats making contributions. Besides Becker and Carlton, this album included guitarists Denny Dias, Elliot Randall, and Dean Parks. The other rhythm section players were a dream roster of drummers Bernard Purdie and Rick Marotta, bassists Chuck Rainey and Mark Davis, and keyboardists Don Grolnick and Paul Griffin. With the further addition of many horn players and background singers, Steely Dan now expanded into a veritable orchestra of session players. Fagen and Becker often recorded a song with as many as six or more different rhythm section combinations, switching players around in endless combinations. The Royal Scam went to number fifteen on the U.S. charts. Among its classic tunes were "Kid Charlemagne," "Green Earrings," "The Fez," and "Haitian Divorce." The album contained story lines about people and events that were both real and fictional. "Kid Charlemagne" was a story set in San Francisco about a drug dealer who had been overtaken by the 1960's psychedelic scene and was left with nothing. "Green Earrings" drew from various musical styles and contained sections built on an interesting rhythmic vamp. This track also featured Dias and Randall, both creating musical guitar solos over Purdie's funky drumset feel. The Royal Scam, with its high level of inspired session musician performances and studio sound mastery, raised the musical bar for Steely Dan.

1977's Aja reached even greater heights of musical achievement, demonstrating Steely Dan's obsessive mastery of the recording studio. Aja reached the top five on the American charts within three weeks of its release. It also gained worldwide respect from musicians in all genres who recognized its high level musicianship, creative and eclectic songwriting, and skillful arranging. It became a multi-platinum Grammy winner and stayed on the U.S. charts for more than a year. Aja's success ran counter to its creator's anti-rock attitude, anti-band approach, and anti-glamour aesthetic. Recorded by Fagen, Becker, and thirty-five of the studio world's finest musicians, Aja provided the listener with modified song forms, mixed meters, and extended solos. It created unique musical experiences as opposed to flashy guitar gymnastics. Fagen said, "We started to get it right around Katy Lied and The Royal Scam…That's when it started to get its own sound. Those records-the bands fourth and fifth-contain the seeds of Aja, not just in their songwriting-plus-sidemen approach, but in specific instrumentation, melodic fragments, harmonic concepts and rhythmic figures that bore repeating." #25

Groundbreaking album Aja
by Steely Dan

For Aja, Fagen and Becker's extensive studio experience allowed them to fully exploit the full potential of the world class musicians they hired. At this point, they had specific musicians in mind for specific parts and solos, even for a song in its preliminary stages. Instead of getting a great player for a song, they got the only player in their mind that could best play that part. The ultimate goal of Aja was to combine world-class musicians with the highest level of production and sound engineering. Aja came to fully realize Fagen and Becker's musical aspirations; to write innovative songs that combined styles with groundbreaking arrangements and sound combinations. Neither Fagen or Becker could anticipate the musical aesthetic of each song until it was complete. Walter Becker's musical sensibilities were felt on virtually every song with his blues guitar parts, solos, and the musical direction that he gave to other studio guitar greats.

Side one opened with "Black Cow," then "Aja," and "Deacon Blues." For "Black Cow," Steely Dan utilized the band's timbral possibilities the way a master classical composer manipulated an orchestra. Like mad scientists, the duo created endless sound combinations of legato horn lines, piano, electric piano, clavinet, lyricon (an electronic wind instrument), saxophones and flute, and background vocals. Guitar and sax solos were woven into the fabric of "Black Cow" with contrasting blues and jazz elements. Tom Scott wrote the horn arrangement for the tune (and entire record). Fagen said, "We consulted with him (Tom Scott) about the sort of thing we wanted; sometimes we'd sing him some lines that we wanted in a certain spot. It was really a collaborative thing, and then he would fill in a lot of the voices. He's a real expert arranger for any kind of band and he took it very seriously...he knew how to match the harmony in the rhythm section with the horn charts." #26

The title track "Aja" was one of the most astounding compositions ever recorded-period. "Aja" was a long, complicated chart that was nailed in only a few takes. The session musicians achieved an exotic sound and an incredible balance of delicate and explosive musical passages. Drummer Steve Gadd delivered one of the greatest drumset performances in recorded music history (this was the only time Steely Dan wanted a drum solo in one of their songs). At the beginning and end of "Aja," a quasi-bossa nova feel was established with acoustic piano, Gadd's soft cymbal timbres, marimba, and temple blocks. The legendary tenor saxophonist Wayne Shorter played a masterful solo in the middle section along with Gadd's explosive soloing over a rhythmic vamp. This section took the listener on a musical adventure that eventually returned to the beginning section. Steely Dan knew (and didn't care) that this would never be a top forty radio song.

"Deacon Blues" did make it to number nineteen on the charts. Fagen's lyrics professed that if a college football team such as the University of Alabama could have a grandiose name like the "Crimson Tide," then the losers and nerds in the world were entitled to a grandiose name as well. In this case, deacon blues. Guitar great Larry Carlton transcribed Fagen's song demo to create rhythm section charts. Tom Scott then wrote the horn arrangements. A smooth Bernard Purdie groove, Walter Becker's bass part, and Victor Feldman's electric piano part combined to build the feel. Larry Carlton and Lee Ritenour played electric guitar while Dean Parks added acoustic guitar. Compositionally, the horn section functioned to extend the feel and groove of the song, not just provide background sounds.

Side two opened with "Peg," then "Home at Last," "I Got the News," and "Josie." Many of the world's best session guitarists played the "Peg" guitar solo, just not to Steely Dans' expectations. Only Jay Graydon satisfied the Fagen and Becker pursuit of perfection. Becker said, "In the past it has been Larry who played most of the guitar solos. We're probably hardest on guitar players...the musicians enjoy getting asked to do something that's challenging...Its diffi-

cult, but it's fun. It's not stupid music." #27 Many of the great session players were often dumbfounded when they knew that they had played a great take but Fagen or Becker would demand more takes or move on to another player. "Home at Last" featured Bernard Purdie and his the famous "Purdie Shuffle," a relaxed half time drumset feel. The acoustic piano part brought a strong gospel feel to the song and the horn lines created smooth legato articulation. "I Got the News" was originally written for the The Royal Scam sessions but Fagen and Becker rewrote it and changed the lyrics. The song still retained the keyboard part, performed by Victor Feldman. "I Got the News" featured the unique funky drumset feel of Ed Greene and the syncopated bassline of Chuck Rainey. Fagen added colorful, dissonant harmonic (avant-garde-like) structures for the piano and composed horn lines. "Josie" ended the album with a funky guitar feel and Chuck Rainey's creative bass playing. Rainey was given a rare written bass part but he improvised on it and employed a palm slapping technique (Steely Dan hated slap bass). For "Josie," studio great drummer Jim Keltner played a brilliant and unorthodox drumset part with the aid of a trash can lid.

To perform on Aja was a barometer of where a musician stood in the L.A. recording session community. Guitarist Lee Ritenour said, " You'd see guys at other sessions, and they'd be asking, Did your solo make it?'" #28 All told, Aja utilized six of the best studio drummers (with only Bernard Purdie playing on two tracks) on the album's seven tracks. Shortly after the release of Aja, jazz great Woody Herman recorded an album of Fagen and Becker compositions in 1978. The Library of Congress selected Aja for inclusion in the United States National Recording Registry based on its artistic, cultural, and historical importance.

Following the release of Aja, ABC Records was bought out by MCA, resulting in a Steely Dan contractual dispute with the label. This would lead to the delay of 1980's masterpiece Gaucho. On Gaucho, Steely Dan continued their pursuit of the highest level of studio and performance perfection. This time the duo used even more musicians (forty-two) for over a year in the studio. They far exceeded the recording budget allotted to them by their record label. The singles released from Gaucho were "Time Out of Mind" and "Hey Nineteen," the latter reaching number ten on the U.S. charts. The other songs on Gaucho were "Babylon Sisters," "Glamour Profession," "Gaucho," "My Rival," and "Third World Man." Unlike Aja, Gaucho utilized more minimal grooves and sought specific moods with less harmonic complexity. The title track utilized typical Fagen and Becker imagery. "Gaucho's" storyline was about two homosexual partners that lived in a luxurious apartment in Manhattan. Their relationship was threatened by the arrival of a handsome young South American cowboy (the Gaucho) wearing a "spangled leather poncho and elevator shoes" (as the lyrics stated).

During the recording sessions for Gaucho, the atmosphere surrounding the studio was tense and uneasy. Fagen was depressed and Becker was dealing with substance abuse issues. The duo was also having some creative differences that led to inconsistencies in maintaining a regular work schedule. However, Steely Dan was still striving for sound perfection as part of their ultimate goal of musical greatness. Longtime Steely Dan engineer Roger Nichols said, "Instead of using EQ on the board to change a drum sound, for instance, we'll bring in 52 different kick or snare drums to try to get the sound

"For some artists, when writers start labeling you a genius, it becomes much too heavy a cross to bear. It's some deep psychological sh**, but I think it's why they (Fagen and Becker) could never finish anything, never let go of anything, never just say, that's enough, lets put it out."

- guitarist Steve Kahn

> "I can't play any instruments in any technically viable sense at all, and it's one of my strengths."
>
> - Brian Eno

we want. We find it's better to make the adjustments at the instrument end rather than try to fix it with EQ and things. So we'll try different instrument and microphone combinations with minimum EQ or no EQ at all to get something that sounds right. #29

The years of stress and self-imposed demands of perfection began to take its toll on Fagen and Becker. After fourteen years of writing and recordings together, the duo split in 1981 to concentrate on solo projects. Fagen released The Nightfly in 1982 and Becker moved to Maui, Hawaii. Becker produced a number of artists in the 1980's including albums by Michael Franks, Fra Lippo Lippi, and Rickie Lee Jones. The first Fagen and Becker reunion occurred in 1986 when they collaborated on Zazu, the debut album by Rosie Vela. In 1991, Becker appeared in Fagen's The New York Rock and Soul Revue, a musical project that evolved from a series of concerts and musical shows that included Michael McDonald, Boz Scaggs, and Phoebe Snow. Steely Dan released Citizen Steely Dan in 1993, a four CD compilation box set.

Donald Fagen didn't record again until 1993, when he called on his old partner's production skills to release 1993's Kamakiriad. It became a transatlantic top ten success on the charts. Steely Dan reunited to promote the album with their first tour in almost twenty years. In 1994, Becker released his solo debut, 11 Tracks of Whack, for which Fagen returned production favors. In 1995, Steely Dan embarked on another reunion tour to support the Steely Dan box set and Becker's Whack album. In 1995, Steely Dan released a live record, Alive in America.

2000's Two Against Nature was Steely Dan's first new studio album in two decades. This album featured a new backing band consisting of guitarist Jon Herrington, bassist Tom Barney and a host of drummers, guitarists, percussionist, horn players, and background singers. Two Against Nature won four Grammies including Album of the Year. Roger Nichols served as executive engineer.

Also in 2000, Steely Dan released Plush TV Jazz-Rock Party, a PBS recording of a concert recorded live in January 2000 at the Sony Studios in New York City. The band recorded a new studio album, Everything Must Go in 2003. In contrast to their earlier approach, Fagen and Becker tried to capture a live feel on this album. Everything Must Go featured fewer session musicians than normal and drummer Keith Carlock played on every track.

Fagen released another solo album in 2006, Morph the Cat, while Becker released Circus Money in 2008. Fagen's band included; pianist Ted Baker, bassist Freddie Washington, drummer Keith Carlock, and saxophonist Walt Weiskopf. In 2009, Steely Dan launched another tour that featured complete performances of either The Royal Scam, Aja, or Gaucho on certain nights. In 2011, long time Steely Dan engineer Roger Nichols unfortunately died of pancreatic cancer. Fagen released a fourth solo album, Sunken Condos in 2012. In 2016, Steely Dan embarked on the The Dan Who Knew Too Much Tour, with Steve Winwood as the opening act.

Steely Dan performed their final shows with Walter Becker in 2017. Sadly, the death of Walter Becker was announced in September 2017. He was sixty-seven years old. Fagen reflected on his musical relationship with Becker and said, "Our writing is intuitive, its nothing much planned about it, in the sense of thinking about the listener…it's a combination of all the things we like." #30 Walter Becker stated that Steely Dan was able to "get away with it…these songs weren't jazz, per se…we just thought that, since we liked them, that other people would like them, in spite of the stylistic difficulties or the arcane lyrics or any of those things. We thought there would be people out there-we didn't know exactly how many, but we figured enough-who would go for this thing." #31

Steely Dan's lyrical content often focused on creating fictional personas that participated in the narrative of their songs. Often characters appeared in songs that evoked images of Los Angeles or New York City. Many of these lyrics were in need of "decoding" to obtain an understanding of their meaning. The starting point for Fagen and Becker was to develop the musical and lyrical framework for a song. Next, they called on state of the art recording techniques, but more importantly, brought in first call studio players in endless combinations to attempt perfection. They studied the specific musical skill sets of these session masters and pursued endless takes of individual tracks until they realized their vision for the potential of a song. This was a process that evolved from their middle period albums and culminated with Aja and Gaucho.

Steely Dan was the vehicle for the songwriting and studio experimentation of Donald Fagen and Walter Becker. They happily defied all rock music conventions with their ironic humor and cryptic and sarcastic lyrics. Steely Dan crafted a sophisticated and unique collection of melodic hooks, complex harmonies, and time signatures. They also conceptualized new rules for how a band could create music. The best musicians were constantly challenged (often to their breaking point) to reach new levels of musicianship. Even thought Steely Dan refused to perform live between 1974 and 1993, their popularity continued to grow throughout the 1970's and early 1980s. Hard to pigeonhole into any one music genre, Steely Dan drew heavily from jazz, blues, R&B, soul, and traditional pop. In the hands of Donald Fagen and Walter Becker, these ingredients didn't just sound like parts of a musical recipe. Together, they realized a musical vision never before heard or conceptualized. Steely Dan was inducted into the Rock and Roll Hall of Fame in 2001.

Brian Eno (1948-) is an English composer/multi-instrumentalist/producer/sound designer from Suffolk, England born in 1948. His musical and artistic career began in the early 1970's with the art rock band Roxy Music (see chapter eight). Eno drew freely from many philosophies of music and art. He was influenced by many genres including R&B, early rock 'n' roll, progressive rock, punk, new wave, African, Middle Eastern, and Asian music. Equally influential to Eno was the music and concepts of minimalism, post-John Cage avant-garde theory, electronic music, and experimental music. Eno was successful in combining music with visual art by way of video and sculptural installations. He has lectured extensively on many music subjects. Eno is the chief inventor of **ambient music** (see ambient music profile). Eno considers the recording studio to be his "real instrument," although he has performed live extensively. Eno has famously referred to himself as a "non-musician." However, he plays keyboards (mostly synthesizers), electric guitar, electric bass, and a variety of percussion instruments. Eno also sings.

As a child, Brian Eno heard early rock, doo-wop, and pop music on American radio broadcasts from a nearby U.S. Air Force base. Eno's family exposed him to a variety of musics, including jazz and old hymns with melancholy qualities that would later influence his musical sensibilities. All through his formative years, Eno was greatly influenced by two specific rock bands, The Who

> "For me, its always contingent on getting a sound-the sound always suggests what kind of melody it should be. So, it's always sound first and then the line afterwards."
>
> - Brian Eno

and The Velvet Underground. As a teenager, Eno studied at the Ipswich Art School from 1964 to 1966 where he experienced a radical art foundation course. This class taught him to question the traditional preconceptions of art. Eno learned to value new strategies of art and creativity through the use of chance operations. He also explored concepts such as behavioral control, conditioned communication, feedback, and systemic relationships that have proven to facilitate higher levels of conceptual thinking. From 1966 to 1969, Eno attended the Winchester School of Art. There, he learned to merge music, sound design, painting, and sculpture in unique combinations. Eno experimented by creating "sound sculptures" and he formed an avant-garde performance group to perform his original works. Eno said, "I had reached a stage in painting where I was actually making a score which I would then carry out in the same way that a musician might. I mean, a score is only a behavior pattern. It says if you do this, this and this, you'll come out with a result of some kind. So it wasn't unnatural to make a transition into music." #32 In the next few years following his time at Winchester, Eno pursued the genre of experimental music. He soon joined the Cardew Scratch Orchestra and Postsmouth Sinfonia, where he played clarinet.

Brian Ferry recruited Eno to play keyboards in Roxy Music in 1971. Eno knew his keyboard skills were limited (at best) but instead focused on utilizing technology to sculpt sounds, thus helping to shape Roxy Music's pre-glam musical approach. Eno was a major force in the creation of Roxy's debut album, Roxy Music, and their second release, For Your Pleasure. Eno and Roxy saxophonist Ian Mackay were able to combine their shared interest in avant-garde composition and electronic music and fuse it to Ferry's artistic tastes. Ferry called the shots when it came to Roxy's musical direction, while a young Eno's electronic contributions were an afterthought. Ferry wrote all the music for their two albums. In Roxy Music, Eno basically played synthesizers and tape machines. However, he also altered the sound colors heard in Roxy's songs, even when they were performing live. Eno was already moving away from a song-based compositional approach and more towards a process-based music. After two years, their was tension in the Eno and Ferry relationship. Eno's eccentric keyboard parts were directly in conflict with Ferry's more straight forward songs. The tension expanded with Eno's penchant for wild costumes and a willingness to talk to the press, drawing increased media attention. Eno left Roxy Music in 1973.

After his departure, Eno produced an album by The Portsmouth Sinfonia, a fifty-piece orchestra work that featured many non-musicians. The sound was pretty shocking and served to illustrate Eno's concept that accidents could have value in music. Then, from 1974 to 1977, Brian Eno recorded and released four progressive rock albums as a solo artist. He first delivered 1974's Here Come the Warm Jets and Taking Tiger Mountain. Next, came 1975's Another Green World and Before and After Science in 1977. On each effort, Eno composed five different types of compositions. He wrote hard driving rock songs that contained distorted electric guitars and shouted vocals with lyrics that exhibited aggressive, futuristic, or sexual topics. A second song type was his pop-styled compositions with a relaxed vocal delivery. Another type was bizarre songs where Eno's imagination ran wild with mixtures of rock, jazz, and pop elements that exhibited dark, irrational verbal imagery. Yet other songs evoked a sense of weird, grotesque and frighting qualities with many strange timbres. Lastly, Eno wrote songs that were very "hymn-like" with slow vocal melodies and harmonic timbres played on synthesizers programmed to sound like a church organ or even a string section. These particular songs harkened back to Eno's childhood when he heard many old hymns. The "hymn-like" compositions would foreshadow his groundbreaking creation of ambient music.

Eno's compositional diversity also revealed a number of instrumental songs that fell into pop, ambient, or more musically adventurous territory. This instrumental approach pointed the way to Eno's later albums including 1982's Ambient 4: On Land and 1983's Apollo: Atmospheres and Soundtracks (see Ambient profile). There were also traces of early American rhythm and blues on these solo recordings. Collectively, this body of work established Eno as an inspired composer and foreshadowed the synth-pop genre.

Eno employed a long list of prominent musicians on the above mentioned four progressive rock albums. They included; drummers Phil Collins and Dave Mattacks, bassists Percy Jones and John Wetton, guitarists Robert Fripp and Fred Frith, viola player John Cale, and many others. Eno was still on good terms with saxophonist Ian Mackey and guitarist Phil Manzanera (from Roxy Music) and now called on them for his budding solo career. As for his self-proclaimed "non-musician" title, Eno played synthesizers, guitar, synth percussion, piano, bells, mini-moog, Yamaha bass pedals, Hammond organ, Peruvian percussion, prepared piano, treated rhythm generator, "electric elements and unnatural sounds," and vocals on his albums. On Here Comes the Warm Jets, Robert Fripp played a brilliant guitar solo on the Eno composition "Baby's on Fire."

Brian Eno came to embrace an open-minded method of spontaneous studio improvisation. His concept of an "additive approach" to recording called for artists to not prepare fully written songs. This approach would lead to his **Oblique Strategies concept**. In 1975, Eno collaborated with artist Peter Schmidt to create the concept of Oblique Strategies, a set of cards with instructions and suggestions that might be applied to a variety of creative situations. For example, Eno would place these cards face down around the room of a recording studio. When a creative issue was presented, Eno would randomly consult one of the one-hundred cards, each offering a different suggestion. One card would say to "Emphasize the flaws," while another would say "Give way to your worst impulse," and yet another stated "Use unqualified people." This would result in unpredictable musical outcomes, sometimes successful and sometimes not. Eno elaborated on his system and said, "The idea of Oblique Strategies was just to dislocate my vision for a while. By means of performing a task that might seem absurd in relation to the picture, one can suddenly come at it from a tangent and possibly reassess it." #33 In March of 1975, Eno gave his first public lecture at the Trent Polytechnic School, reflecting on his educational experience and its relevance to evolving concepts concerning art and music. In this lecture, Eno addressed music as a process and said, "In experimental music the music score is by definition a map of a set of behavior patterns which will produce a result-but on another day that result might be entirely different." #34

The Ambient Music of Brian Eno

In 1975, Brian Eno was hospitalized after being hit by a car. While recovering, Eno was lying in bed listening to an album of harp music a friend had brought to him. Heavily medicated, Eno listened to the music with one of the speakers broken and the other pointed away from him. The rain and wind from outside mixed with the harp sounds, thus giving Eno a sonic mix never before experienced by himself or probably anyone else. Eno remembered, "I started hearing this music as if I'd never heard music before. It was a really beautiful experience. I got the feelings of icebergs. I would occasionally just hear the loudest parts of the music, get a little flurry of notes coming out above the sound of the rain...and then it would drift away again." #35 This bizarre experience would begin to point Eno in a whole new musical direction.

With 1975's Discreet Music, Eno designed music to be heard and ignored simultaneously. The album included two parts, the first involving a pair of synthesizer melodies processed through a system of tape-delay loops. The second part utilized a setting of "Pachelbel's Canon in D Major." Eno then manipulated the tempo of specific instruments to create the desired effect he had envisioned. The results produced a very calm feeling. Subsequent recordings of these sounds eventually would be adapted by hospitals to play during childbirth. Eno realized that this approach was new and unique.

Brian Eno chose the term *"ambient music"* for the above mentioned kind of quiet and atmospheric music he began making in the 1970's. He knew it contained depth and a sense of spaciousness. Ambient sound was purposely designed to approach listeners from all sides and not come straight at them. Ambient music sought to blend with the existing sounds in any environment to create new sonic soundscapes. In Eno's ambient sound design, he took this concept one step further by consciously constructing sounds that gave the impression of a completely new environment. Eno achieved this, in part, by utilizing the recording studio as a compositional tool and part of the music itself.

Between 1978 and 1982, Eno produced four albums that he called the ambient series. The first, 1979's Ambient 1: Music for Airports (broadcast at New York's LaGuardia Airport) and the fourth, 1982's Ambient 4: On Land, contained music mostly composed by Eno. For Ambient 2: The Plateaux of Mirror, he collaborated with composer Harold Budd. For Ambient 3: Day of Radiance, Eno produced compositions by hammer-dulcimer player Laraaji. Eno's ambient music contained soft, lush, and silky sound qualities. These sounds were inspired by specific vocal and instrumental timbres that Eno remembered from his youth.

Brian Eno has created many installations that combined his sound designs with the work of numerous artists. These installations have been shown around the world since 1979. Eno's installations often featured light as a medium, explored in multi-screen configurations. Simultaneously, Eno's accompanying music was designed to blur the boundaries between itself and its surroundings. His goal was to make a distinction between the musician and the audience. As part of his process, Eno experimented with many complex sound combinations. The goal of each music/art installation was to integrate the viewer's perception of space and time within a specific environment.

Eno produced and/or collaborated albums on more ambient albums including: 1978's Music for Films, 1983's Apollo Atmospheres and Soundtracks and More Music for Films Vol. II, 1985's Thursday Afternoon, and 1986's Glint. Eno later recorded more ambient collaborations with various artists including; Fourth World Vol. 1: Possible Musics, and Dream Theory in Malaya: Fourth World Vol. 2. Eno's innovative approach in ambient music was responsible, in part, for the *new age music* movement of the 1980's. This would later inform the style of "ambient techno" dance music that became popular across Europe and America in the 1990's. From the 1990's through 2010, Eno produced many more ambient installation albums including 1997's Extract from Music for White Cube and 2010's Making Space.

Brian Eno's Collaborations and Production Career

Brian Eno's groundbreaking experimental work drew critical acclaim but had not yet yielded any commercial hit singles. He would become *the producer* of choice for many leading artists in the later 1970's and throughout the 1980's. An astounding list of artists that Eno either collaborated with, produced, or co-produced included; Robert Fripp, David Bowie, The Talking Heads and David Byrne, Laurie Anderson, Slowdrive, Grace Jones, Coldplay, James Blake, Ultravox, James, John Cale, Nico, Damon Albarn, and installation artist Jeremy Deller. Eno collaborated with Genesis on the vocal treatments of the songs "In the Cage" and "The Grand Parade of Lifeless Packaging," from their 1974 album, The Lamb Lies Down on Broadway. Eno later added a piano part to the song "Love to Be Loved," from Peter Gabriel's 1992 album Us.

Eno began a collaboration with King Crimson's Robert Fripp that resulted in Fripp's 1973 solo album No Pussyfooting and 1974's Evening Star. Together they developed a concept Fripp would title "Frippertronics." This concept combined a tape loop with a delay and layered Fripp's classic guitar lines into aural landscapes. This was similar to the way a painter could add layers of color to build a rich texture on a canvas. Instead of utilizing the recording studio simply as a place to record music, Eno was employing new recording technology to create music from scratch. The aesthetic of Eno's original songs (based on the old hymns heard in his childhood) would influence his work with Fripp. Both No Pussyfooting and Evening Star were early examples of Eno's ambient music explorations.

From 1977 to 1979, Brian Eno collaborated with David Bowie on three albums known as the Berlin Trilogy. This included 1977's Low and Heroes, and 1979's Lodger. Bowie reached out to Eno because he was searching for new creative ideas and Eno had been impressed with Bowie's 1976 album, Station to Station. On Low, Eno's musical personality was evident throughout, especially on the album's mostly instrumental B side. Eno contributed interesting guitar treatments and an array of metallic and harsh sounds. He also employed many string-like synthesizer lines mixed with flute and Mellotron timbres. Eno and Bowie co-composed the song "Warszawa," a slow and haunting composition based on piano drones and a organ-like synthesizer part. On Heroes, Eno was credited with co-writing four compositions and adding keyboards, synthesizers, and guitar treatments. For the classic Bowie tune "Heroes" (see chapter eight), Eno added massive background synthesizer sounds that he combined with Robert Fripp's distinctive guitar timbres. Eno introduced Bowie to his Oblique Strategies system and they utilized it extensively throughout the making of Heroes, including the song "Sense of Doubt."

"Some bands went to art school...we went to Brian Eno."

- Bono

"Sense of Doubt"
by David Bowie

Brian Eno and David Bowie each pulled out a card from Eno's Oblique Strategies set of cards and kept it a secret from each other. Eno recalled, "It was like a game. We took turns working on it; he'd do one overdub and I'd do the next. The idea was that each was to observe his Oblique Strategy as closely as he could. And as it turned out they were entirely opposed to one another. Effectively mine said 'Try to make everything as similar as possible,' and his said, 'Emphasize differences.'" #36 This conceptual paradox of Eno attempting to smooth out the sound and make it into one continuum was in direct conflict to Bowie's Oblique Strategies directive. This formed the basis for the ambient composition "Sense of Doubt."

"Sense of Doubt" contained a dark mood with a descending four-note piano motif juxtaposed with a Brian Eno composed haunting synthesizer line. Eno was effective in creating a moody and eerie feeling that drew from organic nature timbres such as the sound of wind. Eno was successful in pushing Bowie beyond the limits of rock music.
Esteemed composer Philip Glass covered "Sense of Doubt" on his 1996 release "Heroes" Symphony.

Lodger was the final Eno/Bowie collaboration. This recording was very hard rocking and Bowie influenced, although Eno co-composed six of the ten songs. Eno added "prepared piano," synthesizers, guitar treatments, "horse trumpets," an "Eroica horn," and piano parts. Some of Eno's sound treatments were lost in the busy mix of sound. Eno still employed his Oblique Strategies concept. However, he and Bowie didn't agree on many of the musical decisions and ended up compromising on some of the applications that were utilized. A few of the unusual approaches Eno employed included; playing songs backwards, utilizing identical chord sequences for different songs, and asking the session musicians to play on unfamiliar instruments. Tony Visconti produced the sessions.

Brian Eno produced three album for The Talking Heads from 1978 to 1980. He functioned as an unofficial member of the band during that time. In 1978, Eno moved to Manhattan, New York and immersed himself in the downtown music and performance art scene. Eno was perfectly in his element, surrounded by like-minded artists who exhibited disregard for the traditional distinctions between artistic categories and who made no distinction between classical, avant-garde, and popular music. On the Talking Heads 1978 album, More Songs about Buildings and Food, Eno helped to shape the song's rhythms to create more dance-oriented beats. This included a cover of soul singer Al Green's "Take Me to the River." For 1979's Fear of Music, Eno worked on electronic treatments for many of the tracks once they were written. Eno and David Byrne both became interested in traditional and popular music from all over the world. They both read Robert Farris Thompson's book African Art in Motion and John Chernoff's African Rhythm and Sensibility. These books taught them about the interconnectedness of music, dance, and sculpture. They also explored the integration of these African arts into the everyday lives of the Sub-Saharan Africa people. Eno and Byrne would come to identify the interlocking rhythms of African rhythm. This led to the inclusion of these rhythmic layering concepts in Talking Head's compositions, other Eno/Byrne co-led efforts, and David Byrne's solo albums. The Talking Heads 1980's Remain in Light saw Eno simplify the harmony of the band's songs, often reducing them to one or two chords. This provided a simple underpinning that musically supported numerous percussive and melodic ideas. These songs served as examples for Eno's compositional approach that emphasized a strong pulse and complex subdivisions, combined with repetitive melodic and bass figures. This innovative background material allowed the band to further layer more involved bass, drumset, guitar, and percussion parts. David Byrne loved Eno's approach, although there was some resentment over Eno's involvement by the other Talking Heads band members.

Just before the Remain in Light sessions, Eno and Byrne began an intense collaboration for their co-led My Life in the Bush of Ghosts. Eno was excited to develop "fourth world music" with the above mentioned African music concepts. Eno defined fourth world music as "music that is done in sympathy with the consciousness of music from the rest of the world, rather than just with Western music or just with rock music. It's almost collage music, like grafting a piece of one culture onto a piece of another and trying to make them work as a coherent musical idea, and also trying to make something you can dance to." #37 My Life in the Bush of Ghosts contained compositions with high-tech studio electronics mixed with the sounds of traditional Qu'ran chanting and a huge battery of percussion instruments including West-African djembes and talking drums. Eno and Byrne incorporated found objects like ashtrays, a frying pan, tin cans, and trash cans. This recording occupied a musical place in a broad cultural context beyond the scope of most musicians, rock or otherwise. Eno and Byrne's collaborative union of technology with world rhythms and singing styles was a major source of inspiration for the development of world music. Artists such as Paul Simon and Peter Gabriel would benefit greatly from this groundbreaking work. The song "Moonlight in Glory" revealed some of the innovation from My Life in the Bush of Ghosts.

"Moonlight in Glory"
by Brian Eno and David Byrne

"Moonlight in Glory" featured The Moving Star Hall Singers, a vocal ensemble consisting of the Gullah people who live on Johns Island off the coast of South Carolina. They were descendants of African-American slaves whose distinctive language, culture, and music persists to this day. The Gullah people were discovered by ethnomusicologists Guy Carawan and Alan Lomax in the 1960's. Eno and Byrne combined their vocal styes with other West African rhythmic elements along with funky percussion, bass, and synthesizer lines. This created a very unique sound. Specifically for "Moonlight in Glory," Eno and Byrne sampled three different tracks from the Moving Stars' album Sea Island Folk Festival, all of which dealt with spiritual and supernatural topics. David Byrne said, "It was the *sound* of their vocals-the passion, rhythm and phrasing-that conveyed the emotional content." #38

The phrasing of the Gullah singers music was four-bar repeating cycles in a funky, Afrobeat style. Eno and Byrne constructed a bassline that alternated between two pitches throughout and a guitar doubled the end of each pattern with stepwise parallel fourths. The repetition and regularity of the syncopated congas, bells, and woodblocks created a fixed layer of contrasting length of *six-bar phrases* against a two-measure guitar and synthesizer phrase. This cross-phrasing contained the very West

---

Rock Hard Fact

In 2004, Brian Eno and Peter Gabriel launched a provocative new musicians' alliance ("Magnificent Union of Digitally Downloading Artists" aka MUDDA) to encourage artists to sell their music online instead of only through record labels.

African approach that Eno and Byrne had been listening to and reading about.

Brian Eno also produced David Byrne's 1981 release The Catherine Wheel. On this effort, David Byrne was commissioned by Twyla Tharp to compose a score for her dance ensemble. *The Catherine Wheel* premiered in the fall of 1981 at the Winter Garden Theatre in New York City. Byrne wrote all of the music while Eno produced and added bass, piano, synthesizers, scream sounds, vibraphone, piano, and background vocals. Eno also produced and mixed Devo's 1978 debut album Q: Are We Not Men? A: We Are DEVO!. Tension rose quickly when some of the members of Devo refused to participate in Eno's Oblique Strategies concept.

Brian Eno worked extensively with the band U2 (see chapter sixteen) from 1984 to 2009, producing six of their studio albums. These included; 1984's Unforgettable Fire, 1987's The Joshua Tree, 1990's Achtung Baby, 1993's Zooropa, 2000's All That You Can't Leave Behind, and 2009's No Line On The Horizon. Eno also composed and performed on U2's Original Soundtracks 1 album (released under the name Passengers). On U2's All That You Can't Leave Behind, Eno and his "collaborator in chief partner," Daniel Lanois, worked with the band for a fourth time. Eno convinced U2 to not write much music for the album before going into the studio. He wanted to create a sense of spontaneity and to quickly write songs in the studio environment. The production vision of Eno and Lanois resulted in an album with very musical sound colors and many intricate sonic details.

"Beautiful Day"
by U2

When Brian Eno and Daniel Lanois were helping to shape this future U2 hit, they were building on the song's foundational Bo Diddley rhythm. One day before the U2 band members arrived at the studio to continue working on "Beautiful Day," Eno and Lanois showed up early (as usual) and looked to move the song in a different direction. They both felt frustrated, feeling the song was stuck in the past. Eno soon created a beat-box rhythm and added a piano and string part. Lanois next added a guitar part (a third above the original key) to the chord sequence that U2's guitarist Edge had already established, thus embellishing the harmony.

Lanois was greatly inspired by the presence of Brian Eno in the studio environment. He said, "The beat box gave the song a feeling of speed and travel...Eno is one of the great interpreters. His ability to present a new angle on an already existing theme remains unsurpassed. When the band came in, there was a good mood in the air; everybody could feel the fresh angle." #39 Eno and Lanois recorded Larry Mullen Jr.s' triplet drum part (against the grain of Eno's beat box rhythm) and The Edge's greasy guitar sound in a twenty-minute jam version of the song. From there, Eno and Lanois pulled out a section they referred to as the outro. They also displaced Bono's "beautiful day" vocal shout at different points in the jam section. Together, all of these musical factors fell into place to arrive at the shorter, final version of "Beautiful Day."

The decade of the 1990's saw Eno continue to create ambient music, now fused with an ever expanding combination of musical genres and styles. His 1992 release Nerve Net, explored ambient music concepts with the influence of industrial, trance, techno, and other forms of electronic dance music. Eno followed with 1992's The Shutov Assembly, 1993's Neroli, and 1997's The Drop. The new millennium brought 2005's Another Day on Earth, 2012's Lux, and 2016's The Ship. 2017's Reflection was Eno's twenty-sixth studio album. Also in 2017, his album Sisters was available as an internet download. Brian Eno and musician/software designer Peter Chilvers, while working on the soundtrack for the 2008 video game *Spore*, began to develop generative music for the Apple App format. Their generative music applications for iPhone, iPod Touch, and iPad included the app's *Bloom*, *Trope*, *Scape*, and *Reflection*.

Brian Eno's music is designed to operate on many different levels. From his progressive rock harmonic primitivism to his verbal irony and wordplay to his use of musical nostalgia and futurism, Brian Eno has pushed the boundaries of the compositional process. Eno said, "My role in rock music isn't to come on with new musical ideas in any strict sense. It's to come on with new concepts about how you might generate music. Its always time to question what has become standard and established. I figure that in a way, my contribution...will be more on a theoretical basis, about suggesting greater freedom in the way people approach music." #40

No artist from the 1970's progressive rock or art rock music scene had more impact on the continued development of rock music than Brian Eno. Through his work as a musician, composer, producer and sonic designer; he single-handedly changed the musical direction of some of the biggest rock bands in the world. Within a macro-perspective, Brian Eno has employed breakthroughs in music technology to develop processes rather than final objects. These processes, once set into motion, have produced limitless and constant, non-repeating music and artworks. Eno has profoundly shaped art-rock, progressive rock, new wave, new age, **trance-pop rock**, and other current music genres. Brian Eno is the principle creator of the genre of ambient music and one of music's true innovators.

Peter Gabriel (1950-) first rose to musical prominence with the progressive rock band Genesis (see chapter thirteen) where he explored classical music, indulged in surrealistic fantasy themes, and reached new heights of theatricality. After leaving Genesis in 1975, Gabriel began a five year period that would culminate in his rise to international stardom as a solo artist. In the summer of 1975, the news broke in the British press that Genesis and Gabriel had formally split. That was old news to both Gabriel and Genesis. When Genesis struggled to find his replacement, Gabriel knew that with talent like Rutherford, Collins, and Banks, they would continue to achieve success. Gabriel remembered, "I had more confidence in Genesis continuing than they did themselves. And the reason was because we were a group of songwriters, and the songs would continue coming out of that." #41

After his last performances with Genesis on The Lamb Lies Down On Broadway tour, Gabriel returned home to Bath, England and disappeared into the community. He worked sporadically on several projects including collaborations with lyricist Martin Hall and Charlie Drake. Gabriel even toyed with the possibility of composing tracks for an animated TV show. Gabriel's real commitment to a serious return to recording came when he surprisingly assembled Genesis members Mike Rutherford, Phil Collins, and ex-Genesis member Anthony Phillips (missing was Anthony Banks and Steve Hackett). They recorded demos of new Gabriel tunes including "Howling At the Moon" and "Funny Man." These songs

---

"The worst thing you can say to a creative person is 'You can do anything,' That is the kiss of death. You should say to them, 'You can't do this or you definitely can't do that. And under no circumstances can you do that.' Then they'll start thinking in a different, more creative way."

- Peter Gabriel

Chapter Eighteen: Rock Music Visionaries

would never appear on any Gabriel records. In retrospect, these sessions were about Peter Gabriel pointing the way to his musical future with some help from his most trusted musical friends. Gabriel really didn't know a lot of other musicians outside of this circle just yet.

For his first solo album, Peter Gabriel's first order of business was to contact and secure the well respected producer Bob Ezrin. It was Erzin that hand picked the session musicians for the recording that included; bassist Tony Levin (ex-King Crimson, David Bowie, and John Lennon), drummer Alan Schwartzberg, keyboardist/programmer Larry Fast, and master guitarist Robert Fripp. It was Fast that immediately realized the great potential of Gabriel's evolving musical approach. Fast said, "Freed from his old group...the self-imposed restrictions of the Genesis style-it allowed for some more conventional high-energy rock, world music, minimalist experiments... and unusual time signatures that didn't call attention to themselves. The dynamic changes in musical intensity were used less frequently for shock value and more for guiding the musical journey." #42

1977's debut album Peter Gabriel (Car) (each of his first four solo albums were nameless and referred to by the album cover) delved into dark and cerebral musical territory by infusing electronic and avant-garde approaches in the music. Car achieved moderate success, reaching number seven on the British charts and number thirty-eight in America. The hit single "Solsbury Hill," (later a staple in Gabriel's live performances) was about his departure from Genesis and the idea of letting go. "Solsbury Hill" was in 7/4 with an infectious acoustic guitar-driven folk inspired groove. Gabriel utilized The London Symphony Orchestra for arrangements (by Michael Gibbs) of his compositions "Here Comes the Flood" and "Down the Dolce Vita." Gabriel followed the release of Car with his debut solo tour. He utilized many of the musicians who played on the studio sessions.

1978's Peter Gabriel (Scratch) was critically acclaimed but didn't fare as well as his debut. Scratch went to number ten on the British charts and featured the songs "D.I.Y.," "On the Air," "Exposure," and "Flotsam and Jetsam." Gabriel asked Robert Fripp to produce this album and together they took a more experimental and conceptual approach. Fripp convinced Gabriel to go for a tight, "live" type of sound and keep the production dry. The goal was to encourage spontaneous studio performances. "On the Air" contained layers of synthesizers (utilized less like a string section). "Exposure" added Robert Fripp's Frippertronics that created multi-layers of electric guitar sounds in real time with delays and other effects.

1980's Peter Gabriel (Melt) built on the success of Gabriel's first two solo albums to firmly establish himself as a critically acclaimed cult artist. Gabriel again moved in a new direction, now with producer Steve Lillywhite and engineer Hugh Padgham. This would be a more organic recording that captured Peter's creativity and innovation. Melt would also mark his exploration of highly political issues with the antiwar single "Games Without Frontiers." The anti-apartheid Gabriel classic "Biko" was about the murdered South-African activist, Steven Biko. Also released as singles were "No Self Control" and "I Don't Remember." Melt saw Gabriel move to a new songwriting approach that featured drum machines and an increased interest in experimental sounds. Longtime Gabriel guitarist and collaborator David Rhodes played a key role in the making of Melt. Although not released as a single, "Intruder" became one of Gabriel's defining and groundbreaking compositions.

"Intruder"
by Peter Gabriel

"Intruder" was a sonic breakthrough for Peter Gabriel. As an ex-drummer, Gabriel was inspired to not have any cymbals on the entire Melt album. Gabriel invited his old bandmate, Phil Collins, to come in and experiment with the drum sounds. Gabriel asked Collins to hit a drum whenever he would have instinctively hit a cymbal. The engineer, Hugh Padgham, placed microphones very close to the drums and ran the compressed sound through a noise gate, thus creating a strange and unsettling effect. The result was a stunning gated drum sound. Padgham recalled, "When he (Collins) stopped playing it sucked the big sound of the room into nothing...The revelation that the studio itself could be part of the sound of the record was something that appealed greatly to Gabriel." #43

"Intruder's" use of sound colors opened up a new sonic world without the presence of cymbals. The song embodied a cavernous vacancy that was filled with the eerie and otherworldly timbres of Gabriel's vocal tics, Morris Pert's weird percussion and quirky xylophone solo, Larry Fast's tension filled synth sounds, and David Rhodes' guitar scratching sounds. Gabriel played big block chords on acoustic piano. He added a deranged and monotone whispered vocal quality to his lyrics that described a criminal break-in. This was told through the perspective of the burglar, or "Intruder." Peter Gabriel repeated the phrase "I like..." throughout the narrative, revealing that the intruder was committing a crime for the simple thrill of breaking an entering.

1982's Peter Gabriel (Security), with the commercial success of "Shock the Monkey," moved Gabriel into the mainstream when it became his first top forty hit. "Shock the Monkey" reached number one on the U.S. charts. Around this time, Gabriel was becoming increasingly more interested in world music. He said, "I'm certain the third world is going to have an increasing influence on our culture, and in music, a very vigorous hybrid will be produced which is based on this non-European influence and new technology which is going to get very very cheap and this facility will open up a new age of electronic skiffle." #44

For the Security album, Peter enlisted the production services of David Lord. Gabriel continued his fascination with technology by utilizing multiple synthesizers including; the Prophet 5, Polymoog, Fairlight CMI Series 1, and a Linn LM-1 drum machine. The musicians on Security were bassist Tony Levin, guitarist David Rhodes, synthesizer player Larry Fast, drummer Jerry Marotta, and percussionist Morris Pert. Gabriel explored a wide variety of song topics on this recording. "The Rhythm of the Heat" was inspired by his reading of the Carl Jung book, Symbols And The Interpretation Of Dreams. "San Jacinto" was about the clash of cultures around the San Jacinto American Indians and their relationship with the world in which they lived. "Shock the Monkey" was a sort of warped love song that explored the emotion of jealousy. The monkey became a metaphor for suspicion in a relationship. The song was built on an incessant synth riff that was a catchy melodic hook. The somewhat disturbing video for "Shock the Monkey" received heavy rotation on MTV. It featured Gabriel playing the role of a businessman with a mysterious persona dressed in a white suit, displaying different emotions in various settings.

In 1980, the idea for what would become the organization WOMAD (World Of Music And Dance) came to Peter Gabriel. He imagined a scenario where

Rock Hard Fact

Inspired by the social activism he experienced working with Amnesty, Peter Gabriel co-founded WITNESS in 1992. This is a non-profit organization that equips, trains, and supports locally based organizations worldwide to utilize video and the internet for human rights documentation and advocacy.

musicians from all over the world could come together to collaborate both musically and culturally. Gabriel, with the help of some friends, organized what would become an annual live festival held in various locations around the world. The first WOMAD festival was held in July of 1982 and featured; Peter Gabriel, The Drummers of Burundi, Echo & The Bunnymen, Imrat Khan, Prince Nico Mbarga, Simple Minds, The Chieftains, Don Cherry, and others. (In 2017, the WOMAD Festivals marked their 35th anniversary). The first festival was a great musical success but a financial disaster for Gabriel, who was left with a mountain of debt. The members of Genesis helped Gabriel by together performing a one-off reunion concert to pay all of the outstanding WOMAD debt.

Peter Gabriel next embarked on a world tour titled The Security Tour 1982-83 to promote the Security album. This resulted in the 1983 live album Plays Live. After the tour and live album release, Gabriel worked on a few side projects and was then approached by British film director Alan Parker to compose the music for a major film project to be called *Birdy*. *Birdy* also marked the beginning of Gabriel's work with producer Daniel Lanois. Music from the film *Birdy* was released in the spring of 1985. Gabriel drew from material he had recorded from the past three years. He also wrote seven new compositions that created unique sound collages. Gabriel acknowledged the film score for *Birdy* to be one of his finest efforts in terms of composition. The score for *Birdy* was highly acclaimed and it won the Grand Jury Prize at The Cannes Film Festival in 1985. Also that same year, Gabriel released his Plays Live Highlights album.

The multi-platinum 1986 album So catapulted Gabriel to international stardom. So was accompanied by a series of groundbreaking MTV videos and the number one hit, "Sledgehammer." The R&B styled *Sledgehammer* video was innovative by combining stop-action animation with live action. So reached number two on the U.S. charts and number one in England. So contained six singles and "In Your Eyes" would become one of Gabriel's classic songs. It reached the top thirty on the charts.

Groundbreaking Album So
by Peter Gabriel

Peter Gabriel selected Daniel Lanois to produce and add guitar parts to five of the tracks for the album So. This experience prompted Lanois to say, "I sense the level of obsession I had reached. The intricate details covering every nuance of song arrangements border on forensic...I saw every problem as a personal obstacle to knock down...The core of So was made with only three people: Peter, David Rhodes, and me. No drums or bass were used until much later in the project. It kind of sounds like a backward way of working: shouldn't you start with drums and bass first and then add everything else on top? Yes is the usual answer, except that Peter's songs were not fully written yet, and so my job was to chaperone the songwriting process." #45

The So musicians were a combination of Gabriel's most trusted team and some other esteemed guests. Familiar musicians included; bassist Tony Levin, drummers Jerry Marotta and Manu Katche, guitarist David Rhodes, keyboardist Larry Fast, vocalists Kate Bush and Youssou N'Dour, and violinist L. Shankar. Guests included; drummer Stewart Copeland, pianist Richard Tee, bassist Bill Laswell, guitarist Nile Rodgers, and vocalist Laurie Anderson.

Side one opened with "Red Rain," then "Sledgehammer," "Don't Give Up," and "That Voice Again." The concept for "Red Rain" came from a dream that Gabriel had where he envisioned a big, red sea being divided and glass bottles shaped like humans filling up with blood. "Red Rain" featured drummer Jerry Marotta and hi-hat overdubs by Stewart Copeland. "Sledgehammer's" great popularity would change the course of Gabriel's career. Gabriel said the song was "an attempt to recreate some of the spirit and style of the music that most excited me as a teenager-sixties soul. The lyrics of many of those songs were full of playful sexual innuendo and this is my contribution to that tradition. It is also about the use of sex as a means of getting through a breakdown in communication." #46 Lanois, Rhodes, and Gabriel knew they had a hit. They also made sure that the unexpected jam at the end of "Sledgehammer" remained on the album. The beginning of the song featured a synthesized shakuhachi flute generated with an E-mu Emulator II sampler.

"Don't Give Up" was a duet with the great vocalist Kate Bush. It was about the difficult economic conditions in England at the time. The verses sung by Gabriel personified the real emotions of a man whose unemployment caused himself great despair and a sense of hopelessness. Bush's part offered words of encouragement. "That Voice Again" may be one of Gabriel's most musical and underrated songs. The rhythm section of Katche, Levin, and Rhodes created great chemistry on this track.

Side two opened with "In You Eyes," then "Mercy Street," "Big Time," "We Do What We're Told," and "This Is the Picture (Excellent Birds)." "In Your Eyes," although a marginal hit, may be Gabriel's most popular song among his ardent fans. Gabriel first created a very musical drum machine rhythm track. The innovation of "In Your Eyes" was it's combination of world music elements, great melody, and Gabriel's inspired lyrics of ambiguity between romantic love and a love of God. "In Your Eyes" was both sensitive and powerful with the stunning addition of African star Youssou N'Dour's vocals. N'Dour sang in his native Senegalese Wolof language.

"Mercy Street" was a sensitive track, inspired by the work of American poet Anne Sexton. The percussion parts were recorded in Rio De Janeiro by percussionist Djalma Correa. "Big Time" was a "Sledgehammer-like" pop tune with a story based on a man that breaks out of a small town using his "big" words. "We Do What Were Told" was a story about social psychology and asked the question; how far are people prepared to go to follow an authority figure? "This Is the Picture (Excellent Birds)" was adapted from a track Gabriel had written with Laurie Anderson from her Mister Heartbreak album. So was nominated for four Grammy Awards. So--- Peter Gabriel's masterpiece.

Building on the momentum of So, Peter Gabriel co-headlined the first benefit tour for Amnesty International with U2 and Sting in 1986. In support of the So album, Gabriel also launched a late 1986 tour titled This Way Up. This version of Gabriel's touring band was perhaps his best. It featured Levin, Rhodes, Katche, and E-Street band keyboardist David Sancious. More Amnesty tours followed in 1988 and 1989 and Gabriel continued to champion human rights causes. Also in 1989, Gabriel released Passion: Music for The Last Temptation of Christ, a collection of instrumental tracks he composed for director Martin Scorsese's film, *Passion*. This was

> "There's lots of successful pop which doesn't have much soul to it but I'm drawn to music which does have a passionate spirit. Historically, religion and music have been very close. Ours is probably one of the first cultures to separate the two."
>
> - Peter Gabriel

Gabriel's deepest exploration of world music to date. The album won the 1989 Grammy Award for Best New Age Performance.

The next move for Peter Gabriel was to establish his Real World Studios. It had always been a dream of his to be able to control his own recording schedule. Gabriel also established his own record label (Real World). It would serve to record his future albums and many world music artists and ensembles from all over the world. 1990 saw the release of Shaking the Tree, a compilation of Gabriel hits.

1992's Us was the much anticipated followup to So and was a difficult period for Gabriel personally. Us, a much darker album than So, reflected a painful divorce Gabriel was going through. Only one single, "Steam" reached the top forty, yet the co-produced (with Daniel Lanois) Us yielded some of his strongest material. The album opened with "Come Talk to Me," a personal account of the strained relationship he felt with his first daughter, Melanie. This track utilized African percussion, layers of bagpipes, and background vocals by Sinead O'Connor. "Blood of Eden" contained another vocal interaction with O'Connor. The album's dark and ominous lead single, "Digging In The Dirt" again dealt directly with Gabriel's emotional pain. "Secret World" would become one of Gabriel's signature tunes and a great feature in his live performances.

"Secret World"
by Peter Gabriel

Peter Gabriel said that "Secret World" was "about the private world that two people occupy and the private worlds that they occupy as individuals within that space, and the overlap of their dreams and desires." #47 The song was a powerful portrayal of the lost time between lovers and their collective search for rekindled passion in a decaying relationship. In this secret world of lovers, the couple sets their own rules. Gabriel referenced Adam and Eve (like he did in his song "Blood of Eden") bringing everything back to the first human relationship.

Musically, Daniel Lanois built the song's dynamic intensity slowly and steadily. After a forceful Tony Levin bass run, the song came to a halt and Gabriel whispered the word "Listen" and the groove returned locking in with Rhodes' guitar part. Gabriel ended the song with a question: "In all the places we were hiding love/What was it we were thinking of?" The lyrical answer was "With no guilt and no shame, no sorrow or blame/Whatever it is, we are all the same." Lanois finished the brilliant production with a synthesized cello part by Malcolm Burn. Caroline Lavelle also added a real cello part. Daniel Lanois further contributed to "Secret World" with the sound of a dobro (a wood-bodied, single-cone resonator guitar).

Us was successful in the U.S. selling one million copies and four million in England. The Secret World tour began in the spring of 1993 with a tremendous band that consisted of Katche, Levin, Rhodes, violinist L. Shanker, and keyboardist Jean Claude Naimro. Also Leon Minassian played duduk and vocalist Paula Cole added vocal parts. That same year, Gabriel led this Secret World Tour band and combined it with a WOMAD roster of artists to tour North America and Canada. This roster included; Crowded House, The Drummers of Burundi, Sheila Chandra, and many others. The tour ended in the summer of 1994, and Gabriel released the two-CD set Secret World Live. Later in 1994, Gabriel released a CD-ROM Xplora, one of many projects he developed at his Real World Studios.

Peter Gabriel next ramped up the utilization of his Real World Studio and record label to champion world music artists from all over the world. In 1993, Brian Eno used the studio to record and produce an album for the band James. Around this same time, Gabriel began a long term project he called Real World Week of Recording. Musicians, writers, and producers were offered an opportunity to meet for a week of creative collaboration. In its first incarnation, some seventy-five artists from twenty countries participated in the Real World Week in association with WOMAD. For the rest of the 1990's, Gabriel concentrated on developing more multimedia projects for Real World and he wrote material for a new studio album. Gabriel also took part in preparing reissues of a Genesis box set titled Archive 1967-75. The full Genesis band participated while Gabriel overdubbed some vocal parts.

The new millennium brought to fruition 2000's OVO. This was a multi-media music and video project Gabriel had been working on since 1997 with Mark Fisher. It utilized material Gabriel had composed for Us and featured a number of prominent musicians. Gabriel said, "We were asked to do something that reflects a bit of the past, the present and the future, so I suggested we develop the plot around the struggles of three generations of a family." #48 Gabriel also continued to work on film soundtracks. He released 2002's *Long Walk Home: Music From the Rabbit Proof Fence*. This film score was based on the controversial true story of a stolen generation of Aboriginal children that were taken from their families by the Australian church and state. These children were forced to serve as domestic workers for white society. The exposure of this shocking story was another of Gabriel's humanitarian efforts.

Peter Gabriel worked at a steady rate throughout the decade of the 2000's, although his releases seemed sporadic. Gabriel was often over-extended with commitments to his own studio and record label, interests in technology and multi-media projects, and his charity work. He also devoted a lot of time to composing film scores. This relegated his studio album output to a slower pace. Additionally, Gabriel had recently gotten re-married to a woman named Meabh Flynn and bought a small private hotel in Northern Sardinia.

2002's Up was released a full decade after Gabriel's Us album. Up was cerebral and dense. It reached number nine on the U.S. charts and number eleven in England. Prominent songs included; "Darkness," "Growing Up," "Sky Blue," "I Grieve," "The Barry Williams Show," "More Than This," and "Signal to Noise." Most of Up was recorded at Real World Studios. "Darkness" began with a very quiet synthesized part then exploded into the almost death metal-like assault of David Rhodes' nasty guitar timbres. "Growing Up" was about the cycle of life and became the title of Gabriel's next tour. "Sky Blue" was perhaps the standout track from the album. The Blind Boys of Alabama, one of the great vocal groups Gabriel had championed, added their incredible church-inspired vocal harmonies. Gabriel knew this song was highly emotional and said, "As a teenager I was very influenced by soul and blues and it was my starting point for a lot of music. I think this was definitely an influence on that track." #49 The song "Signal To Noise" was a tribute to the late Nusrat Fateh Ali Khan, a supreme vocal talent and one of Gabriel's close friends. The tour in support of Up began in the fall of 2002. In 2003, Gabriel released a career summation titled Hit: The Definitive Two-CD Collection and a DVD of the Growing Up Tour titled Growing Up: Live.

> "Never lose faith in real rock and roll music. Never lose faith in that. You might have to look a little harder, but its always going to be there."
>
> - Dave Grohl

Over the next few years, Gabriel keep working on various projects and in 2006 was awarded the Man Of Peace award at the Seventh World Summit of Nobel Peace Laureates. This honor was for his commitment to human rights and the spread of principles of peace and solidarity in the world. In 2007, Gabriel performed a set to celebrate the twenty-fifth anniversary of WOMAD. Big Blue Ball, a product of the Real World Recording Weeks, was released in 2008. This recording combined the world music multiculturalism of Music and Rhythm (the first WOMAD compilation) with the production tools of Gabriel's Us recording. Big Blue Ball functioned almost like a secret Peter Gabriel record with his distinctive voice and fingerprints all over it. This album featured a host of world music guests including; Hossam Ramzy, Natacha Atlas, Papa Wemba, Sinead O'Connor, Rossy, and Marta Sebestyen. Also in 2008, Gabriel collaborated with Thomas Newman on music for PIXAR's film, WALL-E.

Gabriel's 2010 release, Scratch My Back, contained orchestral covers of Gabriel singing songs originally performed by his peers including; Paul Simon, David Bowie, Neil Young, Lou Reed, Randy Newman, and David Byrne, and Radiohead. Gabriel added another six covers by younger artists including; Stephin Merritt, Bon Iver, Elbow, Radiohead, Arcade Fire, and Regina Spektor. Scratch My Back was the first of a two-part project where Gabriel would pay homage to some of his favorite artists' songs. Then, those artists in turn would cover Gabriel songs on a 2013 follow-up album tentatively titled, And I'll Scratch Yours. Six Gabriel songs and the artists that recorded them included; "Not One of Us" covered by Stephen Merritt, "Come Talk to Me" covered by Bon Iver, "Biko" covered by Paul Simon, "Solsbury Hill" covered by Lou Reed, "Mercy Street" covered by Elbow, and "I Don't Remember" covered by David Byrne. David Bowie, Neil Young, and Radiohead declined to participate on the And I'll Scratch Yours album.

Gabriel's next project was 2011's New Blood, a collection of Gabriel tracks that were re-recorded by setting them to full orchestral arrangements. The selected tracks were all instrumental versions of songs from the full scope of Gabriel's solo career. Gabriel and arranger John Metcalfe created some incredible orchestrations of Gabriel classics including; "The Rhythm Of the Heat," "Intruder," "Solsbury Hill," "In Your Eyes," and "Red Rain." The DVD New Blood: Live in London was simultaneously released at the time of New Blood. Next came the release of 2012's Live Blood, a live album from The New Blood Tour. Live Blood contained twenty-two tracks.

2016 marked the 25th anniversary of So. To celebrate this, Gabriel launched the 2014 Back to Front tour and performed the entire So album at each concert venue. Gabriel was able to reassemble the original So band of Tony Levin, David Rhodes, Manu Katche, and David Sancious. He added Jennie Abrahamson and Linnea Olsson for background vocals. Gabriel released 2014's Back to Front: Live in London, a live recording from the So anniversary tour. He also released several deluxe editions of the album, the largest being a four-CD-two-DVD-two vinyl album box set. Gabriel's entire recording output is a vast collection that includes; nine studio albums, six live albums, three compilations, eleven video albums, thirty music videos, forty three singles, four movie soundtracks, and numerous guest appearances as a recording artist and producer.

Like other supremely talented and identifiable vocalists such as Freddie Mercury and David Bowie, Peter Gabriel possesses a unique and highly personal voice. Gabriel has many voices. His typical raspy quality can turn into something warm and comforting. He has the ability to not only hit high notes utilizing his falsetto voice but he can phrase intricate melodic ideas there (high falsetto range) as well. He can speak lyrics with great dynamic effectiveness or whisper them for effect. He can also sing with stunning power and force. Gabriel's voice is an instrument that he has fully explored and his musicality has taken him to uncharted expressive places.

Peter Gabriel, beginning with Genesis, created some of progressive rock's most enduring music. This became a launching pad for his remarkable solo career. Gabriel expanded his musical direction with an interest in many diverse music genres, including a great passion for world music. Gabriel's compositions combined dark and sometimes experimental sounds with instrumental and vocal influences from Africa, Asia, and other parts of the world. Peter Gabriel has not only been a visionary for his own music but he made a profound impact as the champion for countless world music artists. Gabriel's ever searching musical appetite merged with his unique vision to synthesize virtually every musical genre; from progressive to soul to heavy metal to orchestral music and beyond. This has informed his sophisticated and never ending musical growth. Peter Gabriel possesses a musical and deeply creative vision unlike any other artist. Daniel Lanois summed up Peter Gabriel with a simple observation. Lanois said, "Peter Gabriel is made of good, he's made of dreams." #50

Peter Gabriel was inducted into the Rock and Roll Hall of Fame twice; first as a member of Genesis in 2010 and then as a solo artist in 2014.

Dave Grohl has become in many ways the current "face of rock 'n' roll." He is in the position to point to the future of rock music. Grohl has made the preservation of rock history a driving passion in his life. His career as ex-Nirvana drummer and Foo Fighter lead vocalist/guitarist and primary songwriter (see chapter sixteen) demonstrates that he is one of rock's elite musicians. Among his other musical associations, Grohl co-founded the rock supergroup Them Crooked Vultures and has recorded and toured frequently with the rock band Queens of the Stone Age. Grohl, along with bandmate Taylor Hawkins, inducted Queen into the Rock and Roll Hall of Fame in 2001. In 2014, Grohl and The Foo Fighters released an eight part HBO documentary mini-series called Foo Fighters: Sonic Highways. This was produced simultaneously with their eighth album, Sonic Highways. Each of the eight HBO episodes sought to explore the unique musical history of different American cities. Grohl and The Foo Fighters visited Washington, D.C., Chicago, Austin, Los Angeles, Nashville, Seattle, New Orleans, and New York with the intention of revealing the musical story of each city. Grohl interviewed major rock artists from each city including; Duff McKagan of Guns N' Roses, Ian MacKaye of Minor Threat and Fugazi, Joe Walsh of The Eagles, Nancy Wilson of Heart, Paul Stanley of Kiss, Rick Nielsen of Cheap Trick, Zac Brown, and Gary Clark, Jr. The Foo Fighters also collaborated with the Preservation Hall Jazz Band from New Orleans. Dave Grohl said, "The thing that will never go away is that connection you make with a band or a song where you're moved by the fact that its real people making music. You make that human connection with a song like 'Let It Be' or 'Long and Winding Road' or a song like 'Bohemian Rhapsody' or 'Roxanne,' any of those songs. They sound like people making music." #51

Rock music is a relatively new art form having been launched in and around the late 1940's. Over the past eighteen chapters, this book has explored how rock 'n' roll was pioneered from the songs of Fats Domino and Little Richard through a myriad of musical influences and styles to arrive at the current trends in rock music. This occurred over (an approximately) seventy year period seen in the creative and innovative output of artists and bands from around the world. The great diversity of rock music is represented by the dozens of rock music sub-genres that fill an entire music styles/genres index at the end of this book. The six artists and bands profiled in this chapter are only a sample of the profound musical genius and visionary innovation inspired by rock music. While some may feel that rock music has run its course, others are optimistic about its continued innovation. No other music genre has been more exciting or has moved in so many unpredictable directions. Rock music has proven itself to be *inspiring*, *resilient*, and above all, *timeless*. Whatever it may bring, the future of rock music has *unlimited potential*.

Discussion Question

There are other rock artists or bands that exhibit similar visionary qualities to those featured in this chapter. Pick an artist or band that you feel belongs in this elite company and describe their musical qualities that makes them special.

Artist/Band Index

The following index contains each major artist or band that was either *mentioned* or *explored in depth* throughout this book. They are cataloged by chapter and page number. Many artists and bands were *listed* but not included in the index. Most artists or bands are usually cited only once and where they could be *most appropriately* placed.

A

Abba	chapter 15	page 288
Accept	chapter 10	page 166
AC/DC	chapter 10	page 185
Bryan Adams	chapter 15	page 288
Aerosmith	chapter 10	page 184
Alabama	chapter 9	page 152
Alice in Chains	chapter 16	page 313
The Allman Brothers Band	chapter 9	page 155
Duane Allman	chapter 9	page 155/156
The Animals	chapter 11	page 191
Paul Anka	chapter 3	page 35
Anthrax	chapter 10	page 177
Apex Twin	chapter 17	page 336
Joan Armatrading	chapter 7	page 118
Armored Saint	chapter 10	page 173
Chet Atkins	chapter 9	page 144
Audioslave	chapter 17	page 332
Frankie Avalon	chapter 3	page 34
The Average White Band	chapter 17	page 334

B

The Babys	chapter 11	page 206
Bachman Turner Overdrive	chapter 11	page 205
Ginger Baker	chapter 4	page 49
Bad Brains	chapter 14	page 264
Bad Company	chapter 11	page 205
Badfinger	chapter 15	page 295
Joan Baez	chapter 1	page 12
The Band	chapter 18	page 351
Tony Banks	chapter 13	page 240/241
Syd Barrett	chapter 8	page 122
David Bartholomew	chapter 3	page 30
Bay City Rollers	chapter 8	page 133
The Beach Boys	chapter 3	page 37
The Beastie Boys	chapter 17	page 329
Beat Happening	chapter 16	page 308
The Beatles	chapter 5	page 57
The Bee Gees	chapter 15	page 288
Jeff Beck	chapter 17	page 342
Walter Becker	chapter 18	page 356
The Bel-Airs	chapter 3	page 39
Chuck Berry	chapter 3	page 27
Dickey Betts	chapter 9	page 156
Big Big Train	chapter 13	page 250
Big Brother and the Holding Company	chapter 6	page 83
Bikini Kill	chapter 14	page 265
Biohazard	chapter 14	page 267
Bjork	chapter 17	page 336
Bill Black	chapter 2	page 16/17
Black Crows	chapter 12	page 222
Black Flag	chapter 14	page 266
The Black Keys	chapter 12	page 222
Black Sabbath	chapter 10	page 167
Blind Faith	chapter 11	page 197
Blink-182	chapter 14	page 269
Blondie	chapter 14	page 272
Blood, Sweat, and Tears	chapter 17	page 333
Blue Cheer	chapter 10	page 166

371

Rock History - the Musician's Perspective

Blue Oyster Cult	chapter 11	page 196
Blues Incorporated	chapter 4	page 43
Blues Traveler	chapter 12	page 222
Blur	chapter 15	page 293
Joe Bonamassa	chapter 12	page 222
John Bonham	chapter 4	page 54
Bon Iver	chapter 7	page 119
Jon Bon Jovi	chapter 12	page 227
Pat Boone	chapter 3	page 34
Boston	chapter 11	page 207
David Bowie	chapter 8	page 129
Billy Bragg	chapter 7	page 118
The Brill Building Songwriters	chapter 3	page 34
James Brown	chapter 17	page 325
Jackson Browne	chapter 12	page 216
Jack Bruce	chapter 4	page 49
Buckethead	chapter 17	page 344
The Buckinghams	chapter 17	page 333
Jeff Buckley	chapter 7	page 118
Tim Buckley	chapter 7	page 118
Buffalo Springfield	chapter 7	page 103
The Buggles	chapter 16	page 305
The Paul Butterfield Blues Band	chapter 6	page 90
Butthole Surfers	chapter 16	page 319
Buzzcocks	chapter 14	page 263
The Byrds	chapter 7	page 99
David Byrne	chapter 8/18	page 128/363

C

John Cage	chapter 8	page 126
J.J. Cale	chapter 7	page 108
Glen Campbell	chapter 9	page 152
Camel	chapter 13	page 240
Canned Heat	chapter 6	page 90
Capercaillie	chapter 7	page 114
Captain Beefheart and his Magic Band	chapter 8	page 127
Caravan	chapter 13	page 240
The Cars	chapter 14	page 272
The Carter Family	chapter 1	page 10
Johnny Cash	chapter 1/2	page 11/19
Harry Chapin	chapter 7	page 114
Tracy Chapman	chapter 7	page 118
The Charlatans	chapter 6	page 78
Ray Charles	chapter 3	page 25
Cheap Trick	chapter 14	page 271
Chubby Checker	chapter 3	page 35
The Chemical Brothers	chapter 17	page 336
Phil and Leonard Chess	chapter 1	page 7
Chicago	chapter 17	page 333
Clannad	chapter 7	page 114
Eric Clapton	chapter 12	page 220
Dick Clark	chapter 3	page 33
Gene Clark	chapter 9	page 144
Kelly Clarkson	chapter 15	page 291
The Clash	chapter 14	page 261
Kurt Cobain	chapter 16	page 310/313
Eddie Cochran	chapter 2	page 21
Joe Cocker	chapter 12	page 213
Leonard Cohen	chapter 7	page 106
Coldplay	chapter 15	page 294
Judy Collins	chapter 7	page 108
Phil Collins	chapter 13/15	page 243/290
Alice Cooper	chapter 10	page 182
Coroner	chapter 10	page 181
Corrosion of Conformity (C.O.C.)	chapter 14	page 268
Elvis Costello	chapter 14	page 271
Counting Crows	chapter 16	page 323
Country Joe and the Fish	chapter 6	page 84
Cream	chapter 4	page 49
Creedence Clearwater Revival	chapter 9	page 149
Jim Croce	chapter 7	page 113
Cro-Mags	chapter 14	page 267

Artist/Band Index

David Crosby	chapter 7	page 108
Crosby, Stills, Nash, and Young	chapter 7	page 104
Crowded House	chapter 15	page 288
The Cult	chapter 10	page 188
Culture Club	chapter 14	page 275
The Cure	chapter 16	page 318
Curved Air	chapter 13	page 240
Cypress Hill	chapter 17	page 329

D

Dick Dale	chapter 3	page 36
Roger Daltrey	chapter 6	page 73
The Damned	chapter 14	page 262
Charlie Daniels Band	chapter 9	page 162
Rick Danko	chapter 18	page 351
Bobby Darin	chapter 3	page 35
Dave Davies	chapter 6	page 72
Ray Davies	chapter 6	page 72
Miles Davis	chapter 17	page 335
The Dead & Company	chapter 12	page 231
The Dead Kennedys	chapter 14	page 267
Deep Purple	chapter 10	page 182
Def Leppard	chapter 10	page 171
Deftones	chapter 17	page 339
Delaney and Bonnie	chapter 11	page 197
Derek and the Dominos	chapter 11	page 199
Devo	chapter 14	page 271
Diamond Head	chapter 10	page 171
Bo Diddley	chapter 3	page 27
The Dillards	chapter 9	page 144
The Dillinger Escape Plan	chapter 13	page 251
Dire Straits	chapter 11	page 207
D.R.I. (Dirty Rotten Imbeciles)	chapter 14	page 268
The Dixie Chicks	chapter 9	page 154
The Dixie Dregs	chapter 17	page 335
Willie Dixon	chapter 1	page 8
Dokken	chapter 10	page 174
Antoine "Fats" Domino	chapter 3	page 29
Donovan	chapter 7	page 114
The Doobie Brothers	chapter 11	page 200
The Doors	chapter 6	page 85
Thomas Dorsey	chapter 1	page 4
Dream Theater	chapter 13	page 249
Duran Duran	chapter 14	page 274
Bob Dylan	chapter 7/9	page 96/151

E

The Eagles	chapter 11	page 203
Duane Eddy	chapter 3	page 36
The Electric Flag	chapter 17	page 334
Electric Light Orchestra	chapter 11	page 201
Emerson, Lake, and Palmer	chapter 13	page 238
Brian Eno	chapter 18	page 360
John Entwistle	chapter 6	page 77
Brian Epstein	chapter 5	page 58
Ahmet Ertegun	chapter 3	page 25
Eurythmics	chapter 14	page 275
Gil Evans	chapter 17	page 335
The Everly Brothers	chapter 3	page 32

F

Fabian	chapter 3	page 34
The Faces/Small Faces	chapter 11	page 193
Donald Fagen	chapter 18	page 356
Fairport Convention	chapter 7	page 102
Faith No More	chapter 16	page 320
Fall Out Boy	chapter 14	page 270
Fear Factory	chapter 17	page 338
Lester Flatt	chapter 1	page 10
The First National Band	chapter 9	page 150
Fleetwood Mac	chapter 4/11	page 44/194
The Flying Burrito Brothers	chapter 9	page 145

Rock History - the Musician's Perspective

Dan Fogelberg	chapter 7	page 117
Foghat	chapter 11	page 203
The Foo Fighters	chapter 16	page 317
Lita Ford	chapter 10	page 175
Foreigner	chapter 11	page 206
Peter Frampton	chapter 12	page 222
Connie Francis	chapter 3	page 35
Aretha Franklin	chapter 3	page 25
Free	chapter 11	page 197
Alan Freed	chapter 3	page 25
Annette Funicello	chapter 3	page 34

G

Peter Gabriel	chapter 18	page 364
Lady Gaga	chapter 8	page 139
Art Garfunkel	chapter 7	page 111
Generation X	chapter 14	page 263
Genesis	chapter 13	page 240
Gentle Giant	chapter 13	page 239
Boy George	chapter 15	page 290
Debbie Gibson	chapter 15	page 288
Philip Glass	chapter 8	page 127
Gary Glitter	chapter 8	page 133
The Glitter Band	chapter 8	page 133
The Glittermen	chapter 8	page 133
Gerry Goffin	chapter 3	page 34
Gov't Mule	chapter 9	page 163
The Grass Roots	chapter 7	page 102
The Grateful Dead	chapter 6	page 78
Green Day	chapter 14	page 269
Howard Greenfield	chapter 3	page 34
Green River	chapter 16	page 308
Dave Grohl	chapter 16/18	page 317/368
Guns 'N' Roses	chapter 10	page 174
Woodie Guthrie	chapter 1	page 13

H

Merle Haggard	chapter 9	page 144
Bill Haley and the Comets	chapter 3	page 26
Hall and Oates	chapter 15	page 287
Emmylou Harris	chapter 9	page 148
George Harrison	chapter 5	page 64
The Hawks	chapter 18	page 351
Heart	chapter 11	page 202
Richard Hell and the Voidoids	chapter 14	page 258
Levon Helm	chapter 18	page 351
Jimi Hendrix	chapter 6	page 87
Herman's Hermits	chapter 6	page 71
John Hiatt	chapter 7	page 117
Hole	chapter 16	page 314
The Hollies	chapter 6	page 71
Buddy Holly	chapter 3	page 32
John Lee Hooker	chapter 1	page 9
Hootie and the Blowfish	chapter 16	page 322
Hot Tuna	chapter 6	page 82
Eddie "Son" House	chapter 1	page 6
Garth Hudson	chapter 18	page 351
Humble Pie	chapter 11	page 196

I

Billy Idol	chapter 14	page 263
Imagine Dragons	chapter 15	page 292
Incubus	chapter 17	page 339
INXS	chapter 16	page 318
Iron Butterfly	chapter 10	page 166
Iron Maiden	chapter 10	page 170

J

Jane's Addiction	chapter 16	page 321
Janet Jackson	chapter 15	page 287
Mahalia Jackson	chapter 1	page 4
Michael Jackson	chapter 15	page 280

Mick Jagger	chapter 4	page 47
The Jam	chapter 14	page 259
Elmore James	chapter 1	page 8
The James Gang	chapter 11	page 194
Jan and Dean	chapter 3	page 39
Blind Lemon Jefferson	chapter 1	page 7
Jefferson Airplane/Starship	chapter 6	page 82
Waylon Jennings	chapter 9	page 144
Jethro Tull	chapter 13	page 244
Joan Jett and the Blackhearts	chapter 10	page 188
Joan Jett and the Runaways	chapter 10	page 187
J. Geils Band	chapter 11	page 196
Billy Joel	chapter 12	page 216
Elton John	chapter 12	page 214
Robert Johnson	chapter 1	page 6
John Paul Jones	chapter 4	page 50
Norah Jones	chapter 7	page 118
Quincy Jones	chapter 15	page 279
Ricky Lee Jones	chapter 7	page 118
Janis Joplin	chapter 6	page 83
Louis Jordan	chapter 3	page 25
Journey	chapter 11	page 205
Judas Priest	chapter 10	page 168

K

Kansas	chapter 11	page 210
Kid Rock	chapter 17	page 329
The Killers	chapter 16	page 322
B.B. King	chapter 1	page 9
Carole King	chapter 7	page 106
King Crimson	chapter 13	page 237
Kings of Leon	chapter 16	page 323
The Kingsman	chapter 16	page 308
The Kinks	chapter 6	page 72
Kiss	chapter 10	page 184
The Knack	chapter 14	page 273
Korn	chapter 17	page 339
Kraftwerk	chapter 17	page 335
Lenny Kravitz	chapter 17	page 328
Kris Kristofferson	chapter 9	page 144

L

Lamb of God	chapter 10	page 180
Adam Lambert	chapter 15	page 292
Cyndi Lauper	chapter 15	page 288
Lead Belly	chapter 1	page 12
Led Zeppelin	chapter 4	page 50
Brenda Lee	chapter 3	page 35
Jerry Leiber	chapter 3	page 35
John Lennon	chapter 5	page 65
Jerry Lee Lewis	chapter 2	page 18
Limp Bizkit	chapter 17	page 331
Linkin Park	chapter 17	page 331
Little Feat	chapter 9	page 160
Living Colour	chapter 17	page 328
Loggins and Messina	chapter 9	page 150
Professor Longhair	chapter 3	page 30
Lyle Lovett	chapter 9	page 153
The Lovin' Spoonful	chapter 7	page 101
Lynyrd Skynyrd	chapter 9	page 158

M

Madonna	chapter 15	page 282
Yngwie Malmsteen	chapter 17	page 343
The Mamas & the Papas	chapter 7	page 101
Richard Manuel	chapter 18	page 351
Marilyn Manson	chapter 8	page 139
Marillion	chapter 13	page 249
Bruno Mars	chapter 7	page 106
The Marshall Tucker Band	chapter 9	page 161
Mars Volta	chapter 13	page 251
George Martin	chapter 5	page 63

Richard Marx	chapter 7	page 106
Matchbox Twenty	chapter 16	page 316
Dave Matthews Band	chapter 12	page 230
John Mayall's Bluesbreakers	chapter 4	page 43
John Mayer	chapter 12	page 229
MC5	chapter 14	page 264
Paul McCartney	chapter 5	page 67
Don McLean	chapter 7	page 114
Meat Puppets	chapter 16	page 319
Medeski, Martin, and Wood	chapter 12	page 231
Megadeth	chapter 10	page 178
John J Mellencamp	chapter 12	page 223
The Melvins	chapter 14	page 265
Men at Work	chapter 15	page 288
Mercyful Fate	chapter 10	page 173
Meshuggah	chapter 10	page 181
Metallica	chapter 10	page 175
The Meters	chapter 3/17	page 30/326
George Michael	chapter 15	page 290
The Steve Miller Band	chapter 6	page 84
Ministry	chapter 17	page 337
Minor Threat	chapter 14	page 264
The Misfits	chapter 14	page 258
Joni Mitchell	chapter 18	page 354
Moby Grape	chapter 6	page 84
The Monkees	chapter 3	page 36
Bill Monroe and His Bluegrass Boys	chapter 1	page 10
The Moody Blues	chapter 13	page 235
Keith Moon	chapter 6	page 77
Scotty Moore	chapter 2	page 16/17
Van Morrison	chapter 7	page 114
Motley Crue	chapter 10	page 174
Motorhead	chapter 10	page 170
Mott the Hoople	chapter 8	page 135
Mountain	chapter 10	page 183
Mudhoney	chapter 16	page 309
Muse	chapter 16	page 321
My Chemical Romance	chapter 14	page 270

N

Graham Nash	chapter 7	page 108
Nazz	chapter 15	page 294
Ricky Nelson	chapter 3	page 35
Willie Nelson	chapter 9	page 144
Mike Nesmith	chapter 9	page 150
Randy Newman	chapter 7	page 117
New Riders of the Purple Sage	chapter 9	page 149
The New Yardbirds	chapter 4	page 50
The New York Dolls	chapter 8	page 138
The Nice	chapter 13	page 236
Nickelback	chapter 16	page 316
Stevie Nicks	chapter 12	page 226
Nico	chapter 8	page 125
Nine Inch Nails	chapter 17	page 337
Nirvana	chapter 16	page 310
Nitty Gritty Dirt Band	chapter 9	page 146
No Doubt	chapter 16	page 322
Ted Nugent	chapter 10	page 188
Laura Nyro	chapter 7	page 116

O

Oasis	chapter 15	page 293
Conor Oberst	chapter 7	page 119
The Offspring	chapter 14	page 269
Opeth	chapter 10	page 181
Roy Orbison	chapter 3	page 33
Ozzy Osbourne	chapter 10	page 172
The Outlaws	chapter 9	page 160
Buck Owens	chapter 9	page 144

P

Jimmy Page	chapter 4	page 51
Robert Palmer	chapter 15	page 286
Pantera	chapter 10	page 179
Gram Parsons	chapter 9	page 145
Charley Patton	chapter 1	page 5
Les Paul	chapter 17	page 341
Pearl Jam	chapter 16	page 315
Carl Perkins	chapter 2	page 19
Peter, Paul, and Mary	chapter 7	page 99
Tom Petty and the Heartbreakers	chapter 12	page 223
Sam Phillips	chapter 2	page 15
Phish	chapter 12	page 230
Pink Floyd	chapter 8	page 121
Gene Pitney	chapter 3	page 35
Robert Plant	chapter 4	page 53
Planxty	chapter 7	page 114
Poco	chapter 9	page 146
Poison	chapter 10	page 174
The Police	chapter 16	page 300
Iggy Pop	chapter 14	page 265
Porcupine Tree	chapter 13	page 249
Elvis Aaron Presley	chapter 2	page 16
The Pretenders	chapter 14	page 273
Primus	chapter 16	page 320
Prince	chapter 15	page 284
Procol Harum	chapter 13	page 236
Prophets of Rage	chapter 17	page 332
Public Image Ltd	chapter 14	page 261
Pure Prairie League	chapter 9	page 150

Q

The Quarrymen	chapter 5	page 57
Queen	chapter 8	page 136
Queens of the Stone Age	chapter 10	page 188
Quicksilver Messenger Service	chapter 6	page 81
Quiet Riot	chapter 10	page 173

R

Radiohead	chapter 16	page 319
Rage Against the Machine	chapter 17	page 330
Rainbow	chapter 10	page 187
Rammstein	chapter 17	page 338
The Ramones	chapter 14	page 257
Ratt	chapter 10	page 173
Raven	chapter 10	page 171
Red Hot Chili Peppers	chapter 17	page 326
Lou Reed	chapter 8	page 126
R.E.M.	chapter 16	page 304
REO Speedwagon	chapter 11	page 196
Little Richard	chapter 3	page 30
Keith Richards	chapter 4	page 45
Robbie Robertson	chapter 18	page 351
Rockpile	chapter 15	page 295
Jimmy Rodgers	chapter 1	page 10
The Rolling Stones	chapter 4	page 44
The Romantics	chapter 15	page 296
Mick Ronson	chapter 8	page 133
Linda Ronstadt	chapter 9	page 148
Johnny Rotten	chapter 14	page 259
Roxy Music	chapter 8	page 135
Todd Rundgren	chapter 15	page 294
Rush	chapter 13	page 247
Leon Russell	chapter 7	page 109
Bobby Rydell	chapter 3	page 34

S

Santana	chapter 6	page 85
Joe Satriani	chapter 17	page 343
Saxon	chapter 10	page 171
Scorpions	chapter 10	page 166
Earl Scruggs	chapter 1	page 10

Sea Level	chapter 17	page 335
Neil Sedaka	chapter 3	page 34
Pete Seeger	chapter 1	page 12
Bob Seger and the Silver Bullet Band	chapter 12	page 217
The Sex Pistols	chapter 14	page 259
Ed Sheeran	chapter 7	page 119
Carly Simon	chapter 7	page 113
Paul Simon	chapter 7	page 112
Simon and Garfunkel	chapter 7	page 102
Siouxsie Sioux	chapter 14	page 266
Slade	chapter 8	page 133
Slayer	chapter 10	page 177
Slipknot	chapter 17	page 341
Smashing Pumpkins	chapter 16	page 320
Patti Smith	chapter 14	page 258
The Smiths	chapter 15	page 292
Soft Machine	chapter 13	page 240
Sonic Youth	chapter 16	page 319
Soundgarden	chapter 16	page 309
Phil Spector	chapter 3	page 39
The Spencer Davis Group	chapter 11	page 192
Spin Doctors	chapter 17	page 328
Spock's Beard	chapter 13	page 250
Bruce Springsteen and the E Street Band	chapter 12	page 218
Ringo Starr	chapter 5	page 68
Steely Dan	chapter 18	page 356
Steppenwolf	chapter 11	page 195
Cat Stevens	chapter 7	page 116
Al Stewart	chapter 7	page 114
Rod Stewart	chapter 12	page 225
Stephen Stills	chapter 7	page 108
Sting	chapter 12	page 227
Mike Stoller	chapter 3	page 35
The Stone Canyon Band	chapter 9	page 150
Stone Temple Pilots	chapter 16	page 314
The Stooges	chapter 14	page 265
Styx	chapter 11	page 204
Suicidal Tendencies	chapter 14	page 268
Supertramp	chapter 11	page 202
The Surfaris	chapter 3	page 39
System of a Down	chapter 17	page 340

T

Talking Heads	chapter 8	page 128
James Taylor	chapter 7	page 110
Tears for Fears	chapter 15	page 290
Tedeschi Trucks Band	chapter 9	page 163
teen idols	chapter 3	page 33
Television	chapter 14	page 256
Thin Lizzy	chapter 11	page 198
George Thorogood	chapter 12	page 222
Tool	chapter 13	page 249
Toto	chapter 11	page 208
Tower of Power	chapter 17	page 334
Pete Townshend	chapter 6	page 73/76
Traffic	chapter 11	page 192
The Traveling Wilburys	chapter 12	page 224
T. Rex	chapter 8	page 133
The Tubes	chapter 8	page 127
The Turtles	chapter 7	page 100
Twisted Sister	chapter 10	page 173
Type O Negative	chapter 10	page 175

U

U2	chapter 16	page 302
UFO	chapter 10	page 166
Uncle Tupelo	chapter 9	page 154
Uriah Heep	chapter 11	page 198

V

Steve Vai	chapter 17	page 343
Richie Valens	chapter 3	page 36

Artist/Band Index

	Van der Graaf Generator	chapter 13	page 237
	Van Halen	chapter 10	page 186
	Vanilla Fudge	chapter 10	page 181
	Stevie Ray Vaughn	chapter 12	page 222
	Bobby Vee	chapter 3	page 35
	Suzanne Vega	chapter 7	page 118
	The Velvet Underground	chapter 8	page 124
	The Ventures	chapter 3	page 37
	The Verve	chapter 15	page 293
	Gene Vincent	chapter 2	page 22
W			
	Tom Waits	chapter 7	page 118
	T-Bone Walker	chapter 1	page 9
	Wang Chung	chapter 15	page 290
	Warrant	chapter 10	page 174
	Muddy Waters	chapter 1	page 7
	Weezer	chapter 15	page 296
	Wham!	chapter 15	page 290
	Jack White	chapter 12	page 222
	Whitesnake	chapter 10	page 174
	White Zombie	chapter 17	page 337
	The Who	chapter 6	page 73
	Wilco	chapter 9	page 154
	Hank Williams Sr.	chapter 1	page 10
	Sonny Boy Williamson #2	chapter 1	page 9
	Bob Wills and His Texas Playboys	chapter 1	page 9
	Brian Wilson	chapter 3	page 37/38
	Wings	chapter 5	page 67
	Johnny Winter	chapter 17	page 343
	Steve Winwood	chapter 12	page 225
	Howlin' Wolf	chapter 1	page 8
	Link Wray	chapter 3	page 37
	The Wrecking Crew	chapter 3	page 39
X			
	X-Pensive Winos	chapter 4	page 47
	X-ray Spex	chapter 14	page 266
Y			
	The Yardbirds	chapter 4	page 48
	Yes	chapter 13	page 245
	Dwight Yoakam	chapter 9	page 153
	La Monte Young	chapter 8	page 126
	Neil Young	chapter 7	page 114
Z			
	Frank Zappa	chapter 18	page 347
	Warren Zevon	chapter 7	page 116
	Rob Zombie	chapter 17	page 337
	ZZ Top	chapter 11	page 199

"Nothing can ever be wrong about music... Develop your talent, man, and leave the world something"

- Duane Allman

Rock Genres, Sub-Genres and Other Musical Styles Index

The following index contains each rock genre, rock sub-genres, and other musical styles that were *mentioned* or *explored in some depth* throughout the book. They are cataloged by chapter and page number. Each musical genre or style was cited only once and where it could be *most appropriately* placed.

A

Afro-Cuban music	chapter 6	page 85
aleatory music	chapter 8	page 126
alternative country rock	chapter 9	page 153
alternative pop	chapter 16	page 322
alternative rock	chapter 16	page 300/318
ambient house	chapter 17	page 337
ambient music	chapter 18	page 360/361
ambient techno	chapter 17	page 336
Americana	chapter 18	page 351
Armenian music	chapter 17	page 341
art rock	chapter 8	page 121
avant-garde	chapter 8	page 126

B

Baroque chamber suite	chapter 6	page 76
black metal	chapter 10	page 180
the blues	chapter 1	page 5
bluegrass	chapter 1	page 10
boogie-woogie	chapter 2	page 18
bossa-nova	chapter 6	page 86
BritPop	chapter 15	page 292
Broadway show songs	chapter 12	page 217

C

cajun	chapter 3	page 30
Celtic rock	chapter 7	page 114
chance music	chapter 8	page 126
the Charleston	chapter 8	page 136
Christian progressive rock	chapter 13	page 251
classic rock	chapter 11	page 191
classical music	chapter 13	page 233
early country music	chapter 1	page 9
country rock	chapter 9	page 143
cowpunk	chapter 9	page 153
crossover-hardcore	chapter 14	page 267
crossover thrash	chapter 10/14	page 180/267

D

deathcore	chapter 10	page 180
death metal	chapter 10	page 180
dixieland	chapter 3	page 30
disco	chapter 15	page 289
doom metal	chapter 10	page 173
doo-wop	chapter 1	page 5
drum and bass	chapter 17	page 335

E

electronica	chapter 17	page 335
electronic dance music (EDM)	chapter 17	page 335
emo	chapter 14	page 270

F

field hollers	chapter 1	page 5
film scores	chapter 18	page 349
folk ballads	chapter 1	page 12
folk music	chapter 1	page 12
English folk music	chapter 7	page 102
folk-rock	chapter 7	page 95
funeral marches	chapter 3	page 29
funk	chapter 17	page 325
funk rock	chapter 17	page 326
fusion music	chapter 17	page 335

G

Gamelan music	chapter 13	page 233
gangsta rap	chapter 17	page 332
garage rock	chapter 16	page 308
glam metal	chapter 10	page 173
glam rock	chapter 8	page 121/129
gospel music	chapter 1	page 3
grindcore	chapter 10	page 181
grunge	chapter 16	page 299/308
guitar slingers	chapter 17	page 341

H

hard rock	chapter 10	page 165/181
hardcord punk	chapter 14	page 264
heavy metal	chapter 10	page 165/166
hillbilly boogie	chapter 1	page 10
Hindu chants	chapter 5	page 65
hip-hop	chapter 17	page 329
honky-tonk	chapter 1	page 10
horn-rock	chapter 17	page 333
horror punk	chapter 14	page 258
house music	chapter 17	page 335
hybrid metal	chapter 10	page 180
hymns	chapter 1	page 4

I

Indian music	chapter 5	page 65
industrial metal	chapter 10/17	page 181/337
intelligent dance music	chapter 17	page 337
isicathamiya	chapter 7	page 112

J

jam band music	chapter 12	page 229
jazz-rock	chapter 17	page 332
jigs	chapter 1	page 9
jug band tunes	chapter 6	page 78
jump blues	chapter 1	page 7

K

Japanese Kabuki Theater	chapter 8	page 130

L

M

Mariachi music	chapter 9	page 149
mathcore	chapter 13	page 251
mbaqanga	chapter 7	page 112
Medieval music	chapter 10	page 187
metalcore	chapter 10	page 180
Mexican folk songs	chapter 3	page 36
Middle Eastern rhythms	chapter 17	page 340
minimalism	chapter 8	page 121
minstrel show tunes	chapter 1	page 5

Rock Genres, Sub-Genres and Other Musical Styles Index

N
new age music	chapter 18	page 362
New Orleans funk	chapter 3	page 30
new romantic pop	chapter 14	page 263
new wave music	chapter 14	page 270
noise rock	chapter 16	page 319
nu metal	chapter 10/17	page 181/339

O
oblique strategies	chapter 18	page 361
opera	chapter 8	page 136
outlaw country	chapter 9	page 144

P
polka	chapter 1	page 9
pop-rock	chapter 15	page 279
post-grunge	chapter 16	page 300/316
power pop	chapter 15	page 294
prison songs	chapter 1	page 12
progressive metal	chapter 10	page 181
progressive rock	chapter 13	page 233
proto-punk	chapter 14	page 264
psychedelic rock	chapter 6	page 78
pub rock	chapter 14	page 259
punk-pop	chapter 14	page 268
punk rock	chapter 14	page 255

Q

R
raga rock	chapter 7	page 100
ragtime songs	chapter 1	page 5
Ranchera music	chapter 9	page 149
rap	chapter 17	page 329
rap-rock	chapter 17	page 329
reels	chapter 1	page 9
reggae	chapter 4	page 47
reggae-punk-new wave	chapter 16	page 301
Renaissance music	chapter 10	page 187
rhythm and blues	chapter 1	page 8
rock concerto	chapter 10	page 182
early rock 'n' roll	chapter 3	page 26
the rock opera	chapter 6	page 75
rockabilly	chapter 2	page 15
roots rock	chapter 9	page 153

S
samba-reggae	chapter 7	page 113
second line	chapter 3	page 30
serial music	chapter 18	page 349
shock rock	chapter 8	page 139
singer/songwriter	chapter 7	page 105
skiffle	chapter 5	page 57
soul	chapter 1	page 5
southern rock	chapter 9	page 155
speed metal	chapter 10	page 173
spirituals	chapter 1	page 3
surf rock	chapter 3	page 36
swamp rock	chapter 9	page 149
symphonic poem	chapter 13	page 234

T
thrash metal	chapter 10	page 173
Tin Pan Alley songs	chapter 1	page 5
township jive	chapter 7	page 112
trance pop-rock	chapter 18	page 364

U

V

    _____

W

    waltz   chapter 1   page 9

    West African music   chapter 1   page 4

    Western swing   chapter 1   page 9

    work songs   chapter 1   page 5

    world music   chapter 7   page 112

X

    _____

Y

    _____

Z

    zydeco   chapter 3   page 30

Sources Cited by Chapter

Chapter One
#1: Bob Dylan from Bob Dylan - Autobiography.
#2: Trent Reznor from Alternative Press, September 2004.

Additional Reading
- Deep Blues by Robert Palmer Penguin Books, New York NY, 1981.
- The Greenwood Encyclopedia of Rock History Vol #1 Greenwood Press 2006.
- The Story of the Blues -The Roots, The Music, The People Francis Davis, Da Capo Press 1995.
- Clapton -The Autobiography Three Rivers Press, 2007.
- American Music: A Panorama Daniel Kingman Schirmer Books 1998.

Chapter Two
#1: Sam Phillips from box set Sun Records Collection Rhineo Records.
#2: Keith Richards from Life - Keith Richards N.Y., Back Bay Books, 2010, pg 73.
#3: Peter Guralnick from the DVD Elvis Presley Classic Albums DVD Classic Albums Series Three limited, 2001.
#4: Levon Helm from This Wheel's On Fire: Levon Helm and The Band N.Y., Morrow Publishing, 1993, pg. 39.
#5: Album review Rolling Stone Magazine, Milo Miles, June, 2002.
#6: Carl Perkins from Go Cat Go! Rockabilly Music and Its Makers, Craig Morrison, Illini Books, 1996
#7: Johnny Cash from Cash: The Autobiography, 1997.
#8: Johnny Cash from Cash: The Autobiography, 1997.
#9: Jimmy Page from When Giants Walked the Earth, Mick Wall, Orion Publishing, 2008.

Chapter Three
#1: Keith Richards, Ibid, pg 134.
#2: Charlie Watts from According to The Rolling Stones, Chronicle Books, 2003, pg 40.
#3: Chuck Berry by Daniel Kreps of Rolling Stone Magazine, 2016.
#4: George Porter Jr., liner notes album Funkify Your Life, Rhino Records, 1995.
#5: Little Richard from A Wopbopaloobop article from The Washington Post, November 12th, 1984.

Chapter Four
#1: Keith Richards from According to The Rolling Stones, Mick Jagger, Keith Richards, Charlie Watts, and Ronnie Wood. Chronicle Books, 2003, pg. 38.
#2: Keith Richards, Ibid., pg 28.
#3: Keith Richards, Ibid., pg 42.
#4: Mick Jagger, Ibid., pg 82.
#5: Keith Richards from Life by Keith Richards, Back Bay Books 2010, pg 241-242.
#6: Keith Richards, Ibid. pg. 240-241.
#7: Keith Richards from Rolling Stone Magazine "Keith Richards-The Ultimate Guide to His Music and Legend" pg 66.
#8: Mick Jagger, According to The Rolling Stones, pg 196.
#9: Mick Jagger, Ibid., pg 217.
#10: Charlie Watts from liner notes album Blue and Lonesome, Interscope Records, 2016.
#11: Mick Jagger from interview Rolling Stone Magazine by Jann S. Wenner, Dec. 1995.
#12: Mick Jagger from According to the Rolling Stones, pg 86
#13: Eric Clapton from Clapton -The Autobiography, Three Rivers Press 2007, pg 48
#14: Jimmy Page from Hammer of the Gods -The Led Zeppelin Saga, Berkeley Publishing, 1976. pg 38
#15: Eric Clapton from Clapton pg 79
#16: Eric Clapton, Ibid, pg 95
#17: Jimmy Page from Hammer of the Gods -The Led Zeppelin Saga, Berkeley Publishing, 1975. pg 51
#18: John Paul Jones, Ibid., pg 55
#19: Jimmy Page, Ibid., pg 55
#20: John Entwistle, Ibid., pg 60
#21: Jimmy Page from The Art of Noise by Daniel Rachel St. Martins Press, 2013, pg 51
#22: Jimmy Page, Ibid.
#23: Jimmy Page on guitars from No Quarter -The Three Lives of Jimmy Page. Martin Power, Omnibus Press, 2016, pg 145
#24: Jimmy Page, No Quarter -The Three Lives of Jimmy Page. Martin Power, Omnibus Press, 2016, pg 130
#25: Jimmy Page from The Art of Noise, pg 49
#26: Jimmy Page from Stairway Hammer of the Gods, pg 151
#27: Robert Plant, Ibid., pg 61
#28: Robert Plant, Ibid., pg 309
#29: Led Zeppelin, Ibid., pg 306

Chapter Five
#1: Paul McCartney from The Beatles - Anthology, Chronicle Books, 2000, pg 116
#2: Ringo Starr, from The Beatles - Anthology, Chronicle Books, 2000, pg 86
#3: John Lennon, Ibid.
#4: John Lennon from interview Maureen Cleave, London Evening Standard, March 1966
#5: Paul McCartney, The Beatles - A Hard Day's Write Carlton Books, New York, 1994
#6: George Martin from Shout! The Beatles in Their Generation, by Philip Martin, Simon and Schuster, New York.,1981, pg 257
#7: Paul McCartney from Mark Lewisohn and George Martin, The Complete Beatles Chronicle. Harmony Book, New York, 1992, pg 99
#8: Jimmy Carter NPR, Debbie Elliott, 2012.
#9: John Lennon from, All We Are Saying: The Last Major Interview with John Lennon and Yoko Ono, David Sheff and Barry Golson, Playboy Press, 1981.
#10: Ringo Starr Starr, Ringo 2007 from the liner notes of Photograph: The Very, 2007.

Additional Reading:
- Norm N Nite Rock on Almanac Harper and Row, New York, 1989.
- Steve Turner The Beatles - A Hard Day's Write Carlton Books, New York, 1994.

Chapter Six
#1: Ray Davies from Ready Steady Kinks! by Nick Hasted, Uncut., 2004, pg 55
#2: Ray Davies from The Art of Noise by Daniel Rachel, St. Martins Press, 2013 pg 7-8
#3: Pete Townshend from Pete Townshend - Who I Am, Harper

Collins Publishing, 2012, pg 59
#4: Random Detours fan from <u>Moon</u>, by Tony Fletcher. Harper Collins Publishing,1999, pg 79
#5: Pete Townshend "I Can't Explain" from <u>Pete Townshend - Who I Am</u>, pg. 75
#6: Bruce Johnston from <u>Moon</u>, pg 170
#7: Pete Townshend, Ibid., pg 172
#8: Pete Townshend, Ibid., pg 162
#9: Pete Townshend from <u>Pete Townshend - Who I Am</u>, pg. 138
#10: Pete Townshend, Ibid., pg 146-147
#11: Pete Townshend, Ibid., pg 57
#12: Pete Townshend, Ibid., pg 157
#13: Pete Townshend, Ibid., pg 152
#14: Pete Townshend, Ibid., pg 146
#15: Pete Townshend, Ibid., pg 67
#16: Jeff Beck <u>Moon - The Life and Death of a Rock Legend</u> by Tony Fletcher, Harper/Collins, NY, 2000, pg 254
#17: John Entwistle, Ibid., pg 207-208
#18: Pete Townshend, Ibid., pg 85
#19: Bill Kreutzmann from <u>Deal</u>, St. Martin Press, New York, NY. 2015.
#20: Phil Lesh <u>Searching for a Sound: My Life with the Grateful Dead</u>, by Phil Lesh, Little, Brown, April 2005.
#21: Jerry Garcia <u>The Rolling Stone Illustrated History of Rock and Roll</u>, Random House, NY., 1992. pg 376
#22: Paul Rothchild from BAM interview with Paul Rothchild, by Jackson Blair, July 1981.
#23 The Institute of Health and Biomedical Innovation and School of public Health, Queensland University of Technology, Brisbane, Australia, published 2011.
#24: Mitch Mitchell <u>Inside the Experience</u> by Mitch Mitchell
#25: Jimi Hendrix unpublished interview by Steve Barker
#26: Chas Chandler from <u>Rolling Stone Magazine</u> interview by Gavin Smith, 1968.
#27: Joe Satriani Internet interview, Jas Obrecht.com, Music Archive

Chapter Seven
#1: David Dalton from <u>Who is That Man? - In Search of The Real Bob Dylan</u>, New York, Hachette Books. pg 23
#2: Bob Dylan from "Hellbound on the Loose-Bob Dylan releases a historic live record album," <u>Time Magazine Archive 126, no 21</u>. 1985.
#3: Roy Silver from <u>Down the Highway - The Life of Bob Dylan.</u>, Grove Press, New York, NY., 2001, pg 120.
#4: John Lennon interview: <u>All We are Saying: The Last Major Interview with John Lennon and Yoko Ono;</u> by David Sheff, New York, St. Martin Press, 2000, pg. 178
#5: Joan Baez, <u>Who is That Man? - In Search of The Real Bob Dylan</u>. pg 102
#6: Kenny Rankin, <u>Down the Highway - The Life of Bob Dylan</u>. pg 171
#7: Al Kooper from <u>Backstage Passes: Rock 'n' Roll in the Sixties</u> New York, Stein and Day, 1977, pg 55
#8: Al Kooper, <u>Who is That Man? - In Search of The Real Bob Dylan</u>, pg 113
#9: Bob Dylan on <u>Blonde on Blonde Who is That Man?</u> pg 154
#10: Paul Simon from <u>Paul Simon: A Life</u>, by Marc Eliot, Wiley and Sons Publishing., pg 40-42
#11: Neil Young from <u>Neil Young Waging Heavy Peace.</u>, Plume Inc, Penguin Group, New York, NY., pg 241-242
#12: Carole King from <u>Carole King - A Natural Woman</u>, Grand Central Publishing., New York, NY, 2012, pg. 41
#13: Carole King, Ibid., pg 42
#14: Carole King, Ibid., pg 60-61
#15: Carole King, Ibid., pg 208
#16: Carole King, Ibid., pg 211
#17: Carole King, Ibid., pg 210
#18: Carole King, Ibid., pg 210
#19: James Taylor from <u>Uncut</u> magazine, 2015.
#20: Steve Gadd from DVD <u>Steve Gadd - Up Close</u>, Alfred Music, 2003.
#21: Paul Simon from <u>Graceland</u> liner notes, 1986.
#22: Paul Simon, Ibid.
#23: Paul Simon, Ibid.
#24: Carly Simon from <u>boys in the trees - a memoir</u> by Flatiron Books, New York, NY., 2015, pg 164
#25: Neil Young from <u>Neil Young Waging Heavy Peace.</u>, Plume Inc, Penguin Group, New York, NY, 2012, pg 229
#26: Neil Young, Ibid., pg 347

Chapter Eight
#1: Roger Waters from <u>Mountains Come Out of The Sky</u>, by Will Romano, Backbeat Books, 2010, pg 25
#2 Roger Waters, Ibid., pg 26
#3: Richard Wright from interview by M. Kriteman <u>www.neptunepinkfloyd.com</u>, 1996.
#4: David Byrne from liner notes of album <u>Once in a Lifetime: The Best of Talking Heads</u>, 1992.
#5: David Bowie from <u>Bowie - A Biography</u> by Marc Spitz, Three Rivers Press, New York, NY., 2009, pg 20
#6: David Bowie, Ibid, pg 88
#7: Rick Wakeman, Ibid , pg 108
#8: David Bowie from <u>Bowie - The Biography</u> by Wendy Leigh. Gallery Books, New York, NY, 2014, pg 115
#9: Woodie Woodmansey, Ibid.
#10: David Bowie, Ibid.
#11: Marc Bolan from interview <u>The Guardian</u> by Keith Altham's Record Mirror, 1971.
#12: Marc Bolan, Ibid.
#13: Freddie Mercury from <u>Queenarchives.com</u>, <u>Interview with Freddie Mercury</u>, Melody Maker, 1981.
#14: Freddie Mercury, Ibid.
#15: Brian May from Brian May Interview from <u>The Telegraph</u>, by Neil Mc Cormick, 2011.
#16: Brian May, Ibid.

Chapter Nine
#1: Gram Parsons from <u>Desperados - The Roots of Country Rock</u>, Cooper Square Press, New York, NY, 2001, pg 44
#2: Keith Richards, Ibid., pg 264
#3: "Sneaky" Pete Kleinow, Ibid., pg 119
#4: Chris Hillman, Ibid., pg 140
#5: "Sneaky" Pete Kleinow, Ibid., pg 141
#6: Chris Hillman, Ibid., pg 181
#7: Richie Furay, Ibid., pg 126
#8: Randy Meisner, Ibid., pg 127
#9: Rusty Young from <u>urockradio.net</u>, 2011.
#10: Stu Cook, <u>Desperados</u>, pg 249
#11: Jerry Garcia, Ibid., pg 188
#12: Mike Nesmith, <u>Desperados</u>, pg 2
#13: Mike Nesmith, Ibid., pg 5
#14: Bob Dylan from <u>Who Is That Man?</u>, Hachette Books, 2016, pg. 215
#15: Bob Johnston from <u>Down the Highway - The Life of Bob Dylan</u>, Grove Press, New York, NY., 2001, pg 241
#16: Duane Allman from <u>One Way Out - The Inside Story of The Allman Brothers Band</u>, by Alan Paul, St. Martin Press, New York, NY, 2014, pg 6
#17: Jai Johanny "Jaimoe" Johanson, Ibid., pg 14-15
#18: Reese Wynans, Ibid., pg 18
#19: Dickey Betts, Ibid., pg 19
#20: Chuck Leavell, Ibid., pg 185
#21: Gregg Allman, Ibid,. pg 21
#22: Gregg Allman from "The Allman Brothers Band - A Decade of Hits 1969-1979," liner notes.
#23 Reese Wynans, <u>One Way Out</u>, pg 22
#24: Dickey Betts from <u>One Way Out</u>, pg 67-68
#25: Duane Allman, Ibid,. pg 62
#26: Duane Allman, Ibid,. pg 62
#27 Tom Dowd, Ibid., pg 123
#28: Dickey Betts, Ibid., pg 73
#29 Dickey Betts, Ibid., pg 117
#30: Gregg Allman, Ibid., pg 176
#31: Gregg Allman, Ibid., pg 178
#32: Bill Payne from interview on <u>Rhino.com</u> March 4th, 2014.
#33: Bill Payne, Ibid.

Chapter Ten
#1: Tony Iommi, <u>Louder That Hell - The Definitive Oral History of Metal</u> by John Wiederhorn and Katherine Turman, Harper/Collins, New York, NY, 2013, pg 36-37
#2 : Ozzy Osbourne, Ibid., pg 39
#3 : Ozzy Osbourne, Ibid., pg 34
#4: Geezer Butler, Ibid., pg 45

#5: Ozzy Osbourne from Classic Albums-Paranoid, Isis Productions/Eagle Rock Entertainment
#6: Iommi from interview Metalhammer.Co.UK, 2013
#7: Glenn Tipton from Louder Than Hell., pg. 56-57
#8: Rob Halford, Ibid., pg 74
#9: Rob Halford, Ibid., pg 87
#10: Rob Halford Ibid., pg 88
#11: Steve Harris, Ibid., pg 91
#12: Ozzy Osbourne, Ibid., pg 84
#13: Ozzy Osbourne from Bang Your Head: The Rise and Fall of Heavy of Heavy Metal, Three Rivers Press, New York, NY, 2002, pg 122
#14: Dimebag Darrell, Ibid., pg 220
#15: James Hetfield, Ibid., pg 246
#16: Scott Ian Ibid., pg 415
#17: Jeff Hanneman, Ibid., pg 252
#18: Tom Araya, Ibid., pg 252
#19: Dave Mustaine, Ibid., pg 222
#20: Dave Ellefson, Ibid., 227-228
#21: Rex Brown, Ibid., pg 324
#22: Ian Gillan from azquotes.com, 2017.
#23: Gene Simmons, Louder Than Hell, pg 51
#24: Angus Young, Ibid., pg 63

Chapter Eleven
#1: Steve Winwood from Rolling Stone Magazine Interview., by Jonathan Cott, 1969.
#2: Peter Frampton from Rockcellar Magazine Interview., by Ken Sharp, 2014.
#3: Eric Clapton from Clapton - The Autobiography, Three Rivers Press, NY., 2007, pg 107
#4: Billy Gibbons from Axs Interview by Victoria Miller, 2017.
#5: Bobby Whitlock from UDiscovermusic.com Interview by Richard Havers, 2015.
#6: Glyn Johns from the documentary History of The Eagles, 2013.
#7: Glenn Frey from BBC Interview by Mark Savage, January 19th, 2016.
#8: Tom Scholz from Guitar Player Magazine Interview by Jude Gold, 2014.
#9: Mark Knopfler from Written In My Soul by Bill Flanagan, Rosetta Books, 1987.
#10: David Paich from Interview with Toto keyboardist and vocalist David Paich, myglobalmind.com, 2015.
#11: Steve Lukather from The Steve Lukather Interview by Shawn Perry, vintagerock.com, 2012.
#12: David Paich, Ibid., 2015.
#13: Jeff Porcaro from Interview from Effingham.com, by Greg Rule, 1991.

Chapter Twelve
#1: Elton John from interview Rolling Stone Magazine, by Paul Gambaccini, August, 1973.
#2: Bernie Taupin, Ibid.
#3: Billy Joel from Interview Newsday Magazine, by Glenn Gamboa, 2015
#4: Billy Joel from interview Rolling Stone Magazine, by Patrick Doyle, June, 2017.
#5: Bruce Springsteen from interview Rolling Stone Magazine, by Dan Epstein, January, 2018.
#6: Eric Clapton from Clapton - The Autobiography, Three Rivers Press, New York, NY, 2007, pg 173-174
#7: Tom Petty from Interview Mojo Magazine, January, 2010
#8: Vinnie Colaiuta from Interview Modern Drummer Magazine, October, 1993. pg 24
#9: Vinnie Colaiuta, Ibid., pg 56
#10: Sting from interview Rolling Stone Magazine, by Stephen Rodrick, December, 2016.

Chapter Thirteen
#1: Chris Squire from Rocking the Classics, pg. 38
#2: Geddy Lee, Ibid., pg. 49
#3: John Lodge from Mountains Come Out, pg. 13
#4: Matthew Fisher, Ibid., pg. 9
#5: Steve Wilson, Ibid., pg. 33
#6: Ian McDonald, Ibid., pg. 34
#7: Bill Bruford, Ibid., pg 41
#8: Keith Emerson, Ibid., pg 51
#9: Greg Lake, Ibid., pg 52
#10: Derek Shulman, Ibid., pg 118
#11: Peter Gabriel from Genesis Chapter and Verse, St. Martin Press, New York. NY, 2007. pg 63
#12: Paul Whitehead, Mountains Come Out. pg 76
#13: Tony Banks, Genesis Chapter and Verse. pg 107
#14: Tony Banks from The Genesis Songbook, 1977.
#15: Tony Banks, Genesis Chapter and Verse. pg 103
#16: Peter Gabriel from a radio interview "Rockline" 92.3 FM KROCK, NYC, June 16th, 1986.
#17: Steve Hackett, Genesis Chapter and Verse. pg 143
#18: Peter Gabriel, Ibid., pg 95
#19: Peter Gabriel, Ibid.
#20: Chester Thompson from Genesis Chapter and Verse, pg 226
#21: Ian Anderson, Ibid., pg 89
#22: Steve Howe, Ibid., pg 62
#23: Eddie Offord, Ibid., pg 64
#24: Terry Brown, Ibid., pg 169
#25: Geddy Lee, Ibid., pg 179
#26: Neil Morse from Mountains Come Out, pg 229
#27 quote Alan Morse, Ibid., pg 229

Additional Reading:
- Rocking the Classics - English Progressive Rock and the Counter-Culture by Edward Macan. Oxford University Press, 1997.
- Mountains Come Out of the Sky -The Illustrated History of Prog Rock by Will Romano, Backbeat Books, 2010

Chapter Fourteen
#1: Mark Perry from Punk Rock - An Oral History by John Robb, PM Press, Oakland, California, 2012, pg 182
#2: John Lydon, Ibid. pg 111
#3: John Lydon from FilmFour Internet Chat Interview, June 30th, 2001.
#4: Mick Jones, Punk Rock - An Oral History, pg 151
#5: Glen Matlock, Ibid., pg 153
#6: John Lydon, Ibid., pg 349
#7: Keith Levene, Ibid., pg 477
#8: Mick Jones, Ibid., pg 126
#9: Mick Jones, Ibid., pg 197
#10: Captain Sensible. Ibid., pg 243
#11: Rat Scabies, Ibid., pg 244
#12: H.R. from Louder That Hell, Harper/Collins, New York, NY, 2013, pg 271
#13: John Joseph, Ibid., pg 274
#14: Billy Graziadei, Ibid., pg 297
#15: Mike Muir, Ibid., pg 279
#16: Reed Mullin, Ibid., pg 282
#17: Debbie Harry from I Want My MTV-The Uncensored Story of The Music Video Revolution, by Craig Marks and Rob Tannenbaum, Dutton Publishing, London., 2011, pg 32
#18: Mick Jones from Punk Rock - An Oral History, pg 153
#19: Chrissie Hynde, Ibid., pg 149

Chapter Fifteen
#1: Michael Jackson from Oprah Winfrey Interview, February 1993.
#2: Quincy Jones from interview for The Library of Congress, June 6th, 2016.
#3: Steve Lukather from interview Guitar Player Magazine by Matt Blackett, July 6th, 2015.
#4: Michael Jackson from Interview with Ian Meldrum, November 1996.
#5: Madonna from Interview Seventeen, October 1986.
#6: Prince from Interview NME.com, December 2012.
#7: Tony Banks from Genesis - Chapter and Verse, St. Martin Press, New York, NY., pg 167
#8: Phil Collins from Interview on DigitalTrends.com by Mike Mettler, 2016.
#9: Phil Collins, Ibid., 2016.

Chapter Sixteen
#1: Sting from Sting - Broken Music, The Dial Press, New York, NY, 2003. pg. 233
#2: Stewart Copeland from Message in a Box, liner notes, 1993, pg 57
#3: Sting, Sting - Broken Music, pg 235
#4: Sting, Ibid., pg 272
#5: Sting, Ibid., pg 292
#6: Sting, Ibid., pg 284

#7: Andy Summers from Message in a Box, pg 58
#8: Sting, Sting - Broken Music, pg 322-323
#9: The Edge from Interview: Playboy Magazine, 1985.
#10: Bono from Interview Rolling Stone Magazine, Andy Greene, 2017.
#11: Jack Schneider, Ibid., pg 81
#12: Billy Gibbons from I Want My MTV, Craig Marks and Rob Tannenbaum, Dutton Press, London, 2011, pg 25
#13: Dave Grohl, Ibid., pg 25
#14: Trevor Horn, Ibid., pg 65
#15: John Landis, Ibid., pg 184
#16: Chris Cornell from Rolling Stone Magazine Interview, January, 1995.
#17: Kurt Cobain from Heavier That Heaven by Charles R. Cross, Hyperion Publishing, New York, NY., 2001, pg 45
#18: Charles R. Cross, Ibid., pg 83.
#19: Kurt Cobain, Ibid., pg 290
#20: Dave Grohl from fooarchive.com interview, 2017.
#21: Chris Shiflett from fooarchive.com interview, 2017.
#22: Paul Lansky from The Rock History Reader, Routledge Publishing, New York, NY., 2013, pg 326
#23: Billy Corgan from Guitar World interview, January 1997.

Chapter Seventeen
#1: Art Neville from The Meters Anthology-Funkify Your Life, Rhino Records Inc., liner notes., pg 7
#2: George Porter Jr., Ibid., pg 13
#3: Leo Nocentelli, Ibid., pg 20
#4: Anthony Kiedis from interview Guitar World Magazine, December 9th, 2011
#5: Flea, Ibid.
#6: Scott Ian from Louder Than Hell, by Jon Wiederhorn and Katherine Turman, Itbooks, Harper/Collins, NY. NY, 2013., pg 416
#7: Trent Reznor, Ibid., pg 366
#8: Trent Reznor, Ibid., pg 385-386
#9: Burton Bell, Ibid., pg 397
#10: Richard Kruspe, Ibid., pg 403
#11: James Shaffer, Ibid., pg 421

Chapter Eighteen
#1: Frank Zappa from Zappa - A Biography by Barry Miles, Grove Press, New York, NY, 2004, pg 382
#2: Frank Zappa from Ibid., pg 277
#3: Frank Zappa from liner notes Joe's Garage-Act I, Munchkin Music, 1979
#4: Frank Zappa, Zappa - A Biography, pg 26-27
#5: Frank Zappa, Ibid., pg 91
#6 quote Levon Helm from This Wheel's on Fire-Hevon Helm and the Story of The Band, Levon Helm and Stephen Davis, A Cappella Book, New York, NY., 1993, pg 44
#7: Ronnie Hawkins, Ibid., pg 68
#8: Ronnie Hawkins, Ibid., pg 82
#9: Levon Helm, Ibid., 86
#10: Rick Danko, Ibid., pg 88
#11: Levon Helm, Ibid., pg 100
#12: Levon Helm, Ibid., pg 165
#13: Levon Helm, Ibid., pg 165
#14: Levon Helm, Ibid., pg 164
#15 quote Arthur Kratzman from Reckless Daughter - A Portrait of Joni Mitchell, by David Yaffe, Sarah Crichton Books, New York, NY, 2017, pg 15
#16: Leonard Cohen, Ibid., pg 61-62
#17: Joni Mitchell from Uncut, pg 26
#18: Joni Mitchell from Uncut, Magazine interview., Time Inc, London. 2015, pg 30
#19 : Larry Carlton, Ibid., pg 32
#20: Donald Fagen from Steely Dan - Reelin in the Years by Brian Sweet, Omnibus Press, New York, 2015, pg 12
#21: Donald Fagen, Ibid., pg 14
#22: Donald Fagen, Ibid., pg 78
#23: Walter Becker, Ibid., 103
#24: Donald Fagen from Steely Dan - Reelin in the Years, pg 121-122
#25: Donald Fagen from Aja - 33 3rd by Don Breithaupt, Bloomsbury Publishing, New York, NY, 2007, pg 9
#26: Donald Fagen from Steely Dan - Reelin in the Years, pg 164
#27: Walter Becker, Ibid.
#28: Lee Ritenour from Aja - 33 3rd, pg 55

#29: Roger Nichols from Steely Dan - Reelin in the Years, pg 202
#30: Donald Fagen from Downbeat Magazine interview, November, 2017, pg 24
#31: Walter Becker from Ibid., pg 24
#32: Brian Eno from interview Creem Magazine, July 1975.
#33: Brian Eno from Brian Eno - Oblique Music by Sean Albiez and David Pattie, Bloomsbury Publishing, New York, NY, 2016, pg 217
#34: Brian Eno, Ibid., pg 143
#35: Brian Eno from Words and Music: A History of Pop in the Shape of a City, by Paul Morley, Athens, University of Georgia Press, 2005, pg 166
#36: Brian Eno from Brian Eno - His Music and the Vertical Color of Sound, by Eric Tamm, De Capo Press, Boston, MA, 1995, pg 158
#37: Brian Eno, Ibid., pg 161
#38: David Byrne, Ibid., pg 202
#39: Daniel Lanois from Soul Mining., pg 112
#40: Brian Eno, Words and Music: A History of Pop in the Shape of a City, pg 55
#41: Peter Gabriel from Without Frontiers - the Life and Music of Peter Gabriel, by Daryl Easlea, Omnibus Press, London, 2014, pg 150
#42: Larry Fast, Ibid., pg 161
#43: Hugh Padgham, Ibid., pg 192
#44: Peter Gabriel, Ibid., pg 211
#45: Daniel Lanois from Soul Mining - A Musical Life by Daniel Lanois, Faber and Faber, New York, NY, 2010, pg 75
#46: Peter Gabriel from Without Frontiers, pg 251
#47: Peter Gabriel, Ibid., pg 295
#48: Peter Gabriel, Ibid., pg 315
#49: Peter Gabriel, Ibid., pg 326
#50: Daniel Lanois, Ibid., pg 245
#51: Dave Grohl from interview Epiphone.com, November 2012.

About the Author

Dr. Robert Brosh has been a music history and drumset faculty member at the University of the Arts in Philadelphia for the past twenty years. There, Rob has taught Rock History, American Music History, World Music, and Jazz History courses. He has taught numerous ensembles including The ECM Jazz ensemble, New Orleans ensemble, Funk ensemble, and Drumset ensemble. Rob has also taught at Rowan University in New Jersey and the New School in New York. Rob received his Master's and Doctor of Arts from New York University. As a performer, Rob has worked the showrooms in Atlantic City as a drummer and percussionist for numerous musical acts and has co-led the Loose Cannon Band and the Raw Deal Band throughout the Philadelphia/New York areas. Rob also leads The Rob Brosh Jazz Group. As a composer, Rob has published a number of jazz/New Orleans funk compositions and has written extensively for the genre of drumset duets with his innovative duo ensemble DrumSquared. Raw Deal has released two CD's titled Raw Deal and Encoded. DrumSquared has released two CD's titled DrumSquared and The Truth. Rob and saxophonist Todd Groves released a duo CD titled Duo and Rob has released a solo jazz CD titled Bartok.

Editor & Musical Consultant

Mark Griffith is a recording artist, educator, author, and a respected drumming historian. He received his Bachelors In Music Performance from William Paterson University. His feature articles have appeared in Modern Drummer, Percussive Notes, UK's Drummer!, and Not So Modern Drummer. Mark collaborated on two best selling instructional DVD's released by Hudson Music: *The Art Of Playing With Brushes*, and J*azz Legacy: Standing on the Shoulders of Giants*. Mark's debut recording, Drumatic, was released on Bluejay Records.

CPSIA information can be obtained
at www.ICGtesting.com
Printed in the USA
FFHW010156300419
52037646-57435FF